GunDigest 2016

Edited by
JERRY LEE

Published by

Gun Digest® Books, an imprint of F+W Media, Inc.
Krause Publications · 700 East State Street · Iola, WI 54990-0001
715-445-2214 · 888-457-2873
www.krausebooks.com

To order books or other products call toll-free 1-800-258-0929
or visit us online at **www.gundigeststore.com**

CAUTION: Technical data presented here, particularly technical data on handloading and on firearms adjustment and alteration, inevitably reflects individual experience with particular equipment and components under specific circumstances the reader cannot duplicate exactly. Such data presentations therefore should be used for guidance only and with caution. Gun Digest Books accepts no responsibility for results obtained using these data.

ISSN 0072-9043

ISBN 13: 978-1-4402-4430-8
ISBN 10: 1-4402-4430-8

Cover & Design by Tom Nelsen

Edited by Jerry Lee & Chris Berens

Printed in the United States of America

10 9 8 7 6 5 4 3 2 1

John T. Amber LITERARY AWARD

I am very pleased to announce that Rick Hacker is the recipient of this year's John T. Amber Literary Award. The award is named in honor of the late John T. Amber, Editor of *Gun Digest* from 1950 to 1979, and is presented each year to an author in recognition of a story published in the previous year's edition. This year's award goes to Rick for his excellent contribution to the 69th edition, "The Holsters of Arvo Ojala," a well-researched and beautifully photographed profile of a man whose leather creations were as much a part of the golden age of Hollywood Westerns as the guns they carried.

Rick Hacker has been a published author since he was 17 when he won the Grand Prize in a writing contest in *Boy's Life* for—what else?—a Western story entitled "The Cowboy and the Steer." He began his gunwriting career in 1976 when the late Robert E. "Pete" Petersen asked him to start writing for *Guns & Ammo*. In 1979 Rick began writing for the NRA's *American Rifleman* and he has been writing for those two publications ever since. His gunwriting and photography skills eventually expanded to other publications, including *Outdoor Life, Sporting Classics, Shooting Illustrated* and *Sports Afield*, in addition to annual publications like *Gun Digest*. Currently, Rick serves as Field Editor for *American Rifleman, Handguns* and *RifleShooter* magazines.

While he is known in these circles as one of the country's top gun writers, Rick is also Contributing Editor for the nation's leading luxury lifestyle magazine, *Robb Report*, where he specializes in whiskies, wines and cigars. (Rick and I have worked together in our writer/editor relationship for many years, and I cannot resist periodically referring to him as Mr. Alcohol, Tobacco and Firearms.)

His byline is also seen in other consumer magazines, both in print and online, and he does a regular International Living column for SCI's *Safari* magazine. Rick is one of the few gunwriters to have bridged the gap between consumer and firearms publications, having written about the Browning Citori in *Playboy*, and Beretta's Marc Newson 486 shotgun in *Robb Report*.

Growing up in Arizona, Rick developed his lifelong hobby of collecting, shooting and hunting with 19th and early 20th century firearms. While in high school he was on the ROTC rifle team, created the Boy Scouts of America's equestrian Mounted Explorer Post

Rick Hacker

Photo by John Fasano

44, and organized a trick shooting and fast draw club, The Arizona Young Guns.

"Although I started out with a .22 rifle," Rick says, "my first handgun was a first generation Colt Single Action Army, chambered in .45 Colt. It had a 4¾-inch barrel, absolutely no finish, but had an action job, stag grips and came with a black Arvo Ojala holster with 25 dummy rounds in the belt. I bought the entire rig for $65 from a young father who needed money. Later, while working my way through college at Arizona State University, I became the one who needed money and reluctantly sold the Colt for $65, but kept everything else. I still have the Ojala rig (which no longer fits me – funny how leather shrinks over the years) and the dummy bullets. And I now have many more Single Action Armies. I think it is the best looking, best balanced and most historically fascinating handgun in the world, slightly ahead of the Government Model 1911."

"Like many from my generation, I grew up watching Westerns on TV. First it was Hopalong Cassidy, Gene Autry and Roy Rogers, who later became a good friend. Then came all the rest, including *Gunsmoke, Have Gun – Will Travel,* and *The Rifleman* with Chuck Connors, who also became a good friend in later years. I watched them all, intently studying the guns and the holsters the actors used. I often practiced my fast

draw in front of the television (with an empty gun, of course, even though we only shot blanks and wax bullets in competition). I became pretty fast and once, while throwing down on Matt Dillon at the beginning of *Gunsmoke*, I cleared leather so rapidly I sent my single action sailing into a vase on top of the TV. From then on I practiced my fast draw over the bed or in the backyard."

Today Rick remains an avid shooter, collector and hunter. In addition, he has written numerous books, including *The Muzzleloading Hunter* (now out of print), *Pipesmoking – A 21st Century Guide*, the recently published *The Ultimate Cigar Book – 4th Edition*, and the recently published *50 Famous Firearms You've Got To Own: Rick Hacker's Bucket List of Guns,* available from Gun Digest Books (www.gundigeststore.com). (An excerpt featuring the Winchester Model 21 shotgun appears in this edition.) Rick is a Benefactor Member of the National Rifle Association, a Life Member of the Single Action Shooting Society, and has been inducted into The National Muzzleloading Rifle Association Hall of Fame.

Congratulations, Rick! And thanks for helping keep the guns of the West alive and well!

Jerry Lee
Editor

WELCOME
to the 2016 70th Edition of *Gun Digest*!

It was 1944 and World War II was raging in Europe and the Pacific when the first edition of *Gun Digest* was published. It would be another year before the war would end.

As editor John T. Amber wrote in a 1968 reprint of the first edition, "Profusely illustrated, and with features that are still timely, the 1944 First Annual Gun Digest alone foresaw the great postwar upsurge of interest that was to develop in guns and shooting as a pastime, sport and hobby."

And it turned out that the timing was certainly right. As soon as the GIs came marching home, a new era in the history of firearms began. Before long, many pre-war Winchesters and Remingtons, Colts and Smith & Wessons were back in production. Roy Weatherby's Magnums were soon redefining high velocity, and Bill Ruger and Alex Sturm were starting an empire. The ammo companies were introducing something new every year, as were the gunmakers. It was indeed an exciting time to be involved in the shooting sports. All the way through the last half of the 20th century until today—amazingly, one-sixth of the way into the 21st—exciting things continue in the world of guns, and *Gun Digest* has been here all along the way to keep the journal.

The dedication in the front of the first edition said, "The *Gun Digest* is dedicated to the millions of American sportsmen who love guns. It is our sincere hope and belief that this book will bring to its readers a greater enjoyment of hunting and shooting—and a deeper appreciation of fine guns and gun lore."

We continue to have that hope and belief today, and hope you enjoy this edition.

Highlights of This Edition

Not many big-game hunters have killed as many elk as Wayne van Zwoll. And certainly, not many have used 36 different calibers to do so. In his "Three Dozen Elk Cartridges," Wayne has a lot to say about the guns and the game. If you want to know about 7mm rifles, Jon Sundra is the man to go to. He calls his relationship with the bore size a "love affair" that has lasted 50 years. Jon has hunted every species of big game all over the world, and in this story he'll tell you why he almost always had a 7mm rifle in his hands. Varmint hunters will enjoy Stan Trzoniec's tale of the long list of .22 centerfires that he

has used in his long career as a writer. Stan also has had a long career as a professional photographer and provides some very nice examples of his work in this story. Phil Massaro is one of the up-and-coming gun and outdoor writers and we are very proud to have him in *Gun Digest*. He writes about putting together a custom 6.5-284, a cartridge that maintains quite a cult following. Other rifle-related articles in this edition include Tom Caceci explaining what an American Rook Rifle is all about, James House comparing two Ruger bolt-action rimfires new and old, Kevin Muramatsu reporting on the state of the AR-style semiautos, and Tom Turpin's annual review of some of the finest examples of the American custom gun.

Gun Digest has long been known for providing a place for articles on the history of great firearms. We continue that tradition in this 70th edition. Purdey is without a doubt the most famous name in the world of fine guns and is now beginning its third century in the British gunmaking trade. Terry Wieland provides a detailed profile of this fine old company and its guns in "James Purdey and the Triumph of Taste." And for an encore, Terry gives us a historic look at some of the early Mannlicher bolt actions that preceded the famous Model 98, the Haenel-Mannlichers, in his "Teutonic Templates" story. Our good friend Garry James is a walking, talking thesaurus on British handguns, as well as guns in the movies. He gives us a great story on the 1884 Mark II Enfield revolver and his quest for a specific gun in his tale, "From the Mounties to the Movies." Of interest to handgunners, we have retired sheriff Jim Wilson unveiling his favorite auto pistols, Paul Scarlata admitting his preference for polymer, Rick Hacker's search for the ultimate single action, and Robert Sadowski's review of the "other" Makarovs.

I hope you will enjoy these and other tales by many other top gun and outdoor writers. And it's nice to have Charlie Petty in *Gun Digest* again. Don't miss his story on the King Gunsight Company.

State of The Industry

The firearms and shooting sports industry continues to prosper and grow. Attendance at the 2015 SHOT Show, which was held in Las Vegas from January 19-22, was approximately 64,000, second only to last year's number of 67,000. NSSF, the National Shooting Sports Foundation

that owns and sponsors the Shooting, Hunting and Outdoor Trade Show, reports that the slight dip in attendance was the result of better pre-screening of attendees in order to weed out those who do not actually work in the industry. The first SHOT Show was held in St. Louis in 1979. The attendance: 5,600. What a difference 36 years can make.

There were approximately 1,600 exhibitors at the latest show spread over about 640,000 square feet, or 13 acres of space, which is why it's almost impossible to see everything, even with the show's four-day schedule.

At the State of the Industry Dinner, NSSF President Steve Sanetti told the crowd that despite what some anti-gun sources have called a decline in the firearms business, the industry is doing very well. He pointed out that gun sales last year were the second highest in history, that the number of FFL dealers is growing, instructors of gun permit classes report long waiting lists, and that apprentice hunting licenses grew to over 1 million in 2014. Gun sales peaked considerably in late 2012 and early 2013 after the rush to ban certain models following the tragic Newtown, Conn., school shooting. In the last couple of years, sales are at a more normal level. Other interesting facts: NSSF Director of Industry Research and Analysis Jim Curcuruto reports that women are now purchasing about 25 percent of industry products. Another growth category is the buyer who is new to firearms; one industry survey shows that more than 20 percent of gun owners bought their first gun in the last five years.

NRA Annual Meetings

The other big annual show in the firearms industry is the NRA Annual Meeting, which was held from April 10-12, 2015, in Nashville. Unlike the SHOT Show, which is open only to persons who work in the industry, the NRA is open to the organization's many members and those in their immediate family. For this reason, NRA attendance figures are higher than the SHOT Show. The Nashville show drew 78,865 attendees. Since the NRA show is usually held about three months after SHOT, it is often where new products that weren't ready in time for the SHOT Show are introduced. Other companies may choose to unveil new things at the NRA show, rather than perhaps get lost among all the new products at SHOT. For whatever reason, Glock chose Nashville as the setting for the introduction of a handgun that is getting a lot of attention—the compact, single-stack 9mm Glock 43. Likewise, Remington introduced the RM380 at the NRA show. It's a compact .380 double-action-only model with a metal frame and hammer-fired action and is being made at Remington's new Huntsville, Ala., plant.

We're told that Beretta introduced a Model 92 full-size pistol chambered in .22 LR at the NRA event, but so far it hasn't appeared on the Beretta website. Meanwhile, back at the SHOT Show, an intriguing and familiar pistol was being shown at the Colt booth, a new-production Model 1903 .32 ACP, also known as the Model M. The model has not been produced for 75 years, since the days of WWII.

Changes and Moves

Since our 2015 edition went to press, several popular gun companies have gone through or are in the process of going through some changes. Speaking of Colt, the company announced in June that they filed for a Chapter 11 bankruptcy reorganization and expected to quickly sell the company. Meanwhile, production continues. Remington has made it official that Para USA's production is being moved to the new Huntsville, Ala., plant, and that the Para brand will soon be no more. Those various 1911s made famous by the old Para-Ordnance company will be rebranded with the Remington name. And in other news, Olympic Arms has suspended its line of 1911-style autos, choosing to focus on its various AR-type rifles that are made in several calibers.

Ruger Challenge

Back in 2012, Ruger made a pledge to the NRA that it would donate a dollar to the group's ILA (Institute for Legislative Action) for every Ruger firearm sold in a 12-month period. The goal was to sell 1 million guns and raise $1 million for ILA. That goal was achieved and Ruger sold 1,114,687 units. This year, Ruger CEO Mike Fifer has doubled down with the pledge, announcing in June that the company will donate to the NRA/ILA two dollars for each gun sold with a goal of selling two million guns in the 12 months between the NRA 2015 and 2016 Annual Meetings. Ruger fans, here's an opportunity to help the NRA continue its fight to preserve the right of law abiding individuals to keep and bear arms. Check out the entire line at www.ruger.com where you're sure to find a Ruger you need.

—Jerry Lee

Acknowledgements

A tip of our hat to Managing Editor Chris Berens for his editorial support, for keeping us on schedule, and on our toes watching out for typos and grammatical no-nos. We want to again this year acknowledge Tom Nelsen's creativity and artistic skills in making Gun Digest look as good as it does.

Gun Digest Staff

Jerry Lee, Editor
Chris Berens, Managing Editor

CONTRIBUTING EDITORS

John Haviland: Shotguns
Kevin Muramatsu: Handguns/Autoloaders
Jeff Quinn: Handguns/Revolvers
Wm. Hovey Smith: Blackpowder

Phil Massaro: Ammunition, Ballistics & Components
Tom Tabor: Optics
Tom Turpin: Custom and Engraved Guns
Wayne van Zwoll: Rifles

TABLE OF CONTENTS
2016 GunDigest®

2016 FIREARMS CATALOG

WHAT THREE DOZEN ELK CARTRIDGES TAUGHT ME

BY **Wayne van Zwoll**

One shot with an iron-sighted Marlin in .32 Special (Hornady ammo) killed this elk at 130 yards.

From the .30-30 to the .375, myths abound. Herewith some observations about what kills elk best.

Many moons ago, in a tight Oregon meadow blackened by lodgepole shadow at dusk, he slipped silently through bleached grass and stood to watch the motionless lump at forest's hem. Dead air kept its scent from him, short yards away. Then the lump shifted…

I had sat out the day's end glassing a distant elk. It had ghosted into the coni-fers without showing me antlers. Time was up. I shifted slightly for a last-minute glance about…

When our eyes met, mine got wide. The bull, seemingly close enough to touch, stared back, antler tips ivory arcs against the inky forest. Slowly, rifle bobbing to my pulse, I cheeked the stock and peered through the scope. Dusk had stolen the dot.

He didn't move.

After a frantic search for the dot against the elk's dark shoulder, I dropped the scope field to the grass. The dot appeared faintly in my peripheral vision. It vanished as I jerked the re-barreled Mauser up onto the elk and pressed the trigger.

A 180-grain Speer handload dropped the bull.

The century-old .30-06 still ranks as a favorite among elk hunters. Modern loads make it deadlier.

A huge success since its 1962 debut, the 7mm Rem. Mag. turns up in elk camps as often as the .30-06.

A big bull rubbed here – a promising sign. That's a Winchester 71 (1935-1957). Its rimmed .348 excels for elk in cover.

Forty-two years later, the .300 Holland & Holland still ranks among my favorite elk rounds. But I've used 36, if memory serves, and carried on elkless hunts rifles chambered to other cartridges. They've all helped shape my views on elk loads. Constrained by the one-bull-per-year-per-state limit imposed on elk hunters everywhere, I've used no cartridge exhaustively. So these notes are hardly authoritative.

Even if by sunny good fortune you were directed to test one cartridge on elk and permitted to take several bulls in a season, you'd have a hard time drawing unassailable conclusions. Each shot is unique. A bullet's effect has less to do with cartridge design, or even the bullet itself, than with range and shot angle, animal size and the missile's track inside. Besides, myriad loads are possible for any one cartridge. The .30-06 appears in about 80 types of factory ammo. Many times that number of handloads can be fashioned, with bullets and powders that continue to proliferate.

Is the .30-06 a good elk cartridge? Land sakes, yes! It's been felling elk for more than a century under a wide range of conditions. Surveys I've taken of thousands of elk hunters put it neck-and-neck with the 7mm Remington Magnum in popularity.

A better choice for elk hunting than Remington's big 7mm is tough to find. Introduced in 1962 with the Model 700 rifle, it featured 150- and 175-grain factory loads. Neither seemed to me ideal for elk, though Wyoming outfitter Les Bowman and the Remington company promoted the round masterfully. Its flat arc and relatively light recoil appealed to hunters. Still, many considered 150 grains on the light side for elk. The 175's weight throttled its muzzle velocity; a nose profile better suited to alder thickets sapped speed and energy downrange. Ballistically, the heavy 7mm load delivered no more reach or punch than a 180-grain spitzer stoked to redline in a .30-06. I asked a Remington troll why Big Green had chosen the 175 over a sleek 160-grain bullet that could be driven much faster but held significant in-flight advantage over a 150 Core-Lokt. "We had a lot of 175s available," was the reply.

Since then, a raft of racy, controlled-expansion 160-grain 7mm bullets have appeared in factory loads and as components. They (and a broader selection of 140s and 150s) have given Remington's iconic magnum more reach, ferocity and versatility.

Some years ago, I followed the echoes of a bull elk into an Oregon canyon. He climbed out ahead but paused on a rim trail. I flopped prone and fired my Model 70. At the crack of that 7mm Magnum he collapsed, spine severed between the shoulders. I'd held a tad high, thinking 300 yards of gravity would tug my bullet into the lungs. Not so. That slippery 160-grain Swift Scirocco lost only a hand's width.

The .300 Winchester appeared a year after Remington's 7mm. Oddly enough, given expectations of the rabble, it was not the .338 Winchester necked down. Its 2.62-inch case and short neck gave it more capacity than other (2.50-inch) short belted magnums of the day. It hurled a 180-grain bullet as fast as the 7mm Remington could a 160. Arcs are nearly identical for the same bullet style, but of course the heavier .30 hits harder. A 160-grain 7mm Core-Lokt Ultra in a current load brings 1,580 foot-pounds to 400 yards – plenty to kill elk, but well shy of the 1,750 delivered by the .300's 180.

One of several .300 Winchester Magnum rifles I've owned was a 1963 Model 70 with tiger-tail walnut – a rare find in those days of fence-post wood before the 70's 1964 overhaul. Accurate and slick-

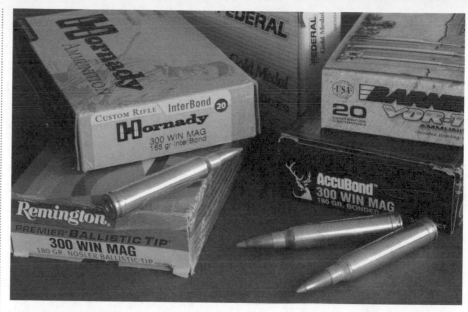

With a 180-grain bullet at 3,100 fps, the popular .300 Win. Mag. shoots very flat and drives bullets deep.

cycling, that Winchester was my go-to elk rifle before I sold it in a fit of insanity. Another pre'64 .300 went the same way. I'd trade my pickup to get them back.

Just as fetching was the Winchester Model 70 Alaskan with a 25-inch barrel in .338 Winchester Magnum. A fellow rimfire competitor used one for elk. I managed to snare a fine example at a gun show and hunted with it. After one singularly unproductive day in the hills, I bounced a herd of elk in a 'pole patch.

The author killed this last-day Colorado elk at 250 yards with a Ruger rifle in .300 Win. Mag.

Left to right: Winchester's .270 is gentle in recoil but lethal. The .270 Weatherby and .270 WSM add punch.

Racing after the thunder, desperate for a wink of antler and a shot alley, I heard a branch snap behind me. I spun to see a bull slipping off to the side. My .338 staggered him; a second shot put him down; I fired a third to finish him. He'd taken more than 7,000 foot-pounds from the first hits, both in the chest. A departing elk can be hard to anchor! The .338 with 225- or 250-grain pointed bullets (Nosler's 210 Partition too) can bring a ton of energy out to 400 yards. In recoil, the .338 reminds you of its horsepower.

The 7mm, .30 and .33 magnums beg the use of stoutly constructed bullets to ensure penetration through thick bone and muscle up close. Once, in Montana's Bob Marshall Wilderness, I chose a 200-grain Winchester Power-Point over stronger missiles because it drilled tighter groups. One dreary afternoon while descending a mountain on horseback, we spied a bull elk across a cut. He was moving by the time I'd swung off Paint and jerked my rifle free. I triggered the Model 70 as he galloped toward cover. The bullet caught him mid-rib, ranged through the heart and balled up, perfectly mushroomed in the far shoulder.

The .338 is a fine pick for quartering shots. Also, its 225-grain bullet flies flatter than a 180 from a .30-06, so it stretches far. Better still by ballistic measure: Weatherby's .340, its 1962 debut buried in the tickertape strewn for the 7mm Remington and .300 Winchester. The .340 is a blown-out,

necked-up .300 H&H, left full length. It blasts a 250-grain bullet downrange faster than an '06 can throw a 150! At 500 steps the .340 hits like a .338 at 400. Shintangle Montana timber in knee-deep snow yielded an elk to my long-limbed Weatherby Mark V in .340. That 250-grain Nosler packed far more foot-pounds than needed.

In truth, many elk hunters are over equipped. To kill an elk you need not land enough energy to rock an armored personnel carrier. But that misconception is common. After years of reading about and dreaming of record-book bulls, we labor up the mountain with visions of cudgel-thick antlers that, upside down on a tall mule, furrow the earth. Said elk will appear at great distance, quartering steeply into a fir jungle, a heartbeat from gone.

While you may get this shot, a powerful cartridge hardly guarantees a kill. Once, when topping a hill, I refused to fire at a magnificent bull, statue-still, facing me at about 300 yards. My rifle: a Lazzeroni bored for the short, stout 8.59 Galaxy, a ballistic match to the .340 Weatherby. Alas, though the air was still and the bull patient, a landform hid the bull when I eased to a sit. In vain I tried to calm the crosswire offhand. Rather than risk a crippling shot, I let the elk walk.

On another morning my Galaxy took a lesser bull. He absorbed the heavy .33 bullet with a slight shudder then moved on into the forest – where he died in seconds. I'd seen the same reaction

in a bull shot with my .375 H&H. The 300-grain softpoint destroyed both lungs at close range. The elk galloped off, nosing into the duff a short distance off. These and other encounters have convinced me that no hunting bullet knocks elk down. Elk fall when they die – when vital organs no longer function – or when bullets strike nerve centers or break supporting bone. One of two bulls I've taken with a .30-30 collapsed when the softnose smashed vertebrae behind his skull. Instant kill. (By the way, that's a shot I take only when very close. A hit in surrounding tissue can doom the animal to a slow death.) Lung-shot elk succumb most quickly when struck by bullets that do the most damage.

Occasionally elk have died more quickly than I expected. One, lung-shot by a client with a .270, reared as might a horse then fell backward, planting its long beams in the ground. No further movement. Another bull, struck mid-rib by a 140-grain .280 bullet, simply crumpled. I can't explain those kills. More often elk hit well will leave as if untouched. Given an accurate shot with an appropriate bullet the trail should be short. But you'll do well to keep firing as long as the elk is upright. One bull trotted off after I drove a .270 bullet into its forward ribs. A second shot to the spine between the shoulders dropped the beast. My first missile had blown a big entrance hole but damaged only the near lung – evidence that bullet was too fragile for elk. Had I not fired again, the animal would doubtless have escaped to die later.

Bullet design can matter more than bullet energy. Shot placement trumps both. Dashing at last light after a bull crippled in the front legs by another hunter, I fired when the elk paused, killing it with a 100-grain softnose from my .250 Savage. While such a bullet is hardly ideal, it's adequate if you take care with each shot. A rancher I know has killed dozens of bulls with his .250. Another friend has used a .25-06 to take 20 elk, without losing one.

Once, a fellow bringing his young son on his first elk hunt asked if he should loan the boy his .30-06. "He has his own 6mm Remington, but isn't that a bit light?" I allowed that it was, but added that the recoil of an '06 might cause flinching. "Accurate shots kill elk." Next morning we climbed into the Utah hills where the boy laced a 6mm Nosler Partition through an elk's heart. The animal died right away.

Sometimes power is comforting. On a stormy morning in the northern Rockies I climbed a ridge across from a herd of elk I'd spied at dawn. Unable to approach the bull on the herd's far flank, I paralleled the animals until the bull moved apart in a logging slash 300 yards out, just shy of timber. When the Swift A-Frame from my .358 Norma Magnum struck the elk crashed as if the earth had been jerked from under it. Essentially a .338 Magnum with a bigger mouth, the .358 Norma can push 250-grain bullets faster. It put an exclamation point on that lung shot.

The main problem with such potent cartridges is that they kick hard in rifles light enough to carry all day in steep places. So I've hunted elk with less ambitious rounds. On a particular Wyoming hunt a pair of bulls piled off a timbered ridge ahead of me and split. I crashed headlong after the left-hand animal hoping for a shot as he lunged down the steep face through the lodgepoles. Suddenly, a sliver of rib came clear. Rifle braced against a tree, I sent a bullet from the 6.5x55 and heard it hit. The bull labored – as did I – through more deadfall. Another glimpse, another 140-grain softpoint, and the elk collapsed.

A year later a 7mm-08 got me an elk in that same canyon. I managed to find one more bull there when the .270 WSM came to market. I believe this was the first elk taken with it. Another stubby powerhouse, the .300 Remington Short Action Ultra Mag, also came my way before I'd heard of it dropping an elk. Again, I was fortunate to bring back a bull.

More recently, with a Montana rifle bored for the largely unsung .280 Remington (circa 1957), I climbed under a bleak, black sky toward timberline. Still-hunting through stunted pines at dawn, I caught the bobbing of an antler tine through the cover. Unaware but alert, the five-point eased up-slope. I angled toward him getting an offhand shot at 60 yards. Two more 140-grain TSX bullets sailed after him as he crashed then rolled into a very steep canyon. Even when you know a hit is fatal, follow-ups make sense – if for nothing more than to limit the climb packing out!

Many elk have fallen to traditional lever-action Winchester and Marlin carbines bored for the likes of the .30-30 and .32 Special. Commonly considered marginal, they're deadly at iron-sight ranges. You must simply decline long

The Seattle Mariners' Willie Bloomquist shot this elk at 160 yards with his powerful .30-378 Weatherby.

In most elk country you'll want a portable rifle. Adding power hikes recoil as you trim rifle weight.

Inset: The author dropped this bull with a 140-grain Nosler from his Zeiss-scoped 6.5/284 at just over 300 yards.

This elk fell to another 6.5, the 6.5 Creedmoor, at very long range. That's a Magnum Research rifle and a GreyBull scope.

shots and quartering pokes – as bullets for such rifles were designed for deer hunting – not to drive the length of a bull elk. Hornady LEVERevolution ammunition, with pointed bullet tips of resilient polymer, offer higher starting velocities and flatter trajectory than flat and roundnose loads. Still, one of my biggest bulls fell to a blunt .30-30 bullet.

A young guide and I had hunted most of the day in sleet, through obnoxious shintangle. Wet and cold, we led the ponies onto a ridge to bellow into the hills at last light. The long, quavering note brought a reply, faint and far off. "We'll hunt there tomorrow," he said, and bugled again. To our astonishment a reply came instantly and louder. "He's coming!"

I scrambled uphill under the pines as the bull brayed again. Short minutes later he crashed into view, charging down toward us. At 55 yards the 170-grain softpoint drove into his chest. He spun and stopped behind a screen of brush as I cycled the Marlin. Silence. I waited, then lizard-slow, crawled to the side. A slot opened to his rib. I fired. He lunged. I fired again. He fell.

On another elk expedition I'd have been lost had the bull appeared at 200 yards. But a well-placed .32 Special bullet – a pointed Hornady – took a Wyoming elk handily for me at 130 steps. I'd muffed a chance earlier in the day, hiked far, then sat to rest near a trail juncture. Glassing the slopes around, in a burn I spied a branch that curved *up*. Odd. Other limbs on those fir skeletons drooped. Then I saw the

PLOWING A PATH TO ELK

The "brush-busting" bullet is a myth. Long, heavy bullets (those of high sectional density) spun fast but exiting at modest speed resist deflection a bit better than do lightweights or short, thick missiles. But all bullets give way to obstructions. In tests with a range of bullet types and weights from quick-stepping smallbore loads to shotgun slugs, I've found none that reliably power straight through sagebrush branches ¼ to ¾ inch in diameter. Targets only a few feet behind show not only significant deflection, but tipping. "Keyholing" occurs even with heavy 35-bore bullets. Best bet for most elk country: a stoutly constructed bullet of sleek form on the heavy edge of midweight for the bore.

In the northern Rockies close shots at elk are the rule – at least for hunters willing to work for them.

A pack train threads the Frank Church Wilderness with a bull taken by a Ruger No. 1 in 7mm WSM.

SIGHTS FOR ELK RIFLES

I've killed elk with iron sights, but my eyes aren't as sharp as when I honed them in smallbore matches. You don't need much magnification for hunting elk. In fact, a fixed 4x scope is my choice. Lighter, shorter, simpler and optically superior (if indistinguishably), it can be mounted low and farther forward than most variables. Only once has a high-power variable helped me take an elk, and that was a special case. I can't recall using more than 6x magnification for other bulls; and I carry variables at 3x or 4x. That's plenty, even for long pokes. Low power boosts brightness and field of view, and tames uncontrollable vibrations that make your reticle dance, delaying the shot. Getting set for a 300-yard kill some years ago I didn't bother to change magnification from 3x on my 3-9x variable. My bullet centered the elk's lungs. On the other hand, I've often had to remind clients to "power down." One had his sight at 8x when a pair of huge bulls appeared. He couldn't find either in the tight view as they made off in the open at 90 yards.

Dating to 1873, the .45-70 can be loaded stiff in modern rifles. It's a deadly elk round in close cover.

ear and backline of the bull. He was staring at me. I centered the bead in the aperture and aimed tight to the tree. At my shot, the elk rocketed off. Apprehensive, I climbed to the trail. A scarlet spray on the snow confirmed a lung hit. The six-point lay dead just 50 yards away.

Hunting with such rifles and loads adds challenge – and thrill – to any hunt. I recall sneaking into a bedded bunch of elk through yellow Colorado aspens. Tension mounted at each step as I skirted cows almost near enough to touch. When my scent detonated the herd I missed with the Marlin 1895 before the departing bull's hide winked one last time in a sun-dappled alley. That .45-70 bullet connected.

Having killed a handful of elk at very close range (one with an arrow at seven yards), I remember well the day I carried a Mark V rifle in 7mm Weatherby Magnum. It had been a frustrating hunt, mostly in rain, in tough country. On the last afternoon my companion spied an elk slipping into hilltop cover far away. We closed on foot to a patch of cedars 340 yards across a brushy valley from the spot. Glassing, I saw brief movement. The elk had bedded, risen, bedded again. With no time left to wait I marked as best I could its location, then stalked in. When cover I had marked vanished from valley-bottom view, I

One of Wayne's biggest bulls fell to a Model Seven Remington in .308. The Core-Lokt Ultra is a top elk bullet.

groped uphill through cedars thicker than they'd appeared. Careful steps put me at the hem of the target thicket. Then – a spot of color! The tip of a tine. Seconds passed. Soon my scent would reach the elk, sending it out the back door. I eased sideways, my movement glacial. A patch of hair in a grapefruit-size gap told me the elk's body position. At a mere 14 yards my TSX zipped through the shoulder.

While a 7mm spitzer at 3,250 fps was hardly necessary there, it was no handicap. In most elk country you can't count on close shots. A .270 Weatherby proved just right for a bull years earlier in the Bob Marshall Wilderness on a

snowy slope with lots of elk and no stalking cover inside 250 yards.

The time I hunted with Middle Fork Outfitters in Idaho's Frank Church Wilderness, I chose a Model 71 Winchester chambered for the wildcat .450 Alaskan. This old lever action had a receiver sight and was ideal for the close cover in which I *almost* got a shot. Alas, a cow winded me and took the herd to another drainage. Some days later at timberline we spied a scattering of elk on a ridge far below. The bull looked big. "Take the Ruger," insisted my pal Ken Nagel, handing me a No. 1 barreled to 7mm WSM. As time was short, I relented, then raced down toward the elk. But the herd beat me to a pass and lined out toward thick forest below. I scurried to a bush on all fours, snugged the sling and searched frantically for antlers as the elk bunched to negotiate deadfalls. I found a slot. The bull paused, but a cow stood behind. I waited. The cow moved. I pressed the trigger, dropped the lever and shoved another round home as the thud of a hit

floated back 330 yards. The bull allowed another hit, then fell. There'd have been no shot at all with the iron-sighted 71.

While I've guided hunters to record-book bulls, most of *my* hunting has happened where any six-point elk is a prize. My two best bulls, both still-hunted, dropped to a Remington CS Model Seven in .308 and a lightweight re-stocked Springfield in .30-06 Improved. Each animal traveled a short distance after a lethal first round. Each required a finisher.

Favorite elk cartridge? I'll confess to several. In a hammerlock, I'd probably howl ".308 Norma!"

It's no better than the .35 Whelen Improved that floored a Washington bull in cover, or the 7mm Dakota that tumbled an Arizona six-point atop a desert plateau, or the mild-mannered 6.5 Creedmoor that killed a New Mexico elk farther than I've shot any other. But if versatility is the gauge, Norma's .308 Magnum with 180-grain spitzers at 3,000 fps is hard to beat. In midweight

rifles its recoil is brisk but not obnoxious. Bullets fly flat as a .270's, but hit much harder. Controlled-upset missiles like Federal's Trophy Bonded, Swift's A-Frame, Norma's Oryx, the Barnes TSX, and Nosler's Partition and Accubond drive to the off-shoulder of quartering elk bounced in thickets. Why not the .300 Winchester? A ballistic twin, it's much more popular. But I prefer the slightly shorter case and longer neck of Norma's round.

Truthfully, such distinctions are meaningless.

Naming runners-up is just as hard. How about the 7mm and .270 Weatherby Magnums, the .300 Holland & Holland, the .300 Ruger Compact Magnum or .300 SAUM? The .30-06? If Remington's 7mm Magnum or some WSM hikes your pulse, or you're enamored of the .280 Improved or a wildcat like the .30 Gibbs, you'll get no quarrel from me. The best elk load for *your* rifle is what's chambered when a bull appears in your sight!

A World Benchmark for 200 Years
JAMES PURDEY
AND THE TRIUMPH OF TASTE

BY **Terry Wieland**

Audley House, at the corner of South Audley and Mount Streets in Mayfair, has been home to James Purdey & Sons since 1881. The building still has bomb scars from the Blitz in 1940.

There is no more respected name in all of gunmaking today than James Purdey & Sons of London. It is not the oldest company, nor the largest, nor the most prolific, but no gunmaker in history has had a greater influence on guns and shooting.

In 2014, Purdey celebrated its 200th anniversary. During those 200 years the world of gunmaking has seen extraordinary changes in technology and society. When James Purdey set up business, the Joseph Manton flintlock was the epitome of the sporting gun. Two hundred years later—two centuries, two world wars, emperors toppled and governments overthrown, to say nothing of the defenestration of Britain's landed class— James Purdey & Sons is still in business, still occupying its famous premises on South Audley Street in London. It is still selling James Purdey's original product: Perfection in gunmaking.

Absolute perfection in anything is impossible, but that reality does not preclude the ambition. It was this ambition that drove Joseph Manton and he passed it on to his craftsmen who, on their own and one by one, created the great London gun trade. These included Charles Lancaster, Thomas Boss and James Purdey.

Before John and Joseph Manton took up the trade in the 1790s, the hunting gun was a crude implement at best, with all the grace, style and workmanship of an ox yoke. They were heavy, dirty and clumsy. The Mantons changed that for all time. Until the Mantons, the one firearm considered worthy of close attention and fine finishing was the duelling pistol, for obvious reasons. Also, duelling with pistols was the province of gentlemen, and gentlemen of taste demanded style and quality.

It should be noted that, stretching back hundreds of years, gunmakers on the continent had produced lavishly engraved, carved and inlaid firearms for kings and emperors, but those show-pieces, which now grace the great museums, are in a different class entirely. A key point is that those guns were little different than the clumsy mechanism carried by the guard on the gate. It was only external glitter.

The duelling pistol, with its emphasis on absolute reliability, had workmanship inside every bit as good as the finishing on the outside. John and Joseph Manton set out to apply the same standards to the sporting gun and, most particularly,

the fowling piece. By reducing weight and making a gun lithe and responsive, they made it possible to shoot flying birds, rather than potting them on the ground.

So we have cause and effect. Which was which, no one today can say. All we know is that the Mantons sparked a revolution that extended beyond mere gunmaking and shaped the habits and tastes of high society.

Through the Regency period in England from 1811 to 1820, the great arbiter of taste was George Bryan "Beau" Brummell. Although the Beau is widely misunderstood—and even more widely misrepresented—his influence on taste was all-encompassing, irrefutable and continues to this day. It extends far beyond men's fashion, although that is where he left his most enduring mark. Frequently referred to as a "dandy," he was actually anything but.

A dandy was a man who dressed in "the pink" of fashion, often outlandishly and even laughingly. At the time men wore powdered wigs, face make-up and elaborately cut clothes of often ludicrous colors. They seldom bathed and compensated by drenching themselves in scent.

Brummell was still a young man when, as a friend of the Prince Regent, he began to move in the highest circles of court and make a name as a man of fashion. The Beau espoused the idea of, first, bathing regularly, and second, eschewing garish ostentation. He wore no wigs or make-up and avoided all but the most sober colors. On the contrary, he emphasized the finest fabrics, perfectly tailored. Understated elegance was his watchword. His coats were black or midnight blue, his neck cloths snowy white and perfectly tied.

Black tie, the classic men's evening dress of today (what Americans call a tuxedo and the English a dinner jacket) owes its existence directly to Beau Brummell.

When Beau Brummell fled London ahead of his creditors—another story entirely—his possessions were put up for auction. The auctioneer, appropriately, was Christie's, and the auction list still exists. Prominent among his collection of Sèvres porcelaine and rare first editions were "Three capital double-barrelled Fowling Pieces by Manton."

Beau Brummell was noted for his unerring taste in all things artistic;

Joseph Manton set a standard for firearms that continues to this day. Of James Purdey, Manton said, "After me, Purdey gets up the best work." James Purdey said of Manton, "But for him, we would have been a parcel of blacksmiths." This exquisite Manton flintlock bears out everything that was said of Joseph Manton.

Colonel Peter Hawker was not. Col. Hawker was the most noted shooter of his day, partly due to his books on field sports. A veteran of the Peninsular Wars against the French under Wellington, Col. Hawker was badly wounded and suffered from the wounds until the end of his days. He did not, however, let that or anything else come between him and his pre-dawn sojourns in wind and rain, awaiting flights of ducks.

An admirer and user of Manton guns, not merely for their artistry but for their perfect handling and absolute reliability, Col. Hawker once asked Joseph Manton who produced the finest guns in London. Manton replied, "After me, Purdey gets up the best work."

James Purdey was born in 1784, into a family of lowland Scots who had immigrated to London. His father was a blacksmith whose brother-in-law was a gunmaker, and Purdey apprenticed under him. In 1805, when he had become a journeyman, he went to work for Joseph Manton. He spent three years in Manton's shop, learning the trade at the highest levels, working beside men with the most exacting standards. Purdey would later say of Manton, "But for him, we would have been a parcel of blacksmiths."

In 1808, Purdey joined the Forsyth Patent Gun Company, a firm set up by the Rev. Alexander Forsyth to exploit his new invention, the percussion ignition system. Purdey was a stockmaker and lock-filer—the Forsyth system required very precise lock manufacture—and was soon promoted to foreman. Sometime between 1814 and 1816 Purdey left Forsyth to set up on his own. He opened

James Purdey the Younger

what Col. Hawker described as "a small shop in Princes Street."

Often overlooked in the histories is what a turbulent time this was for a young gunmaker to go into business for himself. There was a technological change in the transition from flintlock to percussion that was anything but smooth. Although Forsyth had demonstrated how percussion could work—detonating a fulminate with a blow rather than setting powder alight with sparks—exactly how it could be put to practical use was a matter of trial, error and sometimes ruinous litigation.

As well, there was the social and economic upheaval resulting from the French Revolution and the Napoleonic Wars. In some ways, James Purdey picked the worst of times to set up shop, but in others, it turned out to be the best of times. With Napoleon finally defeated at Waterloo in 1815, England was unchallenged as the wealthiest power in Europe. Shooting was popular and the upper classes had money to spend.

Joseph Manton, London's preeminent gunmaker, was embroiled in a lawsuit with Alexander Forsyth and in 1825 declared bankruptcy. The Manton era was over and James Purdey was ideally positioned to fill his shoes. Not that there were not competitors; other Manton craftsmen including Charles Lancaster and Thomas Boss, every bit as able as Purdey, had also struck out on their own. Together, they would define London gunmaking.

James Purdey, however, not only had gunmaking skills and a sense of taste to rival Manton, he was also inventive and an excellent businessman. He had the sense to stay out of the percussion battle, concentrating on the proven flintlock until he established a reputation. He then became associated with the technological advance that allowed percussion to displace the flintlock once and for all. This invention was the percussion cap.

At least one authority credits James Purdey with its invention, but Purdey historian Donald Dallas writes that he found no evidence to support this. James Purdey did embrace it though, and the company's great reputation really dates from this, the real beginning of the percussion revolution.

The percussion era did not last long. Within 30 years it was displaced in its turn by various forms of internal ignition systems – first pinfire cartridges then centerfire. It did last long enough for James Purdey to make the first of several

contributions that would turn out to be pivotal. This was the principle of lighter bullets at higher velocities, or the "Express" system. This was not so much an invention as a change in emphasis.

With black-powder muzzleloaders and round lead balls there was little that could be done to increase velocity. As elongated bullets replaced round balls, Purdey saw how these could be reduced in weight by hollowing out the nose. This resulted in higher velocities and when the hollow-nose bullet struck the target, it expanded violently. Purdey named it for the fast "Express" trains that were then revolutionizing travel in England.

This all occurred as Queen Victoria's consort, Prince Albert, was helping to make shooting ever more popular, and the trains themselves were making it easy for sportsmen to travel to Scotland for stag-stalking. Purdey's express rifles were in exactly the right place at exactly the right time. This development was the beginning of the debate over velocity and killing power that has continued in waves and phases to this very day, and is being argued in hunting magazines around the world.

In 1826, James Purdey left Princes Street and moved to 314½ Oxford Street. This was Joseph Manton's old premises in the highly fashionable and wealthy district of Mayfair near Buckingham Palace, so Purdey was obviously doing well. Two years later after four daughters his wife, Mary, gave birth to a son.

James the Younger, as he became known to the world at large, followed his father into the family business. Throughout his childhood he lived close by the shop, and was immersed in gunmaking; at the age of 14 he began his apprenticeship and completed it in 1850.

The very next year he married and had a son, James III, then later followed by Athol. James III would also go into the business but died of consumption at the age of 36. Eventually, James the Younger was succeeded by Athol Purdey. It was during this period that the company name became James Purdey & Sons, as it remains to this day.

By this time, Purdey was established at the pinnacle of the London gun trade. In 1833, in his famous *Notes to Young Sportsmen*, Col. Hawker noted Joseph Manton's bankruptcy and pronounced that the foremost position in the trade

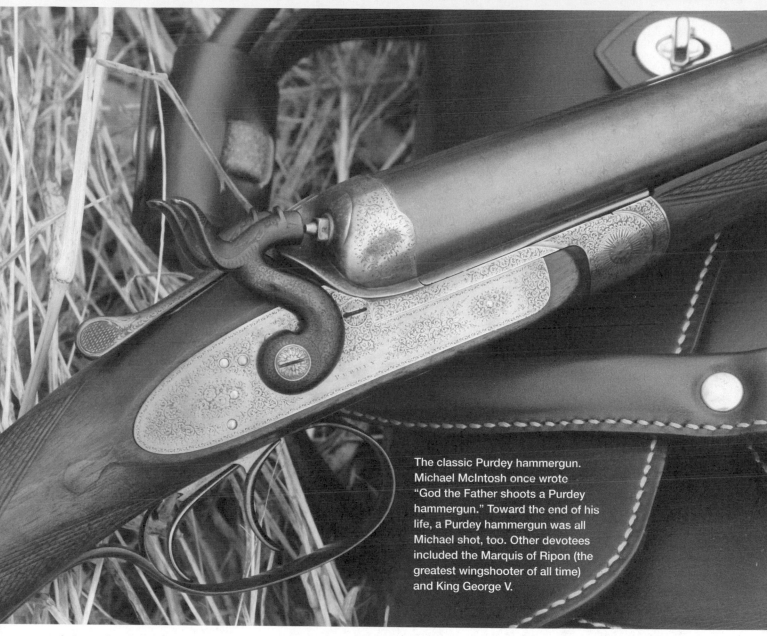

The classic Purdey hammergun. Michael McIntosh once wrote "God the Father shoots a Purdey hammergun." Toward the end of his life, a Purdey hammergun was all Michael shot, too. Other devotees included the Marquis of Ripon (the greatest wingshooter of all time) and King George V.

now belonged to James Purdey. In later years the company would adopt a policy of making only "best" guns, but in the early decades it produced a wide variety of pistols, shotguns and rifles. It also sold every type of shooting accessory including gun cases, powder flasks and shot belts.

As its reputation spread, it attracted business from the aristocracy. Donald Dallas wrote that Purdey's first royal client was the Duke of Gloucester, brother to King George IV, who in 1825 purchased a 16-bore percussion double gun. In 1838, having just ascended to the throne, Queen Victoria placed an order for a pair of pistols for presentation to the Imam of Muscat (a common diplomatic gesture) and two years later her husband,

Prince Albert, made the first of several purchases from Purdey.

Such affiliations further established James Purdey as one of London's premier gunmakers, but even such a stellar clientele could not guarantee indefinite success. Only two things could do that: Innovation and quality.

The company was fortunate in that both James the Founder and James the Younger were talented and inventive gunmakers, and the London trade was about to embark on a half-century that Donald Dallas later described as "the pursuit of perfection." It began in 1851 with the Great Exhibition of London, the first international trade show, held in the Crystal Palace. This was one of Prince Albert's inspirations and it was

an enormous success, drawing exhibits from all over the world.

French gunmaker Casimir Lefaucheux exhibited an early break-action gun. Joseph Lang, James Purdey's son-in-law, is credited with taking the idea and making the first English break-action, which in turn led to the explosion of innovation through the next 40 years.

James Purdey, however, was too shrewd a businessman and too aware of his stellar reputation to risk it immediately on untried technology. As he had with percussion systems 25 years earlier, Purdey continued with the tried-and-true, and watched developments. By the late 1850s it was obvious that the future lay not only in break-action guns, but with breechloaders generally, and that some sort of self-contained cartridge would eventually take over the gunmaking world.

As with percussion, between the Lefaucheux of 1851 and the final perfecting of centerfires in the 1860s lay a number of false starts and short-lived dead ends. These included the pinfire, which worked well but was soon improved upon, and various rimfire designs and paper cartridges.

Purdey steered a careful course. His first pinfire was sold in 1858, but there were considerable obstacles to overcome. It was one thing to embrace the concept of a break-action gun pivoting on a hinge, and quite another to design a system that could withstand the wear and tear of constant shooting, provide a gas seal at the breech, and be fast and convenient to operate.

In that same year James the Younger formally took over the company and immediately faced several difficulties. One was financial, probably due to the aristocracy's notoriously cavalier attitude to paying bills to tradesmen, the second was maintaining the company's dominance during a period of rapid technological change. James the Younger resolved both issues in one stroke.

One of the specific problems of break-action guns was finding a method of bolting them in place. In 1863, Purdey filed what became one of the most famous and lucrative gunmaking patents of all time: patent #1104, for a double underlug. The lugs (or lumps), protruding from the barrel flats pivot down into slots in the action bar and are locked in place by a sliding bolt.

Other systems were designed and adopted at the same time, and some proved quite successful. The Jones underlever, for example, came into wide use and was still made into the 1920s. It was immensely strong but slow to operate, requiring several distinct movements of the hands. Another approach was the rib extension and various designs were patented.

None of these, however, was as elegant, strong, and at the same time convenient, as the Purdey double underlug. This is still the pattern in use today for the vast majority of side-by-side doubles. Although Purdey himself designed a number of latches and levers to manipulate the bolt, it was William Middleditch Scott of Birmingham who invented what came to be known as the Scott spindle. This extended down through the breech behind the triggers, moving the bolt by means of a top lever on the tang. The Scott spindle became the dominant means of operating the Purdey bolt, and is also in use to this day.

Scott and Purdey formed a partnership, allowing each other free use of the other's patent, but each collecting royalties on the combination—Purdey in London, Scott in Birmingham. The royalties from this invention made James Purdey a wealthy man and placed the company on a firm financial footing.

The next major technological change in gunmaking after the general adoption of the centerfire cartridge in the 1860s was the transition from hammer guns to hammerless. Again, Purdey was cautious. There were questions to be answered, and here the choice was as much a matter of taste as anything else. Some shooters—including very prominent ones, such as the future King George V—preferred hammer guns long after the hammerless had become dominant.

Still, in an atmosphere of feverish change and intense competition, Purdey could not afford to fall behind or be seen as old-fashioned. We often forget how much the Victorians admired science, invention, advancement and progress.

A Purdey pinfire from early in the break-action era (1850s). This gun employs the Jones underlever bolting system. During this transitional period Purdey guns came in all shapes and configurations.

Frederick Beesley, the gunmaking genius who designed the Purdey self-opening action and was known as London's "inventor to the trade."

This was no less true of guns than of railroads, electricity and steamships.

In the case of shotguns, there was an additional impetus: The advent of the breechloader had made possible the first driven-bird shooting. Where before the standard method of wingshooting had been walking up birds with dogs, the speed of breechloading allowed the driving of birds to the guns. As driven shooting became almost a mania among the upper classes, so did the demand for guns that were ever faster in loading and reloading.

Every aspect of the game gun was open to improvement. Extractors gave way to ejectors, and speed and ease of opening the gun became important. Invention piled upon invention. So many different inventions and patents were filed between 1850 and 1890 that Crudgington and Baker filled two volumes with them (*The British Shotgun, Vol. 1, 1850-70*, and *Vol. 2, 1870-90*) and later added a third to cover everything in the next 120 years (1891 to 2011).

Theophilus Murcott patented the first "hammerless" gun in 1871. Of course, it was not really hammerless. The hammers were merely reshaped and concealed inside the action, and renamed "tumblers." Obviously, with the hammers out of reach, one of the priorities was developing a method of cocking them. Murcott used an underlever, but the one that became dominant, and remains so to this day, was using the fall of the barrels to apply leverage to cock the tumblers.

Until that method was developed, however, gunmakers tried other approaches. Self-cocking mechanisms had been invented for hammer guns and some of these were adapted to hammerless. A Purdey gunmaker named William Adams invented one underlever action in which the lever cocked the tumblers, and Purdey made some guns to this design. They also used other patents as they searched for one that was perfect. It finally came to them in 1880 in the

hands of Frederick Beesley, a mechanical genius and former Purdey employee who would become known as London's "inventor to the trade."

Frederick Beesley was one of those men who defy categorization, but it is not going too far to use the word genius. The hammerless action he invented and sold to Purdey in 1880 for £55 was so ingenious in its operation that it has since been incorrectly described even by writers familiar with it. In a nutshell, it was a hammerless, sidelock design in which the tumbler mainsprings provided the force to help open the gun as well as to power the tumbler. It was the earliest self-opener.

Four years later Beesley patented a second design in which he simplified the earlier one and rectified what he saw as some of its shortcomings. This later Beesley patent was used by Charles Lancaster, among others, and is among the finest gun designs of all time. It was adaptable to both boxlock and sidelock actions, and could be used with either a straight leaf spring or a V-spring. It never achieved the fame of the Purdey, however, and throughout his career as a gunmaker in London, Beesley's shop window bore the notation "inventor and patentee of Purdey's hammerless gun."

Since 1880, every side-by-side double made by James Purdey & Sons has been on the Beesley patent. It became one of the pillars that supported the firm through every economic and social

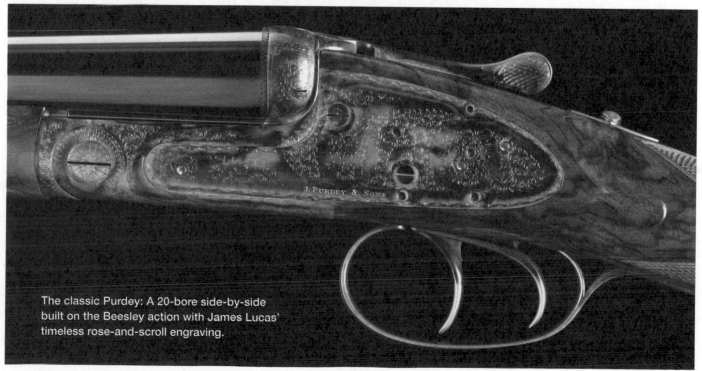

The classic Purdey: A 20-bore side-by-side built on the Beesley action with James Lucas' timeless rose-and-scroll engraving.

upheaval—turmoil that caused the demise of so many other fine London gunmakers.

An important quality of the Beesley action that is often ignored is its extraordinary durability, and the contribution this makes to the longevity of Purdey guns in general. A self-opener does not merely assist the shooter in opening the gun. It also keeps the action under tension when it is closed and absorbs some of the shock of firing. This helps prevent the action from working loose over time and is a major contributor to the Purdey reputation.

By 1881, Purdey was firmly established as one of the top firms in London. That same year, James Purdey undertook to move from his establishment on Oxford Street to a new building he had commissioned at the corner of South Audley and Mount Streets in Mayfair. The land was owned by the Duke of Westminster, then as now one of London's wealthiest landowners.

The resulting building, which the company still occupies, was described in an 1889 magazine article as a "palace among gunmakers," and certainly no other London gunmaker ever enjoyed a more elegant premises.

With its new home on South Audley Street, its new hammerless sidelock establishing a reputation as the best available, and the Purdey sons preparing to continue the family line, the firm was going into the last decades of the 19th century on a firm footing.

The final factor that helped to cement Purdey's position, beyond its mechanical excellence and prominent clientele, was in the ornamentation of its action. By the 1880s London gunmakers were differentiating themselves from their competitors, particularly in Birmingham, by the elegance and good taste of their lines and engraving. In a series of articles beginning in 1889 about London gunmakers in the periodical *Land and Water,* its editor, G.T. Teasdale-Buckell, referred to the "severely plain, Quaker-like quietness of style…a chaste correctness of taste taking the place of any sort of display" in a London gun, compared to the ornate showiness of "country-bred guns." In this, as in every other aspect of gunmaking, James Purdey was a leader.

Beginning in the 1850s, Purdey had developed what we now know as "rose and scroll" engraving, with fine scroll

The legendary Long Room, located upstairs at Audley House, is home to a wonderful collection of Purdey guns and historical artifacts. An invitation to visit the Long Room is prized even by royalty.

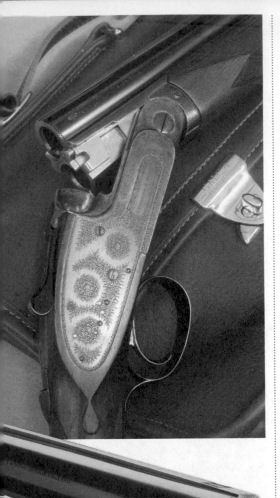

A Purdey over/under 12-bore with a single trigger, made to the Woodward patent. This is a favorite American shotgun configuration.

A new Purdey over/under 12-bore, on the Woodward patent. Over the last 65 years, Purdey has made some improvements to the Woodward action. This combination of game scenes and scroll is very striking on the wide over/under lockplate.

taking the place of the coarser scroll common in earlier guns. With the adoption of the Beesley action, Purdey's engravers were presented with a clean canvas of lock plates and the underside of the frame. James Lucas was Purdey's chief engraver and he is credited with the fine-scroll pattern that became a Purdey trademark. This style has been copied all over the world on all types of guns, and always with one goal: to show that this is a "fine" gun.

While other gunmakers might employ deep carving, game scenes and gold inlay to draw attention, Purdey was content to remain restrained, understated and tasteful—the formula dictated by Beau Brummel a half-century before. Purdey was not unique in having a hallmark engraving pattern. Other notable London companies including Thomas Boss, E.J. Churchill and John Rigby also had their own engraving patterns, and today we still see references to "Boss-style" or "Churchill-style" engraving. None of them, however, achieved the fame and widespread use of the Purdey pattern. In general, when a Spanish or Italian gunmaker wants to show which model is his best, he engraves it with Purdey scroll.

The Great War of 1914-18 put many London gunmakers out of business. It killed tens of thousands of men and irreparably damaged the landed class in England. The subsequent economic hardships, immediately after the war and then again in the Great Depression, culminating in the Second World War, changed English society and the London gunmaking trade almost beyond recognition. Throughout it all, James Purdey & Sons survived. They were able to do so for a number of reasons.

One of these was the fact that as old money faded away new money came along to replace it. After 1918, industrialists with new money took up shooting and knowing that a Purdey was "the best," felt they should shoot a Purdey to denote their status. As with Rolexes and Rolls-Royces, having a name in the stratosphere leads to sales far beyond just the knowledgeable buyers to include the upwardly mobile and social strivers.

This leads to a little known but very interesting side alley in Purdey history. One of their great rivals at the top of the trade for the better part of 75 years was James Woodward & Sons. Woodward was always a small company, but was known as "the gunmaker's gunmaker" because of the quality of its products. Serious, knowledgeable shooters bought Woodwards because of their quality, and shot them frequently and hard. As a result, one sees very few pristine Woodwards, although many of the approximately 5,000 guns and rifles made by the firm are still in existence—itself a tribute to their quality.

A Woodward, except among the cognoscenti, was not a status symbol. A Purdey however, was. Many Purdeys were purchased and then used a little or not at all, and kept purely for display. As a result, many Purdeys available today, out of the 30,000 or so the company has produced, are in beautiful condition. These naturally command a high premium. With Purdey, you do pay for the name, but you are also paying for the unswerving quality the name denotes.

After 1918, English gunmakers realized that their survival lay in courting the shooters of the newly wealthy New World. Americans liked over/unders and companies like Boss and Woodward had excellent over/unders to sell them. Although Purdey worked in this direction, its over/unders were not one of its successes. In 1949, after the ravages of the Blitz and the Second World War, the aging owner of Woodward sold his company to Purdey.

This is the only acquisition or merger Purdey has undertaken in 200 years, and happened solely in order to acquire the Woodward over/under pattern. It became the Purdey over/under, and remains so.

That, however, was the one major change that took place during the 20th century in terms of gun design or technological improvement. The company remained in family hands until 1946 when it was sold to Sir Hugh Seeley (Lord Sher-

A Purdey original, never done before, is this modern all-Damascus over/under built in 2014. With no engraving except the name, this extraordinary gun is decorated only by the natural pattern of its unique Damascus steel construction.

wood), and later in 1994 to Richemont, the Swiss luxury-goods conglomerate. Family involvement effectively ended in 1957 with the death of Tom Purdey. In 1995, Richard Purdey, great-grandson of Athol Purdey, was appointed chairman and he remained in office until 2014. He was succeeded by James Horne.

Today, Purdey remains one of the two major London gunmakers (the other is Holland & Holland) with a large factory and the means to train apprentices. It has adopted considerable modern manufacturing technology, but a great deal of hand-craftsmanship still goes into every Purdey. Many Purdey apprentices leave the company to go on their own after they complete their training, and they have become the backbone of the English gun trade. For this reason alone, Purdey and H&H are immensely valuable to the trade as a whole.

The new chairman, James Horne, took over at a time when Purdey, yet again, faces technological challenges on several fronts. His will be a balancing act between upholding the standards of the past and keeping Purdey relevant in a digital world of rapid change and outlandish fashions.

The company is continuing to adopt modern production methods wherever they can be used without compromising Purdey quality. It will undertake some groundbreaking projects, such as the "all Damascus" over/under that it produced in 2014. Recent new Purdey guns include the reintroduction of the Woodward side-by-side and original over/under, and a new Sporting Gun, as well as rifles – both side-by-side doubles and bolt actions.

None of these will be inexpensive, but no one would expect that. When asked to outline his goals for Purdey products, James Horne replied very simply: "Ultimately clients want craft, beauty and reliability and that is what we seek to provide."

In an article such as this it is possible to touch only the highlights of a fabled company that has been included in and the subject of several dozen books, including more than a few "complete histories."

Any company that survives for 200 years does so for a combination of reasons. Managing this feat in the social and financial upheaval of England since 1814 required business acumen, fine products and more than a little luck.

If there is one strand that runs throughout Purdey's history that accounts for its astonishing longevity and the continuing respect in which it is held, it is adherence to those principles of style and good taste established by Beau Brummell, developed by Joseph Manton, and carried on by the Purdey family, its engravers, and all the craftsmen who combined to make every Purdey a graceful, stylish work of both art and function.

Regarding style, the great former editor of *Gun Digest*, John T. Amber, stated confidently in the 1970 edition (a time when bad taste effused everything from guns to cars to haircuts) "These things too will pass away—or so I keep telling myself!

"Styles and fashions change, though it may take years, but I'm confident that these glittering, glaring guns will eventually disappear—at least in good part—leaving the classic, traditional style once again pre-eminent in the field."

Amber had just taken delivery of a custom-made Perazzi over/under. Perazzi was then a new name in shotguns, made instantly famous by its victories at the 1968 Olympics. Amber's new Perazzi had the graceful lines of a Woodward, and its darkly blued receiver was decorated with Purdey-style, elegant, rose-and-scroll engraving. Daniele Perazzi aspired to be the best, and to be the best, he knew he had to be as good as a Purdey.

It has been that way for 200 years, and there is no sign that will change anytime soon.

The Search For
THE ULTIMATE
SINGLE ACTION

THE NEVER-ENDING PURSUIT OF THE PERFECT PEACEMAKER

This is where the search for the ultimate single action started, with an Ainsworth-inspected U.S. Cavalry issued Colt Single Action Army.

Story and photos by Rick Hacker

It has been said that you can't improve upon perfection. After all, if something is perfect there is nowhere else for it to go. But then again, we are often told that nothing is perfect – everything can be improved upon. Both of these conflicting philosophies certainly come into play in the case of the Colt Single Action Army.

To my mind – and for many others – this 143-year-old design is the epitome of what a sixgun should be: an ergonomically perfect plow-handled grip that flows into the hand, perfectly positioning the barrel into a line of sight that almost metaphysically aligns the gun to the target; a gracefully sculpted hammer that curls under the thumb, requiring just

the slightest twitch of a muscle to cock the gun. I'm sure those thoughts — or some similar —were shared by Colt Patent Firearms factory superintendent William Mason and one of his engineers, Charles B. Richards, when they perfected (there's that word again!) the "Colt New Model Army Metallic Cartridge Revolving Pistol."

But the factory-designed Model P didn't just appear. It had its embryonic beginnings with the Colt Paterson in 1836, which subsequently developed an attached under-barrel rammer and then a triggerguard and some bulk to transform it into the Colt Walker, and then the First, Second and Third Model Dragoons. From there, thanks to better metallurgy, they were scaled down from horse pistols (so called because they were so heavy they had to be carried in saddle pommels on horseback) to belt and holster pistols, most notably the Models 1851 Navy and 1860 Army. The latter of which was a gun that belied its 19th century heritage by appearing as if it had been designed in the 1920s, were it not for its cap and ball countenance.

With the era of the self-contained metallic cartridge and the expiration of Rollin White's patent, which permitted a cylinder to be bored straight through and thus facilitating loading from the breech end, a brief period of cartridge conversions gave way to the Colt Model 1871-72 Open Top. This was a .44-caliber

Above: The 1871-72 Open Top was the direct inspiration for the SAA. This replica Open Top with exhibition engraving and premium walnut grips was custom ordered for the author from Cimarron Firearms.

The dovetailed rear sights on this Bisley Flattop Target Model in .44 S&W was one of Colt's attempts to improve upon their Single Action Army and make it more appealing to shooters. One of only 976 guns produced (and only 64 in .44 S&W caliber), it was shipped to Montgomery Ward in Chicago on Nov. 17, **1898.** Photo courtesy of Justin Davis of Mid-Star Firearms, Middleton, Idaho.

The original owner of this Bisley Flattop Target Model, chambered in .44 S&W and one of only 976 guns produced, replaced the original adjustable nickel silver front sight blade (which may have been lost or damaged) with a cruder one made of ivory. One wonders how this affected accuracy.

Photo courtesy Justin Davis of Mid-Star Firearms.

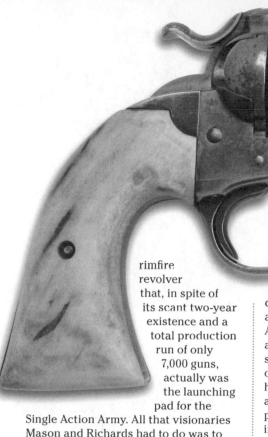

The Colt Bisley was originally called The Model of 1894, but was renamed after its successful showing at the annual British target shooting competitions in Bisley, England. It too, was an attempt by Colt to improve upon the original SAA design.

rimfire revolver that, in spite of its scant two-year existence and a total production run of only 7,000 guns, actually was the launching pad for the Single Action Army. All that visionaries Mason and Richards had to do was to adapt the topstrap concept from Colt's 1855 Sidehammer and stretch it across the 1871-72's cylinder (which they then fluted to reduce weight), and borrow the internal lockwork, plow-handled pistol grip and 7½-inch barrel length from the immensely popular 1851 Navy and – voila! The Colt Single Action Army was born.

Originally the SAA was to be a .44-caliber revolver following the Army's preference for the 1860, their official sidearm at the time. But the government's last-minute insistence on a .45-caliber chambering only added to the Model P's claim as the ultimate sixgun of its era, as the .45 Long Colt (as it was initially called to differentiate it from the shorter .45 cartridge being used concurrently in the Army's Smith & Wesson revolvers) gave it the perfect (oops, there's that word again) combination of balance and firepower. Weighing in at 2½ pounds unloaded, the .45-caliber SAA proved to be the ultimate pairing, as its cartridge packed 40 grains of black powder that propelled a 255-grain soft lead bullet out the barrel at 810 feet per second, and quickly proved itself to be a formidable man-stopper.

Following a precedent set by other Colts before it, the Single Action Army was soon enthusiastically adopted by any serious pistolero who could find and afford one. Contrary to popular belief, these guns didn't suddenly and magically appear all across the country. With the U.S. Army first in the receiving line, it took awhile for the Colt SAA to fill the call of supply and demand. But eventually the old Thumbuster made its way into the hands and holsters of good men and bad, and proving the mantra that "nothing is perfect," the factory heeded the almost immediate call for variations. For those finding fault with the Model P's 7½-inch barrel length, a 5½-inch version was brought out in 1875. To satisfy those wanting more compactness and greater speed in getting the gun into action, a 4¾-inch barrel was introduced four years later. To appease all of those individuals in between, special-order barrel lengths ranging from 2-18 inches were produced, albeit in limited numbers.

Likewise, new calibers were quickly added, the most notable being (in order of popularity) .44-40, .38-40 and .32-20, all three of which permitted the same loadings in either Colt Single Actions or the equally famous Winchester '73, and later the Model 1892 Winchester and Marlin lever actions. But the Model P proved so adaptable that it was eventually chambered for a total of 41 different cartridges, ranging from .22 rimfire to .476 Eley.

Still, the gun wasn't perfect. Otherwise, why was the cylinder base pin changed from a frame-mounted screw to an easier-to-use spring-loaded pushpin in 1892? In retaliation to the shallow groove along the topstrap that served as the SAA's rear sight, from 1888-1896 a total of 925 flattop Target models were produced, sporting a dovetailed notched rear sight that could be drifted for windage, along with a bead and post front sight. Further indication that the Peacemaker needed to be adapted for serious shooters was the fact that in 1894 a total of 976 Bisley Flattop Target Models were manufactured, not to mention the Bisley Model itself, which was a fixed-sight target model that featured an underswept grip so the balance of the gun would "hang" better in the hand, combined with a lowered hammer spur for easier cocking. The only other adaptations that a shooter could make outside the factory was the aftermarket filing down of the overly high front sight, in order to raise the point of impact on a gun that traditionally shot low.

Nonetheless, by the time the 20th century rolled around, it could pretty well be assumed that the Single Action Army, in all its variations, had finally reached perfection. Adding to this assumption was the fact that semiautomatics and double-action revolvers had now unseated the outmoded Peacemaker in the popularity polls. Aside from occasional special order factory engraved and plated guns, the old Model P had just about reached its zenith as a rugged, time-tested handgun that could take abuse, still function with half of its parts broken or missing, and easily able to keep its shots within a pie plate-size circle at 25 yards. But that was about it, thus relegating the Model P to the holsters of outdoorsmen and cowboys who wanted to pack a no-nonsense handgun, as well as for those who were still drawn by its nostalgic link to the Old West.

But things began to change after World War I. Seemingly from out of nowhere, but spurred on by a growing interest in competitive pistol shooting, a new posse was now riding to the SAA's rescue – or rather, its reformation. A small but growing coterie of serious shooters began looking at the Single Action Army not so much for what it had been, but for what it could be. One of the first to rec-

Ted Keith holds his father's famous Keith No. 5 at the James D. Julia pre-auction exhibition held at the Las Vegas Antique Arms Show in January 2015. Just before this photo was taken Keith nonchalantly gave the gun a deft spin, demonstrating its superb balance.

Elmer Keith led the pack when it came to searching for the perfect single action. Many of his innovative guns were auctioned off for his family in March 2015 by James D. Julia, Inc.

ognize the accuracy potential of the old Peacemaker was a San Francisco, Calif., gunsmith named Dean King. His now long gone D.W. King Gun Sight Co. at 171-3 Second Street began outfitting SAA's with full-length ventilated barrel ribs, much in the manner of the future Colt Python. Coinciding with this and affixed to guns as part of the King ventilated rib or simply banded separately onto the barrel, was a variety of ramp front sights. The most notable sight featured a small round mirror inset into a recessed slope to reflect natural light up onto the front sight blade.

Moreover, addressing the Peacemaker's largely inadequate fixed sights, King developed a "micrometer click adjustable" rear sight for the SAA, which was affixed into the back portion of the frame, just forward of the ham-

mer. The hammer itself didn't escape King's analytical scrutiny either, for one of his 1930s catalogs shows a King's "Cockeyed" Hammer. This reshaped hammer spur had the bulk of its re-checkered surface area extending either to the right or left depending on the shooter's preference, thereby enabling the shooter – according to the catalog – to cock the hammer without having to shift his grip on the gun. Others soon copied King's barrel ribs and front sight variations, and they are occasionally encountered on guns from that era today, although I have not come across many "Cockeyed" hammer revisions.

While most collectors cringe at these early 20th century modifications that were done to First Generation Colts, they provide us with some notable SAA variations, and serve as a reminder that

back in those post WWI years a First Generation Colt (although they obviously weren't called that back then) were simply thought of as "working guns." Nor were any of these modifications inexpensive; in the 1930s, when a new-in-the-box Colt Single Action Army had a catalog price of $37.50, the King Gun Sight Company charged $20 for one of their vent ribs. To be sure, you had to be pretty serious about your shooting to even consider such modifications. *(Editor's note: For more on the guns of the King Gun Sight Company, see the article by Charlie Petty in this edition.)*

One such individual, the unavowed leader in the search for the perfect single action, was the late Elmer Keith, a rancher, shooter, big-game guide and trend-setting gun writer who spent a lot of years burning a lot of powder in and around his ranch on the North Fork of the Salmon River near Salmon, Idaho, to try to bring the single action as close to perfection as he could get it. Although Elmer owned and shot many different firearms, he was an unabashed fan of the Single Action Army. At the time of his death in 1984, more than half of the 56 guns in his collection were single actions.

"Dad wasn't big on semiautomatic pistols," said his 79-year-old son, Ted Keith. "'With single actions,' he said, you just cock it and shoot one time and that was it.'" I interviewed Ted at the 2015 Las Vegas Antique Arms Show. It was there that Elmer's collection was on display prior to being auctioned off for the family on March 15-16 of that year by the noted auction house, James D. Julia, Inc.

As early as April 1929, Elmer was writing in *American Rifleman* about Colt employee and famed trick shooter John Henry "Fitz" FitzGerald gently twisting the barrels on Single Action Armies to adjust the front sight blades for windage, and of his friend, S.H. Croft reshaping the grips and tuning the actions.

"The S.A.A. is one of the best-balanced and easiest handled of 6-guns," Elmer wrote in that article. "The regular S.A.A. backstrap, while by far the best shaped of any on the market, and the only one for the slip gun, does not come up as high in back as it should to completely fill the hand. By bending and welding the Bisley backstrap to the same general contour as the S.A.A., and combining with the S.A.A. guard and front strap, we have the No. 3 grip (referring to an earlier Croft-designed

The Grover Improved No. 5 requires a larger-than-normal holster due to its thicker frame. This leather rig was made custom for the author by the old George Lawrence Company.

grip). Needless to say, after playing with Croft's guns for a while I decided to have one of my S.A.A. guns worked over to incorporate some of Croft's improvements, with a few ideas of my own thrown in."

Starting with a standard Colt Peacemaker chambered in .44 Special, Elmer's "few ideas" included involving the talents of a number of noted gunsmiths of the day, not the least of whom was R.F. Sedgley, who welded up the frame and turned the sixgun into a flattop. A sturdier V-shape mainspring, strengthened cylinder locking base pin, sloped Bisley-style hammer, wide checkered trigger, and a greatly beefed-

The elongated and strengthened cylinder base pin of the Keith No. 5, just one of the many improvements Elmer Keith made on the 1873 Colt SAA design. Note the pivoting locking latch for the pin on the frame.

The rear sights of the Keith No. 5 are probably from the D.W. King Gun Sight Company. Note the refitted Colt Bisley hammer.

Above: This was another one of Keith's quests to build a perfect sixgun. It was originally a .45-caliber U.S. Cavalry Colt, with the barrel shortened to 4¾ inches and the frame polished and reblued, though the cylinder still bears the Army's "DFC" inspector's marks. Note the slip-on front sight and the large Bridgeport-style hammer screw for attaching the gun to the Jesse Thompson S.A. Colt Belt Clip on the tooled money belt.

Above right: Proving the practicality of Keith's design, the author (left) dispatched this 350-pound Texas wild boar with his Grover Improved No 5.

Below and opposite page: A 7½-inch barrel .44 Special SAA with Keith lowered and widened hammer spur, and a King's adjustable rear sight arrangement. The barrel shows a King's barrelband with a Keith-designed sighting bar calibrated for his long-range shooting. This is a classic case of Elmer's search for the perfect single action.

up hybrid Bisley backstrap and trigger-guard added to the gun's individualist appearance. Elmer also added King's micro adjustable rear sights and a Patridge-style front sight with a screw in the base that adjusted the blade for elevation. Outfitted with walrus ivory grips (which shrank over the years and were eventually changed to "pre-ban" elephant ivory) and later engraved, Keith referred to this gun as the No. 5, as it was the fifth culmination in his series of cutting edge sixguns. It

has since become the most famous of his experiments in perfecting the single action. Keith called it "the last word" in his attempts to perfect the Single Action Army.

But, perhaps not quite. More than 50 years later, the late Bill Grover of the no-longer-existing Texas Longhorn Arms Company not only duplicated the Keith No. 5, he attempted to improve upon it. Appropriately enough, he called it the Grover Improved No. 5 and chambered it in .44 Magnum, a cartridge that Keith helped create. In addition, he used coil springs. He also gave the Grover Improved No. 5 a unique twist: he made it a reversed mirror image of the original, in the somewhat speculative belief that Sam Colt was left handed and therefore, the Single Action Army was designed for a left-handed shooter. The fact that Sam Colt died in 1862, 10 years before the SAA was created obviously had no bearing for Grover. Thus, the loading gate of Grover's gun was on the left side of the recoil shield and the ejector rod angled to the left side of the barrel. This permitted the Grover Improved No. 5 to be loaded and unloaded without the gun having to leave the right hand by simply flipping open the loading gate with the right hand's thumb and operating the ejector rod with the left hand. I was presented with one of the first guns. After finding it not as awkward to load and unload as one might think, and marveling at its 50-yard accuracy, proceeded to ax a 350-pound wild boar with it at extremely close range during a rather adventurous hunt in the thick brushy hill country near Llano, Texas. But most importantly it gave me the firsthand experience to realize that Elmer knew what he was doing as far as the overall design concept was concerned, especially when I actually got to handle the original No. 5 at the Las Vegas Antique Arms Show.

Not all of Elmer's other single action modifications were as dramatic as the No. 5, but were trendsetting nonetheless, and consisted of folding leaf rear sights and barrel-banded Patridge sights, almost all designed for long-range shooting. These guns were sold for astronomical prices at the James D. Julia auction, which is interesting because back when Elmer was rightfully boasting about dropping a deer at 600 yards with a handgun, very few people understood what he was doing. But times were changing, especially after World War II and Colt's ill-fated decision not to resume production of the SAA.

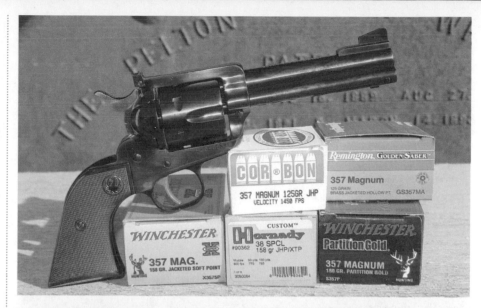

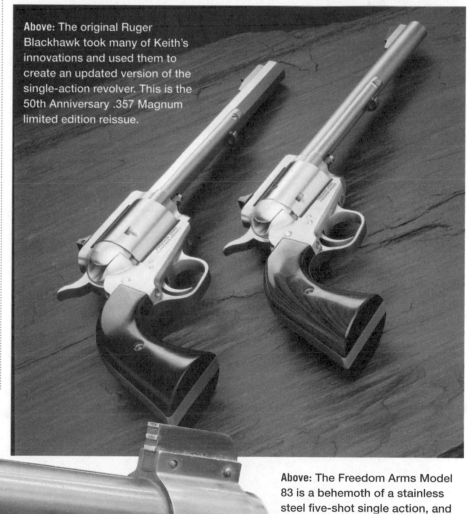

Above: The original Ruger Blackhawk took many of Keith's innovations and used them to create an updated version of the single-action revolver. This is the 50th Anniversary .357 Magnum limited edition reissue.

Above: The Freedom Arms Model 83 is a behemoth of a stainless steel five-shot single action, and it comes with optional octagon barrel and adjustable sights. It's chambered in hard-hitting calibers that include the .454 Casull and the .500 Wyoming Express.
Photo courtesy of Freedom Arms.

The limited-edition Lipsey's Shopkeeper was the distributor's version of an improved stainless steel Ruger New Bearcat, with shortened barrel and ejector, and birds-head grips. The gun quickly sold out and is no longer produced.

The author's attempt at finding the perfect single action, as built for him by Bill Oglesby of Oglesby & Oglesby. This Ruger New Model Super Blackhawk in .44 Magnum features, among many things, case-hardened hammer and frame, high-visibility front sight insert and exclusive one-piece Ivorite grips.

A lifelong fan of the single action, the author found the Lipsey's limited edition Ruger New Model Blackhawk in .44 Special to be on his list for a "perfect" SA.

"Colt wasn't that interested in bringing back the old guns like the single action," recalls Ted. "But (Bill) Ruger would listen to dad. And he told Bill, you just bring them old guns out, sixguns, Dragoons, whatever, and make them with better steel and put coil springs in instead of flat springs, and adjustable rear sights, because you can't shoot without an adjustable sight – at least not accurately."

The result, of course, was the Ruger Blackhawk, which first came out in 1955 and in its own way has become as famous as the Colt Single Action Army. Adroitly chambered in the more power-ful .357 Magnum instead of the legendary

.45 Colt, and made with 4140 chrome molybdenum steel, with a one-piece cast aluminum triggerguard and backstrap assembly, coil mainspring, dramatically beefed up topstrap, and a micro click-adjustable rear sight teamed with a Baughman-style ramp front sight, this was indeed the modern interpretation of many of Elmer Keith's single-action experimentations. A spring-loaded, frame-mounted firing pin and Nylok screws to do away with the Colt's habit of "shooting loose" completed the Ruger's package.

But Bill Ruger wasn't through with his own quest for the perfect single

action. A clamoring for more power resulted in a .44 Magnum chambering, which in 1959 became the Super Blackhawk, sporting elongated grips, heftier frame and nonfluted cylinder. Then came a redefinition of the past with the Bisley models. In 1973, safety concerns turned the entire Blackhawk series into "New Model" Blackhawks, sporting never-before-heard-of transfer bars that made it safe to carry six rounds in a single action for the first time. Had the perfect sixgun finally been achieved?

Some folks, like Wayne Baker and Dick Casull who founded Freedom

Arms in 1978, didn't think so. Their extremely well-built five and six-shot single actions are noted for being chambered in thundering cartridges and are, in many respects, custom guns with a variety of options. For example, the Freedom Arms Model 83 is a behemoth of a stainless steel five-shot single action and it comes with optional octagon barrel and adjustable sights, and is chambered in boulder-bashers like the .454 Casull and the newer .500 Wyoming Express, which I saw take down an American bison in the hands of company honcho Bob Baker. Their smaller (i.e., standard

The author found Colt's reissue of the New Frontier in .44 Special – Elmer Keith's favorite cartridge – to be another viable candidate for the "perfect single action."

portioned) Model 97 is, to my mind, much more user friendly as far as size and weight are concerned. Though it can still digest most of the magnum pistol cartridges as well as some of the big boys like the .475 Linebaugh, which I think is a bit much for a handgun this size, unless you have hands and wrists like The Incredible Hulk. But hey, that's my opinion as a guy with medium-size hands who once put a Butch Cassidy-type gash in my forehead by not maintaining an extra-firm hold on one of these hand cannons stoked with .454 Casulls. Like jumping off a skyscraper, that's something you only do once.

Interestingly, in its search for single-action perfection, Cimarron Firearms has just come out with a compilation of ideas built around the company's standard Italian-made sixguns, most notably The Thunderer. This gun comes with a tuned action, short-stroke hammer (an idea Keith and his cronies experimented with back in the 1920s) and a wider, lowered hammer spur. Cimarron's newest variation of this – called the Short Stroke – is made by Pieta and is available in .357 Magnum or .45 Colt, sports an elongated 1860 Army style checkered grip and 4¾-inch octagon barrel. To be honest, the octagon barrel is the least practical feature of this gun, but it does make it look businesslike and very cool. Perhaps they should have called it The Hired Gun.

Over the years other innovative guns and gunsmithing techniques have emerged in the constant quest to create the perfect single action. Bill Oglesby of Oglesby & Oglesby in Springfield, Ill., (217/487-7100 – no website) began turning out Ruger Blackhawks with cylinders that rotate backwards and hammers that function as both New Model and Old Model guns. Scalloped recoil shields, lift-out simultaneous ejecting cylinders, and

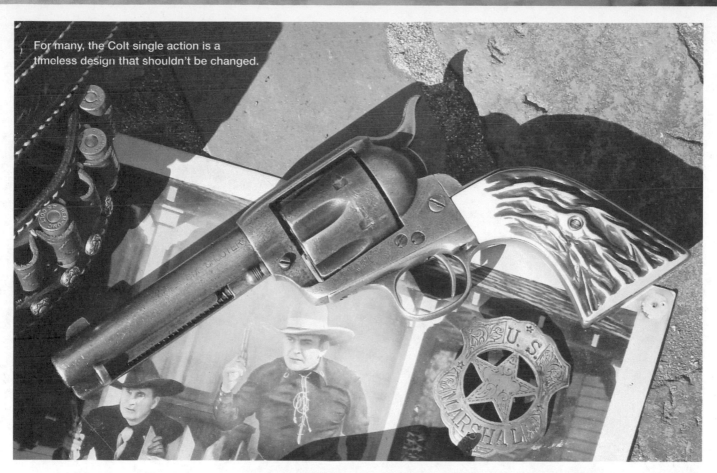

For many, the Colt single action is a timeless design that shouldn't be changed.

recontoured hammers and frames are just a few of the many options offered by Hamilton S. Bowen of Bowen Classic Arms (www.bowenclassicarms. com). John Gallagher of John Gallagher Firearms (www.gallagherfirearms. com) can rebore your .357 Magnum Blackhawk into a .44 Special or turn your sixshooter into a fiveshooter, among other things.

Yet not to be lost among this ongoing plethora of new and improved single actions is the fact that not only did Colt – finally recognizing a good thing when they had it – reintroduce their original Single Action Army in 1955, but even after various interruptions, this legendary gun is still in the line. What is even more interesting is the fact that Colt has now brought back the New Frontier – a Single Action Army with adjustable sights that was introduced in 1961 and then went out of production a few decades later. However, in 2012 it reemerged in limited numbers, but fortunately for us serious shootists it was chambered not only in .45 Colt, but also in Elmer Keith's favorite cartridge, the .44 Special. If anything, the Colt New Frontier in .44 Special is today's out-of-the-box version of many of the

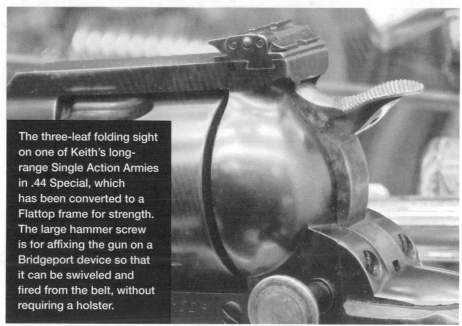

The three-leaf folding sight on one of Keith's long-range Single Action Armies in .44 Special, which has been converted to a Flattop frame for strength. The large hammer screw is for affixing the gun on a Bridgeport device so that it can be swiveled and fired from the belt, without requiring a holster.

innovations that Elmer and his followers were experimenting with back in the early 20th century.

One wonders what Elmer, were he still with us, would do with the well-built and ruggedly handsome Colt New Frontier today. First, I suspect he might opt for

the extra $150 Colt factory action job (yes, they still offer this service). Let's see… then he might lower the hammer spur, shorten the hammer throw and crown the barrel…

Thus, the search for the perfect single action never ends.

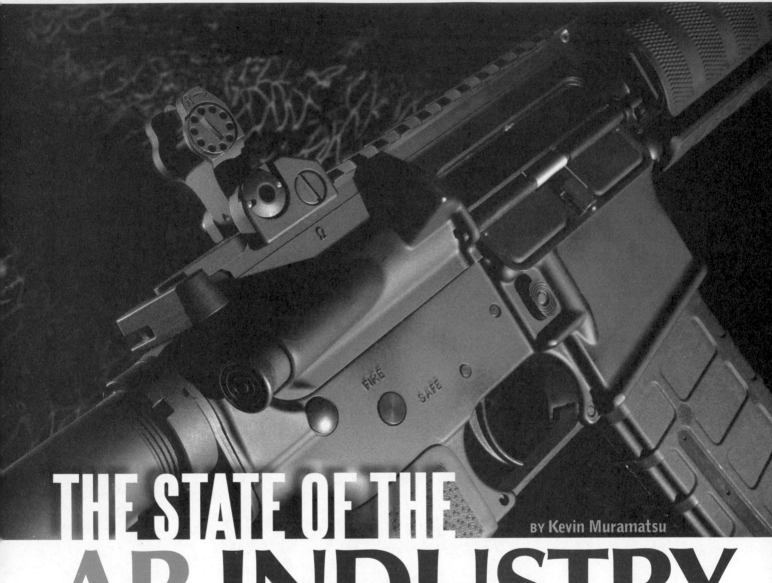

THE STATE OF THE
AR INDUSTRY

BY **Kevin Muramatsu**

A WRITER/DEALER/GUNSMITH PERSPECTIVE

ver the last two election cycles we have seen at least two large-scale buying frenzies (for lack of a better term) in the firearms industry. The first can be directly attributed to the first election of President Obama to the highest office in the nation. Based upon statements that firmly placed him in the "not-friendly-to-ARs" spectrum of firearms politics, Barack Obama's 2008 election spurred the first example of what amounted mostly to panic buying.

In the fortunately errant belief that doom-bringing legislation would be forthcoming the day after the inauguration, the sales of firearms in general, and in MSR's (the shorter way to say "modern sporting rifles") in particular, skyrocketed. We should perhaps examine a little bit of the background to this issue to fully place into perspective what "skyrocketing" means in this case.

After the Clinton "assault weapon" ban expired in 2004, the AR market started to really grow. While the market existed prior

to the expiration, the exploration into the accessory market was limited to relatively few companies. Most people who owned the rifles had to settle for the politically correct versions that manufacturers produced to adhere to the law in effect up to that point. But the law then did expire and companies began to experiment in earnest with concepts designed to enhance the function, appearance, ergonomics and utility of the AR-15 platform.

Fast forward to 2008. In only four years the spectrum of rifles built to the AR-15 pattern had exploded, with the alphabet companies (such as Armalite, Bushmaster, Colt, DPMS, Eagle Arms) being joined by previously unknown entities, and even businesses formerly associated strictly with handguns, such as Wilson Combat and Les Baer. While the production of other firearms receivers such as 1911 frames had existed for some time, the production of AR receivers, in short order, dwarfed any other firearm receiver and the companies manufacturing these receivers started popping up out of nowhere. Many weren't even firearms companies up until that point.

People realized that for less than 200 bucks you could purchase the beginnings of a very good rifle and you

The "assault rifle" ban affected mostly the front of the rifle. There are no muzzle threads, muzzle device or bayonet lug on the gun. It's a good thing, since thousands more would have been killed in road rage incidents if they had been present.

could at any time in the future complete the build on your own time, at home, at your own pace. Small-frame receivers, the AR-15 type, are made by well over 100 different companies. Not even close to all of them produce entire rifles, though many do, on scales small and large. I realize that many readers already know this, but please bear with me as I unpack this.

At this point the accessories and upgrading support structure really came into its own. I can't really pinpoint the first company or companies that definitively started it but I can narrow it down to several that bear some recognition. Magpul Industry's first product was the appropriately named Magpul, a loop that fit around a magazine base and made them easier to pull from a pouch or the rifle. It was one of the first widely sold AR accessories and I'm certain the first

related to AR magazines. From that first product grew the entire Magpul product line which, when multiple colors are included, incorporates over 500 different products ranging from magazines and associated extras through stocks, handguards, apparel and even smartphone covers.

Other companies such as Knight's Armament Company, Surefire and Yankee Hill Manufacturing were later joined by others such as Samson, LaRue, Midwest Industries, Troy Industries, and many more to offer for public consumption a diverse assortment of free-floating handguard tubes, be they smooth, four railed, one railed, or whatever seemed likely to create a demand. Pistol grips also emerged that in this author's opinion were far superior to the mil-spec models that for so long were the only options.

From early on, even back into the ban period, companies such as JP Enterprises and Accuracy Speaks were in differing ways working on refining not just the external appearance of the rifles, but also attempting (with great success, I might add) and refining and improving the function, accuracy and "feel" of the AR. An already inherently accurate

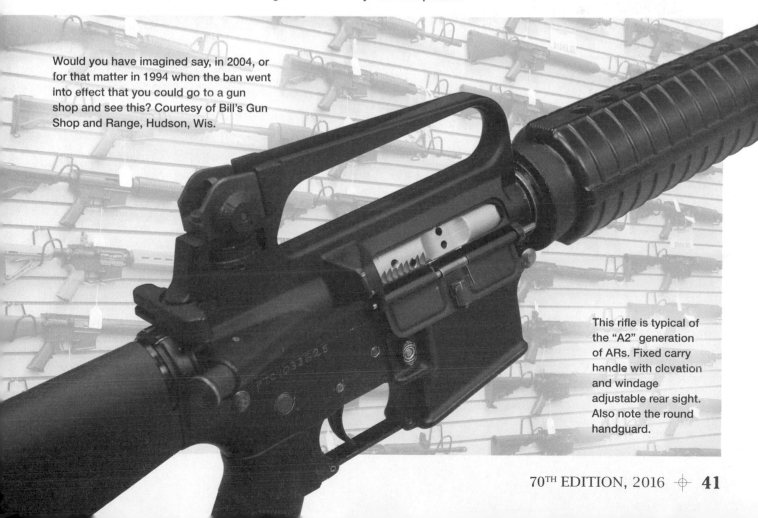

Would you have imagined say, in 2004, or for that matter in 1994 when the ban went into effect that you could go to a gun shop and see this? Courtesy of Bill's Gun Shop and Range, Hudson, Wis.

This rifle is typical of the "A2" generation of ARs. Fixed carry handle with elevation and windage adjustable rear sight. Also note the round handguard.

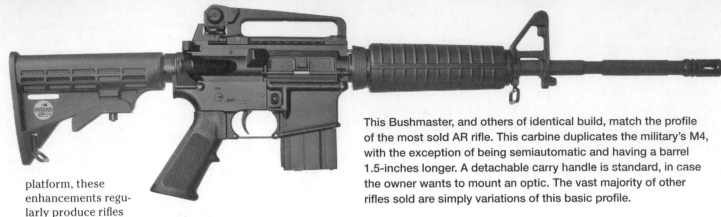

This Bushmaster, and others of identical build, match the profile of the most sold AR rifle. This carbine duplicates the military's M4, with the exception of being semiautomatic and having a barrel 1.5-inches longer. A detachable carry handle is standard, in case the owner wants to mount an optic. The vast majority of other rifles sold are simply variations of this basic profile.

platform, these enhancements regularly produce rifles that shoot inside a dime at 100 yards, are ergonomically and cosmetically superior to the standard factory makes, and have recoil impulses that are so slight that no eye-flinching occurs, allowing the shooter to easily observe the bullet impact, even at the shortest of ranges, whether looking through open sights or a riflescope. Rifles, parts and the concepts incorporated in rifles pioneered by these companies, and a select few others, have allowed them to completely dominate the several competitive shooting sports in which ARs are commonly used.

By 2008, every possible concept of AR usage or upgrading seemed to have been explored; even AR pistols in both small frame and large frame (AR-10, LR-308/SR25, the .308s) were in production in many places. The average price for a starter AR-15, like an M4 clone from one of the alphabet companies was in the $900-1,000 range. The nicer and more refined stuff from the smaller "boutique" companies usually started in the low $2,000s, and some companies like Colt and Knight's that placed a high value on their names, priced their slightly superior M4 clones 30-40 percent higher than the other alphabet companies. M4s became the norm. Twenty-inch barrels became a thing of the past or the stuff of the varmint hunter or the nostalgic. Some progress was made making them more reliable, notably moving the gas system to a mid-length configuration, but the majority of rifles continued to be some variation of the M4 style, with collapsible stock, 16-inch barrel and detachable carry handle or flip-down rear sight (if it had either at all).

This was how it was and everybody made guns and made money selling them, and the consumer base was quite happy with what was being made and what was available, with new things continuing to appear on almost a weekly basis. Then came the 2008 election year.

"Obama's gonna ban guns!!!" was the fighting cry and to a great degree manufacturers were caught off-guard, though it's questionable if there was anything that they could actually do to mitigate the coming shortage in advance. As soon as it was clear that Senator Mc-Cain was hopelessly behind, the buying surge began in earnest. Within only a couple of weeks there wasn't an AR left on the shelves in any store you should care to name. The rifles themselves, for the first time, were now selling at the Manufacturer's Suggested Retail Price (MSRP, which as everyone knows, is in reality a joke, "suggested" being the key word). No, that's understating things.

A rough evolutionary ladder is displayed here in the form of AR-15 bolts. On the bottom is a standard, boring normal factory bolt. This is what we started with, have started with for decades, and is likely to be what we start with for decades to come. Above it is the same thing, but with chrome plating, which has been around for a century. Then we have a low-mass carrier by JP Enterprises. While JP was the first to introduce this by many years, other manufacturers are exploring the low-mass concept. Then we have a normal-mass JP carrier, but unlike the standard carrier it has a QPQ finish, a very hard, high-lubricity oxidation, much like the Tenifer we find on Glock pistols. The second from the top, appearing to be a little yellowish, is a new generation of Nickel Boron plating from WMD Guns. Nickel Boron is harder than Chromium, has a higher lubricity, and when purchased from WMD is highly polished as well. Finally at the top is an example of an excellently made carrier used in a piston-operated rifle, this one from Adams Arms.

They were selling for well over MSRP and 30-round or greater capacity magazines saw a similar increase in price and shortage of availability.

The FBI reported that background checks were far higher than in previous years. Retailers reported far greater AR sales in one month than in the entire previous year. The usual frantic fear mongering of blood in the streets and Old West shootouts came to naught. Ultimately, it took about a year to catch everything back up and by the middle of 2009, with no significant anti-gun legislation appearing, the guns and mags were again plentiful (perhaps too much so from a retailer's perspective), and things settled back down to almost normal.

Almost, until the 2012 election year. Now, this is the beginning of the current state of affairs that you are really reading this article to learn about. As it should by now be clear, even to the least informed, the firearms industry and the political process have become intricately connected and will continue to be integrated for the foreseeable future. There are few issues that are as politically divisive as the right to keep and bear arms, and unfortunately the current times seem to focus squarely on the "assault weapons," a category in which those who would limit that right include many firearms of the AR series. The fallacies behind that term should be well known, but I don't want to get sidetracked because that is an article in and of itself.

Big money is injected into the gun

debate, mostly in the form of publicity and the marketing of ideals and solutions intended to address legislation or to elect or prevent the election of certain public figures. It should be noted that the anti-gun money tends to come from a very few, very wealthy elitists and celebrities like Mike Bloomberg, Warren Buffet, Bill Gates and George Soros, while the pro-gun money tends to come in much smaller packets from the hundreds of thousands of citizens who can't afford the private armed security enjoyed by their opponents.

One of the givens in the U.S. political system is that the nature of the Presidential term limit has the side effect of encouraging the sitting president, after he has been re-elected, to go for broke promoting policies and legislation that he might like to see implemented, particularly if it is not publically popular, and based purely on the political ideology to which he aligns, because he need not fear being fired from his job. He can't run again anyway, so why not? Well, this realization formed a strong undercurrent for the whole of 2012 and running up to the election. Sales increased, and anticipation mounted. At this point, the Sandy Hook school mass murder was perpetrated. The gun-control wing almost experienced an orgasm as they began to shamelessly use this event to push for more gun control (which would have had little or no effect), which was again focused on AR-style rifles (one of which was used as the murder weapon) and certain

This Cobalt Kinetics upper receiver has an extra forward assist. Both buttons also work as bolt releases. This is the kind of innovation seen in the last couple of years, attempting to make the rifle more user-friendly. This kind of innovation however, comes with a cost.

This rifle made by Cobalt Kinetics looks pretty radical (figuratively and literally). It is a mirror-polished piece of art and would be at home on any rock album cover. Note that the pistol grip is integral to the lower receiver.

One of the many versions of rifles used for competition is this home-build using a mix of parts from different manufacturers. It is meant to be used for Service Rifle competition and so has a free-floated barrel, but it's not real evident that it does. Most rifles used in this sport are of the A2 style, or the A4 style like this one. The carry handle is detachable but has a match sight installed in it. The owner (me) didn't want a single-use rifle, so the detachable handle was used. The handle can be removed and replaced with an optic for varminting (it's easily accurate enough for prairie dogs), and then reattached and the rifle re-zeroed for match use. Frankly, it can be used for anything – and that is the benefit of purchasing or home-building a 20-inch barrel AR-15.

Many rifles like this Del-Ton are quite basic. You save money by buying a rifle without rear sights, sometimes without front sights as well. If you want them, you can add them at your leisure and level of expense tolerance. In this case, an ATN night-vision riflescope has been mounted. Optics like this one are under $300 and can make the rifle useful 24 hours a day. This picture was taken at 2:00 in the morning and enhanced... ok, maybe not.

Above Left: These are the most commonly chambered cartridges in the AR platforms: .204 Ruger, .223 Rem. (and 5.56 mm; they look the same), 9mm Luger and .22 Long Rifle. **Above Right:** Less common rounds these are, but growing in popularity. Behold the .300 AAC Blackout, 6.8 Rem. SPC, 6.5 Grendel and the 7.62x39 Russian cartridges. All but the .300 BLK require their own special bolts and magazines. That one uses the same mags and bolt as the .223 and others, such as the .204 Ruger and 6x45mm.

features and accessories associated with them.

The resulting buying frenzy, and there is no more appropriate word for it, was truly fascinating. So once again the shelves were emptied, particularly in the several states that enacted laws to restrict or ban the ownership of MSRs. Lower receivers in particular became very difficult to find as they were ALL bought up. I sold five receivers to one guy at one gun show because he was not going to be caught with his pants down. Fortunately for him I kept the prices reasonable, but many dealers did not and for good reason. For a little while, no one really knew how things would shake out and how much and how soon they could replace their depleted stock.

Unlike in 2008 and 2009 there was a very real threat of widespread anti-gun legislation taking hold, but by this time it seemed that the average American had finally realized that gun laws accomplish nothing more than making criminals out of otherwise law-abiding citizens. Criminals by their very nature do not obey the law, so why would banning a certain type of firearm (based on cosmetics even) stop a determined killer? Even so, this didn't halt the frenzy and again it took a year for the production to catch up, and this has caused a real existing problem that I will discuss in a minute. Even ammunition began to dry up and for a relatively short time the stocks of .223 ammo disappeared. The ammo companies kicked up the production and the ammo reappeared in quantity within six months, and this glut of ammo is still on the shelves as of this writing.

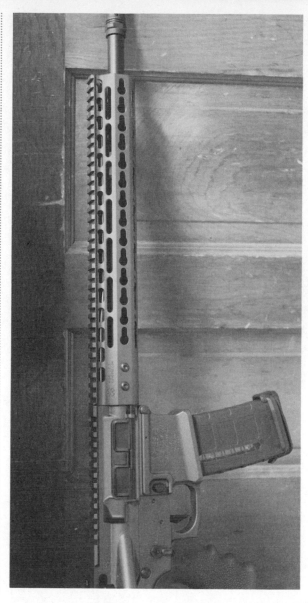

One of the accessory mounting systems currently competing for supremacy is the KeyMod system. The hole and slot attachment points are derived from the ancient method of shelf assembly. The benefit to this system is that the tube can be made thinner than those tubes with tapped holes for screw attachments. A similar method without the slots has been adopted by Magpul called the M-LOK.

Free floating the barrel is always a good thing. New rifles in the second decade of the 21st century often have these enhancements from the factory, and this type of upgrade is often the single most effective part to install on your rifle for an accuracy enhancement. In this case, with a .22 Long Rifle gun, we have a completely extraneous Miculek compensator that is there for the sole purpose of putting clothing on the muzzle.

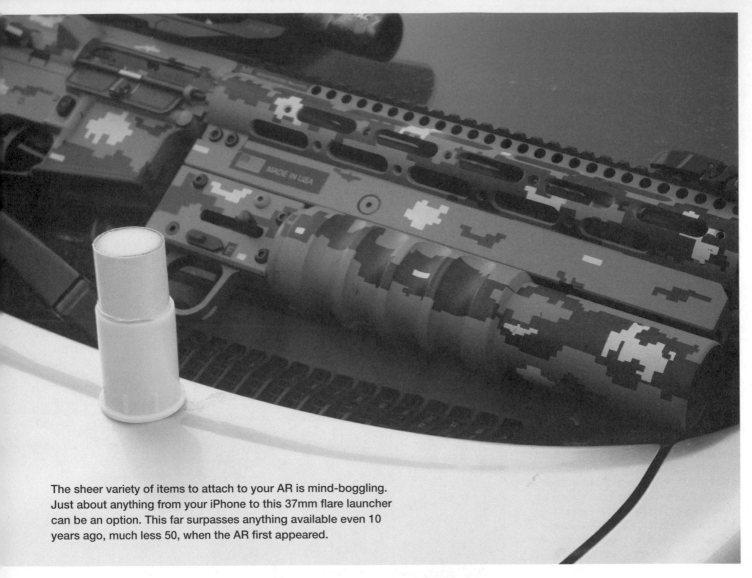

The sheer variety of items to attach to your AR is mind-boggling. Just about anything from your iPhone to this 37mm flare launcher can be an option. This far surpasses anything available even 10 years ago, much less 50, when the AR first appeared.

The other frequent question asked is: "should I get "xxx" caliber?" Start with .223/5.56mm, always. Then if you want to move into something else, start with 9mm. It's cheap and plentiful and just plain fun. If you want to hunt, go to 6.5 Grendel. It is quickly gaining in popularity and draws upon a vast selection of bullets already on the reloading market, and is a very superior cartridge when ballistics are considered. If you want to shoot cheap and a lot, go with .22 LR, 9mm, or 5.45x39 Russian (ammo is still very cheap, if imported). That's just in the small frame. Start with .308 in the large frame and then you can go to 6.5 Creedmoor or .260 Rem. later if you desire. Finally, if you want a good old-fashioned challenge, you can even find muzzle loading upper assemblies to shoot good old-fashioned musket balls.

One of the most peculiar results of this frenzy is the scarcity of .22 LR ammo. Up until the frenzy there was a significant movement pushing the purchase and use of ARs chambered in rimfire cartridges. The idea was you could shoot a rifle virtually identical to the normal AR but in an easy and especially cheap way. Everyone knows, or did up to that point, that .22 is cheap, plentiful, and if you had to you could always make a quick trip to Walmart to pick up a brick or four. You know, shoot more for less. Then the strangest thing happened. The .22 dried up. Disappeared. It still hasn't recovered.

Two years later theories abound as to why, but most chalk it up to paranoia. "If I can't get .223, then I'll get what I can get and .22 is the next best thing." Even now, it's pure good fortune to find any on the shelves, since once a box has been placed there, its retail survival time is inversely proportional to the number of cartridges in the box. Bricks have been known to literally disappear as soon as the store stocker releases his grip on the box, nowhere to be found.

(Clearly the space aliens on the mothership have a preference for rimfire and are working in concert with ATF, the Masons, the Commies and the ammo companies to screw the honest law-abiding American citizen. This is of course, after the Saudis and Nigerians get their first cuts.)

Back to the "problem" I mentioned earlier. There are now so many basic rifles available on store shelves that gun retailers are (generally; there are always a few exceptions) not currently buying them in any quantity. Furthermore, in order to stay productive and, oh… profitable, the manufacturers have to continue making them in order to pay their bills, their loans and their workers. Throw in a crappy economy, and it is crappy despite the executive assurances otherwise, and people aren't as ready to drop $900-1,000 on an AR anymore. The manufacturers are even giving out dealer rebates amounting to 15 percent and more to entice retailers to purchase the guns anyway. Thus, that $1,000 gun is selling for $800, sometimes because the dealer can now afford to lower the prices and still make what he needs to make to support his own business. It remains to be seen whether this will be effective.

About the only manufacturers that seem to be selling on a regular basis are the high-volume, low-margin guys and the boutique companies that sell the expensive, highly specialized units. The low-margin guys tend to take longer to ship and have customer service and ship times that some might gripe about, but are selling product for half or less than the better-known alphabet soup guys. The boutique companies saw less of a swell and less of a downturn since the dude that is ready to drop $3,500 on a rifle, just because he likes how it looks, is likely to still have a job, and thus the $3,500 to spend, even when the average gun purchaser has to cut back on his big-boy toy acquisition. This brings us to now, to this week in February 2015.

I sell thousands of dollars a month worth of parts, especially upgrades. People aren't buying new rifles (I practically have to beg people to buy them), but they are making existing guns nicer, more user-friendly and accurate, and even more importantly, they are building

rifles out of all those stripped lower receivers they purchased in the last six years. They are buying upper assemblies for $300 and getting a good product to boot. They are buying handguards, grips and stocks and personalizing to an insane degree. They are installing new trigger and fire control groups, because for $200 you can get something so much better than the stock factory trigger that it makes you want to cry when you realize you could have bought that trigger sooner and you didn't. People are buying recoil suppression, flash suppression and extraordinarily enough, sound suppression. Legally owned silencers are becoming far more common than they were even five years ago.

Now is the time to stock up on magazines. Five hundred thousand companies are making polymer magazines, most of them superbly, and they are cheap, cheap, cheap. Do what I should have done with .22 ammo. Every paycheck, (if you can afford to) go out and buy a couple magazines or boxes of .223. Then the next time we have a buying frenzy (and we will) you will be ahead of the curve. When you can buy a mil-spec magazine for $6 and every conceivable type of rifle and accessory, you are in a golden age of ARs. Buy an M4 clone for $750 and keep it for the next frenzy; then sell it for the normal $1,000 (or more) price and turn a tidy profit.

There are a host of alternate chamberings. It's just as easy to find a 6.8 SPC or .300 Blackout now as it is .223. Ammo is a little harder to find but not too hard.

6.5 Grendel is popular in the Southwest where you can shoot in the desert in any direction and distance you want. The older caliber upgrades like .50 Beowulf, 7.62x39mm and especially 9mm remain popular. You can even get 5.45x39mm so when the Norks and ChiComs invade you can shoot their ammo out of your AR. There is something for all of the small and large frame ARs to drop any big-game animal in the western hemisphere and most of those in the eastern. From prairie dogs to Kodiaks, the AR platform in some way, shape or form will handle it. Piston upgrades continue to persist, not being just a flash in the pan (nice gun idiom, that), but the vast majority of guns sold or homebuilt continue to operate via Eugene Stoner's original design.

Unless you live in one of the ban states, it is open season on the parts and particularly the rifles and the magazines and the ammo. It is unlikely that this state of affairs will remain for more than a short period. I don't doubt that a more "normal" state will resume within the next two years, and that's assuming another ban threat doesn't reemerge. On the other hand it's entirely possible that there will be no "normality" and we will go forward and experience a repeated cycle of feast and famine.

To end this discussion, I will repeat the old stock-trading maxim. "Buy low and sell high." Right now it's low. If you can afford to do so, and haven't yet caught the AR bug, now is the time to jump in and get infected.

7mm:
A 50-YEAR LOVE AFFAIR

BY **Jon R. Sundra**

Half a century of hunting 'round the world with the Magnificent Sevens

My first 7mm was one I put together using a Herter U9 barreled action chambered in 7mm Rem. Magnum, which I fitted and glass bedded into a Fajen Regent semi-inletted stock. It was 1965, and if memory serves, the BA set me back less than 50 bucks, and the stock about 15.

In those days a "semi-inletted" stock was exactly that. The barrel channel was a uniform ½-inch wide groove running the length of the forearm, and the receiver/bottom metal inletting was about 90 percent done, which left an awful lot of work. My inletting looked like the work of a spastic beaver, but I counted on glass bedding—which I already had some experience with—to bail me out. Long story short, I took that rifle on my first international hunt for caribou in Labrador. I've been a 7mm weenie ever since.

Back in those days, the .30-06 and .270 were the dominant big-game calibers among those who hunted more than just white-tailed deer. Being the iconoclast that I am, I was predisposed to any caliber but a .270 or .30. But let's face it, there aren't that many other calibers to pick from that are versatile enough for general purpose hunting of nondangerous game. To me the 7mm seemed to make the most sense, so when Remington rolled out their sexy new Model 700 rifle along with the equally new 7mm

The author took this mid-Asian ibex in Kyrgyzstan with an H-S Precision rifle chambered in 7mm WSM.

Remington Magnum cartridge in 1962, I was smitten.

At the time I was a sophomore in college and had no immediate use for something as potent as the 7 Mag, but I thought it was the sexiest cartridge I'd ever seen and I simply had to have one. After all, I was planning on becoming a big-time gun writer and hunt all over the world, so I would certainly need something like the 7 Mag sooner or later!

Seriously though, the 7mm has a long and storied history in Europe and the rest of the world, but it took 65 years for it to even begin to be recognized here in the States. The first .284 bore was the 7x57, a cartridge of Mauser design that first appeared in the Spanish Model 1892. The 7x57 (or 7mm Mauser, take your pick) is essentially the German 7.9x57 martial cartridge originally developed for the Commission Rifle of 1888 and necked

down to 7mm. On the 7mm version the shoulder is pushed back a little, resulting in a slightly longer neck and shorter body, but comparing the two side by side it's obvious they share the same case.

For that matter, our own .30-06 is just a slightly lengthened 8mm Mauser. In

The .28 caliber is as diverse as the .30 caliber as far as performance levels are concerned. Here's how they stack up (l. to r.): 7mm-08, 7x57, .284 Win., .280 Rem., 7mm Rem. SA Ultra Mag., 7mm WSM, 7mm Rem. Mag., 7mm Weatherby Mag., 7mm Dakota, 7mm STW, 7mm Ultra Mag. and 7.21 Lazzeroni Firebird.

At far left is an original 7.9x57 Mauser designed for the Commission Rifle of 1888, the parent case for the slightly enlarged, spitzer-bulleted 8x57 adopted in 1904, and the 7x57. Our own .30-06 at right is based on nothing more than a lengthened 8mm Mauser case.

From left: The .280 Rem., .280 RCBS Improved, .280 Ackley and 7mm JRS. Note the 7 JRS pushes the shoulder .150" forward, increasing capacity over the .280 Rem. by about 7 grains.

1927 the famed British gunmaker, John Rigby, adopted the 7x57 and had the temerity to affix his name to it, calling it the .275 Rigby. Another 7mm that still enjoys popularity in Europe today is the 7x64, a cartridge designed by Wilhelm Brenneke in 1917, and one that looks so similar to the .280 Rem. that you have to see them next to each other to tell them apart. In the 1930s the 7x57 was chambered on a very limited basis in the early Model 70 Winchester and Remington Model 30, but other than that only rifle nuts and handloaders were familiar with it or any other 7mms.

The .28 caliber got its real start here in 1957, and it was the result of "Plan A" going sour. From a conversation I had many years ago with Remington's Mike

Walker, who was at the center of the .280 Remington's development, it seems the company wanted to chamber its then 2-year-old Model 740 autoloader for the .270 Winchester, but the pressure level to which commercial .270 ammo was loaded was too punishing on the action. The Remington folks decided that if the Model 740 couldn't handle the .270, then they'd design a cartridge as close to it as possible that would work.

The solution consisted of necking up the oddball .270 Win., with a groove diameter of .277", to the well-established 7mm bore (.284), and load it to a max of 60,000 psi (the .270 is loaded up to 65,000 psi). However, to foil the inevitable dimwit who would sooner or later try to cram a .280 Rem. cartridge into a .270 Win. rifle, Remington increased the head-to-shoulder dimension on the .280 by some .051". The result was a case that had a slightly larger combustion chamber than the .270, enough so that the .280 had the potential of matching the Winchester round. Unfortunately, it couldn't do it in the 22-inch barrel of the Model 740 autoloader. The problem was compounded by the fact that Remington failed to also chamber the round in their bolt-action Model 721 rifle, which would have allowed handloaders to equal or exceed .270 performance. The gun writers of the day were only too happy to point out these shortcomings, and pretty much killed any chance the .280 might have had to gain some headway with America's hunters.

Based on what happened with the .280, it was rather surprising that just five years later Remington had another go at the .284 caliber in the form of its iconic 7mm Rem. Magnum, which is where I came in.

I had that Herter rifle only a couple of years, and though I didn't slay a lot of critters with it — a few whitetails, mule deer, black bear, pronghorn and caribou — everything I pointed it at expired without ceremony. Each positive experience simply reinforced that I had made the right decision. After all, isn't that how most of us come to favor a particular rifle or caliber — the faith and confidence derived from successful experiences? I'm sure that if I had chosen the .30-06 or the .270 for my first big-game rifle and had the same luck with either, I would have been just as big of a fan.

I made my first African safari in the mid-`70s; it was in Rhodesia and by then I had gone through a couple more 7 mags and was now using a Ruger No. 1.

If limited to the cartridge length of factory ammo at far left, bullets over 130 grains deeply infringe on usable powder space. At far right is a 154-grain Hornady bullet seated to what will cycle through the Winchester Model 70 and Montana Model 1999 short actions.

Left: Caribou country is big, making it ideally suited for a flat-shooting 7mm. The author's 7mm JRS on a Sako action accounted for this nice bull.

Below: This South African wildebeest fell to a custom Ruger chambered in what was then a wildcat the author derived by necking down the .300 WSM to 7mm. Shortly thereafter Winchester did the same thing.

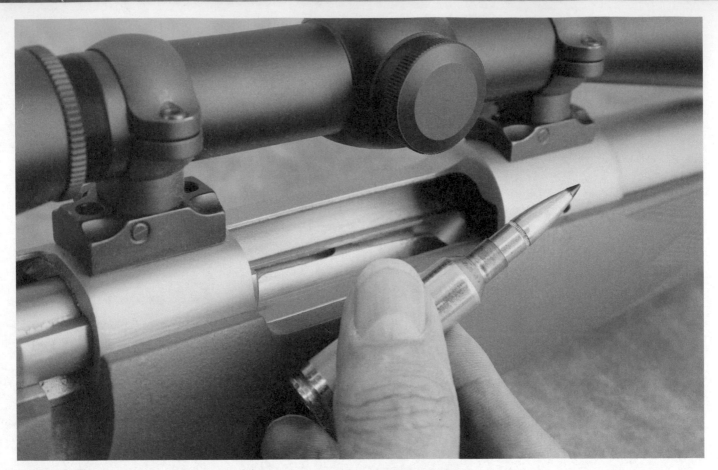

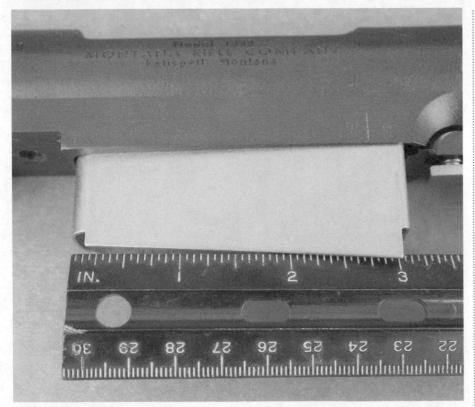

Long-throated short actions of Winchester and Montana Rifle Co. can accommodate WSM cartridges loaded to an overall length of 3.125".

By that time, however, I was becoming disenchanted with the belted magnum case, so I went on safaris to South Africa and Namibia in `78 with a Ruger 77 in .280 Remington. The following year it was Zambia with a custom Ruger 77 chambered in .284 Winchester. Neither, of course, was the equal of the 7 Mag ballistically, but everything fell just as quick and just as dead. I'm talking big, tough critters like zebra, wildebeest, gemsbok, roan, oryx, sable, kudu, and even 1,500-pound eland. Those were the days when we didn't have the plethora of monolithic and bonded core bullets we have today; I was using handloads and plain ol' conventional bullets, mostly Hornady 154-grain spire points.

1980 again found me in Zambia, this time with a wildcat of my own design that I called the 7 JRS, based on the .280 Rem. case. By then I had tried the .280 RCBS Improved and found it didn't improve on the stock .280's velocity by any meaningful amount. The same with the .280 Ackley; by decreasing body taper and sharpening the shoulder angle to 40 degrees it was only marginally better. So I decided to take full advantage of the .280 case by decreasing its body taper to only .015" from head to shoulder, and

reducing the neck length to .300". That allowed me to push a sharper, 35-degree shoulder forward some .150".

The result is a case that held about 70 grains of water compared to the .280's 63 grains.

Over the next 10 years I used my 7 JRS wildcat almost exclusively and took more game than with any other 7mm by far. I ended up building three 7 JRS rifles on magnum length actions (Remington, Sako and Winchester) that allowed me to seat bullets to where they were not seriously infringing on usable powder space. In all three rifles I was able to get more than 3,100 fps using RE22 powder and Norma brass – which holds more than Remington or Winchester hulls. That's 7 Mag performance in rifles that held five rounds in the magazine instead of only three.

But all good things come to an end. When Dakota Arms introduced its 7mm Dakota in the early `90s, I immediately recognized it to be a far better cartridge than my 7 JRS and the 7mm Rem. Mag.

If you compare 7mm and .30-caliber cartridges of similar capacity driving bullets of comparable sectional densities and ballistic coefficients, it requires about 30 percent more recoil to match the trajectory of a 7mm with a .30 caliber. Shown here are pairings of 7mm-08 Rem. and .308 Win.; .280 Rem. and .30-06; 7mm STW and .300 Weatherby; 7mm Ultra Mag. and .300 Ultra Mag.

There's a myriad of component 7mm bullets available and in more bullet weights than the .30 caliber. Shown here are bullets of 120, 125, 139, 140, 145, 150, 154, 160, 162, 170 and 175 grains. Not shown are 100, 130 and 195-grain bullets.

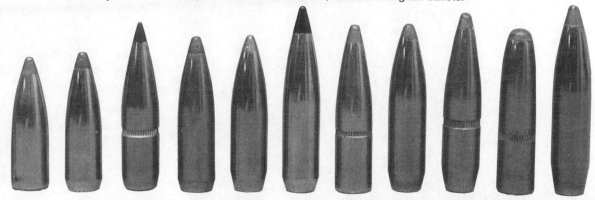

This superb red stag was taken in Argentina using a Bansner custom rifle based on a long throated Winchester Model 70 short action chambered in 7mm WSM.

The author took this sable in old Rhodesia with a Ruger No. 1 in 7mm Remington Magnum.

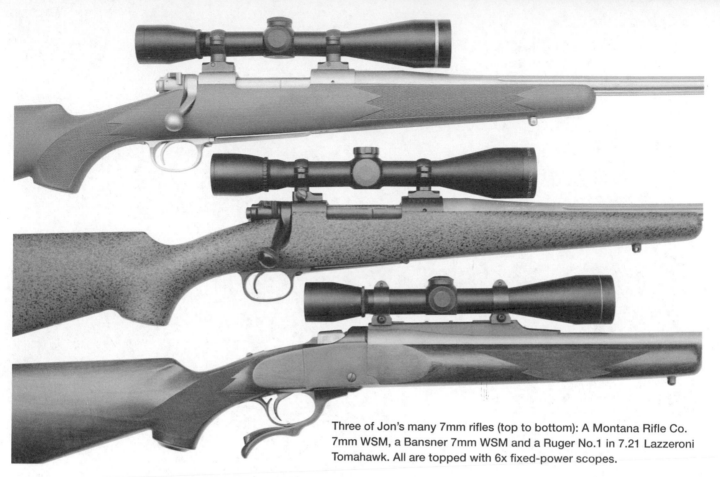

Three of Jon's many 7mm rifles (top to bottom): A Montana Rifle Co. 7mm WSM, a Bansner 7mm WSM and a Ruger No.1 in 7.21 Lazzeroni Tomahawk. All are topped with 6x fixed-power scopes.

It was based on a large-capacity beltless case that had a shorter, fatter powder column, which is where the new technology at the time was starting to go. It had roughly 12 percent more powder capacity than the 7 Mag, and could propel a 140-grain bullet to 3,400 fps. I immediately built a 7mm Dakota on a Ruger No.1 action and with its 26-inch barrel was able to coax 3,350 fps from a 150-grain bullet.

My next fling with the .28 caliber was with John Lazzeroni's short-action magnum line introduced around 1993. His 7.21 Tomahawk (a true 7mm, despite the designation) was based on a drastically shortened .416 Rigby-like case. It's the ultimate example of the short, fat powder-column school of thought. The latter half of the '90s then saw me using the Dakota and Lazzeroni 7mms.

My next epiphany was in 2000 when Winchester announced its .300 Short Magnum. I saw it as the perfect case for a 7mm. So before .300 WSM guns and ammo were even available in the marketplace I had necked it down to 7mm, built a rifle based on a standard-length Ruger 77 action, and taken it to Africa where my son, a buddy and I used it to slay a wide assortment of plains game.

It was no surprise the following year when Winchester introduced a 7mm version of its Short Magnum. To maximize the potential of the WSMs a standard-length action is required to allow seating even bullets of moderate weight no deeper than the body and shoulder juncture. But doesn't that defeat the whole rationale of the short magnums you might ask? Not quite. The Winchester Model 70 and the Montana Model 1999 short actions both have magazines that will accept cartridges of 3.125" in overall length, whereas other short actions are limited to 2.75" or 2.8". I have three such rifles and each one reaches more than 3,150 fps with a 154-grain Hornady bullet out of a 24-inch barrel.

There are those who would say that everything the 7mm can do the .30 can do better. It's true there is nothing inherently superior about the .28 caliber. If you push a .308 bullet over the same trajectory as a .284, the .308 will arrive with about 15 percent more energy. But doing so generates 30 percent more recoil, assuming rifles of equal weight.

Now some may feel that extra 15 percent is worth it. I don't. With a magnum 7 of one variety or another I've shot

from every conceivable position, many times from prone with the toe of the butt on the ground and with just the bony top of my shoulder backing the gun up, I've never suffered a magnum eyebrow. I can't say the same for several .300 magnum guys I've shared camps with or witnessed shooting.

Another thing I particularly like is the fact that, for the handloader, there are more bullet weights offered in 7mm than in .30, and far more than in .270. Consider this: handloaders can choose 7mm bullets from the various manufacturers in 100, 110, 115, 120, 125, 130, 139, 140, 145, 150, 154, 160, 162, 168, 170 and 175 grains. If you've got a particularly finicky rifle with regard to its shooting a specific bullet weight better than others, you've a better chance of finding it if you've got a .284" hole in the barrel.

I guess what I'm trying to say is that based on my experiences over the half century I've been hunting, I've never been disappointed or felt the need for anything larger than a 7mm. Regardless of where I've hunted — from Alaska to Zambia, South Africa to Siberia, the South Pacific to the Arctic Ocean — there's been a 7mm in my hands.

The author wearing a Lightweight Commander in leather from Barranti Leather Co. He calls the whole rig The Border Special.

FAVORITE AUTO PISTOLS

A trip down memory lane with some of the sheriff's favorite semiautos

BY **Jim Wilson**

My affinity for autoloading pistols really began in the early 1970s. The police department I worked for required that we all carry double-action revolvers. However, department regulations did not address the issue of off-duty weapons, except to say that we should be armed when off duty. For that reason, a number of us carried autos when off duty if for no other reason than they were flatter and easier to conceal.

All of that began to change when I was tapped to run the newly formed drug unit. We quickly found that DA revolvers of any useful size were extremely difficult to conceal and we began to campaign our police chief for the authority to carry autos. It was during that time that I switched to carrying a 1911 in .45 ACP and, in all these years since, have pretty much never looked back.

It was my opinion back then, and is now, that a fellow ought to carry the most powerful handgun that he can shoot quickly and accurately Many of us would add that it must also be relatively easy to conceal. For me, all of those requirements came together in the 1911 pistol, particularly in .45 caliber. However,

Right side of the author's engraved Colt Government Model with the Masonic emblem carved in ivory. The pistol is factory D engraved. Stocks are by Gun-Art Co. The left side shows the Mexican eagle & snake carved in ivory.

as you will see, I have owned and still own other types of autos in other calibers. Join me, if you will, for a little trip down memory lane, at least as far as auto pistols are concerned.

The Colt 1911 that has been with me the longest is also my favorite. About 1975, West Texas Wholesale acquired a number of engraved guns from the Colt Custom Shop. Among them was a 70 Series Government Model with full cover engraving and blue finish. As I recall, I bought the gun for something like $750.00. It was accurate, reliable and had one of the nicest triggers of any out-of-the-box pistol I've ever handled.

Of course, an engraved pistol just cries for a nice set of stocks to match. With that in mind, I contacted the Gun-Art Company of New Jersey, and ordered a set of carved ivory stocks. The right panel was to have the Masonic Square & Compass on it and the left panel should display the Scottish Rite double eagle. Well, the folks at Gun-Art got it almost right. The Masonic Square & Compass came out just right, but the left panel turned out to be the eagle and snake emblem as found on the Mexican flag.

When I was sworn in as sheriff of a county near the Mexican border, I had that pistol on my hip. I told my Latino friends that the eagle and snake on the left stock panel was to honor them. After all, I was in politics you know.

I've never looked on handguns, even engraved ones, as wall hangers, so I have carried this one quite a bit over the years. Besides, the holster wear kind of burnishes the engraving and gives the pistol a special look that I appreciate.

One of these days my son can hang it on the wall if he is so inclined.

Also in the 70s, Colt came out with an all-steel version of the Commander pistol and called it the Combat Commander. For some reason I have always liked the Commander version of the 1911, maybe because it seems to bal-

Another view of the author's Colt Lightweight Commander in .45 ACP with silver stocks from Kevin Johnson and XS Express sights.

This all steel Colt Combat Commander is shown with a Yaqui Slide holster from Milt Sparks Leather Co. Combat custom work was done by Novak Sights.

ance better in my hand. At any rate, I acquired two Combat Commanders and made them up as a pair of raid guns for use on drug raids and felony apprehensions. They were fitted with a set of fixed, high-visibility sights and Colt ambidextrous safeties.

After retiring from law enforcement I pretty much retired those two Colts. However, I eventually realized that this was a foolish thing to do. One pistol was given as a gift to a friend and the other was sent off to Novak Sights for an updated defensive remake.

Wayne Novak and his crew replaced some worn parts and fitted the pistol with a set of his low-mount fixed sights. The front sight featured a gold bead and the rear sight had a slightly larger aperture than normal – .140" instead of the standard .125" – as an aid to aging eyes.

The folks at Novak's also fitted the pistol with The Answer, which is a one-piece backstrap that does away with the grip safety. Altering the safety on a pistol is a decision that should not be taken lightly and opens a discussion that is beyond the scope of this article. I will

Border Patrolman Shane Jahn is another fan of the Browning Hi-Power. The author has long been a fan of this 9mm, the first of the high-capacity autos.

simply say that it works for me. Others must decide if it is something that they really need and if they have the training to make use of it safely. Regardless, this old Colt has been the one I used on many trips to Gunsite and other training

schools, and has become a favorite carry piece.

More recently I realized that while I had owned several Lightweight Commanders, I did not currently have one. With its alloy frame, the Lightweight

Smith & Wesson's Model 3913, an excellent midsize 9mm.

Commander weighs a bit less than the all-steel version and is very comfortable for concealed carry. A little trading at a local gun show quickly fixed that and I brought home a like-new Lightweight Commander that had been made in the late 1970s. And, of course, I had to make just a few modifications to it in order to meet my needs.

The slide was shipped off to XS Sights for installation of their Express Sights, with the express-type rear sight and the Big Dot front sight. In defensive shooting, it is critical to see the front sight clearly as the trigger is pressed and that big dot just facilitates that important part of the defensive equation.

Once the pistol was back home, it went off to Colby Brandon, a member of the American Pistolsmiths Guild, for a trigger job. Colby is associated with Virgil Tripp and the good folks at STI. More importantly, he understands 1911s like no person of his young age has any right to. So far so good, I had an accurate pistol with good sights but, of course, I just couldn't stop there.

Through social media I became aware of Kevin Johnson, of Clarendon, Texas,

who engraves guns and makes custom silver stocks for the Texas Rangers. Kevin made me a set of metal stocks with silver overlay that featured my old *cinco peso* badge. This completed project resulted in a nice pistol that I have carried just about every day since the project was completed.

While I like the .45 ACP cartridge, it is not the only horse in the race. I also have to admit to an appreciation of the .38 Super cartridge. It has always been popular with lawmen along this southern border and performs better than the standard 9mm cartridge. For years the cartridge suffered from the fact that Colt had the headspacing wrong and accuracy was not what it should have been.

I have several vintage Colts that are nice guns but really past their prime as carry guns. That oversight in my collection of defensive handguns was solved when I got involved with Mark Stone and

his staff at Nighthawk Custom. At my request, they built an all-steel Commander in .38 Super with a properly headspaced barrel and an integral ramp for more reliable feeding. For sights I chose the same kind of Novak low-mount fixed sights that were on my all-steel Commander, with the .140" opening on the rear sight and the gold dot front sight.

Nighthawk's solution to building sturdy, reliable pistols is quite simple, or complex, depending upon how you want to look at it. They use the best materials available (you won't find any plastic in their guns) and hand fit the parts until they properly mate with the rest of the pistol. Each individual pistol is pretty much built by only one Nighthawk gunsmith. Each one of those gunsmiths is highly trained and takes great pride in the product that his hands have produced. Nighthawk pistols are state-of-the-art in terms of reliability and accuracy. It is easy to find cheaper 1911s, but extremely difficult to find a better 1911 than what comes out of the Nighthawk plant at Berryville, Ark.

While 1911s are certainly a favorite of mine, I have to say that there are quite a number of other good pistols. Not the least of which is the Browning Hi-Power. It is another one of John M. Browning's inventions, though it was finished after his death. I like the pistol for its ruggedness and reliability. While it is a full-size service pistol, it is still thin enough to make a good concealed-carry proposition, even though it is a bit large for the 9mm caliber. The Hi-Power pictured is one I traded for not long ago and is still a work in progress. You can bet that it will go off to one of our quality pistolsmiths, possibly Novaks or Ro-Bar, for some custom work in the near future. Different sights, a trigger job and installation of a single, combat thumb safety will be in order.

There was a time when many of us looked down on the 9mm cartridge as being inadequate for personal defense. It is still not a good choice when full-metal-jacket ammo is mandated. However, the armed citizen can take advantage of the vast improvement in defensive ammunition that is currently available. With these improvements, the 9mm is no longer the wimp that it once was.

A better mate of gun to cartridge is the Smith & Wesson Model 3913. Although this pistol is now discontinued, it makes a very nice defensive carry gun and one that I used as a backup gun for a number of years. The single-stack, eight-round magazine allowed Smith & Wesson to build a pistol that is thin enough to conceal easily. The pistol's alloy frame makes it comfortably lightweight as well. In addition, the pistol has good combat sights just as it came from the factory. The only slight drawback is the double-action trigger pull that requires a good deal of practice to master. But it can be mastered. Altogether, the S&W Model 3913 makes a great little pistol that really doesn't

A first generation Glock Model 17 in 9mm. Not exactly one of the author's favorites, but there's more to that story.

require any custom modifications for concealed carry.

I have to admit that I am as guilty as anyone of making fun of the folks who choose to carry a Glock for personal defense. I have cautioned some against leaving their Glock on the dash of the car because the sun might melt it. I have also suggested that Glocks are easy to engrave because all you need is an old Boy Scout wood-burning kit. And to be honest, I suppose that I will continue to poke fun at those who cleave to this striker-fired wonder of the new age. So just to be fair, let me tell you a little story.

As a Texas Sheriff, I was extremely active in working to get the concealed-carry law passed in our state so that good citizens could protect themselves. Once we were successful in that endeavor, I also took the time to get certified as a licensing instructor and taught a number of classes.

In just about every class there was always at least one person who showed up with a pistol that was just totally inadequate for the task. In some cases it was an el cheapo gun that was better used as a trotline weight. In other situations it was some old relic that was well past its prime and really deserved to be in a museum instead of on a citizen's

hip. Regardless, they were guns that just were not reliable or accurate.

At the same time, due to my other job as handgun editor of a magazine, I had a first generation Glock Model 17 on extended loan. I quickly discovered that I could put this pistol in the hands of those people who had junk guns and get them qualified very easily. They didn't have to remember to squeeze this or flip that, they just had to line up the sight and press the trigger.

Full disclosure also requires me to admit that I really didn't take very good care of this Glock 17. I ran whatever 9mm ammo was available through it and rarely cleaned or lubricated it. The old gun ran like a top in spite of my neglect. In fact, I can't remember a single time that it ever malfunctioned. So I suppose that I will continue to poke fun at Glock users, but now you know the rest of the story.

Throughout my adult life, I have made my living with guns and it has been a satisfying experience. I've met some awfully good people and made lifelong friends along the way. These auto pistols, in their way, have also been good friends. We've had a few adventures that I would just as soon have avoided but they have stuck with me, even in those cases, as good friends will.

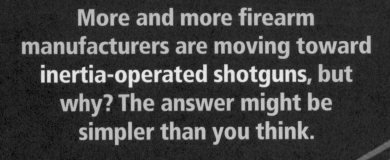

More and more firearm manufacturers are moving toward inertia-operated shotguns, but why? The answer might be simpler than you think.

BY **Brad Fitzpatrick**

THE INERTIA MOVEMENT

Illustration Courtesy Benelli USA

hen John Moses Browning invented the Auto-5 shotgun, which operated on a long-recoil operated system, he revolutionized the scattergun market. Until that time repeating shotguns relied on mechanical operation (primarily a stroke of the fore-end) to cycle the action. There were a number of early semiautos, but Browning's design, wherein the barrel and action moved rearward as one before separating, became the first commercially successful semiauto shotgun on the market. The Auto-5 remained the

king for many years, and even today – almost 20 years after the original A-5 ceased production – the gun still has a loyal following. Its design even spawned a successful variant, Franchi's 48, which has been around for almost seven decades now.

In the mid-20th century, semiauto shotguns underwent a mechanical revolution. Instead of the recoil-operated guns of the past, manufacturers were now looking to gas-operated designs wherein gas from the fired shell provided the energy needed to cycle the action. Regulating gas systems took some time,

but when gas guns took off they were the new dominant force in the market. Winchester, Remington, Mossberg and, yes, even Browning offered effective gas-operated shotguns. Gas guns softened the felt impact of recoil by extending the period of rearward motion, so the guns were more comfortable to shoot, especially guns set up to compensate for heavy turkey and waterfowl loads.

Gas guns were not, however, without their blemishes. Gas operation should, in theory, cycle a whole range of shells, but that isn't always the case. Some gas guns are excellent, but others aren't so reli-

Benelli's Super Black Eagle II was one of the guns that started the inertia revolution in the United States. Waterfowlers adopted the gun quickly and appreciated its weight, superb balance and relentless reliability.

Benelli's Vinci and Super Vinci use a three-piece modular system that allow them to be taken down and reassembled very quickly. The ComforTech stock helps mitigate recoil.

able. In addition, gas guns are generally heavier than recoil guns and the constant flow of gases and debris through the action can cause excessive buildup and compromise reliability.

Benelli, an Italian shotgun maker, had a different idea of how a semiautomatic shotgun should work. The Benelli system, now known as their Inertia-Driven System, consisted of only three parts—a bolt body, inertia spring and rotating bolt head.

Upon firing, the gun moves rearward with the exception of the bolt body, which stays in position until the inertia spring is compressed between the rotating bolt head and the bolt body. When pressures drop, the spring expands and drives the bolt body rearward, unlocking the bolt head and extracting the spent casing from the chamber. When the empty casing strikes the ejector it is driven out of the ejection port and the gun is cocked by the rearward motion of the bolt body. The bolt's movement compresses a recoil spring, which drives the bolt body back forward, chambering another shell. The gun is ready to fire again.

It's a simple action with a minimum of moving parts and no need to rely on

pistons, O-rings or other devices typically associated with a gas-operated gun. In addition, the system actually favors lighter guns, so shotgun makers are motivated to reduce the mass of their inertia guns. Recoil systems are easy to clean and they are extremely reliable with a broad range of loads.

The system is not perfect, though. Gone is the recoil-reducing gas-operation system, so kick is more pronounced, especially with lighter guns. The rotating bolt head also must be locked into the chamber, so it needs to be forcefully dropped to function properly. Still, the inertia system (or, more conventionally, a short-recoil operated system) is a great option and more and more shotgun companies are looking toward the inertia-type system for their firearms. Here's a list of some of the best semiauto inertia guns currently on the market.

Benelli. No discussion of inertia guns is complete without a mention of Benelli's extensive product line. The Italian brand popularized the term "inertia guns," and it offers more variants on the theme than any other manufacturer. The classic Montefeltro is one of the company's earliest and most successful

The Vinci and Super Vinci from Benelli use an in-line inertia system with bolt body, rotating bolt head, inertia spring and recoil spring on one plane. It's a compact and very reliable system.

Above: The Super Black Eagle II has evolved into several different configurations, such as the rifled slug gun shown here and a turkey model with SteadyGrip stock.

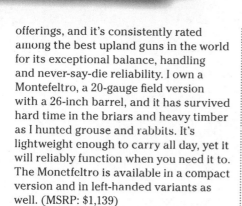

offerings, and it's consistently rated among the best upland guns in the world for its exceptional balance, handling and never-say-die reliability. I own a Montefeltro, a 20-gauge field version with a 26-inch barrel, and it has survived hard time in the briars and heavy timber as I hunted grouse and rabbits. It's lightweight enough to carry all day, yet it will reliably function when you need it to. The Montefeltro is available in a compact version and in left-handed variants as well. (MSRP: $1,139)

The radical-looking Vinci and Super Vinci offer a three-piece modular design, making them perhaps the easiest semi-auto shotguns on the market to assemble and disassemble. The Vinci and Super Vinci utilize Benelli's In-Line Inertia system, where the bolt body, inertia spring, rotating bolt head and recoil spring are all designed along one axis for simplicity of design and improved function. (MSRP from $1,449)

The Super Black Eagle II shotgun is perhaps Benelli's best-known semiauto, still considered by many to be the best waterfowl shotgun of all time. But the SBE II is not just a duck and goose gun; turkey hunters will appreciate the SteadyGrip version of the SBEII, which allows for a firm hold and steady platform when shooting heavy turkey loads. In addition, there's a rifled slug version with a high comb. The SBE II guns are available with Benelli's ComforTech stock, which helps

The Benelli Super Vinci utilizes an in-line inertia system that is effective and efficient. The author used the Super Vinci to down this brace of pintails in Texas.

reduce the impact of recoil. (MSRP for the SBE II starts at $1,899)

The newest offering from Benelli is the Ethos shotgun, which comes with Benelli's new Progressive Comfort stock featuring interlocking buffers that help reduce the impact of recoil. The system works quite well, and after spending a full day hunting with the Ethos I didn't feel any recoil fatigue. Additionally, the Ethos has a two-part carrier latch for rapid loading of shells into the chamber. Owners can choose between an anodized receiver or an engraved, nickel-plated one for an additional $200. (MSRP $1,999 for anodized version)

Browning. Browning resurrected the A5 name in the spring of 2012, but if

shooters hoped to see a long recoil-operated version like the original they were to be disappointed. The rest of the world, however, appreciated the return of the humpback, albeit changed in almost every way except name. Even the distinctive receiver was changed slightly with a lower, less dramatic "hump" that was more familiar to shooters accustomed to rounded receivers. The new A5 is also missing the magazine cutoff switch that was found on the original as well as other guns like the new Browning Maxus. Instead, there's a magazine release button on the bottom of the receiver.

If you've ever wondered why inertia/short recoil-operated guns have a magazine release button, the answer becomes

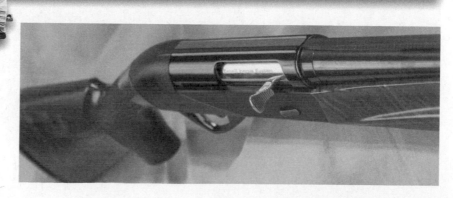

Right: Benelli's Ethos is similar in design to the company's other semiauto inertia guns, and it's available in black anodized (shown here) or an engraved nickel-plated version. It also comes with the company's Progressive Comfort system that helps reduce felt recoil.

The author awaits another group of mallards in the Arkansas timber with the Browning A5 close at hand. The A5 is an excellent all-around gun, and the short-barreled version (26-inch) was ideal for fast shots in the flooded oaks.

Kinematic Drive, but it's basically similar in function to any other short recoil or inertia gun, and Browning is so convinced that the new A5 will last that they back it with a five-year, 100,000-round guarantee. I had a chance to shoot the A5 in Arkansas while chasing mallards in timber, and the gun's svelte fore-end and light weight make it a perfect close-cover waterfowl gun. The large white bead also helps. The A5 is available in a variety of finishes with a variety of stocks, so no matter whether you like basic black, dipped camo or classic walnut with engraving there's an A5 for you. (MSRP $1,499-$1,989)

Franchi. Franchi is the sister company of Benelli and borrows much of its new technology from its larger brandmate. Franchi is also, I believe, one of the most underrated shotgun makers in the industry, and their line of high-quality, attractive, budget-friendly semi-autos continues to grow. The most basic version is the 3-inch Affinity that is available in black, camo, and starting

apparent when the gun is dropped hard on the butt. The light bolt will sometimes slide to the rear, and in such an event you've got a gun that is suddenly and unexpectedly chambered. That's why the magazine release button is in and the mag cutoff is out.

Browning calls the new A5's operating system

Background: The Intensity is Franchi's 3½-inch inertia-operated semiauto. This one was used on an Arkansas snow goose depredation hunt (hence the extended tube) and functioned perfectly through an ice storm.

Franchi's Affinity is now available with a walnut stock, a classy look for this sturdy inertia gun. Available in 12 and 20 gauge, it's a stylish upland gun that is very reliable and affordable.

Franchi's Affinity is a wonderful value in 3-inch inertia guns. New for 2015 is a left-handed version of the popular semiauto.

in 2015, a walnut/blued version. There are compact versions available as well. Step up in chamber size and you'll find the 12-gauge, 3½-inch Intensity, which looks very much like the Affinity with the addition of machined cutouts in the receiver for mounting optics. The Intensity is available in a variety of camo patterns including Realtree Xtra Green and Max-5, and Mossy Oak's classic Bottomlands. There's also a black version available.

For the competitive shooter, there's a Sporting version of the Affinity available with a 3-inch chamber, black synthetic stock and very attractive brushed aluminum anodized receiver that makes it look more expensive than it really is. Plus, it comes with long barrels (30-inch for the 12 gauge, 28 inches for the 20) and a wide target rib for a smooth swing and consistent sight picture. I had a chance to test the Affinity while hunting ducks in Texas and later the Intensity while hunting snow geese in Arkansas. In terms of reliability they were two pretty grueling tests—the Texas hunt involved exposing the guns to corrosive salt water and the Arkansas hunt took place in the middle of an ice storm. On both occasions the guns performed perfectly. The Sporting gun showed up on a hunt I was on in South Dakota, and although I didn't kill any pheasants with it, I dusted a bunch of clays. If I ever have a chance to devote more time to my sporting clays game my first stop will be at the Franchi dealer. (MSRP: $849 for the Affinity, $1,099 for the Intensity and $1,159 for the Sporting)

Stoeger. Like Benelli and Franchi, Stoeger is under the Beretta umbrella of companies. Just like those other two gun companies, Stoeger relies on the Inertia-Driven design Benelli introduced to operate its semiauto shotguns. Stoeger's guns are built for the field and are very budget-friendly. The company offers two different chamber lengths in its 12-gauge guns (coded as the M3000 for the 3-inch version and M3500 for the 3½-inch chamber). There's also a 20-gauge 3020 model as well. If you're a turkey hunter who would like to have a species-specific shotgun but don't want to pay top dollar for a one-season weapon, the M3000 and M3500 turkey models with SteadyGrip are viable options, and they can double as close-range predator and self-defense shotguns. (MSRP: $679-$799)

There is a wide assortment of field guns available for as little as $599, a compact version to fit smaller shooters, and a rifled slug model for big-game hunting. For 2015, Stoeger introduced a new dedicated 3-gun competition version of their M3000, the M3K 3-Gun shotgun. It's based on the standard M3000 but has a shortened (24-inch) barrel with an oversize blue bolt knob and release button. It's a budget-friendly way to get into competitive 3-gun shooting, and the M3K would also double as an excellent defensive and close-quarters hunting shotgun for species like grouse and woodcock in heavy cover. (MSRP is $699)

Weatherby. Roy Weatherby's namesake company will likely always be best known for its high-velocity cartridges and accompanying centerfire rifles. But the Weatherby company has been offering shotguns in their lineup for more than 50 years, so the it knows a thing or two about building scatterguns. Recently, the only shotguns Weatherby

Left: Browning's new A5 shares a similar profile with the original Auto-5, but little else. Its Kinematic Drive System works as a short recoil/inertia system, and is very reliable. This gun is shown in Mossy Oak's new Break-Up Country camo pattern.

offered were the SA-08 and PA-08 gas-operated semiauto and pump guns. They are built in Turkey and consumers have praised the low cost and excellent finish work. The recent addition of two new shotguns represented two very different design concepts. The new Orion is a traditionally styled over/under that is similar, at least in basic function and aesthetic, to the Orion models that Weatherby produced in years past. The new inertia-operated Element, however, is something totally different.

Like the SA-08 and PA-08 before it, the Element is made in Turkey. In the past, Turkish guns were considered to be of a lower quality than guns made elsewhere. That's simply not the case today, and there are Turkish guns rolling off the line that challenge the quality, fit and finish of guns from anywhere else in the world. Case in point: the Element. It's stocked with beautiful, high-gloss AA-grade American walnut and has a lightweight aircraft-grade aluminum alloy receiver with the Weatherby name in gold lettering. The company immediately began offering the Element in 12, 20 and 28 gauge (the subgauge gun will set you back an extra $50). The Element is a very attractive gun and it weighs 6-6¾ pounds, so you can carry it in the field all day without getting tired. The balance is excellent and the gun swings naturally, an overall good value for an inertia-driven gun. (MSRP starts at $1,099)

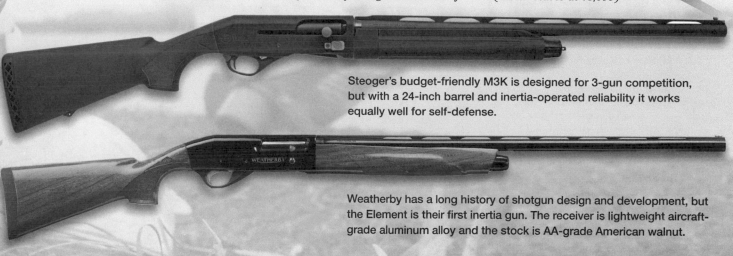

Stoeger's budget-friendly M3K is designed for 3-gun competition, but with a 24-inch barrel and inertia-operated reliability it works equally well for self-defense.

Weatherby has a long history of shotgun design and development, but the Element is their first inertia gun. The receiver is lightweight aircraft-grade aluminum alloy and the stock is AA-grade American walnut.

The King Gun Sight Company

MODERN SIGHTS FOR MODERN ARMS

By Charles E. Petty

A pair of Colt 1911 National Match .45s with King sights and vintage ammo.

If you look at guns made between the two World Wars chances are you've seen some with sights bearing the mark "King." The King Gun Sight Company made replacement sights for a wide variety of rifles of all action types, most notable were tang sights adjustable for both windage and elevation. While there were several companies making improved rifle sights in those days, most pistols and revolvers arrived with fixed sights. Few had any easy way to add adjustable sights and factory target sights of the day were not without their flaws.

That is where King made their breakthrough with sights that could be precisely adjusted for both windage and elevation, and fairly easily installed primarily on revolvers from Colt and Smith & Wesson. Their slogan was, "Modern Sights For Modern Arms." It wasn't until after WWII that others came to swim in what had been King's private pond.

Of course, those earliest handguns didn't have convenient holes drilled by the factory so King installed a lot of them, and along the way became an outstanding gunsmith shop. If you pick up an old revolver with King sights it may also have an awesome trigger action, and you can bet King did that too. It is not an exaggeration to give King credit for advancing the sport of competitive pistol shooting with both their sights and action work.

Dean Wallace King was born Dec. 23, 1869 in Golden, Colo., and first made replacement sights for rifles in Denver. It has been reported that he moved to San Francisco around 1915. By far the best historical reference on King is found in a three-part series of articles entitled "The King Gun Sight Company" by James L. Wallinger and Jim King (no relation) that appeared in the *Journal of the S&W Collectors Association.* Much of their research came from ads that King ran in *American Rifleman* from 1942 to 1952 and interviews with former employees.

From the 1920s until well after WWII, conventional or bull's-eye pistol was the only form of handgun competition, and it wasn't until the 1960s that any form of *practical* pistol match came along. Starting in the '50s, the factories began to offer some guns that were competitive and those were either .22 automatics or revolvers. During the '30s truly

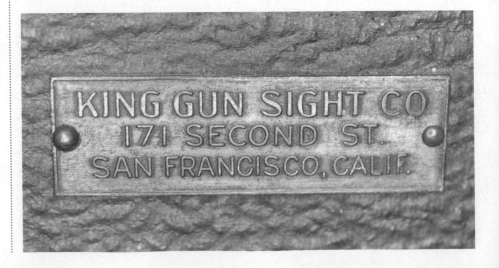

accurate 1911 .45
pistols were either
Colt National Match
models or custom jobs
from the few civilian custom
shops. The military shooting
programs really didn't become
serious players until the U.S. Army
marksmanship training unit (USAMU)
in 1956 or the U.S. Air Force Marksmanship School (USAFMMS) in 1959.

A friend of mine let me copy his copy
of an early King catalog, though it was
far from complete. More recently a
reader, responding to something in a
previous article, referred me to Cornell
Publications (www.cornellpubs.com)
that offers copies of many old catalogs –
including King's No. 19 from 1939. It has
become my wish book.

King's guns have
appealed to me for a
long time and each
one has been a learning
tool, but one of the most
intriguing of all was an
accidental purchase. I was
on the way out the door of a
gun show when I saw one of those
red beacons calling me from a table I
had passed a couple of times earlier. A
conversation with the owner revealed he
had just gotten there and was selling a
few guns that had belonged to his grandfather. One was a Colt Army Special .38
in very nice condition that wore a pair
of Roper thumbrest grips. After a brief
negotiation I bought it, put it in my pack
and hit the road. At home the next day
I cut the tie-wrap off and made several

discoveries. The serial number
was from 1921 and in addition
to the King front and rear sights
it had a wide, checkered hammer.
When I removed the grips I saw that both
front and rear frame straps had been
checkered, as had the trigger.

But the real surprise came when I
found a cylinder latch on the right side
of the frame. Since swing-out cylinders
came along on the S&W Hand Ejector
models and Colt Officers models the
latch has been on the left side. I soon
learned the other one didn't do anything.
Just to be sure I took off the sideplate
and there, plain as day, was a screw
in the right side that held the latch.
The only reasonable conclusion is that
somebody wanted it that way—perhaps
as a thumbrest.

In those days companies would do almost anything as long as it was safe and the customer was willing to pay for it. The workmanship is perfect and it was no simple job to figure out precisely where to drill the hole. While I have no proof, I'd bet the ranch that King did it, because the other work includes a short single-action cocking stroke, and checkering of the trigger, both front and back straps and a wide, checkered hammer. All trademark King jobs. In today's dollars that would be about $525 worth of work, not counting the gun.

Perhaps the most unusual example of King's work is a double-action .38 revolver with King sights that the serial number reveals to be a 1915 vintage Army Special. I had to rely on the number for identification because the 6½-inch barrel is plainly marked, "COLT SINGLE ACTION ARMY." The legend on top of the barrel reads, "COLT'S PT. F.A. MFG. Co HARTF." Really. You can also see where the ejector rod stud was removed and the space filled with a piece often called a "dutchman" that is nearly invisible. The name is presumably for the little Dutch boy plugging the dike.

Another novelty is a .45 SAA that has been converted to .22 Long Rifle. The barrel has been replaced and the cylinder sleeved for the smaller cartridge. Although the gun has King sights and a nice action, there is no proof that the conversion was done by King. In fact another company, Christy Gun Works, in Sacramento was well known for that type of work and may have done this one.

All too often answering one question leads to another, but fortunately this time a plausible explanation

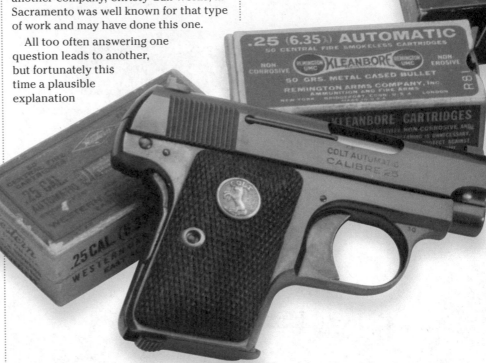

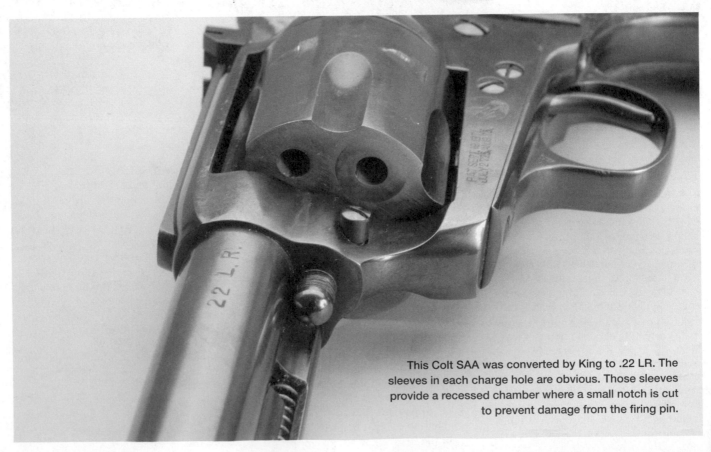

This Colt SAA was converted by King to .22 LR. The sleeves in each charge hole are obvious. Those sleeves provide a recessed chamber where a small notch is cut to prevent damage from the firing pin.

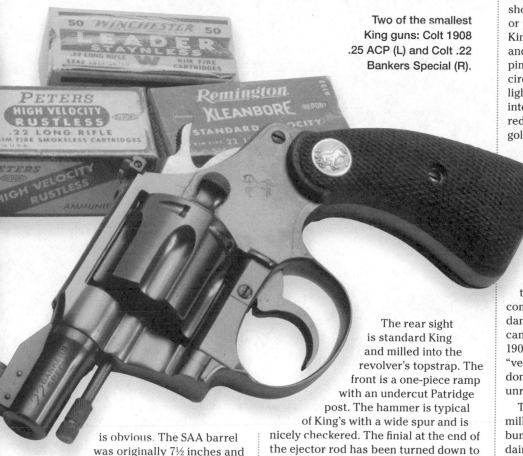

Two of the smallest King guns: Colt 1908 .25 ACP (L) and Colt .22 Bankers Special (R).

The rear sight is standard King and milled into the revolver's topstrap. The front is a one-piece ramp with an undercut Patridge post. The hammer is typical of King's with a wide spur and is nicely checkered. The finial at the end of the ejector rod has been turned down to clear the larger barrel diameter.

There's more: the double-action operation has been removed. If you pull the trigger the cylinder will rotate but that's all. But when you cock it, the trigger pull is a flawless 2 pounds, 3 ounces that really does break without movement; the fabled "glass rod" we hear about but seldom see.

One of the real problems involved

is obvious. The SAA barrel was originally 7½ inches and slightly larger in diameter. After it was modified to fit the Army Special, the SAA barrel adds a few ounces. It is also reasonable to ask "why?" The change is really small but it illustrates the willingness of the gunsmiths to do what the customer wanted. Today an original first-generation SAA .38 barrel would be quite rare and desirable, but at the time that work was done it was just another barrel.

with putting adjustable sights on a pistol is that the front sight is going to be too short, and many are an integral piece or pressed into a slot cut in the barrel. King's sight simply fits over the original and is held in place with one or two small pins. Inlaid into the sight base is a small circle of polished metal that reflects light onto the sight blade. These are interchangeable, but the coolest is the red insert that caught my eye. White and gold inserts were also offered in addition to plain black.

Even though their catalog has a complete menu of services, one of the real adventures in collecting King stuff is to find something totally unexpected. Probably on a whim, someone got King to install adjustable sights on a little Colt Bankers Special in .22 caliber. Surely that couldn't have been for serious competition, but it would have been a dandy fun gun. Still another unlikely candidate is a dainty little Colt Model 1908 .25 ACP pistol, sometimes called the "vest pocket," that must have either been done for show or by someone with highly unrealistic expectations for the .25 ACP.

The little pistol came with a gutter milled in the top of the slide and a tiny bump for a front sight. Now there is a dainty red dot pressed into a little hole drilled into the slide that is virtually invisible from the inside. A small dovetail is milled into the rear of the slide to carry a small rear sight adjustable only for windage by drift, but the sight has five little graduations just like those seen on adjustable sights. It also has a white outline rear and is plainly

A King rear sight on an early Colt National Match 1911.

Top: A first model Woodsman with a ventilated rib and King's Adjustable Balancing Weights. Notice that the triggerguard has been enlarged for shooting with gloves. Below: A second model Woodsman wlth standard King sights and weights.

The spur of the King "cockeyed hammer" was forged to a wider shape then polished and checkered. Not all had the marking.

marked, "King Pat. Pend" There just wasn't enough room for a period to suggest "pending."

The gun's condition is also remarkable. I can find nothing to suggest it has ever been fired, and both the blue and case-hardening look just as they must have when it left the factory in 1932. It is simply a jewel.

There were also options available for the rear sight. The majority are simple notches, but there are also white-outline versions. Those seem to appear in similar numbers, and there is also a U-shaped notch that matches the radius of a standard bull's-eye pistol target.

Another of King's trademark jobs was the "Cockeyed Hammer" for revolvers. Back before autoloaders became the norm, revolvers were used in bull's-eye pistol so the gun had to be cocked for each shot in the timed and rapid-fire events. The wider spur made it easier to cock the gun with the thumb of the shooting hand. These were available for either right- or left-handed shooters, plus there was also a wide-hammer version roughly twice as wide as the standard

Colt hammer. This was done by forging the original spur to the desired width and then polishing and checkering it. They also had several patterns of weight-reducing cuts on the hammer to reduce lock time. Some, but not all, are marked "King Cockeyed Hammer." So if you see a nice wide, finely checkered hammer spur the odds are good King made it.

King's most expensive job was a full-length ventilated rib. Most are found on Colt revolvers and are marked, "Colt-King Super Target," but you might also see, "S&W-King Super Target." More than a few of us suspect that this was the inspiration for Colt's Python. Most ribs are attached by silver solder, but King had an elegant solution that did not require refinishing. The rib was machined from a single piece, finished separately and attached to the front sight with pins. The rear sight was held by the screw that adjusted elevation. The rib was bent so that when both ends were secured it would lie on the barrel with no gaps.

Based on years of observation, by far the greatest number of handguns with King sights are Colt revolvers. S&W revolvers are much less common and estimates suggest that the Colts outnumber S&W by 10 to one. Semiautomatic pistols from Colt and High Standard are even more unusual. One

particularly interesting modification is found within the Colt Woodsman line. In addition to sights or a rib, King installed a tube underneath the barrel to contain a couple of weights. I have observed both brass and steel, and have seen reports of aluminum and a mercury-filled cylinder. King called them, "magazine balancing weights." This added a few ounces of weight and also made the pistol a bit muzzle heavy, which was viewed by some as an asset.

King Gun Sight Co. is best known for handgun sights but that was really only part of their business. My suspicion is that King sold quite a few guns that they bought from Colt or Smith & Wesson. Sadly, there really isn't any way to identify one without a factory letter telling you the gun was sent to King. I've seen a few in other collections and have spent money on fruitless letters. Again, I would have bet that my two Woodsman pistols with King weights would have been, but not so. I finally found a S&W .38/44 Outdoorsman with the rib that was shipped to King in July 1937. Later, I also found a second model .44 Hand Ejector from 1926 with King sights but no rib.

Just when I thought I had seen it all a friend came along with a gun box featuring a placque saying,

"KING GUN SIGHT CO.
171 SECOND ST.
SAN FRANCISCO, CALIF"

Sure enough, there was the gun box on page 60 of the catalog. It was located after all the other rifle sights, so I must have missed that page. Actually they had two models: a four-gun oblong case with a removable ammunition tray and a five-gun model with a swing-up lid to hold a spotting scope. Buyers could choose from a selection of covering material including cordovan leather. There is no indication of who actually made it, but my best guess is an outside vendor.

I was drawn into collecting King guns a long time ago when I first shot a Colt SAA with King sights that belonged to a friend. The first one I ever purchased was a 1917 Colt and the seller lamented that someone had messed up a very collectible revolver. Of course, I thought it had been improved. By far the most distinctive of King's products is the "Ramp Reflector" front sight which is most often seen with a "King Luminous Red" insert. They are like a homing beacon for me and I can literally spot one many rows away at a gun show. The design is wickedly clever and can often be installed without the need for refinishing. It consists of two parts: the ramp base that fits over the original front sight and is held on by one or two small pins that pass through the original sight. The blade is then attached to the

The King ramp reflector front sight is very popular with collectors. It likely served as inspiration for Smith & Wesson's famous red-ramp front and white-outline rear series of sights.

King's popular ramp reflector front sight mounted on a Colt Single Action.

ramp with a small screw. By far the most common is the red insert but they were also available in white, gold or plain steel Patridge style. There were also round bead inserts available in red, white or gold that matched up with a U-shaped rear sight blade.

Five or six years ago I was walking the aisles of a big show and saw the beacon of a red front sight. The gun was absolutely stunning. It went home with me and is now the crown jewel of my collection. It is a .45 Colt Single Action Army with a 5½-inch barrel. It has just about everything: a Colt-King Super Target rib, a short action, wide checkered hammer spur, checkered trigger and three weight-reducing holes in the hammer. There are only a few small marks in the finish to suggest its 81-year life.

I am really surprised that nobody else has copied the reflector sight because not only is it highly functional – it looks very cool too. The design is likely the inspiration for S&W's red ramp front sights and white outline rear. We also have the various fiber-optic designs that use different color filaments. In my opinion those sights are almost too bright. While we want something to draw our attention to the front sight in bright sunlight, there can be a glare that makes it hard to get precise alignment with the rear sight.

The "reflector" is a small circular piece of brightly polished metal mounted at an angle in the base of the front sight to focus light on the insert. It is highly visible. Some say that S&W copied the idea when they introduced the original .44 Magnum, but it's not exactly the same. S&W had long offered to install King sights if the customer wanted them and King actually used a S&W "Fine Tune" rear sight on some installations. Unless the company was installing the ventilated rib, the rear sight required milling a channel for the sight, and some

frames were simply too narrow for the standard sight. I've got a Colt Bankers Special with that arrangement and a friend has a SAA with one too. Some 1911 pistols have the reflector placed in a small hole on top of the slide.

I'm pretty sure one could study King guns until the cows come home and still be finding differences or things to marvel about. I recently found a .38 SAA from those assembled from existing parts during WWII: sometimes called a "Pre-war/Post-war model. When I picked it up something felt unusual about the trigger. A quick look revealed that it was over twice as wide as the normal Colt trigger. It was nicely checkered and then it dawned on me that the window in the trigger guard had to have been enlarged so the new one would fit. It isn't the easiest job to enlarge square holes.

The bottom line here is that every King gun must be studied carefully to see what the company did *this* time. There were so many options that customers could pick and choose either what they liked or could afford. The .38 SAA I mentioned is as close as it gets to a "full house" job with every option King offered. It is one of the few guns I've seen with a checkered backstrap. That was an extra $3.50, but checkering was not nearly as popular back then. The mother of pearl grips were a standard Colt product.

When King died in 1953 his wife took over the company and subsequently hired a manager who eventually came under controversy. He came to the attention of the authorities when it was alleged he had converted a gun to full-auto fire. Furthermore, numerous guns shipped to the company for work were mysteriously lost in the mail. An investigation was launched and a search of the manager's home discovered over 100 of the "lost" guns.

The new manager had also filed suit against Micro Sight Co. for infringing on one of King's patents, and when that suit turned sour, it was the last straw. King Gun Sight Co. went out of business in 1953.

I always thought that was the end of the story until just last year when I came across a gun that obviously had King sights. It was a Colt Woodsman with a top half marked, "Auto-Action." I had once seen a picture of one in Suther-

Pre-war/Post-war model Colt Single Action Army .38 Special with sights, short action, cockeyed hammer, wide checkered trigger and checkered backstrap all from King. Plus, it features original Colt mother of pearl grips.

The author's favorite King revolver was given the "full house" treatment with numerous King options. It's a .45 Colt Single Action Army with a 5½-inch barrel, Colt-King Super Target rib, a short action, wide checkered hammer spur, checkered trigger and three weight-reducing holes in the hammer.

land's book where it was described as an experimental Colt, but my research and then the *S&W Journal* articles provided a different answer. That came in the form of an advertisement in the May 1956 issue of *GUNS Magazine* for the King Auto-Action replacement for the original Colt slide. It provided a stationary rear sight and was sold by Ricky Gunsight Co. of Burlingame, Calif. Ricky had apparently purchased the rights and parts and began to market King sights. The best guess I can make

is that Dean King designed the Auto-Action but did not bring it to market prior to his death.

I'm sure that Dean King had no idea that long after his death guns from his shop would be highly sought after collector's items. As a target shooter I was drawn to them in the early 1980s. In a way, each and every King gun one sees is a mystery because there is no historical record to consult. The copy of an old catalog has become a very valuable reference. I've tried to figure out how to correlate those prices to compare the economy and prices of today. In 1938 the Federal minimum wage was $0.25 per hour and King charged $20 for the full-length rib with a choice of sights installed on a Colt or S&W revolver. You could buy the complete gun for between $54.50 and $72.50. A Colt 5½-inch Single Action Army in a choice of calibers was $59.50. Government statistics say that the average weekly wage in 1938 was about $41, and that inflation has averaged 3.73 percent per year. With all that in mind we would probably classify King's work as "high end."

We do know that King moved a couple of times in San Francisco, presumably to larger quarters, and just from the breadth of the product line

it is safe to say that it was not a small business. The company would have employed machinists, tool & die makers, finishers and gunsmiths, plus shipping clerks and office workers.

King also sold parts, so it is certainly possible to see a gun with King sights that were installed elsewhere. My best advice is to study the gun extremely carefully. King's workmanship was so good that something that looks less than perfect could be a red flag. But as a collector – any King gun you see is a rare gun. For a shooter – the wonderful triggers and sights make them a joy to shoot. While most of us revere King for its work with handguns, the catalog also shows a great variety of both tang and buckhorn sights for rifles, and beads for shotguns.

Every writer will have a story about the boat he missed – and my great regret is learning that the late Jay Postman had worked at King, only after Jay's untimely death. To me, Jay was the voice of RCBS and I sought him out frequently for answers to obscure questions. He had an encyclopedic memory and once told me the exact issue and page of an *American Rifleman* issue where I could find my answer. I remarked that I hadn't heard the click of computer keys, and he replied something to the effect of, "I don' need no stinkin' computer." Of course he was right.

By **Paul Scarlata**
Photos by: **Paul Budde, Becky Scarlata and Dick Cole**

How Springfield's XD family made this shooter a believer

A Preference for POLYMER

Polymer pistols have been around now for more than 30 years. When I first heard about them I thought I was the brunt of some kind of joke. I mean, who ever heard of a pistol made from plastic?

As a member of the firearms media I felt it was my duty to my readers to investigate this new development. The first thing I discovered was that the pistol frame was not made from everyday plastic but of a space-age material known generically as polymer.

Polymer is basically a specially developed, very hard plastic that can replicate the hardness of metal, but is much lighter and in many ways more durable. The low-impact parts of a firearm, particularly the frame, grip, magazine, sights and internal components, can be made out of polymer. Testing showed that polymer is stronger than steel at any given thickness and resists shock, wear, abrasion, salts, solvents, oils and environmental extremes better than metal.

Other advantages of polymer frames are cost, weight and size. Metal pistol frames must be machined—a time consuming and costly process—whereas polymer frames are molded which is quick and inexpensive.

It goes without saying that a pistol with a polymer frame and other parts is going to be considerably lighter than one using the same components made from metal. This makes them more convenient to carry for extended periods of time, an important feature for police officers and military personnel who are already burdened with equipment.

While lighter weight generally means more recoil, when a pistol with a polymer frame is fired the frame actually flexes and absorbs some of the recoil pulse. This means that polymer pistols are often softer shooters than metal-frame pistols of similar size firing the same cartridge.

Lastly we have size. Polymer frame pistols do not require separate grip panels, this reduces the width of the grip frame a considerable degree providing two benefits. It allows the use of high-capacity magazines without making the grip too wide, which means that shooters with small hands don't have trouble handling the pistol. With the increasing number of female police officers and soldiers this was an important consideration.

Well there was only one way to see if this was all true, so in the mid-1980s I bought a Glock 17. I found it to be reliable, accurate, easy to use, easy to carry, and easy to disassemble and clean – all features that led me to use it for concealed carry, home defense and even some informal competitive shooting.

I was not the only shooter who developed an admiration for this new breed of pistol. In fact, so many civilian shooters, police officers and soldiers did that it wasn't long before other handgun manufacturers began adding "plastic" pistols to their product lines. Today, virtually every one of them makes polymer handguns.

For personal and home defense, training, competitive shooting and, in some cases, small-game hunting, the odds are you will see me using a polymer-frame pistol in preference to one with a metal frame. In the last year I have become enamored with a particular line of polymer pistols.

In 1999, the IM Metal Corporation of Croatia introduced a polymer-frame pistol known as the HS-2000. It soon attracted the attention of Springfield Armory, which wanted a product to break into the lucrative police market and saw what they needed in the Croatian pistol.

After some minor changes, the HS-2000 was re-introduced to American shooters in 2002 as the Springfield Armory X-Treme Duty Pistol, better known simply as the XD. The XD lineup quickly earned the respect of shooters and the pistols have become quite popular.

The XD design uses an injection molded polymer frame that provides superior resistance to abuse, wear, oils, solvents and environmental extremes. The grip frame has an ergonomically pleasing shape that provides superior "pointability" over much of the competition. Another innovative feature is the ambidextrous magazine release. No longer is the southpaw shooter forced to

The XD that started it all was the 4-inch barrel 9mm Service Model of 2002. It is also chambered in .357 SIG, .40 S&W and .45 ACP.

release magazines with their trigger finger or swap the release button from port to starboard sides of the pistol.

Machined from solid steel stock, the locking block insert in the frame has integral rails that the slide reciprocates on in addition to housing the lower portion of the feed ramp. Additional slide support is provided by two rails at the rear of the frame, while the dust cover area features a Pictatinny type rail for mounting tactical lights or lasers.

The slide is CNC machined from a solid billet of steel and features front and rear grasping grooves and is protected by Springfield's proprietary Bruniral finish. Locking occurs by way of the barrel hood moving up into, and bearing on the front edge of the ejection port. When the pistol is fired the barrel and slide move

together a short distance before the barrel drops down on the locking block, allowing the slide to continue to the rear extracting and ejecting the spent case. A dual recoil spring located under the barrel then pulls the slide forward, stripping the next round out of the magazine and chambering it. As the slide goes into battery the barrel is pulled up and its hood enters the ejection port locking the two units together.

XD pistols have six separate safety devices: a grip safety at the rear of the frame, a trigger block safety on the face of the trigger, a plunger type firing pin safety, and a disconnector that prevents the pistol from being fired unless to the slide is completely in battery. At the rear of the ejection port is a loaded chamber indicator and, when cocked, the tail of the striker extends out of the end of the slide. Both provide visible and tactical indications of the pistol's condition.

Springfield refers to the XD's trigger system as the USA (Ultra Safe Assurance). When the slide is retracted and released, the wide portion of the striker tail engages a fixed sear in the frame where it's held to the rear. A trip lever for the striker block (or firing pin safety) is positioned along the right side and forward of this sear. Operating together with its own totally independent return spring, the trigger and draw bar have no contact with these parts until pressure is applied to the trigger.

A look at the XD disassembled into its five major components.

The current 9mm and .40-caliber XD 4-inch Service Models are available with the V-10 barrel and slide porting.

Above: This is the 4-inch Compact Service Model, which uses the 3.8-inch compact frame with a 4-inch barrel.

Pulling the XD's trigger depresses the trigger block safety. When it's pulled there is a significant amount of take up before the firing pin safety is depressed and then the sear is tripped. In fact, it feels more like double-action revolver trigger, which is yet another extra margin of safety. The firing pin safety blocks the wide sear portion of the striker on the underside of the slide.

The XD has proved to be a popular item with American civilian shooters, as well as an ever-growing number of law enforcement agencies. As with any new product, Springfield was anxious to get customer feedback and once they did they set about answering the complaints and or suggestions that shooters provided them with. The result was the XD(M).

Introduced in 2008, the XD(M) had all the features of the XD but with a more ergonomically pleasing grip frame featuring interchangeable backstraps, these allowed the shooter to fit the pistol to their particular hand size, while the slide had deeper and longer grasping grooves.

If you check Springfield's website you will find no less than 132 versions (!) of the XD and XD(M) pistols in 9mm, .357 SIG, .40 S&W and .45 ACP – all suitable for police and military service, home and personal defense, concealed carry, competitive shooting and as trail guns.

Over the years I have tested a number of XD and XD(M) pistol for various publications and have found them to be accurate, ergonomically pleasing and utterly reliable. Two years ago I purchased a .40-caliber XD(M) 4.5-inch barrel pistol to use as a backup gun in case my regular USPSA pistol—a customized, high-capacity 1911—choked on me at a match. As these things tend to happen, at a match in 2013 the magazine release on my 1911 locked up solid as I was loading the pistol for the first stage. I returned to my truck, grabbed the XD(M), loaded the magazines and got back into the game.

By the time the match was over I had shot six stages completely clean and finished 1st place in my class in Limited 10 Division. I had just aced a match with an out-of-the-box pistol with which I had only limited experience, and that had cost me a lot less than my custom 1911. Hmmm…

I competed with the XD(M) over the next two months and became increasing enamored with it. In fact, I decided to use it as my regular match pistol and, as we USPSA shooters tend to do, decided to add a few "bells and whistles" to make it even more suitable for competition.

I returned the pistol to Springfield where they installed an extended magazine release and magazine well funnel for fast, fumble-free reloads. Magazine capacity was enlarged to a comforting 19 rounds by using Taylor Freelance magazine extensions with Grams Engineering springs and followers.

A Heinie Ledge rear sight was mated with a fiber-optic front before the pistol was shipped off to Powder River Precision for their Combat Carry Trigger Job. This reduced trigger travel and reset, and gave it a crisp let-off of approximately 3.75 pounds. Lastly, a Canyon Creek Tungsten Guide Rod and spring added about 3 ounces of recoil-reducing weight.

All XD and XD(M) pistols have a loaded chamber indicator on top of the slide to provide a quick visual and tactical indication of the pistol's condition.

The XD 3" Sub-Compact comes with a spare X-Tension magazine and is available with a stainless slide and various colored frames.

I now use my XD(M) exclusively when competing in USPSA Limited and Limited 10 Divisions. When I want to compete in the Production Division all I must do to make it "legal" is remove the magazine well funnel and replace Tungsten Guide Rod with the stock spring and rod. I now have the best of both, or three, worlds for the price of one pistol.

My wife Becky has become an enthusiastic shooter and she recently expressed interest in giving Action Pistol competition a try. She tried a number of pistols until she decided that "...your XD(M)" suited her best. Accordingly I

Below: The author's customized .40-caliber XD(M) 4.5" features Heinie sights, a Springfield magazine well funnel, extended magazine releases, Powder River Precision Combat Carry Trigger kit and a Canyon Creek Tungsten Guide Rod and spring. All add up for three ounces of recoil-reducing weight.

The gaping magazine well that Springfield Armory installed on the author's pistol ensures fast, fumble-free reloads under the pressure of competition shooting. Note the extended magazine release.

The XD(M) 5.25 pistols were designed for Action Pistol competition and have 5.25-inch barrels, Minimal Reset triggers, match-grade barrels, fiber-optic front and adjustable rear sights. They are available in 9mm, .40 and .45 caliber.

obtained a 9mm XD(M) 5.25" Competition Series pistol for Becky to try out.

The XD(M) 5.25" was intended to give the competitor everything they needed to compete in USPSA Production Division right out of the box. It features a match-grade 5.25-inch barrel, which allows the 9mm cartridge to achieve its ballistic potential for enhanced on-target performance. The open-top slide reduces reciprocating mass to lessen muzzle flip, allows for faster cycling and permits the pistol to digest a wide variety of ammunition with reliability. A fully adjustable rear sight and red fiber-optic front sight are standard. Plus, the longer sight radius enhances accuracy.

The XD(M) 9mm 5.25" features Springfield's all-steel "Megazine" which holds 19 rounds of 9mm ammunition. It comes standard with ambidextrous magazine releases, a padded carrying case, three magazines, holster, dual magazine pouch and a magazine loader. All you need is some ammo and you're ready to rock 'n' roll in USPSA's Production Division.

Becky took to the 5.25 like the proverbial duck to water. She really appreciated the excellent sights, longer sight radius, low recoil and, being a southpaw, the ambidextrous magazine release got a big thumbs up the first time she used the pistol.

Since we both needed something to tote our XD(M)s around in at matches I contacted Tommy Campbell at Safariland, who sent me one of their 5197 Open Top holsters with a 567BL-2-150 adjustable belt loop and HDA-KIT-RH two-inch drop kit to move it out and down from my body for an unimpeded draw. For Becky, Tommy sent along a 5197 Holster with the Wedge Belt Loop that adapts the holster to the female shape.

For fans of the original XD who want a longer barreled pistol, Springfield offers the XD 5-inch Tactical model with a 5-inch barrel and the option of ambidextrous thumb safeties.

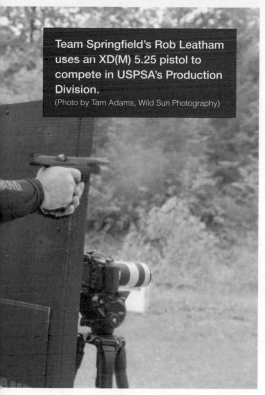

Team Springfield's Rob Leatham uses an XD(M) 5.25 pistol to compete in USPSA's Production Division.
(Photo by Tam Adams, Wild Sun Photography)

The author and his wife both use Safariland 5197 Open Top holsters when competing. She adds a Wedge Belt Loop to adapt it to the female form.

While the XD pistols are replete with safety devices, I feel that thumb safeties have a definite place, especially with pistols used by law enforcement personnel. It is common knowledge that most of the pistols used by police today are not equipped with manual safeties. This means that if an officer's pistol is snatched from him it is instantly usable by his assailant. But, if equipped with a manual safety the criminal will not be able to fire it until they figure out how to take the safety "off," which can give the officer vital time to access a backup gun or take other actions to disable the attacker.

At present Springfield only offers the manual safety option on the .45 caliber 4-inch Service and 5-inch Tactical models. I would like to see this option expanded to cover all models of the XD and XD(M) series.

Springfield also offers an extensive line of compact and subcompact pistols, the smallest of which is the XD-S Single Stack. Available in 9mm and .45 caliber, it is only 6.3 inches long with a 3.3-inch barrel and tips the scales (unloaded) at 23 ounces (21.5 oz. for the .45 model).

New on the XD-S is Springfield's Short Reset trigger. Based upon the earlier USA trigger, it features a shorter take-up, crisper let-off, reduced overtravel and – as its name indicates – a short reset which can be felt and heard by the shooter. The XD-S is small enough that

I can carry it in complete comfort in the front pocket of my cargo pants.

For those wanting a longer sighting radius the XD-S is also available with a 4-inch barrel. Both models come with extended magazines that increase capacity to seven (.45) and nine (9mm) rounds.

If you want a subcompact XD but with higher cartridge capacity you don't need to look any further than Springfield's newest offering, the XD Mod.2. Available in 9mm and .40 S&W, with a 3-inch barrel it is only 6.25 inches long and weighs 26 ounces. Double-column magazines provide a capacity of 13 (9mm) and nine (.40) rounds while the supplied X-Tension magazines up that to 16 and 12 rounds respectively.

The XD Mod.2 also features a reshaped slide and frame. The latter features the GripZone, a set of three distinct textures, each engineered for a specific purpose. The re-contoured, slimmer frame provides a more

natural grip feel, and the High-Hand grip relief and High-Hand beavertail enable the hand to be positioned as high as possible on the pistol to reduce felt recoil. The no-snag triggerguard minimizes possible unintended contact with a holster or clothing. As with the XD(M) 5.25" and XD-S, a fiber-optic front sight is standard equipment.

After examining the XD Mod.2, Becky, who recently obtained her concealed carry license,

Springfield's first single-column (and slimmest) polymer-frame pistol is the XD-S 3.3.

Big-bore lovers will find the .45 ACP XD(M) 3.8" Compact right up their alley.

commented, "I think it would make a wonderful birthday gift for the right person." Hm-mmm... I think I just heard a hint drop?

How would you like to have a pistol that is small enough for concealed carry but large enough for home defense and even police service? If you're in the market for such a multitasking semiauto then you should check out the XD(M) 3.8 Compact.

As with the other pistols, the "3.8" indicates how long the barrel is, and a tube of such length still allows the 9mm, .40 and .45 cartridges to achieve sufficient ballistics while keeping the overall length to a concealable 6.75 inches.

Each pistol comes with a stainless steel X-Tension magazine that not only gives the shooter an extra six, five and four rounds (9mm, .40 and .45), but also provides a full-size grip for enhanced recoil control and makes the pistol large enough for holster carry by law enforcement officers. I guess you could say it "carries like a compact and handles like full-size pistol."

I thought it would be interesting to run several of the pistols mentioned in this article through some drills to see how they handle. Accordingly, Becky and I headed out to the range with my customized .40-caliber XD(M) 4.5, her XD(M) 9mm 5.25", a .40-caliber XD(M) 3.8 Compact, a long-nose XD 5-inch Tactical with thumb safeties and a new 9mm XD Mod.2.

The author and his wife Becky shooting the XD(M) 3.8 Compact in .40 S&W.

Above left: A sampling of the target results with some of the test pistols.

His and hers XD(M)s.

RANGE TESTS			
PISTOL	**AMMUNITION**	**BEST GROUP**	**AVG. GROUP**
XD(M) 4.5 .40 S&W	Winchester 155-gr. Silvertip	1.8"	3"
	Black Hills 180-gr. FMJ	1.5"	2.5"
XD(M) 3.8 .40 S&W	Winchester 155-gr. Silvertip	2.3"	3.0"
	Black Hills 180-gr. FMJ	2"	2.8"
XD(M) 5.25 9mm	CCI Blazer 115-gr. FMJ	1.9"	2.9"
	Black Hills 124-gr. JHP	1.5"	2.3"
XD Mod. 2 9mm	CCI Blazer 115-gr. FMJ	2"	2.5"
	Black Hills 124-gr. JHP	2.3"	2.8"
XD 5" Tactical .45 ACP	Remington 185-gr. Golden Saber	2.8"	3.3"
	Black Hills 230-gr. FMJ	2.8"	3.5"

NOTE: Test firing was conducted from an MTM K-Zone rest.

SPECIFICATIONS – SPRINGFIELD XD(M) 3.8 COMPACT

Caliber:	.40 S&W
Overall length:	6.75 in.
Barrel length:	3.8 in.
Height:	4.75 in.
Weight (unloaded):	28 oz.
Construction:	Slide: forged steel; frame: polymer
Magazine:	11 or 16 rounds
Sights:	Front: white dot
	Rear: dual dots
Features:	Interchangeable backstraps, ambidextrous thumb safeties and magazine release, loaded chamber indicator, cocked striker indicator, two spare magazines, holster, dual magazine pouch, magazine loader, carrying case, cable lock and owner's manual

SPECIFICATIONS – SPRINGFIELD XD MOD.2

Caliber:	9mm Parabellum
Overall length:	6.25 in.
Barrel length:	3 in.
Height:	4.75 in.
Weight (unloaded):	26 oz.
Construction:	Forged steel; frame: polymer
Magazine:	13 or 16 rounds
Sights:	Front: white dot
	Rear: dual dots
Features:	Ambidextrous magazine release, loaded chamber indicator, cocked striker indicator, two spare magazines, holster, dual magazine pouch, magazine loader, carrying case, cable lock and owner's manual

SPECIFICATIONS – SPRINGFIELD XD(M) 4.5

Caliber:	.40 S&W
Overall length:	7.6 in.
Barrel length:	4.5 in.
Height:	4.75 in.
Weight (unloaded):	30 oz.
Construction:	Slide: forged steel; frame: polymer
Magazine:	16 Rounds
Sights:	Front: white dot
	Rear: dual dots
Features:	Interchangeable backstraps, ambidextrous thumb safety and magazine release, loaded chamber indicator, cocked striker indicator, two spare magazines, holster, dual magazine pouch, magazine loader, carrying case, cable lock and owner's manual

SPECIFICATIONS – SPRINGFIELD XD(M) 5.25

Caliber:	9mm Parabellum
Overall length:	8.3 in.
Barrel length:	5.25 in.
Height:	5.875 in.
Weight (unloaded):	29 oz.
Construction:	Slide: forged steel; frame: polymer
Magazine:	19 Rounds
Finish:	Black melonite or bright
Sights:	Front: fiber optic
	Rear: fully adjustable
Grips:	Polymer
Features:	Interchangeable backstraps, ambidextrous thumb safeties and magazine release, loaded chamber indicator, cocked striker indicator, two spare magazines, holster, dual magazine pouch, magazine loader, carrying case, cable lock and owner's manual

SPECIFICATIONS – SPRINGFIELD XD 5" TACTICAL

Caliber:	.45 ACP
Overall length:	8.3 in.
Barrel length:	5 in.
Height:	5.75 in.
Weight (unloaded):	33 oz.
Construction:	Slide: forged steel; frame: polymer
Magazine:	13 Rounds
Sights:	Front: white dot
	Rear: dual dots
Features:	Ambidextrous thumb safety and magazine release, loaded chamber indicator, cocked striker indicator, spare magazine, holster, dual magazine pouch, magazine loader, carrying case, cable lock and owner's manual

Accuracy testing was conducted at 25 yards with the three full-size pistols, 15 yards with the 3.8 Compact and seven yards with the Mod. 2. All five shot to point of aim and produced very impressive results (see the Range Test table on pg.85).

Becky and I then ran our XD(M) 4.5 and 5.25 pistols through a series of drills on 8-inch steel plate racks and static steel targets. We also set up a USPSA-style stage with multiple cardboard targets and ran it several times each.

The three other pistols were run through offhand drills on combat targets

All XD(M) carrying cases include two spare magazines, a holster, dual magazine pouch, magazine loader, interchangeable grip backstraps and cable lock.

from various distances, and all of them performed flawlessly.

By the end of the day we had shot approximately 500 rounds through the five pistols and did not experience a single malfunction. Considering three of them were brand-new, out-of-the-box pistols, this speaks volumes about the quality and innate reliability of the XD/XD(M) platform.

If you're in the market for a modern polymer-frame pistol for police service, competitive shooting, home and personal defense, concealed carry or as a trail gun I'd suggest you check out Springfield's XD/XD(M) series. If you can't find one that meets your needs, well, you're in a lot of trouble!

.22-CALIBER
VARMINT CARTRIDGE
OVERVIEW

By **Stan Trzoniec**
(Photos by the author)

Since a young boy, I've always been drawn to .22-caliber cartridges. After the last day of school for the summer my family would all head up to my Uncle's farm in the southern tier of New York to drop me off for a few months of great outdoor adventures. My buddy from down the road and I would spend time culling woodchucks, fishing in the brook and talking for hours about what we wanted to do when we grew up.

While I had full access to my Uncle's Winchester single-shot .22, it was the sports from around Cooperstown that made me look forward to the various centerfire offerings. Granted at that time the list was few, rifles were too expensive for a young lad like myself. Nevertheless, watching them pick off chucks with custom rifles equipped with Unertl scopes at ranges unheard of by a pair of youthful riflemen still made us daydream of the varmint rigs to come. Looking back, I remember the one cartridge that seemed to overshadow all at that time – the .219 Donaldson Wasp – a cartridge that I would follow up on and eventually chamber in a single-shot Ruger No. 1 rifle.

Sitting on that hill overlooking a couple hundred acres in midsummer was very impressionable on this 10-year-old shooter. During that time, outdoor markets around southern New York were in vogue and I went along with some family members since there was always a bevy of book dealers scattered around the area. While the rest of the family was shopping, I dug deep into the book piles to find the works of Donaldson, Landis, Gebby and Mashburn. Out of those four, Charles Landis seemed to be the most prolific and his books still sit in my library today – a tribute to the longevity of the .22 centerfire cartridge.

Since that time I have had the privilege of working with a host of commercial and wildcat .22 cartridges in a wide array of rifles. I really enjoy the wildcats but do dabble with commercial ammunition as well. All are fun to work with and need plenty of interesting research to get them to that first three-shot group, and they give me an excuse to build a custom rifle using the actions of Thompson Center, Remington, Ruger and Cooper Arms.

It is interesting to note that while most of us will hunt small game with off-the-shelf cartridges, there are the few that are willing to go the wildcat route. For the most part the formula is easy, and while some of these classic cartridges do need some work, others can be fire-formed right in the chamber; neck sized and reloaded to at least a 10 percent advantage in velocities over the commercial brands.

All of the following cartridges are my favorite .22s that I use on a regular basis here in New England for my favorite small game animal – the wily woodchuck. A few have been left out, but for the most part, this list has all of the things necessary to get you out to the north 40 and will supply you with enough work to last a lifetime. The reviews are based on my experiences, the guns I used and the results that gave me the most satisfaction and fun in the field. And I still very much enjoy going to New York for chuck hunts with another friend and hope to for a long time.

.22 Remington Jet

This so-called "handgun" cartridge came about through the resources of the Thompson/Center Custom Shop and their ability to chamber a wide range of now out-of-date .22 cartridges. Starting with the lightweight Contender frame, I added a thumbhole stock and a T/C 3-9x scope with their proprietary ring and one-piece base set. The cartridge itself was developed by Remington and Smith & Wesson in 1961 to be used in the Model

Here are a few common and wildcat .22-caliber varmint cartridges. From left to right you have the .219 Donaldson Wasp, .225 Winchester, .224 Weatherby Magnum, .22-250 Remington, .22-250 Ackley Improved, .220 Swift and the compatible .220 Weatherby Rocket.

Ground squirrels are fair game for year-round shooting fun with some of the smaller .22-caliber cartridges like the .218 Bee or Hornet.

While this rockchuck was photographed in Montana, its kin on the east side of the country is the common woodchuck. With keen senses, they are a challenge to hunt from a distance regardless of the location.

53 revolver. Trouble followed thought as the tapered case was backing out of the cylinder causing lock up problems in the gun. No such problems occurred with the T/C and it makes for a fine varmint gun.

Although cases are available from Huntington Die Specialties (1-866-RE-LOADS), you can make them from virgin .357 Magnum brass with the help of Jet die and form sets from Redding Reloading Equipment. The T/C gun has a barrel sized for the correct .223" bullets, which you can get from Hornady, Sierra and Speer under "Hornet" in weights from 40 to 45 grains. CCI small rifle #500 primers spark the powders that include H-110 and W-296.

The highest velocities recorded were over 3,200 fps with accuracy for some loads averaging .750" for three shots at 100 yards. While you will not see this cartridge in many publications, to me it's a great way to spend a summer afternoon hunting woodchucks.

.22 Hornet

Looking back, the .22 Hornet was the first production cartridge designed especially for varmint hunting. My personal .22 Hornet is a Browning Low Wall; a trim, light rifle that has accompanied me on many varmint trips. The .22 Hornet is truly a walking varminter, and due to its recent upsurge in popularity Savage and Ruger have also chambered guns for this accurate cartridge.

My own experience with the Hornet has been most rewarding, and consider-

ing it holds around 12.2 grains of water – if you use 9.7 grains of 2400 powder per round you will get 721 refills per pound. Brass and loading dies are still available; a neck sizer is a good bet for accuracy and small rifle primers finish off the components.

Groups at 100 yards show the inherent qualities of this vintage cartridge. In testing with a Savage Model 40, bullets from 40 to 55 grains gave me better than average accuracy with some 7/8-inch groups. With that particular rifle and load combination velocities are not record shaking, but 2,901 fps is a good compromise for small game at moderate distances. I'll take it!

.22 K-Hornet

The .22 K-Hornet is the first of what I call "Lazy Wildcats" because it is formed right in the chamber. Starting out with a basic .22 Hornet cast, Lysle Kilbourn modified it for more velocity while improving performance on the terminal end. He was right on both counts.

With his improved version, you will get about 16 percent more velocity over the more common Hornet cartridge. I again turned to Thompson/Center for a barrel assembly, and though taught never to place any cartridge in any gun not so marked for it, you can imagine the unnerving feeling I got when I placed case after case of .22 Hornet ammunition into the chamber of the gun to form it to the improved version. This gave me a perfectly formed K-Hornet, so then all I

had to do was neck size the cases and I was ready to roll.

Velocities approached 3,100 fps with the 40-grain bullets and a bit less with 50-grain Speer bullets at 2,504 fps. With the former, groups ran .875" and with the latter, around .750".

This version still stings. Look into it.

.218 Bee

My pursuit of varmint cartridges and rifles led me to the .218 Bee chambered in a very nice Ruger No. 1 single-shot rifle, then later my adventures with the cartridge took me to a T/C Contender and a Taurus Raging Bull revolver of all things. The cartridge is mild to shoot, forgiving at the loading bench and a joy to shoot for small game. In its original form, this .218 Bee is necked down from the .25-20 cartridge, but today there is enough brass to go around for any dyed-in-the-wool varmint hunter.

My experiences with the No. 1 show that like the Hornet and its relatives, lightweight projectiles from 40 to 50 grains work best. One thing about the Bee is that you have a wider variety of powders at your disposal including W-680, H-322, RL-7, IMR-4227 and 2400. The best ¾-inch groups from the Ruger No. 1 were from a combination of 12.5 grains of IMR-4227 powder under a 50-grain Remington hollowpoint bullet.

With a Redfield 10x scope attached, it was a great gun in the field. I say "was" only because I rechambered the Ruger to the .219 Donaldson Wasp. The beat goes on.

.218 Mashburn Bee

Much like the .22 K-Hornet, the .218 Mashburn Bee is nothing more than the improved version of the parent .218 Bee. It grew from the Gibson Improved to the Ackley Improved, finally to emerge as the Mashburn version discussed here. The Cooper Model 38 rifle is already available in this cartridge.

The best way to make yourself some .218 Mashburn Bee cases is to take commercial .218 Bee ammunition, shoot a bunch of it in the Cooper Mashburn, and bingo, you have a new wildcat to hunt with and reload. Out of the 250 cases I fired off, only a very few showed any problems of the neck or mouth splitting – which speaks well of the Cooper chamber. RCBS supplied the die set, small rifle primers sparked the whole affair and neck sizing kept the cartridge in check

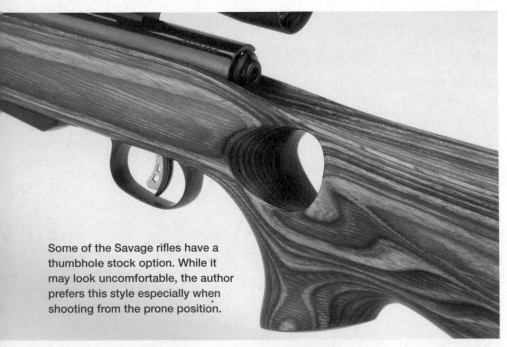

Some of the Savage rifles have a thumbhole stock option. While it may look uncomfortable, the author prefers this style especially when shooting from the prone position.

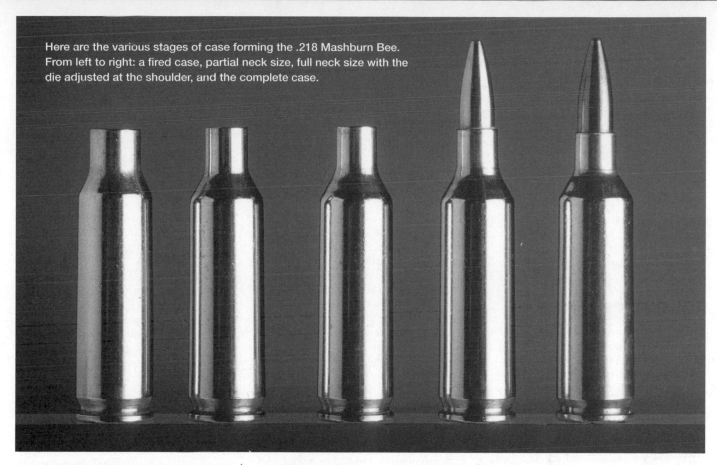

Here are the various stages of case forming the .218 Mashburn Bee. From left to right: a fired case, partial neck size, full neck size with the die adjusted at the shoulder, and the complete case.

during shooting and loading sessions. Finding loads was the only difficult part, but older books from Ness, Landis and Ackley set the parameters when it came to loads. The best performance I found was with a .224" 50-grain Hornady V-Max bullet and 17 grains of H-4198. Three-shot groups at 100 yards never went over 1/4-inch. Perfect.

.219 Zipper

From a handloaders standpoint the Zipper is a very interesting cartridge to load and shoot. Sure, it's a multistep process, but when you have a nice pile of brass to work with it's a pleasure to shoot. Introduced by Winchester around 1937, the Zipper used a .25-35 WCF rimmed case as its foundation, and at the time chambering it in a lever gun seemed like a good idea. The gun was the Winchester Model 64, and with a neat cartridge that hit the high side of 3,300 fps, it was the idea tool for a field full of varmints.

The Custom Shop at Thompson/Center again supplied my barrel, Redding the die set and since I had plenty of .30-30 brass, I was ready to go. The .25-35 case is easier to form and work with, but

since this alternative was never really publicized I went with the .30-30 case.

During case forming the only real problem is pushing the shoulder so far back that you wind up with case dents. Small amounts of lube somewhat solved

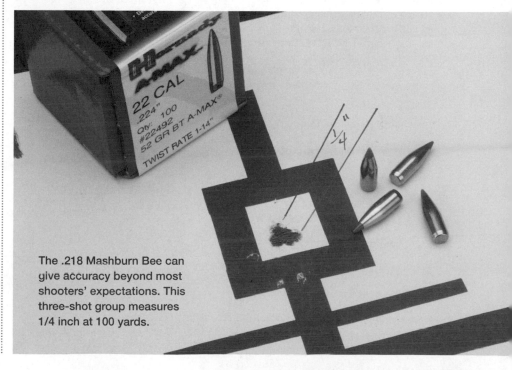

The .218 Mashburn Bee can give accuracy beyond most shooters' expectations. This three-shot group measures 1/4 inch at 100 yards.

the problem, but keep that in mind when working with the Zipper and have some extra cases on the bench.

After a final case forming within the chamber of the T/C with a mild charge of BLC-2, the best groups I shot were

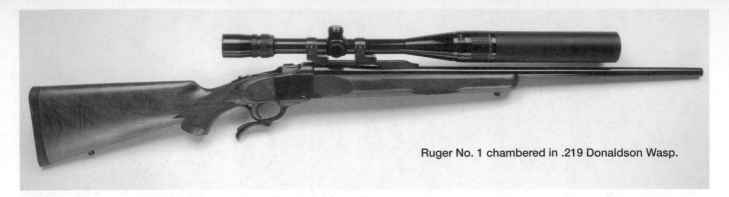

Ruger No. 1 chambered in .219 Donaldson Wasp.

with the Remington 55-grain hollowpoint loaded with 29 grains of H-4895 over Federal 210 primers. Velocity was 3,300 fps, all my groups under an inch and I was a happy guy.

.219 Donaldson Wasp

Watching those guys shooting chucks in New York so many years back made the .219 Donaldson Wasp an itch that had to be scratched! Introduced by Harvey Donaldson in 1935, it went on to be the precursor to many of today's modern cartridges. For this cartridge, I rechambered my Ruger No. 1 from .218 Bee as all Bullberry Barrel Works had to do was recut the chamber, alter the extractor and turn the barrel back a turn or two to compensate for that interior work.

Reloaders beware – this is a labor-intensive cartridge to bring to fruition. You need .30-30 Winchester brass, two sets of dies from RCBS and plenty of muscle power. It is a multistep process – initial forming, cutting to length, chamfering, cleanup – but when completed it's a great cartridge to load and shoot.

Bullet weights ran from 50 to 55 grains with a .224" diameter. Donaldson favored IMR-3031, IMR-4064 and IMR-4320 powders. I would add Hodgdon's popular H-4895, which adds yet another dimension to the loading cycle. In all, this cartridge could do no wrong as 95 percent of all the loadings tested shot 1-inch groups or smaller. If you are looking for a good starting point, the 52-grain Berger hollowpoint over 29 grains of H-4895 produced ¾-inch groups at nearly 3,500 fps. For an updated reference guide, Hornady thought so much of this cartridge that it is included in the latest loading manual.

The itch is gone, but I still have my Ruger No. 1 when I want to spend a pleasant day in the field with the .219 Donaldson Wasp.

.221 Fireball

The .221 Fireball chambered in the famed Remington XP-100 pistol has always been one of my favorites, and when Remington told me that they had taken my suggestion to heart and brought out this round in the Model

700 Classic rifle, I was elated! In the short-barreled handgun the Fireball was good, but in a rifle the cartridge reaches its full potential.

Over the years I shot the Fireball in the Remington, a T/C Contender with an octagon barrel of all things, and the prize jewel – a custom rifle I had made at Cooper Arms. Fancy does not make a gun shoot better, but I added upscale wood, fleur-de-lis checkering and a host of other items to make my Cooper a one-of-a-kind rifle.

Since the Fireball is now fully commercialized, brass and dies can be found from many reloading sources. The drill is simple – fire form a bunch of cases, neck size only and reload them with the best bullets on the market today. The Hornady 50- and 55-grain V-Max do the job with aplomb. With the former, 15.8 grains of IMR-4227 powder hit 3,000 fps; with the latter, 17 grains of AA1680 almost match that. In both cases the groups were less than 1/2 inch!

.222 Remington

The .222 Remington – or Triple Deuce as it is more commonly called – hit the market in 1950 and was an immediate success. Remington, in fact, was in awe that "the onslaught of orders for this ammunition has cleaned out our stock in an amazingly short time," as quoted from an old press release. Target shooters swarmed to it like bees to honey, and once the word was out varmint hunters hit the fields loaded with .222 Remington ammunition.

I wanted something special to test this cartridge and turned to the Remington Custom Shop to build me a Model 700 "C" Grade with a target trigger. I still have the gun today, it is too nice to sell and is a good partner on the chuckin' fields. Even with the advent of newer cartridges, the .222 Remington is still very popular for both small game and varmints.

For the small-game hunter dedicated to the .22 caliber, many bullet varieties are out there for the asking. With all of the products available today, you can take your passion to a lifetime of fun and enjoyment.

Remington Custom Model 700 chambered in .222 Remington.

The cartridge is very tolerant to the whims of any shooter and handloader. This was one of the first cartridges that I could employ the use of only one powder with excellent results with a wide range of bullets. In fact, my records show that using 21 grains of IMR-4198 and 50-grain bullets registered groups rivaling 1/2 inch at 100 yards. My preferred 52-grain Sierra hollowpoint boattails resulted in 3/8-inch groups with a mean velocity of nearly 3,300 fps. Federal nickel cases, RCBS Bench Rest dies and CCI BR-4 primers made up the rest of the components.

.222 Remington Magnum

About the time I became interested in the .222 Remington Magnum, the parent company saw fit not to chamber any rifles for the cartridge. Popularity was waning, the cartridge was not even in the ammunition listing in the back of the catalog, and essentially it seemed like it was a dead issue. However, for the varmint shooter, the .222 Remington Magnum is still a viable cartridge to take afield.

Born in the golden years of the 1950s, the .222 Remington Magnum took part in some field trials in which the military was interested in adopting a new cartridge for the armed forces in conjunction with the Armalite AR-15 rifle. To make a long story short – it was modified and eventually introduced as the .223 Remington. That was one part of its downfall, the other is that it's so close to the .222 and .223 Remington in ballistics that no one seems to pay attention to it anymore.

But, I twisted the arm of then supervisor of the Remington Custom Shop, Tim McCormack, to chamber a production Model 700 in .222 Remington Magnum for testing. He did, I still have that rifle and it has given me much pleasure in the field. It adapts well to a wide range of bullet weights and is fully capable of delivering the goods downrange in groups under an inch with widely available H-4895 powder.

.223 Remington

To be honest, with all of the varmint cartridges around I never really got interested in the .223 Remington until Browning re-introduced the B78 single-shot rifle after a 30-year hiatus. It was a gun that I missed the first time around, and even though this was a limited edition, I managed to get one for my lazy midsummer afternoons in the field.

No question about it, I love single-shot rifles for varmints. This gun was a natural with a heavy 24-inch barrel, strong lockup and high-grade wood. A Leupold Century Limited Edition scope helped it get in shape for the up and coming summer.

Handloading the .223 was next on the list and even though current commercial ammunition is getting to be state-of-the-art accurate, rolling your own has some advantages. One is cost and the other is to have control over bullet weight, velocity and downrange accuracy. For this exercise, and with the warmer weather coming, I used one bullet – the Hornady 52-grain A-Max Match – teamed with Federal brass and Remington's fine #7½ primers. I tested a baker's dozen of powders and BLC-2 emerged as the top contender with ¾-inch groups pushing 3,062 fps.

As the old saying goes, "good things come to those who wait," so 30 years was not that long after all for this Browning rifle. By the way, the .223 Remington is the most popular round that Remington makes.

.22 PPC

Although short lived, it was only a matter of time before the .22 PPC (Pindell-Palmisano Cartridge) and I would meet. When it happened

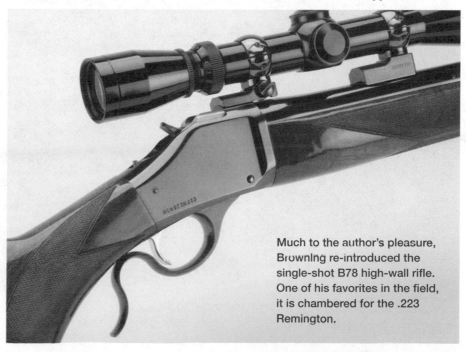

Much to the author's pleasure, Browning re-introduced the single-shot B78 high-wall rifle. One of his favorites in the field, it is chambered for the .223 Remington.

To help develop loads for your special .22-caliber varmint rig, a wide range of propellants from fast to slow burning are available for every cartridge. Primers shown on the right are also made for special applications, and the author favors the BR or bench rest type for the best accuracy.

At the top is the long-action Weatherby Mark V as compared to the short-action .224 Weatherby Magnum below it. While this gun and cartridge are no longer manufactured, the author still enjoys using it in the field with handloaded rounds.

everything seemed to come at once. At the time, Stoeger Arms imported Sako rifles and in the 1994 listing was a neat 6¼-pound rifle they called the Vixen. I field tested a Vixen in .22 PPC and sent it back after the assignment. Regretted that ever since.

According to reference material I have, the .22 PPC "came to be because of one man's passion to design the accuracy/precision cartridge" that would hold its own in both competition and hunting duties. Louis Palmisano had met Ferris Pindell, a well-known tool and die man, and work began in earnest.

There is quite a bit of history with this cartridge, and my experiences with it were most favorable. Sako of Finland supplied the brass for this much-shortened cartridge and employed the use of a Remington #7½ Bench Rest primer for American shooters.

Today the best way to use this cartridge is via handloading, although there is factory ammunition available from Sako. My notes show that the factory 52-grain hollowpoint delivered ¾-inch groups at 3,223 fps, while the best group I could achieve was with a Remington 55-grain hollowpoint over 28.5 grains of AA2520 at 3,202 fps. Average groups circled less than a ½ inch – chucks would never know what hit them.

Darn, I miss that rifle. Should have never sent it back.

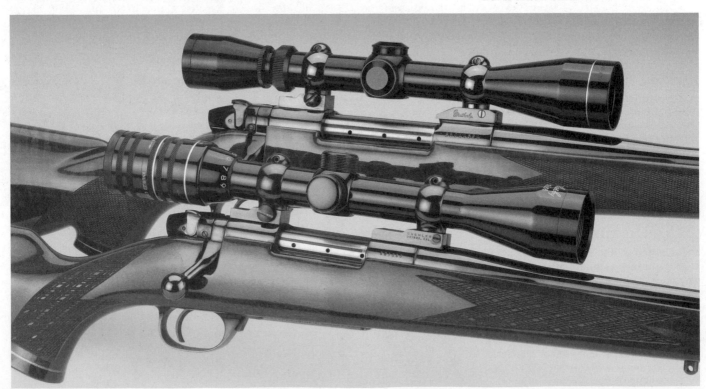

Although the gun and the cartridge have nearly faded away due to new and more improved cartridges, the .224 Weatherby Magnum is right up there when it comes to accuracy. The author considers this cartridge effective right out to 300 yards.

.22 Remington BR

For good reasons I used to call this my "no sweat" wildcat. By simply changing a barrel from E.R. Shaw, my test gun was ready to go. Brass is available from a number of sources and for those who do not want to get involved with the .22 PPC (which uses Russian 7.62 x 39mm brass) this is a big advantage. Lastly, this cartridge is easy to reload, very accurate and very fast.

The rifle I used was a common Remington Model 700 short action. E.R. Shaw installed the barrel, which they polished and blued to match exactly with current Remington barrel contours. The company chambered it for the cartridge, checked the bolt face for the right dimensions, gauged the headspace and shipped it back. Viola! A new rifle completely made to specifications at more than a reasonable price.

You may have some problems getting the brass but a quick Internet search will reveal a few sources. Blue Star Cartridge had enough on hand to fill a truck, so I ordered 500 cases of 6mm BR brass. Then I used the RCBS die set #56034 and simply ran each case into the die, checked for some minor case trimming, trimmed to 1.510" and was set.

Bullets from Nosler, Speer, Remington, Sierra, Hornady and a host of others filled the bill from 40 to 63 grains in a variety of designs. Speer, Hornady and Sierra bullets all resulted in 1-inch groups or less. This .22 Remington BR short-action Model 700 with is certainly a walking rifle suited for all day outings. I like it.

.224 Weatherby Magnum

Many of you might be wondering whatever happened to the .224 Weatherby Magnum? After years of lying by the sidelines, there are few chances that it will ever be a full production rifle cartridge again. I purchased my Weatherby Varmintmaster on Jan. 2, 1981, and still have it, but sorry it's not for sale.

Roy Weatherby was a very personable guy, especially when it came to gun writers. One day we sat down and discussed the .224 WM, a cartridge that he was very proud of. Even though he

The .218 Mashburn Bee is amazingly accurate. This 3-shot 100-tard group measures ³⁄₁₆ of an inch.

already had a design for the cartridge, the action did not come out until 1957, and it was then he went full bore into a rifle that would be the hit of the varmint crowd. "A nice little rifle," he called it.

While I enjoy this rifle and cartridge, his son Ed Weatherby says the .224 WM will probably never see the light of day again. The tooling was lost during a move and the .22-250 Remington put the end to it so there is simply no market for it today. No market, no gun. However, brass is still available from Weatherby, and since it uses popular .224" bullets, there are enough out there to keep you busy forever if you can find a Varmintmaster rifle on the used market.

My tests show that IMR-4895 is a good match for this cartridge. With

Hornady's 55-grain spire point, 31.9 grains of this powder and CCI BR-2 primers, ½-groups and smaller are the order of the day. Velocities hover around 3,600 fps, and woodchucks are hiding from me at 300 yards. The .224 Weatherby… maybe forgotten but never lost in the shuffle of classic varmint cartridges.

.22-250 Remington Ackley Improved

Always working on something new or unique, I took a different track when it came to the .22-250 Remington. Granted, it is rated at number eight on the Remington sales list, but since it is so common and popular I looked at a way to improve it a bit. The answer was the

Although the gun and the cartridge have nearly faded away due to new and more improved cartridges, the .224 Weatherby Magnum is right up there when it comes to accuracy. The author considers this cartridge effective right out to 300 yards.

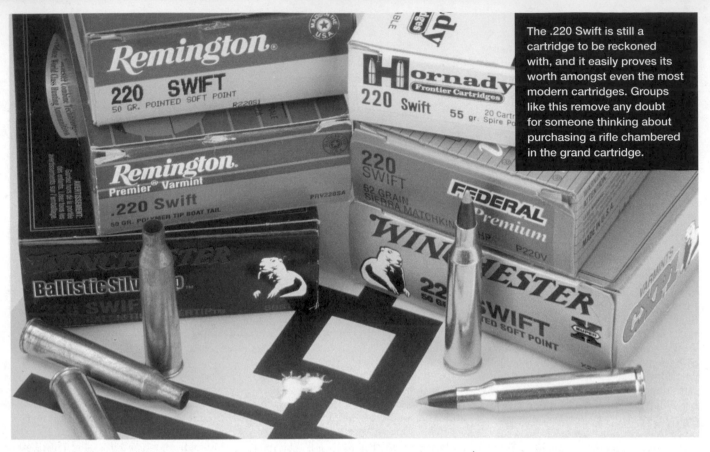

The .220 Swift is still a cartridge to be reckoned with, and it easily proves its worth amongst even the most modern cartridges. Groups like this remove any doubt for someone thinking about purchasing a rifle chambered in the grand cartridge.

Ackley version of the cartridge, or the .22-250 Remington Improved.

You might not want to get involved with this type of wildcat, but like many of my wildcat suggestions, Parker Ackley made it easy to load most of his improved versions. One of his requirements was that they fit and fire in the improved chamber with factory ammunition of the same type. Thus, with this wildcat, case forming is easy and painless for all one has to do is fire common .22-250 ammunition into the improved chamber and have at it. The shoulder angle will change to 40 degrees and you can expect to add about 10 percent more powder for higher velocities.

For this test I again turned to E.R. Shaw for a complete rifle, then fired off factory and handloaded .22-250 Remington cartridges and neck sized everything from there on. While some of the loads with light 40-grain bullets went into ½-inch groups or less, my favored bullet weights hovered around an inch. Not a big deal, and certainly not worthy of concern at the terminal end.

.220 Swift

We cannot finish this story without mentioning the .220 Swift. The Swift occupies a large amount of space in my filing cabinet because over the years I have shot this cartridge in more guns than I can mention here. The Swift has proved itself repeatedly in the field, and accuracy can be quite head turning in my early Ruger M-77 with a sporter-weight barrel.

Winchester offered the Swift beginning in 1935 in the Model 54 bolt-action rifle. The case is based on the semi-rimmed 6mm Lee Navy case and is just necked down to .22 caliber. With a steeper shoulder and less body taper, it is perhaps one of the strongest cartridge cases still on the market. Of course, like all cartridge beginnings, the word got out that it produced excessive and erratic pressures, stretched cases and wore out barrels. With a 4,000 fps record at the time, I think that those folks who had both the gun and cartridge were shooting it so much that they just neglected to pay attention to cleaning the barrel.

My time with the Swift has always been well spent. From shooting it in the Ruger M-77, H-S 2000, Remington 40XB

Weatherby Custom Mark V Varmint chambered in .22-250 Remington.

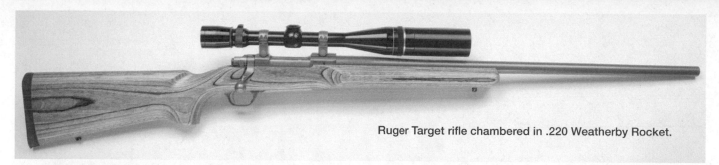

Ruger Target rifle chambered in .220 Weatherby Rocket.

This is the Ruger "Target" type of rifle complete with a custom trigger and stock. The author chambered it for the .220 Weatherby Rocket (kin to the .220 Swift), mounted a high-quality Leupold scope on it, and now it's perfect for long-ranging chucks.

and the Ruger No. 1, I have nothing but praise for this cartridge and its ability to get the job right the first time. One of my favorite loads that seems to agree with most of my rifles (once broken in) is the Hornady 55- grain spire point bullet over 37.1 grains of IMR-4064, for consistent 1/4-inch groups. At 3,500 fps, it gets there fast to dispatch critters within milliseconds.

I could go on and on regarding the subject of varmint cartridges and it would never end. I have also played with the .220 Rocket, another of Roy Weatherby's favorites, but it somehow never made the grade with the Swift barking at its tail for the long haul. Another is the .22-6mm Remington TTH that has some use for

deer, and changing the twist rate and using lighter bullets takes any load up to 4,000 fps with no effort and no pressure signs. I recently had a Ruger No. 1 chambered and modified for the .225 Winchester complete with an octagon barrel, and for a vintage cartridge, bringing it to modern standards has been a blast. There are other projects in the wings, now all I need is the time to try them all out.

Hunters can get a ton of year-round enjoyment from .22 varmint cartridges with a minimum outlay of cash, and sometimes only the simple combination of joining an aftermarket stock to a barreled action. The list is never ending, as is the fun!

After all is said and done, any of the .22-centerfire cartridges offer more than enough power and range to anchor small game or an animal like this portly chuck. For off-season practice, nothing beats this kind of hunting – especially in the summer.

A RUGER

Here's what's new in the Ruger stable

BY **Dick Williams**

The Ruger Single Seven is a dandy new mini-magnum that is perfect for small-game hunting and worth serious consideration as a lightweight, authoritative survival gun.

At the 2015 SHOT Show, there was no doubt as to which gun company won the award for most new products. Despite incredible sales and production demands over the last few years, Ruger's product development guys steadfastly manned their stations and showed up in Vegas with lots of cool new stuff for shooters. Perhaps best of all is that when Ruger announces new guns, the company has production items in stock and ready to ship. Gone are the days when a new product announcement was simply a promise of something good to come at an undetermined future date. Having something new means they have some boxed and ready to travel. If you end up having to wait for product, it's because you were slow to react and initial stocks were gobbled up.

As a longtime handgunner, I have to start with the short-barrel products, and being a big-bore believer, I'm homing in on the new compact Redhawk in .44 Magnum. The stainless steel revolver sports a 2.75-inch barrel, weighs in at just under 3 pounds and holds six rounds of whatever brand and power level of .44 you'd care to load and think you can control. It has the small, fitted wood grips that I remember on the first Redhawks introduced around 1980. It's good looking and compatible with smaller hands (unlike some other magnums,) but with recoil that can become quite unpleasant as the power level of the ammo increases. Sharp edges have been rounded, or dehorned if you prefer, to minimize any damage the Redhawk may inflict on your hands in recoil, but as is the case with all magnums, you will still need to determine what level of performance you can handle.

With .44 Special ammo at 800-900 feet per second, the Redhawk rivals the .45 ACP for fight-stopping potential, at least for the first 6 rounds, and it doesn't get much better than that. Should you want more power or penetration, Buffalo Bore, Corbon and Double Tap offer higher velocity .44 Special ammo loaded with jacketed hollowpoints or heavyweight hard cast bullets. For me, the "lightest load" from Garret Cartridges of Texas featuring a 310-grain hard cast lead bullet that generates around 1,000 fps was about all I wanted to handle, but it will still penetrate anything you might encounter.

ROUNDUP

The Ruger Redhawk in .44 Magnum with 2.75-inch barrel doesn't really qualify as a pocket pistol, but it may be the most effective and decisive CCW weapon ever. Photo by the author.

Given the Redhawk's short sight radius and limited range, I'm more interested in maximizing power with heavier bullets at lower velocities inside 50 yards.

The rear sight is fully adjustable with a white outline surrounding the notch. The front sight has a red plastic insert for enhanced visibility, and is mounted in a slot cut into the heavy rib on top of the barrel.

When a group of writers attended a seminar at Ruger to fire a pre-production model of the compact Redhawk, the only guy "tough enough" to shoot more than a cylinder of full-power 240-grain .44 Magnum factory ammo was a strapping young Border Patrol agent. While I liked the gun on sight and knew it would make a great general-purpose revolver, my happy quotient was fully satisfied after six rounds of the heavy ammo. If you want to flatten the trajectory with higher velocity, you might look at some Magnum loads with the lighter 180-grain bullets and determine at what velocity your tolerance for recoil is reached.

It can be replaced by a different sight simply by pushing in the spring-loaded pin and lifting the sight off. The red plastic insert is nicely visible against a dark background as long as there is adequate ambient light. The red becomes dramatically less visible as light diminishes. I find the factory red insert quite serviceable for general use and as a field gun.

Capable of both single and double-action firing (with a very smooth double-action pull) the Redhawk is better than many magnums in the event things deteriorate and you find yourself in a defensive situation. Mounted in a Galco D.A.O. belt holster, the compact .44 is readily accessible and can be carried for long periods of time with little or no discomfort.

Below: No need to change calibers when transitioning from a full-size service pistol to the classic pocket pistol. Simply put some of your chosen 9mm rounds into the Ruger furnished five-round moon clips and your pocket carried defensive system logistically matches your duty gun.

Two new additions to Ruger's popular line of Light Compact Revolvers include a longer 3-inch barrel with adjustable sights, and a short-barrel 9mm pocket revolver that requires moon clips. Photo by the author.

Ruger has two new models of its popular LCRs, or light compact revolvers. One is a 3-inch barreled .38 Special with adjustable sights, and the other is a 2-inch barreled 9mm with fixed sights. Like other pocket pistols of the modern era, both feature polymer frames and hold five rounds of ammunition. A pocket revolver in 9mm makes a lot of sense both for civilians and law enforcement officers. It allows you to have a backup gun or pocket pistol chambered for the same ammo as your semiauto pistol, and this can greatly simplify your logistics.

Ruger's new LCR in 9mm is the classic pocket revolver with its 2-inch barrel, five-shot cylinder and double-action only hammerless configuration. Keep in mind that Ruger's LCRs have a triggerguard shape slightly different than other manufacturers five-shot revolvers and may require a different holster. My existing hard leather holsters, particularly custom rigs, don't fit the new 9mm. I found one soft, synthetic material pocket holster from Tuff products and

one soft, rough-side-out leather pocket holster from Galco that fit quite well. For belt carry, Galco's Stinger belt holsters work well for the LCRs and are very comfortable.

Firing a rimless cartridge in a double-action revolver requires the use of some kind of moon clip to create an artificial rim against which the extractor can push to eject fired cases. For the old six-shot .45 ACP revolvers you can find three-shot half-moon clips, six-shot full-moon clips or two-shot clips. Since five is an odd number, a five-shot full moon clip would be best, and Ruger provides three of these in the proper size with the little 9mm revolver. In the past, I've had some difficulty loading individual rounds into full moon clips and great difficulty in removing empty brass from them. Ruger has thoughtfully cut long slots in the moon clips between each round, creating some flexibility and making ammo insertion and case removal much simpler. A mooning/de-mooning tool was not necessary.

I had expected to see a larger gap between breach face and the rear of the cylinder to accommodate the extra length of the moon clip. Instead, Ruger extended the circumference of the recess cut into the cylinder face so that the moon clip is fully enclosed and flush with the cylinder face, leaving only the 9mm case "rims" visible from the side. It's difficult telling the difference between the .38 and 9mm frames when the guns are loaded or empty. The extractor teeth are thinner and less beefy on the 9mm than on the .38, but it didn't seem to matter when firing the little guns.

Front sights on both the 9mm and .38 are serrated ramps with a thin white stripe slightly narrower than the ramp itself. The standard black sight picture can be used during daylight engagements while the enhanced visibility of the white strip is helpful in low light. Front sights are pinned so a gunsmith should be able to install a different front sight if you prefer. The rear sight on the short 9mm is a square notch cut into the frame's topstrap, and the 3-inch .38 has an adjustable rear sight recessed into a thicker topstrap. The .38's rear blade also has a square notch so sight pictures are basically the same for both guns. With reading glasses or my prescription shooting glasses, I could acquire a good, conventional sight picture with both guns; without glasses, I could still see the white front sight highlighted against a target.

Grips on both guns are a synthetic material with a stippled effect on the sides to enhance the grip. A soft material high on the backstrap softens felt recoil against the thumb joint and web of the shooting hand. On the more concealable

9mm, the grips are rather short with two finger grooves. On the 3-inch .38, the grips are longer to accommodate all fingers of the firing hand, but have no grooves. Depending on the loads fired, recoil is snappier on the 9mm than on the .38. That's the price you pay when you decrease the size of a cartridge case and try to increase the performance. Recoil isn't painful, but it may pose problems in maintaining control of the gun during rapid or semi-rapid firing, particularly with only two fingers on the grip. New shooters or those more sensitive to recoil might want to avoid +P 9mm loads and stay with the lighter bullets designed for rapid expansion and self-defense. Ruger LCRs I've fired have superb double-action trigger pulls, probably due to the company's friction reducing cam. With either two or three fingers holding the gun, double-action trigger control is excellent.

The loading and reloading procedures are quite different for the two guns. With the moon clip, the five rounds of rimless 9mm ammo are loaded and ejected as a single unit, as all of the rounds are held together by the clip. The rimmed .38 Special rounds can be loaded and ejected simultaneously or individually. This means there are no partial or tactical reloads with the 9mm – whereas the .38 Special can be topped off with a couple of rounds during any lull in the fight. You can replace a partially used 9mm moon clip with a new five rounds if you're concerned about remaining capacity, but it's unlikely you'll be able to reinsert any retained moon clip containing both empty cases and live rounds. That said, many trainers feel that in an actual fight, it's most likely that any five-round revolver will be run dry before a reload is attempted.

A few years back, Ruger chambered its classic Single Six revolver in .32 H&R Magnum. This year, the Single Six is again available in a magnum caliber, only now it holds seven rounds of Federal's .327 Magnum. While the power output is increased by 50 percent over the original .32 Mag., you can still shoot the original .32s for small game and a quieter field trip. Since this is the same size gun as your first Ruger .22 single action, there's no learning curve; you're as good a man as you were when you got that first Ruger .22 at age 16!

Except for its stainless steel, the .327 Fed. Mag. Single Seven is the classic .22 Ruger with larger holes in the barrel and cylinder. Good news is that all three of the "classic" single action barrel lengths are available: 4.75, 5.5 and 7.5 inches. During some very brief range time I was able to shoot all three. My quick conclusion is that the 7.5-inch barrel had slightly more muzzle flip with the more powerful .327 loads, while the 4.75-inch was easiest to carry. The 5.5-inch was a compromise but felt more like the 4.75-inch barrel. Advantage of sight radius goes to the longest barrel, although all of the models have the adjustable black Ruger single-action revolver sights that are quite good for daylight hunting.

The variety of factory ammunition available for the .327 is excellent. Cast and jacketed hollowpoint .32 Mag loads are available from Black Hills and Double Tap, while Hornady offers their Critical Defense FTX bullet load. More powerful .327 Magnum loads come from Federal (jacketed hollowpoints) and Double Tap (both JHPs and heavier 115-grain hard cast solids). Depending on barrel length, you can get anywhere from 800-1,600 fps. This may be the ideal small- or medium-game gun and caliber combination, and if I don't get a chance at jack rabbits and javelina this spring, the .327 and I will go after prairie dogs this summer at the SPUR Ranch in Wyoming.

Also in the Lilliputian category, Ruger has introduced a long awaited variation

While the original .22-caliber Ruger Single Six launched my handgun career back in the 1950s, Ruger's new Single Seven in the multitalented .32 caliber may be the gun with which I ride into the 21st century sunset. Photo by the author.

The Ruger Bearcat is back and better than ever with adjustable sights and your choice of blue or stainless finish. It's the gun you dreamed of as a kid and would still like to have as an adult. Photo by the author.

not sure whether the Bearcat is intended as a first gun for young kids or the final plinking revolver for older guys with fading vision. If this Bearcat had been available when I was young, I would have purchased it as my first handgun, then given it to my kids and taught them how to shoot with it, and finally tried to borrow it back in my "golden years."

Like Ruger's other modern revolvers, the new Bearcat has the two-screw frame and transfer-bar system and also a half-cock position for the hammer. Opening the loading gate does not release the cylinder to turn freely; only putting the hammer at half cock allows you to rotate the cylinder for loading and unloading. Cylinder chambers align perfectly with the ejector rod at the cylinder stop points. Despite the gun's petite size, the hammer is quite wide – much like the Super Blackhawk. With serrations on the spur, it was extremely easy to operate with the thumb of either hand. What a dandy gun for an afternoon walkabout in the country!

Ruger continues to assess and address the needs of the fast-growing CCW community with upgrades on their small autos. The latest one I've handled is their new LC9s Pro in 9mm. Major visible changes from earlier models include

of the Bearcat, this one with adjustable sights. Slightly smaller than the Single Six, the Bearcat is all steel (either blue or stainless), sports a 4.2-inch barrel, weighs 24 ounces and holds six rounds of .22 Long Rifle ammo. The front and rear sight look like the adjustable sight system on the Single Six with a wide ramp front blade and fully adjustable rear blade with a wide notch. Given enough ambient light, even I can get a good sight picture without glasses. I'm

Left: The perfect package for a day afield; a new Ruger Bearcat with adjustable sights, a brick of Federal ammo, a good pocket knife and a handy flashlight in case you want to stay out after dark.

Right: Unlike other Ruger revolvers with two frame screws, the Bearcat has the old-fashioned half-cock position that must be engaged to rotate the cylinder and load ammo.

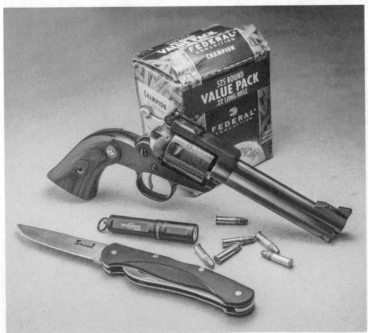

the "LC9s" printed on the left side of the slide, the absence of a loaded bar-indicator pinned into the top of the slide and the missing external safety lever. I'm on the fence about a loading bar indicator on a small auto; it provides an easily checked tactile verification of status, but it also provides an additional nonessential part. Neither am I big on putting an external safety on a pocket-size, striker-fired weapon. De-activating an external safety on a small pistol is difficult during the draw stroke, something worth considering when packing a gun that will probably be carried in pretty deep cover. Keeping the gun contained in a holster that covers the entire trigger and triggerguard should be safe enough, provided you've had some training and have practiced your presentation.

The biggest changes are two major internal improvements on the LC9s Pro. The Pro's trigger is vastly superior to the old model LC9, requiring about half the pressure and traveling perhaps half the distance to fire. With the old model LC9, your hands were starting to tremble about the time the Pro model trigger broke and the pistol fired. In addition, the Pro has no magazine disconnect; it will fire with the magazine removed and a round in the chamber. I think that's an important capability in a serious self-defense pistol. Fumble a reload or drop the magazine and at least you are still in the fight for one additional round.

Finally, the Pro slide locks back after the last round is fired, whereas the older LC9 could be manually locked back but didn't do

so automatically. I wouldn't make a federal case over this feature, but I prefer auto slide lock over nonlock. I doubt it would have much impact on my speed, but almost all of my training has been with service-size pistols having auto slide lock, and you know that they say about trying to learn new skills during an actual gunfight.

Smartly, Ruger's new Pro uses all of the same accessories as the older LC9 including original seven-round magazines and the extended nine-round magazine. While the Pro is delivered with one seven-round magazine, you should absolutely buy a couple of extra mags. Whether these are seven or nine-round capacity can only be decided by you, based on your lifestyle and how you carry the pistol. Separated from the gun, extra magazines can be easily hidden almost anywhere on your person and provide a quick, reassuring reload should you ever find yourself in harm's way. Before deciding you need to carry +P or +P+ ammo, read Ruger's ammunition guidelines in the instruction manual. Carrying additional magazines with standard pressure ammo should serve you better than fewer rounds of hotter ammo.

After more than a century of faithful and successful military service here and abroad, it's no wonder many people consider the Model 1911 as the greatest fighting handgun of all time. Within that circle of admirers, there are those who believe the Commander-size 1911 is the best possible fighting handgun for civilians who carry a concealed weapon. Recognizing the validity of those beliefs, Ruger has maintained the basic Commander line with

some rather small "feature tweaks" that put special custom touches in a mass-produced, factory pistol. The lightweight aluminum frame shaves nearly half a pound off the carry weight without compromising rapid-fire capability. Sights are the legendary Novak Low Mount Carry that provide fast acquisition while allowing precision shot placement. The aluminum skeletonized trigger provides a crisp, no-creep pull with adjustable over-travel stop and quick, positive reset. A standard recoil guide system means quick and easy takedown with no special tools required. Even smaller details like an extended thumb safety and slide stop lever may give that slightly better fit for your hand that allows a more positive manipulation for enhanced speed and confidence. Check the list of features on the Ruger website; it's quite impressive for a machined metal pistol with an MSRP just under $900.

In a shooting world consumed by all things tactical, Ruger has set aside a moment for those of us who still occasionally "stop to smell the roses." The company's Charger Takedown Pistol, basically a 10/22 for us handgunners chambered for the incredible .22 LR, has been modified with a couple of new features. First, the gun is easily taken down into two sections for ease of transport. The Charger also has a standard A2-syle grip than can be swapped for any MSR grip of your choosing. (We are suckers for modularity, even on .22s.) It comes with a Picatinny rail that will accommodate the optic of your choice, and has a threaded barrel (1/2"-28 pattern) that will accept most suppressors and flash hiders, plus it is delivered with a factory-installed protector. The Charger is furnished with a 15-round magazine that is the perfect height match for the factory furnished bipod. Also included is a Ruger hard plastic transport case so you're ready for the impend-

Ruger's new AR-556 Autoloading Rifle features the direct gas impingement design of the military versions rather than the piston design the company uses in its other AR-style rifles. It's the first rifle designed and built in the company's new North Carolina facility and has a very attractive MSRP of $749.

ing apocalypse of an earth overrun with field rats! Or plastic containers! Or dirt clods that need to be reduced in size!

Ruger has not ignored American riflemen this year. Without prioritizing anyone's tastes or preferences, AR-style rifles still dominate the American shooting fraternity. I am definitely not an expert on these rifles, but I was in the military when the M16 was developed and deployed, and my memory seems to recall some priorities as being a lighter weight weapon with more manageable recoil, and more rounds of ammo per pound of weight carried by each soldier. I'm also a tad frugal and a huge fan of simplicity, particularly when it comes to something I'll have to use in moments of great stress, like in a gunfight. Ruger's new AR-556 is an M4-style Modern Sporting Rifle in carbine length with a direct-impingement gas system rather than a piston driven model.

Simple is the gas-impingement system and 1:8 twist rate that will stabilize bullets from 35 to 77 grains. Simple is a front sight adjustable for elevation and a folding rear sight adjustable for windage. Simple is a flat top rail that lets me install whatever optic I want and leave the iron sights in place. Simple is a single-stage trigger with a short pull. And simple is an enlarged triggerguard that will let me shoot with gloves on and not worry about accidental discharges.

Lightweight is a 6-pound rifle rather than a 9-pound rifle festooned with a lot of equipment I may not want. Lightweight is 5.56mm ammo in 30-round magazines. Manageable recoil is not losing sight of your target between rounds. Frugal is an MSRP of $750 and expected street retail closer to $600.

I had a chance to run the AR-556 through some drills at Gunsite, including the Scrambler. What a delight! Using the Ruger pop-up aperture sights and shooting from the standing position, hits on man-size targets out to 130 yards was easy. Working the skinny popper targets at 100 yards was also relatively easy, but shooting prone got rather difficult at 200 yards and pretty much beyond my capabilities at 300. A Trijicon ACOG made the long-range shots much easier, but didn't help the close-range (inside 25 yard) engagements on paper silhouettes. I'm thinking that for general-purpose home defense I'd install one of the smaller dot sights while leaving the Ruger iron sights in place. I'm also thinking about a short piece of rail on the handguard for a small weapon light. Whatever I finally come up with, my youngest daughter has already staked a claim on the Ruger.

Coming from the new Ruger factory in South Carolina is the line of American bolt-action rifles all with an MSRP of under $500. They're light in weight at 6.6 pounds, very handy with barrel lengths of 16 inches for the .300 Blackout and the 5.56/.223, 18 inches in .308 Win. and 22 inches for several other calibers from .204 Ruger to 6.5 Creedmoor. The rifles come from the factory with Ruger's adjustable trigger, a one-piece aluminum scope rail installed, soft rubber recoil pad, integral bedding block system that positively locates the receiver and free-floats the barrel, flush-seating four-shot rotary magazine and easy-to-use tang safety. We had one of the Predator models at Gunsite with a 2x scope mounted. Knowing that Gunsite is a fighting school and not a summer shooting camp, we quickly dialed the gun in at 25 yards putting five shots into one large hole before hitting the Scrambler course and going after the poppers out to 300 yards. Though not as fast on the Scrambler as the AR, hits were easy, even when shooting offhand. Poppers dropped routinely all the way out to 300 yards, but the weather prevented us from claiming the tower on the 400-yard range. While it may be a bit light for a sustained barrage on a prairie dog town, the Predator would make a great walk-and-stalk rifle for anything less than 100 pounds.

For years Ruger has offered a limited selection of their No. 1 single-shot rifles with Mannlicher (full length) wood stocks in a few calibers. This is the Model RSI-International, and production lines do not run year-round, so availability of the different calibers can be restricted. Last year, Ruger introduced a new caliber in the rifle, the .257 Roberts. What a great American caliber choice for a European-style rifle! New this year is the 6.5x55, truly a European caliber for a European/International-type rifle. Guns are an exclusive through Lipsey's Wholesale Firearms Distributor. Lacking

Although perfectly adequate for self-defense as delivered with factory iron sights, our test crew found long-range targets were more easily handled with a good set of optics like those made by Trijicon. Photo by the author.

With scope rings included and scalloped scope ring mounting slots precut at the factory, Ruger No. 1 rifles have always arrived a step closer to field ready than other manufacturers' rifles.

After a quick sight-in from the prone position, the American Ranch Rifle in .223 performed beautifully on Gunsite's Scrambler range. The lightweight bolt-action rifle from the new North Carolina Ruger factory is a dandy walkabout rifle for varmint hunting and the more diminutive size edible creatures. Photos by the author.

an action behind the barrel, these rifles are incredibly compact and handy with their 20-inch barrels. If your shooting objectives are to maximize the number of rounds downrange in the minimum amount of time, this is not the gun for you. But for those of you who like precise shooting and also suffer from my "long stock" affliction, they are irresistible, and Ruger seems interested in making them available in additional calibers. I have the .257 in my vault but have not yet scoped and fired it. If I can obtain a 6.5 and a writing assignment, perhaps a handful of fellow cultists will have some interesting reading next year.

Worthy of mention is that the Red Label over/under shotgun has been taken out of production. It was put on hiatus for a couple of years recently and then made a brief comeback, but this may be the end of the line for the Ruger scatter-gun. Although, no official announcement has been made by the company as of this writing.

Other surprises will be forthcoming from Ruger as the year moves ahead, but in keeping with their "No production quantities, no announcements" policy, we'll have to wait and see. Meanwhile, keep an eye on the Ruger website; if you see it there, it's available.

Ruger's No. 1 RSI-International rifle in .257 Roberts may not be for everyone, but the international touch of a full-length stock has always been able to loosen the author's purse strings.

Custom &

Engraved Guns

Our Annual Review of the Finest Examples of Beauty and Artistry in the World of the Custom Gun

BY **Tom Turpin**

James Anderson

For this recently completed job, James Anderson started with a Brno 21 Mauser action, a Krieger .277-inch barrel and a stick of California English walnut. He fitted the barrel to the action and chambered it for the .270 Winchester cartridge. He then added a customized 1909 Argentine bottom metal unit to the action and sculpted the action bridges. James next created a set of custom scope rings, made and welded on a custom bolt handle, fitted a customized trigger and Dakota three-position safety and shroud, shop-made the quarter rib, front and rear sights, and sling swivels. He then crafted the stock from the very nice blank of walnut from Paul and Sharon Dressel, and added a Biesen checkered steel buttplate. One would be very hard pressed to find a nicer rifle anywhere than this one from Anderson's South Dakota shop. It is superb.

Photos by James Anderson.

John Bolliger

Over the years, Safari Club International has sponsored a few series of rifles dedicated to a certain theme, and usually lasting for five years. The format is that selected builders craft one rifle that is auctioned off as one of the premiere Saturday evening banquet items. The proceeds are shared between the makers and the SCI organization. The first such series that I'm aware of was the Guns of the Big Five in the 1980s, with each rifle in the series commemorating one of the big five of Africa. In the 1990s, there was another similar series commemorating the Dangerous Game Animals of the World. This year, the first in a new series of five rifles was completed and auctioned at the SCI Convention in Las Vegas. The series of rifles is dedicated to the international hunter, the animals that are pursued, and is based on five continents with John Bolliger's Mountain Riflery crafting the first (Africa, shown here) and the last (Americas); John Rigby will do the second (Asia); New England Custom Guns the third (Europe); and Ryan Breeding the fourth (Australia/New Zealand).

Mountain Riflery crafted this first rifle using a new FN Model 70 Winchester action fitted with a full-length ribbed integral barrel from Krieger, along with all the bells and whistles imaginable. It is chambered for the .416 Rigby cartridge. The rifle was extensively engraved and gold inlaid by Master Engraver Mike Dubber. Others involved were Tom Julian who built the display credenza, Peter Werner crafted the elephant leather trunk case, and Dennis Friedley made the companion custom knife. The set sold at the Grand Finale auction and fetched the tidy sum of $140,000.

Photos courtesy of John Bolliger, Mountain Riflery.

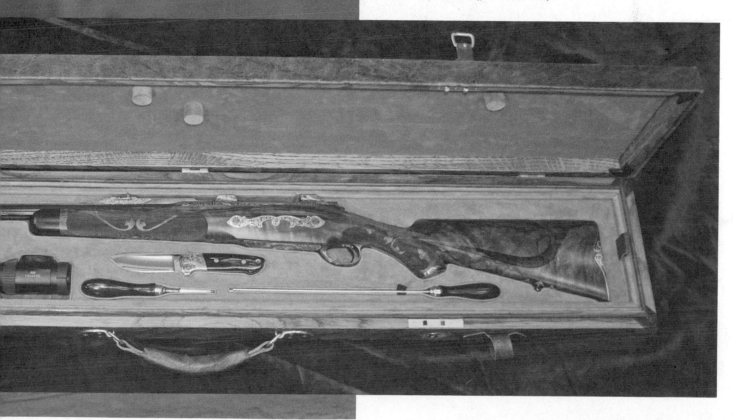

Reto Buehler

The single-shot rifle seen here, dubbed the Model Helvetia, was built by Reto Buehler. With the exception of three "V" springs and the Krieger barrel blank, Buehler created the rest of the rifle. It is a boxlock with an automatic ejector and is chambered for the 8x57JRS cartridge. The rifle is available with a full stock like this one or in a sporter stocked version with the barrel length as the client desires. It is stocked with Turkish walnut and tailored to the owner's dimensions. It features a cartridge magazine on the bottom of the stock and a trapdoor buttplate that holds a peep sight. The half-round, half-octagon 22-inch Krieger barrel has open sights and a quick-detachable swing mount for the scope. This rifle is the ultimate takedown, as the fore-end and barrel can be removed within seconds.

Engraving is by John Vukos & Photos by Bryan Dierks.

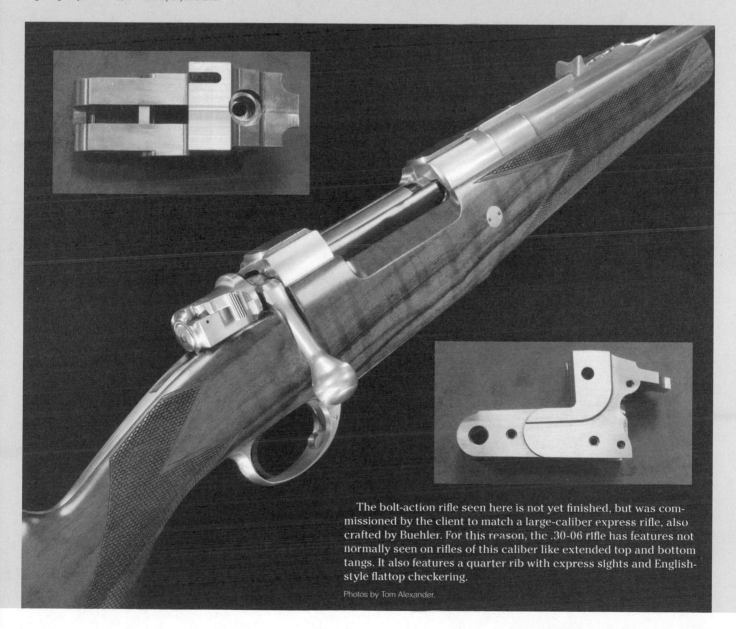

The bolt-action rifle seen here is not yet finished, but was commissioned by the client to match a large-caliber express rifle, also crafted by Buehler. For this reason, the .30-06 rifle has features not normally seen on rifles of this caliber like extended top and bottom tangs. It also features a quarter rib with express sights and English-style flattop checkering.

Photos by Tom Alexander.

D'Arcy Echols

The custom Ruger No.1 seen here is one of the finest custom rifles I have ever been privileged to see and handle. Utah custom maker D'Arcy Echols crafted this rifle a few years ago. All of the work on this rifle was performed in the Echols shop, including milling the octagon barrel, crafting the quarter rib and scope mounts, and whittling out the magnificent stock from a piece of "to-kill-for" English walnut. As the old saying goes, it just doesn't get any better than this.

Photos by Kevin Dilley.

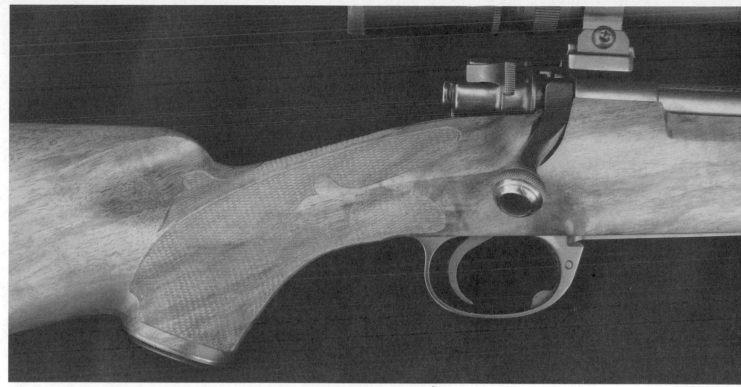

Gary Goudy

Gary Goudy crafted the stock on the .270 shown here with the black background. It was made from the stick of quarter-sawn New Zealand walnut. I chose the blank for its stability and light weight, not for its spectacular figure. The action is a G33/40 Mauser and the barrel is a cut-rifled example of Danny Pedersen's great barrels.

Gary Goudy also stocked the other two rifles shown. The top rifle started as a factory Winchester Model 70 Featherweight chambered for the .30-06 cartridge. I bought it new from Winchester and it served me as a test item for an article I was doing on Hill Country Rifles accurizing service. When I first acquired the rifle I cleaned it, mounted a scope and took it to the range. The best I could get averaged around 1.75 inches for three-shot groups. Contrary to apparently popular belief, however, that is perfectly acceptable accuracy for hunting. I then sent the rifle to Hill Country who performed their accurizing service on it. When they returned it to me, it was averaging groups well under an inch, with a few groups around .5 inch or less using Hornady factory ammo. I took it to Tanzania and Namibia and

shot several animals with it. It served me so well that I sent it off to Gary Goudy, along with a nice stick of European walnut, for one of his wonderful custom stocks.

The bottom rifle is a pre-64 Model 70 action and a Danny Pedersen cut-rifled 7mm barrel with Blackburn bottom metal. I again provided the blank of Circassian walnut. I've taken a few animals with it and my son used it to take his first pronghorn antelope.

Photos by Tom Turpin.

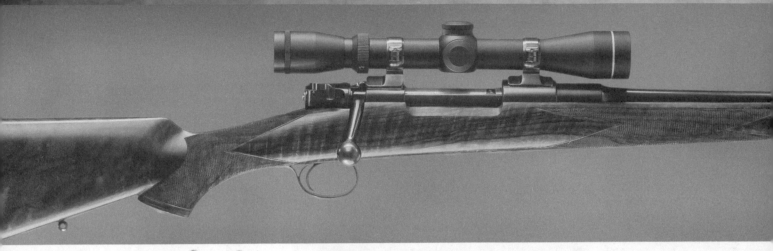

Lee Helgeland

This rifle from Lee Helgeland was crafted as the ninth rifle he made for a longtime client. Before this rifle could be completed, the client, who was also a close friend, was diagnosed with a terminal illness, so Lee arranged to buy the barreled action from him. He promised his friend that he would finish it, take it as his own and hunt with it in his memory. The action was a HVA small ring and the barrel a 25-inch Krieger. Lee added a skeleton grip cap, custom bases and rings, pierced triggerguard, curved leather pad, blind magazine and stocked it with a stick of exhibition California English walnut.

The friend was a wildcatter and experimenter to the tenth degree, and before he passed, he formed 75 rounds of brass and developed loads for a wildcat 7mm using 9.3x64 brass. Helgeland has since named the round the 7mm Strickler, in honor of his friend.

Photos by Victoria Wojciechowski Creative Vision Photography.

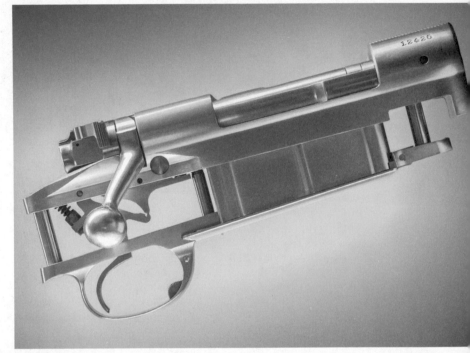

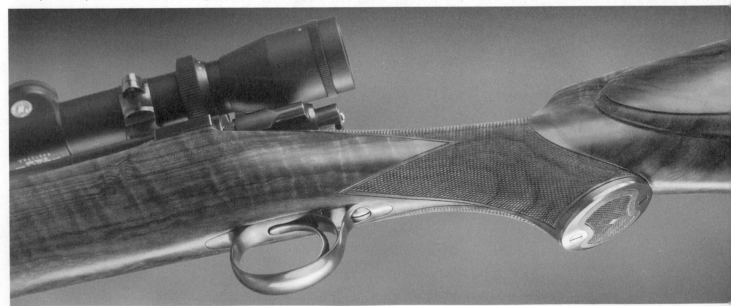

Weldon Lister

This pair of 1911 Colt Commander pistols and the custom crafted knife are the work of Texas engraver Weldon Lister. It's a family thing; Weldon's father was an engraver and is also remembered as Big Bill Lister, a singing cowboy who often toured with Hank Williams Sr. In addition to executing the wonderful scroll engraving on display here, Weldon also provided the excellent photography.

Claus Willig

Claus Willig is one of Germany's finest engravers. For many years, he engraved almost exclusively for Paul Jaeger and later for Paul's nephew, Dietrich Apel. He had to do a bit of scrambling when Dietrich sold the business to Dunn's in Tennessee. Dunn's later closed up shop, leaving Claus without any clients. Since he previously had all the work he could handle from American customers, Willig had not developed a client base in Germany and Europe. He worked his way through that dilemma, but it was terribly difficult for a while. In 2014, after more than six decades in the business, Claus retired. He gave his tools to two colleagues, Hendrik Fruehauf and Manfred Fleischer.

In Claus Willig's honor after so many years in the business after starting as a teenage apprentice to his father, I have devoted considerable space to his work. Not only is he a wonderful engraver, he is also a wonderfully good man, and all that that implies. I won't take up the space necessary to describe the photos shown here, other than to say that the engraved single-action revolvers are from a series on the Old West. In my most recent contact with Claus, he told me that he was getting restless and might start engraving a few more grip caps. Sounds like he may even have to buy some new engraving tools.

Photos courtesy of Claus Willig.

Kevin Wigton

This Remington Model 12 slide-action .22 is one that gunmaker Kevin Wigton put together for his daughter as a graduation gift. Kevin did the stock work and Joe Rundell did the engraving.

Photos courtesy of Kevin Wigton.

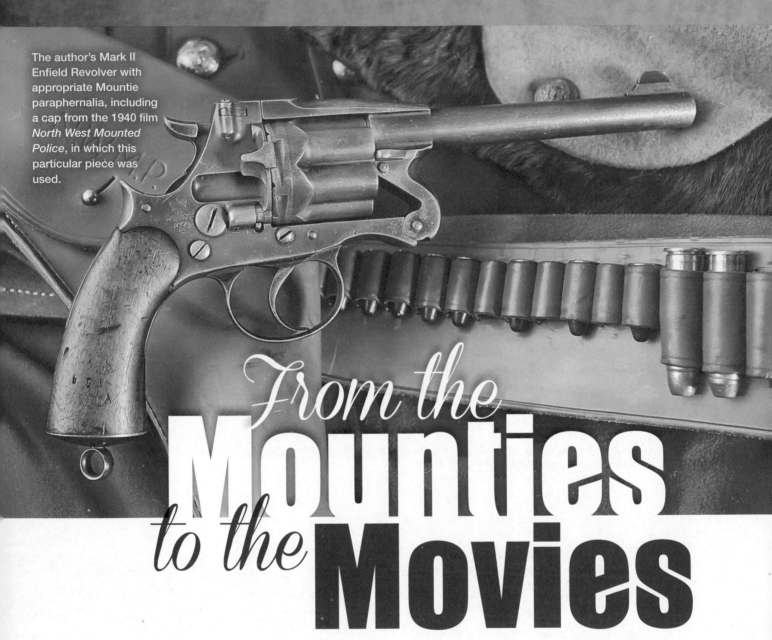

The author's Mark II Enfield Revolver with appropriate Mountie paraphernalia, including a cap from the 1940 film *North West Mounted Police*, in which this particular piece was used.

From the
Mounties
to the Movies

One of the author's favorite guns, this scarce British Enfield Revolver took him almost 40 years to acquire.

BY **Garry James** / PHOTOGRAPHY BY **Jill Marlow**

We firearms enthusiasts, whether we're collectors, shooters or a combination thereof, have a tendency to take our guns pretty personally. It's not a new phenomenon, as witnessed by Davy Crockett's renowned long rifle, "Old Betsy" and Buffalo Bill Cody's favorite buffalo rifle, a Model 1866 Springfield trapdoor rifle, "Lucretia Borgia."

I must admit, I'm no different than most of you out there and do have some favored children in my collection, most particularly a revolver that I have had an almost half-century relationship with, my 1884 British Mark II Enfield "Mountie" revolver.

The gun itself is certainly one of the most unprepossessing military handguns ever designed and is not without its flaws – but to me it's a thing of beauty, an example of patience rewarded, as well as a romantic reminder of the exploits of Canada's intrepid North West Mounted Police, and an evocation of Hollywood's Golden Age of filmmaking. But before we get into this particular paragon of pistolry's tale, perhaps it might not be amiss to give you a bit of the quixotic Enfield revolver's backstory in general.

From Whence It Came

It's probably safe to say the Mark I and Mark II Enfields had what were perhaps the most unusual silhouettes of any military handguns ever—their pouting lower hinges and ungainly mating of barrel to frame made them considerably less than elegant.

Just prior to the appearance of the Enfield, British military handguns involved

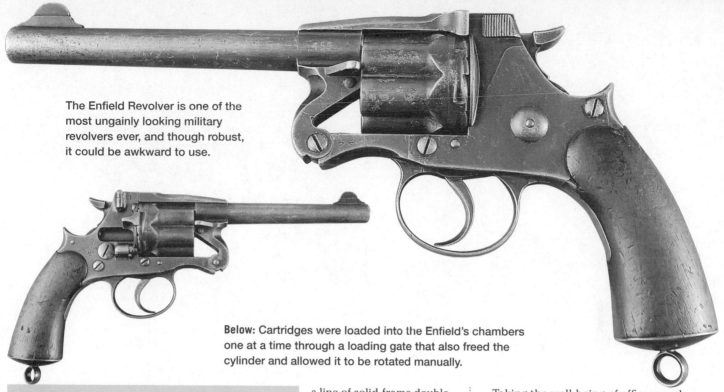

The Enfield Revolver is one of the most ungainly looking military revolvers ever, and though robust, it could be awkward to use.

Below: Cartridges were loaded into the Enfield's chambers one at a time through a loading gate that also freed the cylinder and allowed it to be rotated manually.

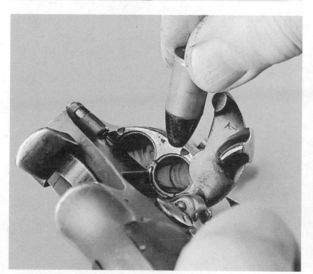

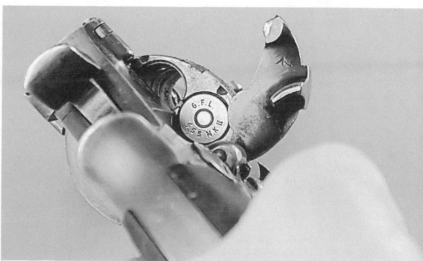

a line of solid-frame double-action Adams revolvers that chambered a rather puny .450 centerfire cartridge. The black-powder round moved its 125-grain lead bullet out at some 650 fps for a muzzle energy of 211 ft-lbs. While it wasn't totally ineffectual, when one considers some of the formidable customers the British were encountering in their quest for empire—Zulus, Afghans, Pathans, etc.—its performance was reckoned to often be less than decisive.

Taking the well-being of officers and men to heart, Queen Victoria's ordnance officials decided a definite upgrade was in order. In August 1880 a revolver was adopted that was totally different from the earlier solid-frames. The gun employed a unique simultaneous extraction system designed by Americanized Welshman Owen Jones and a double-action lockwork with rebounding hammer, patented jointly by Britisher Michael Kaufmann and Belgian Jean Warnant.

The rather schizophrenic setup involved a frontally pivoting hinged frame secured at the rear of the topstrap by a knurled latch. The gun was loaded in the usual manner of most revolvers

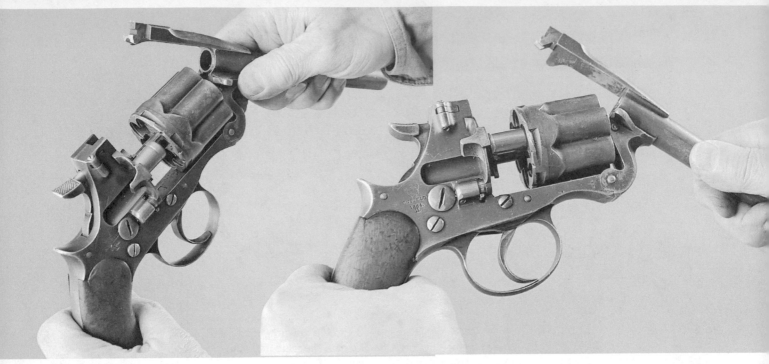

of the era – one round at a time through a side-swinging loading gate. In the original Mark I the cylinder rotated freely clockwise even when the gate was shut, though the later Mark II's cylinder was locked completely and rotated for loading only when the gate was open.

When six rounds had been fired, as instructed by the 1886 *North West Mounted Police Manual and Firing Exercise for the Winchester Carbine and the Enfield Revolver*, "Hold the revolver in the right hand with the barrel pointing upwards to the left front at an angle of 30 to 40 degrees. Place the thumb on the catch and press it back, then with a smart jerk of the wrist, throw the barrel forward when the cartridge cases will fall out… The bottom case may occasionally require to be removed by revolving the cylinder."

What you ended up with was a gun that loaded like a solid-frame revolver but which also featured simultaneous extraction. Besides that, the extraction was even recognized at the time as being not particularly efficient. The star extractor was held captive and the cylinder pulled forward, exposing a thick arbor, which caused the case in the bottom chamber to commonly stick in the action, requiring some fiddling or energetic shaking to dislodge it—especially when the gun was fouled with black-powder residue.

The "Pistol, Revolver, B.L. Enfield (Mark I) Interchangeable" as it was named partially after the arsenal where it was built, originally had the forward portions of the chambers rifled and internal parts nickel-plated, two features which were later eliminated. The 6-inch barrel was rifled with the pattern

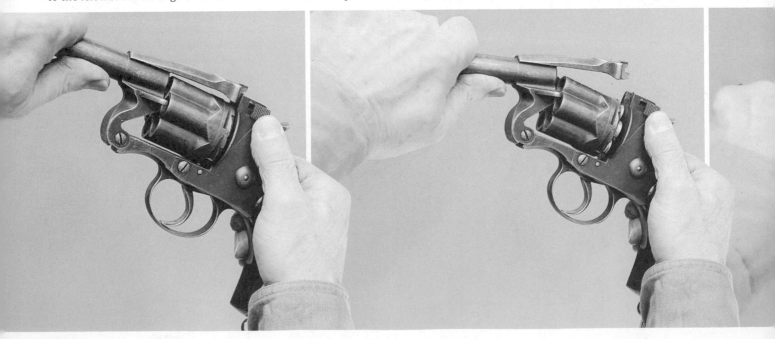

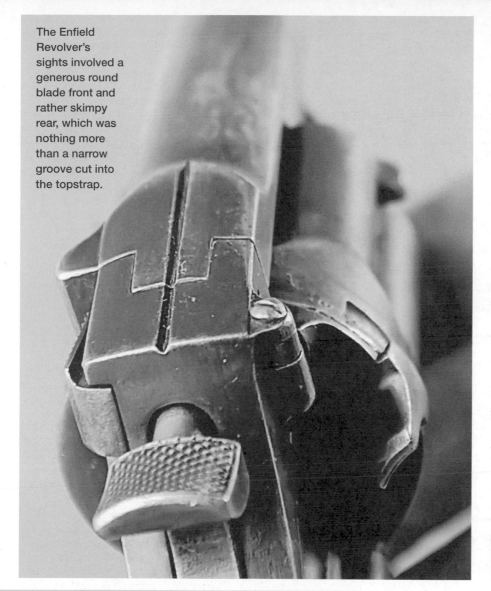

The Enfield Revolver's sights involved a generous round blade front and rather skimpy rear, which was nothing more than a narrow groove cut into the topstrap.

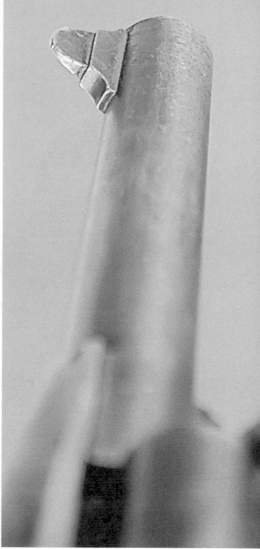

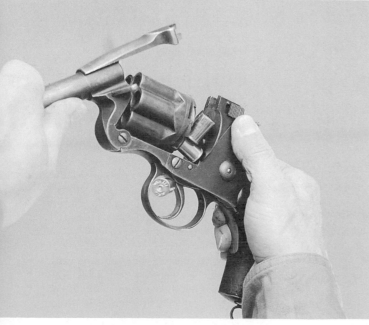

Left & Opposite: Cases were simultaneously ejected by releasing the upper part of the barrel unit by means of a catch, allowing it to be tilted downward. This caused the cylinder to move forward and away from a star extractor, pulling the cases free. They then had to be shaken clear of the gun.

devised by Scottish gunsmith Alexander Henry (of Martini-Henry rifle fame). Overall length of the gun was 11½ inches and it hefted some 2 pounds, 8 ounces.

The topstrap portion of the frame was a separate piece and the foresight of a slightly angular configuration. Grips were checkered walnut, capped with an iron plate that incorporated a lanyard ring.

The cartridge designed for the gun had a 265-grain, .455-inch diameter hollow-base lead bullet and 18 grains of black-powder charge which gave a muzzle energy of 289 ft-lbs. Overall length of the round was 1.47 inches as opposed to the .450's 1.14 inches. As bullet and case diameter of the two rounds were very close, it was stated by the War Department that .450 ammunition could be used in the Enfield in a pinch.

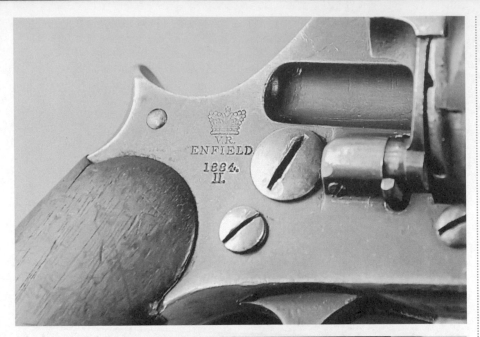

Enfield Revolver markings included the British Crown model designation and date on the frame, and remnants of North West Mounted Police stamping on grip.

In December of 1881, the "Cartridge, S.A. Ball, Pistol, Revolver, Enfield B.L. (Mark III)" was adopted. It differed from its predecessor in having a bullet diameter of .477 and a deeper hollow base inset with a clay expanding plug. The round was designated the ".476."

Field evaluation of the Mark I turned up some shortcomings, so in 1882 a second pattern of Enfield revolver was "sealed." As noted by H.M. War Department, "The main points in which this pistol differs from Mark I are as follows—the topstrap is part of the body. The stock is not checkered, and is secured to the body by means of a stock-cap screw. A locking arrangement has been added to prevent the cylinder revolving accidentally when the pistol is in the holster. This is thrown out of gear when the shield [loading gate] is open. A cam on the shield locks the hammer when the shield is open, and so prevents accidental discharge of the pistol when it is being loaded. This pistol takes the same cartridge as Mark I."

Originally the Enfield was issued to the Royal Navy, Royal Irish Constabulary and the Canadian North West Mounted Police, as well as to troops in India and to several colonial forces. Unfortunately for the Mounties, some shipping anomalies caused the guns to be sent without their proper ammunition and they were forced to load their new Enfields with .450 for a time.

While it was recognized by many that the gun would probably never win a beauty contest, it was nonetheless deemed to be rugged and functional. The .476 cartridge's extra puissance was also welcomed and, when working correctly, the action could certainly be cleared much faster than that of the Adams, which relied on an under-barrel ejector rod.

It Gets Personal

The Mark II shown in this article is an old friend, our star-crossed relationship having extended close to 40 years before we could finally get together permanently. It all started in the early 1970s when I was an associate editor at *Guns & Ammo* magazine and took my first trip to the Paramount Pictures studio since the late 1940s and early 1950s when my dad was a contract actor at Paramount.

The purpose of the excursion was to visit the legendary Stembridge Gun Rentals that, because of its championing by legendary Producer/Director

10 GREAT STARS! 2 GLORIOUS LOVE STORIES! 1000 UNFORGETTABLE THRILLS!

GARY COOPER · MADELEINE CARROLL

with PAULETTE GODDARD · PRESTON FOSTER · ROBERT PRESTON

AKIM TAMIROFF · LYNNE OVERMAN · GEORGE BANCROFT

LON CHANEY, Jr. · WALTER HAMPDEN

Cecil B. DeMille's **NORTH WEST MOUNTED POLICE** in Technicolor

Original Screen Play by Alan Le May, Jesse Lasky, Jr. and C. Gardner Sullivan

Produced and Directed by **CECIL B. DeMILLE** A PARAMOUNT PICTURE

Left: *North West Mounted Police* was Cecil B. DeMille's first Technicolor production. DeMille, a gun enthusiast, went out of his way to make the firearms as correct as possible given availability and compatibility with studio blanks.

After that premier expedition I found myself at Stembridge many times, and always stopped by to see my old friends, the Enfield brothers. Over the years I kept a mental note of the films in which they appeared—the most notable being DeMille's first color film, *North West Mounted Police* (1940), where the director, being a firearms collector and stickler for proper period detail, decreed the Mark II would be the pistol carried by Preston Foster and the Mark I the sidearm of Robert Preston. Early on, I had noticed the faint markings on the grip of the Mark II indicating it was an original Mountie revolver—an extra bonus and an unseen (In the film) stamp of authenticity. Also, the Mark II had an electric pencil mark, ".455," on its barrel indicating that it was to be used with .455 blanks because the longer 5-in-1s normally employed in most .45-caliber revolvers were too long to be properly ejected due to the Enfield's short cylinder throw.

In fact, in some scenes in *NWMP*, Preston Foster can be seen with a Colt New Service cobbled up to look like the Enfield, presumably to take advantage of the 5-in-1s and easier-to-manipulate swing-out cylinder (though in a close-up he is shown ejecting cases from the

Cecil B. DeMille right after World War I, was sited on the Paramount lot. Amassing a remarkable inventory of firearms and associated paraphernalia, Stembridge became the preeminent gun rental business to the movie industry for decades. It is still in business today manufacturing blanks for the cinema.

Needless to say, I was overawed by what I saw. Graciously given a tour by Syd Stembridge, one of the first things I noticed out of the corner of my eye, hanging on a rack, was a brace of Enfield revolvers—a Mark I and a Mark II.

Possessed by a strong penchant for British military firearms and previously having only seen an Enfield revolver once in a museum in the U.K. when I lived in South Wales in the 1960s, I was transfixed. After giving them a good looking-over we moved on, albeit somewhat reluctantly, to other wonderful things.

Though the Enfield revolver was chambered in .476 caliber, it could also handle .450 and .455 rounds. This electric pencil marking on the author's gun was put there by Stembridge Gun Rentals to ensure it would not be loaded with longer 5-in-1 blanks that could not be properly ejected like .455 blanks.

Above: At the author's suggestion, actor John Cleese was armed with the Stembridge Enfield revolver in the western film *Silverado*.

One of the stars of *North West Mounted Police*, Preston Foster (center) carried the revolver shown in this article in the film. Actor Lynne Overman (left) employed an 1886 Winchester carbine in the film that was not in period but would work with available blanks. In one scene he does wield, but not shoot, a '76 carbine.

.455 blank (left) compared to a complete .455 cartridge.

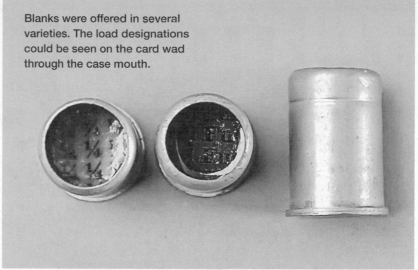

Blanks were offered in several varieties. The load designations could be seen on the card wad through the case mouth.

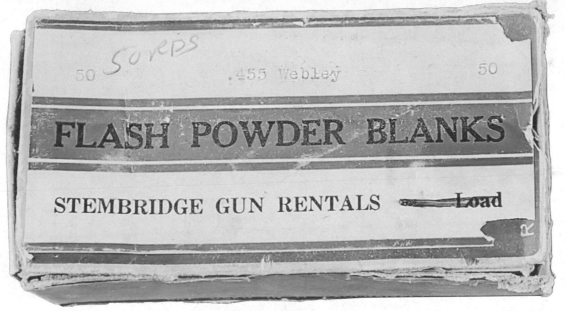

50 *SO RDS* .455 Webley 50

FLASH POWDER BLANKS

STEMBRIDGE GUN RENTALS Load

An original box of Stembridge .455 Blanks.

original Mark II).

Stembridge eventually moved from the Paramount lot to a location in Glendale, Calif. After a number of years operating there the decision was made to dispose of the collection, much of which was purchased by my boss at *Guns & Ammo*, Robert E. Petersen, who had hopes of creating a gun museum with a strong emphasis on the Hollywood angle.

Unfortunately that was not to happen as the powers-that-be in Los Angeles were less than thrilled at the prospect of a firearms museum in their town. After repeated rebuffs, Mr. Petersen ultimately shelved the project and decided to have Little John's Auction Service in Anaheim, Calif., sell a large portion of the Stembridge collection in mid-2007.

It was a stellar affair, featuring guns used by John Wayne, Steve McQueen, James Stewart, etc., and in such films as *Titanic, Star Wars, The Magnificent Seven*… well, you get the picture. The main piece I was interested in was the Mark II Enfield revolver, since I already owned a Mark I. It was listed in the catalog as having been used in *Dracula* (1992), *The Phantom* (1996) and *Mighty Joe Young* (1998).

As well as *North West Mounted Police*, I happened to know the gun was featured in the western *Silverado* (1985), wielded by actor John Cleese. It was actually chosen for this role at my suggestion after Stembridge armorer, Larry Merrill, called me one day to ask if I had an idea what kind of early British revolver might be appropriate for an English-born sheriff.

Fortunately, after some spirited bidding, it was knocked down in my favor and today is one of the focal points of my collection—partly because it is a fine example of an original North West Mounted Police Mark II Revolver, and also because of its great cinema connections—to my mind just about as cool an association as one can get.

TEUTONIC TEMPLATES

Early German bolt-action sporters set a standard

By Terry Wieland

The Sears, Roebuck catalog – the original "wish book" of a century ago – had page after page of guns. There were surplus military Springfields, Belgian doubles, cheap .22s for farm boys, buggy guns, pocket pistols and virtually every fine sporting rifle made in America.

In the years before 1914 one could find, tucked away in a corner, a listing for a bolt-action sporting rifle from Germany. Variously listed as a Mannlicher, or a

Haenel-Mannlicher, or sometimes just a C.G. Haenel (pronounced HY-nul), these rifles were the first steps in a trend that became a deluge: Bolt-action sporting rifles based on military actions.

Generally now known as Haenel-Mannlichers, these rifles were not cheap. In the 1902 Sears catalog, the price was $24.50. By comparison, a Winchester Model 95 listed at only $17.50. What made the German import worth 50 percent more than this state-of-the-art lever rifle? And why, when Model 95s

are prized by collectors, are Haenel-Mannlichers all but forgotten except for a few devotees of early custom rifles?

There are two answers to that question, and relative quality has nothing to do with it. They are both finely made rifles, and some of the Haenels especially so.

For most gun collectors, the era of sporting bolt rifles began with the Mauser 98.

Everything good and modern occurred after that, they believe, and nothing much before. But such was not the case.

Haenel-Mannlicher, circa 1909, fitted with a Lyman Model 36 receiver sight and Lawrence sling. The sight appears to have been fitted at the factory, but it is impossible to say for certain.

In the frenzy of rifle development in Europe between the arrival of smokeless powder in 1886 and the ultimate Mauser in 1898, several good military bolt rifles made their debut. For sporting purposes, the most significant by far was the German Commission rifle of 1888.

For military collectors, the *Gewehr '88* is almost a cult object, and while it has been widely written about, it is also widely misunderstood. It is sometimes described as a Mauser with Mannlicher features, and sometimes the reverse.

Above: In the pages of the Sears, Roebuck wish book ye shall find them. At $24.50, the Haenel-Mannlicher was one of the most expensive rifles in the catalog. A Winchester Model 95 was only $17.50 and a Model 94 in .30-30 was $14.75.

Left: The conversion to a Mauser-style box magazine with hinged floorplate is one of the most beautifully executed floorplate-release mechanisms ever made – far superior to almost any modern rifle, including some ultra-high-dollar custom rifles. It is crisp, positive and unfailing. This rifle also has an excellent double-set trigger.

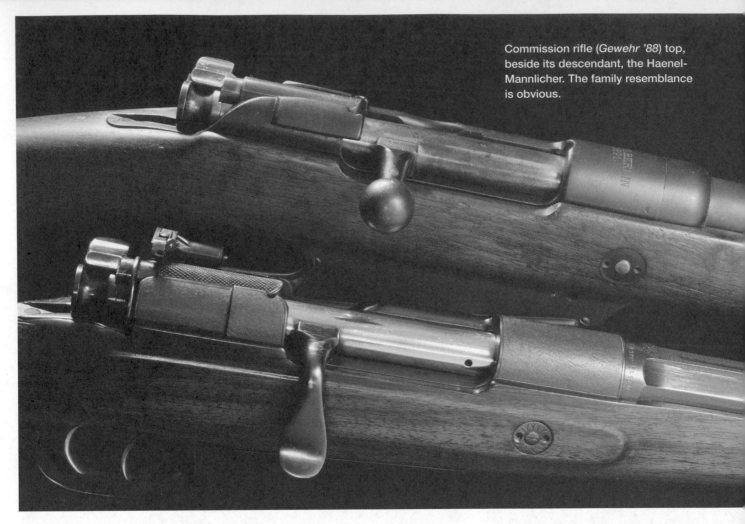

Commission rifle (*Gewehr '88*) top, beside its descendant, the Haenel-Mannlicher. The family resemblance is obvious.

Rifle historian W.H.B Smith includes it in both his history of Mauser and his history of Mannlicher, since a researcher might look for it in either book. In reality, however, the Commission rifle was neither Mauser nor Mannlicher, but that rarest of creatures: A mechanical device designed by committee that was highly successful.

Its stint as the official infantry rifle of the German Army was short-lived – only 10 years – but it went on to a successful career in every corner of the globe as both military rifle and, in its converted form, a hunting rifle. So good was the Commission action that Steyr, in Austria, which manufactured the '88 under contract for Berlin, modified it into a hunting rifle. The result was the famous Mannlicher-Schönauer Model 1903, a design that set the standard for quality hunting rifles for the next 70 years.

Looking at a 1903 Mannlicher action beside a Commission rifle, the similarity is readily apparent. Except for the Mannlicher's butter knife bolt handle

and Schönauer rotary magazine, they are almost identical.

Steyr was not the only company to appreciate the virtues of the Commission rifle. C.G. Haenel, a prominent German gunmaking company in Suhl, also made Commission rifles under contract. Founded by Carl Gottlieb Haenel in 1840, C.G. Haenel & Co. quickly became a force in German gunmaking and, like most German firms, produced sporting weapons when it was not filling military contracts.

Haenel retained its military connections throughout its life. Hugo Schmeisser, of submachine gun fame, was associated with the company (and sometimes listed as an employee) before 1939. After 1945, C.G. Haenel became part of Merkel, and the name survives today on Haenel target and sniper rifles.

Haenel's civilian rifles on the Commission action followed the German hunting rifle style that existed since the advent of centerfire cartridges. Most had half-octagon barrels with full or partial matted ribs, matted receiver ring, folding leaf sights, schnabel fore-ends and

elegant turned-down bolt handles. There was usually a stock-bolt in the fore-end, and sometimes they were fitted with receiver sights. Most had double-set triggers. While the majority were chambered for the standard military 8x57 cartridge (usually the original .318" bullet, rather than the later .323") they were also offered in pure hunting cartridges like the 9x57.

At first Haenel used the original *Gewehr '88* magazine, which consisted of a fixed box forward of the triggerguard, and accepted cartridges in the Mannlicher "packet." A packet was pressed down into the magazine and after the last cartridge was chambered the empty clip dropped out the bottom. On some later rifles, Haenel reworked the magazine completely, installing a Mauser-type box with a hinged floorplate that held the cartridges in staggered rows. This made the rifle more streamlined and easier to carry.

The first importer of Haenel-Mannlichers was Oscar Hesse of New Jersey, who began bringing them into the U.S. in 1894. There was a strong connection be-

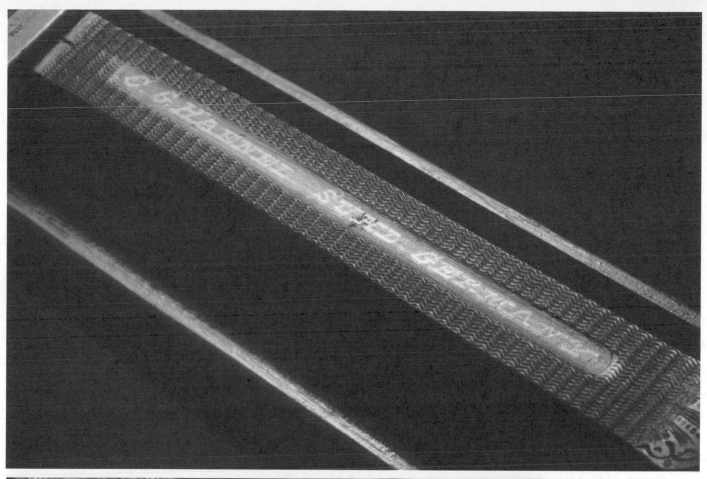

Above: The name "C.G. Haenel – Suhl, Germany" is lightly engraved on the rib.

Left: "Gussstahl Krupp Essen" is engraved around the barrel immediately forward of the receiver ring. Yes, "Gussstahl" has three s's.

The Lyman Model 36 sight was designed for the Mannlicher-Schönauer sporting rifles in 1907 (patented in 1912) with a variation to fit the Haenel-Mannlicher (Model 36H).

The arm pivots out of the way as the bolt is worked through the split bridge. The sight is the early Lyman design with two apertures, the finer of which pivots into place.

The Lyman patent open sight, with two folding leaves, is dovetailed into the full-length, matted rib. Both leaves fold down allowing unimpeded use of the receiver sight. If the open sights are desired the receiver sight can be swung out of the way.

tween German shooting clubs in the U.S., German immigrant gunmakers and the German companies, so more and more importers got into the act, and each, it seemed, stipulated little changes to the overall design. As a result, the number of minor variations seems endless.

This brings us back to the two major reasons there is only minor collector interest in these rifles. The first, of course, is the lack of a famous name such as Winchester. The second is the impossibility of classifying rifles by model and year. Model classification and certifiable originality are the backbone of gun collecting, and with Haenel-Mannlichers and other civilian rifles based on the Commission action,

this is almost impossible. There were too many importers at this end, too many small gunmakers at the other end, and far too many variations in between.

Another factor that worked against the Haenel-Mannlicher was the Great War. Not only did its outbreak in 1914 halt the importation of rifles, it eventually turned Americans against all things German. After 1920, German rifles reappeared on the market, but many were poorly made and confusion about 8x57 ammunition and bullet diameter compounded the problem. Finally, as the American style of hunting rifle took over in the 1920s, based on the Springfield action and, to a lesser degree, the Mauser 98, the Haenel-Mannlichers were forgotten.

For the modern rifle lover though, Haenels in their many guises offer an opportunity to own a rifle of stellar quality for not much money. The materials, workmanship and finishing are comparable to fine, modern, custom rifles.

On the negative side, they are chambered for cartridges like the 8x57 and 9x57 that by today's standards are relatively low velocity and suitable only for short-range hunting. Ammunition and even brass may be difficult to find.

As well, with the split bridge, it's difficult to mount a riflescope. But there's a positive side: These relatively low-power cartridges are comfortable to shoot in a light rifle and, being suited to ranges out to 250 yards, you hardly need a scope.

It's a question of viewing the glass as half empty or half full. Given the way in which white-tailed deer are hunted today from stands over food plots, shot at 150 yards or less, these rifles could have been intended for this purpose. Ironically, this method is similar to traditional hunting in Europe, for which these rifles were designed in the first place. If your preference is still-hunting, prowling along river bottoms and hillsides, they are perfect for that, too.

Hundreds of thousands of Gewehr '88 military rifles and carbines were scattered around the world, and many found their way into the U.S. Here, they were used in their original form or sporterized in styles ranging from the crudest of cutdowns to some really fine custom work. So at first glance a sporterized cavalry carbine can be mistaken for a Haenel, and vice versa.

Genuine civilian Haenels are identifiable in a number of ways. The most obvious is the name *C.G. Haenel – Suhl* engraved on the rib. However, the Haenel name is not deeply engraved and can be worn away through use. Finding the word steel instead of stahl on the barrel shows it was made for export. Neither of these is absolute, however. On my Haenel the words Gussstahl Krupp Essen are engraved around the barrel immediately forward of the receiver ring, and at first appear to be merely some decorative scroll.

Something else to beware of is the lack of caliber marking. My 9x57, for example, does not display its caliber anywhere. Chamber casts and slugging the bore are always a good idea.

The presence (or absence) of old Lyman sights, either the swing-away receiver sight designed for the split-bridge Mannlicher, or folding leaves dovetailed into the rib, does not necessarily prove anything, either. Some were installed at the factory and others after they arrived in the U.S. Since the question of factory originality is moot, however, this is not much of a consideration. In fact, finding one of the Lyman receiver sights is a bonus since they are excellent sights and collectors' items in their own right.

Collecting Haenel-Mannlichers may never make you any money, but it can lead into exploration of a fascinating byway in the history of the sporting rifle. You will find early Mannlichers from Steyr as well as German and Austrian custom makers, and you will find custom-ordered takedown rifles and modified *Gewehr '88s.*

There was life before the Mauser 98 and the evidence lies – as with so much of American life – in the pages of the old Sears, Roebuck wish book.

There are two front sights. One rises when the other is pushed down. One has a slightly larger bead than the other, and is slightly higher (.913" vs. .944"). With two front sights, two different open-sight leaves and a fully adjustable receiver sight, almost any distance or condition can be accommodated. Unlike some German rifles with multiple sights, this one allows any that are not in use to be moved completely out of the way.

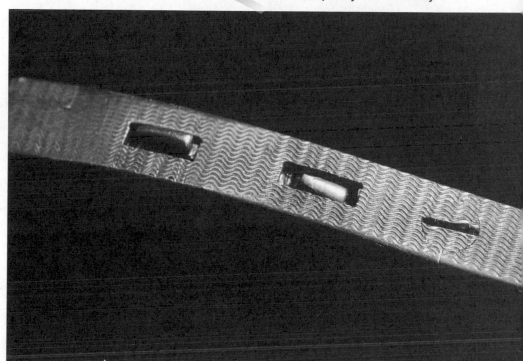

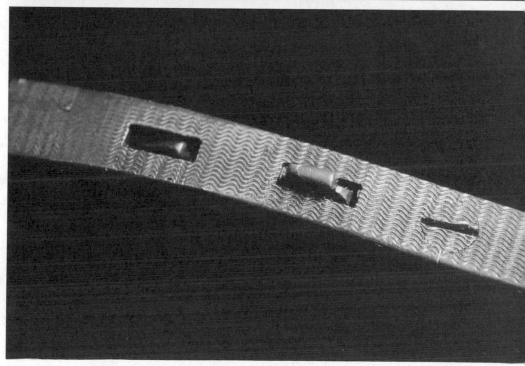

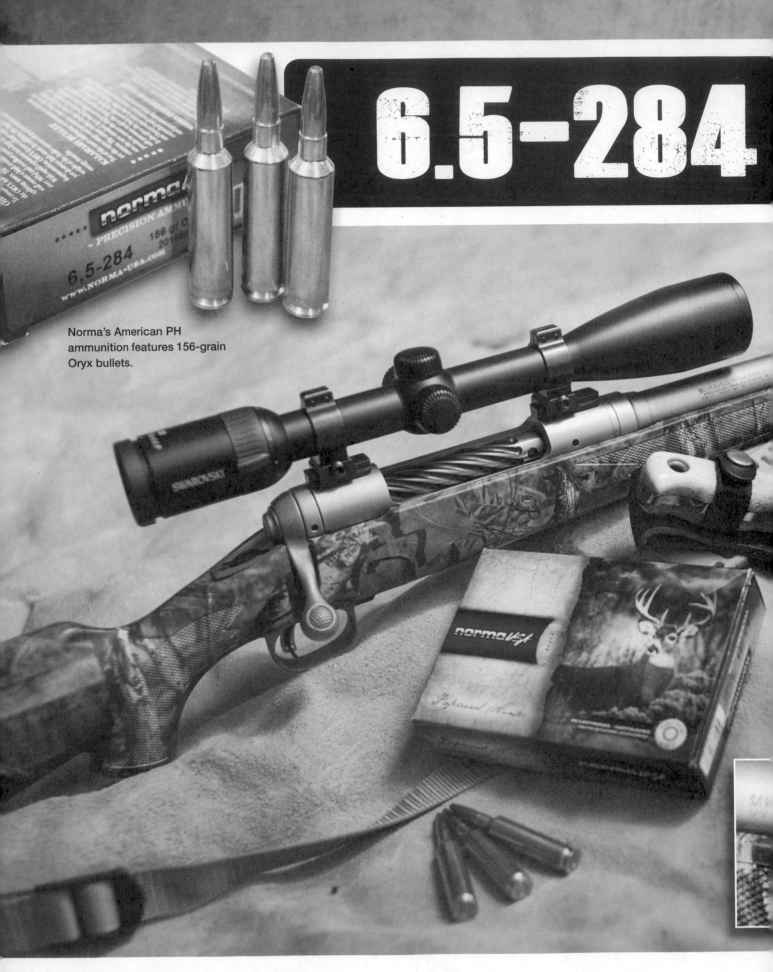

6.5-284

Norma's American PH ammunition features 156-grain Oryx bullets.

norma®

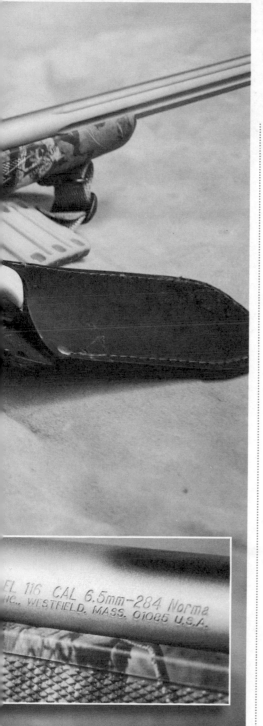

A CUSTOM 6.5-284 NORMA, BRED FOR THE HUNTING FIELDS

BY **Phil Massaro**

I come from a long line of hunters, so even as a young man I was no stranger to hunting rifles. My grandfather, uncles, and especially my dad, were serious deer hunters, and the fall classic was ritualistic. However, my whole family were strict devotees of the sacred .30 caliber for deer; anything else was blasphemy and nearly treasonous for that matter.

To stray from the chosen caliber would be grounds for serious reprimand, so I waited until I was in my 40s (when I started to become a gun writer and my opinion had a little more merit) to fulfill my desire for a sleek 6.5mm caliber. I lusted over a .264 Winchester Magnum for years, but they had become rarer than hen's teeth, well, those with a good barrel anyway, so the more modern 6.5 offerings appealed to me.

Not that there are any flies on the venerable 6.5x55 Swedish Mauser, or the uber-nostalgic 6.5x54 Mannlicher-Schoenauer, but I wanted a little more oomph behind the bullet for long range work and for decent energy figures. The concise package that is the 6.5 Creedmoor had some initial appeal, but the 6.5-284 Norma really tickled my fancy. The ballistic figures put it just shy of the, ahem, barrel burners that are the .264 Mag. and that newcomer the .26 Nosler, and put it pretty well on par with the proven 6.5-06 wildcat. This fact, combined with the wicked array of available 6.5mm bullets on the market, pretty well sealed the deal for me.

The .284 Winchester, parent to our darling little 6.5-284 Norma, was a neat design that just didn't catch on well. Delivering .280 Remington velocities from a short-action cartridge should have been an easy sell, but the gun market is what it is, and the poor .284 faded into obscurity. I'd like to think that the fat case and rebated rim were well ahead of their time, as the more modern Remington Ultra Magnum, Winchester Short Magnum and Nosler family of cartridges all share the same qualities.

It didn't take the wildcat crowd long to start tinkering with that .284 case and the 6.5-284 and 6mm-284 quickly made waves on the benchrest circuits. Norma saw the splash made by the 6.5-284 cartridge and legitimized the wildcat by getting SAAMI approval in 2001. That took any variables out of the case design and gave us all some fantastic factory ammo and brass to move forward with. The 6.5-284 has a case length of 2.170", a neck length of .272", giving plenty of neck tension for good concentricity. Plus it has a shoulder angle of 35.7 degrees, which means there's plenty of shoulder to give good headspacing, yet feed easily.

Another benefit of the design is that it has an overall cartridge length of 3.228", giving those long, lean 6.5mm bullets over an inch outside of the case mouth. Even though it is the darling of the benchrest world, I saw the potential of the cartridge as a hunting round.

From the Ground Up

While chatting with J.J. Reich of Savage Rifles, he explained to me the function of the Savage Custom Shop, which could "Frankenstein" any of the features of nearly any of the rifles that Savage makes into a personalized package. My ears perked up like a chocolate lab at the mention of treats.

"Anything you make?"

"Yup, anything we make."

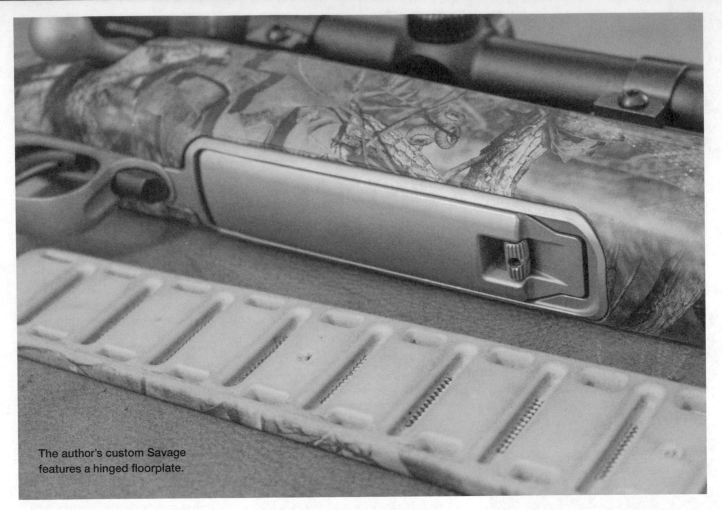

The author's custom Savage features a hinged floorplate.

Well, it didn't take long to pick the caliber (which you can guess), but which rifle? There is a wide array of models and actions to choose from, so it took me a bit to come up with what I thought would be the best blend of hunting rifle and long-range target capability. I wanted an action long enough to give me room to seat the bullets out quite some distance for plenty of case capacity and the ability to use the longer ogive bullets. I also wanted a barrel length that would allow all of the powder to be utilized, yet not so long as to become a hindrance in the woods. Most of the bench rifles chambered for 6.5-284 sport a 28- or even 30-inch barrel, but those lengths don't really translate well in hunting situations. I also wanted a synthetic stock that would be impervious to weather.

I settled on the Savage Model 116 action and Bear Hunter stock in the Mossy Oak Breakup camo pattern. The action is much longer than needed for the 6.5-284 Norma when loaded to SAAMI specifications, but it would easily allow me to use Berger 140-grain VLD bullets and their ilk. Since this was a custom hunting gun

I decided on a 25-inch barrel, medium-heavy contour and fluted. We left muzzlebrake option off though, since my battered ears can't take any more extra noise. I also loved the spiral-fluted bolt featured on the 111 Lightweight Hunter, so I added that as a cool option.

I chose the Bear Hunter's stock for its hinged floorplate, in deference to the standard Savage detachable magazine. To me, it was one less thing to lose while packing for a hunting trip. The AccuTrigger is standard on all the Savage rifles, so that was a no-brainer, but the aluminum bedding block of the AccuStock was an option that I felt was well worthwhile. Good bedding and a good trigger can make or break a rifle and in this case it was definitely a welcome addition.

So, I ended up with a camouflage synthetic stock, stainless steel action and a barrel that was slightly muzzle heavy when pulled up for the shot. The tang three-position thumb safety fit the package like a glove, then it was off to the world of optics to pick some glass that would optimize the potential of both the rifle and the cartridge.

High Class Glass

This rifle would be accompanying me on hunts across the globe, so versatility was my foremost thought. Whitetails in my native New York, caribou on the Alaskan tundra, pronghorn on the Great Plains and a variety of African antelope would all be on the menu, so the magnification range would be the first obstacle. Second, the ability to hit distant targets would be a necessity, as the 6.5-284 Norma is a stellar reach-out-and-touch-'em caliber.

After some research and studying some of the reticles that might mate well with the ballistics of the 6.5-284, I settled on a rather high-end piece of glass: the Swarovski Z5 3.5-18x44mm with a fancy-schmancy side focus knob. This particular scope is fitted with the BRH reticle, which makes long-range shots much easier because it features holdover marks on the lower post and wind drift calibrations to aid the shooter in connecting on targets out past 200 yards. Never in my 43 years have I possessed a scope with this level of clarity, nor have

I ever had a scope that took adjustment this well; when Swarovski says that each click is ¼ MOA, they seriously mean exactly that.

Once the riflescope was nestled into the Talley rings sighting in was not a chore, but was a joy. Seriously, using Norma American PH 156-grain Oryx ammunition I was putting three shots into ½ MOA on the bullseye with less than seven shots fired. I zeroed in at 100 yards for our deer season here in New York, as the longest shot I can muster in our woods is 150 yards. At the maximum power, 18x, I could almost see the bullet rip paper and I felt confident that any feasible shot that presented itself would be a near "gimme", with the shooter being the weak link in the chain. The lower end of the scope, 3.5x, was perfect for shots up close, which are the norm in the woods of Upstate New York.

Home Cooking

I've long been a fan of roundnose bullets and that was part of the selling point of the 6.5mm caliber – the ability to use those high sectional density 156- and 160-grain roundnose slugs to great effect. I've heard it said many times by fans of different 6.5mm cartridges that the 6.5s kill much better than they should. I wanted a cartridge to bridge the gap between my favorite varmint gun, the .22-250 Remington, and my .308 Winchester and .300 Winchester Magnum. There are many good choices like the 6mms, .25s and even the .270s, but they all have limited bullet weights when compared to the 6.5mm.

The ability to use bullets between 85 and 160 grains had a ton of appeal to me, especially when you look at the ballistic coefficient figures for the sleek boattail spitzer bullets weighing between 120 and 140 grains – you have something sort of magical. These bullets offer the wind bucking capabilities of the long proven .30-caliber record-holding bullets, yet at a significant drop in recoil.

So, I chose several of my favorite bullets to arrive at some good handloads. I'm a huge fan of Bill Hober's dynamic duo, the Swift A-Frame and the Scirocco II, so they were definitely on the menu. I'm also a believer in North Fork bullets and their 140-grain hollowpoint bonded-core bullet made it into the party as well. I couldn't exclude the fantastic 160-grain Hornady roundnose bullet, as the lower velocity and high S.D. factor would make this cup-and-core wonder a great deer and black bear bullet in the Catskill and Adirondacks of New York. The Berger 140 VLDs needed to be tested for the accuracy potential alone. Armed with 50 rounds of shiny Norma brass and Federal G210GM Gold Medal primers, my buddy Marty Groppi and I sat down at the bench to cook up some winners.

The cartridge showed a preference for two powders right off the bat: my long-time friend IMR4350 and Hodgdon's H4831-SC. Both have a burn rate on the slower side of the spectrum and are perfect for the case capacity of the 6.5-284. While IMR4350 is known for its temperature fluctuation, it has performed very well in my .300 Winchester Magnum and .375 H&H Magnum, so I'm not surprised that it worked out well here. H4831-SC

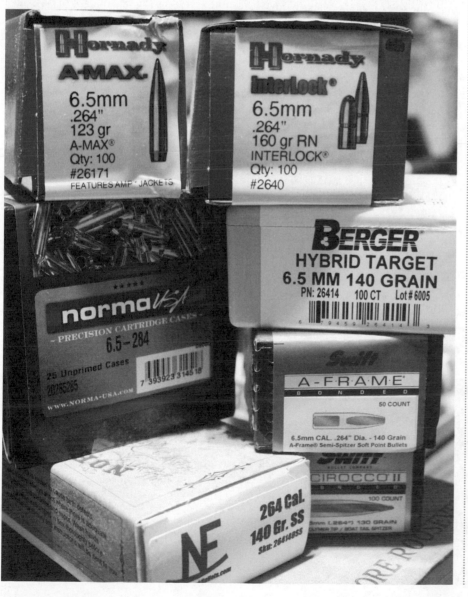

Left: There are many good bullet choices for the 6.5-284 Norma.
Above: The 140-grain Swift A-Frame is a wonderful bonded-core bullet.

Norma brass is widely known as one of the best brands available.

These North Fork 140-grain hollowpoint, bonded-core bullets delivered excellent accuracy in the author's handloads.

(the SC standing for Short Cut) is one of Hodgdon's Extreme powders, engineered for temperature insensitivity, and they're not kidding. It's also a very versatile powder that is equally at home in a cartridge like our darling 6.5 or in magnum cases as big as the .378 Weatherby.

The first loads had my jaw dropping because the rifle printed between ¼ and ½ MOA with five-shot groups. The Bergers were at the top of the heap, no surprise there, but those wicked North Fork 140-grain hollowpoints and the Swift 140-grain A-Frame showed some serious accuracy. Either of these bullets will make a great choice as an all-around medium-game hunting load, and I was grinning ear to ear about having the option of using both in the hunting fields. I'd feel comfortable using these bullets on game up to the size of elk or black bear here in North America, and game up to the size of kudu or sable in Africa. I realize the bullet weight is on the light side of the spectrum, but those 140-grain North Forks and A-Frames are very tough bullets with a sectional density figure of .287, so penetration should be fantastic.

Accuracy was our goal as we tinkered with the handloads, more than wringing every last ounce of velocity that we could out of the rifle. The rifle showed a definite preference for a load of 47 grains of H4831-SC, giving ½ MOA groups using the North Fork 140-grain bullet and the 140-grain Swift A-Frame. Both loads clocked right around 2,650 fps, about 150 fps below what we could've obtained, but with the level of accuracy displayed

I was completely fine with that velocity. Using the same pair of bullets with Reloder-19 (a powder that has served me well for many years), the five-shot groups opened up to just under an inch, but the velocity bumped up to 2,790 fps; a flatter shooting load with more than acceptable hunting accuracy. The Swift A-Frame 140-grain bullet was also happy sitting atop 46.5 grains of IMR4350, printing another ½ MOA group, with an average velocity of 2,700 fps.

The Swift Scirocco II, at 130 grains, proved to be very accurate as well with ¾-inch groups, but for some reason the velocities were well below the published figures by almost 200 fps. As much as I love the Scirocco, I think that this bullet will have to sit the bench during hunting season, unless I can find another powder that will give the accuracy and velocities I'm after to let this bullet do its job for long-range work. The Berger VLD target bullets showed the same tendencies in the velocity department, being plenty accurate but giving less speed than advertised.

I suspect the rifle's barrel, although barely broken in, prefers bullets that are flat based and that give plenty of bearing surface to build pressures. For a hunting rifle, I look for projectiles that will perform well within my self-imposed limit of 350-400 yards, depending on conditions. The North Fork and Swift A-Frame will both deliver the goods at those ranges.

For the close shots, such as those here in the Northeast, the Hornady 160-grain roundnose bullet proved to be an excellent choice with groups just over an inch at the 100-yard mark, cruising along at 2,575 fps. A charge of Winchester WMR, 50.5 grains if you must know, delivered the goods for the long, heavy-for-caliber bullet. This load should prove to be fantastic for whitetails and black bears on shots within 250 yards, as the Sectional Density of that long 160 will guarantee good penetration.

Back to the Beginning

The rifle arrived 10 days before the opening day of our deer season and I had no time to develop the aforementioned handloads, so I procured some Norma American PH factory ammunition loaded with the wonderful 156-grain Norma Oryx bullet. The Oryx is a sound design, being a roundnose bullet, with a jacket that gets thicker toward the base. The Norma engineers

LOADING CHART 6.5-284 NORMA

BULLET	PRIMER= FED GM210M POWDER	NORMA CASES CHARGE	VELOCITY	AVG. GROUP SIZE	C.O.L.
140 gr. North Fork HP	H4831SC	47 grains	2,650 fps	.5"	3.000"
140 gr. North Fork HP	IMR4350	45 grains	2,680 fps	.5"	3.000"
140 gr. North Fork HP	Reloder 19	50 grains	2,790 fps	.9"	3.000"
140 gr. Swift A-Frame	H4831SC	47 grains	2,650 fps	.5"	3.005"
140 gr. Swift A-Frame	IMR4350	46.5 grains	2,700 fps	.5"	3.005"
140 gr. Berger VLD	H4831SC	47 grains	2,510 fps	.4"	3.010"
130 gr. Swift Sciricco II	H4831SC	49.5 grains	2,570 fps	.75"	2.950"
160 gr. Hornady InterLock	Win. WMR	50.5 grains	2,575 fps	1.1"	3.010"
156 gr. Norma Oryx	Factory	Loading	2,730 fps	.6"	2.900"

C.O.L. = cartridge overall length

bonded just the rear portion of the jacket to the core in order to give a blend of great expansion up front, while allowing the rear portion to hold together for reliable penetration. Combine that with a muzzle velocity that registers 2,730 fps, and you've got a great load for all game that is capable of being taken with a 6.5mm caliber.

I was hunting deer with my wife in my native Upstate New York on the second weekend of our three-week season. The morning temperature was a frigid 18 degrees F when I saw the first of three does jog across the little valley I was watching. Behind them were two bucks, following their every move like heat-seeking missiles. Grunting, blowing, lips curled, the bigger of the two was a chocolate-horned 8-pointer, with tines broken from fighting.

The merry little parade of deer ascended my side of the valley and from behind the stone wall I was using to hide my profile, I settled the Swarovski's crosshairs on the inside of his armpit as he quartered toward me. The buck flipped over backward at the shot, never knowing what hit him. The small spike horn that was in tow abandoned all thoughts of the hot doe and stood in awe for several moments, wondering what the heck just happened. The 8-pointer never twitched or moved. The 156-grain roundnose Norma bullet shredded his heart and lungs, and took him in a humane and dramatic fashion. The bullet passed completely through the buck so I didn't get a chance to measure the retained weight, but with a kill that dramatic I wasn't heartbroken.

I was officially sold on the 6.5-284 Norma, even though this wasn't the largest buck I've ever taken, in body or antler size. Mrs. Massaro is preparing the tenderloins as I write these words, and the delicious aroma is making it near impossible to concentrate.

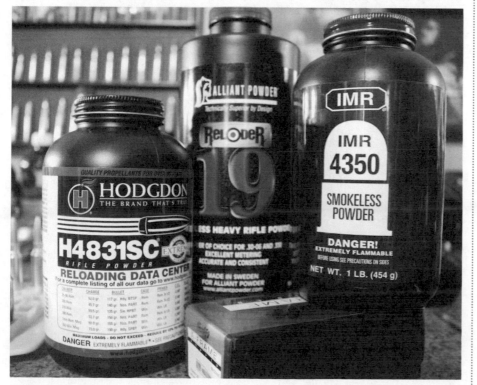

Some of the powders the author tested in his 6.5-284 Norma handloads.

The custom Savage is topped with Swarovski's excellent Z5 3.5-18x44mm scope, mounted with Talley steel rings. **Inset:** The author with the 8-point New York whitetail taken with the custom Savage rifle.

The Rainbow Connection

How does the 6.5-284 do at longer hunting distances? As stated earlier, I limit my shots at unwounded game to 350-400 yards – conditions permitting – so let's examine the trajectory within those ranges. Using a 200-yard zero and the 140-grain Swift A-Frame for demonstrative purposes, the 6.5-284 load moving at 2,700 fps (an average of our attained velocities), you'll find yourself hitting 9 inches low at 300 yards, and 26 inches low at 400, while only being 2 inches high at the 100-yard mark. While not the frozen-rope trajectory of the .264 Winchester Magnum or .26 Nosler, it is still in the category of "flat shooting."

The Swarovski BRH reticle can make the longer shots even easier thanks to wind drift markers and a well-designed holdover system of bars and dots on the lower vertical post. Using the same load I've just described, you will zero the rifle at 200 yards (again 2 inches high at 100) and the first bar below the crosshair will be spot on at 270 yards, the dot below that will hit at 320 yards. The second bar is zeroed for 380 yards and the second dot for 430. For you long-range junkies, the third bar hits at 480 yards, the third dot at 520.

There are a total of five lower crosshairs and four intermediate dots for calibrated holds out to 640 yards with this trajectory. Please note that the BRH reticle is calibrated to function at the maximum power, in this particular case 18x magnification. The use of an accurate rangefinder would allow the shooter to make the most of this trajectory technology.

There are also wind drift markings on the five lower crosshairs with marks for 10 and 20 mph crosswinds. These should come in very handy for caribou and pronghorn hunters, or anyone who hunts wide-open, windy places at long ranges.

The Big Picture

So, what are the advantages of a custom rifle in a not-so-popular caliber? I mean, couldn't we do the same thing with a .270 Winchester? Is it worth the time and trouble? Well, that depends on your outlook on things. If you are a practical person, a more affordable rifle in a caliber that has more choices of factory ammunition might be the way to go for you. Me, I like something a bit different. Obviously, the .270 Winchester and .30-06 Springfield have been heralded as long-range wonders for almost a century, but the magnum cartridges all have their following too, and the shooters' interests in different cartridges seems to know no bounds.

I chose the 6.5-284 Norma because it is different, and I've found it to be a near perfect blend of striking power (the 156-grain Oryx load gives 2,700 ft/lbs of energy at the muzzle) and wonderful shootability. The rifle weighs in at 8¾ pounds fully dressed, so that helps to absorb the recoil, but that aside, I find the 6.5-284 to have much less felt recoil than the numerous .270 Winchesters I've loaded for. Although it is primarily thought of as a paper-punching cartridge, I see the potential for it to be a very useful hunting cartridge that will handle all sorts of medium game on many different continents.

Having a custom rifle is just plain cool. I like the fact that I had a hand in the rifle's creation (by choosing the parts, anyway) and truly enjoy having a rifle that no one else has, at least for now. This modern beauty will be accompanying me on safari this year as my light rifle using the 140-grain North Fork bullets, and I really look forward to all the memories we will create together.

Tanya Faulds, one of the U.K.'s top women shooters with her Syren Tempio Sporting model.

By Nick Sisley

SYREN SHOTGUNS

The ranks of women shooters are on the rise. At the top of the sporting clays category are Desirae Edmonds, Janet McDougall, Diane Sorantino and many others. In Olympic shooting and other clay target work there's the inimitable Kim Rhode. In skeet shooting there's Becky McCumber, Lindsay Plesco, Louise Terry and rising very young stars like Victoria Stellato and Bettina Wohlforth. In the hunting realm the feminine set numbers are rising as fast – if not faster

than in clay target work.

So why no shotguns made especially for women?

That's what Wes Lang of Caesar Guerini USA thought. Evidently so did Giorgio and Antonio Guerini in Italy, the moving engineering and ingenuity forces behind Caesar Guerini and today's Fabarm shotguns. While

STRICTLY FOR THE HUNTRESS

Caesar Guerini might not be a name with the longevity of say a Remington or a Winchester – in a little over a decade Caesar Guerini has taken shotgun-dom by storm.

Why? Maybe a little history would help to answer. Wes Lang's history goes back to

starting in wholesale gun sales, then as Sales Manager at Seminole Gunworks, a stint with Beretta, a publishing role with a major outdoor magazine chain, followed by Sig Arms when the company marketed shotguns. Giorgio and Antonio Guerini had a vision, and they approached Wes Lang with it: make exceptional over/unders for both clay target work and hunting. The company has stuck by its guns, in that they only make over/ unders, and they are very good ones. In time they came out with many models – but all were based on the same super-strong lockup system.

There was no Caesar Guerini factory in those beginning years, so the guns were made in the Fabarm factory in Brescia, the Italian gunmaking Mecca. All engineering and manufacturing were under the scrutinizing eyes of Giorgio and Antonio. Since production started in 2002, this company has sold every gun they have ever produced, obviously a sweet fact to their bottom line. A few years ago Fabarm brass decided it was time to retire. That's when Caesar Guerini bought the factory and the rights to produce Fabarm shotguns.

Some of Caesar Guerini's biggest home runs have been with the Summit Sporting model and the Impact series of high adjustable rib and high adjustable comb models – of which there are now several. With the purchase of Fabarm, a company that had been producing quite a number of semiautos and over/unders, Wes, Giorgio and Antonio were cautious about diving into the figurative deep end of "many" models.

So they took a slow approach. The Impact series was riding an unbelievable high among shotgun buyers so Guerini decided to bring out one semiauto— remember Caesar Guerini only makes over/unders and it's still that way—so why not give that semiauto the same "impact" as the Guerini Impact O/U? Thus, the Fabarm XLR5 was born— the first semiauto with the top-selling high adjustable rib and high adjustable comb. Today there are three models in the Fabarm XLR5 semiauto line up – all are the same save for differing rib and comb configurations. Like the Caesar Guerini over/unders, the Fabarm XLR5 wasn't just a home run, it was a grand slam.

So what to try next? Enter the Syren series. There's not just one model. There are several including over/unders and

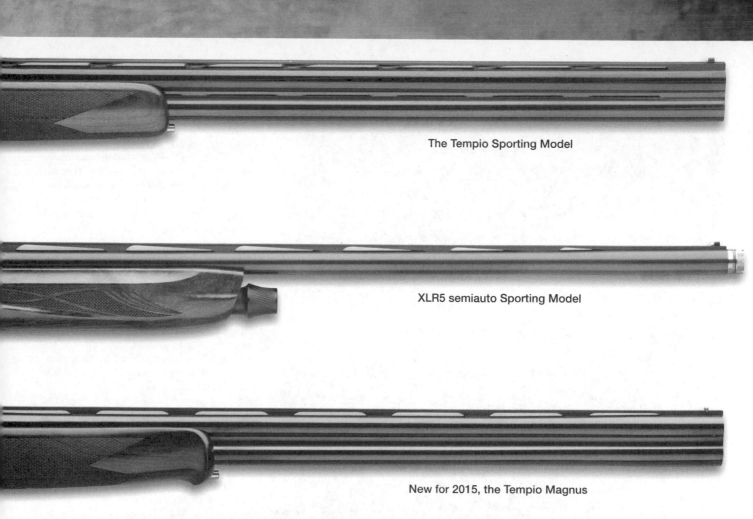

The Tempio Sporting Model

XLR5 semiauto Sporting Model

New for 2015, the Tempio Magnus

Marie Palmer puts the Syren XLR5 12 gauge to the clay bird test.

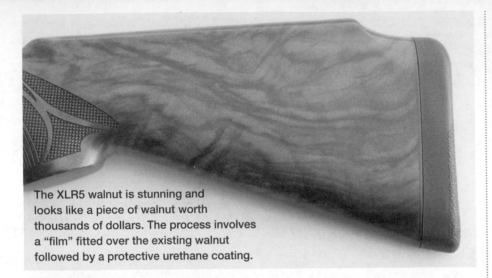

The XLR5 walnut is stunning and looks like a piece of walnut worth thousands of dollars. The process involves a "film" fitted over the existing walnut followed by a protective urethane coating.

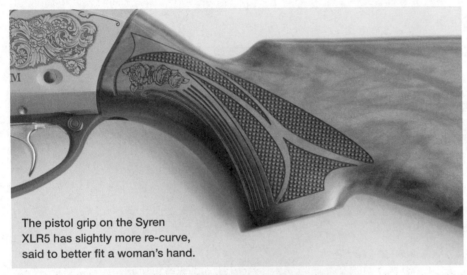

The pistol grip on the Syren XLR5 has slightly more re-curve, said to better fit a woman's hand.

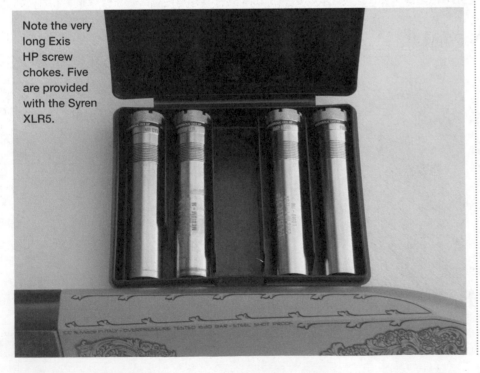

Note the very long Exis HP screw chokes. Five are provided with the Syren XLR5.

a semiauto, all aimed strictly at women shooters. There are Sporting models for virtually all the clay target games and Field models that are ideal for most any feather and furred stuff imaginable.

What makes the Syren series different are different cosmetics, i.e. more feminine looks and less so-called masculine, and different stock dimensions. There's no nuclear science involved in realizing that women are built different than men. First off, ladies are generally smaller; secondly, they're built differently in other obvious ways. A stock that fits a 6-foot, 2-inch tall muscular 200-pounder won't fit a 6-foot, 8-inch tall 300-pounder, or a demure, buxom lady of 5 feet, 6 inches at 110 pounds.

So let's begin by breaking down and inspecting the several Syren models and start with the Syren XLR5 semiauto. Admittedly, this one is aimed more at clay target breaking than quail or ringnecks, though it will do very well for either. Offered only in 12 gauge, the Syren XLR5 weighs in at 7 pounds, 10 ounces on my digital postal scale. The 28-inch barrel (also offered in 30 and 32 inches) hefted 2 pounds, 3.5 ounces. A previous Fabarm XLR5 barrel went 2 pounds, 7 ounces. So was the Syren XLR5 barrel trimmed a tad for a few ounces less weight? The Syren fore-end went 6.5 ounces.

The Syren XLR5 bore takes some explanation. Dubbed Tribore HP, the inner barrel dimensions are like no other. Instead of a traditional forcing cone right in front of the chamber—or a so-called extended (longer) forcing cone—there is no forcing cone. Here's what I measured with my Baker Barrel Reader. Right in front of the chamber area the inner dimension is .737 inch, which is lots of overboring. But that same .737-inch dimension stays the same for about half the length of the barrel. Then a very slow taper starts. It takes the remaining half of the forward part of the barrel to taper from .737" to .728" right before the threads for the screw-in choke tubes. That's only .009" taper in about 14-inches.

How does Tribore HP affect performance?

It's simple. With no forcing cone, no pellets are deformed, as they can be when the shot column is forced into a smaller space, like from the chamber (usually about .800" in 12 gauge) to the squeezing in the forcing cone. In days of yore, forcing cones were a necessity because of fiber and paper wads. Without a sharp forcing cone gases could leak

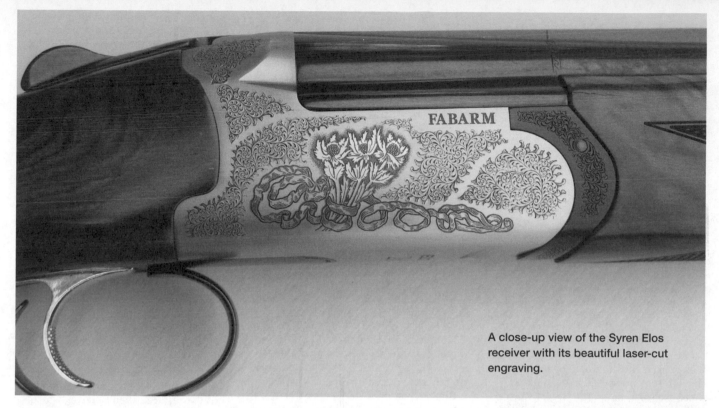

A close-up view of the Syren Elos receiver with its beautiful laser-cut engraving.

past the fiber or paper wad disrupting the shot column and negatively affecting patterns. With plastic wads there is a much better seal so gases can't get past the plastic wad – forcing cone or no forcing cone.

The gun's gas operation is big on recoil reduction. Actually, the recoil is spread over more milleseconds, thus the feel of recoil is much reduced. The XLR5 has a steel gas piston, which may also be instrumental in less felt recoil. I feel that this piston has to be very big in reliable function. These semis just plain work, without malfunction.

Check the close-up of a Syren XLR5 receiver. The finish is called Titanium Silver. Obviously it is corrosion resistant, but the finish is also attractive (though with no sheen) and it allows the laser-cut engraving to show very well. The engraving pattern is different when compared to the Fabarm XLR5 engraving, which is offered in a blued receiver – the Titanium Silver, only for the Syren. The engraving change is meant to have feminine appeal.

Then there's the wood. This is not a wood upgrade but is done through a process called Triwood. Walnut is used with plenty of straight-grain strength at the wrist and grip area. Next a "film" is placed over the walnut that gives the wood that $4,000 walnut look. The "film" is urethane coated. Finally, there's the

handsome hand-rubbed oil finish.

The checkering on the Syren is also a bit different—more lady-like—on both the grip and the fore-end. Without "diamonds," each checkering peak is rounded. How do the stock dimensions differ? Obviously, length of pull is one aspect. Most Guerini and Fabarm stocks are 14.75 inches. The Syren XLR5 stock has 13.75 inches LOP. This is not the only difference. The drop at comb is 1.5 inches, drop at heel (note the Monte Carlo-like step down in the stock photo) is 2.25", cast at heel is .125", cast at toe .375", pitch 6 degrees, reach 4", all measured when the trigger (which is adjustable back and forth) is at its midposition. Further, the grip has slightly more recurve than the masculine model—said to fit a woman's hand better.

The recoil pad is rounded all around to mitigate gun hang-ups during the mount. The vent rib is tapered—metal midbead—white front bead. The screw-in chokes are long at 3¾ inches. Five Exis FP tubes are supplied. The Skeet went .721", the Improved Cylinder .715", the Modified .706", the Improved Modified .701", the Full .691". Recall that the bore size at the start of the choke threads was .728". To finish the package, the XLR5 comes in a nice hard case with a fit interior.

Sticking with the Fabarm side, what about the Syren over/under? Offered in

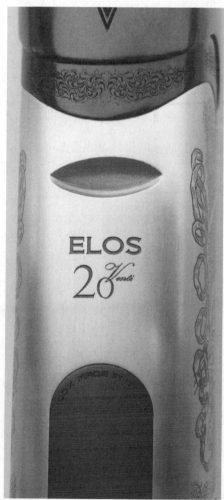

Lindsey Lamagna loves how the Syren Elos 20 gauge points and shoots.

20 and 28 gauges, these are also ideal for the huntress. The base gun is the Fabarm Elos Venti. What makes it a Syren Elos Venti is the different cosmetics and the different stock dimensions. Also, there are roses cut in the stock by laser and these roses are on all of the Syren stocks, another nice touch.

I have a 20-gauge Syren Elos sitting on my lap as I type away on this keyboard. Check the accompanying close-up photo of the receiver for the detailed engraving with gold engraved flowers. The finish is again Titanium Silver, and this bright look does enhance the intricate laser-cut engraving.

This shotgun also features the Tribore HP barrel with .632" in front of the 20-gauge chamber area and running that same measurement for half the barrel length. Then the taper is from .632" to .625" to just in front of the choke threads—more gentle treating of the pellets on the outside of the shot column for the trip down the bore. The recoil pad is thinner, just over ¼-inch, separated from the stock via a thin black spacer. The same Triwood stock that looks like a $4,000 piece of Turkish and the same slight additional re-curve to the pistol grip as the XLR5.

The 10-inch fore-end weighs 8.5 ounces, the 28-inch barrels weighed 2 pounds, 13 ounces, the whole gun 6 pounds, 10.5 ounces. The vent rib is not tapered and there are side panels between the barrels with no vents. In addition to this gun there is also a Syren Elos Venti Light—with an aluminum alloy receiver, so lighter—reportedly at

5 pounds, 11 ounces. Stock dimensions are 13.875 inches length of pull, 1.375" drop at comb, 2.25" drop at heel (again note the Monte Carlo-like step down at the rear of the stock), .125" cast at heel, .375" cast at toe, 6 degrees of pitch, reach 3.5"—all small but subtle stock dimension changes to better fit most women shooters. All Syren over/unders have inertia-type triggers.

Now for the Syren Caesar Guerini over/unders—there are two divisions, Sporting and Field. Both divisions are based on the Tempio model of the Caesar Guerini over/under. So now I'm looking at a 12-gauge Syren Tempio Sporting model on my lap. When I ordered this consignment O/U, I didn't realize that there were 20 and 28 gauge Syren Tempio sporting models as well. With all three gauges, ladies can select from either 28- or 30-inch barrels. My test gun has the latter.

The barrels are overbored on my 12 gauge to .733". Traditionally 12 bores have run about .725", with some European bores sometimes even smaller. These bores are called DuoCon, which means a 5-inch tapered forcing cone. Old forcing cones were in the neighborhood of ¼-inch. In 20 and 28 gauge, the Syren Tempios have 4-inch DuoCon forcing cones.

The gun weighs 8 pounds, 1 ounce; the 30-inch barrels 3 pounds, 6.5 ounces; the 10-inch fore-end 11.3 ounces. Six screw-in chokes are provided. I measured the Cylinder at .734", the Skeet at .729", the two Improved Cylinders were both at .724", the Light Modified at .719", the Modified at .713". Obviously, other chokes are available as aftermarket options. These chokes are extended, just shy of 3¼ total inches in length, so there's lots of room for long taper and parallel sections that treat pellets gently.

The barrels have vented side panels and the top vent rib tapers from 10mm to 6mm. The lockup system for all Guerini and Fabarm over/unders involves barrels pivoting on trunnions, a sliding bolt from the base of the receiver engages the lugs milled into the bottom of the monobloc upon closing, plus recoil lugs milled into the base of the monobloc that nestle into milled away areas in the base of the receiver.

The Syren Tempio receiver is engraved differently than the Guerini Tempio receiver. There's very intricate rose and scroll with engraved gold roses on both receiver sides and just as extensive engraving on the receiver bottom. The

Debra Coulter says the Syren Tempio Sporting 12 gauge is very much to her liking.

Natalie Lamagna puts the Syren Tempio Sporting to work on a skeet field.

engraving design is by Bottega Giovanelli and his signature is on the bottom tang. The receiver finish is Guerini's own Invis-alloy. It looks like a coin-type finish but is very corrosion protective, and it is hand polished. The laser-cut engraving goes up around the fences to the top tang, the triggerguard and the opening lever. The receiver sides have that elegant sculpturing similar to a Perazzi.

The stock dimensions are again tailored for women with a 13.75-inch length of pull, drop at comb 1.375", drop at heel 2.5" (again note the Monte Carlo-like drop at the rear of the stock), cast at heel .125", cast at toe .375", pitch 8 degrees, breech to comb 7", reach 3.5", all measured from the trigger's midposition. The trigger can be moved back and forth so the lady can adjust for her perfect grip-to-trigger distance. Again, while the length of pull is significantly different compared to the standard Guerini Tempio model, the other differences in the stock dimensions are small and subtle.

The stock finish is hand-rubbed oil. There's also that same slight additional re-curve to the grip. There are roses in the stock cut by laser. The cut checkering is also done by laser and at 26 lines-per-inch, which is about as tiny as a huntress will ever see, and the checkering is virtually flawless. The recoil pad

is just shy of 1/3-inch thick, rounded all around with a thin black spacer. Chambers are 2¾ inches—no 3-inch magnums. The same length chambers go for the 20 and 28 gauges. The top rib tapers from 10mm to 6mm on the 12 gauge – nontapered ribs on the 20 and the 28. The small gauge guns will average 8-10 ounces lighter than the 12 gauge in the Sporter versions.

There are also Field versions of the Syren Tempio in 20 and 28 gauges, both with 28-inch barrels. Weights will run about 6½ pounds depending on the gauge. The same Invisalloy protection is on the receivers along with the same beautiful engraving patterns – scroll and engraved gold flowers. There's also the same hand-rubbed oil finish on the stock and 26 lines-per-inch impeccable checkering. Instead of a recoil pad there's a distinctive wood buttplate, a touch I very much like. Chambers are 3 inches in the 20, 2¾ inches in the 28. Ribs are 6mm nontapered. Bores are chrome lined and five screw-in chokes are included. The fore-ends have a different rounded look, say like a Browning Superposed Lightning. The selective trigger is gold plated and the package comes in a hard case, as do all of the Syren models.

Finally, there's the Syren Tempio Light. Most of the gun is the same as the standard Tempio, save for the

lighter aluminum alloy receiver. Weight will be reduced to the 5½-pound range; a bit of weight variation can be expected for gauge and wood density. The stock dimensions will be similar, though probably not exactly the same as the other field models in the Syren line.

An entirely new corporation has been created for the marketing of these women's guns: Syren USA. It's even headed up by a woman, and top shooter, Ann Mauro. Ann is already compiling top lady shooters and sponsoring them to shoot the various Syren models. She's on the ground floor of a new wave in shotgunning.

Suggested retail prices start at $1,995 for the SLR5 semiauto, $2,995 for the Elos Field Gun, $3,995 for the Tempio Field and $4,380 for Tempio Sporting models. Higher grades are available. Expect to see more lady shooters now that they can buy a gun that fits them well – and that cosmetically are sure to please our feminine set. On the web it's www. syrenusa.com.

Readers may be interested in one or more of the author's new e-Books. Three are on shotgun stuff, one on fun single-engine aviation. Go to www.amazon.com. The author welcomes your emails at nicksisley@hotmail.com.

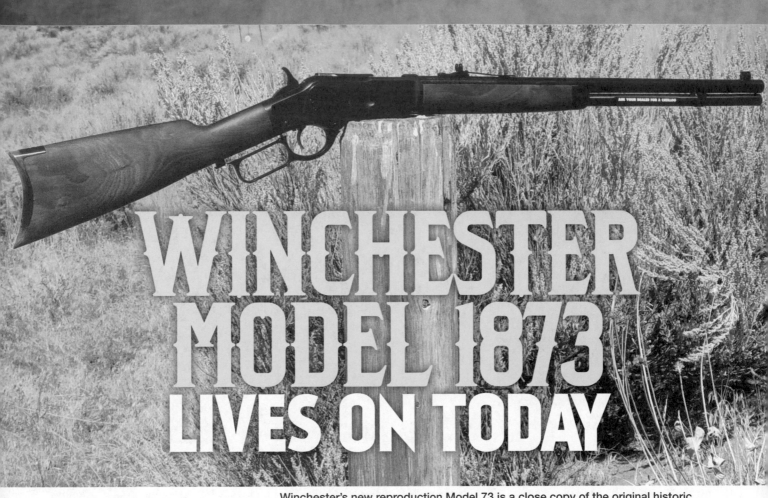

WINCHESTER MODEL 1873 LIVES ON TODAY

Winchester's new reproduction Model 73 is a close copy of the original historic version, some of which were built nearly a century and a half ago.

BY **Tom Tabor**

Many shooters equate the Winchester Model 1873 lever-action rifle as "The gun that won the West." For decades Hollywood has added greatly to fuel that contention through a plethora of movies and television shows depicting Winchesters and specifically the Model 1873 in that role. But like virtually all things in life some folks will disagree, with possibly the vast majority of those individuals arguing that Sharps might be a more deserving candidate for that honor.

Nevertheless, from the time the Winchester '73 was first introduced until production ended in 1920, Winchester had placed nearly 750,000 of these fine rifles in the hands of shooters. A few rifles eventually wound up in other countries, but the vast majority stayed in the United States. Even when viewed by today's production standards that is a tremendous amount of rifles, and when judged against the other rifles of that era, even the Sharps pales in comparison.

Furthermore, when that massive three-quarters of a million figure is placed alongside the 1880 U.S. census, which put the population at that time at only around 50 million, that in itself should be enough to convince everyone that the Winchester Model 73 truly deserves the title of the "The gun that won the West."

The Roots of the Model 1873

Originally Winchester called the rifle the New Model of 1873, but later that name was shortened to merely the Model 73. Of all Winchester lever-action rifles, this particular model is likely the most easily recognizable due to what I would characterize as its distinctive hunchback profile. But aside from this outward and unique appearance, the 73 was distinctive in other ways that clearly set it apart from other rifles of that era and established milestones for both the company, and firearm production in general.

Its predecessor and the very first of the Winchester rifles, the Model 1866, shared some traits with the 73. But the 66 was designed specifically to fire the rimfire cartridges of that era, in particular the .44 Henry. As centerfire ammunition began to appear on the American shooting scene, a new rifle was called for. Winchester took full advantage of that

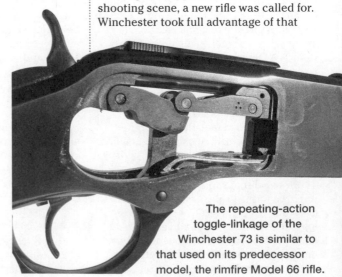

The repeating-action toggle-linkage of the Winchester 73 is similar to that used on its predecessor model, the rimfire Model 66 rifle.

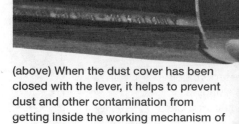

(above) When the dust cover has been closed with the lever, it helps to prevent dust and other contamination from getting inside the working mechanism of the rifle.

(right) As the action of the Model 73 is opened it automatically moves the dust cover to its rearward position in order for the ejection of the empty cartridge case to take place.

opportunity by bringing out the Model 73, the first rifle of the Winchester line to fire centerfire cartridges. Interestingly, later on a limited number of 73s were offered chambered in .22 rimfire, making it also the first repeating-style rifle ever built in the U.S. in that chambering.

The repeating-action toggle linkage, which is the key system utilized for transferring the cartridges from the magazine up and into the chamber of the rifle is similar in both the Model 66 and 73. The firing pin mechanism obviously had to be changed for the 73 in order to accommodate the newly designed centerfire ammunition. Unlike the Model 66, the 73 has a sliding dust cover over the top of the carrier block. This was a simple and very worthwhile feature that helped to prevent dust and debris from accumulating inside the working mechanism of the rifle. Truly this must have been a great benefit when it came to long and dusty days riding the plains on horseback. In order for the dust cover to be effective it is slid forward manually by the shooter, but as the action of the rifle is opened the cover is automatically retracted to the rear permitting the empty brass or cartridge to be ejected.

Winchester also felt it was necessary to veer away from the firing pin design used in the Model 66, and in particular how the firing pin was retracted after the rifle was fired. The Model 66 utilized a spring design, but for the Model 73 a positive action system was used. This change was felt necessary in order to reduce the chances of an accidental discharge from occurring. Winchester

wound up changing back to a spring-based system for the 2013-version Model 73s, but I will get into the reasons behind that change a little later.

At least part of the initial favorability of the Model 73 was the fact that it was chambered for the same cartridges frequently used in the revolvers of the era. This made it easy for the owner who no longer had to carry two types of ammunition – one to be shot in the rifle and one to be used for the sidearm. At the onset, the Model 73 was only offered chambered for .44-40 (.44 WCF), which was loaded to the same specifications as the .44 rimfire ammunition used in the Model 66, that being a 200-grain lead bullet backed by 40 grains of black powder.

Since initially only the .44-40 was offered, Winchester felt it unnecessary to engrave the caliber designation on those very first rifles, but as more caliber choices became available the rifles were

engraved with the appropriate cartridge markings on the bottom of the carrier block. Throughout the 73's reign, the .44-40 (.44 WCF) seemed to remain the most popular caliber, but in 1879 the .38-40 (.38 WCF) was added and in 1882 the .32-30 (.32 WCF) followed. A few takedown version .22 Short and .22 Long rimfire rifles were built in 1884, and on special order there were even a few chambered in .22 Extra Long.

Historically, Winchester offered the Model 73 in three variations that were simply referred to as the Rifle, the Carbine and the Musket, but it is believed that the latter version only accounted for less than 5 or 10 percent of the total production. The rifle version most often came with a 24-inch barrel, but some 30-inch barrels were also offered and the carbine barrel was 20 inches. Likely the carbine was the most popular of these submodels because of the ease of carrying the rifle on horseback.

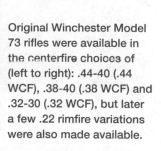

Original Winchester Model 73 rifles were available in the centerfire choices of (left to right): .44-40 (.44 WCF), .38-40 (.38 WCF) and .32-30 (.32 WCF), but later a few .22 rimfire variations were also made available.

Along about the middle or the later part of the 1870s Winchester offered a limited production model referred to as "One of One Thousand," which demands a handsome collectable price today. However, rather than producing 1,000 of these rifles, it is believed that only 136 were ever built, which consisted of two groupings. After assembly all of the rifles within this elite group were test fired and those possessing the best barrels and the highest degree of accuracy went on to be further upgraded. Those enhancements included fancier engraving, higher quality wood, better checkering and they were fitted with set triggers.

It is also believed that only eight of these premium "best of the best rifles" were ever produced, and instead of being engraved "One of One Thousand" those rifles were marked "One of One Hundred" and sold for $100. The remaining rifles making up the "One of One Thousand" grading sold for $20 less.

Winchester '73 Lives On

Over the last 25 years or so cowboy action shooting has become a very popular sport and that is at least partly why there has been a resurgence of interest in the historic firearms of the Wild West. Whether this sport was the main reason why Winchester decided to bring the Model 73 back into production is unknown. The important thing is that this rifle can once again be treasured and used by shooters throughout the world, without having to use a vintage rifle in good enough condition to be shot and enjoyed.

Winchester's Model 73 is being currently offered in three versions called the Short Rifle, the Short Rifle Case Hardened and the Sporter Case Hardened Rifle. The Short and the Short Case Hardened rifles are offered in a choice of three calibers: .38 Special/.357 Magnum, .44-40 Winchester and .45 Colt, but the Sporter Case Hardened Rifle

The new production Model 73 Short Rifle and Short Rifle Case Hardened are available in three caliber choices (left to right): .44-40 Winchester, .45 Colt and .357 Mag./.38 Spl. The Sporter Case Hardened Rifles are not available in .45 Colt.

is only available in .38 Special/.357 Magnum and .44-40 Winchester. Both the Short and the Short Case Hardened rifles come with 20-inch round barrels and the Sporter Case Hardened Rifle has a full octagon 24-inch barrel. The barrel twist rates vary with the cartridge chambering; the .38 Spl./.357 Mag. barrels have a twist rate of 1:18¾" and both the .44-40 and .45 Colt rifles come with a 1:26" twist.

I was anxious to see how Winchester's new 73 would stack up to the older and well-reclaimed historic version, and soon I was holding one of the new Short Rifles chambered for .38/.357 Mag. As the rifle came from the box my initial impression was a good one. Outwardly it appeared to be a near mirror image of the original Model 73. It came equipped with a traditional style semibuckhorn rear sight and a Marble Arms gold bead sight at the muzzle. The heavily curved, blued crescent metal buttplate was clearly a throwback to the past and I considered the semifigured black walnut stock a very pleasant bonus. I thought the brass carrier block added greatly to the overall appearance of the rifle. I also

found the drilled and tapped tang a nice feature in the event the owner might want to install a tang-mounted rear sight.

Clearly a great deal of effort was made by Winchester to produce as close of a representation of the original rifle as possible. While I did find a few of what I would call minor modern-day changes and upgrades, in my opinion those changes only helped to enhance the performance, functionality and safety of the rifle. My gunsmith and friend, Dan Coffin of Victor, Montana's Coffin Gunsmithing, who has a vast amount of experience working on the older Winchesters, brought one of those deviations from the original design to my attention. Having replaced many broken and damaged firing pins on the original 73s, Dan immediately noticed that the new rifle sported a change in that area. No longer was it designed as a positive-action system as on the original rifles, but a spring was now used to retract the firing pin

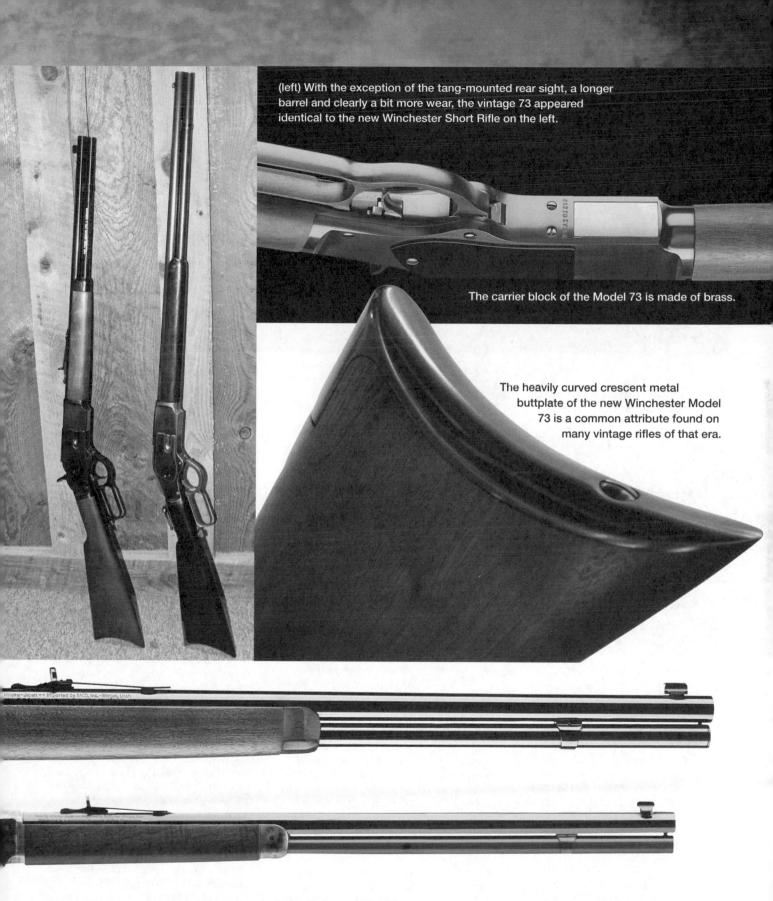

(left) With the exception of the tang-mounted rear sight, a longer barrel and clearly a bit more wear, the vintage 73 appeared identical to the new Winchester Short Rifle on the left.

The carrier block of the Model 73 is made of brass.

The heavily curved crescent metal buttplate of the new Winchester Model 73 is a common attribute found on many vintage rifles of that era.

(top rifle) The Short Rifle Case Hardened version of the new Model 73 comes with the receiver attractively case-colored and like the Short Rifle it is available in: .44-40 Winchester, .45 Colt and .357 Mag./.38 Spl.

(bottom rifle) Available on a limited production basis with only 250 rifles planned, the Sporter Case Hardened Rifle comes equipped with a 24-inch octagon barrel and is only available in .44-40 Winchester and .357 Mag./.38 Spl. calibers.

The new Winchester 73 came from the factory equipped with a traditional semibuckhorn rear sight.

The new Model 73 came with a classic Marble Arms gold bead front sight.

after the rifle had fired.

Dan explained to me that fouling and debris frequently would become lodged inside the firing pin mechanism of the original 73s, and when that occurred it would sometimes prohibit the firing pin from fully retracting. This situation would on occasion result in the cartridge case coming into contact with the partially extended firing pin during the ejection process resulting in either damaging or breaking the firing pin. After replacing many of the older firing pins Dan saw this as a major improvement to the overall rifle design. I did, however, find this change a bit ironic due to the fact that when Winchester originally designed the 73 it was decided that the spring-based system used on the Model 66 would be replaced with a new positive-action design. At the time it was felt that that change was necessary in order to lessen

the chances of an accidental discharge occurring. I must assume that the new design now being used addresses both the concern of safety as well as the ineffective retraction.

Like the original Model 73, Winchester's new '13 version came with a lever lock at the rearmost portion of the finger grip. The purpose of this lock is to prevent the unintentional opening of the action. In order to engage this function you simply rotate the lever lock so it impinges on the bottom of the finger grip. I can see where this feature was an important attribute when the rifle was carried on horseback in the early days, but is possibly less important today for most shooters.

I was very anxious to see how the new 73 would perform on the range, and after running a few patches down the bore in an effort to clean out any possible

residuals left behind by the factory, I headed out back to my private rifle range for a little ceremonial powder burning.

When evaluating a firearm I frequently find that by exposing the weapon to a variety of different ammo provides a better overall assessment of its abilities and performance. In this case I chose to shoot a mixture of both .38 Special and .357 Magnum loads. Those cartridges consisted of: .38 Special +P Federal shells loaded with 125-grain Hi-Shok jacketed hollowpoint bullets, .38 Special American Eagle loads with 158-grain roundnose lead bullets, .357 Magnum Federal Fusion loads with 158-grain Fusion bullets, and .357 Magnum Federal loads with 158-grain jacketed hollowpoint bullets.

The cartridge cases of some of those loads came nickel-plated and others were the more traditional unplated brass. Even though all of the cartridges fed into the magazine easily and effortlessly, due to their exceptionally smooth finish, the nickel-plated rounds seemed to feed into the magazine a tad easier. I did discover, however, that it seemed best when loading the magazine to feed the cartridges in one at a time allowing the spring cover to close behind each cartridge before attempting to feed another round. This would be in lieu of shoving the ammo into the magazine tube in a less continuous fashion as a string of cartridges. The tubular magazine holds 10 rounds of .357 and 11 rounds of .38 Special.

Open sights, while traditional on this style of rifle, aren't always the most accurate when it comes to precise bullet placement, at least when the rifle is against my shoulder. Nevertheless, I

A joint effort by Navy Arms, Winchester and Doug Turnbull's Restoration company, this special model features Turnbull's well-known color case-hardening treatment, a fully checkered Deluxe American Walnut stock and a full octagon barrel.

There are a couple of other companies currently producing and marketing newly manufactured Winchester Model 1873 rifles today. One of those is Navy Arms, which was founded in the 1950s by Val Forgett, Jr. and operated for some time out of the Forgett family basement. Val's son, Val Forgett III eventually took over the company following his father's passing and is carrying on the legacy his father began more than six decades ago.

Working with both Winchester Repeating Arms and Turnbull Restorations, Navy Arms released their own 1873 rifle late in 2014. These rifles are now available and being sold through Navy Arms distributors Lipsey's, Ellett Brothers, Jerry's Sports Center and Zanders Sporting Goods. The receivers are beautifully color case-hardened by Turnbull Restoration and Manufacturing Company. Features include a traditional semibuckhorn rear sight, a gold bead front sight, full octagon barrel in a choice of either 20 or 24¼ inches, and a deluxe American walnut stock with "Winchester Red" finish and full checkering. Rather than being fitted with the crescent metal buttplate, the Navy Arms rifles come equipped with a square shotgun-style buttplate, which is a bit more comfortable that the crescent styling. The Navy Arms Model 1873 rifles are available in a choice of .357 Magnum or .45 Colt and carry a suggested retail price of $2,500.

When rotated to the closed position, the lever latch located at the rearmost portion of the finger grip is intended to prevent the accidental opening of the rifle action.

most area of the triggerguard and ahead of the finger grip area. As the shooter places his or her hand in the normal shooting manner and grips the stock, this button is naturally compressed. This results in retracting an outwardly visible tiny metal block located behind the trigger and allowing the trigger to be pulled.

Even though I can fully understand the need for this system, I must admit that I found it to be a bit irritating when shooting from the bench. In order to disengage the safety blocking mechanism the stock must be gripped, and

A diverse selection of Federal ammunition was used for the live fire review, which consisted of both .38 Special and .357 Magnum cartridges.

found the new 73 and all of the tested ammo produced good groups at 50 and even 100 yards. In my way of thinking, that would constitute the maximum range for which the .38 Special or .357 Magnum would be considered optimum. Obviously the fully loaded .357 Magnum rounds produced a bit more recoil than that of the .38 Special ammo, but none of the cartridges were excessively abusive to my shoulder, even considering the traditional crescent-shape buttplate.

It is important that the breech of the rifle remains completely closed when firing the rifle. In order to ensure that happens, a mechanism called a "trigger stop" is used. This design includes a tiny silver-colored button located in the rear-

The trigger stop mechanism is intended to prevent the firing of the rifle if the action is not completely closed. This system consists of a tiny silver-color button located in the lower tang at the rearmost portion of the triggerguard. When not compressed (as shown here) a tiny metal blockage located behind the trigger prevents the trigger from being moved rearward.

when shooting from the bench I always attempt to be as relaxed as possible, and gripping the stock simply does not come natural to me. Eventually, I forced myself to tighten my grip and everything went well from that point on. This particular issue was only noticeable to me while shooting off the bench; from all other positions it was more natural to grip the stock tightly.

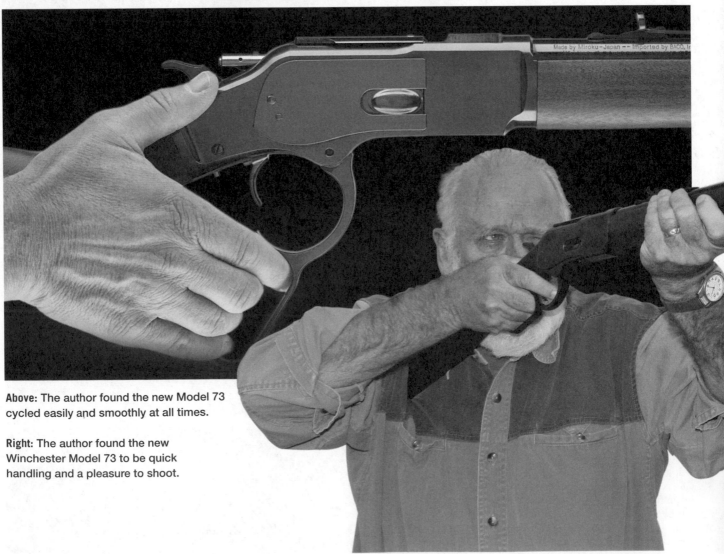

Above: The author found the new Model 73 cycled easily and smoothly at all times.

Right: The author found the new Winchester Model 73 to be quick handling and a pleasure to shoot.

The 73 could be easily cycled while still at the shooter's shoulder – sending the empty cartridge case high into the air.

In my opinion the new Winchester Model 73 is an impressive rifle and is a compliment to both Winchester and the impressive legacy of the original. Overall the rifle functioned very well. I found the wide checkered hammer to be a nice feature that allowed the rifle to be manually cocked and uncocked with little fear of my thumb slipping free. The cycling of the cartridges from the magazine to the chamber was always smooth and consistent. The fired cases ejected perfectly each and every time. Even though Winchester felt it necessary to make a few of what I would consider minor modifications to the original design, most if not all of those slight deviations would likely go unnoticed. Just like my gunsmith spotting the changes to the firing pin mechanism, they would be seen as appropriate and needed improvements. Best of all, for a pittance of what it would cost to purchase an original Model 73 in excellent condition, you can have one of these fine rifles to enjoy and be guaranteed a lifetime of carefree service.

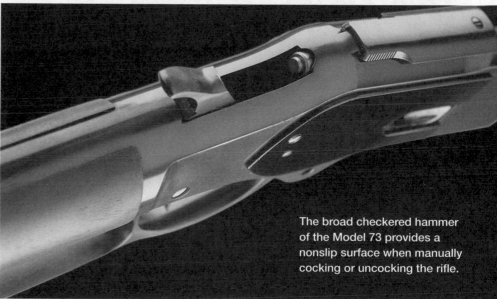

The broad checkered hammer of the Model 73 provides a nonslip surface when manually cocking or uncocking the rifle.

WINCHESTER 73 SHORT RIFLE SPECIFICATIONS	
Manufacturer:	Winchester Repeating Arms built by Miroku of Japan.
Caliber:	.38 Special /.357 Magnum
Weight:	7 pounds, 4 ounces
Sights:	Semibuckhorn rear sight and Marble Arms blade front sight
Stock:	Straight grip, moderately figured walnut stock
Action:	Lever Action
Barrel:	Round 20-inch barrel with a 1:18¾-inch twist rate
Magazine:	Tubular magazine holding 10 rounds of .357 or 11 rounds of .38 Special
Price:	MSRP $1,299.99

The rook is a very common bird in Europe. It's in the same genus as the American crow. Young rooks are considered edible, so long as they have not yet flown. Recipes for rook pie were published in many British cookbooks and can be found even today on cooking websites in the United Kingdom.

An American ROOK RIFLE

By **Tom Caceci**

Great Britain's Crystal Palace Exhibition of 1851 was a stunning display of industrial development, demonstrating to the world what Victorian engineers and manufacturers could do. The Industrial Revolution that had begun a century earlier had made Britain into the world's trading center, expanding the middle class and transforming an agrarian society into "a nation of shopkeepers" and manufacturers.

In the 19th and early 20th centuries the British gun trade was a vibrant industry, serving the world and the needs of the home market on a large scale. Wealthy people – peers, members of the rural squirearchy and barons of industry – sought the delights of the countryside, buying large estates and taking up traditional country pursuits. Respectable gentlemen and ladies of Victorian times enjoyed fox hunting, trout fishing, deerstalking and "shoots"

Inset Above: This *very* exclusive Victorian-era shooting party was hosted by the portly bearded gentleman in the center of the front row: HRH Edward, Prince of Wales, later King Edward VII. "Bertie" was a renowned sportsman and a crack shot. The party has collected several pheasants and hares as part of a "rough shoot." The stern looking gents in the back, who are looking to right and left, were HRH's bodyguards!

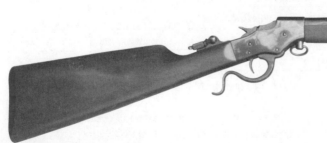

The author's refinished Stevens Favorite, or American Rook Rifle.

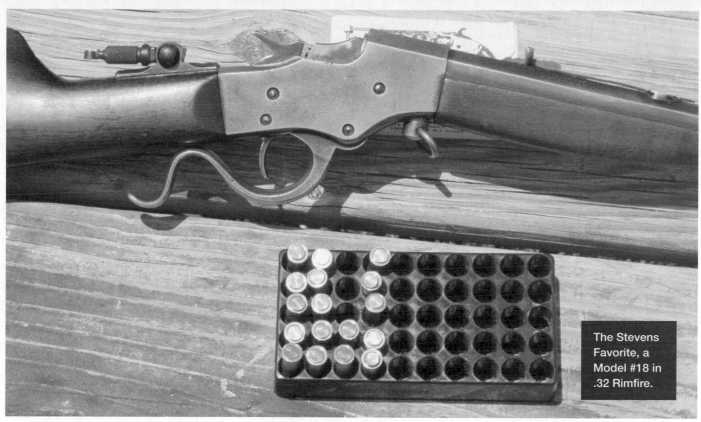

The Stevens Favorite, a Model #18 in .32 Rimfire.

for grouse and pheasant, often as part of elaborate country-house parties. The rich bought finely wrought firearms from the greatest British gunmakers. Their gamekeepers, hired to protect their land and game, also needed shotguns and rifles to do their work. Many members of the middle classes enjoyed shooting, if on a less grand scale than "the quality."

It was also a time of transition in firearms technology as muzzleloaders gave way to breechloaders. Gun designers could work with novel mechanisms and ideas, and along the way produce new types of guns for their clients. Among them was what came to be known as the "rook and rabbit rifle," a dainty gun perfectly adapted to a gentleman's recreational "rough shoot" or a gamekeeper's duty of eliminating pests. The classic rook rifle is a light, small caliber, single-shot firearm made on a break-open, dropping- or falling-block action, almost always in takedown form. The famous firm of Holland and Holland is given credit for introducing the rook rifle in 1883, but many other makers large and small offered them because there was a ready market.

Most small gun shops and lesser-known makers didn't manufacture their products in the literal sense, not even shotguns. While some made the barrels, they bought actions and other parts or even complete guns from a large manufacturer (usually in Birmingham) selling to "the trade." Using those wholesale parts they assembled and stocked a gun to a customer's order, marking it with their own name. This practice was well established for shotguns and naturally was carried over by retailers who had customers in need of a rook rifle for leisure or for a keeper's use.

Rook and rabbit rifles were light enough to be carried on a walk in the country,

accurate and powerful enough for small game, and often very elegant in balance, fit and finish. Calibers included the .22 Long Rifle, but larger bores were made. Classic British rook rifle calibers include the .297/.230 Rook, the .300 Rook, the .300 Sherwood and larger bores up to .380, all of them centerfire rounds. These little guns were used to shoot rooks and the fantastically abundant rabbits found near every country lane and on every estate – hence the name for this rather specialized firearm. Some of the larger calibers were used on roe deer, but most of these guns were primarily for small game.

The rook (*Corvus frugilegus*) is a common British bird in the same genus as the North American crow. Its principal diet consists of earthworms, fruit, cereal grains, game bird eggs and small

Left: The famous gunmakers at Holland & Holland are usually given credit for introducing the concept of the "rook and rabbit rifle." But there are other claimants, and the term became generic; it was used by other "name" makers including Westley Richards. The rapid progress of firearms technology in the mid to late 19th century probably made the rook rifle an inevitable development, as it suited the needs of the time and the place of shooting in British country life.

This advertisement from Nov. 19, 1904, edition of the *Illustrated London News*, a popular paper with the middle and lower middle class of Britain, is the earliest documentation the author has found of Stevens' business presence in the U.K. Leeson's shops were located in a fashionable area of London and he was able to special order guns for his customers.

mammals; unlike American crows, rooks don't principally feed on carrion. Rooks are sometimes regarded as agricultural pests because of the damage they do to crops and new plantings, and because they eat the eggs and young of pheasants and grouse. Surprisingly to Americans, young rooks that have not yet begun to fly ("branchers") are considered edible. English cookbooks still contain recipes for rook pies – the "four and twenty blackbirds baked in a pie" of the nursery rhyme is a reference to eating rooks. Many a cottager or gamekeeper on a large estate ate rook pies as a matter of course; rabbit was another staple of the diet of the working man. A single-shot rifle had no disadvantage in this kind of shooting as the quarry was very skittish and likely to flee as soon as a round was fired.

One maker of quality shotguns who seemed to have had an occasional customer wanting a rook rifle was William Richard Topham Leeson (1851-1934) of Ashford in

Kent, and later London. I am deeply indebted to Mr. Adrian Macer of the United Kingdom, a collector and historian of Leeson's guns. He provided a great deal of information about Leeson and his business, and also alerted me to the existence of a Leeson-marked rook rifle made not in Birmingham, but in Chicopee Falls, Massachusetts!

The rifle in question is a Stevens Favorite, a design well known to Americans. The Favorite was one of the most successful products of the J. Stevens Arms & Tool Company. In various forms it sold well over a million units. The first version was introduced in 1889 and later variations were made for at least a decade after Stevens was bought out by Savage in 1920. Production of the Favorite continued until 1930, and updated models were introduced in the 1970s and 1990s by the present incarnation of the company, Savage Arms. The older Favorites are beautifully crafted, the very epitome of a lightweight small-game gun. They were made in .22, .25 and .32 rimfire; a slightly larger and less commercially successful large-frame version, the Model 44, was chambered in some centerfire calibers as well.

Mr. Macer displays on his website what

is described as – and undoubtedly is – a Stevens Favorite. It has some odd features, which has led us to investigate how this quintessentially American rifle ended up being sold as a rook rifle in Leeson's shop in Edwardian London. Research has uncovered some very interesting information.

Leeson had several addresses for his London business. Between 1904 and 1911 he had shops on Maddox Street, George Street and Harewood Place, the last a prestigious location near Hanover Square. In 1906 he registered his firm as "W.R. Leeson, Ltd." and did business at that location until after World War I, when the post-war depression compelled a move to the company's final address on Warwick Street, where the firm remained until closing in 1933.

While his principal trade was in high-grade shotguns, Leeson could and did supply customers with rook rifles. The Stevens Favorite on Mr. Macer's site is a beautifully finished example with elegant case-coloring on the receiver, a half-octagon barrel, and Lyman tang rear and globe front sights. The barrel is marked

The refinish on the author's Favorite is a beautiful job!

Right: The upper image shows the worn original finish on the receiver of the author's Stevens Favorite. It was refinished to a brilliant high-polish blue. Depending on the reference book consulted, Favorites were made with both blued and case-colored receivers.

The author's American Rook Rifle, cased with its accessories.

with Leeson's name and Maddox Street address, and is a pre-1920 rifle made by the J. Stevens Arms & Tool Company, what is usually called a "Model 1894" design. It is in a custom leather case with accessories, and while it's a .25-caliber rifle, is it *not* in .25 Stevens Rimfire. It is, rather, chambered for the centerfire .297/.230 Rook cartridge!

Guns coming into the U.K. were, and still are, required to be submitted for proof before they could be sold, and this one bears London Proof House markings indicating that this was done. It also has a serial number stamped into the top of the breech – this was clearly a post-import marking because Favorites of that vintage aren't serialized, and the stamping was done rather crudely. Leeson then added his own firm's information.

The rifle is unquestionably a Favorite and not a Model 44. It would appear to be what Stevens' catalog listed as a "#17" that was ordinarily chambered for the .25 Stevens rimfire round. On the face of the receiver there is another marking "17 C" that we think means "No. 17, C(enterfire)."

It would have been a trivial matter to rechamber the rifle to take the .297/.230 Rook round; modifying the breechblock for centerfire ammunition would not have been difficult. Furthermore, Stevens did in fact have a business presence in the U.K. at the time. The company's London agency was located less than a mile from Leeson's shop. Even though Stevens' 1905 United States catalog describes the Favorite as "…not made for centerfire cartridges…" the company understood the British market very well. The earliest advertisement for their guns in the *Il-*

lustrated London News, dated 1904, clearly states that the "Favourite" *was* available in .297/.230 Rook, a classic British center-fire round. In other words, the gun Leeson sold was an export model made specifically for the U.K. market. Leeson's shop records and those of the J. Stevens Arms & Tool Company are not accessible (and may no longer exist) so it's impossible to know for sure how many such "American rook rifles" may have been produced, but they cannot be very common.

Intrigued by the notion of a gun with a style as thoroughly British as could be imagined produced in Massachusetts, I took a look at my own Stevens Favorite. This is a "No. 18" in .32 Rimfire, with identical sights to those on the Leeson gun but with a full octagon barrel, rather than the standard half round and half octagon. I have owned it for years and hunt small game with it. The .32 Rimfire's ballistics are nearly identical to those of the .300 Rook. My rifle was well used when I bought it, but was still tight and accurate with an excellent bore. I have a good source for .32 Rimfire ammunition, so I decided to make my own version of an "American Rook Rifle."

The original finish was completely worn off so I shipped it off for refinishing to Mr. Dave Thomas, who runs Second Amendment Gun Repair in Pinehurst, ID. Dave is a master craftsman and returned it with a dazzling high-polish blue on the receiver and barrel, preserving all of the markings. Depending on what references you read, Favorites were case-colored, like the Leeson gun, but were also available with a blued finish.

Next up for work was the case. I'd

acquired a new hard-sided "motor case" at an auction very cheaply a few years before with the intention of using it for a shotgun, but the barrels wouldn't fit. So it was perfect for the Stevens. With a few added partitions and some green velvet to match the case lining, I had a custom case for my own "American Rook Rifle." As a bit of personal vanity I added a maker's label for my wholly fictitious "New River Armoury."

Having used my Favorite in the field, it's easy for me to understand why rook rifles – wherever they were made – were so popular. Its low weight and perfect balance made it possible to carry along the trail for long periods, its mild calibers didn't disturb anyone in the nearby vicinity and minimized the danger of a bullet carrying too far, and the game pursued was well within the capabilities of the little guns.

The .25 and .32 Rimfire rounds were discontinued in 1942 with America's entry into World War II and production was never resumed. The improvement of the .22 Long Rifle and flagging sales of the larger rimfires doomed them, though they were outstanding small-game calibers, so now there are many, many high-quality rifles languishing in closets for want of ammunition. A casual glance at any gun auction website will bring up dozens of Stevens "American Rook Rifles" for sale at low prices, usually in sound shooting condition. One can hope that someday, someone will do what's needed to bring them out into the field once again, to delight another generation of recreational shooters.

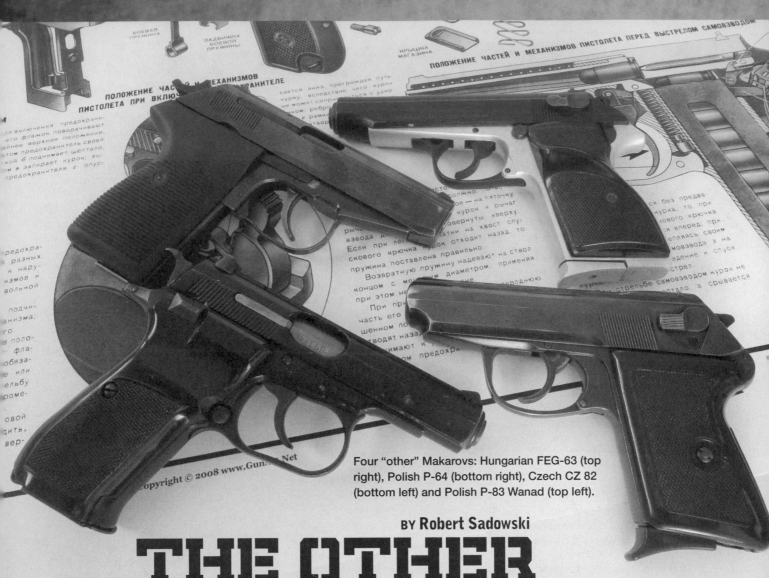

Four "other" Makarovs: Hungarian FEG-63 (top right), Polish P-64 (bottom right), Czech CZ 82 (bottom left) and Polish P-83 Wanad (top left).

BY **Robert Sadowski**

THE OTHER MAKAROVS

Cold War Handguns Chambered in 9x18mm Makarov

The Makarov name has come to include a number of military pistols chambered in the 9x18mm Makarov, but that are not the handgun designed by Nikolai Makarov nor manufactured in Russia. During the Cold War, countries under Soviet influence were required to standardize military calibers. The 7.62x39mm and the AK-47 platform was the caliber and rifle mandated by Moscow, just as the 9x18mm Makarov was the standard pistol cartridge. Some countries like East Germany and Bulgaria adopted

and issued an indigenously manufactured version of the Makarov PM pistol, while other countries like Hungary, Poland and Czechoslovakia opted to develop their own designs chambered in the mandated caliber.

The Makarov story begins shortly after World War II. The Soviet Union was in need of a new sidearm and ran a design competition for a replacement pistol. The winning entrant was a simple blowback pistol designed by Nikolai Makarov chambered in 9x18mm Makarov, the most powerful cartridge that could be safely

fired in a blowback action. The Makarov Pistol, or PM *(Pistolet Makarova),* was officially adopted into service in 1951 and was the standard issue sidearm until 1991. The PM had few parts, was easy to manufacture, simple to use and maintain, and proved to be reliable with reasonable stopping power. At that time in military circles a pistol was more a symbol of rank, and was not meant to be a combat pistol as we have come to define it today.

Generically speaking, pistols made in others countries are called "Polish Makarovs," "Czech Makarovs," among other

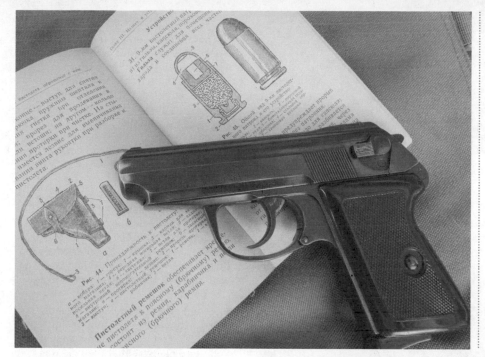

The P-64 and a 1968 vintage copy of an original Makarov PM military manual.

bered in the 9x18mm Makarov.

By 1965, the pistol was rolling off the assembly lines at the Łucznik Arms Factory in Radom, Poland, and officially designated *9 mm pistolet wz. 1964*. More commonly it is called the P-64. Manufactured with a steel slide and frame, it employs a single-stack magazine holding six rounds. Though similar in appearance and function to the Walther PPK, the P-64 has a unique patented disconnector distinctly different from the Walther. In addition to the outward aesthetics, the similarities between the PPK and P-64 include a loaded chamber indicator at the rear of the slide that can felt and seen, the plastic grip panels form the pistol's backstrap, the barrel is fixed to the frame and a thumb-safety

Below: The resemblance to the Walther PPK is uncanny, but the P-64 is a very different design internally.

The safety lever also acts as a decocker.

names. These pistols are chambered in 9x18mm Makarov but the designs are different from the original PM. What is similar to all the Makarovs, in addition to being chambered in 9x18mm, is they share a similar blowback operating system and have common features. These include a double-action/single-action trigger, exposed hammer, fixed sights, external extractor and the barrel is fixed to the frame.

A great influence on these other Makarovs was the Walther PP/PPK, which was used by German officers during WWII and numerous examples of which were captured by the Red Army as spoils of war. When the Soviets occupied Zella-Mehlis in Germany, where the Walther factory was located, the factory's tooling and machinery was disassembled and shipped back to the Soviet Union. Walther pistols clearly influenced pistol design and manufacturing in Poland and Hungary, and while those made in Czechoslovakia look different than Walthers, they too, share some design elements and function in a similar way. Here's a look at four "other Makarovs" from three former Eastern Bloc countries.

P-64: Poland 1951-Present

Similar to the design competition held in the Soviet Union that spawned the PM,

Poland held its own competition during the 1950s for a replacement service pistol. The winning entry was an amalgamation of two pistols from a design team at the Polish Institute for Artillery Research. The team submitted two pistols for evaluation in 1961; a short-barreled Model M chambered in .380 ACP and a Model W chambered in 9x18mm Makarov with a longer barrel. The Model M was selected but cham-

decocker. The two pistols also disassemble in a similar manner. By pulling down on the triggerguard and moving it over slightly, the slide is lifted from the rear of the frame and moved forward and off the barrel.

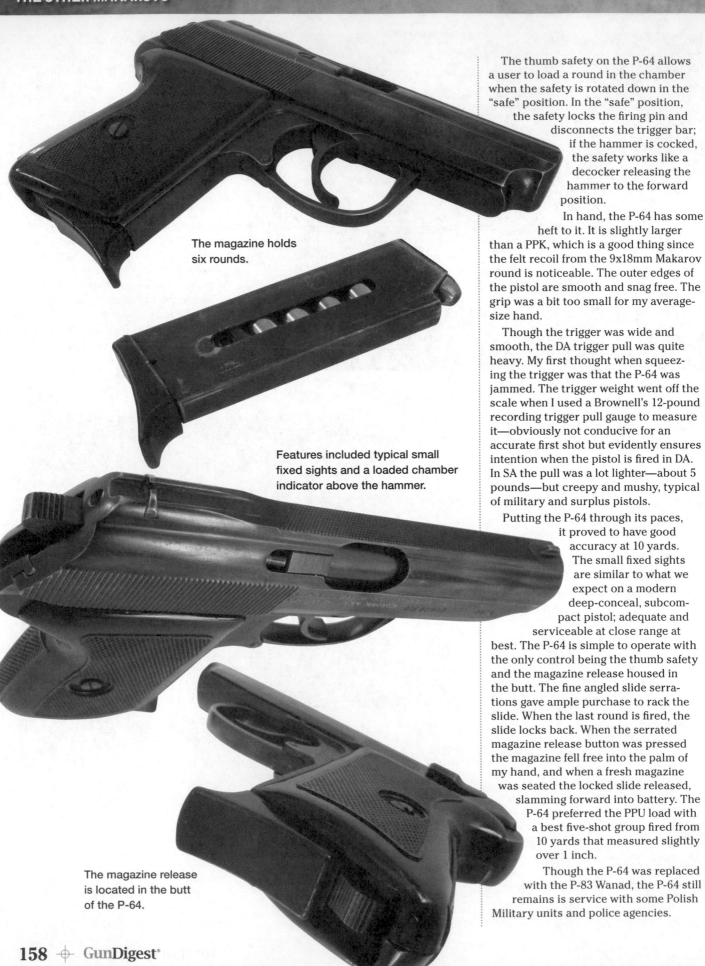

The magazine holds six rounds.

Features included typical small fixed sights and a loaded chamber indicator above the hammer.

The magazine release is located in the butt of the P-64.

The thumb safety on the P-64 allows a user to load a round in the chamber when the safety is rotated down in the "safe" position. In the "safe" position, the safety locks the firing pin and disconnects the trigger bar; if the hammer is cocked, the safety works like a decocker releasing the hammer to the forward position.

In hand, the P-64 has some heft to it. It is slightly larger than a PPK, which is a good thing since the felt recoil from the 9x18mm Makarov round is noticeable. The outer edges of the pistol are smooth and snag free. The grip was a bit too small for my average-size hand.

Though the trigger was wide and smooth, the DA trigger pull was quite heavy. My first thought when squeezing the trigger was that the P-64 was jammed. The trigger weight went off the scale when I used a Brownell's 12-pound recording trigger pull gauge to measure it—obviously not conducive for an accurate first shot but evidently ensures intention when the pistol is fired in DA. In SA the pull was a lot lighter—about 5 pounds—but creepy and mushy, typical of military and surplus pistols.

Putting the P-64 through its paces, it proved to have good accuracy at 10 yards. The small fixed sights are similar to what we expect on a modern deep-conceal, subcompact pistol; adequate and serviceable at close range at best. The P-64 is simple to operate with the only control being the thumb safety and the magazine release housed in the butt. The fine angled slide serrations gave ample purchase to rack the slide. When the last round is fired, the slide locks back. When the serrated magazine release button was pressed the magazine fell free into the palm of my hand, and when a fresh magazine was seated the locked slide released, slamming forward into battery. The P-64 preferred the PPU load with a best five-shot group fired from 10 yards that measured slightly over 1 inch.

Though the P-64 was replaced with the P-83 Wanad, the P-64 still remains is service with some Polish Military units and police agencies.

P-64 SPECIFICATIONS	
Manufacturer:	Łucznik Arms Factory
Caliber:	9x18mm
Barrel Length:	3.3 inches
Overall Length:	6.3 inches
Weight:	22 ounces (empty)
Sights:	Fixed front and rear
Action:	semiauto, blowback
Trigger:	SA/DA
Finish:	Blued
Grip:	Checkered plastic
Capacity:	6+1

Small fixed sights were the norm on Eastern European sidearms during the Cold War.

The similarity of the FEG-63 to the Walther PP is apparent. Though its frame is made of aluminum and left unfinished to lower production costs.

A thumbrest is built into the left grip; the safety also acts as a decocker.

PA-63: Hungary 1963-Present

The FEG PA-63 was Hungary's answer to the 9x18mm Makarov cartridge mandated by Moscow. During WWII in the late 1940s the FEGARMY Arms Factory was building a variant of the Walther PP and PPK called the 48M. After the war Hungary came under Soviet influence and, like other countries, was required to issue a sidearm in 9x18mm Makarov. In 1963 the PA-63 began production, hence the model name, and was produced through 1990. It is still currently used by Hungarian law enforcement.

The PA-63 is very similar to the Walther PP in design and function. What makes the PA-63 distinctly different is the two-tone finish—a blued steel slide and polished aluminum frame, an odd finish choice for a military sidearm but the aluminum frame was inexpensive to manufacture. It also made the pistol lightweight. Like all Eastern Bloc pistols the PA-63 was designed for ease of manufacture, and if the Walther PP is a beauty, the PA-63 is not so much a beast, just less beautiful.

The trigger is wide, nicely curved and serrated, but the heavy DA trigger pull makes an accurate first shot difficult—a trend found with many of these Cold War pistols. In SA the trigger pull is lighter but by no means crisp. Operation of the PA-63 is similar to the PP. The two controls on the pistol are located on the left side: a fairly large and

PA-63 SPECIFICATIONS	
Manufacturer:	FÉGARMY Arms Factory
Caliber:	9x18mm
Barrel Length:	3.9 inches
Overall Length:	6.9 inches
Weight:	21 ounces (empty)
Sights:	Fixed front and rear
Action:	semiauto, blowback
Trigger:	SA/DA
Finish:	Two-tone
Grip:	Checkered plastic
Capacity:	7+1

P-83 Wanad: Poland 1983-Present

The P-83 Wanad was developed in the late 1970s as the successor to the P-64, which users felt had a much too heavy DA trigger pull and limited magazine capacity. With this I concur. Felt recoil was heavy due to its small size. It was also expensive to produce. The P-83 replacement addressed all of these shortcomings and was adopted in 1983. The P-83 used modern cost-effective sheet steel stampings welded together, which made the pistol inexpensive to manufacture – but it is anything but cheap. In fact, the pistol has and continues to be quite effective for Polish military and government operators.

The magazine has a higher capacity—an extra two rounds—than the P-64 and the grip is longer so it is easier for operators with large hands to use. Even though the P-83 is slightly larger than the P-64, the P-83 feels lighter and allows a better grip for more natural pointing. The DA trigger pull weight was also improved. Serrated plastic grips come together in the rear to form the pistol's

grip panel had a thumb rest molded in which made shooting the pistol more comfortable for right-hand shooters. The felt recoil was noticeable with the PA-63, but I was able to get good accuracy in SA. On the last shot the slide locks open.

Due to its popularity and reliability the PA-63 is still in use, especially with the Hungarian Police.

The P-83 Wanad replaced the P-64 as Poland's service sidearm.

Magazine capacity for the PA-63 is seven rounds, plus one in the chamber.

serrated thumb safety/decocker and a round checkered magazine release. To operate the magazine release the user must break hold and reposition their grip. The magazine does not drop free, a characteristic of many European handguns.

The round serrated hammer is a dead ringer for the hammer on the PP. The top of the slide is serrated and the sights are fixed and small, as one would expect on a pistol from this era. The magazine floorplate is made of aluminum and allowed my small finger plenty of room.

The PA-63 is fieldstripped just like a PP or the P-63 by first pulling downward on the triggerguard, then the disassembly steps are the same.

The PA-63 pointed well and the grip was larger giving better control. The left

P-83 WANAD SPECIFICATIONS	
Manufacturer:	Fabryka Broni Lucznik
Caliber:	9x18mm
Barrel Length:	3.5 inches
Overall Length:	6.5 inches
Weight:	26 ounces (empty)
Sights:	Fixed front and rear
Action:	semiauto, straight blowback
Trigger:	SA/DA
Finish:	Blue
Grip:	Ribbed plastic
Capacity:	8+1

The P-83 Wanad was developed for and adopted by the Polish Military in 1983.

The P-83 features a slide-stop release and slide-mounted safety.

backstrap and a lanyard loop is built into the left grip panel.

On the left side of the P-83 there is a disassembly release, slide catch and safety lever. The magazine release is located in the butt of the pistol, and when pressed allows the magazine to fall free from the pistol. Rotate the thumb safety up to decock and put the pistol on "safe," rotate it down to the "fire" position. The slide stop is a feature not commonly found on a blowback pistol.

The hammer of the P-83 also affords a better purchase than the small hammer on the P-64, although it has the potential for snagging, other than that, the outer surface is smooth. A loaded-chamber indicator is located above the thumb safety and protrudes when a round or empty case is in the chamber.

To fieldstrip the P-83, pull down on the disassembly release inside the triggerguard on the left side of the frame, retract the slide rearward to lift it off the frame and allow the slide to move forward and off the barrel. The process is simple and straightforward.

The P-83 has a nice heft in hand and the larger grip gives the user better control. The trigger is nicely curved and smooth. Range time proved the DA trigger pull was heavy but usable. SA was creepy but serviceable. PPU ammo was favored by this Polish pistol, too, and the best five-shot group at 10 yards measured 1.1 inches.

The P-83 still sees limited use with the Polish Military.

CZ 82: Czechoslovakia 1983-1993, Czech Republic 1993-Present, Slovak Republic 1993-Present

In 1983 the CZ 82 or Vz 82—"Vz" is the Czech abbreviation for "model"—replaced the Vz 52 used by Czech forces since 1952. While the full size Vz 52 was chambered in the WWII-era 7.62×25mm Tokarev cartridge, the CZ 82 brought the country in line with Moscow's orders. Chambered in 9x18mm Makarov, the CZ 82 holds a double-stack, high-capacity 12-round magazine, yet is still compact and has a DA/SA trigger.

Out of all the "other Makarovs," the CZ 82 has features found on more modern designs. Controls consist of an ambidextrous thumb safety and a push-button magazine release located next to a right-handed shooter's thumb. The CZ 82 was actually one of the first military pistols to have these ambidextrous controls. A slide release located on the left side of the frame is also something not typically found on a blowback pistol. The thumb safety of the CZ 82 cannot be put in the "safe" mode when the hammer is down, only when the hammer is at full cock. The hammer spur was well textured and large, which made it easy to operate. Also unique to the CZ 82 is a chrome-lined barrel with polygonal rifling. All the other Makarovs use traditional land-and-groove rifling.

The CZ 82 fieldstrips similarly to other Makarovs. Pull down on the triggerguard and it will click into place. But there is no need to move it to one side like with a FEG-63 and P-64. Continue the fieldstripping process like all other Makarovs.

The CZ 82 was developed in Czechoslovakia and adopted in 1983.

The CZ 82 is the most modern of the "other Makarovs" and is shown here with the standard issue ambidextrous holster.

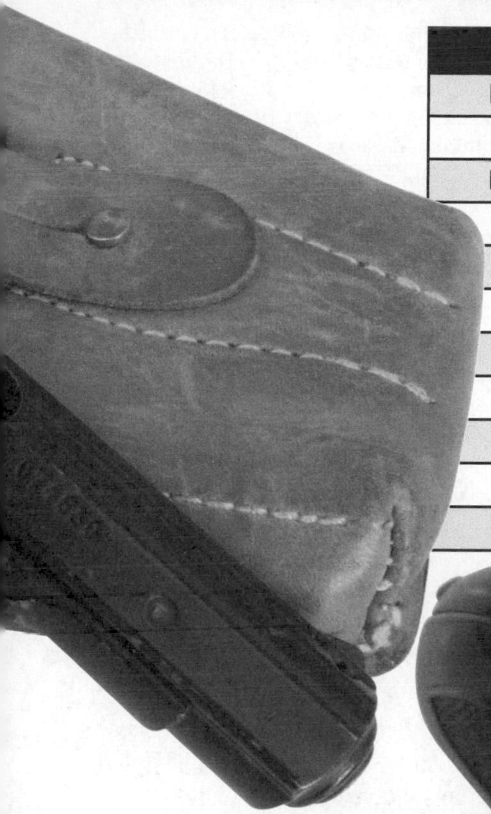

CZ 82 SPECIFICATIONS	
Manufacturer:	Česká zbrojovka
Caliber:	9x18mm
Barrel Length:	3.8 inches
OA Length:	6.8 inches
Weight:	28 ounces (empty)
Sights:	Fixed front and rear
Action:	semiauto, blowback
Trigger:	SA/DA
Finish:	Blued
Grip:	Black checkered plastic
Capacity:	12+1

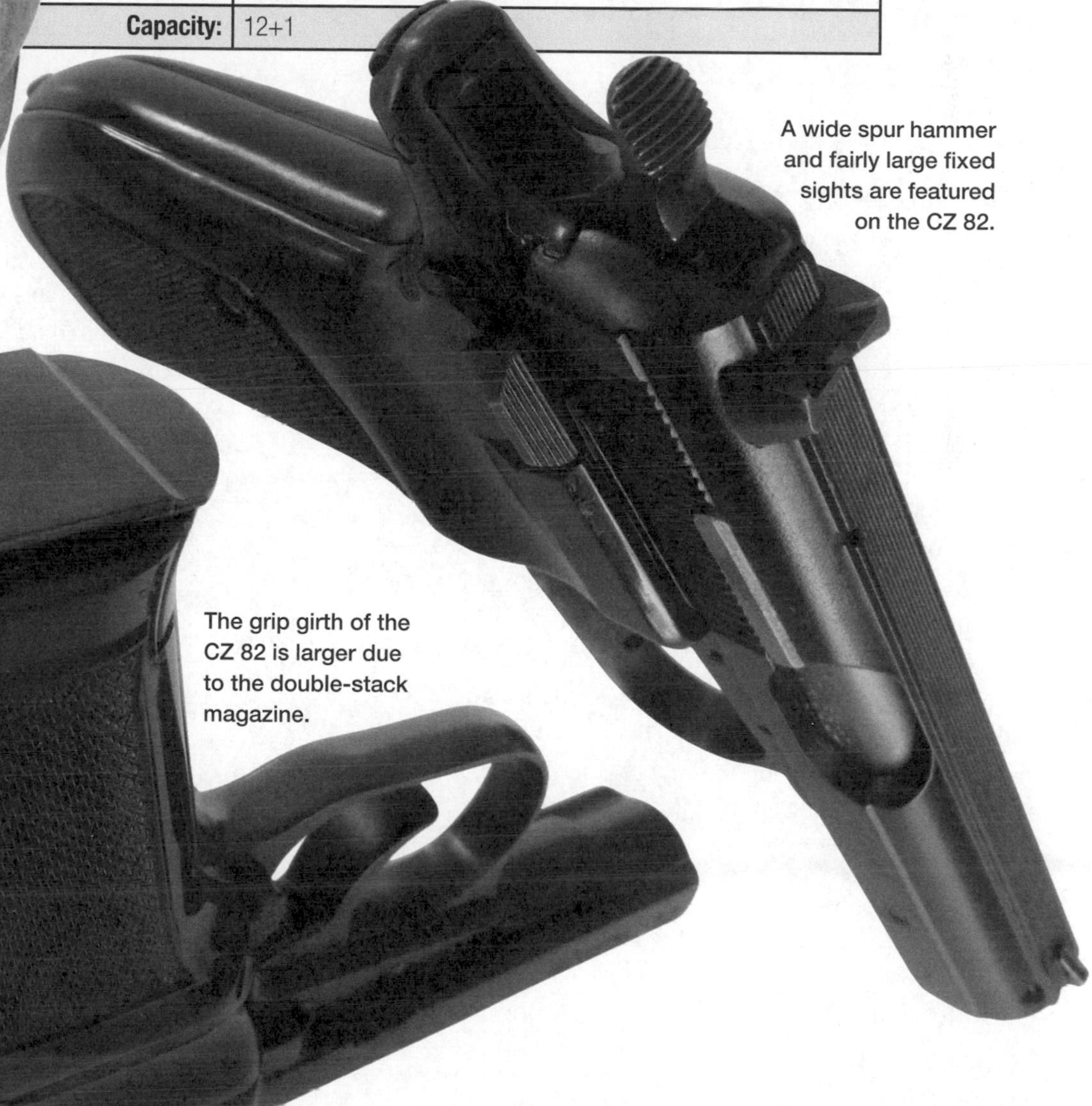

A wide spur hammer and fairly large fixed sights are featured on the CZ 82.

The grip girth of the CZ 82 is larger due to the double-stack magazine.

The double-stack magazine gives the CZ 82 more girth so it feels thicker in the hand. The recoil was also less due to the thicker backstrap that spread felt recoil to more area of the shooter's palm. The sights were also larger, akin to a more modern design. Since the magazine release is inset into the grip you need to reposition the gun in your hand to press the release. Hornady ammunition gave excellent accuracy in the CZ 82 with the best five-shot group at 10 yards measuring .87 inch.

The CZ 82 is the current sidearm of the Czech Army.

Though all of these pistols are relics from the Cold War, they each performed surprising well at close range. None had any issues and functioned as they were designed to be reliable and provide a last ditch defense in time of war.

Special thanks to Eastern Outfitters (easternoutfitter.com) of Hampstead, N.C., for making this story possible, and to gunart.net for use of the vintage Makarov PM poster and original PM manual.

PERFORMANCE:

Pistol	Velocity (fps)	Energy (ft-lbs)	Average Group	Best Group
CZ 82	1017	218	1.95"	1.77"
P-83 Wanad	962	195	1.28"	.87"
P-64	999	211	1.28"	1.1"
PA-63	979	202	1.17"	.99"

PPU 95-Grain JHP

The Red Army's Service Pistol Cartridge

The 9x18mm Makarov – also known as the 9mm Makarov, 9x18 MAK and 9x18 PM – became the standard military pistol cartridge used by the Soviet Union and Eastern Bloc countries beginning in 1951. In ballistic terms, the 9mm Makarov fits between the 9x17mm, which is commonly known to us as the .380 ACP, and the 9x19mm or 9mm Parabellum, normally referred to as the 9mm.

During the 1950s as the Cold War was ramping up, part of the Soviet design specification for a new cartridge was that the round would need to be moderately powerful with the ability to be chambered in a lightweight pistol that was simple to operate and inexpensive to manufacture. Ideally, the round would work in a pistol with a simple blowback mechanism. The round could also not be compatible with NATO firearms so that in the event of a conflict captured Soviet or Eastern Bloc ammunition could not be used in NATO weapons.

The cartridge's designer, B.V. Semin, based the 9x18mm Makarov on a round the German Luftwaffe had been developing during the WWII, the 9x18mm Ultra. This round was built for use in a simple blowback pistol with power between the .380 and 9mm Parabellum. The 9x18mm Makarov and 9x18mm Ultra are not compatible though similar in design and concept.

When directly comparing the 9x18mm Makarov cartridge to the .380 and 9mm the differences become apparent. The 9x18mm Makarov uses a bullet with a diameter of 9.27mm, which is slightly larger than the .380 and the 9mm, both of which use a bullet with a 9.017 mm diameter. The case lengths of the three cartridges are also slightly different: .380 is 17mm, 9mm Makarov is 18mm and 9mm is 19mm.

The 9mm Makarov is a relatively powerful round chambered in a compact pistol that uses a simple blowback action. The round is used in the Makarov pistol and the selective-fire Stechkin machine pistol.

Cartridge Dimension Comparison		
	9x18mm Ultra	9x18mm Makarov
Bullet Diameter	9.00mm	9.25mm
Case Length	18.50mm	18.03mm
Rim Diameter	9.50mm	9.90mm
Base Diameter	9.50mm	9.90mm
Neck	9.50mm	9.85mm
OAL	26.16mm	24.64mm

Hornady Critical Defense 95-Grain FTX				
Pistol	Velocity (fps)	Energy (ft-lbs)	Average Group	Best Group
CZ 82	994	220	1.05"	.87"
P-83 Wanad	931	183	1.58"	1.4"
P-64	931	183	1.75"	1.57"
PA-63	979	202	2.16"	1.98"

Brown Bear 94-Grain FMJ				
Pistol	Velocity (fps)	Energy (ft-lbs)	Average Group	Best Group
CZ 82	1027	220	2.06"	1.88"
P-83 Wanad	998	208	1.33"	1.15"
P-64	971	197	2.41"	2.23"
PA-63	1016	215	2.59"	2.41"

Bullet weight is measured in grains, velocity in feet per second, energy in foot-pounds, taken 15 feet from the muzzle by a ProChrono digital chronograph; accuracy in inches averaged from three, five-shot groups at 10 yards.

The standard military round, designated 57-N-181S, is loaded with a 92.6-grain steel-core, clad metal jacket bullet. The bullet's nose is spherical and the case is made of clad metal, bi-metal or steel with a green lacquer coating. This load produces a muzzle velocity of 978 fps and muzzle energy of 185 ft-lbs, and is designed to penetrate soft and hard targets. Additional military and LE rounds were developed including the RG 028 used to penetrate body armor, and the 7N16 with a lighter, tapered bullet for increased muzzle velocity and soft target penetration. For maximum armor piercing the 7N25 used a tapered bullet with high-strength steel core; the PE hollowpoint was designed for Russian police agencies and others.

What normally is imported into the U.S. from foreign ammunition manufacturers like Priv Partizan, Brown Bear and Wolf are cartridges loaded with 93- or 94-grain FMJ bullets. American ammunition companies like Winchester make a 95-grain FMJ bullet for a military type loading, while Hornady produces a 95-grain FTX HP.

Russia and other countries formerly behind the Iron Curtain like Ukraine, Poland and Bulgaria have since changed to 9mm service sidearms. The 9mm Makarov round is still used by some former satellite nations, notably Vietnam and North Korea, and by Russian police and some rear line supporting military units.

Military style 94-grain FMJ ball ammo by Brown Bear (center) is flanked by modern variants like a 95-grain JHP from PPU (left) and 95-grain FTX by Hornady.

FMJ Bullet Ballistics Comparison			
	.380 ACP	9x18mm Makarov	9mm
Bullet Weight	95-gr. FMJ	95-gr. FMJ	115-gr.
Muzzle Velocity	1000 fps	1050 fps	1300 fps
Muzzle Energy	200 ft-lbs	231 ft-lbs	420 ft-lbs

They are chambered for the same caliber, but the Ruger American (top) and the Model 77/22 are about as different as rimfire rifles can be.

RUGER'S
RIMFIRE BOLT GUNS
Comparing the American Rimfire & the 77/22

BY **James E. House**

Both the 77/22 and the American utilize Ruger's highly reliable rotary magazine.

Alexander M. Sturm and William B. Ruger began a firearm manufacturing company in 1949. The first model produced was an autoloading pistol in .22 LR caliber. That pistol had a retail price of $37.50 and I had one of the early ones. Development of other models followed and in 1964 the legendary Ruger 10/22 was introduced. Configured in somewhat of a carbine style complete with barrel band, one of the unusual features was the 10/22's 10-round magazine.

There seems to be something magical about having a "7" in the model number for a rifle. Perhaps it was established in 1936 when Winchester introduced the Model 70, but that numeral has

certainly been used by others. Classic centerfire sporting rifles such as the Winchester Model 70 and Remington Model 700 have long been popular. Ruger's entry into that market was made in 1968 with the introduction of the Model 77. With the model having two 7s it made a "fashion" statement, and the Ruger 77 has been among the most popular rifles for many years, and a strong rival to such rifles as the Winchester Model 70 and Remington 700. However, the standard model has an MSRP of $939 and many shooters do not wish to spend that much for a rifle to take to the outdoors. Top-of-the-line centerfires produced by other manufacturers are also in that price range.

Introducing Rimfire Sporter Bolt Actions

With rimfire sporting rifles such as the Winchester 75 and Remington 513 out of production, Ruger introduced a rifle in 1983, the Model 77/22, which "was built to centerfire standards of strength, accuracy, and aesthetics." It was patterned along the lines of the Model 77, and the design goals were fully met by the Model 77/22. As a result of the great success of the rotary magazine used in the 10/22, the new rifle also employed that type of magazine. The 77/22 is, indeed, a very handsome and elegant sporting rifle, and I am pleased to say that I have owned one for about 30 years. However, not only is the Ruger 77/22 "built to centerfire standards of strength, accuracy, and aesthetics," but it also carries the same MSRP, $939.

In response to a market in which many shooters seek firearms that give good performance but sell for moderate prices, Ruger introduced the centerfire bolt-action American model in 2012 to compete with comparable offerings from other manufacturers. The American has a composite stock, adjustable trigger, and is available in several versions in several popular calibers. Plus, it features an adjustable trigger known as the Marksman.

The Ruger American has been a huge success, to the effect that the Model 77 offerings have been reduced in number. Since the centerfire version was readily accepted by shooters, the next step would logically be to introduce a lower priced rimfire bolt-action rifle to complement the elegant but expensive Model 77/22. Thus was born the Ruger American Rimfire in 2013, which is now available in .22 LR, .22 WMR and .17 HMR calibers in both standard and compact models. The base price of this innovative rimfire is only $339 and variants have $369 price tags.

The Ruger 77/22 action is a robust unit that resembles the action of a centerfire rifle in construction. It utilizes a three-position safety. When placed in the middle position as shown here, the rifle will not fire but the bolt can be opened.

An elegant triggerguard and floorplate assembly adorns the Ruger 77/22.

Dual extractors are employed on the bolt of the Ruger 77/22.

Ruger 77/22 Overview

The Ruger 77/22 has some features that set it apart from other rimfire rifles. First, the .22 LR versions utilize the 10-round rotary magazine that has been so successfully used in the 10/22, but those used in .22 WMR and .17 HMR versions hold nine rounds. This causes the rifle to be slightly wider in the midsection than I prefer, but not excessively so. However, it gives a rifle that has absolutely no projections on the bottom – and that is the way a sporting rifle should be.

Second, the Ruger 77/22 has a three-position safety that is in the "fire" position when it is forward and on "safe" in the other two positions. In the rear position, the rifle is on "safe" and the bolt is locked, and in the middle position the rifle is on "safe" but the bolt can be opened. This design follows that made famous by the Winchester Model 70, and it has been incorporated in many other rifles. Although not known for having trigger action equivalent to that of a target rifle, I have always been pleased with the trigger on my 77/22. It breaks crisply with a pull of about 4 pounds.

Third, there are numerous desirable features of the action. The receiver is made of steel and incorporates the same type of integral notches on the top that characterize Ruger's method for attaching scope rings to centerfire rifles. The 77/22 utilizes a two-piece bolt of which the rear section rotates as the bolt is opened or closed. The forward end of the rear section has dual locking lugs that rotate into recesses at the top and bottom of the receiver. Dual extractors are located on the front section of the bolt. The result is an incredibly strong action for a rimfire. The same basic action has been utilized on other versions of the Model 77 that are chambered for .22 WMR, .22 Hornet, .357 Magnum and .44 Magnum. It truly is an action built to centerfire levels of strength and rigidity.

Fourth, the barrel is attached to the receiver in the same manner as in the Ruger 10/22. A transverse notch in the bottom of the barrel mates with a wedge that is pulled to the front of the receiver by means of two bolts with 5/32-inch Allen heads. As a result, the owner can

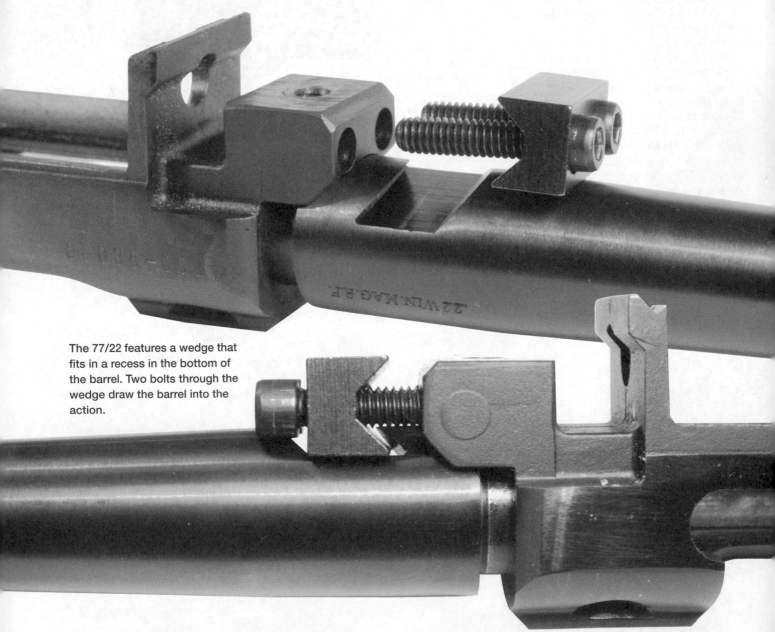

The 77/22 features a wedge that fits in a recess in the bottom of the barrel. Two bolts through the wedge draw the barrel into the action.

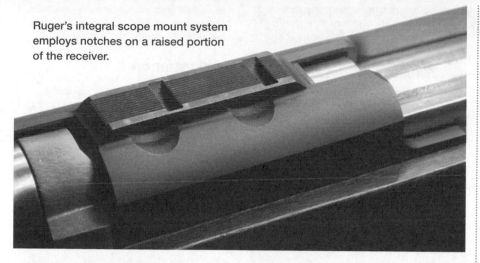

Ruger's integral scope mount system employs notches on a raised portion of the receiver.

remove the barrel and replace it with an aftermarket model if desired. Model 77 rimfires are available with checkered walnut, composite or laminated stocks depending on the model. For example, one popular variant features a heavy stainless steel barrel and laminated stock. Originally, 77/22 rifles were furnished with sights, but none of the current models are.

In my opinion the Ruger 77/22 meets the design parameters that were set forth in the statement that it "was built to centerfire standards of strength, accuracy, and aesthetics."

Ruger American Overview

Although the 10/22 has been a success by any measure, Ruger needed moderately priced bolt-action rifles in both centerfire and rimfire calibers to maintain its position in the marketplace. Given the characteristics described in the previous section, it was clearly necessary to begin with new rifles rather than to simply modify the existing Models 77 and 77/22. Having successfully launched the American in centerfire calibers, it would be only natural to produce a rimfire version.

The Ruger American Rimfire is available in .22 LR, .22 WMR and .17 HMR versions with magazine capacities identical to those of the Model 77 rifles. That is where the similarity between Model 77 and American rifles end. The American

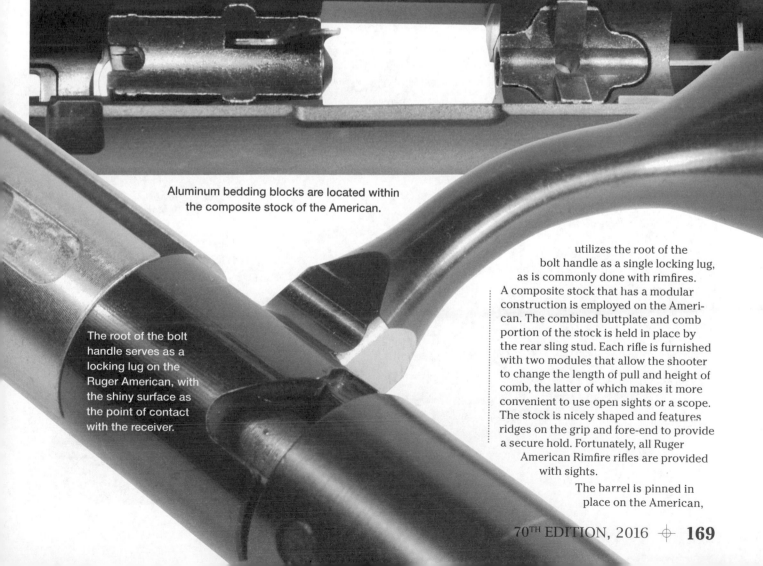

Aluminum bedding blocks are located within the composite stock of the American.

The root of the bolt handle serves as a locking lug on the Ruger American, with the shiny surface as the point of contact with the receiver.

utilizes the root of the bolt handle as a single locking lug, as is commonly done with rimfires. A composite stock that has a modular construction is employed on the American. The combined buttplate and comb portion of the stock is held in place by the rear sling stud. Each rifle is furnished with two modules that allow the shooter to change the length of pull and height of comb, the latter of which makes it more convenient to use open sights or a scope. The stock is nicely shaped and features ridges on the grip and fore-end to provide a secure hold. Fortunately, all Ruger American Rimfire rifles are provided with sights.

The barrel is pinned in place on the American,

RESULTS OF ACCURACY TESTING OF THE RUGER 77/22 AND AMERICAN RIMFIRE

Ammunition	Ruger 77/22 Average Group (inch)	Ruger American Average Group (inch)
CCI Green Tag	.49	.67
CCI Mini Mag	.95	.74
Eley Target	.60	.67
Federal Target	.80	1.35
Remington Game Load	.48	1.02
SK Standard Plus	.61	.85
Winchester Power Point	.86	.53
Winchester SuperX HP	.50	1.81

a customary practice on inexpensive rimfire rifles. However, the barrel and action on my two rifles are beautifully polished and blued, even more so than most Model 77/22 rifles. The bolt has a single extractor. The safety is a push-pull button located on the tang at the rear end of the bolt. When placed in the forward or "fire" position, a large red "F" is clearly visible.

The American also breaks new ground for inexpensive rifles by incorporating an adjustable trigger. Known as the Marksman Adjustable trigger, it provides a crisp let-off that can be adjusted between 3-5 pounds. The barreled action must be removed from the stock to ac-cess the adjustment screw. On my rifle it measures about 4 pounds and I do not intend to change it.

Performance

The Ruger 77/22 has always had a reputation for being an accurate rimfire, so I was really anticipating the chance to pit the new Ruger American against it. I configured the rifles by attaching a Weaver Classic 2-7x rimfire scope on the 77/22 and a Leupold 2-7x VX-1 scope on the American. Testing a rimfire rifle outdoors is always challenging –especially during winter. During the testing it was difficult to maintain a consistent hold with a bunched-up coat and the result was that most groups showed vertical stringing. In order to eliminate some of the human error, I chose to throw out the outlying shot and consider the closest four shots as more correctly indicating the accuracy. The results obtained are shown in the accompanying table.

Some shooters set a rather arbitrary accuracy standard for rimfire rifles at less than 1-inch groups at 50 yards, and this is appropriate except for target rifles.

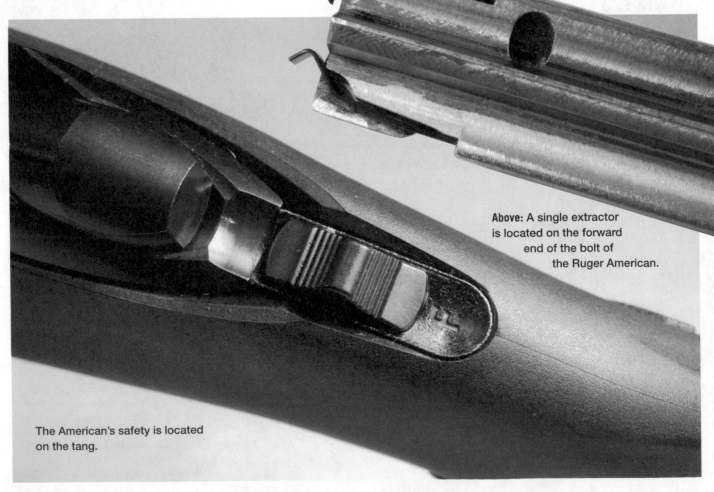

Above: A single extractor is located on the forward end of the bolt of the Ruger American.

The American's safety is located on the tang.

The price of a Ruger 77/22 is almost three times that of the American, but you get what you pay for.

The results shown in the table indicate that both the 77/22 and American are capable of that level of accuracy. The difference is that the 77/22 will perform that well with almost any type of ammunition, and the American will do it with *some* types. With group sizes determined as described earlier, the overall average group sizes were .66 and .96 inches for the 77/22 and American, respectively. Either rifle will serve the small-game hunter and pest shooter extremely well.

As I looked at the targets, it appeared that the American suffered from "first shot blues" in that the first shot after changing to a different type of ammunition seemed to be some distance away from the other four shots. For example, three five-shot groups with SK Standard Plus measured 1.92, 1.41 and 1.26 inches, but for the same three groups the best four shots measured 1, .57 and .97 inch. The results obtained indicate that the owner of a Ruger American should choose ammunition very carefully if maximum accuracy is needed.

The Remington 504 rimfire rifle lasted for only about three years after its introduction in 2004. Kimber's elegant Model 82 sporting rimfires are also defunct. Cooper Firearms of Montana offers superb rimfire rifles, some of which sell for around $2,000. Anschutz produces the outstanding Model 1416 that has a price tag of around $1,000-1,200, and other models are even more expensive. Although relatively expensive, the Ruger 77/22 comes with high-quality rings for scope mounting and can be found in new condition for around $800. It is not a bargain-priced rimfire, but neither is it out of line for such a fine rifle in today's market. I have two other rimfire sporting rifles that could be described as elegant, but the Ruger 77/22 remains my favorite rimfire rifle. Performance of the Ruger American is very good for a rifle with the MSRP of $369 (usually available for around $275), and I could get by nicely with one, but it is not really in the same league as the Model 77/22.

I just hope that the very capable and popularly priced American does not command so much manufacturing space that the Model 77/22 has to be discontinued. Both definitely belong in the rimfire marketplace.

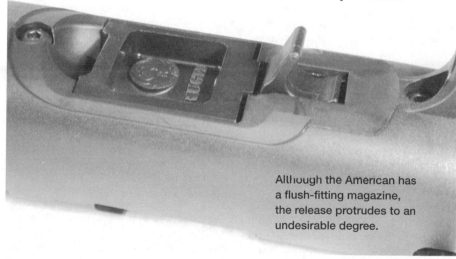

Although the American has a flush-fitting magazine, the release protrudes to an undesirable degree.

The Contemporary·
Longrifle

AN UNBROKEN CHAIN

Flintlock rifles by noted gunmaker and author, Peter Alexander, are indicative of the state-of-the-art of contemporary gunbuilding.

Today's custom muzzleloading gunmakers are keeping tradition alive

BY **Holt Bodinson**

Some of the finest gunmaking going on in the world today is not lavished on big-game rifles or upland shotguns, but on muzzleloading firearms of every conceivable design and style. The contemporary muzzleloading gunmaker has become the master of many arts. He is a metalsmith, stocker, engraver, wood carver, blacksmith and historian. He is a specialized generalist who brings all of these hard-earned and multifaceted skills to bear on a single piece of gunmaking art, and he is probably self-taught.

His canvas is broad. He can pick and choose among centuries, stylistic schools, ignition systems and all types of firearms ranging from 15th century matchlocks to late 19th century target rifles. Contemporary muzzleloading gunmaking today exists in a parallel universe to what we normally think of as the "custom" scene, and because of the simplicity of the tooling involved, it is both the realm of the professional gunmaker and the gifted amateur alike. Here's a brief history.

The making of muzzleloading guns never really did die out. Here and there, particularly in Appalachia and the South, old-time smiths kept the spark alive while turning out a gun or two now and then.

Many of the components they used, like the locks and barrels, were recycled parts from worn out and scrapped guns. Locks were repaired. Barrels were "freshened" or re-bored and re-rifled. Items like triggerguards and buttplates might be salvaged or hand forged from scrap iron. There was always a ready supply of walnut and maple trees, so the availability of stock wood was never a hurdle.

Typical of these transitional gunmakers was Hacker Martin (1895-1970) of Gray's Station, Tenn. Martin owned the "Old Cedar Creek Mill" where grain was milled into flour or corn meal for the farmers of the region. Martin could and did make the whole lock, stock and barrel if he put his mind to it, but just as often used old parts he salvaged and repaired. He encouraged customers to bring in their old guns and trade them for some milling time, and it was said he had a whole room just piled with muzzleloading guns to be salvaged or repaired. He was a mechanical genius and could forge barrels using a 1782-era barrel anvil, or make the complete lock for a fine flint or percussion rifle. His longrifles were elegant and today command premium prices in collector circles.

There were many other muzzleloading gunmakers throughout the country who also bridged that period between the adoption of the cartridge firearm and the renaissance of the muzzleloader, but Hacker Martin stands out as someone who was known nationally and chronicled continually.

The 1930s were a turning point for a revived interest in muzzleloading guns. The Great Depression did not dampen recreational shooting. The watershed event was the formation of the National Muzzleloading Rifle Association (NMLRA) at a small gathering of muzzleloading enthusiasts in Portsmouth, Ohio, in 1933. From the start, the new organization was blessed with the leadership of men like Walter Cline, Red Ferris, Bull Ramsey, Boss Johnson, William Large, Powell Crosley, Jr., Ned Roberts, Adolph Niedner, John G.W. Dillin, Joe Kindig,

Contemporary longrifles are made to be used. Here is the author with a .45-caliber Bedford County style rifle by D. Krauss, and one very dead coyote.

Jr. and others. Once formed, the NMLRA sponsored national matches, encouraged the formation of state and local chapters, published an official journal, *Muzzleblasts,* on an old mimeograph machine, and finally built a national headquarters and the national Walter Cline range in Friendship, Ind.

In the 1930s and 1940s, the predominant muzzleloader still seen on the range was an original that had been well-preserved in shooting condition or else fully restored. By the 1950s the glimmer of a contemporary muzzleloading industry could be seen.

Turner Kirkland established the Dixie Gun Works in Union City, Tenn., to cater to the trade. In 1956 he marketed his "New Model" .40 caliber, a Kentucky rifle built in Italy and retailing for $79.50. For months he could not produce enough to meet the pent-up demand for a contemporary Kentucky rifle. He could, however, furnish parts, separately or as a kit –

While this Jaeger is only Saddler's 12th rifle ever built, it fully demonstrates his mastery of carving and engraving.

The predecessor of the American longrifle was the Germanic Jaeger. This one by contemporary maker, Jeff Saddler.

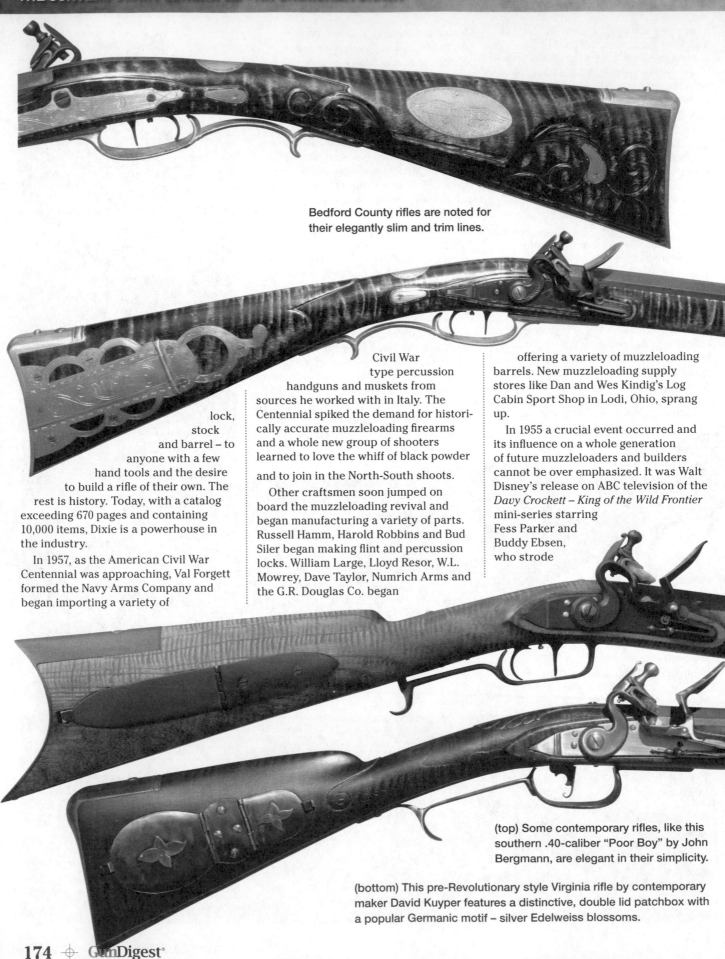

Bedford County rifles are noted for their elegantly slim and trim lines.

lock, stock and barrel – to anyone with a few hand tools and the desire to build a rifle of their own. The rest is history. Today, with a catalog exceeding 670 pages and containing 10,000 items, Dixie is a powerhouse in the industry.

In 1957, as the American Civil War Centennial was approaching, Val Forgett formed the Navy Arms Company and began importing a variety of Civil War type percussion handguns and muskets from sources he worked with in Italy. The Centennial spiked the demand for historically accurate muzzleloading firearms and a whole new group of shooters learned to love the whiff of black powder and to join in the North-South shoots.

Other craftsmen soon jumped on board the muzzleloading revival and began manufacturing a variety of parts. Russell Hamm, Harold Robbins and Bud Siler began making flint and percussion locks. William Large, Lloyd Resor, W.L. Mowrey, Dave Taylor, Numrich Arms and the G.R. Douglas Co. began offering a variety of muzzleloading barrels. New muzzleloading supply stores like Dan and Wes Kindig's Log Cabin Sport Shop in Lodi, Ohio, sprang up.

In 1955 a crucial event occurred and its influence on a whole generation of future muzzleloaders and builders cannot be over emphasized. It was Walt Disney's release on ABC television of the *Davy Crockett – King of the Wild Frontier* mini-series starring Fess Parker and Buddy Ebsen, who strode

(top) Some contemporary rifles, like this southern .40-caliber "Poor Boy" by John Bergmann, are elegant in their simplicity.

(bottom) This pre-Revolutionary style Virginia rifle by contemporary maker David Kuyper features a distinctive, double lid patchbox with a popular Germanic motif – silver Edelweiss blossoms.

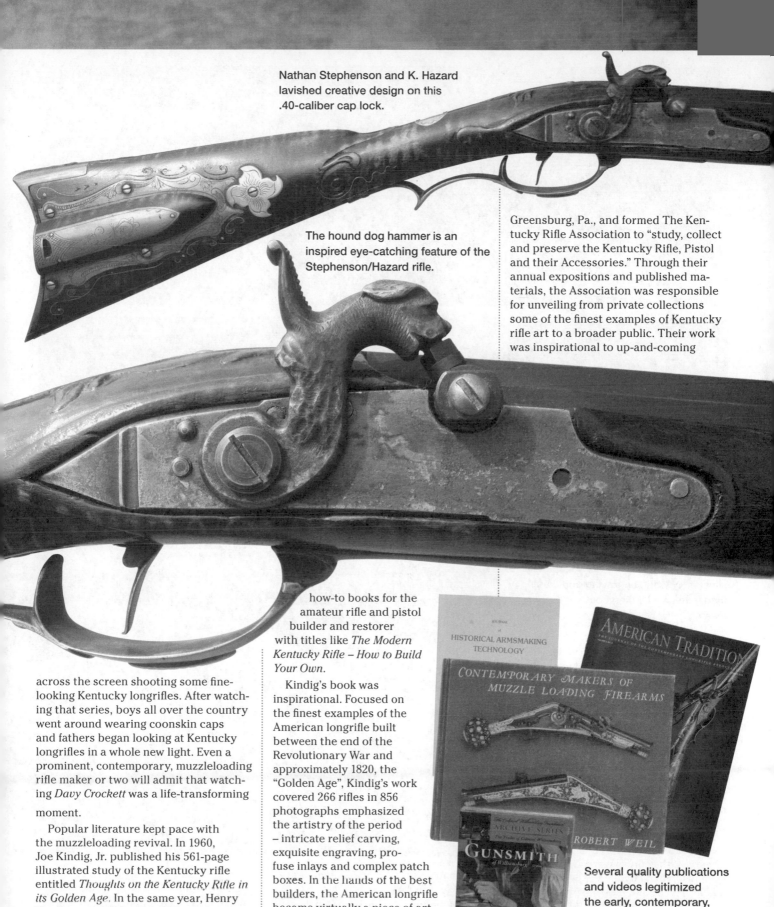

Nathan Stephenson and K. Hazard lavished creative design on this .40-caliber cap lock.

The hound dog hammer is an inspired eye-catching feature of the Stephenson/Hazard rifle.

Greensburg, Pa., and formed The Kentucky Rifle Association to "study, collect and preserve the Kentucky Rifle, Pistol and their Accessories." Through their annual expositions and published materials, the Association was responsible for unveiling from private collections some of the finest examples of Kentucky rifle art to a broader public. Their work was inspirational to up-and-coming

how-to books for the amateur rifle and pistol builder and restorer with titles like *The Modern Kentucky Rifle – How to Build Your Own.*

Kindig's book was inspirational. Focused on the finest examples of the American longrifle built between the end of the Revolutionary War and approximately 1820, the "Golden Age", Kindig's work covered 266 rifles in 856 photographs emphasized the artistry of the period – intricate relief carving, exquisite engraving, profuse inlays and complex patch boxes. In the hands of the best builders, the American longrifle became virtually a piece of art during its Golden Age.

In 1962, a group of advanced Kentucky rifle collectors met in

across the screen shooting some fine-looking Kentucky longrifles. After watching that series, boys all over the country went around wearing coonskin caps and fathers began looking at Kentucky longrifles in a whole new light. Even a prominent, contemporary, muzzleloading rifle maker or two will admit that watching *Davy Crockett* was a life-transforming moment.

Popular literature kept pace with the muzzleloading revival. In 1960, Joe Kindig, Jr. published his 561-page illustrated study of the Kentucky rifle entitled *Thoughts on the Kentucky Rifle in its Golden Age.* In the same year, Henry Kauffman published his 376-page study, *The Pennsylvania-Kentucky Rifle.* At the same time, author and gunsmith R.H. McCrory was self-publishing a series of

Several quality publications and videos legitimized the early, contemporary, longrifle movement.

Contemporary makers can freely choose between centuries, stylistic schools and designs like this 19th century "buggy" rifle made by Leonard Day.

(above and right) A unique matched pair of "His & Hers" rifles in .45 and .50 calibers by Steve Zihn. His spectacular silver inlay work, engraving and carving mark him as a leading contemporary master.

contemporary builders who were hungry to see and examine the finest examples of 18th century gunbuilding.

Another important event occurred in 1963 – the founding of the Colonial Williamsburg Gunshop and the hiring of young and highly talented Wallace Gusler as the first master of the shop. The objective of the Williamsburg Gunshop was to recreate the methods and tooling associated with gunmaking during the 18th century. In short, to make locks, stocks and barrels from basic raw materials and form them into the finest firearms, the equal of any 18th or early 19th century work. Gusler succeeded beyond anyone's expectations, and in 1969 he and his associates were filmed making a complete and elegant "Golden Age" longrifle entirely by hand. The film, *Gunsmith of Williamsburg*, is still available as a DVD and is considered an essential part of every contemporary gunmaker's library.

The Colonial Williamsburg Gunshop was also the spawning ground for a whole generation of highly skilled contemporary makers who served in the shop as journeymen gunsmiths including Gary Brumfield, George Suiter, Jon Laubach, Clay Smith, Dave Wagner and Richard Frazier.

It took until 1980 for the work of increasing numbers of contemporary

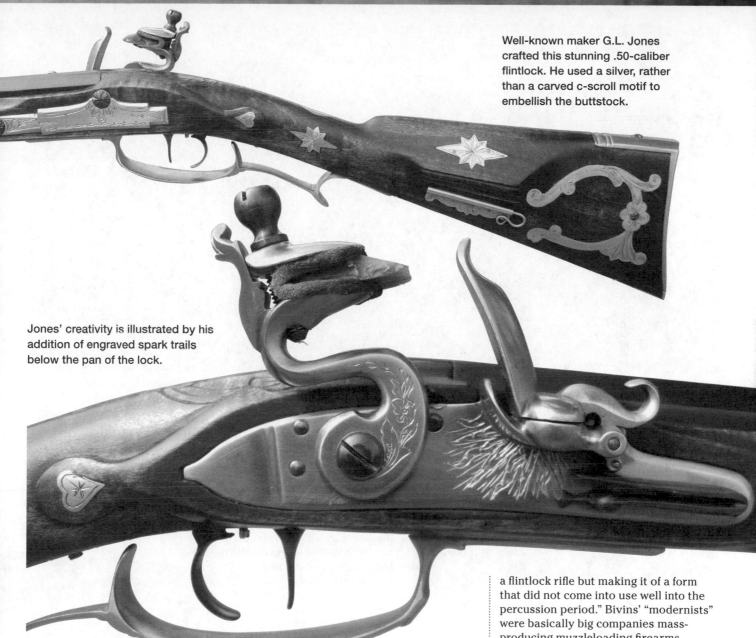

Well-known maker G.L. Jones crafted this stunning .50-caliber flintlock. He used a silver, rather than a carved c-scroll motif to embellish the buttstock.

Jones' creativity is illustrated by his addition of engraved spark trails below the pan of the lock.

builders to be recognized on a national level. In that year, Robert Weil authored a large, coffee table quality book entitled, *Contemporary Makers of Muzzle Loading Firearms*. In 303 pages Weil covered the works and biographies of 31 prominent contemporary makers. The studio quality illustrations of the book were stunning, and the book's introduction by contemporary gunmaker John Bivins established the philosophical basis of the contemporary movement.

In his introduction, Bivins broke out contemporary makers into four groups. There were the "documentarians" – builders who recreate in detail firearms of a specific region, period, style and

possibly of an historical maker. There were the "interpreters" who borrowed the best elements of design from one or more historic schools but kept their work within the parameters of time and place. There were the "new school" makers "who accept the parameters and basic fundamentals of historical design, yet assemble the elements of early design into combinations that are not often identifiable with the work of any single early gunmaker." Finally, there is the "modernist", (whom Bivins despised) who ignores historic design totally and is responsible for "things such as retaining the use of a nosecap but casting it of aluminum; using a brass patchbox on

a flintlock rifle but making it of a form that did not come into use well into the percussion period." Bivins' "modernists" were basically big companies mass-producing muzzleloading firearms.

To his great credit, Bivins took on apprentices who later became prominent gunmakers in their own right, Mark Silver and LaMont "Monte" Mandarino being two outstanding examples.

There was also a high degree of collaboration among this emerging group of skilled, contemporary gunmakers. Gary Brumfield and Wallace Gusler from the Colonial Williamsburg Gunshop, and John Bivins, Lynton McKenzie and Mark Silver created *The Journal of Historical Armsmaking Technology*, a periodic publication that chronicled the methods and tools of 18th century and earlier gunsmakers for a new generation of 20th century contemporary makers. Volume IV, dated 1991, is still available from the

National Muzzleloading Rifle Association.

(above) This contemporary blunderbuss, or coach gun, was crafted by Mike Brooks.

(left) The author used the Brooks gun to compete in the first national blunderbuss match sponsored by the National Muzzleloading Rifle Association.

Still, by the early 1990s, there was no national organization devoted to the contemporary gunmaking world. It took several members of the Kentucky Rifle Association, particularly Mel Hankla and Gordon Barlow, to approach the board in 1995 with a proposal that contemporary longrifle makers be incorporated into their annual meeting and displays. The response from the board was positive but tepid, limiting the number of contemporary items that could be displayed.

In 1996, Gordon Barlow floated the idea of forming a separate organization – an organization devoted exclusively to the contemporary scene to be named the Contemporary Longrifle Association (CLA). Over the next 12 months, a nonprofit corporation was formed, membership development and awards programs initiated and plans drawn up for the first annual meeting and show, which occurred in August in Cincinnati, Ohio. The first meeting and show of the nascent organization was a rousing success. Almost two decades later the final venue for the annual meeting and exposition is now Lexington, Ky., in the month of August, and it's an annual sell-out.

The list of board members who served during the first 10 years of the CLA reads like a who's who of the contemporary world including

Peter A Alexander ~ me fecit Anno~ 2010

Signed pieces identify the maker, the date and often the sequential number of the gun.

names like founder Gordon Barlow, Wallace Gusler, Gary Brumfield, Mark Silver, Jim and Barbie Chambers, Ed Louer, Art Riser, Joe Wood, Earl Lanning, Bob Harn, Bill Surlock, Barry Maxfield, Mel Hankla, Eve Otmar, Bill Ruggie, Ron Ehlet, Jim Wright, Jack Brooks, Alan Hoeweler, Ron Scott, Don Getz, Art DeCamp, H. David Wright, Frank House, Giles Cromwell, Edmund Davidson, Roland Cadle and Lee Larkin.

Today, the CLA projects its message through an *impressive* website, www.longrifle.com, which includes a list of contemporary artisans, an events calendar and a listing of member items for sale, both contemporary and antique. In addition, the CLA publishes a stunning, full-color journal, *American Tradition*, and a quarterly newsletter, the *Broadside*. Recently, the CLA published a virtual history of the organization and the artisans associated with it entitled, *Following the Tradition*, a beautiful coffee table quality book by CLA Founder, Gordon Barlow.

The CLA stands out as a comprehensive organization covering contemporary as well as antique accessories and associated artifacts such as knives, pistols, fowlers, tomahawks, pouches, horns, quillwork, jewelry, paintings and sculptures, and of course longrifles. All these facets of the "tradition" are integrated on their website and in their journals.

Contemporary artisans also have a website at www.americanlongrifles.org where they hang out to "promote, preserve and support the traditional art and craft of building and using the American longrifle." The artisans' website truly complements that of the CLA.

Traditional enthusiasts, collectors, shooters, hunters and amateur makers have their website as well, where the exchanges are lively, often humorous and always informative. With its motto, "Keeping Tradition Alive," it can be found at www.muzzleloadingforum.com.

Digest 2016 Web Directory. It's an extensive jumping-off place to find completed contemporary guns, kits, parts, classes, instructional videos and books.

In closing, Gordon Barlow captured the essence of the contemporary renaissance in his book, *Following the Tradition*, when he included a quotation from Mary Bryan Hood, director of the Owensboro Museum of Fine Art: "Most of the neo-frontier artists have developed a signature style while working within the constraints of an exacting tradition and many have surpassed the aesthetics of the early works creating their own superlative traditions."

The "tradition" is not only being fueled by professional artisans but also by people who simply are drawn to it and enjoy working with their hands to craft something unique, aesthetic and personal.

If you are intrigued, wander through the muzzleloading section of our *Gun*

Peter Alexander's handmade patchboxes are often an artistic blend of silver and brass. He is a master of detailed carving and inlay work.

THUMPER

THE PERFECT
DEER AND HOG RIFLE,
A PROJECT
THE HOME GUNSMITH
CAN ACCOMPLISH

By Walt Hampton

Basic parts, barreled action, buttstock and fore-end.

A couple of years ago my son Wade and I started a project for a friend, a single-shot rifle chambered for that fellow's favorite cartridge, the .35 Remington. Ed Lovette is a retired Green Beret Captain, handgun instructor, gun writer and Southern deer hunter; he is old-school in his technique and hunts for meat and his own spiritual well-being. We met in 1990 and Ed gave me my start in outdoor writing by introducing me to his editor, and since that time we have shared a great friendship and many, many hunts.

Wade and I wanted to finally stop Ed's grousing about not being able to find his "perfect" deer rifle so we thought we would surprise him. We started the effort in 2011, then in 2012 things got sidetracked for personal reasons and gun projects, along with other unimportant things, were put on the back burner. As is so true in all aspects of our lives, time has worked these things out now and after a two-year wait we got the project back on the bench; we call this "gun work therapy" and truly only gun people can know what that means.

If you are a hunter you know what you like. You know what your big-game hunting area has to offer and what conditions you are likely to encounter there, in terms of range and other limitations. If you have been hunting for any period of time and have any ethics whatsoever, you also know your own limitations and under what circumstances you will or will not take a shot. With these things in mind Ed, over a period of many years, and after having used dozens of different rifles and shotguns, formulated in his own mind what the perfect deer and hog rifle would be for his South Carolina and Virginia close quarters, thick cover, stalk-and-stand hunting. There were some factory options that were close to

this dream gun, but all fell short of the mark. The decision was made to build the gun.

If you are going to build a rifle you have to know what you want, how you will use it, how much you want to spend and on what aspects you are willing to compromise. The basic components are action, barrel and stock – simple, right? The complications, and the cost, come in the little things. Since we were building this one "on the cheap" as a gift to a fine friend, we used several "salvaged" components and a few new ones. Let me state for the record that there is nothing presented here that cannot be accomplished by almost every gun person. Here is how the project took shape.

Requirements For The Home Gunsmith

First you will need some reference material. Over many years I have built a fairly extensive gun library that covers those firearms in which I have an interest. I started by buying one book that within it addressed the complete disassembly of one specific firearm. This was in the days long before the personal computer or Internet. The gun information was out there but it was contained in books not usually found in my small-town library. I turned to the best-known gunsmithing supply house at the time, Brownell's. This article is not an advertisement for that company but I'll let you in on 40 years of gun work experience – if you can't find what you want at Brownell's, or if they can't find it for you (all you have to do is ask), then your prize must be obscure indeed.

There are many very good manuals on firearms assembly/disassembly that can be had from Gun Digest Books (www. gundigeststore.com) and the NRA. I know that there are dozens of DVDs and

videos available, but I like a manual that I can have on the bench, and if I spill coffee on it I won't have a stroke. Don't kid yourself, the guts of a gun may look simple, but for most of them there is a procedure that must be followed *to the letter* for properly tearing one down and putting it back together. Working on a particular gun may require repeated assembly and disassembly so it helps to have a reference right there in front of you. On this project I had the Ruger action apart and back together so many times I believe that I can now do it blindfolded. When we were in the gunsmith business I can't count the number of times sheepish clients came in the door with a bag of parts and a sob story – get the books, save the aggravation.

Basic Tools

You need a place to work. You should have a bench with some fixture to hold the firearm securely or a padded space on which to work, and imperative is a good light. The kitchen table might seem appropriate but it will be better if you have your own place to get the job done. Small parts (and guns have lots of tiny parts) have a way of growing legs, and especially in the case of springs, can at the most inopportune time decide to leap into the unknown. Plan for this or I guarantee it will happen to you.

Precision measuring instruments are a must if you are going to install sights or do any drilling. Most of the time I find myself using a good digital or dial caliper and a micrometer. The Smokey Bear ruler your kid brought home from school won't get it done – these are investments that will be used many times for virtually every gun job you do.

Gun screws are made for gun screwdrivers, not the screwdrivers in the drawer by the kitchen sink. Hollow-

ground, straight-sided drivers that fit the screw in question are easily acquired from many, many manufacturers, including Wheeler, Lyman and of course, Brownell's (there are many others). Get the right screwdrivers. The first mark of the amateur job is a boogered-up screw.

Along with screws, guns are held together with pins. You will need drift punches appropriate for the size pin in question and some pins, like roll-pins, require specialized punches. A small hammer (such as a tack hammer) is also a good buy. If you plan to move a sight within a dovetail get a brass drift so you won't mar the finish of the gun. These tools you will use over and over on virtually every gun job you tackle.

For basic stock work such as refinishing or fitting a semifinished stock you will need rasps, files and sandpaper. Some of these files and sandpapers can pull double duty on metal work; look at your project, plan your needs and buy appropriately. Many fine stock-making tools like sandpaper, files and rasps can be found at the big discount hardware stores and at lower prices than you think. I regularly use a couple of orbital sanders I received for Father's Day many years ago, and they save hours of elbow grease and work beautifully.

If you plan to fit stocks to metal, good scrapers of various sizes are very handy, and a hand grinder such as those made

by Dremel can accomplish an amazing amount of work if used properly. If you buy as the need arises and spread out the purchases it will be easier on the pocketbook.

Beyond The Basics

There are some gun jobs that require specialized tools or machinery and the knowledge to use that machinery, such as drilling thru-bolt holes in buttstocks or threading, fitting and chambering a barrel. I would recommend using a professional for these things, then once you have the barreled action in hand you can proceed.

Gunsmith tools need not be expensive, but you must have good measuring instruments, such as a micrometer and caliper. Screwdrivers, files, rasps and orbital sanders make short work of gunstock shaping.

The Metal

For action type we discussed them all and settled on the single shot. Ed wanted a short, Mannlicher-type gun that would be at home in the thicket, quick to the shoulder and look good doing it. And, it had to be chambered for his favorite cartridge, the .35 Remington.

We cannibalized an old and highly modified No. 3 Ruger .45-70 I bought used years ago, because the simple lever arrangement of the No. 3 has more traditional visual appeal than that found on the No. 1 guns. Other than the lever and triggerguard arrangement the No. 3 and

the No. 1 actions are identical; rugged, dependable and rock solid.

To this action Wade used his lathe and mill to mate a new Shilen barrel, and cut the chamber and ejector slot. A new ejector was necessary for the rimless .35 versus the original rimmed-cartridge ejector in the action. If you are looking for cost savings, the barrel is not the place to scrimp. You should buy the best you can afford and Shilen makes outstanding barrels that are surprisingly affordable.

Since this was to be a Mannlicher-style gun the barrel was cut to a length of 19¼ inches from the face of the receiver. The quarter rib was salvaged from a cannibalized Ruger No. 1A and had an open rear sight, just what we wanted, plus with its integral scope ring cuts it satisfied two requirements. Friend and gunsmith Carl Martin of Galax, Va., who later did the blueing on the gun, gave us a hand with rib installation and the cutting/crowning of the barrel (which was done by hand with a hacksaw and Brownell's muzzle cutter).

Since the Mannlicher-style gun looks odd without open sights, and to have them as backup in case of scope problems, we decided to use the New England Gun Masterpiece banded front sight with the interchangeable bead, which would have to be fit to the barrel, stock and nose cap. After ordering the sights

from Brownell's we used a close-fitting chisel shank and some wet-or-dry #220 sandpaper to polish and fit the band to the diameter of the barrel at the muzzle, which was a meaty .650 inch. With a close fit accomplished, we would do the final installation by leveling the front sight base with the quarter rib and fix it in place with Acraglas epoxy.

In keeping with the traditional look, we decided to use a front swivel band instead of the more modern "through-the-stock" swivel loop. For the swivel band I salvaged one from the junk parts box (I have no idea where it came from), did a little heating and bending to get the right contour and made two screws to hold it in place.

The nose cap was a no-brainer—we ordered one from Ruger that fit their International Model No. 1, which

was very close to the diameter we would need. The nose cap was a final fit after the banded front sight was installed using a Dremel tool and coarse sanding band, then rubbed with the same chisel shank and #220 to smooth it up to get a close, tight fit on the front sight band. These little things might seem like insignificant points but a great deal of time was spent to hand fit these parts; you cannot rush this type of work and expect a good result. Take your time on the little things, you will be glad you did.

The Ruger No. 3 action is strong and simple. The lever is plain and classic in style.

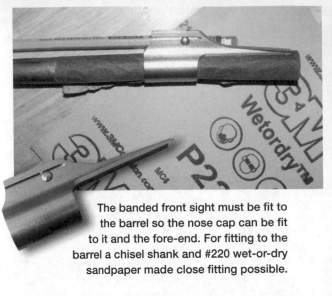

The banded front sight must be fit to the barrel so the nose cap can be fit to it and the fore-end. For fitting to the barrel a chisel shank and #220 wet-or-dry sandpaper made close fitting possible.

In fitting the fore-end furniture, the fore-end has been sealed but not completely finished. This is so parts may be fit and refit as needed to get things right.

The Wood

I had a couple of rough-cut No. 1 buttstocks made from our Grayson County black walnut that were turned on our duplicators before we closed our gun shop, and a Mannlicher-style roughed-out fore-end I had squirreled away. These stocks came from slabs of an ancient tree I had cut way back in 1998 and had stored until they were turned on our duplicator in 2009, after they reached the magic 6 percent moisture level.

I began by fitting the buttstock to the stripped action using hand files, scrapers and rasps, then shaped the stock using rasps and palm sanders with several grits of sandpaper. This is a slow, careful process; the fit must be very close to absorb recoil properly and not crack or shoot loose (and look good too, don't forget that), while at the same time be comfortable for Ed, meeting his pull-length and comb-height requirements.

To finish things off, a Pachmayr Presentation 1/2-inch rifle pad was salvaged from the used parts box and fitted to the stock using an orbital sander, and an old steel grip cap gave the grip that needed finishing touch. Here, the lines are important – to make a buttstock look like it is supposed to look, the lines have to match up. The line from the surface of the grip must meet the heel of the butt, and the line from the toe of the stock needs to hit about where the rear triggerguard/action tang fits.

Fitting the fore-end presented its own unique problems. Not only did it have to fit properly to the receiver front and mainspring hanger, it also had to fully bed the barrel and end at the proper length for the nosecap to be in the proper position on the banded front sight. Now cosmetics comes into play as there were two possibilities for the visual effect of the fore-end: either to make a gradual tapering line from receiver to nose cap (as seen in the No. 1 International), or using a "step" in the wood for the front swivel band, to go back to the old Garcia bolt-action rifle style. Of course we had settled on the band for the front swivel, wanting that extra measure of security for the front

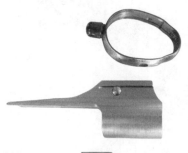

Once the fitting of the banded front sight and nose cap are complete, they may be fit to the fore-end.

sling attachment, and this necessitated the "stepped" look.

Because of the abbreviated barrel length and position of the front swivel band (arrived at by using the traditional "golden ratio" formula), the swivel stud for the butt had to be positioned slightly forward of the traditional 3½ inches from the toe of the stock, so the rifle would ride nearly vertical when on the shoulder. This took some trial and error before drilling to find the right spot for the rear stud. The plan was to use a very simple leather sling (which cost all of $8 at a local gun show) in keeping with the traditional look of the gun, using the ubiquitous Uncle Mike's 1-inch swivel loops. Fitting of the buttstock and fore-end to the metal was accomplished with the metal in the white, before blueing and coating, so that wood and metal could be sanded together for that close fit we look for in a well-handled rifle.

Finish The Wood, Finish The Metal

Once the stock fitting was done to satisfaction, the finishing of the wood and metal could begin. The barreled action was left with Carl Martin for bead blasting and blueing, while the nose cap, front swivel band, quarter rib, lever and front sight band were to be colored with Gun Coat and baked, giving just enough contrast to make things interesting. Ed wanted a matte finish on the rifle as this

was to be a close-quarters hunting gun, without a reflective finish that might spook up-close game.

Carl's work is immaculate. I just hoped that the coating I did on the accessories would measure up to his efforts! The small parts were hand polished, cleaned in TCE and coated according to the manufacturer's instructions, each receiving three coats before baking in a 300-degree oven.

Wood Finishing

Just like every other gunsmith, I have my own way of finishing gunstock wood. For a "real" hunting rifle, first and foremost the finish must be totally and completely waterproof. While I have used Permalyn from Laurel Mountain Forge for many years with wonderful results, lately I have had very good success with polyurethane. Its quick-drying, deep-penetrating and extreme waterproofing qualities are attributes that tend to work very well on a hunting rifle, and particularly on Ed's rifle, since invariably it is raining or snowing when he is hunting.

First, we final-sanded the stocks, using a hard but flexible rubber backing and running through grits of sandpaper beginning with #120 and progressing through #220, #320 and #400, with each change looking to remove any scratches from the previous grit. The backing is necessary to keep the flat surfaces flat and to keep the edges of the flutes

sharp. You can carry this sanding to the extreme, and I have gone all the way down to #1500 paper on other projects, but for this rifle stopping at #400 was fine.

Once this was accomplished, I whiskered the stocks to raise the grain. Here small areas of the stocks were dampened with a clean wet cloth, then were immediately subjected to a heat gun to vaporize the moisture in the wood, causing the grain ends to rise. This must be done to make sure that if moisture ever does reach the wood those ugly grain ends won't rise up through the finish. With the grain raised I gave the stocks a light-handed rub with 0000 oil-free steel wool to pull out the grain ends a bit more.

At this stage under close inspection the surface of the stocks looks pretty bad, and since this was very open-pore walnut, I could see it would require some serious filling to get things smooth. After a 10-minute dip in the poly finish to completely penetrate and seal the wood, I wiped off the excess and after a 24-hour drying period, was ready to fill the pores.

For a filler I combined the fine sanding dust from the catch bag on the orbital sander (which had been used on these stocks) with the poly finish and smeared a thick layer on the entire surface of the stocks, making sure coverage was complete. This was allowed to dry for an additional 24 hours in a warm drying cabinet. Now the stock *really* looked sad, but not to worry, the magic comes next with the first of several wet sandings and rubs.

Wet sanding and rubbing a gunstock is not rocket science, but it does take patience and attention to detail. I started with #320 wet-or-dry paper dipped in the poly finish and started sanding, always with the direction of the grain, not taking off any wood but only taking things down to the finish. As each area was wet sanded, it was gently wiped with a clean lint-free paper towel, leaving a film of finish on the area, before moving on to the next area. I gave the stock two wet rubs with #320, with adequate drying time in between, which succeeded in making sure all the pores were completely filled. Then moved down to #400 and repeated the

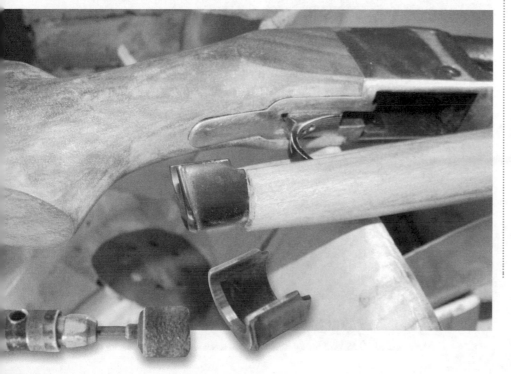

The Dremel hand grinder was used to fit the nose cap to the banded front sight, then hand fitted to the fore-end wood.

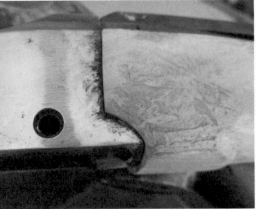

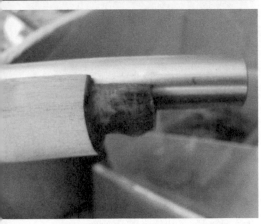

Fitting the wood to the metal is done with the metal in the white. Cheap red lipstick is used for spotting-in. Time must be taken here to assure a good tight fit.

Old friend and gunsmith Carl Martin of Galax, Va., gave us a hand with quarter-rib installation and cutting/crowning the barrel. Carl also did the blueing on the barreled action.

process for three rubs (drying of course between treatments), finishing with two rubs using #600. This process leaves a visual depth to the finish and stable, waterproof protection for the wood. For the inevitable small scratches that may come from future hunts, repair is easy with wet sanding using #600 and the same poly finish.

Polyurethane dries quickly but must be allowed to dry completely before you handle the stock. In my experience a 24-hour drying period after the final wet-rub will do fine.

The Bottom Line: How It Shoots

Many people have asked me, "Why a .35 Remington?" The answer is very simple: it works. For deer and hogs within 150 yards it has the authority and reliable expansion with factory 200-grain ammunition. The .35 Remington has been killing game for many years and

will be so doing long after I am gone.

First, the open sights were regulated to shoot dead on at 50 yards, being backup for the primary scope sight. At this distance with plain-jane Remington 200-grain softpoints, three shots from the bench made a neat cloverleaf just shy of all three shots touching each other. Good enough.

Ed traded me out of a wonderful Burris Mini 6x scope for the rifle, its small objective diameter and short length worked very well with what we wanted to accomplish in relation to the visual impact of the finished gun. Mounted in Ruger medium rings to allow the necessary clearance for breech access, the rifle was bore-sighted, then sighted in with Remington 200-grain softpoint ammunition to strike dead-on at 100 yards. Hornady, Remington and Federal factory ammunition in 150 and 200 grains were shot for groups. Since this is a 150-yard maximum-range gun, and any three-shot group within a 3-inch diameter would have been more than adequate for the intended purpose, imagine our delight when 100-yard groups using Federal Classic 200-grain softpoint loads clustered right around ¾ inch at the widest point. The best

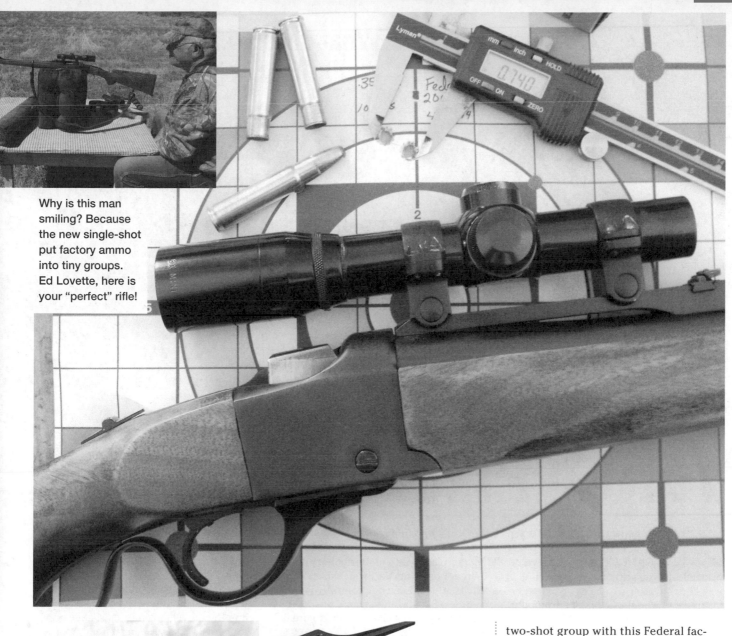

Why is this man smiling? Because the new single-shot put factory ammo into tiny groups. Ed Lovette, here is your "perfect" rifle!

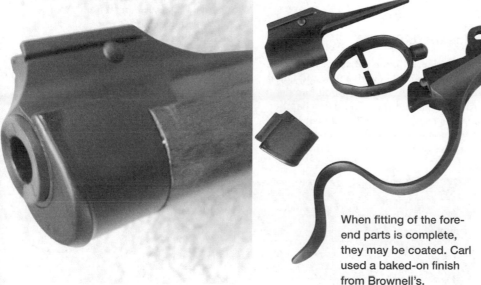

When fitting of the fore-end parts is complete, they may be coated. Carl used a baked-on finish from Brownell's.

two-shot group with this Federal factory ammo sized up at .382 inch, center to center. I don't think one can ask for more than this when shooting factory ammunition.

Shooting from the standing position offhand, the rifle was an absolute joy. From the sitting position, where it will probably see the most use, its slightly short 13¼-inch length of pull was very comfortable. Ed christened the rifle "Thumper" (every good rifle deserves a name) and happily took possession. At 36 inches overall length and weighing in at an even 7 pounds, it is a neat rifle for the serious close-range, thick-cover hunter. I'll have a report on her deer performance when Ed brings her back this fall. I can't wait!

What does $450 get you in today's rifle world?
by Jon R. Sundra

4 Value-Priced Rifles

The author puts a walnut stocked version of the Mossberg Patriot through its paces.

I don't know who it was or when some advertising guru came up with the euphemism "value priced," but you gotta admit it's a kind way of delineating products designed for those to whom price is of paramount consideration. I mean, it does sound better than cheap, inexpensive, budget or entry level, doesn't it?

We've now got a gaggle of bolt-action centerfire rifles to which the term "value priced" can be applied, and for this piece we've set the limit to rifles with an MSRP under $450. Granted, it's an arbitrary figure, but it's also a realistic one. As such, we're talking the Mossberg Patriot, Remington 783, Ruger American and Savage Axis.

Interestingly enough, late last year two rifles that would have been included here were discontinued – Marlin's X7 and Remington's 770. I can see Remington not wanting to have two budget-class rifles competing with one another in the same market niche, but Marlin's dropping of the X7 is a bit more baffling because it was as solid a rifle as any of the others.

I'm just spit-balling now but I suspect the reason the X7 didn't gain traction in the marketplace was a matter of the public's perception tying Marlin so closely to the traditional lever-action rifle. The X7 represented Marlin's second unsuccessful attempt in the last 20 years to break out of that mold.

Mossberg Patriot

New for 2015, the Patriot is simply the existing Model 4x4 with a new and much improved stock and a new bolt handle. Also new is that the .375 Ruger chambering has been added to the caliber lineup, a first for Mossberg and a step that bestows true big-game credibility to the line.

Like the other rifles we're reviewing here, the Patriot is designed for ease and economy of production. As such, it employs a tubular receiver, a barrel lock nut, and a separate, washer-type recoil lug sandwiched between the receiver and the barrel lock nut. This same arrangement is also seen on Remington's 783. While all four rifles under discussion here employ a barrel lock nut, as we shall see, the Ruger American and the Savage Axis do not use the washer-type recoil lug.

There are no flats or facets milled into the receiver, as seen on so many other tubular-receiver rifles, to disguise the fact that it is essentially nothing more than a straight tube with an ejection port and a cut-out in the floor for the magazine. The bolt is comprised of three components: the spiral fluted body to which a separate, floating bolt head is crosspinned at the front end, and a handle collared onto it at the rear. The crosspin that holds the bolt head to the body has a hole in its center to allow passage of the firing pin. This crosspin arrangement allows a few thousandths of an inch of lateral play in the locking lugs so that they self seat, as it were, against their abutment surfaces. It accomplishes the same thing as hand lapping the lugs and a lot less expensively.

The recessed bolt face hosts the familiar plunger-type ejector, while the extractor slides radially within a T-slot at the front of the right-side locking lug. An anti-bind groove in that same right-side locking lug contributes to smooth, wobble-free bolt travel. Mossberg's LBA trigger is user-adjustable from 2-7 pounds, though I can't imagine anyone wanting a trigger even close to 7 pounds.

The stock is the biggest change and what really separates the Patriot from the previous 4x4 models; let's face it, they were downright ugly! The unique bedding system of the 4x4 however, remains unchanged, in that there is a one-piece polymer bedding platform for the receiver that also serves as the well for the detachable magazine. This bedding chassis, if you will, simply drops down into the stock and is not permanently mated to it. This same assembly is found in all three stock types offered for the Patriot—an injection molded synthetic, a traditional walnut stock and a wood laminate.

One of the real strong points of the Patriot is its excellent detachable magazine; it's one piece of molded polymer with integral feed lips. It's feather light, virtually indestructible and one of the easiest loading we've ever encountered. The one thing about this gun we don't like is the unsightly protuberance sticking out on the left side of the bolt shroud. It's a safety thing

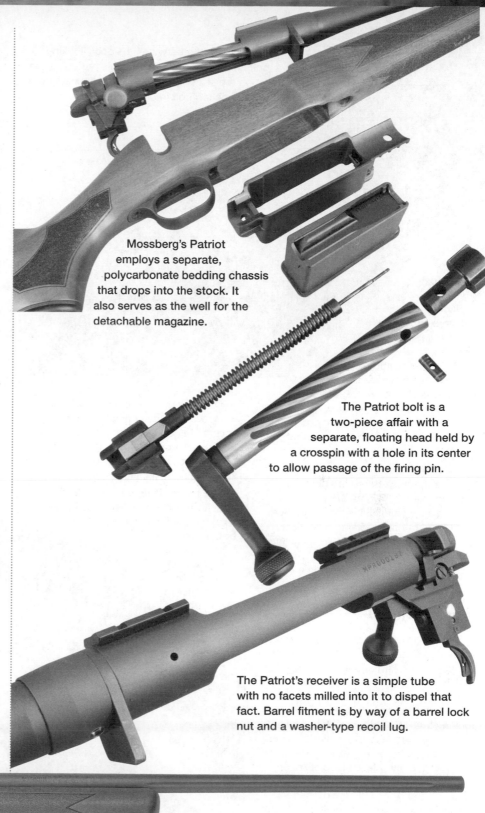

Mossberg's Patriot employs a separate, polycarbonate bedding chassis that drops into the stock. It also serves as the well for the detachable magazine.

The Patriot bolt is a two-piece affair with a separate, floating head held by a crosspin with a hole in its center to allow passage of the firing pin.

The Patriot's receiver is a simple tube with no facets milled into it to dispel that fact. Barrel fitment is by way of a barrel lock nut and a washer-type recoil lug.

New this year is Mossberg's Patriot, shown here with a synthetic stock. Also offered is a traditional walnut stock and a wood laminate with Marinecote metal finish.

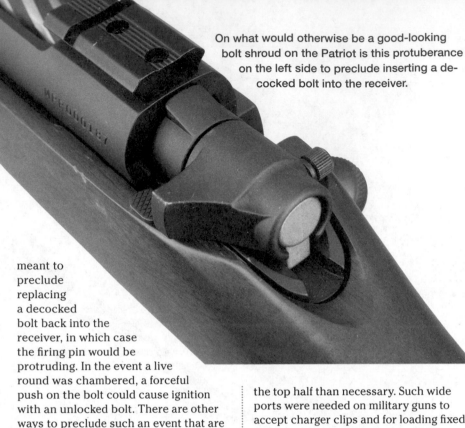

On what would otherwise be a good-looking bolt shroud on the Patriot is this protuberance on the left side to preclude inserting a de-cocked bolt into the receiver.

meant to preclude replacing a decocked bolt back into the receiver, in which case the firing pin would be protruding. In the event a live round was chambered, a forceful push on the bolt could cause ignition with an unlocked bolt. There are other ways to preclude such an event that are far more acceptable both mechanically and cosmetically.

The Patriot is offered in 11 calibers ranging from .22-250 to .375 Ruger. Prices range from $386 for the synthetic stocked version, to $584 for the black/gray wood laminate model with Marine-cote metal finish. Pre-mounted Weaver-type scope mount bases are included. www.mossberg.com

Remington 783

What's already been said about the Mossberg Patriot's bolt design and fab-rication, barrel fitment and receiver can also be said of this rifle, right down to the same extraction, ejection and anti-bind slot at the lower edge of the right locking lug. The bolt shroud, however, is much more attractive on this rifle. Even the bolt stop/release is exactly the same – a pivoting, one-piece blade of sheet steel with an upward extension that juts up just behind the left side of the re-ceiver bridge. A forward push pivots the front end downward out of the left lug raceway allowing bolt removal. It doesn't get any simpler… or more efficient.

The ejection port is of minimal dimen-sions, which makes this receiver substan-tially more rigid than most bolt actions that have far more material removed from the top half than necessary. Such wide ports were needed on military guns to accept charger clips and for loading fixed magazines from above, but most of the newer bolt actions have detachable boxes so those are no longer needed.

The trigger is Remington's user-adjustable CrossFire, which is housed in a robust nonferrous casting that's bolted to the receiver. It has a range of 2.5-5 lbs. and is conceptu-ally similar to Savage's Accutrigger, Ruger's Marksman and Mossberg's LBA. A two-position side safety blocks trigger movement but does not lock the bolt. The bolt stop/release is virtually identical to that described for the Mossberg Patriot, i.e., a one-piece pivoting blade.

The detachable magazine, which sits absolutely flush with the belly of the stock, is a sheet metal box with a polymer boot. The release lever is part of the magazine, not the stock, which we prefer. The stock itself is quite hand-some despite the fact that the shape of the fore-end tip and triggerguard bow are not mainstream. The swivel attachments are molded into the stock, but the triggerguard bow is a separate component. On most other budget rifles with molded stocks, the guard bow is integral.

While several rifles on the market claim to be pillar bedded, the 783 truly is. The only contact points for the entire barreled action are the two aluminum pillars through which the action screws

(below) The 783's ejection port is just large enough to do the job. It makes for a stiffer receiver, which can't hurt accuracy. The magazine is sheet steel with a polymer boot.

Like the Mossberg Patriot, Remington's 783 employs an unfaceted tubular receiver and the same barrel fitment system.

Left: The 783's CrossFire trigger is housed in a sturdy nonferrous casting and is user adjustable from 2.5-5 pounds.

Right: The 783 is a true pillar-bedded rifle in that the receiver does not contact the stock, but rather sits on the two bedding pillars through which the action bolts pass.

pass; their top surface is about .025" higher than the area surrounding them. At the butt end is Remington's SuperCell recoil pad that does a good job of attenuating felt recoil. All in all, the 783 is a sound, good-looking rifle at a rather astounding price. Consider that in 2015 it will be sold only as a package rifle with a pre-mounted and bore-sighted 3-9x40 scope at the almost unbelievable MSRP of $399 in all calibers. That means that realistic street price will be somewhere around $340! Chamberings offered are .223, .22-250, .243 and .308 in the short action, and .270, .30-06, 7mm Rem. and .300 Win. Magnums in long.
www.remington.com

Ruger American

Unlike the other three guns under review here, this is not a Mauser-type twin-lug action requiring a 90-degree bolt rotation. Rather, it's of the "fat bolt" school that employs a larger than normal bolt with forward locking lugs that are formed by machining away material at the head. In other words, measured across the locking lugs, the diameter is the same as that of the bolt body behind.

So instead of two opposed locking lugs, the one-piece American bolt has three, oriented on 120-degree centers, and as such require only a 70-degree handle lift. Dual cocking cams reduce the effort required to cycle the action, which with a shouldered gun makes reloading easier. The recessed bolt face houses the ubiquitous plunger ejector and an extractor very similar to the others in that it slides radially within a T-slot housed in the face of the right side locking lug. The bolt stop/release serves a third function in that it rides a lengthwise groove in the bolt body to prevent free rotation of the bolt when out of battery. Such an arrangement is necessary on fat-bolt actions because there are no protruding locking lugs riding raceways within the receiver.

Instead of employing a washer-type recoil lug, two steel V-blocks imbedded into the stock fore and aft of the magazine well engage matching grooves in the underside of the receiver. It's a clever and very efficient way to transmit recoil to the stock, as well as providing a bedding surface for the receiver. The barrel is, of course, free floating. The receiver is tubular, but two lengthwise facets milled at the 2 and 10 o'clock positions dispel that impression. Like the 783, the ejection port is just large enough to fulfill its function.

The one-piece polycarbonate magazine is among the very best we've seen on any rifle, domestic or foreign, regardless of price. It's a rotary type whereby the spring-loaded follower rotates around a shaft on the left side of the box. As cartridges are loaded, the follower backs up, storing them in a "C" orientation. The bottom of the magazine

The American's bolt at left is totally different from Ruger's flagship Model 77's Mauser-type bolt on the right.

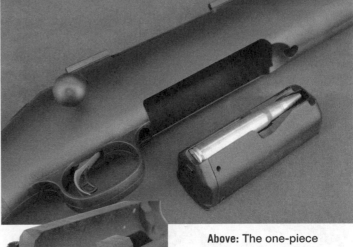

Above: Ruger's American is the only non-Mauser type action of the four rifles discussed in that it is a short-lift, three-lug action with a rotary magazine.

fits absolutely flush with the belly of the stock and is of matching contour. The trigger is Ruger's Marksman, which is user-adjustable from 3-5 pounds. The two-position top tang safety is as ergonomic as it gets; when engaged, it blocks trigger movement.

The American is offered in seven standard calibers ranging from the .223 Rem. to .30-06. If in the future it were to be chambered for magnum calibers, some major changes would have to be made to the bolt because the rim of the recessed face is too thin for the enlargement necessary to accommodate a .532" rim diameter. The American carries an MSRP of $449, which includes pre-mounted Weaver-type scope bases.
www.ruger.com

Right: Instead of a projecting recoil lug, two imbedded steel V-blocks engage slots on the underside of the receiver and provide its only support.

Below: The American exhibits clean lines plus the convenience of a tang safety.

Above: The one-piece polycarbonate rotary magazine of the Ruger American is one of the gun's salient features. It fits perfectly flush and matches the contour of the stock.

Savage Axis

It is somewhat ironic that the Axis series, which is Savage's least expensive centerfire rifle, shares a feature found only on the company's most expensive target/varmint and competition rifles: a minimal-size ejection port. Another unique feature on the Axis is a large scallop machined into the left side of the receiver, which reduces weight and lends some visual interest to what otherwise would be a straight tube.

Yet another difference between this gun and Savage's flagship Model 100-se-

This close-up shows the unique Ruger American bedding system.

ries (as well as all other domestic bolt-action rifles), is that there is no integral rear tang on the receiver. Normally, the rear tang anchors the trigger assembly, and has a deep notch machined into its right side into which the root of the bolt handle lowers, thus acting as a

nonbearing auxiliary safety lug in case of a catastrophic failure. On this rifle, the receiver bridge ends abruptly, and what looks like a rear tang is actually an extension of the trigger housing. Though a different arrangement, the end result is the same tang-mounted safety as found on all Savage 100-series rifles, except that the Axis has a two-position rather than a three-position safety.

With the barreled action removed from the stock, other differences between the 100-series rifles can be seen, differences that cut production costs without materially affecting mechanics

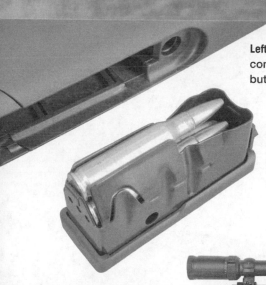

Left: The Axis magazine is comprised of rather thin sheet stock but it works quite well.

Right: Note the lack of a rear tang on the Axis (left) compared to the 100-series Savage rifles (right). What looks like a tang is actually an extension of the trigger housing on which the safety is mounted.

Savage's Axis rifle is the most economical of the four reviewed for this article. Shown here is the Axis II Package Rifle, which comes with a pre-mounted Weaver 3-9x40 scope and AccuTrigger.

or performance. The bolt cap and handle are different, as is the magazine geometry, and the triggerguard is a separate subassembly of the injection-molded polymer stock. Instead of the washer-type recoil lug sandwiched between the barrel and receiver, a steel plate is imbedded in the stock that engages a slot on the underside of the receiver. Both methods are equally effective.

We don't like everything about this rifle, particularly the stock – it's way too thin in the wrist even for our small hands, and the fore-end is too slender as well. The magazine works well enough and fits perfectly flush with the belly of the stock, but it's stamped from sheet stock that's not

Right: The Axis series (top) actually uses a different bedding system and receiver than Savage's flagship Model 100 series.

much thicker than a soup can. But again, none of these affect the rifle's accuracy or function.

The Axis is available in standard calibers ranging from the .204 Ruger to .30-06 at an MSRP of $362.
www.savagearms.com

All four of the rifles reviewed here have more in common than just being value priced – all are embarrassingly accurate! I say that because you can spend double or more for each company's flagship rifle and have them not shoot any better. Granted, you give up some degree of refinement like fit, finish, materials and caliber choice, but if you're interested in performance as well as price, you can't go wrong choosing any one of them.

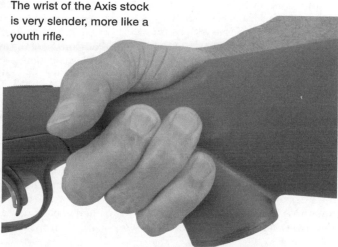

The wrist of the Axis stock is very slender, more like a youth rifle.

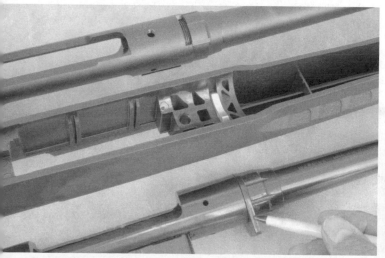

The 100 series (bottom) employs a washer-type recoil lug, whereas the Axis (top) employs steel blocks imbedded into the polymer stock, much like the Ruger American.

America's Enduring Big Bore

AFTER MORE THAN 140 YEARS, THE .45-70 REMAINS AN AMERICAN CLASSIC BY Dick Williams

Growing up a gun enthusiast, I read any firearms material I could find. For a long time I was a bit envious of the legendary, almost mystical treatment accorded to British big-bore rifles used in Africa. For over 100 years, if you didn't have a rifle with a bore size well over .40 inches or, even better, a big-bore double rifle, you might be able to book an African safari, but you would somehow be viewed as a second-class citizen throughout your trip. Admittedly our bison aren't as big as elephant or rhino, but they're bigger than Cape buffalo, and our grizzly bears are bigger and can be every bit as ferocious as the African lion and leopard. American big-bore single-shot rifles and lever actions have certainly proved effective on these creatures. It seemed a case of snob appeal overruling good judgment and com-

mon sense. If there is a prestige award for a classic big-bore rifle cartridge, it should go to America's .45-70.

Introduced in 1873, the .45-70 Government had the advantage of being the U.S. Army's official rifle caliber. Just as they did after the turn of the century with the .30-06, .308 and .223, Americans took advantage of the availability of both rifles and ammo, and continued using both after their military service was completed. As the designation suggests (.45-caliber bullet over 70 grains of black powder), the cartridge was developed and in production before the era of more energetic smokeless powders. But while the military later dropped the cartridge for a more efficient rifle and caliber, Americans not only continued to use the nonbottlenecked cartridge, they continued to build new and stronger rifles in which to shoot it.

The .45-70 was already an old cartridge when I was born, but I've had the pleasure of owning and shooting several different .45-70 rifles in my lifetime, including a couple that are quite modern while still possessing a touch of 19th century character. As a young man in the U.S. Air Force, I traded into a vintage trapdoor Springfield, the rifle initially issued to soldiers in 1873. There was a gravel pit near my house in the Maryland countryside and I did my bit for pollution by donating many pounds of lead back to Mother Earth in the form of home-cast and handloaded 405-grain Lyman bullets. These were delivered at around 1,300 feet per second according to the 43rd Lyman Reloading Handbook, copyright 1964.

The gravel pit was just over 200 yards across at its widest point and I had some great times with the trapdoor's flip-up ladder sight despite never really master-

Modern replicas of the Sharps rifle in .45-70 like this one are favorites of long-range, cast-bullet competitors. The Soule aperture rear sight provides lots of adjustment to compensate for the .45-70's rainbow trajectory.

ing it. Still, having a young man's 20-20 vision, any boxes, rocks or large cans were pretty easy targets at just about any point in the pit. In the hands of a trained 19th century soldier the trapdoor would have been deadly on the first shot, albeit a bit slow on the reload. I never seriously group tested the trapdoor, but in the two or three years I had the rifle, I don't recall a single failure to fire. Neither did I ever attempt to exceed the mild loads recommended for the old gun.

Upon leaving the service, I got lucky and traded into a genuine 1886 Winchester chambered in .45-70. Although the Lyman book offered slightly hotter reloads for the Winchester than the trapdoor, I continued with the 405-grain bullet load at 1,300 fps and thoroughly enjoyed the big repeater. It did not have an alternate sight for long-range shots, but with a full magazine I felt competent to defeat a band of rustlers, beat back a band of savage Indians, or gather buffalo meat for a thousand hungry railroad workers. And, of course, more lead was returned to Mother Earth. Unfortunately, someone smarter than I knew the real value of an '86 Winchester and sweet-talked me out of the gun.

During the '70s, Ruger introduced the No. 3, a carbine version of the company's No. 1 single-shot rifle. The No. 3 looked like the perfect elk gun when I moved to Colorado. Light and compact, yet strong enough to digest .45-70 loads rivaling the power of the .458 Winchester. I got one

and quickly learned that the little rifle was much tougher than I was. While the gun could take any reasonable load I fed it, I could only handle the recoil from the mildest .45-70 loads. In fact, I learned my recoil tolerance limit was reached much more quickly with rifles than with magnum handguns. I parted with the No. 3 and concealed my sissy tendencies.

Sometime in the '90s, Winchester/Browning came out with some newly manufactured 1886 Winchesters, one of which was a takedown model with a 26-inch barrel. This was the answer; a heavy gun to absorb some of the recoil yet storable in a small, inconspicuous case for travel. The takedown '86 and I had some good times and trips together, but not with the heavy loads as planned. The crescent moon shaped steel buttplate was simply not compatible with my aging shoulder. I was back to using

the lighter trapdoor Springfield loads, and even the factory 300-grain jacketed bullet loads quickly became less than enjoyable. Also, I had gotten into pig hunting, and while the lightweight jacketed hollowpoints would work on smaller pigs, I was unsure of how they would handle larger boars carrying some serious gristle plate for armor on their shoulders and sides.

I toyed with the idea of replacing the steel buttplate with a rubber pad, but it just didn't seem right on such a classy rifle. I also contemplated getting a modern bolt action with an absorbent recoil pad chambered in .45-70, but putting that classic cartridge into a bolt gun didn't seem appropriate. Slowly and reluctantly, the takedown Winchester and I eventually parted company.

By now you may be thinking that sometimes I'm not too bright or that I'm addicted to the .45-70 caliber. Frankly, there's some merit in both conclusions, but it's the second thought that speaks to the enduring qualities of the 140-year-old caliber. I can't leave it alone! Plus, in the last few years three things have

Good shooting skills rather than rapid fire make for a successful hunt as this young lady has demonstrated with her single-shot Ruger No. 1 in .45-70.

happened in the .45-70 world that have greatly influenced me.

First, I took another look at Ruger's No. 1 single-shot rifle. Here's a rifle of modern design that fits the shooter (or at least this shooter) better, thus helping to minimize felt recoil. It has a rubber buttplate and some more barrel weight up front to help tame recoil. It will handle ammo of whatever power level you can withstand. It is also designed to accept a scope, which adds a bit more weight and helps old guys see as well as young guys. Should you choose to do some precision shooting at extended ranges (or slightly

extended ranges, since this is a .45-70), the No. 1 has an excellent trigger with which to work. Finally, it is a classic single-shot, which captures the original essence of the .45-70 rifle of 1873.

Second, I've found some ammo that suits my needs perfectly. Garrett Cartridges of Texas makes two loads for .45-70 rifles, both with extremely hard cast bullets that will penetrate any hog that ever walked the planet. It's the lighter load that has my attention because it generates 18,000 CUP and can be fired in all .45-70 rifles –including trapdoors. It puts out a 420-grain bullet at around 1,350 fps, and that spells manageable recoil. That's almost exactly the load I started with five decades ago, except that the bullet is much harder and has a larger meplat for enhanced destruction upon penetration. Going

after soft-skinned quarry? Drop in any 300-grain JHP factory load and you're still within the operating parameters of every .45-70 rifle that's in reasonably good shape.

Third, a couple of new rifles have caught my attention in the last few years. Several years back I was introduced to big-bore Marlin rifles while writing an article on a custom takedown lever gun, called the Co-Pilot, made by Jim West at Wild West Guns of Alaska. It broke down into two pieces for storage under the pilot's seat of a small bush plane for guides or hunters who found themselves on the ground in remote brown bear country, which is basically all of Alaska. The rifle used ammunition even more powerful than .45-70 ammo at 35,000 CUP, and was equipped with a thick rubber buttpad to help absorb recoil.

A customized Marlin using hard cast lead bullets from Garrett Cartridges of Texas is a formidable and thoroughly modern hunting rifle.

Depending on hunting conditions, this custom Marlin can be set up to suit almost any hunter's needs.

Today Marlin makes a few different models of .45-70 lever actions, and I recently acquired a Model 1895 with 26-inch barrel. It balances beautifully and feels much lighter than the replica Winchester takedown I had years ago. Handling characteristics are great, and while the buttplate is hard plastic, its shape is much more friendly than the Winchester's was. I'm more than satisfied with the 420-grain Garret loads, plus I can load these in any .45-70 I happen to be using. If an opportunity for a trip to Alaska or Africa arose, I know the Marlin would be up for the heavier 540-grain Garretts. Whether or not I'd be ready is yet to be determined.

Last year while cruising one of my favorite local gun stores I came upon a used double-barrel rifle in .45-70. No, it was not a Holland & Holland or any other famous English manufacturer. It's made in Russia by Baikal and is called the Model MP-221. It has an attractive walnut stock and fore-end with a thick rubber buttpad. The rear sight is fixed and the front sight can be screwed in or out for elevation changes. The rear sight blade is not elaborate but has a simple U-shape notch that presents a sight picture more than adequate for the ranges at which I expect to be using it. Double triggers go with the double barrels, and the gun came with two sling swivels installed.

Most intriguing is a ratchet device on the bottom of the rifle between the two barrels that allows the barrels to be moved apart or together to regulate their convergence point. This being a tactical world, the gun was getting little attention sitting on the rack, so I was able to pick it up with a trade-in and some coin. We will be going pig hunting together in Texas this spring. As stated, it's not a Holland & Holland, but I'm impressed with the finish and how well it's made, so maybe I'll be getting a little bit snooty in the future.

While recently visiting a friend, he showed me a Harrington & Richardson Trapdoor Springfield Officer's model. I had only seen one of in these in my lifetime, I believe back in the '70s, and have cursed myself ever since for not acquiring it then. I tried to be suave and debonair when asking him if he might sell it, but I was salivating so heavily he saw right through my scheme. I don't think he'll ever sell it, but he did let me shoot it. It's basically a really dressy version of the original rifle from the late 19th century.

Below: A low mounted aperture rear sight and white-striped front blade present a precise sight picture that can be quickly acquired in varying light conditions.

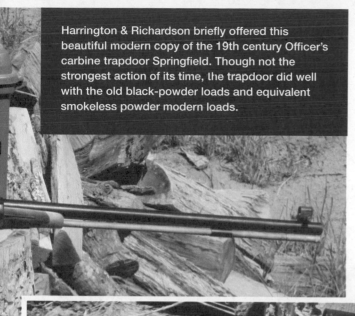

Harrington & Richardson briefly offered this beautiful modern copy of the 19th century Officer's carbine trapdoor Springfield. Though not the strongest action of its time, the trapdoor did well with the old black-powder loads and equivalent smokeless powder modern loads.

There is a very affordable single-shot .45-70 being manufactured today. It's called the Handi-Rifle and it's made by Harrington & Richardson. The top-break action and synthetic stock make it a great gun for new shooters, particularly any who may be taking the gun hunting. It has an external hammer for simplicity, a nice recoil pad and is set up for mounting a scope. Attach it to your ATV or throw it in your truck; it's a superb ranch gun.

As mentioned earlier, the .45-70 is more than 140 years old, yet new rifles continue to appear, as do new shooters interested in owning them. My love affair with the caliber has endured for almost 50 years, and it seems I can always find a "new" .45-70 or regenerate my interest in an older model that I might have once dismissed. Like Al Pacino said in The Godfather Part III, "Every time I almost get away, a .45-70 pulls me back in!" Or something like that.

The H&R Handi-Rifle .45-70 single shot is an excellent and inexpensive hunting rifle for big game. "Make every shot count" is the credo of hunting, and the single-shot Handi-Rifle is a great way to impress this on young hunters.

TOM BURGESS
Metalsmith Extraordinaire

Remembering a legend in the art of the custom rifle

BY Tom Turpin

here is an old saying that "the cream always rises to the top." The meaning is pretty simple. In every field of endeavor, regardless of what it is, there are always a few individuals that are so gifted, so motivated and so determined to do nothing less than their very best, that they slowly surpass their colleagues and rise to the top.

It has been said that luck plays a big role as well. I suppose it does play a role, but the importance of luck is overblown, at least when it comes to gunmakers. The really gifted ones tend to make their own luck, rather than sitting around on their backsides waiting for the tooth fairy to show up.

Tom Burgess was just such a craftsman and perfectionist. As a custom gun metalsmith he had few, if any, peers. As but one example of his tenacity, he needed a fixture to help him do a couple of milling cuts for the sights on an Enfield P17 action. He had no peers when converting military Enfield actions to large-caliber express rifles. He told

D'Arcy Echols that he spent 1,800 hours figuring out how to do the task of setting up and installing his iron sights, consisting of a fold-up peep rear and a pop-up front blade and making fixtures to accomplish it. Once he figured it out, it took him three hours to make the fixtures. They are still in use today.

Burgess was a native Washingtonian, born in Spokane, where he lived and worked until moving to Kalispell, Mont., in 1971. He lived in Kalispell until his passing. Tom took up gunmaking at an early age, building his first gun from scrap wood and metal at the ripe old age of 13. He started working at Columbia Gun Company while still in high school at Gonzaga High. He also attended Spokane Trade School while still in high school. Needless to say, he was a pretty busy youngster.

He continued that trait into adulthood, working both at building custom rifles and in the machine trade, mostly as a tool and die maker. Beginning in 1966, when he was 37 years old, he devoted his efforts solely to custom rifle work. All of us who appreciate the finest in custom rifle work owe debts of gratitude to Tom

Burgess for making that decision. We owe him not only for his own superlative craftsmanship, but also for setting the standard of excellence very high for all those after him to try to emulate. A friend of his told me that Burgess was extremely proud of some craftsmen that he helped along the way, Herman Waldron in particular. Burgess told Waldron that

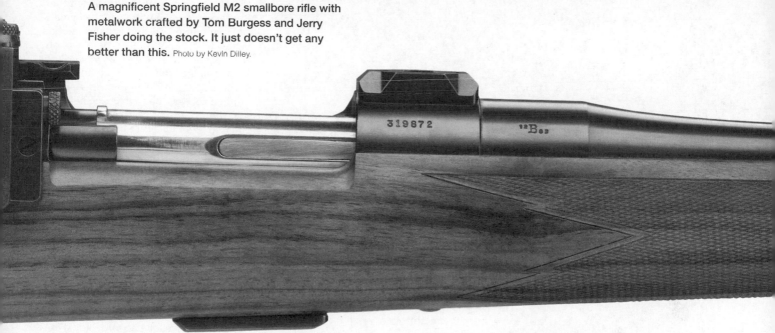

A magnificent Springfield M2 smallbore rifle with metalwork crafted by Tom Burgess and Jerry Fisher doing the stock. It just doesn't get any better than this. Photo by Kevin Dilley.

in his case, the student had surpassed the instructor—high praise indeed. Alas, Waldron is now gone as well as his instructor.

I am very pleased to have some of the last work coming out of the Waldron shop. Gary Goudy, a fantastic stockmaker and good friend of mine, used Herman for most of his metalwork. Gary was stocking a rifle for me and he found a couple things on the metalwork that he didn't like. He called me and told me about it and suggested that he would have Waldron correct the issues if I approved. Naturally, I agreed and that was done. Alas, Waldron passed away shortly after completing the work on my barreled action.

Once Burgess began devoting all of his time to his chosen craft, recognition for his excellence soon followed. Publications such as *Gun Digest* and *American Rifleman* published features on his work, along with many others. Jack O'Connor, the late and great dean of outdoor writers and certainly the most influential of his era, had a number of rifles that Burgess had worked on. He also wrote that a rifle that Burgess had crafted for Prince Abdorreza Pahlavi of Iran, brother of the Shah, had probably killed more big game around the world than any other rifle.

As with many highly talented and intelligent people, to the ordinary man like me, they seem rather odd in some aspects of their personalities. Burgess was no exception. He could, and did, ramble on in a conversation among his friends for lengthy periods of time, and after awhile it was readily apparent that only he understood what was being discussed. The other participants had not the foggiest idea of what the voluminous

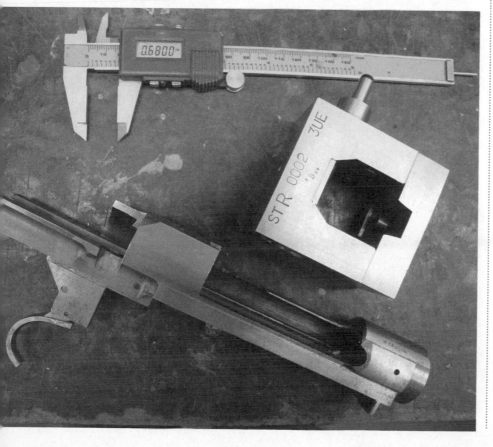

This is the fixture that took Tom Burgess 1,800 hours to figure out how he wanted it to work, and once that was done, he only needed three hours to build it. Photo by Tom Turpin.

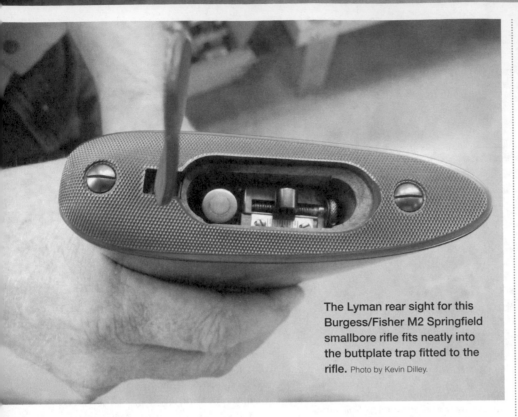

The Lyman rear sight for this Burgess/Fisher M2 Springfield smallbore rifle fits neatly into the buttplate trap fitted to the rifle. Photo by Kevin Dilley.

clue that the height of the front ramp on the M2 was not at all random. I felt that Burgess had planned to use the Lyman Globe intentionally and I confirmed this yesterday. I cut off the knurled head on the attachment screw for a Lyman Globe, made a simple fixture to then hold that screw so I could clean up the screws cupped recess, round over the head, and then slot this screw. As I suspected, the rear sight aperture bar just barely cleared the rear scope base and allowed the sight system to be perfectly zeroed. There is no latitude at all to make a lower, more svelte looking front sight as you would run out of any elevation correction to zero the currently installed irons. There is no doubt in my mind that when Burgess made the modified scope base system, he damn well engineered

amount of data Tom was dispensing meant or referred to. I personally never had the opportunity to sit in on one of Tom's dissertations, but I have listened to several audio tapes that he made. After a minute or so, he might as well have been conversing in Athabaskan, as I had no earthly idea what he was talking about.

In addition, the condition of his shop was mentioned by just about everyone I spoke with about him, not in a negative way, but simply as a matter of fact. It was apparently a disaster to everyone except Tom. That reminded me of a very fine custom gunmaker friend of mine who had a similar shop. He spent the majority of his time looking for a part or a tool. Outwardly, Tom's shop apparently looked very much like my friend's. The difference was that Burgess knew exactly where every item was in what to everyone else was a mess. My pal didn't.

Fantastic custom rifle maker D'Arcy Echols knew Burgess well. When I visited with Echols in his shop a year ago, he had a custom Springfield M2 .22 rimfire rifle in the shop that had been built by Burgess and stocked by Jerry Fisher several years earlier. As one might expect from such notable artisans, it was spectacular. When crafted, it was set up with both a scope and mounts and Lyman iron sights. Unfortunately, the front sight was missing. The owner of the rifle

was in a quandary as to what to do and brought it to Echols to determine a fix.

Echols told me, "I have learned all too well that when T. Burgess did something it was done with forethought and purpose. With this in mind I had a

Below: The rifle on the left was originally built for Jack O'Connor by Tom Burgess (metal) and Russell Leonard (stock) in 1951. Chambered for the 7x57 cartridge, O'Connor's wife Eleanor took a liking to the rifle and absconded with it. It was her primary hunting rifle for the rest of her life. The rifle on the right is a custom .30-06 built specifically for Eleanor by Lenard Brownell. It was her "heavy" rifle and she even shot an elephant with it.
Photos by Tom Turpin.

the Lyman sight heights in this manner."

As a premiere metalsmith, Burgess tended to work with a few select stockmakers. The first rifle I came across that Burgess had metalsmithed was a 7x57 custom Czech VZ24 Mauser that was made for Jack O'Connor in 1951. Eleanor O'Connor took a liking to the rifle and took it as her own, doing the vast majority of her hunting with it from then on. The rifle was stocked by Russell Leonard, a Spokane stockmaker. Whether he worked with Leonard on any other projects, I can't say, but since they were both Spokane based at the time, I suspect that they probably did. He worked several projects with Earl Milliron, as well as Maurice Ottmar and Jerry Fisher. D'Arcy Echols has also stocked a few Burgess barreled actions.

As his reputation grew, he did work for commoners, Princes, CEOs and outdoor writers. As already mentioned, he did several rifles for Jack O'Connor, including what became Eleanor's rifle. Not long after the 7×57, Burgess joined forces with Harvey Anderson and Alvin Oslin, both from Washington state, in building a custom .450 Watts Mauser for Jack's 1953 safari to Kenya and Tanganyika. Ander-son fitted the barrel and Oslin did the stockwork. Burgess did the rest. In 1966 Burgess did a Brevex Magnum Mauser action barreled and chambered for the .416 Rigby cartridge, and stocked by Bob Johnson for O'Connor who used it on a safari to Zambia in 1969. These two craftsmen also built a Mauser custom chambered in .338 Winchester for O'Connor around 1966.

Burgess joined forces with Earl Milliron to do at least three other O'Connor rifles that I am aware of. In 1966, Burgess did the metal work on a Mauser square-bridge action, installing the barrel and fabricating special scope mounts for the rifle. It was chambered in the .280 Remington cartridge. Milliron made the stock. Another was a Winchester Model 70 completed in 1968 chambered for the .338 Winchester round with Milliron creating the stock. The last one that I'm aware of was a prewar square-bridge Magnum Mauser in .375 H&H completed in 1971. Again the duo of Burgess and Milliron created the work.

Burgess had several items that somewhat became his trademarks. Among other things, he designed and made quick-detachable scope mounts that were as finely made as a Swiss watch. They functioned flawlessly. He also developed a front sight ramp that featured a pop-up front sight blade and a fold-down rear peep sight fitted into the scope mount base. He was an absolute master at converting military 1917 Enfield rifles into superb large-caliber

One of Burgess's famous Enfield conversions of a rough military rifle to a magnificent Express rifle chambered for the .416 Rigby cartridge. Burgess did all of the metalwork and D'Arcy Echols stocked the rifle. Photo by Kevin Dilley.

One of the trademark features of many Tom Burgess metalsmithing jobs was a front sight ramp with a spring-loaded flip-up front sight blade. He often paired this feature with a flip-up rear peep sight fitted into the rear scope base.
Photo by Victoria Wojciechowski of Creative Visions.

Tom Burgess really liked the G33/40 small-ring action. This one was well on its way to completion in his shop.
Photo by Tom Turpin.

express rifles. His version of these rifles bore no resemblance to the ugly military actions he started with.

Tom Burgess had six children, four boys and two girls. He set aside actions to build each of his kids a rifle. He also wanted his kids to participate in the building process, doing things such as grinding and polishing the action once it was set in the machinery. He also wanted them to even do some of the machining of some of the staple parts like sling swivels, safety levers, bolt handles and the like. All of the boys' rifles were built on Mauser G33/40 actions, Halfmoon barrels, Canjar triggers, along with Burgess bolt handles, safeties and other shop-made parts. To permit the rifles to be used before they were actually finished, they were stocked and glass bedded into whatever excess stocks happened to be lying around in the shop, usually a military Mauser stock. In a case or two, the metal was spray painted when there wasn't enough time to do a proper blue job. The bluing came later. Sometimes, much later.

The first of the boys' rifles to be actually finished was stocked by Maurice Ottmar, one of the last rifles he stocked before passing. Shortly after it was completed, it was used to take a moose and then an elk. Two other rifles were completed after Tom's passing by an outstanding rifle maker, Lee Helgeland. Lee completed the metalwork on the two rifles, installing Burgess trademark flip-up front sights and fabricating rear sights similar to what Burgess would have crafted. Lee then stocked

the rifles. The other son has not yet had his rifle finished as he actively uses it as a hunting rifle. He plans to have Lee finish it up in the near future. He also owns Tom's hunting rifle that was at one time finished, but over time Burgess cannibalized parts from it to complete customer rifles. It currently sports unfinished bottom metal, a scope with Burgess rings that does not fit the action, an unblued barrel and other odds and ends. It will also get finished one of these days.

The actions set aside for the two girls are still

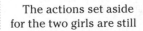

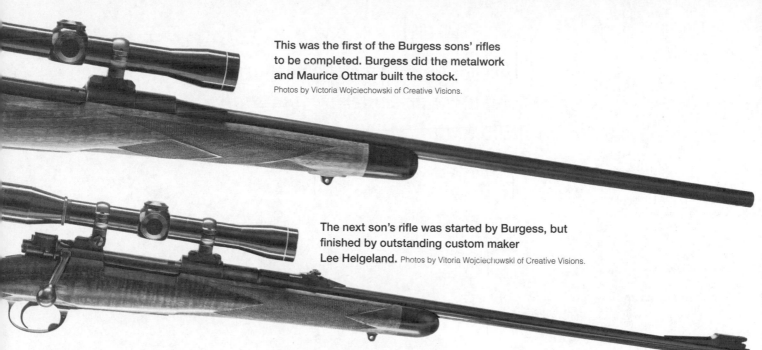

This was the first of the Burgess sons' rifles to be completed. Burgess did the metalwork and Maurice Ottmar built the stock. Photos by Victoria Wojciechowski of Creative Visions.

The next son's rifle was started by Burgess, but finished by outstanding custom maker Lee Helgeland. Photos by Vitoria Wojciechowski of Creative Visions.

there, but until rather recently they showed little interest in finishing them or hunting with them. With the work on the boys' rifles progressing, there is now renewed interest in the project and serious talk about finishing them up. Hopefully, they will get built over the next few years.

Tom Burgess may have been a bit eccentric around the edges, but he certainly knew exactly what he was doing with a Bridgeport in front of him.

Very few artisans, then or now, could equal his work, let alone better it. His rifles and his fixtures are works of art. Several that I know of are still in use every day, a tribute to the excellence of his engineering and fabrication skills. His quick-detachable scope mounts are unique and worth their weight in gold when a set can be found. His ability to diagnose problems and devise solutions to those problems was legendary. Echols

once drove almost 10 hours each way from Utah to Montana and back, to get Tom's help in fixing an issue that had him completely buffaloed. Echols is no dummy at figuring out gun problems, but this one stumped him. Burgess figured it out, fixed it in very short order, and had Echols on his way back to Utah.

The likes of Tom Burgess are not soon apt to pass this way again. He was one-of-a-kind.

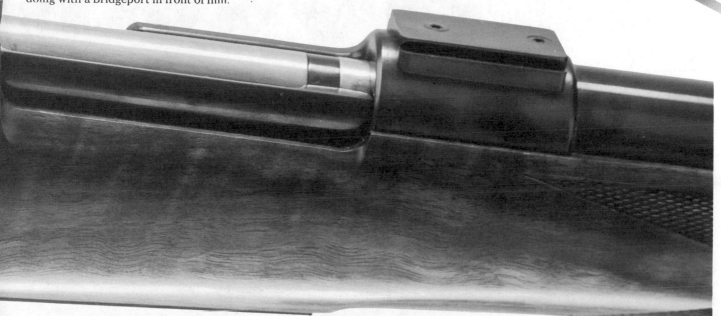

This son's rifle was also started by Burgess and finished by Lee Helgeland. Note the trademark folding rear peep sight that fits into the rear scope mount base when not in use. Photos by Victoria Wojciechowski of Creative Visions.

This company makes a vast array of rimfire, metallic centerfire and shotgun ammunition, and tailors its products to the needs of specific groups of shooters.

Fabulous FIOCCHI

BY Steve Gash

Fiocchi is a familiar name to most American shooters, and for good reason. The company was started in 1876 when Giulio Fiocchi took over a small black-powder factory in Lecco, Italy. Fiocchi USA was founded in 1983 and in 1987 a large modern plant was constructed in Ozark, Mo., where millions of rounds of ammunition are made annually.

Recently, Fiocchi USA invited a gaggle of gun scribes to the Desert Lakes Shooting Club near Las Vegas to demonstrate the company's shotshell line. Marketing VP Carlo Fiocchi, grandson of founder Giulio, summarized the strategy behind their products. Carlo pointed out that Fiocchi provides American shooters with "something just a little different, but with a European flair," and that "shotshells are the backbone

of the company." He emphasized that there is considerable family pride in the business. After all, he said, "Our name is on every box."

Clay-target shooters have diverse but definite ideas on what load should be applied to a particular target. To that end, Fiocchi makes a comprehensive caboodle of target loads that vary both in shot size and velocity within charge weights, with a few specialty loads thrown in. Shot sizes are mostly 7½ and 8, although 8½ and 9 are available in several loads, and the results are shown in the corresponding tables. I used an Oehler M-35P chronograph system to check velocities, as does the Fiocchi lab in Ozark, so the results are pretty much an apples-to-apples comparison. The velocities I recorded were pretty close to the listed velocities. In

my experience, measured shotshell velocities are always lower than those listed.

The traditional clay target load is a 3-dram equivalent charge under 1-⅛ ounces of shot at a nominal 1,200 fps, and it works very well. But there is the omnipresent recoil, which gradually contributes to the "fatigue factor," and on a 100-round or longer course it makes a difference. Many sporting targets are neither super-fast nor long-range, however, so 1-⅛ ounces of lead is a bit of overkill.

For those close ones, try the 1-ounce loads. The 12TL load at a velocity of 1,150 fps doesn't beat you up, but still convincingly crushes targets. As ranges lengthen, that same charge can be launched at 1,200 (12TH) or 1,250 (12TX) fps. The 12CRSR Crusher at 1,300 fps and

Fiocchi makes a bewildering array of target loads in virtually all gauges. These 12-gauge shells include the low-recoiling 1-ounce loads, the versatile 1-1/16-ounce ammo and the powerful 1-1/8-ounce fodder.

the 12SCRS Super Crusher at a sizzling 1,400 fps are great long-range choices for the fastest targets.

Should conditions warrant, one can go up a shot size and to the 1-1/16-ounce loads to maintain the appropriate pattern density. This unique weight is relatively new and is making inroads in the clay-target world.

Here there are three power levels: 1,175, 1,225 or 1,275 fps. The advantages of the 1 1/16-ounce load are twofold: more pellets than 1 ounce, but less recoil than the 1 1/8-ounce ammo. My personal favorite is the load known as the Target Lite 16. At 1,175 fps it recoils lightly, and 1 1/16 ounces of #7½ has 372 pellets, only 38 less than 1 ounce of #8.

Target loads with 1-1/8 ounces of shot are well represented. The light recoiling 12VIPL at 1,150 fps is always a good

SHOTSHELLS

The quantity of components in the plant is staggering. Here, a bin of new primed 20-gauge shotshell hulls await transfer to the other side of the building where they'll be loaded onto automated machines.

FIOCCHI TARGET SHOTSHELL CHRONOGRAPH DATA

LOAD NUMBER	LOAD TYPE	OUNCES OF SHOT	SHOT SIZE	LISTED VEL. (FPS)	MEASURED VEL. (FPS)	SD
1278OZ	12 Ga. Trainer	⅞	7½	1,200	1,142	8
12TL	Target Lite 1	1	8	1,150	1,148	10
12 TH	Target Heavy 1	1	7½	1,200	1,206	8
12TX	Little Rino	1	8	1,250	1,220	8
12CRSR	Crusher	1	8	1,300	1,262	14
12SCRS	Super Crusher	1	8	1,400	1,312	7
12TL16	Target Lite 16	1 1⁄16	7½	1,175	1,126	16
12TH16	Target Heavy 16	1 1⁄16	7½	1,225	1,177	31
12TX16	New Rino 16	1 1⁄16	8	1,275	1,218	17
12VIPL	VIP Light	1 ⅛	8	1,150	1,129	12
12VIPH	VIP Heavy	1 ⅛	7½	1,200	1,174	16
12WRNO	White Rino	1 ⅛	7½	1,250	1,258	13
12HEL	Nickel Helice	1 ¼	7-N	1,350	1,266	31

Note: The test gun was a 12 gauge Browning Lightning Citori Special Sporting Clays Model with 28-inch barrels and skeet chokes. All shells were 2¾ inches in length.

The Fiocchi Helice load is a real thumper: 1¼ ounces of nickel-plated #7 registered 1,266 fps over the chronograph.

choice, as is 12VIPH zipping along at the traditional 3-dram equivalent velocity of 1,200 fps. The White Rhino load achieves top velocity of 1,250 fps.

But for a lot of sporting clays and about 99 percent of all skeet shooting, a 12-gauge shell with ⅞ ounce of shot is nigh on to perfect. In this case Fiocchi's 1278OZ at 1,200 fps is just the ticket.

At the other end of the power continuum is Fiocchi's 12HEL load. "HEL" stands for Helice, in which the unique targets simulate the flight of live birds and are unbelievably difficult. Fiocchi's Helice load features 1¼ ounces of #7, 7½ or 8 nickel-plated shot at a blistering 1,350 fps. Sure, it kicks, but anything centered with it usually eats dirt. I might add that it is a great hunting load, too. Helice must really be catching on, as Fiocchi sells a lot of Helice ammunition here in the USA.

I was also able to tour Fiocchi's ultra-modern facility in southwest Missouri. The plant is nestled in the heart of the Ozarks, where deer and turkeys wander the scenic glades of the large fenced property with complete impunity.

I was very impressed with the efficient layout of the plant and production procedures. Mark Halstead directs production, which is logically divided into two parts: centerfire and shotshell. Randy Russell

watches over the former and Wesley Swafford takes care of the shotshell line. Throughout both plants production folks were in good cheer and obviously enjoying their jobs of producing high-quality ammo. Tour guide and Chief Operations Officer Donna Swafford mentioned that the company has been working four 10-hour days for 10 years – long before it was politically correct – and that this schedule really contributes to employee morale.

Fiocchi uses plastic cases, their own No. 616 primers and American powders in their shotshells. Cases are manufactured in Italy. Shotshell hulls (about 7 million annually) arrive primed, but metallic cases are primed at the plant. Shotshell cases are made by the Reifenhauser process, and feature a 10.5mm plastic basewad. The head is either brass or brass-plated steel. The ribbed plastic tube is lightly skived at the mouth to aid crimping. Shells are finished with either a six-point or an eight-point crimp, depending on the load.

The firm buys lead-alloy shot in this country, but the nickel-plated shot is imported from Italy. The lead shot has either a 3 or 5 percent antimony content, depending on its intended use, and nickel-plated shot has 3.2 percent. A variety of loads with treated steel

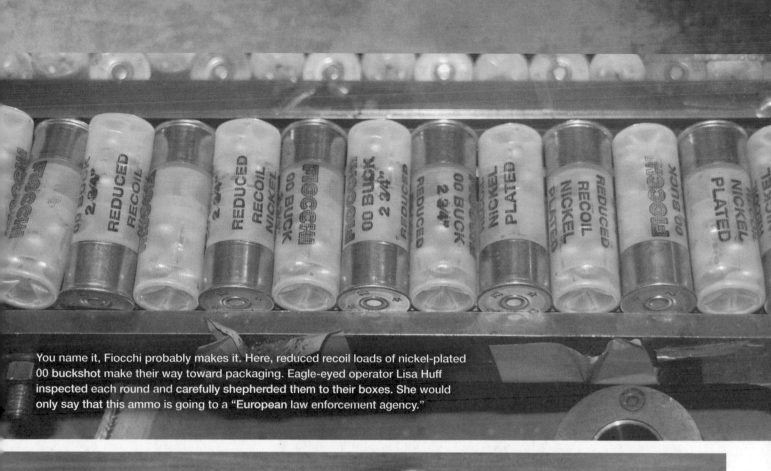

You name it, Fiocchi probably makes it. Here, reduced recoil loads of nickel-plated 00 buckshot make their way toward packaging. Eagle-eyed operator Lisa Huff inspected each round and carefully shepherded them to their boxes. She would only say that this ammo is going to a "European law enforcement agency."

Many shooters use Fiocchi No. 616 primers for their target ammo. The plastic cases make perfect handloads with a variety of readily available components, and form solid, tight crimps for consistent ballistics.

FAVORITE FIOCCHI HANDLOADS

POWDER	CHARGE (GRAINS)	WAD	SHOT WEIGHT & SIZE	VELOCITY (FPS)	SD (FPS)
Red Dot	16.5	WAA-12SL	⅞-oz. #7½	1,197	21
CLAYS	18.8	CB-1100	1-oz. #8	1,198	12
CLAYS	20	Fed-12S3	1 1⁄16-oz. #7½	1,237	11
Inter'l. Clays	18	WAA-12	1 ⅛-oz. #8	1,149	13

Notes: The test gun was a 12-gauge Browning Lightning Citori Special Sporting Clays Model with 28-inch barrels and skeet chokes. All cases were Fiocchi plastic 2¾ inches in length.

At the range, Vice President of Marketing Carlo Fiocchi described the upcoming shot, and described each type of ammo to be tested.

The author shooting skeet with Fiocchi 20VIP 20-gauge loads with ⅞ ounce of #8 in a 1970 vintage Browning Superposed. At a velocity of 1,152 fps, this ammo easily broke targets and the recoil was not a factor. (R. Gash photo)

shot (both target and hunting) are also produced. Fiocchi uses top-of-the-line Baschieri & Pellagri or Gualandi one-piece plastic wads, which are also imported from Italy. For the reloading purists, it should be noted that these wads can be obtained from Ballistic Products, Inc., the well-known purveyor of all things shotshell.

The production lines are relatively short and hence quite flexible. Loads within gauge can be changed in about 35 minutes; a switch to another gauge takes only a little longer. Fiocchi makes many different target loads and also produces specialized hunting rounds. The Golden Pheasant loads are extremely popular in the cornfields of Kansas.

On the production line, finished shotshells roll down a trough toward the packaging station, where a metal disk grabs every other shell and turns it 180 degrees so the brass heads end up in the familiar alternating pattern in the 25-round boxes. Each round is hand inspected as it makes its journey down the line.

During the tour I noticed the shotshell building is set up with a very interesting layout. Production machines are on one side of a dividing wall and component storage on the other. Over on the component side, huge bins of cases and wads are neatly stacked at the ready, and a series of colored lights above the production floor signal when a particular component at a certain production machine is running low. When the appropriately colored light comes on, a forklift operator quickly hoists a bin high atop the ceiling over the production side where it's needed, and gravity takes over from there. It was pretty slick. Seeing multiple pallets of finished cases of ammo in the warehouse almost made me light headed. A large inventory is kept on hand so that orders can be filled quickly. The plant is environmentally friendly, and everything reusable is recycled.

After finishing the factory tour I visited the nearby Ozark Shooters Sports Complex near Branson, Mo., and shot sporting clays and skeet with Fiocchi

ammo. All that fun shooting produced quite a lot of empties. It always pains a dedicated reloader to throw away a perfectly good hull, and Fiocchi hulls reload beautifully. Even with component prices on the rise, a fellow can still economize with reloads, and I have developed several good recipes with Fiocchi hulls and their No. 616 primers, shown in the accompanying chart. They are loosely patterned after the multiweight charges pioneered by the company. Rather than order the Italian wads, I just used what I had on hand, and everything worked out fine. Crimps were near picture-perfect, and ballistic uniformity was good.

Scattergunners are fortunate that Fiocchi "invaded" the USA over 20 years ago, as their distinct product line serves large portions of the shotshell market. The next time you're at a sporting clay, skeet or trap range, keep an eye out for those colorful blue Fiocchi hulls. Chances are that you'll see lots of them.

ESSENTIAL RELOADING TOOLS

For safe, successful handloading,
it's critical to have the right equipment

By **Philip Massaro**

For most of his reloading work, the author prefers a single-stage press.
Massaro Media Group & J.D. Fielding Photography Photos

Once you have an understanding of what a cartridge is made of, from a handloading perspective, the next important step is to look at the tools you'll need to reform and assemble a cartridge. There's a long list of tools available to the reloader; some are a necessity and some simply make life easier. The setup you choose can be as simple or complex as you'd like, so long as it is effective, and by effective I mean that whether you're using all new components or brass cases that have been previously fired, you will need to be able to control the dimensions and weights of the components you are going to use.

First thing you're going to need is a clean, quiet place, one removed from distraction, in which to do your loading. A workbench with good lighting is what I prefer. Beyond that, let's look at each of the necessary tools individually.

Reloading Presses

Your reloading press is the important piece of gear used to obtain a leveraged mechanical advantage, something that's needed for resizing brass from its fired dimensions back to its original specifications, and also for properly seating a bullet in a sized case. Presses come in many shapes and sizes and are produced by a number of companies.

For most of my rifle loading work, I prefer a "single-stage" press. The single stage press performs only one operation of the various reloading steps each time the handle is worked. For me, the single-stage allows me to "feel" the resizing operation and ensures the bullets are seated the same exact way every time I pull the handle. Most single-stage presses are of the "C"-type or the "O"-type, named for the shape of their respective frames.

In addition to progressive presses, many companies offer a turret press. While still technically a single-stage by definition, the top portion of the press contains a rotating turret, which can hold three or more reloading dies at once (we'll get to dies in a minute). This turret allows the reloader to perform three or four operations without changing the dies, as you would have to do in a straight-forward single-stage press. Some folks have frowned upon the turret press, for having too much play in the turret and not holding to the tight tolerances found in a true single-stage press. I have a Redding T7 turret press that I dearly love and I can attest to using a Lee turret press with my dad to load tens of thousands of very accurate rounds. To each their own. Whatever press you choose, make sure it is securely bolted to your bench, in a comfortable place, and that you are thoroughly familiar with its operation before you set your first case in the first die.

Reloading Dies

Your reloading dies are the screw-in tools that reform spent brass into its proper dimensions, punch out the spent primer (the process known as "decapping"), flare the case mouth in the case of straight-walled cartridges and seat the bullet into the case. A set of dies is specific to the cartridge you are reloading and, save for a few pistol cartridges, are not interchangeable. Reloading dies are a precisely machined image of a cartridge's specified shape within the tolerances allowed by SAAMI specifications.

So what happens with the dies? The first die you'll use is the resizing die. The press (using its mechanical advantage) squeezes the fired brass into the die and, because brass is a malleable metal, the steel (or carbide) die reforms it back into proper shape. The resizing die also has a centered decapping pin, used to remove the spent primer, and this pin is located below the expander ball.

The process of resizing and decapping works like this. On the upstroke of the press's ram (the ram moves up when you lower the handle of the press), the brass case is driven up into the die body and the neck or mouth portion (depending on whether it is a bottleneck cartridge or straight-walled cartridge) is squeezed down to a dimension smaller than caliber size. On the downstroke of the ram (when you raise the press handle back up), the case is drawn over the expander ball to open the case neck or mouth to a dimension of .001- or .002-inch less than the bullet diameter so that, when the bullet is seated into the reformed case, there is proper tension between the bullet "shank" (its sides) and the sidewalls of the case.

Next up is the bullet seating die. This die is used for the final step in cartridge assembly. It has a depth-adjustable cup, centered in the die, that pushes on the bullet's nose (its "ogive") when the ram is raised. This allows for precise adjustment of the seating of a bullet into the case. This die is also capable of installing a crimp of the case mouth onto the bullet, to further hold the bullet in place. Whether or not you want to put a crimp on a cartridge depends on the case you are loading and the situation at hand. Your reloading manual and the cartridge's specifications should dictate which policy is correct for your round and load. Straight-walled cartridges require a third die that will flare the case mouth to receive the new bullet. There is also a fourth kind of die known as a neck-sizing die. This is a special die, one usually reserved for bolt-action rounds. It resizes only the neck portion of the cartridge and is used in lieu of the full-length resizing die.

Shellholders

Shellholders are another tool you will need. These are variously sized attachments that usually slide into the mouth of the press's ram. They are machined to hold the head of a particular cartridge and are numbered according to the size of the case head. Thus, one shellholder will often fit many different cartridges.

It is very important that you have the proper shellholder for the cartridge you are loading, or you can easily tear off a rim or stick a case in a resizing die—not good times I assure you!

Priming Tools

There are two ways to reprime the cartridge case, either in a handheld priming tool or in a priming device attached to a reloading press. Using the handheld primer, the case is loaded into the device, a new primer inserted, and a lever is squeezed to seat the primer into the case. When the priming tool is attached to the reloading press, the primer is inserted into the priming cup and, on the upstroke of the press handle, the primer is seated into the case.

I most often use a priming tool attached to my press. It allows for a more efficient and faster operation, and I can still "feel" the primer seat to the slightly recessed level I prefer. Primer seating should be flush to the case or a little bit deeper, which is what I prefer, but be careful about going too deep. Your press can create a whole bunch of force, sometimes more than you need and something that will seat your primer too deep in the case. I have also used handheld priming tools to great effect.

Powder Measuring Tools

Measuring powder is a process that requires the utmost and serious attention. An undercharge or overcharge can result in destruction and death. Nope, I'm not trying to scare you into taking up quilt-

Reloading dies are specific to the cartridge you are loading and are used to reform brass, remove spent primers, flare case mouth and seat the bullet into the case.

ing instead, just being up front about what can go wrong. If you take what I say to heart, the chances of destruction (or worse) are remote at best. So, with that in mind, an accurate means of measuring powder is a *necessity*.

The traditional method for weighing powder and the one I most often employ is via the beam scale. It is capable of measuring weights down to a tenth of a grain. Gravity never wears out, and a well-calibrated beam scale will become an old friend. My RCBS 505 scale has been with me for a long time and it is a great value. I also love the Redding Model No. 2 for its durable construction. I doubt you would wear out the hardened chrome bearing surfaces in a lifetime of loading. Whatever make or model you choose, a set of calibrating weights can help to keep things in working order.

There are also many good digital scales. They display to the nearest tenth of a grain and can be easily calibrated. But, because they work on piezo pressure, rather than true gravitational weight, digital scales tend to need to be zeroed often. I have an RCBS ChargeMaster that

is among the best of the digital scales, and though I verify its reading often with a reweigh on a balance beam scale, it has yet to give me an erroneous reading.

Should you decide to purchase a mechanical powder dispenser—there are both mechanical dispensers and hand "tricklers" that allow you to control the finest increments of a powder charge—to make the loading process quicker, the powder scale should be used to check the charge being dispensed at frequent intervals.

Case Trimmers

Another tool you will need is a "case trimmer." Brass is malleable and, over repeated firings, will stretch or "flow." When the cartridge case becomes too long, it must be trimmed back to the proper length. It is *crucial* that the brass you intend to load be trimmed to the correct, specified length.

Trimming the brass is an important step in making good ammunition. It ensures the proper dimensions of a reloaded cartridge. Some case trimmers are hand-cranked affairs, the devices

bolted down to the reloading bench and carefully set to the proper measured length. Others are machined tools of specific length and diameter, screwed into a cutting piece and inserted into the case to then trim it to proper length. Several flicks of the wrist will do the trick. There are also some great motorized trimmers, like the RCBS Case Preparation Station, which can be fine-tuned to trim to very precise dimensions and take the wear and tear off of your hands and wrists. They cost a bit more than the hand-powered models, but if you get the loading bug (and you will!), they save an appreciable amount of time and give wonderful results.

Being able to observe the dimensions of your resized case is necessary. A micrometer is a precise measuring tool designed to measure in inches and decimal portions of an inch. Case length, cartridge overall length (COL for short), neck diameter and rim diameter are a few of the dimensions you will want to be able to verify. A micrometer capable of measuring to the ten-thousandth of an inch is what you want to own.

Chamfer/Deburring Tool

The chamfer/deburring tool is a little brass cutting wonder designed to remove any burrs on the inside and outside of the case mouth, while, at the same time, putting a nice, beveled edge on the inside of the case mouth. This bevel is referred to as a "chamfer." The chamfer tool has a tapering diameter, so as to be used in case mouths from .17-inch to .500-inch or bigger.

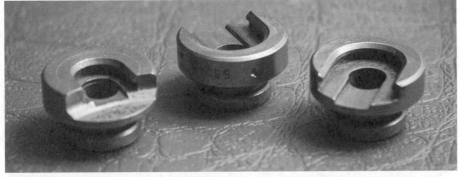

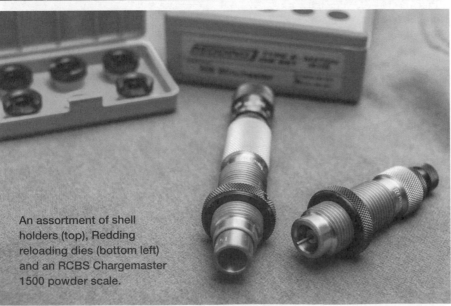

An assortment of shell holders (top), Redding reloading dies (bottom left) and an RCBS Chargemaster 1500 powder scale.

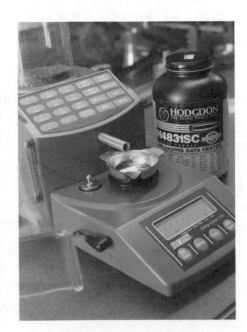

A few twists will clean up the outside of a burred case mouth easily. A clean, well-chamfered and -deburred case mouth will aid in seating the new bullet and in the chambering of a cartridge. There are handheld models that work very well, but they can give you blisters and sore wrists, if you're loading a lot at one time. Some models mount to motor-driven case prep stations and not only speed up the process, but save hand fatigue. The chamfer process is usually only necessary on bottlenecked cases, but I like to deburr all my cases, including the straight-walled rifle and pistol cartridges.

Primer Pocket Cleaner

The primer pocket cleaner is a steel scraping tool that removes the burnt residue left behind by the fired primer that was in residence before you decapped your case. Many of these cleaners are dual-sided, with one side for large primer pockets and the other for small. Some other models are constructed of small steel wire brushes, which will clean the pocket in a rotary action, rather than scrape the debris away. Cleaning the primer pocket will ensure that the spark of the new primer can easily reach the fresh powder charge and help to see the new primer is properly seated.

Case Cleaning Tumbler Tools

Brass is a malleable metal, yet tarnishes very easily. It must be cleaned before being resized to make sure your resizing dies give you a lifetime of good service. Using an abrasive media, such as ground corncobs or crushed walnut shells, the case tumbler vibrates a load of dirty brass in its vessel until that brass is once again shiny and clean.

There are also many chemical solutions that can hasten the brass cleaning process, and I often use these in conjunction with corncob or walnut media. Tumblers come in a variety of sizes, with some capable of holding up to 1,000 pistol cases at a time. The type of reloading you intend to do should dictate the size tumbler you require.

There are ultra-sonic cleaners available, like the Lyman Turbo Sonic Cleaner, which vibrate the cases in a solution. These work much faster than traditional media tumblers. The big thing I like about cleaning ultrasonically is the way these machines clean the *inside* of the brass cases.

Having the *inside* of the case cleaned can greatly affect the accuracy potential of your cases, in a good way, as the case volume becomes more uniform when the burnt residue from the previous firing is removed from fired cases. An added benefit to ultrasonic cleaners is that they can also be used to periodically remove the grit, brass, lube, and other accumulated dirt from your reloading dies. (You'd be shocked to see what comes out of them!)

I found a chemical cleaning solution available from Iosso, which removes almost all the residue from your dirty brass. The kit comes with a cheesecloth-style pouch. You place the dirty brass in the pouch, dunk it in the chemical cleaner for 20 to 60 seconds, and then rinse in clean water. Simple, easy, and effective, though I'd recommend a light tumbling after any chemical or ultra-sonic cleaning, to put a nice shine on your cases. Neatness counts.

Case Lube

Before squeezing a fired case into a reloading die, that case must be lubricated. If not, you risk having the case getting wedged in the resizing die during the process. Case lubricants come in waxes, sprays, gels, etc. There are lots of good options.

Most gels and sprays are required if you choose to use a lube pad, a sponge-like material upon which the cases are rolled, the lube in the pad thereby evenly dispersing itself on the entire case. This process of lubrication is a fickle thing.

Too much lubricant and you will have hydraulic dents in the shoulder section of a bottlenecked case. Too little will result in a stuck case. I have always used the RCBS Case Lube and a lube pad in my work. I know how much to use, and the lube comes off the cases rather easily, with just a light wiping after sizing.

Case Brush

These little gems, of varying calibers, will help remove any excess lube or media from inside the case neck of your clean cases so they are good to go. They're kind of self-explanatory.

Case Loading Blocks

Case loading blocks can be a great aid. They are designed to hold the cartridges you are loading, simple as that. Case blocks are a small platform or tray in which holes have been drilled or formed to a specific rim diameter, so that the cases don't fall over or roll off the reloading bench. They can be made of pre-formed plastic, or you may make your own by drilling properly sized holes into a wood block.

Flash Hole Reamer

The flash hole is the only means of getting the primer's flame into the powder charge. While most of today's cases are manufactured to high tolerances, sometimes small burrs or slightly out-of-round flash holes appear. A reamer or a drill bit of exact flash hole diameter (0.08-inch) can clean up the flash hole and make sure you get consistent ignition.

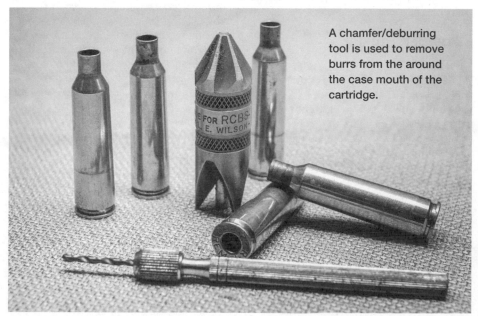

A chamfer/deburring tool is used to remove burrs from the around the case mouth of the cartridge.

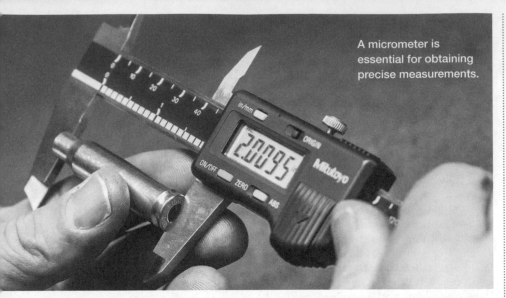

A micrometer is essential for obtaining precise measurements.

Powder Funnel

Once the powder charge has been weighed, getting it into the case requires a funnel. I like a quality plastic funnel that resists static electricity. Such a funnel eliminates any powder clinging to the funnel walls. Most of the common funnels are dimensioned for use in cases of .22-caliber through .45-caliber, though there are specialty funnels, too.

Loading the diminutive .17 Remington (as Col. Le Frogg has me load so often), requires a special funnel with a smaller hole in the end, to make sure the powder doesn't spill out around the mouth of the tiny case. If you load any of big .470s or .500s, you will need a bigger-mouthed funnel. Some cases, such as the Winchester Short Magnums and Remington Ultra Magnums, have a very sharp shoulder and short neck, so the most common funnels available will give you headache. Because of the length of the common funnel's mouth, powder can easily spill around the cartridge shoulder.

Powder Thrower

A powder thrower is a dispenser of powder. It uses a large plastic vial to hold the store of powder and has a mechanism to throw a predetermined, measured amount of powder. The hand-operated variety works like this: On the up crank of the handle, the adjustable chamber is filled with powder; on the down crank, that charge is dispensed out of the lower tube and onto the pan of the scale.

The electronic age has seen the development of automated powder measurers with digital displays. The operator punches in the desired charge weight and, via an electronic motor, the machine dispenses the powder onto a digital scale until the exact amount has been poured out. I do appreciate and use the digitized devices, but I am still a fan of hand-weighed charges and beam scales.

The Redding Model No. 3 powder measure and the RCBS UniFlow powder measure are a couple of my favorite models, as they are easy to use and throw a very accurate amount of powder. The Redding LR-1000 is designed for the shooter who loads powder charges upwards of 100 grains, and it can be a great asset to the shooter who is loading for the big safari magnums or something like the .338 Lapua. It sure beats scooping out 100-plus grains of powder for each case!

Powder Trickler

I mentioned a powder trickler before, but here's more on what this tool does. While weighing powder charges, whether you scoop the powder out or use a powder measure to throw powder onto the scale's pan, you will need to add in that last little bit to make the charge weight perfect. This is where the powder trickler comes in. Shaped a bit like an hourglass, it has a longitudinal tube threaded like a worm screw, which delivers small amounts of powder when you twist the knob. The last few tenths of a grain are precisely delivered into the pan. I have a well-worn RCBS powder trickler that has served me very well for more than 20 years of reloading.

Primer Tray

Primer trays are designed to hold the primers you intend to seat in the cases. A handy tool like this eliminates the awful chore of picking up primers off the floor on hands and knees once you've dropped them. I've done it and, inevitably, you will, too. There are better ways to pass the time than searching under the bench for the last three or four lost primers, so the cost of these simple trays is a good investment.

Reloading Manuals

I use the plural in this title because, sooner or later, you will need more than one. Nearly all the manufacturers of component bullets and/or powder offer a reloading manual for sale; for those produced by bullet makers, those manuals are specific to each company's bullets. The loads are developed and researched on high-tech pressure testing machines, using a variety of powders that are viable with a particular cartridge. Such data can tell you which powder performed best during the company's testing and provide you with the velocities obtained in the test rifle. Each cartridge covered usually comes with a brief history, and some will provide some helpful loading instructions.

Note that not every powder that can perform well is tested by every company. Most often, the ballisticians choose what they feel are the powders that should perform well in a given case and test those.

This can pose a problem, if you have a great quantity of a powder that you like, yet the Whiz-Bang Bullet Company's manual didn't test its new 154-grain polymer-tip-bonded-core-blessed-by-the-gods-boat-tail bullet with that powder you so love. If you have a different manual that provides load data with a comparably shaped projectile of the same exact weight, you can use the starting load and *carefully* increase the charge, looking for the first slight sign of pressure and stopping your shooting immediately if it occurs.

The same idea applies to older versions of annual and semi-annual manuals. They are well worth keeping around, because they can provide data for powders that are no longer produced, but that you still have a supply of (and is still safe to shoot). I have found several very accurate loads hiding within manuals that are older than I. Personally, I hoard them for their inherent value and actually enjoy reading them (this might be a touch of geekdom) for the insight they provide. They are also a valuable source of loading data for cartridges that have or will become obsolete.

When you pick a bullet and powder charge for the cartridge you intend to load, compare the test firearm data to the firearm you are loading for. The difference between the barrel length of the test gun and your gun may result in a change in the velocity you receive from the published data. I load many different types and makes of bullets, so I like to have as many of the different company manuals on hand as I can, be they in hard copy or digital form.

Data Notebooks

A means of keeping an accurate record of your loading trials and errors, successes, and overall results is very important. I use two methods. I keep my very precious notebook, in which I describe all the load data and notes regarding each load, so that I may replicate it at any point in time, and I also keep an ".xl" file on my computer, along with a well-organized backup version of my loading data. This recorded data should include the cartridge, brand of case, number of firings through that case, the bullet make, model, and weight, the primer used, the type of powder and charge weight, and the cartridge overall length (COL).

Stuck Case Remover

Sooner or later, it will happen to you. A case too lightly lubed will stick in a

A case prep station makes preparing cases for loading a cinch.

resizing die and, on the down stroke of the press arm, the rim of the case will rip off.

The stuck case remover can heal your woes. It is a simple tool set, but with it you can drill and tap a large hole through the flash hole and web of the case. Then, using a large screw, the tool draws the case out of the sizing die.

A quick tip for use with this tool. Be sure to back the expander ball and rod all the way out of the die, or as far as

possible, so the drill bit doesn't break the decapping pin or damage the expander ball when it drills through the cartridge's web. I've forgotten to do this and broken the pin and damaged the ball to the point where I've had to order a new one.

Bullet Puller

Let's say you've seated your bullet too deep in the case or, worse, forgotten to install a primer into a case in which you've charged and seated a bullet. What now, throw it away? Nope, not at all. The bullet puller erases this mistake in short order.

There are two common types of bullet pullers: The inertia-hammer and the press-mounted model. The hammer model looks like a hammer, with a screw cap on the rear portion. An appropriate collet is placed around the cartridge rim, the cap screwed back on and you swing the hammer down onto a block of wood. A couple swings later and the bullet pops out, along with the powder. The press-mounted model uses a collet in the same location where you would screw in a reloading die. The collet bites on the bullet and the down stroke of the press separates bullet from case. *Voila!* You're back in business!

* Originally published in *Gun Digest – The Magazine*, January 1, 2015 edition.

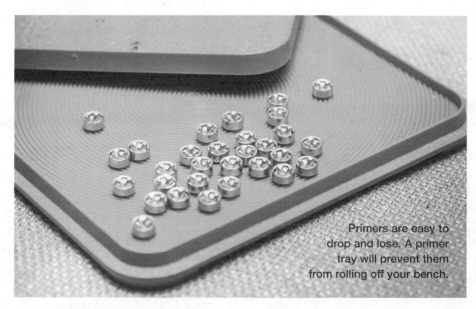

Primers are easy to drop and lose. A primer tray will prevent them from rolling off your bench.

The downsized 1911 semi-auto pistol is made for carry.

Springfield Armory
Range Officer Compact

By **Dick Jones**

My first experience with large caliber semi-auto pistols was with a 1911. For many years, a 1911 was the only centerfire semi-auto I owned, and I learned to love John Browning's remarkable design. Try to imagine any other mechanical design that's still at the zenith of its life after more than 100 years of use. 1911s have been the mainstay of competition pistols since a few years after their introduction, and they're still at the top.

Last year, I reviewed Springfield Armory's Range Officer in 9mm. One of my friends who's competed in almost every imaginable kind of competition and shot dozens of 1911s during his shooting career remarked that the 9mm Range Officer was one of the nicest out-of-the-box pistols he's ever shot. He even proclaimed it to perhaps be the best bargain in modern firearms. Originally a candidate in a Defense Department trial to find a lighter service pistol for

officers, the Colt Commander was the first lightweight 1911. Chambered in 9mm and with an aluminum alloy frame and a 4¼-inch barrel, Colt put the Commander into production in 1950.

When I found out Springfield Armory was making a compact version, I knew I had to try one out and emailed Springfield Armory that same day requesting a test gun. The Range Officer Compact is a smaller gun than the Colt Commander of my youth. It has a 4-inch barrel and an aluminum alloy frame, and an Officer-length grip. The front strap is smooth and the flat back strap is checkered in a high-grip, fine checkering pattern. There's an extended beavertail grip safety with a generous bump at the bottom to allow shooters with thin hands to engage the grip safety. My hands are slender enough that I can't rest my thumb on the thumb safety of guns without the bump and still be sure I'll keep the grip safety engaged. The thumb safety is oversized and on the right side only. I think this is a

good idea on a carry 1911. While I haven't carried a 1911 as a daily CCH gun, I've had friends in law enforcement advise me that an ambidextrous safety might not be a good idea on a carry 1911 because it can be disengaged by seat belts and other objects the shooter comes in contact with. If you need a left-hand safety, it's an easy and economical add on.

The trigger is a long, lightweight speed trigger. On my test gun the trigger broke with a slight amount of creep at just over 5 pounds, reasonable for a concealed carry defense gun. There are angled, generous cocking serrations on the rear area of the slide. The hammer is a skeletonized Commander style. Sights are a combat style two-dot rear and a high-visibility front with both green and red replacement material provided. The slide sports a flat Parkerized finish, and the aluminum frame is black Hardcoat anodized and matches well. The grips are thin cocobolo with double diamonds at the attachment screws and the familiar

The author produced extremely tight groups with the Range Officer Compact using Winchester Target and Win 1911 loads.

Author Photo

crossed cannons Springfield Armory logo.

A Bull-Barreled Gun

While the standard Range Officer is straight laced all the way, the design of the Range Officer is drastically different from the build of older 1911s. The Compact is a bull-barreled gun without a barrel bushing. The stainless steel match-grade barrel features a fully supported ramp, and there's a full-length recoil spring guide rod and dual recoil springs.

Shooting the Range Officer Compact is similar to shooting an old style Commander except with better sights and more ergonomic controls. Recoil with 230-grain hardball and +P defense loads is snappy but manageable. It's my theory that you carry a gun more than you shoot it, and if you use the gun to defend yourself, you'll never feel the recoil. Obviously, second shot recovery is always an issue with hard kicking guns, but no one will argue the potential of the .45 ACP round, and heavy guns often get left at home.

Accuracy was more than adequate, though it seemed to take 50 or so rounds for it to settle down. Of course, this might have

SPRINGFIELD ARMORY RANGE OFFICER COMPACT

CALIBER:	.45 ACP
CAPACITY:	6 + 1
MAGAZINES:	Blued steel with witness holes
BARREL:	4-in. stainless steel, ramped match grade
SIGHTS:	Two-dot combat style rear and high-visibility front
FRAME:	Aluminum alloy with anodized matte finish
SLIDE:	Forged steel, Parkerized
LENGTH:	7.6 in.
HEIGHT:	5 in.
WEIGHT:	28.5 oz.
OPTIONS:	Comes with a hard plastic case, holster, magazine pouch, two six-round magazines, tools and extra sight insert material
SRP:	$970
WEBSITE:	springfield-armory.com

The RO Compact breaks down simply like any 1911. The stainless steel barrel works with a full-length recoil spring guide rod and dual recoil springs.
Author Photo

The Range Officer Compact boasts a combat-style two-dot rear and high-visibility front sight with replaceable red and green dots.
Author Photo

been me. After a couple hundred rounds, I managed a pretty respectable 10-shot group at 10 yards. Slow fire and rapid fire were both manageable and plenty accurate. It wasn't a problem running the plate machine at 10 yards while staying on the standard six-second time limit.

Most of my shooting was done with Winchester 230-grain Target and Win 1911 230-grain Target. I also ran a couple of boxes of 185-grain Silvertips, and there wasn't a single malfunction.

Like the standard Range Officer, the Range Officer Compact is a lot of gun for the money. If I were to voice a suggestion, it would be to include at least one slightly longer magazine for pocket carry or perhaps to extend the magazine just a bit to allow for seven rounds. Of course, longer magazines for 1911s are not difficult to find. Extra magazine capacity is always a good thing. The RO Compact functions flawlessly and is more than accurate enough for the purpose intended. There's a hard plastic case with a holster, magazine pouch, two six-round magazines, tools and extra sight insert material. As is the usual case for Springfield Armory, it's a lot of gun and an excellent value.

* Originally published in *Gun Digest – The Magazine*, Spring 2015 Concealed Carry issue.

After a long quest by the author, this Model 21 is finally back in the field. The hand-checkered buttstock is protected by a Galco recoil pad, which also adds a half-inch to the length of pull.

WINCHESTER'S
MODEL 21
A QUEST FOR A CLASSIC SHOTGUN FULFILLED

BY Rick Hacker

I suspect I'm not the only one who does this, but sometimes I lie awake at night thinking about certain guns that I simply must have, no matter how costly or rare they may be. As a matter of fact, that's how this book got started. As an example, for decades I felt this way about the Winchester Model 21, technically and aesthetically the finest shotgun ever created by American craftsmen and perfected by American ingenuity.

Produced by Winchester Repeating Arms Company from 1930 until 1988 (after 1981, it was under the auspices of U.S. Repeating Arms Company), this side-by-side boxlock was the ultimate smoothbore for serious upland and waterfowl hunters, as well as for highly competitive trap and skeet shooters.

It took seven years of development by T.C. Johnson, Winchester's chief

designer, and further refinement by Edwin Pugsley, their factory manager who would go on to become its vice president, but the company had created a masterpiece. Interestingly, it was the first double-barreled shotgun Winchester ever produced, as all of its previous side-by-sides had been imported.

The Winchester 21 owed its fame to a number of manufacturing techniques and design features that had never before been incorporated in a side-by-side shotgun. For one, the action broke open at an unusually shallow angle, to reduce ejecting and reloading time. Moreover, the Model 21 ignored traditional shotgun manufacturing techniques by foregoing the standard practice of brazing the twin barrels together, a process that often weakened the steel. Instead, the right and left tubes were each forged with an integral chopper lump lug, which, in turn,

was cut with a dovetail that locked into the corresponding dovetail of the matching barrel and then soldered. Winchester referred to this as its "interlocking grip." Because of the incredible strength of these dovetailed barrels, the Model 21 didn't require a rib extension. To give additional strength to this already muscular design, the receiver and barrels were forged of Winchester's proprietary chrome molybdenum "Proof Steel," which was developed especially for the Model 21, but, because of its unprecedented durability, ended up being used for other Winchester firearms, as well.

The entire shotgun was so well machined and the parts matched to such close tolerances that it could easily withstand over 2,000 high-velocity "proof loads," a feat that, in an actual field test, completely *decimated* the actions of other top-grade American shotguns, including the sidelock L.C. Smith and the venerable Parker boxlock. Only the Model 21 emerged unscathed from this grueling trial, a fact that was subsequently touted in ads featuring the surviving rock-solid Model 21 resting atop a stack of spent proof load casings, dramatic testimony to the gun's mechanical superiority.

Of course, all these innovations came with a high price tag. Making its ill-timed appearance on the eve of The Great Depression, the Model 21 was an extremely expensive shotgun to produce and sell. In fact, if not for John Olin, whose Western Cartridge Company purchased Winchester Repeating Arms in 1931, the Model 21 would have been discontinued because of its unprofitability, its unsurpassed excellence as a sporting arm notwithstanding. But Olin was an avid wingshooter who knew a good thing when he saw it, and he devoted the rest of his life not only to keeping the Model 21 in the line, but improving and upgrading it. Under his direction, the original double triggers were replaced with a sturdy single trigger that featured a push-button barrel selector, a faultless inertia-driven design that was regulated to the trigger pull (thus making "doubling" impossible), and which was the brainchild of Louis Stiennon, one of Winchester's research and development men. That innovation has since been copied by numerous other companies.

In addition, the Model 21's splinter fore-end was reshaped into a more hand-filling beavertail, first offered as an option in 1934, but becoming standard by 1941. Whether it was the plain Field Grade, the specialized Trap, Tournament, Skeet, or Duck (Magnum) models or, in later years, the more elaborately engraved and artistically checkered Custom Built, Deluxe, and Custom Deluxe grades and the stratospherically priced Pigeon Grade and Grand American showpieces, the Winchester 21 had evolved into the epitome of a classic, side-by-side American shotgun. And, in the true spirit of American equality, no matter what its grade or price tag, internally every Model 21 exhibited the same superb degree of mechanical perfection and workmanship. When that boxlock action softly snapped shut, it locked up tighter than the hatch on a Bradley Fighting Vehicle.

Even back in my early pre-gun writing days, I sensed this shotgun was unique. My hunting buddies often spoke of it in hushed tones, as if it were something sacred. In gun stores, there were nod-

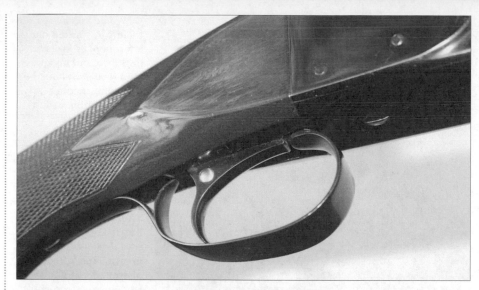

The Model 21's inertia-driven single selective trigger prevents doubling and enables the shooter to choose either right or left barrel by pushing the button to the right or left. Originally developed by Louis Stiennon, one of Winchester's research and development men, it has never been improved upon.

Because of the incredible strength of the "interlocking grip" dovetailed barrels, the Model 21 does not require a rib extension.

ding heads and murmurs of reverence among customers of the fabled Winchester 21. Clearly, I wasn't the only one to come under this double gun's spell, and, as I learned more of the Model 21's attributes, it only increased my desire to own one.

My acquisition of this shotgun was perpetually thwarted by its high price tag, always just out of reach of my meager budget. By the 1980s, when my income had finally risen to a point where I thought I could afford a Model 21, I was shocked to discover that the cost of a new plain Field Grade had also risen. It was now over $5,000, and an engraved Custom Grade would break the bank (my

bank, for sure), at more than $11,000. Once the gun was discontinued, prices on the higher grades and rarer 20- and 28-gauges and the scarce .410-bore rose even more. Besides, with only an estimated 32,500 guns having been made, there just weren't that many Winchester Model 21s around; they never wore out, and shooters who owned them obviously were in no hurry to get rid of them.

Occasionally, I would find a used Model 21, but they invariably featured options that priced them well out of any negotiating range. At one point, I lucked into a Field Grade 12-gauge in the used gun racks of a favorite sporting goods store. Even though the gun had been reblued

Hacker proudly poses with his Model 21, after taking these Nebraska pheasants.

and featured a non-factory Simmons ventilated rib, the price was $4,500 (the Model 21 is one of the few collectibles in which wear and refinishing don't seem to affect value as dramatically as they do with other guns). *A bit steep*, I thought, as I left the shop and drove home. Then something snapped: What was I *thinking*? Here was my dream gun, the first one I had seen for sale in years. *Go back and buy it, you idiot!* The next day, I returned to the shop, armed with a bevy of credit cards. As I entered, an empty spot in the gun rack confirmed my fears. During my brief absence, the gun had been sold! As my long-suffering wife can attest, that was a sad day at Hacker House.

Undaunted, I continued my search. At one point, I discovered that my friend, the late cowboy movie star Roy Rogers, had an exquisite two-gun set of Grand Americans, each with a separate set of barrels.

"Would you like to see them?" Roy asked one afternoon, as I was telling him about my quest for a Model 21. I began mumbling incoherently and salivating, which Roy took to mean "Yes." Years ago, he had visited the Winchester factory to be measured for the stocks and to select engraving patterns for these fabulous guns. After all, no matter what its grade, the Model 21 was always a hand-built firearm, and Winchester offered any option the customer wanted and could afford. Each of Roy's Grand Americans sported finely figured, *fleur de lis*-carved, black walnut stocks and was fully engraved with gold inlays of Roy, Trigger, his dog Bullet, and other western and hunting motifs. Roy was an excellent shotgunner and occasionally competed with these showpieces. I, of course, would have been settled for a plain 12-gauge Field Grade, should I ever again stumble onto one that was affordable.

A few years later, at the Wally Beinfeld International Sporting Arms Show held each year in Las Vegas, I thought that day had finally arrived. It's worth the price of admission just to see some of the world's finest rifles and shotguns on display and for sale. And it was here that I discovered the Mecca of Winchester Model 21s—every grade, gauge, and barrel length, with price tags to match. Entranced, I was able to cover only half the show and decided to return the next day to continue my quest. On the way back to my hotel, I shared a cab with a fellow who seemed remarkably happy.

"Get anything good at the show?" I asked, curious as to the cause of his beaming countenance.

"You bet!" he enthused. "I just bought the shotgun of my dreams."

"What was it?" I had a bad feeling about this.

"A Model 21!"

I was immediately filled with a mixture of admiration and blatant envy. "What did you have to give for it?" I dreaded asking, but I had to.

Wide-eyed, he turned to me and said, "Only $2,500. Can you believe it?"

Don't get me wrong; I was happy this guy had struck the mother lode. But I couldn't help thinking that, if I'd walked the show a little bit longer or a little bit faster, that gun could have been *mine!* Needless to say, there were no other $2,500 Model 21s at the International Sporting Arms Show the next day. Or the next year.

Then, once again fate dealt me a hand that made me believe ownership of a Winchester 21 might become a possibility. At the annual Shooting Hunting Outdoor Trade (SHOT) Show, a trade event for firearms dealers and manufacturers, I met Anthony Galazan, owner of Connecticut Shotgun Manufacturing Company. Tony had purchased all the remaining inventory of Model 21 parts and machinery when USRC ceased manufacturing the shotgun. CSMS is now the official factory repair center for Winchester 21s and has resurrected the production of custom Model 21s but, of course, without the Winchester logo. Naturally, I told Tony of my eternally frustrating pursuit of this fabled and elusive shotgun.

"Come on down and visit my factory," Tony offered. "I've got the largest selection of Model 21s anywhere."

Indeed he had, for Tony has been buying up all the Model 21s he can find (contributing, I might add, to their scarcity on the open market). As it just so happened, a few months later I was in Connecticut on a business trip. I extended my stay an extra day to visit the Galazan operation. Tony's factory is a beehive of activity, with craftsmen busily hand-building Model 21s just, I imagined, as they must have done at the Winchester plant many years ago. Bluing, engraving, hand fitting of parts—it was like stepping into a time warp. But the best part was the showroom, a wood paneled shrine of shotguns that lined the walls—Parkers, Remingtons, L.C. Smiths, indeed, double guns of all vintages and descriptions. And there, taking up one whole wall, was a case full of Winchester 21s, some all original, others reconditioned by CSMC to "factory mint."

"Why don't you look around and see if there's something you like," Tony offered.

Left alone in the room, I began to hyperventilate as I picked up and examined virtually every Winchester 21 in the place. By this time I knew what I wanted: a single trigger, pistol-grip gun with open chokes for upland wingshooting (no way was I going to take a shotgun like the Model 21 into a wet, muddy duck blind). After a couple hours, I had selected three Model 21s that fit me and my criteria. I laid each of them on a table and called for Tony to come in, all set to do some hard and fast wheeling and dealing for one of them. This was as close as I had ever gotten and I was fully prepared to max out my credit cards and end my quest that very day. But, after hearing me out and glancing at the three shotguns on the table, Tony said, "Listen, you've waited so long for a Model 21, why don't you let me build a gun for you? That way you'll have exactly what you want—chokes, beads, everything. It will be made to measure and I'll even put some fancy wood on it."

By golly, he was right—why shouldn't I have the ultimate custom-made shotgun? Okay, so I wouldn't leave Connecticut with my goals finally attained, but I would, eventually, get a Model 21, even though it wouldn't have the Winchester name stamped on the barrels. So I agreed. We never discussed price, but CSMC Model 21s are not cheap. However, I rationalized the decision by thinking this would probably be the only shotgun I would ever need. And so I got professionally measured for the stock: length of pull, cast on, cast off, drop at heel, grip at comb, all the same criteria Winchester called for on its original Model 21 order forms. If I was going to plunge into debt, I was going to do it in style.

I sent my measurements to Tony, along with my choice of chokes, WS-1 and WS-2, Winchester's well-researched Skeet combination known for its superb close-range patterning. And then I waited. And waited. Bird season came and went. Twice. At the next SHOT Show, I caught up with Tony. To his credit, he was trying to save me money by looking for an original Model 21 receiver, which evidently was harder to find than original guns. Of course, he was also busy filling orders for his A.H. Fox doubles, as well as his Galazan Over & Under and Round Body Sidelock, both of which feature no visible screws or pins. Another year passed, and this time I saw Tony at the Las Vegas show. He had Model 21s on his table, but he had convinced me: after so many years, I wasn't going

to settle for anything that wasn't exactly to my specifications. Again I was advised that the wait would be worth it. I had to admit, CSMC's Model 21s looked every bit as good as the original Winchesters. The problem was, I began to fear that if I ever I got the gun, I would be too old to shoot it.

Then, one day, as I was perusing Cabela's latest catalog, I noticed a blurb on the order form for the Cabela's Gun Library. I must have glanced over this innocuous announcement numerous times, always thinking it was a listing for gun books. This time I read it. "We Buy Guns, Antique and Modern," it said. Of course, it was just like wine libraries. Older, high-end collectibles. I immediately got on the phone to Cabela's flagship store in Sidney, Nebraska. With trepidation, I asked if they had any Model 21s in stock. The Gun Library manager pulled up his computer listings for all seven Cabela's stores. They had 16 of them! But, by now, my lengthy search had made me even more specific about the gun I wanted.

"Listen," I said, "it's got to be a 12-gauge, with a pistol grip, and have 26-inch barrels with a ventilated rib, and choked WS-1 and WS-2. And another thing; it's got to have above average wood."

A moment passed while the manager searched through the 16 guns on his computer screen. "Well, look at this!" he exclaimed. "Our Michigan store has a Model 21 in 12-gauge with a pistol grip, factory vent rib, 26-inch barrels choked Skeet 1 and Skeet 2 … and its got the prettiest wood you ever saw!"

I had him e-mail me a jpeg image of the gun, which I used as a screensaver for weeks afterwards. Cabela's Gun Library manager was more than accommodating. Learning I had a December deer hunt scheduled in Nebraska, he offered to have the gun shipped from their Michigan store to Sydney. They would hold it for me so that I could see it firsthand after my hunt. Was that service or what?

From Cabela's, I obtained the Model 21's serial number and contacted the Buffalo Bill Historical Center, where, for a fee, they can supply information from Winchester factory records. It turned out that this particular Skeet model was shipped on December 12, 1946. Unfortunately, it was not only used but abused, for it was returned to Winchester on February 28, 1979, for a complete overhaul, which

The author's Skeet Model 21, with 26-inch barrels and ventilated rib, was shipped from the factory on December 12, 1946.

included rebuilding the receiver, rebluing the barrels, and refinishing the wood. Then it went off to a new owner, who took much better care of it, until he finally sold it to Cabela's. In short, to use the Gun Library manager's words, it was "as close to a factory new Winchester 21 as you're likely to get." In addition to this research, I paid a modest fee to verify the approximate value by contacting the Preferred Customer Service division of Steve Fjestad's *Blue Book Publications*. After all, in spite of Cabela's extremely competitive prices, this was still going to be a major purchase for me. *The Blue Book* report was money well spent for the peace of mind it brought.

Cabela's store in Sidney is huge, but, after my hunt, I rushed past the racks of outdoor gear, stuffed wildlife dioramas, and Christmas decorations and headed straight for the Gun Library, a separate area from the regular sporting guns department. Inside the gun-filled room, the manager and his assistant were waiting with the Model 21. I took it from them like a long lost friend and threw it up to my shoulder. As expected, the factory's standard 14-inch length of pull was a little short for me, but, when they slipped on a leather Galco recoil pad (which also protected the hand-checkered butt), the fit was perfect.

"Maybe you'd like to take it out and shoot some pheasants," the manager joked. Plenty of time for that, I thought, as we wrote up the sales receipt and arranged for an FFL delivery. Later on, I called Tony and changed my order. I now wanted one of his new Model 21 Over & Unders, which he had just started building at a very competitive introductory price. It would be a perfect companion double. But for now, almost 70 years since it was originally shipped from the New Haven factory, my quest for a Winchester Model 21 was over.

* Originally published in *50 Famous Firearms You've Got to Own* by Rick Hacker, Gun Digest Books, 2014.

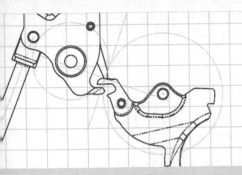

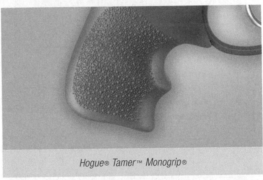

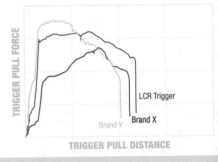

BY **Wayne van Zwoll**

RIFLES

FEW NEW MODELS ARE TRADITIONAL "CLASSICS." BUT SURELY SOME WILL BE REMEMBERED THAT WAY!

Roughly six centuries ago gunmakers latched onto the idea of spinning a ball for better accuracy. Rifling and rifles have taken many forms since. Such notions as oval and funnel bores have been pruned away, but rifling dimensions and twist rates still vary according to purpose. Ditto rifle actions and stocks. New materials and manufacturing methods have delivered lighter, stronger rifles that cycle more reliably, better resist rust and absorb recoil more effectively.

For those of us enamored of French walnut and mechanisms dating to the Boer War or the Great Depression, not all change is welcome. But bolt rifles have never been more affordable, self-loaders never more accurate, the reach of hunters never greater. Look at what's new for 2015, and you'll see why sales curves for sporting rifles arc ever upward.

Bergara

You might know the name for its barrels. But Bergara now has bolt-action rifles too. The B-14 comes in two action lengths: short for the 6.5 Creedmoor and .308 (22-inch chrome-moly barrels), long for the .270, .30-06 and .300 Winchester (24-inch). The mechanism features a coned bolt nose, sliding plate extractor,

two-position safety, adjustable trigger, traditional hinged floorplate. Choose a checkered walnut (Timber) or synthetic stock with grip panels (Hunter) in the Performance series ($950 and $825). BPR-16 Premier rifles are upgrades in wood (Classic) and synthetic (Stalker) versions ($2,199). The 13¾-inch pull seems to me an improvement over standard 13½-inch. From 7 to 8 pounds, B-14 and BPR-16 rifles have aim-steadying heft but aren't burdensome. There's a Tactical BPR-17 too. The Bergara brand belongs to the BPI Outdoors family. (www.bergarausa.com)

Blaser

Blaser (it's blah'-zer, not blay'-zer) was founded in 1957. This German firm is best known for straight-pull R93 and R8 rifles—the R8 an improved R93, introduced in 2008. Both have an improbably short receiver with telescoping bolt. The radial bolt-head locks into a circumferential groove. A thumb-operated switch cocks the rifle; there's no safety. The R93 and R8 are the only bolt rifles you can carry safely loaded, as they're not cocked until you thumb that switch. The trigger is crisp, consistent, adjustable. A featherlight single-stack magazine feeds smoothly and reliably. Interchangeable barrels and magazine innards afford

chamberings from .223 to .500 Jeffery. New versions of the R8 include, most notably, the Professional S, with synthetic stock. At just $2,895, it has all the features of costlier R8s, save a quick-detach magazine. Barrels and all other R8 components interchange, even those eye-popping walnut stocks. (www.blaser-usa.com)

Browning

Alas, the rifle-festooned walls towering above the Browning booth at the 2015 SHOT Show displayed nothing really new. Last year there was the X-Bolt Eclipse Hunter rifle (laminated thumbhole, .243 to .300 Winchester) and the AB3, a synthetic-stocked A-Bolt-style rifle at $600 (.270, .30-06, 7mm Remington and .300 Winchester). My favorite, then and now: a fetching maple-stocked T-Bolt .22 rifle. Introduced in 1965 then built for a decade in Browning's Belgian FN plant, the T-Bolt was costly to make and vanished. It re-appeared, with changes, in 2006. In 2008 Browning offered the new Miroku-built T-Bolt in .17 HMR and .22 WMR, as well as .22 LR. It boasts a clever 10-shot "double helix" detachable box magazine. The maple stock was announced as a limited-run option. Your dealer will know if any are available. But even in walnut, you'll look hard to find a more appealing rimfire. (www.browning.com)

Cooper

The Bitterroot Valley's most celebrated shop has tweaked its line of bolt rifles for 2015. Cooper Firearms of Montana began life producing .22 rimfires. About a decade ago, founder Dan Cooper came up with a beautiful centerfire. My .270 Model 52 drilled 3/4-minute groups. The short-action 54 followed, a .250 Savage sending my 87-grain Sierras into even smaller knots. The Model 56 magnum arrived next. All feature a flush, single-stack, detachable magazine of thick steel. Cartridges march smoothly off the dished follower. The trigger adjusts from 1½-5 pounds. Synthetic stocks are available, but Cooper's crew keeps the warehouse full of figured walnut. For 2015 the Model 52 action now handles short belted magnums (to .300 Winchester). The 56 is the heart of a new long-range rifle. (www.cooperfirearms.com)

CZ

Last year the Czech maker of the rugged 550 bolt-action rifle announced its replacement. The push-feed 557 action supplants the 550 in all but safari-class rifles, for which CZ will keep the magnum-length 550 and its Mauser extractor. The push-feed 557 has a bolt-face extractor, plunger ejector. But in many aspects, it's the 550's twin. Machined from a steel billet, the receiver has 19mm dovetails for CZ bases. Bottom metal is steel, a hinged floorplate securing a four-shot magazine. A two-detent safety permits bolt cycling on "safe." The trigger adjusts for weight, take-up and overtravel. The hammer-forged barrels (22 inches) are lapped for smooth bore finish. Short-action chamberings are .243 and .308. Long-action: 6.5x55, .270, .30-06. The walnut stock has a straight comb, machine-

In three models, new Nesika rifles bring benchrest features, long-range potential to mid-tier pricing.

Wayne settles in with a new Nesika rifle, manufactured and marketed by Dakota Arms in Sturgis, S.D.

CZ will keep the 550 action for safari rifles. Lesser loads get the 557. The author is a fan of this 557 Carbine.

cut checkering. Just out is the 557 Carbine (20½-inch barrel). Enamored of its cat-like balance and iron sights that align instantly, I bought a .30-06. It delivers fine accuracy. A Manners Sporter trims 8 ounces from my 7¼-pound walnut version, but hikes the price from around $800 to over $1,250. The wood looks better, handles nimbly. (www.cz-usa.com)

Dakota

When pilot/stockmaker/entrepreneur Don Allen founded Dakota Arms, he had in mind a rifle that would look and function like early M70 Winchesters but offer refinements, better fit and finish. The Dakota 76 does.

The later 97, similar in form but with a tubular receiver, undercut escalating 76 prices. New in the 76 stable is a synthetic-stocked Professional Hunter, with quarter-rib, banded front sight and swivel. Chamberings: .375 H&H to .450 Dakota. The 76 Alpine stock resembles that of the current M70 Featherweight, as Don Allen designed both. Hunters are just now discovering the Alpine. The 97 series has a new Varminter, with Claro walnut that makes this heavy rifle look downright racy. I like its blind magazine – same as on the 97 Outfitter (with iron sights). The Nesika brand, born in Benchrest circles, is now in the Dakota family. Nesika actions have been modified for midpriced Sporter, Tactical and Long Range rifles with Douglas stainless air-gauged barrels, Bell and Carlson stocks, Leupold QRW bases or 1913 Picatinny rails with 15-minute elevation gain. Chamberings run to .338 Lapua. Nesika also

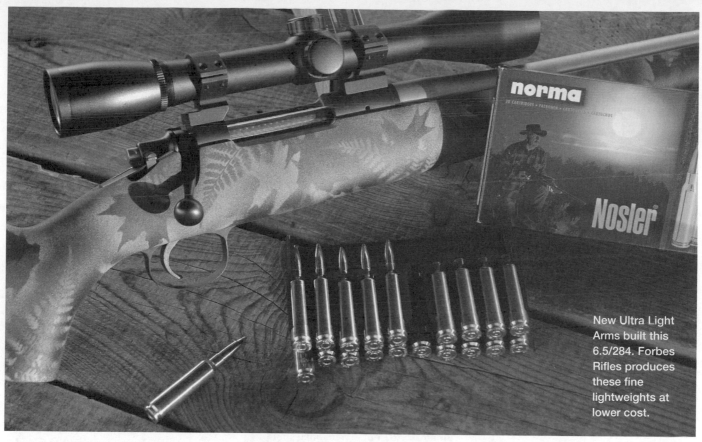

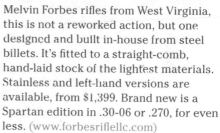

New Ultra Light Arms built this 6.5/284. Forbes Rifles produces these fine lightweights at lower cost.

sells actions only. (www.dakotaarms.com and www.nesikafirearms.com)

Forbes Rifle

When Melvin Forbes sold me an Ultra Light rifle many years ago, it was clearly the best lightweight sporter around. His Models 24 and short-action 20, recently under the banner of New Ultra Light Arms, are now more affordable as the Forbes 24B and 20B. Teaming with the Westbrook, Maine, firm of Titan Machine Works, Melvin and his crew at Forbes, LLC offer a 5½-pound rifle with blind magazine, Timney trigger, two-position/three-function safety, Talley scope rings and E.R. Shaw barrel. Like the original Melvin Forbes rifles from West Virginia, this is not a reworked action, but one designed and built in-house from steel billets. It's fitted to a straight-comb, hand-laid stock of the lightest materials. Stainless and left-hand versions are available, from $1,399. Brand new is a Spartan edition in .30-06 or .270, for even less. (www.forbesriflellc.com)

H-S Precision

Founded in 1978 in Arizona, H-S has grown into a unique enterprise, producing not only actions and barrels, but the hand-laid synthetic stocks of its fine hunting and competition rifles. Options in barrel contours, finishes and magazines yield "millions of possible configurations." I don't doubt this claim. An H-S action is cylindrical and trued, its heavy recoil lug secured by the cut-rifled barrel. Twin bolt lugs and an enclosed face bring to mind a Remington 700. But the side-swing safety has three detents; there's a tang-side bolt release. The Kevlar-fiberglass-carbon fiber stock has a full-length alloy bedding block. H-S

As usual, H-S Precision manufactures all major components for its classy new rimfire in .17 WSM.

Clean lines, precise fit, flawless finish and exceptional accuracy distinguish H-S rifles, here a .30-06.

offers detachable and floorplate-style magazines, plus, praise be, a blind box that holds four magnum rounds. H-S Precision lost its founder, Tom Houghton, in 2014; but it remains a family-owned company under the leadership of Tom Jr. and a capable staff in Rapid City, S.D. (www.HSprecision.com)

Heym

It's a carriage-class rifle, one you heft between sips of costly bourbon, under the catatonic gaze of a super slam of the world's antlered game in a trophy room the size of a gymnasium. "A stunning slab of Turkish," you observe, adjusting your monocle. Your host corrects you: "Actually, it's Circassian, old boy." Spared such embarrassment because I don't frequent these man caves, I did find a Heym rifle in my hands in an African hunting camp. The owner was no snob. "Take it tomorrow." I complied, cradling it as my first-born. A kudu appeared. I killed it over iron sights with the left barrel of that .470 double and was instantly in love. Besides a stout, svelte and arguably affordable side-by-side, Heym offers a bolt-action Express rifle, to my eye one of the most fetching of its type. The refined 98 Mauser action is machined from a steel billet, then fitted to a hammer-forged barrel and a made-to-measure stock of fine, seductively shaped, checkered walnut. Express sights and barrelband swivel. Per the original Mauser design, action and magazine are cartridge specific for perfect function. Thunderous big-bore rounds get a .785-inch bolt face (compared to the standard .700" and Brevex's .750"). Costly, yes. But that wad

of cash buys a rifle you'll be proud to flaunt in anyone's trophy room. (www.heymusa.com)

Hill Country Rifles

Its hometown, New Braunfels, Texas, produced one of our greatest exhibition shooters. Ad Topperwein once shot at 72,500 tossed 2¼-inch wood blocks and missed just nine. He ran 14,500 straight…. But I digress. Hill Country Rifles, founded in 1996, specializes in centerfire bolt guns that would impress even Ad. It's a semicustom shop, using Remington 700 actions for synthetic-stocked Harvester hunting rifles (from $2,000), but also Stiller actions for walnut-stocked sporters. Dangerous Game rifles are built on the Dakota 76, an "old school classic" based on the controlled-feed M70 Winchester. HCR

installs top-end barrels from Schneider, Krieger, Benchmark and others, with triggers from Timney and Jewell. Choose hand-laid synthetic stocks or hand-checkered walnut. All are pillar- and glass-bedded. Fit and finish on rifles I've used have been exceptional. Dozens of chamberings include popular wildcats. Half-minute accuracy guarantees apply to many. (www.hillcountryrifles.com)

Howa

Used by Weatherby and other firms as the heart of sturdy bolt guns, the Howa action is sold by its real name under the shingle of Legacy Sports International. Legacy packages it with scopes. To the Hunter Zeiss Walnut Package, Howa has added the Alpine, a trim new rifle that weighs 6¾ pounds with a 3-9x42 Vortex Viper. You can also get this rifle without a scope. The push-feed action has a twin-lug bolt, three-position safety and two-stage trigger that on my .308 breaks at just over 3 pounds. The magazine is a straight-stack detachable box I don't like because it protrudes well below the rifle's belly, impeding one-hand carry in difficult places. The latch protrudes in front, where you're forced to shift your grip. With gloves on, I dumped a magazine crossing a beaver dam. Legacy says Alpines will come with a floorplate and a box, so you can choose or change. I do like the rifle's High Tech stock. Chamberings include the .243, 7mm-08 and 6.5 Creedmoor. Also new for 2015 is the Howa Mini Action series, with a mechanism an inch shorter and thus lighter than standard short actions. Chamberings: .204 Ruger and .223 (20-inch barrel). A protruding polymer single-stack magazine holds five rounds.

Howa's latest rifle (from Legacy Sports) is the lightweight Alpine, a nimble, short-action sporter.

The new 5½-pound Howa Alpine has an enclosed, twin-lug bolt head – a proven design for accuracy.

The Hogue stock comes in black, green or Highlander. A Nikko Stirling scope package is available too. (www.legacysports.com)

Kilimanjaro

More than a decade ago, Serengeti Rifles appeared. Erik Eike followed its progress, and in 2007 explored a new line of rifles based on those of Serengeti's Mel Smart. Two years and 20 prototypes later, he bought the name and its equipment to form Kilimanjaro Rifles. He recruited the best craftsmen in the industry to build semicustom rifles in their shops under the Kilimanjaro shingle. Erik settled on eight styles in chamberings from .22-250 to .500 Jeffery, including wildcats. Since then, Tigercat and Leopard models have dominated as lightweights. Kodiak and

African rifles equip hunters for dangerous game. So does the Doctari, a big-bore with a rounded grip. It's become a best seller. The Artemis is a svelte rifle proportioned for women. While built on established patterns, Kilimanjaro rifles are truly custom projects – components, measurements and styling tweaks decided by each client. Erik uses barrels from PacNor, Douglas, Shilen, Lilja and Krieger. I specified a Dakota 76 action for a middleweight Walkabout rifle in 7mm Weatherby. The PacNor barrel wears a banded NECG front sight to match the pop-up aperture below a 6x Zeiss. The walnut blank I chose responded beautifully to shaping, finishing, Diamond Fleur full-wrap checkering. This Kilimanjaro is ideal for big game on western landscapes or the African veldt. (www.kilimanjarorifles.com)

Kimber

With four actions (for .308, .30-06, WSM and belted-magnum cartridge sizes), Kimber rifles fit perfectly their 22 different chamberings. The new Adirondack weighs just 4 pounds, 13 ounces with an 18-inch fluted barrel threaded for a Kimber brake. This year it's available in .300 Blackout and 6.5 Creedmoor (the .300 Blackout with standard threads for aftermarket brakes). Its synthetic stock has a classy gray camo Forest finish. The Mountain Ascent weighs very little more with its 84L action and 24-inch barrel. It has Open Country stock camo and for 2015 comes with Model 8400 actions in

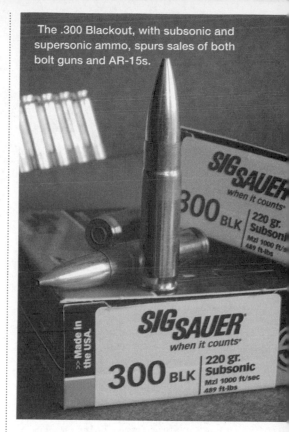

The .300 Blackout, with subsonic and supersonic ammo, spurs sales of both bolt guns and AR-15s.

.270 and .300 WSM, plus 7mm Rem. and .300 Win. Magnums. Both the Adirondack and Mountain Ascent include lightweight Talley scope rings. The Montana employs 84M, 84L and 8400 actions for a broad suite of chamberings, as do the walnut-stocked Classic and Classic Select. All Kimbers feature a two-lug bolt with Mauser-style extractor for controlled feed, and a three-position M70-type safety. That bolt, with modifications, appears in three Tactical rifles. The Patrol Tactical II, Advanced Tactical II and Advanced Tactical SOC are all bored to .308 and .300 Win. Mag., and the latter two this year, 6.5 Creedmoor. Also new for 2015 is an Advanced Tactical SRC with a 16-inch barrel in .308 only. It's a shorter, lighter version of the SOC with a black, not desert-tan, stock. Advanced Tactical models accept detachable box magazines. Kimber has not changed its Talkeetna and Caprivi dangerous-game rifles. Ditto the four Varmint and LongMaster models. (www.kimberamerica.com)

Legendary Arms Works

It's new, but it isn't. Pennsylvanian Mark Bansner has built semicustom rifles for, well, decades. His High Tech rifle stocks are industry favorites. Now he, with partners, has his own action. Legendary Rifle Works debuts with three rifles. The Model

Kimber's stable adds beautifully trim, super-lightweight rifles in new chamberings, a new "tactical."

This new rifle from Legendary Arms Works has a High-Tech stock, fresh action from Mark Bansner.
Lower right: Legendary Arms receivers of 416 stainless steel have features of Winchester 70s and Remington 700s.

704 LAW action features the best of Remington's popular 700, common on Bansner rifles. LAW refinements include a beefier, .250-inch recoil lug, an extractor for controlled feed and a Model 70-style safety that works with the Timney trigger. The tubular receiver, of 416 stainless, is CNC machined true with the bolt's axis. It has 8-40 thread scope base holes. A stainless follower brings each round to the same place. Hinged bottom metal is alloy for The Closer and The Professional models, steel for The Big Five. Stocks are High Tech. A prototype impressed me with its handling and accuracy. Pick from 18 chamberings in Closer and Professional versions (each in short- and long-action form); choose .375 H&H, .416 Remington or .458 Lott in the Big Five version. The latter two rifles have muzzlebrakes; the Big Five wears iron sights. Prices: $1,600, $1,829 and $2,743, respectively. LAW rifles are built in Pennsylvania, with components designed in-house to specific purpose. (www.legendaryarmsworks.com)

Mauser and Sauer

It's back! If any hunting rifle has up-staged those built on Paul Mauser's bolt action of 1898, it's the double-square-bridge Magnum Mauser. Essentially a grown-up '98, it can swallow the longest rimless dangerous-game rounds. Heart of archetypal sporters from the middle of the 20th century, it's now available in classic-style rifles from Mauser. The new 98 Magnum has a three-detent side-swing safety, deep magazine, pillar bedding with double recoil lugs. Its 24½-inch barrel wears an express rear sight (three leaves on an island) and a height-adjustable, barrelband front sight. Barrelband swivel too. The black fore-end tip and steel grip cap accent a straight-comb stock with point-pattern checkering, shadow-line cheekpiece. Walnut on rifles I've seen is of very fine quality. Choose .375 H&H or .416 Rigby; five- and four-shot magazines, with a heavy-barrel option in .416. No, they're not inexpensive. But do you really want to live without a Magnum Mauser?

Since Mauser shares its manufacturing site in Germany, and a marketing team in the U.S., I'll here hail a new Sauer 101. This smooth-shucking action appears in eight rifles, all with straight-comb stocks that resemble Winchester's Featherweight. Handsome. Nimble in hand. Choose synthetic, walnut or laminate with various barrel contours and many chamberings. I like the new Scandic carbine, 6½ pounds with iron sights on a 20-inch barrel, in a green/brown laminated stock. It points like a shotgun and fires the potent 9.3x62. Or pick an American round, .243 to .30-06. (www.mauser.com and www.sauer.de)

Mossberg

In my youth, Mossberg made .22 rimfire rifles, from bolt actions to self-loaders. Later, the firm came up with the Model 500 shotgun, a hugely successful smoothbore. A couple of centerfire rifle lines followed and the 464 lever action, after America's .30-30 "deer rifle." For 2015 Mossberg has extended its MVP series of 5.56 and 7.62 (.223 and .308) bolt rifles with Scout, Tactical and Patrol Thunder Ranch models. All accept AR-15 or AR-10 and M1A/M14 magazines. So does a new MVP Light Chassis, with AR-style buttstock and grip. Mossberg's flag-ship big-game rifles have now evolved into the Patriot, with fluted bolt and a detachable box that fits flush. Mossberg did its homework with this line, which includes a laminate-stocked .375 Ruger with iron sights. Stocks (walnut and synthetic too) feature straight combs and stippled grips. Those I've shouldered align my eye quickly with a low-mounted scope. Choose from 11 chamberings. I like the Lighting adjustable trigger, but prefer 24-inch barrels for long-action rifles in .25-06 and .270, and in 7mm, .300 and .338 Magnums. Mossberg uses 22-inch tubes for all Patriots. The rifles also come in combo packages with Vortex scopes. (www.mossberg.com)

While heavy bolt guns and AR-15s have a place, so do lightweight sporters (here a Mauser M12).

Nosler

The 48 Heritage rifle recently chambered to Nosler's new, quick .26 cartridge is the company's own, with traditional push-feed, twin-lug bolt action. It's available in 18 other chamberings too. Its side-mounted extractor and plunger ejector permit an enclosed bolt face. The two-position thumb safety does not lock the bolt. The adjustable trigger is properly positioned to the rear of the guard, floorplate button outside up front. The box is long enough for the huge .26 case with 129-grain Long Range spitzers or 140 Partitions. Bottom metal is alloy. The stainless, hand-lapped 26-inch barrel has a slender, but not whippy profile. Its 1-in-8 rifling should stabilize the heaviest 6.5mm bullets. All steel parts are Cerakoted satin black. The well-figured, conservatively shaped walnut stock is checkered in 20-lpi point patterns. It wears a shadow-line cheek-piece, palm swell and 1-inch Decelerator pad. Besides the Heritage, Nosler offers the M48 in two synthetic-stocked versions, both pillar- and glass-bedded with alloy bedding rail. Save for its stock, the Patriot is identical to the Heritage, in 17 chamberings (.22-250 to .35 Whelen). The Outfitter is designed for dangerous game with open sights and a blind magazine, in seven chamberings, .308 to .458. M48s list for $1,695 (Patriot) and $1,895. The Heritage I used for handloading the .26 Nosler wrung out just over 3,400 fps from 81 grains of H1000 driving 129-grain AccuBond LR bullets. They drilled an .8-inch group. With 78 grains of Retumbo, I got 3,320 fps from 140-grain Partitions.

On the horizon: a .28 Nosler. This 7mm on the .26 hull actually makes more sense than its parent. That huge case can wring more speed from 140-grain bullets and use heavier bullets efficiently. Neither rifles nor cartridges are available at this writing, but the .28 is slated for the same Model 48s as the .26, and RCBS already has dies. Stay tuned! (www.nosler.com)

Quarter Minute Magnums

Scott and Vickie Harrold moved from Pennsylvania, the home of long-range benchrest shooting, to Idaho, the home range of elk. In Lewiston, Scott started building rifles, but not for IBS matches. His lightest weighs less than 8 pounds with a No. 5 Krieger barrel and HTG McMillan stock. He calls them Quarter Minute Magnums. That's his accuracy standard—1/2-inch groups at 200 yards!

The Nosler .26, essentially a super .264 Magnum, will soon spawn a .28. Nosler makes rifles for both.

Nosler's 48 Heritage, a twin-lug, push-feed rifle in 18 chamberings, has a 26-inch barrel in .26 Nosler.

The face of this Nosler 48 bolt shows the large diameter of the .26 (and coming soon, .28) Nosler.

Scott Harrold builds long-range Quarter Minute Magnum rifles in Lewiston, Idaho, on BAT actions.

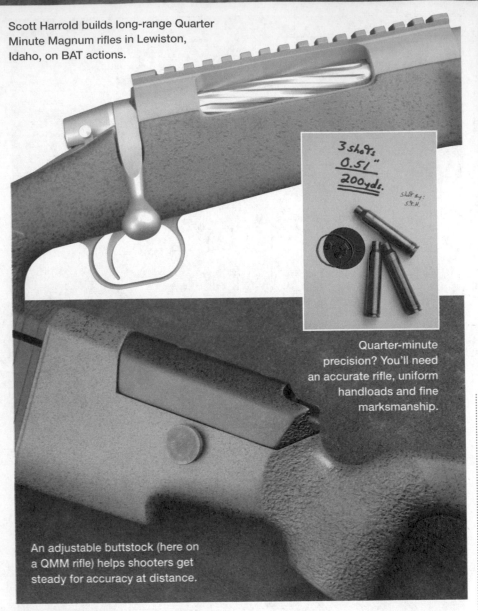

3 shots 0.51" 200 yds.

Quarter-minute precision? You'll need an accurate rifle, uniform handloads and fine marksmanship.

An adjustable buttstock (here on a QMM rifle) helps shooters get steady for accuracy at distance.

Remington now lists 24 versions of the 700. This lightweight stainless is handsome – and deadly!

Half a mile off, he expects softball-size knots. Scott uses Remington 700 actions but prefers BATs from Bruce A. Thorne. The integral rail has 20 minutes gain for long shots. Scott installs top-quality barrels, cut-rifled and lapped, twist rates matched to the long bullets "but as slow as will make them fly straight." Though he'll ream for factory ammo, Scott wants chambers snug around neck-turned hulls. He has Dave Manson reamers for more than 40 cartridges. The most popular – the .300 Winchester Magnum. He finishes throats so long the bullets kiss the rifling. Since many clients want them, he installs muzzlebrakes, allowing that they can affect accuracy. To ensure concentricity, Scott buys BAT brakes undersize, then bores them .020" over groove diameter. He makes another concession for magazines because hunters prefer repeaters to single-shots. "Solid-bottom actions are stiffer." Most Quarter Minute Magnum rifles wear McMillan stocks—A-3s for midweight rifles, A-5s for heavies. Trigger choice is the client's. (www.quarterminutemagnums.com)

Remington

For the first time in the decades I've covered Remington the company has not published a hard copy catalog. You'll have to go online to see what's new at Big Green. There's not much – at least in rifles. Headlines go to a self-loading pistol and auto shotgun. Sure, variations of the Model 700 pop up annually. In fact, Remington now lists 24. This year there's a VTR (Varmint-Tactical Rifle): stainless with a tan synthetic stock, or chrome-moly with black. The short action wears a stiff, triangular barrel with integral brake. At $930, it comes in .223, .22-250, .260 and .308. The new 700 Long Range has an M40 Bell & Carlson stock with alloy bedding block. In .25-06 to .300 Ultra Mag., it retails for $829. The Tactical Chassis model has an AR-style adjustable stock on a stainless barreled action in .308, .300 Winchester, .338 Lapua. It wears a full-length rail and ratchet brake, and is priced for taxpayer-funded agencies at $2,900. While some quarters apply "the modern sporting rifle" label to AR-15s, you'll see many more Model 700s afield. Since their 1962 debut, 700s have sold briskly. My pick? The Classic, or Titanium, or... (www.remington.com)

Rifle Inc.

I've known Lex Webernick almost as long as he's been building trim rifles on Remington 700 and Winchester 70 actions—like the 6.5x55 in my rack. A couple of visits to his rural Texas machine shop showed me how this soft-spoken hunter and machinist produces such lightweight, beautifully fitted rifles that shoot as accurately as benchrest guns. Lex designed his own hand-laid stocks. Ditto the muzzlebrakes that seem integral, so seamless is their fit. (He used acoustical instruments to test the effectiveness of myriad brake designs.) Rifles Inc. has offered "special edition" rifles like the Pear Flat with distinctive graphics. But it's the sub-minute accuracy, glass-smooth function and wand-like handling of all its rifles—even

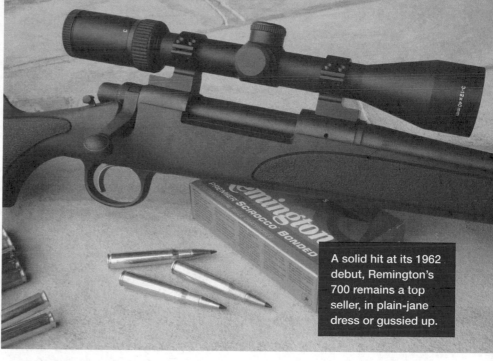

A solid hit at its 1962 debut, Remington's 700 remains a top seller, in plain-jane dress or gussied up.

in the popular .300 Winchester—that keep orders coming from all over the world. (www.riflesinc.com)

Rigby

At age 17 in Dublin in 1775, John Rigby started building firearms. Dueling pistols and flintlock smoothbores preceded long-range target rifles and doubles for heavy game. Generations later, around the turn of the 20th century, Thomas Bissell and Paul Mauser collaborated on a Rigby magazine rifle. It would become the most celebrated of classic African bolt actions. In 1912 the .416 Rigby cartridge gave it even more appeal. Since then, the company has endured a tortuous history. But now the classic Rigby big-bore has returned. It's built in Germany on Magnum Mauser actions and marketed by the Blaser/Mauser/Sauer triumvirate. A Single Square Bridge model, in .416 or .450 Rigby, wears a 22-inch barrel and is designed for use with its express sights. This 10½-pound rifle has a three-position flag safety. The Double Square Bridge model in .375 H&H or .416 weighs a ½ pound less. It has a 24-inch barrel and Winchester M70-style safety for use under scopes. Sights, quarter-rib, barrelband swivel and deep magazine are the same. Ditto the point-pattern checkering and fine walnut stock. Upgrades? Of course! (www.johnrigbyandco.com)

Rock River Arms

How many AR-style rifles can you design before you run out of ideas? Rock River isn't there yet. No other manufacturer on my radar builds more or better ARs. The LAR-15 (5.56) and LAR-8 (7.62) models boast myriad barrel options, and a wide range of accoutrements like the firm's Beast and Hunter muzzlebrakes. Full-length Picatinny rails on floating handguards above low-profile gas blocks permit countless sight options. The LAR-15 X-1 has a cryo-treated barrel with Wylde chamber for both .223 and 5.56 loads. Its 1-in-8 rifling delivers subminute accuracy with heavy bullets. The 9½-pound LAR-8 X-1 offers that precision in .308. The X-1 rifles, tan and black, now come in 6.8 SPC and .458 SOCOM chamberings. RRA has hunters in mind with its Varmint, Coyote, Predator HP, Predator Pursuit models. You needn't bleed Junior's college fund to fire some of the best ARs around. Most from Rock River list for between $1,000 and $1,500. (www.rockriverarms.com)

New Ruger Americans are coming! The author used, then loaned a Magnum prototype. It passed muster!

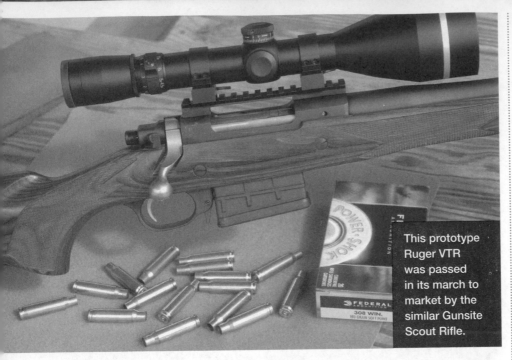

This prototype Ruger VTR was passed in its march to market by the similar Gunsite Scout Rifle.

is heavier than the original. But at 6.62 pounds, the Predator is hardly ponderous. Also in .204 Ruger, .223, .22-250, .243 and .308, the Predator has a threaded muzzle. In place of Weaver-style scope blocks, it comes with a rail. New for '15 is an FTW version (for the Texas ranch of the same name catering to long-range shooters). It has an adjustable stock. I wept when Ruger announced its No. 1 single-shot would be sold only through Lipsey's, one of the firm's distributors. All five versions will be made, one chambering each. Why didn't I buy more in 1968? (www.ruger.com)

Ruger

The American rifle is a big design departure from Ruger's Model 77 series. At a debut price of just $449, it costs less, but it's good too. A three-lug, full-diameter bolt has a 70-degree lift and minimum wobble. Ruger attacked the steep-cam-angle issue with dual cocking cams. A detachable rotary magazine fits flush. The trigger, with front tab, adjusts from 3-5 pounds. The tang safety does not lock the bolt. Bedding? Steel V-blocks in the stock engage angled action mortises. The barrel floats. Long and short actions wear 22-inch barrels. The newest versions are the midweight Predator and the American Rimfire. My Predator in 6.5 Creedmoor prints tiny groups. The 22-inch barrel, .665" at the muzzle,

Sako

Sako – it's not "Sayko" or "Sacko," but "Socko." At least, if you're in Finland. There, Suojeluskuntain yliesikunnan asepaja was founded the first day of April, 1919. Nearly a century later, it hawks two main rifle lines. The 85, in eight versions and chamberings from .22-250 to .375 H&H, boasts a three-lug bolt with controlled feed, fixed ejector, flush detachable box and hammer-forged barrel. Stocks include the new angular, checkered-walnut option on the Finn Bear. Retro! Laminated stocks on the Grey Wolf and safari-style Kodiak (with banded swivel and iron sights) fit me perfectly. In my view, the Kodiak is one of the best .375s available, at any price. The walnut-stocked Bavarian

Ruger's No. 1 has slipped from the catalog. Ruger now builds it only for Lipsey's, one of its distributors.

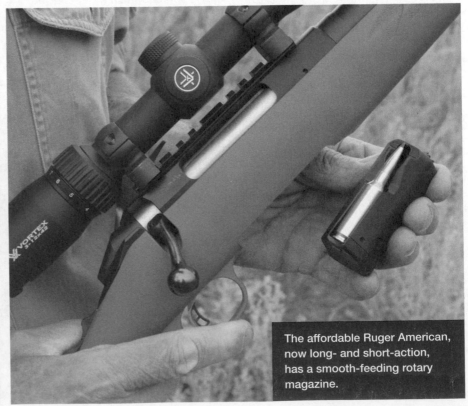

The affordable Ruger American, now long- and short-action, has a smooth-feeding rotary magazine.

After firing this group with a Savage 11, Wayne used it on three deer hunts. Confidence!

has irons too. The Finnlight stainless rifle in a carbon-fiber stock hews to Sako's tradition of sizing actions to cartridge families. Choose from four action lengths. The new A7 Roughteck has features of the 85, in five chamberings. Its synthetic stock boasts an alloy skeleton. Sako still makes its sleek Finnfire rimfire (.22 LR and .17 HMR). But R&D has followed the market to powerful "tactical" rifles. The TRG 22 in .308, and TRG 42 in .338 Lapua have heavy, braked barrels, adjustable stocks. Magazines: 10-shot detachable boxes in the 22, five-shot in the 42. The TRG M10 is tricked out as a sniper rifle, with interchangeable bolts, magazines and barrels (.308, .300 Winchester, .338 Lapua), a fully adjustable buttstock and an alloy forestock with rail attachments all around. Ambidextrous controls too! Sako rifles are marketed in the U.S. through Beretta. (www.sako.fi & www.beretta.com)

Savage

Sometimes a good cartridge gets ignored. The .338 Federal has languished but Savage has now added the chambering to its short-action Model 10, 11 and (stainless) 16 bolt rifles. Also new are the Law Enforcement line extensions with 20- and 24-inch heavy-barreled .308 rifles. They have 10-shot detachable boxes and double front swivels. The 11 Scout with aperture sight, brake and midstation rail on its 20-inch barrel is similar. It has a tan stock with adjustable comb. I used a Savage Long-Range Hunter rifle with this comb in the Vortex Extreme match last summer and liked it very much. In the Target Series you'll find a new 112 Magnum with laminated prone stock and single-shot action behind a braked 26-inch barrel in .338 Lapua.

Savage's biggest news for 2015, however, is a smallbore. The A17 autoloader handles the .17 HMR with a

hard-chromed bolt in a case-hardened receiver. Trying to perfect self-cycling mechanisms that digest the high-pressure .22 WMR and .17 HMR has driven otherwise sane engineers into therapy, and traditional blowback actions designed for magnums are piled deep in rifle boneyards. The synthetic-stocked A17 has a delayed blowback action with a rising lug to hold the bolt closed "just long enough." Its 10-round rotary box gives you plenty of fast fun. AccuTrigger too! (www.savagearms.com)

Shiloh Sharps

Charles E. Overbaugh, Sharps Rifle Company's chief traveling salesman and exhibition shooter in 1876, had an idea for an action like the Model 1874's, but lighter. His inspiration – the 1,000-yard Creedmoor match. Shooters favored long, heavy barrels for their generous sight radius and recoil-absorbing mass. Also, a .45 bore with a 520-grain bullet driven by 105 grains of black powder required thick barrel walls for adequate stiffness. The 10-pound weight ceiling thus limited barrel length. A lighter action permitted a longer barrel. Overbaugh's 1877 Sharps is now in the Shiloh Sharps catalog, faithful in all details from the trim hammer and action plates to plain hinge pin. The Big Timber, Mont., company has pared delivery time to 18 months, I'm told. Choose from heavy and standard-weight barrels in 26- to 34-inch lengths, in 10 chamberings from .38-55 to .45/100. Specify straight wrist or pistol grip. At around $2,150, the price seems very reasonable. But you'll want figured Turkish walnut instead of plain American. Probably a tang sight with front globe. A Rigby rib would look good, and a cheek-rest. (www.shilohrifle.com)

Springfield Armory

Like me, the Reese family is fond of U.S. military rifles that predate polymer and sub-.30 bullets. In 1974 the Reese's firm, Springfield Armory, began offering a semiauto version of the M14. Renamed the M1A, it has evolved over four decades without losing its soul. For 2015 the Geneseo, Ill., company has seven new rifles and carbines on the M14 action. Distinctions include some that are only camo-color deep. Two new SOCOM rifles, with braked 16¼-inch barrels have Flat Dark Earth and Multi-Cam stock finishes. Like their black and green predecessors, still cataloged, they pair .135"-aperture rear sights with XS posts (tritium inserts) up front. Scout carbines with 18-inch barrels now offer a Flat Dark Earth option, as does the Standard (22-inch) group, with flash hider in place of a brake. New Highlander Camo brings the Standard stable to six. National Match and Super Match lines are unchanged. I'm sweet on the Super Match with oversize walnut stock and heavy stainless barrel. At just over 11 pounds it is hardly ponderous, but the stock's long, steep wrist and beefy fore-end add control. The Loaded M1A series has a new 9¾-pound member with adjustable polymer stock.

(www.springfield-armory.com)

Tikka

You could say Tikkas are bargain-priced Sakos. They're built at the same Finnish plant, though Tikka's history predates Sako's by 26 years. Established in 1893, Tikka has manufactured many products. During WWII it produced sewing machines and submachine guns. Then it turned to hunting rifles. After it

Tikka's slick T3, with straight-stack feed, remains a top buy in bolt guns. It's made in the Sako plant.

collaborated with Sako on a 555 Tikka rifle, Sako acquired Tikka and Valmet, a shotgun firm. By 1989 production at Tikkakoski Works had moved to Sako's Riihimaki plant. Few U.S. shooters had heard of Tikka before its Whitetail model in the 1990s. Then, in 2003, Tikka began importing a T3, with features of the Sako 75. Still Tikka's flagship, the T3 comes in several versions from .204 Ruger to .300 Winchester. One of the most appealing, the T3 Lite, scales at 6¼ pounds. It's fed by a single-stack, three-shot polymer box. Trigger pull adjusts from 2-4 pounds. The two-position safety locks the bolt and trigger. Early on, the T3 brought me to Finland where I trudged into the forest behind a Norwegian elkhound and its handler. Our job: move moose toward standers. But then I spied a wink of moose hide. A cow eased across our front. When the Tikka boomed, my Fail Safe blew steam into the shadows. The moose sprinted in a tight circle and collapsed. The next day, a young bull crossed my path and for a moment came clear of the poplars. I fired offhand. The moose dropped instantly. Tikka rifles are handled Stateside by Beretta. (www.tikka.fi and www.beretta.com)

Volquartsen

In 1974 Tom Volquartsen began bluing firearms part time. Soon he was rebarreling rifles and handguns. After 12 years, he jumped into full-time gunsmithing and building custom firearms. Still a family-owned business, Volquartsen Custom continues to grow, CNC and wire-EDM machines turning steel into beautifully fitted, slick-cycling autoloading pistols and rifles. Most are rimfire, including a new rifle in .17 WSM.

This Vanguard is a .240, but the new .375 with iron sights has the same rugged, sure-handling stock.

Its stainless receiver wears an integral rail. The tungsten alloy bolt yields to a center-mounted recoil spring and rod. With beefy 20-inch stainless barrel, laminated stock and a full eight-shot magazine, the .17 WSM weighs just over 9½ pounds. It's the only self-loading rifle I know that chambers this hot new rimfire (3,000 fps!). Volquartsen's big stable of .22 autoloaders includes a WMR with birch stock, a takedown with tubular AR-style handguard, and a suite of racy sporters in colored laminate stocks. You can also buy barreled actions and components, even compensators and carbon-fiber barrels. New on my radar is Volquartsen's 6¼-pound Evolution centerfire self-loader, in .204 Ruger and .223. Its stainless receiver is paired with black-nitrided bolt, carrier and extractor. A 20-inch barrel rifled 1-in-9 is standard (24-inch available in .204). (www.volquartsen.com)

Weatherby

The predictable news on its 70th anniversary: Weatherby will build a 70th Anniversary Mark V rifle. But only 70 will come off the line, complete with a fine leather case and a handmade knife and sheath by Roy's grandson, Dan Weatherby. Both rifle and knife will wear exhibition-grade walnut. Also on the production schedule is a new Mark V Arroyo RC (Range Certified) in 14 chamberings up to the .338-378 Weatherby and .338 Lapua. I'm most taken by a new Vanguard Synthetic, a nimble .375 with iron sights and a field-worthy stock. It joins a full roster of Vanguard Synthetics, .223 to .300 Weatherby. At under $800, this .375 is one of the best buys out there! The Vanguard Back Country, with hand-laid stock and attractive gray finish, ranks among my favorite open-country rifles. New for 2015 is the .308 chambering (I'm stuck on my .240). The Weatherby-X Vanguard line, for shooters younger than me, boasts new stock cosmetics: The Saratoga (24-inch barrel) has an American flag motif; the Volt (20-inch barrel) features green webbing on black. Both offer standard chamberings from .223 and up. (www.weatherby.com)

John Browning designed lever rifles with vertical lugs. Here: a current 1886 Winchester from Miroku.

Winchester

In 1937 it gave us the Model 70, progeny of the Model 54, announced in 1925. Now there's a new bolt-action centerfire from Winchester. The XPR is a synthetic-stocked, push-feed, long-action rifle with detachable polymer single-stack box. In .270 and .30-06 (24-inch barrels) it scales 7 pounds. In .300 and .338 Winchester Magnum (26-inch barrels), 7¼ pounds. The M.O.A. trigger adjusts for weight and overtravel, but not sear engagement. Claims of "zero take-up, zero creep and zero overtravel" are not exactly precise. But I've found the trigger as good as most. The two-position safety has a button that permits unloading with the safety "on." At $550, the XPR shoulders into a crowd of entry-level rifles from competitors. The Model 70 starts at $800. My pick of that stable is still the M70 Featherweight and the recently revived Alaskan.

The firm's lever actions now hail from Japan's Miroku plant, which has faithfully reproduced 1873 and John Browning-designed 1886 and 1892 Winchesters, plus the 1895 stack-fed rifle favored by T.R. Also cataloged: 1885 High Wall and Low Wall single-shots. This year the 1873 comes in case-colored Sporter Octagon (24-inch barrel) dress, and the Low Wall Hunter Rimfire chambers the .17 WSM. New 94s are produced Stateside, with angled ejection and a trigger decidedly unlike the original. (www.winchesterguns.com)

NEW SHOTGUNS

BY **John Haviland**

This shooter is waiting for clay targets with a Winchester SX3 Ultimate Sporting Adjustable in hand.

his year's new shotgun models run the gamut from elegant guns for targets and game to everyday mainstays that get the job done in the slush and the swamps while accommodating shooters from small to tall.

Benelli

Benelli has always been known for its autoloading shotguns. So it's a surprise to see a Benelli over/under. The 828U over/under has a distinct look with smooth receiver walls that taper to the rear and flow into a slim wrist. The head of the receiver also has flat face, allowing 40 different settings of fit and sight picture with shims. The Progressive Comfort System shock-absorber recoil reducer, introduced by Benelli last year, is contained inside the walnut buttstock. Benelli has always been big on a rotating bolt head that locks into the barrel of its

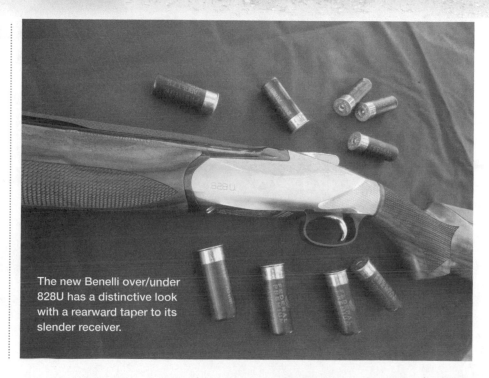

The new Benelli over/under 828U has a distinctive look with a rearward taper to its slender receiver.

Benelli 828U Anodized Receiver

Benelli 828U Engraved,
Nickel Plated Receiver

autoloaders and continued that feature in the 828U. Other elements of the 12-gauge gun include an auto safety, easy-operating opening lever, steel-on-steel hinges and lockplate opening system, and recoil activated ejection to keep unfired shells in the chamber. The 828U comes in nickel-engraved and black anodized models with 26- or 28-inch barrels. The 828U weighs about 6.5 pounds and that light weight comes from no side rib, a carbon-fiber top rib and aluminum receiver. The trigger assembly detaches for easy cleaning.

I shot an 828U at clay targets and, if I do say so myself, shot quite well with the gun. The targets floated ever so slightly above rib in their rising arc and the gun seemed to fire on its own. By the way, "U" stands for upland.

The Benelli Performance Shop 20-Gauge Turkey Edition is based on the belief a hat-full of shot is not required to kill a turkey. The Turkey is based on the M2 Field autoloader with its Inertia Driven system and a weight of 5.9 pounds. A full choke and lengthened forcing cone contribute to tight and uniform patterns, and the barrel is ported to reduce kick and muzzle flip. The Turkey comes with a ComforTech stock in Realtree APG camo. A Burris FastFire II red-dot sight is mounted and ready for opening day.

The 20-Gauge Waterfowl Edition is also based on the M2 Field with a lighter trigger pull, large bolt handle, and longer and wider bolt release. The Waterfowl comes with a sling and a set of Rob Roberts Custom Triple Threat choke tubes for short, medium and long-range shooting. A ComforTech stock reduces felt recoil. The barrel wears a HiViz Comp front sight with a variety of colored fiber-optic inserts.

The M4 Tactical, employed by armed forces and law enforcement units around the country, is now available with Cerakote coating. The M4 Cerakote resists corrosion and scratches from some of the harshest conditions around. (www.benelliusa.com)

Browning

The demand for 16-gauge shotguns builds to the point every half dozen years or so that it's worthwhile for gun companies to chamber a gun to meet the call. It has been even longer, 25 years in fact, since Browning chambered the

Benelli M2 Performance Shop
Waterfowl Edition 20 Gauge

Benelli M2 Performance Shop
Turkey Edition 20 Gauge

Benelli M4 Cerakote
Tactical Shotgun

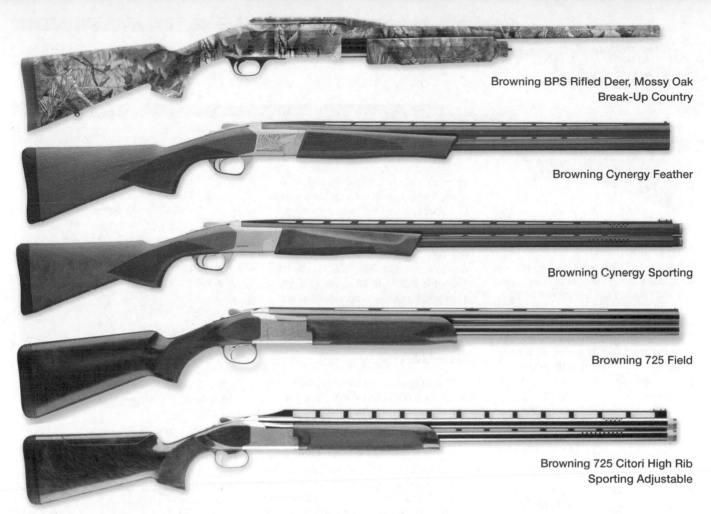

Browning BPS Rifled Deer, Mossy Oak Break-Up Country

Browning Cynergy Feather

Browning Cynergy Sporting

Browning 725 Field

Browning 725 Citori High Rib Sporting Adjustable

popular Citori over/under in 16 gauge, but now it is back in style as the Citori Gran Lightning. The Lightning wears a satin-finished walnut buttstock and fore-end complemented with a ventilated rib on 26- or 28-inch blued barrels and high-relief engraved steel receiver. The barrel selector/safety is on the tang and full, modified and improved cylinder choke tubes are included. Weight is a rather heavy at 7 pounds, 5 ounces.

The Citori White Lightning over/under is also chambered in 16 gauge, as well as 12, 20 and 28 gauge, and .410 bore. The White Lightning has a silver nitride finished steel receiver with high-relief engraving, contrasting polished blued barrels and oil-finish walnut. The round knob grip and fore-end go nicely together. A curved grip is also available. The .410 weighs 6½ pounds with 26-inch barrels. The 12 gauge weighs 8 pounds, also with 26-inch barrels.

Browning's BT-99 Plus trap gun has a polished blued finish, high-relief engraving and a stock made of Grade III/IV walnut with a gloss oil finish. The Plus

has a ported barrel, Midas Grade Invector Plus choke tubes, adjustable comb and a high-post rib.

The company has also released two new versions of its pump shotgun. The BPS 12-gauge National Wild Turkey Federation (NWTF) model is veiled in Mossy Oak Break-Up Country camouflage. The composite stock is covered with Dura-Touch armor coating. Three choke tubes are included, as well as a HiViz 4-in-1 fiber-optic front sight. The BPS Rifled Deer, in 20 and 12 gauge, is also covered in Mossy Oak Break-Up Country camo.

The Cynergy has become Browning's flagship over/under and new variations of the gun continue. The Cynergy Classic Trap Unsingle Combo with Adjustable Comb has a gray laminated Monte Carlo buttstock with right-hand palm swell, adjustable comb, semibeavertail fore-end with finger grooves, two barrel sets (30/34 inches, 32/32 inches or 32/34 inches) that all fit in a green canvas and leather case. The Cynergy Feather Composite Charcoal Gray weighs as little as 5 pounds, 15 ounces in .410 bore and

up to 7 pounds, 11 ounces in 12 gauge. The light weight comes from a composite stock with black overmolding. The Cynergy Field's wood is finished in satin varnish to contrast with a silver nitride finish on the receiver and matte blued barrels. The gun is available in 12, 20, 28 and .410. The Cynergy Micro Midas 20-gauge has a 13-inch length of pull and 24- or 26-inch barrels for smaller shooters. The 6-pound gun has a satin-varnish finish walnut stock, silver nitride low-profile receiver and matte blued barrels. Full, modified and improved cylinder choke tubes are included. The 30- or 32-inch ported barrels on the Cynergy Sporting 12 gauge have a HiViz Pro-Comp fiber-optic sight, full, modified and skeet choke tubes, and Grade I/II walnut stock. The stock is also available with a comb that is adjustable for a custom fit.

The Silver NWTF 12-gauge autoloader has a rifle-style HiViz 4-in-1 fiber-optic sight, Mossy Oak Break-Up Country camo and Invector Plus choke tubes, including a Full Strut tube for its 24-inch barrel. The Silver Rifled Deer 12 and 20

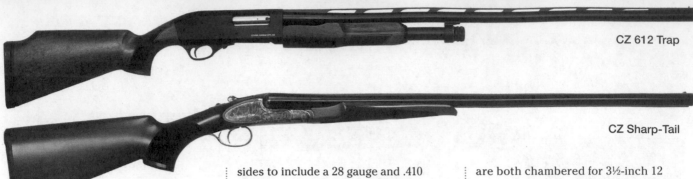

CZ 612 Trap

CZ Sharp-Tail

gauge are also camo covered and have a cantilever base for optics.

A couple of Citori over/unders are now chambered in smaller gauges. The Citori 725 Feather is chambered in 20 gauge and weighs 5 pounds, 12 ounces. The Citori 725 Field and Sporting are new in 28 gauge and .410 bore. The 725 Pro Sporting 12 and 20 gauge each have an adjustable comb and extended full, improved modified, modified, improved cylinder and skeet choke tubes. Sights are HiViz Pro-Comp front and ivory midbead on 30- or 32-inch barrels. The Pro Balance system allows shooters to customize gun balance with an adjustable weight in the buttstock. Another 725 version has a long 16-inch length of pull. The Citori 725 Sporting Grade VII is embellished with deep-relief hand engraving and select high-grade walnut. It has a HiViz Pro-Comp fiber-optic front bead sight and its barrel is ported. The Citori Crossover Target is made with a blue/black laminated buttstock and fore-end and throws shot slightly high in a 60/40 pattern. (www.browning.com)

Cabela's

Cabela's has expanded its Turkish-made Dickinson Estate Grade side-by-

sides to include a 28 gauge and .410 bore. A two-barrel set combination gun has also been added, one with 20- and 28-gauge barrels on a 20-gauge frame, and another with 28-gauge and .410 barrels on a 28-gauge frame. The Plantation Grade is an upgrade of the Estate. It's available in 20 and 28 gauge and .410. This gun has case-colored sideplates and upgraded Turkish Walnut stock and fore-end. (www.cabelas.com)

CZ –USA

The Ringneck has been replaced by the Sharp-Tail side-by-side. The Sharp-Tail is a new action that is smaller overall and features coil springs instead of leaf springs. Its single trigger mates with newly designed sears and floating firing pins. Stocks are Turkish walnut and five choke tubes are included for the 28-inch barrels. The Sharp-Tail is chambered in 12, 20 and 28 gauges, and .410 bore. The Sharp-Tail Target 12 gauge has 30-inch barrels, a semibeavertail fore-end and a raised rib. It comes equipped with six Kicks extended stainless steel choke tubes.

CZ also has three new 612 pumps this year. The 612 Trap wears a 32-inch ported barrel with five extended choke tubes and a Monte Carlo buttstock. It's chambered in 3-inch 12 gauge. The 612 Magnum Turkey and Magnum Waterfowl

are both chambered for 3½-inch 12 gauge. The Turkey comes with modified and extra-full choke tubes for its 26-inch barrel, and is finished in Realtree Xtra Green camo. The Waterfowl has a 28-inch barrel with five choke tubes. It's wrapped in Realtree MAX-4 camo. (cz-usa.com)

Mossberg

Mossberg has been busy building shotguns with new sights, left-hand shotguns, and shotguns that accept the Mossberg FLEX system to increase their utility.

The 930 and 935 Magnum DC Pro Series shotguns feature gas pistons, piston rings, magazine tubes, hammers, sears, return spring plungers and return spring tubes that are all nickel-boron coated for corrosion resistance and easy cleaning. The stainless steel return spring ensures reliable operation of the recoil system. These shotguns feature full Realtree MAX-5 camo, TRUGLO Tru•bead Dual Color front fiber-optic sight, Uni-Line soft-angled receiver design for proper eye and sight alignment, and full, modified and improved cylinder choke tubes. The 12-gauge, 3½-inch 935 Magnum DC Pro Series shotgun has a 28-inch overbored, vent-rib barrel. The 930 DC Pro Series 12-gauge, 3-inch shotgun

Mossberg 930 DC
Pro-Series Autoloader

Mossberg 935 Magnum DC
Pro-Series

Mossberg 500
20-Gauge Slugster

Mossberg 930 SPX 8-Shot
With XS Ghost Ring Sights

features a 28-inch vent-rib barrel. Both have an easy quick-empty release button that provides for convenient unloading of shells from the magazine.

The 835 Ulti-Mag and 535 ATS Turkey 12-gauge 3½-inch pumps both have Marble Arms Bullseye Sights for low-light conditions of early morning and evening hunts. The double-ring design of the Bullseye rear sight is combined with its light-gathering, fiber-optic front sight. When the rear sight is misaligned, the front sight drifts out of the smaller center ring and reminds hunters to keep their head tight on the comb. Other standard features include a 24-inch

ventilated rib barrel with Accu-Mag, Ulti-Full choke tubes, a drilled and tapped receiver and sling swivel studs.

The 12-gauge 3½-inch 535 ATS pump action builds on the 835 Ulti-Mag and 500 pump-action guns with its lighter weight and shortened magazine tube. The soft-angled, Uni-Line receiver of the 535 marries perfectly with the stock for correct sight alignment and quick target acquisition. The 535 ATS features a 22-inch vent-rib barrel with a XX-Full choke tube.

The Mossberg 500/590/590A1 L Series of 20 and 12-gauge pumps are available in left-handed models in 15

versions. Nine versions of the 500 L Series can easily be reconfigured using Mossberg's FLEX TLS accessory fore-ends, buttstocks and recoil pads. The 500 All-Purpose, Slugster, Turkey, Waterfowl, Field/Deer Combo and 500 Super Bantam also get the left-hand treatment.

XS Express or XS Ghost Ring sights on a receiver-mounted Picatinny rail are featured on seven pumps and autoloaders. The XS Express sight consists of a white dot front sight that aligns with a shallow V rear sight. The XS Ghost Ring has a post front sight that centers in a large diameter rear aperture. Express

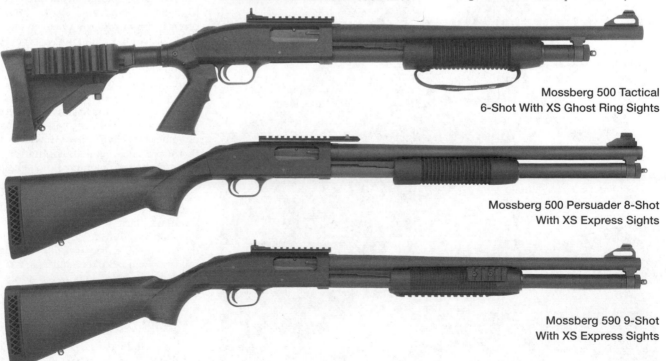

Mossberg 500 Tactical
6-Shot With XS Ghost Ring Sights

Mossberg 500 Persuader 8-Shot
With XS Express Sights

Mossberg 590 9-Shot
With XS Express Sights

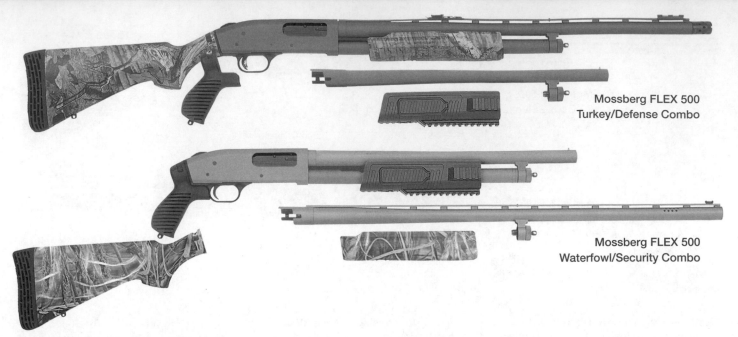

Mossberg FLEX 500
Turkey/Defense Combo

Mossberg FLEX 500
Waterfowl/Security Combo

sights are included on the 500 Persuader, 590 9-Shot and 930 5-Shot. Ghost Ring sights are incorporated on the 590A1 Tri-Rail 9-Shot, 500 Tri-Rail 8-Shot, 500 Tactical ADJ 6-Shot and 930 SPX 8-Shot.

Three hunting and security combination guns are available featuring FLEX Tool-less Locking System (TLS) components. FLEX TLS equipped stocks, fore-ends and recoil pads are designed with simple, strong connectors for easy switching. The combination guns include the Turkey/Security, Waterfowl/Security and Slug/Security. A multi-compartment FLEX soft case comes with each. (www.mossberg.com)

Remington

The V3 is the smaller brother of VERSA MAX 12-gauge 3½-inch autoloader, but with a few changes. The V3 has a 3-inch 12-gauge chamber, and like the VERSA MAX, it readily cycles light target loads on up to magnum shells. The V3's short piston stroke provides for a more compact gas system located directly forward of the receiver, and therefore allows a bit shorter receiver. Versaport technology that leaves various numbers of gas ports open, depending on the length of the shell, ensures just the right amount of gas is bled to cycle various shells. In addition, pressure-compensating valves in gas chambers on each side of the barrel further reduce recoil and optimize performance of magnum 3-inch shells. The V3 has no recoil spring in the stock, which allows the use of folding and tactical stocks. It's available with a walnut, black or camo synthetic fore-end and buttstock with cast and drop shims. The receiver finish is black oxide or camo. Barrel lengths are 26 or 28 inches and it weighs 7.25 pounds. (www.remington.com)

Stoeger

Stoeger Industries has taken its M3000 autoloader line to the next level with the

Remington V3
Field Sport Synthetic

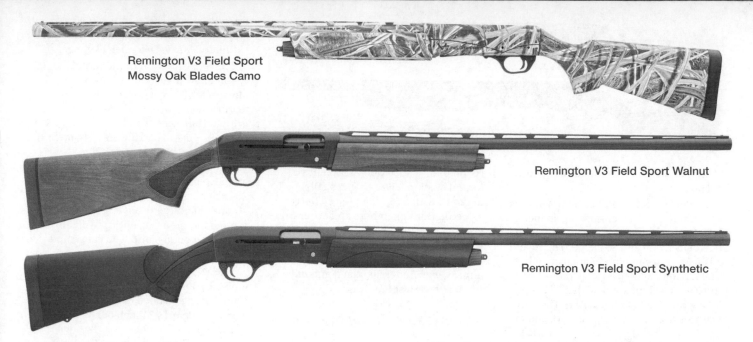

Remington V3 Field Sport
Mossy Oak Blades Camo

Remington V3 Field Sport Walnut

Remington V3 Field Sport Synthetic

creation of the M3K 3-Gun shotgun. The M3K relies on the fast, dependable Inertia Driven operating system and adds an extended bolt handle and an oversized aluminum bolt release and safety. An elongated carrier and large loading port make for quicker reloading. The 12-gauge has a 24-inch barrel with cylinder, improved cylinder and modified choke tubes, fiber-optic red-bar front sight and a weight of 7.3 pounds. (www.stoegerindustries.com)

Weatherby

Shotguns for turkey, waterfowl and upland birds, and a compact pump are new guns from Weatherby this year. The SA-459 Turkey auto, and PA-459 Turkey and PA-08 Turkey pumps are covered in Realtree Xtra Green camo pattern. The SA-459 12 and 20 gauge both feature a 22-inch vent-rib chrome-lined barrel, extended and fluted extra-full choke tube, and sporting-style fore-end and pistol grip. A fiber-optic front sight is standard, and the receiver is drilled and tapped for an included Picatinny rail to mount optics. The PA-459 12 gauge has a

pistol grip, 22-inch chrome-lined barrel, fiber-optic front sight, an extended and fluted extra-full choke tube, and is drilled and tapped for an included Picatinny rail. The 12-gauge PA-08 Turkey offers a 22-inch vent-rib chrome-lined barrel, brass bead front sight and flush-mounted full choke tube.

The 12-gauge SA-08 Waterfowler and PA-08 Waterfowler shotguns have an injection-molded stock dip-coated in

Realtree Max-5 camouflage. The 12-gauge guns have a 3-inch chamber and either a 26- or 28-inch vented top rib barrel with improved cylinder, modified and full choke tubes included.

The 20-gauge PA-08 Synthetic Compact (22-inch barrel), WBY-X SA-08 Kryptek Compact and SA-08 Volt Compact shotguns (24-inch barrels) all have a 12½-inch length of pull. Other features include a lightweight, black synthetic

Weatherby SA-459 Turkey

Weatherby PA-08 Waterfowler Max-5

Weatherby SA-08 Waterfowler Max-5

Weatherby SA-459 TR

Weatherby Element Deluxe

Weatherby PA-08 Synthetic Compact

stock and matte black metal. Weight is 5¾ pounds.

The new Element Deluxe auto features an aluminum receiver housing an inertia-operated action with a 26- or 28-inch barrel in 12, 20 and 28 gauge. The 12 and 20 have a chrome-lined 3-inch chamber. The Element sports an AA Grade American walnut stock with 22 lines-per-inch wrap-around checkering. The gun features a ventilated top rib with a fiber-optic green bead, and a drop-out trigger assembly. The 12 and 20-gauge models have Weatherby's Integral Multi Choke System of improved cylinder, modified and full tubes. The 28 gauge offers the Beretta Mobil pattern choke tubes. Weights are slightly less than 7 pounds.

Orion over/under shotguns have returned to the Weatherby line in 12 gauge with 26- or 28-inch barrels, 3-inch chambers and a weight of 7 pounds. The Orion wears a Grade A walnut stock with a high-gloss finish and a rounded grip, featuring 22 lines-per-inch checkering and Pachmayr Decelerator

recoil pad. The boxlock action has a forged steel receiver that is shallow in depth with a top tang safety/barrel selector. Both chambers and bores are chrome lined and have automatic shell ejectors. A matte ventilated top rib has a brass bead front sight. Chokes include improved cylinder, modified and full tubes. (www.weatherby.com)

Winchester Repeating Arms

Winchester now offers its SX3 auto and SXP pump in 20 gauge. The Field and Field Compact 20 gauge models will feature a satin-finished wood stock and fore-end and black matte finish on the aluminium receiver. The Black Shadow wears a black matte synthetic stock and fore-end with textured gripping surfaces. The Turkey Hunter as a 24-inch barrel with a TRUGLO fiber-optic front bead and adjustable rear sight, and Inflex Technology recoil pad. A rear ghost ring sight integrated into a Picatinny base, a side-mounted rail and

Door Breacher choke tube have been added to the SXP Ultimate Defender and Ultimate Marine Defender 12 gauge.

The SX3 Universal Hunter autoloader 12- and 20-gauge models are covered in Mossy Oak Break-Up Country camo and feature synthetic stocks with textured gripping surfaces. The 12-gauge model has a chrome-plated 3½-inch chamber with a 26- or 28-inch barrel. The 20-gauge model has a 3-inch chamber and also has the choice of a 26- or 28-inch barrel. A TRUGLO front sight is standard and the receiver is drilled and tapped for mounting optics. Weight is 7 to 7-1/8 pounds for the 12 gauge and 6-5/8 to 6¾ pounds for the 20 gauge.

The SX3 Long Beard Turkey features a pistol grip stock and Briley Extra-Full Long Beard extended choke tube. The Long Beard's 24-inch barrel has a chrome-plated chamber for 12-gauge 3½-inch shells and its synthetic stock and fore-end are covered in Mossy Oak Break-Up Country camo. Choose an Inflex Technology recoil pad of three thicknesses. Sights consist of a TRUGLO fiber-optic front with an adjustable rear sight. Optics can be mounted on a Weaver-style cantilever rail. Three comb inserts fine-tune eye alignment behind the sights. The SX3 Ultimate Sporting Adjustable is the tried-and-true SX3 Sporting with an oversized red Briley operating handle and magazine release button. (www.winchesterguns.com)

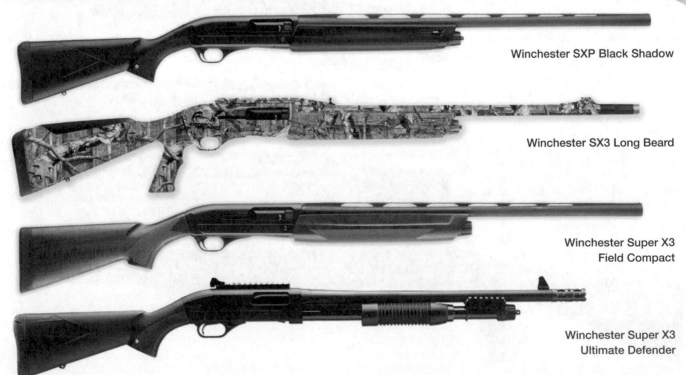

Winchester SXP Black Shadow

Winchester SX3 Long Beard

Winchester Super X3 Field Compact

Winchester Super X3 Ultimate Defender

New Semi-Auto Handguns

BY Kevin Muramatsu

A s in previous years, firearms manufacturers continue to produce new products for the American consumer. Those new products are sometimes brand-new items, but the majority are variations on already produced models. Most companies do a pretty good job when it comes to releasing a new firearm, and then in the next two or three years if the platform is well accepted, of also adding variations to that platform's line to increase its appeal to more shooters and gun owners.

Most often, this involves some sort of cosmetic change or improvement. For example, a frequent – universal actually – example of this concept relates to pistols with a polymer frame. The frames are black to start with, but with successful sales comes the introduction of green frames next year, followed by a desert tan or flat dark earth color. While it is certainly not restricted to polymer-framed pistols, it certainly is the most common there. This pattern is as old as the Glock and that was arguably the first mass-marketed and successful pistol to receive this treatment. Several guns in this article will follow this pattern. I for one, rather like

this pattern. Black is so boring, and even the presence of another earthy color like olive drab adds a little character to an otherwise mass-produced handgun. There are even brightly colored frames with metal flakes embedded in them; the best example of this type would be the EAA Witness Pavona, which is directly marketed to new women shooters.

Almost as frequent is the addition of a special plating to the frame or the slide, usually the slide. The use of materials such as nickel and chrome has been around for a century or more and continues to be used regularly. However, newer external coverings come in the form of Titanium nitride, RoBar, Nickel-Boron or Teflon, in addition to the sprayed-on coatings like Cerakote or DuraCoat. Conveniently, while most of these surface treatments are more functionally intended, to act to prevent corrosion for example, they also tend to add some cosmetic enhancement to the firearm to some degree or another. A good example of this would be the Nickel-Boron craze currently enveloping much of the firearms industry. It is a very hard material with high lubricity and is generally somewhat gold colored, and can be polished to a high sheen. It looks pretty

good and it's very easy to clean. Mostly you find it on rifle bolts, but several pistols have been subject to it recently as well. Contrast this to Titanium nitride that can be displayed in very colorful ways. Traditionally it was only gold colored, but now it can attain any color of the rainbow. The use is mostly driven by cosmetic demands but it also is a good corrosion preventative as well.

Truly new firearms are less common and the big companies tend to only come out with new models every few years. Smaller companies have a hard time getting into the game, but with names like Kel-Tec, Kahr and Diamondback making it big in relatively short order, it does happen. Also very common lately is the specialization of full-size firearms into compact and even subcompact versions more suitable for concealed carry. The legal carry market is the only one really showing some energy right now and manufacturers know this and continue to release new, small models for the concealed carry crowd.

So we are going to look at a decent selection of companies and what they released in late 2014 and very early 2015, all of which should be in full production by the latter end of 2015.

ATI
Firepower
Extreme:
FXH Series

ATI

ATI has expanded their Firepower Xtreme line of 1911 pistols with the new Hybrid. Mirroring the Omni Hybrid AR receivers that utilize polymer receivers with aluminum reinforcing, the Xtreme Hybrid uses a polymer frame with steel inserts for support and interfacing with the slide. The look has been changed considerably. Though quite clearly derived from the famous 1911, the frame has finger grooves, which is somewhat unusual, and the slide has been "sleekified" and is marginally lower than is normal in a 1911 to assist in mitigating muzzle flip when firing. They will be available in full-size, Commander and Officer versions as well. The FXH series all have an MSRP of $660. (www.americantactical.us)

Bersa

Last year saw the introduction of the BPCC series of pistols in 9mm and .40 S&W. This year Bersa has unveiled the BPCC in .380 ACP. It has the same size frame and slide as the 9s and 40s and is fed with an eight-round magazine. This is a small gun but still allows most users to get their pinkie finger on the frame, which helps with recoil control. (bersa.eagleimportsinc.com)

Browning

The 1911-22 has been out for a couple of years now. As one of the first 85 percent rimfire clones, it is a nice little .22 for small hands to shoot. This year, Browning introduced the same pistol but upgraded to .380 ACP. The .22 and the .380 pistols are the exact same size, though more steel is used in the .380 and is a bit heavier. Multiple variants are currently available for the .22, but the 1911-380 has only one model on

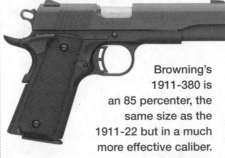

Browning's 1911-380 is an 85 percenter, the same size as the 1911-22 but in a much more effective caliber.
Photo courtesy Browning.

The new Browning 1911-380 below the slightly older 1911-22. The new .380 is more of a Commander style with all the bells and whistles on it.

the market right now with the usual full-out 1911 frills like an ambidextrous safety, skeletonized trigger and extended beavertail grip safety. Browning is clearly aiming at the .380 concealed carry market and I think it will be very successful version. The current MSRP is $670. (www.browning.com)

Caracal

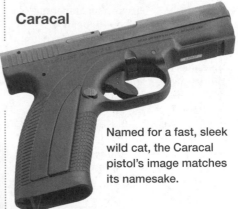

Named for a fast, sleek wild cat, the Caracal pistol's image matches its namesake.

The Caracal pistol was introduced several years ago and deserves a new release entry now since it disappeared for a bit and has since returned. It is a full-size 9mm pistol with an 18-round magazine and tactical rail made in the United Arab Emirates, a new player on the domestic arms scene. A compact model with a 15-round magazine is also anticipated. (www.caracal-usa.com)

CZ-USA

CZ-USA has several new pistols available this year. Perhaps the most

The Bersa BPCC pistols now come in all three flavors of 9, 40, and 380, all in the same size.

The CZ Scorpion is back. It's just spelled different and is a completely different gun.
Photo courtesy CZ-USA.

Yet another pistol variant of a former rifle, the Bren from CZ-USA joins other such samples from other manufacturers.
Photo courtesy CZ-USA.

sidearm, and as part of NATO, the AR-15 magazine is the standard used. The MSRP is quite a bit higher than that for the Scorpion at $1,982.

The CZ 75 has been around for a long time now, but CZ continues to tweak and modify it for the current customer base. The newest is a commemorative model called the CZ 75 B 40th Anniversary Limited Edition. A high-polish blue finish with hand engraving is the first feature. This is backed up with controls that are titanium nitride plated in a rainbow color effect. The plastic or plain wood grips are replaced with custom birds-eye maple grips that have a number of hues including blue, black and gold/yellow. Very attractive grips. This $1,500 pistol is limited to 1,000 pieces and is sure to be a fine collectible for those interested in such.

CZ has also entered the 1911 market with a basic model reminiscent of the 1911A1, but with a few small improvements, such as taller and easier-to-see sights and a stainless steel barrel. The controls are also checkered and the grip panels are walnut. The company is also making the slide-to-frame fit a bit tighter than the original 1911A1 for better accuracy. There are other minor improvements that, as a whole, are designed to give a quality custom pistol feel to a gun with 90-year-old clothing. This pistol also has an $849 MSRP and, allowing for the taller sights, looks almost exactly like the original. It is also the first CZ pistol made in the USA. (cz-usa.com)

Dan Wesson

Several different 1911-type models have been made by Dan Wesson Firearms for some time now and this line has again expanded. The Silverback is available in .45 ACP and 10mm with night sights and eight-round magazines. In fit and finish it is similar to the Valor

well-received handgun has been their new Scorpion Evo 3 S1 Pistol. Recently approved for import, the Scorpion Evo 3 is nothing like the original and famous CZ Skorpion vz. 61 machine pistol. First of all, so far it's chambered only in 9mm instead of the old vz. 61 options of .32 ACP, .380, 9mm and 9x18. Hopefully the CZ will offer some additional calibers in the near future. Secondly, it's a totally different animal in appearance and size. The gun ships with clear 20-round magazines, has ambidextrous controls and rugged adjustable sights, and has rails on it so you can make it heavier by adding things you don't need to it. You can even attach a sling to the back of the

receiver or use a separate adaptor for mounting a pistol stabilizing brace. The MSRP is well under a thousand bucks at $849, which makes it as affordable as the average AR-15.

To accompany the Scorpion, is the pistol version of the Bren rifle, called the CZ 805 Bren S1. The Bren, like the Scorpion, has ambidextrous controls and the ability to mount a sling or pistol brace at the back of the receiver. Semiauto and chambered in 5.56mm/.223, it also uses AR-15 type of magazine, of course, which is a pretty universal thing to do with modern firearms chambered for that cartridge. Since the Bren was designed to be the Czech Republic's new standard

The CZ 75 turned 40 with a Limited Edition model. This anniversary edition has many eye-catching cosmetic enhancements.
Photo courtesy CZ-USA.

CZ's new 1911. It looks "original retro," but has useful high-quality enhancements.
Photo courtesy CZ-USA.

The full-size high-end Silverback from Dan Wesson.
Photo courtesy Dan Wesson.

Like the Silverback, the Valkyrie is a top-notch Commander/Officer hybrid-size pistol.
Photo courtesy Dan Wesson.

line of pistols but is two-tone rather than all black. The grips are G10 – and if you don't have something with G10 grip panels you are missing out. They really look sharp and enhance the appearance of any pistol they are mounted to, just as they do the Silverback. This pistol is the pinnacle of the Dan Wesson line and they are sold for $2,012.

Similar in quality and price is the new Valkyrie. This is an Officer-size frame under a Commander-size slide and barrel – a true mix granting the concealability of an Officer model but with the accuracy potential of a Commander. Tritium sights are standard, as is the $2,012 MSRP. (cz-usa.com/product-category/dan-wesson-2/)

Diamondback

The DB FS Nine is the full-size version of Diamondback Firearms' DB9. This is definitely full size, with a nice long rail

under the frame big enough to mount a machete to it. The barrel is a rather uncommon 4.75 inches long and the magazine has a large extension/base pad on it for positive control. This pistol just looks skinny, sleek and low slung, and is only an inch wide. MSRP is only $483, and therefore quite affordable. (diamondbackfirearms.com)

FNH

FNH-USA has introduced a compact version of the FNS pistol, named simply the FNS Compact. Available with a manual safety, or if you prefer, no manual safety, it is somewhat shorter and not quite as tall as the parent FNS pistol. It is chambered in 9mm or .40 S&W and has a 3.6-inch barrel compared to the full-size gun's 4 inches, or last year's introduction, the long slide at 5 inches. A large front sight rounds out the mix, giving this fully ambidextrous pistol a rapid acquisition feature for concealed carry. MSRP is $599. (www.fnhusa.com)

Glock

After being in the rumor-mill for years, Glock has finally given shooters a single-stack 9mm. Introduced at the NRA Annual Meeting in Nashville in April of 2015, the 43 is slimmer and trimmer in the grip, as one would expect. The Model 43's slide width is just .87 inch, compared to the Model 26's 1.2 inches. Designed for more comfortable concealed-carry, this should be a very popular model. Magazine capacity is reduced to six rounds, plus one in the chamber.

Left: The DB FS Nine is a full-size handgun from Diamondback Firearms. It has a very low bore axis and is very competitively priced.

Right: Glock "perfection" continues to change. The new Glock 40, designed for big-game hunting, can be accessorized with a micro-red-dot sight mounted to a cut-out in the slide.

Glock is one of those companies that makes something new or improved every single year. For decades, there were few pistol owners that had optics on their handguns. Then some of the big-bore revolvers started to sport them (usually for big-game hunting), and after that they became quite common on competition handguns. Still, optics remain uncommon on the average pistol owner's property, and it is virtually unheard of for them to be mounted on handguns from the factory. For that matter, the ability to mount optics to pistols is usually only gained after a trip to the local gunsmith, and 3-gunners started the trend of cutting slides to mount micro red-dot sights to their guns. Glock has now added this feature to several existing firearms and one new model this year.

Glock calls it the MOS configuration. It involves taking a standard slide and taking out a chunk right in front of the rear sight. This leaves a footprint that fits a Leupold DeltaPoint or similar sight to sit below the top of the slide. This is mostly done in order to lower the overall height to co-witness the iron sights with the red dot, or to at least allow the shooter to

The new single-stack 9mm Glock 43.

still see and use the iron sights through the glass. A filler piece, or cover, is standard in the slide until you decide to mount your optic. Glock has done this with the Gen4 models of the G34, G35 and G41 (9mm, .40 and .45 respectively), and finally on the new Gen4 G40 in 10mm. The new G40 is billed as an ideal hunting pistol, and certainly with a red dot mounted can be a very fast-acquiring tool for smaller big game like whitetails and feral pigs. It has a full 6-inch barrel and 15-round capacity. As with other Gen4 models, the G40 has additional backstraps to lengthen the grip according to the individual user's desires (as if Glock grips weren't big enough already!). The other MOS versions are clearly marketed for the competitive crowd, which already commonly use Glock pistols in a variety of disciplines. Thin adapter plates are included for the most commonly used micro red dots such as the Docter, Trijicon, C-More and Leupold models. (www.glock.com)

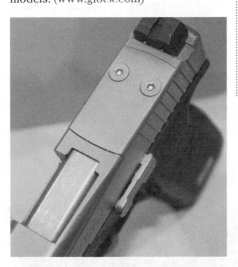

Heckler & Koch

Heckler & Koch in mid-2014 introduced their first polymer-frame striker-fired pistol in 30 years. The VP9 bears the HK look and feel but has a double-action-only trigger, like most striker-fired guns. The trigger is quite smooth and has a good overall feel. The VP9 is not quite full size, and almost could be classified as a semifull or some other similar mix of words. It has a 15-round magazine and the MSRP is comparable to many of its competitors at $719. An ambidextrous slide stop, and replaceable backstraps and palm swells make the gun very user friendly. Unusual, though welcome, is a cocking enhancer at the back of the slide that makes it a little easier to grasp and pull. (hk-usa.com)

Kahr

The Gen2 Premium line of pistols has been released for 2015. Like several other companies' handguns, the slide is cut out on the 5- and 6-inch barrel pistols for the mounting of a micro red-dot sight, such as the Leupold DeltaPoint. Tall iron sights are paired with this cut-out slide so that the red dot can be co-witnessed. A trigger safety and 30 percent shorter

Left: This Kahr TP-45 close-up shows the cover in place over the red-dot sight mount.

Below: The Gen2 Kahr pistols display more cosmetic machining than in the previous generation, and many bear the now famous red-dot sight cut-out in the slide.

Kimber's Solo Sapphire at the range. The blue slide is striking.

trigger travel length also makes the pull feel a lot nicer. Other minor redesigns on the Gen2 models include front slide serrations and accessory rails. Some models are available with compensated barrels. It's almost not a concealed carry pistol any longer. (www.kahr.com)

Kimber

Where to start? 2015 has brought the release of a number of Kimber pistols with either a significant cosmetic upgrade, or the addition of a very useful item.

The cosmetic area deals with two totally fantastic finishes. The first is a glossy, deep black PVD finish that Kimber is calling "Onyx." You can see your reflection in it and it reminds this author of a black lacquered katana scabbard. It is also backed up with some minor engraving to give the finish an accent. The second finish is similar, but is a bright blue "Sapphire." This is an attractive finish and instantly one is reminded of the nitre blueing so popular on high-end pistols at the onset of the 20th century. The same scrollwork engraving is present on the Sapphire as on the Onyx and both have matching grips, blue machined G-10 for the Sapphire and black machined aluminum for the Onyx.

The Sapphire finish and grip combo is available on the Pro II version of Kimber's 1911 and on the Solo Sapphire, both in 9mm only. The Solo is Kimber's addition to the subcompact 9mm striker-fired market and has been around for several years now. The Onyx upgrade can be applied to the Ultra II pistol in both .45 ACP and 9mm. Both of the 1911s have an

MSRP of $1,652, and the Solo Sapphire has a $1,291 price tag.

Another addition to the Solo line is the Solo Crimson Carry. A black slide with a Crimson Trace Lasergrip with the appearance of wood grain makes a nice three-tone gun, and the presence of a laser will reassure many a concealed carry gun owner.

A stainless Raptor version of the Micro pistol is also coming out. This mustang-size handgun now can be had with the scalloped "feathered" slide serrations and grip panels. In .380 Auto and at $960, it is also equipped with a set of Tritium night sights.

Now an option on the Warrior SOC, the Desert Warrior and Pro TLE II is the wonderful extended barrel with a threaded muzzle. Kimber calls it the TFS (threaded for suppression) barrel, it is definitely intended to exploit the rapidly growing sound suppressor market and the increasing amount of Americans buying into the coolness of reduced muzzle blast, sound, recoil mitigation and general entertainment enhancement found in using sound suppressors. They range in price from $1,153 for the TLE II up to $1,738 for the Warrior SOC (which also sports a Crimson Trace Rail Master laser unit).

The Eclipse series of 1911s is also now available with Crimson Trace Lasergrips under the LG descriptor. (www.kimberamerica.com)

Les Baer

The GT Monolith Stinger is the newest addition to Les Baer's collec-

The Monolith Stinger series is Les Baer Custom's newest inclusion. They are heavyweights in .45 ACP and .38 Super.

tion of 1911-style pistols. Featuring a round-bottom, full-length dust cover on the front end of the frame allows the Monolith Stinger to reduce muzzle flip because of the additional forward mass. The slide and barrel are Commander size, and the frame is Officer size, following the trend of many 1911 makers by combining the best features of the Commander and Officer pistols into one assembly. Fully adjustable night sights are standard, with three magazines and an MSRP of $2,915 for the .45 ACP and $3,090 for the .38 Super. The GT Monolith Stinger Heavyweight models are almost identical, but retain a squared-off frame bottom for a little more weight. $3,015 and $3,190 for those, respectively. (www.lesbaer.com)

Magnum Research

The new Baby Desert Eagle II is an evolution from the old Baby Eagle and sports more Desert Eagle-ish

appearance and other mostly cosmetic improvements, another example of the current trend of gun manufacturers universally branding their products by common visual identification. It is available in steel or polymer frames; in full-size, semicompact and compact versions; and in 9mm, .40 and .45. Prices start at $629. (www.magnumresearch.com)

Rock Island Armory/Armscor

In a similar move to Browning's 1911-380, RIA has made an 85 percenter to its normal-size 1911. It's called the Baby Rock .380 and it has more styling changes than are evident on the other example. It weighs a pound and a half, give or take, whether loaded or unloaded with a seven-round magazine. It fires straight blowback. MSRP is $460. (us.armscor.com)

This is the full-size polymer frame Magnum Research Baby Eagle II.

The new striker-fired Ruger LC9s has a much-improved trigger over the original LC9. The Pro model, shown here, has no external safety and no magazine disconnect.

Ruger

Ruger has done something with its 1911 that someone should have thought about doing a long time ago. One of the arguable faults in an aluminum-frame 1911 is that the front top of the magazine well, essentially the feed

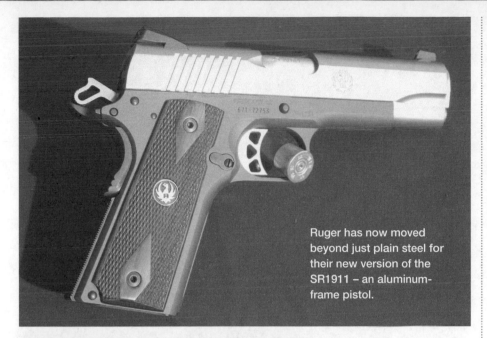

Ruger has now moved beyond just plain steel for their new version of the SR1911 – an aluminum-frame pistol.

Looking closely you can see the light-blueish giveaway of the titanium feed ramp on the Ruger SR1911.

ramp in the frame, gets chewed up from the hollowpoint bullet noses. This is why most aluminum-frame guns have some sort of feed ramp attached to the barrel (either Wilson/Nowlin or Para/Clark usually) with the frame cut out to fit it; then the nose doesn't chew up the frame. What Ruger has done is add a titanium feed ramp insert at the front of the magazine well. It is inserted into a hole and screwed down prior to final machining in the mag well. The result is that after machining there is a seamless, high-durability frame feed ramp for the otherwise all aluminum frame. This Ruger 1911 also has a titanium firing pin for reduced lock time and drop fire chances. It has all the usual other Ruger features and is a Commander-size pistol, which

means it has a full-size frame but with a shorter 4.25-inch barrel.

The Ruger Charger is a pistol version of the venerable 10/22 rifle. Two new models are here. Both of these guns come with threaded and protected muzzles for use with suppressors. Both guns are supplied with an adjustable bipod and both use standard AR-15 pistol grips, so there are many other options out there if you don't like the grip that is supplied. Both models are also shipped with BX-15 15-round magazines. The "standard" model is clothed in a brown laminate stock and the second model has what is called a Green Mountain laminate stock. Even better, on this second model, Ruger has used the 10/22 Takedown system to ensure that the Charger

Takedown can utilize storage space more efficiently. MSRP for the brown laminate model is $309 and for the Takedown model, it is $409.

Ruger LCPs can now be purchased in a model with a red skeletonized aluminum trigger and photoluminescent night sights for $419. Also new is a striker-fired variation of the popular LC9 called the LC9s for shooters who favor the feel of a striker-fired gun. The GP100 Match Champion is now available with either fixed or adjustable sights, and since it is meant for competitive use, it has a tuned action for the perfectionists that might use it in a match. (www.ruger.com)

Smith & Wesson

The M&P line of Smith & Wesson pistols has quite a history. In recent years a .22 LR version of the M&P 9mm was introduced, in the exact same size as the centerfire pistol. Like other manufacturers, S&W has now taken that full-sized pistol and shrunk it down to about 85 percent of its original size. In this case, it became the M&P22 Compact. The grip is reduced in size along with the rest of the frame and the slide so it is a very comfortable gun for small-handed adults and even adolescents. It has the usual 10-round magazine and was released in mid-2014. A threaded muzzle, and manual safety and magazine safety are present on these models, adding to the appropriateness for a semiauto training pistol with an MSRP of $389.

The M&P9 also is available with a "carbon-fiber finish." It's not really carbon

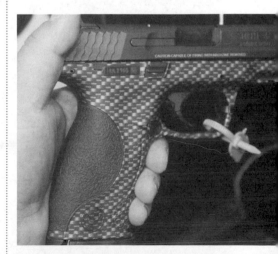

This is the new "carbon fiber" finish on the Smith & Wesson M&P pistols. The look is popular and becoming common on guns even when there is no actual carbon fiber on the gun.

The S&W M&P22 Compact. You can get both a standard-size pistol and a pint-size pistol. Small hands rejoice.

The S&W Pro Series C.O.R.E. is now ported. It can also mount a red dot on the slide.

fiber, though it does a good job of appearing so, but is rather a printed-on graphic. Similarly, a flat dark earth finish is new this year on the same pistols. Also, riding the bandwagon, 9mm and .45 pistols can be purchased with a threaded barrel kit that contains an extra barrel with those wonderful muzzle threads for suppressor attachment. Swap barrels as needed as the guns come with both. $669 and $719 are the factory asking prices for the 9mm and .45 respectively.

The handy little Shield subcompact can be purchased this year with a factory-installed Crimson Trace Green Laserguard. I think they should call it "emerald trace" since it isn't red, but I'm not in charge. It is a front activation conformal mount that sits just in front of the triggerguard. Hopefully accommodating holsters will be forthcoming shortly. With the laser, the Shield MSRPs for $589.

The M&P Pro C.O.R.E. has been updated with a more versatile micro red-dot sight cut, and decorative, lightening cuts in the slide, with barrel ports under

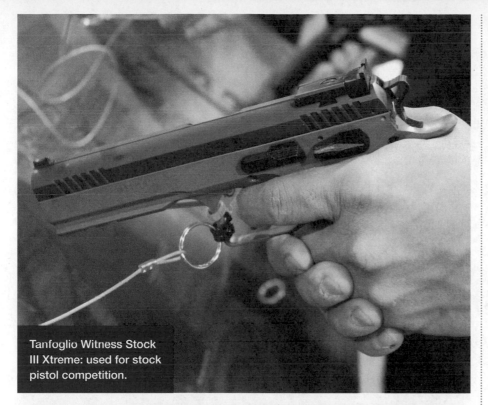

Tanfoglio Witness Stock III Xtreme: used for stock pistol competition.

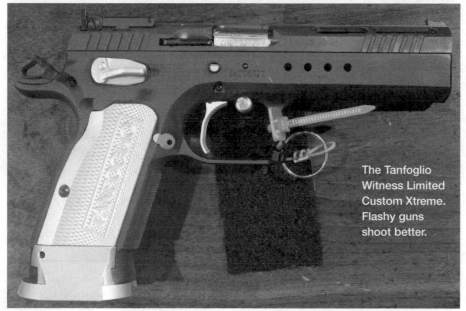

The Tanfoglio Witness Limited Custom Xtreme. Flashy guns shoot better.

rest, with a "normal" barrel and adjustable iron sights. A 2-pound trigger pull caused by sear and hammer redesign makes for a fine shooter, even lighter than the Open's 2.5-pound trigger. $2,799 is a pretty good price for a Limited match handgun like this one. Both models sport a heavily textured grip that will certainly enhance control in rapid-fire competition strings. (stiguns.com)

Tanfoglio

European American Armory Corporation (EAA Corp.) has been importing the Tanfoglio Witness pistol for years now. Now available in 2015 are the Witness Xtreme series of pistols. These Xtremes are heavily tuned match pistols, most of which also sport some intensive cosmetic bling. Typical of the Witness series is the double action/single action means of trigger pulling. The Gold Team, Limited Custom and Match models of the Xtreme are fitted with a very nice single-action-only trigger – as this is the norm for pistols used in many competitive arenas, as well as lightened slides, ceramic finishes, adjustable sights, polygonally rifled barrels and machined aluminum grip panels; the Gold Team also ships with a C-More red-dot sight. The Stock II and III models, meant for "stock" competition retain the DA/SA trigger of standard Witness models yet still retain many of the other options present on the match models. Customers expressed a desire for the same Witness pistols fielded by high-end competitors and Tanfoglio responded with this line of handguns. The Gold Team full-bore race gun has an MSRP of $5,313. The Stock II Xtreme goes for $2,254, and the other models' prices are between those two. (eaacorp.com)

Taurus

Taurus just pulled a "why didn't I think of that" idea and turned it into what may well be solid gold bars. One of the largest impediments to carrying a concealed firearm is that guns aren't really shaped to conform to the human body. So Taurus just did the obvious thing and designed a pistol that has a curvature to it that will blend with the contours of the human hip structure. Then in a groundbreaking feat of product naming, christened it the Curve.

It is small, a .380 ACP pistol with only a six-round magazine. However, it also can be purchased with an integral LED and laser sight that are encased in front

the front cuts. This, combined with its aggressive grip texture, should be popular on the competitive circuit. It is available from the Performance Center with an MSRP of around $775, and the red dot is most definitely not included. (www.smith-wesson.com)

STI

The DVC line of competition guns was introduced this year. Both are built on the 2011 frame of double-stack magazine

1911-type pistol. The Open model is very open, shipped with a C-More sight and a bevy of internal and external enhancements. A very efficient compensator is attached to a titanium nitride plated barrel inside a heavily modified, almost skeletonized slide. This is just the beginning of the cool internal stuff. A hard chrome finish is applied to these 9mm and .38 Super pistols for hardcore open IPSC competition. MSRP is $3,699.

The Limited model subtracts the compensator and red dot but retains the

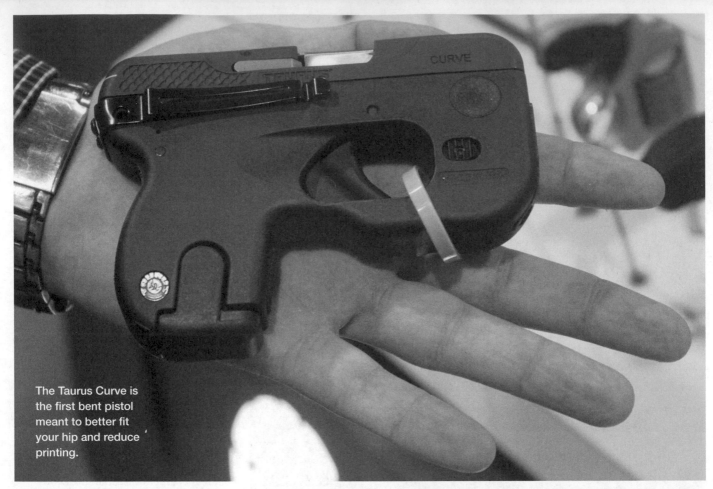

The Taurus Curve is the first bent pistol meant to better fit your hip and reduce printing.

of the triggerguard. Designed to reduce visible pistol printing, with the light and laser, it will have an MSRP of $392. The Curve also has a clip on its side for hooking onto your pants, theoretically obviating the need for an expensive and bulky holster. At less than three-quarters of a pound, even beltless pants should effectively conceal the Curve on most occasions.

Taurus has also introduced several models of Millennium G2 pistols to add to the collection. The Models 111 and 140 are chambered in 9mm and .40 S&W, and in either all-black or black frame with stainless slide. Plus, these small and thin subcompacts have the usual large profile sights like the larger G2 pistols. (www.taurususa.com)

Walther

Walther Arms is importing from Germany the new CCP, or Concealed Carry Pistol. It takes advantage of a little-used method of operation. Most small 9mm pistols operate on the short-recoil method, where recoil from the barrel to the rear and downward unlocks the slide and allows the slide to continue rearward to extract and eject the fired case, and then to feed a new live round from the magazine into the chamber as it moves forward. Small .380 pistols usually use a straight-blowback design that uses stiff springs and the relatively heavy mass of the slide to keep the slide closed long enough for pressure to reach safe levels. The CCP uses what is known as gas-delayed blowback. It taps gas from the barrel to keep the slide closed for a period of time. This method allows the pistol to use a much lighter recoil spring than recoil-operated and especially straight-blowback operated guns. It also allows a lower barrel axis (since the barrel need not move) and overall smaller profile, and some felt recoil reduction as well. This is important in a carry gun, particularly for women, who tend to avoid pistols that are difficult to operate; those with heavy or standard, really, recoil springs. This gun will likely become popular with female concealed carry permit holders who want a small,

Walther should sell a whole lot of the gas-delayed blowback pistol known as the CCP.
Photo courtesy Walther Arms.

accurate, easy-to-operate pistol. Available currently in all-black or stainless steel two-tone, the MSRP is $469 or $499. Also note Walther's attention to branding, with the P22, PK380 and CCP looking virtually identical and all very similar to their larger PPQ brother. (www.waltherarms.com)

The author fires a couple rounds from the Bond Snake Slayer.

REVOLVERS & OTHERS

BY **Jeff Quinn**

The revolver, while being pronounced as obsolete by many "experts" for decades, is alive and well, with more variations being introduced by companies that understand some of us do not live in a world of plastic semiautomatic pistols. Sure, there is a place for the modern plastic pistols. They are tools, and most work well, but not many gun enthusiasts sit around admiring the beauty and graceful lines of a Glock. This is not meant to slam the plastic pistols. I own several of them. They serve a purpose, but there will always be situations in which a good revolver is the better choice. While a plastic pistol seems cold and utilitarian, a classic single-action sixgun stirs the soul as no other handgun can. However, there are still precious few new revolvers introduced each year, compared to the vast number of plastic semiauto pistols produced.

There are a few new variations of existing revolver models coming out, particularly from Ruger. Here, we will look at a few new introductions from Ruger, and there are at least two more dandy Ruger revolvers in the works that I cannot mention at this time. Taylor's and Cimarron have a couple of new variations on the classic Colt design, and S&W has a couple of Performance Center variations on their production models. Taurus continues to try new things with their compact revolvers, and Rossi has also extended their line to include a couple of new models.

For those of us who love Old West history, the times have never been better to enjoy historical firearms, both real and imagined, as importers bring in more versions of the guns from the 19th century, as well as replicas of sixguns that were used as movie props.

When it comes to handgun power, nothing is better than a good single-shot or revolver. While there are a couple of semiautomatic pistols that are chambered for magnum cartridges, they do not carry nor handle as well as a revolver, and for the class of cartridges such as the .475 and .500 magnums, the autoloader just cannot compete.

As always, we will go down the list of interesting and available revolvers, single-shots and derringers from some of the companies currently producing these fine handguns, so let's get started.

American Derringer

New from American Derringer this year is a replica of a cane gun. At this time at least, it is a nonfiring replica, so no paperwork is needed to purchase one, but it is built on a black-powder-style frame, and has been selling quite well. American Derringer also produces an extensive line of derringers chambered for cartridges from the .22 rimfire up through the powerful .45 Colt/.410 shotshell combination. I really like their slim double-action derringers, reminiscent of the old High Standard derringer, and earlier designs from the late 19th century. American Derringer firearms are built right, and built in the USA. (www.amderringer.com)

Armscor

Armscor has expanded their line of double-action revolvers this year, adding a 4-inch barreled version of their six-shot revolver to the lineup. Armscor entered the revolver market a few years ago with a .38 Special six-shot revolver that is reminiscent of the old Colt double-action revolver design. Marketed under their Rock Island brand, the Armscor sixgun is a durable, well-built and very affordable double-action revolver with a Parkerized finish and black polymer grip. It is rugged and reliable, and serves well for carry or bedside protection, while maintaining an economical price. (us.armscor.com)

Bond Arms

The big news from Bond Arms this year is that they have derringers that are approved for sale in California. While California is a huge firearms market, the Bond derringers were on the banned list as they could be fitted with a .410 shotshell barrel set, and in the Golden State, that is not allowed. The new California guns will not accept .410 shotshell barrel sets, so they are now on the approved list for sale in the state. Bond Arms makes some of the best two-shot single-action derringers ever built. Crafted from stainless steel, the Bond line of derringers are fitted to close tolerances, and any set of barrels will fit on any Bond frame, without individual fitting, excepting the aforementioned California guns. Bond offers an extensive variety of chamberings, from .22 Long Rifle up through .45 Colt/.410 shotshell, covering many popular chamberings in between.

These derringers come in a variety of barrel lengths, and with or without triggerguards. In addtion to being ideal to use for protection from venomous

Cimarron Outlaw
.45 Colt Revolvers

reptiles, the .410 models are also a good choice for use against carjackers and other two-legged predators. Loaded with 000 buckshot or Winchester's combination PDX-1 load, that compact two-barrel would be a very effective close-range defensive weapon, and many who buy the Bond carry them for just that purpose. Up close and personal, a load of buckshot or one of the specialty combat loads is very effective. Those who carry the two-shot derringers do not seem to worry about having only two shots ready to go, because if needed, the Bond can be reloaded pretty quickly. Bond Derringers are built entirely in the state of Texas. (bondarms.com)

Charter Arms

Charter Arms has been producing affordable and reliable revolvers for decades. The newest are their lightweight Pathfinder revolvers. These six-shot .22 Long Rifle and .22 Magnum revolvers can now be had with lightweight aluminum frames for easier carry and concealment. I have owned many Charter revolvers throughout the years, and one favorite that I carried for a long time was a .44 Bulldog, a lightweight, five-shot .44 Special. The various Charter .38 Special revolvers are fine for personal protection but some of us like a bigger, heavier bullet.

Charter revolvers are available in blued steel or stainless, and some models have alloy frames. Among the lighter weight alloy models are some featuring colorful finishes, which are directed at the women's market. Charter also makes a true left-handed snubnose revolver called the Southpaw, chambered for the .38 Special cartridge. The Southpaw is a mirror image of the standard revolver design with the cylinder latch is on the right side, and the cylinder swings out to the right as well.

The Pit Bull uses a patented spring-loaded rim engagement assembly to allow the weapon to function with rimless pistol cartridges such as the 9x19mm and .40 S&W cartridges. As the cartridges are loaded into the chambers, they push the extractor out of the way. As the cartridge is fully chambered, the extractor, a sliding piece of stainless steel about 3/16-inch wide, snaps into the rim solidly. Upon ejection, as the ejector rod is operated as is normal with a double-action revolver, the extractor rod system ejects all five rounds at once, positively and quickly.

The execution of the system is a very good design, but why build a revolver for a rimless cartridge when plenty of rimmed cartridges exist? The answer to that lies in the performance, availability and popularity of the 9mm and .40 S&W cartridges. These pistol cartridges are

some of the most popular in the United States. As such, availability is excellent, being available almost anywhere that ammunition is sold. Also due to its popularity the cost of the ammo is reasonable, compared to many other popular revolver cartridges. No matter which caliber or finish is chosen, the Charter revolvers are reliable and effective weapons. (www.charterfirearms.com)

Chiappa

Chiappa Firearms now has the Rhino revolver in full production, after a couple of delays. Built upside down compared to other revolvers, the Rhino fires from the lowest chamber in the cylinder, instead of the uppermost. This design lowers the axis of recoil, greatly reducing muzzle flip upon firing, lessening felt recoil. This makes the Rhino quick to get back on target between shots. I have had the opportunity to briefly fire a Rhino revolver, but not yet the chance to do a full review on one. However, I do like the concept.

Chiappa also has a line of muzzleloading single-shot pistols, including the .36-caliber and .45-caliber Rochatte design, as well as both percussion and flintlock Kentucky-style pistols. Also, the Napoleon LePage pistols are offered individually or in cased sets with accessories. In the single-action revolver line, Chiappa has a very affordable Colt Single Action Army replica chambered for the .22 Long Rifle cartridge, which is very affordable and shoots well. (www. chiappafirearms.com)

Cimarron

For many years shooters have looked to Cimarron Firearms of Fredericksburg, Texas, for quality firearms that replicate the guns of the Old West. Cimarron has an extensive line of Pietta and Uberti cartridge revolvers such as the 1875 and 1890 Remingtons, along with the Colt Single Action Army, derringers and various cartridge conversion firearms of the transition period from cap-and-ball to self-contained cartridge revolvers. The company has engraved revolvers and various finishes including nickel, blued, case-hardened and antiqued. New for this year are a couple of fine short-stroke sixguns, built at the request of Cowboy Action competitors. These revolvers feature very smooth actions, and are built to withstand the rigors of competition. (www.cimarron-firearms.com)

Cobra

Cobra manufactures and markets some very affordable small and reliable two-shot single-action derringers under the Cobra name, as well as making those derringers for other firearms brands. These compact derringers are made in .22 Long Rifle, .22 Magnum, .25 ACP,

.38 Special, 9mm Luger, .32 Auto, .380 Auto and .32 H&R Magnum. Its larger Titan model is built of stainless steel and offered in 9mm Luger or .45 Colt/.410 shotshell. The Cobra derringers are available in a variety of finishes.

Cobra also has a line of compact double-action revolvers, offered in a multitude of finish colors. These five-shot pocket revolvers are similar in size and design to the Smith & Wesson J-frame models. (www.cobrapistols.net)

Colt

Except for the period from 1940 to 1955, the Colt Single Action Army has been in production almost continuously since 1873. It is probably the most recognized revolver in the world, and the ones being made today are as good as any to ever leave the Colt factory. The SAA is still available in the same three popular barrel lengths: 4.75, 5.5 and 7.5 inches, and with blued/case-hardened or nickel finishes. It is currently chambered in .357 Magnum or .45 Colt with other chamberings available through the Colt Custom Shop. Other options are also available through the Custom Shop, such as nonstandard barrel lengths and hand engraving.

The New Frontier SAA remains in the Colt lineup. It was originally introduced in 1961. The frame was "flat-topped" and a fully adjustable rear sight was installed with a long ramped front sight. The combo made for a sight picture that was

much improved over the traditional SAA fixed sights. The New Frontier was the classiest, most elegant single action Colt had ever produced with its deep bluing on the barrel, triggerguard, cylinder and grip frame, which contrasted nicely with the case-hardened cylinder frame. The gun was taken out of production in 1974, but returned in 1978 with the Third Generation models. The New Frontier went away again in 1981 with a few trickling out of the factory over the next few years. The current model was introduced in 2011 in .44 Special and .45 Colt, and in the standard SAA barrel lengths of 4.75, 5.5 and 7.5 inches. These New Frontiers are every bit as beautiful as the originals, and in my opinion, better built. (www.colt.com)

DoubleTap Defense

DoubleTap is continuing to produce its unique two-shot pistol in both .45 ACP and 9x19mm. The break-open pocket gun is available with either an aluminum or titanium frame. The pistol fires the upper and lower barrel alternately, and carries two spare cartridges in the butt of the grip. The pistol is lightweight, reliable and very easy to conceal in a pocket, plus it is made in the USA. (www. doubletapdefense.com)

European American Armory Corporation

EAA Corp. offers both single-action and double-action revolvers. The double-action Windicator revolvers are chambered for the .38 Special cartridge with an alloy frame, or the all-steel .357 Magnum version. Both revolvers have a synthetic rubber grip and a business-like matte blue finish, with a choice of 2-inch or 4-inch barrel lengths. These double-action revolvers are well-built and affordable – nothing fancy, but they work and work well.

The company imports a Single Action Army replica called the Bounty Hunter. These guns are available in rimfire versions, with an alloy or steel frame and a choice of six, eight, or 10-round cylinders. There is also a centerfire Bounty Hunter chambered in .357 Magnum, .44 Magnum and .45 Colt. The centerfires have all-steel frames in a choice of nickel, blued or case-hardened finishes. All have the traditional half-cock loading feature, and a modern transfer-bar safety action that permits carrying fully loaded. (eaacorp.com)

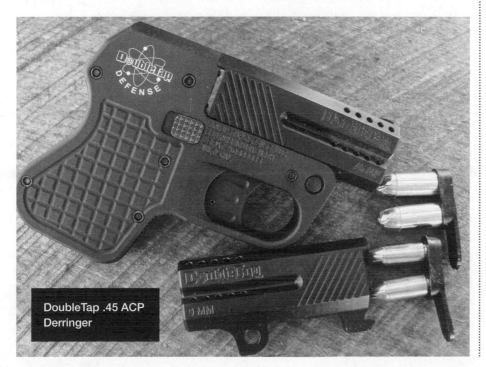

DoubleTap .45 ACP Derringer

Freedom Arms

The Freedom Arms Model 2008 Single Shot pistol has been on the market for several years. It is a high-quality single-shot handgun that is made for hunting and long-range target shooting. It is offered chambered for 11 different cartridges from .223 Remington up through .45-70 Government, with many high-performance cartridges in between. Weighing in at around four pounds, depending upon the chosen chambering and barrel length. Standard barrel length options are 10, 15 or 16 inches, and nonstandard lengths are available for a nominal extra cost. What makes this single-shot so comfortable to shoot is the single-action revolver grip style. This grip allows the gun to recoil comfortably, with no pain at all to the hands like is encountered with some single-shot pistols. The barrels are interchangeable, with extra fitted barrels available, allowing the shooter to switch among any of the barrel and caliber options all on one frame. The barrel is drilled for a Freedom Arms scope mount, and the scope stays with the barrel so there is no need for sight adjustment. The Model 2008 wears beautiful, expertly fitted laminated wood grips and fore-end, and are the best-feeling, most comfortable single-shot handgun grips that I have ever handled.

Heading up the Freedom Arms revolver line is the large-frame Model 83. The Model 83 is chambered for the .454 Casull and .475 Linebaugh cartridges, in addition to the .357 Magnum, .500 Wyoming Express, .41 Magnum and .44 Magnum cartridges. You can also get the Model 83 chambered for the .22 rimfire cartridges, if desired. They are available with fixed sights or rugged adjustable sights. The adjustable-sight guns will also accept a variety of scope mounts. The fixed sight models have a dovetail front sight to retain a low profile and rugged durability.

The Model 97 is Freedom's compact-frame single-action revolver. Built to the same tight tolerances as the Model 83 revolvers, the Model 97 is a bit handier to carry all day, and is chambered in .17 HMR, .22 Long Rifle or Magnum, .327 Federal, .357 Magnum, .41 Magnum, .44 Special and .45 Colt. In addition to these standard handgun cartridges, the Model 97 is also available in Freedom Arms' own .224-32 cartridge, which is a fast-stepping .22 centerfire based on the .327 Federal cartridge case.

Additional cylinders are available for other cartridges, as well as several different sight options. Freedom Arms revolvers are widely known as premium revolvers, built for those who appreciate high-quality and hand-fitted workmanship. You never regret buying the best. (www.freedomarms.com)

Heizer Defense

Heizer Defense is the manufacturer of the PS1 Pocket Shotgun, a single-shot pistol that is flat, thin and chambered for the .45 Colt/.410 shotshell. I have fired a couple of these and they work very well. The PS1 is very easy to conceal, and carries well in the pocket. New for this year is the Pocket AR, which is like the Pocket Shotgun, but chambered for the .223 Remington cartridge. This little flamethrower is only .7 inch thick, and weighs just 23 ounces. I also hear that Heizer has a .308 Winchester version in the works. (www.heizerdefense.com)

Henry Repeating Arms

Henry is well-known for their extensive line of American-made rimfire and centerfire rifles, but they also make a "Mare's Leg" version of their lever-action rifle. The Mare's Leg has a shortened barrel, magazine and buttstock, making this firearm legally a lever-action pistol. It's available in .22 Long Rifle, .357 Magnum, .44 Magnum and .45 Colt. The .22 version will also cycle and fire .22 Short and .22 Long cartridges. The .357 Magnum will function with .38 Special, and the .44 Magnum will also function with .44 Special ammunition. (www.henryrifles.com)

Heritage Manufacturing

Heritage Manufacturing produces some very good replicas of the legendary Single Action Army revolver with parts imported from Pietta in Italy, then fitted, finished and assembled in the USA. The Heritage Big Bore Rough Rider sixguns are available in .357 Magnum, .44 WCF and .45 Colt cartridges. These handsome revolvers are fitted with one-piece wood grips, and have a modern frame-mounted firing pin with transfer-bar safety, so they can be safely carried with a fully loaded cylinder.

Heritage Small Bore Rough Rider revolvers are chambered for the .22 Long Rifle and .22 Magnum, and are smaller in size than their Big Bore revolvers. Currently, Heritage lists 21 different versions of their Small Bore revolvers, with various barrel lengths and grips. (www.heritagemfg.com)

Magnum Research

Magnum Research of Minneapolis, part of the Kahr family of firearms, is well-known for the Desert Eagle line of semiauto pistols, but they also have some very powerful, rugged and accurate revolvers. The revolver offered by Magnum Research is called the BFR. Built for hunting the largest, most dangerous game on the planet, the BFR is available in .44 Magnum, .45 Colt/.410, .454 Casull, .475 Linebaugh, .480 Ruger, .50 Action

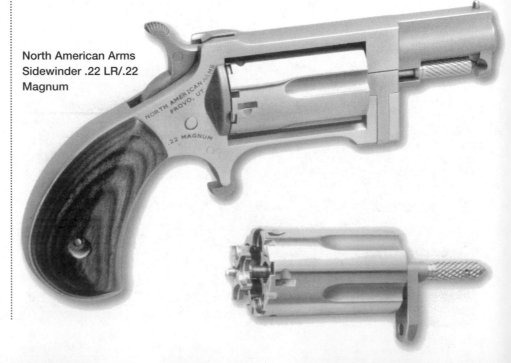

North American Arms Sidewinder .22 LR/.22 Magnum

Express and the .460 and .500 Smith & Wesson Magnums. It is also chambered for the .30-30 Winchester, .444 Marlin and .45-70 rifle cartridges. Using a modern transfer-bar safety system, the BFR can be safely carried with the cylinder fully loaded. The revolver is made primarily of stainless steel and is built in the USA. (www.magnumresearch.com)

North American Arms

North American Arms makes a compact, reliable .380 semiauto pistol, but they are best known for their miniature revolvers. NAA offers several versions of their excellent high-quality mini revolvers that have been in production for a long time now, and seem to be more popular than ever. These little five-shot miniature revolvers are small enough to fit into most any pocket and are chambered for the .22 Short, .22 Long Rifle or .22 Magnum cartridges, as well as a cap-and-ball version. There are several grip options available, in addition to a couple of sight options. Most wear short barrels, though the dandy little Earl is a fine mini revolver with a 4-inch barrel, and is reminiscent of the old Remington revolvers of the late 19th century. The little revolvers are fun to shoot, and made in the USA. (northamericanarms.com)

Rossi

The Rossi Ranch Hand is Rossi's version of the Mare's Leg lever-action design, which is basically a shortened Model 92 Winchester replica, in pistol form. It has a polished, blued steel finish and wears a walnut-stained hardwood stock. The abbreviated buttstock features a blued steel buttplate. The lever loop is of the large style and has ample room for the largest gloved hand, just right for twirling the lever gun to work the action, if that is your thing. The left side of the receiver wears a traditional saddle ring with a short leather thong attached. The magazine holds six cartridges, plus one up the spout for a total loaded capacity of seven. Currently, the Ranch Hand is available in .357 Magnum, .44 WCF (.44-40) and .45 Colt. It weighs in at four pounds, nine ounces unloaded on my scale. It wears a 12-inch tapered, round barrel that measures .64 inch at the muzzle. The overall length measures 24 inches. The rear sight is of buckhorn style, and is ladder adjustable for elevation and drift adjustable for windage correction.

The front sight is a brass bead on a blued steel blade, and is adjustable for windage correction in its dovetail. The blued steel magazine tube is attached to the barrel by both a screw near the muzzle and a barrelband about 1/2 inch aft of that. Cartridges are loaded into the magazine tube through the loading gate on the right side of the receiver and working the lever fully chambers a round from the magazine tube, and the magazine can be topped-off at any time that the bolt is closed just like most full-size lever-action rifles. The locking bolts are of the traditional '92 Winchester style, and securely lock the bolt from movement during the firing of the weapon.

Rossi has been producing reliable and affordable revolvers for many years. These double-action sixguns are available chambered for the .22 Long Rifle, .38 Special and .357 magnum cartridges, in either blued steel or stainless finishes. They are good-looking, reliable revolvers built for concealed carry, duty or as hunting guns. Rossi now has 14 different versions of their revolvers listed, with the line expanding every year. (www.rossiusa.com)

Ruger

Ruger has been very busy with new revolver variations. Of particular importance in the single-action line is the introduction of the .327 Federal cartridge as the Single-Seven. Ruger managed to

shoehorn the .327 into the Single-Six rimfire frame, machining an extra hole in the process for seven chambers in the cylinder. The cylinder is plenty long enough to handle even the 130-grain class of bullets. The Single-Seven is just the right size revolver for this dandy little magnum cartridge. I have fired several of them, and they all shot very well. This is a distributor exclusive model, available through Lipsey's.

The double-action SP101 in .327 Federal is back. The chambering was available several years ago but was dropped in 2011. This version has the 4.2-inch full-lug barrel and adjustable fiber-optic sights. It's good to see the .327 Federal back in the Ruger line. For a while it looked like it might be gone for good. It's a fine cartridge and revolvers chambered for it can also fire .32 H&R Magnum, .32 S&W and .32 S&W Long ammunition.

Also new from Ruger is a snubnose version of the Redhawk .44 Magnum. This is a special version made exclusively for the TALO group. TALO is an association of several firearms distributors, giving the group the buying power needed to have special versions of firearms built solely for distribution by the individual distributors in the association. The standard model Redhawk is offered through all distributors with a 4.2-, 5.5- or 7.5-inch barrel, but this TALO exclusive wears a nominal 2.75-inch barrel. Also differentiating this TALO sixgun from the standard Redhawk

Ruger Single-Seven .327 Federal Revolvers

Ruger GP100 Match Champion .357 Magnum

is that this short-barrel version has a round-butt grip instead of the usual squared version, making this special edition easier to carry comfortably and easier to conceal. The Redhawk is a very strong design. It has been around for more than 35 years and I have never seen a worn-out Redhawk. They can withstand a lifetime of shooting and never miss a beat. At the top of the Ruger double-action category is the Super Redhawk, which is chambered for the .44 Magnum, .454 Casull and .480 Ruger. It

comes supplied with scope mounts, and is a superb choice for hunting large game including the big bears.

Ruger introduced its polymer-frame LCR five-shot .38 Special revolver a few years ago, and it has been a runaway success. Ruger sold many thousands of these little pocket revolvers the first year and demand is still outpacing supply, as the company has added other chamberings and features over the years. I own a few LCR revolvers, and each of mine has proven to be strong,

reliable and accurate. The latest, and the one riding in my pocket right now, is the LCR that is chambered for the 9x19mm pistol cartridge. Using full moon clips, the revolver is easy to load and unload quickly, and the gun offers impressive performance from such a short barrel. Another new addition to the LCR line is the LCRx 3-Inch, a .38 Special model with adjustable sights and 3-inch barrel. Weight is just under a pound.

Ruger also continues to produce variations on their rugged and reliable GP100

Ruger Redhawk TALO Edition

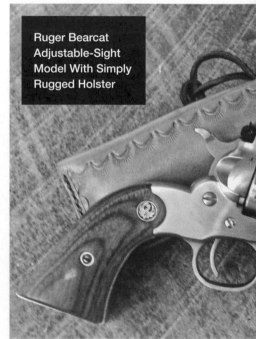

Ruger Bearcat Adjustable-Sight Model With Simply Rugged Holster

Ruger 3-inch LCRx

line of .357 Magnum sixguns – such as my favorite – the Match Champion. An adjustable-sighted Match Champion was added this year. Look for other additions to the Ruger defensive revolver line this year. They have some promising new handguns in the works.

Right: Smith & Wesson 929 9mm Revolver

Back to the single-action line, Ruger has added an adjustable-sighted version of its little Bearcat .22 rimfire sixgun. That addition transforms this classic little beauty from a great plinker into an excellent little trail gun, making the revolver much easier for most to shoot accurately, with a better sight picture and the ability to use the ammo of the owner's choice. (www.ruger.com)

Smith & Wesson

Smith & Wesson has been making revolvers since the 1850s, before the Civil War. Today it is safe to say that S&W is the most prolific producer of double-action revolvers in the world, from the .17 HMR to the massive .500 Smith & Wesson Magnum. The last time I checked, the company listed well over 100 different variations of double-action revolvers in production. The most recent additions to the category are two models that were

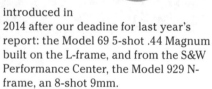

introduced in 2014 after our deadline for last year's report: the Model 69 5-shot .44 Magnum built on the L-frame, and from the S&W Performance Center, the Model 929 N-frame, an 8-shot 9mm.

The Model 69 is the first .44 Magnum to be built on Smith & Wesson's L frame. It weighs 36.6 ounces, about four ounces less than the Model 29/629 N-frame guns. The barrel length is 4.23 inches. It has a satin stainless steel finish and is quite attractive with black screws, sights, grip, hammer, trigger and cylinder release. The rear sight is fully adjustable and there is a red plastic insert in the ramp front sight. With its lighter weight and shorter barrel, the Model 69 will be popular as a carry gun for hunting or personal defense.

The 929 is meant primarily to be used as a competition gun. It is designed for full-moon 8-shot clips, although it will function without them. However, that will mean the empty cases have to be

ejected individually. This is a 44-ounce gun with a 6.5-inch barrel and has Jerry Miculek's signature of approval on the frame. Jerry is one of the best and fastest revolver shooters in the world and helped design the Model 929. He has been timed emptying a five-shot revolver in .57 seconds and six shots in .60. Features for this Performance Center model include a removable compensator, satin stainless finish, chrome-plated hammer and trigger, and of course, fully adjustable sights.

Taking a brief overview of the S&W revolver line, the small J-frame five-shot .38 Special revolvers are some of the most popular self-defense guns ever produced, and remain so today. The Model 642 is said to be the best-selling revolver in the S&W line. It is a compact, reliable five-shot revolver with a concealed hammer and a lightweight frame. Among the other 40 or so J-frames currently in production and in addition to the .38 Specials are models in .22 LR, .22 WMR and even .357 Magnum.

Moving up in size, the K-frame and L-frame revolvers are the mainstay of the Smith & Wesson duty line. These revolvers have served well for generations of sixgun users, both for defense and hunting.

The larger N-frame guns are the epitome of what a Smith & Wesson revolver should be. The Models 27 and 29 are still in the lineup of the Classic Series, and are beautiful and functional examples of the timeless double-action revolver. Among the most popular of the current N-frames is the big Governor model that fires both .45 Colt and .410 bore 2.5-inch shotshells.

Moving up now to the massive X-frame guns, are the most powerful double-action revolvers ever made. The .460 and .500 S&W Magnums are at the upper limits of what most would ever consider possible in a handheld firearm and are capable of taking any game animal on the planet. A generation ago, the .44 Magnum was considered to be the "most powerful handgun in the world, and would blow your head clean off," as Dirty Harry Callahan phrased it. Even though the state-

Taurus No View

Continuing to be some of the hottest-selling revolvers currently in production are the many variations of the Taurus Judge. Folks have really taken to these versatile handguns. They are available in all-steel or lightweight versions with 2-, 3-, or 6-inch barrels and are chambered for the 2½- or 3-inch .410 shotshell, and also the .45 Colt cartridge. These are formidable close-range defensive weapons, firing .45 Colt, .410 birdshot or .410 buckshot loads. They will also fire .410 slugs, but if a solid projectile is desired, the .45 Colt is a much better choice. I really like the personal defense loads that are now being sold by Winchester, Hornady and Federal. These loads are tailor-made for the Judge series, and are very effective for defensive situations. The lightest in the Taurus Judge series of revolvers is the Judge Poly, with a short barrel and polymer frame that make for a relatively lightweight and compact package. (www.taurususa.com)

ment was not quite correct, it made for good theatre. (www.smith-wesson.com)

Taurus

The newest revolver from Taurus USA is the No View, very similar to their diminutive View revolver from last year, but without the clear Lexan sideplate that allowed shooters to see into the internal workings of the revolver. When brand new, the View's clear sideplate looked like an interesting idea, but as the oil inside became dirty, the sideplate covered with oil inside, and the Lexan was scratched, the view into the View was nothing close to clear. I guess Taurus figured out that, like most sausages, looking inside might not be the best idea. Anyway, the revolver is now the No View with a solid sideplate, and is as small a five-shot .38 Special one can get.

Taurus has dozens of revolvers designed for every purpose from concealed carry, personal protection, formal and

informal target shooting and for hunting small, medium and large game. From their small, lightweight pocket revolvers up through their .454 Raging Bull, Taurus has a wide selection of revolvers from which to choose. The small-frame models come in .22 LR, .22 WMR, .38 Special and .357 Magnum, and even a couple of auto pistol calibers—.380 ACP and 9mm. Middle-frame service type revolvers are chambered for .38 Special or .357 Magnum, and the large-frame models are in .357 and .44 Mag. The hunting series like the Tracker, Raging Bull and Family of Hunters come in all of the above plus the .17 HMR and .454 Casull.

Taylor's & Company

Taylor's imports high-quality replicas of some of our most historic revolvers. Its percussion revolvers replicate the Colt 1851 Navy, 1860 Army and 1858 Remington sixguns. They also import replicas of the lesser-known revolvers of the 19th century, such as the 1836 Paterson, 1849 Pocket Colt and the huge 1847 Walker. These quality

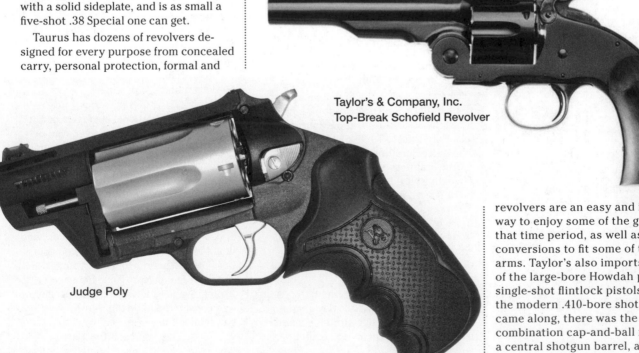

Taylor's & Company, Inc.
Top-Break Schofield Revolver

Judge Poly

revolvers are an easy and inexpensive way to enjoy some of the guns from that time period, as well as cartridge conversions to fit some of those arms. Taylor's also imports replicas of the large-bore Howdah pistols and single-shot flintlock pistols. Before the modern .410-bore shotshell pistols came along, there was the Lemat combination cap-and-ball revolver with a central shotgun barrel, and a replica

Traditions Performance
Firearms Josey Wales
.36-Caliber Sixgun

of that unique weapon is available from Taylor's & Company as well. Moving into the more modern stuff, the company has variations of the legendary Colt Single Action Army sixgun, the Remington cartridge revolvers, as well as one of my favorites – the Smith & Wesson Schofield. (www.taylorsfirearms.com)

Thompson/Center Arms

Thompson/Center is responsible for making the modern single-shot hunting pistol popular. Starting with their Contender model decades ago, T/C pistols have evolved into the Encore Pro Hunter and Contender G2 designs. Both are really just improvements and refinements of the original Contender pistol. The Encore Pro Hunter is currently offered in .223 Rem. or .308 Win., but replacement barrels are available in several other popular calibers. The Contender G2 comes only in .22 Long Rifle or .357 Magnum, with barrels offered in .44 Mag., .45-70, and the popular .45 Colt/.410 shotshell combination.

Thompson/Center offers wood and synthetic stocks, and a variety of barrel lengths. The barrels are interchangeable within the same frame group, and these hand-rifles come pre-drilled for scope mounts to take full advantage of their power and accuracy potential. (www. tcarms.com)

Traditions Performance Firearms

Traditions imports replicas of the Colt Single Action Army called the Frontier Series, chambered for the .38 Special/.357 Magnum and the .45 Colt. The company also sells several historic replica black-powder revolvers, including a unique .36-caliber Josey Wales Navy revolver from the classic Clint Eastwood film. These are all well-made and

smooth-running revolvers. (traditions-firearms.com)

Uberti

Uberti has been producing quality replicas of 19th century American firearms for decades now. While manufacturing replica rifles and handguns for other companies like Taylor's and Cimarron, Uberti also markets their own line of replica firearms, and have a variety of revolver designs. The Uberti Stallion is a slightly scaled-down version of the Colt Single Action Army, and is chambered in a choice of six-shot .22 Long Rifle or .38 Special, or a 10-shot .22 Long Rifle. There are also Bisley and birdshead grip models available.

The Cattleman series replicates the Colt SAA design and includes the Callahan Model that is chambered for the .44 Magnum cartridge. This Magnum is offered with original-style fixed sights or as a flattop style with adjustable target sights. There are several other 1873-style sixguns chambered for the .45 Colt, .357 Magnum and .44 WCF (.44-40) cartridges. Finish options run from a standard blued/case-hardened to nickel, and even a bright charcoal blue finish.

The Italian company also has fans of the old Remington revolvers covered with its Outlaw, Police and Frontier models, replicating the 1875 and 1890 Remington models. Uberti has several variations of the S&W top-break revolver, including the Number 3 Second Model and the Russian, in both nickel and blued finishes. It also offers them in fully hand-engraved models. These are available in .38 Special, .44 Russian and .45 Colt. And finally, Uberti has not forgotten the fans of the early cap-and-ball sixguns and offers authentic replicas of Colt and Remington models. (www.uberti.com)

That pretty much covers the revolver offerings from within the firearms industry this year, as well as the quality derringer and single-shot pistols available. The interest in revolvers is growing once again. While plastic auto pistols are still much more popular, many shooters are discovering – or rediscovering – the advantages that are unique to the revolver, as well as the performance available in a high-powered single-shot pistol. As stated at the beginning of this piece, the revolver has been pronounced dead by man so-called "experts" within the industry many times. These folks are usually the "tactical" types with barbed wire tattoos, three-day beard and a bad attitude, but they have been proven wrong time and time again. The revolver is just as important and just as powerful today as it has ever been, and most are a lot more accurate than a plastic autoloader with a fistful of ammo in the magazine. In a fight or in the field, only the hits count, and today's revolvers can deliver the accuracy and power necessary to get the job done.

Uberti 1873
Stallion Birdshead

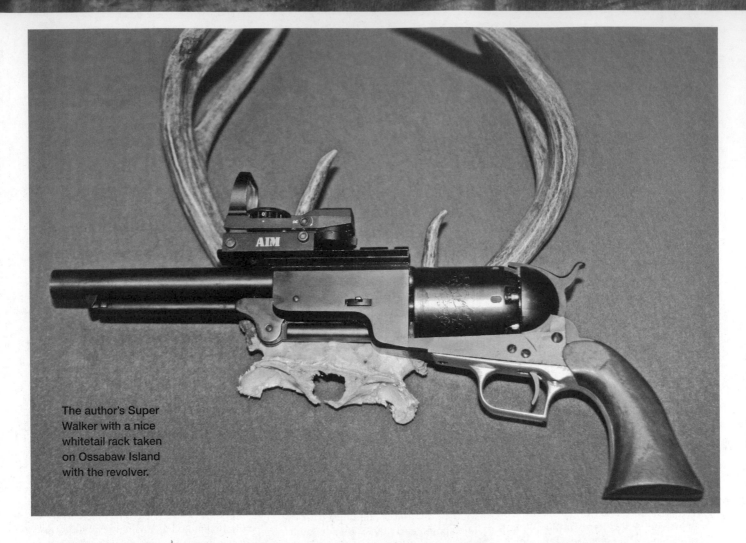

The author's Super Walker with a nice whitetail rack taken on Ossabaw Island with the revolver.

MUZZLE LOADERS

BUILDING ON OLD FOUNDATIONS

BY WM. Hovey Smith

How could I have missed a shot at that doe at 15 yards with my Super Walker percussion revolver? Even though this was a one-handed shot from a strained position as I shot behind me, the 5-pound gun had steadied down and the AIM Red Dot sight's crosshairs were well centered in the lower chest cavity of the deer. The trigger pull was smooth, and the shot felt good.

Nonetheless, the small doe showed no sign of impact from the shot. It stood for a fraction of a second then ran out of my field of view. Sitting in my treestand, I could not turn to watch what sounded like a rapidly departing deer. It seemed that the deer ran, stopped about 30 yards away, and then I heard a small rustling of the dried leaves as it apparently moved farther away.

There was nothing wrong with the load. Although the pistol had been loaded for more than a month, the load of 37 grains of Hodgdon's Triple Se7en and Kaido Ojamaa's 220-grain cast lead bullet had been sealed in the Walker's chamber by a plug of hard-setting beeswax lube, separated from the powder by a hand-cut Styrofoam wad, and protected in the rear by a tight-fitting No. 10 Remington cap. This had proved to be a strong, accurate and good-functioning load that developed over 500 ft-lbs of energy at 15 yards.

I thought that with a reasonable hit there should have been more physical indications of the shot. I stood in the stand and turned around to look at the area where I had last heard the deer. Although I could not see enough of it through the leaves to be absolutely sure, it looked like there was a long form lying on the pine straw. Either that was my deer or I was seeing a piece of rotten log.

The Super Walker Revolver

Samuel Colt's second major development in percussion revolvers was the Colt Walker, so named because it was developed in consultation with Col. Samuel Hamilton Walker of the U.S. Mounted Rifles. Walker had used the earlier Paterson model revolver, but thought that a bigger, less delicate pistol was what his troopers needed. His

basic requirements were that the gun's chambers contain a powder charge that would bring down a horse if necessary, and the revolver's cylinder, frame and barrel were lengthened accordingly.

As these pistols were to be carried in pairs in holsters suspended from horse's saddle, their size was not too significant, so long as a man could reasonably shoot it with one hand. The single-shot pistols usually issued to horsemen in the world's armies of the day were often .75 caliber and could've been over 2 feet long. Barrel length was needed to burn the black-powder charge and weight was required to make the gun controllable.

The pistol Walker had in mind could be big and heavy while retaining the multishot capacity that he had found so valuable when fighting the Comanche Indians in Texas. With a load of 60 grains of black powder and a .454-inch round ball, the Walker remained the most powerful revolver in existence until

the development of magnum handgun cartridges in the mid-20th century.

My past experiences with two replica Walker revolvers demonstrated that they were powerful. My problems with the guns were that the loading lever dropped with nearly every shot, which locked up the cylinder, and the gun had such poor sights that precision shot placement was very difficult. Due to these factors I wrote off the Walker and all percussion revolvers as being nearly useless for hunting big game. I could see them as backup guns on muzzleloading hunts, but not as primary hunting handguns.

With the advent of more powerful powders, such as Hodgdon's Triple Se7en, Keith-style semiwadcutter bullets developed by Kaido Ojamaa, and the availability of modernized replica guns with adjustable sights and longer barrels, I began to see that these guns had the potential of being more useful

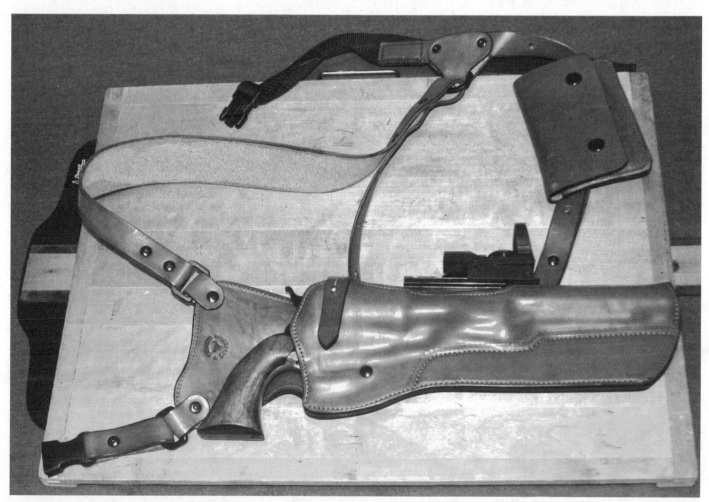

K-Bar-J's leather carry outfit for the Super Walker includes shoulder straps, a pouch for an extra cylinder and a cut-away along the top of the barrel to allow for the AIM Red Dot sight mounted on Weaver bases.

than I had previously thought. Several people corresponded with me about their favorable experiences with percussion revolvers on deer and hogs.

I found that I could obtain nearly 500 ft-lbs of energy from Cabela's Pietta-made Buffalo revolver's 12-inch barrel using the new powder and bullets. Taking advantage of the Buffalo's adjustable sights, I killed three hogs with four shots on Georgia's Cumberland Island, which was a practical demonstration that these guns could kill. This was reported in *Gun Digest 2014* and a series of YouTube videos.

Last year I finished a Uberti Walker kit gun and converted it into a Super Walker by having gunsmith Dykes Reber of North Little Rock, Ark., attach a more secure loading lever and Weaver sight bases to the barrel. Then I sent the gun to H&M Metal Processing of Akron, Ohio, for a matte black nitride finish.

Subsequent work with the gun showed that it would shoot well with the load that I had developed and sealed with an over-bulled wad of hard-setting beeswax lube. These loads lasted for months without losing their potency when loaded in chambers that were lightly lubricated with Thompson/Center's Bore Butter, and in front of similarly cleaned and lubed nipples with tight-fitting caps.

A remaining problem was how to carry this outside pistol since I am a relatively small guy. Belt holsters were available but pretty cumbersome when I was climbing into a treestand. The solution was to use a custom leather holster made by K Bar J Enterprises of Newell, S.D. I met owner Jack Gully at the Atlanta Blade Show and he created a fine holster to fit the gun and red-dot sight. The result was that my Super Walker had a holster that I could comfortably carry across the front of my chest with a leather accessory pouch to contain a spare cylinder.

This was the gun and rig I had used to shoot at the doe. When I walked over to confirm the results of my shot, I found the doe stretched out on the pine straw. The hard-cast bullet penetrated the animal, apparently causing little immediate

shock, and had punctured a .45-caliber hole right through the doe's heart.

Super Walker on the Islands

Georgia's coastal islands have abundant populations of deer and hogs, and I hunt Ossabaw and Cumberland islands as often as possible. In preparation for taking the Super Walker on the Ossabaw hunt, I used a homemade multistation loading stand to charge the cylinder with weighed charges of powder and weight-matched bullets.

With my reloading stand I can load cylinders for my Colt Walker, Remington 1858 and Colt 1851 by repositioning the plunger on the loading lever. By using the stand for reloading, the costs of modifying the loading lever on the Walker pistol can be saved as the lever could be detached while hunting.

No reloading components went to Ossabaw. With six rounds in the Walker's chamber and another six in the Remington 1858 Sheriff's model that I used as a backup gun, I saw no need to take extra loads on the trip. Hunters may shoot two deer and an unlimited number of hogs on this hunt, and 12 shots should be enough to get the job done, even if I took two deer and two hogs.

I saw no game during the first two days of the hunt. On the third and final day, I moved my stand to another location and busted hogs in the dark as I walked in. I sat in my stand until about 8:30 a.m., then decided to get down from my treestand and look for hogs.

The parcel that I hunted was a triangular piece of land that necked down to a

narrow strip with marshes on both sides. I was about a half-mile from the road and hunted across the strip to the marsh on the other side. When I got to where I could see the marsh, a buck walked through the middle of a water-flooded grassy patch. I already had the gun in hand. I dialed up the No. 1 setting on the AIM sight, cocked the pistol and raised it in a two-handed off-hand position.

At the shot, the deer disappeared in a cloud of smoke. It was if the earth had gobbled it up. Indeed, it nearly had. When I walked over to the deer it was down in the water and was partly covered with duck weed and black mud. It was still struggling some, so I finished if off with a shot in the neck.

With my off-hand shot, I had apparently pulled the shot to the right as it had hit the neck and not the front shoulder where I aimed. This reminded me to use a rest whenever possible. Before I headed home, I emptied the gun by shooting at two water bottles at 25 yards. Both were hit well that indicates that the sighting-in was adequate. I had just made a sloppy shot on the buck.

These island deer are small due to a lack of food caused by overpopulation and competition with wild hogs. The buck that I took on Ossabaw had a live weight of about 100 pounds, even though it had eight points and was 4½ years old. Although my deer had the highest scoring horns, the largest buck taken during the hunt was 5½ years old and weighed 130 pounds. Both were mature bucks that were hard earned. You can see a video of this hunt on YouTube at: http://youtu.be/2PwgPwPkSdQ.

Fired and unfired (left to right) 255-, 240- and 220-grain bullets by Kaido Ojamaa are designed for muzzleloading revolvers. The 255-grain bullet is for the Ruger Old Army revolver, and the 240- and 220-grain bullets were tried in the Super Walker. The lighter 220-grain bullet was the best compromise between power and accuracy.

UBERTI SUPER WALKER SAMPLE LOADS

Bullet	Powder	Velocity	Energy	Comments
.457 Round Ball	37 grains of Hodgdon's TripleSe7en FFg (wt)/57 (vol)	1,062 fps	343 ft-lbs	
220-grain Kaido Ojamaa	37 grains 3/7 (wt)	1,036 fps	535 ft-lbs	Most accurate hunting load
240-grain Kaido Ojamaa	35 grains 3/7 (wt)	887 fps	419 ft-lbs	

In the final development of my hunting load I used 37 grains of Hodgdon's FFg Triple Se7en, a cut Styrofoam wad between the bullet and the powder, and an over-bullet wad made from hard-setting beeswax bullet lubricant. A No. 10 Remington cap provided a long-lasting nearly weatherproof load.

The weak design of the Colt Walker will cause the barrel wedge to deform and the cylinder pin to pull if fed a steady diet of top-end loads. A competent gunsmith can repair this by replacing the cylinder pin retaining pin and wedge, and the gun can be returned to service.

NEW BLACK-POWDER GUNS AND PRODUCTS FOR 2015

The number of new products offered by major manufacturers and importers has been scaled back from previous years, but there are still some very interesting developments to report.

CVA (BPI) International

CVA's best-selling line remains its midpriced Optima drop-barreled muzzle-loaders. This year CVA will be offering a nitride coating process to protect the barrels of some Accura and Optima rifles to guarantee that the barrels will not rust. This extra-cost option, unlike a coating or plating, does not change the internal dimensions of the barrel, but bonds with the steel to make a chemically impervious coating. Nonetheless, muzzleloading barrels will still need to be cleaned to remove the physical debris from the barrel so the next shot can be more easily reloaded.

A Long Range (LR) version of the Accura has been added with a 30-inch barrel to get higher velocities from three-pellet loads, and the entry level striker-fired Buckhorn has been dropped. Some are still on dealers' shelves at an MSR of about $177. (cva.com)

Davide Pedersoli

Pedersoli is the only company to introduce a new replica Civil War-era firearm. This is the Artillery Model of the Cook & Brothers rifle that was made in Athens, Ga., and joins the carbine-length gun that was introduced last year. Pedersoli uses CNC machining and hand finishing to produce the largest selection of replica muzzleloading and early cartridge guns that exist. Options

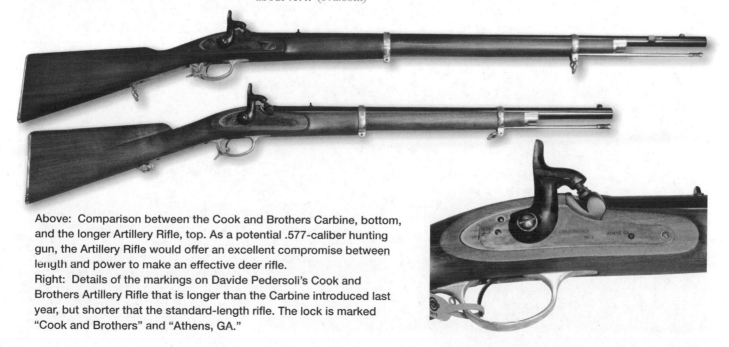

Above: Comparison between the Cook and Brothers Carbine, bottom, and the longer Artillery Rifle, top. As a potential .577-caliber hunting gun, the Artillery Rifle would offer an excellent compromise between length and power to make an effective deer rifle.
Right: Details of the markings on Davide Pedersoli's Cook and Brothers Artillery Rifle that is longer than the Carbine introduced last year, but shorter that the standard-length rifle. The lock is marked "Cook and Brothers" and "Athens, GA."

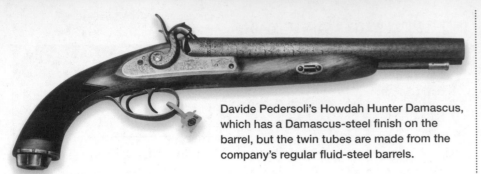

Davide Pedersoli's Howdah Hunter Damascus, which has a Damascus-steel finish on the barrel, but the twin tubes are made from the company's regular fluid-steel barrels.

include engraving, special finishing and special target models for international competition. Pedersoli now also has a full-line distributor in the U.S., the Italian Firearms Group (IFG), located in Amarillo, Texas. (www.davide-pedersoli.com)

Dixie Gun Works

Dixie remains a one-stop shop for almost anything imaginable for users of replica muzzleloading and early historic cartridge guns. Here is where you will not only find the latest offerings from Uberti, Pietta, Davide Pedersoli and others, but also the almost nearly impossible to find bullet molds for Civil War carbines, period clothing and a catalog jammed full of useful information. (www.dixiegunworks.com)

Knight

The only thing new in the Knight line is an interesting horn-pattern finish called "Skull Works Camouflage." This pattern features renditions of skulls and horns of North American deer and elk. Now that Knight has relocated to Athens, Tenn., the company has returned the major Knight striker-fired, bolt-action and drop-barreled guns into full production. Intentions are to reintroduce the KPX combo model as a .50-caliber muzzleloader with interchangeable .444 Marlin and .45-70 barrels, and the gun is being readied for production. Since the Revolution and Rolling Block models were complex and had a relatively poor reception, there are currently no plans to reintroduce these guns. (www.knightrifles.com)

LHR Sporting Arms

LHR Sporting Arms has thoughts of expanding the .50-caliber Redemption line of muzzleloading rifles from its three initial variants with walnut, black synthetic and G2 camouflage stocks, to include a 20-inch barrel carbine and 20-gauge muzzleloading shotgun. Several prototype shotguns took turkeys last year, and consideration is being given to bringing the guns into production. These will feature the rust-preventative nitride finish, external threaded breech plug attachment that holds the 209 primer, and thumb-activated cocking mechanisms that distinguish the original rifle. (603) 335-8091

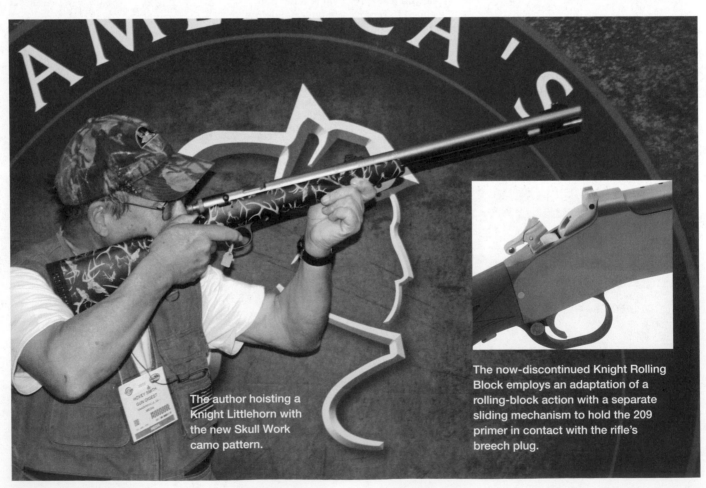

The author hoisting a Knight Littlehorn with the new Skull Work camo pattern.

The now-discontinued Knight Rolling Block employs an adaptation of a rolling-block action with a separate sliding mechanism to hold the 209 primer in contact with the rifle's breech plug.

Typical of PowerBelt Bullets, the 295-grain hollowpoint expanded to nearly 1-inch diameter and drove through both shoulders of a 120-pound doe to be recovered from just under the hide on the off-side of the deer. The bullet was fired from a Knight Rolling Block rifle using a 100-grain charge of Hodgdon's Triple Se7en pellets.

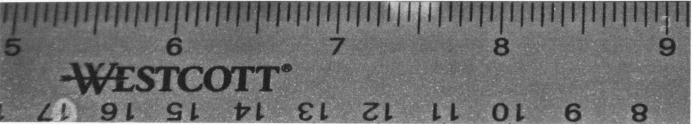

Pietta

A pepperbox-inspired pistol made on an 1851 Colt frame is the Navy Yank Pepperbox, which consists of a standard-length frame with a 3.1-inch six-shot cylinder that serves as both firing chambers and barrel. The result is a 7-inch, six-shot, .36-caliber pistol with a weight of 2.3 lbs.

This pepperbox fits into my "fun gun" category. It has a chunky, solid feeling in the hand, and the cylinder is long enough to hold double balls, or shot. The pistol would have solid creds as a nonauthentic, but useful, part of a cowboy action shooter's concealed defensive armament. If you happened to be on the other end of this thing, looking at those six chambers/barrels would very likely

provoke thought as to whether you really wanted to continue whatever you were doing. (www.pietta.us)

Remington

The Model 700 Ultimate Muzzleloader is Remington's fourth muzzleloader. There was a one-year limited run of a replica of an 1816 flintlock made by

The business end of the Pietta Navy Yank Pepperbox. Those six .36-caliber barrels look very intimidating from the front end of the revolver. This gun fires its six shots sequentially, as any revolver, but the thought that all might go off at once comes immediately to mind.

Pietta's Navy Yank .36-caliber Pepperbox compares favorably in size to modern pocket pistols, such as this .44 Special Charter Arms revolver.

Eliphalet Remington in 1995. That was followed a year later by a fairly simple adaptation of the Model 700 by adding a .50-caliber barrel with a breech plug and ramrod pipes. The 700 ML shot very accurately, but fouling in the bolt mechanism required periodic cleaning. This was more trouble than many shooters were willing to undertake, and the gun was withdrawn from production. The 700 ML was replaced from 2006-2008 by a Spanish-made side-swinging-block rifle called the Genesis.

After 2008, Remington didn't offer any muzzleloaders until the introduction of the 700 Ultimate Muzzleloader in mid-2014. To overcome the fouling problems of the 700 ML, the 700 UML uses a brass case primed with a large magnum rifle primer to seal the gasses in the 26-inch barrel. This case is designed to fit the contours of a fixed breech plug, which has a long flash channel to conduct the primer flame to ignite up to four 50-grain powder pellets.

Remington advertises this gun to have a 300-yard killing range with a four-pellet (or 200-grain) load and a 150-grain saboted Barnes copper bullet. Factory testing indicates that when the gun is zeroed at 150 yards its drop at 300 yards is 23.5-inches, which can be accommodated by either holdover or with gun-matched telescopic sights that may be available in 2016.

With the load of four of Hodgdon's Triple Se7en pellets the bullet leaves the muzzle at 2,400 fps. This load is flat shooting out to 150 yards and drops only 4 inches at 200 yards. For most shooters this will extend their point-blank range out to 200 yards, but 300-yard shots will require significant

Remington Model 700 Ultimate Muzzleloader shown in Laminated Stock and Synthetic Stock versions.

The Remington UML's receiver has an effective loading trough. If the priming cartridge case is dropped into the trough, the bolt will automatically center the case on the bolt face and perfectly seat it against the specially designed breech plug. The interior of the reloadable case (takes a Remington large magnum primer) is contoured to match the nonremovable breech plug.

Hodgdon's Triple Se7en pellets with Remington's recommended four-pellet load for the UML. Although generating considerable recoil and advertised as a 300-yard load, with a 150-yard zero it still drops 23 inches at 300 yards, so requires either holdover or a special crosshair placement in a scope.

FACTORY DATA FOR THE REMINGTON MODEL 700 ULTIMATE MUZZLELOADER, 26-INCH BARREL

Four 50-grain Hodgdon Triple Se7en Pellets, 250-grain Remington (Barnes) Premier Accutip Copper						
Range (yards)	0 (Muzzle)	50	100	150	200	300
Velocity (fps)	2,400	2,188	1,987	1,792	1,621	1,319
Energy (ft-lbs)	3,198	2,656	2,191	1,793	1,459	9,66
Trajectory (inches)	–1.5	.095	1.49	0	-4.28	-23.57

IS MY MUZZLELOADER LEGAL?

My muzzleloading revolvers equipped with adjustable sights and using modern powders and bullets, have killed or mortally struck three deer and three hogs with seven shots. The largest weighed 150 pounds and all were taken within 30 yards, a typical range for the thick habitats that I hunt. Even so, one hunter reported to me that he had been told that muzzleloading revolvers were not legally "muzzleloaders" in Georgia because they loaded from cylinders and not through the muzzle of the gun.

I can see the logic behind this restrictive definition of muzzleloading firearms, but it is not supported by historical fact or customary usage. If a state wishes to restrict the use of multishot muzzleloaders for their primitive weapons seasons that is certainly a legislative option. Georgia's game booklet states that legal muzzleloaders for deer and hogs are ".44-caliber or larger, or muzzleloading shotguns 20 gauge or larger" and does not restrict the use of multishot muzzleloaders.

Any hunter could logically assume from reading of these regulations that .44-caliber muzzleloading revolvers are legal. If I were called as a witness to defend a person who was accused of using an illegal percussion revolver during Georgia's muzzleloading season my argument would proceed as follows:

Many muzzleloaders do indeed load from the muzzle, but not all. Historically there have been many multibarreled muzzleloaders, sometimes with clusters of barrels that rotated as well as volley guns that fired them all simultaneously. The pepperbox pistol utilized a cluster of barrels that were loaded from the muzzle, but fired them one at a time each time the trigger was pulled, in the manner of a double-action revolver. The percussion revolver shortened this cluster of barrels, made a cylinder and discharged multiple chambers through a single barrel. The cylinder's chambers are individually loaded from the front, or muzzle if you like, and so are muzzleloading arms. They were always considered so, and in even in

today's catalogs are listed as muzzleloading guns. Therefore, these percussion revolvers are loaded with loose components, use an external source of ignition, load from the front of the cylinder and therefore can be nothing but muzzleloading arms. There is no other category in present or historical usage into which these arms can logically fit.

That takes care of revolvers and harmonica guns, which used a horizontally sliding group of chambers. But what about breechloading arms like the Ferguson flintlock rifle, Sharps percussion carbines and others like the Maynard that used a cartridge-like subchamber that held the powder and ball, yet fired it with an external percussion cap? Are these also muzzleloaders?

The Ferguson rifle used loose powder and ball that were loaded after a few turns of the triggerguard dropped down a breech plug to allow access to the barrel. The Sharps used paper cartridges, which were cut off when the breech was closed to expose the loose powder to hot gasses from the percussion cap. The Maynard, Smith and some other carbines used subchambers with center-positioned holes to allow musket caps to fire the guns. It is noteworthy that a very similar technology is employed on the new Remington Ultra Muzzleloader, although it uses a brass case with a large rifle primer cap to fire a charge of loose or pelletized powder, which is loaded from the muzzle.

A comprehensive definition of muzzleloaders that resolves these difficulties is as follows: A muzzleloading gun either loads from the muzzle of the gun, from a series of chambers or employs a separate priming component that fires a charge in a manually loaded chamber. Use of this definition would allow the owners of Sharps percussion rifles to use these guns for taking big game without fear that they might be prosecuted under an incorrect interpretation of their state's laws, provided that the gun also meets any caliber and energy requirements required by the state.

holdover. In comparison, using a 150-grain charge of powder in a 28-inch Knight Rolling Block, a 295-grain PowerBelt HP bullet will drop about 19.6 inches at 250 yards, again giving about a 50-yard increase in range for the four-pellet load from the Model 700 ML.

I received a test gun the afternoon before the close of Georgia's deer season and, using the iron sights, sighted in the gun. With the recommended four-pellet load and factory supplied bullets, I found that this gun generated more recoil from the 8.5-pound rifle than the .458 Lott and similar African cartridges. I was unsuccessful in taking a deer with it, but with new sights and reduced loads plan to try it on small game, turkeys, deer and hogs. I loved the gun, but hated the recoil from the four-pellet loads. Watch a video of me shooting the gun on YouTube at: http://youtu.be/pMgiRTcGSMA. (www.remington.com)

Traditions

The only new product enhancements from Traditions is a new stock with an expanded fore-end for the Pursuit and a Quick T-Handle Accessory. This handle fits almost any inline ramrod and extends its length and allows for easier loading and cleaning. The hollow T-shaped handle enables it to slip onto the rod and be carried on the gun. This

Tradition's Quick-T-Handle is available on new guns and as an accessory. When purchased separately, it is threaded to fit most ramrods and will extend their length to allow a firm grip to pull a tight patch.

is also sold as a separate accessory item. (traditionsfirearms.com)

Bullets, Primers and Accessories

Federal has introduced a .50-caliber 270-grain Premium Muzzleloading Trophy Copper bullet that features a hard plastic base for breaking through the "crud ring" left by pelletized powders, a polymer driving band, and protected-point solid-copper bullet for reliable expansion and deep penetration.

CCI also joined the muzzleloading effort with a new 209 In-Line Muzzleloading Primer specifically designed for black-powder shooting.

Another product worth mention, although a bit older, is the Power Pack Pro

made by the Shoot Straight Company, which uses a spring-loaded compression chamber in a wood cylinder to exert uniform pressure on the ramrod when loading loose powder. I found this particularly useful when loading granular Triple Se7en, which is unusually pressure sensitive.

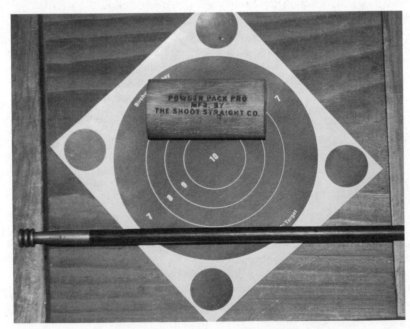

The Straight Shoot Company's Power Pack Pro wooden loading tool has an interior spring that enables even pressure to be applied to loads of loose powder, which is particularly significant to pressure-sensitive powders like Black Powder and Triple Se7en granular powders.

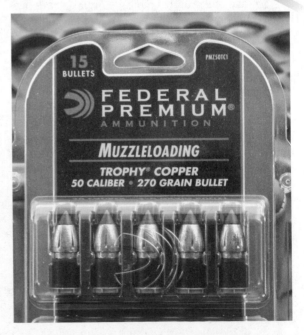

Federal's new Premium Muzzleloading Trophy Copper bullets have a hard base for breaking through the "crud ring" left by many powder pellets, and a plastic driving band around the bullets.

OPTICS

BY **Tom Tabor**

Clarity and precision are a large part of good shot placement whether shooting from the bench or in the field. High-quality optics are essential for good performance.

I am always surprised at the innovation coming from the optics manufacturers. Each year an impressive array of creative new products are developed that have the potential to make our lives afield better, easier and more productive. But in addition to those new products, the manufacturers continue to improve their existing optic lines by incorporating new state-of-the-art developments and ingenious new design modifications. This year the popularity of the "modern sporting rifle" has shown up in a big way with some manufacturers focusing more heavily on the development of better sights and scopes for those AR-type firearms.

The newly acquired technology to marry range-finding capabilities with the binocular has clearly intensified as has the diversity and choices in reticles. So extensive are these developments, I can only hope to tantalize you here with a mere spattering of what is available. From there I would encourage all outdoor enthusiasts and shooters to look deeper into these and the many other favorable optics in order to obtain a more thorough understanding of how they might help you in the field.

Aimpoint

Aimpoint introduced their new Micro compact reflex sight in 2007, which quickly became a rousing success story for the company. Law enforcement and military personnel found this sight to be extremely beneficial due to its compact size, durability and long battery life. Soon feedback began to roll in with suggestions on potential product enhancements that have now been incorporated into Aimpoint's new Micro T-2 sight. But instead of merely making im-

Aimpoint's new Micro T-2 sight is favored by many law enforcement and military personnel because of its compact size, durability and long battery life.

provements to an existing product, Aimpoint decided on a complete redesign for the new Micro T-2. In this case, heavy emphasis was placed on improving the optical performance through such things as a newly designed front lens and a new breakthrough in the reflective lens coatings, which help to increase the clarity and performance properties of the sight. Many of the favorable traits and characteristics have also been carried over from the previous unit. The Aimpoint Micro T-2 can be mounted on nearly any individual weapon platform and can be used with all existing mounts that fit the Micro T-1. It is also compatible with all generations of night-vision devices and it works well with Aimpoint's wide range of accessories, including the 3x Magnifier and the Concealed Engagement Unit (CEU). With a single CR-2032 battery the Micro T-2 can operate up to five years of constant use. MSRP for the Aimpoint Micro T-2 is $846.

Also new at Aimpoint is the Carbine Optic (ACO), which was designed specifically for use on modern sporting rifles and in particular the AR-15 and M4 carbines. Right out of the box the new ACO is ready to mount and shoot and comes with a full suite of branded accessories such as front and rear flip-up covers and an anti-reflective filter. The ACO pairs a 30mm aluminum alloy sight tube with a rugged fixed-height mount designed to provide absolute co-witness with AR-15 backup iron sights. The ACO comes equipped with a two-MOA red dot and is guaranteed to be completely waterproof. Power is provided by a single 1/3N battery that provides up to one year of constant usage. MSRP for the ACO is $393.

(www.aimpoint.com)

Alpen

Alpen Optics, winner of seven Great Buy Awards from *Outdoor Life Magazine*, has introduced the new top-of-the-line Apex XP AR 1-6x24 30mm series riflescopes. These scopes come fully loaded with "Xtreme Performance" (XP) features that are intended to provide the ultimate in shooting performance. Both the 4065 and 4069 models are available with the company's new AR-BDC reticle. The AR-BDC reticle was designed

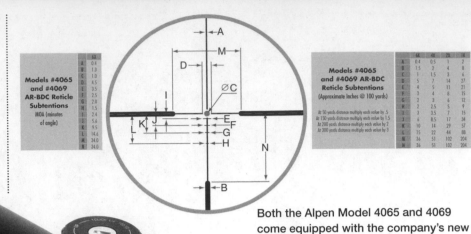

Models #4065 and #4069 AR-BDC Reticle Subtentions MOA (minutes of angle)	6X
A	0.4
B	1.3
C	1.0
D	4.5
E	3.5
F	2.5
G	2.0
H	1.5
I	2.4
J	5.6
K	9.5
L	14.6
M	34.0
N	34.0

Models #4065 and #4069 AR-BDC Reticle Subtentions (Approximate Inches @ 100 yards)	6X	4X	2X	1X
A	0.4	0.5	1	2
B	1.5	2	4	8
C	1	1.5	3	4
D	5	7	14	27
E	4	5	11	21
F	3	4	8	15
G	3	4	6	12
H	2	2.5	5	9
I	3	3.5	7	15
J	6	8.5	17	34
K	10	14	29	57
L	15	22	44	88
M	36	51	102	204
N	36	51	102	204

At 50 yards distance multiply each value by .5
At 150 yards distance multiply each value by 1.5
At 200 yards distance multiply each value by 2
At 300 yards distance multiply each value by 3

specifically for modern rifle use and in particular the .223 loaded with 55- to 70-grain bullets. Nevertheless, any bullet combination can be used. When set on 6x magnification and used in conjunction with the included Subtension Chart, it allows the shooter to match whatever range they are shooting with the anticipated trajectory drop of the bullet. The center crosshair can also be used for any magnification. The Model 4069 comes with the added feature of an illuminated red center dot and all of the scopes in this series are shock tested to 1,000 Gs. They are also fully waterproof, fogproof and shockproof, and come backed by the company's "no-blame, no-fault, no-problem" lifetime warranty. (www.alpenoptics.com)

BSA

In order to complement the innovative new .17 Winchester Super Magnum (WSM) rimfire cartridge, BSA has designed a scope series it appropriately refers to as the BSA 17 Super Mag Scope Series. These new scopes were designed specifically to match the performance of the .17 WSM cartridges when loaded with either 20-grain or 25-grain bullets. This new scope series includes three models to select from including an illuminated red, green and blue reticle version. Features include a fast focus ring on

Both the Alpen Model 4065 and 4069 come equipped with the company's new sophisticated AR-BDC reticle. The AR-BDC reticle was designed specifically for modern rifle use and in particular the .223 loaded with 55- to 70-grain bullets.

The new Alpen Optics Apex XP AR 1-6x24mm riflescope is considered to be the top of the Alpen line and comes fully loaded with "Xtreme Performance" features.

the adjustable objective lens, two-piece aluminum body, haze filter and limited lifetime warranty. The ultimate eye relief distance has been set at the factory at 3 inches. The MSRPs for the new BSA 17 Super Mag Scope Series range from $139.95 up to $159.95.

BSA has also launched a new tactical weapon 30mm scope series that has been designed specifically with military and law enforcement applications in mind. The features include 30mm main tubes, mil-dot reticle, 3.5-inch eye relief, multicoated optics, fast focus ring, two-piece aluminum construction, haze filters and limited lifetime warranty. Parallax has been set to 100 yards and the scopes come waterproof, shockproof and fogproof. MSRP: TW 1-4x24/30mm, $117.95; TW 2.5-8x36mm, $149.95; TW 3-16x44mm, $169.95; and TW 3.5-10x40mm, $184.95.

Also with military and law enforcement applications in mind, BSA is offering a new Tactical Weapon .223 Scope Series that comes with two sets of interchangeable turret dials, one for the .223 and one for .300 AAC Blackout. The turret dials are each marked with specific click markings for three different bullet weight settings. For the .223 that includes settings for 55-, 69- and 75-grain bullets; and in the .300 AAC those settings are for 115-, 125- and 220-grain bullets. The scopes come with mil-dot reticles, fully coated optics, two-piece aluminum body, haze filters and limited lifetime warranty. The scopes are set with an eye relief of 3.5 inches. MSRP: TW223-14x24CP, $89.95; TW223-4x30CP, $89.95; TW223-27x32CP, $104.95; TW223-312x40AOCP, $119.95; and TW223-618x40AOCP, $139.95.

(www.bsaoptics.com)

Burris

Burris Optics has added to its already extensive line of shooting optics with a new 4.5-14x42mm riflescope designed specifically for AR-platforms. It comes with a customized elevation turret that matches the ballistics when shooting either the 5.56mm or the 7.62mm round, and includes a WindMap to assist in determining the proper windage adjustment. This new scope features a 1-inch main tube and comes with what the company calls their Cartridge Calibrated Custom Clicker, which allows the shooter to simply dial in the range of the shot. The reticle design has MOA marks extending out to 10 MOA on each side of the horizontal crosshairs to provide wind drift adjustments based on 10 mph crosswind increments. Included with each sight is a removable anti-reflection device. MSRP for the new AR riflescope is $570.

Also new at Burris is the XTR II series of next generation tactical riflescopes. This line features sophisticated reticles, advanced windage and elevation adjustments in a 5:1 zoom ratio, which range from 1-5x24mm up to 8-40x50mm. All scope adjustment knobs come with a zero-click stop that permits the shooter to easily revert back to the baseline zero setting point. Each scope is also equipped with a side parallax adjustment. (www.burrisoptics.com)

Bushnell

Bushnell recently became part of the shooting industry conglomerate ATK. So far there seems to be little outward sign of changes affecting the consumer, and the product lines within the Bushnell brand continue to expand offering exciting new additions. One of those products is the new Bushnell Elite Long Range Hunter Scope (LRHS). As the name would seem to indicate, this versatile 3-12x44mm scope was specifically designed for those hunters who have a need to shoot long distances.

It is the first hunting riflescope produced under the Bushnell name that offers a first focal plane reticle. The new G2H milliradian-based reticle is designed to give hunters the ability to range targets at virtually any magnification setting. It comes with .5-mil hash marks with 8 mils of holdover and 6 mils of windage adjustment. The center of the reticle features a Vital Bracket that has a diameter of 3 mils at any range, which would be the equivalent of 7.2 inches at 100 yards. The LRHS is constructed with a forged aluminum, one-piece 30mm main tube, is 13 inches long and weighs 26 ounces. It features low-profile, tactical-style turrets that are calibrated in .1-mil clicks with 10 mils of adjustment per revolution. The RevLimiter zero stop allows the hunter to easily return to the preset zero point without the possibility of passing that point. The Elite LRHS 3-12x44mm riflescope is available for a MAP (Minimum Advertised Price) of $1,500.

Also part of Bushnell's Elite Tactical Line is a new Professional Grade Red Dot Sight called the Elite Tactical Close Quarters Tactical Sight (CQTS). This sight comes with a fixed-power illuminated red-dot system designed specifically to provide quick target acquisition and can be mounted on any Picatinny rail or a normal Weaver-style base. The new 1x32mm Elite Tactical CQTS comes with fully multicoated optics, 30mm main tube and features a 3-MOA red dot and eight brightness settings (three of which are designed for use with night-vision devices). MSRP is $349.

There simply isn't a better example of Bushnell's long tenure of sporting optics than the Banner series of scopes. For many of us old-timers, the name Bushnell Banner has the ability to conjure up visions of our youth and frequently was the very first scope we owned. Bushnell has now introduced an improved version of that classic series that features a sleek cosmetic redesign, but still is priced reasonably. The new design includes fingertip reticle adjustment, ¼-MOA knobs and a new rubber-coated fast-focus eyepiece. The Banner family of riflescopes includes a total of 19 models in 12 different configurations. Whether you are looking for a scope to use on a centerfire, rimfire or slug gun, there is likely a Banner riflescope that will fit your needs. The higher magnification models in the line feature an adjustable objective to eliminate parallax and give better overall image clarity. MSRPs run from a low of $108.95 up to $279.95.

A combination of quality and value is inherent in Bushnell's new Excursion HD Binoculars. Available in two popular configurations, 8x42mm and 10x42mm, they feature BaK-4 prisms, PC-3 Phase Coating, fully multicoated optics and a roof-prism open-bridge design. The Excursion HD 8x42mm and 10x42mm Binos carry a MAP (Minimum Advertised Price) of $179.99 and $199.99 respectively.

(www.bushnell.com)

EOTech

EOTech has announced two new additions to their Holographic Weapons Sights (HWS), the Model 518 and 558. In response to their customer demands, EOTech took all the best features of its HWS products and combined them into these two new models. Both the 518 and 558 feature adjustable locking, quick-release bases and side-button functionality, and operate on two common AA batteries (lithium or alkaline). Both models are compatible with the G33 Magnifier and the recently released EOTech Laser Battery Caps (LBCs), which essentially doubles the aiming capabilities of the sight. The 518 comes with 20 brightness setting and the 558 has 30 settings (10 of which are for night vision capabilities). Simply remove the standard cap and replace it with the drop-in LBC visible laser or the LBC2 with both visible and infrared lasers. Both models come with a 65-MOA ring and a 1-MOA dot reticle. The Model 518 has an MSRP of $539 and the Model 558 is $629.

(www.eotechinc.com)

Firefield

New to the Firefield line of illuminated reticle riflescopes are the Agility 3-9x40IR and 4x32IR models. Both of these scopes were designed

The EOTech Model 558 Holographic Weapons Sight is compatible with all Gen I-III night-vision devices and features an adjustable, locking, quick-detach mount that will hold zero to 1 MOA.

to offer dependable performance in all types of weather extremes including temperatures below zero and up to 120 degrees. They come with an IPX6-rated weatherproof tube, fully multicoated lens systems and are nitrogen filled. These scopes are acceptable for use on centerfire, rimfire or even airguns, and are available with either a green or red illuminated duplex reticle. The fast-focus design allows the shooter to simply rotate the eyepiece to bring the reticle and target into quick and clear focus. MSRPs run $71.99 for the 3-9x40IR and $35.99 for the 4x32IR.

(www.fire-field.com)

Hi-Lux

Hi-Lux has built a solid reputation on the construction of historic reproduction riflescopes, which include classic designs from the days of the Wild West and long past military campaigns. It also produces optics more attuned for use on modern weaponry like the company's new M40 Tactical Hunter. This scope was first introduced at the 2014 SHOT Show and combines simplicity with modern technology. Each scope comes with an easy-to-use ranging system that was used by Marine Corps snipers in Vietnam. Once the range is known the shooter uses the bullet drop holdover

Firefield has recently added two new riflescopes possessing illuminated duplex reticles, the Agility 3-9x40IR and the 4x32IR models. These scopes are usable on centerfire, rimfire and even airguns.

marks to provide accurate shot placement out to 600 yards. These aiming points have been calibrated for .308 Winchester and .223 Remington, but also work very well with the ballistics of many other popular hunting cartridges. The 12.5-inch long, 1-inch diameter scope weighs considerably less than many comparable riflescopes at only 16.2 ounces. MSRP for the 3-9x40mm M40 Tactical Hunter is $419.

The Hi-Lux Max-Tac Dot (MTD) sight is said to be one of the toughest electronic red-dot sights built today. The rugged machined aluminum housing comes with a solid Picatinny mount machined right into the scope housing. The 30mm lenses are fully multicoated to ensure clear and bright sight pictures, and the digital illumination can be operated either manually or set to automatic. In auto mode the sight relies on a built-in light sensor to automatically adjust to the intensity of the ambient light. When set on the manual mode, the shooter can adjust the brightness of the illuminated red dot to meet his or her specific needs at the time. An automatic shut off occurs after one hour in order to save on the CR2032 battery life. The TMD-30 is acceptable for use on tactical-style rifles, hunting rifles, slug-shooting shotguns, handguns or muzzleloaders. MSRP for the TMD-30 is $149.

(www.hi-luxoptics.com)

Konus

Konus has expanded their line to include several intriguing new products for the shooter. There are two new F30 riflescopes: 6-24x50mm and 8-32x56mm. These scopes are built on a 30mm one-piece main tube body and come with side parallax wheel that permits focusing as close as 10 yards and out to infinity. Also included is an internal bubble level that helps to limit rifle canting and encourage a higher degree of shooting accuracy. Each comes with dual illumination (red/blue) to assist in low-light situations. The first or front focal plane reticle allows ranging at all magnification settings, and because the reticles are glass etched it makes them essentially impervious to damage or breakage. MSRP for the 6-24x50mm F30 is $1,139.99. The 8-32x56mm carries an MSRP of $1,279.99.

The new Konus Sight-Pro R8 electronic sight comes with eight different reticle patterns making it a versatile choice for shooters. A great advantage lies in the fact that the battery powering the sight is rechargeable, and each unit comes with its own charging unit and a plug for both USA and a European use. Dot sizes are available in either 2 MOA or 5 MOA and include both red and green colors. Brightness is adjustable to five rheostat settings and elevation and windage adjustment are made in 1 MOA increments. MSRP for the Sight-Pro R8 is $309.99.

Spotting scopes are typically very expensive, but not so in the case of the new Konus KonuSpot 60 15-45x60mm. This scope carries an impressively low MSRP of only $169.99 and comes with multicoated optics, is designed with a comfortable viewing angle of 45 degrees, has a sliding sunshade and 60mm objective lens. It is capable of focusing as close as 10 meters and comes with a tabletop tripod, lens covers and carrying case.

The Konus 15-45x60 KonuSpot 60 spotting scope provides versatility of use at a very reasonable price.

(www.konuspro.com)

Leica

Leica has been manufacturing state-of-the-art quality lenses for more than a century and a half, and now has a couple of exciting new products specifically meant for the world's outdoorsmen. One of those products is the Ultravid HD-Plus 42mm binoculars, which combines a long list of great new enhancements with all of the attributes inherent in the company's earlier Ultravid HD 42 binos. The new Ultravid HD-Plus 42mm binoculars contain newly developed objective HD/HT glass elements that encourage the best possible crystal clear viewing thorough the lens. The prisms are made from SCHOTT HT glasses, which are created using a new high-temperature plasma coating process, which deposits thin films of high-quality materials on the lens surface to encourage higher contrast and near perfect image color. These enhanced elements combine to provide up to 92 percent better light transmission. There are three models available – all with 42mm lenses. Those include magnifications of 7x, 8x and 10x. MSRP for the new Ultravid HD-Plus 42mm binoculars runs $2,399; $2,449; and $2,499 respectively.

Leica has now joined the fast-growing number of manufacturers that are incorporating rangefinding capabilities within their binoculars. The company's new Leica Geovid HD-R binoculars include all of the great features of the Geovid HD series, but come with the added bonus of an innovative ballistic function, capable of calculating the ballistically relevant distance (EHR = Equivalent Horizontal Range). This feature is particularly beneficial when adjusting for bullet trajectory drop at steep angles. The algorithm developed by Leica takes not only takes the linear distance and the angle into account, but also includes a ballistic curve, which the company believes results in greater accuracy than the Rifleman's Rule (cosine-function). Just press the button and the display will appear without any need of presetting or preprogramming and the LED display automatically adjusts to the ambient light conditions present at that time. Four models of the Leica Geovid HD-R are available: 8x42, 10x42, 8x56 and 15x56. MSRPs run $2,449; $2,499; $2,949; and $3,149 respectively.

(www.leica.com)

Leica's Geovid HD-R binos come with the added bonus of rangefinding capabilities and are available in four models: 8x42, 10x42, 8x56 and 15x56.

Leupold's new VX-R 1.5-5x33mm Scout Riflescope comes equipped with the company's popular FireDot reticle and was designed to be mounted ahead of the rifle receiver.

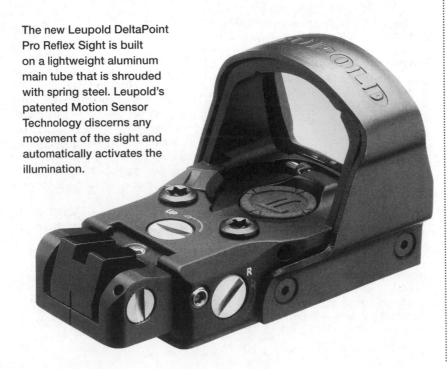

The new Leupold DeltaPoint Pro Reflex Sight is built on a lightweight aluminum main tube that is shrouded with spring steel. Leupold's patented Motion Sensor Technology discerns any movement of the sight and automatically activates the illumination.

Leupold

Leupold has added a scope to their popular VX-R riflescope series that combines a long list of favorable features that shooters frequently find beneficial. The new VX-R 1.5-5x33mm Scout FireDot was designed to be mounted forward of the receiver. A scope mounted in this fashion typically provides quicker target acquisition, encourages shooting with both eyes open for better peripheral vision and enhanced depth perception. When used on rifles possessing heavy recoil it lessens the chances of having the rim of the scope coming back into the shooters face. The optimum eye relief is 153mm-181mm (approximately 6-7 inches). It comes with Leupold's Quantum Optical System, which incorporates Index Matched lens coatings with lead-free, edge-blackened lenses for enhanced brightness, clarity, contrast and resolution. The DiamondCoat lens coatings on the exterior lens surfaces are abrasion resistant and boost light transmission by up to 94 percent. Other features include a lockable, fast-focus eyepiece for quick and easy reticle focus, finger adjustable ¼-MOA windage and elevation dials, an all-new main tube design, an advanced power selector design with a tactile power indicator and easy-to-read numbers, and it comes argon/krypton gas blend filled. The 30mm VX-R 1.5-5x33mm Scout FireDot is 12 inches long and weighs 14.2 ounces. MSRP is $749.99.

Leupold has also added a new reflex-style sight to their line called the Delta-Point Pro. This is a lightweight, rugged sight built on an aluminum housing that is shrouded by spring steel. Leupold's patented Motion Sensor Technology discerns any movement of the sight and automatically activates the illumination accordingly. Its built-in Auto-Brightness sensor immediately and continuously samples the current lighting conditions in order to provide the optimal reticle intensity, but those sensors can be easily overridden if the shooter prefers. The DeltaPoint Pro can be mounted and used on any firearm from .22 to .458 Magnum and comes fully covered by Leupold's Golden Ring Full Lifetime Warranty and the electronics are covered by Leupold's Golden Ring Electronics Warranty. MSRP for the Deltapoint Pro is $749.99.

(www.leupold.com)

Meopta

The Meopta Group is a U.S. family owned, multinational company with

Above: Meopta has recently expanded their 1-inch MeoPro Riflescope Line that now includes hunting and target versions. These additions were specifically designed with long-range hunters and shooters in mind and come with an impressive array of features.

Left: New to the Meopta line of products are the MeoPro HD Binocular Series, which features fluoride HD optics and are available in 8x32, 10x32, 8x42 and 10x42 models.

facilities in the United States as well as Europe. The company was founded in 1933 in Czechoslovakia (now the Czech Republic). In its Czech facility Meopta designs, develops and manufactures precision optical and electro/optical systems for the semiconductor, medical, aerospace and military industries as well as markets to individual consumers. Meopta's U.S. facility is based in New York where it manufacturers and assembles the company's precision optical products for marketing to military, industrial and individual consumers.

Meopta USA has recently introduced several new models within the 1-inch riflescope series, which includes both hunting and target versions. These new scopes are offered in 3-9x40mm, 4.5-14x44mm and 4.5-14x50mm. Within the 3-9x40mm line there are two models to choose from, one intended for use on centerfire rifles and the other, the R/M Model, for use on rimfires and muzzleloaders. In this latter case the parallax has been set to 50 yards in order to be better suited for the typically closer range of those firearms. Reticle choices include: #4, Z-Plex and BDC, which are all designed in the second focal plane. Weight is 15.2 ounces and optimum eye relief has been set at 4 inches.

The 4.5-14x44mm model is available in both a hunting and target version with the latter choice identified by a "T"

following the optic designation. Reticle choices include: #4, McWhorter and BDC, which are also designed in the second focal plane. Weight is 17.1 ounces, parallax adjustment is set at 30 yards to infinity and optimum eye relief has been set at 3.5 inches. The 4.5-14x50mm is also available in either hunting or target versions and comes with a reticle choice of: #4, Z-Plex and BDC and are of the second focal plane design. Weight is 19.75 ounces; parallax adjustment is set at 30 yards to infinity with the optimum eye relief of 3.5 inches. MSRPs run from $517.49-$574.99 for the 3-9x40mm series scopes, $804.99- $919.99 for the 4.5-14x44mm series and $862.49-$919.99 for the 4.5-14x50mm series.

Also freshly introduced by Meopta is the new MeoPro® HD Binocular Series, which features fluoride HD optics and are available in 8x32, 10x32, and 8x42 or 10x42. As Meopta's General Manager, Reinard Seipp puts it: "Our newly designed optical system, combined with SCHOTT fluoride HD glass and improved ergonomics, makes our new MeoPro HD binocular an exceptional performer. In high-contrast light situations, chromatic aberrations are completely suppressed while resolution and clarity are maximized. The new MeoPro HD series offers top level HD performance to hunters looking for a true value." Weight is an important consideration in binoculars

and the Meopta MeoPro HD Series excels in this area with the 8x32mm Model tipping the scale at only 21.1 ounces, the 10x32mm at 21.1, the 8x42mm at 24.6 and 10x42mm at only a mere 24.3 ounces. MSRPs run $747.49, $804.99, $977.49 and $1,034.99 respectively.

(www.meoptasportsoptics.com/us)

Nikon

Nikon has developed an all-new 30mm riflescope specifically designed to maximize the effectiveness of the .300 AAC Blackout cartridge. Appropriately called the M-300 BLK this new addition was developed around both supersonic and subsonic ammunition. Currently it is only available in 1.5-6x42mm magnification and features Nikon's own BDC SuperSub reticle with open circle aiming points out to 600 yards in 100-yard increments and with additional hash marks at 50-yard intervals. This scope is also available with an illuminated reticle adjustable to different brightness settings and up to 32 different intensity settings for the orange center dot. The MSRP for the M-300 BLK 1.5-6x42 BDC SuperSub is $699.95 and the M-300 BLK 1.5-6x42 BDC SuperSub Illuminated Is $899.95.

The company's new PROSTAFF 7S binocular series is flagged by Nikon as being the most advanced of the Nikon PROSTAFF line. They come with fully

Nikon's new M-300 BLK 30mm riflescope was specifically designed to maximize the effectiveness of shooting supersonic and subsonic .300 AAC Blackout cartridges. It is available in 1.5-6x42mm magnification and features Nikon's own BDC SuperSub reticle with open circle aiming points out to 600 yards in 100-yard increments.

Right: Nikon considers their new PROSTAFF 7S binocular series to be the most advanced of their PROSTAFF line and includes five models to choose from: 8x42mm, 10x42mm, 10x42mm Xtra Green®, 8x30mm and 10x30mm. Shown here is the 10x42mm with a black finish.

multilayer coated lenses and phase-correction coated prisms intended to provide sharp images with very high resolution and clarity. They are nitrogen filled and O-ring sealed in order to provide waterproof and fogproof performance. The line includes five submodels to choose from: 8x42mm, 10x42mm, 10x42mm Xtra Green®, 8x30mm and 10x30mm, and carry MSRPs of $189.95, $199.95, $219.95, $189.95 and $199.95 respectively.

(www.NikonSportOptics.com)

Redfield

Redfield's Battlefield 10x42mm roof prism binoculars are now available featuring the same TAC-MOA reticle offered in the Battlezone and Revolution/TAC riflescopes. These binos combine lightweight, ranging capabilities and the ability to place your shots more precisely in a low-cost, economical package. They come with fully multicoated lenses and premium BAK4 prisms for enhanced brightness and high resolution, and feature stadia lines in the vertical and horizontal crosshairs set in 2-MOA increments. Twist-up eyepieces accommodate both eyeglass users and nonusers. They

Right: The Nikon PROSTAFF 7S 8x42mm binocular includes the advanced features of the new series, but in a slightly smaller package.

Above: Redfield's Battlefield 10x42mm roof prism binoculars now are available featuring the TAC-MOA reticle.

Above: Sightmark's new Ultra Shot M-Spec Reflex Sight is the latest addition to the company's Ultra-Shot family. It features six variable brightness settings for use in daytime and six settings in night-vision mode, and has a magnesium alloy housing.

Above: For shooters looking for a more compact and even lighter weight binoculars there are a couple of Redfield Rebel® roof prism models that would fit that desire very nicely. Shown here is the 8x25mm, and there is also a 10x25mm model.

Right: Sightmark's new AR platform Wolfhound 3x24 Prismatic Weapon Sight is favored by hunters, law enforcement officers and 3-gun competitors. The design was inspired by the military and features longer eye relief, horseshoe dot reticle and bullet drop compensation.

come with a tripod adaptable mount, MOLLE case, neoprene neck strap, lens covers and are attractively colored in a Desert Digital finish. MSRP for the Redfield Battlefield 10x42mm binos is $249.99.

For those shooters looking for a more compact and even lighter weight binocular, the new Redfield Rebel roof prism 8x25mm and the 10x25mm could be a good choice. Both models are only 5 inches long and weigh only 9.8 ounces. They come with fully multicoated lenses and premium BAK4 prisms to offer bright resolution and edge clarity. They have a polycarbonate body to provide guaranteed toughness and durability, and are backed by Redfield's "no excuses, full lifetime" warranty. The Redfield Rebel 8x25mm carries an MSRP of $159.99 and the 10x25mm come in at only $5 higher at $164.99.

(www.redfield.com)

Sightmark

Sightmark has introduced a new member to their Ultra Shot family – the Ultra Shot M-Spec Reflex Sight. The digital switch control features six variable brightness settings for use in daytime and six settings in its night-vision mode. Its magnesium alloy housing provides a high degree of durability and its single CR2 battery source provides up to 1,000 hours of use. The shockproof frame design is intended to stand up to the massive recoil produced from a .50-caliber rifle, and its protective hood helps to shield the sight from abusive impacts.

The Ultra Shot M-Spec is fully submersible in down to 40 feet of water. It is equipped with dual-pane glass and its parallax-corrected lens system allows the shooter to sight accurately from 10 yards to infinity. MSRP for the Ultra Shot M-Spec Reflex Sight is $239.99.

Designed specifically for AR platform use, the new Sightmark Wolfhound 3x24 Prismatic Weapon Sight would possibly be the perfect choice when it comes to 3-gun competitions, hunting or law enforcement applications. The design was military inspired and features longer-than-average eye relief and an advanced Horseshoe Dot reticle with bullet drop compensation. The reticle is ballistically matched to a .223-caliber shooting 55- and 62-grain bullets with holdovers from 300-900 yards. Focusing capabilities can be as close as 10 yards. It is equipped with a 5-MOA central aiming point for long-range shooting capabilities and a 7.5-MOA outer circle when shots become close and personal. The Sightmark Wolfhound 3x24 Prismatic Weapon Sight has a rubber armor finish and includes a built-in aluminum Picatinny mount. MSRPs for the Wolfhound Prismatic Weapon Sights are $419.99 for

the 3x24 and $479.99 for the 6x44.
(www.sightmark.com)

Swarovski

Swarovski is frequently recognized by outdoorsmen throughout the world for building some of the finest optics available anywhere. Recently, the North American subsidiary division announced a new binocular series intended specifically for hunters and wildlife watchers heading to the Dark Continent. The new CL Companion Africa series is available in two magnification choices, 8x with a 30mm objective diameter weighing only 17.6 ounces, and a 10x, 30mm objective diameter model that weighs 18.2 ounces. The compact size and rugged armor construction of these binoculars make them a perfect choice when traveling long distances and facing harsh environments. Both models are colored in an elegant dark brown to blend into the natural surroundings of the African environment. They come accessorized with a handcrafted bag made from waxed canvas by ONA, practical hand strap, cleaning cloth and an exclusive certificate signed by Swarovski's Chairwoman of the Executive Board, Carina

The author used his new 10x30mm Swarovski CL Companion Africa Binoculars on a recent hunt for gray squirrels in Alabama, and found the optics to be excellent. The light weight is a real advantage over other hunting optics.

Right: Swarovski's new lightweight compact CL Companion Africa Binoculars are colored to match the Dark Continent environment and come in either 8x30mm or 10x30mm.

Above: Swarovski's DCB II Digital Camera Base allows the user to attach a video or still camera to the STR 80 Spotting Scope to easily and effectively capture extended range images of wildlife or other subject matter.

Right: Swarovski's STR 80 spotting scopes come with HD optics and illuminated MOA or MRAD reticle. Eyepieces are available in either 20-60x or 25-50x.

Fans of the Trijicon AccuPoint riflescope series can now harness the maximum range potential with new custom laser-engraved adjustable turrets, which are available from Kenton Industries.

Schiestl-Swarovski. MSRP for the CL Companion Africa Binos is $1,380 for the 8x30 and $1,443 for the 10x30.

After learning that some long-range hunters were seeking a spotting scope that not only had the ability of visual observation, but included an integrate reticle, Swarovski listened. The result came in the form of the company's new STR 80. This scope combines high-quality HD optics with ranging capabilities and are available with either an MOA or MRAD-style illuminated reticle. Fifteen different reticle brightness levels are provided, 10 for day use and five for nighttime, and the reticle size adjusts as the magnification changes. If the reticle is not needed, it can be easily removed from the view. Two magnification eyepieces are currently available: 20-60x and 25-50xW (wide). Further adding to the flexibility and usefulness of the STR 80 Spotting Scope, it can be used in conjunction with Swarovski's DCB II Digital Camera Base, which allows the user to capture long-range digital still or video images on camera. MSRPs: STR 80 with the illuminated reticle is $3,689; STR 80 with the 20-60x eyepiece is $4,332; or the STR 80 with the 25-50xW eyepiece is $4,499.

(www.swarovskioptik.us)

Trijicon

Trijicon, Inc. has introduced new reticle choices for their Advanced Combat Optical Gunsight (ACOG) 4x32 LED riflescopes. These battery powered LED scopes now come in a choice of Horseshoe, Chevron or Crosshair .223

illuminated reticles (red and green), all of which are powered by a single AA battery. These sights are mil-spec constructed and come with a forged aluminum main tube that is both waterproof and fogproof with reticle adjustments of ½ inch per click.

Fans of the Trijicon AccuPoint riflescope series can now harness the maximum range potential with new custom laser-engraved adjustable turrets, which are available from Kenton Industries. A complete selection of these custom turrets is available for the AccuPoint 3-9x40mm, 2.5-10x50mm and 5-20x50mm models in Speed Dial, Long Range Hunter or Military configuration, which are appropriate for a variety of long-range shooting styles and scenarios and feature easy-to-read numbering for quick, intuitive adjustments.

There is a new Trijicon line of Reflex sights now available with a green dot reticle. The green color offers a highly visible reference for close-range shooting without obscuring the target at extended ranges. This new option is available in 4.5-MOA and 6.5-MOA dot sizes. The Reflex is powered by Trijicon's dual-illuminated technology that combines Tritium illumination with advanced fiber optics. They come in a durable aluminum alloy housing that is designed to withstand the rigors of hard use under the most severe environmental conditions.

(www.trijicon.com)

Weaver

Weaver has been producing optics and mounting systems for over 80 years.

Recently it was announced that two of their tactical scopes had received the prestigious "Member Tested and Recommended" seal of approval from the National Tactical Officers Association (NTOA). After extensive testing by law enforcement officials, the Weaver 1-5x24mm Illuminated Close-Intermediate Range Scope (CIRS) and 2-10x36mm 1/10 Mil Tactical Scope received a score of 4.32 and 4.27 out of a possible 5, respectively. Both of these scopes are part of the Weaver Super Slam series.

The Weaver 1-5x24mm Tactical Scope with the Illuminated Close-Intermediate Range Tactical Reticle fits a wide variety of shooting applications. With its 5x zoom capabilities it fits well in CQB scenarios or out to 600-plus yard extended range shooting. It comes in a durable one-piece construction and features a first-focal plane reticle for accurate mil units at all magnifications, and can be illuminated in red or green. The unique "reset-to-zero" function turrets eliminate the need to loosen caps when on-the-fly adjustments become necessary. MSRP of the Weaver 1-5x24mm CIRT reticle scope is $1,069.95.

The Weaver 2-10x36mm 1/10 Tactical Scope with the Enhanced MilDot Ranging reticle features fully multicoated lenses with an extra-hard coating on the exterior lenses to help ensure long durability. The greater range of magnification in the 2-10x36mm provides a high degree of flexibility of use that works equally well at either close or long range. MSRP for the Weaver 2-10x36mm EMDR reticle is $1,197.95.

With the recent popularity of scout

A major trend today lies in the resurrection of scout-style scope mounting. Savage's new 10FCM Scout rifle is shown here topped with a Weaver Classic K-Series 4x28mm long eye relief scope.

Right: For longer ranges, use the Weaver 2-10x36mm 1/10 Tactical Scope that features the Enhanced MilDot Ranging Reticle.

Below: The Weaver 1-5x24mm Tactical Scope with the Illuminated Close-Intermediate Range Tactical Reticle fits a wide range of applications from CQB scenarios to extended shots out to 600-plus yards.

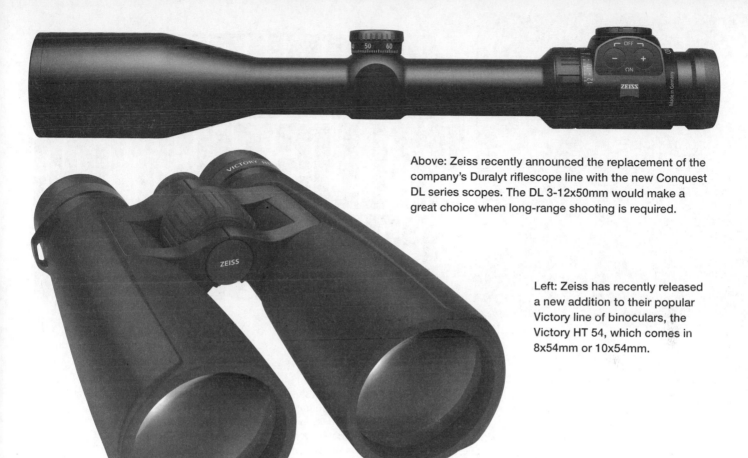

Above: Zeiss recently announced the replacement of the company's Duralyt riflescope line with the new Conquest DL series scopes. The DL 3-12x50mm would make a great choice when long-range shooting is required.

Left: Zeiss has recently released a new addition to their popular Victory line of binoculars, the Victory HT 54, which comes in 8x54mm or 10x54mm.

scope mounting, the extended eye relief Weaver Classic K-Series Model 849417 could provide the perfect option for those situations. The Scout 4x28mm comes in matte finish, has a Dual-X reticle and is set at the factory to be parallax free at 50 yards. MSRP for the Classic K-Series 4x28mm is $273.49.

(www.weaveroptics.com)

Zeiss

Zeiss has recently released a new addition to its popular Victory line of binoculars – the Victory HT 54. The 8x54mm and 10x54mm are light in weight and compact in design, and are said to be even brighter than any comparable standard 56mm binocular. The 20 percent lighter weight of the Victory HT54 is a characteristic that comes from a new and unique lens diameter, yet image brightness is not sacrificed due to the HD glass. The weight of the 8x54mm is 36.5 ounces and the 10x54mm is only a half an ounce heavier at 37 ounces. Both models deliver

95 percent light transmission. That is achieved by virtue of their SCHOTT High Transmission (HT) glass, enhanced ZEISS T* multicoating and their Abbe-König-prism system. Their double-link bridge made of super-light magnesium helps to couple lightweight with a maximum degree of mechanical precision and serviceability. MSRPs for the Victory HT 54 8x54mm and 10x54mm are $2,722.21 and $2,777.77 respectively.

Zeiss recently announced the replacement of the company's Duralyt riflescope line with their new Conquest DL series scopes. This new DL line features three models: 1.2-5x35mm, 2-8x42mm and 3-12x50mm. All three models are available in a choice of illuminated reticle #60 or nonilluminated reticle #6. Todd Pearson, Vice President of Carl Zeiss Sports Optics, characterized this change by saying: "The new design of the DL is loaded with features that optimize operation and performance that will continue the international success of the Duralyt." Made in Germany, the new Conquest DL line of scopes deliver the same standard

of quality as their predecessors did, but with a higher degree of improved performance capabilities. For the hunter, the fine illuminated red dot provides minimum target coverage whether that is by day or when shooting under extremely low-light situations. For the target shooter the optional ASV target turrets should be of great interest. Other features include LotuTec protective coatings and larger buttons to simplify adjustments of the illumination system. MSRP for the Conquest DL 1.2-5x36mm with the #60 illuminated reticle is $1,444.43. The Conquest DL 2-8x42mm equipped with the #60 illuminated reticle runs $1,499.99 and the Conquest DL 3-12x50mm with the #60 illuminated reticle is $1,555.54.

(www.zeiss.com/sports)

A final note to keep in mind: In some locales the use of night-vision equipment is considered illegal for hunting purposes, or restricted to the hunting of certain species. For this reason it is strongly recommended that anyone contemplating the use of any night-vision enhancing equipment for hunting purposes should check with their local game department to determine the legality.

AMMUNITION, BALLISTICS AND COMPONENTS

BY **Phil Massaro**

here's lots of new stuff being introduced for 2016, from new cartridges like the 28 Nosler to a rippin' new turkey load from Federal, to some factory loaded rifle ammunition featuring the longtime favorite of reloaders, Berger bullets. It seems that the great ammo crunch of 2013 and 2014 is slowly loosening up, and there are some fantastic new reloading tools for those who've decided to roll their own. Let's take a look at them!

Accurate Powder

New from Accurate Powder is the LT-30 smokeless powder, designed for smaller

capacity, benchrest-style cartridges. The burn rate is similar to H-4198 (yet not interchangeable, not at all!) and has shown fantastic accuracy in the .30BR Remington cartridge, and is suitable for the popular .223 Remington and .308 Winchester we all love. Western Powders have been a favorite of mine for years, and are often an overlooked source of great accuracy and consistency. If you're a fan of those loveable short, stubby cartridges like the 6.5 Grendel and the 6mm PPC, or varmint cartridges like the .17 Remington Fireball and .222 Remington, this may be a powder for you. Also, you .308 shooters may want to take a look at the data for LT-30 for lighter loads, as they would be great for close-range work or for teaching good marksmanship skills to a new shooter. The LT-32 powder is a bit slower burning, and will work very well in the .223 Remington/5.56 NATO, 6mm BR Norma and .204 Ruger. Both of these powders are just about perfect for the venerable .45-70 Government, giving the classic velocities in an easy-to-meter powder. (www.WesternPowders.com)

Alliant

The Reloder series of powders dates back to the old Hercules Powder Co., and they've had a great lineup for decades. I routinely use Reloder powder

for my own rifle cartridges; RL-15 in the .308 Winchester and .375 H&H, RL-19 in my .300 Winchester Magnum, RL-25 in the .300 Remington Ultra Magnum, and I've been overheard referring to Reloder-22 as "a miracle in a can." They are very consistent, not to mention their accuracy potential. The new offerings from Alliant are no exception and there are some improvements, especially in the realm of temperature sensitivity. As much as I love these older powders, they are susceptible to temperature fluctuations, losing a bit of velocity on the colder extremes and gaining some

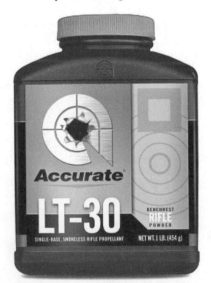

Accurate Powder LT-30

Alliant Reloder 23

Alliant Reloder 26

in the hotter temperatures, and pressures change accordingly. Alliant has changed the game with these two new releases. Both Reloder 23 and 26 are designed to be extremely consistent across the full range of temperatures, minimizing the velocity and pressure deviation associated with temperature extremes. Reloder 23 has a burn rate similar (but again, not interchangeable) to Reloder 22, and Reloder 26 burns a bit slower than Reloder 25, so those of you who love the huge-cased super magnums should make a couple of new friends here, rather quickly. I know my beloved .300 Winchester Magnum will appreciate the new all-weather propellants!

(www.Alliantpowder.com)

ASYM

The brainchild of famous custom 1911 maker Stan Chen is now a separate entity under new management, but still delivering the same quality products. Loaded in .45 ACP, 9mm Luger, .223 Remington and .308 Winchester, ASYM produces premium ammunition using the best components, held to tight tolerances for excellent accuracy. Defense loads feature the Barnes TAC-XP bullet, while rifle loads utilize the Barnes TSX for hunting and Sierra MatchKing for target accuracy, in addition to proprietary loads for match-grade accuracy. Note to reloaders: ASYM loads with match-grade brass for their target loads, so you might want to hang on to that spent brass.

(www.Asym-ammo.com)

Barnes

If you enjoy range time with your AR, Barnes has a new line of ammunition just for you. The Range AR ammunition features a new bullet: a copper jacket and zinc core in an open-tip, flat-base configuration. The Range AR is made in 5.56mm with a 52-grain bullet, and in .300 Blackout in a 90-grain load. While not a hunting bullet, it is perfect for training, competition or target work. The zinc core works well with the faster twist rates associated with ARs in these calibers, and they are completely lead free so as to be compliant with all lead restricted areas.

(www.BarnesBullets.com)

Berger

Berger bullets are no stranger to the handloading world – they've been target shooters' favorites for quite some time. With few exceptions, the long, sleek bullets and their high Ballistic Coefficients have required handloading to be used, but all that is changed. Applied Ballistic Munitions (ABM) has solved that problem. Offering factory loaded ammo in .308 Winchester, .300 Winchester Magnum and the mighty .338 Lapua, you can choose between hunting bullets and target bullets, in several different weights and configurations of Berger Bullets. ABM offers three grades: Mission Ready, Target Ready and Hunt Ready, each loaded with the appropriate style of Berger bullet for the job at hand. I liked the .300 Winchester Magnum load featuring the 230-grain Berger Hybrid Target Match, showing sub-MOA accuracy. If you're serious about hair-splitting accuracy, give this ammunition a whirl and experience the incredible potential of the designs of Walt Berger and Bryan Litz.

(www.bergerbullets.com)

Cutting Edge Bullets

The popularity of the .300 Blackout continues to grow and components grow with it. The team at Cutting Edge Bullets

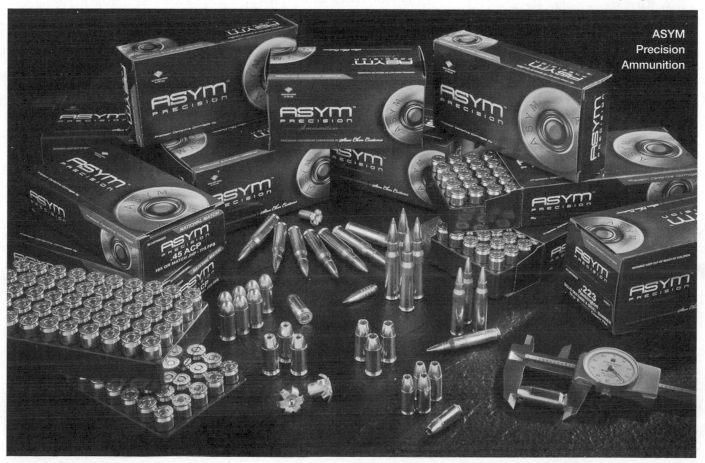

ASYM
Precision
Ammunition

has produced their lathe-turned copper bullets for a while now, but the new 190-grain flat-base Raptor is designed around the subsonic performance of the .300 Blackout and Whisper. The bullet features a skived hollowpoint that will give good expansion at velocities as low as 900 fps – perfect for the Blackout velocity. Upon impact the frontal section of the bullet breaks into blades that provide good impact trauma, while the remaining caliber-size slug continues on for good penetration. This is the standard Cutting Edge design, but brought to you in 2015 designed for the Blackout's velocity range.

(www.CuttingEdgeBullets.com)

Falcon Bullet Company

Since ammunition has been hard to come by for the last couple of years, many shooters have turned to reloading their ammunition as a means to keep shooting. With the price of copper going through the roof, and with components even becoming a rarity, cast lead bullets have been an affordable alternative. Folks like Elmer Keith touted the virtues of the classic lead bullet, and it's well known that they are highly accurate. But with lead bullets, as we also know, comes the chore of cleaning a leaded barrel. Not so with the new FalCoated bullets from Falcon Bullet Company. A proprietary polymer coating (in a really cool crimson color) coats the meplat and sides of the bullets to reduce lead fouling. The FalCoated .45 ACP 230-grain

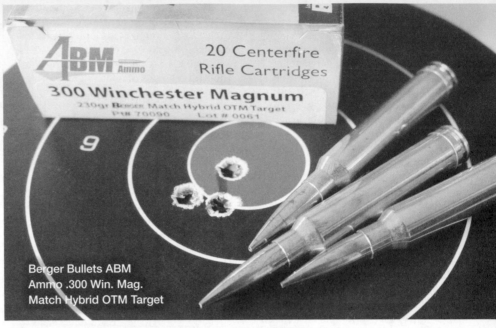

Berger Bullets ABM Ammo .300 Win. Mag. Match Hybrid OTM Target

bullet mimics the profile of the highly popular ball ammunition projectile, and has shot very well from our test guns. My own .38 Special absolutely loves the .357-inch diameter 158-grain semiwadcutter, and I've had good results in the .357 Magnum with this bullet as well. There have been no feed problems in the autoloaders we've tested, making the FalCoated bullets a great economical choice for the gun games as well as for those high-volume plinkers. For convenience they come in bulk boxes of 500 and 2,000. Available in most popular pistol calibers from .380 ACP to .45 ACP.

(www.FalconBullets.com)

Federal

For those of us who like to head afield with a 10mm Auto in hand, such as Razor Dobbs and Uncle Ted Nugent, Federal Premium has given us a great 180-grain hunting bullet: the Trophy Bonded jacketed softpoint. I had the privilege of being able to test this load for penetration and expansion in ballistic gelatin this past November at the Federal Plant in Anoka and I can attest to the integrity of this load; I wouldn't hesitate to take it hunting for medium game at sane distances. The 180-grain bullet should prove worthy of deer and hog hunting, at the very least. With

Cutting Edge Bullets 190-grain .300 Blackout

Falcon FalCoated Bullets

a muzzle velocity of 1, 275 fps, and a bullet based on the hugely successful Trophy Bonded Bear Claw, it uses a bonded core to prevent jacket and core separation and to ensure deep penetration. The accuracy of these loads proved to be very good as well, printing 2-inch groups at 25 yards. You'll want to give these a try in your Big Ten.

Look, I love the long-range target game, but the ammunition involved with hitting a target at 1,000 yards can be cost prohibitive, especially when we're talking about the .338 Lapua Magnum. It can burn over 100 grains of powder and has a huge case that often demands a price commensurate with its size. Not so any longer, as I had the opportunity to shoot Federal's American Eagle .338 Lapua Magnum and can testify that it's much more accurate than its price point. At the range I was ringing steel at 935 yards with no problems at all, putting together a group that even raised my own eyebrows. Featuring a 250-grain jacketed spitzer and a tag of less than $70 per box of 20, it's difficult to turn away from a deal like this. Those of you who reload for the .338 Lapua will find it almost worth the cost just to have the brass. It makes me want to order a .338 Lapua of my own!

Turkey hunters have long looked for a balance of shot patterns that will kill birds at long distance when the tom hangs up for apparently no reason, yet still will open wide enough at close ranges for those times the tom doesn't present a shot until he's right up on top of you. The good folks at Federal have given us just that with their 3rd Degree turkey Ammo. Available in 12 gauge, 3-inch length, they've designed a new shotshell that blends three different types of shot to deliver a

Federal 10mm Trophy Bonded 180-grain JSP

good killing pattern at ranges from, "I can literally smell Thanksgiving," to "What in the heck made him stop at 50 yards?" The shot column consists of 20 percent Flitestopper No. 6 shot (the cool ones that look like the planet Saturn) to open up for close shots, 40 percent copper-plated No. 6 shot giving the traditional turkey load performance, and 40 percent No. 7 Heavyweight shot for the distant toms. The 3rd Degree loads have been proven in the game fields from 8 yards out past 50 yards, and I can't wait to try them this spring!

Federal's American Eagle .338 Lapua Ammo

3RD DEGREE™

12 GAUGE 3"
5-6-7 SHOT

Federal 3rd Degree Turkey shotshells

The .30-30 Winchester seems to be getting quite a facelift these days, first from the Hornady LEVERevolution line, and now from the Federal Trophy Copper 150-grain bullet. The Trophy Copper bullet is a monometal design, and in a flatpoint configuration it will give the .30-30 fans a bullet with fantastic weight retention and penetration. The rounded polymer tip will ensure that there will be no risk of primer detonation in a tubular magazine. I'm thinking this load will be fantastic for a bear hunt in the spring where shots are relatively close and a short, handy carbine will make a whole lot of sense. This load will make the .30-30 Winchester come to life, giving fantastic penetration on the biggest of black bears. The Trophy Copper comes loaded in nickel-plated cases and should be well received among the lever-gun aficionados.

For a carry gun, we'd all like a pistol the size and weight of a credit card,

but those guns usually lack the throw weight we'd like to have to stop a threat. That's just a simple matter of physics. So, the best possible projectiles are definitely warranted with the smaller calibers like .380 Auto. Federal's HST, now loaded in a 90-grain configuration for the .380, is one of the best defensive bullets I've ever seen. I had the opportunity to put the HST through some serious testing at the Federal Premium plant, and it expanded and penetrated reliably through bare gel, clothing and sheet rock. The .380 Auto falls into the category of what I call a "belly gun," meaning that it is for close-quarters work, and certainly isn't any sort of a long-distance round. For this purpose, you'll want a bullet with the best characteristics to quell the situation if need be, and see that you keep your own anatomy in its current configuration. I love the HST in the bigger sidearms like the .40 S&W and the .45 ACP, but

it is even more crucial when the bullet diameter and weight are diminished to match a concealable handgun – as is the case with the .380 Auto. Were I to carry a .380, I'd load it with Federal's HST, with confidence.

Another new Federal gem is for the smokepole crowd. The Trophy Copper Muzzleloader projectile system is designed for .50-caliber rifles using a polymer-tipped 270-grain spitzer bullet, of all-copper construction. The B.O.R. LOCK system uses a fiber-reinforced polymer cup that snaps onto the base of the bullet to both seal the gases in the bore for better velocity, and to scrape fouling from the bore to reduce cleaning. This cup also reduces the amount of pressure required to load the muzzleloader when compared to a saboted bullet, making reloading quicker than you're used to. Accuracy with this bullet is good out to 250 yards and beyond. Another revolutionary new

Federal HST .380 ACP cartridges

Federal Trophy Copper Muzzleloader Bullets

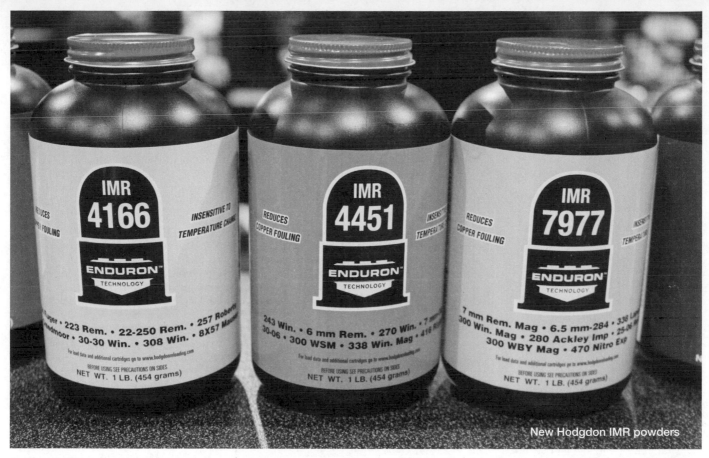

New Hodgdon IMR powders

design, Federal continues to show its innovation. (www.FederalPremium.com)

Hodgdon

Hodgdon 2015 Reloading Manual. This year's manual from Hodgdon gives the reloader data for the new IMR Enduron powders, in addition to our favorite stuff from Winchester, IMR and Hodgdon. The trio of Enduron powders – IMR 4166,

IMR 4451 and IMR 7977 – is tested in 41 different cartridges within the Hodgdon Manual. These new powders are designed to be temperature insensitive and are of the "short cut" grain structure to flow well through powder throwers and auto dispensers. All of the classic powder offerings from this powerhouse trio of companies are included in centerfire pistol and rifle, as well as shotgun loads. Any cartridge, any caliber and a

great diversity of bullet types are tested – there's a good load in this manual for you. (www.hodgdon.com)

Hornady

Reduced recoil ammunition is a great tool for teaching good marksmanship to new shooters, or for those who can be recoil sensitive, especially in a life-threatening situation. Hornady's

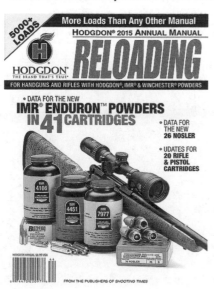

Left: Hodgdon Reloading Manual

Right: Hornady Critical Defense Lite

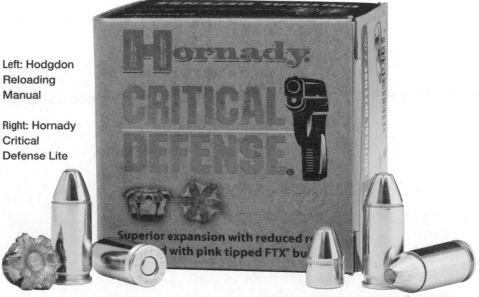

Above:
100-grain
GMX Hornady

Right: Hornady
American
Whitetail
12-gauge
slug

Critical Defense Lite ammunition makes a great choice for the smaller carry guns, especially the compact 9mm Lugers. Using a 100-grain FTX bullet, this load generates 1,125 fps at the muzzle from a 4-inch barrel and carries 1,000 fps out to 50 yards. The FTX is a hollowpoint design and the hollow cavity filled with a pliable material that helps to initiate expansion through many types of material. Felt recoil is reduced by 27 percent, which will make this ammo absolutely perfect for the shooter who is new to the handgun game, or those who are recoil sensitive. As if the ammo wasn't cool enough, for those boxes that come with the pink tip and box, Hornady sends a portion of the proceeds to breast cancer research. Now, there's a valid reason to buy more ammo!

Those shooters who enjoy the .270 Winchester, .270 WSM, .270 Weatherby Magnum and 6.8 SPC cartridges now have a new toy to play with – the 100-grain GMX bullet from Hornady. The concept of monometal construction goes back a few decades, and though it took a bit of wrangling to set things right, Hornady seems to have a design that works well. All of the GMX designs that I have worked with have proved to be very accurate, whether in the 6mm calibers or the .375s. One of the distinguishing characteristics of all-copper bullets is that they are longer for caliber

than are their lead-core counterparts, and one could say that the lighter weight copper bullets will perform on par with a cup-and-core bullet of slightly heavier weight. The 100-grain weight in .277-inch diameter should prove to be a bullet that will perform close to a cup-and-core 130-grain bullet within this caliber. It can be revved up to over 3,400 fps in the magnum cartridges, or loaded sedately in the 6.8 SPC with equal success. No worries of jacket and core separation, because there is no core. The entire bullet is constructed of jacket metal (hence the name Gilding Metal eXpanding, or GMX) so simply put, this bullet will hold together. Weight retention ranges between 85-95 percent and depending upon impact velocity, expansion can be one and a half times the original caliber. This particular bullet would make a great choice for white-tailed deer and pronghorn antelope, as well as the smaller African plains game.

The Hornady GMX (Gilding Metal eXpanding) bullet has been a staple in the Hornady line for a while, but the new Full Boar ammo lets the hunter who uses factory ammunition take full advantage of it. Being a monometal bullet with a red polymer tip, you'll get the fantastic reputation associated with all-copper bullets. The polymer tip fills a hollow cavity and acts as a wedge to promote expansion upon impact, so you get a great blend of deep penetration and the wide expansion of the hollowpoint copper bullets, all the while increasing the Ballistic Coefficient of the overall package. While they are perfect for those of the porcine persuasion,

these bullets are also great for deer, elk, moose and even bears in the appropriate calibers. Available in .223 Remington, .243 Winchester, 6.8mm SPC, .270 Winchester, 7mm Remington Magnum, .308 Winchester, .30-06 Springfield and .300 Winchester Magnum.

Some folks like to use their "old-school" shotguns to hunt deer. Sometimes it's too difficult to set Ol' Betsy aside for the new-fangled shotguns with the rifled bores and doodads that come along with them, and that's not a bad thing. I've seen some old-timers make some shots with an old 12 gauge that would put the rifle guys on their heels. Hornady has introduced the American Whitetail, an affordable slug for smoothbore shotgun shooters designed to give good accuracy from those who choose not to use a rifled slug barrel. With a 1-ounce Foster rifled slug pushed to a muzzle velocity of 1,600 fps, whitetail hunters can confidently head afield with a traditional shotgun barrel. Hornady used a compression-style wad to protect the rear portion of the slug from deformation and seal the burning gases to maximize velocity from the shotgun.

The new .17 WSM is all the rimfire rage, being at the top of the velocity heap among the .17-caliber rimfire cartridges. The .17 rimfire world is relatively new and this is the third in the line, being faster than the .17 Mach II (based on the CCI Stinger-length .22 LR case) and the .17 Hornady Magnum Rimfire (based on the .22 Winchester Magnum Rimfire case). Hornady's load drives their proven 20-grain jacketed V-Max bullet to an even 3,000 fps, and in terms of velocity, the .17 WSM falls in between the .17 HMR and the centerfire .17 Hornet. Based on

Hornady Full Boar Ammuntion

Hornady .17
Winchester
Super Magnum

my experience with that 20-grain V-Max in other .17 cartridges, varmints and other small game don't stand a chance. The red polymer tip and thin jacket form a dynamic duo of expansion, and the speed of the .17 WSM should easily indoctrinate this Hornady load into the Brotherhood of the Red Mist.

(www.Hornady.com)

Norma

Norma adds three 6.5mm cartridges to their excellent lineup of brass cases for 2015: 6.5 Grendel, 6.5 Creedmoor and .26 Nosler. We're all aware of the accuracy potential of the 6.5mm cases, and with Norma brass that accuracy will be even easier to obtain. Norma cases have been an integral part of my accuracy equation for decades, and for target competitions or expensive hunts there is really no reason to skimp on cartridge cases. Norma anneals their case necks, making the brass softer where it is worked the most to extend the case life considerably, and keep things uniform for much longer.

Norma's cases are extremely consistent, and consistency is a huge part of achieving that hair-splitting accuracy we're all seeking.

(www.Norma-usa.com)

Nosler

After the shockwave created by last year's unveiling of the .26 Nosler, which is based on a modified Remington Ultra Magnum case (itself being a blown out version of the .404 Jeffery), it only made sense for the Nosler folks to open that case to hold 7mm bullets. Both the .26 and .28 Nosler are designed to blend

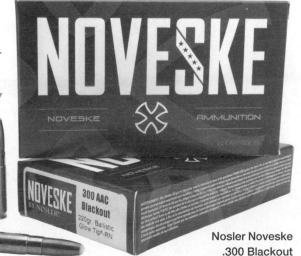

Nosler Noveske
.300 Blackout

the case diameter and rebated rim of the Remington Ultra Mag. series in a case short enough to fit in a .30-06 length action. Pushing a 160-grain AccuBond bullet to 3,300 fps, and a 175-grain AccuBond Long Range bullet to just over 3,100 fps, this is going to be a winner. In terms of speed and power, it lies just south of the huge 7mm RUM and 7mm STW, but well above the über-popular 7mm Remington Magnum, while still able to be housed in a long-action rifle. The beltless design will give better case life than the Holland & Holland design, as there will be less of the stretching that occurs just north of the belt. By launching the 7mm bullets that are so popular with big-game hunters, the .28 Nosler will be in many trophy pictures to come. I can't wait to test drive this big Seven.

The 28 Nosler

(www.28nosler.com)

Designed to perform in modern sporting rifles, Nosler's Noveske line of ammunition features a slick-looking black oxide finish on both bullet and casing, and a tip that glows in the dark. Yes, I said that, they glow in the dark, and you know you want some of this ammo just for this reason. Seriously, this is good stuff, optimized for the AR platform that these cartridges work within. Within each caliber is a Varmegeddon loading and a ballistic tip offering, making each of the three calibers loaded worthy of both varmint and deer hunts with your modern sporting rifle. The ammunition is manufactured by Nosler, but features the Noveske headstamp on the casings. Offered in 5.56 NATO, .300 Blackout and 7.62x51 NATO.

(www.nosler.com/noveske-ammunition)

RCBS

For you high-volume shooters who appreciate the benefits of a progressive press, you'd do well to take a look at the new RCBS seven-station ProChucker 7. Auto-indexing, with a removable die plate, the option of seven stations gives the reloader plenty of flexibility. Gone are the plastic APS primer strips of the RCBS Pro2000 AutoIndex progressive (that nearly drove me insane!); the Pro-Chucker comes with a standard primer pickup tube and a safety shield. The press comes with the Quick Change powder measure, with larger powder capacity to reduce the number of times you'll need to refill the hopper, and a drain tube allows you to rapidly empty the hopper when your session is over. It's never a good idea to leave powder in the hopper of your press, as the possibility of someone fooling around and spilling it certainly exists, but also for the fact that some pistol powders have been known to have a chemical reaction with the plastic material and sort of "melt" the plastic if left for prolonged periods of time – and that's never a good thing. Its seven stations will allow you to seat and crimp in separate functions, and use a bullet feeder and lock-out die without issue. With that removable die plate you can quickly change calibers by removing two pins and swapping out plates and shell plates. Output capacity is roughly 600 rounds per hour, so this makes a solid choice for those of you who participate in the gun games or those who have fun making huge piles of empty brass at the range. (www.rcbs.com)

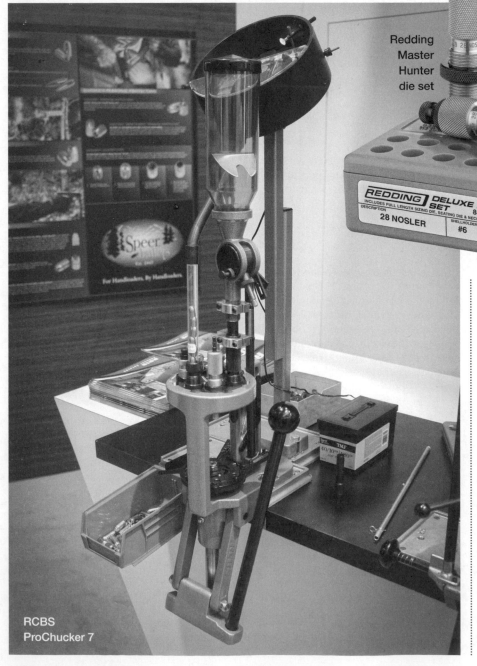

Redding Master Hunter die set

RCBS ProChucker 7

Redding

The .26 and .28 Nosler are fantastic new cartridges, but if you can't handload for them, that takes half the fun out of it. Not to worry – the team at Redding Reloading has you covered. New for '15, the Master Hunter series uses a standard full-length sizing die and a Competition seating die. If you're unfamiliar with Redding Competition dies, this is the cool one with the micrometer adjustable bullet seater. When seating depth gets critical, having micrometer adjustable seating depth is a definite advantage to a traditional seating die, where you screw the seating adjustment up or down a bit, and hope you've got it close. You can load those new Nosler cartridges with any brand of bullet you choose, then start working up your custom loads with the high tolerances and repeatability of Redding die sets.

(www.Redding-reloading.com)

Remington

Big Green announces a new load for waterfowlers this year, the HyperSonic Steel shotshells. By now, we are all familiar with the shortcomings of the early steel shot loads and how they paled in comparison to the lead shot loads that hunters were accustomed to. Steel, being

Right: SIG SAUER .300 Blackout Ammunition

Below: Remington HyperSonic Steel

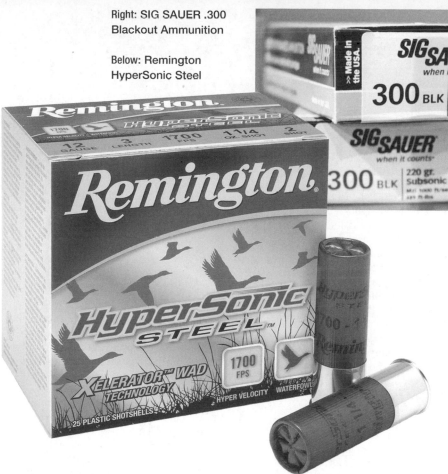

lighter than lead, doesn't hold velocity as well downrange, so if we can push the payload faster we can minimize the amount of lead necessary, allowing you to fill your limit faster (or in my case, to hit a wood duck at all coming by at

Mach II!) Using a hotter primer, the higher velocity will cut your lead down by up to 8 inches at 40 yards. HyperSonic Steel is available in 10, 12 and 20 gauge in popular waterfowl shot sizes.

(www.Remington.com)

Sierra

Who doesn't love shooting Sierra MatchKing bullets? I know I do, and now that they feature a green polymer tip to protect the meplat and increase the Ballistic Coefficient – so they're even cooler than they ever were. Available in 69 and 77 grains in .224-inch diameter, and 125, 155, 168 and 175 grains in .308-inch diameter, all you benchrest shooters can enjoy the industry standard tolerances of the MatchKing line, now with vibrant color! The .223 weights should prove perfect for the .223 Remington and 5.56mm NATO, however, they'll prove a bit too long for the standard twist rates of my pet .22-250 Remington and the .220 Swift, much to my chagrin. But, the .308 weights will work in any and all of the .30-caliber cartridges including the big honkin' magnum cases. The tipped MatchKings feature the same standards of the traditional MatchKing – the +/- 0.3 grain weight differential and the tight jacket concentricity that have put them at the top of the heap.

(www.sierrabullets.com)

Sig Sauer Ammunition

The prestigious firm of SIG SAUER has answered the .300 Blackout calling, offering Match Grade ammunition in both subsonic and supersonic configurations. Both loads feature the time-tested Sierra MatchKing bullets; the subsonic load is centered around the 220-grain MatchKing and the supersonic load uses the 125-grain MatchKing. SIG loads both of these cartridges into match-grade brass cases to maximize the accuracy of the Blackout round. The supersonic load has a muzzle velocity of 2,200 fps, giving a dead-flat trajectory from the muzzle out to 100 yards, and even the subsonic load, with its heavy and slow bullet, will be 3.2 inches high

Sierra Tipped MatchKing Bullets

at 50 yards to be zeroed at 100 yards. This gives the .300 Blackout fans a very diverse pair of factory match-grade loads for their ARs, using one of the best bullets available on the market. (www.sigsauer.com)

Sinter Fire

Ammunition designed for self-defense is always a tricky proposition. You want a bullet that will do its job, that is, give adequate expansion and penetration to neutralize the threat to life and limb. However, we all want a bullet that won't go sailing through walls and trees and concrete barriers. The balance is a tough one. Sinter Fire has done very well at meeting that balance in their Special Duty line of handgun ammunition. Using a proven combination of a light, frangible bullet delivered at a higher velocity, the Special Duty ammunition will minimize the risk of over penetration as the bullet is designed to break up when it impacts a surface or substance harder than it is. The hollowpoint design will initiate the expansion, and that expansion should be devastating. Special Duty is available in 75-grain .380 ACP; 110-grain .38 Special; 100-grain 9mm Luger; 125-grain .40 S&W; and 155-grain .45 ACP. (www.sinterfire.com)

Snake River

Snake River Shooting Products has teamed up with U.S. Navy SEAL Marcus Lutrell and Taya Kyle, widow of Navy SEAL Chris Kyle, to offer "Team Never Quit" ammunition in .45 ACP and .300 Blackout. The ammunition is due out mid-2015, and while I don't have a ton of details on the specifications at this moment, I think the central point is the news that these great American patriots have teamed together to form an ammunition company celebrating the spirit of those who have given so much for our freedom. (www.snakerivershootingproducts.com)

Swift Bullets

OK, I'll admit it. I'm a geek who enjoys reading reloading manuals and I get

Swift Bullet Company *Reloading Manual Number Two*

excited when a new one comes out. It didn't take 10 seconds after finding out that Swift published *Reloading Manual Number Two,* before I was on the phone ordering mine. *Number Two* covers all of the new developments from Swift, like the .22-caliber Scirocco II bullets, as well as new calibers like the .300 Ruger Compact Magnum, and data for the many new powders on the market. There are more powders tested per caliber, and energy and trajectory tables are included, optimized for the performance level of each cartridge. All of our old favorites are still there, and if you are a lover of Swift Bullets like I am, this manual is a must have. (www.SwiftBullets.com)

Winchester

Everybody loves a good deer bullet – let's face it – it's the number one game animal of all time. The new Winchester Deer Season XP ammo features a flat-base, cup-and-core bullet with a larger-than-normal polymer tip to initiate expansion for large amounts of hydrostatic shock. This translates into a bullet that is designed to give optimum performance on the relatively thin-skinned white-tailed deer. Is it a good choice for an elk or moose bullet? Probably not, but it should be perfect for the deer woods. The folks at Winchester assure me it will give performance similar to the older Power Point model, but with a bit better expansion to switch that big bruiser's power supply to "off." Available in deer-worthy calibers: .243 Winchester, .270 Winchester, 7mm Remington Magnum, .308 Winchester, .30-06 Springfield and .300 Winchester Magnum.

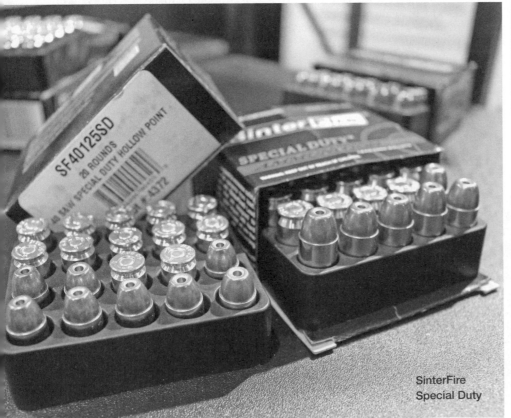

SinterFire Special Duty

Winchester Deer Season XP ammo

Winchester has offered a solution to shot deformation and premature pattern expansion with its new Rooster XR series of shotshells. The shot column of the Rooster XR is held together with a hard-

Winchester Long Beard XR and "Winchester Rooster XR shotshells with a cut-away view of featuring Shot-Lok™ Technology

ened resin, so that the shot at the rear of the column does not become deformed from the violent impact of the ignition of the powder charge. The resin keeps the column protected until free of the bore, where it breaks apart and falls away, leaving a virtually perfect group of shot that will fly well and deliver the goods at farther distances than will deformed shot. That equals more hits at long

ranges and better patterns throughout the range of shots. Available in 12 gauge, 2¾-inch length with 1¼ ounces of No. 4, 5 or 6 shot; or 3-inch length, 1½ ounces of No. 4, 5 or 6 shot. Both loads have a muzzle velocity of 1,300 fps. Pheasants, consider yourselves warned!
(www.winchester.com)

No matter how justified the shooting was, some will mourn the slain criminal and seek revenge in court. Here, from one of author's cases years after the shooting, is a shrine to a man who died trying to kill a cop.

STANDARDS
OF DEADLY FORCE

BY **Massad Ayoob**

If forty-some years working and teaching in the justice system has taught me anything, it is this: If you act to the standards by which you know you will be judged, you should not be found wanting in the judgment.

No two use of force incidents will be exactly the same in every respect. There is a virtually infinite potential for branching of circumstances. Because of this, the courts will hold us to standards, to a formula if you will. For the same reasons, it behooves all of us to use a formula to analyze each situation we face to determine whether lethal force is justified.

Lethal force (or deadly force; the terms are interchangeable) is that degree of force which a reasonable and prudent person would consider capable of causing death or great bodily harm. Various laws use the terminology "great bodily harm," "grave bodily harm," "serious bodily harm," etc.; the easiest

Warren on Homicide is widely considered the "bible" of homicide law.

way to remember it in layman's terms is "crippling injury."

The set of circumstances that justifies the use of deadly force is a *situation of immediate danger of death or great bodily harm to oneself or other innocent persons*. Since deadly force is normally only allowed as a last resort, the danger should be otherwise unavoidable and not created by the defender himself. This brings in an element called

preclusion, which can vary according to jurisdiction and circumstances, and will be discussed separately in this book.

That situation of immediate danger of death or crippling injury is normally determined by the simultaneous presence of three criteria. Different schools use different terminology, but the most widely used and court-proven standard has been in use for decades: *ability/ opportunity/jeopardy*. "Ability" means

that the assailant possesses the power to kill or cripple. "Opportunity" means he is capable of immediately employing that power. "Jeopardy" means that his actions and/or words indicate to a reasonable, prudent person that he intends to do so and is about to do so. We will discuss each of these in great detail in this book.

Throughout, the law-abiding armed citizen must maintain *the mantle of*

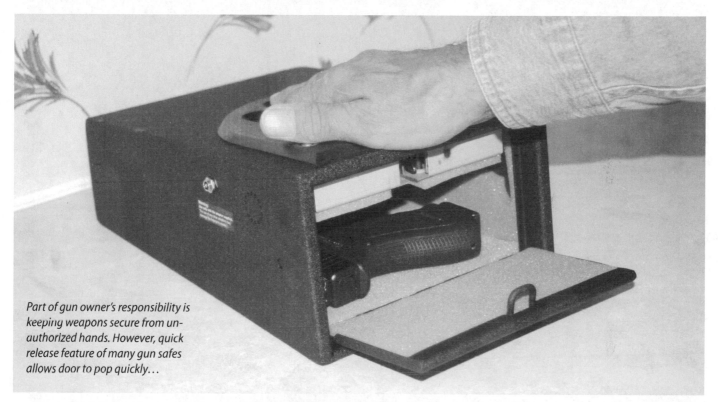

Part of gun owner's responsibility is keeping weapons secure from un-authorized hands. However, quick release feature of many gun safes allows door to pop quickly…

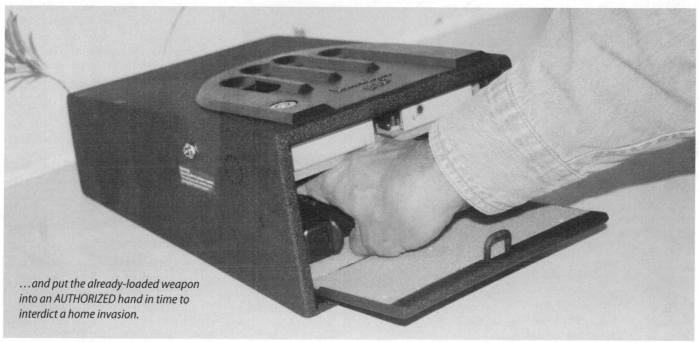

…and put the already-loaded weapon into an AUTHORIZED hand in time to interdict a home invasion.

Experience in court has taught author, "If you act to the standard by which you know you will be judged, you should not be found wanting in the judgment."

Those who don't know their rights to self-defense, or are unprepared and unequipped to defend themselves, can end up here.

innocence. Think of the mantle of innocence as a legal cloak that shields the wearer from successful accusation of wrong-doing. The defender must not have provoked the encounter, must not have started the fight, or an element

Think of the mantle of innocence as a legal cloak that shields the wearer from successful accusation of wrong-doing.
"

of guilt and wrong-doing will accrue. If it lay within the defender's power to end the argument or abjure from the conflict, but instead he "kept the ball rolling" and things predictably escalated, he may very likely be held to have been at least partially at fault.

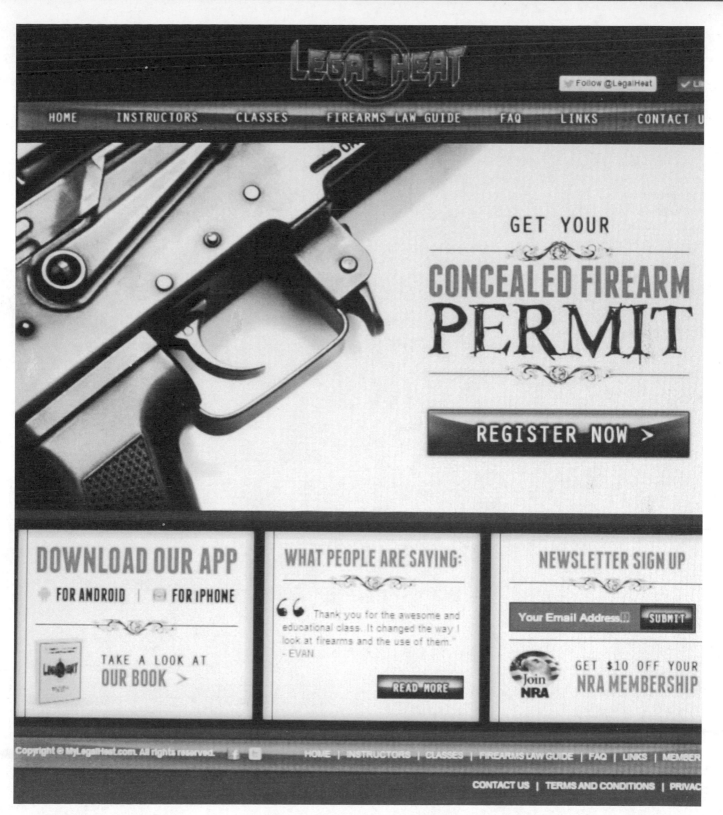

Some states, but not all, have provisions for *excusable homicide* as well as *justifiable homicide*. In essence, a finding of excusable homicide means that the deceased probably shouldn't have been killed, but any reasonable and prudent person under identical circumstances would likely have made the same mistake as the person who killed him. By contrast, a finding of justifiable homicide says in essence that the person who killed the deceased acted correctly in doing so. In either case, the person who is responsible for the killing is held harmless.

Know the laws where you go. This Legal Heat app is useful for checking that on handheld electronic devices.

Author's CLE teaching partner Jim Fleming, a veteran criminal defense lawyer, notes sagely, "You don't have to like reality, but you do have to face it."

We must have *reasonable fear* of death or grave bodily harm when we employ this level of force. Reasonable fear is starkly distinct from what the law calls *bare fear,* which never justifies harming another. Bare fear is naked panic, a blind and unreasoning fear. It is understood that when panic comes in, reason departs. The necessary reasonable fear doesn't mean you're soiling your pants or running away screaming; reasonable fear is simply that apprehension of danger which any reasonable, prudent person would experience if they were in the same situation as you, knowing what you know at the time.

Seasoned criminal defense lawyer Jim Fleming tells a class of attorneys how to handle a deadly force case.

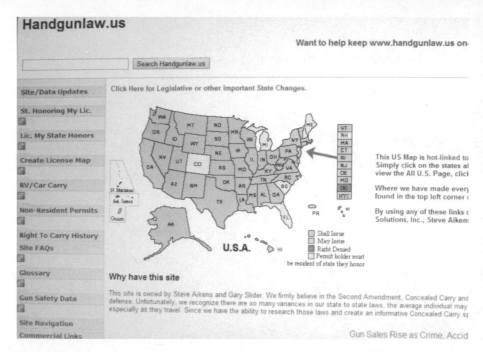

Website handgunlaw.us is author's favorite internet site for up to date state-by-state gun laws, including reciprocity.

Much – but not all—about deadly force law can be learned on-line.

Lawyer, police chief, and tactician Jeff Chudwin reminds his students, "You don't have to be right, you have to be reasonable."

General Rules of Engagement

Each state has its own statutes and codes, colloquially known as "black letter law." The laws are interpreted through the prism of case law, decisions by appellate courts which essentially nail down the fine points. Some of the clearest, most easily understood legal definitions and interpretations may be found in the given state's recommended jury instructions on the various issues. All of these may be researched at a legal library. In every county seat, at or near the county courthouse, you will find a legal library that is open to the public. The legal librarians, I've found as a rule, are delighted to help ordinary citizens look up these things.

Because ours is the most mobile society on Earth, we are constantly moving between jurisdictions. No lawyer can memorize the vastness of The Law in its entirety; that's why every law office has its own legal library. No police officer can memorize them all; that's why the patrol car has a mobile data terminal with the capability of looking things up. It follows that the law-abiding armed citizen can't hold all the laws in his head, either. For that reason, in this book as in my classes, I teach generic principles that are common to the law of all fifty states.

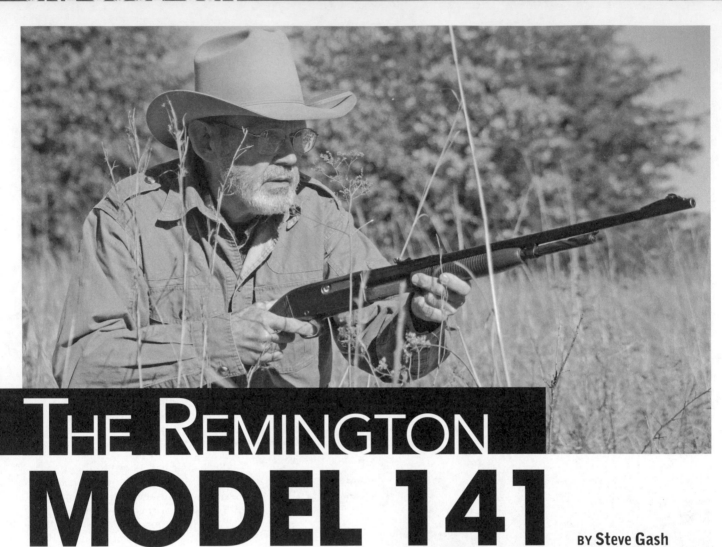

THE REMINGTON
MODEL 141

BY **Steve Gash**

s I perused the tables recently at a modest-size gun show, I spied a rifle I did not recognize. It was a sleek little pump that was in such nice condition that it looked out of place among the rusty clunkers on the table. It seemed to call to me, like a secret friend. I asked for and received permission to pick it up. The left side of the receiver revealed it was a Remington Model 141, "The Gamemaster." While I was vaguely aware of the model, I didn't know a lot about it.

The M-141's caliber marking on the barrel was most intriguing. Just ahead of the receiver was stamped ".30 REM," and a cartridge case head was imbedded in the receiver. The little gun was in excellent condition and I knew I had to have it. The vendor and I

The name "Gamemaster" was stamped on the left side of the receiver, and a case head of the cartridge for which the rifle was chambered was imbedded in the front of the receiver.

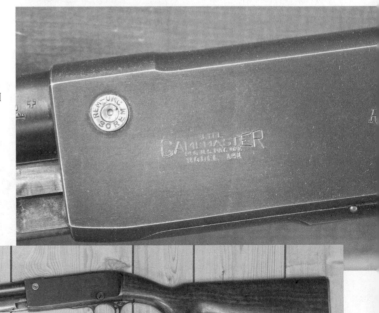

The slide-action Remington Model 141 was made from 1935 to 1950 and chambered for the .25, .30, .32 and .35 Remington cartridges. It offered competition to Winchester's lever-action Model 94.

The M-141's tubular magazine moves back with the slide when the action is cycled, and has spiral flutes that supposedly allow the use of pointed bullets. The metal piece at the front of the magazine is a "brush guard."

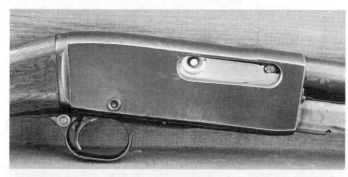

The M-141's sleek receiver has a push-button safety at the rear of the triggerguard. The action release button was at the rear of the action block.

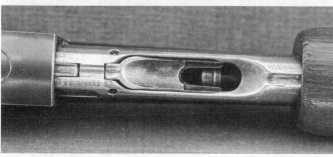

Cartridges are inserted into the magazine via this port ahead of the receiver. Capacity is five rounds.

engaged in a brief and friendly negotiation, a price was determined, paperwork was completed, and the M-141 had a new and loving home.

As it turned out, the Model 141 has a fascinating history. In the early 1900s, Winchester pretty much had the "deer gun" market sewed up. The new Model 1894 lever action was available in several calibers and the .30 WCF (Winchester Central Fire), what we now call the .30-30 Winchester, was by far the most popular.

Compact, light and handy, the M-94 in .30-30 was the go-to gun for multitudes of hunters.

This popularity was not lost on Remington as the brisk sales of M-94s, to say nothing of the Marlin and Savage lever guns, took a big bite out of Big Green's bottom line. Rather than try to compete with Winchester with another lever action, Remington took a different road.

The Model 8 semiauto was introduced in 1906 in four new rimless cartridges:

the .25, .30, .32 and .35 Remingtons. Next, the pump-action Model 14 came along in 1913. Designed by John Pederson, it was chambered for the same cartridges as the Model 8. The Model 14½ came along a year later in .38-40 and .44-40 Winchester. Then in 1935, the slide-action series evolved into the Model 141, which was offered in the four Remington cartridges.

Winchester's Model 94 cartridges all had .506-inch rims, and these were not suitable for the pump-action M-141, so the Remington lineup was rimless. All had a rim diameter of .421 inch except for the .35 Remington, which had an odd .460-inch rim.

In 1935 the retail price of a standard-grade M-141A was $46. The 14, 14½ and 141 had a host of innovative features including a spiral magazine tube that (presumably) prevented the tip of a spitzer bullet from setting off the primer of the cartridge ahead of it when the gun was fired. Magazine capacity in all models is five rounds.

Cartridges are inserted into the magazine in front of the bottom of the receiver. The first round then zips backward, ready to be lifted into position as the action is cycled. Interestingly, the unique magazine tube moves back and forth when the action is cycled. The action release is a small button on the action block itself.

Possibly the slickest feature of the M-141 is the takedown. By unscrewing a large knurl-headed screw on the left side of the action, the receiver and barrel-magazine assembly can be easily and quickly separated from the buttstock and triggerguard.

The date code "UU" on the barrel indicates that my rifle was one of 8,311 made in 1949. Before the M-141 was discontinued in 1950, a total of 76,881 were produced. A new pump gun was on the horizon that was simpler and more economical to make, and in 1952 the Model 760 was introduced, variations of which are made to this day. The M760 would handle the modern cartridges of the day, i.e., the .30-06, .270, as well as the then very popular .300 Savage.

As my friend Garry James says, old or new, antique or modern, "guns are made to be shot," so that was the next phase of the adventure.

It was an adventure, all right. Ammunition for it hasn't been made since about 1997, and what I found on the Internet had serious "collector" prices. So reloading was the answer.

Above: The caliber was marked on the left rear of the barrel. The date code of "UU" indicates a production date of 1949.

Above: The M-141 can be taken down into two pieces for easy cleaning or transport by removing the takedown screw from the left side of the receiver.

Right: The receiver easily lifts off of the triggerguard; no parts fall off, and the action block can be removed so the barrel can be cleaned from the breech.

.30 Remington and .30-30 Winchester cases (from left): Primed and unprimed .30-30 Winchester cases converted to .30 Remington, unaltered .30-30 Winchester case and .30 Remington case from Quality Cartridge.

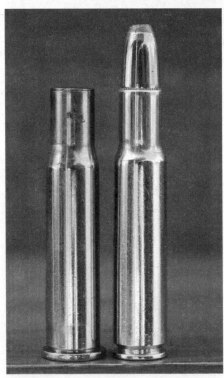

Cases for the .30 Remington (right) can be made from .30-30 Winchester brass (left) by turning off the rim and cutting an extractor groove.

Handloading the .30 Remington is actually pretty straightforward – once you have cases. Bob Hayley of Seymour, Texas, makes cases for all manner of obscure and rare cartridges out of other cases. He converts .30-30 cases to .30 Remington by turning off the rims and cutting an exact extractor groove. The result is picture-perfect brass that slithers through the M-141's action slick as scum off a Louisiana swamp. The cost is a reasonable $1.00 per case, plus return shipping.

I sent 50 Winchester .30-30 cases to Mr. Hayley, and in short order I had .30 Remington cases. In the interim I ordered dies and a shellholder from RCBS. (An interesting aside: The 6.8mm SPS was developed around a beefed-up .30 Remington case, so shellholder no. 19 for the 6.8 also fits the older round, and is readily available.)

Quality Cartridge, Inc. in Hollywood, Md., makes new cases for dozens of obsolete cartridges, including the .30 Remington, that are the spittin' image of

Converted .30-30 cases for the .30 Remington are available from Bob Hayley, and Quality Cartridge makes brand new ones.

Test loads were prepared with a new die set from RCBS. The Lee Factory Crimp Die for the .30-30 (right) actually works well for the .30 Remington, too.

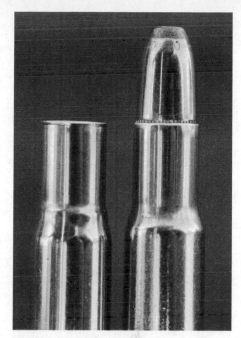

The .30 Remington's shoulder is a bit farther forward than the parent .30-30 case, so a secondary shoulder should be formed to control headspace on the first firing (see text). The difference is easily visible on this formed case (left) and a loaded round (right).

Due to the continued popularity of the .30-30 Winchester, there is a good variety of .30-caliber flatnose and roundnose hunting bullets also suitable for use in the .30 Remington.

the originals. They even have the correct headstamp. They aren't cheap, but they are top-notch, and I used some along with the converted .30-30 cases for load development.

The M-141 has a 24-inch barrel with a seven groove, 12-inch right-hand twist. While the listed bullet diameter of the .30 Remington is .307 inch, modern-day .308-inch bullets intended for the .30-30 work just fine. Period literature on the

M-141 notes that pointed bullets can be used in the gun because the design of the spiral magazine keeps the point of a bullet from resting on the primer ahead of it. However, more than one contemporary manual cautions against the use of spitzers in any tubular magazine, so I stuck with flatpoint .30-30 bullets for most test loads, except for the new Hornady 160-grain FTX bullet.

While the case body and neck of the .30-30 and .30 Remington are similar in size, the shoulder is about .057 inch farther forward than for the .30-30. Thus, if you full-length resize a modified .30-30 case in a .30-30 die, you'll end up with a case with excessive headspace. So careful sizing to produce a "secondary shoulder" is the key. First, expand the necks of your reformed .30-30 cases with a .32-caliber expander, then run the cases over a .338-caliber expander. Doing the expansion all in one step tends to produce "lopsided" case necks. I used stainless steel expander mandrels in a "Generation II Die" from Sinclair International. These tools are very high quality, modest in cost and work perfectly.

Then by trial and error, size the cases a little at a time in your .30 Remington resizer to form a "secondary shoulder."

Keep sizing until the case will just chamber in your rifle. Upon firing, the shoulder will iron out and the case will be custom fitted to your rifle. After you get a few fired cases you can double check the shoulder position with a Hornady Lock-N-Load headspace gauge. Remember that for reliable functioning, the overall length of loaded rounds needs to be about to 2.535 inches.

Starting loads for the .30-30 can be used, then increased as indicated, if desired. S.A.A.M.I MAP (maximum average pressure) for the .30 Remington is 35,000 CUP, and for the .30-30, it's 38,000 CUP. I used Hodgdon's .30-30 data as a guide, watching for signs of excessive pressure. All of the loads shown in the accompanying table appeared perfectly safe in my Remington Model 141.

Factory loads can be easily duplicated with handloads. Powders that work in the .30-30 obviously are the first choices for the .30 Remington, too. Hodgdon-Hornady's LEVERevolution (LVR) powder is a real boon for the lever-action reloader. LVR was designed to boost velocities about 100 fps in lever-action cartridges, and that it does. IMR-8208XBR, CFE-223, Varget and H-4895 also work well. Actually, just about any powder in this burn-

.30 REMINGTON LOAD DATA

Case	Powder	Charge (grains)	Bullet Make & Type	Bullet Weight (grains)	Vel. (fps)	SD (fps)	M.E. (ft-lb.)	Group (inches)	COL (inches)
Win.	CFE-223	35.4	Sierra FN	150	2,219	6	1,640	1.51	2.510
Q.C.	CFE-223	35.4	Sierra FN	150	2,178	25	1,580	1.65	2.510
Win.	CFE-223	36.8	Sierra FN	150	2,317	27	1,789	1.04	2.510
Win.	Varget	32.8	Sierra FN	150	2,131	26	1,513	2.63	2.510
Win.	Varget	34.5	Sierra FN	150	2,226	15	1,651	2.20	2.510
Win.	IMR-8208	30.0	Sierra FN	150	2,056	49	1,408	0.82	2.510
Win.	IMR-8208	32.3	Sierra FN	150	2,262	37	1,705	2.68	2.510
Win.	LVR	35.0	Sierra FN	150	2,283	15	1,736	1.22	2.510
Win.	LVR	36.8	Sierra FN	150	2,374	15	1,878	1.63	2.510
Win.	H-4895	30.5	Sierra FN	150	2,096	3	1,464	1.73	2.510
Win.	H-4895	32.3	Sierra FN	150	2,260	53	1,702	1.14	2.510
Win.	IMR-4166	31.2	Sierra FN	150	2,097	5	1,465	2.48	2.510
Win.	IMR-4166	32.6	Sierra FN	150	2,202	18	1,615	1.08	2.510
Win.	IMR-4064	32.2	Sierra FN	150	2,173	12	1,573	0.94	2.510
Win.	IMR-4064	33.3	Sierra FN	150	2,251	7	1,688	1.36	2.510
Win.	LVR	36.0	Sierra FN	170	2,346	12	2,078	1.24	2.512
Q.C.	CFE-223	34.0	Sierra FN	170	2,141	33	1,731	1.73	2.512
Win.	LVR	34.0	Barnes TSX-FN	150	2,208	22	1,624	0.94	2.462
Win.	Varget	34.5	Speer DC	150	2,222	21	1,645	1.00	2.495
Win.	LVR	35.0	Hornady FTX	160	2,371	10	1,998	1.77	2.540
Win.	CFE-223	34.0	Hornady FTX	160	2,213	2	1,740	2.32	2.540
Win.	IMR-4166	30.0	Hornady FP	170	2,032	16	1,559	1.14	2.525
Win.	Ball-C(2)	35.5	Nosler BST	150	2,325	32	1,801	1.81	2.513
Q.C.	Ball-C(2)	34.5	Nosler Partition	170	2,197	6	1,822	0.75	2.500
Q.C.	IMR-4320	32.0	Nosler Partition	170	2,116	26	1,691	1.24	2.500
Winchester Factory Load			Silvertip	170	2,044	54	1,577	2.04	

Notes: Federal No. 210 primers used for all handloads. Balllistic data are for at least two, three-shot groups at 50 yards from a rest. Mid point of chronograph screens was 10 feet from the gun's muzzle.

Abbreviations: Q.C., Quality Cartridge; FN, Flat Nose; FP, Flat Point; HP, Hollow Point; TSX-FN, Triple Shock-X Flat Nose; DC, Deep Curl; FTX, Flex Tip eXpanding; BST, Ballistic Silvertip; COL, cartridge overall length.

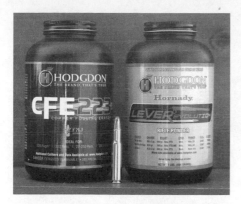

Ammunition for the .30 Remington hasn't been made for years, so handloading is about the only way to get one up and shooting. CFE-223 and LEVERevolution powders from Hodgdon are optimum for most loads.

Representative bullets for .30 Remington handloads are, from left: 125-grain Sierra Hollow Point Flat Nose, 150-grain Sierra Flat Nose, 170-grain Sierra Flat Nose, 170-grain Hornady Flat Point, 150-grain Barnes Triple Shock-X Flat Nose, 150-grain Speer Deep Curl and 170-grain Nosler Partition Round Nose.

ing range such as IMR's 3031, 4064 and 4320 will make up fine loads. Standard large rifle primers are appropriate for the .30 Remington.

The deer hunter can hardly go wrong with the traditional 150- and 170-grain flatpoint bullets designed for the .30-30. But a couple of newcomers merit some attention. Hornady's 160-grain FTX can be pushed with LVR to some pretty spiffy speeds that flatten trajectories and boost remaining downrange energy a bit. Plus, the accuracy of all of these bullets was more than acceptable, coming in at around 1½-2½ inches at 50 yards; with open sights.

As for the "best" powder, it's a no-brainer: LVR wins by a landslide. Not only does it deliver the highest velocities, it also produces excellent accuracy. But IMR-8208, CFE-223 and Varget should not be overlooked. If you can't find them, 3031 and 4320 from IMR and H-4895 are usually available, and also work well.

One can never go wrong with the traditional cup-and-core 150- and 170-grain flatpoints, the Speer 150-grain Deep Curl or the Nosler 150-grain Ballistic Silvertip. For the deepest penetration, the 170-grain Partition and Barnes 150-grain TSX-FN are especially designed for .30-30 velocities.

Working with the little M-141 was a refreshing step back in time. I envisioned the engineers who designed the gun, the draftsmen who labored over the drawing boards conjuring up new parts, and the machinists who then skillfully crafted them, all with great pride in their work. Then there are the legions of hunters who bought these rifles and put them to their intended purpose.

REMINGTON MODEL 141 "GAMEMASTER" SPECIFICATIONS

Years of Production	1935-1950
Total production	76,881
Calibers	.25, .30, .32 and .35 Remington (.25 made in 1935 only)
Action	Slide-action repeater
Weight	7½ pounds
Overall length	42¾ inches
Barrel length	24 inches
Rifling	7 grooves, twist: .25 cal., 8- or 10-inch; .30 cal., 12-inch; .32 cal., 14-inch; .35 cal., 16-inch
Stock & fore-end	American walnut
Trigger pull	4-6 pounds
Magazine capacity	5
Maximum pressure	35,000 CUP (current S.A.A.M.I. MAP)
Proof load	45,500 CUP (min.), 50,750 CUP (max.)
Accuracy at 100 yards	3½ inches (max.) for 5-shot group, 4 inches for 10-shot group

I wonder if, after another 80 years, some other septuagenarian will be pondering these same mysteries? I certainly hope so.

Acknowledgements
I am indebted to several folks who graciously supplied literature, materials and pertinent information for this article. Special thanks to Gene Myszkowski and Al Petrillo of Excalibur Publications; Scott Nichols of Remington; Fred Supry, formerly of Remington; Ken Sakamato with RCBS; J.J. Riech with ATK/Federal; Ron Rieber and Chris Hodgdon, Hodgdon Powder Co.; Lane Pearce and Lee Guthrie.

References and Resources
"Remington Model 141 Carbines," by Ken Blauch, 2008. Remington Society of America Journal, 3rd Quarter, 2008, pp. 3-1 to 3-11.

"Remington Autoloading & Pump-Action Rifles," by Gene Myszkowski, 2002, 132 pp.

Excalibur Publications, P.O. Box 35369, Tucson, Arizona 85740, 520-575-9057; excalibureditor@earthlink.net.

"The History of Remington Firearms," by Roy Marcot, 2005, 128 pp. Lyons Press, P.O. Box 480, Guilford, Connecticut 06437; LyonsPress.com.

"Instructions for Operation and Care of the Remington Model 141," Facsimile of owner's manual, circa 1936, available from Remington Arms Co., 870 Remington Drive, Madison, North Carolina, 800-243-9700; remington.com.

Bob Hayley (custom-made cartridge cases), 211 North River, P.O. Box 889, Seymour, Texas 76380; 940-888-3352.

Quality Cartridge (new cartridge cases), P.O. Box 445, Hollywood, Maryland, 20636; qual-cart.com.

The
AMERICAN EAGLE
LUGER

BY Rick Hacker
All photos by the author

The author's pristine 1906 American Eagle Luger, which was purchased from Lock, Stock And Barrel Investments (www.LSBauctions.com).

o paraphrase Will Rogers, I never met a gun I didn't like. Of course, the noted American author and humorist was referring to people, not firearms. But just the same, as with people, there are certain guns I like more than others. Although it is arguably one of the world's most notable pistols, over the years I've had a difficult time reconciling with the *Pistole Parabellum,* or as it is more commonly called, the P08 German Luger. After all, here was a prolific weapon of two world wars with more than three million made in various factories between 1900 and 1945—and beyond, for that matter. But it was a gun that spent much of the first half of the 20th century being aimed at American soldiers. So yes, there is a stigma about the P08, as far as I am concerned.

Yet, from a strictly objective viewpoint, there can be no denying the Luger's appeal. It is a marvel of German ingenuity and workmanship, with each of its 37 components

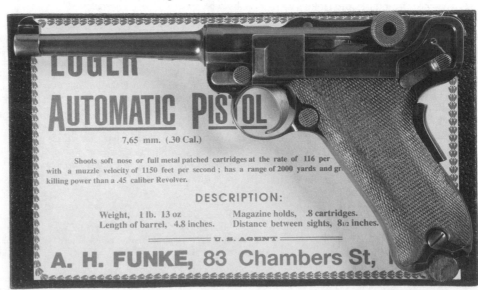

LUGER
AUTOMATIC PISTOL
7,65 mm. (.30 Cal.)

Shoots soft nose or full metal patched cartridges at the rate of 116 per with a muzzle velocity of 1150 feet per second; has a range of 2000 yards and gr killing power than a .45 caliber Revolver.

DESCRIPTION:

Weight, 1 lb. 13 oz   Magazine holds, .8 cartridges.
Length of barrel, 4.8 inches.   Distance between sights, 8½ inches.

═════ U. S. AGENT ═════
A. H. FUNKE, 83 Chambers St,

Model 1906 American Eagle Luger Semi-Automatic Pistol with Retailer Box.
Photo Courtesy Rock Island Auction Co.

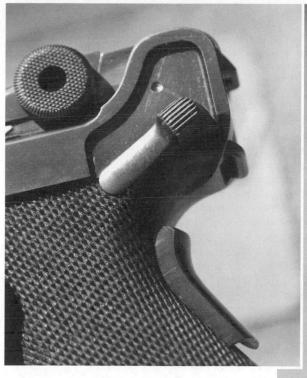

Above: Safeties include a thumb and grip safety.

Right: The elegant script is found on the toggle of all DWM-manufactured Lugers, including this American Eagle version.

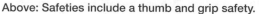

fitting precisely, and with a unique grip-to-barrel axis that proved to be an ergonomic natural for point shooting. In fact, the late Bill Ruger once told me the Luger had provided him with the inspiration for the grip angle and tapered barrel design of Sturm Ruger's first successful handgun, the .22-caliber semiautomatic Standard. And I'm sure I wasn't the first to note the ironic similarities between the Luger and Ruger surnames of their respective inventors.

Georg Johann Luger was born in Austria in 1849. With a natural gift for marksmanship and a penchant for firearms design, he eventually went to work for Ludwig Loewe & Company. The company was ultimately reorganized to become the German Weapons and Munitions company, or *Deutsche Waffen und Munitionsfabriken Aktien-Gesellschaft,* whose DWM scripted initials would soon become a familiar sight on Luger's pistols.

In 1894 Luger was sent to America by DWM to try to convince the United States Army to adopt the clunky Borchardt C-93 semiautomatic pistol, which was based upon the recoil-operated Maxim

machine gun. The army rightfully turned down the C-93 but eventually adopted the Maxim. Luger, however, found favor with both guns and ended up combining the Maxim's recoil principle of operation with a much more refined version of the C-93's toggle-link system. Out of this came the Pistole Parabellum, a 4-7/8-inch tapered barrel semiautomatic handgun that was an anomaly in a shooting world still dominated by revolvers. Along with an eight-round detachable magazine, Luger chambered his new pistol for the 7.65×21mm Parabellum, also known as the .30 Luger, a cartridge he had previously developed with Hugo Borchardt for the C-93.

Although the German Luger was groundbreaking at the time of its introduction in 1900, it was the Swiss who were the first to recognize its advantages as a military weapon, and the *Bundersrate* promptly placed an initial order for 3,000 guns (additional orders soon followed, enough to keep the guns in the Swiss ranks until 1970). The DWM reciprocated by roll stamping the nationalistic Swiss cross and sunburst emblem across the top of the Luger's receiver chamber.

But it wasn't until 1904 that the Imperial German Navy adopted a 6-inch barrel version of the Luger. Acquiescing to the German army's demand for a more powerful caliber, Georg Luger came up with the 9x19mm Parabellum, or as it is better known today, the 9mm Luger, a cartridge that has become even more prolific than the gun for which it was designed. As a result of its 9mm chambering, the semiautomatic Luger became the official sidearm of the Germany Army in 1908. It was rechristened the Pistole 08, or as it is more commonly abbreviated, the P08.

But prior to all of this, the United States Army had been readying itself for their field trials in 1907 to attempt to replace their dated arsenal of .45- and .38-caliber revolvers with a semiautomatic pistol. Sensing an opportunity, Georg Luger hit upon a unique marketing scheme with a long-range hope of securing a U.S. military contract. It was well known that the U.S. was a viable market for the civilian sales of European-made firearms. Thus, it is my theory that Luger reasoned if he could get his pistol firmly established in the hands of American shooters, the Luger

would have a better chance of being accepted by the U.S. Army when it came time for testing.

Thus, as early as 1900, DWM began exporting Lugers with a rather commendable image of the Great Seal of the United States roll stamped across the top of the receiver just forward of the toggle bolt. No doubt there was inspiration from placing a nationalistic symbol on the earlier Swiss army contract guns. But unlike some of the very first Swiss Lugers, in which slightly less than 100 had their "sunburst and cross" emblems hand engraved, the U.S. seal was always roll stamped (so beware of fakes!).

Consequently, these guns – and their subsequent successors – are known as American Eagle Lugers. Approximately 12,000 of the first version, the Model 1900 American Eagle in .30 Luger, were produced between 1900 and 1902, a sizeable number for a two-year period. Nonetheless, this was the gun that launched a whole new variation for today's Luger aficionados, as American Eagle Lugers have become highly coveted as part of the myriad subcategories of Luger collecting.

"You don't see any American Eagle Lugers prior to serial number 2,000, going chronologically from number one," says Michael Krause of Krausewerk Collectables (www.krausewerk.com), a firearms and militaria specialist and dealer in San Mateo, Calif. "The Lugers were immediately successful commercially in the U.S. and then when they put the American Eagle on them, well, that was just icing on the cake."

The P08 went on to be adopted by the armies of more than 15 countries, and over the years was manufactured by other factories in addition to DWM including W+F Bern, Krieghoff, Simson, Vickers and Mauser (with countless minor variations as military and police sidearms). But it was the American Eagle Luger that initially only came from Germany and was

The receiver over the chamber is deeply roll-marked with the American Eagle seal of the United States.

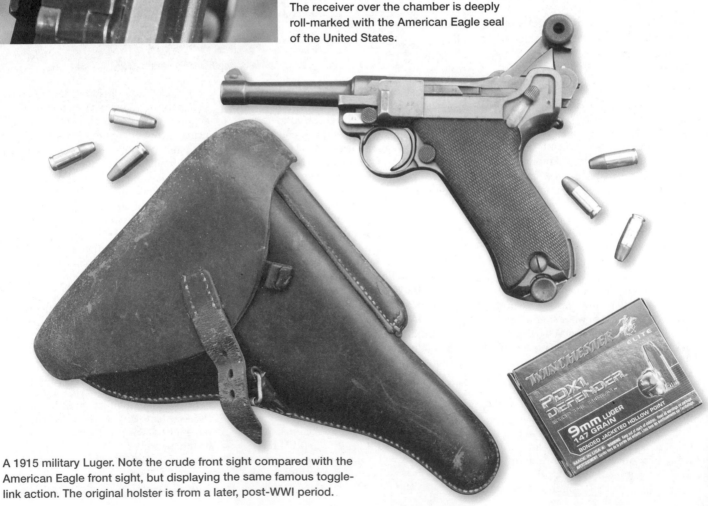

A 1915 military Luger. Note the crude front sight compared with the American Eagle front sight, but displaying the same famous toggle-link action. The original holster is from a later, post-WWI period.

One of the criticisms of the Luger has always been the thumb-shredding difficulty in loading the magazine. A P08 loading tool, which was originally supplied with each gun, made the job easier. Note the wood-capped magazine, which is proper for this gun.

Right: The front of the frame of this American Eagle Luger is marked "Germany," indicating the gun was made for export.

Left: The proper period ivory bead front sight on the author's 1906 American Eagle Luger was clearly made for the civilian market, rather than for military use.

strictly manufactured for both pre-war and post-war America.

So here at last was a Luger I could identify with, one that was not made to be used against our doughboys in World War I, nor our GIs in World War II. One can only surmise what would have happened had the Luger been adopted by the U.S. Army during its 1907 field trials. As it turned out, the Luger (and others) lost out to the Browning-designed Colt 1911, a gun that was made in America by an American company with a formidable American reputation. However, in spite of the failure of the two known examples of the P08 that were especially chambered in .45 ACP for the Army trials (one of which sold in 2010 for $494,500 – including a 15 percent buyer's premium – at Greg Martin Auctions in Anaheim,

Calif.), the Army was impressed enough to ask for additional guns for additional testing.

But for reasons that have become lost in the smoke and rubble of two world wars, the DWM factory refused to participate further with the U.S. government. No doubt these reasons included the fact that Germany was already working at full capacity to supply guns to other nations. Plus, international tension was brewing in Europe, a political cauldron that would soon boil over into WWI. Certainly Germany was aware of this, and consequently thought better of trying to get their official Army pistol adopted by one of the countries they would soon be battling. Nonetheless, in 1901 the U.S. Army purchased approximately 1,000 Lugers for our cavalry to experiment

The author's 1906 American Eagle Luger still retains much of its original straw-color finish on the trigger and other small parts, which makes it especially desirable.

Rather than the DWM scroll, later post-war Mauser-made American Eagles had the Mauser logo.

The stamping on a 1970s-era Mauser-made American Eagle Luger.

with in field tests. These guns were military models and not factory-stamped American Eagles, and were eventually sold off after WWI by Bannerman's as war surplus.

Owing to its initial success, the American Eagle Luger continued to be produced and imported into the U.S. After the Model 1900 came the Model 1902, the first to be chambered in 9mm Parabellum, and approximately 600 guns were made. Even rarer yet was the American Eagle 1902 "Fat Barrel" variation, a standard American Eagle fitted with a thicker barrel in deference to the more powerful (a relative term, to be sure) 9mm chambering. No more than 700 guns were made, a rarity matched only by an even smaller number of "cartridge counter" open-sided magazines for the Model 1902. Then the Model 1906 American Eagle came out featuring a slightly recontoured safety, and offered in 9mm (3,000 guns manufactured) and 7.65mm (8,000 guns produced), making it one of the more readily encountered versions; both were made until 1912.

I suspect most of these pre-WW I guns were purchased by shooters more or less out of curiosity. I think many were taken out to the back 40, shot at tin cans and rapid-fired at scampering rabbits to see how fast the action would cycle. Then they were cleaned and put away and forgotten as their U.S. owners – perhaps becoming disenfranchised with the "foreign" German design – turned their handgunning interests to more U.S.-friendly hardware such as the Smith & Wesson Triple Lock and the Colt "Hammerless" Model 1903 Pocket Pistol. This is the only explanation I can come up with for so many early American Eagle Lugers being found today in relatively pristine condition, with most of the handsome rust bluing and straw-colored small parts still in good shape. After all, unlike other Lugers, the American Eagle pistols were not carried into battle.

Obviously The War To End All Wars (as WWI was optimistically called) halted further manufacture of American Eagle Lugers, but by 1920 – two years after the Armistice – the importation of war surplus P08s began to flood the market, led by firms such as Pacific Arms and the Stoeger Arms Company of New York. In 1923, Stoeger Arms hit upon the idea of trademarking the Luger name. This had never been done before and Stoeger became the first to actually put the word "Luger" on the German-made P08 pistols they imported. Next came

This mint condition American Eagle Luger was made by Mauser in 1970, and while these guns do not have the collector appeal of pre-war guns, they are excellent shooters and are especially desirable when found with all of their original accessories, as shown here.

the 1920 and 1923 "reworked" American Eagle Stoeger-marked Lugers (with "A.F. Stoeger Inc./New York" stamped on the right side of the barrel extension) that were made by DWM from reconditioned WWI surplus guns. These are considered quite scarce, with only slightly more than 1,000 made. After that came the Stoeger-marked 1930 American Eagle, which was made by DWM and featured 4 7/8-inch (Standard), 6-inch (Navy) and the rare 8-inch (Artillery) barrels.

In 1930 Mauser acquired DWM and continued producing both military and commercial Lugers (but no American Eagles) in their Oberndorf factory until 1945, when World War II ended. In the 1970s, with the war well behind it, Mauser resumed American Eagle production. Numerous variations were also made by other firms including a U.S.-made stainless steel American Eagle by Stoeger and others, such as Mitchell Arms, under license to Stoeger.

But clearly it is the earlier, pre-WWII American Eagles that hold the most interest to collectors.

"There's just enough of them to bring a premium (on the used gun and collector's market)," says Krause, "not a tremendous amount, but slightly more than a plain chamber-marked gun, just because of the desirability and demand factor. Eagles are rare, but they are not super rare."

Nonetheless, it took quite a bit of searching for me to finally find an American Eagle Luger that not only was in decent condition, but one that I could purchase without seeing my credit card burst into flames, although we're still talking about a four-digit price tag. But the 7.65mm Model 1906 American Eagle

Luger that I finally acquired at Lock, Stock And Barrel Investments (www. LSBauctions.com) in NRA Excellent condition is the epitome of what this gun could and should be. The hand-fitted close tolerances of its parts – one of the factors that doomed it in the Army trials – function flawlessly, as long as the action is kept clean. Although it is not meant for anything other than roundnose bullets, accuracy at 25 yards, even with fixed sights and my poor eyes, can easily keep all rounds within the diameter of an eight ring. But most importantly to my mind, it is a gun that was meant to be owned and shot by an American shooter. That makes it not just "One Good Gun," but specifically "one good Luger."

DICK'S MODEL 700
WALKING VARMINTER

By Wayne van Zwoll

Between NASA projects, he used rifles that satisfied his engineer's eye for form and function.

Wayne likes the "hunting" profile and weight of Dick's 700 in .22-250 – a "walking varminter."

Dick's rifle is a midweight, late '60s Remington 700 sporter with a 24-inch barrel. The rear sight gave way to the Weaver scope.

"Until that reversal, they were going in like trained pigs!" Dick Nelson's metaphor was clear to us, trying to keep .22 bullets in the X-ring. How quickly wind shift can scuttle a score! Smallbore prone competition was in Dick's blood, and he fired some good aggregates. More importantly, I remember him as a gentleman on the line, as ready to compliment fellow shooters as to beat them.

A great, round-bellied presence, he laughed through an impish grin that belied his age and occupation. In Seattle, I believe Dick worked with Boeing for NASA. Don't hold me to that, because his projects were, indeed, rocket science. One was the first moon vehicle. Having worked my way through college math milking Holsteins, I had a tenuous grasp of space exploration.

But at smallbore matches, Dick was no smarter than me. Gusts that grabbed my bullets took his as readily. Dick's pulse bounced to a nine as often as did mine. In part because my eyes were then young and sharp, I stayed higher on the board at most events. When I snared a couple of state prone titles, Dick was among the first to congratulate me. Warmly. Sincerely. He enjoyed seeing other people succeed. When asked about his pioneer-

ing work in air and space travel, he downplayed it. "I'm a slave to physics," he'd chuckle. No conspiratorial wink, so common now among lesser minds engaged in projects "classified." I concluded early on that Dick had not a self-important bone in his body. He was genuinely modest.

On Seattle's range, the evening before a two-day match, he stepped over to the bench where I was snugging iron sights on my Anschutz. "I see you're on the first relay with me," he grinned. Then, leaning forward, he whispered. "We get a bit of fog here first thing, but no wind. They'll go in like trained pigs!"

And they did.

A couple of years later, after another shoot, Dick and his lovely wife invited me to their home for lunch. Over tomato soup and sandwiches I caught an unfamiliar tension in his smile. "I'm peddling a few guns," he said. "Thought you might like one."

He didn't have many. They were solid rifles, all obviously fired but carefully tended. I picked up a Remington 700, a standard-weight BDL I reckoned dated to the late '60s. It was a .22-250.

"That's a very accurate rifle," said Dick. I knew then that it was. I bought it.

A year later, Dick was gone. The next Seattle match seemed eerily silent

without his boisterous laugh. "...Ready on the firing line... Commence firing!" As I crushed the final ounce from the trigger, a column of pigs ghosted with absurd grace through the ragged hole in the X-ring...

Remington's 700 is, as much as Winchester's 70, a rifleman's rifle. And Dick's .22-250 has the profile and features I've come to appreciate even more since his passing. Its 24-inch barrel wrings more speed from bullets – regardless of chambering – than do the 22-inch barrels of lightweights. At the same time, it gives the rifle a slight tilt to muzzle. That's the balance I prefer. It helps bring the muzzle on target quickly and loads my left arm a bit to deaden pulse bounce. The barrel is of medium contour, stiff enough to resist walking after a few shots. Iron sights give it a finished look (though the rear has made way for a Weaver 6-20x scope).

Dick Nelson's 700 weighs 7¾ pounds. Though light enough for easy all-day carry, it has the heft for a steady hold. Bluing has thinned slightly in places. The stock shows a few light handling scuffs. It's the standard BDL version with pressed grip and fore-end panels, white spacers at the butt, grip cap and fore-end tip.

While Dick's .22-250 came off the line early in Model 700 production, it wasn't a first-year rifle. And the 700 was hardly Remington's first bolt-action.

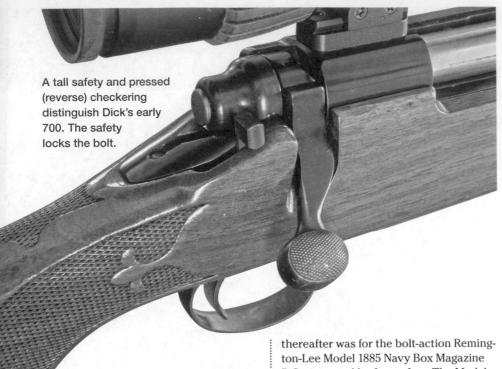

A tall safety and pressed (reverse) checkering distinguish Dick's early 700. The safety locks the bolt.

As early as the 1870s, on the heels of Winchester's famous '73 lever rifle, Remington pursued repeaters. John Keene, a New Jersey inventor, offered a tube-fed bolt gun in .45-70. But it was costly to build and the Army rejected it in 1881. Hartley and Graham, which owned Union Metallic Cartridge Co., bought E. Remington & Sons when it went into receivership five years later. The first military contract thereafter was for the bolt-action Remington-Lee Model 1885 Navy Box Magazine Rifle, invented by James Lee. The Model 1899 sporting version didn't reach the market until Winchester's controlling interest in Remington (1888-1896) ended. Remington-Lee sporters came in 7x57 and 7.35mm Mauser, .236 Remington, .30-30 Winchester and .30-40 Krag.

Twelve years after these rifles went away in 1909 Remington announced its 30S, derived from the 1917 Enfield that Remington had manufactured during the Great War. Heavy and expensive, the 30S sold poorly. In 1926 it was replaced by the Model 30 Express chambered in .30-06 and Remington's .25, .30, .32 and .35. The 7x57 and .257 Roberts came later. The 30 Express, initially priced at $45.75, expired in 1940.

The Model 720 High Power Rifle, developed by Oliver Loomis and A.H. Lowe, replaced the 30 Express in 1941. It chambered the .30-06, .270 and .257 Roberts. After only 4,000 rifles Remington put its muscle into military hardware. The Navy acquired many of the first 720s. Those not issued during the war were presented, beginning in 1964, as marksmanship trophies by the Navy and Marine Corps.

Rather than build more 720s in the late '40s, Remington adopted a low-cost bolt-action designed by engineers Merle "Mike" Walker and Homer Young. A Benchrest shooter, Walker insisted on features that enhanced accuracy. The Models 721 and short-action 722 appeared early in 1948, with receivers cut from cylindrical tubing. Recoil lugs were thick steel washers sandwiched between the receiver face and barrel shoulder. The clip-ring extractor, plunger ejector, self-contained trigger group and stamped-steel bottom metal trimmed costs. The bolt head with twin lugs was brazed (as was the bolt handle) to the bolt body. A recessed face enabled Remington to claim the case was supported by "three rings of steel."

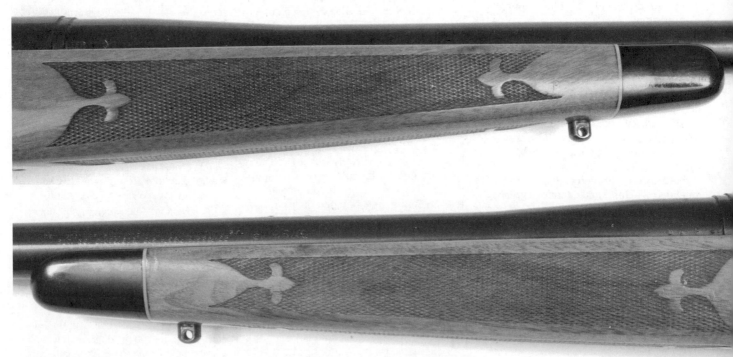

Classic fleur-de-lis checkering graces many a 700, including Dick's "walking varminter".

The 721 (top) spawned the 700. Stamped steel bottom metal eventually changed to a hinged alloy floorplate.

A 1969 .22-250 Remington 700BDL Varmint Special with factory blued finish and jeweled bolt.

In the March 1948 *American Rifleman*, Julian Hatcher called the 721 the strongest, safest rifle available. In .270 or .30-06, a 721 listed for $79.95, $5 more than a 722 in .257 Roberts or .300 Savage. Other chamberings came later. High-grade A and B versions of both rifles were replaced in 1955 with ADL and BDL designations. The Model 725, a 1958 upgrade, featured a hinged floorplate and checkered walnut stock, a hooded front sight and adjustable rear. In December 1961, Remington dropped the 721/722 series and the 725.

In 1962 Remington announced a new rifle on the 721/722 mechanism. The Model 700 offered refinements: trim tang, swept bolt with checkered knob, cast (not stamped) bottom metal. The stock had a higher, scope-friendly comb. Mike Walker gave the 700 faster lock time (3.2 milliseconds), shortened the leade in the bore and tightened bore and chamber tolerances.

The Model 700 came in two action lengths and two grades. Barrels wore iron

The 50-year 700 has grip panels like early BDLs (but cut-checkered). White spacers, iron sights too.

sights. The ADL in .222, .222 Magnum, .243, 6mm, .270, .280, .308 and .30-06 retailed for $114.95. It had a blind magazine and pressed, point-pattern "checkering." The BDL cost $139.95; it featured white-line spacers and fleur-de-lis checkering. Magnum versions listed for $129.95 (ADL) and $154.95 (BDL). The 700 got a boost from the concurrent introduction of Remington's 7mm Magnum cartridge. The only other magnum slated for early production was Winchester's similar but less ably presented .264. Both of those calibers and the .300 Winchester Magnum that followed wore 24-inch barrels – as did rifles in .222 and .222 Magnum. The 20-inch barrels, standard for the .243, 6mm, .270, .280, .308 and .30-06, were replaced by 22-inch tubes in 1964.

The 700 got its first facelift in 1969 when Remington installed a longer bolt shroud and jeweled the bolt body. A restyled stock wore a buttplate of black plastic, supplanting anodized alloy. Machine-cut checkering supplanted pressed panels. By the mid-'70s Remington had replaced the satin stock finish with RKW gloss. Model 700 sales gained steam as shooters lashed out at Winchester for its 1964 overhaul of the Model 70. A left-bolt, left-stock 700 arrived in 1973 chambered in .270, .30-06 and 7mm Magnum. By then the Varmint Special had arrived with heavy barrel *sans* sights. Chamberings included the .22-250.

Many new Model 700s have arrived over recent decades. Only a handful carry the appeal of Dick Nelson's .22-250. The walnut stocks I prefer have been largely replaced by synthetics and current wood lacks both the figure and clean contours of earlier models. Machine-cut checkering has, mercifully, replaced the stamped patterns of 40 years ago, but stock-to-metal fit hasn't improved. I mourn too the passing of iron sights. While scopes make sense on accurate, flat-shooting rifles, iron sights seem, well, *necessary*. Without sights a rifle is useless. If you plan to equip your new pickup with a brush guard and oversize rubber, you still expect the truck to come with a bumper and tires.

While some have criticized the 700's beryllium clip extractor, its longevity is undeniable. Unlike the Mauser claw, it requires no cut in the receiver or barrel. Gunsmiths have installed Sako-style hooks; but the Remington clip has won in shear tests and contacts more of the case rim. In 40 years I've never had a Model 700 extractor fail. No, it does not allow controlled-round feed.

For most of its life the 700 trigger could be adjusted for weight of pull (lower front screw), sear engagement (rear screw) and over-travel (upper front screw). Drops of sealant prevented accidental screw rotation and discouraged incompetents from fiddling with the adjustments. In 2005 Remington replaced that trigger with its "X Mark Pro" and a fixed pull of 3½ pounds. Four years later it was re-engineered, the pull adjustable from 2½ to 4½ pounds.

Initially, Remington used stainless steel in magnum 700s. Stainless can't be blued, so those early barrels were plated with copper, then tin, *then* blued! In 1967 Remington changed to chrome-moly steel for 700 barrels. Stainless steel later returned, but unblued. Ceramic and other coatings added color and protection. TriNyte coating was introduced in 2005. Rifling in 700 barrels is hammer-forged.

The Model 700 has been bored to nearly every centerfire round practical in a bolt action. Indeed, it might be easier to list popular chamberings *not* offered in 700s! The two action lengths suit rounds as dainty as the .17 Remington (1971), as big as the .338 Lapua Magnum (2011). High-performance rounds include the 8mm Remington Magnum (1978) and 7mm STW (Shooting Times Westerner, 1996), plus the Remington Ultra Mags: 7mm, .300, .338 and .375 (1999-2002). The 7mm and .300 Short Action Ultra Mags (2001 and 2002) appeal to me. An Idaho elk I shot was likely the first taken with the .300 SAUM. Top-sellers in the 700 are still the .30-06 and .270, the 7mm Remington and .300 Winchester Magnums.

Dick's choice of the .22-250 chambering was no surprise. Steeped in high-performance hardware, but a smallbore shooter at heart, he picked the hottest .22 going – a wildcat dating to the Great War but still new as a factory cartridge. By the time Remington adopted it in 1965, the .22-250 had logged more field time than the .270 Winchester or .300 H&H Magnum! It had won buckets of Benchrest medals and probably accounted for more 'chucks, foxes and coyotes than any other centerfire .22.

The .22-250's parent is the .250 Savage, developed by Charles Newton in 1913 for short actions like Savage's 1899. The company boasted its 87-grain missile could achieve 3,000 fps – so was born the .250/3000. Later the 87-grain load bowed to the 100 in commercial ammo, prompting a name change to .250 Savage. Smallbore enthusiasts also hailed Newton's .22 High Power, fashioned in 1911 from the .25-35. Hunters hurled the

High Power's .227-inch bullets (clocking at 2,800 fps) at game as big as deer and even tigers! By the 1930s wildcatters J.E. Gebby, J.B. Smith, Harvey Donaldson, Grosvenor Wotkyns and John Sweaney had come up with a fast-stepping .22 on the .250 hull. A 1937 version by Gebby and Smith became the "Varminter," a name copyrighted by Gebby.

It's truly astonishing that for 30 years the .22-250 trundled along as a wildcat, while in 1936 the .220 Swift made the charter list of chamberings in Winchester's Model 70. The Swift's roomy case held enough powder to drive 48-grain bullets at 4,110 fps. But the Varminter nipped at its hocks. Nearly 80 years later the Swift has faded, while the .22-250 is chambered in every varmint-class rifle I can think of.

With 50-grain bullets at 3,800 fps, the .22-250 brings more than 500 ft-lbs of energy to 400 yards. That bullet starts as fast as a 40-grain spitzer from a .223 but bucks wind better. Four football fields hence it outpaces the .223's by 270 fps. While the world is full of better deer cartridges, 55- and 60-grain bullets in .22-250s have taken boatloads of whitetails. A 60-grain spitzer kicked from the Varminter at 3,600 fps exits 200 fps faster than a 75-grain .243 bullet, and is still faster at 400 yards, where it delivers 600 ft-lbs.

Dick handloaded for his Model 700, though I don't have his notes. Myriad bullets in a wide range of weights and styles suit the .22-250. Ditto dozens of propellants midrange in burn rate. Think AA2520, H335, IMR 4320, Winchester 748, BL-C(2), RL-15, Vihtavuori 140, Varget and TAC. Faster fuels like RL-7 and IMR 3031, even 4198 work with lighter missiles. Powder that began as WC852 got a new

Remington adopted the wildcat .22-250 in 1965. It has since become hugely popular, in many forms.

name when Bruce Hodgdon found it excelled in his .22-250. Ron Reiber told me Bruce "used 38 grains behind a 50-grain bullet to reach 3,800 fps. That propellant became H380."

Dick's 700 is my only Remington in .22-250. I've owned many other 700s. Most endearing: a 5½-pound 700ti in .30-06, with titanium receiver and 24-inch barrel. A long, stainless, laminate-stocked rifle in .300 Ultra Mag accompanied me to the Arctic. My rack has several Classics and a 1978 series with conservative walnut stocks checkered "full-wrap" up front. In 1981 Remington began chambering Classic rifles to just one cartridge per year. Alas, that program and the rifle expired in 2005.

None of my other 700s out-shoot Dick's. This .22-250, with its clean, traditional profile, its lively feel but comforting heft, nips tiny groups. It's the ideal "walking varminter" and a champ on paper. Send one bullet through the middle, and, if you dope wind and squeeze the trigger like Dick Nelson, your next shots follow like trained pigs.

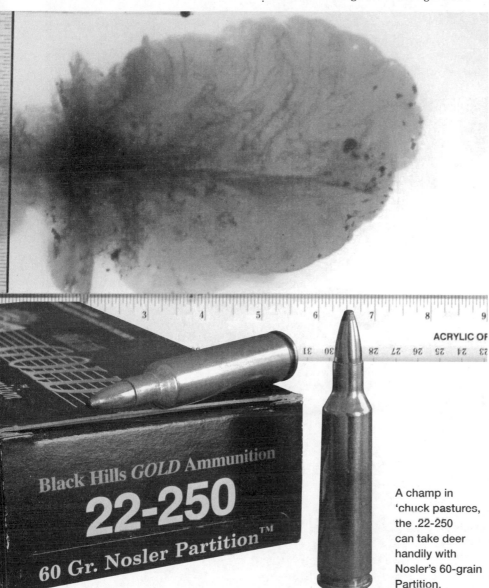

A champ in 'chuck pastures, the .22-250 can take deer handily with Nosler's 60-grain Partition.

The Heckler and Koch

P7M8

An Iconic Handgun

BY Robert K. Campbell

The HK P7M8 is a classic handgun with tremendous appeal both as a shooter and a historical piece.

When you examine the Heckler and Koch P7M8 handgun, it has a fantastic look that no other handgun can match. The 110-degree backstrap, hand-filling grip, cocking lever and relatively low-riding slide are all distinctive.

Many handguns that have been different have also been odd. There is nothing odd about the P7M8. This is a credible defensive handgun, relentlessly reliable and more than accurate enough for any task. HK's G3 is one milestone, and as many of you know the adoption of the Spanish CETME into the HK 91 was a case of German technology coming home. The MP5 submachine gun remains universally respected.

Modern shooters have voted with their cash and made the HK USP a popular handgun. My personal favorite of all HK designs is the P7M8. The original PSP or Police Service Pistol was a product of West German police trials in the 1970s. The pistol adopted had to be reliable, accurate enough for hostage rescue and

The author has quite a bit of experience with numerous HK designs. The P7M8 is his favorite.

simple to operate. Safety features were desirable – but a manual safety was not. Special teams would rely primarily upon the rifle. Tactical doctrine of the time called for a handgun that was simple to bring into action and operate.

SIG responded with the immensely popular P220, Walther warmed over the P38 and Heckler and Koch gave us the P7. The P7 was the most radical of the three. It was also the most expensive, perhaps the reason the pistol was not widely adopted for institutional use. However, the design and execution of the pistol has won critical acclaim. The slide and barrel of the P7 are lower in relation to the firing grip than most handguns. The P7 and the later P7M8 are not locked-breech, tilting-barrel handguns in the manner of practically every other service handgun in the world. These handguns feature a fixed barrel.

This was accomplished by use of a gas retarded blowback action. A small hole in the forward section of the chamber is used to bleed gas on firing. This gas is bled into a piston that rides under the barrel. This pressure prevents the rapid opening of the slide in recoil. Rather than operating the action as with the AR-15 rifle, the operation is tuned to keep the action closed until pressure dissipates.

From the 110-degree grip angle to the squeeze-cocking action – the P7M8 is an immensely interesting design.

This system allows for a fixed barrel. This is one reason the HK P7M8 is so accurate. The barrel is polygonal rifled for an excellent gas seal, which is really needed with the HK P7M8 action.

Let's get the designations out of the way. The original P7 uses a heel-type magazine release. The pistol illustrated uses the Americanized HK type paddle magazine release, hence the P7M8. There were later high-capacity variants as well, including the P7M13 that is fairly rare today.

Safety and speed into action are

OBERNDORF/N MADE IN GERMAN

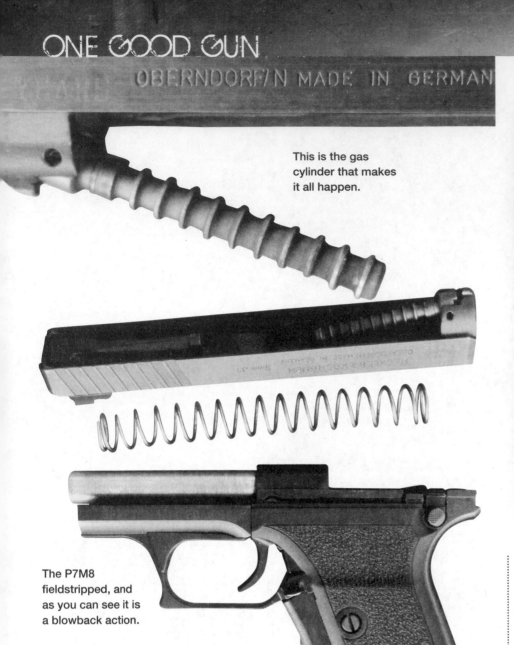

This is the gas cylinder that makes it all happen.

The P7M8 fieldstripped, and as you can see it is a blowback action.

HK P7 M8

addressed with the cocking lever. When the pistol is at rest the striker is locked in place by a firing pin block and the trigger is inert. A cocking lever on the front strap is pressed to cock the striker. At the same time the drawbar to the trigger is engaged. A few pounds of pressure cocks the pistol. Once the striker is cocked, little pressure is needed to keep the lever depressed – simply maintain a firing grip.

Trigger compression is light and crisp, usually breaking at less than 4 pounds. My personal example boasts a perfectly balanced 2.8-pound trigger release.

If dropped or the lever released, the striker is released, the firing pin block is engaged and the trigger disengaged. The striker protrudes from the rear of the slide when the striker is in the cocked position. Overall, a brilliantly designed system that is well executed. At no time is the striker partially cocked or prepped.

The HK P7M8 paddle-type magazine release works well. Press the lever downward and the magazine is released. This is one of the fastest combat handguns ever designed to speed load. The slide locks to the rear on an empty magazine.

The magazine release is hit and the spent magazine drops free of the receiver. Insert another magazine and press the cocking lever and the slide drops, loading the chamber.

The P7M8 also features excellent service-grade combat-type sights and this 9mm proved popular with professionals the world over. One limiting factor though, is the time and skilled labor needed to produce such a complicated but durable design. Some have stated that the HK P7M8 is the most reliable handgun in the world. Considering the service record of first-quality handguns such as the Beretta 92 and the SIG P226, not to mention the CZ 75, this is a strong statement. Just the same – there is much validity to the claim.

The HK P7M8 is no longer in production and listed at well over $1,300 during its last few years in production. Today it brings top dollar on the used market, with good clean examples beginning at $1,500 or more.

The test gun is a well-maintained example of the Heckler and Koch "squeeze cocker." For the purposes of this review, the handgun was field stripped and lubricated prior to firing. Since the

The European proof marks are German, the import stamp American.

unique gas-retarded action precludes the use of +P ammunition as well as lead bullets, the pistol was evaluated with several standard-pressure loadings using jacketed bullets. The overall impression is one of excellent control while firing. Not only that, the pistol clears leather quickly due to the 110-degree grip design, plus it fits the hand well and the natural pointability is excellent.

The pistol was carried primarily in a first-class leather inside-the-waistband holster from Wright Leatherworks during the evaluation. This holster features dual belt loops and high-quality molding to the individual handgun. As the hand grasps the handle the lever is cocked as the pistol comes on target. The trigger finger does not engage the trigger until you fire. The pistol lines up on target quickly with an intuitive point – the first shot hit probability of the handgun is very high. Once the first shot is fired, recoil is easily controlled and the pistol settles back in for quick follow-up shots. The slim eight-round magazine is easily changed to keep the pistol in action.

Initial range work was accomplished with the Black Hills Ammunition 115-grain FMJ loading. This cartridge ran well with positive function and gave

The P7M8 nicely fits in this custom Garrity's Gunleather Triskel Holster. The holster can be worn as a conventional IWB, clipped onto the belt as an easy on/easy off OWB strong-side belt holster or serve as a 'tuckable' holster and conceals with your shirt tucked in.

Photo courtesy http://www.garritysgunleather.com

more than adequate combat accuracy. The P7M8 was also fired with the Black Hills 124-grain JHP. This load also gave excellent function and good accuracy. Perhaps the best choice for personal defense in this handgun is the Black Hills 115-grain EXP, or Extra Power loading. This 9mm Luger cartridge is designed for the maximum velocity and energy possible without resorting to +P pressure. For many reasons handgun users should not rush to stress their 9mm handgun with a heavy load, and the Black Hills Ammunition 115-grain EXP is the ideal choice for just the right amount of performance.

The HK P7M8 left nothing to be desired in a demanding combat course. Its all-steel construction results in excellent

The HK P7M8 is often carried in this Wright Leatherworks IWB holster. It doesn't get any better – comfortable, discreet and secure.

LOAD	FIVE-SHOT GROUPS @ 25 YARDS
Black Hills Ammunition 115–grain FMJ	2.5 inches
Black Hills Ammunition 124–grain JHP	1.5 inches
Speer 124–grain Gold Dot	1.8 inches
SIG SAUER 124–grain JHP	2 inches

Above: This is the takedown button. Press the button and simply pull the slide to the rear, then forward off of the barrel. **Right:** The author did not simply fire at fixed targets. The HK 9mm was given a good tactical run.

control. The pistol is fast on target. The low bore axis and crisp, its short and light trigger action results in excellent hit probability. From my experience, there is no handgun faster into action and more controllable in 9mm.

One consideration to keep in mind is that due to the gas-retarded operation, the front of the dust cover heats up during firing. The gun can handle about 150 rounds comfortably until you need to wear gloves. Another interesting note is that this handgun was designed to allow top-grade accuracy in case it was used in hostage rescue duty. Even though the P7M8 has a short sight radius, the sights and trigger action are excellent examples of a superior design and the pistol exhibited first class accuracy from a sandbag rest at 25 yards. See accompanying table for the accuracy results of the tested cartridges.

The P7M8 is clearly more than accurate enough for any foreseeable threat engagement. The pistol is a classic – a treasure to those that own and use it, and a very credible defensive handgun.

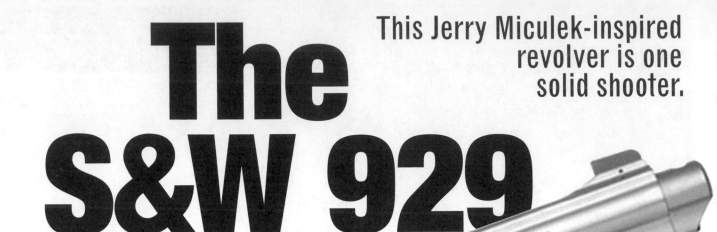

The S&W 929

This Jerry Miculek-inspired revolver is one solid shooter.

BY **Dick Jones**

My first target revolver was a Smith & Wesson Model 28 Highway Patrolman. Of course, it was designed for service use, but the excellent adjustable sights and 6-inch barrel allowed me to achieve the AA classification in the NRA Hunter's Pistol category in the late '70s. The Model 28 was accurate and had a great trigger. I'm not sure what caused me to let that one slide, but I've wished I had it back dozens of times. More recently, I tested the Smith & Wesson R8, an eight-shot .357 revolver on that same N-sized frame. I shot some plate matches with it, and my wife, Cherie, shot the 2013 Bianchi Cup with that revolver. The exceptional accuracy and butter-smooth trigger have inspired almost everyone

who's shot that gun to make an offer for it, but it still rests comfortably in my safe. Through a dozen decades, Smith & Wesson has created some of the best revolvers ever made, and when I saw the 929, I knew they had another winner. While the size, sights and trigger are reminiscent of my old Highway Patrolman, the resemblance ends there. The Model 929 has a full-length ejector rod shroud with a removable muzzle compensator. The frame is matte-finished stainless steel with a titanium alloy cylinder.

The same excellent rear sight that graced my Model 28 is there along with a larger Patridge front sight. It's a visually striking gun because the extended ejector rod shroud tapers towards the end of the barrel.

The author's wife, Cherie, checks out the .38 Super Cliff Walsh used at the 2012 Bianchi Cup.
Author Photo

The S&W 929 is a factory version of the guns guys like Jerry Miculek and Cliff Walsh have been using for years. Those guns are highly modified to make them more suitable for action and tactical shooting competitions. They have super slick, honed actions, match barrels, and have been converted to .38 Super to allow use of full moon clips for faster reloading. I suspect S&W chose 9mm instead of .38 Super for better availability and lower cost of the ammunition.

Other than the eight-shot 9mm cylinder, there's little internal difference between the 929 and the earlier N-frame Performance Center guns. The new gun has the same smooth double action and crisp single-action trigger as my old Model 28, but now with an adjustable over-travel screw. One area I prefer on the old guns was the grip. Older N frames almost all had square butts, and while the Model 28 came with the standard grip panels, many were upgraded to the oversized grip that just feels better to me. It's probably a personal preference and I'm sure some folks like the round

butt and finger grooved rubber grips; I just like the feel of the old N-frame, oversized target grip better.

Of course, the question one might ask is, "Why make a 9mm revolver when you already have a great .38 Special revolver?" Fact is, there are several good reasons, and I think we need more 9mm revolvers, but more on that later. The first good reason is speed of loading and unloading for tactical and action shooting. While speed loaders and full moon clips are available for rimmed pistol calibers like .38 Special, the moon clips are somewhat flimsy. Also, the length of the .38 Special round makes fast ejection an iffy proposition. If you've ever watched Jerry Miculek shoot a Smith & Wesson .45 ACP with moon clips 12 times in less than three seconds, you can understand the value of moon-clipped rimless rounds in revolvers.

Another advantage of the 9mm over the .38 Special is power level. Obviously, guns like the R8 eight-shot .357 Magnum have more power than the 9mm, but no one is likely to shoot a .357 in an

action pistol competition because of recoil. The Bianchi requires a power factor of 120,000. Few commercial loads provide that level of power, yet almost all commercial 9mm loads make 120,000 easily. The third advantage is cost and availability since 9mm loads are almost always cheaper than .38 Special and generally more available.

Shooting Impressions

For the sake of comparison, the S&W R8 is a similar revolver to the 929. The R8 is a .38/.357 eight-shot N-frame revolver with similar sights and the same grip as the 929. I've shot mine extensively, and Cherie used it while competing in the 2013 Bianchi Cup. It's seven ounces lighter and has a 5-inch barrel, but otherwise it's comparable to the 929. Both are great pistols, but for action pistol competition, the 929 has advantages, hands down, and the R8 is a very good competition revolver.

Although the power factor of the 929 with standard 115-grain 9mm am-

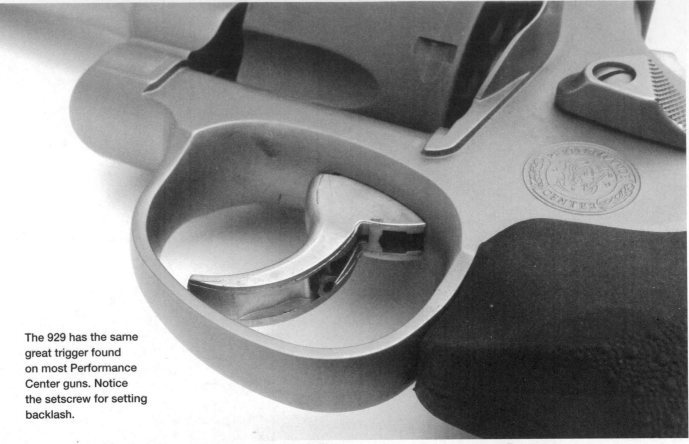

The 929 has the same great trigger found on most Performance Center guns. Notice the setscrew for setting backlash.

SMITH & WESSON MODEL 929

CALIBER:	9mm Luger
CAPACITY:	8 rounds
BARREL:	6.5" in. with a full-length under-lug and removable muzzle compensator
SIGHTS:	Adjustable rear with white outline and Patridge front
FRAME:	Matte stainless steel N frame
LENGTH:	12.25 in.
HEIGHT:	6.25 in.
WEIGHT:	44.2 oz.
OPTIONS:	Extra moon clips
SRP:	$1,189
WEBSITE:	smith-wesson.com

Ten shots, 25 yards, standing, single action, my group measured just under 2.5 inches.

Author Photo

The TC Custom full moon clips can be loaded without a tool, but the tool makes life much easier and reduces the chances of tweaking a clip. I found a .300 Winchester Magnum case worked great for unloading the clips.

TK CUSTOM MOON CLIPS

Moon clips or full moon clips are so named after the half moon clips used to allow the Army's 1917 Colt and S&W revolvers to shoot .45 ACP ammunition when .45 Auto Rim wasn't available. Half moon clips held three rounds of .45 ACP together and provided a surface for extraction. While it's possible to load and unload moon clips without the aid of a loader, it can wear your fingers out. TK Custom is a small shop that makes moon clips and a tool for loading moon clips. They also do conversions to relieve the rear of the cylinder of guns to allow use of moon clips. Converting defense firearms to use moon clips makes sense, but converting a .38 Special to 9mm moon clip capability makes even more sense.

munition is well over the power factor of 120,000, and the 130 .38 Special load isn't, I could discern no difference in recoil. I'm quite sure the extra seven ounces of weight and the muzzle compensator are the main reasons. In fact, the 929 seems to have less muzzle rise than the less-powerful .38. The 929 is very controllable in fast shooting (or at least, what's fast shooting for me) and the trigger and grip are identical.

Accuracy is excellent and should be with good ammunition. The sight picture is exceptional with the large and blocky Patridge front sight, leaving a narrow line of light on either side of the rear notch with the gun extended. Of course, the extra sight radius of the 6.5-inch barrel doesn't hurt. I'd be just as happy without the white outline of the rear sight blade, but a little sight black will resolve that distraction. Shooting standing single action at 25 yards, I shot a 10-shot group that measured 2.46 inches overall with eight shots within just over 1.5 inches.

I'm pretty sure that's better performance than my old Highway Patrolman, and I made AA classification with it shooting as far out as 100 yards in the Hunter's Pistol category. I ran my plate machine, and staying within match times, managed a 44 of 48, which is about as well as I ever shoot. I've only cleaned a string of 48 plates once and that was with an optic-equipped race gun.

With every advantage in a firearm, there is a disadvantage. The R8 is designed to be used as a duty gun, hence the lighter weight, and .357 Magnum is a better caliber for duty use. The 929 is primarily a competition/recreational pistol, and 9mm makes sense for those uses. While the full moon clips work well for managing the rimless cartridges, they aren't a panacea. While you can fire the 929 without moon clips (the 9mm round headspaces on the case mouth), you can't extract them. Loading the moon clips can be done with fingers, but it works better with a loading tool.

Removing spent cases from the clips is harder than loading. I found a fired .300 Winchester Magnum case worked great as a removal tool, and the case mouth of the .300 fit the inside of the 9mm cases almost perfectly. Another disappointment was that there was only one full moon clip included with my gun.

I would have liked to see the top rib drilled and tapped for an optic, and there is the matter of only one full moon clip and my grip preference. The chambers need to be chamfered to allow faster loading, but most of this is either personal preference or the kinds of things that are accomplished in match preparation for high-level competition guns. Smith & Wesson has done an excellent job on the 929, both in conception and execution. While it isn't race ready right out of the box, this is the best revolver I've tested in a long time and one that will certainly stay in my safe.

* Originally published in *Gun Digest – The Magazine,* February 15, 2015 edition.

The CZ American Safari Magnum is offered in several classic calibers, including everybody's favorite – the .375 H&H Magnum. It is appropriately styled, sized and priced to fit into just about any rifleman's shooting or hunting plans.

The comprehensive line of CZ rifles includes the 550 in various medium-game calibers, as well as in safari cartridges, both modern and old.

TEST FIRE

CZ AMERICAN
SAFARI MAGNUM

BY **Steve Gash**

The classic safari battery has changed considerably over the past few decades. In days of yore, it was fashionable to take three rifles to Africa: A "light," a "medium" and a "heavy." The light was usually something in the .30-06 to .300 magnum class or, if you hailed from the continent, a .303 or 8mm. The heavy rifle was either a bolt gun or, if you were really loaded, a luscious side-by-side chambering some exotic

banana-sized round. Both types of heavy rifles were expensive in those days, as the budding African hunter had to rely on a custom bolt action made stateside, or a European "best quality" repeater (probably used) from a famous English or German maker.

This changed in 1955 when Winchester introduced the Model 70 "African" in .458 Winchester Magnum. Suddenly, anyone who could afford an African safari could certainly afford a real heavy rifle. In

1957, for example, a Winchester Model 70 in .30-06 retailed for $129.95. The M70 African in .458 was $295, but this was the "Supergrade."

But then as now, there is little consternation over the choice of the medium rifle. Anyone with half a brain gravitates to the .375 Holland & Holland Magnum. Jack O'Connor referred to it as the "queen of the medium bores," and for good reason.

These days, the impact of persnickety customs officials, obtuse baggage han-

TESTFIRE

dlers, anti-gun security agents, and various fees have significantly affected what we travel with on airplanes. Now, quite a few hunters travel Africa with only two rifles; the medium and the light. In fact, it is not unheard of to go with just one. I'll let you guess what that might be.

Which leads full circle back to the wonderful .375 H&H. As Craig Boddington succinctly put it, "The .375-bore remains what it was nearly a century ago: the single most useful rifle any African hunter could carry."

Of course, one need not be bound for Africa to need a quality .375. The versatile round is functional almost anywhere game is hunted.

The .375 H&H was introduced in 1912, and is still going strong. There are some new .375-caliber rounds, and while they're fine in their own right,

they in no way diminish the greatness of the .375 H&H. It is flat-shooting and powerful enough for almost any game encountered anywhere, on any continent. From short ranges to long, and from small game to large, it's simply the best all-around cartridge ever invented. And while many different rifle actions have been wrapped around the wonderful .375, the classic bolt action clears the path to nostalgic nirvana.

CZ has a proud and inspiring history on the world stage. CZ stands for Ceska Zbrojovka, or "Czech Weapons Factory." The facility has been in operation since 1936 in what is now the Czech Republic. CZ was originally a subsidiary of Ceska Zbrojovka Strakonice in the hamlet of Uhersky Brod, Czechoslovakia. This location was strategic because it was located

farther away from German bombers. But in 1936-1939, Germany seized control of Czechoslovakia and the country was dissected and ravaged. In one of his more prescient remarks, Winston Churchill said at the time, "Czechoslovakia recedes into the darkness."

But light follows darkness, and it is refreshing to report that the new democratic Czech Republic is thriving, and more importantly for us riflemen, so is the modern CZ production facility.

CZ has kept the allure of the classic European Mauser "best rifle" alive with its extensive line of bolt guns. From the diminutive 527 for varmints, the 550 for all manner of big game, the 550 Safari and the Safari Classic Express Rifles from the CZ Custom Shop, CZ has it covered.

The 550's barrel roll mark of "CAL. 375 H&H MAG." is sure to stir the hearts of serious riflemen everywhere.

Left: The origin of the CZ 550 ASM is the "Safari Classic" series, and is made in the Czech Republic. CZ's U.S. offices are located in Kansas City, Kansas.

Below: Three cartridges for which the 550 American Safari Magnum is chambered (from left): .375 H&H Magnum, .404 Jeffery and .505 Gibbs.

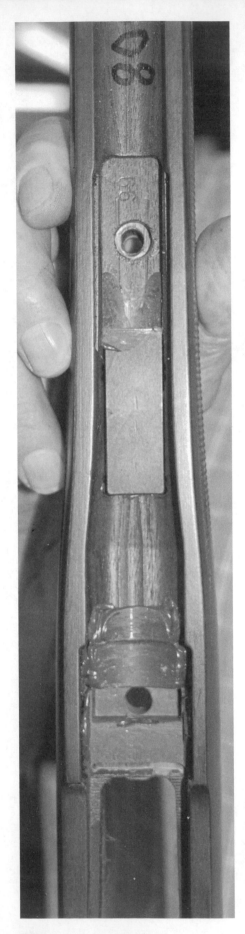

Left: One of the most functional features of the 550 .375 is what is called the "F Block," a steel lug dovetailed into the barrel that is glass-bedded to the stock to better distribute the recoil of heavy calibers.

Right: The stock is secured to the F Block via this escutcheon screw through the bottom of the fore-end.

Below: The rear sight is exactly what you'd expect on a "safari" rifle – a solid express sight with a fixed 100-yard leaf and two folding leafs, one for 200 yards and the other for 300 yards.

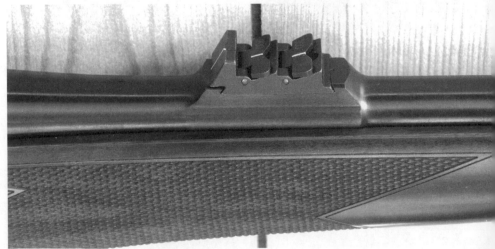

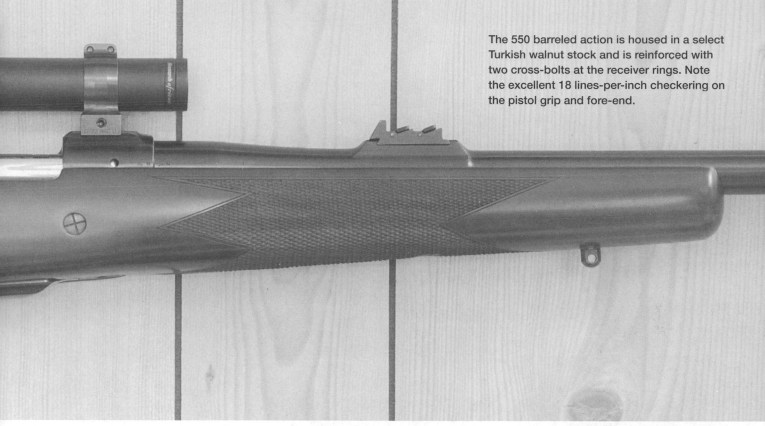

The 550 barreled action is housed in a select Turkish walnut stock and is reinforced with two cross-bolts at the receiver rings. Note the excellent 18 lines-per-inch checkering on the pistol grip and fore-end.

A recent addition to the 550 line is a version specifically tailored to American tastes called the American Safari Magnum. It's sure to stir the hearts of those who are on their way to Africa, or wish they were, as well as shooters who just appreciate a fine, classic rifle. The American Safari is available in .404 Jeffery, .458 Winchester, .458 Lott, .416 Rigby, .505 Gibbs, and of course, the .375 H&H.

Everybody needs a quality .375, and when I first saw the test gun, I was smitten. I immediately sold the .375 of another make I owned at the time and purchased this one. Every detail of this rifle exudes restrained elegance, and evokes images of the best-quality English bolt guns of old. The stock is of Turkish walnut, and, like a beautiful woman, is full-figured and plump in all the right places. The color is so dark it's almost black, and jet-black swirls course through the wood like a subtle yet powerful ocean current.

The metal finish is midway between gloss and matte. Whatever you call it, it perfectly complements the stock to complete the look. The buttstock is finished with a nice, functional solid recoil pad, and the excellent 18 line-per-inch cut checkering is in a point pattern on both sides of the pistol grip, and wraps all the way around the fore-end. There is no

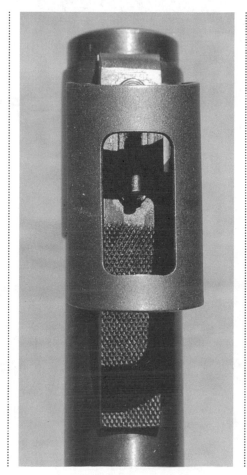

Above: The .375's muzzle means business on any continent. The open top of the front sight hood is clearly visible.

Left: The front sight is a brass bead, and is easily removable, if desired. The hood is open at the top for better visibility of the front sight in poor light.

A fine rifle deserves a fine scope, and this Nikon African Monarch 1-4x20 with the traditional German No. 4 reticle fits that description perfectly. It is attached to the receiver with quick-detachable steel rings from Alaska Arms, LLC.

The CZ 550 ASM has dual reinforcing crossbolts at the receiver rings, a hinged floorplate and an adjustable single-set trigger.

The enduring popularity of the .375 H&H makes fine factory loads like these universally available just about anywhere game is hunted.

grip cap or fore-end tip to distract from the classic elegance of the stock. Sling swivels are provided, and the only slight faux pas that I could find is that the front swivel stud is in the stock, instead of on a barrel band. (The CZ custom shop can add this feature, but it's rather expensive.)

The action is a genuine full magnum length and easily handles the .375, as well as the other rounds listed. It is a true controlled-feed action: to load the chamber, fill the magazine and close the bolt. The magazine holds five cartridges in .375, .458 Winchester and .458 Lott, four in .416 Rigby, and three in the gargantuan .505 Gibbs. A hinged floorplate allows emptying the magazine without disturbing the chambered round, and the spring-loaded floorplate release button is powered by a stout spring at the front of the triggerguard, where inertia keeps it from dumping your ammo in the dirt during recoil. The two-position safety locks both the sear and the bolt.

The single-set trigger is fully adjustable and can only be described as delightful and imminently practical. Unset, it breaks at 3 pounds, 10.3 ounces. Set, it lets off at a dazzling 15.1 ounces. Unset is, of course, perfect if

you're facing a petulant pachyderm or belligerent bovine, but the set feature is just the ticket for range testing and for zeroing, and it would be great for the occasional longer shot over a rest in the savannah.

The 25-inch barrel is hammer-forged and hydraulically lapped for ultra smoothness. This keeps barrel fouling to a minimum, and this, in turn, enhances accuracy.

Here's an interesting touch: An extra recoil lug called the "F block" is dovetailed into the underside of the barrel about 5¼ inches back from the fore-end tip. It is glass-bedded to the stock and is essentially an extra recoil lug that further strengthens the wood-to-metal interface for recoil distribution. It is secured by an escutcheon screw through the stock. The action has two crossbolts at the front and rear receiver rings, and the action is likewise glass-bedded.

The rear sight is the classic three-leaf that is exactly as you'd expect on your safari rifle. The fixed blade is for 100 yards, with two folding leaves for 200 and 300 yards. All have shallow Vs that give you a good view of the front sight. The front sight itself is a ramp that holds a white bead on a blade that is

easily removable, should you wish to replace it with another size or style. A small spring-loaded plunger at the front of the front blade can be depressed, and out pops the front sight.

The front sight is protected by a sturdy hood. For many rifles, these are usually removed (and lost), but this is not necessary on the American Safari Magnum. The CZ folks cleverly made the hood with a fat "window" on the top to let in plenty of light for fast iron-sight shooting in poor light. It's a really neat and functional feature. Most shooters will probably opt for scope sights, and the CZ 550 action comes equipped with 19mm dovetail cutouts and 1-inch rings.

For sighting, I mounted a tough new Nikon "Monarch African" 1-4x20 scope. This excellent scope has the traditional German #4 reticle that stands out nicely against most targets. The rings used are the quick-detachable models from Alaska Arms (available from CZ) that attach to the 19mm dovetails in the 550's receiver. These rings are top drawer, and allow the scope to be removed and replaced in a flash with no loss of zero. As a package, the scope, rings and rifle were literally made for each other.

Testfire Results — .375 H&H Magnum, Factory Loads

This is all very informative, but how'd it shoot? That's easy: great! I tested 10 representative factory loads at 50 yards, and nine handloads, and the results are shown in the accompanying table. All loads shot pretty well—I wouldn't hesitate to go on safari with any of them. The exception is my "deer load" with the Sierra 200-grain flatpoint. This bullet was designed for the .375 Winchester. When loaded over 41 grains of SR-4759, the velocity of 2,285 fps perfectly duplicates the lever-action round. I took a plump whitetail buck a few years ago with this load. I called it my "backyard safari."

The best .375 factory load tested was the Nosler 260-grain Partition load that went into an amazing .60-inch group. Velocity was 2,586 fps. Remington's 270-grain roundnose load grouped a

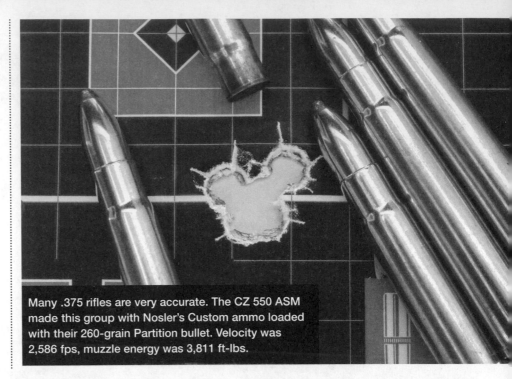

Many .375 rifles are very accurate. The CZ 550 ASM made this group with Nosler's Custom ammo loaded with their 260-grain Partition bullet. Velocity was 2,586 fps, muzzle energy was 3,811 ft-lbs.

TESTFIRE RESULTS –.375 H&H MAGNUM

Factory Loads Brand	Load No.	Bullet	Velocity (fps)	SD (fps)	Group (inches)
Federal	P375B	Soft Point 300-gr.	2,495	25	1.45
Winchester Supreme Safari SLSP	P375	Nosler 300-gr. Partition	2,417	5	2.2
Barnes Vortex	22014	Triple Shock-X 300-gr.	2,484	12	2
Nosler Trophy Grade	60090	Partition 260-gr.	2,586	8	.60
Nosler Trophy Grade	34005	Partition 300-gr.	2,414	12	1.85
Remington Express	R375M1	Soft Point 270-gr.	2,718	8	1.55
Federal Premium High Energy	P375T3	Trophy Bonded Bear Claw 300-gr.	2,541	6	2.2
Federal Premium	P375A1	Nosler AccuBond 260 gr.	2,586	16	1.83
Hornady DGS	8213	Hornady 270-gr. SP-RP	2,596	12	1.56
Hornady DGS	82332	Hornady DGX 300-gr. Expanding	2,484	15	1.48

SELECTED HANDLOADS

Case	Primer	Powder	Charge (grains)	Bullet	Velocity (fps)	SD (fps)	Group (inches)
Win.	F-210	Varget	65	Speer 235-gr. Semi-Spitzer	2,481	20	1.24
Rem.	WLRM	H-4895	67	Speer 235-gr. Semi-Spitzer	2,574	23	2.18
Rem.	WLR	SR-4759	41	Sierra 200-gr. Flat Point	2,285	19	1.1
Rem.	WLRM	H-4895	66.5	Sierra 250-gr. Spitzer BT	2,551	15	1.32
Rem.	WLRM	H-4895	66	Speer 270-gr. Spitzer BT	2,523	20	2.11
Win.	CCI-250	CFE-223	72	Hornady 225-gr. Soft Point	2,611	21	1.5
Win.	Fed-215	IMR-4064	67	Sierra 250-gr. Spitzer BT	2,607	12	1.21
Win.	Fed-215	IMR-4350	74	Speer 270-gr. Spitzer BT	2,622	13	2.6
Win.	Fed-215	IMR-4350	73	Hornady Spitzer BT	2,492	5	1.22

NOTES: All loads fired in a CZ American Safari Magnum with a 25-inch barrel. Sight was a Nikon Monarch African 1-4x20 set at 4x. Data are for five shots at 100 yards from a Lead Sled. Midpoint of Oehler M-35P chronograph screens was 10 feet from the gun's muzzle. Range temperatures varied from 44-56 degrees Fahrenheit.

DISCLAIMER: Any and all loading data found in this article or previous articles is to be taken as reference material *only*. The publishers, editors, authors, contributors and their entities bear no responsibility for the use by others of the data included in this article or others that came before it.

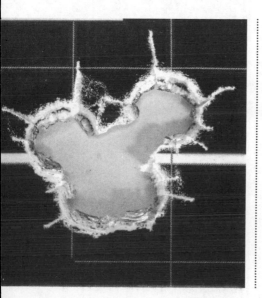

little over 1½ inches, and at 2,718 fps, produced a punishing 4,430 ft-lbs, the most muzzle energy of any load tested. Groups with the various 300-grain versions were only slightly larger, and muzzle energies ranged from 3,800-4,100 ft-lbs. Thanks to the well-designed stock and the rifle's weight of 10½ pounds, recoil was an authoritative shove, rather that an unpleasant punch.

All in all, it's hard to envision a better-balanced package for a .375 than the new CZ American Safari Magnum. It is not inappropriate to call it a "classic," as it embodies the best qualities required for a .375 H&H: appropriate heft, superb accuracy and total reliability. The impeccable attention to detail in styling results in an aesthetically pleasing package that perfectly fits the mold of the "medium" bore, whether you're going on safari to Africa or just to your backyard.

References

While reams have been (and, I fervently hope, will still be) written on the .375 H&H, I would be remiss if I did not reference these two volumes. With no intended slight to any other expert, I respectively refer the reader to two of Craig Boddington's many books on Africa, which relate excellent firsthand experience on the use of the .375 H&H.

Safari Rifles II, 2009. Safari Press, Long Beach, California, 594 pp.

Buffalo!, 2006, Safari Press, Long Beach, California, 248 pp.

TEST⊕FIRE

FRANKLIN

BY **L.P. Brezny**

ARMORY F17-L
An AR Platform for the World's Fastest Rimfire

First introduced during the 2014 SHOT Show, the arrival of a fully gas-operated .17 WSM has become a reality. This high-intensity, increased-chamber-pressure round makes use of a fully functional gas operating system and rotating locking bolt, instead of the common rimfire blowback semiauto system.

Last September I took possession of one of the very first F17-L series rifles to come off Franklin Armory's production line. With warm varmint targets almost at my front door, getting this new rimfire

The F17-L is the first of its kind – the .17 WSM in an AR platform.

into real-time test mode was very little trouble at all.

In terms of basic nomenclature, the magazine, bolt size and length, as well as the gas system itself, are all redesigned around the .17 WSM, which is much smaller than the popular AR/M-16 .223/5.56 NATO cartridge used in the big brothers to this rimfire creation. The magazine makes use of an almost-standard-size AR housing, but at the top retains a down-sized housing and follower to allow 10 rounds of WSM to be top-loaded, just like the basic full-size .223 round. The magazine is bent forward, giving it a look much like the AK-47's curved design, due to the bottlenecked rimfire round. This makes for a bit shorter magazine when shooting over bags or prone. Sighting slits on both the right and left side of the magazine housing allow the shooter to keep track of rounds remaining, as well as being a safety factor of sorts. When working the magazine for function I found it to be easy to use, solid in the mag well, and it functioned nicely with the Winchester WSM rounds.

The upper receiver is an AR look-alike to the last pin and part. We are seeing a rifle that makes use of a Franklin Armory Libertas proprietary billet-machined receiver. This receiver is not stamped, but fully cut from a single block of 7075 T6 aluminum. The anodized olive drab upper and lower are in contrast to the black surfaces over the rest of the rifle's barrel, fore-end and buttstock. Clean, sharp and great-looking surfaces come to mind when looking over this new shooter. It is very hard to come up with a

true signature AR today — there are over 180 of them in the marketplace — but the folks at Franklin Armory have done a fine job of creating a very unique and original AR platform.

The barrel in this rifle is made of 4140 chrome moly, with a salt bath nitride chamber and bore. It features a 20-inch bull barrel with no step. The bore has a 1.9-inch twist and an 11-degree target crown that is recessed. Zeroing accuracy prior to field review resulted

in a .763-inch, five-shot group at 50 yards. The rifle also held easily to one minute-of-angle at 100 yards. The rifle's gas system uses a piston design with a custom-designed bolt carrier group.

Function right out of the box was almost flawless during warm-up, bore cleaning and target-zeroing range work. The handguard design is from Franklin Armory and is a free-floating system that can use bipods as well as other equipment adaptors, and is threaded

The magazine modified to fit a standard AR mag well. Functioning was positive.

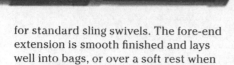

for standard sling swivels. The fore-end extension is smooth finished and lays well into bags, or over a soft rest when shooting for long-range targets.

The rifle's lower receiver is built exactly like the material used in the upper. It retains all the controls found in most fully equipped ARs and I found its controls to work with ease during all the test shooting I undertook. With a cold-weather triggerguard, a memory-indexed point for the shooting finger, and a special tension screw that eliminates any upper and lower flex or play, the rifle becomes a dream to shoot. The trigger is a Franklin Armory design, and was set with a let-off of a crisp 3 pounds. With a total weight, including scope, coming in at 11.6 pounds, this is a static position, light-duty dog rifle – not a long-haul carry gun.

In the stock department, the rifle makes use of an ERGO Ambi Sure Grip behind the triggerguard and a Magpul MOE buttstock. The buttstock is designed to be a snag-free system and all I can say about that is this: It is about

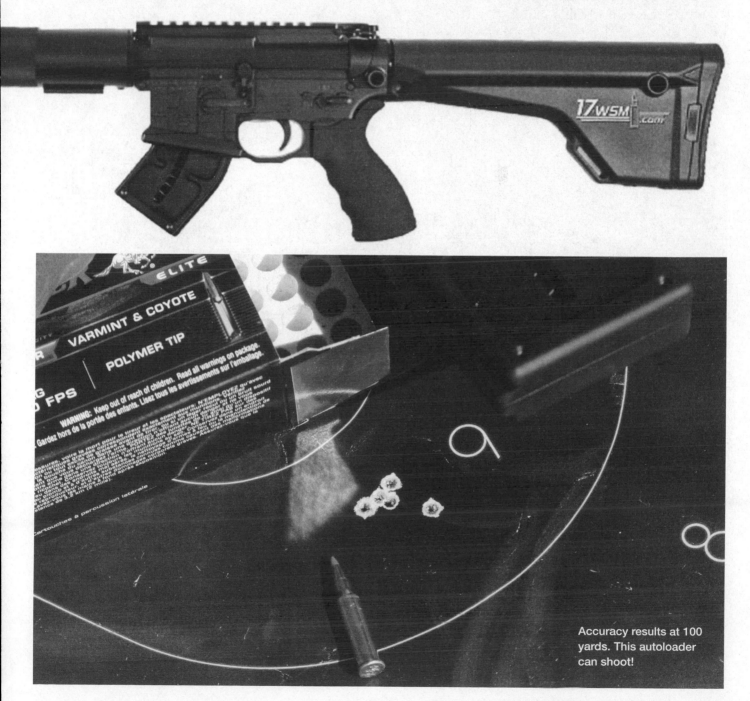

Accuracy results at 100 yards. This autoloader can shoot!

The Franklin Armory AR is a full-size platform and can accept other uppers.

time someone got after the sharp edges and angles associated with the standard M4 or full-size AR/M16 rifle platform.

The Ammunition

You can't talk about the new F17-L without paying some attention to the new Winchester-developed .17 WSM cartridge. While the rifle – with modifications – can take on any of the high-intensity rounds in use today on AR platforms by way of a different upper, the .17 WSM falls into a specialized group of cartridges. As such, it will appeal to shooters who want a particular round for special-purpose events. Its power is a

step ahead of the .17 HMR, which leaves the muzzle running at 2,270 fps; the .17 WSM picks up the velocity to 3,000 fps, enough to make it the fastest rimfire round in existence today.

With the exception of a very lucky hit on a song dog or badger, all of the .17s save for the Hornady .17 Hornet, are in my estimation relegated to midrange prairie dog or gopher gunning service. Want a coyote rifle? This, my friends, ain't it. Oh yes, when it rolled out in late 2013 it was all the rage, as observed by the desktop gun writers who seemingly don't shoot much of anything. We active field writers and a large group of engineers shot Remington .17 centerfires on song

dogs in Wyoming during several industry hunts with rotten results, so what makes anyone think a much-reduced velocity load in a 20-grain, .17-caliber pill is going to do any better? Answer, it won't. For the most part, I like the .17 Hornet a whole lot as a fall turkey rifle here in the hills. Possibly the .17 WSM could fit that role if a good turkey-shooting rifleman is behind the buttstock.

Warm Targets

The next step in testing was to get this little flat-shooting midrange varmint rig out and onto some real-world warm targets. Grass rats were getting large and fat by the first part of September, and when hit, some of them could give workable information as to the general damage this V-Max 20-grain pill would deliver downrange. I have been informed that this cartridge has a second offering in a 25-grain pill, but to date none of them have showed up at my door for evaluation.

I got my chance to test shoot this little bullet a day after I had taken possession of the F17-L rifle. I went to work on the dead air side of late afternoon, and was able to maintain some very strict control as to exactly how far I was shooting on live prairie dogs, and able to send bullets in perfect weather conditions as well. Shooting into a low-angle sunset, I could see my bullets' dust clouds with ease as they floated over the impact areas. It was a chance to play with elevation adjustments, as I took on a number of large grass rats as they were sitting out on their lodges for the evening.

My first round downrange illustrated that I was a mil high at 100 yards, so I dropped a mil-dot off in the crosshairs and touched off a second round that caught the dog dead center. There is no question that the .17 WSM is a very flat-shooting rifle cartridge out to 200 yards. With the great shooting conditions I was experiencing, and the fact that the test rifle had a basic weight above 11 pounds with a heavy bull barrel to make for a very accurate platform, I decided to push the limits of the little rat killer just a bit more. After locating a second dog at the 223-yard mark I sent a round downrange that caught it in the front shoulder, but entered and came to a stop. No exit wound at all, save for a very pronounced "plop" that carried well up-range to my ears. That dog rolled off the mound stone dead with no chance at making a run for its den hole.

Shooting the Franklin Armory rifle for the next hour resulted in my first impressions of the total gunning system. In terms of malfunctions, I did have a few, but all of them came after almost 50 rounds had been sent down

SPECIFICATIONS	
Overall Length:	38.25"
Weight:	9 lbs. (Without magazine)
Barrel:	Chambered in 17 Winchester Super Magnum Rimfire 4140 Chrome Moly, Salt Bath Nitride Chamber, Bore, & Finish, 20" Bull Barrel, 11 Degree Target Crown with Recessed Muzzle Crown, 1/9-Inch Twist
Upper Receiver:	Franklin Armory™ Libertas™ Proprietary Billet Upper Receiver, Machined From 7075-T6 Aluminum, Hard Coat Type III Anodized Olive Drab Green, Franklin Armory™ Free Float Handguard (Fluted & Vented, M-Lok compatible, and an Integral Bi-pod & Tri-pod Adapter), Forward Assist, Custom Designed 17 WSM Bolt Carrier Group, Gas Piston System Design
Lower Receiver:	Franklin Armory™ Libertas™ Proprietary Billet Lower Receiver, Machined From 7075-T6 Aluminum, Hard Coat Type III Anodized Olive Drab Green, Flared Magazine Well for Quick Magazine Changes, Ambidextrous Push Button QD Sling Mounts, Integral Cold Weather Trigger Guard, Serrated Memory Index Point for Shooting Finger, Textured Front Area for Offhand Grip, Specialized Tension Screw – Eliminates Upper/Lower Play, Franklin Armory™ Factory Custom Tuned Trigger, Ergo Ambi Sure Grip
Magazine:	10 Round Capacity – Custom Design, Metal Feed Lips Metal Follower, Hard Coat Anodized Black, Fits Standard AR15 Magazine Well
Stock:	Magpul MOE Rifle Stock, Snag Free Design, Sling Mountable
Additional Features:	Comprehensive Safety Manual, California Certified Cable Lock, Complimentary Lockable Case

The complete .17 rimfire family, from left: CCI .17 Mach II, Hornady .17 WMR, Winchester .17 WSM.

the bore. True to form in the AR/M16 community of rifles, the action went dry and the system started to double feed and hang up unfired bullets just behind the chamber feed ramp. In the accuracy area the rifle was spot on deadly, being a tack driver for sure.

When I folded up for the evening, I was hell-bent on locating the problem with the new rifle. Upon reaching home I went to work and took down the receiver, and finding nothing wrong whatsoever, I proceeded to soak the action both upper and lower with my favorite gunsmith-in-a-can. Simple, effective and cheap Liquid Wrench was coming to the rescue, and a second try the following morning would be the proof as to AR-style rifles requiring a wet action, at least during break-in.

When taken afield on the second day, the rifle never skipped a single beat over the 30 rounds that went downrange. It was like the previous evening's issues had never taken place at all.

There is no question that by mounting the BSA target glass and Rock River cantilever all-steel mount and bases onto this rifle the weight equation went up

substantially. However it would be nice to see this rifle with a deep-fluted barrel that would remain stiff while reducing heat and weight. The use of a tube fore-end in carbon fiber would also be a nice addition to a second model in this rifle. We have used this approach here at Ballistics Research and Development by way of 7.62 NATO (.308) centerfire varmint and big-game rifles with some very positive results.

As many of you well know, the LR series on AR-style rifles can become a bit bulky as field-carry rifles. This new rifle as a static varmint rig is clearly very workable, but it can become a bit much as a walking varmint rig, at least as I had it set up for my needs.

Overall, as a shooting system, the Franklin Armory F-17 returned some very positive results in the field. Keeping a new rifle firing "wet" seems to be some good advice, and by watching out for proper lubrication, will allow the system to run quite well. This .17-caliber gunning system is well made of quality materials and is right in line with the better quality AR systems in other cartridge offerings.

The .17 WSM was introduced with 20-grain bullets, shown here. A new load with a 25-grain bullet was recently announced.

THE SPHINX SDP

An Exceptional Handgun

BY **Robert K. Campbell**

The Sphinx 9mm pistol is well made of the finest materials and exhibits first-class performance.

The handgun covered in this report is arguably among the finest finished and fitted handguns in the world. It is manufactured by Sphinx Systems Ltd. of Switzerland, a firm that is enjoying more than 140 years as a tool and precision manufacturing company. The 9mm Sphinx is a product of a desire to produce a world-class handgun, a goal that has been achieved.

The present pistol is the result of long experience in producing quality handguns, including the original Sphinx and a number of CZ 75-inspired clone guns. These handguns have proven accurate and reliable. However, for many reasons including currency trades, the pistols are often very expensive. Quality handguns are not inexpensive, but as the price reaches $2,000 or more, buyers are few. Sphinx set out to develop a handgun with excellent performance but which might be sold for a price in middle range—in this case about $1,350. Sphinx developed the SDP series to fill this role.

The handguns are well-finished by any standard and offer excellent performance. They are not inexpensive but they are affordable.

There is much that is familiar with the Sphinx pistol. It uses the proven short recoil system and a locked breech design that began with the Browning patents. The pistol's construction is interesting. While the slide, barrel and critical parts are of steel, the upper portion of the frame is aluminum. The

lower receiver is of a modern polymer. This is an unusual construction. While polymer is lighter than steel and less expensive, this mix of materials isn't easily mastered.

The appearance of the slide is a clue to the pride with which this handgun was produced. In a day when many gunmakers are attempting to cut corners and limit machine work, the Sphinx slide requires extensive machine

work. The bevels are very well done. The slide features forward cocking serrations and the ejection port machine work is artfully accomplished.

Another feature is that the slide rides inside of the frame. This gives the

The Sphinx 9mm features a front rail to allow the use of a modern combat light such as the Viridian.

The only controls are the slide lock and the de-cocking lever. There is no manual safety.

Left: The Sphinx is supplied with a total of three magazines and three grip inserts along with other accessories.

Below: Three supplied grip inserts allow the shooter to find a comfortable, custom fit.

In rapid fire the Sphinx 9mm is very controllable.

The author found the Sphinx lively in the hand.

practiced eye a clue to the lineage of the Sphinx handgun. It is based upon the durable and well-respected CZ 75 handgun. The slide's position inside of the frame limits muzzle flip, as the bore axis remains low. This is a difficult feat to achieve with a double-action handgun. The contact between the slide and frame is tight, resulting in high accuracy potential.

As for the sights, the rear sight is dovetailed in place. The front sight is not a common dovetail, but firmly attached in a trough that runs from the forward section of the slide to the rear of the front sight. This is an excellent setup that anchors the sights well. The rear sight may be drifted to adjust the point of impact for windage. The sights provide a good sight picture.

The action is contained in the aluminum section of the receiver. The double-action first-shot trigger is similar to that of the CZ 75, with a recurved trigger offering good leverage. The double-action trigger pull is tight, long and heavy, as these often are,

breaking the sear at about 14 pounds. The single-action trigger is clean at 5.5 pounds with the modest backlash common to the CZ 75 and its variants.

Controls include a slide lock, a frame-mounted de-cocker and a magazine release. The hammer is bobbed with no hammer spur. The de-cocker is ambidextrous. There is no manual safety and no provision for carrying the pistol cocked and locked. The frame is bobbed to prevent snagging on covering garments. The frame features a light rail for mounting laser aiming devices or a combat light.

Unlike most CZ 75-based handguns, the Sphinx can be adjusted for hand fit. This is due to the inclusion of the polymer grip frame component. Additional grip inserts are included in the hard plastic box supplied with the Sphinx.

The polymer grip frame feels good in the hand, with the heft consistent with a quality CZ 75 handgun. When you look at the de-cocker and the magazine release, it is obvious that a lot of care goes into producing high-grade checkering on each of these parts. The grip frame offers plenty of abrasion as the result of a serrated finish. There is

The gun's magazine release button provides a quick extraction, and rapid reloads are very fast. When firing the powerful Black Hills Ammunition 124-grain +P load, recoil was more noticeable but not painful.

In single-action mode the trigger pull is short and crisp.

a removable backstrap that allows for good hand-to-gun fit. There is a total of three straps. The front strap features slight finger grooves.

Three steel magazines that hold 15 rounds of 9mm Luger ammunition are provided.

The Sphinx in every detail is an impressive piece of Swiss workmanship. No corners have been cut. It exhibits high precision in the detail work and excellent slide-to-frame fit. This is a tight handgun. The slide rides in the frame with excellent lockup. Lateral play is practically non-existent. The frame feels good and the pistol is well balanced. The slide is short, giving the

pistol a squat appearance. The 3.7-inch barrel is well fitted into the slide, and locks up by butting the barrel hood into the slide.

The heft and balance of the handgun is good, coming in at 28 ounces unloaded. When beginning the firing sessions, I loaded the magazines with Black Hills 115-grain Blue Box remanufactured loads. These loads are an excellent resource for training and practice. I fired at man-size targets at five, seven and 10 yards. I started the drills in the double-action mode. After the first shot, I fired the subsequent single-action shots as quickly as I could reacquire the sight picture and the Sphinx gave

excellent results. The sights are good combat sights that were quickly picked up by the eye.

The grip frame is comfortable while firing. I am not a fan of finger grooves in the front strap, but have to admit in this case the modest grooves seem to be an aid in control. The pistol proved to be more than combat accurate. During one session, firing at seven yards, I put a magazine of 15 rounds into the same ragged hole. Double taps were easily delivered and the pistol is easily the most capable double-action/first-shot handgun I have fired in some time. During the initial firing tests there were no failures to feed, chamber, fire or eject. Felt recoil was light.

Moving to personal defense loads, a number of popular JHP loads were fired in the Sphinx with good function. Among these was the Black Hills Ammunition 115-grain EXP. This load isn't loaded to +P pressure and instead for the greatest velocity possible, hence the term, Extra Power. At well over 1,200 fps this load gave good function and control, virtually the same as the 115-grain practice load. I also fired a quantity of the Black Hills Ammunition 124-grain +P service load. If I were back

ACCURACY RESULTS, TWO 5-SHOT GROUPS AT 25 YARDS

Load	Average Group Size
HPR 115-grain JHP	2.5 inches
Fiocchi 124-grain EXTREMA	1.9 inches
Black Hills 124-gr. JHP +P	2.25 inches
Remington 124-grain Golden Saber	2.5 inches

in uniform, this would be my favored 9mm service load. The slight difference in recoil was noticeable, but the Sphinx remained controllable.

A good test for any handgun and shooter is firing at small targets at known and unknown ranges. The Sphinx proved accurate at long range, connecting on the Innovative Targets steel gong at a long 50 yards. This target is an excellent training resource that I use often. (Innovativetargets.net)

Moving to bench rest firing, I collected a number of loads that have proven accurate in the past. Taking a careful rest, with attention to every detail, I fired two 5-shot groups with four different loads. These loads were from four manufacturers and in four different bullet weights, so the results were excellent by any standard. The single most accurate load, the Fiocchi

124-grain Extrema, produced a 5-shot group of 1.9 inches. That is target-grade accuracy. The Black Hills 124-grain +P is about 100 fps faster and posted a group of 2.25 inches.

The Sphinx is indeed an accurate handgun. Remember, this is a compact handgun designed for concealed carry or all-day uniformed carry. The Sphinx isn't inexpensive, but it is clearly worth its price.

SPECIFICATIONS

Manufacturer:	Sphinx Arms
Distributor:	Kriss USA
Model:	SDP Compact Alpha
Action:	Double-Action/Single-Action
Caliber:	9mm
Slide:	Steel, Matte Black
Upper Frame:	Anodized Aluminum
Grip Frame:	Black Polymer
Grips:	Polymer/Synthetic Inserts
Sights:	White Dot Front, Drift Adjustable Rear
External Safety:	None, De-cocking Lever
Barrel Length:	3.7 inches
Overall Length:	7.4 inches
Height:	5.35 inches
Width:	1.06 inches
Weight:	28 ounces
Capacity:	15 rounds
Accessories:	Pistol is provided with three magazines, magazine loader, cleaning kit, hard case, lock, owner's manual and grip inserts.

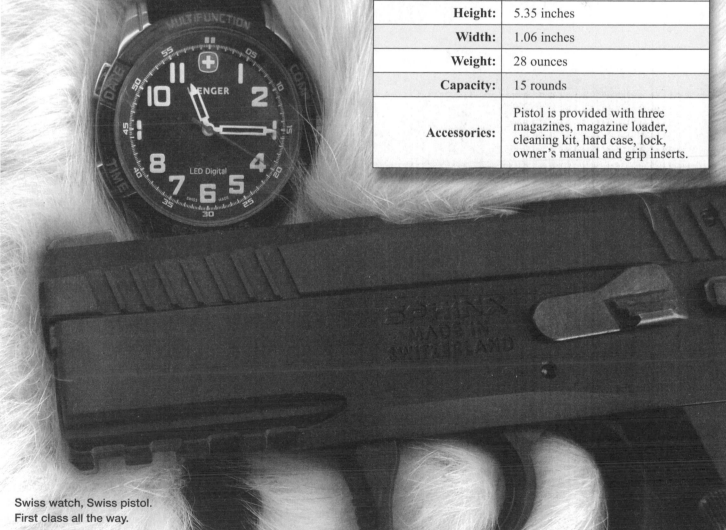

Swiss watch, Swiss pistol.
First class all the way.

A unique and economical way to more smallbore shooting fun.

MCA SPORTS BARREL INSERTS

TEST FIRE

BY **Al Doyle**

In a world of 30-round magazines and high-velocity ammunition, the idea of a single-shot rifle chambered for low-powered centerfire pistol calibers seems amusing and quaint. Who would want a gun that is just right for tossing in the back seat of a Model T?

Those who appreciate single-shots would say that to handle and use these sleek rifles (whether recently made or vintage) is to love them. The workmanship, colorful case-hardening, skilled engraving and eye-pleasing wood stocks often found on old British Rook rifles can be a delight to behold. With a little attitude adjustment, the limited capacity becomes an enjoyable challenge rather than a hindrance.

Making every round count – especially the first one – rather than pouring lead downrange is the name of the single-shot

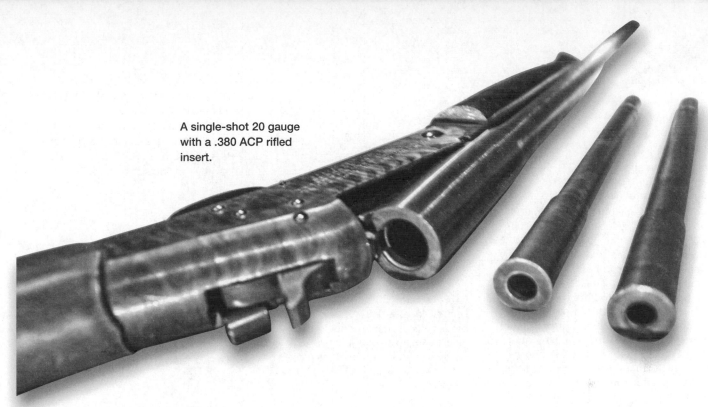

A single-shot 20 gauge with a .380 ACP rifled insert.

game. This philosophy also applies in hunting, regardless of what kind of rifle is being used.

If the siren song of Rook-style rifles is so strong, why not pick up a few or build a larger collection? Even a well-worn example could cost $1,000 or more, and pristine pieces command much higher prices. Obtain an original Rook long gun in a British/Australian caliber such as .295 Rook, .297/.230 Rook, .310 Cadet or .360, and it means adding the cost of rechambering, and possibly relining the barrel, to the original purchase price. For many shooters (myself included), wanting a nice Rook is a futile exercise of having Ralph Lauren tastes on a Ralph Kramden budget.

Stevens Favorite rifles of the early 1900s are a less expensive variation on the theme, but these American-made

products come in obsolete calibers such as .25 rimfire and .32 rimfire. Plan on spending a minimum of $2 per round for vintage ammo.

Is there a more affordable and practical option? Modern single-shot rifles by H&R 1871 and Rossi are typically chambered in deer hunting calibers. The Rook (as in the British term for a crow or raven) rifle is intended for smaller game, so another solution is needed. Enter the wide range of chamber inserts that are made in Alaska by MCA Sports.

The firm's website (www.mcace. com) offers an incredible assortment of cartridge adapters, along with rifled barrel inserts in lengths of 10 and 18 inches. Single-shots in 12, 16 and 20 gauge, along with the .410, are as common as dirt, so many gun owners won't

have to purchase another firearm to experiment with shooting pistol calibers from a long gun. If a person needs to obtain a platform for chamber inserts, used single-shots can often be found for $100 or less, and new-in-the-box versions shouldn't exceed $175.

MCA Sports owner and machinist Ace Dube supplied a pair of 10-inch rifled inserts in .32 H&R Magnum/.32 S&W Long along with a .380 ACP for an early 1990s vintage H&R 20 gauge. The first thing I noticed while installing these all-steel devices was how tightly both inserts fit into the shotgun. No sloppy tolerances here.

Once the insert is in place, load a round, aim and fire away. While the concept of turning a shotgun into a rifle in seconds is appealing, there is one problem. Trying to aim with just

The MCA chamber inserts aren't fancy, but they are solid and well made.

a front shotgun bead and no rear sight is quite an adjustment, especially for middle-age and older eyes.

There was one other unanticipated problem. I had a decent supply of .380 ACP on hand, but no .32 S&W Long or .32 H&R Magnum was available at a nearby Cabela's or at the popular regional chain store (Fleet Farm). The folks at Salmon, Idaho-based Buffalo Bore (www.buffalobore.com) saved the day by providing a supply of both calibers. Since Buffalo Bore is known for large-diameter ammo (the firm's motto is "Strictly Big Bore – Strictly Business"), it was a surprise to see their selection of various .32-caliber rounds.

The smaller Buffalo Bore rounds worked flawlessly in testing. As expected, the .32 S&W Long was a quiet performer, and the .32 H&R is ideal for those who want more punch and range while game hunting or dealing with four-legged pests and feral animals. I later pounced on 50-round boxes of Sellier & Belliot .32 S&W wadcutters and Fiocchi roundnose when they turned up at a local gun show.

It's obvious that the MCA inserts are inherently accurate, as two- and three-shot groups at minute of groundhog – or an inch – at 25 yards can be achieved with regularity. That changes with five-round strings. The obvious solution is to add a traditional rear rifle sight or peep sight to the barrel, but what can be done if you want to retain the bead-only setup for shotgun usage?

Long-time gun writer Ed Harris has done a good deal of experimenting with single-shot rifles in handgun calibers, and he provided a creative solution for this problem.

"Take a quarter-inch copper washer and use a little Loctite for a temporary rear sight," Harris advised. "It can easily be removed."

The H&R ejector becomes an extractor with an MCA rifled insert, but it takes some breaking in. Initially, I had to remove the 10-inch sleeve after every shot and punch out the fired brass or use a longer rod to get the job done, but things

improved after 30 rounds. Ideally, the brass will come out of the insert enough so that it can easily be plucked out with fingers before a fresh round is loaded.

What's the big deal about shooting .32s or .380 ACPs from a working-class shotgun? The experience was one of the most relaxing times I have ever had on the range. The moderate pace of one round at a time combined with minimal recoil made the shooting sessions a real pleasure. The history buff might feel like he has been transported back to a simpler time. Those on a budget will appreciate the smaller number of rounds fired as compared to more "sophisticated" weapons.

Harris moved the barrel insert concept to the next level when he took an old H&R .410 frame and had a pair of barrels fashioned into .32 ACP and .32 H&R Magnum/.32 S&W Long tubes complete with rifle sights. The results of his project can be found at www.grantcunningham.com. He is sold on .32s for logical reasons.

"I live in settled farm country, and the .32 Long is delightful because it keeps the noise level low," he said. "If you have a 24-inch barrel and use a fast-burning powder like Bullseye, the noise level is no greater than an Eley .22 out of a Winchester 61. Groundhogs, raccoons and possums are anchored much better with a .32 than they are with a .22. If you have a free source of lead and reload, you can shoot .32s as cheaply or cheaper than .22s at current prices." Likewise, the .380 ACP is a quiet option out of an MCA barrel insert, and it's a cost-effective caliber for bullet casting and reloading.

Dube's customers are an eclectic lot.

Originally purchased at Wal-Mart for $65, this humble H&R 20 gauge becomes an extremely versatile firearm with a MCA Sports chamber insert. It is shown with a .32 H&R Magnum/.32 S&W Long insert, and another in .380 ACP.

"It's everything from the guy who says he lives in back of the stinky trading post in West Virginia to Ph.D.s at big-name colleges," he said. "They are gun cranks who are into oddball stuff. Some dads buy adapters to train young shooters."

Take that old single-shot that is gathering dust and go to the MCA Sports website for some pleasant day-dreaming. How about a .45 ACP insert for a 12 gauge? Can't beat that combo. Why not a .30 Carbine, .32 ACP, .38 Special or .44 Special? Those and many other calibers are made to order for $95 apiece for a 10-inch insert.

Many manufacturers do not supply suggested retail prices. Others did not get their pricing to us before press time. All pricing can vary dependent on the exact brand and style of ammo selected and/or the retail outlet from which you make your purchase. Pricing has been rounded to the nearest dollar and represents our best estimate of average pricing. An * after the cartridge means these loads are available with Nosler Partition or Swift A-Frame bullets. Listed pricing may or may not reflect this bullet type. ** = these are packed 50 to box, all others are 20 to box. Wea. Mag.= Weatherby Magnum. Spfd. = Springfield. A-Sq. = A-Square N.E.–Nitro Express.

Cartridge	Bullet Wgt. Grs.	VELOCITY (fps)					ENERGY (ft. lbs.)					TRAJ. (in.)				Est. Price/box
		Muzzle	100 yds.	200 yds.	300 yds.	400 yds.	Muzzle	100 yds.	200 yds.	300 yds.	400 yds.	100 yds.	200 yds.	300 yds.	400 yds.	
17, 22																
17 Hornet	15.5	3860	2924	2159	1531	1108	513	294	160	81	42	1.4	0.0	-9.1	-33.7	NA
17 Hornet	20	3650	3078	2574	2122	1721	592	421	294	200	131	1.10	0.0	-6.4	-20.6	NA
17 Remington Fireball	20	4000	3380	2840	2360	1930	710	507	358	247	165	1.6	1.5	-2.8	-13.5	NA
17 Remington Fireball	25	3850	3280	2780	2330	1925	823	597	429	301	206	0.9	0.0	-5.4	NA	NA
17 Remington	20	4200	3544	2978	2477	2029	783	558	394	272	183	0	-1.3	-6.6	-17.6	NA
17 Remington	25	4040	3284	2644	2086	1606	906	599	388	242	143	+2.0	+1.7	-4.0	-17.0	$17
4.6x30 H&K	30	2025	1662	1358	1135	1002	273	184	122	85	66	0	-12.7	-44.5	—	NA
4.6x30 H&K	40	1900	1569	1297	1104	988	320	218	149	108	86	0	-14.3	-39.3	—	NA
204 Ruger (Hor)	24	4400	3667	3046	2504	2023	1032	717	494	334	218	0.6	0	-4.3	-14.3	NA
204 Ruger (Fed)	32 Green	4030	3320	2710	2170	1710	1155	780	520	335	205	0.9	0.0	-5.7	-19.1	NA
204 Ruger	32	4125	3559	3061	2616	2212	1209	900	666	486	348	0	-1.3	-6.3	—	NA
204 Ruger	32	4225	3632	3114	2652	2234	1268	937	689	500	355	.6	0.0	-4.2	-13.4	NA
204 Ruger	40	3900	3451	3046	2677	2336	1351	1058	824	636	485	.7	0.0	-4.5	-13.9	NA
204 Ruger	45	3625	3188	2792	2428	2093	1313	1015	778	589	438	1.0	0.0	-5.5	-16.9	NA
5.45x39mm	60	2810	2495	2201	1927	1677	1052	829	645	445	374	1.0	0.0	-9.2	-27.7	NA
221 Fireball	40	3100	2510	1991	1547	1209	853	559	352	212	129	0	-4.1	-17.3	-45.1	NA
221 Fireball	50	2800	2137	1580	1180	988	870	507	277	155	109	+0.0	-7.0	28.0	0.0	$14
22 Hornet (Fed)	30 Green	3150	2150	1390	990	830	660	310	130	65	45	0.0	-6.6	-32.7	NA	NA
22 Hornet	34	3050	2132	1415	1017	852	700	343	151	78	55	+0.0	-6.6	-15.5	-29.9	NA
22 Hornet	35	3100	2278	1601	1135	929	747	403	199	100	67	+2.75	0.0	-16.9	-60.4	NA
22 Hornet	40	2800	2397	2029	1698	1413	696	510	366	256	177	0	-4.6	-17.8	-43.1	NA
22 Hornet	45	2690	2042	1502	1128	948	723	417	225	127	90	+0.0	-7.7	-31.0	0.0	$27**
218 Bee	46	2760	2102	1550	1155	961	788	451	245	136	94	+0.0	-7.2	-29.0	0.0	$46**
222 Rem.	35	3760	3125	2574	2085	1656	1099	759	515	338	213	1.0	0.0	-6.3	-20.8	NA
222 Rem.	50	3345	2930	2553	2205	1886	1242	953	723	540	395	1.3	0	-6.7	-20.6	NA
222 Remington	40	3600	3117	2673	2269	1911	1151	863	634	457	324	+1.07	0.0	-6.13	-18.9	NA
222 Remington	50	3140	2602	2123	1700	1350	1094	752	500	321	202	+2.0	-0.4	-11.0	-33.0	$11
222 Remington	55	3020	2562	2147	1773	1451	1114	801	563	384	257	+2.0	-0.4	-11.0	-33.0	$12
222 Rem. Mag.	40	3600	3140	2726	2347	2000	1150	876	660	489	355	1.0	0	-5.7	-17.8	NA
222 Rem. Mag.	50	3340	2917	2533	2179	1855	1238	945	712	527	382	1.3	0	-6.8	-20.9	NA
222 Rem. Mag.	55	3240	2748	2305	1906	1556	1282	922	649	444	296	+2.0	-0.2	-9.0	-27.0	$14
22 PPC	52	3400	2930	2510	2130	NA	1335	990	730	525	NA	+2.0	1.4	-5.0	0.0	NA
223 Rem.	35	3750	3206	2725	2291	1899	1092	799	577	408	280	1.0	0	-5.7	-18.1	NA
223 Rem.	35	4000	3353	2796	2302	1861	1243	874	607	412	269	0.8	0	-5.3	-17.3	NA
223 Rem.	64	2750	2368	2018	1701	1427	1074	796	578	411	289	2.4	0	-11	-34.1	NA
223 Rem.	75	2790	2562	2345	2139	1943	1296	1093	916	762	629	1.5	0	-8.2	-24.1	NA
223 Remington	40	3650	3010	2450	1950	1530	1185	805	535	340	265	+2.0	+1.0	-6.0	-22.0	$14
223 Remington	40	3800	3305	2845	2424	2044	1282	970	719	522	371	0.84	0.0	-5.34	-16.6	NA
223 Remington (Rem)	45 Green	3550	2911	2355	1865	1451	1259	847	554	347	210	2.5	2.3	-4.3	-21.1	NA
223 Remington	50	3300	2874	2484	2130	1809	1209	917	685	504	363	1.37	0.0	-7.05	-21.8	NA
223 Remington	52/53	3330	2882	2477	2106	1770	1305	978	722	522	369	+2.0	+0.6	-6.5	-21.5	$14
223 Remington (Win)	55 Green	3240	2747	2304	1905	1554	1282	921	648	443	295	1.9	0.0	-8.5	-26.7	NA
223 Remington	55	3240	2748	2305	1906	1556	1282	922	649	444	296	+2.0	-0.2	-9.0	-27.0	$12
223 Remington	60	3100	2712	2355	2026	1726	1280	979	739	547	397	+2.0	+0.2	-8.0	-24.7	$16
223 Remington	62	3000	2700	2410	2150	1900	1240	1000	800	635	495	1.60	0.0	-7.7	-22.8	NA
223 Remington	64	3020	2621	2256	1920	1619	1296	977	723	524	373	+2.0	-0.2	-9.3	-23.0	$14
223 Remington	69	3000	2720	2460	2210	1980	1380	1135	925	750	600	+2.0	+0.8	-5.8	-17.5	$15
223 Remington	75	2790	2554	2330	2119	1926	1296	1086	904	747	617	2.37	0.0	-8.75	-25.1	NA
223 Rem. Super Match	75	2930	2694	2470	2257	2055	1429	1209	1016	848	703	1.20	0.0	-6.9	-20.7	NA
223 Remington	77	2750	2584	2354	2169	1992	1293	1110	948	804	679	1.93	0.0	-8.2	-23.8	NA
223 WSSM	55	3850	3438	3064	2721	2402	1810	1444	1147	904	704	0.7	0.0	-4.4	-13.6	NA
223 WSSM	64	3600	3144	2732	2356	2011	1841	1404	1001	789	574	1.0	0.0	-5.7	-17.7	NA
5.50 NATO	55	3130	2740	2382	2051	1750	1196	917	693	514	372	1.1	0	-7.3	-23.0	NA
5.56 NATO	75	2910	2676	2543	2242	2041	1410	1192	1002	837	693	1.2	0	-7.0	-21.0	NA
224 Wea. Mag.	55	3650	3192	2780	2403	2057	1627	1244	943	705	516	+2.0	+1.2	-4.0	-17.0	$32
225 Winchester	55	3570	3066	2616	2208	1838	1556	1148	836	595	412	+2.0	+1.0	-5.0	-20.0	$19

Cartridge	Bullet Wgt. Grs.	VELOCITY (fps)					ENERGY (ft. lbs.)					TRAJ. (in.)				Est. Price/box
		Muzzle	100 yds.	200 yds.	300 yds.	400 yds.	Muzzle	100 yds.	200 yds.	300 yds.	400 yds.	100 yds.	200 yds.	300 yds.	400 yds.	
22-250 Rem.	35	4450	3736	3128	2598	2125	1539	1085	761	524	351	6.5	0	-4.1	-13.4	NA
22-250 Rem.	40	4000	3320	2720	2200	1740	1420	980	660	430	265	+2.0	+1.8	-3.0	-16.0	$14
22-250 Rem.	40	4150	3553	3033	2570	2151	1530	1121	817	587	411	0.6	0	-4.4	-14.2	NA
22-250 Rem.	45 Green	4000	3293	2690	2159	1696	1598	1084	723	466	287	1.7	1.7	-3.2	-15.7	NA
22-250 Rem.	50	3725	3264	2641	2455	2103	1540	1183	896	669	491	0.89	0.0	-5.23	-16.3	NA
22-250 Rem.	52/55	3680	3137	2656	2222	1832	1654	1201	861	603	410	+2.0	+1.3	-4.0	-17.0	$13
22-250 Rem.	60	3600	3195	2826	2485	2169	1727	1360	1064	823	627	+2.0	+2.0	-2.4	-12.3	$19
22-250 Rem.	64	3425	2988	2591	2228	1897	1667	1269	954	705	511	1.2	0	-6.4	-20.0	NA
220 Swift	40	4200	3678	3190	2739	2329	1566	1201	904	666	482	+0.51	0.0	-4.0	-12.9	NA
220 Swift	50	3780	3158	2617	2135	1710	1586	1107	760	506	325	+2.0	+1.4	-4.4	-17.9	$20
220 Swift	50	3850	3396	2970	2576	2215	1645	1280	979	736	545	0.74	0.0	-4.84	-15.1	NA
220 Swift	50	3900	3420	2990	2599	2240	1688	1298	992	750	557	0.7	0	-4.7	-14.5	NA
220 Swift	55	3800	3370	2990	2630	2310	1765	1390	1090	850	650	0.8	0.0	-4.7	-14.4	NA
220 Swift	55	3650	3194	2772	2384	2035	1627	1246	939	694	506	+2.0	+2.0	-2.6	-13.4	$19
220 Swift	60	3600	3199	2824	2475	2156	1727	1364	1063	816	619	+2.0	+1.6	-4.1	-13.1	$19
22 Savage H.P.	70	2868	2510	2179	1874	1600	1279	980	738	546	398	0	-4.1	-15.6	-37.1	NA
22 Savage H.P.	71	2790	2340	1930	1570	1280	1225	860	585	390	190	+2.0	-1.0	-10.4	-35.7	NA
6mm (24)																
6mm BR Rem.	100	2550	2310	2083	1870	1671	1444	1185	963	776	620	+2.5	-0.6	-11.8	0.0	$22
6mm Norma BR	107	2822	2667	2517	2372	2229	1893	1690	1506	1337	1181	+1.73	0.0	-7.24	-20.6	NA
6mm PPC	70	3140	2750	2400	2070	NA	1535	1175	895	665	NA	+2.0	+1.4	-5.0	0.0	NA
243 Winchester	55	4025	3597	3209	2853	2525	1978	1579	1257	994	779	+0.6	0.0	-4.0	-12.2	NA
243 Win.	58	3925	3465	3052	2676	2330	1984	1546	1200	922	699	0.7	0	-4.4	-13.8	NA
243 Winchester	60	3600	3110	2660	2260	1890	1725	1285	945	680	475	+2.0	+1.8	-3.3	-15.5	$17
243 Win.	70	3400	3020	2672	2350	2050	1797	1418	1110	858	653	0	-2.5	-9.7	—	NA
243 Winchester	70	3400	3040	2700	2390	2100	1795	1435	1135	890	685	1.1	0.0	-5.9	-18.0	NA
243 Winchester	75/80	3350	2955	2593	2259	1951	1993	1551	1194	906	676	+2.0	+0.9	-5.0	-19.0	$16
243 Win.	80	3425	3081	2763	2468	2190	2984	1686	1357	1082	852	1.1	0	-5.7	-17.1	NA
243 Win.	87	2800	2574	2359	2155	1961	1514	1280	1075	897	743	1.9	0	-8.1	-23.8	NA
243 Win.	95	3185	2908	2649	2404	2172	2140	1784	1480	1219	995	1.3	0	-6.3	-18.6	NA
243 W. Superformance	80	3425	3080	2760	2463	2184	2083	1684	1353	1077	847	1.1	0.0	-5.7	-17.1	NA
243 Winchester	85	3320	3070	2830	2600	2380	2080	1770	1510	1280	1070	+2.0	+1.2	-4.0	-14.0	$18
243 Winchester	90	3120	2871	2635	2411	2199	1946	1647	1388	1162	966	1.4	0.0	-6.4	-18.8	NA
243 Winchester*	100	2960	2697	2449	2215	1993	1945	1615	1332	1089	882	+2.5	+1.2	-6.0	-20.0	$16
243 Winchester	105	2920	2689	2470	2261	2062	1988	1686	1422	1192	992	+2.5	+1.6	-5.0	-18.4	$21
243 Light Mag.	100	3100	2839	2592	2358	2138	2133	1790	1491	1235	1014	+1.5	0.0	-6.8	-19.8	NA
243 WSSM	55	4060	3628	3237	2880	2550	2013	1607	1280	1013	794	0.6	0.0	-3.9	-12.0	NA
243 WSSM	95	3250	3000	2763	2538	2325	2258	1898	1610	1359	1140	1.2	0.0	-5.7	-16.9	NA
243 WSSM	100	3110	2838	2583	2341	2112	2147	1789	1481	1217	991	1.4	0.0	-6.6	-19.7	NA
6mm Remington	80	3470	3064	2694	2352	2036	2139	1667	1289	982	736	+2.0	+1.1	-5.0	-17.0	$16
6mm R. Superformance	95	3235	2955	2692	2443	3309	2207	1841	1528	1259	1028	1.2	0.0	-6.1	-18.0	NA
6mm Remington	100	3100	2829	2573	2332	2104	2133	1777	1470	1207	983	+2.5	+1.6	-5.0	-17.0	$16
6mm Remington	105	3060	2822	2596	2381	2177	2105	1788	1512	1270	1059	+2.5	+1.1	-3.3	-15.0	$21
240 Wea. Mag.	87	3500	3202	2924	2663	2416	2366	1980	1651	1370	1127	+2.0	+2.0	-2.0	-12.0	$32
240 Wea. Mag.	100	3150	2894	2653	2425	2207	2202	1860	1563	1395	1082	1.3	0	-6.3	-18.5	NA
240 Wea. Mag.	100	3395	3106	2835	2581	2339	2559	2142	1785	1478	1215	+2.5	+2.8	-2.0	-11.0	$43
25-20 Win.	86	1460	1194	1030	931	858	407	272	203	165	141	0.0	-23.5	0.0	0.0	$32**
25-45 Sharps	87	3000	2677	2385	2112	1859	1739	1384	1099	862	668	1.1	0	-7.4	-22.6	$25
25-35 Win.	117	2230	1866	1545	1282	1097	1292	904	620	427	313	+2.5	-4.2	-26.0	0.0	$24
250 Savage	100	2820	2504	2210	1936	1684	1765	1392	1084	832	630	+2.5	+0.4	-9.0	-28.0	$17
257 Roberts	100	2980	2661	2363	2085	1827	1972	1572	1240	965	741	+2.5	-0.8	-5.2	-21.6	$20
257 Roberts	122	2600	2331	2078	1842	1625	1831	1472	1169	919	715	+2.5	0.0	-10.6	-31.4	$21
257 Roberts+P	100	3000	2758	2529	2312	2105	1998	1689	1421	1187	984	1.5	0	-7.0	-20.5	NA
257 Roberts+P	117	2780	2411	2071	1761	1488	2009	1511	1115	806	576	+2.5	-0.2	-10.2	-32.6	$18
257 Roberts+P	120	2780	2560	2360	2160	1970	2060	1750	1480	1240	1030	+2.5	+1.2	-6.4	-23.6	$22
257 R. Superformance	117	2946	2705	2478	2265	2057	2253	1901	1595	1329	1099	1.1	0.0	-5.7	-17.1	NA
25-06 Rem.	87	3440	2995	2591	2222	1884	2286	1733	1297	954	686	+2.0	+1.1	-2.5	-14.4	$17
25-06 Rem.	90	3350	3001	2679	2378	2098	2243	1790	1434	1130	879	1.2	0	-6.0	-18.3	NA
25-06 Rem.	90	3440	3043	2680	2344	2034	2364	1850	1435	1098	827	+2.0	+1.8	-3.3	-15.6	$17
25-06 Rem.	100	3230	2893	2580	2287	2014	2316	1858	1478	1161	901	+2.0	+0.8	-5.7	-18.9	$17
25-06 Rem.	117	2990	2770	2570	2370	2190	2320	2000	1715	1465	1246	+2.5	+1.0	-7.9	-26.6	$19
25-06 Rem.*	120	2990	2730	2484	2252	2032	2382	1985	1644	1351	1100	+2.5	+1.2	-5.3	-19.6	$17

Cartridge	Bullet Wgt. Grs.	VELOCITY (fps)					ENERGY (ft. lbs.)					TRAJ. (in.)				Est. Price/box
		Muzzle	100 yds.	200 yds.	300 yds.	400 yds.	Muzzle	100 yds.	200 yds.	300 yds.	400 yds.	100 yds.	200 yds.	300 yds.	400 yds.	
25-06 Rem.	122	2930	2706	2492	2289	2095	2325	1983	1683	1419	1189	+2.5	+1.8	-4.5	-17.5	$23
25-06 R. Superformance	117	3110	2861	2626	2403	2191	2512	2127	1792	1500	1246	1.4	0.0	-6.4	-18.9	NA
25 WSSM	85	3470	3156	2863	2589	2331	2273	1880	1548	1266	1026	1.0	0.0	-5.2	-15.7	NA
25 WSSM	115	3060	2844	2639	2442	2254	2392	2066	1778	1523	1398	1.4	0.0	-6.4	-18.6	NA
25 WSSM	120	2990	2717	2459	2216	1987	2383	1967	1612	1309	1053	1.6	0.0	-7.4	-21.8	NA
257 Wea. Mag.	87	3825	3456	3118	2805	2513	2826	2308	1870	1520	1220	+2.0	+2.7	-0.3	-7.6	$32
257 Wea. Mag.	90	3550	3184	2848	2537	2246	2518	2026	1621	1286	1008	1.0	0	-5.3	-16.0	NA
257 Wea. Mag.	100	3555	3237	2941	2665	2404	2806	2326	1920	1576	1283	+2.5	+3.2	0.0	-8.0	$32
257 Wea. Mag.	110	3330	3069	2823	2591	2370	2708	2300	1947	1639	1372	1.1	0	-5.5	-16.1	NA
257 Scramjet	100	3745	3450	3173	2912	2666	3114	2643	2235	1883	1578	+2.1	+2.77	0.0	-6.93	NA

6.5

Cartridge	Bullet Wgt. Grs.	Muzzle	100 yds.	200 yds.	300 yds.	400 yds.	Muzzle	100 yds.	200 yds.	300 yds.	400 yds.	100 yds.	200 yds.	300 yds.	400 yds.	Price/box
6.5 Grendel	123	2590	2420	2256	2099	1948	1832	1599	1390	1203	1037	1.8	0	-8.6	-25.1	NA
6.5x47 Lapua	123	2887	NA	2554	NA	2244	2285	NA	1788	NA	1380	NA	4.53	0.0	-10.7	NA
6.5x50mm Jap.	139	2360	2160	1970	1790	1620	1720	1440	1195	985	810	+2.5	-1.0	-13.5	0.0	NA
6.5x50mm Jap.	156	2070	1830	1610	1430	1260	1475	1155	900	695	550	+2.5	-4.0	-23.8	0.0	NA
6.5x52mm Car.	139	2580	2360	2160	1970	1790	2045	1725	1440	1195	985	+2.5	0.0	-9.9	-29.0	NA
6.5x52mm Car.	156	2430	2170	1930	1700	1500	2045	1630	1285	1005	780	+2.5	-1.0	-13.9	0.0	NA
6.5x52mm Carcano	160	2250	1963	1700	1467	1271	1798	1369	1027	764	574	+3.8	0.0	-15.9	-48.1	NA
6.5x55mm Swe.	93	2625	2350	2090	1850	1630	1425	1140	905	705	550	2.4	0.0	-10.3	-31.1	NA
6.5x55mm Swe.	123	2750	2570	2400	2240	2080	2065	1810	1580	1370	1185	1.9	0.0	-7.9	-22.9	NA
6.5x55mm Swe.*	139/140	2850	2640	2440	2250	2070	2525	2170	1855	1575	1330	+2.5	+1.6	-5.4	-18.9	$18
6.5x55mm Swe.	140	2550	NA	NA	NA	NA	2020	NA	NA	NA	NA	0.0	0.0	0.0	0.0	$18
6.5x55mm Swe.	140	2735	2563	2397	2237	2084	2325	2041	1786	1556	1350	1.9	0	-8.0	-22.9	NA
6.5x55mm Swe.	156	2650	2370	2110	1870	1650	2425	1950	1550	1215	945	+2.5	0.0	-10.3	-30.6	NA
260 Rem.	100	3200	2917	2652	2402	2165	2273	1889	1561	1281	1041	1.3	0	-6.3	-18.6	NA
260 Rem.	130	2800	2613	2433	2261	2096	2262	1970	1709	1476	1268	1.8	0	-7.7	-22.2	NA
260 Remington	125	2875	2669	2473	2285	2105	2294	1977	1697	1449	1230	1.71	0.0	-7.4	-21.4	NA
260 Remington	140	2750	2544	2347	2158	1979	2351	2011	1712	1448	1217	+2.2	0.0	-8.6	-24.6	NA
6.5 Creedmoor	120	3020	2815	2619	2430	2251	2430	2111	1827	1574	1350	1.4	0.0	-6.5	-18.9	NA
6.5 Creedmoor	120	3050	2850	2659	2476	2300	2479	2164	1884	1634	1310	1.4	0	-6.3	-18.3	NA
6.5 Creedmoor	140	2550	2380	2217	2060	1910	2021	1761	1527	1319	1134	2.3	0	-9.4	-27.0	NA
6.5 Creedmoor	140	2710	2557	2410	2267	2129	2283	2033	1805	1598	1410	1.9	0	-7.9	-22.6	NA
6.5 Creedmoor	140	2820	2654	2494	2339	2190	2472	2179	1915	1679	1467	1.7	0.0	-7.2	-20.6	NA
6.5 C. Superformance	129	2950	2756	2570	2392	2221	2492	2175	1892	1639	1417	1.5	0.0	-6.8	-19.7	NA
6.5x52R	117	2208	1856	1544	1287	1104	1267	895	620	431	317	0	-8.7	-32.2	—	NA
6.5x57	131	2543	2295	2060	1841	1638	1882	1532	1235	986	780	0	-5.1	-18.5	-42.1	NA
6.5-284 Norma	142	3025	2890	2758	2631	2507	2886	2634	2400	2183	1982	1.13	0.0	-5.7	-16.4	NA
6.5-284 Norma	156	2790	2531	2287	2056	-	2697	2220	1812	1465	-	1.9	0	-8.6	-	NA
6.71 (264) Phantom	120	3150	2929	2718	2517	2325	2645	2286	1969	1698	1440	+1.3	0.0	-6.0	-17.5	NA
6.5 Rem. Mag.	120	3210	2905	2621	2353	2102	2745	2248	1830	1475	1177	+2.5	+1.7	-4.1	-16.3	Disc.
264 Win. Mag.	100	3400	3104	2828	2568	2322	2566	2139	1775	1464	1197	1.1	0	-5.4	-16.1	NA
264 Win. Mag.	125	3200	2978	2767	2566	2373	2841	2461	2125	1827	1563	1.2	0	-5.8	-16.8	NA
264 Win. Mag.	130	3100	2900	2709	2526	2350	2773	2427	2118	1841	1594	1.3	0	-6.1	-17.6	NA
264 Win. Mag.	140	3030	2782	2548	2326	2114	2854	2406	2018	1682	1389	+2.5	+1.4	-5.1	-18.0	$24
6.5 Nosler	129	3400	3213	3035	2863	2698	3310	2957	2638	2348	2085	0.9	0	-4.7	-13.6	NA
6.5 Nosler	140	3300	3118	2943	2775	2613	3119	2784	2481	2205	1955	1.0	0	-5.0	-14.6	NA
6.71 (264) Blackbird	140	3480	3261	3053	2855	2665	3766	3307	2899	2534	2208	+2.4	+3.1	0.0	-7.4	NA
6.8 REM SPC	90	2840	2444	2083	1756	1469	1611	1194	867	616	431	2.2	0	-3.9	-32.0	NA
6.8 REM SPC	110	2570	2338	2118	1910	1716	1613	1335	1095	891	719	2.4	0.0	-6.3	-20.8	NA
6.8 REM SPC	120	2460	2250	2051	1863	1687	1612	1349	1121	925	758	2.3	0	-10.5	-31.1	NA
6.8mm Rem.	115	2775	2472	2190	1926	1683	1966	1561	1224	947	723	+2.1	0.0	-3.7	-9.4	NA

27

Cartridge	Bullet Wgt. Grs.	Muzzle	100 yds.	200 yds.	300 yds.	400 yds.	Muzzle	100 yds.	200 yds.	300 yds.	400 yds.	100 yds.	200 yds.	300 yds.	400 yds.	Price/box
270 Win. (Rem.)	115	2710	2482	2265	2059	NA	1875	1485	1161	896	NA	0.0	4.8	-17.3	0.0	NA
270 Win.	120	2675	2288	1935	1619	1351	1907	1395	998	699	486	2.6	0	-12.0	-37.4	NA
270 Win.	140	2940	2747	2563	2386	2216	2687	2346	2042	1770	1526	1.8	0	-6.8	-19.8	NA
270 Win. Supreme	130	3150	2881	2628	2388	2161	2865	2396	1993	1646	1348	1.3	0.0	-6.4	-18.9	NA
270 Win. Supreme	150	2930	2693	2468	2254	2051	2860	2416	2030	1693	1402	1.7	0.0	-7.4	-21.6	NA
270 W. Superformance	130	3200	2984	2788	2582	2393	2955	2570	2228	1924	1653	1.2	0.0	-5.7	-16.7	NA
270 Winchester	100	3430	3021	2649	2305	1988	2612	2027	1557	1179	877	+2.0	+1.0	-4.9	-17.5	$17
270 Winchester	130	3060	2776	2510	2259	2022	2702	2225	1818	1472	1180	+2.5	+1.4	-5.3	-18.2	$17
270 Winchester	135	3000	2780	2570	2369	2178	2697	2315	1979	1682	1421	+2.5	+1.4	-6.0	-17.6	$23
270 Winchester*	140	2940	2700	2480	2260	2060	2685	2270	1905	1590	1315	+2.5	+1.8	-4.6	-17.9	$20

Cartridge	Bullet Wgt. Grs.	VELOCITY (fps)					ENERGY (ft. lbs.)					TRAJ. (in.)				Est. Price/box
		Muzzle	100 yds.	200 yds.	300 yds.	400 yds.	Muzzle	100 yds.	200 yds.	300 yds.	400 yds.	100 yds.	200 yds.	300 yds.	400 yds.	
270 Winchester*	150	2850	2585	2336	2100	1879	2705	2226	1817	1468	1175	+2.5	+1.2	-6.5	-22.0	$17
270 WSM	130	3275	3041	2820	2609	2408	3096	2669	2295	1564	1673	1.1	0.0	-5.5	-16.1	NA
270 WSM	140	3125	2865	2619	2386	2165	3035	2559	2132	1769	1457	1.4	0.0	-6.5	-19.0	NA
270 WSM	150	3000	2795	2599	2412	2232	2997	2601	2250	1937	1659	1.5	0	-6.6	-19.2	NA
270 WSM	150	3120	2923	2734	2554	2380	3242	2845	2490	2172	1886	1.3	0.0	-5.9	-17.2	NA
270 Wea. Mag.	100	3760	3380	3033	2712	2412	3139	2537	2042	1633	1292	+2.0	+2.4	-1.2	-10.1	$32
270 Wea. Mag.	130	3375	3119	2878	2649	2432	3287	2808	2390	2026	1707	+2.5	-2.9	-0.9	-9.9	$32
270 Wea. Mag.	130	3450	3194	2958	2732	2517	3435	2949	2525	2143	1828	1.0	0	-4.9	-14.5	NA
270 Wea. Mag.*	150	3245	3036	2837	2647	2465	3507	3070	2681	2334	2023	+2.5	+2.6	-1.8	-11.4	$47

7mm

Cartridge	Bullet Wgt. Grs.	Muzzle	100 yds.	200 yds.	300 yds.	400 yds.	Muzzle	100 yds.	200 yds.	300 yds.	400 yds.	100 yds.	200 yds.	300 yds.	400 yds.	Est. Price/box
7mm BR	140	2216	2012	1821	1643	1481	1525	1259	1031	839	681	+2.0	-3.7	-20.0	0.0	$23
7mm Mauser*	139/140	2660	2435	2221	2018	1827	2199	1843	1533	1266	1037	+2.5	0.0	-9.6	-27.7	$17
7mm Mauser	139	2740	2556	2379	2209	2046	2317	2016	1747	1506	1292	1.9	0	-8.1	-23.3	NA
7mm Mauser	154	2690	2490	2300	2120	1940	2475	2120	1810	1530	1285	+2.5	+0.8	-7.5	-23.5	$17
7mm Mauser	175	2440	2137	1857	1603	1382	2313	1774	1340	998	742	+2.5	-1.7	-16.1	0.0	$17
7x30 Waters	120	2700	2300	1930	1600	1330	1940	1405	990	685	470	+2.5	-0.2	-12.3	0.0	$18
7mm-08 Rem.	120	2675	2435	2207	1992	1790	1907	1579	1298	1057	854	2.2	0	-9.4	-27.5	NA
7mm-08 Rem.	120	3000	2725	2467	2223	1992	2398	1979	1621	1316	1058	+2.0	0.0	-7.6	-22.3	$18
7mm-08 Rem.	139	2840	2608	2387	2177	1978	2489	2098	1758	1463	1207	1.8	0	-7.9	-23.2	NA
7mm-08 Rem.*	140	2860	2625	2402	2189	1988	2542	2142	1793	1490	1228	+2.5	+0.8	-6.9	-21.9	$18
7mm-08 Rem.	154	2715	2510	2315	2128	1950	2520	2155	1832	1548	1300	+2.5	+1.0	-7.0	-22.7	$23
7-08 R. Superformance	139	2950	2857	2571	2393	2222	2686	2345	2040	1768	1524	1.5	0.0	-6.8	-19.7	NA
7x64mm	173	2526	2260	2010	1777	1565	2452	1962	1552	1214	941	0	-5.3	-19.3	-44.4	NA
7x64mm Bren.	140	2950	2710	2483	2266	2061	2705	2283	1910	1597	1320	1.5	0.0	-2.9	-7.3	$24.50
7x64mm Bren.	154	2820	2610	2420	2230	2050	2720	2335	1995	1695	1430	+2.5	+1.4	-5.7	-19.9	NA
7x64mm Bren.*	160	2850	2669	2495	2327	2166	2885	2530	2211	1924	1667	+2.5	+1.6	-4.8	-17.8	$24
7x64mm Bren.	175	2650	2445	2248	2061	1883	2728	2322	1964	1650	1378	2.2	0	-9.1	-26.4	$24.50
7x65mmR	173	2608	2337	2082	1844	1626	2613	2098	1666	1307	1015	0	-4.9	-17.9	-41.9	NA
275 Rigby	139	2680	2456	2242	2040	1848	2217	1861	1552	1284	1054	2.2	0	-9.1	-26.5	NA
284 Winchester	150	2860	2595	2344	2108	1886	2724	2243	1830	1480	1185	+2.5	+0.8	-7.3	-23.2	$24
280 R. Superformance	139	3090	2890	2699	2516	2341	2946	2578	2249	1954	1691	1.3	0.0	-6.1	-17.7	NA
280 Rem.	139	3090	2891	2700	2518	2343	2947	2579	2250	1957	1694	1.3	0	-6.1	-17.7	NA
280 Remington	140	3000	2758	2528	2309	2102	2797	2363	1986	1657	1373	+2.5	+1.4	-5.2	-18.3	$17
280 Remington*	150	2890	2624	2373	2135	1912	2781	2293	1875	1518	1217	+2.5	+0.8	-7.1	-22.6	$17
280 Remington	160	2840	2637	2442	2556	2078	2866	2471	2120	1809	1535	+2.5	+0.8	-6.7	-21.0	$20
280 Remington	165	2820	2510	2220	1950	1701	2913	2308	1805	1393	1060	+2.5	+0.4	-8.8	-26.5	$17
280 Ack. Imp.	140	3150	2946	2752	2566	2387	3084	2698	2354	2047	1772	1.3	0	-5.8	-17.0	NA
280 Ack. Imp.	150	2900	2712	2533	2360	2194	2800	2450	2136	1855	1603	1.6	0	-7.0	-20.3	NA
280 Ack. Imp.	160	2950	2751	2561	2379	2205	3091	2686	2331	2011	1727	1.5	0	-6.9	-19.9	NA
7x61mm S&H Sup.	154	3060	2720	2400	2100	1820	3200	2520	1965	1505	1135	+2.5	+1.8	-5.0	-19.8	NA
7mm Dakota	160	3200	3001	2811	2630	2455	3637	3200	2808	2456	2140	+2.1	+1.9	-2.8	-12.5	NA
7mm Rem. Mag.	139	3190	2986	2791	2605	2427	3141	2752	2405	2095	1817	1.2	0	-5.7	-16.5	NA
7mm Rem. Mag. (Rem.)	140	2710	2482	2265	2059	NA	2283	1915	1595	1318	NA	0.0	-4.5	-1.57	0.0	NA
7mm Rem. Mag.*	139/140	3150	2930	2710	2510	2320	3085	2660	2290	1960	1670	+2.5	+2.4	-2.4	-12.7	$21
7mm Rem. Mag.	150/154	3110	2830	2568	2320	2085	3221	2667	2196	1792	1448	+2.5	+1.6	-4.6	-16.5	$21
7mm Rem. Mag.*	160/162	2950	2730	2520	2320	2120	3090	2650	2250	1910	1600	+2.5	+1.8	-4.4	-17.8	$34
7mm Rem. Mag.	165	2900	2699	2507	2324	2147	3081	2669	2303	1978	1689	+2.5	+1.2	-5.9	-19.0	$28
7mm Rem Mag.	175	2860	2645	2440	2244	2057	3178	2718	2313	1956	1644	+2.5	+1.0	-6.5	-20.7	$21
7 R.M. Superformance	139	3240	3033	2836	2648	2467	3239	2839	2482	2163	1877	1.1	0.0	-5.5	-15.9	NA
7 R.M. Superformance	154	3100	2914	2736	2565	2401	3286	2904	2560	2250	1970	1.3	0.0	-5.9	-17.2	NA
7mm Rem. SA ULTRA MAG	140	3175	2934	2707	2490	2283	3033	2676	2277	1927	1620	1.3	0.0	-6	-17.7	NA
7mm Rem. SA ULTRA MAG	150	3110	2828	2563	2313	2077	3221	2663	2188	1782	1437	2.5	2.1	-3.6	-15.8	NA
7mm Rem. SA ULTRA MAG	160	2850	2676	2508	2347	2192	2885	2543	2235	1957	1706	1.7	0	-7.2	-20.7	NA
7mm Rem. SA ULTRA MAG	160	2960	2762	2572	2390	2215	3112	2709	2350	2029	1743	2.6	2.2	-3.6	-15.4	NA
7mm Rem. WSM	140	3225	3008	2801	2603	2414	3233	2812	2438	2106	1812	1.2	0.0	-5.6	-16.4	NA
7mm Rem. WSM	160	2990	2744	2512	2081	1883	3176	2675	2241	1864	1538	1.6	0.0	-7.1	-20.8	NA
7mm Wea. Mag.	139	3300	3091	2891	2701	2519	3361	2948	2580	2252	1958	1.1	0	-5.2	-15.2	NA
7mm Wea. Mag.	140	3225	2970	2729	2501	2283	3233	2741	2315	1943	1621	+2.5	+2.0	-3.2	-14.0	$35
7mm Wea. Mag.	140	3340	3127	2925	2732	2546	3467	3040	2659	2320	2016	0	-2.1	-8.2	-19	NA
7mm Wea. Mag.	150	3175	2957	2751	2553	2364	3357	2913	2520	2171	1861	0	-2.5	-9.6	-22	NA
7mm Wea. Mag.	154	3260	3023	2799	2586	2382	3539	3044	2609	2227	1890	+2.5	+2.8	-1.5	-10.8	$32
7mm Wea. Mag.*	160	3200	3004	2816	2637	2464	3637	3205	2817	2469	2156	+2.5	+2.7	-1.5	-10.6	$47

Cartridge	Bullet Wgt. Grs.	VELOCITY (fps)					ENERGY (ft. lbs.)					TRAJ. (in.)				Est. Price/box
		Muzzle	100 yds.	200 yds.	300 yds.	400 yds.	Muzzle	100 yds.	200 yds.	300 yds.	400 yds.	100 yds.	200 yds.	300 yds.	400 yds.	
7mm Wea. Mag.	165	2950	2747	2553	2367	2189	3188	2765	2388	2053	1756	+2.5	+1.8	-4.2	-16.4	$43
7mm Wea. Mag.	175	2910	2693	2486	2288	2098	3293	2818	2401	2033	1711	+2.5	+1.2	-5.9	-19.4	$35
7.21(.284) Tomahawk	140	3300	3118	2943	2774	2612	3386	3022	2693	2393	2122	2.3	3.2	0.0	-7.7	NA
7mm STW	140	3300	3086	2889	2697	2513	3384	2966	2594	2261	1963	0	-2.1	-8.5	-19.6	NA
7mm STW	140	3325	3064	2818	2585	2364	3436	2918	2468	2077	1737	+2.3	+1.8	-3.0	-13.1	NA
7mm STW	150	3175	2957	2751	2553	2364	3357	2913	2520	2171	1861	0	-2.5	-9.6	-22	NA
7mm STW	175	2900	2760	2625	2493	2366	3267	2960	2677	2416	2175	0	-3.1	-11.2	-24.9	NA
7mm STW Supreme	160	3150	2894	2652	2422	2204	3526	2976	2499	2085	1727	1.3	0.0	-6.3	-18.5	NA
7mm Rem. Ultra Mag.	140	3425	3184	2956	2740	2534	3646	3151	2715	2333	1995	1.7	1.6	-2.6	-11.4	NA
7mm Rem. Ultra Mag.	160	3225	3035	2854	2680	2512	3694	3273	2894	2551	2242	0	-2.3	-8.8	-20.2	NA
7mm Rem. Ultra Mag.	174	3040	2896	2756	2621	2490	3590	3258	2952	2669	2409	0	-2.6	-9.9	-22.2	NA
7mm Firehawk	140	3625	3373	3135	2909	2695	4084	3536	3054	2631	2258	+2.2	+2.9	0.0	-7.03	NA
7.21 (.284) Firebird	140	3750	3522	3306	3101	2905	4372	3857	3399	2990	2625	1.6	2.4	0.0	-6.0	NA
.28 Nosler	160	3300	3114	2930	2753	2583	3883	3444	3049	2693	2371	1.1	0	-5.1	-14.9	$78
30																
300 ACC Blackout	110	2150	1886	1646	1432	1254	1128	869	661	501	384	0	8.3	-29.6	-67.8	NA
300 AAC Blackout	125	2250	2031	1826	1636	1464	1404	1145	926	743	595	0	-7	-24.4	-54.8	NA
300 AAC Blackout	220	1000	968	-	-	-	488	457	-	-	-	0	-	-	-	-
30 Carbine	110	1990	1567	1236	1035	923	977	600	373	262	208	0.0	-13.5	0.0	0.0	$28**
30 Carbine	110	2000	1601	1279	1067	—	977	626	399	278	—	0	-12.9	-47.2	—	NA
300 Whisper	110	2375	2094	1834	1597	NA	1378	1071	822	623	NA	3.2	0.0	-13.6	NA	NA
300 Whisper	208	1020	988	959	NA	NA	480	451	422	NA	NA	0.0	34.10	NA	NA	NA
303 Savage	190	1890	1612	1327	1183	1055	1507	1096	794	591	469	+2.5	-7.6	0.0	0.0	$24
30 Remington	170	2120	1822	1555	1328	1153	1696	1253	913	666	502	+2.5	-4.7	-26.3	0.0	$20
7.62x39mm Rus.	123	2360	2049	1764	1511	1296	1521	1147	850	623	459	3.4	0	-14.7	-44.7	NA
7.62x39mm Rus.	123/125	2300	2030	1780	1550	1350	1445	1125	860	655	500	+2.5	-2.0	-17.5	0.0	$13
30-30 Win.	55	3400	2693	2085	1570	1187	1412	886	521	301	172	+2.0	0.0	-10.2	-35.0	$18
30-30 Win.	125	2570	2090	1660	1320	1080	1830	1210	770	480	320	-2.0	-2.6	-19.9	0.0	$13
30-30 Win.	140	2500	2198	1918	1662	—	1943	1501	1143	858	—	2.9	0	-12.4	—	NA
30-30 Win.	150	2390	2040	1723	1447	1225	1902	1386	989	697	499	0.0	-7.5	-27.0	-63.0	NA
30-30 Win. Supreme	150	2480	2095	1747	1446	1209	2049	1462	1017	697	487	0.0	-6.5	-24.5	0.0	NA
30-30 Win.	160	2300	1997	1719	1473	1268	1879	1416	1050	771	571	+2.5	-2.9	-20.2	0.0	$18
30-30 Win. Lever Evolution	160	2400	2150	1916	1699	NA	2046	1643	1304	1025	NA	3.0	0.2	-12.1	NA	NA
30-30 PMC Cowboy	170	1300	1198	1121	—	—	638	474	—	—	—	0.0	-27.0	0.0	0.0	NA
30-30 Win.*	170	2200	1895	1619	1381	1191	1827	1355	989	720	535	+2.5	-5.8	-23.6	0.0	$13
300 Savage	150	2630	2354	2094	1853	1631	2303	1845	1462	1143	886	+2.5	-0.4	-10.1	-30.7	$17
300 Savage	150	2740	2499	2272	2056	1852	2500	2081	1718	1407	1143	2.1	0	-8.8	-25.8	NA
300 Savage	180	2350	2137	1935	1754	1570	2207	1825	1496	1217	985	+2.5	-1.6	-15.2	0.0	$17
30-40 Krag	180	2430	2213	2007	1813	1632	2360	1957	1610	1314	1064	+2.5	-1.4	-13.8	0.0	$18
7.65x53mm Arg.	180	2590	2390	2200	2010	1830	2685	2280	1925	1615	1345	+2.5	0.0	-27.6	0.0	NA
7.5x53mm Argentine	150	2785	2519	2269	2032	1814	2583	2113	1714	1376	1096	+2.0	0.0	-8.8	-25.5	NA
308 Marlin Express	140	2800	2532	2279	2040	1818	2437	1992	1614	1294	1207	2.0	0	-8.7	-25.8	NA
308 Marlin Express	160	2660	2430	2226	2026	1836	2513	2111	1761	1457	1197	3.0	1.7	-6.7	-23.5	NA
307 Winchester	150	2760	2321	1924	1575	1289	2530	1795	1233	826	554	+2.5	-1.5	-13.6	0.0	Disc.
7.5x55 Swiss	180	2650	2450	2250	2060	1880	2805	2390	2020	1700	1415	+2.5	+0.6	-8.1	-24.9	NA
7.5x55mm Swiss	165	2720	2515	2319	2132	1954	2710	2317	1970	1665	1398	+2.0	0.0	-8.5	-24.6	NA
30 Remington AR	123/125	2800	2465	2154	1867	1606	2176	1686	1288	967	716	2.1	0.0	-9.7	-29.4	NA
308 Winchester	55	3770	3215	2726	2286	1888	1735	1262	907	638	435	-2.0	+1.4	-3.8	-15.8	$22
308 Win.	110	3165	2830	2520	2230	1960	2447	1956	1551	1215	938	1.4	0	-6.9	-20.9	NA
308 Win. PDX1	120	2850	2497	2171	NA	NA	2164	1662	1256	NA	NA	0.0	-2.8	NA	NA	NA
308 Winchester	150	2820	2533	2263	2009	1774	2648	2137	1705	1344	1048	+2.5	+0.4	-8.5	-26.1	$17
308 W. Superformance	150	3000	2772	2555	2348	1962	2997	2558	2173	1836	1540	1.5	0.0	-6.9	-20.0	NA
308 Win.	155	2775	2553	2342	2141	1950	2650	2243	1887	1577	1308	1.9	0	-8.3	-24.2	NA
308 Win.	155	2850	2640	2438	2247	2064	2795	2398	2047	1737	1466	1.8	0	-7.5	-22.1	NA
308 Winchester	165	2700	2440	2194	1963	1748	2670	2180	1763	1411	1199	+2.5	0.0	-9.7	-28.5	$20
308 Winchester	168	2680	2493	2314	2143	1979	2678	2318	1998	1713	1460	+2.5	0.0	-8.9	-25.3	$18
308 Win. Super Match	168	2870	2647	2462	2284	2114	3008	2613	2261	1946	1667	1.7	0.0	-7.5	-21.6	NA
308 Win. (Fed.)	170	2000	1740	1510	NA	NA	1510	1145	860	NA	NA	0.0	0.0	0.0	0.0	NA
300 Winchester	178	2620	2415	2220	2034	1857	2713	2306	1948	1635	1363	+2.5	0.0	-9.6	-27.6	$23
308 Win. Super Match	178	2780	2609	2444	2285	2132	3054	2690	2361	2064	1797	1.8	0.0	-7.6	-21.9	NA
308 Winchester*	180	2620	2393	2178	1974	1782	2743	2288	1896	1557	1269	+2.5	-0.2	-10.2	-28.5	$17
30-06 Spfd.	55	4080	3485	2965	2502	2083	2033	1483	1074	764	530	+2.0	+1.9	-2.1	-11.7	$22

Cartridge	Bullet Wgt. Grs.	VELOCITY (fps)					ENERGY (ft. lbs.)					TRAJ. (in.)				Est. Price/box
		Muzzle	100 yds.	200 yds.	300 yds.	400 yds.	Muzzle	100 yds.	200 yds.	300 yds.	400 yds.	100 yds.	200 yds.	300 yds.	400 yds.	
30-06 Spfd. (Rem.)	125	2660	2335	2034	1757	NA	1964	1513	1148	856	NA	0.0	-5.2	-18.9	0.0	NA
30-06 Spfd.	125	2700	2412	2143	1891	1660	2023	1615	1274	993	765	2.3	0	-9.9	-29.5	NA
30-06 Spfd.	125	3140	2780	2447	2138	1853	2736	2145	1662	1279	953	+2.0	+1.0	-6.2	-21.0	$17
30-06 Spfd.	150	2910	2617	2342	2083	1853	2820	2281	1827	1445	1135	+2.5	+0.8	-7.2	-23.4	$17
30-06 Superformance	150	3080	2848	2617	2417	2216	3159	2700	2298	1945	1636	1.4	0.0	-6.4	-18.9	NA
30-06 Spfd.	152	2910	2654	2413	2184	1968	2858	2378	1965	1610	1307	+2.5	+1.0	-6.6	-21.3	$23
30-06 Spfd.*	165	2800	2534	2283	2047	1825	2872	2352	1909	1534	1220	+2.5	+0.4	-8.4	-25.5	$17
30-06 Spfd.	168	2710	2522	2346	2169	2003	2739	2372	2045	1754	1497	+2.5	+0.4	-8.0	-23.5	$18
30-06 M1 Garand	168	2710	2523	2343	2171	2006	2739	2374	2048	1758	1501	2.3	0	-8.6	-24.6	NA
30-06 Spfd. (Fed.)	170	2000	1740	1510	NA	NA	1510	1145	860	NA	NA	0.0	0.0	0.0	0.0	NA
30-06 Spfd.	178	2720	2511	2311	2121	1939	2924	2491	2111	1777	1486	+2.5	+0.4	-8.2	-24.6	$23
30-06 Spfd.*	180	2700	2469	2250	2042	1846	2913	2436	2023	1666	1362	-2.5	0.0	-9.3	-27.0	$17
30-06 Superformance	180	2820	2630	2447	2272	2104	3178	2764	2393	2063	1769	1.8	0.0	-7.6	-21.9	NA
30-06 Spfd.	220	2410	2130	1870	1632	1422	2837	2216	1708	1301	988	+2.5	-1.7	-18.0	0.0	$17
30-06 High Energy	180	2880	2690	2500	2320	2150	3315	2880	2495	2150	1845	+1.7	0.0	-7.2	-21.0	NA
30 T/C	150	2920	2696	2483	2280	2087	2849	2421	2054	1732	1450	1.7	0	-7.3	-21.3	NA
30 T/C Superformance	150	3000	2772	2555	2348	2151	2997	2558	2173	1836	1540	1.5	0.0	-6.9	-20.0	NA
30 T/C Superformance	165	2850	2644	2447	2258	2078	2975	2560	2193	1868	1582	1.7	0.0	-7.6	-22.0	NA
300 Rem SA Ultra Mag	150	3200	2901	2622	2359	2112	3410	2803	2290	1854	1485	1.3	0.0	-6.4	-19.1	NA
300 Rem SA Ultra Mag	165	3075	2792	2527	2276	2040	3464	2856	2339	1898	1525	1.5	0.0	-7	-20.7	NA
300 Rem SA Ultra Mag	180	2960	2761	2571	2389	2214	3501	3047	2642	2280	1959	2.6	2.2	-3.6	-15.4	NA
300 Rem. SA Ultra Mag	200	2800	2644	2494	2348	2208	3841	3104	2761	2449	2164	0	-3.5	-12.5	-27.9	NA
7.82 (308) Patriot	150	3250	2999	2762	2537	2323	3519	2997	2542	2145	1798	+1.2	0.0	-5.8	-16.9	NA
300 RCM	150	3265	3023	2794	2577	2369	3550	3043	2600	2211	1870	1.2	0	-5.6	-16.5	NA
300 RCM Superformance	150	3310	3065	2833	2613	2404	3648	3128	2673	2274	1924	1.1	0.0	-5.4	-16.0	NA
300 RCM Superformance	165	3185	2964	2753	2552	2360	3716	3217	2776	2386	2040	1.2	0.0	-5.8	-17.0	NA
300 RCM Superformance	180	3040	2840	2649	2466	2290	3693	3223	2804	2430	2096	1.4	0.0	-6.4	-18.5	NA
300 WSM	150	3300	3061	2834	2619	2414	3628	3121	2676	2285	1941	1.1	0.0	-5.4	-15.9	NA
300 WSM	180	2970	2741	2524	2317	2120	3526	3005	2547	2147	1797	1.6	0.0	-7.0	-20.5	NA
300 WSM	180	3010	2923	2734	2554	2380	3242	2845	2490	2172	1886	1.3	0	-5.9	-17.2	NA
300 WSM	190	2875	2729	2588	2451	2319	3486	3142	2826	2535	2269	0	3.2	-11.5	-25.7	NA
308 Norma Mag.	180	2975	2787	2608	2435	2269	3536	3105	2718	2371	2058	0	-3	-11.1	-25.0	NA
308 Norma Mag.	180	3020	2820	2630	2440	2270	3645	3175	2755	2385	2050	+2.5	+2.0	-3.5	-14.8	NA
300 Dakota	200	3000	2824	2656	2493	2336	3996	3542	3131	2760	2423	+2.2	+1.5	-4.0	-15.2	NA
300 H&H Mag.	180	2870	2678	2494	2318	2148	3292	2866	2486	2147	1844	1.7	0	-7.3	-21.6	NA
300 H&H Magnum*	180	2880	2640	2412	2196	1990	3315	2785	2325	1927	1583	+2.5	+0.8	-6.8	-21.7	$24
300 H&H Mag.	200	2750	2596	2447	2303	2164	3357	2992	2659	2355	2079	1.8	0	-7.6	-21.8	NA
300 H&H Magnum	220	2550	2267	2002	1757	NA	3167	2510	1958	1508	NA	-2.5	-0.4	-12.0	0.0	NA
300 Win. Mag.	150	3290	2951	2636	2342	2068	3605	2900	2314	1827	1424	+2.5	+1.9	-3.8	-15.8	$22
300 WM Superformance	150	3400	3150	2914	2690	2477	3850	3304	2817	2409	2043	1.0	0.0	-5.1	-15.0	NA
300 Win. Mag.	165	3100	2877	2665	2462	2269	3522	3033	2603	2221	1897	+2.5	+2.4	-3.0	-16.9	$24
300 Win. Mag.	178	2900	2760	2568	2375	2191	3509	3030	2606	2230	1897	+2.5	+1.4	-5.0	-17.6	$29
300 Win. Mag.	178	2960	2770	2588	2413	2245	3463	3032	2647	2301	1992	1.5	0	-6.7	-19.4	NA
300 WM Super Match	178	2960	2770	2587	2412	2243	3462	3031	2645	2298	1988	1.5	0.0	-6.7	-19.4	NA
300 Win. Mag.*	180	2960	2745	2540	2344	2157	3501	3011	2578	2196	1859	+2.5	+1.2	-5.5	-18.5	$22
300 WM Superformance	180	3130	2927	2732	2546	2366	3917	3424	2983	2589	2238	1.3	0.0	-5.9	-17.3	NA
300 Win. Mag.	190	2885	1691	2506	2327	2156	3511	3055	2648	2285	1961	+2.5	+1.2	-5.7	-19.0	$26
300 Win. Mag.	195	2930	2760	2596	2438	2286	3717	3297	2918	2574	2262	1.5	0	-6.7	-19.4	NA
300 Win. Mag.*	200	2825	2595	2376	2167	1970	3545	2991	2508	2086	1742	-2.5	+1.6	-4.7	-17.2	$36
300 Win. Mag.	220	2680	2448	2228	2020	1823	3508	2927	2424	1993	1623	+2.5	0.0	-9.5	-27.5	$23
300 Rem. Ultra Mag.	150	3450	3208	2980	2762	2556	3964	3427	2956	2541	2175	1.7	1.5	-2.6	-11.2	NA
300 Rem. Ultra Mag.	150	2910	2686	2473	2279	2077	2820	2403	2037	1716	1436	1.7	0.0	-7.4	-21.5	NA
300 Rem. Ultra Mag.	165	3350	3099	2862	2938	2424	4110	3518	3001	2549	2152	1.1	0	-5.3	-15.6	NA
300 Rem. Ultra Mag.	180	3250	3037	2834	2640	2454	4221	3686	3201	2786	2407	2.4	0.0	-3.0	-12.7	NA
300 Rem. Ultra Mag.	180	2960	2774	2505	2294	2093	3501	2971	2508	2103	1751	2.7	2.2	-3.8	-16.4	NA
300 Rem. Ultra Mag.	200	3032	2791	2562	2345	2138	4083	3459	2916	2442	2030	1.5	0.0	-6.8	-19.9	NA
300 Rem. Ultra Mag.	210	2920	2790	2665	2543	2424	3975	3631	3311	3015	2740	1.5	0	-6.4	-18.1	NA
300 Wea. Mag.	100	3900	3441	3038	2652	2305	3714	2891	2239	1717	1297	+2.0	+2.6	-0.6	-8.7	$32
300 Wea. Mag.	150	3375	3126	2892	2670	2459	3794	3255	2786	2374	2013	1.0	0	-5.2	-15.3	NA
300 Wea. Mag.	150	3600	3307	3033	2776	2533	4316	3642	3064	2566	2137	+2.5	+3.2	0.0	-8.1	$32
300 Wea. Mag.	165	3140	2921	2713	2515	2325	3612	3126	2697	2317	1980	1.3	0	-6.0	-17.5	NA
300 Wea. Mag.	165	3450	3210	3000	2792	2593	4360	3796	3297	2855	2464	+2.5	+3.2	0.0	-7.8	NA

Cartridge	Bullet Wgt. Grs.	VELOCITY (fps)					ENERGY (ft. lbs.)					TRAJ. (in.)				Est. Price/box
		Muzzle	100 yds.	200 yds.	300 yds.	400 yds.	Muzzle	100 yds.	200 yds.	300 yds.	400 yds.	100 yds.	200 yds.	300 yds.	400 yds.	
300 Wea. Mag.	178	3120	2902	2695	2497	2308	3847	3329	2870	2464	2104	+2.5	-1.7	-3.6	-14.7	$43
300 Wea. Mag.	180	3330	3110	2910	2710	2520	4430	3875	3375	2935	2540	+1.0	0.0	-5.2	-15.1	NA
300 Wea. Mag.	190	3030	2830	2638	2455	2279	3873	3378	2936	2542	2190	+2.5	+1.6	-4.3	-16.0	$38
300 Wea. Mag.	220	2850	2541	2283	1964	1736	3967	3155	2480	1922	1471	+2.5	+0.4	-8.5	-26.4	$35
300 Pegasus	180	3500	3319	3145	2978	2817	4896	4401	3953	3544	3172	+2.28	+2.89	0.0	-6.79	NA
31																
32-20 Win.	100	1210	1021	913	834	769	325	231	185	154	131	0.0	-32.3	0.0	0.0	$23**
303 British	150	2685	2441	2211	1993	1789	2401	1985	1628	1323	1066	2.2	0	-9.3	-27.4	NA
303 British	180	2460	2124	1817	1542	1311	2418	1803	1319	950	687	+2.5	-1.8	-16.8	0.0	$18
303 Light Mag.	150	2830	2570	2325	2094	1884	2667	2199	1800	1461	1185	+2.0	0.0	-8.4	-24.6	NA
7.62x54mm Rus.	146	2950	2730	2520	2320	NA	2820	2415	2055	1740	NA	+2.5	+2.0	-4.4	-17.7	NA
7.62x54mm Rus.	174	2800	2607	2422	2245	2075	3029	2626	2267	1947	1664	1.8	0	-7.8	-22.4	NA
7.62x54mm Rus.	180	2580	2370	2180	2000	1820	2650	2250	1900	1590	1100	+2.5	0.0	-9.8	-28.5	NA
7.7x58mm Jap.	150	2640	2399	2170	1054	1752	2321	1916	1568	1271	1022	+2.3	0.0	-9.7	-28.5	NA
7.7x58mm Jap.	180	2500	2300	2100	1920	1750	2490	2105	1770	1475	1225	+2.5	0.0	-10.4	-30.2	NA
8mm																
8x56 R	205	2400	2188	1987	1797	1621	2621	2178	1796	1470	1196	+2.9	0.0	-11.7	-34.3	NA
8x57mm JS Mau.	165	2850	2520	2210	1930	1670	2965	2330	1795	1360	1015	+2.5	+1.0	-7.7	0.0	NA
32 Win. Special	165	2410	2145	1897	1669	NA	2128	1685	1318	1020	NA	2.0	0.0	-13.0	-19.9	NA
32 Win. Special	170	2250	1921	1626	1372	1175	1911	1393	998	710	521	+2.5	-3.5	-22.9	0.0	$14
8mm Mauser	170	2360	1969	1622	1333	1123	2102	1464	993	671	476	+2.5	-3.1	-22.2	0.0	$18
8mm Mauser	196	2500	2338	2182	2032	1888	2720	2379	2072	1797	1552	2.4	0	-9.8	-27.9	NA
325 WSM	180	3060	2841	2632	2432	2242	3743	3226	2769	2365	2009	+1.4	0.0	-6.4	-18.7	NA
325 WSM	200	2950	2753	2565	2384	2210	3866	3367	2922	2524	2170	+1.5	0.0	-6.8	-19.8	NA
325 WSM	220	2840	2605	2382	2169	1968	3941	3316	2772	2300	1893	+1.8	0.0	-8.0	-23.3	NA
8mm Rem. Mag.	185	3080	2761	2464	2186	1927	3896	3131	2494	1963	1525	+2.5	+1.4	-5.5	-19.7	$30
8mm Rem. Mag.	220	2830	2581	2346	2123	1913	3912	3254	2688	2201	1787	+2.5	+0.6	-7.6	-23.5	Disc.
33																
338 Federal	180	2830	2590	2350	2130	1930	3200	2670	2215	1820	1480	1.8	0.0	-8.2	-23.9	NA
338 Marlin Express	200	2565	2365	2174	1992	1820	2922	2484	2099	1762	1471	3.0	1.2	-7.9	-25.9	NA
338 Federal	185	2750	2550	2350	2160	1980	3105	2660	2265	1920	1615	1.9	0.0	-8.3	-24.1	NA
338 Federal	210	2630	2410	2200	2010	1820	3225	2710	2265	1880	1545	2.3	0.0	-9.4	-27.3	NA
338 Federal MSR	185	2680	2459	2230	2020	1820	2950	2460	2035	1670	1360	2.2	0.0	-9.2	-26.8	NA
338-06	200	2750	2553	2364	2184	2011	3358	2894	2482	2118	1796	+1.9	0.0	-8.22	-23.6	NA
330 Dakota	250	2900	2719	2545	2378	2217	4668	4103	3595	3138	2727	+2.3	+1.3	-5.0	-17.5	NA
338 Lapua	250	2900	2685	2481	2285	2098	4668	4002	2416	2899	2444	1.7	0	-7.3	-21.3	NA
338 Lapua	250	2963	2795	2640	2493	NA	4842	4341	3881	3458	NA	+1.9	0.0	-7.9	0.0	NA
338 Lapua	285	2745	2616	2491	2369	2251	4768	4331	3926	3552	3206	1.8	0	-7.4	-21	NA
338 Lapua	300	2660	2544	2432	2322	-	4715	4313	3940	3592	-	1.9	0	-7.8	-	NA
338 RCM Superformance	185	2980	2755	2542	2338	2143	3647	3118	2653	2242	1887	1.5	0.0	-6.9	-20.3	NA
338 RCM Superformance	200	2950	2744	2547	2358	2177	3846	3342	2879	2468	2104	1.6	0.0	-6.9	-20.1	NA
338 RCM Superformance	225	2750	2575	2407	2245	2089	3778	3313	2894	2518	2180	1.9	0.0	-7.9	-22.7	NA
338 WM Superformance	185	3080	2850	2632	2424	2226	3896	3337	2845	2413	2034	1.4	0.0	-6.4	-18.8	NA
338 Win. Mag.	200	3030	2820	2620	2429	2246	4077	3532	3049	2621	2240	1.4	0	-6.5	-18.9	NA
338 Win. Mag.*	210	2830	2590	2370	2150	1940	3735	3130	2610	2155	1760	+2.5	+1.4	-6.0	-20.9	$33
338 Win. Mag.*	225	2785	2517	2266	2029	1808	3871	3165	2565	2057	1633	+2.5	+0.4	-8.5	-25.9	$27
338 WM Superformance	225	2840	2758	2582	2414	2252	4318	3798	3331	2911	2533	1.5	0.0	-6.8	-19.5	NA
338 Win. Mag.	230	2780	2573	2375	2186	2005	3948	3382	2881	2441	2054	+2.5	+1.2	-6.3	-21.0	$40
338 Win. Mag.*	250	2660	2456	2261	2075	1898	3927	3348	2837	2389	1999	+2.5	+0.2	-9.0	-26.2	$27
338 Ultra Mag.	250	2860	2645	2440	2244	2057	4540	3882	3303	2794	2347	1.7	0.0	-7.6	-22.1	NA
338 Lapua Match	250	2900	2760	2625	2494	2366	4668	4229	3825	3452	3108	1.5	0.0	-6.6	-18.8	NA
338 Lapua Match	285	2745	2623	2504	2388	2275	4768	4352	3966	3608	3275	1.8	0.0	-7.3	-20.8	NA
8.59(.338) Galaxy	200	3100	2899	2707	2524	2347	4269	3734	3256	2829	2446	3	3.8	0.0	-9.3	NA
340 Wea. Mag.*	210	3250	2991	2746	2515	2295	4924	4170	3516	2948	2455	+2.5	+1.9	-1.8	-11.8	$56
340 Wea. Mag.*	250	3000	2806	2621	2443	2272	4995	4371	3812	3311	2864	+2.5	+2.0	-3.5	-14.8	$56
338 A-Square	250	3120	2799	2500	2220	1958	5403	4348	3469	2736	2128	+2.5	+2.7	-1.5	-10.5	NA
338-378 Wea. Mag.	225	3180	2974	2778	2591	2410	5052	4420	3856	3353	2902	3.1	3.8	0.0	-8.9	NA
338 Titan	225	3230	3010	2800	2600	2409	5211	4524	3916	3377	2898	+3.07	+3.0	0.0	-8.95	NA
338 Excalibur	200	0000	3361	3134	2920	2715	5755	5015	4363	3785	3274	+2.23	+2.87	0.0	-6.99	NA
338 Excalibur	250	3250	2922	2618	2333	2066	5863	4740	3804	3021	2370	+1.3	0.0	-6.35	-19.2	NA
34, 35																
348 Winchester	200	2520	2215	1931	1672	1443	2820	2178	1656	1241	925	+2.5	-1.4	-14.7	0.0	$42

Cartridge	Bullet Wgt. Grs.	VELOCITY (fps)					ENERGY (ft. lbs.)					TRAJ. (in.)				Est. Price/box
		Muzzle	100 yds.	200 yds.	300 yds.	400 yds.	Muzzle	100 yds.	200 yds.	300 yds.	400 yds.	100 yds.	200 yds.	300 yds.	400 yds.	
357 Magnum	158	1830	1427	1138	980	883	1175	715	454	337	274	0.0	-16.2	-33.1	0.0	$25**
35 Remington	150	2300	1874	1506	1218	1039	1762	1169	755	494	359	+2.5	-4.1	-26.3	0.0	$16
35 Remington	200	2080	1698	1376	1140	1001	1921	1280	841	577	445	+2.5	-6.3	-17.1	-33.6	$16
35 Remington	200	2225	1963	1722	1505	—	2198	1711	1317	1006	—	3.8	0	-15.6	—	NA
35 Rem. Lever Evolution	200	2225	1963	1721	1503	NA	2198	1711	1315	1003	NA	3.0	-1.3	-17.5	NA	NA
356 Winchester	200	2460	2114	1797	1517	1284	2688	1985	1434	1022	732	+2.5	-1.8	-15.1	0.0	$31
356 Winchester	250	2160	1911	1682	1476	1299	2591	2028	1571	1210	937	+2.5	-3.7	-22.2	0.0	$31
358 Winchester	200	2475	2180	1906	1655	1434	2720	2110	1612	1217	913	2.9	0	-12.6	-37.9	NA
358 Winchester	200	2490	2171	1876	1619	1379	2753	2093	1563	1151	844	+2.5	-1.6	-15.6	0.0	$31
358 STA	275	2850	2562	2292	2039	NA	4958	4009	3208	2539	NA	+1.9	0.0	-8.6	0.0	NA
350 Rem. Mag.	200	2710	2410	2130	1870	1631	3261	2579	2014	1553	1181	+2.5	-0.2	-10.0	-30.1	$33
35 Whelen	200	2675	2378	2100	1842	1606	3177	2510	1958	1506	1145	+2.5	-0.2	-10.3	-31.1	$20
35 Whelen	200	2910	2585	2283	2001	1742	3760	2968	2314	1778	1347	1.9	0	-8.6	-25.9	NA
35 Whelen	225	2500	2300	2110	1930	1770	3120	2650	2235	1870	1560	+2.6	0.0	-10.2	-29.9	NA
35 Whelen	250	2400	2197	2005	1823	1652	3197	2680	2230	1844	1515	+2.5	-1.2	-13.7	0.0	$20
358 Norma Mag.	250	2800	2510	2230	1970	1730	4350	3480	2750	2145	1655	+2.5	+1.0	-7.6	-25.2	NA
358 STA	275	2850	2562	229*2	2039	1764	4959	4009	3208	2539	1899	+1.9	0.0	-8.58	-26.1	NA
9.3mm																
9.3x57mm Mau.	286	2070	1810	1590	1390	1110	2710	2090	1600	1220	955	+2.5	-2.6	-22.5	0.0	NA
370 Sako Mag.	286	3550	2370	2200	2040	2880	4130	3570	3075	2630	2240	2.4	0.0	-9.5	-27.2	NA
9.3x62mm	232	2625	2302	2002	1728	-	2551	2731	2066	1539	-	2.6	0	-11.3	-	NA
9.3x62mm	250	2550	2376	2208	2048	—	3609	3133	2707	2328	—	0	-5.4	-17.9	—	NA
9.3x62mm	286	2360	2155	1961	1778	1608	3537	2949	2442	2008	1642	0	-6.0	-21.1	-47.2	NA
9.3x62mm	286	2400	2163	1941	1733	—	3657	2972	2392	1908	—	0	-6.7	-22.6	—	NA
9.3x64mm	286	2700	2505	2318	2139	1968	4629	3984	3411	2906	2460	+2.5	+2.7	-4.5	-19.2	NA
9.3x72mmR	193	1952	1610	1326	1120	996	1633	1112	754	538	425	0	-12.1	-44.1	—	NA
9.3x74mmR	250	2550	2376	2208	2048	—	3609	3133	2707	2328	—	0	-5.4	-17.9	—	NA
9.3x74Rmm	286	2360	2136	1924	1727	1545	3536	2896	2351	1893	1516	0.0	-6.1	-21.7	-49.0	NA
375																
375 Winchester	200	2200	1841	1526	1268	1089	2150	1506	1034	714	527	+2.5	-4.0	-26.2	0.0	$27
375 Winchester	250	1900	1647	1424	1239	1103	2005	1506	1126	852	676	+2.5	-6.9	-33.3	0.0	$27
376 Steyr	225	2600	2331	2078	1842	1625	3377	2714	2157	1694	1319	2.5	0.0	-10.6	-31.4	NA
376 Steyr	270	2600	2372	2156	1951	1759	4052	3373	2787	2283	1855	2.3	0.0	-9.9	-28.9	NA
375 Dakota	300	2600	2316	2051	1804	1579	4502	3573	2800	2167	1661	+2.4	0.0	-11.0	-32.7	NA
375 N.E. 2-1/2"	270	2000	1740	1507	1310	NA	2398	1815	1362	1026	NA	+2.5	-6.0	-30.0	0.0	NA
375 Flanged	300	2450	2150	1886	1640	NA	3998	3102	2369	1790	NA	+2.5	-2.4	-17.0	0.0	NA
375 Ruger	250	2890	2675	2471	2275	2088	4636	3973	3388	2873	2421	1.7	0	-7.4	-21.5	NA
375 Ruger	260	2900	2703	2514	2333	—	4854	4217	3649	3143	—	0	-4.0	-13.4	—	NA
375 Ruger	270	2840	2600	2372	2156	1951	4835	4052	3373	2786	2283	1.8	0.0	-8.0	-23.6	NA
375 Ruger	300	2660	2344	2050	1780	1536	4713	3660	2800	2110	1572	2.4	0.0	-10.8	-32.6	NA
375 H&H Magnum	250	2890	2675	2471	2275	2088	4636	3973	3388	2873	2421	1.7	0	-7.4	-21.5	NA
375 H&H Magnum	250	2670	2450	2240	2040	1850	3955	3335	2790	2315	1905	+2.5	-0.4	-10.2	-28.4	NA
375 H&H Magnum	270	2690	2420	2166	1928	1707	4337	3510	2812	2228	1747	+2.5	0.0	-10.0	-29.4	$28
375 H&H Mag.	270	2800	2562	2337	2123	1921	4700	3936	3275	2703	2213	1.9	0	-8.3	-24.3	NA
375 H&H Magnum*	300	2530	2245	1979	1733	1512	4263	3357	2608	2001	1523	+2.5	-1.0	-10.5	-33.6	$28
375 H&H Mag.	300	2660	2345	2052	1782	1539	4713	3662	2804	2114	1577	2.4	0	-10.8	-32.6	NA
375 H&H Hvy. Mag.	270	2870	2628	2399	2182	1976	4937	4141	3451	2150	1845	+1.7	0.0	-7.2	-21.0	NA
375 H&H Hvy. Mag.	300	2705	2386	2090	1816	1568	4873	3793	2908	2195	1637	+2.3	0.0	-10.4	-31.4	NA
375 H&H Mag.	350	2300	2052	1821	-	-	4112	3273	2578	-	-	0	-6.7	-	-	NA
375 Rem. Ultra Mag.	270	2900	2558	2241	1947	1678	5041	3922	3010	2272	1689	1.9	2.7	-8.9	-27.0	NA
375 Rem. Ultra Mag.	260	2950	2750	2560	2377	—	5023	4367	3783	3262	—	0	-3.8	-12.9	—	NA
375 Rem. Ultra Mag.	300	2760	2505	2263	2035	1822	5073	4178	3412	2759	2210	2.0	0.0	-8.8	-26.1	NA
375 Wea. Mag.	260	3000	2798	2606	2421	—	5195	4520	3920	3384	—	0	-3.6	-12.4	—	NA
375 Wea. Mag.	300	2700	2420	2157	1911	1685	4856	3901	3100	2432	1891	+2.5	-.04	-10.7	0.0	NA
378 Wea. Mag.	260	3100	2894	2697	2509	—	5547	4834	4199	3633	—	0	-4.2	-14.6	—	NA
378 Wea. Mag.	270	3180	2976	2781	2594	2415	6062	5308	4635	4034	3495	+2.5	+2.6	-1.8	-11.3	$71
378 Wea. Mag.	300	2929	2576	2252	1952	1680	5698	4419	3379	2538	1881	+2.5	+1.2	-7.0	-24.5	$77
375 A-Square	300	2920	2626	2351	2093	1850	5679	4594	3681	2917	2281	+2.5	+1.4	-6.0	-21.0	NA
38-40 Win.	180	1160	999	901	827	764	538	399	324	273	233	0.0	-33.9	0.0	0.0	$42**
40, 41																
400 A-Square DPM	400	2400	2146	1909	1689	NA	5116	2092	3236	2533	NA	2.98	0.0	-10.0	NA	NA
400 A-Square DPM	170	2980	2463	2001	1598	NA	3352	2289	1512	964	NA	2.16	0.0	-11.1	NA	NA

Cartridge	Bullet Wgt. Grs.	VELOCITY (fps)					ENERGY (ft. lbs.)					TRAJ. (in.)				Est. Price/box
		Muzzle	100 yds.	200 yds.	300 yds.	400 yds.	Muzzle	100 yds.	200 yds.	300 yds.	400 yds.	100 yds.	200 yds.	300 yds.	400 yds.	
408 CheyTac	419	2850	2752	2657	2562	2470	7551	7048	6565	6108	5675	-1.02	0.0	1.9	4.2	NA
405 Win.	300	2200	1851	1545	1296		3224	2282	1589	1119		4.6	0.0	-19.5	0.0	NA
450/400-3"	400	2050	1815	1595	1402	NA	3732	2924	2259	1746	NA	0.0	NA	-33.4	NA	NA
416 Ruger	400	2400	2151	1917	1700	NA	5116	4109	3264	2568	NA	0.0	-6.0	-21.6	0.0	NA
416 Dakota	400	2450	2294	2143	1998	1859	5330	4671	4077	3544	3068	+2.5	-0.2	-10.5	-29.4	NA
416 Taylor	400	2350	2117	1896	1693	NA	4905	3980	3194	2547	NA	+2.5	-1.2	15.0		NA
416 Hoffman	400	2380	2145	1923	1718	1529	5031	4087	3285	2620	2077	+2.5	-1.0	-14.1	0.0	NA
416 Rigby	350	2600	2449	2303	2162	2026	5253	4661	4122	3632	3189	+2.5	-1.8	-10.2	-26.0	NA
416 Rigby	400	2370	2210	2050	1900	NA	4990	4315	3720	3185	NA	+2.5	-0.7	-12.1	0.0	NA
416 Rigby	400	2400	2115	1851	1611	—	5115	3973	3043	2305	—	0	-6.5	-21.8	—	NA
416 Rigby	400	2415	2156	1915	1691	—	5180	4130	3256	2540	—	0	-6.0	-21.6	—	NA
416 Rigby	410	2370	2110	1870	1640	NA	5115	4050	3165	2455	NA	+2.5	-2.4	-17.3	0.0	$110
416 Rem. Mag.*	350	2520	2270	2034	1814	1611	4935	4004	3216	2557	2017	+2.5	-0.8	-12.6	-35.0	$82
416 Rem. Mag.	400	2400	2142	1901	1679	—	5116	4076	3211	2504	—	3.1	0	-12.7	—	NA
416 Rem. Mag.	450	2150	1925	1716	-	-	4620	3702	2942	-	-	0	-7.8	-	-	NA
416 Wea. Mag.*	400	2700	2397	2115	1852	1613	6474	5104	3971	3047	2310	+2.5	0.0	-10.1	-30.4	$96
10.57 (416) Meteor	400	2730	2532	2342	2161	1987	6621	5695	4874	4147	3508	+1.9	0.0	-8.3	-24.0	NA
500/416 N.E.	400	2300	2092	1895	1712	—	4697	3887	3191	2602	—	0	-7.2	-24.0	—	NA
404 Jeffrey	400	2150	1924	1716	1525	NA	4105	3289	2614	2064	NA	+2.5	-4.0	-22.1	0.0	NA
404 Jeffrey	400	2300	2053	1823	1611	—	4698	3743	2950	2306	—	0	-6.8	-24.1	—	NA
404 Jeffery	400	2350	2020	1720	1458	—	4904	3625	2629	1887	—	0	-6.5	-21.8	—	NA
404 Jeffery	450	2150	1946	1755	-	-	4620	3784	3078	-	-	0	-7.6	-	-	NA
425, 44																
425 Express	400	2400	2160	1934	1725	NA	5115	4145	3322	2641	NA	+2.5	-1.0	-14.0	0.0	NA
44-40 Win.	200	1190	1006	900	822	756	629	449	360	300	254	0.0	-33.3	0.0	0.0	$36**
44 Rem. Mag.	210	1920	1477	1155	982	880	1719	1017	622	450	361	0.0	-17.6	0.0	0.0	$14
44 Rem. Mag.	240	1760	1380	1114	970	878	1650	1015	661	501	411	0.0	-17.6	0.0	0.0	$13
444 Marlin	240	2350	1815	1377	1087	941	2942	1753	1001	630	472	+2.5	-15.1	-31.0	0.0	$22
444 Marlin	265	2120	1733	1405	1160	1012	2644	1768	1162	791	603	+2.5	-6.0	-32.2	0.0	Disc.
444 Mar. Lever Evolution	265	2325	1971	1652	1380	NA	3180	2285	1606	1120	NA	3.0	-1.4	-18.6	NA	NA
444 Mar. Superformance	265	2400	1976	1603	1298	NA	3389	2298	1512	991	NA	4.1	0.0	-17.8	NA	NA
45																
45-70 Govt.	250	2025	1616	1285	1068	—	2276	1449	917	634	—	6.1	0	-27.2	—	NA
45-70 Govt.	300	1810	1497	1244	1073	969	2182	1492	1031	767	625	0.0	-14.8	0.0	0.0	$21
45-70 Govt. Supreme	300	1880	1558	1292	1103	988	2355	1616	1112	811	651	0.0	-12.9	-46.0	-105.0	NA
45-70 Govt.	325	2000	1685	1413	1197	—	2886	2049	1441	1035	—	5.5	0	-23.0	—	NA
45-70 Lever Evolution	325	2050	1729	1450	1225	NA	3032	2158	1516	1083	NA	3.0	-4.1	-27.8	NA	NA
45-70 Govt. CorBon	350	1800	1526	1296			2519	1810	1307			0.0	-14.6	0.0	0.0	NA
45-70 Govt.	405	1330	1168	1055	977	918	1590	1227	1001	858	758	0.0	-24.6	0.0	0.0	$21
45-70 Govt. PMC Cowboy	405	1550	1193	—	—	—	1639	1280	—	—	—	0.0	-23.9	0.0	0.0	NA
45-70 Govt. Garrett	415	1850	—	—	—	—	3150	—	—	—	—	3.0	-7.0	0.0	0.0	NA
45-70 Govt. Garrett	530	1550	1343	1178	1062	982	2828	2123	1633	1327	1135	0.0	-17.8	0.0	0.0	NA
450 Bushmaster	250	2200	1831	1508	1480	1073	2686	1860	1262	864	639	0.0	-9.0	-33.5	0.0	NA
450 Marlin	325	2225	1887	1587	1332	—	3572	2570	1816	1280	—	4.2	0	-18.1	—	NA
450 Marlin	350	2100	1774	1488	1254	1089	3427	2446	1720	1222	922	0.0	-9.7	-35.2	0.0	NA
450 Mar. Lever Evolution	325	2225	1887	1585	1331	NA	3572	2569	1813	1278	NA	3.0	-2.2	-21.3	NA	NA
457 Wild West Magnum	350	2150	1718	1348	NA	NA	3645	2293	1413	NA	NA	0.0	-10.5	NA	NA	NA
450/500 N.E.	400	2050	1820	1609	1420	—	3732	2940	2298	1791	—	0	-9.7	-32.8	—	NA
450 N.E. 3-1/4"	465	2190	1970	1765	1577	NA	4952	4009	3216	2567	NA	+2.5	-3.0	-20.0	0.0	NA
450 N.E.	480	2150	1881	1635	1418	—	4927	3769	2850	2144	—	0	-8.4	-29.8	—	NA
450 N.E. 3-1/4"	500	2150	1920	1708	1514	NA	5132	4093	3238	2544	NA	+2.5	-4.0	-22.9	0.0	NA
450 No. 2	465	2190	1970	1765	1577	NA	4952	4009	3216	2567	NA	+2.5	-3.0	-20.0	0.0	NA
450 No. 2	500	2150	1920	1708	1514	NA	5132	4093	3238	2544	NA	+2.5	-4.0	-22.9	0.0	NA
450 Ackley Mag.	465	2400	2169	1950	1747	NA	5947	4857	3927	3150	NA	+2.5	-1.0	-13.7	0.0	NA
450 Ackley Mag.	500	2320	2081	1855	1649	NA	5975	4085	3820	3018	NA	+2.5	-1.2	-15.0	0.0	NA
450 Rigby	500	2350	2139	1939	1752	—	6130	5079	4176	3408	—	0	-6.8	-22.9	—	NA
458 Win. Magnum	400	2380	2170	1960	1770	NA	5030	4165	3415	2785	NA	+2.5	-0.4	-13.4	0.0	373
458 Win. Magnum	465	2220	1999	1791	1601	NA	5088	4127	3312	2646	NA	+2.5	-2.0	-17.7	0.0	NA
458 Win. Magnum	500	2040	1823	1623	1442	1237	4620	3689	2924	2308	1839	+2.5	-3.5	-22.0	0.0	$61
458 Win. Mag.	500	2140	1880	1643	1432	—	5084	3294	2996	2276	—	0	-8.4	-29.8	—	NA
458 Win. Magnum	510	2040	1770	1527	1319	1157	4712	3547	2640	1970	1516	+2.5	-4.1	-25.0	0.0	$41
458 Lott	465	2380	2150	1932	1730	NA	5848	4773	3855	3091	NA	+2.5	-1.0	-14.0	0.0	NA

Cartridge	Bullet Wgt. Grs.	VELOCITY (fps)					ENERGY (ft. lbs.)					TRAJ. (in.)				Est. Price/box
		Muzzle	100 yds.	200 yds.	300 yds.	400 yds.	Muzzle	100 yds.	200 yds.	300 yds.	400 yds.	100 yds.	200 yds.	300 yds.	400 yds.	
458 Lott	500	2300	2029	1778	1551	—	5873	4569	3509	2671	—	0	-7.0	-25.1	—	NA
458 Lott	500	2300	2062	1838	1633	NA	5873	4719	3748	2960	NA	+2.5	-1.6	-16.4	0.0	NA
460 Short A-Sq.	500	2420	2175	1943	1729	NA	6501	5250	4193	3319	NA	+2.5	-0.8	-12.8	0.0	NA
460 Wea. Mag.	500	2700	2404	2128	1869	1635	8092	6416	5026	3878	2969	+2.5	+0.6	-8.9	-28.0	$72
475																
500/465 N.E.	480	2150	1917	1703	1507	NA	4926	3917	3089	2419	NA	+2.5	-4.0	-22.2	0.0	NA
470 Rigby	500	2150	1940	1740	1560	NA	5130	4170	3360	2695	NA	+2.5	-2.8	-19.4	0.0	NA
470 Nitro Ex.	480	2190	1954	1735	1536	NA	5111	4070	3210	2515	NA	+2.5	-3.5	-20.8	0.0	NA
470 N.E.	500	2150	1885	1643	1429	—	5132	3945	2998	2267	—	0	-8.9	-30.8	—	NA
470 Nitro Ex.	500	2150	1890	1650	1440	1270	5130	3965	3040	2310	1790	+2.5	-4.3	-24.0	0.0	$177
475 No. 2	500	2200	1955	1728	1522	NA	5375	4243	3316	2573	NA	+2.5	-3.2	-20.9	0.0	NA
50, 58																
50 Alaskan	450	2000	1729	1492	NA	NA	3997	2987	2224	NA	NA	0.0	-11.25	NA	NA	NA
500 Jeffery	570	2300	1979	1688	1434	—	6694	4958	3608	2604	—	0	-8.2	-28.6	—	NA
505 Gibbs	525	2300	2063	1840	1637	NA	6166	4922	3948	3122	NA	+2.5	-3.0	-18.0	0.0	NA
505 Gibbs	570	2100	1893	1701	-	-	5583	4538	3664	-	-	0	-8.1	-	-	NA
505 Gibbs	600	2100	1899	1711	-	-	5877	4805	3904	-	-	0	-8.1	-	-	NA
500 N.E.	570	2150	1889	1651	1439	—	5850	4518	3450	2621	—	0	-8.9	-30.6	—	NA
500 N.E.-3"	570	2150	1928	1722	1533	NA	5850	4703	3752	2975	NA	+2.5	-3.7	-22.0	0.0	NA
500 N.E.-3"	600	2150	1927	1721	1531	NA	6158	4947	3944	3124	NA	+2.5	-4.0	-22.0	0.0	NA
495 A-Square	570	2350	2117	1896	1693	NA	5850	4703	3752	2975	NA	+2.5	-1.0	-14.5	0.0	NA
495 A-Square	600	2280	2050	1833	1635	NA	6925	5598	4478	3562	NA	+2.5	-2.0	-17.0	0.0	NA
500 A-Square	600	2380	2144	1922	1766	NA	7546	6126	4920	3922	NA	+2.5	-3.0	-17.0	0.0	NA
500 A-Square	707	2250	2040	1841	1567	NA	7947	6530	5318	4311	NA	+2.5	-2.0	-17.0	0.0	NA
500 BMG PMC	660	3080	2854	2639	2444	2248	13688		500 yd. zero			+3.1	+3.9	+4.7	+2.8	NA
577 Nitro Ex.	750	2050	1793	1562	1360	NA	6990	5356	4065	3079	NA	+2.5	-5.0	-26.0	0.0	NA
577 Tyrannosaur	750	2400	2141	1898	1675	NA	9591	7633	5996	4671	NA	+3.0	0.0	-12.9	0.0	NA
600, 700																
600 N.E.	900	1950	1680	1452	NA	NA	7596	5634	4212	NA	NA	+5.6	0.0	0.0	0.0	NA
700 N.E.	1200	1900	1676	1472	NA	NA	9618	7480	5774	NA	NA	+5.7	0.0	0.0	0.0	NA
50 BMG																
50 BMG	624	2952	2820	2691	2566	2444	12077	11028	10036	9125	8281	0	-2.9	-10.6	-23.5	NA
50 BMG Match	750	2820	2728	2637	2549	2462	13241	12388	11580	10815	10090	1.5	0.0	-6.5	-18.3	NA

Notes: Blanks are available in 32 S&W, 38 S&W and 38 Special. "V" after barrel length indicates test barrel was vented to produce ballistics similar to a revolver with a normal barrel-to-cylinder gap. Ammo prices are per 50 rounds except when marked with an ** which signifies a 20 round box; *** signifies a 25-round box. Not all loads are available from all ammo manufacturers. Listed loads are those made by Remington, Winchester, Federal, and others. DISC. is a discontinued load. Prices are rounded to the nearest whole dollar and will vary with brand and retail outlet.

Cartridge	Bullet Wgt. Grs.	VELOCITY (fps)			ENERGY (ft. lbs.)			Mid-Range Traj. (in.)		Bbl. Lgth. (in.)	Est. Price/ box
		Muzzle	50 yds.	100 yds.	Muzzle	50 yds.	100 yds.	50 yds.	100 yds.		
22, 25											
221 Rem. Fireball	50	2650	2380	2130	780	630	505	0.2	0.8	10.5"	$15
25 Automatic	35	900	813	742	63	51	43	NA	NA	2"	$18
25 Automatic	45	815	730	655	65	55	40	1.8	7.7	2"	$21
25 Automatic	50	760	705	660	65	55	50	2.0	8.7	2"	$17
30											
7.5mm Swiss	107	1010	NA	NA	240	NA	NA	NA	NA	NA	NEW
7.62x25 Tokarev	85	1647	1458	1295	512	401	317	0	-3.2	4.75	
7.62mmTokarev	87	1390	NA	NA	365	NA	NA	0.6	NA	4.5"	NA
7.62 Nagant	97	790	NA	NA	134	NA	NA	NA	NA	NA	NEW
7.63 Mauser	88	1440	NA	NA	405	NA	NA	NA	NA	NA	NEW
30 Luger	93	1220	1110	1040	305	255	225	0.9	3.5	4.5"	$34
30 Carbine	110	1790	1600	1430	785	625	500	0.4	1.7	10"	$28
30-357 AeT	123	1992	NA	NA	1084	NA	NA	NA	NA	10"	NA
32											
32 NAA	80	1000	933	880	178	155	137	NA	NA	4"	NA
32 S&W	88	680	645	610	90	80	75	2.5	10.5	3"	$17
32 S&W Long	98	705	670	635	115	100	90	2.3	10.5	4"	$17
32 Short Colt	80	745	665	590	100	80	60	2.2	9.9	4"	$19
32 H&R	80	1150	1039	963	235	192	165	NA	NA	4"	NA
32 H&R Magnum	85	1100	1020	930	230	195	165	1.0	4.3	4.5"	$21
32 H&R Magnum	95	1030	940	900	225	190	170	1.1	4.7	4.5"	$19
327 Federal Magnum	85	1400	1220	1090	370	280	225	NA	NA	4-V	NA
327 Federal Magnum	100	1500	1320	1180	500	390	310	-0.2	-4.50	4-V	NA
32 Automatic	60	970	895	835	125	105	95	1.3	5.4	4"	$22
32 Automatic	60	1000	917	849	133	112	96			4"	NA
32 Automatic	65	950	890	830	130	115	100	1.3	5.6	NA	NA
32 Automatic	71	905	855	810	130	115	95	1.4	5.8	4"	$19
8mm Lebel Pistol	111	850	NA	NA	180	NA	NA	NA	NA	NA	NEW
8mm Steyr	112	1080	NA	NA	290	NA	NA	NA	NA	NA	NEW
8mm Gasser	126	850	NA	NA	200	NA	NA	NA	NA	NA	NEW
9mm, 38											
380 Automatic	60	1130	960	NA	170	120	NA	1.0	NA	NA	NA
380 Automatic	75	950	NA	NA	183	NA	NA	NA	NA	3"	$33
380 Automatic	85/88	990	920	870	190	165	145	1.2	5.1	4"	$20
380 Automatic	90	1000	890	800	200	160	130	1.2	5.5	3.75"	$10
380 Automatic	95/100	955	865	785	190	160	130	1.4	5.9	4"	$20
38 Super Auto +P	115	1300	1145	1040	430	335	275	0.7	3.3	5"	$26
38 Super Auto +P	125/130	1215	1100	1015	425	350	300	0.8	3.6	5"	$26
38 Super Auto +P	147	1100	1050	1000	395	355	325	0.9	4.0	5"	NA
38 Super Auto +P	115	1130	1016	938	326	264	225	1	-9.5	-	NA
9x18mm Makarov	95	1000	930	874	211	182	161	NA	NA	4"	NEW
9x18mm Ultra	100	1050	NA	NA	240	NA	NA	NA	NA	NA	NEW
9x21	124	1150	1050	980	365	305	265	NA	NA	4"	NA
9x21 IMI	123	1220	1095	1010	409	330	281	-3.15	—	5.0	NA
9x23mm Largo	124	1190	1055	966	390	306	257	0.7	3.7	4"	NA
9x23mm Win.	125	1450	1249	1103	583	433	338	0.6	2.8	NA	NA
9mm Steyr	115	1180	NA	NA	350	NA	NA	NA	NA	NA	NEW
9mm Luger	88	1500	1190	1010	440	275	200	0.6	3.1	4"	$24
9mm Luger	90	1360	1112	978	370	247	191	NA	NA	4"	$26
9mm Luger	92	1325	1117	991	359	255	201	-3.2	—	4.0	NA
9mm Luger	95	1300	1140	1010	350	275	215	0.8	3.4	4"	NA
9mm Luger	100	1180	1080	NA	305	255	NA	0.9	NA	4"	NA
9mm Luger Guard Dog	105	1230	1070	970	355	265	220	NA	NA	4"	NA
9mm Luger	115	1155	1045	970	340	280	240	0.9	3.9	4"	$21
9mm Luger	123/125	1110	1030	970	340	290	260	1.0	4.0	4"	$23

Cartridge	Bullet Wgt. Grs.	VELOCITY (fps)			ENERGY (ft. lbs.)			Mid-Range Traj. (in.)		Bbl. Lgth. (in).	Est. Price/ box
		Muzzle	50 yds.	100 yds.	Muzzle	50 yds.	100 yds.	50 yds.	100 yds.		
9mm Luger	124	1150	1040	965	364	298	256	-4.5	—	4.0	NA
9mm Luger	135	1010	960	918	306	276	253	—	—	4.0	NA
9mm Luger	140	935	890	850	270	245	225	1.3	5.5	4"	$23
9mm Luger	147	990	940	900	320	290	265	1.1	4.9	4"	$26
9mm Luger +P	90	1475	NA	NA	437	NA	NA	NA	NA	NA	NA
9mm Luger +P	115	1250	1113	1019	399	316	265	0.8	3.5	4"	$27
9mm Federal	115	1280	1130	1040	420	330	280	0.7	3.3	4"V	$24
9mm Luger Vector	115	1155	1047	971	341	280	241	NA	NA	4"	NA
9mm Luger +P	124	1180	1089	1021	384	327	287	0.8	3.8	4"	NA
38											
38 S&W	146	685	650	620	150	135	125	2.4	10.0	4"	$19
38 S&W Short	145	720	689	660	167	153	140	-8.5	—	5.0	NA
38 Short Colt	125	730	685	645	150	130	115	2.2	9.4	6"	$19
39 Special	100	950	900	NA	200	180	NA	1.3	NA	4"V	NA
38 Special	110	945	895	850	220	195	175	1.3	5.4	4"V	$23
38 Special	110	945	895	850	220	195	175	1.3	5.4	4"V	$23
38 Special	130	775	745	710	175	160	120	1.9	7.9	4"V	$22
38 Special Cowboy	140	800	767	735	199	183	168			7.5" V	NA
38 (Multi-Ball)	140	830	730	505	215	130	80	2.0	10.6	4"V	$10**
38 Special	148	710	635	565	165	130	105	2.4	10.6	4"V	$17
38 Special	158	755	725	690	200	185	170	2.0	8.3	4"V	$18
38 Special +P	95	1175	1045	960	290	230	195	0.9	3.9	4"V	$23
38 Special +P	110	995	925	870	240	210	185	1.2	5.1	4"V	$23
38 Special +P	125	975	929	885	264	238	218	1	5.2	4"	NA
38 Special +P	125	945	900	860	250	225	205	1.3	5.4	4"V	#23
38 Special +P	129	945	910	870	255	235	215	1.3	5.3	4"V	$11
38 Special +P	130	925	887	852	247	227	210	1.3	5.50	4"V	NA
38 Special +P	147/150	884	NA	NA	264	NA	NA	NA	NA	4"V	$27
38 Special +P	158	890	855	825	280	255	240	1.4	6.0	4"V	$20
357											
357 SIG	115	1520	NA	NA	593	NA	NA	NA	NA	NA	NA
357 SIG	124	1450	NA	NA	578	NA	NA	NA	NA	NA	NA
357 SIG	125	1350	1190	1080	510	395	325	0.7	3.1	4"	NA
357 SIG	135	1225	1112	1031	450	371	319	—	—	4.0	NA
357 SIG	147	1225	1132	1060	490	418	367	—	—	4.0	NA
357 SIG	150	1130	1030	970	420	355	310	0.9	4.0	NA	NA
356 TSW	115	1520	NA	NA	593	NA	NA	NA	NA	NA	NA
356 TSW	124	1450	NA	NA	578	NA	NA	NA	NA	NA	NA
356 TSW	135	1280	1120	1010	490	375	310	0.8	3.5	NA	NA
356 TSW	147	1220	1120	1040	485	410	355	0.8	3.5	5"	NA
357 Mag., Super Clean	105	1650									NA
357 Magnum	110	1295	1095	975	410	290	230	0.8	3.5	4"V	$25
357 (Med.Vel.)	125	1220	1075	985	415	315	270	0.8	3.7	4"V	$25
357 Magnum	125	1450	1240	1090	585	425	330	0.6	2.8	4"V	$25
357 Magnum	125	1500	1312	1163	624	478	376	—	—	8.0	NA
357 (Multi-Ball)	140	1155	830	665	420	215	135	1.2	6.4	4"V	$11**
357 Magnum	140	1360	1195	1075	575	445	360	0.7	3.0	4"V	$25
357 Magnum FlexTip	140	1440	1274	1143	644	504	406	NA	NA	NA	NA
357 Magnum	145	1290	1155	1060	535	430	360	0.8	3.5	4"V	$26
357 Magnum	150/158	1235	1105	1015	535	430	360	0.8	3.5	4"V	$25
357 Mag. Cowboy	158	800	761	725	225	203	185				NA
357 Magnum	165	1290	1189	1108	610	518	450	0.7	3.1	8-3/8"	NA
357 Magnum	180	1145	1055	985	525	445	390	0.9	3.9	4"V	$25
357 Magnum	180	1180	1088	1020	557	473	416	0.8	3.6	8"V	NA
357 Mag. CorBon F.A.	180	1650	1512	1386	1088	913	767	1.66	0.0		NA
357 Mag. CorBon	200	1200	1123	1061	640	560	500	3.19	0.0		NA
357 Rem. Maximum	158	1825	1590	1380	1170	885	670	0.4	1.7	10.5"	$14**
40, 10mm											
40 S&W	120	1150	-	-	352	-	-	-	-	-	$38
40 S&W	125	1265	1102	998	444	337	276	-3.0	—	4.0	NA
40 S&W	135	1140	1070	NA	390	345	NA	0.9	NA	4"	NA

Cartridge	Bullet Wgt. Grs.	VELOCITY (fps)			ENERGY (ft. lbs.)			Mid-Range Traj. (in.)		Bbl. Lgth. (in).	Est. Price/ box
		Muzzle	50 yds.	100 yds.	Muzzle	50 yds.	100 yds.	50 yds.	100 yds.		
40 S&W Guard Dog	135	1200	1040	940	430	325	265	NA	NA	4"	NA
40 S&W	155	1140	1026	958	447	362	309	0.9	4.1	4"	$14***
40 S&W	165	1150	NA	NA	485	NA	NA	NA	NA	4"	$18***
40 S&W	175	1010	948	899	396	350	314	—	—	4.0	NA
40 S&W	180	985	936	893	388	350	319	1.4	5.0	4"	$14***
40 S&W	180	1000	943	896	400	355	321	4.52	—	4.0	NA
40 S&W	180	1015	960	914	412	368	334	1.3	4.5	4"	NA
400 Cor-Bon	135	1450	NA	NA	630	NA	NA	NA	NA	5"	NA
10mm Automatic	155	1125	1046	986	436	377	335	0.9	3.9	5"	$26
10mm Automatic	155	1265	1118	1018	551	430	357	—	—	5.0	NA
10mm Automatic	170	1340	1165	1145	680	510	415	0.7	3.2	5"	$31
10mm Automatic	175	1290	1140	1035	650	505	420	0.7	3.3	5.5"	$11**
10mm Auto. (FBI)	180	950	905	865	361	327	299	1.5	5.4	4"	$16**
10mm Automatic	180	1030	970	920	425	375	340	1.1	4.7	5"	$16**
10mm Auto H.V.	180	1240	1124	1037	618	504	430	0.8	3.4	5"	$27
10mm Automatic	200	1160	1070	1010	495	510	430	0.9	3.8	5"	$14**
10.4mm Italian	177	950	NA	NA	360	NA	NA	NA	NA	NA	NEW
41 Action Exp.	180	1000	947	903	400	359	326	0.5	4.2	5"	$13**
41 Rem. Magnum	170	1420	1165	1015	760	515	390	0.7	3.2	4"V	$33
41 Rem. Magnum	175	1250	1120	1030	605	490	410	0.8	3.4	4"V	$14**
41 (Med. Vel.)	210	965	900	840	435	375	330	1.3	5.4	4"V	$30
41 Rem. Magnum	210	1300	1160	1060	790	630	535	0.7	3.2	4"V	$33
41 Rem. Magnum	240	1250	1151	1075	833	706	616	0.8	3.3	6.5V	NA
44											
44 S&W Russian	247	780	NA	NA	335	NA	NA	NA	NA	NA	NA
44 Special	210	900	861	825	360	329	302	5.57	—	6.0	NA
44 Special FTX	165	900	848	802	297	263	235	NA	NA	2.5"	NA
44 S&W Special	180	980	NA	NA	383	NA	NA	NA	NA	6.5"	NA
44 S&W Special	180	1000	935	882	400	350	311	NA	NA	7.5"V	NA
44 S&W Special	200	875	825	780	340	302	270	1.2	6.0	6"	$13**
44 S&W Special	200	1035	940	865	475	390	335	1.1	4.9	6.5"	$13**
44 S&W Special	240/246	755	725	695	310	285	265	2.0	8.3	6.5"	$26
44-40 Win.	200	722	698	676	232	217	203	-3.4	-23.7	4.0	NA
44-40 Win.	205	725	689	655	239	216	195	—	—	7.5	NA
44-40 Win.	210	725	698	672	245	227	210	-11.6	—	5.5	NA
44-40 Win.	225	725	697	670	263	243	225	-3.4	-23.8	4.0	NA
44-40 Win. Cowboy	225	750	723	695	281	261	242				NA
44 Rem. Magnum	180	1610	1365	1175	1035	745	550	0.5	2.3	4"V	$18**
44 Rem. Magnum	200	1296	1193	1110	747	632	548	-.5	-6.2	6.0	NA
44 Rem. Magnum	200	1400	1192	1053	870	630	492	0.6	NA	6.5"	$20
44 Rem. Magnum	200	1500	1332	1194	999	788	633	—	—	7.5	NA
44 Rem. Magnum	210	1495	1310	1165	1040	805	635	0.6	2.5	6.5"	$18**
44 Rem. Mag. FlexTip	225	1410	1240	1111	993	768	617	NA	NA	NA	NA
44 (Med. Vel.)	240	1000	945	900	535	475	435	1.1	4.8	6.5"	$17
44 R.M. (Jacketed)	240	1180	1080	1010	740	625	545	0.9	3.7	4"V	$18**
44 R.M. (Lead)	240	1350	1185	1070	970	750	610	0.7	3.1	4"V	$29
44 Rem. Magnum	250	1180	1100	1040	775	670	600	0.8	3.6	6.5"V	$21
44 Rem. Magnum	250	1250	1148	1070	867	732	635	0.8	3.3	6.5"V	NA
44 Rem. Magnum	275	1235	1142	1070	931	797	699	0.8	3.3	6.5"	NA
44 Rem. Magnum	300	1150	1083	1030	881	781	706	—	—	7.5	NA
44 Rem. Magnum	300	1200	1100	1026	959	806	702	NA	NA	7.5"	$17
44 Rem. Magnum	330	1385	1297	1220	1406	1234	1090	1.83	0.00	NA	NA
44 Webley	262	850	—	—	—	—	—	—	—	—	NA
440 CorBon	260	1700	1544	1403	1669	1377	1136	1.58	NA	10"	NA
45, 50											
450 Short Colt/450 Revolver	226	830	NA	NA	350	NA	NA	NA	NA	NA	NEW
45 S&W Schofield	180	730	NA	NA	213	NA	NA	NA	NA	NA	NA
45 S&W Schofield	230	730	NA	NA	272	NA	NA	NA	NA	NA	NA
45 G.A.P.	165	1007	936	879	372	321	283	-1.4	-11.8	5.0	NA
45 G.A.P.	185	1090	970	890	490	385	320	1.0	4.7	5"	NA
45 G.A.P.	230	880	842	NA	396	363	NA	NA	NA	NA	NA

Cartridge	Bullet Wgt. Grs.	VELOCITY (fps)			ENERGY (ft. lbs.)			Mid-Range Traj. (in.)		Bbl. Lgth. (in).	Est. Price/ box
		Muzzle	50 yds.	100 yds.	Muzzle	50 yds.	100 yds.	50 yds.	100 yds.		
45 Automatic	150	1050	NA	NA	403	NA	NA	NA	NA	NA	$40
45 Automatic	165	1030	930	NA	385	315	NA	1.2	NA	5"	NA
45 Automatic Guard Dog	165	1140	1030	950	475	390	335	NA	NA	5"	NA
45 Automatic	185	1000	940	890	410	360	325	1.1	4.9	5"	$28
45 Auto. (Match)	185	770	705	650	245	204	175	2.0	8.7	5"	$28
45 Auto. (Match)	200	940	890	840	392	352	312	2.0	8.6	5"	$20
45 Automatic	200	975	917	860	421	372	328	1.4	5.0	5"	$18
45 Automatic	230	830	800	675	355	325	300	1.6	6.8	5"	$27
45 Automatic	230	880	846	816	396	366	340	1.5	6.1	5"	NA
45 Automatic +P	165	1250	NA	NA	573	NA	NA	NA	NA	NA	NA
45 Automatic +P	185	1140	1040	970	535	445	385	0.9	4.0	5"	$31
45 Automatic +P	200	1055	982	925	494	428	380	NA	NA	5"	NA
45 Super	185	1300	1190	1108	694	582	504	NA	NA	5"	NA
45 Win. Magnum	230	1400	1230	1105	1000	775	635	0.6	2.8	5"	$14**
45 Win. Magnum	260	1250	1137	1053	902	746	640	0.8	3.3	5"	$16**
45 Win. Mag. CorBon	320	1150	1080	1025	940	830	747	3.47			NA
455 Webley MKII	262	850	NA	NA	420	NA	NA	NA	NA	NA	NA
45 Colt FTX	185	920	870	826	348	311	280	NA	NA	3"V	NA
45 Colt	200	1000	938	889	444	391	351	1.3	4.8	5.5"	$21
45 Colt	225	960	890	830	460	395	345	1.3	5.5	5.5"	$22
45 Colt + P CorBon	265	1350	1225	1126	1073	884	746	2.65	0.0		NA
45 Colt + P CorBon	300	1300	1197	1114	1126	956	827	2.78	0.0		NA
45 Colt	250/255	860	820	780	410	375	340	1.6	6.6	5.5"	$27
454 Casull	250	1300	1151	1047	938	735	608	0.7	3.2	7.5"V	NA
454 Casull	260	1800	1577	1381	1871	1436	1101	0.4	1.8	7.5"V	NA
454 Casull	300	1625	1451	1308	1759	1413	1141	0.5	2.0	7.5"V	NA
454 Casull CorBon	360	1500	1387	1286	1800	1640	1323	2.01	0.0		NA
460 S&W	200	2300	2042	1801	2350	1851	1441	0	-1.60	NA	NA
460 S&W	260	2000	1788	1592	2309	1845	1464	NA	NA	7.5"V	NA
460 S&W	250	1450	1267	1127	1167	891	705	NA	NA	8.375-V	NA
460 S&W	250	1900	1640	1412	2004	1494	1106	0	-2.75	NA	NA
460 S&W	300	1750	1510	1300	2040	1510	1125	NA	NA	8.4-V	NA
460 S&W	395	1550	1389	1249	2108	1691	1369	0	-4.00	NA	NA
475 Linebaugh	400	1350	1217	1119	1618	1315	1112	NA	NA	NA	NA
480 Ruger	325	1350	1191	1076	1315	1023	835	2.6	0.0	7.5"	NA
50 Action Exp.	300	1475	1251	1092	1449	1043	795	-	-	6"	NA
50 Action Exp.	325	1400	1209	1075	1414	1055	835	0.2	2.3	6"	$24**
500 S&W	275	1665	1392	1183	1693	1184	854	1.5	NA	8.375	NA
500 S&W	300	1950	1653	1396	2533	1819	1298	—	—	8.5	NA
500 S&W	325	1800	1560	1350	2340	1755	1315	NA	NA	8.4-V	NA
500 S&W	350	1400	1231	1106	1523	1178	951	NA	NA	10"	NA
500 S&W	400	1675	1472	1299	2493	1926	1499	1.3	NA	8.375	NA
500 S&W	440	1625	1367	1169	2581	1825	1337	1.6	NA	8.375	NA
500 S&W	500	1300	1178	1085	1876	1541	1308	—	—	8.5	NA
500 S&W	500	1425	1281	1164	2254	1823	1505	NA	NA	10"	NA

RIMFIRE AMMUNITION BALLISTICS

Note: The actual ballistics obtained with your firearm can vary considerably from the advertised ballistics. Also, ballistics can vary from lot to lot with the same brand and type load.

Cartridge	Bullet Wt. Grs.	Velocity (fps) 22-1/2" Bbl.		Energy (ft. lbs.) 22-1/2" Bbl.		Mid-Range Traj. (in.)	Muzzle Velocity
		Muzzle	100 yds.	Muzzle	100 yds.	100 yds.	6" Bbl.
17 Aguila	20	1850	1267	NA	NA	NA	NA
17 Hornady Mach 2	15.5	2050	1450	149	75	NA	NA
17 Hornady Mach 2	17	2100	1530	166	88	0.7	NA
17 HMR Lead Free	15.5	2550	1901	NA	NA	.90	NA
17 HMR TNT Green	16	2500	1642	222	96	NA	NA
17 HMR	17	2550	1902	245	136	NA	NA
17 HMR	20	2375	1776	250	140	NA	NA
17 Win. Super Mag.	20 Tipped	3000	2504	400	278	0.0	NA
17 Win. Super Mag.	20 JHP	3000	2309	400	237	0.0	NA
17 Win. Super Mag.	25 Tipped	2600	2230	375	276	0.0	NA
5mm Rem. Rimfire Mag.	30	2300	1669	352	188	NA	24
22 Short Blank	—	—	—	—	—	—	—
22 Short CB	29	727	610	33	24	NA	706
22 Short Target	29	830	695	44	31	6.8	786
22 Short HP	27	1164	920	81	50	4.3	1077
22 Colibri	20	375	183	6	1	NA	NA
22 Super Colibri	20	500	441	11	9	NA	NA
22 Long CB	29	727	610	33	24	NA	706
22 Long HV	29	1180	946	90	57	4.1	1031
22 LR Pistol Match	40	1070	890	100	70	4.6	940
22 LR Shrt. Range Green	21	1650	912	127	NA	NA	NA
CCI Quiet 22 LR	40	710	640	45	36	NA	NA
22 LR Sub Sonic HP	38	1050	901	93	69	4.7	NA
22 LR Segmented HP	40	1050	897	98	72	NA	NA
22 LR Standard Velocity	40	1070	890	100	70	4.6	940
22 LR AutoMatch	40	1200	990	130	85	NA	NA
22 LR HV	40	1255	1016	140	92	3.6	1060
22 LR Silhoutte	42	1220	1003	139	94	3.6	1025
22 SSS	60	950	802	120	86	NA	NA
22 LR HV HP	40	1280	1001	146	89	3.5	1085
22 Velocitor GDHP	40	1435	0	0	0	NA	NA
22 LR Segmented HP	37	1435	1080	169	96	2.9	NA
22 LR Hyper HP	32/33/34	1500	1075	165	85	2.8	NA
22 LR Expediter	32	1640	NA	191	NA	NA	NA
22 LR Stinger HP	32	1640	1132	191	91	2.6	1395
22 LR Lead Free	30	1650	NA	181	NA	NA	NA
22 LR Hyper Vel	30	1750	1191	204	93	NA	NA
22 LR Shot #12	31	950	NA	NA	NA	NA	NA
22 WRF LFN	45	1300	1015	169	103	3	NA
22 Win. Mag. Lead Free	28	2200	NA	301	NA	NA	NA
22 Win. Mag.	30	2200	1373	322	127	1.4	1610
22 Win. Mag. V-Max BT	33	2000	1495	293	164	0.60	NA
22 Win. Mag. JHP	34	2120	1435	338	155	1.4	NA
22 Win. Mag. JHP	40	1910	1326	324	156	1.7	1480
22 Win. Mag. FMJ	40	1910	1326	324	156	1.7	1480
22 Win. Mag. Dyna Point	45	1550	1147	240	131	2.60	NA
22 Win. Mag. JHP	50	1650	1280	300	180	1.3	NA
22 Win. Mag. Shot #11	52	1000	—	NA	—	—	NA

NOTES: * = 10 rounds per box. ** = 5 rounds per box. Pricing variations and number of rounds per box can occur with type and brand of ammunition.
Listed pricing is the average nominal cost for load style and box quantity shown. Not every brand is available in all shot size variations.
Some manufacturers do not provide suggested list prices. All prices rounded to nearest whole dollar.
The price you pay will vary dependent upon outlet of purchase. # = new load spec this year; "C" indicates a change in data.

10 Gauge 3-1/2" Magnum

Dram Equiv.	Shot Ozs.	Load Style	Shot Sizes	Brands	Avg. Price/box	Velocity (fps)
Max	2-3/8	magnum blend	5, 6, 7	Hevi-shot	NA	1200
4-1/2	2-1/4	premium	BB, 2, 4, 5, 6	Win., Fed., Rem.	$33	1205
Max	2	premium	4, 5, 6	Fed., Win.	NA	1300
4-1/4	2	high velocity	BB, 2, 4	Rem.	$22	1210
Max	18 pellets	premium	00 buck	Fed., Win.	$7**	1100
Max	1-7/8	Bismuth	BB, 2, 4	Bis.	NA	1225
Max	1-3/4	high density	BB, 2	Rem.	NA	1300
4-1/4	1-3/4	steel	TT, T, BBB, BB, 1, 2, 3	Win., Rem.	$27	1260
Mag	1-5/8	steel	T, BBB, BB, 2	Win.	$27	1285
Max	1-5/8	Bismuth	BB, 2, 4	Bismuth	NA	1375
Max	1-1/2	hypersonic	BBB, BB, 2	Rem.	NA	1700
Max	1-1/2	heavy metal	BB, 2, 3, 4	Hevi-Shot	NA	1500
Max	1-1/2	steel	T, BBB, BB, 1, 2, 3	Fed.	NA	1450
Max	1-3/8	steel	T, BBB, BB, 1, 2, 3	Fed., Rem.	NA	1500
Max	1-3/8	steel	T, BBB, BB, 2	Fed., Win.	NA	1450
Max	1-3/4	slug, rifled	slug	Fed.	NA	1280
Max	24 pellets	Buckshot	1 Buck	Fed.	NA	1100
Max	54 pellets	Super-X	4 Buck	Win.	NA	1150

12 Gauge 3-1/2" Magnum

Dram Equiv.	Shot Ozs.	Load Style	Shot Sizes	Brands	Avg. Price/box	Velocity (fps)
Max	2-1/4	premium	4, 5, 6	Fed., Rem., Win.	$13*	1150
Max	2	Lead	4, 5, 6	Fed.	NA	1300
Max	2	Copper plated turkey	4, 5	Rem.	NA	1300
4.34	2	-	5, 6, 7	-	NA	1250
Max	18 pellets	premium	00 buck	Fed., Win., Rem.	$7**	1100
Max	1-7/8	Wingmaster HD	4, 6	Rem.	NA	1225
Max	1-7/8	heavyweight	5, 6	Fed.	NA	1300
Max	1-3/4	high density	BB, 2, 4, 6	Rem.		1300
Max	1-7/8	Bismuth	BB, 2, 4	Bis.	NA	1225
Max	1-5/8	blind side	Hex, 1, 3	Win.	NA	1400
Max	1-5/8	Hevi-shot	T	Hevi-shot	NA	1350
Max	1-5/8	Wingmaster HD	T	Rem.	NA	1350
Max	1-5/8	high density	BB, 2	Fed.	NA	1450
Max	1-5/8	Blind side	Hex, BB, 2	Win.	NA	1400
Max	1-3/8	Heavyweight	2, 4, 6	Fed.	NA	1450
Max	1-3/8	steel	T, BBB, BB, 2, 4	Fed., Win., Rem.	NA	1450
Max	1-1/2	FS steel	BBB, BB, 2	Fed.	NA	1500
Max	1-1/2	Supreme H-V	BBB, BB, 2, 3	Win.	NA	1475
Max	1-3/8	H-speed steel	BB, 2	Rem.	NA	1550

12 Gauge 3-1/2" Magnum (cont.)

Dram Equiv.	Shot Ozs.	Load Style	Shot Sizes	Brands	Avg. Price/box	Velocity (fps)
Max	1-1/4	Steel	BB, 2	Win.	NA	1625
Max	24 pellets	Premium	1 Buck	Fed.	NA	1100
Max	54 pellets	Super-X	4 Buck	Win.	NA	1050

12 Gauge 3" Magnum

Dram Equiv.	Shot Ozs.	Load Style	Shot Sizes	Brands	Avg. Price/box	Velocity (fps)
4	2	premium	BB, 2, 4, 5, 6	Win., Fed., Rem.	$9*	1175
4	1-7/8	premium	BB, 2, 4, 6	Win., Fed., Rem.	$19	1210
4	1-7/8	duplex	4x6	Rem.	$9*	1210
3.96	1-3/4	-	5, 6, 7	-	NA	1250
Max	1-3/4	turkey	4, 5, 6	Fed., Fio., Win., Rem.	NA	1300
Max	1-3/4	high density	BB, 2, 4	Rem.	NA	1450
Max	1-5/8	high density	BB, 2	Fed.	NA	1450
Max	1-5/8	Wingmaster HD	4, 6	Rem.	NA	1227
Max	1-5/8	high velocity	4, 5, 6	Fed.	NA	1350
4	1-5/8	premium	2, 4, 5, 6	Win., Fed., Rem.	$18	1290
Max	1-1/2	Wingmaster HD	T	Rem.	NA	1300
Max	1-1/2	Hevi-shot	T	Hevi-shot	NA	1300
Max	1-1/2	high density	BB, 2, 4	Rem.	NA	1300
Max	1-1/2	slug	slug	Bren.	NA	1604
Max	1-5/8	Bismuth	BB, 2, 4, 5, 6	Bis.	NA	1250
4	24 pellets	buffered	1 buck	Win., Fed., Rem.	$5**	1040
4	15 pellets	buffered	00 buck	Win., Fed., Rem.	$6**	1210
4	10 pellets	buffered	000 buck	Win., Fed., Rem.	$6**	1225
4	41 pellets	buffered	4 buck	Win., Fed., Rem.	$6**	1210
Max	1-3/8	heavyweight	5, 6	Fed.	NA	1300
Max	1-3/8	high density	B, 2, 4, 6	Rem. Win.	NA	1450
Max	1-3/8	slug	slug	Bren.	NA	1476
Max	1-3/8	blind side	Hex, 1, 3, 5	Win.	NA	1400
Max	1-1/4	slug, rifled	slug	Fed.	NA	1600
Max	1-3/16	saboted slug	copper slug	Rem.	NA	1500
Max	7/8	slug, rifled	slug	Rem.	NA	1875
Max	1-1/8	low recoil	BB	Fed.	NA	850
Max	1-1/8	steel	BB, 2, 3, 4	Fed., Win., Rem.	NA	1550
Max	1-1/16	high density	2, 4	Win.	NA	1400
Max	1	steel	4, 6	Fed.	NA	1330
Max	1-3/8	buckhammer	slug	Rem.	NA	1500
Max	1	TruBall slug	slug	Fed.	NA	1700
Max	1	slug, rifled	slug, magnum	Win., Rem.	$5**	1760

Dram Equiv.	Shot Ozs.	Load Style	Shot Sizes	Brands	Avg. Price/ box	Velocity (fps)
12 Gauge 3" Magnum *(cont.)*						
Max	1	saboted slug	slug	Rem., Win., Fed.	$10**	1550
Max	385 grs.	partition gold	slug	Win.	NA	2000
Max	1-1/8	Rackmaster	slug	Win.	NA	1700
Max	300 grs.	XP3	slug	Win.	NA	2100
3-5/8	1-3/8	steel	BBB, BB, 1, 2, 3, 4	Win., Fed., Rem.	$19	1275
Max	1-1/8	snow goose FS	BB, 2, 3, 4	Fed.	NA	1635
Max	1-1/8	steel	BB, 2, 4	Rem.	NA	1500
Max	1-1/8	steel	T, BBB, BB, 2, 4, 5, 6	Fed., Win.	NA	1450
Max	1-1/8	steel	BB, 2	Fed.	NA	1400
Max	1-1/8	FS lead	3, 4	Fed.	NA	1600
Max	1-3/8	Blind side	Hex, BB, 2	Win.	NA	1400
4	1-1/4	steel	T, BBB, BB, 1, 2, 3, 4, 6	Win., Fed., Rem.	$18	1400
Max	1-1/4	FS steel	BBB, BB, 2	Fed.	NA	1450
12 Gauge 2-3/4"						
Max	1-5/8	magnum	4, 5, 6	Win., Fed.	$8*	1250
Max	1-3/8	lead	4, 5, 6	Fiocchi	NA	1485
Max	1-3/8	turkey	4, 5, 6	Fio.	NA	1250
Max	1-3/8	steel	4, 5, 6	Fed.	NA	1400
Max	1-3/8	Bismuth	BB, 2, 4, 5, 6	Bis.	NA	1300
3-3/4	1-1/2	magnum	BB, 2, 4, 5, 6	Win., Fed., Rem.	$16	1260
Max	1-1/4	blind side	Hex, 2, 5	Win.	NA	1400
Max	1-1/4	Supreme H-V	4, 5, 6, 7-1/2	Win. Rem.	NA	1400
3-3/4	1-1/4	high velocity	BB, 2, 4, 5, 6, 7-1/2, 8, 9	Win., Fed., Rem., Fio.	$13	1330
Max	1-1/4	high density	B, 2, 4	Win.	NA	1450
Max	1-1/4	high density	4, 6	Rem.	NA	1325
3-1/4	1-1/4	standard velocity	6, 7-1/2, 8, 9	Win., Fed., Rem., Fio.	$11	1220
Max	1-1/8	Hevi-shot	5	Hevi-shot	NA	1350
3-1/4	1-1/8	standard velocity	4, 6, 7-1/2, 8, 9	Win., Fed., Rem., Fio.	$9	1255
Max	1-1/8	steel	2, 4	Rem.	NA	1390
Max	1	steel	BB, 2	Fed.	NA	1450
3-1/4	1	standard velocity	6, 7-1/2, 8	Rem., Fed., Fio., Win.	$6	1290
3-1/4	1-1/4	target	7-1/2, 8, 9	Win., Fed., Rem.	$10	1220
3	1-1/8	spreader	7-1/2, 8, 8-1/2, 9	Fio.	NA	1200
3	1-1/8	target	7-1/2, 8, 0, 7-1/2x8	Win., Fed., Rem., Fio.	$7	1200
2-3/4	1-1/8	target	7-1/2, 8, 8-1/2, 9, 7-1/2x8	Win., Fed., Rem., Fio.	$7	1145

Dram Equiv.	Shot Ozs.	Load Style	Shot Sizes	Brands	Avg. Price/ box	Velocity (fps)
12 Gauge 2-3/4" *(cont.)*						
2-3/4	1-1/8	low recoil	7-1/2, 8	Rem.	NA	1145
2-1/2	26 grams	low recoil	8	Win.	NA	980
2-1/4	1-1/8	target	7-1/2, 8, 8-1/2, 9	Rem., Fed.	$7	1080
Max	1	spreader	7-1/2, 8, 8-1/2, 9	Fio.	NA	1300
3-1/4	28 grams (1 oz)	target	7-1/2, 8, 9	Win., Fed., Rem., Fio.	$8	1290
3	1	target	7-1/2, 8, 8-1/2, 9	Win., Fio.	NA	1235
2-3/4	1	target	7-1/2, 8, 8-1/2, 9	Fed., Rem., Fio.	NA	1180
3-1/4	24 grams	target	7-1/2, 8, 9	Fed., Win., Fio.	NA	1325
3	7/8	light	8	Fio.	NA	1200
3-3/4	8 pellets	buffered	000 buck	Win., Fed., Rem.	$4**	1325
4	12 pellets	premium	00 buck	Win., Fed., Rem.	$5**	1290
3-3/4	9 pellets	buffered	00 buck	Win., Fed., Rem., Fio.	$19	1325
3-3/4	12 pellets	buffered	0 buck	Win., Fed., Rem.	$4**	1275
4	20 pellets	buffered	1 buck	Win., Fed., Rem.	$4**	1075
3-3/4	16 pellets	buffered	1 buck	Win., Fed., Rem.	$4**	1250
4	34 pellets	premium	4 buck	Fed., Rem.	$5**	1250
3-3/4	27 pellets	buffered	4 buck	Win., Fed., Rem., Fio.	$4**	1325
		PDX1	1 oz. slug, 3-00 buck	Win.	NA	1150
Max	1 oz	segmenting, slug	slug	Win.	NA	1600
Max	1	saboted slug	slug	Win., Fed., Rem.	$10**	1450
Max	1-1/4	slug, rifled	slug	Fed.	NA	1520
Max	1-1/4	slug	slug	Lightfield		1440
Max	1-1/4	saboted slug	attached sabot	Rem.	NA	1550
Max	1	slug, rifled	slug, magnum	Rem., Fio.	$5**	1680
Max	1	slug, rifled	slug	Win., Fed., Rem.	$4**	1610
Max	1	sabot slug	slug	Sauvestre		1640
Max	7/8	slug, rifled	slug	Rem.	NA	1800
Max	400	plat. tip	sabot slug	Win.	NA	1700
Max	385 grains	Partition Gold Slug	slug	Win.	NA	1900
Max	385 grains	Core-Lokt bonded	sabot slug	Rem.	NA	1900
Max	325 grains	Barnes Sabot	slug	Fed.	NA	1900
Max	300 grains	SST Slug	sabot slug	Hornady	NA	2050
Max	3/4	Tracer	#8 + tracer	Fio.	NA	1150

12 Gauge 2-3/4" *(cont.)*

Dram Equiv.	Shot Ozs.	Load Style	Shot Sizes	Brands	Avg. Price/box	Velocity (fps)
Max	130 grains	Less Lethal	.73 rubber slug	Lightfield	NA	600
Max	3/4	non-toxic	zinc slug	Win.	NA	NA
3	1-1/8	steel target	6-1/2, 7	Rem.	NA	1200
2-3/4	1-1/8	steel target	7	Rem.	NA	1145
3	1#	steel	7	Win.	$11	1235
3-1/2	1-1/4	steel	T, BBB, BB, 1, 2, 3, 4, 5, 6	Win., Fed., Rem.	$18	1275
3-3/4	1-1/8	steel	BB, 1, 2, 3, 4, 5, 6	Win., Fed., Rem., Fio.	$16	1365
3-3/4	1	steel	2, 3, 4, 5, 6, 7	Win., Fed., Rem., Fio.	$13	1390
Max	7/8	steel	7	Fio.	NA	1440

16 Gauge 2-3/4"

Dram Equiv.	Shot Ozs.	Load Style	Shot Sizes	Brands	Avg. Price/box	Velocity (fps)
3-1/4	1-1/4	magnum	2, 4, 6	Fed., Rem.	$16	1260
3-1/4	1-1/8	high velocity	4, 6, 7-1/2	Win., Fed., Rem., Fio.	$12	1295
Max	1-1/8	Bismuth	4, 5	Bis.	NA	1200
2-3/4	1-1/8	standard velocity	6, 7-1/2, 8	Fed., Rem., Fio.	$9	1185
2-1/2	1	dove	6, 7-1/2, 8, 9	Fio., Win.	NA	1165
2-3/4	1		6, 7-1/2, 8	Fio.	NA	1200
Max	15/16	steel	2, 4	Fed., Rem.	NA	1300
Max	7/8	steel	2, 4	Win.	$16	1300
3	12 pellets	buffered	1 buck	Win., Fed., Rem.	$4**	1225
Max	4/5	slug, rifled	slug	Win., Fed., Rem.	$4**	1570
Max	.92	sabot slug	slug	Sauvestre	NA	1560

20 Gauge 3" Magnum

Dram Equiv.	Shot Ozs.	Load Style	Shot Sizes	Brands	Avg. Price/box	Velocity (fps)
3	1-1/4	premium	2, 4, 5, 6, 7-1/2	Win., Fed., Rem.	$15	1185
Max	1-1/4	Wingmaster HD	4, 6	Rem.	NA	1185
3	1-1/4	turkey	4, 6	Fio.	NA	1200
Max	1-1/4	Hevi-shot	2, 4, 6	Hevi-shot	NA	1250
Max	1-1/8	high density	4, 6	Rem.	NA	1300
Max	18 pellets	buck shot	2 buck	Fed.	NA	1200
Max	24 pellets	buffered	3 buck	Win.	$5**	1150
2-3/4	20 pellets	buck	3 buck	Rem.	$4**	1200
Max	1	hypersonic	2, 3, 4	Rem.	NA	Rem.

20 Gauge 3" Magnum *(cont.)*

Dram Equiv.	Shot Ozs.	Load Style	Shot Sizes	Brands	Avg. Price/box	Velocity (fps)
3-1/4	1	steel	1, 2, 3, 4, 5, 6	Win., Fed., Rem.	$15	1330
Max	1	blind side	Hex, 2, 5	Win.	NA	1300
Max	7/8	steel	2, 4	Win.	NA	1300
Max	7/8	FS lead	3, 4	Fed.	NA	1500
Max	1-1/16	high density	2, 4	Win.	NA	1400
Max	1-1/16	Bismuth	2, 4, 5, 6	Bismuth	NA	1250
Mag	5/8	saboted slug	275 gr.	Fed.	NA	1900
Max	3/4	TruBall slug	slug	Fed.	NA	1700

20 Gauge 2-3/4"

Dram Equiv.	Shot Ozs.	Load Style	Shot Sizes	Brands	Avg. Price/box	Velocity (fps)
2-3/4	1-1/8	magnum	4, 6, 7-1/2	Win., Fed., Rem.	$14	1175
2-3/4	1	high velocity	4, 5, 6, 7-1/2, 8, 9	Win., Fed., Rem., Fio.	$12	1220
Max	1	Bismuth	4, 6	Bis.	NA	1200
Max	1	Hevi-shot	5	Hevi-shot	NA	1250
Max	1	Supreme H-V	4, 6, 7-1/2	Win. Rem.	NA	1300
Max	1	FS lead	4, 5, 6	Fed.	NA	1350
Max	7/8	Steel	2, 3, 4	Fio.	NA	1500
2-1/2	1	standard velocity	6, 7-1/2, 8	Win., Rem., Fed., Fio.	$6	1165
2-1/2	7/8	clays	8	Rem.	NA	1200
2-1/2	7/8	promotional	6, 7-1/2, 8	Win., Rem., Fio.	$6	1210
2-1/2	1	target	8, 9	Win., Rem.	$8	1165
Max	7/8	clays	7-1/2, 8	Win.	NA	1275
2-1/2	7/8	target	8, 9	Win., Fed., Rem.	$8	1200
Max	3/4	steel	2, 4	Rem.	NA	1425
2-1/2	7/8	steel - target	7	Rem.	NA	1200
1-1/2	7/8	low recoil	8	Win.	NA	980
Max	1	buckhammer	slug	Rem.	NA	1500
Max	5/8	Saboted Slug	Copper Slug	Rem.	NA	1500
Max	20 pellets	buffered	3 buck	Win., Fed.	$4	1200
Max	5/8	slug, saboted	slug	Win.,	$9**	1400
2-3/4	5/8	slug, rifled	slug	Rem.	$4**	1580
Max	3/4	saboted slug	copper slug	Fed., Rem.	NA	1450

20 Gauge 2-3/4" (cont.)

Dram Equiv.	Shot Ozs.	Load Style	Shot Sizes	Brands	Avg. Price/box	Velocity (fps)
Max	3/4	slug, rifled	slug	Win., Fed., Rem., Fio.	$4**	1570
Max	.9	sabot slug	slug	Sauvestre		1480
Max	260 grains	Partition Gold Slug	slug	Win.	NA	1900
Max	260 grains	Core-Lokt Ultra	slug	Rem.	NA	1900
Max	260 grains	saboted slug	platinum tip	Win.	NA	1700
Max	3/4	steel	2, 3, 4, 6	Win., Fed., Rem.	$14	1425
Max	250 grains	SST slug	slug	Hornady	NA	1800
Max	1/2	rifled, slug	slug	Rem.	NA	1800
Max	67 grains	Less lethal	2/.60 rubber balls	Lightfield	NA	900

28 Gauge 3"

Dram Equiv.	Shot Ozs.	Load Style	Shot Sizes	Brands	Avg. Price/box	Velocity (fps)
Max	7/8	tundra tungsten	4, 5, 6	Fiocchi	NA	TBD

28 Gauge 2-3/4"

Dram Equiv.	Shot Ozs.	Load Style	Shot Sizes	Brands	Avg. Price/box	Velocity (fps)
2	1	high velocity	6, 7-1/2, 8	Win.	$12	1125
2-1/4	3/4	high velocity	6, 7-1/2, 8, 9	Win., Fed., Rem., Fio.	$11	1295
2	3/4	target	8, 9	Win., Fed., Rem.	$9	1200
Max	3/4	sporting clays	7-1/2, 8-1/2	Win.	NA	1300
Max	5/8	Bismuth	4, 6	Bis.	NA	1250

28 Gauge 2-3/4" (cont.)

Dram Equiv.	Shot Ozs.	Load Style	Shot Sizes	Brands	Avg. Price/box	Velocity (fps)
Max	5/8	steel	6, 7	NA	NA	1300
Max	5/8	slug		Bren.	NA	1450

410 Bore 3"

Dram Equiv.	Shot Ozs.	Load Style	Shot Sizes	Brands	Avg. Price/box	Velocity (fps)
Max	11/16	high velocity	4, 5, 6, 7-1/2, 8, 9	Win., Fed., Rem., Fio.	$10	1135
Max	9/16	Bismuth	4	Bis.	NA	1175
Max	3/8	steel	6	NA	NA	1400
		judge	5 pellets 000 Buck	Fed.	NA	960
		judge	9 pellets #4 Buck	Fed.	NA	1100
Max	Mixed	Per. Defense	3DD/12BB	Win.	NA	750

410 Bore 2-1/2"

Dram Equiv.	Shot Ozs.	Load Style	Shot Sizes	Brands	Avg. Price/box	Velocity (fps)
Max	1/2	high velocity	4, 6, 7-1/2	Win., Fed., Rem.	$9	1245
Max	1/5	slug, rifled	slug	Win., Fed., Rem.	$4**	1815
1-1/2	1/2	target	8, 8-1/2, 9	Win., Fed., Rem., Fio.	$8	1200
Max	1/2	sporting clays	7-1/2, 8, 8-1/2	Win.	NA	1300
Max		Buckshot	5-000 Buck	Win.	NA	1135
		judge	12-bb's, 3 disks	Win.	NA	TBD
Max	Mixed	Per. Defense	4DD/16BB	Win.	NA	750
Max	42 grains	Less lethal	4/.41 rubber balls	Lightfield	NA	1150

ACCU-TEK AT-380 II ACP
Caliber: 380 ACP, 6-shot magazine. **Barrel:** 2.8" **Weight:** 23.5 oz.
Length: 6.125" overall. **Grips:** Textured black composition. **Sights:** Blade front, rear adjustable for windage. **Features:** Made from 17-4 stainless steel, has an exposed hammer, manual firing-pin safety block and trigger disconnect. Magazine release located on the bottom of the grip. American made, lifetime warranty. Comes with two 6-round stainless steel magazines and a California-approved cable lock. Introduced 2006. Made in U.S.A. by Excel Industries.
Price: Satin stainless $289.00

ACCU-TEK HC-380
Simlar to AT-380 II except has a 13-round magazine.
Price: $330.00

ACCU-TEK LT-380
Simlar to AT-380 II except has a lightweight aluminum frame.
Weight: 15 ounces.
Price: $324.00

AKDAL GHOST SERIES
Caliber: 9x19mm 15-round double stacked magazine. **Barrel:** 4.45" **Weight:** 29.10 oz. **Length:** 7.5" overall. **Grips:** Polymer black polycoat. **Sights:** Fixed, open type with notched rear sight dovetailed into the slide. Adjustable sight also available. **Features:** Compact single action pre-cocked, semiautomatic pistol with short recoil operation and locking breech. It uses modified Browning-type locking, in which barrel engages the slide with single lug, entering the ejection window. Pistol also has no manual safeties; instead, it has automatic trigger and firing pin safeties. The polymer frame features removable backstraps (of different sizes), and an integral accessory Picatinny rail below the barrel.
Price: $499.00

AMERICAN CLASSIC 1911-A1
Caliber: .45 ACP. 7+1 magazine capacity. **Barrel:** 5" **Grips:** Checkered walnut. **Sights:** Fixed. **Finish:** Blue or hard chromed. A .22 LR version is also available. Other variations include Trophy model with adjustable sights, two-tone finish.
Price: .... $579.00 to $811.00

AMERICAN CLASSIC COMMANDER
Caliber: .45 ACP. Same features as 1911-A1 model except is Commander size with 4.25" barrel.
Price: $616.00

AMERICAN TACTICAL IMPORTS MILITARY 1911
Caliber: .45 ACP. 7+1 magazine capacity. **Barrel:** 5" **Grips:** Textured mahogany. **Sights:** Fixed military style. **Finish:** Blue. Also offered in Commander and Officer's sizes and Enhanced model with additional features.
Price: .... $500.00 to $585.00

ARMALITE AR-24
Caliber: 9mm Para., 10- or 15-shot magazine. **Barrel:** 4.671" 6-groove, right-hand cut rifling. **Weight:** 34.9 oz. **Length:** 8.27" overall. **Grips:** Black polymer. **Sights:** Dovetail front, fixed rear, 3-dot luminous design. **Features:** Machined slide, frame and barrel. Serrations on forestrap and backstrap, external thumb safety and internal firing pin box, half cock. Two 15-round magazines, pistol case, pistol lock, manual and cleaning brushes. Manganese phosphate finish. Compact comes with two 13-round magazines, 3.89 barrel, weighs 33.4 oz. Made in U.S.A. by ArmaLite.
Price: AR-24 Full Size $550.00
Price: AR-24K Compact $550.00

ARMSCOR/ROCK ISLAND ARMORY 1911A1-45 FS GI
1911-style semiauto pistol chambered in .45 ACP (8 rounds), 9mm Parabellum, .38 Super (9 rounds). Features include checkered plastic or hardwood grips, 5-inch barrel, parkerized steel frame and slide, drift adjustable sights.
Price: $500.00

Prices given are believed to be accurate at time of publication however, many factors affect retail pricing so exact prices are not possible.

ARMSCOR/ROCK ISLAND ARMORY 1911A1-45 CS GI
1911-style Officer's-size semiauto pistol chambered in .45 ACP. Features plain hardwood grips, 3.5-inch barrel, parkerized steel frame and slide, drift adjustable sights.
Price: $500.00

ARMSCOR/ROCK ISLAND ARMORY 1911A2-.22 TCM
Caliber: .22 TCM, 17-round magazine. **Barrel:** 5 inches. **Weight:** 36 oz. **Length:** 8.5 inches. **Grips:** Polymer. **Sights:** Adjustable rear. **Features:** Chambered for high velocity .22 TCM rimfire cartridge.
Price: $660.00

ARMSCOR/ROCK ISLAND ARMORY 1911 TACTICAL II FS
Caliber: 10mm, 8-round magazine. **Barrel:** 5 inches. **Weight:** 40 oz. **Length:** 8.5 inches. **Grips:** VZ G10. **Sights:** Fiber optic front, adjustable rear. **Features:** Parkerized finish, comes with two magazines, lock and lockable hard case. Accessory rail available.
Price: $660.00

ARMSCOR/ROCK ISLAND ARMORY MAP1 & MAPP1
Caliber: 9mm, 16-round magazine. Browning short recoil action style pistols with: integrated front sight; Snag-free rear sight (police standard); Tanfoglio barrel; Single & double-action trigger; automatic safety on firing pin & manual on rear lever; standard hammer; side extractor; standard or ambidextrous rear safety; combat slide stop; parkerized finish for nickel steel parts; polymer frame with accessory rail.
Price: $400.00

ARMSCOR/ROCK ISLAND ARMORY XT22
Caliber: .22 LR, 15-round magazine std. **Barrel:** 5" **Weight:** 38 oz. The XT-22 is a combat 1911 .22 pistol. Unlike most .22 1911 conversions, this pistol is built as a complete gun. Designed for durability, it is the only .22 1911 with a forged 4140 steel slide and the only .22 1911 with a one piece 4140 chrome moly barrel.
Price: $473.99

ARMSCOR/ROCK ISLAND ARMORY BABY ROCK 380
Caliber: .380 ACP, 7-round magazine. Blowback operation. An 85 percent-size version of 1911-A1 design with features identical to full-size model.
Price: $460.00

AUTO-ORDNANCE 1911A1
Caliber: 45 ACP, 7-shot magazine. **Barrel:** 5" **Weight:** 39 oz. **Length:** 8.5" overall. **Grips:** Brown checkered plastic with medallion. **Sights:** Blade front, rear drift-adjustable for windage. **Features:** Same specs as 1911A1 military guns-parts interchangeable. Frame and slide blued; each radius has non-glare finish. Introduced 2002. Made in U.S.A. by Kahr Arms.
Price: 1911PKZSE Parkerized, plastic grips $668.00
Price: 1911PKZSEW Parkerized, wood grips........................$685.00
Price: 1911TC Stainless...$813.00

BAER H.C. 40
Caliber: 40 S&W, 18-shot magazine. **Barrel:** 5" **Weight:** 37 oz. **Length:** 8.5" overall. **Grips:** Wood. **Sights:** Low-mount adjustable rear sight with hidden rear leaf, dovetail front sight. **Features:** Double-stack Caspian frame, beavertail grip safety, ambidextrous thumb safety, 40 S&W match barrel with supported chamber, match stainless steel barrel bushing, lowered and flared ejection port, extended ejector, match trigger fitted, integral mag well, bead blast blue finish on lower, polished sides on slide. Introduced 2008. Made in U.S.A. by Les Baer Custom, Inc.
Price: $2,960.00

BAER 1911 BOSS .45
Caliber: .45 ACP, 8+1 capacity. **Barrel:** 5" **Weight:** 37 oz. **Length:** 8.5" overall. **Grips:** Premium Checkered Cocobolo Grips. **Sights:** Low-Mount LBC Adj Sight, Red Fiber Optic Front. **Features:** Speed Trgr, Beveled Mag Well, Rounded for Tactical. Rear cocking serrations on the slide, Baer fiber optic front sight (red), flat mainspring housing, checkered at 20 lpi, extended combat safety, Special tactical package, chromed complete lower, blued slide, (2) 8-round premium magazines.
Price: $2,560.00

BAER 1911 CUSTOM CARRY
Caliber: .45 ACP, 7- or 10-shot magazine. **Barrel:** 5" **Weight:** 37 oz. **Length:** 8.5" overall. **Grips:** Checkered walnut. **Sights:** Baer

improved ramp-style dovetailed front, Novak low-mount rear.
Features: Baer forged NM frame, slide and barrel with stainless bushing. Baer speed trigger with 4-lb. pull. Partial listing shown. Made in U.S.A. by Les Baer Custom, Inc.
Price: Custom Carry 5, blued $2,190.00
Price: Custom Carry 5, stainless $2,290.00
Price: Custom Carry 4 Commanche length, blued $2,190.00
Price: Custom Carry 4 Commanche length, .38 Super $2,550.00

BAER 1911 ULTIMATE RECON
Caliber: .45 ACP, 7- or 10-shot magazine. **Barrel:** 5" **Weight:** 37 oz. **Length:** 8.5" overall. **Grips:** Checkered cocobolo. **Sights:** Baer improved ramp-style dovetailed front, Novak low-mount rear. **Features:** NM Caspian frame, slide and barrel with stainless bushing. Baer speed trigger with 4-lb. pull. Includes integral Picatinny rail and Sure-Fire X-200 light. Made in U.S.A. by Les Baer Custom, Inc. Introduced 2006.
Price: Bead blast blued $2,650.00
Price: Bead blast chrome $2,910.00

BAER 1911 PREMIER II
Caliber: .38 Super, 400 Cor-Bon, .45 ACP, 7- or 10-shot magazine. **Barrel:** 5" **Weight:** 37 oz. **Length:** 8.5" overall. **Grips:** Checkered rosewood, double diamond pattern. **Sights:** Baer dovetailed front, low-mount Bo-Mar rear with hidden leaf. **Features:** Baer NM forged steel frame and barrel with stainless bushing, deluxe Commander hammer and sear, beavertail grip safety with pad, extended ambidextrous safety; flat mainspring housing; 30 lpi checkered front strap. Made in U.S.A. by Les Baer Custom, Inc.
Price: 5" .45 ACP $2,180.00
Price: 5" 400 Cor-Bon $2,380.00
Price: 5" .38 Super $2,620.00
Price: 6" .45 ACP, 400 Cor-Bon, .38 Super, from $2,390.00
Price: Super-Tac, .45 ACP, 400 Cor-Bon, .38 Super, from $2,650.00

BAER 1911 S.R.P.
Caliber: .45 ACP. **Barrel:** 5" **Weight:** 37 oz. **Length:** 8.5" overall. **Grips:** Checkered walnut. **Sights:** Trijicon night sights. **Features:** Similar to the F.B.I. contract gun except uses Baer forged steel frame. Has Baer match barrel with supported chamber, complete tactical action. Has Baer Ultra Coat finish. Introduced 1996. Made in U.S.A. by Les Baer Custom, Inc.
Price: Government or Commanche length $2,840.00

BAER 1911 STINGER
Caliber: .45 ACP or .38 Super, 7-round magazine. **Barrel:** 5" **Weight:** 34 oz. **Length:** 8.5" overall. **Grips:** Checkered cocobolo. **Sights:** Baer dovetailed front, low-mount Bo-Mar rear with hidden leaf. **Features:** Baer NM frame. Baer Commanche slide, Officer's style grip frame, beveled mag well. Made in U.S.A. by Les Baer Custom, Inc.
Price: .45 ACP ....$2,240.00 to $2,310.00
Price: .38 Super $2,840.00

BAER 1911 PROWLER III
Caliber: .45 ACP, 8-round magazine. **Barrel:** 5" **Weight:** 34 oz. **Length:** 8.5" overall. **Grips:** Checkered cocobolo. **Sights:** Baer dovetailed front, low-mount Bo-Mar rear with hidden leaf. **Features:** Similar to Premier II with tapered cone stub weight, rounded corners. Made in U.S.A. by Les Baer Custom, Inc.
Price: Blued $2,910.00

BERETTA M92/96 A1 SERIES
Caliber: 9mm, 15-round magazine; .40 S&W, 12 rounds (M96 A1). **Barrel:** 4.9 inches. **Weight:** 33-34 oz. **Length:** 8.5 inches. **Sights:** Fiber optic front, adjustable rear. **Features:** Same as other models in 92/96 family except for addition of accessory rail.
Price: $775.00

BERETTA MODEL 92FS
Caliber: 9mm Para., 10-shot magazine. **Barrel:** 4.9" **Weight:** 34 oz. **Length:** 8.5" overall. **Grips:** Checkered black plastic. **Sights:** Blade front, rear adjustable for windage. Tritium night sights available. **Features:** Double action. Extractor acts as chamber loaded indicator, squared trigger guard, grooved front and backstraps, inertia firing pin. Matte or blued finish. Introduced 1977. Made in U.S.A.
Price: $675.00
Price: Inox $775.00
Price: With LaserMax $1,074.00

BERETTA MODEL 21 BOBCAT
Caliber: .22 LR or .25 ACP. Both double action. **Barrel:** 2.4" **Weight:** 11.5 oz.; 11.8 oz. **Length:** 4.9" overall. **Grips:** Plastic. **Features:** Available in matte black or stainless. Introduced in 1985.
Price: Black matte $410.00
Price: Stainless $450.00

BERETTA MODEL 3032 TOMCAT
Caliber: .32 ACP, 7-shot magazine. **Barrel:** 2.45" **Weight:** 14.5 oz. **Length:** 5" overall. **Grips:** Checkered black plastic. **Sights:** Blade front, drift-adjustable rear. **Features:** Double action with exposed hammer; tip-up barrel for direct loading/unloading; thumb safety; polished or matte blue finish. Made in U.S.A. Introduced 1996.
Price: Matte $390.00
Price: Inox $485.00

Prices given are believed to be accurate at time of publication however, many factors affect retail pricing so exact prices are not possible.

BERETTA MODEL U22 NEOS
Caliber: .22 LR, 10-shot magazine. **Barrel:** 4.5" and 6" **Weight:** 32 oz.; 36 oz. **Length:** 8.8"/ 10.3" **Sights:** Target.
Features: Integral rail for standard scope mounts, light, perfectly weighted, 100 percent American made by Beretta.
Price: Blue $325.00
Price: Inox $350.00

BERETTA MODEL PX4 STORM
Caliber: 9mm Para., 40 S&W. **Capacity:** 17 (9mm Para.); 14 (40 S&W). **Barrel:** 4" **Weight:** 27.5 oz. **Grips:** Black checkered w/3 interchangeable backstraps. **Sights:** 3-dot system coated in Superluminova; removable front and rear sights. **Features:** DA/SA, manual safety/hammer decocking lever (ambi) and automatic firing pin block safety. Picatinny rail. Comes with two magazines (17/10 in 9mm Para. and 14/10 in 40 S&W). Removable hammer unit. American made by Beretta. Introduced 2005.
Price: 9mm or .40 .... $575.00
Price: .45 ACP $650.00
Price: .45 ACP SD (Special Duty) $1,150.00

BERETTA MODEL PX4 STORM SUB-COMPACT
Caliber: 9mm, 40 S&W. **Capacity:** 13 (9mm); 10 (40 S&W). **Barrel:** 3" **Weight:** 26.1 oz. **Length:** 6.2" overall. **Grips:** NA. **Sights:** NA.
Features: Ambidextrous manual safety lever, interchangeable backstraps included, lock breech and tilt barrel system, stainless

steel barrel, Picatinny rail.
Price: $600.00

BERETTA MODEL M9
Caliber: 9mm Para. **Capacity:** 15. **Barrel:** 4.9" **Weight:** 32.2-35.3 oz. **Grips:** Plastic. **Sights:** Dot and post, low profile, windage adjustable rear. **Features:** DA/SA, forged aluminum alloy frame, delayed locking-bolt system, manual safety doubles as decocking lever, combat-style trigger guard, loaded chamber indicator. Comes with two magazines (15/10). American made by Beretta. Introduced 2005.
Price: $650.00

BERETTA MODEL M9A1
Caliber: 9mm Para. **Capacity:** 15. **Barrel:** 4.9" **Weight:** 32.2-35.3 oz. **Grips:** Plastic. **Sights:** Dot and post, low profile, windage adjustable rear. **Features:** Same as M9, but also includes integral Mil-Std-1913 Picatinny rail, has checkered frontstrap and backstrap. Comes with two magazines (15/10). American made by Beretta. Introduced 2005.
Price: $750.00

BERETTA NANO
Caliber: 9mm Para. Six-shot magazine. **Barrel:** 3.07". **Weight:** 17.7 oz. **Length:** 5.7" overall. **Grips:** Polymer. **Sights:** 3-dot low profile.
Features: Double-action only, striker fired. Replaceable grip frames.
Price: $475.00

BERSA THUNDER 9 ULTRA COMPACT/40 SERIES
Caliber: 9mm Para., 40 S&W. **Barrel:** 3.5" **Weight:** 24.5 oz. **Length:** 6.6" overall. **Features:** Otherwise similar to Thunder 45 Ultra Compact. 9mm Para. High Capacity model has 17-round capacity. 40 High Capacity model has 13-round capacity. Imported from Argentina by Eagle Imports, Inc.
Price: $500.00

BERSA THUNDER 22
Caliber: .22 LR, 10-round magazine. **Weight:** 19 oz. **Features:** Similar to Thunder .380 Series except for caliber. Alloy frame and slide. Finish: Matte black, satin nickel or duo-tone.
Price: $349.00

BERETTA PICO
Caliber: .380 ACP, 6 rounds. **Barrel:** 2.7" **Weight:** 11.5 oz. **Length:** 5.1" overall. **Grips:** Integral with polymer frame. Interchangeable backstrap. **Sights:** White outline rear. **Features:** Adjustable, quick-change. Striker-fired, double-action only operation. Ambidextrous magazine release and slide release. Ships with two magazines, one flush, one with grip extension. Made in the USA.
Price: $399.00

BERSA THUNDER 45 ULTRA COMPACT
Caliber: .45 ACP. **Barrel:** 3.6" **Weight:** 27 oz. **Length:** 6.7" overall. **Grips:** Anatomically designed polymer. **Sights:** White outline rear. **Features:** Double action; firing pin safeties, integral locking system. Available in matte, satin nickel, gold, or duo-tone. Introduced 2003. Imported from Argentina by Eagle Imports, Inc.
Price: Thunder 45, matte blue $500.00
Price: Thunder 45, duo-tone $550.00

BOBERG XR9-S
Caliber: 9mm, 7-round magazine. **Barrel:** 3.35 inches. XR9-L has 4.2 inch barrel. **Weight:** 17.4 oz. **Length:** 5.1 inches, 5.95 (XR9-L). **Sights:** Fixed low profile. **Features:** Unique rotating barrel, locked-breech operation, with "pull-push" feeding system utilizing a claw-type loader attached to the slide to pull rounds from the magazine. Black polymer frame with stainless steel barrel. Available with all black or platinum finish.
Price: $1,099.00
Price: (XR-9L)...$1,349.00

BERSA THUNDER 380 SERIES
Caliber: .380 ACP, 7 rounds. **Barrel:** 3.5" **Weight:** 23 oz. **Length:** 6.6" overall. **Features:** Otherwise similar to Thunder 45 Ultra Compact. 380 DLX has 9-round capacity. 380 Concealed Carry has 8-round capacity. Imported from Argentina by Eagle Imports, Inc.
Price: Thunder Matte $335.00
Price: Thunder Satin Nickel $355.00
Price: Thunder Duo-Tone $355.00
Price: Thunder Duo-Tone with Crimson Trace Laser Grips $555.00

BROWNING 1911-22 COMPACT
Caliber: .22 L.R.,10-round magazine. **Barrel:** 3.625" **Weight:** 15 oz. **Length:** 6.5" overall. **Grips:** Brown composite. **Sights:** Fixed.

Prices given are believed to be accurate at time of publication however, many factors affect retail pricing so exact prices are not possible.

Features: Slide is machined aluminum with alloy frame and matte blue finish. Blowback action and single action trigger with manual thumb and grip safetys. Works, feels and functions just like a full size 1911. It is simply scaled down and chambered in the best of all practice rounds: .22 LR for focus on the fundamentals.
Price: $600.00

BROWNING 1911-22 A1
Caliber: .22 L.R.,10-round magazine. **Barrel:** 4.25" **Weight:** 16 oz. **Length:** 7.0625" overall. **Grips:** Brown composite. **Sights:** Fixed. **Features:** Slide is machined aluminum with alloy frame and matte blue finish. Blowback action and single action trigger with manual thumb and grip safetys. Works, feels and functions just like a full size 1911. It is simply scaled down and chambered in the best of all practice rounds: .22 LR for focus on the fundamentals.
Price: $600.00

BROWNING 1911-380
Caliber: ..380 ACP. 8-round magazine. **Barrel:** 4.25" **Weight:** 18 oz.
Features: Aluminum slide, polymer frame. Features are virtually identical to those on the 1911-22.
Price: $670.00

BROWNING 1911-22 POLYMER WITH RAIL
Caliber: .22 L.R.,10-round magazine. **Barrel:** 4.25" or 3.625" (Compact model, shown). **Weight:** 14 oz. overall. **Features:** Other features are similar to standard 1911-22 except for this model's composite/polymer frame, extended grip safety, stipled black laminated grip, skeleton trigger and hammer. Available with accessory rail (shown).
Price: $640.00
Price: With Rail $670.00

BROWNING HI-POWER
Caliber: 9mm, 13-round magazine. **Barrel:** 4.625 inches. **Weight:** 32 oz. **Length:** 7.75 Inches. **Grips:** Checkered walnut (standard model), textured and grooved polymer (Mark III). **Sights:** Fixed low-profile 3-dot (Mark III), fixed or adjustable low profile (standard model).
Features: Single-action operation with ambidextrous thumb safety, forged steel frame and slide. Made in Belgium.
Price: Mark III...$1,070.00
Price: Fixed Sights...$1,080.00

Price: Standard, Adjustable sights $1,160.00

BROWNING 1911-22 POLYMER DESERT TAN
Caliber: .22 L.R.,10-round magazine. **Barrel:** 4.25" or 3.625" **Weight:** 13-14 oz. overall. **Features:** Other features are similar to standard 1911-22 except for this model's composite/polymer frame. Also available with pink composite grips.
Price: $580.00

BROWNING BUCK MARK CAMPER UFX
Caliber: .22 LR with 10-shot magazine. **Barrel:** 5.5" tapered bull.
Weight: 34 oz. **Length:** 9.5" overall. **Grips:** Overmolded Ultragrip Ambidextrous. **Sights:** Pro-Target adjustable rear, ramp front.
Features: Matte blue receiver, matte blue or stainless barrel.
Price: Camper UFX $390.00
Price: Camper UFX stainless $430.00

BROWNING BUCK MARK HUNTER

Caliber: .22 LR with 10-shot magazine. **Barrel:** 7.25" heavy tapered bull. **Weight:** 38 oz. **Length:** 11.3" overall. **Grips:** Cocobolo target. **Sights:** Pro-Target adjustable rear, Tru-Glo/Marble's fiber-optic front. Integral scope base on top rail. Scope in photo is not included. **Features:** Matte blue.
Price: $500.00

BROWNING BUCK PRACTICAL URX

Caliber: .22 LR with 10-shot magazine. **Barrel:** 5.5" tapered bull. **Weight:** 34 oz. **Length:** 9.5" overall. **Grips:** Ultragrip RX Ambidextrous. **Sights:** Pro-Target adjustable rear, Tru-Glo/Marble's fiber-optic front. **Features:** Matte gray receiver, matte blue barrel.
Price: $440.00

BROWNING BUCK MARK PLUS UDX

Caliber: .22 LR with 10-shot magazine. **Barrel:** 5.5" slab sided. **Weight:** 34 oz. **Length:** 9.5" overall. **Grips:** Walnut Ultragrip DX Ambidextrous. **Sights:** Pro-Target adjustable rear, Tru-Glo/Marble's fiber-optic front. **Features:** Matte blue.
Price: $540.00

BUSHMASTER XM-15 PATROLMAN'S AR PISTOL

Caliber: 5.56/223, 30-round. **Barrel:** 7" or 10.5" stainless steel with A2-type flash hider, knurled free-float handguard. **Weight:** 5.2 to 5.7 lbs. (4.9 to 5.5 lbs., Enhanced model). **Length:** 23" to 26.5" **Grips:** A2 pistol grip with standard triggerguard. **Features:** AR-style semi-auto pistol. Enhanced model has Barnes Precision free-float lightweight quad rail, Magpul MOE pistol grip and triggerguard.
Price: $973.00
Price: Enhanced... $1,229.00

CHIAPPA 1911-22

A faithful replica of the famous John Browning 1911A1 pistol.
Caliber: .22 LR. **Barrel:** 5". **Weight:** 33.5 oz. **Length:** 8.5". **Grips:** Two-piece wood. **Sights:** Fixed. **Features:** Fixed barrel design, 10-shot magazine. Available in black, OD green or tan finish. Target and Tactical models have adjustable sights.
Price: .... $300 to $419

CHIAPPA M9-22 STANDARD

Caliber: .22 LR. **Barrel:** 5" **Weight:** 2.3 lbs. **Length:** 8.5" **Grips:** Black molded plastic or walnut. **Sights:** Fixed front sight and windage adjustable rear sight. **Features:** The M9-9mm has been a U.S. standard-issue service pistol since 1990. Chiappa's M9-22 is a replica of this pistol in 22 LR. The M9-22 has the same weight and feel as its 9mm counterpart but has an affordable 10 shot magazine for the 22 long rifle cartridge which makes it a true rimfire reproduction. Comes standard with steel trigger, hammer assembly and a 1/2-28 threaded barrel.
Price: $369.00

CHIAPPA M9-22 TACTICAL

Caliber: .22 LR. **Barrel:** 5" **Weight:** 2.3 lbs. **Length:** 8.5" **Grips:** Black molded plastic. **Sights:** Fixed front sight and Novak style rear sites. **Features:** The M9-22 Tactical model has Novak style rear sites and comes with a fake suppressor (this ups the "cool factor" on the range

Prices given are believed to be accurate at time of publication however, many factors affect retail pricing so exact prices are not possible.

and extends the barrel to make it even more accurate). It also has a 1/2 x 28 thread adaptor which can be used by those with a legal suppressor.

Price: $419.00

CHRISTENSEN ARMS 1911 SERIES

Caliber: .45 ACP, .40 S&W, 9mm. **Barrel:** 3.7", 4.3", 5.5" **Features:** All models are built on a titanium frame with hand-fitted slide, match-grade barrel, tritium night sights, G10 Operator grip panels.

Price: $3,195

CITADEL M-1911

Caliber: .45 ACP, .38 Super, 9mm, .22 LR. **Capacity:** 7 (.45), 8 (9mm, .38), or 10 rounds (.22). **Barrel:** 5 or 3.5 inches (.45 & 9mm only). **Weight:** 2.3 lbs. **Length:** 8.5" **Grips:** Checkered wood or Hogue wrap-around polymer. **Sights:** Low-profile combat fixed rear, blade front. **Finish:** Matte black, brushed or polished nickel. **Features:** Extended grip safety, ambidextrous safety and slide release. Built by Armscor (Rock Island Armory) in the Philippines and imported by Legacy Sports.

Price: Matte black..$592.00
Price: Matte black, Hogue grips $630.00
Price: Brushed nickel..$681.00
Price: Polished nickel..$700.00
Price: Matte black, .22 LR $310.00
Price: Matte black, .22 LR, Hogue grips, fiber-optic sights......$592.00

CIMARRON MODEL 1911

Caliber: .45 ACP **Barrel:** 5 inches. **Weight:** 37.5 oz. **Length:** 8.5" overall. **Grips:** Checkered walnut. **Features:** A faithful reproduction of the original pattern of the Model 1911 with Parkerized finish and lanyard ring.

Price: $541.00

COBRA ENTERPRISES FS32, FS380

Caliber: .32 ACP, .380 ACP, 7-shot magazine. **Barrel:** 3.5" **Weight:** 2.1 lbs. **Length:** 6-3/8" overall. **Grips:** Black composition. **Sights:** Fixed. **Features:** Choice of bright chrome, satin nickel or black finish. Introduced 2002. Made in U.S.A. by Cobra Enterprises of Utah, Inc.

Price: .... $129.00 to $165.00

COBRA ENTERPRISES PATRIOT SERIES

Caliber: .380, 9mm or .45 ACP; 6, 7, or 10-shot magazine. **Barrel:** 3.3" **Weight:** 20 oz. **Length:** 6" overall. **Grips:** Black polymer. **Sights:** Rear adjustable. **Features:** Stainless steel or black melonite slide with load indicator; Semi-auto locked breech, DAO. Made in U.S.A. by Cobra Enterprises of Utah, Inc.

Price: .... $349.00 to $395.00

COBRA ENTERPRISES CA32, CA380

Caliber: .32 ACP, .380 ACP. **Barrel:** 2.8" **Weight:** 17 oz. **Length:** 5.4" **Grips:** Black molded synthetic. **Sights:** Fixed. **Features:** Choice of black, satin nickel, or chrome finish. Made in U.S.A. by Cobra Enterprises of Utah, Inc.

Price: $157.00

COBRA DENALI

Caliber: .380 ACP, 5 rounds. **Barrel:** 2.8" **Weight:** 22 oz. **Length:** 5.4" **Grips:** Black molded synthetic integral with frame. **Sights:** Fixed. **Features:** Made in U.S.A. by Cobra Enterprises of Utah, Inc.

Price: $179.00

COLT MODEL 1991 MODEL O

Caliber: .45 ACP, 7-shot magazine. **Barrel:** 5" **Weight:** 38 oz. **Length:** 8.5" overall. **Grips:** Checkered black composition. **Sights:** Ramped blade front, fixed square notch rear, high profile. **Features:** Matte finish. Continuation of serial number range used on original G.I. 1911A1 guns. Comes with one magazine and molded carrying case. Introduced 1991.

Price: Blue $974.00
Price: Stainless $1,038.00

COLT XSE SERIES MODEL O

Caliber: .45 ACP, 8-shot magazine. **Barrel:** 5" **Grips:** Checkered, double diamond rosewood. **Sights:** Drift-adjustable 3-dot combat. **Features:** Brushed stainless finish; adjustable, two-cut aluminum trigger; extended ambidextrous thumb safety; upswept beavertail with palm swell; elongated slot hammer. Introduced 1999. From Colt's Mfg. Co., Inc.

Price: XSE Government $1,104.00

COLT XSE LIGHTWEIGHT COMMANDER

Caliber: .45 ACP, 8-shot. **Barrel:** 4.25" **Weight:** 26 oz. **Length:** 7.75" overall. **Grips:** Double diamond checkered rosewood. **Sights:** Fixed, glare-proofed blade front, square notch rear; 3-dot system. **Features:** Brushed stainless slide, nickeled aluminum frame; McCormick elongated slot enhanced hammer, McCormick two-cut adjustable aluminum hammer. Made in U.S.A. by Colt's Mfg. Co., Inc.

Price: $1,104.00

COLT DEFENDER

Caliber: .45 ACP (7-round magazine), 9mm (8-round). **Barrel:** 3" **Weight:** 22-1/2 oz. **Length:** 6.75" overall. **Grips:** Pebble-finish rubber wraparound with finger grooves. **Sights:** White dot front, snag-free Colt competition rear. **Features:** Stainless finish; aluminum frame; combat-style hammer; Hi Ride grip safety, extended manual safety, disconnect safety. Introduced 1998. Made in U.S.A. by Colt's Mfg. Co., Inc.

Price: 07000D, stainless $1,098.00

COLT SERIES 70
Caliber: .45 ACP. **Barrel:** 5" **Weight:** 37.5 oz. **Length:** 8.5" **Grips:** Rosewood with double diamond checkering pattern. **Sights:** Fixed. **Features:** Custom replica of the Original Series 70 pistol with a Series 70 firing system, original rollmarks. Introduced 2002. Made in U.S.A. by Colt's Mfg. Co., Inc.
Price: Blued **$1,075.00**
Price: Stainless **$1,110.00**

COLT 38 SUPER
Caliber: .38 Super. **Barrel:** 5" **Weight:** 36.5 oz. **Length:** 8.5" **Grips:** Checkered rubber (stainless and blue models); wood with double diamond checkering pattern (bright stainless model). **Sights:** 3-dot. **Features:** Beveled magazine well, standard thumb safety and service-style grip safety. Introduced 2003. Made in U.S.A. by Colt's Mfg. Co., Inc.
Price: Blued **$999.00**
Price: Stainless **$1,377.00**

COLT MUSTANG POCKETLITE
Caliber: .380 ACP. Six-shot magazine. **Barrel:** 2.75". **Weight:** 12.5 oz. **Length:** 5.5". **Grips:** Black composite. **Finish:** Brushed stainless. **Features:** Thumb safety, firing-pin safety block. Introduced 2012.
Price: **$698.00**

COLT MUSTANG XSP
Caliber: .380 ACP. **Features:** Similar to Mustang Pocketlite except has polymer frame, black diamond or bright stainless slide, squared triggerguard, accessory rail, electroless nickel finished controls.
Price: Bright Stainless................................. **$528.00**
Price: Black Diamond-Like Carbon finish............... **$672.00**

COLT NEW AGENT
Caliber: .45 ACP (7+1), 9mm (8+1). **Barrel:** 3" **Weight:** 25 oz. **Length:** 6.75" overall. **Grips:** Double diamond slim fit. **Sights:** Snag free trench style. **Features:** Semi-auto pistol with blued finish and enhanced black anodized aluminum receiver. Skeletonized aluminum trigger, series 80 firing system, front strap

serrations, beveled magazine well. Also available in a double-action-only version (shown), in .45 ACP only.
Price: **$1,078.00**

COLT RAIL GUN
Caliber: .45 ACP (8+1). **Barrel:** NA. **Weight:** NA. **Length:** 8.5" **Grips:** Rosewood double diamond. **Sights:** White dot front and Novak rear. **Features:** 1911-style semi-auto. Stainless steel frame and slide, front and rear slide serrations, skeletonized trigger, integral; accessory rail, Smith & Alexander upswept beavertail grip palm swell safety, tactical thumb safety, National Match barrel.
Price: .... **$1,141.00 to $1,223.00**

COLT SPECIAL COMBAT GOVERNMENT CARRY MODEL
Caliber: .45 ACP (8+1), .38 Super (9+1). **Barrel:** 5" **Weight:** NA. **Length:** 8.5". **Grips:** Black/silver synthetic. **Sights:** Novak front and rear night. **Features:** 1911-style semi-auto. Skeletonized three-hole trigger, slotted hammer, Smith & Alexander upswept beavertail grip palm swell safety and extended magazine well, Wilson tactical ambidextrous safety. Available in blued, hard chrome, or blue/satin nickel finish, depending on chambering. Marine Pistol has Desert Tan Cerakoted stainless steel finish, lanyard loop.
Price: **$2,095.00**
Price: Marine Pistol... **$1,995.00**

COLT GOVERNMENT MODEL 1911A1 .22
Caliber: .22 LR. 12-round magazine. **Barrel:** 5" **Weight:** 36 oz. **Features:** Made in Germany by Walther under exclusive arrangement with Colt Manufacturing Company. Blowback operation. All other features identical to original including manual and grip safeties, drift-adjustable sights.
Price: **$399.00**

CZ 75 B
Caliber: 9mm Para., .40 S&W, 10-shot magazine. **Barrel:** 4.7" **Weight:** 34.3 oz. **Length:** 8.1" overall. **Grips:** High impact

checkered plastic. **Sights:** Square post front, rear adjustable for windage; 3-dot system. **Features:** Single action/double action design; firing pin block safety; choice of black polymer, matte or high-polish blue finishes. All-steel frame. B-SA is a single action with a drop-free magazine. Imported from the Czech Republic by CZ-USA.

Price: 75 B $625.00
Price: 75 B, stainless $783.00
Price: 75 B-SA $661.00

CZ 75 BD DECOCKER

Similar to the CZ 75B except has a decocking lever in place of the safety lever. All other specifications are the same. Introduced 1999. Imported from the Czech Republic by CZ-USA.
Price: 9mm Para., black polymer $612.00

CZ 75 B COMPACT

Similar to the CZ 75 B except has 14-shot magazine in 9mm Para., 3.9 barrel and weighs 32 oz. Has removable front sight, non-glare ribbed slide top. Trigger guard is squared and serrated; combat hammer. Introduced 1993. Imported from the Czech Republic by CZ-USA.
Price: 9mm Para., black polymer $631.00
Price: 9mm Para., dual tone or satin nickel $651.00
Price: 9mm Para. D PCR Compact, alloy frame $651.00

CZ P-07 DUTY

Caliber: .40 S&W, 9mm Luger (16+1). **Barrel:** 3.8" **Weight:** 27.2 oz. **Length:** 7.3" overall. **Grips:** Polymer black polycoat. **Sights:** Blade front, fixed groove rear. **Features:** The ergonomics and accuracy of the CZ 75 with a totally new trigger system. The new Omega trigger system simplifies the CZ 75 trigger system, uses fewer parts and improves the trigger pull. In addition, it allows users to choose between using the handgun with a decocking lever (installed) or a manual safety (included) by a simple parts change. The polymer frame design of the Duty and a new sleek slide profile (fully machined from bar stock) reduce weight, making the P-07 Duty a great choice for concealed carry.
Price: $524.00

CZ P-09 DUTY

High-capacity version of P-07. **Caliber:** 9mm, .40 S&W. **Magazine capacity:** 19 rounds (9mm), 15 (.40). **Features:** Accessory rail, interchangeable grip backstraps, ambidextrous decocker can be converted to manual safety.
Price: $544.00

CZ 75 TACTICAL SPORT

Similar to the CZ 75 B except the CZ 75 TS is a competition ready pistol designed for IPSC standard division (USPSA limited division). Fixed target sights, tuned single-action operation, lightweight polymer match trigger with adjustments for take-up and overtravel, competition hammer, extended magazine catch, ambidextrous manual safety, checkered walnut grips, polymer magazine well, two tone finish. Introduced 2005. Imported from the Czech Republic by CZ-USA.
Price: 9mm Para., 20-shot mag. $1,310.00
Price: .40 S&W, 16-shot mag. $1,310.00

CZ 75 SP-01

Similar to NATO-approved CZ 75 Compact P-01 model. Features an integral 1913 accessory rail on the dust cover, rubber grip panels, black polycoat finish, extended beavertail, new grip geometry with checkering on front and back straps, and double or single action operation. Introduced 2005. The Shadow variant designed as an IPSC "production" division competition firearm. Includes competition hammer, competition rear sight and fiber-optic front sight, modified slide release, lighter recoil and main spring for use with "minor power factor" competition ammunition. Includes polycoat finish and slim walnut grips. Finished by CZ Custom Shop. Imported from the Czech Republic by CZ-USA.
Price: SP-01 9mm Para., black polymer, 19+1, Standard $680.00
Price: SP-01 9mm Para., black polymer, 19+1, Shadow $1,710.00

CZ 85 B/85 COMBAT

Same gun as the CZ 75 except has ambidextrous slide release and safety levers; non-glare, ribbed slide top; squared, serrated trigger guard; trigger stop to prevent overtravel. Introduced 1986. The CZ 85 Combat features a fully adjustable rear sight, extended magazine release, ambidextrous slide stop and safety catch, drop free magazine and overtravel adjustment. Imported from the Czech Republic by CZ-USA.
Price: 9mm Para., black polymer $628.00
Price: Combat, black polymer $702.00
Price: Combat, dual-tone, satin nickel $732.00

Prices given are believed to be accurate at time of publication however, many factors affect retail pricing so exact prices are not possible.

70TH EDITION, 2016 ⊕ **387**

CZ 97 B
Caliber: .45 ACP, 10-shot magazine. **Barrel:** 4.85" **Weight:** 40 oz. **Length:** 8.34" overall. **Grips:** Checkered walnut. **Sights:** Fixed. **Features:** Single action/double action; full-length slide rails; screw-in barrel bushing; linkless barrel; all-steel construction; chamber loaded indicator; dual transfer bars. Introduced 1999. Imported from the Czech Republic by CZ-USA.
Price: Black polymer $707.00
Price: Glossy blue $727.00

CZ 97 BD DECOCKER
Similar to the CZ 97 B except has a decocking lever in place of the safety lever. Tritium night sights. Rubber grips. All other specifications are the same. Introduced 1999. Imported from the Czech Republic by CZ-USA.
Price: 9mm Para., black polymer $816.00

CZ 2075 RAMI/RAMI P
Caliber: 9mm Para., .40 S&W. **Barrel:** 3". **Weight:** 25 oz. **Length:** 6.5" overall. **Grips:** Rubber. **Sights:** Blade front with dot, white outline rear drift adjustable for windage. **Features:** Single-action/double-action; alloy or polymer frame, steel slide; has laser sight mount. Imported from the Czech Republic by CZ-USA.
Price: 9mm Para., alloy frame, 10 and 14-shot magazines $671.00
Price: 40 S&W, alloy frame, 8-shot magazine $671.00
Price: RAMI P, polymer frame, 9mm Para., 40 S&W $612.00

CZ P-01
Caliber: 9mm Para., 14-shot magazine. **Barrel:** 3.85". **Weight:** 27 oz. **Length:** 7.2" overall. **Grips:** Checkered rubber. **Sights:** Blade front with dot, white outline rear drift adjustable for windage. **Features:** Based on the CZ 75, except with forged aircraft-grade aluminum alloy frame. Hammer forged barrel, decocker, firing-pin block, M3 rail, dual slide serrations, squared triggerguard, recontoured trigger, lanyard loop on butt. Serrated front and back strap. Introduced 2006. Imported from the Czech Republic by CZ-USA.
Price: CZ P-01 ....$627.00

CZ 1911A1
Caliber: .45 ACP. 7+1 capacity. **Barrel:** 5 inches. **Grips:** Checkered walnut. **Sights:** High profile fixed. **Features:** Made in the USA, this model pays homage to the classic 1911 A1. Other features and dimensions identical to the original Colt Government Model.
Price: $849.00

CZ SCORPION EVO
Caliber: : 9mm Para. 20-round magazine. Semi-automatic version of CZ Scorpion Evo submachine gun. **Features:** Ambidextrous controls, adjustable sights, accessory rails.
Price: $849.00

DAN WESSON DW RZ-10
Caliber: 10mm, 9-shot. **Barrel:** 5". **Grips:** Diamond checkered cocobolo. **Sights:** Bo-Mar style adjustable target sight. **Weight:** 38.3 oz. **Length:** 8.8" overall. **Features:** Stainless-steel frame and serrated slide. Series 70-style 1911, stainless-steel frame, forged stainless-steel slide. Commander-style match hammer. Reintroduced 2005. Made in U.S.A. by Dan Wesson Firearms, distributed by CZ-USA.
Price: 10mm, 8+1 ....$1,350.00

DAN WESSON DW RZ-45 HERITAGE
Similar to the RZ-10 Auto except in .45 ACP with 7-shot magazine. Weighs 36 oz., length is 8.8" overall.
Price: 10mm, 8+1 ....$1,298.00

DAN WESSON VALOR 1911
Caliber: .45 ACP, 8-shot. **Barrel:** 5". **Grips:** Slim Line G10. **Sights:** Heinie ledge straight eight adjustable night sights. **Weight:** 2.4 lbs. **Length:** 8.8" overall. **Features:** The defensive style Valor, is a base stainless 1911 with our matte black "Duty" finish. This finish is a ceramic base coating that has set the standard for all coating tests. Other features include forged stainless frame and match barrel with

Prices given are believed to be accurate at time of publication however, many factors affect retail pricing so exact prices are not possible.

25 LPI checkering and undercut triggerguard, adjustable defensive night sites, and Slim line VZ grips. Silverback model has polished stainless slide and matte black frame Made in U.S.A. by Dan Wesson Firearms, distributed by CZ-USA.

Price: $2,012.00
Price: Silverback..$2,012.00

DAN WESSON SPECIALIST

Caliber: .45 ACP, 8-shot magazine. **Barrel:** 5". **Grips:** G10 VZ Operator II. **Sights:** Single amber tritium dot rear, green lamp with white target ring front sight. **Features:** Integral Picatinny rail, 25 lpi front strap checkering, undercut triggerguard, ambidextrous thumb safety, extended mag release and detachable two-piece mag well.

Price: $1,870.00

DAN WESSON V-BOB

Caliber: .45 ACP 8-shot magazine. **Barrel:** 4.25". **Weight:** 34 oz. **Length:** 8". **Grips:** Slim Line G10. **Sights:** Heinie Ledge Straight-Eight Night Sights. **Features:** Black matte or stainless finish. Bobtail forged grip frame with 25 lpi checkering front and rear.

Price: $2,077.00

DAN WESSON VALKYRIE

Caliber: .45 ACP. **Barrel:** 4.25". **Length:** 7.75". **Grips:** Slim Line G10. **Sights:** Tritium Night Sights. **Features:** Similar to V-Bob except has Commander-size slide on Officer-size frame.

Price: $2,012.00

DESERT EAGLE 1911 G

Caliber: .45 ACP 8-shot magazine. **Barrel:** 5" or 4.33" (DE1911C

Commander size), or 3.0" (DE1911U Undercover). **Grips:** Double diamond checkered wood. **Features:** Extended beavertail grip safety, checkered flat mainspring housing, skeletonized hammer and trigger, extended mag release and thumb safety, stainless full-length guide road, enlarged ejection port, beveled mag well and high profile sights. Comes with two 8-round magazines.

Price: $904.00
Price: Undercover $1,019.00

DESERT EAGLE MARK XIX

Caliber: .357 Mag., 9-shot; .44 Mag., 8-shot; .50 AE, 7-shot. **Barrel:** 6", 10", interchangeable. **Weight:** .357 Mag.-62 oz.; .44 Mag.-69 oz.; .50 AE-72 oz. **Length:** 10.25" overall (6" bbl.). **Grips:** Polymer; rubber available. **Sights:** Blade on ramp front, combat-style rear. Adjustable available. **Features:** Interchangeable barrels; rotating three-lug bolt; ambidextrous safety; adjustable trigger. Military epoxy finish. Satin, bright nickel, chrome, brushed, matte or black-oxide finishes available. 10 barrel extra. Imported from Israel by Magnum Research, Inc.

Price: Black-6, 6" barrel....................................$1,742.00
Price: Black-10, 10" barrel $1,793.00

MICRO DESERT EAGLE

Caliber: .380 ACP, 6-rounds. **Barrel:** 2.22. **Weight:** 14 oz. **Length:** 4.52 overall. **Grips:** NA. **Sights:** Fixed low-profile. **Features:** Small-frame DAO pocket pistol. Steel slide, aluminum alloy frame, nickel-teflon finish.

Price: $467.00

DESERT BABY EAGLE II

Caliber: 9mm Para., .40 S&W, .45 ACP, 10- or 15-round magazines. **Barrel:** 3.64", 3.03", 4.52" **Weight:** 26.0 to 39.8 oz. **Length:** 7.25" to 8.25" overall. **Grips:** Polymer. **Sights:** Drift-adjustable rear, blade front. **Features:** Steel slide; choice of steel or polymer frame; slide-mounted decocking safety. Reintroduced in 2011. Imported from Israel by Magnum Research, Inc.

Price: .... $619.00 to $656.00

Prices given are believed to be accurate at time of publication however, many factors affect retail pricing so exact prices are not possible.

70TH EDITION, 2016 ◈ **389**

DESERT EAGLE MR9, MR40
Caliber: 9mm Para., (15-round magazine) or .40 S&W (11 rounds). **Barrel:** 4.5". **Weight:** 25 oz. **Length:** 7.6" overall. **Sights:** Three-dot rear sight adjustable for windage, interchangeable front sight blades of different heights. **Features:** Polymer frame, locked breech, striker-fired design with decocker/safety button on top of slide, three replaceable grip palm swells, Picatinny rail. Made in Germany by Walther and imported by Magnum Research. Introduced in 2014.
Price: $559.00

DIAMONDBACK DB380
Caliber: .380, 6+1-shot capacity. **Barrel:** 2.8". **Weight:** 8.8 oz. **Features:** A "ZERO-Energy" striker firing system with a mechanical firing pin block, steel magazine catch, windage-adjustable sights.
Price: $394.00

DIAMONDBACK DB9
Caliber: 9mm, 6+1-shot capacity. **Barrel:** 3". **Weight:** 11 oz. **Length:** 5.60". **Features:** Other features similar to DB380 model.
Price: $431.00

DOUBLESTAR 1911
Caliber: .45 ACP, 8-shot magazine. **Barrel:** 5". **Weight:** 40 oz. **Grips:** Cocobolo wood. **Sights:** Novak LoMount 2 white-dot rear, Novak white-dot front. **Features:** Single-action, M1911-style with forged frame and slide of 4140 steel, stainless steel barrel machined from bar stock by Storm Lake, funneled mag well, accessory rail, black Nitride or nickel plated finish.
Price: Black..$2,000.00
Price: Nickel plated...$2,150.00

EAA WITNESS FULL SIZE
Caliber: 9mm Para., .38 Super, 18-shot magazine; .40 S&W, 10mm, 15-shot magazine; .45 ACP, 10-shot magazine. **Barrel:** 4.5". **Weight:** 35.33 oz. **Length:** 8.1" overall. **Grips:** Checkered rubber. **Sights:** Undercut blade front, open rear adjustable for windage. **Features:** Double-action/single-action trigger system; round triggerguard; frame-mounted safety. Available with steel or polymer frame. Also available with interchangeable .45 ACP and .22 LR slides. Steel frame introduced 1991. Polymer frame introduced 2005. Imported from Italy by European American Armory.
Price: Steel frame $607.00
Price: Polymer frame $571.00
Price: 45/22 .22 LR, full-size steel frame, blued $752.00

EAA WITNESS COMPACT
Caliber: 9mm Para., 14-shot magazine; .40 S&W, 10mm, 12-shot magazine; .45 ACP, 8-shot magazine. **Barrel:** 3.6" **Weight:** 30 oz. **Length:** 7.3" overall. **Features:** Available with steel or polymer frame

Prices given are believed to be accurate at time of publication however, many factors affect retail pricing so exact prices are not possible.

(shown). All polymer frame Witness pistols are capable of being converted to other calibers. Otherwise similar to Full Size Witness. Imported from Italy by European American Armory.

Price: Polymer frame $571.00
Price: Steel frame $607.00

EAA WITNESS-P CARRY

Caliber: 9mm, 17-shot magazine; 10mm, 15-shot magazine; .45 ACP, 10-shot magazine. **Barrel:** 3.6". **Weight:** 27 oz. **Length:** 7.5" overall. **Features:** Otherwise similar to Full Size Witness. Polymer frame introduced 2005. Imported from Italy by European American Armory.

Price: $691.00

EAA WITNESS PAVONA COMPACT POLYMER

Caliber: .380 ACP (13-round magazine), 9mm (13) or .40 S&W (9). **Barrel:** 3.6". **Weight:** 30 oz. **Length:** 7" overall. **Features:** Designed primarily for women with fine-tuned recoil and hammer springs for easier operation, a polymer frame with integral checkering, contoured lines and in black, charcoal, blue, purple, or magenta with silver or gold sparkle.

Price: .... $476.00 to $528.00

EAA WITNESS ELITE 1911

Caliber: .45 ACP (8-round magazine). **Barrel:** 5". **Weight:** 32 oz. **Length:** 8.58" overall. **Features:** Full-size 1911-style pistol with either steel or polymer frame.

Price: $580.00

ED BROWN CLASSIC CUSTOM

Caliber: .45 ACP, 7 shot. **Barrel:** 5". **Weight:** 40 oz. **Grips:** Cocobolo

wood. **Sights:** Bo-Mar adjustable rear, dovetail front. **Features:** Single-action, M1911 style, custom made to order, stainless frame and slide available. Special mirror-finished slide.

Price: $3,695.00

ED BROWN KOBRA AND KOBRA CARRY

Caliber: .45 ACP, 7-shot magazine. **Barrel:** 5" (Kobra); 4.25" (Kobra Carry). **Weight:** 39 oz. (Kobra); 34 oz. (Kobra Carry). **Grips:** Hogue exotic wood. **Sights:** Ramp, front; fixed Novak low-mount night sights, rear. **Features:** Has snakeskin pattern serrations on forestrap and mainspring housing, dehorned edges, beavertail grip safety.

Price: Kobra K-SS $2,695.00
Price: Kobra Carry $2,945.00

ED BROWN KOBRA CARRY LIGHTWEIGHT

Caliber: .45 ACP, 7-shot magazine. **Barrel:** 4.25" (Commander model slide). **Weight:** 27 oz. **Grips:** Hogue exotic wood. **Sights:** 10-8 Performance U-notch plain black rear sight with .156 notch, for fast aquisition of close targets. Fixed dovetail front night sight with high visibility white outlines. **Features:** Aluminum frame and Bobtail™ housing. Matte finished Gen III coated slide for low glare, with snakeskin on rear of slide only. Snakeskin pattern serrations on forestrap and mainspring housing, dehorned edges, beavertail grip safety. "LW" insignia on slide, which stands for "Lightweight".

Price: Kobra Carry Lightweight $3,320.00

ED BROWN EXECUTIVE

Similar to other Ed Brown products, but with 25-lpi checkered frame and mainspring housing.

Price: .... $2,895.00 - $3,145.00

ED BROWN SPECIAL FORCES

Similar to other Ed Brown products, but with ChainLink treatment on forestrap and mainspring housing. Entire gun coated with Gen

III finish. "Square cut" serrations on rear of slide only. Dehorned. Introduced 2006.
Price: From $2,695.00

ED BROWN SPECIAL FORCES CARRY
Similar to the Special Forces basic models. Features a 4.25" Commander model slide, single stack commander Bobtail frame. Weighs approx. 35 oz. Fixed dovetail 3-dot night sights with high visibility white outlines.
Price: From $2,945.00

ED BROWN SPECIAL FORCES BRONZE
Caliber: .45 ACP, 8+1 capacity. **Grips:** Black G10. **Sights:** Novak 3-dot Night Sights. **Features:** Full size Special Forces variation with black Gen4 slide, Battle Bronze Gen4 frame. .
Price: From $2,445.00

EXCEL ARMS ACCELERATOR MP-22
Caliber: .22 WMR, 9-shot magazine. **Barrel:** 8.5" bull barrel. **Weight:** 54 oz. **Length:** 12.875" overall. **Grips:** Textured black composition. **Sights:** Fully adjustable target sights. **Features:** Made from 17-4 stainless steel, comes with aluminum rib, integral Weaver base, internal hammer, firing-pin block. American made, lifetime warranty. Comes with two9-round stainless steel magazines and a California-approved cable lock. .22 WMR Introduced 2006. Made in U.S.A. by Excel Arms.
Price: $455.00

FN FNS SERIES
Caliber: 9mm, 17-shot magazine, .40 S&W (14-shot magazine). **Barrel:** 4" or 3.6" (Compact). **Weight:** 25 oz. (9mm), 27.5 oz. (.40). **Length:** 7.25". **Grips:** Integral polymer with two interchangeable backstrap inserts. **Features:** Striker-fired, double action with manual safety, accessory rail, ambidextrous controls, 3-dot Night Sights.
Price: $699.00

FN FNX SERIES
Caliber: 9mm, 17-shot magazine, .40 S&W (14-shot), .45 ACP (10 or 14-shot). **Barrel:** 4" (9mm and .40), 4.5" .45. **Weight:** 22 to 32 oz (.45). **Length:** 7.4, 7.9" (.45). **Features:** Double-action/single-action operation with decocking/manual safety lever. Has external extractor with loaded-chamber indicator, front and rear cocking serrations, fixed 3-dot combat sights.
Price: $699.00

FN FNX .45 TACTICAL
Similar to standard FNX .45 except with 5.3" barrel with threaded muzzle, polished chamber and feed ramp, enhanced high-profile night sights, slide cut and threaded for red-dot sight (not included), MIL-STD 1913 accessory rail, ring-style hammer.
Price: $1,400.00

FN FIVE-SEVEN
Caliber: 5.7x28mm, 10- or 20-round magazine capacity. **Barrel:** 4.8". **Weight:** 23 oz. **Length:** 8.2" **Features:** Adjustable three-dot system. Single-action polymer frame model chambered for low-recoil 5.7x28mm cartridge.
Price: $1,329.00

GLOCK 17/17C
Caliber: 9mm Para., 17/19/33-shot magazines. **Barrel:** 4.49". **Weight:** 22.04 oz. (without magazine). **Length:** 7.32" overall. **Grips:** Black polymer. **Sights:** Dot on front blade, white outline rear adjustable for windage. **Features:** Polymer frame, steel slide; double-action trigger with "Safe Action" system; mechanical firing pin safety, drop safety; simple takedown without tools; locked breech, recoil operated action. ILS designation refers to Internal Locking System. Adopted by Austrian armed forces 1983. NATO approved 1984. Imported from Austria by Glock, Inc. USA.
Price: From $599.00

GLOCK GEN4 SERIES
In 2010 a new series of Generation Four pistols was introduced with several improved features. These included a multiple backstrap system offering three different size options, short, medium or large frame; reversible and enlarged magazine release; dual recoil springs; and RTF (Rough Textured Finish) surface. As of 2012, the following models were available in the Gen4 series: Models 17, 19, 21, 22, 23, 26, 27, 31, 32, 34, 35, 37. Price: Same as standard models
Price: ....N/A

Prices given are believed to be accurate at time of publication however, many factors affect retail pricing so exact prices are not possible.

GLOCK 19/19C
Caliber: 9mm Para., 15/17/19/33-shot magazines. **Barrel:** 4.02".
Weight: 20.99 oz. (without magazine). **Length:** 6.85" overall.
Compact version of Glock 17. Pricing the same as Model 17.
Imported from Austria by Glock, Inc.
Price: $699.00
Price: 19C Compensated $675.00

GLOCK 20/20C 10MM
Caliber: 10mm, 15-shot magazines. **Barrel:** 4.6". **Weight:** 27.68 oz.
(without magazine). **Length:** 7.59" overall. **Features:** Otherwise similar
to Model 17. Imported from Austria by Glock, Inc. Introduced 1990.
Price: From $700.00

GLOCK MODEL 20 SF SHORT FRAME
Caliber: 10mm. **Barrel:** 4.61" with hexagonal rifling. **Weight:** 27.51 oz.
Length: 8.07" overall. **Sights:** Fixed. **Features:** Otherwise similar to
Model 20 but with short-frame design, extended sight radius.
Price: $664.00

GLOCK 21/21C
Caliber: .45 ACP, 13-shot magazines. **Barrel:** 4.6". **Weight:** 26.28
oz. (without magazine). **Length:** 7.59" overall. **Features:** Otherwise
similar to Model 17. Imported from Austria by Glock, Inc. Introduced
1991. SF version has tactical rail, smaller diameter grip, 10-round
magazine capacity. Introduced 2007.
Price: Fixed sight, from $700.00

GLOCK 22/22C
Caliber: .40 S&W, 15/17-shot magazines. **Barrel:** 4.49". **Weight:**
22.92 oz. (without magazine). **Length:** 7.32" overall. **Features:**
Otherwise similar to Model 17, including pricing. Imported from
Austria by Glock, Inc. Introduced 1990.
Price: Fixed sight, from $641.00

GLOCK 23/23C
Caliber: .40 S&W, 13/15/17-shot magazines. **Barrel:** 4.02". **Weight:**
21.16 oz. (without magazine). **Length:** 6.85" overall. **Features:**
Otherwise similar to Model 22, including pricing. Compact version
of Glock 22. Imported from Austria by Glock, Inc. Introduced 1990.
Price: $641.00
Price: 23C Compensated $694.00

GLOCK 26
Caliber: 9mm Para. 10/12/15/17/19/33-shot magazines. **Barrel:**
3.46". **Weight:** 19.75 oz. **Length:** 6.29" overall. Subcompact version
of Glock 17. Pricing the same as Model 17. Imported from Austria
by Glock, Inc.
Price: $599.00

GLOCK 27
Caliber: .40 S&W, 9/11/13/15/17-shot magazines. **Barrel:** 3.46".
Weight: 19.75 oz. (without magazine). **Length:** 6.29 overall.
Features: Otherwise similar to Model 22, including pricing.
Subcompact version of Glock 22. Imported from Austria by Glock,
Inc. Introduced 1996.
Price: $750.00

GLOCK 29
Caliber: 10mm, 10/15-shot magazines. **Barrel:** 3.78". **Weight:** 24.69
oz. (without magazine). **Length:** 6.77" overall. **Features:** Otherwise
similar to Model 20, including pricing. Subcompact version of Glock
20. Imported from Austria by Glock, Inc. Introduced 1997.
Price: Fixed sight $672.00

GLOCK MODEL 29 SF SHORT FRAME
Caliber: 10mm. **Barrel:** 3.78" with hexagonal rifling. **Weight:** 24.52 oz.
Length: 6.97" overall. **Sights:** Fixed. **Features:** Otherwise similar to
Model 29 but with short-frame design, extended sight radius.
Price: $660.00

GLOCK 30
Caliber: .45 ACP, 9/10/13-shot magazines. **Barrel:** 3.78". **Weight:**
23.99 oz. (without magazine). **Length:** 6.77" overall. **Features:**
Otherwise similar to Model 21, including pricing. Subcompact
version of Glock 21. Imported from Austria by Glock, Inc. Introduced
1997. SF version has tactical rail, octagonal rifled barrel with a
1:15.75 rate of twist, smaller diameter grip, 10-round magazine
capacity. Introduced 2008.
Price: $700.00

GLOCK 30S
Variation of Glock 30 with a Model 36 slide on a Model 30SF frame
(short frame). **Caliber:** .45 ACP, 10-round magazine. **Barrel:** 3.78
inches. **Weight:** 20 oz. **Length:** 7 inches.
Price: $637.00

GLOCK 31/31C
Caliber: .357 Auto, 15/17-shot magazines. **Barrel:** 4.49". **Weight:**
23.28 oz. (without magazine). **Length:** 7.32" overall. **Features:**
Otherwise similar to Model 17. Imported from Austria by Glock, Inc.
Price: From $641.00

GLOCK 32/32C
Caliber: .357 Auto, 13/15/17-shot magazines. **Barrel:** 4.02". **Weight:**
21.52 oz. (without magazine). **Length:** 6.85" overall. **Features:**
Otherwise similar to Model 31. Compact. Imported from Austria by
Glock, Inc.
Price: $669.00

GLOCK 33
Caliber: .357 Auto, 9/11/13/15/17-shot magazines. **Barrel:** 3.46".
Weight: 19.75 oz. (without magazine). **Length:** 6.29" overall.
Features: Otherwise similar to Model 31. Subcompact. Imported
from Austria by Glock, Inc.
Price: From $641.00

GLOCK 34
Caliber: 9mm Para. 17/19/33-shot magazines. **Barrel:** 5.32". **Weight:**
22.9 oz. **Length:** 8.15" overall. **Features:** Competition version of
Glock 17 with extended barrel, slide, and sight radius dimensions.
Available with MOS (Modular Optic System).
Price: Adjustable sight, from $648.00
Price: MOS $840.00

GLOCK 35

Caliber: .40 S&W, 15/17-shot magazines. **Barrel:** 5.32. **Weight:** 24.52 oz. (without magazine). **Length:** 8.15 overall. **Sights:** Adjustable. **Features:** Otherwise similar to Model 22. Competition version of Glock 22 with extended barrel, slide, and sight radius dimensions. Available with MOS (Modular Optic System). Introduced 1996.
Price: $648.00
Price: MOS $840.00

GLOCK 36

Caliber: .45 ACP, 6-shot magazines. **Barrel:** 3.78. **Weight:** 20.11 oz. (without magazine). **Length:** 6.77 overall. **Sights:** Fixed. **Features:** Single-stack magazine, slimmer grip than Glock 21/30. Subcompact. Imported from Austria by Glock, Inc. Introduced 1997.
Price: $616.00

GLOCK 37

Caliber: .45 GAP, 10-shot magazines. **Barrel:** 4.49. **Weight:** 25.95 oz. (without magazine). **Length:** 7.32 overall. **Features:** Otherwise similar to Model 17. Imported from Austria by Glock, Inc. Introduced 2005.
Price: $614.00

GLOCK 38

Caliber: .45 GAP, 8/10-shot magazines. **Barrel:** 4.02. **Weight:** 24.16 oz. (without magazine). **Length:** 6.85 overall. **Features:** Otherwise similar to Model 37. Compact. Imported from Austria by Glock, Inc.
Price: $614.00

GLOCK 39

Caliber: .45 GAP, 6/8/10-shot magazines. **Barrel:** 3.46. **Weight:** 19.33 oz. (without magazine). **Length:** 6.3 overall. **Features:** Otherwise similar to Model 37. Subcompact. Imported from Austria by Glock, Inc.
Price: $614.00

GLOCK 42

Caliber: .380 ACP, 6-round magazine capacity. **Barrel:** 3.25" **Weight:** 13.8 oz. **Length:** 5.9" overall. **Features:** This single-stack, slimline sub-compact is the smallest pistol Glock has ever made. This is also the first Glock pistol made in the USA.
Price: $637.00

GLOCK 43

Caliber: 9mm. 6+1 capacity. **Barrel:** 3.39" **Weight:** 17.95 oz. **Length:** 6.26". **Height:** 4.25". **Width:** 1.02". **Features:** Newest member of Glock's Slimline series with single-stack magazine.
Price: $589.00

GLOCK 41

Caliber: .45 ACP, 13-round magazine capacity. **Barrel:** 5.31". **Weight:** 27 oz. **Length:** 8.9" overall. **Features:** This is a long-slide .45 ACP Gen4 model introduced in 2014. Operating features are the same as other Glock models. Available with MOS (Modular Optic System).
Price: $775.00
Price: MOS $840.00

GUNCRAFTER INDUSTRIES NO. 1

Caliber: .45 ACP or .50 GI. **Features:** 1911-style series of pistols best known for the proprietary .50 GI chambering. Offered in several common 1911 variations. No. 1 has 5-inch heavy match-grade barrel, 7-round magazine, Parkerized or hard chrome finish, checkered grips and front strap, Heinie slant tritum sights, 7-round magazine. Other models include Commander style, Officer's Model, Long Slide w/6-inch barrel and several 9mm versions.
Price: ....$2,695.00 to $4,125.00

Prices given are believed to be accurate at time of publication however, many factors affect retail pricing so exact prices are not possible.

HECKLER & KOCH USP

Caliber: 9mm Para., 15-shot magazine; .40 S&W, 13-shot magazine; 45 ACP, 12-shot magazine. **Barrel:** 4.25-4.41. **Weight:** 1.65 lbs. **Length:** 7.64-7.87 overall. **Grips:** Non-slip stippled black polymer. **Sights:** Blade front, rear adjustable for windage. **Features:** New HK design with polymer frame, modified Browning action with recoil reduction system, single control lever. Special "hostile environment" finish on all metal parts. Available in SA/DA, DAO, left- and right-hand versions. Introduced 1993. 45 ACP Introduced 1995. Imported from Germany by Heckler & Koch, Inc.
Price: USP .45 ....$1,033.00
Price: USP .40 and USP 9mm $952.00

HECKLER & KOCH USP COMPACT

Caliber: 9mm Para., 13-shot magazine; .40 S&W and .357 SIG, 12-shot magazine; .45 ACP, 8-shot magazine. Similar to the USP except the 9mm Para., 357 SIG, and 40 S&W have 3.58 barrels, measure 6.81 overall, and weigh 1.47 lbs. (9mm Para.). Introduced 1996. 45 ACP measures 7.09 overall. Introduced 1998. Imported from Germany by Heckler & Koch, Inc.
Price: USP Compact .45 ....$1,040.00
Price: USP Compact 9mm
    Para., .40 S&W $992.00

HECKLER & KOCH USP45 TACTICAL

Caliber: .40 S&W, 13-shot magazine; .45 ACP, 12-shot magazine.

Barrel: 4.90-5.09. **Weight:** 1.9 lbs. **Length:** 8.64 overall. **Grips:** Non-slip stippled polymer. **Sights:** Blade front, fully adjustable target rear. **Features:** Has extended threaded barrel with rubber O-ring; adjustable trigger; extended magazine floorplate; adjustable trigger stop; polymer frame. Introduced 1998. Imported from Germany by Heckler & Koch, Inc.
Price: USP Tactical .45 ....$1,352.00
Price: USP Tactical .40 ....$1,333.00

HECKLER & KOCH USP COMPACT TACTICAL

Caliber: .45 ACP, 8-shot magazine. Similar to the USP Tactical except measures 7.72 overall, weighs 1.72 lbs. Introduced 2006. Imported from Germany by Heckler & Koch, Inc.
Price: USP Compact Tactical $1,352.00

HECKLER & KOCH HK45

Caliber: .45 ACP, 10-shot magazine. **Barrel:** 4.53". **Weight:** 1.73 lbs. **Length:** 7.52" overall. **Grips:** Ergonomic with adjustable grip panels. **Sights:** Low profile, drift adjustable. **Features:** Polygonal rifling, ambidextrous controls, operates on improved Browning linkless recoil system. Available in Tactical and Compact variations.
Price: USP Tactical .45 .... **$1,193.00 to $1,392.00**

HECKLER & KOCH MARK 23 SPECIAL OPERATIONS

Caliber: .45 ACP, 12-shot magazine. **Barrel:** 5.87. **Weight:** 2.42 lbs. **Length:** 9.65 overall. **Grips:** Integral with frame; black polymer. **Sights:** Blade front, rear drift adjustable for windage; 3-dot. **Features:** Civilian version of the SOCOM pistol. Polymer frame; double action; exposed hammer; short recoil, modified Browning action. Introduced 1996. Imported from Germany by Heckler & Koch, Inc.
Price: $2,253.00

HECKLER & KOCH P30 AND P30L

Caliber: 9mm and .40 S&W with 13 or 15-shot magazines. **Barrel:** 3.86" or 4.45" (P30L). **Weight:** 26 to 27.5 oz. **Length:** 6.95, 7.56" overall. **Grips:** Interchangeable panels. **Sights:** Open rectangular notch rear sight with contrast points (no radioactive). **Features:** Ergonomic features include a special grip frame with interchangeable backstraps inserts and lateral plates, allowing the pistol to be individually adapted to any user. Browning type action with modified short recoil operation. Ambidextrous controls include dual slide releases, magazine release levers, and a serrated decocking button located on the rear of the frame (for applicable variants). A Picatinny rail molded into the front of the frame. The extractor serves as a loaded-chamber indicator.

Price: P30 .... **$1,054.00**
Price: P30L Variant 2 Law Enforcement Modification
 (LEM) enhanced DAO **$1,108.00**
Price: P30L Variant 3 Double Action/Single Action
 (DA/SA) with Decocker **$1,108.00**

HECKLER & KOCH P2000

Caliber: 9mm Para., 13-shot magazine; .40 S&W and .357 SIG, 12-shot magazine. **Barrel:** 3.62. **Weight:** 1.5 lbs. **Length:** 7 overall. **Grips:** Interchangeable panels. **Sights:** Fixed Patridge style, drift adjustable for windage, standard 3-dot. **Features:** Incorporates features of HK USP Compact pistol, including Law Enforcement Modification (LEM) trigger, double-action hammer system, ambidextrous magazine release, dual slide-release levers, accessory mounting rails, recurved, hook trigger guard, fiber-reinforced polymer frame, modular grip with exchangeable back straps, nitro-carburized finish, lock-out safety device. Introduced 2003. Imported from Germany by Heckler & Koch, Inc.
Price: **$992.00**

HECKLER & KOCH P2000 SK

Caliber: 9mm Para., 10-shot magazine; .40 S&W and .357 SIG, 9-shot magazine. **Barrel:** 3.27. **Weight:** 1.3 lbs. **Length:** 6.42 overall. **Sights:** Fixed Patridge style, drift adjustable. **Features:** Standard accessory rails, ambidextrous slide release, polymer frame, polygonal bore profile. Smaller version of P2000. Introduced 2005. Imported from Germany by Heckler & Koch, Inc.
Price: **$1,037.00**

HECKLER & KOCH VP9

Caliber: 9mm Para., 10 or 15-shot magazine. **Barrel:** 4.09". **Weight:** 25.6 oz. **Length:** 7.34 overall. **Sights:** Fixed 3-dot, drift adjustable.

Features: Striker-fired system with HK enhanced light pull trigger. Ergonomic grip design with interchangeable backstraps and side panels.
Price: **$719.00**

HELLCAT II

Caliber: .380 ACP, magazine capacity 6 rounds. **Barrel:** 2.75 inches. **Weight:** 9.4 oz. **Length:** 5.16 inches. **Grips:** Integral polymer. **Sights:** Fixed. **Features:** Polymer frame, double-action only. Several finishes available including black, desert tan, pink, blaze orange. Made in U.S.A. by I.O., Inc.
Price: **$250.00**

HI-POINT FIREARMS MODEL 9MM COMPACT

Caliber: 9mm Para., 8-shot magazine. **Barrel:** 3.5. **Weight:** 25 oz. **Length:** 6.75 overall. **Grips:** Textured plastic. **Sights:** Combat-style adjustable 3-dot system; low profile. **Features:** Single-action design; frame-mounted magazine release; polymer frame. Scratch-resistant matte finish. Introduced 1993. Comps are similar except they have a 4 barrel with muzzle brake/compensator. Compensator is slotted for laser or flashlight mounting. Introduced 1998. Made in U.S.A. by MKS Supply, Inc.
Price: C-9 9mm **$189.00**

HI-POINT FIREARMS MODEL 380 POLYMER

Similar to the 9mm Compact model except chambered for .380 ACP, 8-shot magazine, adjustable 3-dot sights. Weighs 25 oz. Polymer frame. Action locks open after last shot. Includes 10-shot and 8-shot magazine; trigger lock.
Price: CF-380 .... **$151.00**

HI-POINT FIREARMS 40 AND 45 SW/POLY

Caliber: .40 S&W, 8-shot magazine; .45 ACP (9-shot). **Barrel:** 4.5. **Weight:** 32 oz. **Length:** 7.72 overall. **Sights:** Adjustable 3-dot. **Features:** Polymer frames, last round lock-open, grip mounted magazine release, magazine disconnect safety, integrated accessory rail, trigger lock. Introduced 2002. Made in U.S.A. by MKS Supply, Inc.
Price: **$199.00**

HIGH STANDARD VICTOR .22

Caliber: .22 Long Rifle (10 rounds) or .22 Short (5 rounds). **Barrel:** 4.5"-5.5". **Weight:** 45 oz.-46 oz. **Length:** 8.5"-9.5" overall. **Grips:** Freestyle wood. **Sights:** Frame mounted, adjustable. **Features:** Semi-auto with drilled and tapped barrel, tu-tone or blued finish.
Price: **$965.00**

HIGH STANDARD 10X CUSTOM .22

Similar to the Victor model but with precision fitting, black wood grips, 5.5 barrel only. High Standard Universal Mount, 10-shot magazine, barrel drilled and tapped, certificate of authenticity. Overall length is 9.5". Weighs 44 oz. to 46 oz. From High Standard Custom Shop.
Price: **$1,375.00**

HIGH STANDARD SUPERMATIC TROPHY .22

Caliber: .22 Long Rifle (10 rounds) or .22 Short (5 rounds/Citation version), not interchangable. **Barrel:** 5.5", 7.25". **Weight:** 44 oz., 46 oz. **Length:** 9.5", 11.25" overall. **Grips:** Wood. **Sights:** Adjustable. **Features:** Semi-auto with drilled and tapped barrel, tu-tone or blued finish with gold accents.
Price: 5.5 .... **$965.00**

HIGH STANDARD OLYMPIC MILITARY .22

Similar to the Supermatic Trophy model but in .22 Short only with 5.5" bull barrel, five-round magazine, aluminum alloy frame, adjustable sights. Overall length is 9.5", weighs 42 oz.
Price: **$1,050.00**

HIGH STANDARD SUPERMATIC CITATION SERIES .22

Similar to the Supermatic Trophy model but with heavier trigger pull, 10" barrel, and nickel accents. 22 Short conversion unit available. Overall length 14.5", weighs 52 oz.
Price: **$975.00**

HIGH STANDARD SUPERMATIC TOURNAMENT .22

Caliber: .22 LR. **Barrel:** 5.5" bull barrel. **Weight:** 44 oz. **Length:** 9.5" overall. **Features:** Limited edition; similar to High Standard Victor model but with rear sight mounted directly to slide.
Price: **$1,025.00**

HIGH STANDARD SPORT KING .22

Caliber: .22 LR. **Barrel:** 4.5" or 6.75" tapered barrel. **Weight:** 40 oz. to 42 oz. **Length:** 8.5" to 10.75". **Features:** Sport version of High Standard Supermatic. Two-tone finish, fixed sights.
Price: **$835.00**

HI-STANDARD SPACE GUN

Semiauto pistol chambered in .22 LR. Recreation of famed competition "Space Gun" from 1960s. Features include 6.75- 8- or 10-inch barrel; 10-round magazine; adjustable sights; barrel weight; adjustable muzzle brake; blue-black finish with gold highlights.
Price: **$1,350.00**

ITHACA 1911

Caliber: .45 ACP, 7-round capacity. **Barrel:** 5". **Weight:** 41 oz. **Length:** 8.75" **Sights:** Fixed combat or fully adjustable target. **Grips:** Checkered cocobolo with Ithaca logo. **Features:** Classic 1911A1-style pistol with enhanced features including match-grade barrel, lowered and flared ejection port, skeletonized hammer and trigger, full-length two-piece guide rod, hand-fitted barrel bushing, extended beavertail grip safety, checkered front strap. Made 100 percent in the U.S.A.
Price: **$1,799.00**
Price: Adjustable sights, ambidextrous safety **$1,949.00**

IVER JOHNSON EAGLE

Series of 1911-style pistols made in typical variations including full-size (Eagle), Commander (Hawk), Officer's (Thrasher) sizes in .45 ACP and 9mm. Many finishes available including Cerakote, polished stainless, pink and several "snakeskin" variations.
Price: .... **$608.00 to $959.00**

KAHR CM SERIES
Caliber: 9mm (6+1), .40 S&W (6+1). .45 ACP (5+1). CM45 Model is shown. **Barrel:** 3", 3.25"(45). **Weight:** 15.9 to 17.3 oz. **Length:** 5.42 overall. **Grips:** Textured polymer with integral steel rails molded into frame. **Sights:** CM9093 - Pinned in polymer sight; PM9093 - Drift adjustable, white bar-dot combat. **Features:** A conventional rifled barrel instead of the match grade polygonal barrel on Kahr's PM series; the CM slide stop lever is MIM (metal-injection-molded) instead of machined; the CM series slide has fewer machining operations and uses simple engraved markings instead of roll marking and finally the CM series are shipped with one magazine instead of two magazines. The slide is machined from solid 416 stainless slide with a matte finish, each gun is shipped with one 6-round stainless steel magazine with a flush baseplate. Magazines are USA made, plasma welded, tumbled to remove burrs and feature Wolff Gunsprings. The magazine catch in the polymer frame is all metal and will not wear out on the stainless steel magazine after extended use.
Price: **$460.00**

KAHR CT40/CT45 SERIES
Caliber: .40 S&W (6+1) .45 ACP (7+1). **Barrel:** 4 inches. **Weight:** 23.7 oz. **Length:** 5.42 overall. **Grips:** Textured polymer with integral steel rails molded into frame. **Sights:** Drift adjustable, white bar-

dot combat. **Features:** A conventional rifled barrel instead of the match grade polygonal barrel on Kahr's PM series; the CM slide stop lever is MIM (metal-injection-molded) instead of machined; the CM series slide has fewer machining operations and uses simple engraved markings instead of roll marking and finally the CM series are shipped with one magazine instead of two magazines. The slide is machined from solid 416 stainless slide with a matte finish, each gun is shipped with one 6-round stainless steel magazine with a flush baseplate. Magazines are USA made, plasma welded, tumbled to remove burrs and feature Wolff Gunsprings. The magazine catch in the polymer frame is all metal and will not wear out on the stainless steel magazine after extended use
Price: **$460.00**

KAHR K SERIES
Caliber: K9: 9mm Para., 7-shot; K40: .40 S&W, 6-shot magazine. **Barrel:** 3.5. **Weight:** 25 oz. **Length:** 6 overall. **Grips:** Wraparound textured soft polymer. **Sights:** Blade front, rear drift adjustable for windage; bar-dot combat style. **Features:** Trigger-cocking double-action mechanism with passive firing pin block. Made of 4140 ordnance steel with matte black finish. Contact maker for complete price list. Introduced 1994. Made in U.S.A. by Kahr Arms.
Price: K9093C K9, matte stainless steel **$855.00**
Price: K9093NC K9, matte stainless steel w/tritium night sights **$985.00**
Price: K9094C K9 matte blackened stainless steel **$891.00**
Price: K9098 K9 Elite 2003, stainless steel **$932.00**
Price: K4043 K40, matte stainless steel **$855.00**
Price: K4043N K40, matte stainless steel w/tritium night sights **$985.00**
Price: K4044 K40, matte blackened stainless steel **$891.00**
Price: K4048 K40 Elite 2003, stainless steel **$932.00**

KAHR MK SERIES MICRO
Similar to the K9/K40 except is 5.35 overall, 4 high, with a 3.08 barrel. Weighs 23.1 oz. Has snag-free bar-dot sights, polished feed ramp, dual recoil spring system, DA-only trigger. Comes with 5-round flush baseplate and 6-shot grip extension magazine. Introduced 1998. Made in U.S.A. by Kahr Arms.
Price: M9093 MK9, matte stainless steel **$855.00**
Price: M9093N MK9, matte stainless steel, tritium night sights **$958.00**
Price: M9098 MK9 Elite 2003, stainless steel **$932.00**
Price: M4043 MK40, matte stainless steel **$855.00**
Price: M4043N MK40, matte stainless steel, tritium night sights **$958.00**
Price: M4048 MK40 Elite 2003, stainless steel **$932.00**

KAHR P SERIES
Caliber: 380 ACP, 9x19, 40 S&W, 45 ACP. Similar to K9/K40 steel frame pistol except has polymer frame, matte stainless steel slide. Barrel length 3.5"; overall length 5.8"; weighs 17 oz. Includes two 7-shot magazines, hard polymer case, trigger lock. Introduced 2000. Made in U.S.A. by Kahr Arms.
Price: KP9093 9mm Para. **$739.00**
Price: KP4043 .40 S&W **$739.00**
Price: KP4543 .45 ACP... **$805.00**
Price: KP3833 .380 ACP (2008)... **$649.00**

Prices given are believed to be accurate at time of publication however, many factors affect retail pricing so exact prices are not possible.

KAHR PM SERIES

Caliber: 9x19, .40 S&W, .45 ACP. Similar to P-Series pistols except has smaller polymer frame (Polymer Micro). Barrel length 3.08"; overall length 5.35"; weighs 17 oz. Includes two 7-shot magazines, hard polymer case, trigger lock. Introduced 2000. Made in U.S.A. by Kahr Arms.

Price: PM9093 PM9 ....$786.00
Price: PM4043 PM40 ....$786.00
Price: PM4543 (2007) $855.00

KAHR T SERIES

Caliber: T9: 9mm Para., 8-shot magazine; T40: .40 S&W, 7-shot magazine. **Barrel:** 4". **Weight:** 28.1-29.1 oz. **Length:** 6.5" overall. **Grips:** Checkered Hogue Pau Ferro wood grips. **Sights:** Rear: Novak low profile 2-dot tritium night sight, front tritium night sight. **Features:** Similar to other Kahr makes, but with longer slide and barrel upper, longer butt. Trigger cocking DAO; lock breech; "Browning-type" recoil lug; passive striker block; no magazine disconnect. Comes with two magazines. Introduced 2004. Made in U.S.A. by Kahr Arms.

Price: KT9093 T9 matte stainless steel $831.00
Price: KT9093-NOVAK T9, "Tactical 9," Novak night sight $968.00
Price: KT4043 40 S&W $831.00

KAHR TP SERIES

Caliber: TP9: 9mm Para., 7-shot magazine; TP40: 40 S&W, 6-shot magazine. **Barrel:** 4". **Weight:** 19.1-20.1 oz. **Length:** 6.5-6.7" overall. **Grips:** Textured polymer. Similar to T-series guns, but with polymer frame, matte stainless slide. Comes with two magazines. TP40s introduced 2006. Made in U.S.A. by Kahr Arms.

Price: TP9093 TP9 ....$697.00
Price: TP9093-Novak TP9
(Novak night sights) $838.00
Price: TP4043 TP40 ....$697.00
Price: TP4043-Novak (Novak night sights) $838.00
Price: TP4543 (2007) $697.00
Price: TP4543-Novak (4.04 barrel, Novak night sights) $838.00

KAHR CW SERIES

Caliber: 9mm Para., 7-shot magazine; .40 S&W and .45 ACP, 6-shot magazine. **Barrel:** 3.5-3.64". **Weight:** 17.7-18.7 oz. **Length:** 5.9-6.36" overall. **Grips:** Textured polymer. Similar to P-Series, but CW Series have conventional rifling, metal-injection-molded slide stop lever, no front dovetail cut, one magazine. CW40 introduced 2006. Made in U.S.A. by Kahr Arms.

Price: CW9093 CW9 ....$449.00
Price: CW4043 CW40 ....$449.00
Price: CW4543 CW45 ....$449.00

KAHR P380

Very small double action only semiauto pistol chambered in .380 ACP. Features include 2.5-inch Lothar Walther barrel; black polymer frame with stainless steel slide; drift adjustable white bar/dot combat/ sights; optional tritium sights; two 6+1 magazines. Overall length 4.9 inches, weight 10 oz. without magazine.

Price: Standard sights $649.00

KAHR CW380

Caliber: .380 ACP, six-round magazine. **Barrel:** 2.58 inches. **Weight:** 11.5 oz. **Length:** 4.96 inches. **Grips:** Textured integral polymer. **Sights:** Fixed white-bar combat style. **Features:** Double-action only. Black or purple polymer frame, stainless slide.

Price: $419.00

KEL-TEC P-11

Caliber: 9mm Para., 10-shot magazine. **Barrel:** 3.1. **Weight:** 14 oz. **Length:** 5.6 overall. **Grips:** Checkered black polymer. **Sights:** Blade front, rear adjustable for windage. **Features:** Ordnance steel slide, aluminum frame. Double-action-only trigger mechanism. Introduced 1995. Made in U.S.A. by Kel-Tec CNC Industries, Inc.
Price: From $340.00

KEL-TEC PF-9

Caliber: 9mm Para.; 7 rounds. **Weight:** 12.7 oz. **Sights:** Rear sight adjustable for windage and elevation. **Barrel Length:** 3.1. **Length:** 5.85. **Features:** Barrel, locking system, slide stop, assembly pin, front sight, recoil springs and guide rod adapted from P-11. Trigger system with integral hammer block and the extraction system adapted from P-3AT. MIL-STD-1913 Picatinny rail. Made in U.S.A. by Kel-Tec CNC Industries, Inc.
Price: From $340.00

KEL-TEC P-32

Caliber: .32 ACP, 7-shot magazine. **Barrel:** 2.68. **Weight:** 6.6 oz. **Length:** 5.07 overall. **Grips:** Checkered composite. **Sights:** Fixed. **Features:** Double-action-only mechanism with 6-lb. pull; internal slide stop. Textured composite grip/frame.
Price: From $326.00

KEL-TEC P-3AT

Caliber: .380 ACP; 7-rounds. **Weight:** 7.2 oz. **Length:** 5.2. **Features:** Lightest .380 ACP made; aluminum frame, steel barrel.
Price: From $331.00

KEL-TEC PLR-16

Caliber: 5.56mm NATO; 10-round magazine. **Weight:** 51 oz. **Sights:** Rear sight adjustable for windage, front sight is M-16 blade. **Barrel:** 9.2. **Length:** 18.5. **Features:** Muzzle is threaded 1/2-28 to accept standard attachments such as a muzzle brake. Except for the

barrel, bolt, sights, and mechanism, the PLR-16 pistol is made of high-impact glass fiber reinforced polymer. Gas-operated semi-auto. Conventional gas-piston operation with M-16 breech locking system. MIL-STD-1913 Picatinny rail. Made in U.S.A. by Kel-Tec CNC Industries, Inc.
Price: Blued $682.00

KEL-TEC PLR-22

Semi-auto pistol chambered in .22 LR; based on centerfire PLR-16 by same maker. Blowback action, 26-round magazine. Open sights and picatinny rail for mounting accessories; threaded muzzle. Overall length is 18.5", weighs 40 oz.
Price: $400.00

KEL-TEC PMR-30

Caliber: .22 Magnum (.22WMR) 30-rounds. **Barrel:** 4.3. **Weight:** 13.6 oz. **Length:** 7.9 overall. **Grips:** Glass reinforced Nylon (Zytel). **Sights:** Dovetailed aluminum with front & rear fiber optics. **Features:** Operates on a unique hybrid blowback/locked-breech system. It uses a double stack magazine of a new design that holds 30 rounds and fits completely in the grip of the pistol. Dual opposing extractors for reliability, heel magazine release to aid in magazine retention, Picatinny accessory rail under the barrel, Urethane recoil buffer, captive coaxial recoil springs. The barrel is fluted for light weight and effective heat dissipation. PMR30 disassembles for cleaning by removal of a single pin.
Price: $436.00

KIMBER MICRO CDP

Caliber: .380 ACP, 6-shot magazine. **Barrel:** 2.75". **Weight:** 17 oz. **Grips:** Double diamond rosewood. Mini 1911-style single action with no grip safety.
Price: $951.00

KIMBER MICRO CARRY

Caliber: .380 ACP, 6-round magazine. **Barrel:** 2.75 inches. **Weight:** 13.4 oz. **Length:** 5.6 inches **Grips:** Black synthetic, double diamond. **Sights:** Fixed low profile. **Finish:** Blue or stainless. **Features:**

Aluminum frame, steel slide, carry-melt treatment, full-length guide rod.

Price: **$651.00**

KIMBER MICRO RAPTOR

Caliber: .380 ACP, 6-round magazine. **Sights:** Tritium night sights. **Finish:** Stainless. **Features:** Variation of Micro Carry with Raptor style scalloped "feathered" slide serrations and grip panels.

Price: **$960.00**

KIMBER AEGIS II

Caliber: 9mm (9-shot magazine, 8-shot (Ultra model). **Barrel:** 3", 4" or 5". **Weight:** 25 to 38 oz. **Grips:** Scale-textured zebra wood. **Sights:** Tactical wedge 3-dot green night sights. **Features:** Made in the Kimber Custom Shop. Two-tone satin silver/matte black finish. Service Melt treatment that rounds and blends edges. Available in three frame sizes: Custom (shown), Pro and Ultra.

Price: **$1,331.00**

KIMBER COVERT II

Caliber: .45 ACP (7-shot magazine). **Barrel:** 3", 4" or 5". **Weight:** 25 to 31 oz. **Grips:** Crimson Trace laser with camo finish. **Sights:** Tactical wedge 3-dot night sights. **Features:** Made in the Kimber Custom Shop. Desert tan frame and matte black slide finishes. Available in three frame sizes: Custom, Pro (shown) and Ultra.

Price: **$1,657.00**

KIMBER CUSTOM II

Caliber: .45 ACP. **Barrel:** 5". **Weight:** 38 oz. **Length:** 8.7" overall. **Grips:** Checkered black rubber, walnut, rosewood. **Sights:** Dovetailed front and rear, Kimber low profile adj. or fixed sights. **Features:** Slide, frame and barrel machined from steel or stainless

steel. Match grade barrel, chamber and trigger group. Extended thumb safety, beveled magazine well, beveled front and rear slide serrations, high ride beavertail grip safety, checkered flat mainspring housing, kidney cut under triggerguard, high cut grip, match grade stainless steel barrel bushing, polished breech face, Commander-style hammer, lowered and flared ejection port, Wolff springs, bead blasted black oxide or matte stainless finish. Introduced in 1996. Custom TLE II (Tactical Law Enforcement) has tritium night sights, threaded barrel. Made in U.S.A. by Kimber Mfg., Inc.

Price: Custom II **$871.00**
Price: Custom TLE II...**$905.00**

KIMBER STAINLESS II

Same features as Custom II except has stainless steel frame.

Price: Stainless II .45 ACP **$998.00**
Price: Stainless II 9mm Para. **$1,016.00**
Price: Stainless II .45 ACP w/night sights...........**$1,141.00**
Price: Stainless II Target .45 ACP (stainless, adj. sight) **$1,108.00**

KIMBER PRO CARRY II

Similar to Custom II, has aluminum frame, 4 bull barrel fitted directly to the slide without bushing. Introduced 1998. Made in U.S.A. by Kimber Mfg., Inc.

Price: Pro Carry II, .45 ACP **$919.00**
Price: Pro Carry II, 9mm **$969.00**
Price: Pro Carry II
w/night sights **$1,039.00**

KIMBER SAPPHIRE PRO II

Similar to Pro Carry II, chambered in 9mm with 9-shot magazine, 4-inch match-grade barrel. Striking two-tone appearance with satin silver aluminum frame and high polish bright blue slide. Grips are blue/black G-10 with grooved texture. Fixed Tactical Edge night sights.

Price: **$1,652.00**

KIMBER RAPTOR II

Caliber: .45 ACP (8-shot magazine, 7-shot (Ultra and Pro models).

Barrel: 3", 4" or 5". **Weight:** 25 to 31 oz. **Grips:** Thin milled rosewood. **Sights:** Tactical wedge 3-dot night sights. **Features:** Made in the Kimber Custom Shop. Matte black or satin silver finish. Available in three frame sizes: Custom (shown), Pro and Ultra.
Price: .... $1,434.00 to $1,568.00

KIMBER SOLO CARRY

Caliber: 9mm, 6-shot magazine. **Barrel:** 2.7. **Weight:** 17 oz. **Length:** 5.5 overall. **Grips:** Black synthetic, Checkered/smooth. **Sights:** Fixed low-profile dovetail-mounted 3-dot system. **Features:** Single action striker-fired trigger that sets a new standard for small pistols. A premium finish that is self-lubricating and resistant to salt and moisture. Ergonomics that ensure comfortable shooting. Ambidextrous thumb safety, slide release lever and magazine release button are pure 1911 – positive, intuitive and fast. The thumb safety provides additional security not found on most small pistols. Available with Crimson Trace Laser grips. Also available in stainless.
Price: $815.00

KIMBER COMPACT STAINLESS II

Similar to Pro Carry II except has stainless steel frame, 4-inch bbl., grip is .400 shorter than standard, no front serrations. Weighs 34 oz. 45 ACP only. Introduced in 1998. Made in U.S.A. by Kimber Mfg., Inc.
Price: $1,052.00

KIMBER ULTRA CARRY II

Lightweight aluminum frame, 3 match grade bull barrel fitted to slide without bushing. Grips .4 shorter. Low effort recoil spring. Weighs 25 oz. Introduced in 1999. Made in U.S.A. by Kimber Mfg., Inc.
Price: Stainless Ultra Carry II .45 ACP.................................... $919.00
Price: Stainless Ultra Carry II 9mm Para. $1,016.00
Price: Stainless Ultra Carry II .45 ACP
    with night sights $1,039.00

KIMBER GOLD MATCH II

Similar to Custom II models. Includes stainless steel barrel with match grade chamber and barrel bushing, ambidextrous thumb safety, adjustable sight, premium aluminum trigger, hand-checkered double diamond rosewood grips. Barrel hand-fitted for target accuracy. Made in U.S.A. by Kimber Mfg., Inc.
Price: Gold Match II $1,393.00
Price: Gold Match Stainless II .45 ACP $1,574.00
Price: Gold Match Stainless II
    9mm Para. (2008) $1,653.00

KIMBER CDP II SERIES

Similar to Custom II, but designed for concealed carry. Aluminum frame. Standard features include stainless steel slide, fixed Meprolight tritium 3-dot (green) dovetail-mounted night sights, match grade barrel and chamber, 30 LPI front strap checkering, two-tone finish, ambidextrous thumb safety, hand-checkered double diamond rosewood grips. Introduced in 2000. Made in U.S.A. by Kimber Mfg., Inc.
Price: Ultra CDP II 9mm Para. (2008) $1,359.00
Price: Ultra CDP II .45 ACP $1,318.00
Price: Compact CDP II .45 ACP $1,318.00
Price: Pro CDP II .45 ACP... $1,318.00
Price: Custom CDP II
    (5" barrel, full length grip) $1,318.00

KIMBER ECLIPSE II SERIES

Caliber: .45 ACP, 10mm (Target II only). Similar to Custom II and other stainless Kimber pistols. Stainless slide and frame, black oxide, two-tone finish. Gray/black laminated grips. 30 lpi front strap checkering. All models have night sights; Target versions have Meprolight adjustable Bar/Dot version. Made in U.S.A. by Kimber Mfg., Inc.
Price: Eclipse Ultra II (3" barrel, short grip) $1,279.00
Price: Eclipse Pro II (4" barrel, full-length grip) $1,279.00
Price: Eclipse Pro Target II (4" barrel, full-length grip,
    adjustable sight) $1,279.00
Price: Eclipse Custom II 10mm $1,299.00
Price: Eclipse Target II (5" barrel, full-length grip,
    adjustable sight) $1,393.00

KIMBER TACTICAL ENTRY II

Caliber: 45 ACP, 7-round magazine. **Barrel:** 5". **Weight:** 40 oz. **Length:** 8.7" overall. **Features:** 1911-style semiauto with checkered frontstrap, extended magazine well, night sights, heavy steel frame, tactical rail.
Price: $1,490.00

Prices given are believed to be accurate at time of publication however, many factors affect retail pricing so exact prices are not possible.

KIMBER TACTICAL CUSTOM HD II
Caliber: .45 ACP, 7-round magazine. **Barrel:** 5" match-grade. **Weight:** 39 oz. **Length:** 8.7" overall. **Features:** 1911-style semiauto with night sights, heavy steel frame.
Sights: Night sights with cocking shoulder radius (inches): 4.8.
Features: Rugged stainless steel slide and frame with KimPro II finish. Aluminum match grade trigger with a factory setting of approximately 4-5 pounds.
Price: $1,387.00

Sights: Night sights with cocking shoulder radius (inches): 4.8.
Features: Rugged stainless steel slide and frame with KimPro II finish. Aluminum match grade trigger with a factory setting of approximately 4-5 pounds.
Price: $1,699.00

KIMBER SUPER CARRY PRO
1911-syle semiauto pistol chambered in .45 ACP. Features include 8-round magazine; ambidextrous thumb safety; carry melt profiling; full length guide rod; aluminum frame with stainless slide; satin silver finish; super carry serrations; 4-inch barrel; micarta laminated grips; tritium night sights.
Price: $1,596.00

KIMBER SUPER CARRY HD SERIES
Designated as HD (Heavy Duty), each is chambered in .45 ACP and features a stainless steel slide and frame, premium KimPro II™ finish and night sights with cocking shoulder for one-hand operation. Like the original Super Carry pistols, HD models have directional serrations on slide, front strap and mainspring housing for unequaled control under recoil. A round heel frame and Carry Melt treatment make them comfortable to carry and easy to conceal.

KIMBER SUPER CARRY PRO HD™
Caliber: .45 ACP, 8-shot magazine. **Barrel:** 4. **Weight:** 35 oz. **Length:** 7.7 overall. **Grips:** G-10, Checkered with border.
Sights: Night sights with cocking shoulder radius (inches): 5.7.
Features: Rugged stainless steel slide and frame with KimPro II finish. Aluminum match grade trigger with a factory setting of approximately 4-5 pounds.
Price: $1,699.00

KIMBER SUPER CARRY ULTRA HD™
Caliber: .45 ACP, 7-shot magazine. **Barrel:** 3. **Weight:** 32 oz. **Length:** 6.8 overall. **Grips:** G-10, Checkered with border.

KIMBER SUPER CARRY CUSTOM HD™
Caliber: .45 ACP, 8-shot magazine. **Barrel:** 5. **Weight:** 38 oz. **Length:** 8.7 overall. **Grips:** G-10, Checkered with border.
Sights: Night sights with cocking shoulder radius (inches): 4.8.
Features: Rugged stainless steel slide and frame with KimPro II finish. Aluminum match grade trigger with a factory setting of approximately 4-5 pounds.
Price: $1,625.00

KIMBER ULTRA CDP II

Compact 1911-syle pistol chambered in .45 ACP or 9mm. Features include 7-round magazine (9 in 9mm); ambidextrous thumb safety; carry melt profiling; full length guide rod; aluminum frame with stainless slide; satin silver finish; checkered frontstrap; 3-inch barrel; rosewood double diamond Crimson Trace lasergrips grips; tritium 3-dot night sights.
Price: $1,603.00

KIMBER STAINLESS ULTRA TLE II

1911-syle semiauto pistol chambered in .45 ACP. Features include 7-round magazine; full-length guide rod; aluminum frame with stainless slide; satin silver finish; checkered frontstrap; 3-inch barrel; tactical gray double diamond grips; tritium 3-dot night sights.
Price: $1,210.00

KIMBER ROYAL II

Caliber: .45 ACP, 7-shot magazine. **Barrel:** 5". **Weight:** 38 oz.

Length: 8.7" overall. **Grips:** Solid bone-smooth. **Sights:** Fixed low profile. **Features:** A classic full-size pistol wearing a charcoal blue finish complimented with solid bone grip panels. Front and rear serrations. Aluminum match-grade trigger with a factory setting of approximately 4-5 pounds.
Price: $1,938.00

KIMBER MASTER CARRY PRO

Caliber: .45 ACP, 8-round magazine. **Barrel:** 4 inches. **Weight:** 28 oz. **Length:** 7.7 inches **Grips:** Crimson Trace Laser. **Sights:** Fixed low profile. **Features:** Matte black KimPro slide, aluminum round heel frame, full-length guide rod.
Price: $1,568.00

KIMBER WARRIOR SOC

Caliber: .45 ACP, 7-round magazine. **Barrel:** 5 inches threaded for suppression. **Sights:** Fixed Tactical Wedge tritium. **Finish:** Dark Green frame, Flat Dark Earth slide. **Features:** Full-size 1911 based on special series of pistols made for USMC. Service melt, ambidextrous safety.
Price: $1,738.00

LIONHEART LH9 MKII

Caliber: 9mm, 15-round magazine. LH9C Compact, 10 rounds. **Barrel:** 4.1 inches. **Weight:** 26.5 oz. **Length:** 7.5 inches **Grips:** One piece black polymer with textured design. **Sights:** Fixed low profile. Novak LoMount sights available. **Finish:** Cerakote Graphite Black or Patriot Brown. **Features:** Hammer-forged heat-treated steel slide, hammer-forged aluminum frame. Double-action PLUS action.
Price: $695.00
Price: Novak sights...$749.00

NIGHTHAWK CUSTOM T4

Manufacturer of a wide range of 1911-style pistols in Government Model (full-size), Commander and Officer's frame sizes. **Caliber:** .45 ACP, 7 or 8-round magazine; 9mm, 9 or 10 rounds; 10mm, 9 or 10 rounds. **Barrel:** 3.8, 4.25 or 5 inches. **Weight:** 28 to 41 ounces, depending on model. Shown is T4 model, introduced in 2013 and available only in 9mm.
Price: From .... **$2,995.00 to $3,995.00**

NORTH AMERICAN ARMS GUARDIAN DAO

Caliber: .25 NAA, .32 ACP, .380 ACP, .32 NAA, 6-shot magazine. **Barrel:** 2.49. **Weight:** 20.8 oz. **Length:** 4.75 overall. **Grips:** Black polymer. **Sights:** Low profile fixed. **Features:** Double-action only mechanism. All stainless steel construction. Introduced 1998. Made in U.S.A. by North American Arms.
Price: From **$402.00**

OLYMPIC ARMS OA-93 AR

Caliber: 5.56 NATO. **Barrel:** 6.5" button-rifled stainless steel. **Weight:** 4.46 lbs. **Length:** 17" overall. **Sights:** None. **Features:** Olympic Arms integrated recoil system on the upper receiver eliminates the

buttstock, flat top upper, free floating tubular match handguard, threaded muzzle with flash suppressor. Made in U.S.A. by Olympic Arms, Inc.
Price: **$1,202.00**

OLYMPIC ARMS K23P AR

Caliber: 5.56 NATO. **Barrel:** 6.5" button-rifled chrome-moly steel. **Length:** 22.25" overall. **Weight:** 5.12 lbs. **Sights:** Adjustable A2 rear, elevation adjustable front post. **Features:** A2 upper with rear sight, free floating tubular match handguard, threaded muzzle with flash suppressor, receiver extension tube with foam cover, no bayonet lug. Made in U.S.A. by Olympic Arms, Inc. Introduced 2007.
Price: **$973.70**

OLYMPIC ARMS K23P-A3-TC AR

Caliber: 5.56 NATO. **Barrel:** 6.5" button-rifled chrome-moly steel. **Length:** 22.25" overall. **Weight:** 5.12 lbs. **Sights:** Adjustable A2 rear, elevation adjustable front post. **Features:** Flat-top upper with detachable carry handle, free floating FIRSH rail handguard, threaded muzzle with flash suppressor, receiver extension tube with foam cover, no bayonet lug. Made in U.S.A. by Olympic Arms, Inc. Introduced 2007.
Price: **$1,118.20**

OLYMPIC ARMS WHITNEY WOLVERINE

Caliber: .22 LR, 10-shot magazine. **Barrel:** 4.625" stainless steel. **Weight:** 19.2 oz. **Length:** 9" overall. **Grips:** Black checkered with fire/safe markings. **Sights:** Ramped blade front, dovetail rear. **Features:** Polymer frame with natural ergonomics and ventilated rib. Barrel with 6-groove 1x16 twist rate. All metal magazine shell. Made in U.S.A. by Olympic Arms.
Price: **$291.00**

PARA USA BLACK OPS SERIES

Caliber: .45 ACP, single (8 round) or double-stack magazine (14 rounds). **Barrel:** 5 inches. **Weight:** 39 oz. **Grips:** VZ G10. **Sights:** Fixed night sights or adjustable. Stainless receiver with IonBond finish.
Price: .... **$1,257.00 to $1,325.00**

Prices given are believed to be accurate at time of publication however, many factors affect retail pricing so exact prices are not possible.

70TH EDITION, 2016 ⊕ **405**

2-dot rear combat, Green fiber optic front. **Features:** Double-stack aluminum frame, adjustable skeletonized trigger, black nitride or satin stainless finish. Comes with two 10-round magazines.
Price: (black) $884.00
Price: (stainless)...$919.00

PARA USA BLACK OPS RECON
Caliber: 9mm, 18-round double-stack magazine. **Barrel:** 4.25 inches. **Weight:** 34 oz. **Grips:** VZ G10. **Sights:** Trijicon night sights. **Features:** Stainless receiver with IonBond finish.
Price: $1,299.00

PARA USA EXPERT SERIES
Caliber: .45 ACP, 7+1-round capacity, 9mm (8+1). **Barrel:** 5" stainless. **Weight:** 39 oz. **Length:** 8.5" overall. **Grips:** Checkered Polymer. **Sights:** Dovetail Fixed, 3-White Dot. **Features:** The Para "Expert" is an entry level 1911 pistol that will allow new marksmen to own a pistol with features such as, Lowered and flared ejection port, beveled magazine well, flat mainspring housing, grip safety contoured for spur hammer. Model 1445 has double-stack frame, 14-round magazine.
Price: $663.00
Price: Carry $799.00
Price: Commander..$799.00
Price: 1445 Model...................... $884.00 to $919.00

PARA ELITE SERIES
Caliber: .45 ACP, 9mm (Elite LS Hunter only). **Capacity:** 6, 7 or 8 rounds; 9 rounds (9mm LS Hunter). **Barrel:** 3, 4 or 5 inches (.45 models), 6 inches (9mm LS Hunter). **Features:** Pro Model has Ed Brown mag well, HD extractor, checkered front strap and mainspring housing, Trijicon sights.
Price: Elite Standard $949.00
Price: Agent 3.5"...$949.00
Price: Officer 4" $949.00
Price: Commander 4.5" $949.00
Price: Target $949.00
Price: Pro, LS Hunter $1,249.00
Price: Pro Stainless...$1,249.00

PARA USA LDA SERIES
Caliber: 9mm, .45 ACP. **Capacity:** 9 rounds (9mm), 7 rounds (.45) for Officer model; 8 and 6 round capacity for Agent model, which has shorter grip. Double-action only design with PARA's exclusive LDA (Light Double Action) trigger. **Barrel:** 3 inches. **Sights:** Trijicon night sights. **Grips:** VZ Gator.
Price: Officer $1,025.00
Price: Agent $1,025.00

PARA EXECUTIVE CARRY
Caliber: .45 ACP, 8-round magazine. **Capacity:** 8-round magazine. **Barrel:** 3 inches **Sights:** Trijicon Night Sights. **Features:** Ed Brown Bobtail mainspring housing, adjustable skeletonized trigger, Ionbond anodized finish, V7 grips. Full-size grip frame with 3-inch barrel. Comes with two 8-round magazines.
Price: $1,399.00

PARA CUSTOM SERIES
Caliber: .45 ACP, .40 S&W, 9mm. Magazine capacity: 8 to 18 rounds, depending on model. **Barrel:** 3" (Executive Carry), 5". **Weight:** 26 or 40 oz. **Grips:** Polymer. **Sights:** Night sights or adjustable rear with fiber optic front. **Finish:** Stainless steel.
Price: Executive Carry $1,399.00
Price: Pro Comp 9, Pro Comp 40 ....$1,299.00
Price: Pro Custom 14.45 ....$1,449.00
Price: Pro Custom 16.40 ....$1,449.00

PARA USA WARTHOG
Caliber: .45 ACP, 10-round magazine. **Barrel:** 3 inches. **Sights:**

Prices given are believed to be accurate at time of publication however, many factors affect retail pricing so exact prices are not possible.

Other features include forward slide serrations, fiber optic front sight. Available with threaded barrel.
Price: $940.00
Price: Threaded barrel ....$ 940.00 to $1,140.00

PHOENIX ARMS HP22, HP25

Caliber: .22 LR, 10-shot (HP22), .25 ACP, 10-shot (HP25). **Barrel:** 3". **Weight:** 20 oz. **Length:** 5.5" overall. **Grips:** Checkered composition. **Sights:** Blade front, adjustable rear. **Features:** Single action, exposed hammer; manual hold-open; button magazine release. Available in satin nickel, matte blue finish. Introduced 1993. Made in U.S.A. by Phoenix Arms.
Price: With gun lock $130.00
Price: HP Range kit with 5" bbl., locking case
and accessories (1 Mag) $171.00
Price: HP Deluxe Range kit with 3" and 5" bbls.,
2 mags, case $210.00

REMINGTON R1

Caliber: .45 (7-shot magazine). **Barrel:** 5". **Weight:** 38.5 oz. **Grips:** Double diamond walnut. **Sights:** Fixed, dovetail front and rear, 3-dot. **Features:** Flared and lowered ejection port. Comes with two magazines.
Price: $729.00
Price: (stainless) ....$ 729.00 to 789.00

REMINGTON R1 ENHANCED

Same features as standard R1 except 8-shot magazine, stainless satin black oxide finish, wood laminate grips and adjustable rear sight.

REMINGTON R1 CARRY

Caliber: .45 ACP. **Barrel:** 5 or 4.25 inches (Carry Commander). **Weight:** 35 to 39 oz. **Grips:** Cocobolo. **Sights:** Novak-type drift-adjustable rear, tritium-dot front sight. **Features:** Skeletonized trigger. Comes with one 8-round and one 7-round magazine.
Price: $1,299.00

REMINGTON R51

Caliber: 9mm+P rated, 6-shot magazine. **Barrel:** 3.4". **Weight:** 22 oz. **Length:** 6.6" overall **Grips:** Black synthetic, checkered/smooth. **Sights:** Fixed low-profile 3-dot system. Skeletonized trigger. **Features:** Grip safety only, fixed barrel/locked breech operating system allows a lighter recoil spring, which is placed around the barrel. This is the reason for the gun's thin design. Width of the frame is one inch. Based on the Pedersen design of the original Model 51 .32/.380 pistol made from 1918 to 1926, with numerous improvements. Introduced in 2014. **NOTE:** Due to performance issues production of the R51 ceased in July 2014. According to Remington, the problems were rectified and production was expected to resume in mid 2015. Owners of an original R51 should return their pistol to Remington and it will be replaced by one of the new models. For more information contact Remington at 800-243-9700.
Price: $420.00

REMINGTON RM380

Caliber: .380 ACP, 6-shot magazine + 1. **Barrel:** 2.9", **Length:** 5.27". **Height:** 3.86". **Weight:** 12.2 oz. **Sights:** Fixed and contoured. **Grips:** Glass-filled nylon with replaceable panels. **Features:** Double-action-only operation, all-metal construction with aluminum frame, stainless steel barrel, light dual recoil spring system, extended beavertail. Introduced in 2015.
Price: $417.00

Prices given are believed to be accurate at time of publication however, many factors affect retail pricing so exact prices are not possible.

70TH EDITION, 2016 ✦ **407**

REPUBLIC FORGE 1911

Caliber: .45 ACP, 9mm, .38 Super, .40 S&W, 10mm. A manufacturer of custom 1911-style pistols offered in a variety of configurations, finishes and frame sizes, including single and double-stack models with many options. Made in Texas.
Price: From **$2,795.00**

ROBERTS DEFENSE 1911 SERIES

Caliber: : .45 ACP (8+1 rounds). **Barrel:** 5, 4.25 or 3.5 inches. **Weight:** 26 to 38 oz. **Sights:** Novak-type drift-adjustable rear, tritium-dot or fiber optic front sight. **Features:** Skeletonized trigger. Offered in three model variants with many custom features and options. Made in Wisconsin by Roberts Defense.
Price: Recon **$1,499.00**
Price: Super Grade **$1,549.00**
Price: Operator **$1,649.00**

ROCK RIVER ARMS LAR-15/LAR-9

Caliber: .223/5.56mm NATO or 9mm Para. **Barrel:** 7", 10.5". Wilson chrome moly, 1:9 twist, A2 flash hider, 1/2-28 thread. **Weight:** 5.1 lbs. (7" barrel), 5.5 lbs. (10.5" barrel). **Length:** 23" overall. **Stock:** Hogue rubber grip. **Sights:** A2 front. **Features:** Forged A2 or A4 upper, single stage trigger, aluminum free-float tube, one magazine. Similar 9mm Para. LAR-9 also available. From Rock River Arms, Inc.
Price: LAR-15 7" A2 AR2115 .... **$955.00**
Price: LAR-15 10.5" A4 AR2120 .... **$945.00**
Price: LAR-9 7" A2 9mm2115 .... **$1,125.00**

ROCK RIVER ARMS 1911 POLY

Caliber: .45 ACP, 7-round magazine. Full-size 1911-style model with polymer frame and steel slide. **Barrel:** 5". **Weight:** 33 oz. **Sights:** Fixed.
Price: **$925.00**

ROHRBAUGH R9

Caliber: 9mm Parabellum, .380 ACP. **Barrel:** 2.9". **Weight:** 12.8 oz. **Length:** 5.2" overall. **Features:** Very small double-action-only semiauto pocket pistol. Stainless steel slide with matte black aluminum frame. Available with or without sights. Available with all-black (Stealth) and partial Diamond Black (Stealth Elite) finish.
Price: **$1,149.00**

RUGER SR9 /SR40

Caliber: 9mm Para. (17 round magazine), .40 S&W (15). **Barrel:** 4.14". **Weight:** 26.25, 26.5 oz. **Grips:** Glass-filled nylon in two color options—black or OD Green, w/flat or arched reversible backstrap. **Sights:** Adjustable 3-dot, built-in Picatinny-style rail. **Features:** Semi-auto in six configurations, striker-fired, through-hardened stainless steel slide, brushed or blackened stainless slide with black grip frame or blackened stainless slide with OD Green grip frame, ambidextrous manual 1911-style safety, ambi. mag release, mag disconnect, loaded chamber indicator, Ruger camblock design to absorb recoil, comes with two magazines. 10-shot mags available. Introduced 2008. Made in U.S.A. by Sturm, Ruger & Co.
Price: SR9 (17-Round), SR9-10 (SS) **$529.00**

RUGER SR9C /SR40C COMPACT

Caliber: 9mm or .40 S&W. **Barrel:** 3.4 " (SR9C), 3.5" (SR40C). **Features:** Features include 1911-style ambidextrous manual safety; internal trigger bar interlock and striker blocker; trigger safety; magazine disconnector; loaded chamber indicator; two magazines, one 10-round and the other 17-round; 3.5-inch barrel; 3-dot sights; accessory rail; brushed stainless or blackened allow finish. Weight 23.40 oz.
Price: **$525.00**

RUGER 9E

Caliber: 9mm. A value-priced variation of the SR9 with black oxide finish, drift-adjustable sights. Other features similar to SR9.
Price: **$429.00**

RUGER SR45

Caliber: .45 ACP, 10-round magazine. **Barrel:** 4.5 inches. **Weight:** 30 oz. **Length:** 8 inches. **Grips:** Glass-filled nylon with reversible flat/

arched backstra. **Sights:** Adjustable 3-dot. **Features:** Same features as SR9.
Price: $529.00

RUGER LC9

Caliber: 9mm luger, 7+1 capacity. **Barrel:** 3.12 **Weight:** 17.10 oz. **Grips:** Glass-filled nylon. **Sights:** Adjustable 3-dot. **Features:** Double-action-only, hammer-fired, locked-breech pistol with a smooth trigger pull. Control and confident handling of the Ruger LC9 are accomplished through reduced recoil and aggressive frame checkering for a positive grip in all conditions. The Ruger LC9 features smooth "melted" edges for ease of holstering, carrying and drawing. Made in U.S.A. by Sturm, Ruger & Co.
Price: $449.00

RUGER LC9S

Caliber: 9mm luger, 7+1 capacity. **Barrel:** 3.12 **Grips:** Glass-filled nylon. **Sights:** Adjustable 3-dot. **Features:** Identical to the LC9 but with a striker-fired design.
Price: $449.00

RUGER LC380

Caliber: .380 ACP. Other specifications and features identical to LC9.
Price: $449.00

Price: LaserMax laser grips $529.00
Price: Crimson Trace Laserguard $629.00

RUGER LCP

Caliber: .380 (6-shot magazine). **Barrel:** 2.75". **Weight:** 9.4 oz. **Length:** 5.16". **Grips:** Glass-filled nylon. **Sights:** Fixed, drift adjustable or integral Crimson Trace Laserguard.
Price: Blued $389.00
Price: Stainless steel slide $429.00
Price: Crimson Trace Laserguard $575.00
Price: Custom w/drift adjustable rear sight $419.00

RUGER CHARGER

Caliber: .22 LR, 10-shot BX-15 magazine. Based on famous 10/22 rifle design with pistol grip stock and fore-end, scope rail, bipod. Brown laminate (standard model) or Green Mountain laminate stock (takedown model). Reintroduced with improvements and enhancements in 2015.
Price: Standard $409.00
Price: Takedown $509.00

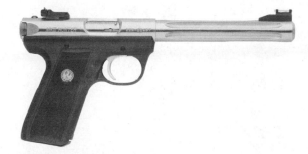

RUGER MARK III SERIES

Caliber: .22 LR, 10-shot magazine. **Barrel:** 4.5, 4.75, 5.5, 6, or 6-7/8". **Weight:** 33 oz. (4.75" bbl.). **Length:** 9" (4.75" bbl.). **Grips:** Checkered composition grip panels. **Sights:** Fixed, fiber-optic front, fixed rear. **Features:** Updated design of original Standard Auto and Mark II series. Hunter models have lighter barrels. Target models

Prices given are believed to be accurate at time of publication however, many factors affect retail pricing so exact prices are not possible.

70TH EDITION, 2016 **409**

have cocobolo grips; bull, target, competition, and hunter barrels; and adjustable sights. Introduced 2005. Modern successor of the first Ruger pistol of 1949.

Price: Standard $389.00
Price: Target (blue) $459.00
Price: Target (stainless) $569.00
Price: Hunter $679.00
Price: Hunter (target grips)..$729.00
Price: Competition $659.00

RUGER 22/45 MARK III PISTOL

Similar to other .22 Mark III autos except has Zytel grip frame that matches angle and magazine latch of Model 1911 .45 ACP pistol. Available in 4.0, 4.4, 4.5, 5.5 inch bull barrels. Comes with extra magazine, plastic case, lock. Molder polymer or replaceable laminate grips. **Weight:** 31 to 33 oz. **Sights:** Adjustable.

Price: Target model, 4" bull barrel, adjustable sights $465.00
Price: 4.5" bull threaded barrel w/rails or adj. sights $465.00
Price: Lite w/rail and adj. sights $515.00

RUGER SR22

Caliber: .22 LR (10-shot magazine). **Barrel:** 3.5". **Weight:** 17.5 oz. **Length:** 6.4". **Sights:** Adjustable 3-dot. **Features:** Ambidextrous manual safety/decocking lever and mag release. Comes with two interchangeable rubberized grips and two magazines. Black or silveranodize finish. Available with threaded barrel.

Price: Black $415.00
Price: Silver $429.00
Price: Threaded barrel $449.00

RUGER SR1911

Caliber: .45 (8-shot magazine). **Barrel:** 5". **Weight:** 39 oz. **Length:** 8.6". **Grips:** Slim checkered hardwood. **Sights:** Novak LoMount Carry rear, standard front. **Features:** Based on Series 70 design. Flared and lowed ejection port. Extended mag release, thumb safety and slide-stop lever, oversized grip safety, checkered

backstrap on the flat mainspring housing. Comes with one 7-shot and one 8-shot magazine.

Price: $859.00

RUGER SR1911 CMD

Commander-size version of SR1911. **Caliber:** .45 ACP. **Barrel:** 4.25 inches. **Weight:** 29.3 (aluminum), 36.4 oz. (stainless). Other specifications and features are identical to SR1911.

Price: Low glare stainless $859.00
Price: Anodized aluminum two tone.............................$899.00

SCCY CPX

Caliber: 9mm, 10-round magazine. **Barrel:** 3.1". **Weight:** 15 oz. **Length:** 5.7" overall. **Grips:** Integral with polymer frame. **Sights:** 3-dot system, rear adjustable for windage. **Features:** Zytel polymer frame, steel slide, aluminum alloy receiver machined from bar stock. Double-action only with consistent 9-pound trigger pull. Concealed hammer. Available with (CPX-1) or without (CPX-2) manual thumb safety. Introduced 2014. Made in U.S.A. by SCCY Industries.

Price: Black carbon $334.00
Price: Stainless/blue two-tone..................................$339.00

SEECAMP LWS 32/380 STAINLESS DA

Caliber: .32 ACP, .380 ACP Win. Silvertip, 6-shot magazine. **Barrel:** 2", integral with frame. **Weight:** 10.5 oz. **Length:** 4-1/8" overall. **Grips:** Glass-filled nylon. **Sights:** Smooth, no-snag, contoured slide and barrel top. **Features:** Aircraft quality 17-4 PH stainless steel. Inertia-operated firing pin. Hammer fired double-action-only. Hammer automatically follows slide down to safety rest position after each shot, no manual safety needed. Magazine safety disconnector. Polished stainless. Introduced 1985. From L.W. Seecamp.

Price: .32..$446.25
Price: .380..$795.00

SIG SAUER 250 COMPACT

Caliber: 9mm Para. (16-round magazine), 357 SIG, .40 S&W and .45 ACP. **Weight:** 24.6 oz. **Length:** 7.2" overall. **Grips:** Interchangeable polymer. **Sights:** Siglite night sights. **Features:** Modular polymer frame design allows for immediate change in caliber. Available in full, compact and subcompact sizes. Six different grip combinations for each size. Introduced 2008. From SIG Sauer, Inc.

Price: P250 ....$717.00
Price: Black Nitron Finish $769.00

SIG SAUER 1911

Caliber: .45 ACP, .40 S&W. 8-10 shot magazine. **Barrel:** 5". **Weight:** 40.3 oz. **Length:** 8.65" overall. **Grips:** Checkered wood

Prices given are believed to be accurate at time of publication however, many factors affect retail pricing so exact prices are not possible.

grips. **Sights:** Novak night sights. Blade front, drift adjustable rear for windage. **Features:** Single-action 1911. Hand-fitted dehorned stainless-steel frame and slide; match-grade barrel, hammer/sear set and trigger; 25-lpi front strap checkering, 20-lpi mainspring housing checkering. Beavertail grip safety with speed bump, extended thumb safety, firing pin safety and hammer intercept notch. Introduced 2005. XO series has contrast sights, Ergo Grip XT textured polymer grips. Target line features adjustable target night sights, match barrel, custom wood grips, non-railed frame in stainless or Nitron finishes. TTT series is two-tone 1911 with Nitron slide and black controls on stainless frame. Includes burled maple grips, adjustable combat night sights. STX line available from Sig Sauer Custom Shop; two-tone 1911, non-railed, Nitron slide, stainless frame, burled maple grips. Polished cocking serrations, flat-top slide, magwell. Carry line has Novak night sights, lanyard attachment point, gray diamondwood or rosewood grips, 8+1 capacity. Compact series has 6+1 capacity, 7.7 OAL, 4.25" barrel, slim-profile wood grips, weighs 30.3 oz. RCS line (Compact SAS) is Customs Shop version with anti-snag dehorning. Stainless or Nitron finish, Novak night sights, slim-profile gray diamondwood or rosewood grips. 6+1 capacity. 1911 C3 (2008) is a 6+1 compact .45 ACP, rosewood custom wood grips, two-tone and Nitron finishes. Weighs about 30 ounces unloaded, lightweight alloy frame. Length is 7.7. Now offered in more than 30 different models with numerous options for frame size, grips, finishes, sight arrangements and other features. From SIG SAUER, Inc.

Price: Nitron	$1,200.00
Price: Tacops	$1,213.00
Price: XO Black	$1,050.00
Price: STX	$1,213.00
Price: Nightmare	$1,242.00
Price: CarryNightmare	$1,242.00
Price: Compact C3	$1,042.00
Price: Max	$1,712.00
Price: Spartan	$1,356.00
Price: Scorpion	$1,213.00
Price: 1911-22-B .22 LR w/custom rosewood grips	$460.00

SIG SAUER P210
Caliber: 9mm, 8-shot magazine. **Barrel:** 4.7". **Weight:** 37.4 oz.

Length: 8.5" overall. **Grips:** Custom wood. **Sights:** Post and notch and adjustable target sights. **Features:** The carbon steel slide, machined from solid billet steel, now features a durable Nitron® coating, and the improved beavertail adorns the Nitron coated, heavy-style, carbon steel frame. The P210 Legend also offers an improved manual safety, internal drop safety, side magazine release, and custom wood grips.
Price: P210-9-LEGEND $2,428.00
Price: P210-9-LEGEND-TGT
w/adjustable target sights $2,642.00

SIG SAUER P220
Caliber: .45 ACP, (7- or 8-shot magazine). **Barrel:** 4.4". **Weight:** 27.8 oz. **Length:** 7.8" overall. **Grips:** Checkered black plastic. **Sights:** Blade front, drift adjustable rear for windage. Optional Siglite night sights. **Features:** Double action. Stainless-steel slide, Nitron finish, alloy frame, M1913 Picatinny rail; safety system of decocking lever, automatic firing pin safety block, safety intercept notch, and trigger bar disconnector. Squared combat-type trigger guard. Slide stays open after last shot. Introduced 1976. P220 SAS Anti-Snag has dehorned stainless steel slide, front Siglite Night Sight, rounded trigger guard, dust cover, Custom Shop wood grips. Equinox line is Custom Shop product with Nitron stainless-steel slide with a black hard-anodized alloy frame, brush-polished flats and nickel accents. Truglo tritium fiber-optic front sight, rear Siglite night sight, gray laminated wood grips with checkering and stippling. From SIG SAUER, Inc.
Price:	$1,108.00
Price: P220 Combat	$1,316.00
Price: P220 Elite Stainless	$1,396.00
Price: P220 Equinox	$1,253.00
Price: P220 Elite Dark	$1,253.00
Price: P220 Elite Dark, threaded barrel	$1,305.00
Price: P220 .22 LR	$642.00

SIG SAUER P220 CARRY
Caliber: .45 ACP, 8-shot magazine. **Barrel:** 3.9". **Weight:** NA. **Length:** 7.1" overall. **Grips:** Checkered black plastic. **Sights:** Blade front, drift adjustable rear for windage. Optional Siglite night sights. **Features:** Similar to full-size P220, except is "Commander" size. Single stack, DA/SA operation, Nitron finish, Picatinny rail, and either post and dot contrast or 3-dot Siglite night sights. Introduced

2005. Many variations availble. From SIG SAUER, Inc.
Price: P220 Carry, from $1,108.00
w/night sights $1,166.00
Price: P220 Carry Elite Stainless $1,396.00

SIG SAUER P224

Caliber: 9mm, .357 SIG, .40 S&W. **Magazine Capacity:** 11 rounds (9mm), 10 rounds (.357 and .40). **Barrel:** 3.5" inches. **Weight:** 25 oz. **Length:** 6.7" inches. **Grips:** Hogue G-10. **Sights:** SIGlite night sights. **Features:** Ultra-compact, double-stack design with features and operating controls of other SIG models. Available in SAS, nickel, Equinox and Extreme variations.
Price: .... $1,108.00 to $1,243.00

SIG SAUER P226

Similar to the P220 pistol except has 4.4 barrel, measures 7.7 overall, weighs 34 oz. Chambered in 9mm, .357 SIG, or .40 S&W. X-Five series has factory tuned single-action trigger, 5 slide and barrel, ergonomic wood grips with beavertail, ambidextrous thumb safety and stainless slide and frame with magwell, low-profile adjustable target sights, front cocking serrations and a 25-meter factory test target. Many variations available. Snap-on modular grips. From SIG SAUER, Inc.
Price: $1,108.00
Price: Elite from $1,243.00

Price: X Series... $2,245.00
Price: X Super Match....................................... $3,042.00
Price: .22 LR $636.00

SIG SAUER P227

Same general specifications and features as P226 except chambered for .45 ACP and has double-stack magazine. **Magazine Capacity:** 10 rounds.
Price: .... $1,108.00 to $1,250.00

SIG SAUER P228

Caliber: 9mm. **Capacity:** 15 rounds. Single/double action. **Sights:** Siglite night sights. Black nitron or Flat Dark Earth finish. Threaded barrel available. Reintroduced in 2013.
Price: .... $1,149.00 to $1,220.00

SIG SAUER P229 DA

Similar to the P220 except chambered for 9mm Para. (10- or 15-round magazines), .40 S&W, (10- or 12-round magazines). Has 3.86" barrel, 7.1" overall length and 3.35" height. Weight is 32.4 oz. Introduced 1991. Snap-on modular grips. Frame made in Germany, stainless steel slide assembly made in U.S.; pistol assembled in U.S. Many variations available. From SIG SAUER, Inc.
Price: P229, from $1,085.00
Price: P229 Stainless Elite................................ $1,396.00
Price: P229 Scorpion Elite $1,312.00

SIG SAUER SP2022

Caliber: 9mm Para., .357 SIG, .40 S&W, 10-, 12-, or 15-shot magazines. **Barrel:** 3.9". **Weight:** 30.2 oz. **Length:** 7.4" overall. **Grips:** Composite and rubberized one-piece. **Sights:** Blade front, rear adjustable for windage. Optional Siglite night sights. **Features:** Polymer frame, stainless steel slide; integral frame accessory rail; replaceable steel frame rails; left- or right-handed magazine release; two interchangeable grips. From SIG SAUER, Inc.
Price: $642.00

SIG SAUER P232

Caliber: .380 ACP, 7-shot. **Barrel:** 3.6". **Weight:** 17.6-22.4 oz. **Length:** 6.6" overall. **Grips:** Checkered black composite. **Sights:** Blade front, rear adjustable for windage. **Features:** Double action/ single action or DAO. Blow-back operation, stationary barrel. Introduced 1997. From SIG SAUER, Inc.
Price: $809.00
Price: Stainless $889.00

SIG SAUER P238

Caliber: .380 ACP, 6-7-shot magazine. **Barrel:** 2.7". **Weight:** 15.4

oz. **Length:** 5.5" overall. **Grips:** Hogue® G-10 and Rosewood grips. **Sights:** Contrast / SIGLITE night sights. **Features:** All metal beavertail-style frame.

Price: $723.00
Price: Gambler w/rosewood grip $752.00
Price: Extreme w/X-Grip extended magazine.......................$752.00
Price: Equinox..$752.00

SIG SAUER P290 RS

Caliber: 9mm, 6/8-shot magazine. **Barrel:** 2.9". **Weight:** 20.5 oz. **Length:** 5.5" overall. **Grips:** Polymer. **Sights:** Contrast / SIGLITE night sights. **Features:** Unlike many small pistols, the P290 features drift adjustable sights in the standard SIG SAUER dovetails. This gives shooters the option of either standard contrast sights or SIGLITE® night sights. The slide is machined from a solid billet of stainless steel and is available in a natural stainless or a durable Nitron® coating. A reversible magazine catch is left-hand adjustable. Interchangeable grip panels allow for personalization as well as a custom fit. In addition to the standard polymer inserts, optional panels will be available in aluminum, G10 and wood.

Price: Model 290 RS $570.00
Price: Model 290 RS Enhanced...............................$613.00
Price: Model 290 RS Two-Tone with laser sight $685.00
Price: Model 290 RS Rainbow or Pink with
laser sights..$613.00

SIG SAUER P239

Caliber: 9mm Para., 8-shot, .357 SIG, .40 S&W, 7-shot magazine.

Barrel: 3.6". **Weight:** 25.2 oz. **Length:** 6.6" overall. **Grips:** Checkered black composite. **Sights:** Blade front, rear adjustable for windage. Optional Siglite night sights. **Features:** SA/DA or DAO; blackened stainless steel slide, aluminum alloy frame. Introduced 1996. Made in U.S.A. by SIG SAUER, Inc.
Price: P239, from $1,108.00

SIG SAUER P320

Caliber: 9mm, .357 SIG, .40 S&W. Magazine capacity 15 or 16 rounds (9mm), 13 or 14 rounds (.357 or .40). **Barrel:** 3.9 (Carry model) or 4.7" (Full size). **Weight:** 26 to 30 oz. **Length:** 7.2 or 8.0 inches overall. **Grips:** Interchangeable black composite. **Sights:** Blade front, rear adjustable for windage. Optional Siglite night sights. **Features:** Striker-fired double-action only, Nitron finish slide, black polymer frame. Frame size and calibers are interchangeable. Introduced 2014. A .45 ACP version is expected by 2015. Made in U.S.A. by SIG SAUER, Inc.
Price: Full size $713.00
Price: Carry (shown) $713.00

SIG SAUER MOSQUITO

Caliber: .22 LR, 10-shot magazine. **Barrel:** 3.9". **Weight:** 24.6 oz. **Length:** 7.2" overall. **Grips:** Checkered black composite. **Sights:** Blade front, rear adjustable for windage. **Features:** Blowback operated, fixed barrel, polymer frame, slide-mounted ambidextrous safety. Introduced 2005. Made in U.S.A. by SIG SAUER, Inc.
Price: Mosquito, from $408.00

SIG SAUER P522

Semiauto blowback pistol chambered in .22 LR. Pistol version of SIG522 rifle. Features include a 10-inch barrel; lightweight polymer lower receiver with pistol grip; ambi mag catch; aluminum upper; faux gas valve; birdcage; 25-round magazine; quad rail or "clean" handguard; optics rail
Price: From $587.00

SIG SAUER P556 SWAT

Caliber: 5.56 NATO. Pistol version of P556 rifle. **Barrel:** 10 inches. **Capacity:** 10 rounds. **Weight:** 7.2 lbs. **Length:** 27.25 inches.
Price: From $1,471.00

SIG SAUER MPX
Caliber: 9mm, .357 SIG, .40 S&W. **Capacity:** 10, 20 or 30 rounds. **Barrel:** 8 inches. Semi-auto AR-style gun with closed, fully locked short-stroke pushrod gas sytem. **Weight:** 5 lbs.

Price: **$2,199.00**

SIG SAUER P938
Caliber: 9mm (6-shot magazine), .22 LR (10). **Barrel:** 3.0". **Weight:** 16 oz. **Length:** 5.9". **Grips:** Rosewood, Blackwood, Hogue Extreme, Hogue Diamondwood. **Sights:** Siglite night sights or Siglite rear with Tru-Glo front. **Features:** Slightly larger version of P238.
Price: .... **$809.00 to $823.00**
Price: .22 LR **$656.00**

SPHINX
Caliber: 9mm Para., .45 ACP, 10-shot magazine. **Barrel:** 4.43". **Weight:** 39.15 oz. **Length:** 8.27" overall. **Grips:** Textured polymer. **Sights:** Fixed Trijicon Night Sights. **Features:** CNC engineered from stainless steel billet; grip frame in stainless steel, titanium or high-strength aluminum. Integrated accessory rail, high-cut beavertail, decocking lever. Made in Switzerland. Imported by Sabre Defence Industries.
Price: .45 ACP (2007) **$2,990.00**
Price: 9mm Para. Standard, titanium w/decocker **$2,700.00**

SPHINX SDP
Caliber: 9mm (15-shot magazine). **Barrel:** 3.7". **Weight:** 27.5 oz.

Length: 7.4". **Sights:** Defiance Day & Night Green fiber/tritium front, tritium 2-dot red rear. **Features:** Double/single action with ambidextrous decocker, integrated slide postion safety, aluminum MIL-STD 1913 Picatinny rail, Blued alloy/steel or stainless. Aluminum and polymer frame, machined steel slide. Offered in several variations. Made in Switzerland
Price: **$1,295.00**

SMITH & WESSON M&P SERIES
Caliber: .22 LR, 9mm, .357 Sig, .40 S&W. **Magazine capacity, full-size models:** 12 rounds (.22), 17 rounds (9mm), 15 rounds (.40). **Compact models:** 12 (9mm), 10 (.40). **Barrel:** 4.25, 3.5 inches. **Weight:** 24, 22 oz. **Length:** 7.6, 6.7 inches. **Grips:** Polymer with three interchangeable palmswell grip sizes. **Sights:** 3 white-dot system with low-profile rear. **Features:** Zytel polymer frame with stainless steel slide, barrel and structural components. VTAC (Viking Tactics) model has Flat Dark Earth finish, VTAC Warrior sights. Compact models available with Crimson Trace Lasergrips.
Price: (VTAC) .... **$569.00 to $779.00**
Price: (CT) **$809.00**
Price: M&P 22 ....**$419.00**

SMITH & WESSON M&P PRO SERIES C.O.R.E.
Caliber: 9mm, .40 S&W. Magazine capacity: 17 rounds (9mm), 15 rounds (.40). **Barrel:** 4.25" (M&P9, M&P40), or 5" (M&P9L, M&P40L.) **Features:** Based on the Pro series line of competition-ready firearms, the C.O.R.E. models (Competition Optics Ready Equipment) feature a slide engineered to accept six popular competition optics (Trijicon RMR, Leupold Delta Point, Jpoint, Doctor, C-More STS, Insight MRDS). Sight not included. Other features identical to standard M&P9 and M&P40 models.
Price: **$769.00**

Prices given are believed to be accurate at time of publication however, many factors affect retail pricing so exact prices are not possible.

SMITH & WESSON M&P 45

M&P model offered in three frame sizes and chambered in .45 ACP. **Magazine capacity:** 8 or 10 rounds. **Barrel length:** 4 or 4.5 inches. **Weight:** 26, 28 or 30 oz. Available with or without thumb safety. **Finish:** Black or Dark Earth Brown. Available with Crimson Trace Lasergrips.
Price: .... $599.00 to $619.00
Price: CT (Crimson Trace) $829.00

SMITH & WESSON M&P SHIELD

Ultra-compact, single-stack variation of M&P series. **Caliber:** 9mm, .40 S&W. Comes with one 7 and one 8-round magazine (9mm), one 6-round and one 7-round magazine (.40). **Barrel:** 3.1 inches. **Length:** 6.I inches. **Weight:** 19 oz. **Sights:** 3-white-dot system with low-profile rear.
Price: $449.00

SMITH & WESSON MODEL SD9 VE/SD40 VE

Caliber: .40 S&W and 9mm, 10+1, 14+1 and 16+1 round capacities. **Barrel:** 4 inches. **Weight:** 39 oz. **Length:** 8.7". **Grips:** Wood or rubber. **Sights:** Front: Tritium Night Sight, Rear: Steel Fixed 2-Dot. **Features:** SDT™ - Self Defense Trigger for optimal, consistent pull first round to Last, standard picatinny-style rail, slim ergonomic textured grip, textured finger locator and aggressive front and back strap texturing with front and rear slide serrations.
Price: From $389.00

SMITH & WESSON MODEL SW1911

Caliber: .45 ACP, 9mm. **Magazine capacity:** 8 rounds (.45), 7 rounds

(sub compact .45), 10 rounds (9mm). **Barrel:** 3, 4.25, 5 inches. **Weight:** 26.5 to 41.7 oz. **Length:** 6.9 to 8.7 inches. **Grips:** Wood, wood laminate or synthetic. Crimson Trace Lasergrips available. **Sights:** Low profile white dot, tritium night sights or adjustable. **Finish:** Black matte, stainless or two-tone. **Features:** Offered in three different frame sizes. Skeletonized trigger. Accessory rail on some models. Compact models have round butt frame. Pro Series have 30 lpi checkered front strap, oversized external extractor, extended mag well, full-length guide rod, ambidextrous safety.
Price: Standard model .... $919.00 to $1,319.00
Price: Compact SC series .... $1,369.00 to $1,389.00
Price: Crimson Trace grips $1,454.00
Price: Pro Series .... $1,159.00 to $1,519.00

SMITH & WESSON BODYGUARD® 380

Caliber: .380 Auto, 6+1 round capacity. **Barrel:** 2.75". **Weight:** 11.85 oz. **Length:** 5.25". **Grips:** Polymer. **Sights:** Integrated laser plus drift-adjustable front and rear. **Features:** The frame of the Bodyguard is made of reinforced polymer, as is the magazine base plate and follower, magazine catch, and the trigger. The slide, sights, and guide rod are made of stainless steel, with the slide and sights having a Melonite hard coating.
Price: $449.00

SPRINGFIELD ARMORY EMP ENHANCED MICRO

Caliber: 9mm Para., 40 S&W; 9-round magazine. **Barrel:** 3" stainless steel match grade, fully supported ramp, bull. **Weight:** 26 oz. **Length:** 6.5" overall. **Grips:** Thinline cocobolo hardwood. **Sights:** Fixed low profile combat rear, dovetail front, 3-dot tritium. **Features:** Two 9 round stainless steel magazines with slam pads, long aluminum match-grade trigger adjusted to 5 to 6 lbs., forged aluminum alloy frame, black hardcoat anodized; dual spring full-length guide rod, forged satin-finish stainless steel slide. Introduced 2007. From Springfield Armory.
Price: 9mm Para. Compact Bi-Tone $1,345.00
Price: 40 S&W Compact Bi-Tone.......................................$1,345.00

Prices given are believed to be accurate at time of publication however, many factors affect retail pricing so exact prices are not possible.

70TH EDITION, 2016 ◆ **415**

SPRINGFIELD ARMORY XD SERIES
Caliber: 9mm Para., .40 S&W, .45 ACP. **Barrel:** 3, 4, 5 inches. **Weight:** 20.5-31 oz. **Length:** 6.26-8 overall. **Grips:** Textured polymer. **Sights:** Varies by model; Fixed sights are dovetail front and rear steel 3-dot units. **Features:** Three sizes in X-Treme Duty (XD) line: Sub-Compact (3" barrel), Service (4" barrel), Tactical (5" barrel). Three ported models available. Ergonomic polymer frame, hammer-forged barrel, no-tool disassembly, ambidextrous magazine release, visual/tactile loaded chamber indicator, visual/tactile striker status indicator, grip safety, XD gear system included. Introduced 2004. XD 45 introduced 2006. Compact line introduced 2007. Compact is shipped with one extended magazine (13) and one compact magazine (10). XD Mod.2 Sub-Compact has newly contoured slide and redesigned serrations, stippled grip panels, fiber-optic front sight. From Springfield Armory.

SPRINGFIELD ARMORY XDM SERIES
Calibers: 9mm, .40 S&W, .45 ACP. **Barrel:** 3.8 or 4.5". **Sights:** Fiber optic front with interchangeable red and green filaments, adjustable target rear. **Grips:** Integral polymer with three optional backstrap designs. **Features:** Variation of XD design with improved ergonomics, deeper and longer slide serrations, slightly modified grip contours and texturing. Black polymer frame, forged steel slide. Black and two-tone finish options.
Price: .... **$697.00 to $732.00**

SPRINGFIELD ARMORY XD-S
Caliber: 9mm, .45 ACP. Same features as XDM except has single-stack magazine for thinner profile. **Capacity:** 7 rounds (9mm), 5 rounds (.45). An extra extended-length magazine is included (10 rounds, 9mm; 7 rounds, .45). **Barrel:** 3.3 inches. **Weight:** 21.5 oz. **Features:** Black or two-tone finish.
Price: (two-tone) .... **$599.00 to $669.00**

Price: Sub-Compact OD Green 9mm Para./40 S&W,
    fixed sights **$549.00**

SPRINGFIELD ARMORY MIL-SPEC 1911A1
Caliber: 9mm, 9-shot magazines; .45 ACP, 7-shot magazine. **Barrel:** 5". **Weight:** 35.6- 39 oz. **Length:** 8.5-8.625" overall. **Features:** Similar to Government Model military .45.
Price: Mil-Spec Parkerized, 7+1, 35.6 oz. **$785.00**
Price: Mil-Spec Stainless Steel, 7+1, 36 oz. **$889.00**

SPRINGFIELD ARMORY 1911A1 LOADED

Similar to standard 1911A1, slide and barrel are 4". 7.5" OAL. Available in .45 ACP only. Novak Night Sights. Delta hammer and cocobolo grips. Parkerized or stainless. Introduced 1989..
Price: Stainless, 34 oz. **$1,118.00**
Price: Lightweight, 28 oz. **$1,076.00**

STEYR M-A1 SERIES

Caliber: 9mm (15 or 17-round capacity) or .40 S&W (10-12). **Barrel:** 3.5" (MA-1), 4.5" (L-A1), 3" (C-A1). **Weight:** 27 oz. **Sights:** Fixed with white outline triangle. **Grips:** Black synthetic. Ergonomic low-profile for reduced muzzle lift. DAO striker-fired operation.
Price: M-A1...**$560.00**
Price: C-A1 compact model **$560.00**
Price: L-A1 full-size model...**$560.00**

SPRINGFIELD ARMORY TACTICAL RESPONSE

Similar to 1911A1 except .45 ACP only, checkered front strap and main-spring housing, Novak Night Sight combat rear sight and matching dove-tailed front sight, tuned, polished extractor, oversize barrel link; lightweight speed trigger and combat action job, match barrel and bushing, extended ambidextrous thumb safety and fitted beavertail grip safety. Checkered cocobolo wood grips, comes with two Wilson 7-shot magazines. Frame is engraved "Tactical" both sides of frame with "TRP." Introduced 1998. TRP-Pro Model meets FBI specifications for SWAT Hostage Rescue Team. From Springfield Armory.
Price: Black Armory Kote finish, fixed Trijicon night sights ..**$1,867.00**

STOEGER COMPACT COUGAR

Caliber: 9mm, 13+1 round capacity. **Barrel:** 3.6". **Weight:** 32 oz. **Length:** 7". **Grips:** Wood or rubber. **Sights:** Quick read 3-dot. **Features:** Double/single action with a matte black finish. The ambidextrous safety and decocking lever is easily accessible to the thumb of a right-handed or left-handed shooter.
Price: **$469.00**

SPRINGFIELD ARMORY RANGE OFFICER

Caliber: 9mm or .45 ACP. **Barrel:** 5" stainless match grade. Compact model has 4" barrel. **Sights:** Adjustable target rear, post front. **Grips:** Double diamond checkered walnut. **Weight:** 40 oz.
Price: **$977.00**

STI DUTY ONE SERIES

This company manufactures a wide selection of 1911-style semiauto pistols chambered in .45 ACP, 9mm, .357 SIG, 10mm and .38 Super. Barrel lengths are offered from 3.0 to 6.0 inches. Listed here are several of the company's more than 20 current models. Numerous finish, grip and sight options are available. Duty One series features include government size frame with integral tactical rail and 30 lpi checkered front strap; milled tactical rail on the dust cover of the frame; ambidextrous thumb safeties; high rise beavertail grip safety; lowered and flared ejection port; fixed rear sight; front and rear cocking serrations; 5-inch fully supported STI International ramped bull barrel.

Price: $1,384.00

STI EAGLE

1911-style semiauto pistol chambered in .45 ACP, .38 Super, .357 SIG, 9mm, .40 S&W. Features include modular steel frame with polymer grip; high capacity double-stack magazines; scalloped slide with front and rear cocking serrations; dovetail front sight and STI adjustable rear sight; stainless steel STI hi-ride grip safety and stainless steel STI ambi-thumb safety; 5- or 6-inch STI stainless steel fully supported, ramped bull barrel or the traditional bushing barrel; blued or stainless finish.

Price: $2,123.00

STI TOTAL ECLIPSE

Compact 1911-style semiauto pistol chambered in 9x19, .40 S&W, and .45 ACP. Features include 3-inch slide with rear cocking serrations, oversized ejection port; 2-dot tritium night sights recessed into the slide; high-capacity polymer grip; single-sided blued thumb safety; bobbed, high-rise, blued, knuckle relief beavertail grip safety; 3-inch barrel.

Price: $1,870.00

STI ESCORT

Similar to STI Eclipse but with aluminum alloy frame and chambered in .45 ACP only.

Price: $1,233.00

TAURUS CURVE

Caliber: .380 ACP. 6+1 capacity. Unique curved design to fit contours of the body for comfortable concealed carry with no visible "printing" of the firearm. **Barrel:** 2.5 inches. **Weight:** 10.2 oz. **Length:** 5.2 inches. Double-action only. Light and laser are integral with frame.

Price: $392.00

Prices given are believed to be accurate at time of publication however, many factors affect retail pricing so exact prices are not possible.

TAURUS MODEL 1911

Caliber: .45 ACP, 8+1 capacity, 9mm, 9+1 capacity. **Barrel:** 5".
Weight: 33 oz. **Length:** 8.5". **Grips:** Checkered black. **Sights:**
Heinie straight 8. **Features:** SA. Blue, stainless steel, duotone blue,
and blue/gray finish. Standard/picatinny rail, standard frame, alloy
frame, and alloy/picatinny rail. Introduced in 2007. Imported from
Brazil by Taurus International.

Price: 1911B, Blue $719.00
Price: 1911B, Walnut grips $866.00
Price: 1911SS, Stainless Steel $907.00
Price: 1911SS-1, Stainless Steel w/rail $945.00
Price: 1911 DT, Duotone Blue $887.00

TAURUS MODEL PT-22/PT-25

Caliber: .22 LR, 8-shot (PT-22); .25 ACP, 9 shot (PT-25). **Barrel:** 2.75".
Weight: 12.3 oz. **Length:** 5.25" overall. **Grips:** Smooth rosewood
or mother-of-pearl. **Sights:** Fixed. **Features:** Double action. Tip-up
barrel for loading, cleaning. Blue, nickel, duo-tone or blue with gold
accents. Introduced 1992. Made in U.S.A. by Taurus International.

Price: PT-22B or PT-25B, checkered
wood grips...$282.00

TAURUS PT2011 DT

Caliber: 9mm, .40 S&W. **Magazine capacity:** 9mm (13 rounds),
.40 S&W (11 rounds). **Barrel:** 3.2 inches. **Weight:** 24 oz. **Features:**
Single/double-action with trigger safety.

Price: $589.00
Price: (stainless).. $605.00

TAURUS MODEL 22PLY SMALL POLYMER FRAME

Similar to Taurus Models PT-22 and PT-25 but with lightweight
polymer frame. Features include .22 LR (9+1) or .25 ACP (8+1)
chambering. 2.33" tip-up barrel, matte black finish, extended
magazine with finger lip, manual safety. Overall length is 4.8".
Weighs 10.8 oz.

Price: $276.00

TAURUS 24/7 G2 SERIES

Double/single action semiauto pistol chambered in 9mm Parabellum
(15+1), .40 S&W (13+1), and .45 ACP (10+1). Features include
blued or stainless finish; "Strike Two" capability; new trigger
safety; low-profile adjustable rear sights for windage and elevation;
ambidextrous magazine release; 4.2-inch barrel; Picatinny rail;
polymer frame; polymer grip with metallic inserts and three
interchangeable backstraps. Also offered in compact model with
shorter grip frame and 3.5-inch barrel.

Price: .... $523.00 to $543.00

TAURUS MODEL 92

Caliber: 9mm Para., 10- or 17-shot mags. **Barrel:** 5". **Weight:** 34
oz. **Length:** 8.5" overall. **Grips:** Checkered rubber, rosewood,
mother-of-pearl. **Sights:** Fixed notch rear. 3-dot sight system.
Also offered with micrometer-click adjustable night sights.
Features: Double action, ambidextrous 3-way hammer drop
safety, allows cocked & locked carry. Blue, stainless steel, blue
with gold highlights, stainless steel with gold highlights, forged
aluminum frame, integral key-lock. .22 LR conversion kit available.
Imported from Brazil by Taurus International.

Price: 92B $638.00
Price: 92SS $653.00

TAURUS MODEL 111 G2

Caliber: 9mm Para., 10- or 12-shot mags. **Barrel:** 3.25. **Weight:** 18.7
oz. **Length:** 6-1/8 overall. **Grips:** Checkered polymer. **Sights:** 3-dot
fixed; night sights available. Low profile, 3-dot combat. **Features:**
Double action only, polymer frame, matte stainless or blue steel
slide, manual safety, integral key-lock. Deluxe models with wood
grip inserts.

Price: Blued $436.00
Price: Stainless $450.00

TAURUS SLIM 700 SERIES

Compact double/single action semiauto pistol chambered in 9mm
Parabellum (7+1), .40 S&W (6+1), and .380 ACP (7+1). Features
include polymer frame; blue or stainless slide; single action/double
action trigger pull; low-profile fixed sights. Weight 19 oz., length 6.24
inches, width less than an inch.

Price: $404.00
Price: Stainless $504.00

Prices given are believed to be accurate at time of publication however, many factors affect retail pricing so exact prices are not possible.

70TH EDITION, 2016 ✦ **419**

TAURUS MODEL 709 G2 SLIM

Caliber: 9mm., 7+1-shot magazine. **Barrel:** 3". **Weight:** 19 oz.
Length: 6" overall. **Grips:** Black. **Sights:** Low profile. **Features:**
Single-action only operation.
Price: Matte black $404.00
Price: Stainless $504.00

TAURUS SLIM 740

Caliber: .40 cal., 6+1-shot magazine. **Barrel:** 3.2". **Weight:** 19 oz.
Length: 6.24" overall. **Grips:** Polymer Grips. **Features:** Double
action with stainless steel finish.
Price: $504.00

THOMPSON CUSTOM 1911A1

Caliber: .45 ACP, 7-shot magazine. **Barrel:** 4.3". **Weight:** 34 oz.
Length: 8" overall. **Grips:** Checkered laminate grips with a
Thompson bullet logo inlay. **Sights:** Front and rear sights are
black with serrations and are dovetailed into the slide. **Features:**
Machined from 420 stainless steel, matte finish. Thompson
bullet logo on slide. Flared ejection port, angled front and rear
serrations on slide, 20-lpi checkered mainspring housing and
frontstrap. Adjustable trigger, combat hammer, stainless steel
full-length recoil guide rod, extended beavertail grip safety;
extended magazine release; checkered slide-stop lever. Made in
U.S.A. by Kahr Arms.
Price: 1911TC $866.00

THOMPSON TA5 1927A-1 LIGHTWEIGHT DELUXE

Caliber: .45 ACP, 50-round drum magazine. **Barrel:** 10.5", 1:16 right-
hand twist. **Weight:** 94.5 oz. **Length:** 23.3" overall. **Grips:** Walnut,
horizontal foregrip. **Sights:** Blade front, open rear adjustable.
Features: Based on Thompson machine gun design. Introduced
2008. Made in U.S.A. by Kahr Arms.
Price: TA5 (2008)..$1,323.00

TRISTAR 100 /120 SERIES

Caliber: 9mm, .40 S&W (C-100 only). **Magazine capacity:** 15
(9mm), 11 (.40). **Barrel:** 3.7 to 4.7 inches. **Weight:** 26 to 30 oz.
Grips: Checkered polymer. **Sights:** Fixed. **Finish:** Blue or chrome.
Features: Alloy or steel frame. Single/double action. A series of
pistols based on the CZ-75 design. Imported from Turkey.
Price: $459.00

TURNBULL MODEL 1911

Caliber: .45 ACP. An accurate reproduction of 1918-era Model 1911
pistol. **Features:** Forged slide with appropriate shape and style.
Later style sight with semi-circle notch. Early style safety lock
with knurled undercut thumb piece. Short, wide checkered spur
hammer. Hand checkered double-diamond American Black Walnut
grips. Hand polished with period correct Carbonia charcoal bluing.
Custom made to order with many options. Made in the USA by
Doug Turnbull Manufacturing Co.
Price: $2,250.00

WALTHER P99 AS

Caliber: 9mm, .40 S&W. Offered in two frame sizes, standard
and compact. **Magazine capacity:** 15 or 10 rounds (9mm), 10
or 8 rounds (.40). **Barrel:** 3.5 or 4 inches. **Weight:** 21 to 26 oz.
Length: 6.6 to 7.1 inches. **Grips:** Polymer with interchangeable
backstrap inserts. **Sights:** Adjustable rear, blade front with three
interchangeable inserts of different heights. **Features:** Double action

Prices given are believed to be accurate at time of publication however, many factors affect retail pricing so exact prices are not possible.

with trigger safety, decocker, internal striker safety, loaded chamber indicator. Made in Germany.
Price: $629.00

WALTHER PK380
Caliber: .380 ACP (8-shot magazine). **Barrel:** 3.66". **Weight:** 19.4 oz. **Length:** 6.5". **Sights:** Three-dot system, drift adjustable rear. **Features:** Double action with external hammer, ambidextrous mag release and manual safety. Picatinny rail. Black frame with black or nickel slide.
Price: $399.00
Price: Nickel slide $449.00

WALTHER PPK
Caliber: .380 ACP. **Capacity:** 6+1. **Barrel:** 3.3 inches **Weight:** 22 oz. **Length:** 6.1 inches **Grips:** Checkered plastic. **Sights:** Fixed. **Features:** Available in blue or stainless finish. Made in the U.S.A.
Price: $699.00

WALTHER PPK/S
Caliber: .22 LR or .380 ACP. **Capacity:** 10+1 (.22), 7+1 (.380). Made in Germany. **Features:** identical to PPK except for grip length and magazine capacity.
Price: (.380)..$699.00
Price: (.22 blue)...$400.00
Price: (.22 stainless)..$430.00

WALTHER PPQ M2
Caliber: 9mm, (15 round magazine), .40 S&W (11). 22 LR (PPQ M2 .22). 12-shot magazine. **Barrel:** 4 or 5". **Weight:** 24 oz. **Length:** 7.1, 8.1". **Sights:** Drift adjustable. **Features:** Quick Defense trigger, firing pin block, ambidextrous slide lock and mag release, Picatinny rail. Comes with two extra magazines, two interchangeable frame backstraps and hard case. Navy SD model has threaded 4.6" barrel. M2 .22 has aluminum slide, blowback operation, weighs 19 ounces.
Price: $649.00
Price: M2 .22...$429.00

WALTHER CCP
Caliber: 9mm, 8-shot magazine. **Barrel:** 3.5 inches. **Weight:** 22 oz. **Length:** 6.4 inches. **Features:** Thumb operated safety, reversible mag release, loaded chamber indicator. Delayed blowback gas-operated action provides less recoil and muzzle jump, and easier slide operation. Available in all black or black/stainless two-tone finish.
Price: From .... $469.00 to $499.00

WALTHER PPS
Caliber: 9mm Para., 40 S&W. 6-, 7-, 8-shot magazines for 9mm Para.; 5-, 6-, 7-shot magazines for 40 S&W. **Barrel:** 3.2". **Weight:** 19.4 oz. **Length:** 6.3" overall. **Stocks:** Stippled black polymer. **Sights:** Picatinny-style accessory rail, 3-dot low-profile contoured sight. **Features:** PPS-"Polizeipistole Schmal," or Police Pistol Slim. Measures 1.04 inches wide. Ships with 6- and 7-round magazines. Striker-fired action, flat slide stop lever, alternate backstrap sizes. QuickSafe feature decocks striker assembly when backstrap is removed. Loaded chamber indicator. Introduced 2008.
Price: $629.00

WALTHER PPX
Caliber: 9mm, .40 S&W. **Capacity:** 16 rounds (9mm), 14 rounds (.40). **Barrel:** 4 inches. **Weight:** 27.2 oz. **Length:** 7.3 inches. **Grips:**

Textured polymer integral with frame. **Sights:** Fixed. **Finish:** Black or black/stainless two-tone. Threaded barrel is optional. Made in Ulm, Germany.

Price: **$449.00**
Price: (threaded barrel) **$499.00**

WALTHER P22

Caliber: .22 LR. **Barrel:** 3.4, 5". **Weight:** 19.6 oz. (3.4), 20.3 oz. (5). **Length:** 6.26, 7.83". **Sights:** Interchangeable white dot, front, 2-dot adjustable, rear. **Features:** A rimfire version of the Walther P99 pistol, available in nickel slide with black frame, or Desert Camo or Digital Pink Camo frame with black slide.

Price: From **$379.00**
Price: Nickel slide/black frame, or black slide/camo frame **$449.00**

WILSON COMBAT ELITE PROFESSIONAL

Caliber: 9mm Para., .38 Super, .40 S&W; .45 ACP. **Barrel:** Compensated 4.1" hand-fit, heavy flanged cone match grade. **Weight:** 36.2 oz. **Length:** 7.7" overall. **Grips:** Cocobolo. **Sights:** Combat Tactical yellow rear tritium inserts, brighter green tritium front insert. **Features:** High-cut front strap, 30-lpi checkering on front strap and flat mainspring housing, High-Ride Beavertail grip safety. Dehorned, ambidextrous thumb safety, extended ejector, skeletonized ultralight hammer, ultralight trigger, Armor-Tuff finish on frame and slide. Introduced 1997. Made in U.S.A. by Wilson Combat. This manufacturer offers more than 100 different 1911 models ranging in price from about $2,800 to $5,000. XTAC and Classic 6-inch models shown.

Price: From **$3,650.00**

Prices given are believed to be accurate at time of publication however, many factors affect retail pricing so exact prices are not possible.

BAER 1911 ULTIMATE MASTER COMBAT

Caliber: .38 Super, 400 Cor-Bon, .45 ACP (others available), 10-shot magazine. **Barrel:** 5, 6"; Baer NM. **Weight:** 37 oz. **Length:** 8.5" overall. **Grips:** Checkered cocobolo. **Sights:** Baer dovetail front, low-mount Bo-Mar rear with hidden leaf. **Features:** Full-house competition gun. Baer forged NM blued steel frame and double serrated slide; Baer triple port, tapered cone compensator; fitted slide to frame; lowered, flared ejection port; Baer reverse recoil plug; full-length guide rod; recoil buff; beveled magazine well; Baer Commander hammer, sear; Baer extended ambidextrous safety, extended ejector, checkered slide stop, beavertail grip safety with pad, extended magazine release button; Baer speed trigger. Made in U.S.A. by Les Baer Custom, Inc.
Price: .45 ACP Compensated $2,880.00
Price: .38 Super Compensated $3,140.00

BAER 1911 NATIONAL MATCH HARDBALL

Caliber: .45 ACP, 7-shot magazine. **Barrel:** 5". **Weight:** 37 oz. **Length:** 8.5" overall. **Grips:** Checkered walnut. **Sights:** Baer dovetail front with under-cut post, low-mount Bo-Mar rear with hidden leaf. **Features:** Baer NM forged steel frame, double serrated slide and barrel with stainless bushing; slide fitted to frame; Baer match trigger with 4-lb. pull; polished feed ramp, throated barrel; checkered front strap, arched mainspring housing; Baer beveled magazine well; lowered, flared ejection port; tuned extractor; Baer extended ejector, checkered slide stop; recoil buff. Made in U.S.A. by Les Baer Custom, Inc.
Price: $1,960.00

BAER 1911 PPC OPEN CLASS

Designed for NRA Police Pistol Combat matches. **Caliber:** .45 ACP, 9mm. **Barrel:** 6 inches, fitted to frame. **Sights:** Adjustable PPC rear, dovetail front. **Grips:** Checkered cocobola. **Features:** Lowered and flared ejection port, extended ejector, polished feed ramp, throated barrel, front strap checkered at 30 lpi, flat serrated mainspring housing, Commander hammer, front and rear slide serrations. 9mm has supported chamber.
Price: $2,350.00

BAER 1911 BULLSEYE WADCUTTER

Similar to National Match Hardball except designed for wadcutter loads only. Polished feed ramp and barrel throat; Bo-Mar rib on slide; full length recoil rod; Baer speed trigger with 3-1/2-lb. pull; Baer deluxe hammer and sear; Baer beavertail grip safety with pad; flat mainspring housing checkered 20 lpi. Blue finish; checkered walnut grips. Made in U.S.A. by Les Baer Custom, Inc.
Price: From $2,140.00

COLT GOLD CUP SERIES

Caliber: .45 ACP, 8-shot + 1 magazine. **Barrel:** 5-inch National Match. **Weight:** 37 oz. **Length:** 8.5. **Grips:** Checkered wraparound rubber composite with silver-plated medallions or checkered walnut grips with gold medallions. **Sights:** Target post dovetail front, Bomar fully adjustable rear. **Features:** Adjustable aluminum wide target trigger, beavertail grip safety, full length recoil spring and target recoil spring, available in blued finish or stainless steel.
Price: (blued) $1,217.00
Price: (stainless) $1,250.00

COLT SPECIAL COMBAT GOVERNMENT

Caliber: .45 ACP, .38 Super. **Barrel:** 5". **Weight:** 39 oz. **Length:** 8.5". **Grips:** Rosewood w/double diamond checkering pattern. **Sights:** Clark dovetail, front; Bo-Mar adjustable, rear. **Features:** A competition-ready pistol with enhancements such as skeletonized trigger, upswept grip safety, custom tuned action, polished feed ramp. Blue or satin nickel finish. Introduced 2003. Made in U.S.A. by Colt's Mfg. Co.
Price: $2,095.00

COMPETITOR SINGLE-SHOT

Caliber: .22 LR through .50 Action Express, including belted magnums. **Barrel:** 14" standard; 10.5" silhouette; 16" optional. **Weight:** About 59 oz. (14 bbl.). **Length:** 15.12" overall. **Grips:** Ambidextrous; synthetic (standard) or laminated or natural wood. **Sights:** Ramp front, adjustable rear. **Features:** Rotary cannon-type action cocks on opening; cammed ejector; interchangeable barrels, ejectors. Adjustable single stage trigger, sliding thumb safety and trigger safety. Matte blue finish. Introduced 1988. From Competitor Corp., Inc.
Price: 14, standard calibers, synthetic grip $660.00

Prices given are believed to be accurate at time of publication however, many factors affect retail pricing so exact prices are not possible.

70TH EDITION, 2016 ⊕ **423**

CZ 75 TS CZECHMATE

Caliber: 9mm Luger, 20-shot magazine. **Barrel:** 130mm. **Weight:** 1360 g **Length:** 266 mm overall. **Features:** The handgun is custom-built, therefore the quality of workmanship is fully comparable with race pistols built directly to IPSC shooters wishes. Individual parts and components are excellently match fitted, broke-in and tested. Every handgun is outfitted with a four-port compensator, nut for shooting without a compensator, the slide stop with an extended finger piece, the slide stop without a finger piece, ergonomic grip panels from aluminium with a new type pitting and side mounting provision with the C-More red dot sight. For the shooting without a red dot sight there is included a standard target rear sight of Tactical Sports type, package contains also the front sight.
Price: $3,317.00

CZ 75 TACTICAL SPORTS

Caliber: 9mm Luger and .40 S&W, 17-20-shot magazine capacity. **Barrel:** 114mm. **Weight:** 1270 g **Length:** 225 mm overall. **Features:** semi-automatic handgun with a locked breech. This pistol model is designed for competition shooting in accordance with world IPSC (International Practical Shooting Confederation) rules and regulations. The pistol allow rapid and accurate shooting within a very short time frame. The CZ 75 TS pistol model design stems from the standard CZ 75 model. However, this model feature number of special modifications, which are usually required for competitive handguns: - single-action trigger mechanism (SA) - match trigger made of plastic featuring option for trigger travel adjustments before discharge (using upper screw), and for overtravel (using bottom screw). The adjusting screws are set by the manufacturer - sporting hammer specially adapted for a reduced trigger pull weight - an extended magazine catch - grip panels made of walnut wood - guiding funnel made of plastic for quick inserting of the magazine into pistol's frame. Glossy blue slide, silver polycoat frame. Packaging includes 3 pcs of magazines.
Price: $1,310.00

CZ 85 COMBAT

Caliber: 9mm Luger, 16-shot magazine. **Barrel:** 114mm. **Weight:** 1000 g **Length:** 206 mm overall. **Features:** The CZ 85 Combat modification was created as an extension to the CZ 85 model in its standard configuration with some additional special elements. The rear sight is adjustable for elevation and windage, and the trigger for overtravel regulation. An extended magazine catch, elimination of the magazine brake and ambidextrous controlling elements directly predispose this model for sport shooting competitions. Characteristic features of all versions A universal handgun for both left-handers and right-handers,. The selective SA/DA firing mechanism, a large capacity double-column magazine, a comfortable grip and balance in either hand lead to good results at instinctive shooting (without aiming). Low trigger pull weight and high accuracy of fire. A long service life and outstanding reliability - even when using various types of cartridges. The slide stays open after the last cartridge has been fired, suitable for COMBAT shooting. The sights are fitted with a three-dot illuminating system for better aiming in poor visibility conditions. The COMBAT version features an adjustable rear sight by means of micrometer screws.
Price: $664.00

DAN WESSON CHAOS

Caliber: 9mm Luger, 21-shot magazine capacity. **Barrel:** 5". **Weight:** 3.20 lbs. **Length:** 8.75" overall. **Features:** A double-stack 9mm designed for three-gun competition.
Price: $3,829.00

DAN WESSON HAVOC

Caliber: 9mm Luger & .38 Super, 21-shot magazine capacity. **Barrel:** 4.25". **Weight:** 2.20 lbs. **Length:** 8" overall. **Features:** The HAVOC is based on an "All Steel" Hi-capacity version of the 1911 frame. It comes ready to dominate Open IPSC/USPSA division. The C-more mounting system offers the lowest possible mounting configuration possible, enabling extremely fast target acquisition. The barrel and compensator arrangement pairs the highest level of accuracy with the most effective compensator available.
Price: $4,299.00

DAN WESSON MAYHEM

Caliber: .40 S&W, 18-shot magazine capacity. **Barrel:** 6". **Weight:** 2.42 lbs. **Length:** 8.75" overall. **Features:** The MAYHEM is based on an "All Steel" Hi-capacity version of the 1911 frame. It comes ready to dominate Limited IPSC/USPSA division or fulfill the needs of anyone looking for a superbly accurate target grade 1911. Taking weight away from where you don't want it and adding it to where you do want it was the first priority in designing this handgun. The 6" bull barrel and the tactical rail add to the static weight "good weight". We wanted a 6" long slide for the added sight radius and the enhanced pointability, but that would add to the "bad weight" so the 6" slide has been lightened to equal the weight of a 5". The result is a 6" long slide that balances and feels like a 5" but shoots like a 6". The combination of the all steel frame with industry leading parts delivers the most well balanced, softest shooting 6" limited gun on the market.
Price: $3,899.00

DAN WESSON TITAN

Caliber: 10mm, 21-shot magazine capacity. **Barrel:** 4.25". **Weight:** 1.62 lbs. **Length:** 8" overall. **Features:** The TITAN is based on an "All Steel" Hi-capacity version of the 1911 frame. Turning the most well known defensive pistol "1911" into a true combat handgun was

no easy task. The rugged HD night sights are moved forward and recessed deep in the slide yielding target accuracy and extreme durability. The Snake Scale serrations' aggressive 25 lpi checkering, and the custom competition G-10 grips ensure controllability even in the harshest of conditions. The combination of the all steel frame, bull barrel, and tactical rail enhance the balance and durability of the most formidable target grade Combat handgun on the market.
Price: **$3,829.00**

EAA WITNESS ELITE GOLD TEAM
Caliber: 9mm Para., 9x21, .38 Super, .40 S&W, .45 ACP. **Barrel:** 5.1". **Weight:** 44 oz. **Length:** 10.5" overall. **Grips:** Checkered walnut, competition-style. **Sights:** Square post front, fully adjustable rear. **Features:** Triple-chamber cone compensator; competition SA trigger; extended safety and magazine release; competition hammer; beveled magazine well; beavertail grip. Hand-fitted major components. Hard chrome finish. Match-grade barrel. From E.A.A. Custom Shop. Introduced 1992. Limited designed for IPSC Limited Class competition. Features include full-length dust-cover frame, funneled magazine well, interchangeable front sights. Stock (2005) designed for IPSC Production Class competition. Match introduced 2006. Made in Italy, imported by European American Armory.
Price: Gold Team **$2,336.00**
Price: Pro Limited, 4.75" barrel..............................**$1,216.00**
Price: Stock, 4.5" barrel, hard chrome finish.........................**$1,102.00**
Price: Match, 4.75" barrel, two-tone finish..............................**$778.00**

FREEDOM ARMS MODEL 83 .22 FIELD GRADE SILHOUETTE CLASS
Caliber: .22 LR, 5-shot cylinder. **Barrel:** 10". **Weight:** 63 oz. **Length:** 15.5" overall. **Grips:** Black micarta. **Sights:** Removable Patridge front blade; Iron Sight Gun Works silhouette rear, click adjustable for windage and elevation (optional adj. front sight and hood). **Features:** Stainless steel, matte finish, manual sliding-bar safety system; dual firing pins, lightened hammer for fast lock time, pre-set trigger stop. Introduced 1991. Made in U.S.A. by Freedom Arms.
Price: Silhouette Class **$2,376.00**

FREEDOM ARMS MODEL 83 CENTERFIRE SILHOUETTE MODELS
Caliber: 357 Mag., .41 Mag., .44 Mag.; 5-shot cylinder. **Barrel:** 10", 9" (.357 Mag. only). **Weight:** 63 oz. (41 Mag.). **Length:** 15.5", 14.5" (.357 only). **Grips:** Pachmayr Presentation. **Sights:** Iron Sight Gun Works silhouette rear sight, replaceable adjustable front sight blade with hood. **Features:** Stainless steel, matte finish, manual sliding-

bar safety system. Made in U.S.A. by Freedom Arms.
Price: Silhouette Models, from **$2,091.00**

HIGH STANDARD SUPERMATIC TROPHY TARGET
Caliber: .22 LR, 9-shot mag. **Barrel:** 5.5" bull or 7.25" fluted. **Weight:** 44-46 oz. **Length:** 9.5-11.25" overall. **Stock:** Checkered hardwood with thumbrest. **Sights:** Undercut ramp front, frame-mounted micro-click rear adjustable for windage and elevation; drilled and tapped for scope mounting. **Features:** Gold-plated trigger, slide lock, safety-lever and magazine release; stippled front grip and backstrap; adjustable trigger and sear. Barrel weights optional. From High Standard Manufacturing Co., Inc.
Price: 5.5", adjustable sights **$935.00**
Price: 7.25", adjustable sights **$985.00**

HIGH STANDARD VICTOR TARGET
Caliber: .22 LR, 10-shot magazine. **Barrel:** 4.5" or 5.5" polished blue; push-button takedown. **Weight:** 46 oz. **Length:** 9.5" overall. **Stock:** Checkered walnut with thumbrest. **Sights:** Undercut ramp front, micro-click rear adjustable for windage and elevation. Also available with scope mount, rings, no sights. **Features:** Stainless steel frame. Full-length vent rib. Gold-plated trigger, slide lock, safety-lever and magazine release; stippled front grip and backstrap; polished blue slide; adjustable trigger and sear. Comes with barrel weight. From High Standard Manufacturing Co., Inc.
Price: 4.5" or 5.5" barrel, vented sight rib,
universal scope base **$1,050.00**

KIMBER SUPER MATCH II
Caliber: .45 ACP, 8-shot magazine. **Barrel:** 5". **Weight:** 38 oz. **Length:**

Prices given are believed to be accurate at time of publication however, many factors affect retail pricing so exact prices are not possible.

70TH EDITION, 2016 ✛ **425**

8.7" overall. **Grips:** Rosewood double diamond. **Sights:** Blade front, Kimber fully adjustable rear. **Features:** Guaranteed to shoot 1" groups at 25 yards. Stainless steel frame, black KimPro slide; two-piece magazine well; premium aluminum match-grade trigger; 30 lpi front strap checkering; stainless match-grade barrel; ambidextrous safety; special Custom Shop markings. Introduced 1999. Made in U.S.A. by Kimber Mfg., Inc.
Price: $2,313.00

KIMBER RIMFIRE TARGET
Caliber: .22 LR, 10-shot magazine. **Barrel:** 5". **Weight:** 23 oz. **Length:** 8.7" overall. **Grips:** Rosewood, Kimber logo, double diamond checkering, or black synthetic double diamond. **Sights:** Blade front, Kimber fully adjustable rear. **Features:** Bumped beavertail grip safety, extended thumb safety, extended magazine release button. Serrated flat top slide with flutes, machined aluminum slide and frame, matte black or satin silver finishes, 30 lines-per-inch checkering on frontstrap and under trigger guard; aluminum trigger, test target, accuracy guarantee. No slide lock-open after firing the last round in the magazine. Introduced 1999. Made in U.S.A. by Kimber Mfg., Inc.
Price: $871.00

RUGER MARK III TARGET
Caliber: .22 LR, 10-shot magazine. **Barrel:** 5.5" to 6-7/8". **Weight:** 41 to 45 oz. **Length:** 9.75" to 11-1/8" overall. **Grips:** Checkered cocobolo/laminate. **Sights:** .125 blade front, micro-click rear, adjustable for windage and elevation, loaded chamber indicator; integral lock, magazine disconnect. Plastic case with lock included.
Price: (bull barrel, blued) $459.00
Price: (bull barrel, stainless) $569.00
Price: Competition (stainless slabside barrel) $659.00

SMITH & WESSON MODEL 41 TARGET
Caliber: .22 LR, 10-shot clip. **Barrel:** 5.5", 7". **Weight:** 41 oz. (5.5" barrel). **Length:** 10.5" overall (5.5" barrel). **Grips:** Checkered walnut with modified thumbrest, usable with either hand. **Sights:** 1/8" Patridge on ramp base; micro-click rear adjustable for windage and elevation. **Features:** 3/8" wide, grooved trigger; adjustable trigger stop drilled and tapped.
Price: .... $1,369.00 to $1,619.00

SMITH & WESSON MODEL 22A
Caliber: .22 LR, 10-shot magazine. **Barrel:** 4", 5.5" bull. **Weight:** 28-39 oz. **Length:** 9.5" overall. **Grips:** Dymondwood with ambidextrous

thumbrests and flared bottom or rubber soft touch with thumbrest. **Sights:** Patridge front, fully adjustable rear. **Features:** Sight bridge with Weaver-style integral optics mount; alloy frame, stainless barrel and slide; blue/black finish. Introduced 1997. The 22S is similar to the Model 22A except has stainless steel frame. Introduced 1997. Made in U.S.A. by Smith & Wesson.
Price: from $339.00
Price: Realtree APG camo finish....................... $369.00

SPRINGFIELD ARMORY TROPHY MATCH
Similar to Springfield Armory's Full Size model, but designed for bullseye and action shooting competition. Available with a Service Model 5 frame with matching slide and barrel in 5" and 6" lengths. Fully adjustable sights, checkered frame front strap, match barrel and bushing. In .45 ACP only. From Springfield Inc.
Price: $1,605.00

STI APEIRO
1911-style semiauto pistol chambered in 9x19, .40 S&W, and .45 ACP. Features include Schuemann "Island" barrel; patented modular steel frame with polymer grip; high capacity double-stack magazine; stainless steel ambidextrous thumb safeties and knuckle relief high-rise beavertail grip safety; unique sabertooth rear cocking serrations; 5-inch fully ramped, fully supported "island" bull barrel, with the sight milled in to allow faster recovery to point of aim; custom engraving on the polished sides of the (blued) stainless steel slide; stainless steel magwell; STI adjustable rear sight and Dawson fiber optic front sight; blued frame.
Price: $2,934.00

STI EAGLE 5.0, 6.0
Caliber: 9mm Para., 9x21, .38 & .40 Super, .40 S&W, 10mm, .45 ACP, 10-shot magazine. **Barrel:** 5", 6" bull. **Weight:** 34.5 oz. **Length:** 8.62" overall. **Grips:** Checkered polymer. **Sights:** STI front, Novak or Heinie rear. **Features:** Standard frames plus 7 others; adjustable match trigger; skeletonized hammer; extended grip safety with locator pad. Introduced 1994. Made in U.S.A. by STI International.
Price: (5.0 Eagle) $2,123.00
Price: (6.0 Eagle) $2,243.00

STI EXECUTIVE
Caliber: .40 S&W. **Barrel:** 5" bull. **Weight:** 39 oz. **Length:** 8-5/8".

Prices given are believed to be accurate at time of publication however, many factors affect retail pricing so exact prices are not possible.

Grips: Gray polymer. **Sights:** Dawson fiber optic, front; STI adjustable rear. **Features:** Stainless mag. well, front and rear serrations on slide. Made in U.S.A. by STI.
Price: $2,638.00

STI STEELMASTER

Caliber: 9mm minor, comes with one 126mm magazine. **Barrel:** 4.15". **Weight:** 38.9 oz. **Length:** 9.5" overall. **Features:** Based on the renowned STI race pistol design, the SteelMaster is a shorter and lighter pistol that allows for faster target acquisition with reduced muzzle flip and dip. Designed to shoot factory 9mm (minor) ammo, this gun delivers all the advantages of a full size race pistol in a smaller, lighter, faster reacting, and less violent package. The Steelmaster is built on the patented modular steel frame with polymer grip. It has a 4.15" classic slide which has been flat topped. Slide lightening cuts on the front and rear further reduce weight while "Sabertooth" serrations further enhance the aesthtics of this superior pistol. It also uses the innovative Trubor compensated barrel which has been designed to eliminate misalignment of the barrel and compensator bore or movement of the compensator on the barrel. The shorter Trubor barrel system in the SteelMaster gives an even greater reduction in muzzle flip, and the shorter slide decreases overall slide cycle time allowing the shooter to achieve faster follow up shots. The SteelMaster is mounted with a C-More, 6-minute, red-dot scope with blast shield and thumb rest. Additional enhancements include aluminum magwell, stainless steel ambidextrous safeties, stainless steel high rise grip safety, STI's "Spur" hammer, STI's RecoilMaster guide rod system, and checkered front strap and mainspring housing.
Price: $3,048.00

STI TROJAN

Caliber: 9mm Para., .38 Super, .40 S&W, .45 ACP. **Barrel:** 5", 6". **Weight:** 36 oz. **Length:** 8.5". **Grips:** Rosewood. **Sights:** STI front with STI adjustable rear. **Features:** Stippled front strap, flat top slide, one-piece steel guide rod.
Price: (Trojan 5) $1,222.00
Price: (Trojan 6, not available in .38 Super) $1,555.00

STI TRUBOR

Caliber: 9mm 'Major', 9x23, .38 Super - USPSA, IPSC. **Barrel:** 5" with integrated compensator. **Weight:** 41.3 oz. (including scope and mount) **Length:** 10.5" overall. **Features:** Built on the patented modular steel frame with polymer grip, the STI Trubor utilizes the Trubor compensated barrel which is machined from ONE PIECE of 416, Rifle Grade, Stainless Steel. The Trubor is designed to eliminate misalignment of the barrel and compensator bore or movement of the compensator along the barrel threads, giving the shooter a more consistent performance and reduced muzzle flip. True to 1911 tradition, the Trubor has a classic scalloped slide with front and rear cocking serrations on a forged steel slide (blued) with polished sides, aluminum magwell, stainless steel ambidextrous safeties, stainless steel high rise grip safety, full length guide rod, checkered front strap, and checkered mainspring housing. With mountedC-More Railway sight included with the pistol.
Price: $3,350.00

Grip: Crimson Trace™. **Sights:** Fixed. **Features:** Stainless finish & frame. American made by Charter Arms.
Price: $560.00

CHARTER ARMS BULLDOG
Caliber: .44 Special. **Barrel:** 2.5". **Weight:** NA. **Sights:** Blade front, notch rear. **Features:** 5-round cylinder, soft-rubber pancake-style grips, shrouded ejector rod, wide trigger and hammer spur. American made by Charter Arms.
Price: Blued $414.00
Price: Stainless $436.00
Price: Target Bulldog, 4 barrel, 23 oz. $479.00

CHARTER ARMS POLICE BULLDOG
Caliber: .38 Special, 6-shot cylinder. **Barrel:** 4" tapered or bull. **Weight:** 23 oz. **Sights:** Blade front, notch rear. Large frame version of Bulldog design.
Price: Blued $421.00

CHARTER ARMS OFF DUTY
Caliber: .38 Spec. **Barrel:** 2". **Weight:** 12.5 oz. **Sights:** Blade front, notch rear. **Features:** 5-round cylinder, aluminum casting, DAO. American made by Charter Arms.
Price: Aluminum $410.00
Price: Crimson Trace Laser grip $570.00

CHARTER PANTHER BRONZE & BLACK CAMO STANDARD
Caliber: .22 Mag.- 5-round cylinder. **Barrel:** 1-1/8". **Weight:** 6 oz. **Grip:** Compact. **Sights:** Fixed. **Features:** 2-tone bronze & black with aluminum frame. American made by Charter Arms.
Price: $443.00

CHARTER ARMS PINK LADY
Caliber: .32 H&R Magnum, .38 Special +P. **Barrel:** 2". **Weight:** 12 oz. **Grips:** Rubber Pachmayr-style. **Sights:** Fixed. **Features:** Snubnose, five-round cylinder. Pink anodized aluminum alloy frame.
Price: $410.00
Price: Lavender Lady, lavender frame $410.00
Price: Goldfinger, gold anodized frame, matte black barrel and cylinder assembly $410.00

CHARTER ARMS CHIC LADY & CHIC LADY DAO
Caliber: .38 special - 5-round cylinder. **Barrel:** 2". **Weight:** 12 oz. **Grip:** Combat. **Sights:** Fixed. **Features:** 2-tone pink & stainless with aluminum frame. American made by Charter Arms.
Price: Chic Lady $481.00
Price: Chic Lady DAO... $492.00

CHARTER COUGAR UNDERCOVER LITE
Caliber: .38 special +P - 5-round cylinder. **Barrel:** 2". **Weight:** 12 oz. **Grip:** Full. **Sights:** Fixed. **Features:** 2-tone pink & stainless with aluminum frame. Constructed of tough aircraft-grade aluminum and steel, the Undercover Lite offers rugged reliability and comfort. This ultra-lightweight 5-shot .38 Special features a 2" barrel, fixed sights and traditional spurred hammer. American made by Charter Arms.
Price: $443.00

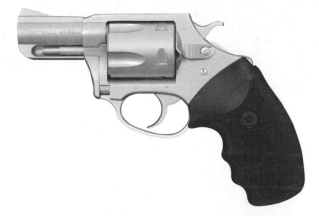

CHARTER ARMS PIT BULL
Caliber: .9mm, 6-round cylinder; .40 S&W, 5-round cylinder. **Barrel:** 21.3". **Weight:** 20 oz. **Sights:** Fixed rear, ramp front. **Grips:** Rubber. **Features:** Matte stainless steel frame. Five-shot cylinder does not require moon clips.
Price: 9mm...$496.00
Price: .40 S&W..$484.00

CHARTER ARMS SOUTHPAW
Caliber: .38 Special +P. **Barrel:** 2". **Weight:** 12 oz. **Grips:** Rubber Pachmayr-style. **Sights:** NA. **Features:** Snubnose, five-round cylinder, matte black aluminum alloy frame with stainless steel cylinder. Cylinder latch and crane assembly are on right side of frame for convenience to left-hand shooters.
Price: $427.00

CHARTER ARMS CRIMSON UNDERCOVER
Caliber: .38 special +P - 5-round cylinder. **Barrel:** 2". **Weight:** 16 oz.

Prices given are believed to be accurate at time of publication however, many factors affect retail pricing so exact prices are not possible.

CHARTER ARMS UNDERCOVER
Caliber: .38 Spec. +P. **Barrel:** 2". **Weight:** 12 oz. **Sights:** Blade front, notch rear. **Features:** 6-round cylinder. American made by Charter Arms.
Price: Blued $352.00

CHARTER ARMS UNDERCOVER SOUTHPAW
Caliber: .38 Spec. +P. **Barrel:** 2". **Weight:** 12 oz. **Sights:** NA. **Features:** Cylinder release is on the right side and the cylinder opens to the right side. Exposed hammer for both single and double-action firing. 5-round cylinder. American made by Charter Arms.
Price: Aluminum...$428.00
Price: Pink SS..$447.00

CHIAPPA RHINO
Caliber: .357 Magnum, 9mm, .40 S&W. **Features:** 2-, 4-, 5- or 6-inch barrel; fixed or adjustable sights; visible hammer or hammerless design. **Weight:** 24 to 33 oz. Walnut or synthetic grips with black frame; hexagonal-shaped cylinder. Unique design fires from bottom chamber of cylinder.
Price: From $990.00
Price: Gold finish...$1,458.00

COBRA SHADOW
Caliber: .38 Spec. +P. **Capacity:** 5 rounds. **Barrel:** 1-7/8". **Weight:** 15 oz. Aluminum frame with stainless steel barrel and cylinder. **Length:** 6 3/8". **Grips:** Rosewood, black rubber or Crimson Trace Laser. **Features:** Black anodized, titanium anodized, or custom colors including gold, red, pink and blue.
Price: $369.00
Price: Rosewood grips $434.00
Price: Crimson Trace Laser grips....................$625.00

COMANCHE II-A
Caliber: .38 Special, 6 shot. **Barrel:** 3 or 4". **Weight:** 33, 35 oz. **Length:** 8, 8.5" overall. **Grips:** Rubber. **Sights:** Fixed. **Features:** Blued finish, alloy frame. Distributed by SGS Importers.
Price: $236.95

DAN WESSON 715
Caliber: .357 Magnum, 6-shot cylinder. **Barrel:** Six-inch heavy barrel with full lug. **Weight:** 38 oz. **Length:** 8, 8.5" overall. **Grips:** Hogue rubber with finger grooves. **Sights:** Adjustable rear, interchangeable front blade. **Features:** Stainless steel. Interchangeable barrel assembly. Reintroduced in 2014.
Price: $1,168.00

EAA WINDICATOR
Caliber: .38 Spec., 6-shot; .357 Mag., 6-shot. **Barrel:** 2", 4". **Weight:** 30 oz. (4"). **Length:** 8.5" overall (4" bbl.). **Grips:** Rubber with finger grooves. **Sights:** Blade front, fixed rear. **Features:** Swing-out cylinder; hammer block safety; blue or nickel finish. Introduced 1991. Imported from Germany by European American Armory.
Price: .38 Spec. 2" barrel, alloy frame $325.00
Price: .38 Spec. 4" barrel, alloy frame $342.00
Price: .357 Mag. 2" barrel, steel frame $343.00
Price: .357 Mag. 4" barrel, steel frame $360.00
Price: .357 Mag. 2" barrel, steel frame, nickel finish $405.00
Price: .357 Mag. 4" barrel, steel frame, nickel finish $422.00

KORTH USA
Caliber: .22 LR, .22 WMR, .32 S&W Long, .38 Spec., .357 Mag., 9mm Para. **Barrel:** 3", 4", 5.25", 6". **Weight:** 36-52 oz. Grips, Combat, Sport: Walnut, Palisander, Amboinia, Ivory. Grips, Target: German Walnut, matte with oil finish, adjustable ergonomic competition style. **Sights:** Adjustable Patridge (Sport) or Baughman (Combat), interchangeable and adjustable rear w/Patridge front (Target) in blue and matte. **Features:** DA/SA, 3 models, over 50 configurations, externally adjustable trigger stop and weight, interchangeable cylinder, removable wide-milled trigger shoe on Target model. Deluxe models are highly engraved editions. Available finishes include high polish blue finish, plasma coated in high polish or matted silver, gold, blue, or charcoal. Many deluxe options available. 6-shot. From Korth USA.
Price: From $8,000.00
Price: Deluxe Editions, from $12,000.00

ROSSI R461/R462
Caliber: .357 Mag. **Barrel:** 2". **Weight:** 26-35 oz. **Grips:** Rubber. **Sights:** Fixed. **Features:** DA/SA, +P rated frame, blue carbon or high polish stainless steel, patented Taurus Security System, 6-shot.
Price: Blue carbon finish..................................$391.00
Price: Stainless finish......................................$455.00

Prices given are believed to be accurate at time of publication however, many factors affect retail pricing so exact prices are not possible.

70TH EDITION, 2016 ✦ **429**

RUGER GP-100
Caliber: .357 Mag., 6-shot cylinder. **Barrel:** 3" full shroud, 4" full shroud, 6" full shroud. **Weight:** 36 to 45 oz. **Sights:** Fixed; adjustable on 4" and 6" full shroud barrels. **Grips:** Ruger Santoprene Cushioned Grip with Goncalo Alves inserts. **Features:** Uses action, frame features of both the Security-Six and Redhawk revolvers. Full length, short ejector shroud. Satin blue and stainless steel.
Price: Blued $729.00
Price: Satin stainless $779.00

ROSSI MODEL R971/R972
Caliber: 357 Mag. +P, 6-shot. **Barrel:** 4", 6". **Weight:** 32 oz. **Length:** 8.5 or 10.5" overall. **Grips:** Rubber. **Sights:** Blade front, adjustable rear. **Features:** Single/double action. Patented key-lock Taurus Security System; forged steel frame. Introduced 2001. Made in Brazil by Amadeo Rossi. Imported by BrazTech/Taurus.
Price: Model R971 (blued finish,
    4" bbl.) $455.00
Price: Model R972 (stainless steel finish, 6" bbl.) $511.00

ROSSI MODEL 851
Similar to Model R971/R972, chambered for .38 Spec. +P. Blued finish, 4-inch barrel. Introduced 2001. Made in Brazil by Amadeo Rossi. From BrazTech/Taurus.
Price: $389.00

RUGER GP-100 MATCH CHAMPION
Caliber: .357 Mag., 6-shot cylinder. **Barrel:** 4.2" half shroud, slab sided. **Weight:** 38 oz. **Sights:** Fixed rear, fiber optic front. **Grips:** Hogue Stippled Hardwood. **Features:** Satin stainless steel finish.
Price: Blued $929.00

RUGER LCR
Caliber: .22 LR (8-shot cylinder), .22 WMR, .38 Special and .357 Mag., 5-shot cylinder. **Barrel:** 1-7/8". **Weight:** 13.5 oz. –17.10 oz.

Prices given are believed to be accurate at time of publication however, many factors affect retail pricing so exact prices are not possible.

Length: 6-1/2" overall. **Grips:** Hogue® Tamer™ or Crimson Trace® Lasergrips®. **Sights:** Pinned ramp front, U-notch integral rear. **Features:** The Ruger Lightweight Compact Revolver (LCR), a 13.5 ounce, small frame revolver with a smooth, easy-to-control trigger and highly manageable recoil. Packed with the latest technological advances and features required by today's most demanding shooters.

Price: .22 LR, .22 WMR, .38 Spl., iron sights $545.00
Price: Above with Crimson Trace Laser grip $825.00
Price: 9mm, .357, iron sights $619.00
Price: 9mm, .357, Crimson Trace Laser grip $899.00

RUGER LCRX

.38 Special+P, Barrel: 1 7/8 or 3 inches. Features similar to LCR except this model has visible hammer, adjustable rear sight. Three-inch barrel model has longer grip.
Price: $545.00

RUGER SP-101

Caliber: .22 LR (6 shot); .327 Federal Mag. (6-shot), .38 Spl, .357 Mag. (5-shot). **Barrel:** 2.25, 3-1/16, 4.2 inches (.327 Mag.). **Weight:**

25-30 oz. **Sights:** Adjustable or fixed, rear; fiber-optic or black ramp front. **Grips:** Ruger Cushioned Grip with inserts. **Features:** Compact, small frame, double-action revolver. Full-length ejector shroud. Stainless steel only.
Price: Fixed sights $679.00
Price: Adjustable rear, fiber optic front sights $719.00

RUGER REDHAWK

Caliber: .44 Rem. Mag., .45 Colt, 6-shot. **Barrel:** 2.75, 4.2, 5.5, 7.5 inches. (.45 Colt in 4.2" only.) **Weight:** 54 oz. (7.5 bbl.). **Length:** 13 overall (7.5 barrel). **Grips:** Square butt cushioned grip panels. TALO Distributor exclusive 2.75" barrel stainless model has round butt, wood grips. **Sights:** Interchangeable Patridge-type front, rear adjustable for windage and elevation. **Features:** Stainless steel, brushed satin finish, blued ordnance steel. 9.5 sight radius. Introduced 1979.
Price: $1,029.00
Price: Hunter Model 7.5" bbl. $1,089.00
Price: TALO 2.75" model $1,019.00

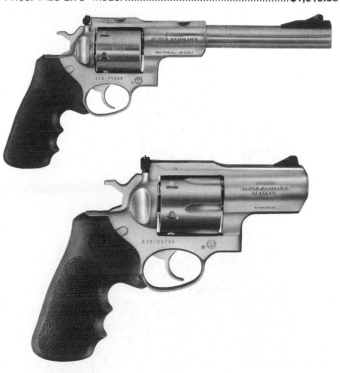

RUGER SUPER REDHAWK

Caliber: .44 Rem. Mag., .454 Casull, .480 Ruger, 5 or 6-shot. **Barrel:** 2.5" (Alaskan), 5.5" 7.5" or 9.5". **Weight:** 44 to 58 oz. **Length:** 13" overall (7.5" barrel). **Grips:** Hogue Tamer Monogrip. **Features:** Similar to standard Redhawk except has heavy extended frame with Ruger Integral Scope Mounting System on wide topstrap. Wide hammer spur lowered for better scope clearance. Incorporates mechanical design features and improvements of GP-100. Ramp front sight base has Redhawk-style Interchangeable Insert sight blades, adjustable rear sight. Alaskan model has 2.5-inch barrel. Satin stainless steel and low-glare stainless finishes. Introduced 1987.
Price: .44 Magnum $1,079.00
Price: .454 Casull, .480 Ruger $1,199.00

SMITH & WESSON GOVERNOR™

Caliber: .410 Shotshell (2 1/2"), .45 ACP, .45 Colt; 6 rounds. **Barrel:** 2.75". **Length:** 7.5", (2.5" barrel). **Grip:** Synthetic. **Sights:** Front: Dovetailed tritium night sight or black ramp, rear: fixed. **Grips:** Synthetic. **Finish:** Matte Black or matte silver (Silver Edition). **Weight:** 29.6 oz. **Features:** Capable of chambering a mixture of .45 Colt, .45 ACP and .410 gauge 2½-inch shotshells, the Governor is suited for both close and distant encounters, allowing users to customize the load to their preference. Scandium Alloy frame, stainless steel cylinder. Packaged with two full-moon clips and three 2-shot clips.
Price: Silver Edition... $809.00
Price: Matte black with Tritium night sights $869.00
Price: Matte black w/Crimson Trace® Laser Grip $1,119.00

SMITH & WESSON J-FRAME

The smallest S&W wheelguns come in a variety of chamberings, barrel lengths, and materials, as noted in the individual model listings.

SMITH & WESSON 60LS/642LS LADYSMITH

Caliber: .38 Spec. +P, .357 Mag., 5-shot. **Barrel:** 1-7/8" (642LS); 2-1/8" (60LS) **Weight:** 14.5 oz. (642LS); 21.5 oz. (60LS); **Length:** 6.6" overall (60LS). **Grips:** Wood. **Sights:** Black blade, serrated ramp front, fixed notch rear. 642 CT has Crimson Trace Laser Grips. **Features:** 60LS model has a Chiefs Special-style frame. 642LS has Centennial-style frame, frosted matte finish, smooth combat wood grips. Introduced 1996. Comes in a fitted carry/storage case. Introduced 1989. Made in U.S.A. by Smith & Wesson.
Price: (642LS) $499.00
Price: (60LS) $759.00
Price: (642 CT) $699.00

SMITH & WESSON MODEL 63

Caliber: .22 LR, 8-shot. **Barrel:** 3". **Weight:** 26 oz. **Length:** 7.25" overall. **Grips:** Black synthetic. **Sights:** Hi-Viz fiber optic front sight, adjustable black blade rear sight. **Features:** Stainless steel construction throughout. Made in U.S.A. by Smith & Wesson.
Price: $769.00

SMITH & WESSON MODEL 442/637/638/642 AIRWEIGHT

Caliber: .38 Spec. +P, 5-shot. **Barrel:** 1-7/8", 2-1/2". **Weight:** 15 oz. **Length:** 6-3/8" overall. **Grips:** Soft rubber. **Sights:** Fixed, serrated ramp front, square notch rear. **Features:** A family of J-frame .38 Special revolvers with aluminum-alloy frames. Model 637; Chiefs Special-style frame with exposed hammer. Introduced 1996. Models 442, 642; Centennial-style frame, enclosed hammer. Model 638, Bodyguard style, shrouded hammer. Comes in a fitted carry/storage case. Introduced 1989. Made in U.S.A. by Smith & Wesson.
Price: From $469.00

SMITH & WESSON MODELS 637 CT/638 CT/642 CT

Similar to Models 637, 638 and 642 but with Crimson Trace Laser Grips.
Price: $699.00

Prices given are believed to be accurate at time of publication however, many factors affect retail pricing so exact prices are not possible.

SMITH & WESSON MODEL 317 AIRLITE
Caliber: .22 LR, 8-shot. **Barrel:** 1-7/8". **Weight:** 10.5 oz. **Length:** 6.25" overall (1-7/8" barrel). **Grips:** Rubber. **Sights:** Serrated ramp front, fixed notch rear. **Features:** Aluminum alloy, carbon and stainless steels, Chiefs Special-style frame with exposed hammer. Smooth combat trigger. Clear Cote finish. Model 317 Kit Gun has adjustable rear sight, fiber optic front. Introduced 1997.
Price: $699.00
Price: Kit Gun $759.00

SMITH & WESSON MODEL 340/340PD AIRLITE SC CENTENNIAL
Caliber: .357 Mag., 38 Spec. +P, 5-shot. **Barrel:** 1-7/8". **Weight:** 12 oz. **Length:** 6-3/8" overall (1-7/8" barrel). **Grips:** Rounded butt rubber. **Sights:** Black blade front, rear notch **Features:** Centennial-style frame, enclosed hammer. Internal lock. Matte silver finish. Scandium alloy frame, titanium cylinder, stainless steel barrel liner. Made in U.S.A. by Smith & Wesson.
Price: Model 340 ....$1,019.00

SMITH & WESSON MODEL 351PD
Caliber: .22 Mag., 7-shot. **Barrel:** 1-7/8". **Weight:** 10.6 oz. **Length:** 6.25" overall (1-7/8" barrel). **Sights:** HiViz front sight, rear notch. **Grips:** Wood. **Features:** Seven-shot, aluminum-alloy frame. Chiefs Special-style frame with exposed hammer. Nonreflective matte-black finish. Internal lock. Made in U.S.A. by Smith & Wesson.
Price: $759.00

SMITH & WESSON MODEL 360/360PD AIRLITE CHIEF'S SPECIAL
Caliber: .357 Mag., .38 Spec. +P, 5-shot. **Barrel:** 1-7/8". **Weight:** 12 oz. **Length:** 6-3/8" overall (1-7/8" barrel). **Grips:** Rounded butt rubber. **Sights:** Black blade front, fixed rear notch. **Features:** Chief's Special-style frame with exposed hammer. Internal lock. Scandium

alloy frame, titanium cylinder, stainless steel barrel. Made in U.S.A. by Smith & Wesson.
Price: 360PD $1,019.00

SMITH & WESSON BODYGUARD® 38
Caliber: .38 S&W Special +P; 5 rounds. **Barrel:** 1.9". **Weight:** 14.3 oz. **Length:** 6.6". **Grip:** Synthetic. **Sights:** Front: Black ramp, Rear: fixed, integral with backstrap. Plus: Integrated laser sight. **Grips:** Synthetic. **Finish:** Matte Black. **Features:** The first personal protection series that comes with an integrated laser sight.
Price: $509.00

SMITH & WESSON MODEL 640 CENTENNIAL DA ONLY
Caliber: .357 Mag., .38 Spec. +P, 5-shot. **Barrel:** 2-1/8". **Weight:** 23 oz. **Length:** 6.75" overall. **Grips:** Uncle Mike's Boot grip. **Sights:** Serrated ramp front, fixed notch rear. **Features:** Stainless steel. Fully concealed hammer, snag-proof smooth edges. Internal lock.
Price: $729.00

SMITH & WESSON MODEL 649 BODYGUARD
Caliber: .357 Mag., .38 Spec. +P, 5-shot. **Barrel:** 2-1/8". **Weight:** 23 oz. **Length:** 6-5/8" overall. **Grips:** Uncle Mike's Combat. **Sights:** Black pinned ramp front, fixed notch rear. **Features:** Stainless steel construction, satin finish. Internal lock. Bodyguard style, shrouded hammer. Made in U.S.A. by Smith & Wesson.
Price: $729.00

SMITH & WESSON K-FRAME/L-FRAME
The K-frame series are mid-size revolvers and the L-frames are slightly larger.

SMITH & WESSON MODEL 10 CLASSIC
Caliber: .38 Special, 6-round cylinder. Features include a bright blue steel frame and cylinder, checkered wood grips, 4-inch barrel, and

Prices given are believed to be accurate at time of publication however, many factors affect retail pricing so exact prices are not possible.

70TH EDITION, 2016 ✦ **433**

fixed sights. The oldest model in the Smith & Wesson line, its basic design goes back to the original Military & Police Model of 1905.
Price: $739.00

SMITH & WESSON MODEL 17 MASTERPIECE CLASSIC
Caliber: .22 LR. **Capacity:** 6 rounds. **Barrel:** 6 inches. **Weight:** 40 oz. **Grips:** Checkered wood. **Sights:** Pinned Patridge front, Micro Adjustable rear. Updated variation of K-22 Masterpiece of the 1930s.
Price: $989.00

SMITH & WESSON MODEL 48 CLASSIC
Same specifications as Model 17 excet chambered in .22 Magnum (.22 WMR) and is available with a 4 or 6-inch barrel.
Price: .... $949.00 to $989.00

SMITH & WESSON MODEL 64/67
Caliber: .38 Spec. +P, 6-shot. **Barrel:** 3". **Weight:** 33 oz. **Length:** 8-7/8" overall. **Grips:** Soft rubber. **Sights:** Fixed, 1/8 serrated ramp front, square notch rear. Model 67 issimilar to Model 64 except for adjustable sights. **Features:** Satin finished stainless steel, square butt.
Price: From .... $689.00 to $749.00

SMITH & WESSON MODEL 66
Caliber: .357 Magnum. **Capacity:** 6 rounds. **Barrel:** 4.25". **Weight:** 36.6 oz. **Grips:** Synthetic. **Sights:** White outline adjustable rear, red ramp front. **Features:** Return in 2014 of the famous K-frame "Combat Magnum" with stainless finish.
Price: $849.00

SMITH & WESSON MODEL 69
Caliber: ..44 Magnum. **Capacity:** 5 rounds. **Barrel:** 4.25". **Weight:** 37 oz. **Grips:** Checkered wood. **Sights:** White outline adjustable rear, red ramp front. **Features:** L-frame with stainless finish, 5-shot cylinder, introduced in 2014.
Price: $989.00

SMITH & WESSON MODEL 617
Caliber: .22 LR, 10-shot cylinder **Barrel:** 6". **Weight:** 44 oz. **Length:** 11-1/8". **Grips:** Soft rubber. **Sights:** Patridge front, adjustable rear. Drilled and tapped for scope mount. **Features:** Stainless steel with satin finish. Introduced 1990.
Price: From $829.00

SMITH & WESSON MODEL 620
Caliber: .38 Spec. +P; 357 Mag., 7 rounds. **Barrel:** 4. **Weight:** 37.5 oz. **Grips:** Rubber. **Sights:** Integral front blade, fixed rear notch on the 619; adjustable white-outline target style rear, red ramp front on 620. **Features:** Replaces Models 65 and 66.

Two-piece semi-lug barrel. Satin stainless frame and cylinder. Made in U.S.A. by Smith & Wesson.
Price: From $893.00

SMITH & WESSON MODEL 386 XL HUNTER
Single/double action L-frame revolver chambered in .357 Magnum. Features include 6-inch full-lug barrel, 7-round cylinder, Hi-Viz fiber optic front sight, adjustable rear sight, scandium frame, stainless steel cylinder, black matte finish, synthetic grips.
Price: $1,019.00

SMITH & WESSON MODEL 686/686 PLUS
Caliber: .357 Mag., .38 S&W Special; 6 rounds. **Barrel:** 2.5", 4", 6". **Weight:** 35 oz. (2.5" barrel). **Length:** 7.5", (2.5" barrel). **Grips:** Rubber. **Sights:** White outline adjustable rear, red ramp front. **Features:** Satin stainless frame and cylinder. Plus series guns have 7-shot cylinders. Introduced 1996. Powerport (PP) has Patridge front, adjustable rear sight. Introduced early 1980s. Stock Service Revolver (SSR) intr. 2007. **Capacity:** 6. **Barrel:** 4". **Sights:** Interchangeable front, adjustable rear. **Grips:** Wood. **Finish:** Satin stainless frame and cylinder. **Weight:** 38.3 oz. **Features:** Chamfered charge holes, custom barrel w/recessed crown, bossed mainspring. High-hold ergonomic grip. Made in U.S.A. by Smith & Wesson.
Price: 686 ....$829.00
Price: Plus, 7 rounds $849.00
Price: SSR $999.00

SMITH & WESSON MODEL 686 PLUS PRO SERIES
Single/double-action L-frame revolver chambered in .357 Magnum. Features include 5-inch barrel with tapered underlug, 7-round cylinder, satin stainless steel frame and cylinder, synthetic grips, interchangeable and adjustable sights.
Price: $1,059.00

Prices given are believed to be accurate at time of publication however, many factors affect retail pricing so exact prices are not possible.

SMITH & WESSON MODEL 986 PRO

Single/double-action L-frame revolver chambered in 9mm. Features similar to 686 PLUS Pro Series including 7-round cylinder, 5-inch tapered underlug barrel, satin stainless finish, synthetic grips, adjustable rear and Patridge blade front sight.
Price: $1,149.00

SMITH & WESSON M&P R8

Caliber: .357 Mag., 8-round cylinder. **Barrel:** 5", half lug with accessory rail. **Weight:** 36.3 oz. **Length:** 10.5" **Grips:** Black synthetic. **Sights:** Adjustable v-notch rear, interchangeable front. **Features:** Scandium alloy frame, stainless steel cylinder.
Price: $1,329.00

SMITH & WESSON N-FRAME

These large-frame models introduced the .357, .41 and .44 Magnums to the world.

SMITH & WESSON MODEL 25 CLASSIC

Caliber: .45 Colt. **Capacity:** Six rounds. **Barrel:** 6.5 inches. **Weight:** 45 oz. **Grips:** Checkered wood. **Sights:** Pinned Patridge front, Micro Adjustable rear.
Price: $1,019.00

SMITH & WESSON MODEL 27 CLASSIC

Caliber: .357 Magnum. **Capacity:** Six rounds. **Barrel:** 4 or 6.5 inches. **Weight:** 41.2 oz. **Grips:** Checkered wood. **Sights:** Pinned Patridge front, Micro Adjustable rear. Updated variation of the first magnum revolver, the .357 Magnum of 1935.
Price: (4") $1,019.00
Price: (6.5") $1,059.00

SMITH & WESSON MODEL 57 CLASSIC

Caliber: .41 Magnum. Six rounds. **Barrel:** 6 inches. **Weight:** 48 oz. **Grips:** Checkered wood. **Sights:** Pinned red ramp, Micro Adjustable rear.
Price: $1,009.00

SMITH & WESSON MODEL 29 CLASSIC

Caliber: .44 Mag, 6-round. **Barrel:** 4 or 6.5". **Weight:** 48.5 oz. **Length:** 12". **Grips:** Altamont service walnut. **Sights:** Adjustable white-outline rear, red ramp front. **Features:** Carbon steel frame, polished-blued or nickel finish. Has integral key lock safety feature to prevent accidental discharges. Original Model 29 made famous by "Dirty Harry" character created in 1971 by Clint Eastwood.
Price: .... $999.00 to $1,169.00

SMITH & WESSON MODEL 329PD ALASKA BACKPACKER

Caliber: .44 Mag., 6-round. **Barrel:** 2.5". **Weight:** 26 oz. **Length:** 9.5". **Grips:** Synthetic. **Sights:** Adj. rear, HiViz orange-dot front. **Features:** Scandium alloy frame, blue/black finish, stainless steel cylinder.
Price: From $1,159.00

SMITH & WESSON MODEL 625/625JM

Caliber: .45 ACP, 6-shot. **Barrel:** 4", 5". **Weight:** 43 oz. (4" barrel). **Length:** 9-3/8" overall (4" barrel). **Grips:** Soft rubber; wood optional. **Sights:** Patridge front on ramp, S&W micrometer click rear adjustable for windage and elevation. **Features:** Stainless steel construction with .400 semi-target hammer, .312 smooth combat trigger; full lug barrel. Glass beaded finish. Introduced 1989. Jerry Miculek Professional (JM) Series has .265-wide grooved trigger, special wooden Miculek Grip, five full moon clips, gold bead Patridge front sight on interchangeable front sight base, bead blast finish. Unique serial number run. Mountain Gun has 4" tapered barrel, drilled and tapped, Hogue Rubber Monogrip, pinned black ramp front sight, micrometer click-adjustable rear sight, satin stainless frame and barrel, weighs 39.5 oz.
Price: 625JM $1,074.00

SMITH & WESSON MODEL 629

Caliber: .44 Magnum, .44 S&W Special, 6-shot. **Barrel:** 4", 5", 6.5". **Weight:** 41.5 oz. (4" bbl.). **Length:** 9-5/8" overall (4" bbl.). **Grips:** Soft rubber; wood optional. **Sights:** 1/8 red ramp front, white outline rear, internal lock, adjustable for windage and elevation. Classic similar to standard Model 629, except Classic has full-lug 5" barrel, chamfered front of cylinder, interchangeable red ramp front sight with adjustable white outline rear, Hogue grips with S&W monogram, drilled and tapped for scope mounting. Factory accurizing and endurance packages. Introduced 1990. Classic Power Port has Patridge front sight and adjustable rear sight. Model 629CT has 5" barrel, Crimson Trace Hoghunter Lasergrips, 10.5 OAL, 45.5 oz. weight. Introduced 2006.
Price: From $949.00

Prices given are believed to be accurate at time of publication however, many factors affect retail pricing so exact prices are not possible.

70TH EDITION, 2016 ✦ **435**

SMITH & WESSON MODEL 329 XL HUNTER

Similar to Model 386 XL Hunter but built on large N-frame and chambered in .44 Magnum. Other features include 6-round cylinder and 6.5"-barrel.

Price: $1,138.00

SMITH & WESSON X-FRAME

These extra-large X-frame S&W revolvers push the limits of bigbore handgunning.

SMITH & WESSON MODEL 500

Caliber: 500 S&W Mag., 5 rounds. **Barrel:** 4", 6-1/2", 8-3/8". **Weight:** 72.5 oz. **Length:** 15" (8-3/8" barrel). **Grips:** Hogue Sorbothane Rubber. **Sights:** Interchangeable blade, front, adjustable rear. **Features:** Recoil compensator, ball detent cylinder latch, internal lock. 6.5"-barrel model has orange-ramp dovetail Millett front sight, adjustable black rear sight, Hogue Dual Density Monogrip, .312 chrome trigger with over-travel stop, chrome tear-drop hammer, glassbead finish. 10.5"-barrel model has red ramp front sight, adjustable rear sight, .312 chrome trigger with overtravel stop, chrome tear drop hammer with pinned sear, hunting sling. Compensated Hunter has .400 orange ramp dovetail front sight, adjustable black blade rear sight, Hogue Dual Density Monogrip, glassbead finish w/black clear coat. Made in U.S.A. by Smith & Wesson.

Price: From $1,249.00

SMITH & WESSON MODEL 460V

Caliber: 460 S&W Mag., 5-shot. Also chambers .454 Casull, .45 Colt. **Barrel:** 7-1/2", 8-3/8" gain-twist rifling. **Weight:** 62.5 oz. **Length:** 11.25". **Grips:** Rubber. **Sights:** Adj. rear, red ramp front. **Features:** Satin stainless steel frame and cylinder, interchangeable compensator. 460XVR (X-treme Velocity Revolver) has black blade

front sight with interchangeable green Hi-Viz tubes, adjustable rear sight. 7.5"-barrel version has Lothar-Walther barrel, 360-degree recoil compensator, tuned Performance Center action, pinned sear, integral Weaver base, non-glare surfaces, scope mount accessory kit for mounting full-size scopes, flashed-chromed hammer and trigger, Performance Center gun rug and shoulder sling. Interchangeable Hi-Viz green dot front sight, adjustable black rear sight, Hogue Dual Density Monogrip, matte-black frame and shroud finish with glass-bead cylinder finish, 72 oz. Compensated Hunter has tear drop chrome hammer, .312 chrome trigger, Hogue Dual Density Monogrip, satin/matte stainless finish, HiViz interchangeable front sight, adjustable black rear sight. XVR introduced 2006.

Price: 460V $1,519.00
Price: 460XVR, from $1,519.00

SUPER SIX CLASSIC BISON BULL

Caliber: .45-70 Government, 6-shot. **Barrel:** 10" octagonal with 1:14 twist. **Weight:** 6 lbs. **Length:** 17.5"overall. **Grips:** NA. **Sights:** Ramp front sight with dovetailed blade, click-adjustable rear. **Features:** Manganese bronze frame. Integral scope mount, manual crossbolt safety.

Price: $1,500.00

TAURUS MODEL 17 TRACKER

Caliber: .17 HMR, 7-shot. **Barrel:** 6.5". **Weight:** 45.8 oz. **Grips:** Rubber. **Sights:** Adjustable. **Features:** Double action, matte stainless, integral key-lock.

Price: From $539.00

TAURUS MODEL 992 TRACKER

Caliber: .22 LR with interchangeable .22 WMR cylinder. 9-shot capacity. **Barrel:** 4 or 6.5 inches with ventilated rib, adjustable rear sight, blue or stainless finish.

Price: Blue $591.00
Price: Stainless $627.00

TAURUS MODEL 44SS

Caliber: .44 Mag., 5-shot. **Barrel:** 4" ported. **Weight:** 34 oz. **Grips:** Rubber. **Sights:** Adjustable. **Features:** Double-action. Integral key-lock. Introduced 1994. Finish: Matte stainless. Imported from Brazil by Taurus International Manufacturing, Inc.

Price: From $648.00

TAURUS MODEL 65

Caliber: .357 Mag., 6-shot. **Barrel:** 4" full underlug. **Weight:** 38 oz. **Length:** 10.5" overall. **Grips:** Soft rubber. **Sights:** Fixed. **Features:** Double action, integral key-lock. Matte blue or stainless. Imported by Taurus International.

Price: Blue $488.00
Price: Stainless $536.00

TAURUS MODEL 66

Similar to Model 65, 4" or 6" barrel, 7-shot cylinder, adjustable rear sight. Integral key-lock action. Imported by Taurus International.

Price: Blue $543.00
Price: Stainless $591.00

TAURUS MODEL 82 SECURITY

Caliber: .38 Spec., 6-shot. **Barrel:** 4", heavy. **Weight:** 36.5 oz. **Length:** 9-1/4" overall. **Grips:** Soft black rubber. **Sights:** Serrated ramp front, square notch rear. **Features:** Double action, solid rib,

Prices given are believed to be accurate at time of publication however, many factors affect retail pricing so exact prices are not possible.

integral key-lock. Imported by Taurus International.
Price: From $481.00

TAURUS MODEL 85 FS

Caliber: .38 Spec., 5-shot. **Barrel:** 2". **Weight:** 16.5-21 oz. **Grips:** Rubber. **Sights:** Ramp front, square notch rear. **Features:** Blue, stainless, two-tone. Alloy, aluminum or polymer frame. Rated for +P ammo. Integral keylock. Imported by Taurus International.
Price: From $299.00

TAURUS MODEL 85 "NO VIEW"

Caliber: .38 Special, 5-shot cylinder. Similar to the Model 85 View that was in production only in 2014. Instead of thermoplastic clear sideplate, this model has blue aluminum sideplate. **Barrel:** 1.41". **Weight:** 9.1 oz. **Grips:** Rubber. **Sights:** Fixed.
Price: $599.00

TAURUS 380 MINI

Caliber: .380 ACP (5-shot cylinder w/moon clip). **Barrel:** 1.75". **Weight:** 15.5 oz. **Length:** 5.95". **Grips:** Rubber. **Sights:** Adjustable rear, fixed front. **Features:** Double-action-only. Available in blued or stainless finish. Five Star (moon) clips included.
Price: Blued $443.00
Price: Stainless $447.00

TAURUS RAGING JUDGE MAGNUM

Single/double-action revolver chambered for .454 Casull, .45 Colt, 2.5-inch and 3-inch .410. Features include 3- or 6-inch barrel; fixed sights with fiber-optic front; blued or stainless steel finish; vent rib for scope mounting (6-inch only); cushioned Raging Bull grips.
Price: $1,038.00

TAURUS MODEL 627 TRACKER

Caliber: .357 Mag., 7-shot. **Barrel:** 4 or 6.5". **Weight:** 28.8, 41 oz. **Grips:** Rubber. **Sights:** Fixed front, adjustable rear. **Features:** Double-action. Stainless steel, Shadow Gray or Total Titanium; vent rib (steel models only); integral key-lock action. Imported by Taurus International.
Price: From $670.00

TAURUS MODEL 45-410 JUDGE

Caliber: 2-1/2"-.410/.45 LC, 3"-.410/.45 LC. **Barrel:** 3", 6.5" (blued finish). **Weight:** 35.2 oz., 22.4 oz. **Length:** 7.5". **Grips:** Ribber rubber. **Sights:** Fiber Optic. **Features:** DA/SA. Matte Stainless and Ultra-Lite Stainless finish. Introduced in 2007. Imported from Brazil by Taurus International.
Price: From $653.00

TAURUS JUDGE PUBLIC DEFENDER POLYMER

Single/double action revolver chambered in .45 Colt/.410 (2-1/2"). Features include 5-round cylinder; polymer frame; Rubber rubber-feel grips; fiber-optic front sight; adjustable rear sight; blued or stainless cylinder; shrouded hammer with cocking spur; blued finish; 2.5-inch barrel. Weight 27 oz.
Price: .... $515.00 to $653.00

TAURUS MODEL 444 ULTRA-LIGHT

Caliber: .44 Mag, 5-shot. **Barrel:** 2.5 or 4". **Weight:** 28.3 oz. **Grips:** Cushioned inset rubber. **Sights:** Fixed red-fiber optic front, adjustable rear. **Features:** UltraLite titanium blue finish, titanium/alloy frame built on Raging Bull design. Smooth trigger shoe, 1.760 wide, 6.280 tall. Barrel rate of twist 1:16, 6 grooves. Introduced 2005. Imported by Taurus International.
Price: $792.00

Prices given are believed to be accurate at time of publication however, many factors affect retail pricing so exact prices are not possible.

70TH EDITION, 2016 ⊕ **437**

TAURUS MODEL 444/454 RAGING BULL SERIES
Caliber: .44 Mag., .454 Casull. **Barrel:** 2.25, 5, 6.5, 8-3/8". **Weight:** 53-63 oz. **Length:** 12" overall (6.5" barrel). **Grips:** Soft black rubber. **Sights:** Patridge front, adjustable rear. **Features:** Double-action, ventilated rib, integral key-lock. Most models have ported barrels. Introduced 1997. Imported by Taurus International.
Price: 444 ....$753.00
Price: 454..$1,055.00

TAURUS MODEL 605 PLY
Caliber: .357 Mag., 5-shot. **Barrel:** 2". **Weight:** 20 oz. **Grips:** Rubber. **Sights:** Fixed. **Features:** Polymer frame steel cylinder. Blued or stainless. Introduced 1995. Imported by Taurus International.
Price: Blue $460.00
Price: Stainless $507.00

TAURUS MODEL 608
Caliber: .357 Mag., 38 Spec., 8-shot. **Barrel:** 4, 6.5, 8-3/8". **Weight:** 44-57 oz. **Length:** 9-3/8" overall. **Grips:** Soft black rubber. **Sights:** Adjustable. **Features:** Double-action, integral key-lock action. Available in blue or stainless. Introduced 1995. Imported by Taurus International.
Price: From $608.00

TAURUS MODEL 617
Caliber: .357 Mag., 7-shot. **Barrel:** 2". **Weight:** 28.3 oz. **Length:** 6.75" overall. **Grips:** Soft black rubber. **Sights:** Fixed. **Finish:** Stainless steel. **Features:** Double-action, polished or matte stainless steel, integral key-lock. Available with porting, concealed hammer. Introduced 1998. Imported by Taurus International.
Price: $560.00

TAURUS MODEL 650 CIA
Caliber: .357 Mag., or .38 Special +P only. 5-shot. **Barrel:** 2". **Weight:** 24.5 oz. **Grips:** Rubber. **Sights:** Ramp front, square notch rear. **Features:** Double-action only, blue finish, integral key-lock, internal hammer. Introduced 2001. From Taurus International.
Price: : From $513.00

TAURUS MODEL 941
Caliber: .22 WMR, 8-shot. **Barrel:** 2", 4", 5". **Weight:** 27.5 oz. (4" barrel). **Grips:** Soft black rubber. **Sights:** Serrated ramp front, rear adjustable. **Features:** Double-action, integral key-lock. Blued or stainless finish. Introduced 1992. Imported by Taurus International.
Price: From $465.00

TAURUS MODEL 970 TRACKER
Caliber: .22 LR, 7-shot. **Barrel:** 6". **Weight:** 53.6 oz. **Grips:** Rubber. **Sights:** Adjustable. **Features:** Double barrel, heavy barrel with ventilated rib; matte stainless finish, integral key-lock. Introduced 2001. From Taurus International.
Price: $472.00

TAURUS MODEL 905
Caliber: 9mm, 5-shot. **Barrel:** 2". Small-frame revolver with rubber boot grips, fixed sights, choice of exposed or concealed hammer Blue or stainless finish.
Price: Blue $481.00
Price: Stainless $528.00

Prices given are believed to be accurate at time of publication however, many factors affect retail pricing so exact prices are not possible.

CIMARRON 1872 OPEN TOP
Caliber: .38, .44 Special, .44 Colt, .44 Russian, .45 LC, .45 S&W Schofield. **Barrel:** 5.5" and 7.5". **Grips:** Walnut. **Sights:** Blade front, fixed rear. **Features:** Replica of first cartridge-firing revolver. Blue finish; Navy-style brass or steel Army-style frame. Introduced 2001 by Cirnarron F.A. Co.
Price: Navy model...$508.00
Price: Army $550.00

CIMARRON 1875 OUTLAW
Caliber: .357, .38 Special, .44 W.C.F., .45 Colt, .45 ACP. **Barrel:** 5-1/2" and 7-1/2". **Weight:** 2.5-2.6 lbs. **Grip:** 1-piece walnut. **Features:** Standard blue finish with color case hardened frame. Replica of 1875 Remington model. Available with dual .45 Colt/.45 ACP cylinder.
Price: $578.00
Price: Dual Cyl. $686.00

CIMARRON MODEL 1890
Caliber: .357, .38 special, .44 W.C.F., .45 Colt, .45 ACP. **Barrel:** 5-1/2". **Weight:** 2.4-2.5 lbs. **Grip:** 1-piece walnut. **Features:** Standard blue finish with standard blue frame. Replica of 1890 Remington model. Available with dual .45 Colt/.45 ACP cylinder.
Price: $606.00
Price: Dual Cyl. $702.00

CIMARRON BISLEY MODEL SINGLE-ACTION
Caliber: .357 Mag., .44 WCF, .44 Spl., .45. Similar to Colt Bisley, special grip frame and triggerguard, knurled wide-spur hammer, curved trigger. Introduced 1999. Imported by Cimarron F.A. Co.
Price: From $615.00

CIMARRON LIGHTNING SA
Caliber: .22 LR, .32-20/32 H&R dual cyl. combo, .38 Special, .41 Colt. **Barrel:** 3.5", 4.75", 5.5". **Grips:** Smooth or checkered walnut. **Sights:** Blade front. **Features:** Replica of the Colt 1877 Lightning DA. Similar to Cimarron Thunderer, except smaller grip frame to fit smaller hands. Standard blue, charcoal blue or nickel finish with forged, old model, or color case-hardened frame. Dual cylinder model available with .32-30/.32 H&R chambering. Introduced 2001. From Cimarron F.A. Co.
Price: From .... $503.00 to $565.00
Price: .32-20/.32 H&R dual cylinder $649.00

CIMARRON MAN WITH NO NAME
Caliber: .45 LC. **Barrel:** 4-3/4" and 5-1/2". **Weight:** 2.66-2.76 lbs. **Grip:** 1-piece walnut with silver rattle snake inlay in both sides.

Features: Standard blue finish with case hardened pre-war frame. An accurate copy of the gun used by our nameless hero in the classic Western movies "Fist Full Of Dollars" & "For A Few Dollars More".
Price: Conversion Model $818.00
Price: SAA Model...$774.00

CIMARRON MODEL P SAA
Caliber: .32 WCF, .38 WCF, .357 Mag., .44 WCF, .44 Spec., .45 Colt, and .45 ACP. **Barrel:** 4.75, 5.5, 7.5". **Weight:** 39 oz. **Length:** 10" overall (4.75" barrel). **Grips:** Walnut. **Sights:** Blade front. **Features:** Old model black-powder frame with Bullseye ejector, or New Model frame. Imported by Cimarron F.A. Co.
Price: From $550.00

CIMARRON MODEL "P" JR.
Caliber: .32-20, .32 H&R. **Barrel:** 3.5, 4.75, 5.5". **Grips:** Checkered walnut. **Sights:** Blade front. **Features:** Styled after 1873 Colt Peacemaker, except 20 percent smaller. Blue finish with color case-hardened frame; Cowboy action. Introduced 2001. From Cimarron F.A. Co.
Price: $550.00

CIMARRON ROOSTER SHOOTER
Caliber: .357, .45 Colt and .44 W.C.F. **Barrel:** 4-3/4". **Weight:** 2.5 lbs. **Grip:** 1-piece orange finger grooved. **Features:** A replica of John Wayne's Colt Single Action Army model used in many of his great Westerns including his Oscar winning performance in "True Grit", where he brings the colorful character Rooster Cogburn to life.
Price: $909.00

CIMARRON THUNDERER
Caliber: .357 Mag., .44 WCF, .45 Colt, 6-shot. Combo comes with leather shoulder holster, ivory handled dagger. Gun and knife have matching serial numbers. Made by Uberti.
Price: .... $723.00 to $948.00
Price: Combo..$1,754,00

CIMARRON THUNDERSTORM
Caliber: .45 Colt. **Barrel:** 3.5 or 4.75 inches. **Grips:** Model P or Thunderer, checkered wood. **Finish:** Blue or stainless. Action job including U.S. made competition springs. Designed for Cowboy Action Shooting. Available with Short Stroke action.
Price: Blue $753.00

Price: Stainless $948.00
Price: Short Stroke Action $779.00

CIMARRON FRONTIER

Caliber: .357 Mag., .44 WCF, .45 Colt. **Barrel:** 3.5, 4.75, 5.5 or 7.5 inches. Basic SAA design. Choice of Old Model or Pre-War frame. Blue or stainless finish. Available with Short Stroke action.
Price: Blue $530.00
Price: Stainless $723.00
Price: Short Stroke Action $598.00

CIMARRON U.S.V. ARTILLERY MODEL SINGLE-ACTION

Caliber: .45 Colt. **Barrel:** 5.5". **Weight:** 39 oz. **Length:** 11.5" overall. **Grips:** Walnut. **Sights:** Fixed. **Features:** U.S. markings and cartouche, case-hardened frame and hammer. Imported by Cimarron F.A. Co.
Price: Blue finish $594.00
Price: Original finish $701.00

COLT NEW FRONTIER

Caliber: .44 Special and .45 Colt. **Barrel:** 4-3/4", 5-1/2",and 7-1/2". **Grip:** Walnut. **Features:** The legend of Colt continues in the New Frontier®, Single Action Army. From 1890 to 1898, Colt manufactured a variation of the venerable Single Action Army with a uniquely different profile. The "Flattop Target Model" was fitted with an adjustable leaf rear sight and blade front sights. Colt has taken this concept several steps further to bring shooters a reintroduction of a Colt classic. The New Frontier has that sleek flattop design with an adjustable rear sight for windage and elevation and a target ready ramp style front sight. The guns are meticulously finished in Colt Royal Blue on both the barrel and cylinder, with a case-colored frame.
Price: $1,528.00

COLT SINGLE-ACTION ARMY

Caliber: .357 Mag., .45 Colt, 6-shot. **Barrel:** 4.75", 5.5", 7.5".

Weight: 40 oz. (4.75" barrel). **Length:** 10.25" overall (4.75" barrel). **Grips:** Black Eagle composite. **Sights:** Blade front, notch rear. **Features:** Available in full nickel finish with nickel grip medallions, or Royal Blue with color case-hardened frame. Reintroduced 1992. Sheriff's Model and Frontier Six introduced 2008, available in nickel in 2010.
Price: Blue $1,416.00
Price: Stainless $1,629.00

EAA BOUNTY HUNTER SA

Caliber: .22 LR/.22 WMR, .357 Mag., .44 Mag., .45 Colt, 6-shot. 10-shot cylinder available for .22LR/.22WMR. **Barrel:** 4.5", 7.5". **Weight:** 2.5 lbs. **Length:** 11" overall (4-5/8" barrel). **Grips:** Smooth walnut. **Sights:** Blade front, grooved topstrap rear. **Features:** Transfer bar safety; 3-position hammer; hammer-forged barrel. Introduced 1992. Imported by European American Armory
Price: Centerfire, blue or case-hardened $478.00
Price: Centerfire, nickel $515.00
Price: .22 LR/.22 WMR, blue $343.00
Price: .22LR/.22WMR, nickel $380.00
Price: .22 LR/.22WMR, 10-round cylinder $465.00

EMF GREAT WESTERN II PONY EXPRESS SINGLE-ACTION

Same as the regular model except uses grip of the Colt Lightning revolver. Barrel lengths of 4.75". Introduced 2006. Imported by E.M.F. Co.
Price: Stainless, Ultra Ivory grips $820.00
Price: Walnut grips $779.00

EMF 1875 OUTLAW

Caliber: .357 Mag., .44-40, .45 Colt. **Barrel:** 7.5", 9.5". **Weight:** 46 oz. **Length:** 13.5" overall. **Grips:** Smooth walnut. **Sights:** Blade front, fixed groove rear. **Features:** Authentic copy of 1875 Remington with firing pin in hammer; color case-hardened frame, blue cylinder, barrel, steel backstrap and triggerguard. Also available in nickel, factory engraved. Imported by E.M.F. Co.
Price: All calibers $520.00
Price: Laser Engraved $800.00

EMF 1873 GREAT WESTERN II

Caliber: .357, .45 Colt, .44/40. **Barrel:** 3.5, 4.75, 5.5, 7.5". **Weight:** 36 oz. **Length:** 11" (5.5" barrel). **Grips:** Walnut. **Sights:** Blade front, notch rear. **Features:** Authentic reproduction of the original 2nd Generation Colt single-action revolver. Standard and bone case hardening. Coil hammer spring. Hammer-forged barrel.
Price: 1873 Californian .... $545.00 to $560.00
Price: 1873 Custom series, bone or nickel, ivory-like grips ... $689.90

Prices given are believed to be accurate at time of publication however, many factors affect retail pricing so exact prices are not possible.

Price: 1873 Stainless steel, ivory-like grips $589.90
Price: 1873 Paladin $560.00
Price: Deluxe Californian with checkered walnut grips $660.00
Price: Buntline with stag grips $810.00

EMF 1873 DAKOTA II
Caliber: .357, 45 Colt. **Barrel:** 4¾ inches. **Grips:** Walnut. **Finish:** black.
Price: $400.00

FREEDOM ARMS MODEL 97 PREMIER GRADE
Caliber: .17 HMR, .22 LR, .32 H&R, .327 Federal, .357 Mag., 6-shot; .41 Mag., .44 Special, .45 Colt, 5-shot. **Barrel:** 4.25", 5.5", 7.5", 10" (.17 HMR, .22 LR, .32 H&R). **Weight:** 40 oz. (5.5" .357 Mag.). **Length:** 10.75" (5.5" bbl.). **Grips:** Impregnated hardwood; Micarta optional. **Sights:** Adjustable rear, replaceable blade front. Fixed rear notch and front blade. **Features:** Stainless steel construction, brushed finish, automatic transfer bar safety system. Introduced in 1997. Lifetime warranty. Made in U.S.A. by Freedom Arms.
Price: From $2,055.00

FREEDOM ARMS MODEL 83 PREMIER GRADE
Caliber: .357 Mag., 41 Mag., .44 Mag., .454 Casull, .475 Linebaugh, .500 Wyo. Exp., 5-shot. **Barrel:** 4.75", 6", 7.5", 9" (.357 Mag. only), 10" (except .357 Mag. and 500 Wyo. Exp.) **Weight:** 53 oz. (7.5" bbl. in .454 Casull). **Length:** 13" (7.5" bbl.). **Grips:** Impregnated hardwood. **Sights:** Adjustable rear with replaceable front sight. Fixed rear notch and front blade. **Features:** Stainless steel construction with brushed finish; manual sliding safety bar. Micarta grips optional. 500 Wyo. Exp. Introduced 2006. Lifetime warranty. Made in U.S.A. by Freedom Arms, Inc.
Price: From $2,436.00

HERITAGE ROUGH RIDER
Caliber: .17 HMR, .22 LR, 22 LR/22 WMR combo, .32 H&R, .357 Mag, .45 Colt, 6-shot. **Barrel:** 2.75, 3.5, 4.75, 5.5, 6.5, 7.5, 9. **Weight:** 31 to 38 oz. **Grips:** Exotic cocobolo laminated wood or mother-of-pearl; bird's-head models offered. **Sights:** Blade front, fixed rear. Adjustable sight on 4, 6 and 9 models. **Features:** Hammer block safety. Transfer bar with Big Bores. High polish blue, black satin, silver satin, case-hardened and stainless finish. Introduced 1993. Made in U.S.A. by Heritage Mfg., Inc.
Price: Rimfire calibers, from $301.00
Price: Centerfire calibers, from $467.00

FREEDOM ARMS MODEL 83 FIELD GRADE
Caliber: .22 LR, .357 Mag., 41 Mag., .44 Mag., .454 Casull, .475 Linebaugh, .500 Wyo. Exp., 5-shot. **Barrel:** 4.75", 6", 7.5", 9" (.357 Mag. only), 10" (except .357 Mag. and .500 Wyo. Exp.) **Weight:** 56 oz. (7.5" bbl. in .454 Casull). **Length:** 13.1" (7.5" bbl.). **Grips:** Pachmayr standard, impregnated hardwood or Micarta optional. **Sights:** Adjustable rear with replaceable front sight. Model 83 frame. All stainless steel. Introduced 1988. Made in U.S.A. by Freedom Arms Inc.
Price: From $2,074.00
Price: Varmint Grade .22 LR $1,525.00

LEGACY SPORTS PUMA M-1873
Caliber: .22 LR / .22 Mag. **Barrel:** 4.75", 5.5" and 7.5". **Weight:** 2.2 lbs. - 2.4 lbs. **Grips:** Wood or plastic. **Features:** With the frame size and weight of a Single Action Army revolver, the M-1873 makes a great practice gun for Cowboy Action or an ideal carry gun for camping, hiking or fishing. The M-1873 loads from a side gate and at the half cock position just like a centerfire "Peacemaker", but is chambered for .22 LR or .22 magnum rounds. The hammer is made

Prices given are believed to be accurate at time of publication however, many factors affect retail pricing so exact prices are not possible.

70TH EDITION, 2016 ✛ **441**

to traditional SAA appearance and feel. A key-operated, hammer block safety is standard on the left side of the recoil shield. The M-1873 is offered in matte black or antiqued finish. Construction is of alloy and steel.

Price: .... $189.00 to $340.00

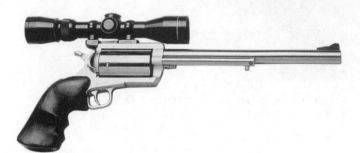

MAGNUM RESEARCH BFR SINGLE ACTION

Caliber: .44 Magnum, .444 Marlin, .45/70, .45 Colt/.410, .450 Marlin, .454 Casull, .460 S&W Magnum, .480 Ruger/.475 Linebaugh, .500 S&W, .30/30 Winchester. **Barrel:** 6.5", 7.5" and 10". **Weight:** 3.6 lbs. - 5.3 lbs. **Grips:** Black rubber. **Sights:** Rear sights are the same configuration as the Ruger revolvers. Many aftermarket rear sights will fit the BFR. Front sights are machined by Magnum in four heights and anodized flat black. The four heights accommodate all shooting styles, barrel lengths and calibers. All sights are interchangeable with each BFR's. **Features:** Crafted in the U.S.A., the BFR single action 5-shot stainless steel revolver frames are CNC machined inside and out from a "pre-heat treated" investment casting. This is done to prevent warping and dimensional changes or shifting that occurs during the heat treat process. Magnum Research designed the frame with large calibers and large recoil in mind, built to close tolerances to handle the pressure of true big-bore calibers. The BFR is equipped with a transfer bar safety feature that allows the gun to be carried safely with all five chambers loaded.

Price: $1,050.00

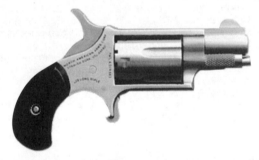

NORTH AMERICAN ARMS MINI

Caliber: .22 Short, 22 LR, 22 WMR, 5-shot. **Barrel:** 1-1/8", 1-5/8". **Weight:** 4 to 6.6 oz. **Length:** 3-5/8" to 6-1/8" overall. **Grips:** Laminated wood. **Sights:** Blade front, notch fixed rear. **Features:** All stainless steel construction. Polished satin and matte finish. Engraved models available. From North American Arms.

Price: .22 Short, .22 LR $209.00
Price: .22 WMR $219.00

NORTH AMERICAN ARMS MINI-MASTER

Caliber: .22 LR, .22 WMR, 5-shot cylinder. **Barrel:** 4" **Weight:** 10.7

oz. **Length:** 7.75" overall. **Grips:** Checkered hard black rubber. **Sights:** Blade front, white outline rear adjustable for elevation, or fixed. **Features:** Heavy vented barrel; full-size grips. Non-fluted cylinder. Introduced 1989.

Price: .... $284.00 to $349.00

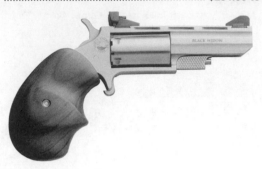

NORTH AMERICAN ARMS BLACK WIDOW

Similar to Mini-Master, 2" heavy vent barrel. Built on .22 WMR frame. Non-fluted cylinder, black rubber grips. Available with Millett Low Profile fixed sights or Millett sight adjustable for elevation only. Overall length 5-7/8", weighs 8.8 oz. From North American Arms.

Price: Adjustable sight, .22 LR or .22 WMR $309.00
Price: Fixed sight, .22 LR or .22 WMR $274.00

NORTH AMERICAN ARMS "THE EARL" SINGLE-ACTION

Caliber: .22 Magnum with .22 LR accessory cylinder, 5-shot cylinder. **Barrel:** 4" octagonal. **Weight:** 6.8 oz. **Length:** 7-3/4" overall. **Grips:** Wood. **Sights:** Barleycorn front and fixed notch rear. **Features:** Single-action mini-revolver patterned after 1858-style Remington percussion revolver. Includes a spur trigger and a faux loading lever that serves as cylinder pin release.

Price: ....$289.00 (.22 Magnum only); $324.00 (convertible)

RUGER NEW MODEL SINGLE-SIX SERIES

Caliber: .22 LR, .17 HMR. **Capacity:** Six rounds. Convertible and Hunter models come with extra cylinder for .22 WMR. **Barrel:** 4.62, 5.5, 6.5 or 9.5 inches. **Weight:** 35 to 42 ounces. **Finish:** Blue or stainless. **Grips:** Black checkered hard rubber, black laminate or hardwood (stainless model only). Single-Six .17 Model available only with 6.5-inch barrel, blue finish, rubber grips. Hunter Model available only with 7.5-inch barrel, black laminate grips and stainless finish.

Price: (blue).. $589.00
Price: (stainless)... $659.00
Price: (Hunter) $829.00

RUGER SINGLE-TEN AND RUGER SINGLE-NINE SERIES

Caliber: .22 LR, .22 WMR. **Capacity:** 10 (.22 LR Single-Ten), 9 (.22 Mag Single-Nine). **Barrel:** 5.5 inches (Single-Ten), 6.5 inches (Single-Nine). **Weight:** 38 to 39 ounces. **Grips:** Hardwood Gunfighter. **Sights:** Williams Adjustable Fiber Optic.

Price: $659.00

RUGER NEW MODEL BLACKHAWK

Caliber: .30 Carbine, .357 Mag./.38 Spec., .41 Mag., .44 Special, .45 Colt, 6-shot. **Barrel:** 4-5/8", 5.5", 6.5", 7.5" (.30 carbine and .45 Colt). **Weight:** 36 to 45 oz. **Lengths:** 10-3/8" to 13.5" **Grips:** Rosewood or black checkered. **Sights:** 1/8 ramp front, micro-click rear adjustable for windage and elevation. **Features:** Rosewood grips, Ruger transfer bar safety system, independent firing pin, hardened chrome-moly steel frame, music wire springs through-out. Case and lock included. Convertibles come with extra cylinder.

Price: (blue) .... $609.00 to $625.00
Price: (Convertible, .357/9mm) $699.00
Price: (Convertible, .45 Colt/.45 ACP) $699.00
Price: (stainless, .357 only) $749.00

RUGER BISLEY SINGLE-ACTION

Similar to standard Blackhawk, hammer is lower with smoothly curved, deeply checkered wide spur. The trigger is strongly curved with wide smooth surface. Longer grip frame. Adjustable rear sight, ramp-style front. Unfluted cylinder and roll engraving, adjustable sights. Chambered for .44 Mag. and .45 Colt; 7.5" barrel; overall length 13.5"; weighs 48-51 oz. Plastic lockable case. Orig. fluted cylinder introduced 1985; discontinued 1991. Unfluted cylinder introduced 1986.
Price: RB-44W (.44 Mag.), RB45W (.45 Colt) $825.00

RUGER NEW MODEL SUPER BLACKHAWK

Caliber: .44 Mag., 6-shot. **Barrel:** 4-5/8", 5.5", 7.5", 10.5" bull.
Weight: 45-55 oz. **Length:** 10.5" to 16.5" overall. **Grips:** Rosewood.
Sights: 1/8 ramp front, micro-click rear adjustable for windage and elevation. **Features:** Ruger transfer bar safety system, fluted or unfluted cylinder, steel grip and cylinder frame, round or square back trigger guard, wide serrated trigger, wide spur hammer. With case and lock.
Price: $769.00

RUGER NEW MODEL SUPER BLACKHAWK HUNTER

Caliber: .44 Mag., 6-shot. **Barrel:** 7.5", full-length solid rib, unfluted cylinder. **Weight:** 52 oz. **Length:** 13-5/8" **Grips:** Black laminated

wood. **Sights:** Adjustable rear, replaceable front blade. **Features:** Reintroduced Ultimate SA revolver. Includes instruction manual, high-impact case, set 1 medium scope rings, gun lock, ejector rod as standard. Bisley-style frame available.
Price: (Hunter, Bisley Hunter) $889.00

RUGER NEW VAQUERO SINGLE-ACTION

Caliber: .357 Mag., .45 Colt, 6-shot. **Barrel:** 4-5/8", 5.5", 7.5".
Weight: 39-45 oz. **Length:** 10.5" overall (4-5/8" barrel). **Grips:** Rubber with Ruger medallion. **Sights:** Fixed blade front, fixed notch rear. **Features:** Transfer bar safety system and loading gate interlock. Blued model color case-hardened finish on frame, rest polished and blued. Engraved model available. Gloss stainless. Introduced 2005.
Price: $769.00

RUGER NEW MODEL BISLEY VAQUERO

Similar to New Vaquero but with Bisley-style hammer and grip frame. Chambered in .357 and .45 Colt. Features include a 5.5" barrel, simulated ivory grips, fixed sights, six-shot cylinder. Overall length is 11.12", weighs 45 oz.
Price: $835.00

RUGER NEW BEARCAT SINGLE-ACTION

Caliber: .22 LR, 6-shot. **Barrel:** 4" **Weight:** 24 oz. **Length:** 9" overall. **Grips:** Smooth rosewood with Ruger medallion. **Sights:** Blade front, fixed notch rear. Distributor special edition available with adjustable sights. **Features:** Reintroduction of the Ruger Bearcat with slightly lengthened frame, Ruger transfer bar safety system. Available in blue only. Rosewood grips. Introduced 1996 (blued), 2003 (stainless). With case and lock.
Price: SBC-4, blued $589.00
Price: KSBC-4, satin stainless $639.00

UBERTI 1851-1860 CONVERSION

Caliber: .38 Spec., .45 Colt, 6-shot engraved cylinder. **Barrel:** 4.75, 5.5, 7.5, 8" **Weight:** 2.6 lbs. (5.5" bbl.). **Length:** 13" overall (5.5" bbl.). **Grips:** Walnut. **Features:** Brass backstrap, triggerguard; color case-hardened frame, blued barrel, cylinder. Introduced 2007. Imported from Italy by Stoeger Industries.
Price: 1851 Navy $569.00
Price: 1860 Army $589.00

UBERTI 1871-1872 OPEN TOP

Caliber: .38 Spec., .45 Colt, 6-shot engraved cylinder. **Barrel:** 4.75, 5.5, 7.5". **Weight:** 2.6 lbs. (5.5" bbl.). **Length:** 13" overall (5.5" bbl.). **Grips:** Walnut. **Features:** Blued backstrap, triggerguard; color case-hardened frame, blued barrel, cylinder. Introduced 2007. Imported from Italy by Stoeger Industries.

Price: .... **$539.00 to $569.00**

UBERTI 1873 CATTLEMAN SINGLE-ACTION

Caliber: .45 Colt; 6-shot fluted cylinder. **Barrel:** 4.75, 5.5, 7.5". **Weight:** 2.3 lbs. (5.5" bbl.). **Length:** 11" overall (5.5" bbl.). **Grips:** Styles: Frisco (pearl styled); Desperado (buffalo horn styled); Chisholm (checkered walnut); Gunfighter (black checkered), Cody (ivory styled), one-piece walnut. **Sights:** Blade front, groove rear. **Features:** Steel or brass backstrap, triggerguard; color case-hardened frame, blued barrel, cylinder. NM designates New Model plunger style frame; OM designates Old Model screw cylinder pin retainer. Imported from Italy by Stoeger Industries.

Price: 1873 Cattleman Frisco $809.00
Price: 1873 Cattleman Desperado (2006) $819.00
Price: 1873 Cattleman Chisholm (2006) $549.00
Price: 1873 Cattleman NM, blued 4.75" barrel $619.00
Price: 1873 Cattleman NM, Nickel finish, 7.5" barrel $819.00
Price: 1873 Cattleman Cody...................................$819.00

UBERTI 1873 CATTLEMAN BIRD'S HEAD SINGLE ACTION

Caliber: .357 Mag., .45 Colt; 6-shot fluted cylinder. **Barrel:** 3.5, 4,

---

4.75, 5.5". **Weight:** 2.3 lbs. (5.5" bbl.). **Length:** 10.9" overall (5.5" bbl.). **Grips:** One-piece walnut. **Sights:** Blade front, groove rear. **Features:** Steel or brass backstrap, triggerguard; color case-hardened frame, blued barrel, cylinder. Imported from Italy by Stoeger Industries.

Price: **$569.00**

UBERTI CATTLEMAN .22

Caliber: .22 LR. **Capacity:** 6 or 12 rounds. **Barrel:** 5.5 inches **Grips:** One-piece walnut. **Sights:** Fixed. **Features:** Blued and case hardened finish, steel or brass backstrap/triggerguard.

Price: (brass backstrap, triggerguard) **$509.00**
Price: (steel backstrap, triggerguard).......................**$529.00**
Price: (12-shot model, steel backstrap, triggerguard) **$559.00**

UBERTI 1873 BISLEY SINGLE-ACTION

Caliber: .357 Mag., .45 Colt (Bisley); .22 LR and .38 Spec. (Stallion), both with 6-shot fluted cylinder. **Barrel:** 4.75, 5.5, 7.5". **Weight:** 2 to 2.5 lbs. **Length:** 12.7" overall (7.5" barrel). **Grips:** Two-piece walnut. **Sights:** Blade front, notch rear. **Features:** Replica of Colt's Bisley Model. Polished blue finish, color case-hardened frame. Introduced 1997. Imported by Stoeger Industries.

Price: 1873 Bisley, 7.5" barrel **$599.00**

UBERTI 1873 BUNTLINE AND REVOLVER CARBINE SINGLE-ACTION

Caliber: .357 Mag., .44-40, .45 Colt; 6-shot fluted cylinder **Barrel:** 18" **Length:** 22.9 to 34" **Grips:** Walnut pistol grip or rifle stock. **Sights:** Fixed or adjustable. **Features:** Imported from Italy by Stoeger Industries.

Price: 1873 Revolver Carbine, 18" barrel, 34" OAL **$729.00**
Price: 1873 Catttleman Buntline Target, 18" barrel, 22.9" OAL **$639.00**

UBERTI OUTLAW, FRONTIER, AND POLICE

Caliber: .45 Colt, 6-shot fluted cylinder. **Barrel:** 5.5", 7.5". **Weight:** 2.5 to 2.8 lbs. **Length:** 10.8" to 13.6" overall. **Grips:** Two-piece smooth walnut. **Sights:** Blade front, notch rear. **Features:** Cartridge version of 1858 Remington percussion revolver. Nickel and blued finishes. Imported by Stoeger Industries.

Price: 1875 Outlaw, nickel finish **$629.00**
Price: 1875 Frontier, blued finish **$539.00**
Price: 1890 Police, blued finish **$549.00**

UBERTI 1870 SCHOFIELD-STYLE TOP BREAK

Caliber: .38, .44 Russian, .44-40, .45 Colt, 6-shot cylinder. **Barrel:** 3.5, 5, 7". **Weight:** 2.4 lbs. (5" barrel) **Length:** 10.8" overall (5" barrel). **Grips:** Two-piece smooth walnut or pearl. **Sights:** Blade front, notch rear. **Features:** Replica of Smith & Wesson Model 3 Schofield. Single-action, top break with automatic ejection. Polished blue finish (first model). Introduced 1994. Imported by Stoeger Industries.

Price: No. 3-2nd Model, nickel finish **$1,369.00**

AMERICAN DERRINGER MODEL 1

Caliber: All popular handgun calibers plus .45 Colt/.410 Shotshell. **Capacity:** Two rounds, (.45-70 model is single shot). **Barrel:** 3 inches. **Overall length:** 4.82 inches. **Weight:** 15 oz. **Features:** Manually operated hammer-block safety automatically disengages when hammer is cocked.
Price: .... $635.00 to $735.00
Price: Texas Commemorative..$835.00

AMERICAN DERRINGER MODEL 8

Caliber: .45 Colt/.410 shotshell. **Capacity:** Two rounds. **Barrel:** 8 inches. **Weight:** 24 oz.
Price: $915.00
Price: High polish finish $1,070.00

AMERICAN DERRINGER DA38

Caliber: .38 Special, .357 Magnum, 9mm Luger. **Barrel:** 3.3 inches. **Weight:** 14.5 oz. **Features:** Double-action operation with hammer-block thumb safety. Barrel, receiver and all internal parts are made from stainless steel.
Price: .... $690.00 to $740.00

BOND ARMS TEXAS DEFENDER DERRINGER

Caliber: Available in more than 10 calibers, from .22 LR to .45 LC/.410 shotshells. **Barrel:** 3". **Weight:** 20 oz. **Length:** 5". **Grips:** Rosewood. **Sights:** Blade front, fixed rear. **Features:** Interchangeable barrels, stainless steel firing pins, cross-bolt safety, automatic extractor for rimmed calibers. Stainless steel construction, brushed finish. Right or left hand.
Price: $440.00
Price: Interchangeable barrels, .22 LR thru .45 LC, 3 ......$139.00
Price: Interchangeable barrels, .45 LC, 3.5 ..... $159.00 to $189.00

BOND ARMS RANGER

Caliber: .45 LC/.410 shotshells. **Barrel:** 4.25" **Weight:** 23.5 oz. **Length:** 6.25" **Features:** Similar to Snake Slayer except no triggerguard. Intr. 2008. From Bond Arms.
Price: $673.00

BOND ARMS CENTURY 2000 DEFENDER

Caliber: .45 LC/.410 shotshells. **Barrel:** 3.5" **Weight:** 21 oz. **Length:** 5.5". **Features:** Similar to Defender series.
Price: $435.00

BOND ARMS COWBOY DEFENDER

Caliber: From .22 LR to .45 LC/.410 shotshells. **Barrel:** 3". **Weight:** 19 oz. **Length:** 5.5". **Features:** Similar to Defender series. No trigger guard.
Price: $440.00

BOND ARMS SNAKE SLAYER

Caliber: .45 LC/.410 shotshell (2.5" or 3"). **Barrel:** 3.5". **Weight:** 21 oz. **Length:** 5.5". **Grips:** Extended rosewood. **Sights:** Blade front, fixed rear. **Features:** Single-action; interchangeable barrels; stainless steel firing pin. Introduced 2005.
Price: $519.00

BOND ARMS SNAKE SLAYER IV

Caliber: .45 LC/.410 shotshell (2.5" or 3"). **Barrel:** 4.25". **Weight:** 22 oz. **Length:** 6.25". **Grips:** Extended rosewood. **Sights:** Blade front, fixed rear. **Features:** Single-action; interchangeable barrels; stainless steel firing pin. Introduced 2006.
Price: $551.00

CHARTER ARMS DIXIE DERRINGERS

Caliber: .22 LR, .22 WMR. **Barrel:** 1.125". **Weight:** 6 oz. **Length:** 4" overall. **Grips:** Black polymer. **Sights:** Blade front, fixed notch rear. **Features:** Stainless finish. Introduced 2006. Made in U.S.A. by Charter Arms.
Price: $215.00

COBRA BIG-BORE DERRINGERS

Caliber: .22 WMR, .32 H&R Mag., .38 Spec., 9mm Para., .380 ACP. **Barrel:** 2.75". **Weight:** 14 oz. **Length:** 4.65" overall. **Grips:** Textured black or white synthetic or laminated rosewood. **Sights:** Blade front, fixed notch rear. **Features:** Alloy frame, steel-lined barrels, steel breech block. Plunger-type safety with integral hammer block. Black, chrome or satin finish. Introduced 2002. Made in U.S.A. by Cobra Enterprises of Utah, Inc.
Price: $187.00

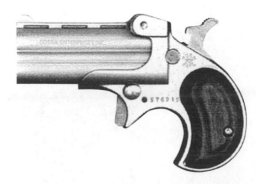

COBRA STANDARD SERIES DERRINGERS

Caliber: .22 LR, .22 WMR, .25 ACP, .32 ACP. **Barrel:** 2.4". **Weight:** 9.5 oz. **Length:** 4" overall. **Grips:** Laminated wood or pearl. **Sights:** Blade front, fixed notch rear. **Features:** Choice of black powder coat, satin nickel or chrome finish. Introduced 2002. Made in U.S.A. by Cobra Enterprises of Utah, Inc.
Price: $169.00

COBRA LONG-BORE DERRINGERS

Caliber: .22 WMR, .38 Spec., 9mm Para. **Barrel:** 3.5". **Weight:** 16 oz. **Length:** 5.4" overall. **Grips:** Black or white synthetic or rosewood. **Sights:** Fixed. **Features:** Chrome, satin nickel, or black Teflon finish. Introduced 2002. Made in U.S.A. by Cobra Enterprises of Utah, Inc.
Price: $187.00

COBRA TITAN
.45 LC/.410 DERRINGER

Caliber: .45 LC, .410 or 9mm, 2-round capacity. **Barrel:** 3-1/2". **Weight:** 16.4 oz. **Grip:** Rosewood. **Features:** The Titan is a powerhouse derringer designed to shoot a .45 Long Colt or the wide range of personal protection .410 shells with additional calibers to follow soon. Standard finshes include: satin stainless, black stainless, and brushed stainless. Made in U.S.A. by Cobra Enterprises of Utah, Inc.
Price: $419.00

COMANCHE SUPER SINGLE-SHOT

Caliber: .45 LC/.410 **Barrel:** 10". **Sights:** Adjustable. **Features:** Blue finish, not available for sale in CA, MA. Distributed by SGS Importers International, Inc.
Price: $225.00

DOUBLETAP DERRINGER

Caliber: .45 Colt or 9mm **Barrel:** 3". **Weight:** 12 ozs. **Length:** 5.5" **Sights:** Adjustable. **Features:** Over/under, two-barrel design. Rounds are fired individually with two separate trigger pulls. Tip-up design, aluminum or titanium frame.
Price: Aluminum. $499.00
Price: Titanium. $799.00

HEIZER PS1 POCKET SHOTGUN

Caliber: .45 Colt or .410 shotshell. Single-shot. **Barrel:** Tip-up, 3.25 inches. **Weight:** 22 oz. **Length:** 5.6 inches. **Width:** .742 inches **Height:** 3.81 inches. **Features:** Available in several finishes. Standard model is matte stainless or black. Also offered in Hedy Jane series for the women in pink or in two-tone combinations of stainless and pink, blue, green, purple. Made in the U.S.A. by Heizer Industries.
Price: $499.00

HEIZER POCKET AR

Caliber: : .223 Rem./5.56 NATO. Similar to PS1 Pocket Shotgun but chambered for .223/5.56 rifle cartridge. Single shot. **Length:** 6-3/8 inches. **Weight:** 23 oz.
Price: $499.00

HENRY MARE'S LEG

Caliber: : .22 LR, .22 WMR, .357 Mag., .44 Mag., .45 Colt. **Capacity:** 10 rounds (.22 LR), 8 rounds (.22 WMR), 5 rounds (others). **Barrel:** 12.9 inches. **Length:** 25 inches. **Weight:** 4.5 lbs (rimfire) to 5.8 lbs. (centerfire calibers). Lever-action operation based on Henry rifle series and patterned after gun made famous in Steve McQueen '50s TV show, "Wanted: Dead or Alive." Made in the U.S.A. .
Price: .22 LR. $440.00
Price: .22 WMR. $450.00
Price: Centerfire calibers $957.00

MAXIMUM SINGLE-SHOT

Caliber: .22 LR, .22 Hornet, .22 BR, .22 PPC, 223 Rem., 22-250, 6mm BR, 6mm PPC, 243, 250 Savage, 6.5mm-35M, 270 MAX, 270 Win., 7mm TCU, 7mm BR, 7mm-35, 7mm INT-R, 7mm-08, 7mm Rocket, 7mm Super-Mag., 30 Herrett, 30 Carbine, 30-30, 308 Win., 30x39, 32-20, 350 Rem. Mag., .357 Mag., .357 Maximum, 358 Win., 375 H&H, .44 Mag., .454 Casull. **Barrel:** 8.75", 10.5", 14". **Weight:** 61 oz. (10.5" bbl.); 78 oz. (14" bbl.). **Length:** 15", 18.5" overall (with 10.5"

Prices given are believed to be accurate at time of publication however, many factors affect retail pricing so exact prices are not possible.

and 14" bbl., respectively). **Grips:** Smooth walnut stocks and fore-end. Also available with 17-finger-groove grip. **Sights:** Ramp front, fully adjustable open rear. **Features:** Falling block action; drilled and tapped for M.O.A. scope mounts; integral grip frame/receiver; adjustable trigger; Douglas barrel (interchangeable). Introduced 1983. Made in U.S.A. by M.O.A. Corp.

Price: $1,062.00

ROSSI MATCHED PAIR , "DUAL THREAT PERFORMER"

Caliber: .22LR, .44 Mag., .223, .243. .410, 20 gauge, single shot. Interchangeable rifle and shotgun barrels in various combinations. **Sights:** Fiber optic front sights, adjustable rear. **Features:** Two-in-one pistol system with sinle-shot simplicity. Removable choke and cushioned grip with a Taurus Security System.

Price: .22/.410 from $245.00
Price: .44 Mag/20 ga. from $352.00

ROSSI RANCH HAND

Caliber: .38/.357, .45 Colt or .44 magnum, 6-shot. **Weight:** 4 lbs. **Length:** 24" overall. **Stock:** Brazilian hardwood. **Sights:** Adjustable buckhorn. **Features:** Matte blue or case hardened finish with oversized lever loop to accomodate gloved hands. Equipped with classic buckhorn sights for fast target aquisition and a Taurus Security Sytem.

Price: .... $597.00 to $661.00

THOMPSON/CENTER ENCORE

Calibers: .17 HMR, .22 LR, .204 Ruger, .223, .22-250, .243, .270., 7mm-08, .308, .20-06, .44 Mag., .45 Colt/.410, .45-70 Govt., .460 S&W, .500 S&W. Single shot, break-open design. **Barrel:** 15 inches, 12 inches (.44 Mag., .45 Colt). **Weight:** 4.25 to 4.5 lbs. **Grip:** Walnut on blued models, rubber on stainless. Matching fore-end. **Sights:** Adjustable rear, ramp front. **Features:** Interchangeable barrels, adjustable trigger. Pro Hunter has "Swing Hammer" to allow reaching the hammer when the gun is scoped. Other Pro Hunter features include fluted barrel.

Price: From $779.00

THOMPSON/CENTER G2 CONTENDER

A second generation Contender pistol maintaining the same barrel interchangeability with older Contender barrels and their corresponding forends (except Herrett fore-end). The G2 frame will not accept old-style grips due to the change in grip angle. Incorporates an automatic hammer block safety with built-in interlock. Features include trigger adjustable for overtravel, adjustable rear sight; ramp front sight blade, blued steel finish.

Price: From $729.00

Prices given are believed to be accurate at time of publication however, many factors affect retail pricing so exact prices are not possible.

70TH EDITION, 2016 ✦ 447

ALEXANDER ARMS AR SERIES

Caliber: .17 HMR, 5.56 NATO, 6.5 Grendel, .300 AAC, .338 Lapua Mag., .50 Beowulf. This manufacturer produces a wide range of AR-15 type rifles and carbines. **Barrel:** 16, 18, 20 or 24 inches. Models are available for consumer, law enforcement and military markets. Depending on the specific model, features include forged flattop receiver with Picatinny rail, button-rifled stainless steel barrels, composite free-floating handguard, A2 flash hider, M4 collapsible stock, gas piston operating system.

Price: .17 HMR $1,210.00
Price: 5.56 NATO $1,349.00
Price: 6.5 Grendel .... $1,540.00 to $1,750.00
Price: .300 AAC $1,349.00
Price: .50 Beowulf .... $1,375.00 to $1,750.00

ALEXANDER ARMS ULFBERHT

Caliber: .338 Lapua Mag. Custom-designed adjustable gas-piston operating system. **Barrel:** 27.5-inch chrome moly with three-prong flash hider. **Stock:** Magpul PRS. **Length:** 41.25 inches (folded), 50 inches (extended stock). **Weight:** 19.8 lbs.
Price: Ulfberht .338 Lapua Mag. $6,850.00

ARMALITE M15A4 CARBINE

Caliber: .223 Rem., 30-round magazine. **Barrel:** 16" heavy chrome lined; 1:7" twist, flash suppressor. **Weight:** 6.8 lbs. **Length:** 36" overall. **Stock:** Green or black composition. **Sights:** Standard A2. **Features:** Forged flattop receiver with Picatinny rail, 8-inch handguard, anodize aluminum supper/lower receiver, flip-up sights.
Price: $1,073.00

ARMALITE AR-10A4 SPECIAL PURPOSE

Caliber: .243, .308 Win., 10- and 20-round magazine. **Barrel:** 20" chrome-lined, 1:11.25" twist. **Weight:** 9.6 lbs. **Length:** 41" overall. **Stock:** Green or black composition. **Sights:** Detachable handle, front sight, or scope mount available; comes with international style flattop receiver with Picatinny rail. **Features:** Forged upper receiver with case deflector. Receivers are hard-coat anodized. Introduced 1995. Made in U.S.A. by ArmaLite, Inc.
Price: $1,557.00

ARMALITE AR-10A2

Utilizing the same 20" double-lapped, heavy barrel as the ArmaLite AR10A4 Special Purpose Rifle. Offered in .308 Win. only. Made in U.S.A. by ArmaLite, Inc.
Price: AR-10A2 rifle or carbine $1,561.00

ARSENAL, INC. SLR-107F

Caliber: 7.62x39mm. **Barrel:** 16.25". **Weight:** 7.3 lbs. **Stock:** Left-side folding polymer stock. **Sights:** Adjustable rear. **Features:** Stamped receiver, 24mm flash hider, bayonet lug, accessory lug, stainless steel heat shield, two-stage trigger. Introduced 2008. Made in U.S.A. by Arsenal, Inc.
Price: SLR-107FR, includes scope rail $1,099.00

ARSENAL, INC. SLR-107CR

Caliber: 7.62x39mm. **Barrel:** 16.25". **Weight:** 6.9 lbs. **Stock:** Left-side folding polymer stock. **Sights:** Adjustable rear. **Features:** Stamped receiver, front sight block/gas block combination, 500-meter rear sight, cleaning rod, stainless steel heat shield, scope rail, and removable muzzle attachment. Introduced 2007. Made in U.S.A. by Arsenal, Inc.
Price: SLR-107CR $1,119.00

ARSENAL, INC. SLR-106CR

Caliber: 5.56 NATO. **Barrel:** 16.25", Steyr chrome-lined barrel, 1:7 twist rate. **Weight:** 6.9 lbs. **Stock:** Black polymer folding stock with cutout for scope rail. Stainless-steel heatshield handguard. **Sights:** 500-meter rear sight and rear sight block calibrated for 5.56 NATO. Warsaw Pact scope rail. **Features:** Uses Arsenal, Bulgaria, Mil-Spec receiver, two-stage trigger, hammer and disconnector. Polymer magazines in 5- and 10-round capacity in black and green, with Arsenal logo. Others are 30-round black waffles, 20- and 30-round versions in clear/smoke waffle, featuring the "10" in a double-circle logo of Arsenal, Bulgaria. Ships with 5-round magazine, sling, cleaning kit in a tube, 16" cleaning rod, oil bottle. Introduced 2007. Made in U.S.A. by Arsenal, Inc.
Price: SLR-106CR $1,200.00

AUTO-ORDNANCE 1927A-1 THOMPSON

Caliber: .45 ACP. **Barrel:** 16.5". **Weight:** 13 lbs. **Length:** About 41" overall (Deluxe). **Stock:** Walnut stock and vertical fore-end. **Sights:** Blade front, open rear adjustable for windage. **Features:** Recreation of Thompson Model 1927. Semiauto only. Deluxe model has finned barrel, adjustable rear sight and compensator; Standard model has plain barrel and military sight. Available with 100-round drum or 30-round stick magazine. From Auto-Ordnance Corp
Price: Deluxe w/stick magazine $1,461.00
Price: Deluxe w/drum magazine $2,061.00
Price: Lightweight model w/stick mag $1,325.00

AUTO-ORDNANCE THOMPSON M1/M1-C

Similar to the 1927 A-1 except is in the M-1 configuration with side cocking knob, horizontal fore-end, smooth unfinned barrel, sling swivels on butt and fore-end. Matte-black finish. Introduced 1985.
Price: M1 semiauto carbine $1,375.00
Price: M1-C lightweight semiauto $1,241.00

AUTO-ORDNANCE 1927 A-1 COMMANDO

Similar to the 1927 A-1 except has Parkerized finish, black-finish wood butt, pistol grip, horizontal fore-end. Comes with black nylon sling. Introduced 1998. Made in U.S.A. by Auto-Ordnance Corp.
Price: T1-C $1,393.00

AUTO ORDNANCE M1 CARBINE

Caliber: .30 Carbine (15-shot magazine). **Barrel:** 18". **Weight:** 5.4 to 5.8 lbs. **Length:** 36.5". **Stock:** Wood or polymer. **Sights:** Blade front, flip-style rear. A faithful recreation of the military carbine.
Price: $846.00

BARRETT MODEL 82A-1 SEMI-AUTOMATIC

Caliber: .416 Barret, 50 BMG, 10-shot detachable box magazine. **Barrel:** 29". **Weight:** 28.5 lbs. **Length:** 57" overall. **Stock:**

Prices given are believed to be accurate at time of publication however, many factors affect retail pricing so exact prices are not possible.

Composition with energy-absorbing recoil pad. **Sights:** Scope optional. **Features:** Semiautomatic, recoil operated with recoiling barrel. Three-lug locking bolt; muzzle brake. Adjustable bipod. Introduced 1985. Made in U.S.A. by Barrett Firearms.
Price: From $8,900.00

BARRETT M107A1
Caliber: 50 BMG. 10-round detachable magazine. **Barrel:** 20 or 29 inches. **Sights:** 27-inch optics rail with flip-up iron sights. **Weight:** 30.9 lbs. **Finish:** Flat Dark Earth. Features: Four-port cylindrical muzzle brake. Quick-detachable Barrett QDL Suppressor. Adjustable bipod and monopod.
Price: $12,000.00

BARRETT MODEL REC7 GEN II
Caliber: 5.56 (.223), 6.8 Rem. SPC. 30-round magazine. **Barrel:** 16 inches. **Sights:** ARMS rear, folding front. Weight: 28.7 lbs. **Features:** AR-style configuration with standard 17-4 stainless piston system, two-position forward venting gas plug, chrome-lined gas block, A2 flash hider, 6-postion MOE stock.
Price: $2,759.00

BENELLI R1
Caliber: .30-06 (4+1), .300 Win Mag (3+1), .338 Win Mag (3+1). **Weight:** 7.1 lbs. **Length:** 43.75" to 45.75". **Stock:** Select satin walnut or synthetic. **Sights:** None. **Features:** Auto-regulating gas-operated system, three-lug rotary bolt, interchangeable barrels, optional recoil pads. Introduced 2003. Imported from Italy by Benelli USA.
Price: .... $1,379.00 to $1,689.00

BENELLI MR1
Gas-operated semiauto rifle chambered in 5.56 NATO. Features include 16-inch, 1:9 twist, hard chrome-lined barrel, synthetic stock with pistol grip, rotating bolt, military-style aperture sights with picatinny rail. Comes equipped with 5-round detachable magazine but accepts M16 magazines.
Price: $1,339.00

BERETTA CX4/PX4 STORM CARBINE
Caliber: 9mm Para., .40 S&W, .45 ACP. **Weight:** 5.75 lbs. **Barrel Length:** 16.6", chrome lined, rate of twist 1:16 (.40 S&W) or 1:10 (9mm Para.). **Length:** NA. **Stock:** Black synthetic. **Sights:** Ghost ring. **Features:** Introduced 2005. Imported from Italy by Beretta USA.
Price: $900.00

BROWNING BAR SAFARI AND SAFARI W/BOSS SEMI-AUTO
Caliber: Safari: .25-06 Rem., .270 Win., 7mm Rem. Mag., .30-06 Spfl., .308 Win., .300 Win. Mag., .338 Win. Mag. Safari w/BOSS: .270 Win., 7mm Rem. Mag., .30-06 Spfl., .300 Win. Mag., .338 Win. Mag. **Barrel:** 22-24" round tapered. **Weight:** 7.4-8.2 lbs. **Length:** 43-45" overall. **Stock:** French walnut pistol grip stock and fore-end, hand checkered. **Sights:** No sights. **Features:** Has new bolt release lever; removable trigger assembly with larger triggerguard; redesigned gas and buffer systems. Detachable 4-round box magazine. Scroll-engraved receiver is tapped for scope mounting. BOSS barrel vibration modulator and muzzle brake system available. Mark II Safari introduced 1993. Made in Belgium.
Price: BAR MK II Safari, from $1,300.00
Price: BAR Safari w/BOSS, from $1,500.00

BROWNING BAR SHORTTRAC/LONGTRAC
Caliber:(ShortTrac models) .270 WSM, 7mm WSM, .300 WSM, .243 Win., .308 Win., .325 WSM; (LongTrac models) .270 Win., .30-06 Spfl., 7mm Rem. Mag., .300 Win. Mag. **Barrel:** 23". **Weight:** 6 lbs. 10 oz. to 7 lbs. 4 oz. **Length:** 41.5" to 44". **Stock:** Satin-finish walnut, pistol-grip, fluted fore-end. **Sights:** Adj. rear, bead front standard, no sights on BOSS models (optional). **Features:** Designed to handle new WSM chamberings. Gas-operated, blued finish, rotary bolt design (LongTrac models).
Price: BAR ShortTrac, .243 Win., .308 Win. from $1,230.00
Price: BAR ShortTrac Left-Hand, intr. 2007, from $1,270.00
Price: BAR ShortTrac Mossy Oak New Break-up
.... **$1,260.00 to $1,360.00**
Price: BAR LongTrac Left Hand, .270 Win., .30-06 Spfl.,
from $1,270.00
Price: BAR LongTrac, from $1,200.00
Price: BAR LongTrac Mossy Oak Break Up, from $1,360.00

BROWNING BAR STALKER
Caliber: .243 Win., 7mm-08, .308 Win., .270 Win., .30-06 Spfl., .270 WSM, 7mm WSM, .300 WSM, .300 Win. Mag., .338 Win. Mag. **Barrel:** 20-24". **Weight:** 7.1-7.75 LBS. **Length:** 41-45" overall. **Stock:** Black composite stock and forearm. **Sights:** Hooded front and adjustable rear. **Features:** Gas-operated action with seven-lug rotary bolt; dual action bars; 2-, 3- or 4-shot magazine (depending on cartridge). Introduced 2001. Imported by Browning.
Price: BAR ShortTrac or LongTrac Stalker, from $1,350.00
Price: BAR Lightweight Stalker, from......,.......................$1,260.00

BUSHMASTER 300 AAC BLACKOUT
Caliber: .300 AAC. M4-style AR platform chambered for cartridge that duplicates 7.62x39 ballistics. **Features:** Utilizes regular AR magazines at full capacity. Muzzlebrake. Magpul stock and grip.
Price: $1,471.00

Prices given are believed to be accurate at time of publication however, many factors affect retail pricing so exact prices are not possible.

70TH EDITION, 2016 ✛ **449**

BUSHMASTER 308 HUNTER

Caliber: .308 Win / 7.62 NATO., 5-round magazine. **Barrel:** 20". **Weight:** 8-1/2 lbs. **Length:** 38-1/4" overall. **Stock:** Standard A2 stock with Hogue® rubberized pistol grip. **Sights:** Two ¾" mini-risers for optics mounting. **Features:** Bushmaster .308 Rifles were developed for the Hunter who intends to immediately add optics (scope, red dot or holographic sight) to the rifle. The premium 20" heavy fluted profile barrel is chrome lined in both bore and chamber to provide Bushmaster accuracy, durability and maintenance ease.
Price: .308 Hunter. $1,685.00

BUSHMASTER ACR

Caliber: 5.56mm, 6.5mm, 6.8mm., 30-round polymer magazine. **Barrel:** All three calibers are availaible with 10-1/2", 14-1/2", 16-1/2" and 18" barrels. **Weight:** 14-1/2" bbl. 7 lbs.. **Length:** 14-1/5" bbl. with stock folded: 25-3/4", with stock deployed (mid) 32-5/8", 10.5" bbl. with stock folded: 21-5/16", with stock deployed (mid): 27-7/8", with stock deployed and extended: 31-3/4". Folding Stock Length of Pull - 3". **Stock:** Fixed high-impact composite A-frame stock with rubber buttpad and sling mounts (ORC & A-TACS®) **Features:** Cold hammer-forged barrels with melonite coating for extreme long life. A2 birdcage-type hider to control muzzle flash and adjustable, two-position, gas piston-driven system for firing suppressed or unsuppressed, supported by hardened internal bearing rails. The Adaptive Combat Rifle (ACR) features a tool-less, quick-change barrel system available in 10.5", 14.5" and 16.5" and in multiple calibers. Multi-caliber bolt carrier assembly quickly and easily changes from .223/5.56mm NATO to 6.8mm Rem SPC (spec II chamber). Free-floating MIL-STD 1913 monolithic top rail for optic mounting. Fully ambidextrous controls including magazine release, bolt catch and release, fire selector and nonreciprocating charging handle. High-impact composite handguard with heat shield – accepts rail inserts. High-impact composite lower receiver with textured magazine well and modular grip storage. Fire Control – Semi and Full Auto two-stage standard AR capable of accepting drop-in upgrade. Magazine – Optimized for MagPul PMAG Accepts standard NATO/M-16 magazines.
Price: Basic ORC Configuration $2,343.00
Price: A-TACS Basic Configuration $2,604.00
Price: Designated Marksman Rifle $2,800.00
Price: Basic Folder Configuration $2,553.00
Price: ACR Enhanced $2,766.00

BUSHMASTER VARMINTER

Caliber: .223 Rem., 5-shot. **Barrel:** 24", 1:9" twist, fluted, heavy, stainless. **Weight:** 8.75 lbs. **Length:** 42.25". **Stock:** Rubberized pistol grip. **Sights:** 1/2" scope risers. **Features:** Gas-operated, semiauto, two-stage trigger, slotted free floater fore-end, lockable hard case.
Price: $1,430.00

BUSHMASTER 6.8 SPC/7.62X39 PATROLMAN'S CARBINE

Caliber: 6.8 SPC, 26-shot mag. **Barrel:** 16" M4 profile. **Weight:** 6.57 lbs. **Length:** 32.75" overall. **Features:** Semiauto AR-style with Izzy muzzlebrake, six-position telestock. Available in A2 (fixed carry handle) or A3 (removable carry handle) configuration. Quad rail system.
Price: $1,391.00

BUSHMASTER ORC CARBINE

Caliber: 5.56/.223. **Barrel:** 16" M4 profile. **Weight:** 6 lbs. **Length:** 32.5" overall. **Features:** AR-style carbine with chrome-lined barrel, fixed carry handle, receiver-length picatinny optics rail, heavy oval M4-style handguards.
Price: $1,391.00

BUSHMASTER 11.5" BARREL CARBINE

Caliber: 5.56/.223, 30-shot mag. **Barrel:** 11.5". **Weight:** 6.46 lbs. or 6.81 lbs. **Length:** 31.625" overall. **Features:** AR-style carbine with chrome-lined barrel with permanently attached BATF-approved 5.5" flash suppressor, fixed or removable carry handle, optional optics rail.
Price: $1,406.00

BUSHMASTER HEAVY-BARRELED CARBINE

Caliber: 5.56/.223. **Barrel:** 16". **Weight:** 6.93 lbs. to 7.28 lbs. **Length:** 32.5" overall. **Features:** AR-style carbine with chrome-lined heavy profile vanadium steel barrel, fixed or removable carry handle, six-position telestock.
Price: $1,215.00

BUSHMASTER MODULAR CARBINE

Caliber: 5.56/.223, 30-shot mag. **Barrel:** 16". **Weight:** 7.3 lbs. **Length:** 36.25" overall. **Features:** AR-style carbine with chrome-lined chrome-moly vanadium steel barrel, skeleton stock or six-position telestock, clamp-on front sight and detachable flip-up dual aperature rear.
Price: $1,745.00

BUSHMASTER 450 RIFLE AND CARBINE

Caliber: .450 Bushmaster. **Barrel:** 20" (rifle), 16" (carbine), five-round mag. **Weight:** 8.3 lbs. (rifle), 8.1 lbs. (carbine). **Length:** 39.5" overall (rifle), 35.25" overall (carbine). **Features:** AR-style with chrome-lined chrome-moly barrel, synthetic stock, Izzy muzzlebrake.
Price: Carbine $1,485.00
Price: Rifle $1,500.00

BUSHMASTER TARGET

Caliber: 5.56/.223, 30-shot mag. **Barrel:** 20 or 24-inch heavy or standard. **Weight:** 8.43 lbs. to 9.29 lbs. **Length:** 39.5" or 43.5" overall. **Features:** Semiauto AR-style with chrome-lined or stainless steel 1:9" twist barrel, fixed or removable carry handle, manganese phosphate finish.
Price: $1,195.00

BUSHMASTER M4A3 TYPE CARBINE

Caliber: 5.56/.223, 30-shot mag. **Barrel:** 16". **Weight:** 6.22 to 6.7 lbs. **Length:** 31 to 32.5 inches overall. **Features:** AR-style carbine with chrome-moly vanadium steel barrel, Izzy-type flash hider, six-position telestock, various sight options, standard or multi-rail handguard, fixed or removable carry handle.
Price: $1,270.00
Price: Patrolman's Carbine: Standard mil-style sights $1,270.00
Price: State Compliance Carbine $1,270.00

CENTURY INTERNATIONAL AES-10 HI-CAP

Caliber: 7.62x39mm. 30-shot magazine. **Barrel:** 23.2". **Weight:** NA. **Length:** 41.5" overall. **Stock:** Wood grip, fore-end. **Sights:** Fixed notch rear, windage-adjustable post front. **Features:** RPK-style, accepts standard double-stack AK-type mags. Side-mounted scope mount, integral carry handle, bipod. Imported by Century Arms Int'l.
Price: AES-10, from $450.00

CENTURY INTERNATIONAL GP WASR-10 HI-CAP

Caliber: 7.62x39mm. 30-shot magazine. **Barrel:** 16.25", 1:10 right-hand twist. **Weight:** 7.2 lbs. **Length:** 34.25" overall. **Stock:** Wood laminate or composite, grip, forend. **Sights:** Fixed notch rear, windage-adjustable post front. **Features:** Two 30-rd. detachable box magazines, cleaning kit, bayonet. Version of AKM rifle; U.S.-parts added for BATFE compliance. Threaded muzzle, folding stock, bayonet lug, compensator, Dragunov stock available. Made in Romania by Cugir Arsenal. Imported by Century Arms Int'l.
Price: GP WASR-10, from $450.00

Prices given are believed to be accurate at time of publication however, many factors affect retail pricing so exact prices are not possible.

CENTURY INTERNATIONAL M70AB2 SPORTER

Caliber: 7.62x39mm. 30-shot magazine. **Barrel:** 16.25". **Weight:** 7.5 lbs. **Length:** 34.25" overall. **Stocks:** Metal grip, wood fore-end. **Sights:** Fixed notch rear, windage-adjustable post front. **Features:** Two 30-rd. double-stack magazine, cleaning kit, compensator, bayonet lug and bayonet. Paratrooper-style Kalashnikov with under-folding stock. Imported by Century Arms Int'l.
Price: M70AB2, from $480.00

COLT LE6920

Caliber: 5.56 NATO. **Barrel:** 16.1-inch chrome lined. **Sights:** Adjustable. Based on military M4. Features include Magpul MOE handguard, carbine stock, pistol grip, vertical grip. Direct gas/locking bolt operating system.
Price: From **$1,155.00**
Price: OEM 1, OEM 2 no sights................................**$793.00**

COLT LE6940

Caliber: 5.56 NATO. Similar to LE1920 with Magpul MBUS backup sight, folding front, four accessory rails. One-piece monolithic upper receiver has continuous Mil Spec rail from rear of upper to the front sight. Direct gas (LE6940) or articulating link piston (LE6940P) system.
Price: LE6940 ....**$1,546.00**
Price: LE6940P **$2,105.00**

COLT CARBINE

Caliber: .223, 9mm. Capacity 10, 20 or 30 rounds. **Barrel:** 16.1 or 20 inches. Offered in a wide range of AR configurations and finishes.
Price: From...**$1,136.00**

COLT LE901

Caliber: .308. Capacity 20 rounds. **Barrel:** 16.1" heavy. **Weight:** 9.4 lbs. **Stock:** 4-position collapsible. **Sights:** Mil-Spec Flip-Up. **Features:** One piece upper receiver, fully floated barrel, ambidextrous controls, bayonet lug and flash hider.
Price: **$2,544.00**

DANIEL DEFENSE AR SERIES

Caliber: 5.56 NATO/.223. 20-round Magpul PMAG magazine. **Barrel:** 16 or 18 inches. Flash suppressor. **Weight:** 7.4 lbs. **Length:** 34.75" to 37.85" overall. **Stock:** Glass-filled polymer with Soft Touch overmolding. Pistol grip. **Sights:** None. **Features:** Lower receiver is Mil Spec with enhanced and flared magazine well, QD swivel attachment point. Upper receiver has M4 feed ramps. Lower and upper CNC machined of 7075-T6 aluminum, hard coat anodized. Shown is MK12, one of many AR variants offered by Daniel Defense. Made in the U.S.A.
Price: From **$1,599.00**

DPMS VARMINT SERIES

Caliber: .204 Ruger, .223. **Barrel:** 16", 20" or 24" bull or fluted profile. **Weight:** 7.75 to 11.75 lbs. **Length:** 34.5" to 42.25" overall. **Stock:** Black Zytel composite. **Sights:** None. **Features:** Flattop receiver with Picatinny top rail; hardcoat anodized receiver; aluminum free-float tube handguard; many options. From DPMS Panther Arms.
Price: ....**$1,059.00 to $1,269.00**

DPMS PRAIRIE PANTHER

Semiauto AR-style rifle chambered in 5.56 NATO or 6.8 SPC. Features include 20-inch 416 stainless fluted heavy 1:8" barrel; phosphated steel bolt; free-floated carbon fiber handguard; flattop upper with Picatinny rail; aluminum lower; two 30-round magazines; skeletonized Zytel stock; Choice of matte black or one of several camo finishes.
Price: ....**$1,269.00 to $1,289.00**

DPMS REPR

Semiauto AR-style rifle chambered in .308 Win./7.62 NATO. Features include 18-inch 416 stainless steel 1:10" twist barrel; phosphated steel bolt; 4-rail free-floated handguard; no sights; aluminum lower; bipoad; two 19-round magazines; Coyote Brown camo finish overall. Scope not included.
Price: **$2,549.00**

DPMS MK12

Caliber: .308 Win./7.62 NATO. **Barrel:** 18 inches. **Weight:** 8.5 lbs. **Sights:** Midwest Industry flip-up. **Features:** 4-rail free floating handguard, flash hider, extruded 7029 T6 A3 Flattop receiver.
Price: **$1,759.00**

DPMS 3G2

Caliber: .223/5.56. **Barrel:** 16 inches. **Weight:** 7.1 lbs. **Stock:** Magpul STR with Hogue rubber pistol grip. **Sights:** Magpul Gen 2 BUS. **Features:** Miculek Compensator, two-stage fire control. M111 Modular handguard allows placement of sights on top rail or 45-degree angle.
Price: **$1,239.00**

DPMS LITE HUNTER

Caliber: .243, .260 Rem., .308, .338 Federal. **Barrel:** 20 inches, stainless. **Weight:** 8 pounds. **Stock:** Standard A2. **Features:** Two-stage match trigger. Hogue pistol grip. Optics ready top rail.

Prices given are believed to be accurate at time of publication however, many factors affect retail pricing so exact prices are not possible.

70TH EDITION, 2016 ✦ **451**

Price: $1,499.00

DPMS .300 AAC BLACKOUT
Caliber: .300 AAC Blackout. **Barrel:** 16-inch heavy 4150 chrome-lined. **Weight:** 7 pounds. **Stock:** Adjustable 6-position.

Price: $1,199.00

DPMS GII SERIES
Caliber: .308 Win./7.62 NATO. **Barrel:** 16, 18 inches. **Weight:** From 7.25 lbs., promoted as the lightest .308 AR available. Features include new extractor and ejector systems, and improved steel feed ramp. New bolt geometry provides better lock-up and strength. Offered in several configurations.

Price: AP4 (shown)... $1,499.00
Price: Recon $1,759.00
Price: SASS $2,379.00
Price: Hunter $1,699.00
Price: Bull.. $1,759.00
Price: MOE... $1,599.00

DSA SA58 CONGO, PARA CONGO
Caliber: .308 Win. **Barrel:** 18" w/short Belgian short flash hider. **Weight:** 8.6 lbs. (Congo); 9.85 lbs. (Para Congo). **Length:** 39.75" **Stock:** Synthetic w/military grade furniture (Congo); Synthetic with nonfolding steel para stock (Para Congo). **Sights:** Elevation adjustable protected post front sight, windage adjustable rear peep (Congo); Belgian type Para Flip Rear (Para Congo). **Features:** FAL-style rifle with fully adjustable gas system, high-grade steel upper receiver with carry handle. Made in U.S.A. by DSA, Inc.

Price: Congo.. $1,975.00
Price: Para Congo $2,200.00

DSA SA58 STANDARD
Caliber: .308 Win. **Barrel:** 21" bipod cut w/threaded flash hider. **Weight:** 8.75 lbs. **Length:** 43". **Stock:** Synthetic, X-Series or optional folding para stock. **Sights:** Elevation-adjustable post front, windage-adjustable rear peep. **Features:** Fully adjustable short gas system, high-grade steel or 416 stainless upper receiver. Made in U.S.A. by DSA, Inc.

Price: From $1,700.00

DSA SA58 CARBINE
Caliber: .308 Win. **Barrel:** 16.25" bipod cut w/threaded flash hider. **Features:** Carbine variation of FAL-style rifle. Other features identical to SA58 Standard model. Made in U.S.A. by DSA, Inc.

Price: $1,700.00

DSA SA58 TACTICAL CARBINE
Caliber: .308 Win. **Barrel:** 16.25" fluted with A2 flash hider. **Weight:** 8.25 lbs. **Length:** 36.5". **Stock:** Synthetic, X-Series or optional folding para stock. **Sights:** Elevation-adjustable post front, windage-adjustable match rear peep. **Features:** Shortened fully adjustable short gas system, high grade steel or 416 stainless upper receiver. Made in U.S.A. by DSA, Inc.

Price: $1,975.00

DSA SA58 MEDIUM CONTOUR
Caliber: .308 Win. **Barrel:** 21" w/threaded flash hider. **Weight:** 9.75 lbs. **Length:** 43". **Stock:** Synthetic military grade. **Sights:** Elevation-adjustable post front, windage-adjustable match rear peep. **Features:** Gas-operated semiauto with fully adjustable gas system, high grade steel receiver. Made in U.S.A. by DSA, Inc.

Price: $1,700.00

DSA ZM4 AR SERIES
Caliber: .223/5.56 NATO. Standard Flattop rifle features include 20-inch, chrome moly heavy barrel with A2 flash hider. **Weight:** 9 pounds. **Features:** Mil-Spec forged lower receiver, forged flattop or A2 upper. Fixed A2 stock. Carbine variations are also available with 16-inch barrels and many options.

Price: .... From $788.00

EXCEL ARMS ACCELERATOR
Caliber: .17 HMR, .22 WMR, 5.7x28mm, 9-shot magazine. **Barrel:** 18" fluted stainless steel bull barrel. **Weight:** 8 lbs. **Length:** 32.5" overall. **Grips:** Textured black polymer. **Sights:** Fully adjustable target sights. **Features:** Made from 17-4 stainless steel, aluminum shroud w/ Weaver rail, manual safety, firing-pin block, last-round bolt-hold-open feature. Four packages with various equipment available. American made, lifetime warranty. Comes with one 9-round stainless steel magazine and a California-approved cable lock. Introduced 2006. Made in U.S.A. by Excel Arms.

Price: MR-17 .17 HMR $672.00
Price: MR-22 .22 WMR $538.00

EXCEL ARMS X-SERIES
Caliber: .22 LR, 5.7x28mm (10 or 25-round); .30 Carbine (10 or 20-round magazine). **Barrel:** 18". **Weight:** 6.25 lbs. **Length:** 34 to 38".

Prices given are believed to be accurate at time of publication however, many factors affect retail pricing so exact prices are not possible.

Features: Available with or without adjustable iron sights. Blow-back action (5.57x28) or delayed blow-back (.30 Carbine).
Price: .22 LR **$504.00**
Price: 5.7x28 ....**$795.00 to $916.00**

FNH FNAR COMPETITION
Caliber: .308 Win., 10-shot magazine. **Barrel:** 20" fluted. **Weight:** 8.9 lbs. **Length:** 41.25" overall. **Sights:** None furnished. Optical rail atop receiver, three accessory rails on fore-end. **Stock:** Adjustable for comb height, length of pull, cast-on and cast-off. Blue/gray laminate. Based on BAR design.
Price: **$1,767.00**

FNH SCAR 16S
Caliber: 5.56mm/.223. **Capacity:** 10 or 30 rounds. **Barrel:** 16.25". **Weight:** 7.25 lbs. **Length:** 27.5 to 37.5 " (extended stock). **Stock:** Telescoping, side-folding polymer. Adjustable cheekpiece, A2 style pistol grip. **Sights:** Adjustable folding front and rear. **Features:** Hard anodized aluminum receiver with four accessory rails. Ambidextrous safety and mag release. Charging handle can be mounted on right or left side. Semiauto version of newest service rifle of U.S. Special Forces.
Price: **$2,995.00**

FNH SCAR 17S
Caliber: 7.62x51mm/.308. **Capacity:** 10 or 30 rounds. **Barrel:** 16.25". **Weight:** 8 lbs. **Length:** 28.5 to 38.5 " (extended stock). **Features:** Other features the same as SCAR 16S.
Price: **$3,349.00**

FRANKLIN ARMORY 3 GR-L
Caliber: 5.56mm/.223. **Capacity:** 10 or 30 rounds. **Barrel:** 18" fluted with threaded muzzle crown. **Weight:** 7.25 lbs. **Stock:** Magpul PRS. Adjustable comb and length of pull. **Features:** Hard anodized Desert Smoke upper receiver with full length Picatinny rail. One of many AR type rifles and carbines offered by this manufacturer. Made in the U.S.A.
Price: **$2,310.00**

HECKLER & KOCH MODEL MR556A1
Caliber: .223 Remington/5.56 NATO, 10+1 capacity. **Barrel:** 16.5". **Weight:** 8.9 lbs. **Length:** 33.9"-37.68". **Stock:** Black Synthetic Adjustable. **Features:** Uses the gas piston system found on the HK 416 and G26, which does not introduce propellant gases and carbon fouling into the rifle's interior.
Price: **$3,295.00**

HECKLER & KOCH MODEL MR762A1
Caliber: Similar to Model MR556A1 except chambered for 7.62x51mm/.308 Win. cartridge. **Weight:** 10 lbs. w/empty magazine. **Length:** 36 to 39.5". Variety of optional sights are available. Stock has five adjustable positions.
Price: **$3,995.00**

HI-POINT 9MM CARBINE
Caliber: 9mm Para. .40 S&W, (10-shot magazine); .45 ACP (9-shot). **Barrel:** 16.5" (17.5" for .40 S&W and .45). **Weight:** 4.5 lbs. **Length:** 31.5" overall. **Stock:** Black polymer, camouflage. **Sights:** Protected post front, aperture rear. Integral scope mount. **Features:** Grip-mounted magazine release. Black or chrome finish. Sling swivels. Available with laser or red-dot sights, RGB 4X scope, forward grip. Introduced 1996. Made in U.S.A. by MKS Supply, Inc.
Price: 9mm (995TS) from **$286.00**
Price: .40 S&W (4095TS) from **$315.00**
Price: .45 ACP (4595TS) from **$319.00**

JP ENTERPRISES LRP-07
Caliber: .308 Win, .260 Rem., 6.5 Creedmoor, .338 Federal. **Barrel:** 16 to 22 inches, polished stainless with compensator. **Buttstock:** A2, ACE ARFX, Tactical Tactical Intent Carbine, Magpul MOE. **Grip:** Hogue Pistol Grip. **Features:** Machined upper and lower receivers with left-side charging system. MKIII Hand Guard. Adjustable gas system.
Price: From **$3,299.00**

JP ENTERPRISES JP-15
Caliber: .223, .204 Ruger, 6.5 Grendel, .300 Blackout, .22 LR. **Barrel:** 18 or 24-inches. **Buttstock:** Synthetic modified thumbhole or laminate thumb-hole. **Grip:** Hogue Pistol grip. Basic AR-type general-purpose rifle with numerous options.
Price: From **$1,999.00**

KEL-TEC RFB
Caliber: 7.62 NATO/.308. 20-round FAL-type magazine. **Barrel:** 18" with threaded muzzle, A2-style flash hider. **Weight:** 8 lbs. **Features:** A bullpup short-stroke gas piston operated carbine with ambidextrous controls, reversible operating handle, Mil-Spec Picatinny rail.
Price: **$1,927.00**

KEL-TEC SU-16 SERIES
Caliber: 5.56 NATO/.223. 10-round magazine capacity. **Barrel:** 16 or 18.5". **Weight:** 4.5 to 5 lbs. **Features:** Offering in several rifle and carbine variations.
Price: From **$682.00**

LARUE TACTICAL OBR
Caliber: 5.56 NATO/.223, 7.62 NATO/.308 Win. **Barrel:** 16.1, 18 or 20 inches. **Weight:** 7.5 to 9.25 lbs. **Features:** Manufacturer of several models of AR-style rifles and carbines. Optimized Battle Rifle (OBR) series is made in both NATO calibers. Many AR-type options available. Made in the U.S.A.
Price: OBR 5.56 ....**$2,245.00**
Price: OBR 7.62 ....**$3,370.00**

LEWIS MACHINE & TOOL (LMT)
Caliber: 5.56 NATO/.223, 7.62 NATO/.308 Win. **Barrel:** 16.1, 18 or 20 inches. **Weight:** 7.5 to 9.25 lbs. **Features:** Manufacturer of a wide

range of AR-style carbines with many options. SOPMOD stock, gas piston operating system, monolithic rail platform, tactical sights. Made in the U.S.A. by Lewis Machine & Tool.

Price: Standard 16 ....$1,594.00
Price: Comp 16, flattop receiver $1,685.00
Price: CQB Series from $2,100.00
Price: Sharpshooter Weapons System $5,198.00

LES BAER CUSTOM ULTIMATE AR 223
Caliber: .223. **Barrel:** 18", 20", 22", 24". **Weight:** 7.75 to 9.75 lb. **Length:** NA. **Stock:** Black synthetic. **Sights:** None furnished; Picatinny-style flattop rail for scope mounting. **Features:** Forged receiver; Ultra single-stage trigger (Jewell two-stage trigger optional); titanium firing pin; Versa-Pod bipod; chromed National Match carrier; stainless steel, hand-lapped and cryo-treated barrel; guaranteed to shoot 1/2 or 3/4 MOA, depending on model. Made in U.S.A. by Les Baer Custom Inc.

Price: Super Varmint Model.......................$2,640.00 to $2870.00
Price: Super Match Model ....$2,740.00 to $2960.00
Price: M4 Flattop model $2,590.00
Price: Police Special 16" (2008) $1,790.00
Price: IPSC Action Model $2,890.00
Price: LBC-AR (.264 LBC-AR) $2,640.00

LES BAER UTIMATE MATCH/SNIPER
Caliber: .308 Win. **Barrel:** 18 or 20 in. Magpul stock, Enforcer muzzlebrake.
Price: $3,940.00

LR 300S
Caliber: 5.56 NATO, 30-shot magazine. **Barrel:** 16.5"; 1:9" twist. **Weight:** 7.4-7.8 lbs. **Length:** NA. **Stock:** Folding. **Sights:** YHM flip front and rear. **Features:** Flattop receive, full length top picatinny rail. Phantom flash hider, multi sling mount points, field strips with no tools. Made in U.S.A. from Z-M Weapons.
Price: AXL, AXLT $2,139.00
Price: NXL $2,208.00

LWRC INTERNATIONAL M6 SERIES
Caliber: 5.56 NATO or 6.8 SPC, 30-shot magazine. REPR (Rapid Engagement Precision Rifle) chambered in 7.62 NATO/.308 Win. Barrel: 16.1 inches (16, 18, 20 inches, REPR). This company makes a complete line of AR-15 type rifles operated by a short-stroke, gas piston system. A wide variety of stock, sight and finishes are available. Colors include black, Flat Dark Earth, Olive Drab Green, Patriot Brown.
Price: M6A2 (shown)...$2,217.00
Price; M6-SPR (Special Purpose Rifle)...............................$2,479.00
Price: REPR (7.62 NATO) $3,600.00

MERKEL MODEL SR1 SEMI-AUTOMATIC
Caliber: .223, .308 Win., .30-06, .300 Win Mag., 7x64, 8x57IS, 9.3x62. **Features:** Streamlined profile, checkered walnut stock and fore-end, 19.7" (308) or 20.8" (300 SM) barrel, two- or five-shot detachable box magazine. Adjustable front and rear iron sights with Weaver-style optics rail included. Imported from Germany by Merkel USA.
Price: $1,995.00

OLYMPIC ARMS K9, K10, K40, K45 PISTOL-CALIBER AR15 CARBINES
Caliber: 9mm Para., 10mm, .40 S&W, .45 ACP; 32/10-shot modified magazines. **Barrel:** 16" button rifled stainless steel, 1x16" twist rate. **Weight:** 6.73 lbs. **Length:** 31.625" overall. **Stock:** A2 grip, M4 6-point collapsible stock. **Features:** A2 upper with adjustable rear sight, elevation adjustable front post, bayonet lug, sling swivel, threaded muzzle, flash suppressor, carbine length handguards. Made in U.S.A. by Olympic Arms, Inc.

Price: K9GL, 9mm Para., Glock lower..................................$1,157.00
Price: K10, 10mm, modified 10-round Uzi magazine............$1,006.20
Price: K40, .40 S&W, modified 10-round Uzi magazine $1,006.20
Price: K45, .45 ACP, modified 10-round Uzi magazine $1,006.20

OLYMPIC ARMS K3B SERIES AR15 CARBINES
Caliber: 5.56 NATO, 30-shot magazines. **Barrel:** 16" button rifled chrome-moly steel, 1x9" twist rate. **Weight:** 5-7 lbs. **Length:** 31.75" overall. **Stock:** A2 grip, M4 6-point collapsible buttstock. **Features:** A2 upper with adjustable rear sight, elevation adjustable front post, bayonet lug, sling swivel, threaded muzzle, flash suppressor, carbine-length handguards. Made in U.S.A. by Olympic Arms, Inc.

Price: K3B base model, A2 upper $815.00
Price: K3B-M4 M4 contoured barrel & handguards $1,103.70
Price: K3B-M4-A3-TC A3 upper, M4 barrel, FIRSH rail handguard $1,246.70
Price: K3B-CAR 11.5" barrel with 5.5" permanent flash suppressor..$1,033.50
Price: K3B-FAR 16" featherweight contoured barrel.............$1,071.20

OLYMPIC ARMS PLINKER PLUS AR15 MODELS

Caliber: 5.56 NATO, 30-shot magazine. **Barrel:** 16" or 20" button-rifled chrome-moly steel, 1x9" twist. **Weight:** 7.5-8.5 lbs. **Length:** 35.5"-39.5" overall. **Stock:** A2 grip, A2 buttstock with trapdoor. **Sights:** A1 windage rear, elevation-adjustable front post. **Features:** A1 upper, fiberlite handguards, bayonet lug, threaded muzzle and flash suppressor. Made in U.S.A. by Olympic Arms, Inc.
Price: Plinker Plus $727.00
Price: Plinker Plus 20 ....$908.00

OLYMPIC ARMS GAMESTALKER

Sporting AR-style rifle chambered in 5.56 NATO, 6.8 SPC, .243 WSSM, .25 WSSM, .300 WSSM or 7.62x39. Features include forged aluminum upper and lower; flat top receiver with Picatinny rail; gas block front sight; 22-inch stainless steel fluted barrel; free-floating slotted tube handguard; camo finish overall; ACE FX skeleton stock.
Price: $1,364.00

OLYMPIC ARMS ULTIMATE MAGNUM AR

Sporting AR-style rifle chambered in .22-250, .223 WSSM, .243 WSSM, .25 WSSM and .300 WSSM. **Weight:** 9.4 lbs. Features include forged aluminum upper and lower; flat top gas block receiver with Picatinny rail; 24-inch heavy match-grade bull barrel; free-floating slotted-tube handguard; camo finish overall.
Price: $1,359.00

REMINGTON MODEL R-15 MODULAR REPEATING

Caliber: .204 Ruger, .223 and .30 Rem. AR, five-shot magazine. **Barrel:** 18" (carbine), 22", 24". **Weight:** 6.75 to 7.75 lbs. **Length:** 36.25" to 42.25". **Stock:** Camo. **Features:** AR-style with optics rail, aluminum alloy upper and lower.
Price: R-15 Hunter: .30 Rem. AR, 22" barrel, Realtree AP HD
camo $1,327.00
Price: R-15 VTR SS Varmint, 24" stainless steel barrel $1,529.00
Price: R-14 Hunter .450 Bushmaster....................................$1,631.00

REMINGTON MODEL R-25 MODULAR REPEATING

Caliber: .243, 7mm-08, .308 Win., four-shot magazine. **Barrel:** 20" chrome-moly. **Weight:** 7.75 lbs. **Length:** 38.25" overall. **Features:** AR-style semiauto with single-stage trigger, aluminum alloy upper and lower, Mossy Oak Treestand camo finish overall.
Price: $1,697.00

REMINGTON MODEL 750 WOODSMASTER

Caliber: .243 Win., .270 Win., .308 Win., .30-06 Spfl., 4-shot magazine. **Barrel:** 22" round tapered, 18.5" (carbine version). **Weight:** 7.2 to 7.5 lbs. **Length:** 42.6" overall. **Stock:** Restyled American walnut fore-end and stock with machine-cut checkering. Satin finish. **Sights:** Gold bead front sight on ramp; step rear sight with windage adjustable. **Features:** Gas-operated action, SuperCell recoil pad. Positive cross-bolt safety. Receiver tapped for scope mount. Introduced 2006. The latest variation of the classic semiauto Remington 740 of 1955. Made in U.S.A. by Remington Arms Co.
Price: 750 Woodsmaster $1,024.00
Price: 750 Woodsmaster Carbine (18.5" bbl.) $902.00

ROCK RIVER ARMS LAR SERIES

Caliber: .223/5.56, .308/7.62, 6.8 SPC, .458 SOCOM, 9mm and .40 S&W. These AR-15 type rifles and carbines are available with a very wide range of options. Virtually any AR configuration is offered including tactical, hunting and competition models. Some models are available in left-hand versions.
Price: .... $1,010.00 to $1,600.00

RUGER AR-556

Caliber: 5.56 NATO. Basic AR M4-style Modern Sporting Rifle with direct impingement operation, forged aluminum upper and lower receivers, and cold hammer-forged chrome-moly steel barrel with M4 feed ramp cuts. Other features include Ruger Rapid Deploy folding rear sight, milled F-height gas block with post front sight, telescoping 6-postion stock and one 30-round Magpul magazine. Introduced in 2015.
Price: $759.00

RUGER SR-556

AR-style semiauto rifle chambered in 5.56 NATO. Feature include two-stage piston; quad rail handguard; Troy Industries sights; black synthetic fixed or telescoping buttstock; 16.12-inch 1:9" twist steel barrel with birdcage; 10- or 30-round detachable box magazine; black matte finish overall.

Price: $2,049.00
Price: SR-762 ....$2,269.00

RUGER MINI-14

Caliber: .223 Rem., 5-shot or 20-shot detachable box magazine. Tactical Rifle is also available in .300 AAC Blackout. **Barrel:** 18.5". Rifling twist 1:9". **Weight:** 6.75 to 7 lbs. **Length:** 37.25" overall. **Stock:** American hardwood, steel reinforced, or synthetic. **Sights:** Protected blade front, fully adjustable Ghost Ring rear. **Features:** Fixed piston gas-operated, positive primary extraction. New buffer system, redesigned ejector system. Ruger S100RM scope rings included on Ranch Rifle. Heavier barrels added in 2008, 20-round magazine added in 2009.
Price: Mini-14/5, Ranch Rifle, blued, wood stock **$939.00 to $990.00**
Price: K-Mini-14/5, Ranch Rifle, stainless, scope rings $999.00
Price: Mini-14 Target Rifle: laminated thumbhole stock,
heavy crowned 22" stainless steel barrel, other
refinements $1,199.00
Price: Mini-14 ATI Stock: Tactical version of Mini-14 but with
six-position collapsible stock or folding stock, grooved
pistol grip. Multiple picatinny optics/accessory rails . $1,019.00
Price: Mini-14 Tactical Rifle: Similar to Mini-14 but with 16.12"
barrel with flash hider, black synthetic stock, adjustable
sights $1,019.00

RUGER MINI THIRTY
Similar to the Mini-14 rifle except modified to chamber the 7.62x39 Russian service round. **Weight:** 6.75 lbs. Has 6-groove barrel with 1:10" twist, Ruger Integral Scope Mount bases and protected blade front, fully adjustable Ghost Ring rear. Detachable 5-shot staggered box magazine. 20-round magazines available. Stainless or matte black alloy w/synthetic stock. Introduced 1987.
Price: Matte black finish $999.00
Price: Stainless $1,075.00

SIG-SAUER SIG516 GAS PISTON
AR-style rifle chambered in 5.56 NATO. Features include 14.5-, 16-, 18- or 20-inch chrome-lined barrel; free-floating, aluminum quad rail fore-end with four M1913 Picatinny rails; threaded muzzle with a standard (0.5x28TPI) pattern; aluminum upper and lower receiver is machined; black anodized finish; 30-round magazine; flattop upper; various configurations available.
Price: .... $1,719.00 to $2,371.00

SIG SAUER M400 VARMINTER/PREDATOR SERIES
Caliber: .223/5.56 NATO. AR Flattop design. **Barrel:** 18 or 22-inch heavy stainless match grade with Hogue free-floated fore-end. **Features:** Two-stage Geissele match trigger, Hogue grip, ambidextrous controls, Magpul MOE stock.
Price: Predator...$1,384.00
Price: Varminter $1,395.00

SIG-SAUER SIG716 TACTICAL PATROL
AR-10 type rifle chambered in 7.62 NATO/.308 Winchester. Features include gas-piston operation with 3-round-position (4-position optional) gas valve; 16-, 18- or 20-inch chrome-lined barrel with threaded muzzle and nitride finish; free-floating aluminum quad rail fore-end with four M1913 Picatinny rails; telescoping buttstock; lower receiver is machined from a 7075-T6 Aircraft grade aluminum forging; upper receiver, machined from 7075-T6 aircraft grade aluminum with integral M1913 Picatinny rail.
Price: .... $2,066.00 to $2,970.00

SMITH & WESSON M&P15
Caliber: 5.56mm NATO/.223, 30-shot steel magazine. **Barrel:** 16", 1:9" twist. **Weight:** 6.74 lbs., w/o magazine. **Length:** 32-35" overall. **Stock:** Black synthetic. **Sights:** Adjustable post front sight, adjustable dual aperture rear sight. **Features:** 6-position telescopic stock, thermo-set M4 handguard. 14.75" sight radius. 7-lbs. (approx.) trigger pull. 7075 T6 aluminum upper, 4140 steel barrel. Chromed barrel bore, gas key, bolt carrier. Hard-coat black-anodized receiver and barrel finish. OR (Optics Ready) model has no sights. TS model has Magpul stock and folding sights. Made in U.S.A. by Smith & Wesson.
Price: Sport Model..$739.00
Price: OR Model $1,069.00
Price: TS model $1,569.00

SMITH & WESSON M&P15-300
Caliber: .300 Whisper/.300 AAC Blackout. Other specifications the same of 5.56 models.
Price: $1,119.00

SMITH & WESSON MODEL M&P15 VTAC
Caliber: .223 Remington/5.56 NATO, 30-round magazine. **Barrel:** 16". **Weight:** 6.5 lbs. **Length:** 35" extended, 32" collapsed, overall. **Features:** Six-position CAR stock. Surefire flash-hider and G2 light

with VTAC light mount; VTAC/JP handguard; JP single-stage match trigger and speed hammer; three adjustable picatinny rails; VTAC padded two-point adjustable sling.
Price: $1,949.00

SMITH & WESSON M&P15PC CAMO
Caliber: 223 Rem/5.56 NATO, A2 configuration, 10-round mag. **Barrel:** 20" stainless with 1:8" twist. **Weight:** 8.2 lbs. **Length:** 38.5" overall. **Features:** AR-style, no sights but integral front and rear optics rails. Two-stage trigger, aluminum lower. Finished in Realtree Advantage Max-1 camo.
Price: $1,589.00

SMITH & WESSON M&P10
Caliber: .308 Win. **Capacity:** 10 rounds. **Barrel:** 18 inches. **Weight:** 7.7 pounds. **Features:** 6-position CAR stock, black hard anodized finish. Camo finish hunting model available w/5-round magazine.
Price: $1,619.00
Price: (Camo) $1,729.00

SPRINGFIELD ARMORY M1A
Caliber: 7.62mm NATO (.308), 5- or 10-shot box magazine. **Barrel:** 25-1/16" with flash suppressor, 22" without suppressor. **Weight:** 9.75 lbs. **Length:** 44.25" overall. **Stock:** American walnut with walnut-colored heat-resistant fiberglass handguard. Matching walnut handguard available. Also available with fiberglass stock. **Sights:** Military, square blade front, full click-adjustable aperture rear. **Features:** Commercial equivalent of the U.S. M-14 service rifle with no provision for automatic firing. From Springfield Armory
Price: SOCOM 16 ....$1,893.00
Price: SOCOM II, from..$2,399.00
Price: Scout Squad, from $1,761.00
Price: Standard M1A, from $1,640.00
Price: Loaded Standard, from $1,794.00
Price: National Match, from $2,318.00
Price: Super Match (heavy premium barrel) about $2,905.00
Price: Tactical, from $3,780.00

STAG ARMS AR-STYLE SERIES
Caliber: 5.56 NATO/.223, 6.8 SPC, 9mm Parabellum. Ten, 20 or 30-shot magazine capacity. This manufacturer offers more than 25 AR-style rifles or carbines with many optional features including barrel length and configurations, stocks, sights, rail systems and both direct impingement and gas piston operating systems. Left-hand models are available on some products. Listed is a sampling of Stag Arms models.
Price: Model 1 .... $949.00
Price: Model 2T Carbine (Tactical).........................$1,130.00
Price: Model 3 Carbine (shown)................................$895.00
Price: Model 3G Rifle...$1,459.00
Price: Model 5 Carbine (6.8) $1,045.00
Price: Stag 7 Hunter (6.8)..$1,055.00
Price: Model 9 (9mm)..$990.00

STONER SR-15 M-5
Caliber: .223. **Barrel:** 20". **Weight:** 7.6 lbs. **Length:** 38" overall. **Stock:** Black synthetic. **Sights:** Post front, fully adjustable rear (300-meter sight). **Features:** Modular weapon system; two-stage trigger. Black finish. Introduced 1998. Made in U.S.A. by Knight's Mfg.
Price: $2,207.00

STONER SR-25 CARBINE
Caliber: 7.62 NATO, 10-shot steel magazine. **Barrel:** 16" free-floating. **Weight:** 7.75 lbs. **Length:** 35.75" overall. **Stock:** Black synthetic.

Prices given are believed to be accurate at time of publication however, many factors affect retail pricing so exact prices are not possible.

Sights: Integral Weaver-style rail. Scope rings, iron sights optional.
Features: Shortened, nonslip handguard; removable carrying handle. Matte black finish. Introduced 1995. Made in U.S.A. by Knight's Mfg. Co.
Price: **$3,597.00**

STONER SR-30
Caliber: .300 Blackout. **Barrel:** 16" **Weight:** 7.75 lbs. **Features:** QDC flash suppressor, micro front and rear iron sights, ambidextrous controls, fully adjustable stock.
Price: **$2,723.00**

TAURUS CT G2 CARBINE
Caliber: .40 S&W, 9 mm and .45 ACP. Capacity is 10 rounds. **Barrel:** 16". **Weight:** 6.6 lbs. **Length:** 36" overall. **Stock:** Aluminum & Polymer. **Sights:** Adjustable rear sight and fixed front sight. **Features:** Full length Picatinny rail, ambidextrous slide catch, two-position safety. Made in U.S.A. by Knight's Mfg. Co.
Price: **$879.00**

WILSON COMBAT TACTICAL
Caliber: 5.56mm NATO, accepts all M-16/AR-15 Style Magazines, includes one 20-round magazine. **Barrel:** 16.25", 1:9" twist, match-grade fluted. **Weight:** 6.9 lbs. **Length:** 36.25" overall. **Stock:** Fixed or collapsible. **Features:** Free-float ventilated aluminum quad-rail handguard, Mil-Spec parkerized barrel and steel components, anodized receiver, precision CNC-machined upper and lower receivers, 7075 T6 aluminum forgings. Single stage JP Trigger/ Hammer Group, Wilson Combat Tactical Muzzle Brake, nylon tactical rifle case. M-4T version has flat-top receiver for mounting optics, OD green furniture, 16.25" match-grade M-4 style barrel. SS-15 Super Sniper Tactical Rifle has 1-in-8 twist, heavy 20" match-grade fluted stainless steel barrel. Made in U.S.A by Wilson Combat.
Price: .... **$2,225.00 to $2,450.00**

Prices given are believed to be accurate at time of publication however, many factors affect retail pricing so exact prices are not possible.

70TH EDITION, 2016 ⊕ **457**

BIG HORN ARMORY MODEL 89 RIFLE AND CARBINE

Lever action rifle or carbine chambered for .500 S&W Magnum. Features include 22-or 18-inch barrel; walnut or maple stocks with pistol grip; aperture rear and blade front sights; recoil pad; sling swivels; enlarged lever loop; magazine capacity 5 (rifle) or 7 (carbine) rounds.

Price: **$2,424.00**

BROWNING BLR

Action: Lever action with rotating bolt head, multiple-lug breech bolt with recessed bolt face, side ejection. Rack-and-pinion lever. Flush-mounted detachable magazines, with 4+1 capacity for magnum cartridges, 5+1 for standard rounds. **Barrel:** Button-rifled chrome-moly steel with crowned muzzle. **Stock:** Buttstocks and forends are American walnut with grip and forend checkering. Recoil pad installed. **Trigger:** Wide-groove design, trigger travels with lever. Half-cock hammer safety; fold-down hammer. **Sights:** Gold bead on ramp front; low-profile square-notch adjustable rear. **Features:** Blued barrel and receiver, high-gloss wood finish. Receivers are drilled and tapped for scope mounts, swivel studs included. Action lock provided. Introduced 1996. Imported from Japan by Browning.

BROWNING BLR LIGHTWEIGHT W/PISTOL GRIP, SHORT AND LONG ACTION; LIGHTWEIGHT '81, SHORT AND LONG ACTION

Calibers: Short Action, 20" Barrel: .22-250 Rem., .243 Win., 7mm-08 Rem., .308 Win., .358, .450 Marlin. Calibers: Short Action, 22" Barrel: .270 WSM, 7mm WSM, .300 WSM, .325 WSM. Calibers: Long Action 22" Barrel: .270 Win., .30-06. Calibers: Long Action 24" Barrel: 7mm Rem. Mag., .300 Win. Mag. **Weight:** 6.5-7.75 lbs. **Length:** 40-45" overall. **Stock:** New checkered pistol grip and Schnabel forearm. Lightweight '81 differs from Pistol Grip models with a Western-style straight grip stock and banded forearm. Lightweight w/Pistol Grip Short Action and Long Action introduced 2005. Model '81 Lightning Long Action introduced 1996.

Price: Lightweight w/Pistol Grip Short Action, from **$1,020.00**
Price: Lightweight w/Pistol Grip Long Action **$1,100.00**
Price: Lightweight '81 Short Action **$960.00**
Price: Lightweight '81 Long Action **$1,040.00**
Price: Lightweight '81 Takedown Short Action, from **$1,040.00**
Price: Lightweight '81 Takedown Long Action, from **$1,120.00**
Price: Lightweight stainless .... **$1,100.00 to $1,180.00**
Price: Stainless Takedown .... **$1,230.00 to $1,300.00**
Price: Gold Medallion w/nickel finish,
engraving .... **$1,470.00 to $1,550.00**

CHIAPPA MODEL 1892 RIFLE

Caliber: .38 Spec./357 Mag., .38-40, .44-40, .44 Mag., .45 Colt. **Barrel:** 16" (Trapper), 20" round and 24" octagonal (Takedown). **Weight:** 7.7 lbs. **Stock:** Walnut. **Sights:** Blade front, buckhorn. Trapper model has interchangeable front sight blades. **Features:** Finishes are blue/case colored. Magazine capacity is 12 rounds with 24" bbl.; 10 rounds with 20" barrel; 9 rounds in 16" barrel.

Price: **$1,053.00**
Price: Takedown **$1,299.00**
Price: Trapper **$1,169.00**

CIMARRON 1860 HENRY CIVIL WAR MODEL

Caliber: .44 WCF, .45 LC; 12-shot magazine. **Barrel:** 24" (rifle). **Weight:** 9.5 lbs. **Length:** 43" overall (rifle). **Stock:** European walnut. **Sights:** Bead front, open adjustable rear. **Features:** Brass receiver and buttplate. Uses original Henry loading system. Copy of the original rifle. Charcoal blue finish optional. Introduced 1991. Imported by Cimarron F.A. Co.

Price: From **$1,579.78**

CIMARRON 1866 WINCHESTER REPLICAS

Caliber: .38 Spec., .357, .45 LC, .32 WCF, .38 WCF, .44 WCF. **Barrel:** 24" (rifle), 20" (short rifle), 19" (carbine), 16" (trapper). **Weight:** 9 lbs. **Length:** 43" overall (rifle). **Stock:** European walnut. **Sights:** Bead front, open adjustable rear. **Features:** Solid brass receiver, buttplate,

fore-end cap. Octagonal barrel. Copy of the original Winchester '66 rifle. Introduced 1991. Imported by Cimarron F.A. Co.
Price: 1866 Sporting Rifle, 24" barrel, from **$1,177.00**
Price: 1866 Short Rifle, 20" barrel, from **$1,177.00**
Price: 1866 Carbine, 19" barrel, from **$1,190.00**
Price: 1866 Trapper, 16" barrel, from **$1,104.00**

CIMARRON 1873 SHORT

Caliber: .357 Mag., .38 Spec., .32 WCF, .38 WCF, .44 Spec., .44 WCF, .45 Colt. **Barrel:** 20" tapered octagon. **Weight:** 7.5 lbs. **Length:** 39" overall. **Stock:** Walnut. **Sights:** Bead front, adjustable semi-buckhorn rear. **Features:** Has half "button" magazine. Original-type markings, including caliber, on barrel and elevator and "Kings" patent. From Cimarron F.A. Co.
Price: **$1,272.00**

CIMARRON 1873 DELUXE SPORTING

Similar to the 1873 Short Rifle except has 24" barrel with half-magazine.
Price: **$1,378.00**

CIMARRON 1873 LONG RANGE

Caliber: .44 WCF, .45 Colt. **Barrel:** 30", octagonal. **Weight:** 8.5 lbs. **Length:** 48" overall. **Stock:** Walnut. **Sights:** Blade front, semi-buckhorn ramp rear. Tang sight optional. **Features:** Color case-hardened frame; choice of modern blue-black or charcoal blue for other parts. Barrel marked "Kings Improvement." From Cimarron F.A. Co.
Price: **$1,325.10**

EMF 1866 YELLOWBOY LEVER ACTIONS

Caliber: .38 Spec., .44-40, .45 LC. **Barrel:** 19" (carbine), 24" (rifle). **Weight:** 9 lbs. **Length:** 43" overall (rifle). **Stock:** European walnut. **Sights:** Bead front, open adjustable rear. **Features:** Solid brass frame, blued barrel, lever, hammer, buttplate. Imported from Italy by EMF.
Price: Rifle..**$1,175.00**

EMF MODEL 1873 LEVER-ACTION

Caliber: .32/20, .357 Mag., .38/40, .44-40, .45 Colt. **Barrel:** 18", 20", 24", 30". **Weight:** 8 lbs. **Length:** 43.25" overall. **Stock:** European walnut. **Sights:** Bead front, rear adjustable for windage and elevation. **Features:** Color case-hardened frame (blue on carbine). Imported by EMF.
Price: **$1,250.00**

HENRY ORIGINAL RIFLE

Caliber: .44-40 (13-round magazine). **Barrel:** 24". **Weight:** 9 lbs. **Stock:** Straight-grip fancy American walnut with hardened brass buttplate. **Sights:** Folding ladder rear with blade front. **Finish:** Hardened brass receiver with blued steel barrel. **Features:** Virtually identical to the original 1860 version except for the caliber. Each serial number has prefix "BTH" in honor of Benjamin Tyler Henry, the inventor of the lever-action repeating rifle that went on to become the most legendary firearm in American history. Introduced in 2014 by Henry Repeating Arms. Made in the U.S.A.
Price: **$2,300.00**

HENRY .45-70

Caliber: .45-70 (4-shot magazine). **Barrel:** 18.5". **Weight:** 7 lbs. **Stock:** Pistol grip walnut. **Sights:** XS Ghost Rings with blade front.
Price: **$850.00**

Prices given are believed to be accurate at time of publication however, many factors affect retail pricing so exact prices are not possible.

HENRY BIG BOY LEVER-ACTION CARBINE

Caliber: .44 Magnum, standard model; .357 Magnum, .45 Colt, Deluxe II only. 10-shot tubular magazine. **Barrel:** 20" octagonal, 1:38" right-hand twist. **Weight:** 8.68 lbs. **Length:** 38.5" overall. **Stock:** Straight-grip American walnut, brass buttplate. **Sights:** Marbles full adjustable semi-buckhorn rear, brass bead front. **Features:** Brasslite receiver not tapped for scope mount. Made in U.S.A. by Henry Repeating Arms.

Price: .44 Magnum, walnut, blued barrel **$899.95**
Price: Deluxe II .45 Colt, .357 Mag., engraved receiver **$1,995.95**

HENRY .30/30 LEVER-ACTION CARBINE

Same as the Big Boy except has straight grip American walnut, .30-30 only, 6-shot. Receivers are drilled and tapped for scope mount. Made in U.S.A. by Henry Repeating Arms.

Price: H009 Blued receiver, round barrel **$749.95**
Price: H009B Brass receiver, octagonal barrel **$949.95**

MARLIN MODEL 336C LEVER-ACTION CARBINE

Caliber: .30-30 or .35 Rem., 6-shot tubular magazine. **Barrel:** 20" Micro-Groove. **Weight:** 7 lbs. **Length:** 38.5" overall. **Stock:** Checkered American black walnut, capped pistol grip. Mar-Shield finish; rubber buttpad; swivel studs. **Sights:** Ramp front with Wide-Scan hood, semi-buckhorn folding rear adjustable for windage and elevation. **Features:** Hammer-block safety. Receiver tapped for scope mount, offset hammer spur; top of receiver sandblasted to prevent glare. Includes safety lock. The latest variation of Marlin's classic lever gun that originated in 1937.

Price: **$610.00**

MARLIN MODEL 336SS LEVER-ACTION CARBINE

Same as the 336C except receiver, barrel and other major parts are machined from stainless steel. .30-30 only, 6-shot; receiver tapped for scope. Includes safety lock.

Price: **$749.00**

MARLIN MODEL 336W LEVER-ACTION

Similar to the Model 336C except has walnut-finished, cut-checkered Maine birch stock; blued steel barrel band has integral sling swivel; no front sight hood; comes with padded nylon sling; hard rubber butplate. Introduced 1998. Includes safety lock. Made in U.S.A. by Marlin.

Price: **$515.00**

MARLIN 336BL

Lever action rifle chambered for .30-30. Features include 6-shot full length tubular magazine; 18-inch blued barrel with Micro-Groove rifling (12 grooves); big-loop finger lever; side ejection; blued steel receiver; hammer block safety; brown laminated hardwood pistol-grip stock with fluted comb; cut checkering; deluxe recoil pad; blued swivel studs.

Price: **$641.00**

MARLIN MODEL XLR LEVER-ACTION RIFLES

Similar to Model 336C except has an 24" stainless barrel with Ballard-type cut rifling, stainless steel receiver and other parts, laminated hardwood stock with pistol grip, nickel-plated swivel studs. Chambered for .30-30 Win. with Hornady spire-pointed Flex-Tip cartridges. Includes safety lock. Introduced 2006.

Price: Model 336XLR **$932.00**

MARLIN MODEL .308 MX, .338 MX

Caliber: .308 Marlin Express or .338 Marlin Express. **Barrel:** 24" stainless steel. **Weight:** 7.5 lbs. **Length:** 42.5" overall. **Features:** Stainless steel receiver, lever and magazine tube. American black walnut stock and fore-end. .338 MXLR model has black/gray

laminated checkered stock and fore-end. Hooded ramp front sight and adjustable semibuckhorn rear; drilled and tapped for scope mounts. Receiver-mounted crossbolt safety.

Price: .338 MXLR **$905.00**
Price: .308 or .338 MX **$686.00**

MARLIN MODEL 1894

Caliber: .44 Spec./.44 Mag., 10-shot tubular magazine. **Barrel:** 20" Ballard-type rifling. **Weight:** 6 lbs. **Length:** 37.5" overall. **Stock:** Checkered American black walnut, straight grip and forend. Mar-Shield finish. Rubber rifle buttpad; swivel studs. **Sights:** Wide-Scan hooded ramp front, semibuckhorn folding rear adjustable for windage and elevation. **Features:** Hammer-block safety. Receiver tapped for scope mount, offset hammer spur, solid top receiver sand blasted to prevent glare. Includes safety lock.

Price: **$730.00**

MARLIN MODEL 1894C CARBINE

Similar to the standard Model 1894 except chambered for .38 Spec./.357 Mag. with full-length 9-shot magazine, 18.5" barrel, hammer-block safety, hooded front sight. Introduced 1983. Includes safety lock.

Price: **$730.00**

MARLIN MODEL 1894 COWBOY

Caliber: .357 Mag., .44 Mag., .45 Colt, 10-shot magazine. **Barrel:** 20" tapered octagon, deep cut rifling. **Weight:** 7.5 lbs. **Length:** 41.5" overall. **Stock:** Straight grip American black walnut, hard rubber buttplate, Mar-Shield finish. **Sights:** Marble carbine front, adjustable Marble semibuckhorn rear. **Features:** Squared finger lever; straight grip stock; blued steel fore-end tip. Designed for Cowboy Shooting events. Introduced 1996. Includes safety lock. Made in U.S.A. by Marlin.

Price: **$1,040.00**

MARLIN MODEL 1894SS

Similar to Model 1894 except has stainless steel barrel, receiver, lever, guard plate, magazine tube and loading plate. Nickel-plated swivel studs.

Price: **$829.00**

MARLIN 1894 DELUXE

Lever action rifle chambered in .44 Magnum/.44 Special. Features include 10-shot tubular magazine; squared finger lever; side ejection; richly polished deep blued metal surfaces; solid top receiver; hammer block safety; #1 grade fancy American black walnut straight-grip stock and forend; cut checkering; rubber rifle buttpad; Mar-Shield finish; blued steel fore-end cap: swivel studs; deep-cut Ballard-type rifling (6 grooves).

Price: **$950.00**

MARLIN 1894CSS

Lever action rifle chambered in .357 Magnum/.38 Special. Features include 9-shot tubular magazine; stainless steel receiver, barrel, lever, trigger and hammer; squared finger lever; side ejection; solid top receiver; hammer block safety; American black walnut straight-grip stock and fore-end; cut checkering; rubber rifle buttpad; Mar-Shield finish.

Price: **$829.00**

MARLIN MODEL 1895 LEVER-ACTION

Caliber: .45-70 Govt., 4-shot tubular magazine. **Barrel:** 22", round.

Prices given are believed to be accurate at time of publication however, many factors affect retail pricing so exact prices are not possible.

70TH EDITION, 2016 ◆ **459**

Weight: 7.5 lbs. **Length:** 40.5" overall. **Stock:** Checkered American black walnut, full pistol grip. Mar-Shield finish; rubber buttpad; quick detachable swivel studs. **Sights:** Bead front with Wide-Scan hood, semibuckhorn folding rear adjustable for windage and elevation. **Features:** Hammer-block safety. Solid receiver tapped for scope mounts or receiver sights; offset hammer spur. Includes safety lock.
Price: $696.00

MARLIN MODEL 1895G GUIDE GUN LEVER-ACTION
Similar to Model 1895 with deep-cut Ballard-type rifling; straight-grip walnut stock. Overall length is 37", weighs 7 lbs. Introduced 1998. Includes safety lock. Made in U.S.A. by Marlin.
Price: $701.00

MARLIN MODEL 1895GS GUIDE GUN
Similar to Model 1895G except receiver, barrel and most metal parts are machined from stainless steel. Chambered for .45-70 Govt., 4-shot, 18.5" barrel. Overall length is 37", weighs 7 lbs. Introduced 2001. Includes safety lock. Made in U.S.A. by Marlin.
Price: $837.00

MARLIN MODEL 1895 SBLR
Similar to Model 1895GS Guide Gun but with stainless steel barrel (18.5"), receiver, large loop lever and magazine tube. Black/gray laminated buttstock and forend, XS ghost ring rear sight, hooded ramp front sight, receiver/barrel-mounted top rail for mounting accessory optics. Chambered in .45-70 Government. Overall length is 42.5", weighs 7.5 lbs.
Price: $1,070.00

MARLIN MODEL 1895 COWBOY LEVER-ACTION
Similar to Model 1895 except has 26" tapered octagon barrel with Ballard-type rifling, Marble carbine front sight and Marble adjustable semi-buckhorn rear sight. Receiver tapped for scope or receiver sight. Overall length is 44.5", weighs about 8 lbs. Introduced 2001. Includes safety lock. Made in U.S.A. by Marlin.
Price: $840.00

MARLIN 1895GBL
Lever action rifle chambered in .45-70 Government. Features include 6-shot, full-length tubular magazine; 18-1/2-inch barrel with deep-cut Ballard-type rifling (6 grooves); big-loop finger lever; side ejection; solid-top receiver; deeply blued metal surfaces; hammer block safety; pistol-grip two-tone brown laminate stock with cut checkering; ventilated recoil pad; Mar-Shield finish, swivel studs.
Price: $734.00

MOSSBERG 464 LEVER ACTION
Caliber: .30-30 Win., 6-shot tubular magazine. **Barrel:** 20" round. **Weight:** 6.7 lbs. **Length:** 38.5" overall. **Stock:** Hardwood with straight or pistol grip, quick detachable swivel studs. **Sights:** Folding rear sight, adjustable for windage and elevation. **Features:** Blued receiver and barrel, receiver drilled and tapped, two-position top-tang safety. Available with straight grip or semi-pistol grip. Introduced 2008. From O.F. Mossberg & Sons, Inc.
Price: $530.00
Price: SPX Model w/tactical stock and features $569.00

NAVY ARMS 1873 RIFLE
Caliber: .357 Mag., .45 Colt, 12-shot magazine. **Barrel:** 20", 24.25", full octagonal. **Stock:** Deluxe checkered American walnut. **Sights:** Gold bead front, semi-buckhorn rear. **Features:** Turnbull color case-hardened frame, rest blued. Full-octagon barrel. Available exclusively from Navy Arms.

REMINGTON MODEL 7600 PUMP ACTION
Caliber: .243 Win., .270 Win., .30-06 Spfl., .308. **Barrel:** 22" round tapered. **Weight:** 7.5 lbs. **Length:** 42.6" overall. **Stock:** Cut-checkered walnut pistol grip and fore-end, Monte Carlo with full cheekpiece. Satin or high-gloss finish. Also, black synthetic. **Sights:** Gold bead front sight on matted ramp, open step adjustable sporting rear. **Features:** Redesigned and improved version of the Model 760. Detachable 4-shot magazine. Crossbolt safety. Receiver tapped for scope mount. Introduced 1981.
Price:7600 Wood $918.00
Price:7600 Synthetic..$771.00

ROSSI R92 LEVER-ACTION CARBINE
Caliber: .38 Special/.357 Mag, .44 Mag., .44-40 Win., .45 Colt, .454 Casull. **Barrel:** 16" or 20" with round barrel, 20" or 24" with octagon barrel. **Weight:** 4.8 lbs. to 7 lbs. **Length:** 34 to 41.5 inches. **Features:** Blued or stainless finish. Various options available in selected chamberings (large lever loop, fiber-optic sights, cheekpiece, etc.).
Price: Blued $624.00
Price: Stainless $650.00
Price: .454 Casull $754.00

ROSSI RIO GRANDE
Caliber: .30-30 or .45-70 or .410 shotshell. **Barrel:** 20". **Weight:** 7 lbs. **Sights:** Adjustable rear, post front. **Stock:** Hardwood or camo.
Price: $643.00

UBERTI 1873 SPORTING RIFLE
Caliber: .357 Mag., .44-40, .45 Colt. **Barrel:** 16.1" round, 19" round or 20", 24.25" octagonal. **Weight:** Up to 8.2 lbs. **Length:** Up to 43.3" overall. **Stock:** Walnut, straight grip and pistol grip. **Sights:** Blade front adjustable for windage, open rear adjustable for elevation. **Features:** Color case-hardened frame, blued barrel, hammer, lever, buttplate, brass elevator. Imported by Stoeger Industries.
Price: Carbine 19" bbl. $1,219.00
Price: Trapper 16.1" bbl. $1,259.00
Price: Carbine 18" half oct. bbl. $1,309.00
Price: Short Rifle 20" bbl. $1,259.00
Price: Sporting Rifle, 24.25" bbl. $1,259.00
Price: Special Sporting Rifle, A-grade walnut $1,399.00

UBERTI 1866 YELLOWBOY CARBINE, SHORT, RIFLE
Caliber: .38 Spec., .44-40, .45 Colt. **Barrel:** 24.25", octagonal. **Weight:**

CENTERFIRE RIFLES Lever & Slide

8.2 lbs. **Length:** 43.25" overall. **Stock:** Walnut. **Sights:** Blade front adjustable for windage, rear adjustable for elevation. **Features:** Frame, buttplate, fore-end cap of polished brass, balance charcoal blued. Imported by Stoeger Industries.
Price: 1866 Yellowboy Carbine, 19" round barrel **$1,119.00**
Price: 1866 Yellowboy Short Rifle, 20" octagonal barrel **$1,169.00**
Price: 1866 Yellowboy Rifle, 24.25" octagonal barrel **$1,169.00**

UBERTI 1860 HENRY
Caliber: .44-40, .45 Colt. **Barrel:** 24.25", half-octagon. **Weight:** 9.2 lbs. **Length:** 43.75" overall. **Stock:** American walnut. **Sights:** Blade front, rear adjustable for elevation. Imported by Stoeger Industries.
Price: 1860 Henry Trapper, 18.5" barrel, brass frame............**$1,429.00**
Price: 1860 Henry Rifle Iron Frame, 24.25" barrel **$1,459.00**

UBERTI LIGHTNING
Caliber: .357 Mag., .45 Colt, 10+1. Slide action operation. **Barrel:** 20" to 24.25". **Stock:** Satin-finished walnut. **Finish:** Case-hardened. Introduced 2006. Imported by Stoeger Industries.
Price: **$1,259.00**

WINCHESTER MODEL 94 SHORT RIFLE
Caliber: .30-30, .38-55. **Barrel:** 20". **Weight:** 6.75 lbs. **Sights:** Semi-buckhorn rear, gold bead front. **Stock:** Walnut with straight grip. Fore-end has black grip cap. Also available in Trail's End takedown design in .450 Marlin or .30-30.
Price: **$1,230.00**
Price: (Takedown)..**$1,460.00**

WINCHESTER MODEL 94 CARBINE
Same general specifications as M94 Short Rifle except for curved buttplate and fore-end barrelband.
Price: **$1,200.00**

WINCHESTER MODEL 94 SPORTER
Caliber: .30-30, .38-55. **Barrel:** 24". **Weight:** 7.5 lbs. **Features:**

Same features of Model 94 Short Rifle except for crescent butt and steel buttplate, 24" half-round, half-octagon barrel, checkered stock.
Price: **$1,400.00**

WINCHESTER 1873 SHORT RIFLE
Caliber: .357 Magnum, .44-40, .45 Colt. Tubular magazine holds 10 rounds (.44-40, .45 Colt), 11 rounds (.38 Special). **Barrel:** 20 inches. **Weight:** 7.25 lbs. **Sights:** Marble semi-buckhorn rear, gold bead front. Tang is drilled and tapped for optional peep sight. **Stock:** Satin finished, straight-grip walnut with steel crescent buttplate and steel fore-end cap. Tang safety. A modern version of the "Gun That Won the West."
Price: **$1,300.00**

WINCHESTER MODEL 1886 SHORT RIFLE
Caliber: .45-70 or .49-90. **Barrel:** 24". **Weight:** 8.4 lbs. **Sights:** Adjustable buckhorn rear, blade front. **Stock:** Grade 1 walnut with crescent butt.
Price **$1,340.00**

WINCHESTER MODEL 1892 CARBINE
Caliber: .357 Mag., .44 Mag., .44-40, .45 Colt. **Barrel:** 20 inches. **Weight:** 6 lbs. **Stock:** Satin finished walnut with straight grip, steel fore-end strap. **Sights:** Marble semi-buckhorn rear, gold bead front. Other features include saddle ring and tang safety. Available with large loop lever.
Price: Large loop lever.......................................**$1,260.00**
Price: 1892 Short Rifle.......................................**$1,070.00**

Prices given are believed to be accurate at time of publication however, many factors affect retail pricing so exact prices are not possible.

ARMALITE AR-30A1

Caliber: .300 Win. Mag., .338 Lapua. Bolt-action with five-round capacity. **Barrel:** 24 inches (.300 Win.), 26 inches (.338 Lapua), competition grade. **Weight:** 12.8 lbs. **Length:** 46 inches. **Stock:** Standard fixed. **Sights:** None. Accessory top rail included. **Features:** Muzzlebrake, ambidextrous magazine release, large ejection port makes single loading easy, V-block patented bedding system, bolt-mounted safety locks firing pin. Target versions have adjustable stock.
Price: .... **$3,264.00 to $3,599.00**

ARMALITE AR-50A1

Caliber: .50 BMG, .416 Barrett. Bolt-action single-shot. **Barrel:** 30 inches with muzzlebrake. National Match model (shown) has 33-inch fluted barrel. **Weight:** 34.1 lbs. **Stock:** Three-section. Extruded fore-end, machined vertical grip, forged and machined buttstock that is vertically adjustable. National Match model (.50 BMG only) has V-block patented bedding system, Armalite Skid System to ensure straight-back recoil.
Price: **$3,359.00**
Price: National Match **$4,230.00**

BARRETT MODEL 95

Caliber: 50 BMG, 5-shot magazine. **Barrel:** 29". **Weight:** 23.5 lbs. **Length:** 45" overall. **Stock:** Energy-absorbing recoil pad. **Sights:** Scope optional. **Features:** Bolt-action, bullpup design. Disassembles without tools; extendable bipod legs; match-grade barrel; muzzlebrake. Introduced 1995. Made in U.S.A. by Barrett Firearms Mfg., Inc.
Price: From **$6,500.00**

BARRETT MODEL 98B

Caliber: .338 Lapua Magnum (10-shot magazine). **Barrel:** 27" fluted or 20". **Weight:** 13.5 lbs. **Length:** 49.8". Comes with two magazines, bipod, monopod, side accessory rail, hard case.
Price: **$4,850.00**

BARRETT MODEL 99 SINGLE SHOT

Caliber: .50 BMG., .416 Barrett. **Barrel:** 33". **Weight:** 25 lbs. **Length:** 50.4" overall. **Stock:** Anodized aluminum with energy-absorbing recoil pad. **Sights:** None furnished; integral M1913 scope rail. **Features:** Bolt action; detachable bipod; match-grade barrel with high-efficiency muzzlebrake. Introduced 1999. Made in U.S.A. by Barrett Firearms.
Price: From .... **$3,999.00 to $4,199.00**

BARRETT MRAD

Caliber: .338 Lapua Magnum. **Magazine capacity:** 10 rounds.

Barrel: 20, 24 or 26 inches, fluted or heavy. **Features:** User interchangeable barrel system, folding stock, adjustable cheekpiece, 5-position length of pull adjustment button, match-grade trigger, 22-inch optics rail.
Price: .... **$5,850.00 to $6,000.00**

BLASER R93 PROFESSIONAL

Caliber: .22-250 Rem., .243 Win., 6.5x55, .270 Win., 7x57, 7mm-08 Rem., .308 Win., .30-06 Spfl., .257 Wby. Mag., 7mm Rem. Mag., .300 Win. Mag., .300 Wby. Mag., .338 Win. Mag., .375H&H, 416 Rem. Mag. **Barrel:** 22" (standard calibers), 26" (magnum). **Weight:** 7 lbs. **Length:** 40" overall (22" barrel). **Stock:** Two-piece European walnut. **Sights:** None furnished; drilled and tapped for scope mounting. **Features:** Straight pull-back bolt action with thumb-activated safety slide/cocking mechanism; interchangeable barrels and bolt heads. LRS (Long Range Sporter) is competition model with many competition features including fluted barrel, adjustable trigger and stock. Imported from Germany by Blaser USA.
Price: From **$3,145.00**
Price: LRS from **$4,405.00**
Price: R-93 Synthetic from **$1,800.00**

BROWNING AB3 COMPOSITE STALKER

Caliber: .270, 7mm Rem. Mag., .30-06, .300 Win. Mag. or .308 Win. **Barrel:** 22 inches, 26 for magnums. **Weight:** 6.8 lbs. **Stock:** Matte black synthetic. **Sights:** None. Picatinny rail scope mount included. **Features:** Based on A-Bolt action. General specifications are the same as A-Bolt Medallion.
Price: **$600.00**

BROWNING A-BOLT MEDALLION

Calibers: 7mm Rem. Mag., .300 Win. Mag. **Barrel:** 26" **Weight:** 7.1 lbs. **Length:** 46.75" overall. **Stock:** Select walnut with rosewood grip cap and fore-end cap. Checkered grip and fore-end. Gloss finish. **Features:** High polish blue metal finish. Sixty-degree bolt lift, top tang safety.
Price: **$700.00**

BROWNING X-BOLT HOG STALKER

Caliber: .223 or .308 Win. **Barrel:** 20 inches, medium heavy, threaded for suppressor. **Weight:** 6.8 to 7 pounds. **Stock:** Composite black or Realtree Max-1 camo. **Sights:** None. Picatinny rail scope mount included.
Price: **$1,200.00**

BROWNING X-BOLT HUNTER

Calibers: .223, .22-250, .243 Win., .25-06 Rem., .270 Win., .270 WSM, .280 Rem., 7mm Rem. Mag., 7mm WSM, 7mm-08 Rem., .308 Win., .30-06 Spfl., .300 Win. Mag., .300 WSM, .325 WSM, .338 Win. Mag., .375 H&H Mag. **Barrels:** 22", 23", 24", 26", varies by model. Matte blued or stainless free-floated barrel, recessed muzzle crown. **Weight:** 6.3-7 lbs. **Stock:** Hunter and Medallion models have black walnut stocks; Composite Stalker and Stainless Stalker models have composite stocks. Inflex Technology recoil pad. **Sights:** None, drilled and tapped receiver, X-Lock scope mounts. **Features:** Adjustable three-lever Feather Trigger system, polished hard-chromed steel components, factory pre-set at 3.5 lbs., alloy trigger housing. Bolt unlock button, detachable rotary magazine, 60-degree bolt lift, three locking lugs, top-tang safety, sling swivel studs. Introduced 2008.
Price: Standard calibers **$900.00**
Price: Magnum calibers **$950.00**

Prices given are believed to be accurate at time of publication however, many factors affect retail pricing so exact prices are not possible.

CENTERFIRE RIFLES Bolt-Action

BROWNING X-BOLT MICRO HUNTER
Similar to Browning X-Bolt Hunter but with compact dimensions. **Calibers:** .22-250, .243, .7mm-08, .308 Win., .270 WSM, .300 WSM. **Barrel:** 20" or 22". **Weight:** 5.9 lbs. Length of pull: 13-15/16".
Price: Standard chamberings **$900.00**
Price: Magnum **$950.00**

BROWNING X-BOLT MICRO MIDAS
Caliber: .243 Win., 7mm-08 Rem., .308 Win., .22-250 Rem. **Barrel:** 20". **Weight:** 6 lbs.1 oz. **Length:** 37-5/8" to 38-1/8" overall. **Stock:** Satin finish checkered walnut stock. **Sights:** Hooded front and adjustable rear. **Features:** Steel receiver with low-luster blued finish. Glass bedded, drilled and tapped for scope mounts. Barrel is free-floating and hand chambered with target crown. Bolt-action with adjustable Feather Trigger™ and detachable rotary magazine. Compact 12-1/2" length of pull for smaller shooters, designed to fit smaller-framed shooters like youth and women. This model has all the same features as the full-size model with sling swivel studs installed and Inflex Technology recoil pad. (Scope and mounts not included).
Price: **$860.00**

BROWNING X-BOLT VARMINT STALKER
Similar to Browning X-Bolt Stalker but with medium-heavy free-floated barrel, target crown, composite stock. Chamberings available: .223, .22-250, .243 Winchester and .308 Winchester only
Price: **$1,170.00**

BUSHMASTER BA50 BOLT-ACTION
Caliber: .50 Browning BMG. **Barrel:** 30" (rifle), 22" (carbine), 10-round mag. **Weight:** 30 lbs. (rifle), 27 lbs. (carbine). **Length:** 58" overall (rifle), 50" overall (carbine). **Features:** Free-floated Lothar Walther barrel with muzzlebrake, Magpul PRS adjustable stock.
Price: **$5,657.00**

CHEYTAC M-200
Caliber: 408 CheyTac, 7-round magazine. **Barrel:** 30". **Length:** 55", stock extended. **Weight:** 27 lbs. (steel barrel); 24 lbs. (carbon-fiber barrel). **Stock:** Retractable. **Sights:** None, scope rail provided. **Features:** CNC-machined receiver, attachable Picatinny rail M-1913, detachable barrel, integral bipod, 3.5-lb. trigger pull, muzzlebrake. Made in U.S. by CheyTac, LLC.
Price: **$13,795.00**

COOPER FIREARMS OF MONTANA
This company manufacturers bolt-action rifles in a variety of styles and in almost any factory or wildcat caliber. Features of the major model sub-category/styles are listed below. Several other styles and options are available.

Classic: Available in all models. AA Claro walnut stock with 4-panel hand checkering, hand-rubbed oil-finished wood, Pachmayr pad, steel grip cap and standard sling swivel studs. Barrel is chrome-moly premium match grade Wilson Arms. All metal work has matte finish.
Custom Classic: Available in all models. AAA Claro walnut stock with shadow-line beaded cheek-piece, African ebony tip, Western fleur wrap-around hand checkering, hand-rubbed oil-finished wood, Pachmayr pad, steel grip cap and standard sling swivel studs. Barrel is chrome-moly premium match grade Wilson Arms. All metal work has high gloss finish.
Western Classic: Available in all models. AAA+ Claro walnut stock. Selected metal work is highlighted with case coloring. Other features same as Custom Classic.
Mannlicher: Available in all models. Same features as Western Classic with full-length stock having multi-point wrap-around hand checkering.
Varminter: Available in Models 21, 22, 38, 52, 54 and 57-M. Same features as Classic except heavy barrel and stock with wide fore-end, hand-checkered grip.

COOPER MODEL 21
Caliber: Virtually any factory or wildcat chambering in the .223 Rem. family is available including: .17 Rem., .19-223, Tactical 20, .204 Ruger, .222 Rem, .222 Rem. Mag., .223 Rem, .223 Rem A.I., 6x45, 6x47. Single shot. **Barrel:** 22" or 24" in Classic configurations, 24"-26" in Varminter configurations. **Weight:** 6.5-8.0 lbs., depending on type. **Stock:** AA-AAA select claro walnut, 20 lpi checkering. **Sights:** None furnished. **Features:** Three front locking-lug, bolt-action, single-shot. Action: 7.75" long, Sako extractor. Button ejector. Fully adjustable single-stage trigger. Options include wood upgrades, case-color metalwork, barrel fluting, custom LOP, and many others.
Price: Classic **$2,195.00**
Price: Custom Classic. **$2,495.00**
Price: Western Classic. **$3,355.00**
Price: Varminter **$2,195.00**
Price: Mannlicher **$4,395.00**

COOPER MODEL 22
Caliber: Virtually any factory or wildcat chambering in the mid-size cartridge length including: .22-250 Rem., .22-250 Rem. AI, .25-06 Rem., .25-06 Rem. AI, .243 Win., .243 Win. AI, .220 Swift, .250/3000 AI, .257 Roberts, .257 Roberts AI, 7mm-08 Rem., 6mm Rem., .260 Rem., 6x284, 6.5x284, .22 BR, 6mm BR, .308 Win. Single shot. **Barrel:** 24" or 26" stainless match in Classic configurations. 24" or 26" in Varminter configurations. **Weight:** 7.5 to 8.0 lbs. depending on type. **Stock:** AA-AAA select claro walnut, 20 lpi checkering. **Sights:** None furnished. **Features:** Three front locking-lug bolt-action single shot. Action: 8.25" long, Sako-style extractor. Button ejector. Fully adjustable single-stage trigger. Options include wood upgrades, case-color metalwork, barrel fluting, custom LOP, and many others.
Price: Classic **$2,195.00**
Price: Custom Classic. **$2,595.00**
Price: Western Classic. **$3,455.00**
Price: Varminter **$2,195.00**
Price: Mannlicher **$4,495.00**

COOPER MODEL 38
Caliber: .22 Hornet family of cartridges including the.17 Squirrel, 17 He Bee, 17 Ackley Hornet, 17 Mach IV, 19 Calhoon, 20 VarTarg, 221 Fireball, .22 Hornet, .22 K-Hornet, .22 Squirrel, 218 Bee, 218 Mashburn Bee. Single shot. **Barrel:** 22" or 24" in Classic configurations, 24" or 26" In Varminter configurations. **Weight:** 6.5-8.0 lbs. depending on type. **Stock:** AA-AAA select claro walnut, 20 lpi checkering. **Sights:** None furnished. **Features:** Three front locking-lug bolt-action single shot. Action: 7" long, Sako-style extractor. Button ejector. Fully adjustable single-stage trigger. Options include wood upgrades, case-color metalwork, barrel fluting, custom LOP, and many others.
Price: Classic **$2,195.00**
Price: Custom Classic. **$2,495.00**
Price: Western Classic. **$3,895.00**
Price: Varminter **$2,195.00**
Price: Mannlicher **$4,395.00**

COOPER MODEL 52
Caliber: .30-06, .270 Win., .280 Rem, .25-06, .284 Win.,.257 Weatherby Mag., .264 Win. Mag., .270 Weatherby Mag., 7mm Remington Mag., 7mm Weatherby Mag., 7mm Shooting Times Westerner, .300 Holland & Holland, .300 Winchester Mag., .300

Weatherby Mag., .308 Norma Mag., 8mm Rem. Mag., .338 Win. Mag., .340 Weatherby V. Three-shot magazine. **Barrel:** 22" or 24" in Classic configurations, 24" or 26" in Varminter configurations. **Weight:** 7.75 - 8 lbs. depending on type. **Stock:** AA-AAA select claro walnut, 20 lpi checkering. **Sights:** None furnished. **Features:** Three front locking-lug bolt-action single shot. Action: 7" long, Sako style extractor. Button ejector. Fully adjustable single-stage trigger. Options include wood upgrades, case-color metalwork, barrel fluting, custom LOP, and many others.

Price: Classic. $2,275.00
Price: Custom Classic. $3,195.00
Price: Western Classic. $3,895.00
Price: Jackson Game. $2,295.00
Price: Jackson Hunter $2,155.00
Price: Excalibur. $2,155.00
Price: Mannlicher $4,995.00

COOPER MODEL 54

Caliber: .22-250, .243 Win., .250 Savage, .260 Rem., 7mm-08, .308 Win. and similar length cartridges. Features are similar to those of the Model 52.

Price: Classic. $2,275.00
Price: Custom Classic. $2,495.00
Price: Western Classic. $3,895.00
Price: Jackson Game. $2,295.00
Price: Jackson Hunter $2,155.00
Price: Excalibur. $2,155.00
Price: Mannlicher $4,995.00

COOPER MODEL 57-M

Caliber: .17 HMR, .22 LR, .22 WMR. Capacity 3 or 4 rounds. Cooper Firearms series of rimfire rifles, available in most of the company's popular styles.

Price: Classic $2,245.00
Price: Custom Classic $2,595.00
Price: Western Classic $3,445.00
Price: Schnabel $2,395.00
Price: Jackson Squirrel $2,355.00
Price: Jackson Hunter $2,195.00
Price: Mannlicher $4,395.00

CZ 527 LUX BOLT-ACTION

Caliber: .17 Hornet, .204 Ruger, .22 Hornet, .222 Rem., .223 Rem., detachable 5-shot magazine. **Barrel:** 23.5"; standard or heavy barrel. **Weight:** 6 lbs., 1 oz. **Length:** 42.5" overall. **Stock:** European walnut with Monte Carlo. **Sights:** Hooded front, open adjustable rear. **Features:** Improved mini-Mauser action with non-rotating claw extractor; single set trigger; grooved receiver. Imported from the Czech Republic by CZ-USA.

Price: Brown laminate stock $733.00
Price: Model FS, full-length stock, cheekpiece $827.00

CZ 527 AMERICAN BOLT-ACTION

Similar to the CZ 527 Lux except has classic-style stock with 18 lpi checkering; free-floating barrel; recessed target crown on barrel. No sights furnished. Introduced 1999. Imported from the Czech Republic by CZUSA.

Price: From $733.00

CZ 550 FS MANNLICHER

Caliber: .22-250 Rem., .243 Win., 6.5x55, 7x57, 7x64, .308 Win., 9.3x62, .270 Win., 30-06. **Barrel:** Free-floating barrel; recessed target

crown. **Weight:** 7.48 lbs. **Length:** 44.68" overall. **Stock:** American classic style stock with 18 lpi checkering or FS (Mannlicher). **Sights:** No sights furnished. **Features:** Improved Mauser-style action with claw extractor, fixed ejector, square bridge dovetailed receiver; single set trigger. Introduced 1999. Imported from the Czech Republic by CZ-USA.

Price: FS (full stock) $894.00
Price: American, from $827.00

CZ 550 SAFARI MAGNUM/AMERICAN SAFARI MAGNUM

Similar to CZ 550 American Classic. Chambered for .375H&H Mag., .416 Rigby, .458 Win. Mag., .458 Lott. Overall length is 46.5"; barrel length 25"; weighs 9.4 lbs., 9.9 lbs (American). Hooded front sight, express rear with one standing, two folding leaves. Imported from the Czech Republic by CZ-USA.

Price: Safari Magnum $1,215.00
Price: American Safari Field .... $1,215.00 to $1,348.00
Price: American Kevlar $1,714.00

CZ 550 VARMINT

Similar to CZ 550 American Classic. Chambered for .308 Win. and .22-250. Kevlar, laminated stocks. Overall length is 46.7"; barrel length 25.6"; weighs 9.1 lbs. Imported from the Czech Republic by CZ-USA.

Price: $865.00
Price: Kevlar $1,037.00
Price: Laminated $966.00

CZ 550 MAGNUM H.E.T.

Similar to CZ 550 American Classic. Chambered for .338 Lapua, .300 Win. Mag., .300 RUM. Overall length is 52"; barrel length 28"; weighs 14 lbs. Adjustable sights, satin blued barrel. Imported from the Czech Republic by CZ-USA.

Price: $3,929.00

CZ 550 ULTIMATE HUNTING

Similar to CZ 550 American Classic. Chambered for .300 Win Mag. Overall length is 44.7"; barrel length 23.6"; weighs 7.7 lbs. Kevlar stock. Nightforce 5.5-20x50mm scope included. Imported from the Czech Republic by CZ-USA.

Price: $4,242.00

CZ 557

Caliber: .243 Win., 6.5x55, .270 Win., .308 Win., .30-06. **Capacity:** 5+1. **Barrel:** 20.5". **Stock:** Satin finished walnut or Manners carbon fiber with textured grip and fore-end. **Sights:** None on Sporter model; Carbine has fixed rear and fiber optic front. Forged steel receiver has integral scope mounts. Magazine has hinged floorplate. Trigger is adjustable. Push-feed action features short extractor and plunger style ejector.

Price: Carbine, walnut stock (shown) $812.00
Price: Sporter, walnut stock $792.00
Price: Sporter, carbon fiber stock $1,268.00

CZ 750 SNIPER

Caliber: .308 Winchester, 10-shot magazine. **Barrel:** 26". **Weight:** 11.9 lbs. **Length:** 48" overall. **Stock:** Polymer thumbhole. **Sights:** None furnished; permanently attached Weaver rail for scope mounting. **Features:** 60-degree bolt throw; oversized triggerguard and bolt handle for use with gloves; full-length equipment rail on fore-end; fully adjustable trigger. Introduced 2001. Imported from the Czech Republic by CZ-USA.

Price: $1,999.00

DAKOTA 76 TRAVELER TAKEDOWN

Caliber: .257 Roberts, .25-06 Rem., 7x57, .270 Win., .280 Rem., .30-06 Spfl., .338-06, .35 Whelen (standard length); 7mm Rem. Mag., .300 Win. Mag., .338 Win. Mag., .416 Taylor, .458 Win. Mag. (short

Prices given are believed to be accurate at time of publication however, many factors affect retail pricing so exact prices are not possible.

magnums); 7mm, .300, .330, .375 Dakota Magnums. **Barrel:** 23". **Weight:** 7.5 lbs. **Length:** 43.5" overall. **Stock:** Medium fancy-grade walnut in classic style. Checkered grip and fore-end; solid buttpad. **Sights:** None furnished; drilled and tapped for scope mounts. **Features:** Threadless disassembly. Uses modified Model 76 design with many features of the Model 70 Winchester. Left-hand model also available. Introduced 1989. African chambered for .338 Lapua Mag., .404 Jeffery, .416 Rigby, .416 Dakota, .450 Dakota, 4-round magazine, select wood, two stock cross-bolts. 24" barrel, weighs 9-10 lbs. Ramp front sight, standing leaf rear. Introduced 1989. Made in U.S.A. by Dakota Arms, Inc.

Price: Classic **$7,240.00**
Price: Safari **$9,330.00**
Price: African **$10,540.00**

DAKOTA 76 CLASSIC
Caliber: .257 Roberts, .270 Win., .280 Rem., .30-06 Spfl., 7mm Rem. Mag., .338 Win. Mag., .300 Win. Mag., .375H&H, .458 Win. Mag. **Barrel:** 23". **Weight:** 7.5 lbs. **Length:** 43.5" overall. **Stock:** Medium fancy grade walnut in classic style. Checkered pistol grip and fore-end; solid buttpad. **Sights:** None furnished; drilled and tapped for scope mounts. **Features:** Has many features of the original Winchester Model 70. One-piece rail triggerguard assembly; steel gripcap. Model 70-style trigger. Many options available. Left-hand rifle available at same price. Introduced 1988. From Dakota Arms, Inc.

Price: From **$6,030.00**

DAKOTA MODEL 97 BOLT-ACTION
Caliber: .22-250 to .330. **Barrel:** 22" to 24". **Weight:** 6.1 to 6.5 lbs. **Length:** 43" overall. **Stock:** Fiberglass. **Sights:** Optional. **Features:** Matte blue finish, black stock. Right-hand action only. Introduced 1998. Made in U.S.A. by Dakota Arms, Inc.

Price: From **$3,720.00**
Price: All Weather (stainless)....................................**$4,050.00**

HOWA M-1500 RANCHLAND COMPACT
Caliber: .223 Rem., .22-250 Rem., .243 Win., .308 Win. and 7mm-08. **Barrel:** 20" #1 contour, blued finish. **Weight:** 7 lbs. **Stock:** Hogue Overmolded in black, OD green, Coyote Sand colors. 13.87" LOP. **Sights:** None furnished; drilled and tapped for scope mounting. **Features:** Three-position safety, hinged floorplate, adjustable trigger, forged one-piece bolt, M-16 style extractor, forged flat-bottom receiver. Also available with Nikko-Stirling Nighteater 3-9x42 riflescope. Introduced in 2008. Imported from Japan by Legacy Sports International.

Price: Rifle Only, (2008)...**$585.00**
Price: Rifle with 3-9x42 Nighteater scope (2008) **$700.00**

HOWA M-1500 THUMBHOLE SPORTER
Caliber: .204, .223 Rem., .22-250 Rem., .243 Win., 6.5x55 (2008) .25-06 Rem., .270 Win., 7mm Rem. Mag., .308 Win., .30-06 Spfl., .300 Win. Mag., .338 Win. Mag., .375 Ruger. Similar to Camo Lightning except stock. **Weight:** 7.6 to 7.7 lbs. **Stock:** S&K laminated wood in nutmeg (brown/black) or pepper (grey/black) colors, raised comb with forward taper, flared pistol grip and scalloped thumbhole. **Sights:** None furnished; drilled and tapped for scope mounting. **Features:** Three-position safety, hinged floorplate, adjustable trigger, forged one-piece bolt, M-16 style extractor, forged flat-bottom receiver. Introduced in 2001. Imported from Japan by Legacy Sports International.

Price: Blue/Nutmeg, standard calibers..................**$649.00 to $669.00**
Price: Stainless/Pepper, standard calibers............**$749.00 to $769.00**

HOWA M-1500 VARMINTER SUPREME AND THUMBHOLE VARMINTER SUPREME
Caliber: .204, .223 Rem., .22-250 Rem., .243 Win., .308 Win. **Stock:** Varminter Supreme: Laminated wood in nutmeg (brown) pepper

(grey) colors, raised comb and rollover cheekpiece, full pistol grip with palm-filling swell and broad beavertail forend with six vents for barrel cooling. Thumbhole Varminter Supreme similar, adds a high, straight comb, more vertical pistol grip. **Sights:** None furnished; drilled and tapped for scope mounting. **Features:** Three-position safety, hinged floorplate, adjustable trigger, forged one-piece bolt, M-16 style extractor, forged flat-bottom receiver, hammer forged bull barrel and recessed muzzle crown; overall length, 43.75", 9.7 lbs. Introduced 2001. Barreled actions imported by Legacy Sports International; stocks by S&K Gunstocks.

Price: Varminter Supreme, Blue/Nutmeg.................**$679.00**
Price: Varminter Supreme, Stainless/Pepper..........**$779.00**
Price: Thumbhole Varminter Supreme, Blue/Nutmeg.....**$773.00**
Price: Thumbhole Varminter Supreme, Stainless/Pepper **$813.00**

HOWA/HOGUE M-1500 COMPACT HEAVY BARREL VARMINTER
Chambered in .223 Rem., .22-250, 308 Win., has 20" #6 contour and fluted heavy barrel, recessed muzzle crown. **Stock:** Hogue Overmolded, black, or OD green; ambidextrous palm swells. **Sights:** None furnished; drilled and tapped for scope mounting. **Length:** 44.0" overall. **Features:** Three-position safety, hinged floorplate, adjustable trigger, forged one-piece bolt, M-16 style extractor, forged flat bottom receiver, aluminum pillar bedding and free-floated barrels. **Weight:** 9.3 lbs. Introduced 2008. Imported from Japan by Legacy Sports International.

Price: From **$631.00**

HOWA/AXIOM M-1500 VARMINTER
Caliber: .204, .223 Rem., .22-250 Rem., .243 Win., 6.5x55 (2008), .25-06 Rem. (2008), .270 Win., .308 Win., .30-06 Spfl., 7mm Rem., .300 Win. Mag., .338 Win. Mag., .375 Ruger standard barrel; .204, .223 Rem., .243 Win. and .308 Win. heavy barrel. **Barrel:** Howa barreled action, 22" contour standard barrel, 20" #6 contour heavy barrel, and 24" #6 contour heavy barrel. **Weight:** 8.6-10 lbs. **Stock:** Knoxx Industries Axiom V/S synthetic, black or camo. Adjustable length of pull from 11.5" to 15.5". **Sights:** None furnished; drilled and tapped for scope mounting. **Features:** Three-position safety, adjustable trigger, hinged floorplate, forged receiver with large recoil lug, forged one-piece bolt with dual locking lugs. Introduced in 2007. Standard-barrel scope packages come with 3-10x42 Nikko-Stirling Nighteater scope, rings, bases (2008). Heavy barrels come with 4-16x44 Nikko-Stirling scope. Imported from Japan by Legacy Sports International.

Price: Axiom 20" and 24" Varminter, black or camo stock, from **$853.00**
Price: Axiom 20" and 24" Varminter, camo stock w/scope (2008), from.................................**$993.00**

HOWA/HOGUE KRYPTEK RIFLE
Caliber: Most popular calibers from .204 Ruger to .375 Ruger. **Barrel:** 20, 22 or 24", blue or stainless. Hogue overmolded stock in Kryptek Camo. Features include three-position safety, two-stage match trigger, one piece bolt with two locking lugs.

Price: **$626.00**
Price: Magnum calibers **$652.00**
Price: Stainless from **$736.00**

HOWA ALPINE MOUNTAIN RIFLE
Caliber: .243 Win., 6.5 Creedmoor, 7mm-08, .308 Win. **Barrel:** 20". **Weight:** 5.7 lbs. **Stock:** OD Green synthetic. **Features:** Two-stage HACT trigger, Cerakote finish on barrel and action, Pachmyr Decelerator pad.

Price: Stainless from..**$1,188.00**

H-S PRECISION PRO-SERIES 2000
Caliber: Offered in about 30 different chamberings including virtually all popular calibers. Made in hunting, tactical and competition styles with many options. **Barrel:** 20", 22", 24" or 26", depending on model and caliber. Hunting models include the Pro-Hunter Rifle (PHR) designed for magnum calibers with built-in recoil reducer and heavier barrel; Pro-Hunter Lightweight (PHL) with slim, fluted barrel; Pro-Hunter Sporter (SPR) and Pro-Hunter Varmint (VAR). Takedown, Competition and Tactical variations are available. **Stock:** H-S Precision synthetic stock in many styles and colors with full-length bedding block chassis system. Made in U.S.A.

Price: PHR **$3,695.00**

Price: PHL...$3,795.00
Price: SPR...$3,395.00
Price: SPL Sporter $3,495.00
Price: VAR...$3,495.00
Price: PTD Hunter Takedown.....................$3,495.00
Price: STR Short Tactical...........................$3,795.00
Price: HTR Heavy Tactical $3,795.00
Price: Competition.....................................$3,795.00

KENNY JARRETT RIFLES

Caliber: Custom built in virtually any chambering including .223 Rem., .243 Improved, .243 Catbird, 7mm-08 Improved, .280 Remington, .280 Ackley Improved, 7mm Rem. Mag., .284 Jarrett, .30-06 Springfield, .300 Win. Mag., .300 Jarrett, .323 Jarrett, .338 Jarrett, .375 H&H, .416 Rem., .450 Rigby, other modern cartridges. Numerous options regarding barrel type and weight, stock styles and material. **Features:** Tri-Lock receiver. Talley rings and bases. Accuracy guarantees and custom loaded ammunition. Newest series is the Shikar featuring 28-year aged American Black walnut hand-checkered stock with Jarrett-designed stabilizing aluminum chassis. Accuracy guaranteed to be ½ MOA with standard calibers, 7/10 MOA with magnums.

Price: Shikar Series.....................................$9,640.00
Price: Signature Series $7,640.00
Price: Long Ranger Series...........................$7,640.00
Price: Ridge Walker Series..........................$7,640.00
Price: Wind Walker $7,380.00
Price: Original Beanfield (customer's receiver) $5,380.00
Price: Professional Hunter $10,400.00
Price: SA/Custom $6,630.00

KIMBER MODEL 8400

Caliber: .25-06 Rem., .270 Win., 7mm, .30-06 Spfl., .300 Win. Mag., .338 Win. Mag., or .325 WSM, 4 shot. **Barrel:** 24". **Weight:** 6 lbs., 3 oz. to 6 lbs., 10 oz. **Length:** 43.25". **Stock:** Claro walnut or Kevlar-reinforced fiberglass. **Sights:** None; drilled and tapped for bases. **Features:** Mauser claw extractor, two-position wing safety, action bedded on aluminum pillars and fiberglass, free-floated barrel, match-grade adjustable trigger set at 4 lbs., matte or polished blue or matte stainless finish. Introduced 2003. Sonora model (2008) has brown laminated stock, hand-rubbed oil finish, chambered in .25-06 Rem., .30-06 Spfl., and .300 Win. Mag. Weighs 8.5 lbs., measures 44.50" overall length. Front swivel stud only for bipod. Stainless steel bull barrel, 24" satin stainless steel finish. Made in U.S.A. by Kimber Mfg. Inc.

Price: Classic...$1,223.00
Price: Classic Select Grade, French walnut stock (2008)......$1,427.00
Price: SuperAmerica, AAA walnut stock.............$2,240.00
Price: Patrol Tactical $2,447.00
Price: Montana $1,359.00

KIMBER MODEL 8400 ADVANCED TACTICAL II

Caliber: 6.5 Creedmoor, .308 Win., .300 Win Mag. Five-round detachable box. **Barrel:** 22", 27", threaded and fitted with SureFire muzzlebrake/suppressor adaptor. **Stock:** Manners MCS-TS4 Folding. Weight: 10.6 to 11.3 lbs.

Price: $4,351.00

KIMBER MODEL 8400 CAPRIVI

Similar to 8400 bolt rifle, but chambered for .375 H&H, .416 Remington and .458 Lott, 4-shot magazine. Stock is Claro walnut or Kevlar-reinforced fiberglass. Features twin steel crossbolts in stock, AA French walnut, pancake cheekpiece, 24 lines-per-inch wrap-around checkering, ebony forend tip, hand-rubbed oil finish, barrel-mounted sling swivel stud, 3-leaf express sights, Howell-type rear sling swivel stud and a Pachmayr Decelerator recoil pad

in traditional orange color. Introduced 2008. Made in U.S.A. by Kimber Mfg. Inc.

Price: From $3,263.00
Price: Special Edition from $5,031.00

KIMBER MODEL 8400 TALKEETNA

Similar to 8400 bolt rifle, but chambered for .375 H&H, 4-shot magazine. Weighs 8 lbs., overall length is 44.5". Stock is synthetic. Features free-floating match-grade barrel with tapered match-grade chamber and target crown, three-position wing safety acts directly on the cocking piece for greatest security, and Pachmayr Decelerator. Made in U.S.A. by Kimber Mfg. Inc

Price: $2,175.00

KIMBER MODEL 84M

Caliber: .22-250 Rem., .204 Ruger, .223 Rem., .243 Win., .257 Robts., .260 Rem., 7mm-08 Rem., .308 Win., 5-shot. **Barrel:** 22", 24", 26". **Weight:** 5 lbs., 10 oz. to 10 lbs. **Length:** 41" to 45". **Stock:** Claro walnut, checkered with steel gripcap; synthetic or gray laminate. **Sights:** None; drilled and tapped for bases. **Features:** Mauser claw extractor, three-position wing safety, action bedded on aluminum pillars, free-floated barrel, match-grade trigger set at 4 lbs., matte blue finish. Includes cable lock. Introduced 2001. Montana (2008) has synthetic stock, Pachmayr Decelerator recoil pad, stainless steel 22" sporter barrel. Adirondak has Kevlar white/black Optifade Forest camo stock, 18" barrel with threaded muzzle, weighs less than 5 lbs. Made in U.S.A. by Kimber Mfg. Inc.

Price: Classic...$1,223.00
Price: Varmint $1,291.00
Price: Montana $1,359.00
Price: Classic Stainless, matte stainless steel receiver and barrel $1,495.00
Price: Adirondak $1,768.00

KIMBER MODEL 84L CLASSIC

Bolt-action rifle chambered in .270 Win. and .30-06. Features include 24-inch sightless matte blue sporter barrel; hand-rubbed A-grade walnut stock with 20 lpi panel checkering; pillar and glass bedding; Mauser claw extractor; 3-position M70-style safety; 5-round magazine; adjustable trigger.

Price: $1,223.00

KIMBER MODEL 84M WSM SERIES

Caliber: .270 WSM, .300 WSM, .325 WSM. Other features similar to Model 84M and Model 84L Classic.

Price: Classic...$1,223.00
Price: Classic Select Grade $1,427.00
Price: SuperAmerica, AAA walnut stock.............$2,240.00
Price Montana $1,359.00

MARLIN XL7

Caliber: .223, .243 Win., .25-06 Rem., .270 Win., .30-06 Spfl., 4-shot magazine. **Barrel:** 22" 1:10" right-hand twist, recessed barrel crown. **Weight:** 6.5 lbs. **Length:** 42.5" overall. **Stock:** Black synthetic or Realtree APG-HD camo, Soft-Tech recoil pad, pillar bedded. **Sights:** None. **Features:** Pro-Fire trigger is user adjustable down to 2.5 lbs. Fluted bolt, steel sling swivel studs, high polished blued steel, checkered bolt handle, molded checkering, one-piece scope base. Introduced in 2008. From Marlin Firearms, Inc.

Price: Black Synthetic..................................$402.00
Price: Varmint w/heavy bbl. $409.00
Price: X7Y Youth model $403.00

MARLIN XS7 SHORT-ACTION

Similar to Model XL7 but chambered in 7mm-08, .243 Winchester and .308 Winchester.

Price: $391.00

Prices given are believed to be accurate at time of publication however, many factors affect retail pricing so exact prices are not possible.

Price: XS7Y Youth $402.00
Price: XS7C Camo, Realtree APG HD camo stock $426.00
Price: XS7S Stainless $500.00

MERKEL RX HELIX

Caliber: .223 Rem., .243 Rem., 6.5x55, 7mm-08, .308 Win., .270 Win., .30-06, 9.3x62, 7mm Rem. Mag., .300 Win. Mag., .270 WSM, .300 WSM, .338 Win. Mag. **Features:** Straight-pull bolt action. Synthetic stock on Explorer model. Walnut stock available in several grades. Factory engraved models available. Takedown system allows switching calibers in minutes.
Price: Explorer, synthetic stock, from $3,295.00
Price: Walnut stock, from $3,795.00

MOSSBERG MVP SERIES

Caliber: .223/5.56 NATO. 10-round capacity. Uses AR-style magazines. **Barrel:** 16.25 inches medium bull, 20-inch fluted sporter. **Weight:** 6.5 to 7 lbs. **Stock:** Classic black textured polymer. **Sights:** Adjustable folding rear, adjustable blade front. **Features:** Available with factory mounted 3-9x32mm scope, (4-16x50mm on Varmint model). FLEX model has 20-inch fluted sporter barrel, FLEX AR-style 6-position adjustable stock. Varmint model has laminated stock, 24-inch barrel. Thunder Ranch model has 18-inch bull barrel, OD Green synthetic stock.
Price: Patrol model $709.00
Price: Patrol model w/scope.. $863.00
Price: FLEX model $966.00
Price: FLEX MODEL w/scope....................................... $1,142.00
Price: Thunder Ranch model $748.00
Price: Predator model $709.00
Price: Predator model w/scope...................................... $758.00
Price: Varmint Model... $732.00
Price: Varmint Model w/scope....................................... $912.00

MOSSBERG PATRIOT

Caliber: .22-250, .243 Win., .25-06, .270 Win., 7mm-08, .7mm Rem., .308 Win., .30-06, .300 Win. Mag., .38 Win. Mag., .375 Ruger. **Capacity:** 4 or 5 rounds. Detachable box magazine. **Barrel:** 22" sporter or fluted. **Stock:** Walnut, laminate, camo or synthetic black. **Weight:** 7.5 - 8 lbs. **Finish:** Matte blue. **Sights:** Adjustable or none. Some models available with 3-9x40mm scope. Other features include patented Lightning Bolt Action Trigger adjustable from 2 to 7 pounds, spiral-fluted bolt. Not all variants available in all calibers. Introduced in 2015.
Price: Walnut stock.. $438.00
Price: Walnut with premium Vortex Crossfire scope $649.00
Price: Synthetic stock... $386.00
Price: Synthetic stock with standard scope $426.00
Price: Laminate stock w/iron sights................................ $584.00
Price: Deer THUG w/Mossy Oak Infinity Camo stock $500.00

MOSSBERG PATRIOT NIGHT TRAIN

Caliber: .308 Win. or .300 Win. Mag. Tactical model with Silencerco Saker Muzzlebrake, 6-24x50mm scope with tactical turrets, green synthetic stock with Neoprene comb-raising kit. **Weight:** 9 lbs.
Price: Night Train with 6-24x50mm $811.00

NESIKA SPORTER RIFLE

Caliber: .260 Rem., 6.5x284, 7mm-08, .280 Rem., 7mm Rem. Mag., .308 Win., .30-06, .300 Win. Mag. **Barrel:** 24 or 26" Douglas air-gauged stainless. **Stock:** Composite with aluminum bedding block. **Sights:** None, Leupold QRW bases. **Weight:** 8 lbs. **Features:** Timney trigger set at 3 pounds, receiver made from 15-5 stainless

steel, one-piece bolt from 4340 CM steel. Guaranteed accuracy at 100 yards.
Price: $3,499.00
Price: Long Range w/heavy bbl., varmint stock $3,999.00
Price: Tactical w/28î bbl., muzzle brake, adj. stock $4,499.00

NOSLER MODEL 48 SERIES

Caliber: Offered in most popular calibers including .280 Ackley Improved and 6.5-284 wildcats. **Barrel:** 24". **Weight:** 7.25 to 8 lbs. **Stock:** Walnut or composite. Custom Model is made to order with several optional features.
Price: Patriot $1,795.00
Price: Heritage $1,895.00
Price: Custom Model from.. $3,795.00

REMINGTON MODEL 700 CDL CLASSIC DELUXE

Caliber: .223 Rem., .243 Win., .25-06 Rem., .270 Win., 7mm-08 Rem., .280 Remington, 7mm Rem. Mag., 7mm Rem. Ultra Mag., .30-06 Spfl., .300 Rem. Ultra Mag., .300 Win. Mag. **Barrel:** 24" or 26" round tapered. **Weight:** 7.4 to 7.6 lbs. **Length:** 43.6" to 46.5" overall. **Stock:** Straight-comb American walnut stock, satin finish, checkering, right-handed cheekpiece, black fore-end tip and grip cap, sling swivel studs. **Sights:** None. **Features:** Satin blued finish, jeweled bolt body, drilled and tapped for scope mounts. Hinged-floorplate magazine capacity: 4, standard calibers; 3, magnum calibers. SuperCell recoil pad, cylindrical receiver, integral extractor. Introduced 2004. CDL SF (stainless fluted) chambered for .260 Rem., .257 Wby. Mag., .270 Win., .270 WSM, 7mm-08 Rem., 7mm Rem. Mag., .30-06 Spfl., .300 WSM. Left-hand versions introduced 2008 in six calibers. Made in U.S. by Remington Arms Co., Inc.
Price: Standard Calibers from .... **$1,029.00 to $1,089.00**
Price: CDL SF from **$1,226.00**

REMINGTON MODEL 700 BDL

Caliber: .243 Win., .270 Win., 7mm Rem. Mag., .30-06 Spfl., .300 Rem Ultra Mag. **Barrel:** 22, 24, 26" round tapered. **Weight:** 7.25-7.4 lbs. **Length:** 41.6-46.5" overall. **Stock:** Walnut. Gloss-finish pistol grip stock with skip-line checkering, black forend tip and gripcap with white line spacers. Quick-release floorplate. **Sights:** Gold bead ramp front; hooded ramp, removable step-adjustable rear with windage screw. **Features:** Side safety, receiver tapped for scope mounts, matte receiver top, quick detachable swivels.
Price: Standard Calibers $994.00
Price: Magnum Calibers $1,020.00
Price: 50th Anniversary Edition, 7mm Rem. Mag. $1,399.00

REMINGTON MODEL 700 SPS

Caliber: .22-250 Rem., 6.8 Rem SPC, .223 Rem., .243 Win., .270 Win., .270 WSM, 7mm-08 Rem., 7mm Rem. Mag., 7mm Rem. Ultra Mag., .30-06 Spfl., .308 Win., .300 WSM, .300 Win. Mag., .300 Rem. Ultra Mag. **Barrel:** 20", 24" or 26" carbon steel. **Weight:** 7 to 7.6 lbs. **Length:** 39.6" to 46.5" overall. **Stock:** Black synthetic, sling swivel studs, SuperCell recoil pad. Woodtech model has walnut decorated synthetic stock with overmolded grip patterns. Camo stock available. **Sights:** None. Introduced 2005. SPS Stainless replaces Model 700 BDL Stainless Synthetic. **Barrel:** Bead-blasted 416 stainless steel. **Features:** Plated internal fire control component. SPS DM features detachable box magazine. SPS Varmint includes X-Mark Pro trigger, 26" heavy contour barrel, vented beavertail fore-end, dual front sling swivel studs. Made in U.S. by Remington Arms Co., Inc.
Price: From .... $724.00 to $838.00

REMINGTON 700 SPS TACTICAL

Caliber: .223 .300 AAC Blackout and .308 Win. **Features:** Features include 20-inch heavy-contour tactical-style barrel; dual-point pillar

CENTERFIRE RIFLES Bolt-Action

bedding; black synthetic stock with Hogue overmoldings; semi-beavertail fore-end; X-Mark Pro adjustable trigger system; satin black oxide metal finish; hinged floorplate magazine; SuperCell recoil pad.
Price: From .... **$788.00 to $842.00**

REMINGTON 700 VTR A-TACS CAMO
Caliber: :.223 and .308 Win. **Features:** Features include ATACS camo finish overall; triangular contour 22-inch barrel has an integral muzzlebrake; black overmold grips; 1:9" twist (.223 caliber), or 1:12" (.308) twist.
Price: **$930.00**

REMINGTON MODEL 700 VLS
Caliber: .204 Ruger, .223 Rem., .22-250 Rem., .243 Win., .308 Win. **Barrel:** 26" heavy contour barrel (0.820" muzzle O.D.), concave target-style barrel crown. **Weight:** 9.4 lbs. **Length:** 45.75" overall. **Stock:** Brown laminated stock, satin finish, with beavertail fore-end, gripcap, rubber buttpad. **Sights:** None. **Features:** Introduced 1995. Made in U.S. by Remington Arms Co., Inc.
Price: **$1,056.00**

REMINGTON MODEL 700 SENDERO SF II
Caliber: 7mm Rem. Mag., .300 Win. Mag., .300 Rem. Ultra Mag. **Barrel:** Satin stainless 26" heavy contour fluted. **Weight:** 8.5 lbs. **Length:** 45.75" overall. **Stock:** Black composite reinforced with aramid fibers, beavertail fore-end, palm swell. **Sights:** None. **Features:** Aluminum bedding block, drilled and tapped for scope mounts, hinged floorplate magazines. Introduced 1996. Made in U.S. by Remington Arms Co., Inc.
Price: **$1,465.00**

REMINGTON MODEL 700 TARGET TACTICAL
Caliber: .308 Win. **Barrel:** 26" triangular counterbored, 1:11-1/2" rifling. **Weight:** 11.75 lbs. **Length:** 45-3/4" overall. **Features:** Textured green Bell & Carlson varmint/tactical stock with adjustable comb and length of pull, adjustable trigger, satin black oxide finish on exposed metal surfaces, hinged floorplate, SuperCell recoil pad, matte blue on exposed metal surfaces.
Price: **$2,138.00**

REMINGTON MODEL 700 VTR SERIES
Caliber: .204 Ruger, .22-250, .223 Rem., .243 Win., .308 Win. **Barrel:** 22" triangular counterbored with integrated muzzlebrake. **Weight:** 7.5 lbs. **Length:** 41-5/8" overall. **Features:** Olive drab overmolded or Digital Tiger TSP Desert Camo stock with vented semi-beavertail fore-end, tactical-style dual swivel mounts for bipod, matte blue on exposed metal surfaces.
Price: From .... **$825.00 to $980.00**

REMINGTON MODEL 700 VARMINT SF
Caliber: .22-250, .223, .220 Swift, .308 Win. **Barrel:** 26" stainless steel fluted. **Weight:** 8.5 lbs. **Length:** 45.75 inches. **Features:** Synthetic stock with ventilated forend, stainless steel/triggerguard/floorplate, dual tactical swivels for bipod attachment.
Price: **$991.00**

REMINGTON MODEL 700 MOUNTAIN SS
Calibers: .25-06, .270 Win., .280 Rem., 7mm-08, .308 Win., .30-06. **Barrel:** 22". **Length:** 40.6". **Weight:** 6.5 lbs. Satin stainless finish, Bell & Carlson Aramid Fiber stock.
Price: **$1,135.00**

REMINGTON MODEL 770 BOLT-ACTION
Caliber: .243 Win., .270 Win., 7mm Rem. Mag., 7mm-08 Rem., .308 Win., .30-06 Spfl., .300 Win. Mag. **Barrel:** 22" or 24", button rifled. **Weight:** 8.5 lbs. **Length:** 42.5" to 44.5" overall. **Stock:** Black synthetic. **Sights:** Bushnell Sharpshooter 3-9x scope mounted and bore-sighted. **Features:** Upgrade of Model 710 introduced 2001. Unique action locks bolt directly into barrel; 60-degree bolt throw; 4-shot dual-stack magazine; all-steel receiver. Introduced 2007. Stainless Camo model has Realtree camo stock, stainless metal finish. Made in U.S.A. by Remington Arms Co.
Price: **$383.00**
Price: Youth, .243 Win. **$375.00**
Price: Stainless Camo **$467.00**

REMINGTON MODEL 783
Calibers: .270 Win., 7mm Rem. Mag., .308 Win., .30-06 Sprg. **Barrel:** 22 inches. **Stock:** Synthetic. **Weight:** 7 to 7.25 lbs. **Finish:** Matte black. **Features:** Adjustable trigger with two-position trigger-block safety, magnum contour button-rifle barrel, cylindrical receiver with minimum-size ejection port, pillar-bedded stock, detachable box magazine, 90-degree bolt throw.
Price: **$451.00**
Price: Camo stock **$503.00**

REMINGTON MODEL SEVEN CDL
Calibers: .243, .260 Rem., 7mm-08, .308 Win. **Barrel:** 20". **Weight:** 6.5 lbs. **Length:** 39.25". **Stock:** Walnut with black fore-end tip, satin finish. Predator model in .223, .22-250 and .243 has Mossy Oak Brush camo stock, 22" barrel.
Price: CDL **$1,039.00**
Price: Predator **$895.00**
Price: Synthetic stock **$731.00**

REMINGTON 40-XB TACTICAL
Caliber: .308 Winchester. **Features:** Features include stainless steel bolt with Teflon coating; hinged floorplate; adjustable trigger; 27-1/4-inch tri-fluted 1:14" twist barrel; H-S precision pro series tactical stock, black color with dark green spiderweb; two front swivel studs; one rear swivel stud; vertical pistol grip. From the Remington Custom Shop.
Price: **$2,995.00**

REMINGTON 40-XB RANGEMASTER
Caliber: Almost any caliber from .22 BR Rem. to .300 Rem. Ultra Mag. Single-shot or repeater. **Features:** Features include stainless steel bolt with Teflon coating; hinged floorplate; adjustable trigger; 27-1/4-inch tri-fluted 1:14" twist barrel; walnut stock. From the Remington Custom Shop.
Price: **$2,595.00**

REMINGTON 40-XS TACTICAL - 338LM SYSTEM
Caliber: .338 Lapua Magnum. **Features:** Features include 416 stainless steel Model 40-X 24-inch 1:12" twist barreled action;

black polymer coating; McMillan A3 series stock with adjustable length of pull and adjustable comb; adjustable trigger and Sunny Hill heavy-duty, all-steel triggerguard; Harris bipod with quick adjust swivel lock; Leupold Mark IV 3.5-10x40mm long-range M1 scope with Mil Dot reticle; Badger Ordnance all-steel Picatinny scope rail and rings. From the Remington Custom Shop.

Price: **$4,950.00**

ROCK ISLAND ARMORY TCM

Caliber: .22 TCM. 5-round capacity magazine, interchangeable with .22 TCM 17-round pistol magazine. **Barrel:** 22.75 inches. **Weight:** 6 pounds. Chambered for .22 TCM cartridge introduced in 2013. Manufactured in the Philippines and imported by Armscor Precision International.

Price: **$450.00**

RUGER AMERICAN RIFLE

Caliber: .22-250, .243, 7mm-08, .308, .270 Win., .30-06 (4-shot rotary magazine). **Barrel:** 22" or 18" (Compact). **Length:** 42.5". **Weight:** 6.25 lbs. **Stock:** Black composite. **Finish:** Matte black or matte stainless (All Weather model). **Features:** Tang safety, hammer-forged free-floating barrel. Available with factory mounted Redfield Revolution 4x scope. Ranch model has Flat Dark Earth composite stock, Predator has Moss Green composite stock, both chambered in several additional calibers to standard model.

Price: Standard or compact....................................**$459.00**
Price: All-weather model, standard or compact.......**$595.00**
Price: With scope..**$699.00**
Price: Ranch or Predator model **$499.00**

RUGER GUNSITE SCOUT RIFLE

Caliber: .308 Win., 10-shot magazine capacity. **Barrel:** 16.5". **Weight:** 7 lbs. **Length:** 38-39.5". **Stock:** Black laminate. **Sights:** Front post sight and rear adjustable. **Features:** Gunsite Scout Rifle is a credible rendition of Col. Jeff Cooper's "fighting carbine" Scout Rifle. The Ruger Gunsite Scout Rifle is a platform in the Ruger M77 family. While the Scout Rifle has M77 features such as controlled round feed and integral scope mounts (scope rings included), the 10-round detachable box magazine is the first clue this isn't your grandfather's Ruger rifle. The Ruger Gunsite Scout Rifle has a 16.5 medium contour, cold hammer-forged, alloy steel barrel with a Mini-14 protected nonglare post front sight and receiver mounted, adjustable ghost ring rear sight for out-of-the-box usability. A forward mounted Picatinny rail offers options in mounting an assortment of optics – including Scout Scopes available from Burris and Leupold, for "both eyes open" sighting and super-fast target acquisition.

Price: **$1,075.00**
Price: (stainless)..**$1,139.00**

RUGER ROTARY MAGAZINE RIFLE

Caliber: .17 Hornet, .22 Hornet, .357 Magnum, . 44 Magnum (capacity 4 to 6 rounds). **Barrel:** 18.5" (.357 and .44 Mag,), 20 or 24" (.17 Hornet and .22 Hornet). **Weight:** 5.5 to 7.5 lbs. **Stock:** American walnut, black synthetic, Next G1 Vista Camo or Green Mountain laminate.

Price: 77/17, Green Mtn. Laminate stock **$969.00**

Price: 77/22, Green Mtn. Laminate stock **$969.00**
Price: 77/22, walnut stock **$939.00**
Price: 77/357, 77/44, black synthetic stock **$999.00**
Price: 77/44, Next G1 Vista Camo.........................**$1,060.00**

RUGER GUIDE GUN

Calibers: .30-06, .300 Ruger Compact Mag., .300 Win. Mag., .338 RCM, .338 Win. Mag., .375 Ruger. **Capacity:** 3 or 4 rounds. **Barrel:** 20 inches with barrelband sling swivel and removable muzzlebrake. **Weight:** 8 to 8.12 pounds. **Stock:** Green Mountain Laminate. **Finish:** Hawkeye matte stainless. **Sights:** Adjustable rear, bead front. Introduced 2013.

Price: **$1,240.00**

RUGER HAWKEYE

Caliber: .204 Ruger, .223 Rem., .22-250 Rem., .243 Win., .25-06 Rem., .270 Win., .280 Rem., 6.5 Creedmoor, 7mm/08, 7mm Rem. Mag., .308 Win., .30-06 Spfl., .300 Win. Mag., .338 Win. Mag., 4-shot magazine, except 3-shot magazine for magnums; 5-shot magazine for .204 Ruger and .223 Rem. **Barrel:** 22", 24". **Weight:** 6.75 to 8.25 lbs. **Length:** 42-44.4" overall. **Stock:** American walnut, laminate or synthetic. Magnum Hunter has Green Hogue stock. **Sights:** None furnished. Receiver has Ruger integral scope mount base, Ruger 1" rings. **Features:** Includes Ruger LC6 trigger, new red rubber recoil pad, Mauser-type controlled feeding, claw extractor, 3-position safety, hammer-forged steel barrels, Ruger scope rings. Walnut stocks have wrap-around cut checkering on the forearm, and more rounded contours on stock and top of pistol grips. Matte stainless all-weather version features synthetic stock. Hawkeye African chambered in .375 Ruger and has 23" blued barrel, checkered walnut stock, windage-adjustable shallow "V" notch rear sight, white bead front sight. Introduced 2007.

Price: Standard, right- and left-hand.......................**$939.00**
Price: All-Weather **$939.00**
Price: Compact **$939.00**
Price: Laminate Compact **$999.00**
Price: Compact Magnum **$969.00**
Price: Magnum Hunter **$1,139.00**

Prices given are believed to be accurate at time of publication however, many factors affect retail pricing so exact prices are not possible.

Price: VT Varmint Target $1,069.00
Price: Predator $1,069.00

SAKO TRG-22 TACTICAL RIFLE
Caliber: .308 Winchester (TRG-22). **Features:** Features include target grade Cr-Mo or stainless barrels with muzzlebrake; three locking lugs; 60° bolt throw; adjustable two-stage target trigger; adjustable or folding synthetic stock; receiver-mounted integral 17mm axial optics rails with recoil stop-slots; tactical scope mount for modern three-turret tactical scopes (30 and 34 mm tube diameter); optional bipod.
Price: TRG-22 .... **$3,495.00**
Price: TRG-42 .... **$4,445.00**

SAKO MODEL 85
Caliber: .22-250 Rem., .243 Win., .25-06 Rem., .260, 6.5x55mm, .270 Win., .270 WSM, 7mm-08 Rem., 7x64, .308 Win., .30-06; 7mm WSM, .300 WSM, .338 Federal, 8x57IS, 9.3x62. **Barrel:** 22.4", 22.9", 24.4". **Weight:** 7.75 lbs. **Length:** NA. **Stock:** Polymer, laminated or high-grade walnut, straight comb, shadow-line cheekpiece. **Sights:** None furnished. **Features:** Controlled-round feeding, adjustable trigger, matte stainless or nonreflective satin blue. Offered in a wide range of variations and models. Introduced 2006. Imported from Finland by Beretta USA.
Price: Grey Wolf **$1,600.00**
Price: Black Bear **$1,850.00**
Price: Kodiak **$1,925.00**
Price: Varmint Laminated **$2,000.00**
Price: Classic **$2,200.00**
Price: Bavarian .... **$2,200.00 - $2,300.00**
Price: Bavarian carbine, Full-length stock **$2,400.00**
Price: Brown Bear **$2,175.00**

SAKO 85 FINNLIGHT
Similar to Model 85 but chambered in .243 Win., .25-06, .260 Rem., .270 Win., .270 WSM, .300 WSM, .30-06, .300 WM, .308 Win., 6.5x55mm, 7mm Rem Mag., 7mm-08. Weighs 6 lbs., 3 oz. to 6 lbs. 13 oz. Stainless steel barrel and receiver, black synthetic stock
Price: **$1,725.00**

SAVAGE AXIS SERIES
Caliber: .243 WIN., 7mm-08 REM., .308 WIN., .25-06 REM., .270 WIN, .30-06 SPFLD., .223 REM., .22-250 REM. **Barrel:** 22". **Weight:** 6.5 lbs. **Length:** 43.875". **Stock:** Black synthetic or camo, including pink/black Muddy Girl. **Sights:** Drilled and tapped for scope mounts. Several models come with factory mounted Weaver Kaspa 3-9x40 scope. **Features:** Available with black matte or stainless finish
Price: From .... **$363.00 to $525.00**

SAVAGE MODEL 25
Caliber: .17 Hornet, .22 Hornet, .222 Rem., .204 Ruger, .223 Rem., 4-shot magazine. **Barrel:** 24", medium-contour fluted barrel with recessed target crown, free-floating sleeved barrel, dual pillar bedding. **Weight:** 8.25 lbs. **Length:** 43.75" overall. **Stock:** Brown laminate with beavertail-style fore-end. **Sights:** Weaver-style bases installed. **Features:** Diameter-specific action built around the .223 Rem. bolthead dimension. Three locking lugs, 60-degree bolt lift, AccuTrigger adjustable from 2.5 to 3.25 lbs. Model 25 Classic Sporter has satin lacquer American walnut with contrasting fore-end tip, wraparound checkering, 22" blued barrel. **Weight:** 7.15 lbs. **Length:** 41.75". Introduced 2008. Made in U.S.A. by Savage Arms, Inc.
Price: From .... **$600.00 to $800.00**

SAVAGE CLASSIC SERIES MODEL 14/114
Caliber: .243 Win., 7mm-08 Rem., .308 Win., .270 Win., 7mm Rem. Mag., .30-06 Spfl., .300 Win. Mag., 3- or 4-shot magazine. **Barrel:** 22"

or 24". **Weight:** 7 to 7.5 lbs. **Length:** 41.75" to 43.75" overall (Model 14 short action); 43.25" to 45.25" overall (Model 114 long action). **Stock:** Satin lacquer American walnut with ebony fore-end, wraparound checkering, Monte Carlo Comb and cheekpiece. **Sights:** None furnished. Receiver drilled and tapped for scope mounting. **Features:** AccuTrigger, matte blued barrel and action, hinged floorplate.
Price: **$922.00**

SAVAGE MODEL 12 VARMINT/TARGET SERIES
Caliber: .204 Ruger, .223 Rem., .22-250 Rem.; 4-shot magazine. **Barrel:** 26" stainless barreled action, heavy fluted, free-floating and button-rifled barrel. **Weight:** 10 lbs. **Length:** 46.25" overall. **Stock:** Dual pillar bedded, low profile, black synthetic or laminated stock with extra-wide beavertail fore-end. **Sights:** None furnished; drilled and tapped for scope mounting. **Features:** Recessed target-style muzzle. AccuTrigger, oversized bolt handle, detachable box magazine, swivel studs. Model 112BVSS has heavy target-style prone laminated stock with high comb, Wundhammer palm swell, internal box magazine. Model 12VLP DBM has black synthetic stock, detachable magazine, and additional chamberings in .243, .308 Win., .300 Win. Mag. Model 12FV has blued receiver. Model 12BTCSS has brown laminate vented thumbhole stock. Made in U.S.A. by Savage Arms, Inc.
Price: 12 FV **$732.00**
Price: 12 FCV **$904.00**
Price: 12 BVSS **$1,021.00**
Price: 12 Varminter Low Profile (VLP) **$1,113.00**
Price: 12 Long Range Precision **$1,215.00**
Price: 12 BTCSS **$1,219.00**
Price: 12 Long Range Precision Varminter **$1,465.00**
Price: 12 F Class **$1,600.00**

SAVAGE MODEL 16/116 WEATHER WARRIORS
Caliber: .204 Ruger, .223 Rem., .22-250 Rem., .243 Win., 6.5 Creedmoor, 6.5-284 Norma, 7mm-08 Rem., .308 Win., .270 WSM, 7mm WSM, .300 WSM (short action Model 16), 2- or 4-shot magazine; .270 Win., 7mm Rem. Mag., .30-06 Spfl., .300 Win. Mag., .338 Win. Mag. (long action Model 114), 3- or 4-shot magazine. **Barrel:** 22", 24"; stainless steel with matte finish, free-floated barrel. **Weight:** 6.5 to 6.75 lbs. **Length:** 41.75" to 43.75" overall (Model 16); 42.5" to 44.5" overall (Model 116). **Stock:** Graphite/fiberglass filled composite. **Sights:** None furnished; drilled and tapped for scope mounting. **Features:** Quick-detachable swivel studs; laser-etched bolt. Left-hand models available. Model 116FSS introduced 1991; 116FSAK introduced 1994. Made in U.S.A. by Savage Arms, Inc.
Price: From .... **$885.00 to $966.00**

SAVAGE MODEL 11/111 HUNTER SERIES
Caliber: .223 Rem., .22-250 Rem., .243 Win., 6.5 Creedmoor, .260 Rem., 6.5x284 Norma, .338 Lapua, 7mm-08 Rem., .308 Win., 2- or 4-shot magazine; .25-06 Rem., .270 Win., 7mm Rem. Mag., .30-06 Spfl., .300 Win. Mag., (long action Model 111), 3- or 4-shot magazine. **Barrel:** 20", 22" or 24"; blued free-floated barrel. **Weight:** 6.5 to 6.75 lbs. **Length:** 41.75" to 43.75" overall (Model 11); 42.5" to 44.5" overall (Model 111). **Stock:** Graphite/fiberglass filled composite or hardwood. **Sights:** Ramp front, open fully adjustable rear; drilled and tapped for scope mounting. **Features:** Three-position top tang safety, double front locking lugs. Introduced 1994. Made in U.S.A. by Savage Arms, Inc.
Price: From .... **$560.00 to $1,104.00**

SAVAGE MODEL 10 BAS LAW ENFORCEMENT
Caliber: .308 Win., (10 BAS), .300 Win., .338 Lapua (110 BA). **Barrel:** 24" or 26" fluted heavy with muzzlebrake **Weight:** 13.4 to 15.6 lbs. **Length:**

Prices given are believed to be accurate at time of publication however, many factors affect retail pricing so exact prices are not possible.

45". **Features:** Bolt-action repeater based on Model 10 action but with M4-style collapsible buttstock, pistol grip with palm swell, all-aluminum Accustock, Picatinny rail for mounting optics.
Price: $2,375.00
Price: 110 BA.. $2,561.00

SAVAGE MODEL 10FP/110FP LAW ENFORCEMENT SERIES

Caliber: .223 Rem., .308 Win. (Model 10), 4-shot magazine; .25-06 Rem., .300 Win. Mag., (Model 110), 3- or 4-shot magazine. **Barrel:** 24"; matte blued free-floated heavy barrel and action. **Weight:** 6.5 to 6.75 lbs. **Length:** : 41.75" to 43.75" overall (Model 10); 42.5" to 44.5" overall (Model 110). **Stock:** Black graphite/fiberglass composition, pillar-bedded, positive checkering. **Sights:** None furnished. Receiver drilled and tapped for scope mounting. **Features:** Black matte finish on all metal parts. Double swivel studs on the forend for sling and/or bipod mount. Right- or left-hand. Model 110FP introduced 1990. Model 10FP introduced 1998. Model 10FCPXP has HS Precision black synthetic tactical stock with molded alloy bedding system, Leupold 3.5-10x40mm black matte scope with Mil Dot reticle, Farrell Picatinny Rail Base, flip-open lens covers, 1.25" sling with QD swivels, Harris bipod, Storm heavy-duty case. Made in U.S.A. by Savage Arms, Inc.
Price: Model 10FP, 10FLP (left hand), 110FP $775.00
Price: Model 10FP folding Choate stock................................ $896.00
Price: Model 10FCP McMillan, McMillan fiberglass tactical
  stock $1,545.00
Price: Model 10FCP-HS HS Precision, HS Precision tactical
  stock $1,277.00
Price: Model 10FPXP-HS Precision.................................... $2,715.00
Price: Model 10FCP $925.00
Price: Model 10FLCP, left-hand model, standard stock
  or Accu-Stock $975.00
Price: Model 10FCP SR $1,250.00
Price: Model 10 Precision Carbine $952.00

SAVAGE MODEL 10 PREDATOR SERIES

Caliber: .204 Ruger. .223, .22-250, .243, .260 Rem., 6.5 Creedmoor, 6.5x284 Norma. **Barrel:** 22", medium-contour. **Weight:** 7.25 lbs. **Length:** 43" overall. **Stock:** Synthetic with rounded fore-end and oversized bolt handle. **Features:** Entirely covered in either Mossy Oak Brush or Realtree Hardwoods Snow pattern camo. Also features AccuTrigger, AccuStock, detachable box magazine.
Price: $971.00

SAVAGE MODEL 12 PRECISION TARGET SERIES BENCHREST

Caliber: .308 Win., 6.5x284 Norma, 6mm Norma BR. **Barrel:** 29" ultra-heavy. **Weight:** 12.75 lbs. **Length:** 50" overall. **Stock:** Gray laminate. **Features:** New Left-Load, Right-Eject target action, Target AccuTrigger adjustable from approx 6 oz. to 2.5 lbs, oversized bolt handle, stainless extra-heavy free-floating and button-rifled barrel.
Price: $1,629.00

SAVAGE MODEL 12 PRECISION TARGET PALMA

Similar to Model 12 Benchrest but in .308 Win. only, 30" barrel, multi-adjustable stock, weighs 13.3 lbs.
Price: $2,085.00

SAVAGE MODEL 12 F CLASS TARGET RIFLE

Similar to Model 12 Benchrest but chambered in 6 Norma BR, 30" barrel, weighs 13.3 lbs.
Price: $1,600.00

SAVAGE MODEL 12 F/TR TARGET RIFLE

Similar to Model 12 Benchrest but in .308 Win. only, 30" barrel, weighs 12.65 lbs.
Price: $1,381.00

STEYR MANNLICHER CLASSIC

Caliber: .222 Rem., .223 Rem., .243 Win., .25-06 Rem., .308 Win., 6.5x55, .270 Win., .270 WSM, 7x64 Brenneke, 7mm-08 Rem., .30-06 Spfl., 8x57IS, 9.3x62, 7mm Rem. Mag., .300 WSM, .300 Win. Mag., .330 Wby. Mag.; 4-shot magazine. **Barrel:** 23.6" standard; 26" magnum; 20" full stock standard calibers. **Weight:** 7 lbs. **Length:** 40.1" overall. **Stock:** Hand-checkered fancy European oiled walnut with standard fore-end. **Sights:** Ramp front adjustable for elevation, V-notch rear adjustable for windage. **Finish:** Deep blue with case colors. **Features:** Single adjustable trigger; 3-position roller safety with "safe-bolt" setting; drilled and tapped for Steyr factory scope mounts. Introduced 1997. Imported from Austria by Steyr Arms, Inc.
Price: Half stock, standard calibers...................................... $3,799.00
Price: Half stock, standard calibers, no case color................. $2,799.00
Price: Full stock, standard calibers....................................... $4,199.00
Price: Full stock, standard calibers, no case colors.............. $2,999.00

STEYR PRO HUNTER

Similar to the Classic Rifle except has ABS synthetic stock with adjustable butt spacers, straight comb without cheekpiece, palm swell, Pachmayr 1" swivels. Special 10-round magazine conversion kit available. Introduced 1997. Imported from Austria by Steyr Arms, Inc.
Price: From .... **$1,150.00 to $1,377.00**

STEYR SCOUT

Caliber: .308 Win., 5-shot magazine. **Barrel:** 19", fluted. **Weight:** NA. **Length:** NA. **Stock:** Gray Zytel. **Sights:** Pop-up front & rear, Leupold M8 2.5x28 IER scope on Picatinny optic rail with Steyr mounts. **Features:** luggage case, scout sling, two stock spacers, two magazines. Introduced 1998. Imported from Austria by Steyr Arms, Inc.
Price: From $2,199.00

Prices given are believed to be accurate at time of publication however, many factors affect retail pricing so exact prices are not possible.

70TH EDITION, 2016 ✛ **471**

STEYR SSG08
Caliber: 7.62x51mmNATO (.308Win) or 7.62x63B (.300 Win Mag)., 10-shot magazine capacity. **Barrel:** 508mm or 600mm. **Weight:** 5.5 kg - 5.7 kg. **Length:** 1090mm - 1182mm. **Stock:** Dural aluminium foldingstock black with .280 mm long UIT-rail and various Picatinny rails. **Sights:** Front post sight and rear adjustable. **Features:** The STEYR SSG 08 features high-grade alumnium folding stock, adjustable cheekpiece and buttplate with height marking, and an ergonomical exchangeable pistol grip. The STEYR SSG 08 also features a Versa-Pod, a muzzlebrake, a Picatinny rail, a UIT rail on stock and various Picatinny rails on fore-end, and a 10-round HC-magazine. SBSrotary bolt action with four frontal locking lugs, arranged in pairs. Cold-hammer-forged barrels are available in standard or compact lengths.
Price: **$5,899.00**

STEYR SSG 69 PII
Caliber: .22-250 Rem., .243 Win., .308 Win., detachable 5-shot rotary magazine. **Barrel:** 26". **Weight:** 8.5 lbs. **Length:** 44.5" overall. **Stock:** Black ABS Cycolac with spacers for length of pull adjustment. **Sights:** Hooded ramp front adjustable for elevation, V-notch rear adjustable for windage. **Features:** Sliding safety; NATO rail for bipod; 1" swivels; Parkerized finish; single or double-set triggers. Imported from Austria by Steyr Arms, Inc.
Price: **$1,889.00**

THOMPSON/CENTER DIMENSION
Caliber: .204 Ruger, .223 Rem., .22-250 Rem., .243 Win., .270 Win., 7mm Rem. Mag., .308 Win., .30-06 Springfield, .300 Win. Mag., 3-round magazine. **Barrel:** 22 or 24". **Weight:** NA. **Length:** NA. **Stock:** Textured grip composite with adjustment spacers. **Features:** Calibers are interchangeable between certain series or "families" – .204/.223; .22-250/.243/7mm-08/.308; .270/.30-06; 7mm Rem. Mag./.300 Win. Mag. Introduced in 2012.
Price: **$689.00**

THOMPSON/CENTER VENTURE
Caliber: .270 Win., 7mm Rem. Mag., .30-06 Springfield, .300 Win. Mag. Standard length action with 3-round magazine. **Barrel:** 24", 20" (Compact). **Weight:** 7.5 lbs. **Stock:** Composite. **Sights:** None, Weaver-style base. **Features:** Nitride fat bolt design, externally adjustable trigger, two-position safety, textured grip. Introduced 2009.
Price: **$537.00**

THOMPSON/CENTER VENTURE MEDIUM ACTION
Bolt action rifle chambered in .204, .22-250, .223, .243, 7mm-08, .308 and 30TC. Features include a 24-inch crowned medium weight barrel, classic styled composite stock with inlaid traction grip panels, adjustable 3.5 to 5-pound trigger along with a drilled and tapped receiver (bases included). 3+1 detachable nylon box magazine. **Weight:** 7 lbs. **Length:** 43.5 inches.
Price: **$537.00**

THOMPSON/CENTER VENTURE PREDATOR PDX
Bolt action rifle chambered in .204, .22-250, .223, .243, .308. Similar to Venture Medium action but with heavy, deep-fluted 22-inch barrel and Max-1 camo finish overall. **Weight:** 8 lbs. **Length:** 41.5 inches.
Price: From **$638.00**

TIKKA T3 HUNTER
Caliber: .243 Win., .270 Win., 7mm Rem. Mag., .308 Win., .30-06 Spfl., .300 Win. Mag. **Stock:** Walnut. **Sights:** None furnished. **Barrel:** 22-7/16", 24-3/8". **Features:** Detachable magazine, aluminum scope rings. Left-hand model available. Introduced 2005. Imported from Finland by Beretta USA.
Price: **$775.00**

TIKKA T3 STAINLESS SYNTHETIC
Similar to the T3 Hunter except stainless steel, synthetic stock. Available in .243 Win., .25-06, .270 Win., .308 Win., .30-06 Spfl., .270 WSM, .300 WSM, 7mm Rem. Mag., .300 Win. Mag., .338 Win. Mag. Introduced 2005.
Price: **$675.00**

TIKKA T3 LITE
Similar to the T3 Hunter, available in .204 Ruger, .222 Rem., .223 Rem., .22-250 Rem., .243 Win., .25-06 Rem., .260 Rem., 6.5x66, 7mm-08, 7x64, 7mm. Rem. Mag., 8x57IS, .270 Win., .270 WSM, .308 Win., .30-06 Sprg., .300 Win. Mag., .300 WSM, .338 Federal, .338 Win. Mag., 9.3x62. Synthetic stock. Barrel lengths vary from 22-7/16" to 24-3/8". Made in Finland by Sako. Imported by Beretta USA.
Price: **$775.00**
Price: Left-hand **$825.00**

ULTRA LIGHT ARMS
Caliber: Custom made in virtually every current chambering. **Barrel:** Douglas, length to order. **Weight:** 4.75 to 7.5 lbs. **Length:** Varies. **Stock:** Kevlar graphite composite, variety of finishes. **Sights:** None furnished; drilled and tapped for scope mounts. **Features:** Timney trigger, hand-lapped action, button-rifled barrel, hand-bedded action, recoil pad, sling-swivel studs, optional Jewell trigger. Made in U.S.A. by New Ultra Light Arms.
Price: Model 20 (short action) **$3,500.00**
Price: Model 24 (long action) **$3,600.00**
Price: Model 28 (magnum action) **$3,900.00**
Price: Model 32 (long action magnum action) **$3,900.00**
Price: Model 40 (.416 Rigby) **$3,900.00**

WEATHERBY MARK V
Caliber: Deluxe version comes in all Weatherby calibers plus .243 Win., .270 Win., 7mm-08 Rem., .30-06 Spfl., .308 Win. **Barrel:** 24", 26", 28". **Weight:** 6.75 to 10 lbs. **Length:** 44" to 48.75" overall. **Stock:** Walnut, Monte Carlo with cheekpiece; high luster finish; checkered pistol grip and fore-end; recoil pad. **Sights:** None furnished. **Features:** 4 models with Mark V action and wood stocks; other common elements include cocking indicator; adjustable trigger; hinged floorplate, thumb safety; quick detachable sling swivels. Ultramark has hand-selected exhibition-grade walnut stock, maplewood/ebony spacers, 20-lpi checkering. Chambered for .257 and .300 Wby Mags. Lazermark same as Mark V Deluxe except stock has extensive oak leaf pattern laser carving on pistol grip and fore-end; chambered in Wby. Magnums—.257, .270 Win., 7mm., .300, .340, with 26" barrel. Introduced 1981. Sporter is same as the Mark V Deluxe without the embellishments. Metal

Prices given are believed to be accurate at time of publication however, many factors affect retail pricing so exact prices are not possible.

has low-luster blue, stock is Claro walnut with matte finish, Monte Carlo comb, recoil pad. Chambered for these Wby. Mags: .257, .270 Win., 7mm, .300, .340. Other chamberings: 7mm Rem. Mag., .300 Win. Introduced 1993. Six Mark V models come with synthetic stocks. Ultra Lightweight rifles weigh 5.75 to 6.75 lbs.; 24", 26" fluted stainless barrels with recessed target crown; Bell & Carlson stock with CNC-machined aluminum bedding plate and tan "spider web" finish, skeletonized handle and sleeve. Available in .243 Win., Wby. Mag., .25-06 Rem., .270 Win., 7mm-08 Rem., 7mm Rem. Mag., .280 Rem., .308 Win., .30-06 Spfl., .300 Win. Mag. Wby. Mag chamberings: .240, .257, .270 Win., 7mm, .300. Introduced 1998. Accumark uses Mark V action with heavy-contour 26" and 28" stainless barrels with black oxidized flutes, muzzle diameter of .705". No sights, drilled and tapped for scope mounting. Stock is composite with matte gel-coat finish, full-length aluminum bedding Hasblock. Weighs 8.5 lbs. Chambered for these Wby. Mags: .240, .257, .270, 7mm, .300, .340, .338-378, .30-378. Other chamberings: .22-250, .243 Win., .25-06 Rem., .270 Win., .308 Win., 7mm Rem. Mag., .300 Win. Mag. Introduced 1996. SVM (Super Varmint Master) has 26" fluted stainless barrel, spiderweb-pattern tan laminated synthetic stock, fully adjustable trigger. Chambered for .223 Rem., .22-250 Rem., .243. Mark V Synthetic has lightweight injection-molded synthetic stock with raised Monte Carlo comb, checkered grip and fore-end, custom floorplate release. Weighs 6.5-8.5 lbs., 24-28" barrels. Available in .22-250 Rem., .243 Win., .25-06 Rem., .270 Win., 7mm-08 Rem., 7mm Rem. Mag, .280 Rem., .308 Win., .30-06 Spfl., .300 Win. Mag., .375 H&H Mag., and these Wby. Magnums: .240, .257, .270 Win., 7mm, .300, .30-378, .338-378, .340. Introduced 1997. Fibermark composites are similar to other Mark V models except has black Kevlar and fiberglass composite stock and bead-blast blue or stainless finish. Chambered for 9 standard and magnum calibers. Introduced 1983; reintroduced 2001. SVR comes with 22" button-rifled chrome-moly barrel, .739" muzzle diameter. Composite stock w/bedding block, gray spiderweb pattern. Made in U.S.A. From Weatherby.

Price: Mark V Deluxe **$2,400.00**
Price: Mark V Ultramark...**$3,200.00**
Price: Mark V Lazermark...**$2,600.00**
Price: Mark V Sporter **$1,600.00**
Price: Mark V Ultra Lightweight...............................**$2,100.00**
Price: Mark V Accumark .... **$2,100.00 to $2,400.00**
Price: Mark V Fibermark...**$1,500.00**

WEATHERBY VANGUARD II SERIES

Caliber: .240, .257, and .300 Wby Mag. **Barrel:** 24" barreled action, matte black. **Weight:** 7.5 to 8.75 lbs. **Length:** 44" to 46-3/4" overall. **Stock:** Raised comb, Monte Carlo, injection-molded composite stock. **Sights:** None furnished. **Features:** One-piece forged, fluted bolt body with three gas ports, forged and machined receiver, adjustable trigger, factory accuracy guarantee. Vanguard Stainless has 410-Series stainless steel barrel and action, bead blasted matte metal finish. Vanguard Deluxe has raised comb, semi-fancy-grade Monte Carlo walnut stock with maplewood spacers, rosewood fore-end and grip cap, polished action with high-gloss-blued metalwork. Vanguard Synthetic Package includes Vanguard Synthetic rifle with Bushnell Banner 3-9x40mm scope mounted and boresighted, Leupold Rifleman rings and bases, Uncle Mikes nylon sling, and Plano PRO-MAX injection-molded case. Sporter has Monte Carlo walnut stock with satin urethane finish, fineline diamond point checkering, contrasting rosewood fore-end tip, matte-blued metalwork. Sporter SS metalwork is 410 Series bead-blasted stainless steel. Vanguard Youth/Compact has 20" No. 1 contour barrel, short action, scaled-down nonreflective matte black hardwood stock with 12.5" length of pull, and full-size, injection-molded composite stock. Chambered for .223 Rem., .22-250 Rem., .243 Win., .308 Win. Weighs 6.75 lbs.; OAL 38.9". Sub-MOA Matte and Sub-MOA Stainless models have pillar-bedded Fiberguard composite stock (Aramid, graphite unidirectional fibers and fiberglass) with 24" barreled action; matte black metalwork, Pachmayr Decelerator recoil pad. Sub-MOA Stainless metalwork is 410 Series bead-blasted stainless steel. Sub-MOA Varmint guaranteed to shoot 3-shot group of .99" or less when used with specified Weatherby factory or premium (non-Weatherby calibers) ammunition. Hand-laminated, tan Monte Carlo composite stock with black spiderwebbing; CNC-machined aluminum bedding block, 22" No. 3 contour barrel, recessed target crown. Varmint Special has tan injection-molded Monte

Carlo composite stock, pebble grain finish, black spiderwebbing. 22" No. 3 contour barrel (.740" muzzle dia.), bead blasted matte black finish, recessed target crown. Back Country has two-stage trigger, pillar-bedded Bell & Carlson stock, 24-in. fluted barrel, three-position safety. WBY-X Series comes with choice of several contemporary camo finishes (Bonz, Black Reaper, Kryptek, Hog Reaper, Whitetail Bonz, Blaze, GH2 "Girls Hunt Too") and is primarily targeted to younger shooters. Made in U.S.A. From Weatherby.

Price: Vanguard Synthetic **$649.00**
Price: Vanguard Synthetic DBM .... **$749.00 to $899.00**
Price: Vanguard Stainless...**$799.00**
Price: Vanguard Deluxe, 7mm Rem. Mag., .300 Win. Mag. ..**$1,149.00**
Price: Vanguard Synthetic Package, .25-06 Rem.................**$999.00**
Price: Vanguard Sporter **$849.00**
Price: Vanguard Youth/Compact **$599.00**
Price: Vanguard S2 Back Country **$1,399.00**
Price: Vanguard WBY-X Series **$749.00**
Price: Vanguard Black Reaper...**$749.00**
Price: Vanguard RC (Range Certified)...............................**$1,199.00**
Price: Vanguard Varmint Special **$849.00**

WINCHESTER MODEL 70

Caliber: Varies by model. Available in virtually all popular calibers. **Barrel:** Blued, or free-floating, fluted stainless hammer-forged barrel, 22", 24", 26". Recessed target crown. **Weight:** 6.75 to 7.25 lbs. **Length:** 41" to 45.75 " overall. **Stock:** Walnut (three models) or Bell and Carlson composite; textured charcoal-grey matte finish, Pachmayr Decelerator recoil pad. Super Grade offered with maple stock. **Sights:** None. **Features:** Claw extractor, three-position safety, M.O.A. three-lever trigger system, factory-set at 3.75 lbs. Super Grade features fancy grade walnut stock, contrasting black fore-end tip and pistol grip cap, and sculpted shadowline cheekpiece. Featherweight Deluxe has angled-comb walnut stock, Schnabel fore-end, satin finish, cut checkering. Extreme Weather SS has composite stock, drop @ comb, 0.5"; drop @ heel, 0.5". Made in U.S.A. From Winchester Repeating Arms.

Price: Extreme Weather SS...**$1,270.00**
Price: Super Grade **$1,360.00**
Price: Super Grade Maple stock .... **$1,600.00 to $1,640.00**

WINCHESTER MODEL 70 COYOTE LIGHT

Caliber: .22-250, .243 Winchester, .308 Winchester, .270 WSM, .300 WSM and .325 WSM, five-shot magazine (3-shot in .270 WSM, .300 WSM and .325 WSM). **Barrel:** 22" fluted stainless barrel (24" in .270 WSM, .300 WSM and .325 WSM). **Weight:** 7.5 lbs. **Length:** NA. **Features:** Composite Bell and Carlson stock, Pachmayr Decelerator pad. Controlled round feeding. No sights but drilled and tapped for mounts.
Price: .... **$1,200.00 to $1,240.00**

WINCHESTER MODEL 70 FEATHERWEIGHT

Caliber: .22-250, .243, 7mm-08, .308, .270 WSM, 7mm WSM, .300 WSM, .325 WSM, .25-06, .270, .30-06, 7mm Rem. Mag., .300 Win. Mag., .338 Win. Mag. Capacity 5 rounds (short action) or 3 rounds (long action). **Barrel:** 22" blued barrel (24" in magnum chamberings). **Weight:** 6-1/2 to 7-1/4 lbs. **Length:** NA. **Features:** Satin-finished checkered Grade I walnut stock, controlled round feeding. Pachmayr Decelerator pad. No sights but drilled and tapped for scope mounts.
Price: .... **$940.00 to $980.00**

WINCHESTER MODEL 70 SPORTER

Caliber: .270 WSM, 7mm WSM, .300 WSM, .325 WSM, .25-06, .270, .30-06, 7mm Rem. Mag., .300 Win. Mag., .338 Win. Mag. Capacity 5 rounds (short action) or 3 rounds (long action). **Barrel:** 22", 24" or

26" blued. **Weight:** 6-1/2 to 7-1/4 lbs. **Length:** NA. **Features:** Satin-finished checkered Grade I walnut stock with sculpted cheekpiece, controlled round feeding. Pachmayr Decelerator pad. No sights but drilled and tapped for scope mounts.
Price: .... $940.00 to $980.00

WINCHESTER MODEL 70 ULTIMATE SHADOW
Caliber: .243, .308, .270 WSM, 7mm WSM, .300 WSM, .325 WSM, .270, .30-06, 7mm Rem. Mag., .300 Win. Mag. Capacity 5 rounds (short action) or 3 rounds (long action). **Barrel:** 22" matte stainless (24" or 26" in magnum chamberings). **Weight:** 6-1/2 to 7-1/4 lbs. **Length:** NA. **Features:** Synthetic stock with WinSorb recoil pad, controlled round feeding. Pachmayr Decelerator pad. No sights but drilled and tapped for scope mounts.
Price: .... $760.00 to $1,040.00

WINCHESTER MODEL 70 ALASKAN
Caliber: .30-06, .300 Win. Mag., .338 Win. Mag., .375 H&H Magnum. **Barrel:** 25 inches. **Weight:** 8.8 pounds. **Sights:** Folding adjustable rear, hooded brass bead front. **Stock:** Satin finished Monte Carlo with cut checkering. **Features:** Integral recoil lug, Pachmayr Decelerator recoil pad.
Price: $1,270.00

WINCHESTER MODEL 70 SAFARI EXPRESS
Caliber: .375 H&H Magnum, .416 Remington, .458 Winchester. **Barrel:** 24 inches. **Weight:** 9 pounds. **Sights:** Fully adjustable rear,

hooded brass bead front. **Stock:** Satin finished Monte Carlo with cut checkering, deluxe cheekpiece. **Features:** Forged steel receiver with double integral recoil lugs bedded front and rear, dual steel crossbolts, Pachmayr Decelerator recoil pad.
Price: $1,420.00

WINCHESTER XPR
Caliber: .270 Win., .30-06, .300 Win. Mag., .338 Win. Mag. Detachable box magazine holds 3 to 5 rounds. **Barrel:** 24 or 26". **Stock:** Black polymer with Inflex Technology recoil pad. **Weight:** Approx. 7 lbs. **Finish:** Matte blue. **Features:** Bolt unlock button, nickel coated Teflon bolt.
Price: $549.99
Price: Mossy Oak Break-Up Country camo stock................... $600.00
Price: With Vortex II 3-9x40 scope $710.00

ARMALITE AR-50
Caliber: .50 BMG **Barrel:** 31". **Weight:** 33.2 lbs. **Length:** 59.5" **Stock:** Synthetic. **Sights:** None furnished. **Features:** A single-shot bolt-action rifle designed for long-range shooting. Available in left-hand model. Made in U.S.A. by Armalite.
Price: $3,359.00

BALLARD 1875 1 1/2 HUNTER
Caliber: Various calibers. **Barrel:** 26-30". **Weight:** NA **Length:** NA. **Stock:** Hand-selected classic American walnut. **Sights:** Blade front, Rocky Mountain rear. **Features:** Color case-hardened receiver, breechblock and lever. Many options available. Made in U.S.A. by Ballard Rifle & Cartridge Co.
Price: $3,250.00

BALLARD 1875 #3 GALLERY SINGLE SHOT
Caliber: Various calibers. **Barrel:** 24-28" octagonal with tulip. **Weight:** NA. **Length:** NA. **Stock:** Hand-selected classic American walnut. **Sights:** Blade front, Rocky Mountain rear. **Features:** Color case-hardened receiver, breechblock and lever. Many options available. Made in U.S.A. by Ballard Rifle & Cartridge Co.
Price: $3,300.00

BALLARD 1875 #4 PERFECTION
Caliber: Various calibers. **Barrel:** 30" or 32" octagon, standard or heavyweight. **Weight:** 10.5 lbs. (standard) or 11.75 lbs. (heavyweight bbl.) **Length:** NA. **Stock:** Smooth walnut. **Sights:** Blade front, Rocky Mountain rear. **Features:** Rifle or shotgun-style buttstock, straight grip action, single or double-set trigger, "S" or right lever, hand polished and lapped Badger barrel. Made in U.S.A. by Ballard Rifle & Cartridge Co.
Price: $3,950.00

BALLARD 1875 #7 LONG RANGE
Caliber: .32-40, .38-55, .40-65, .40-70 SS, .45-70 Govt., .45-90, .45-110. **Barrel:** 32", 34" half-octagon. **Weight:** 11.75 lbs. **Length:** NA. **Stock:** Walnut; checkered pistol grip shotgun butt, ebony fore-end cap. **Sights:** Globe front. **Features:** Designed for shooting up to 1,000 yards. Standard or heavy barrel; single or double-set trigger; hard rubber or steel buttplate. Introduced 1999. Made in U.S.A. by Ballard Rifle & Cartridge Co.
Price: From $3,600.00

BALLARD 1875 #8 UNION HILL
Caliber: Various calibers. **Barrel:** 30" half-octagon. **Weight:** About 10.5 lbs. **Length:** NA. **Stock:** Walnut; pistol grip butt with cheekpiece. **Sights:** Globe front. **Features:** Designed for 200-yard offhand shooting. Standard or heavy barrel; double-set triggers; full loop lever; hook Schuetzen buttplate. Introduced 1999. Made in U.S.A. by Ballard Rifle & Cartridge Co.
Price: From $4,175.00

BALLARD MODEL 1885 LOW WALL SINGLE SHOT RIFLE
Caliber: Various calibers. **Barrel:** 24-28". **Weight:** NA. **Length:** NA. **Stock:** Hand-selected classic American walnut. **Sights:** Blade front, sporting rear. **Features:** Color case-hardened receiver, breechblock and lever. Many options available. Made in U.S.A. by Ballard Rifle & Cartridge Co.
Price: $3,300.00

BALLARD MODEL 1885 HIGH WALL STANDARD SPORTING SINGLE SHOT
Caliber: Various calibers. **Barrel:** Lengths to 34". **Weight:** NA. **Length:** NA. **Stock:** Straight-grain American walnut. **Sights:** Buckhorn or flattop rear, blade front. **Features:** Faithful copy of original Model 1885 High Wall; parts interchange with original rifles; variety of options available. Introduced 2000. Made in U.S.A. by Ballard Rifle & Cartridge Co.
Price: $3,300.00

BALLARD MODEL 1885 HIGH WALL SPECIAL SPORTING SINGLE SHOT
Caliber: Various calibers. **Barrel:** 28-30" octagonal. **Weight:** NA. **Length:** NA. **Stock:** Hand-selected classic American walnut. **Sights:** Blade front, sporting rear. **Features:** Color case-hardened receiver, breechblock and lever. Many options available. Made in U.S.A. by Ballard Rifle & Cartridge Co.
Price: $3,600.00

BROWN MODEL 97D SINGLE SHOT
Caliber: Available in most factory and wildcat calibers from .17 Ackley Hornet to .375 Winchester. **Barrel:** Up to 26", air gauged match grade. **Weight:** About 5 lbs., 11 oz. **Stock:** Sporter style with pistol grip, cheekpiece and Schnabel fore-end. **Sights:** None furnished; drilled and tapped for scope mounting. **Features:** Falling-block action gives rigid barrel-receiver matting; polished blue/black finish. Hand-fitted action. Standard and custom made-to-order rifles with many options. Made in U.S.A. by E. Arthur Brown Co., Inc.
Price: Standard model..$1,695.00

C. SHARPS ARMS MODEL 1875 TARGET & SPORTING RIFLE
Caliber: .38-55, .40-65, .40-70 Straight or Bottlenecks, .45-70, .45-90. **Barrel:** 30" heavy tapered round. **Weight:** 11 lbs. **Length:** NA. **Stock:** American walnut. **Sights:** Globe with post front sight. **Features:** Long Range Vernier tang sight with windage adjustments. Pistol grip stock with cheek rest; checkered steel buttplate. Introduced 1991. From C. Sharps Arms Co.
Price: Without sights...$1,325.00
Price: With blade front & Buckhorn rear barrel sights $1,420.00
Price: With standard Tang & Globe w/post & ball front
    sights $1,615.00
Price: With deluxe vernier Tang & Globe w/spirit level &
    aperture sights $1,730.00
Price: With single set trigger, add $125.00

C. SHARPS ARMS 1875 CLASSIC SHARPS
Similar to New Model 1875 Sporting Rifle except 26", 28" or 30" full octagon barrel, crescent buttplate with toe plate, Hartford-style fore-end with cast German silver nose cap. Blade front sight, Rocky Mountain buckhorn rear. Weighs 10 lbs. Introduced 1987. From C. Sharps Arms Co.
Price: $1,670.00

C. SHARPS ARMS 1874 BRIDGEPORT SPORTING
Caliber: .38-55 to .50-3.25. **Barrel:** 26", 28", 30" tapered octagon. **Weight:** 10.5 lbs. **Length:** 47". **Stock:** American black walnut; shotgun butt with checkered steel buttplate; straight grip, heavy fore-end with Schnabel tip. **Sights:** Blade front, buckhorn rear. Drilled and tapped for tang sight. **Features:** Double-set triggers. Made in U.S.A. by C. Sharps Arms.
Price: $1,895.00

CENTERFIRE RIFLES Single Shot

C. SHARPS ARMS NEW MODEL 1885 HIGHWALL
Caliber: .22 LR, .22 Hornet, .219 Zipper, .25-35 WCF, .32-40 WCF, .38-55 WCF, .40-65, .30-40 Krag, .40-50 ST or BN, .40-70 ST or BN, .40-90 ST or BN, .45-70 Govt. 2-1/10" ST, .45-90 2-4/10" ST, .45-100 2-6/10" ST, .45-110 2-7/8" ST, .45-120 3-1/4" ST. **Barrel:** 26", 28", 30", tapered full octagon. **Weight:** About 9 lbs., 4 oz. **Length:** 47" overall. **Stock:** Oil-finished American walnut; Schnabel-style forend. **Sights:** Blade front, buckhorn rear. Drilled and tapped for optional tang sight. **Features:** Single trigger; octagonal receiver top; checkered steel buttplate; color case-hardened receiver and buttplate, blued barrel. Many options available. Made in U.S.A. by C. Sharps Arms Co.
Price: From $1,850.00

CIMARRON U.S. SHOOTING TEAM CREEDMOOR SHARPS
Caliber: .45-70. **Barrel:** 34" round. **Weight:** 11.5 pounds. **Length:** NA. **Stock:** European walnut. **Sights:** Blade front, Creedmoor rear. **Features:** Color case-hardened frame, blued barrel. Hand-checkered grip and fore-end; hand-rubbed oil finish. A percentage of the sale of this rifle that was used to win the first organized shooting event in the United States, will be given to the USA Shooting Team to support their efforts to continue the country's legacy in international shooting sports. Made in Italy by Chiappa. Imported by Cimarron F.A. Co.
Price: From $1,559.70

CIMARRON BILLY DIXON 1874 SHARPS SPORTING
Caliber: .45-70, .45-90, .50-70. **Barrel:** 32" tapered octagonal. **Weight:** NA. **Length:** NA. **Stock:** European walnut. **Sights:** Blade front, Creedmoor rear. **Features:** Color case-hardened frame, blued barrel. Hand-checkered grip and fore-end; hand-rubbed oil finish. Made by Pedersoli. Imported by Cimarron F.A. Co.
Price: From $2,079.70

CIMARRON MODEL 1885 HIGH WALL
Caliber: .38-55, .40-65, .45-70 Govt., .45-90, .45-120, .30-40 Krag, .348 Winchester, .405 Winchester. **Barrel:** 30" octagonal. **Weight:** NA. **Length:** NA. **Stock:** European walnut. **Sights:** Bead front, semi-buckhorn rear. **Features:** Replica of the Winchester 1885 High Wall rifle. Color case-hardened receiver and lever, blued barrel. Curved buttplate. Optional double-set triggers. Introduced 1999. Imported by Cimarron F.A. Co.
Price: From $1,065.00
Price: With pistol grip, from $1,250.00

CIMARRON MODEL 1885 LOW WALL
Caliber: .22 Hornet, .32-20, .38-40, .44-40, .45 Colt. **Barrel:** 30" octagonal. **Weight:** NA. **Length:** NA. **Stock:** European walnut. **Sights:** Bead front, semi-buckhorn rear. **Features:** Replica of the Winchester 1885 Low Wall rifle. Color case-hardened receiver, blued barrel. Curved buttplate. Optional double-set triggers. Introduced 1999. Imported by Cimarron F.A. Co.
Price: From $1,003.00

CIMARRON ADOBE WALLS ROLLING BLOCK
Caliber: .45-70 Govt. **Barrel:** 30" octagonal. **Weight:** 10-1/3 lbs. **Length:** NA. **Stock:** Hand-checkered European walnut. **Sights:** Bead front, semi-buckhorn rear. **Features:** Color case-hardened receiver, blued barrel. Curved buttplate. Double-set triggers. Made by Pedersoli. Imported by Cimarron F.A. Co.
Price: From $1,805.00

DAKOTA ARMS MODEL 10
Caliber: Most rimmed and rimless commercial calibers. **Barrel:** 23". **Weight:** 6 lbs. **Length:** 39.5" overall. **Stock:** Medium fancy grade walnut in classic style. Standard or full-length Mannlicher-style. Checkered grip and fore-end. **Sights:** None furnished. Drilled and

tapped for scope mounting. **Features:** Falling block action with underlever. Top tang safety. Removable trigger plate for conversion to single set trigger. Introduced 1990. Made in U.S.A. by Dakota Arms.
Price: From $5,260.00
Price: Deluxe from $6,690.00

DAKOTA ARMS SHARPS
Calibers: Virtually any caliber from .17 Ackley Hornet to .30-40 Krag. Features include a 26" octagon barrel, XX-grade walnut stock with straight grip and tang sight. Many options and upgrades are available.
Price: From $4,490.00

EMF PREMIER 1874 SHARPS
Caliber: .45-70, .45-110, .45-120. **Barrel:** 32", 34". **Weight:** 11-13 lbs. **Length:** 49", 51" overall. **Stock:** Pistol grip, European walnut. **Sights:** Blade front, adjustable rear. **Features:** Superb quality reproductions of the 1874 Sharps Sporting Rifles; case-hardened locks; double-set triggers; blue barrels. Imported from Pedersoli by EMF.
Price: Business Rifle...$1,499.90
Price: Down Under Sporting Rifle, Patchbox, heavy barrel ..$2,249.90
Price: Silhouette, pistol-grip $1,799.90
Price: Super Deluxe Hand Engraved $3,500.00

EMF ROLLING BLOCK SPORTING TARGET
Caliber: .45/70. **Barrel:** 30" octagonal. **Weight:** 9 lbs. **Finish:** Polished blue with case hardened frame. Accurate reproduction of Remington Rolling Block rifle. Imported from Pedersoli by EMF.
Price: $1,350.00

EMF ROLLING BLOCK SUPER MATCH
Caliber: .45/70. **Barrel:** 34" round. **Weight:** 12 lbs. **Sights:** Adjustable Creedmoor rear, adjustable front with interchangeable inserts. **Stock:** Checkered walnut. **Finish:** Polished blue with case hardened frame. Imported from Pedersoli by EMF.
Price: $1,635.00

EMF SPRINGFIELD TRAPDOOR RIFLE/CARBINE
Caliber: .45/70. **Barrel:** Round 22" (Carbine) or 26" (Officer's Model). **Weight:** 7 or 8 lbs. **Features:** Officer's Model has Creedmoor adjustable sight, checkered walnut stock, steel fore-end cap. Carbine has saddle ring, oil-finished walnut stock. Both models have single set trigger, case hardened frame, blued barrel. Imported from Pedersoli by EMF.
Price: Carbine $1,540.00
Price: Officer's $1,890.00

H&R BUFFALO CLASSIC
Caliber: .45 Colt or .45-70 Govt. **Barrel:** 32" heavy. **Weight:** 8 lbs. **Length:** 46" overall. **Stock:** Cut-checkered American black walnut. **Sights:** Williams receiver sight; Lyman target front sight with 8 aperture inserts. **Features:** Color case-hardened Handi-Rifle action with exposed hammer; color case-hardened crescent buttplate; 19th century checkering pattern. Introduced 1995. Made in U.S.A. by H&R 1871, Inc.
Price: Buffalo Classic Rifle..$479.00

H&R HANDI-RIFLE
Caliber: .204 Ruger, .22 Hornet, .223 Rem., .243 Win., .30-30, .270 Win., .280 Rem., 7mm-08 Rem., .308 Win., 7.62x39 Russian, .30-06 Spfl., .357 Mag., .35 Whelen, .44 Mag., .45-70 Govt., .500

Prices given are believed to be accurate at time of publication however, many factors affect retail pricing so exact prices are not possible.

S&W. **Barrel:** From 20" to 26", blued or stainless. **Weight:** 5.5 to 7 lbs. **Stock:** Walnut-finished hardwood or synthetic. **Sights:** Vary by model, but most have ramp front, folding rear, or are drilled and tapped for scope mount. **Features:** Break-open action with side-lever release. Swivel studs on all models. Blue finish. Introduced 1989. From H&R 1871, Inc.

Price:	$314.00
Price: Synthetic stock	$323.00
Price: Thumbhole stock	$341.00
Price: Superlight model	$323.00

H&R SURVIVOR
Caliber: 223 Rem., .308 Win. **Barrel:** 20" to 22" bull contour. **Weight:** 6 lbs. **Length:** 34.5" to 36" overall. **Stock:** Black polymer, thumbhole design. **Sights:** None furnished; scope mount provided. **Features:** Receiver drilled and tapped for scope mounting. Stock and fore-end have storage compartments for ammo, etc.; comes with integral swivels and black nylon sling. Introduced 1996. Made in U.S.A. by H&R 1871, Inc.
Price: Blue or nickel finish $327.00

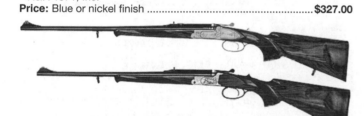

KRIEGHOFF HUBERTUS SINGLE-SHOT
Caliber: .222, .22-250, .243 Win., .270 Win., .308 Win., .30-06 Spfl., 5.6x50R Mag., 5.6x52R, 6x62R Freres, 6.5x57R, 6.5x65R, 7x57R, 7x65R, 8x57JRS, 8x75RS, 9.3x74R, 7mm Rem. Mag., .300 Win. Mag. **Barrel:** 23.5". Shorter lengths available. **Weight:** 6.5 lbs. **Length:** 40.5" **Stock:** High-grade walnut. **Sights:** Blade front, open rear. **Features:** Break-open loading with manual cocking lever on top tang; takedown; extractor; Schnabel forearm; many options. Imported from Germany by Krieghoff International Inc.
Price: Hubertus single shot, from $6,995.00
Price: Hubertus, magnum calibers $7,995.00

MERKEL K1 MODEL LIGHTWEIGHT STALKING
Caliber: .243 Win., .270 Win., 7x57R, .308 Win., .30-06 Spfl., 7mm Rem. Mag., .300 Win. Mag., 9.3x74R. **Barrel:** 23.6". **Weight:** 5.6 lbs. unscoped. **Stock:** Satin-finished walnut, fluted and checkered; sling-swivel studs. **Sights:** None (scope base furnished). **Features:** Franz Jager single-shot break-open action, cocking/uncocking slide-type safety, matte silver receiver, selectable trigger weights, integrated, quick detach 1" or 30mm optic mounts (optic not included). Extra barrels are an option. Imported from Germany by Merkel USA.
Price: Jagd Stalking Rifle $3,795.00
Price: Jagd Stutzen Carbine $4,195.00
Price: Extra barrels $1,195.00

MILLER ARMS
Calibers: Virtually any caliber from .17 Ackley Hornet to .416

Remington. Falling block design with 24" premium match-grade barrel, express sights, XXX-grade walnut stock and fore-end with 24 lpi checkering. Made in several styles including Classic, Target and Varmint. Many options and upgrades are available. From Dakota Arms.
Price: From $5,590.00

ROSSI SINGLE-SHOT SERIES
Caliber: .223 Rem., .243 Win., .44 Magnum. **Barrel:** 22" **Weight:** 6.25 lbs. **Stocks:** Black Synthetic Synthetic with recoil pad and removable cheek piece. **Sights:** Adjustable rear, fiber optic front, scope rail. Some models have scope rail only. **Features:** Single-shot break open, positive ejection, internal transfer bar mechanism, manual external safety, trigger block system, Taurus Security System, Matte blue finish.
Price: $307.00

ROSSI MATCHED PAIRS
Gauge/Caliber: 20 gauge shotgun barrel with interchangeable rifle barrel in either .223 Rem. or .243 caliber. **Barrel:** 23" shotgun, 28" rifle. **Weight:** 5-6.3 lbs. **Stock:** Black synthetic. **Sights:** Bead front on shotgun barrel, fully adjustable front and rear on rifle barrel, top rail mounted for scope, fully adjustable fiber optic sights. **Features:** Single-shot break open, internal transfer bar mechanism, manual external safety, blue finish, trigger block system, Taurus Security System. Rimfire models are also available.
Price: $352.00

RUGER NO. 1-A LIGHT SPORTER
Caliber: 7mm-08 Rem. **Barrel:** 22". **Weight:** 7.25 lbs. **Length:** 38.5". **Stock:** Checkered American walnut with Alexander Henry style fore-end. **Sights:** Adjustable rear, bead front. **Features:** Under-lever falling-block design with automatic ejector, top tang safety. Ruger currently chambers each No. 1 variation only in one caliber, which will change every year.
Price: $1,449.00

RUGER NO. 1-V VARMINTER
Caliber: .223 Rem. **Barrel:** 26" heavy barrel. **Weight:** 8.5 lbs. **Length:** 38.5". **Stock:** Checkered American walnut with semi-beaver-tail fore-end. **Sights:** None. Barrel ribbed for target scope block, with 1" Ruger scope rings. **Features:** Under-lever falling-block design with automatic ejector, top tang safety. Ruger currently chambers each No. 1 variation only in one caliber, which will change every year.
Price: $1,449.00

RUGER NO. 1 RSI INTERNATIONAL
Caliber: 6.5x55mm. **Barrel:** 20 inches. **Weight:** 7 lbs. **Length:** 38.5".

Prices given are believed to be accurate at time of publication however, many factors affect retail pricing so exact prices are not possible.

70TH EDITION, 2016 ✛ **477**

Stock: Checkered American walnut with full-length International-style fore-end with loop sling swivel. **Sights:** Adjustable folding leaf rear sight on quarter-rib, ramp front with gold bead. **Features:** Under-lever falling-block design with automatic ejector, top tang safety. Ruger currently chambers each No. 1 variation only in one caliber, which will change every year.
Price: $1,449.00

RUGER NO. 1-H TROPICAL RIFLE
Caliber: .375 H&H Magnum. **Barrel:** 24" heavy contour. **Weight:** 9.25 lbs. **Length:** 38.5". **Stock:** Checkered American walnut with Alexander Henry-style fore-end. **Sights:** Adjustable folding leaf rear sight on quarter-rib, ramp front with dovetail gold bead. **Features:** Under-lever falling-block design with automatic ejector, top tang safety. Ruger currently chambers each No. 1 variation only in one caliber, which will change every year.
Price: $1,449.00

RUGER NO. 1-S MEDIUM SPORTER
Caliber: .30-06. **Barrel:** 20" **Weight:** 7.25 lbs. **Length:** 38.5". **Stock:** Checkered American walnut with Alexander Henry-style fore-end. **Sights:** Adjustable folding leaf rear sight on quarter-rib, ramp front sight base and dovetail-type gold bead front sight. **Features:** Under-lever falling-block design with automatic ejector, top tang safety. Ruger currently chambers each No. 1 variation only in one caliber, which will change every year.
Price: $1,449.00

NO. 1-B STANDARD
Caliber: .257 Weatherby. **Barrel:** 28". **Stock:** Checkered American walnut with Alexander Henry-style fore-end, **Sights:** None. **Barrel:** Ribbed for target scope block, with 1" Ruger scope rings. **Weight:** 8.5 lbs. Under-lever falling-block design with automatic ejector, top tang safety. Ruger currently chambers each No. 1 variation only in one caliber, which will change every year.
Price: $1,449.00

SHILOH CO. SHARPS 1874 LONG RANGE EXPRESS
Caliber: .38-55, .40-50 BN, .40-70 BN, .40-90 BN, .40-70 ST, .40-90 ST, .45-70 Govt. ST, .45-90 ST, .45-110 ST, .50-70 ST, .50-90 ST. **Barrel:** 34" tapered octagon. **Weight:** 10.5 lbs. **Length:** 51" overall. **Stock:** Oil-finished walnut (upgrades available) with pistol grip, shotgun-style butt, traditional cheek rest, Schnabel forend. **Sights:** Customer's choice. **Features:** Re-creation of the Model 1874 Sharps rifle. Double-set triggers. Made in U.S.A. by Shiloh Rifle Mfg. Co.
Price: $2,018.00
Price: Sporter Rifle No. 1 (similar to above except with 30" barrel, blade front, buckhorn rear sight) $2,018.00
Price: Sporter Rifle No. 3 (similar to No. 1 except straight-grip stock, standard wood) $1,910.00

SHILOH CO. SHARPS 1874 QUIGLEY
Caliber: .45-70 Govt., .45-110. **Barrel:** 34" heavy octagon. **Stock:**

Military-style with patch box, standard-grade American walnut. **Sights:** Semi-buckhorn, interchangeable front and midrange vernier tang sight with windage. **Features:** Gold inlay initials, pewter tip, Hartford collar, case color or antique finish. Double-set triggers.
Price: $3,464.00

SHILOH CO. SHARPS 1874 SADDLE
Caliber: .38-55, .40-50 BN, .40-65 Win., .40-70 BN, .40-70 ST, .40-90 BN, .40-90 ST, .44-77 BN, .44-90 BN, .45-70 Govt. ST, .45-90 ST, .45-100 ST, .45-110 ST, .45-120 ST, .50-70 ST, .50-90 ST. **Barrel:** 26" full or half octagon. **Stock:** Semi-fancy American walnut. Shotgun style with cheek rest. **Sights:** Buckhorn and blade. **Features:** Double-set trigger, numerous custom features can be added.
Price: $1,964.00

SHILOH CO. SHARPS 1874 MONTANA ROUGHRIDER
Caliber: .38-55, .40-50 BN, .40-65 Win., .40-70 BN, .40-70 ST, .40-90 BN, .40-90 ST, .44-77 BN, .44-90 BN, .45-70 Govt. ST, .45-90 ST, .45-100 ST, .45-110 ST, .45-120 ST, .50-70 ST, .50-90 ST. **Barrel:** 30" full or half octagon. **Stock:** American walnut in shotgun or military style. **Sights:** Buckhorn and blade. **Features:** Double-set triggers, numerous custom features can be added.
Price: $2,018.00

SHILOH CO. SHARPS CREEDMOOR TARGET
Caliber: .38-55, .40-50 BN, .40-65 Win., .40-70 BN, .40-70 ST, .40-90 BN, .40-90 ST, .44-77 BN, .44-90 BN, .45-70 Govt. ST, .45-90 ST, .45-100 ST, .45-110 ST, .45-120 ST, .50-70 ST, .50-90 ST. **Barrel:** 32", half round-half octagon. **Stock:** Extra fancy American walnut. Shotgun style with pistol grip. **Sights:** Customer's choice. **Features:** Single trigger, AA finish on stock, polished barrel and screws, pewter tip.
Price: $2,966.00

THOMPSON/CENTER ENCORE PROHUNTER PREDATOR RIFLE
Caliber: .204 Ruger, .223 Remington, .22-250 and .308 Winchester. **Barrel:** 28-inch deep-fluted interchangeable. **Length:** 42.5 inches. **Weight:** 7 3/4 lbs. **Stock:** Composite buttstock and fore-end with non-slip inserts in cheekpiece, pistol grip and fore-end. Realtree Advantage Max-1 camo finish overall. Scope is not included.
Price: $882.00

THOMPSON/CENTER ENCORE PRO HUNTER KATAHDIN CARBINE
Caliber: .45-70 Govt., .460 S&W Mag., .500 S&W Mag. **Barrel:** 28-inch deep-fluted interchangeable. **Length:** 34.5 inches. **Weight:** 7 lbs. **Stock:** Flex-Tech with Simms recoil pad. Grooved and textured grip surfaces. **Sights:** Adjustable rear peep, fiber optic front.
Price: $852.00

THOMPSON/CENTER G2 CONTENDER
Caliber: .204 Ruger, .223 Rem., 6.8 Rem. 7-30 Waters, .30-30 Win. **Barrel:** 23-inch interchangeable with blued finish. **Length:** 36.75 inches. **Stock:** Walnut. **Sights:** None. **Weight:** 5.5 pounds. Reintroduced in 2015. Interchangeable barrels available in several centerfire and rimfire calibers.
Price: $729.00

UBERTI 1874 SHARPS SPORTING
Caliber: .45-70 Govt. **Barrel:** 30", 32", 34" octagonal. **Weight:** 10.57 lbs. with 32" barrel. **Length:** 48.9" with 32" barrel. **Stock:** Walnut. **Sights:** Dovetail front, Vernier tang rear. **Features:** Cut checkering, case-colored finish on frame, buttplate, and lever. Imported by Stoeger Industries.
Price: Standard Sharps...$1,809.00
Price: Special Sharps $2,019.00
Price: Deluxe Sharps $3,129.00
Price: Down Under Sharps $2,579.00
Price: Long Range Sharps.......................................$2,579.00

Price: Buffalo Hunter Sharps $2,469.00
Price: Sharps Cavalry Carbine...............................$1,809.00
Price: Sharps Extra Deluxe $4,999.00
Price: Sharps Hunter $1,639.00

UBERTI 1885 HIGH-WALL SINGLE-SHOT
Caliber: .45-70 Govt., .45-90, .45-120. **Barrel:** 28" to 32". **Weight:** 9.3 to 9.9 lbs. **Length:** 44.5" to 47" overall. **Stock:** Walnut stock and fore-end. **Sights:** Blade front, fully adjustable open rear. **Features:** Based on Winchester High-Wall design by John Browning. Color case-hardened frame and lever, blued barrel and buttplate. Imported by Stoeger Industries.
Price: From .... $1,009.00 to $1,279.00

UBERTI SPRINGFIELD TRAPDOOR RIFLE/CARBINE
Caliber: .45-70 Govt., single shot **Barrel:** 22 or 32.5 inches. **Features:** Blue steel receiver and barrel, case-hardened breechblock and buttplate. **Sights:** Creedmoor style.
Price: Springfield Trapdoor Carbine, 22" barrel $1,669.00
Price: Springfield Trapdoor Army, 32.5" barrel $1,949.00

BAIKAL MP94 COMBO GUN

Caliber/Gauge: Over/under style with 12-gauge shotgun barrel over either a .223 or .308 rifle barrel. **Barrels:** 19.7". **Stock:** Checkered walnut. **Sights:** Adjustable rear, ramp front with bead. Picatinny or 11mm scope rail. **Features:** Four choke tubes for shotgun barrel. Double triggers. Made in Russia by Baikal and imported by U.S. Sporting Goods Inc.
Price: $592.00

BAIKAL MP221 DOUBLE RIFLE

Caliber: .30-06 or .45-70 side-by-side double rifle. **Barrels:** 23.5". **Stock:** Checkered walnut. **Sights:** Adjustable rear, ramp front with bead. Picatinny or 11mm scope rail. **Features:** Double triggers, extractors, adjustable barrel regulation. Made in Russia by Baikal and imported by U.S. Sporting Goods Inc.
Price: $1,155.00

BERETTA S686/S689 O/U RIFLE SERIES

Calibers: .30-06, 9.3x74R. **Barrels:** 23 inches. O/U boxlock action. Single or double triggers. EELL Grade has better wood, moderate engraving.
Price: .... $4,200.00 to $9,000.00
Price: EELL Diamond Sable grade, from $12,750.00

BRNO MODEL 802 COMBO GUN

Caliber/Gauge: .243 Win./12 ga. Over/under. **Barrels:** 23.6". **Weight:** 7.6 lbs. **Length:** 41". **Stock:** European walnut. **Features:** Double trigger, shotgun barrel is improved-modified chokes. Imported by CZ USA.
Price: $2,181.00

FAUSTI CLASS EXPRESS

Caliber: .30-06, .30R Blaser, 8x57 JRS, 9.3x74R, .444 Marlin, .45-70 Govt. Over/under. **Barrels:** 24". **Weight:** 7.5 lbs. **Length:** 41". **Stock:** Oil-finished Grade A walnut. Pistol grip, Bavarian or Classic. **Sights:** Folding leaf rear, fiber optic front adjustable for elevation. **Features:** Inertia single or double trigger, automatic ejectors. Made in Italy and imported by Fausti USA.
Price: $4,990.00
Price: SL Express w/hand engraving, AA wood $7,600.00

HOENIG ROTARY ROUND ACTION DOUBLE

Caliber: Most popular calibers. Over/under design. **Barrel:** 22" to 26". **Stock:** English Walnut; to customer specs. **Sights:** Swivel hood front with button release (extra bead stored in trap door gripcap), express-style rear on quarter-rib adjustable for windage and elevation; scope mount. **Features:** Round action opens by rotating barrels, pulling forward. Inertia extractor system, rotary safety blocks strikers. Single lever quick-detachable-e scope mount. Simple takedown without removing fore-end. Introduced 1997. Custom rifle made in U.S.A. by George Hoenig.
Price: From $22,500.00

HOENIG ROTARY ROUND ACTION COMBINATION

Caliber: Most popular calibers and shotgun gauges. Over/under design with rifle barrel atop shotgun barrel. **Barrel:** 26". **Weight:** 7 lbs. **Stock:** English Walnut to customer specs. **Sights:** Front ramp with button release blades. Foldable aperture tang sight windage and elevation adjustable. Quarter-rib with scope mount. **Features:** Round action opens by rotating barrels, pulling forward. Inertia extractor; rotary safety blocks strikers. Simple takedown without removing forend. Custom rifle made in U.S.A. by George Hoenig.
Price: $27,500.00

HOENIG VIERLING FOUR-BARREL COMBINATION

Caliber/gauge: Two 20-gauge shotgun barrels with one rifle barrel chambered for .22 Long Rifle and another for .223 Remington. Custom rifle made in U.S.A. by George Hoenig.
Price: $50,000.00

KRIEGHOFF CLASSIC DOUBLE

Caliber: 7x57R, 7x65R, .308 Win., .30-06 Spfl., 8x57 JRS, 8x75RS, 9.3x74R, 375NE, 500/416NE, 470NE, 500NE. **Barrel:** 23.5". **Weight:** 7.3 to 11 lbs. **Stock:** High grade European walnut. Standard model has conventional rounded cheekpiece, Bavaria model has Bavarian-style cheekpiece. **Sights:** Bead front with removable, adjustable wedge (.375 H&H and below), standing leaf rear on quarter-rib. **Features:** Boxlock action; double triggers; short opening angle for fast loading; quiet extractors; sliding, self-adjusting wedge for secure bolting; Purdey-style barrel extension; horizontal firing pin placement. Many options available. Introduced 1997. Imported from Germany by Krieghoff International.
Price: $10,995.00
Price: Engraved sideplates, add................................$4,000.00
Price: Extra set of rifle barrels, add $6,300.00
Price: Extra set of 20-ga., 28" shotgun barrels, add $4,400.00

KRIEGHOFF CLASSIC BIG FIVE DOUBLE RIFLE

Similar to the standard Classic except available in .375 H&H, .375 Flanged Mag. N.E., .416 Rigby, .458 Win., 500/416 NE, 470 NE, 500 NE. Has hinged front trigger, nonremovable muzzle wedge, Universal Trigger System, Combi Cocking Device, steel trigger-guard, specially weighted stock bolt for weight and balance. Many options available. Introduced 1997. Imported from Germany by Krieghoff International.
Price: $13,995.00
Price: Engraved sideplates, add $4,000.00
Price: Extra set of 20-ga. shotgun barrels, add....................$5,000.00
Price: Extra set of rifle barrels, add $6,300.00

LEBEAU-COURALLY EXPRESS SXS

Caliber: 7x65R, 8x57JRS, 9.3x74R, .375 H&H, .470 N.E. **Barrel:** 24" to 26". **Weight:** 7.75 to 10.5 lbs. **Stock:** Fancy French walnut with cheekpiece. **Sights:** Bead on ramp front, standing left express rear on quarter-rib. **Features:** Holland & Holland-type sidelock with automatic ejectors; double triggers. Built to order only. Imported from Belgium by Wm. Larkin Moore and Griffin & Howe.
Price: $45,000.00

MERKEL DRILLINGS

Caliber/Gauge: : 12, 20, 3" chambers, 16, 2-3/4" chambers; .22 Hornet, 5.6x50R Mag., 5.6x52R, .222 Rem., .243 Win., 6.5x55, 6.5x57R, 7x57R, 7x65R, .308 Win., .30-06 Spfl., 8x57JRS, 9.3x74R, .375 H&H. **Barrel:** 25.6". **Weight:** 7.9 to 8.4 lbs. depending upon caliber. **Stock:** Oil-finished walnut with pistol grip; cheekpiece on 12-, 16-gauge. **Sights:** Blade front, fixed rear. **Features:** Double barrel locking lug with Greener crossbolt; scroll-engraved, case-hardened receiver; automatic trigger safety; Blitz action; double triggers. Imported from Germany by Merkel USA.
Price: Model 96K (manually cocked rifle system), from.........$8,495.00
Price: Model 96K engraved (hunting series on receiver) $9,795.00

MERKEL BOXLOCK DOUBLE

Caliber: 5.6x52R, .243 Winchester, 6.5x55, 6.5x57R, 7x57R, 7x65R, .308 Win., .30-06 Springfield, 8x57 IRS, 9.3x74R. **Barrel:** 23.6". **Weight:** 7.7 oz. **Length:** NA. **Stock:** Walnut, oil finished, pistol grip. **Sights:** Fixed 100 meter. **Features:** Anson & Deeley boxlock action with cocking indicators, double triggers, engraved color case-hardened receiver. Introduced 1995. Imported from Germany by Merkel USA.
Price: Model 140-2, from.....................................$11,995.00
Price: Model 141 Small Frame SXS Rifle; built on smaller frame, chambered for 7mm Mauser, .30-06, or 9.3x74R $8,195.00
Price: Model 141 Engraved; fine hand-engraved hunting scenes on silvered receiver $9,495.00

RIZZINI EXPRESS 90L

Caliber: .308 Win., .30-06 Spfl., 7x65R, 9.3x74R, 8x57 JRS, .444 Marlin. **Barrel:** 24". **Weight:** 7.5 lbs. **Length:** 40" overall.

Prices given are believed to be accurate at time of publication however, many factors affect retail pricing so exact prices are not possible.

Stock: Select European walnut with satin oil finish; English-style cheekpiece. **Sights:** Ramp front, quarter-rib with express sight. **Features:** Over/under with color case-hardened boxlock action; automatic ejectors; single selective trigger; polished blue barrels. Extra 20-gauge shotgun barrels available. Imported from Italy by Fierce Products.
Price: With case...$4,500.00

SAVAGE MODEL 42
Caliber/Gauge: Break-open over/under design with .22 LR or .22 WMR barrel over a .410 shotgun barrel. Under-lever operation. **Barrel:** 20 inches. **Stock:** Synthetic black matte. **Weight:** 6.1 lbs. **Sights:** Adjustable rear, bead front. Updated variation of classic Stevens design from the 1940s.
Price: $485.00

ANSCHUTZ RX22
Caliber: .22 LR. AR-style semiautomatic rifle with blowback operation. **Barrel:** 16.5". **Features:** Available in several styles and colors including black, Desert Tan. Fixed or folding stock, adjustable trigger, military-type folding iron sights. Made in Germany and imported by Steyr Arms Inc.
Price: $895.00

AMERICAN TACTICAL IMPORTS GSG-522
Semiauto tactical rifle chambered in .22 LR. Features include 16.25-inch barrel; black finish overall; polymer fore-end and buttstock; backup iron sights; receiver-mounted Picaatinny rail; 10-round magazine. Several other rifle and carbine versions available.
Price: $451.00

BROWNING BUCK MARK SEMI-AUTO
Caliber: .22 LR, 10+1. **Action:** A rifle version of the Buck Mark Pistol; straight blowback action; machined aluminum receiver with integral rail scope mount; manual thumb safety. **Barrel:** Recessed crowns. **Stock:** Stock and forearm with full pistol grip. **Features:** Action lock provided. Introduced 2001. Four model name variations for 2006, as noted below. **Sights:** FLD Target, FLD Carbon, and Target models have integrated scope rails. Sporter has Truglo/Marble fiber-optic sights. Imported from Japan by Browning.
Price: FLD Target, 5.5 lbs., bull barrel, laminated stock $720.00
Price: Target, 5.4 lbs., blued bull barrel, wood stock $700.00
Price: Sporter, 4.4 lbs., blued sporter barrel w/sights $700.00

BROWNING SA-22 SEMI-AUTO 22
Caliber: .22 LR. Tubular magazine in buttstock hold 11 rounds. **Barrel:** 19.375". **Weight:** 5 lbs. 3 oz. **Length:** 37" overall. **Stock:** Checkered select walnut with pistol grip and semi-beavertail fore-end. **Sights:** Gold bead front, folding leaf rear. **Features:** Engraved receiver with polished blue finish; crossbolt safety; easy takedown for carrying or storage. The Grade VI is available with either grayed or blued receiver with extensive engraving with gold-plated animals: right side pictures a fox and squirrel in a woodland scene; left side shows a beagle chasing a rabbit. On top is a portrait of the beagle. Stock and fore-end are of high-grade walnut with a double-bordered cut checkering design. . Introduced 1956. Made in Belgium until 1974. Currently made in Japan by Miroku.
Price: Grade I, scroll-engraved blued receiver $700.00
Price: Grade VI BL, gold-plated engraved blued receiver $1,580.00

COLT TACTICAL RIMFIRE M4 OPS CARBINE
Blowback semiauto rife chambered in .22 LR, styled to resemble Colt M16. Features include 16.2-inch barrel; front sight adjustable for elevation; adjustable rear sight; alloy lower; adjustable telestock; flattop receiver with removable carry handle; 10- or 30-round detachable magazine. Made in Germany by Walther, under license from Colt, and imported by Umarex.
Price: $599.00

COLT TACTICAL RIMFIRE M4 CARBINE
Blowback semiauto rifle chambered in .22 LR, styled to resemble

Colt M4. Features include 16.2-inch barrel; front sight adjustable for elevation; adjustable rear sight; alloy lower; adjustable telestock; flattop receiver with optics rail; 10- or 30-round detachable magazine. M4 Ops model has four-position collapsible stock, muzzle brake, inline design. Made in Germany by Walther under license from Colt, and imported by Umarex.
Price: $569.00

CITADEL M-1 CARBINE
Caliber: .22LR., 10-round magazines. **Barrel:** 18". **Weight:** 4.8 lbs. **Length:** 35". **Stock:** Wood or synthetic in black or several camo patterns. **Features:** Built to the exacting specifications of the G.I. model used by U.S. infantrymen in both WWII theaters of battle and in Korea. Used by officers as well as tankers, drivers, artillery crews, mortar crews, and other personnel. Weight, barrel length and OAL are the same as the "United States Carbine, Caliber .30, M1," its official military designation. Made in Italy by Chiappa. Imported by Legacy Sports.
Price: Synthetic stock, black. $316.00
Price: Synthetic stock, camo..................................... $368.00
Price: Wood stock. $400.00

CZ MODEL 512
Caliber: .22 LR/.22 WMR, 5-round magazines. **Barrel:** 20.5". **Weight:** 5.9 lbs. **Length:** 39.3". **Stock:** Beech. **Sights:** Adjustable. **Features:** The modular design is easily maintained, requiring only a coin as a tool for field stripping. The action of the 512 is composed of an aluminum alloy upper receiver that secures the barrel and bolt assembly and a fiberglass reinforced polymer lower half that houses the trigger mechanism and detachable magazine. The 512 shares the same magazines and scope rings with the CZ 455 bolt-action rifle.
Price: .22 LR $480.00
Price: .22 WMR.. $510.00

H&K 416-22
Blowback semiauto rife chambered in .22 LR, styled to resemble H&K 416. Features include metal upper and lower receivers; rail interface system; retractable stock; pistol grip with storage compartment; on-rail sights; rear sight adjustable for wind and elevation; 16.1-inch barrel; 10- or 20-round magazine. Also available in pistol version with 9-inch barrel. Made in Germany by Walther under license from Heckler & Koch and imported by Umarex.
Price: $599.00

H&K MP5 A5
Blowback semiauto rife chambered in .22 LR, styled to resemble H&K MP5. Features include metal receiver; compensator; bolt catch; NAVY pistol grip; on-rail sights; rear sight adjustable for wind and elevation; 16.1-inch barrel; 10- or 25-round magazine. Also available in pistol version with 9-inch barrel. Also available with SD-type fore-end. Made in Germany by Walther under license from Heckler & Koch. Imported by Umarex.
Price: $499.00
Price: MP5 SD $599.00

HENRY U.S. SURVIVAL AR-7 22
Caliber: .22 LR, 8-shot magazine. **Barrel:** 16" steel lined. **Weight:** 2.25 lbs. **Stock:** ABS plastic. **Sights:** Blade front on ramp, aperture rear. **Features:** Takedown design stores barrel and action in hollow stock. Light enough to float on water. Dark gray or camo finish. Comes with

Prices given are believed to be accurate at time of publication however, many factors affect retail pricing so exact prices are not possible.

two magazines. Introduced 1998. From Henry Repeating Arms Co.
Price: H002B Black finish $290.00
Price: H002C Camo finish $350.00

KEL-TEC SU-22CA
Caliber: .22 LR. 26-round magazine. **Barrel:** 16.1". **Weight:** 4 lbs.
Length: 34" **Features:** Blowback action, crossbolt safety, adjustable
front and rear sights with integral picatinny rail. Threaded muzzle,
26-round magazine.
Price: $440.00

MAGNUM RESEARCH MAGNUMLITE
Caliber: .22 WMR or .22 LR, 10-shot magazine. **Barrel:** 17" graphite.
Weight: 4.45 lbs. **Length:** 35.5" overall. **Stock:** Hogue OverMolded
synthetic or walnut. **Sights:** Integral scope base. **Features:** Magnum
Lite graphite barrel, French grey anodizing, match bolt, target trigger.
.22 LR rifles use factory Ruger 10/22 magazines. 4-5 lbs. average
trigger pull. Graphite carbon-fiber barrel. Introduced: 2007. From
Magnum Research, Inc.
Price: .22 LR $665.00
Price: .22 WMR..$791.00

MARLIN MODEL 60
Caliber: .22 LR, 14-shot tubular magazine. **Barrel:** 19" round tapered.
Weight: About 5.5 lbs. **Length:** 37.5" overall. **Stock:** Press-checkered,
laminated Maine birch with Monte Carlo, full pistol grip; black synthetic
or Realtree Camo. **Sights:** Ramp front, open adjustable rear. Matted
receiver is grooved for scope mount. **Features:** Last-shot bolt hold-
open. Available with factory mounted 4x scope.
Price: Laminate..$199.00
Price: Model 60C camo $232.00
Price: Synthetic $191.00

MARLIN MODEL 60SS SELF-LOADING RIFLE
Same as the Model 60 except breech bolt, barrel and outer magazine
tube are made of stainless steel; most other parts are either nickel-
plated or coated to match the stainless finish. Monte Carlo stock is of
black/gray Maine birch laminate, and has nickel-plated swivel studs,
rubber buttpad. Introduced 1993.
Price: $300.00

MARLIN 70PSS PAPOOSE STAINLESS
Caliber: .22 LR, 7-shot magazine. **Barrel:** 16.25" stainless steel,
Micro-Groove rifling. **Weight:** 3.25 lbs. **Length:** 35.25" overall.
Stock: Black fiberglass-filled synthetic with abbreviated forend,
nickel-plated swivel studs, molded-in checkering. **Sights:** Ramp
front with orange post, cut-away Wide Scan hood; adjustable open
rear. Receiver grooved for scope mounting. **Features:** Takedown
barrel; crossbolt safety; manual bolt hold-open; last shot bolt hold-
open; comes with padded carrying case. Introduced 1986. Made in
U.S.A. by Marlin.
Price: $345.00

MARLIN MODEL 795
Caliber: .22. **Barrel:** 18" with 16-groove Micro-Groove rifling. **Sights:**
Ramp front sight, adjustable rear. Receiver grooved for scope mount.
Stock: Black synthetic, hardwood, synthetic thumbhole, solid pink,
pink camo, or Mossy Oak New Break-up camo finish. **Features:**
10-round magazine, last shot hold-open feature. Introduced 1997. SS
is similar to Model 795 except stainless steel barrel. Most other parts
nickel-plated. Adjustable folding semi-buckhorn rear sights, ramp front
high-visibility post and removable cutaway wide scan hood. Made in
U.S.A. by Marlin Firearms Co.
Price: $183.00
Price: Stainless $262.00

MOSSBERG MODEL 702 PLINKSTER
Caliber: .22 LR, 10-round detachable magazine. **Barrel:** 18" free-
floating. **Weight:** 4.1 to 4.6 lbs. **Sights:** Adjustable rifle. Receiver
grooved for scope mount. **Stock:** Solid pink or pink marble finish
synthetic. **Features:** Ergonomically placed magazine release and
safety buttons, crossbolt safety, free gun lock. Made in U.S.A. by O.F.
Mossberg & Sons, Inc.
Price: $182.00

MOSSBERG MODEL 702 PLINKSTER AUTOLOADING RIFLE WITH MUZZLE BRAKE
Semiauto rifle chambered in .22 LR. Features include a black synthetic
stock with Schnabel, 10-round detachable box magazine, 21-inch
matte blue barrel with muzzlebrake, receiver grooved for scope
mount.
Price: $294.00

MOSSBERG MODEL 702 PLINKSTER DUCK COMMANDER
Caliber: .22 LR. Similar to standard model except synthetic stock has
Realtree Max-5 camo finish, Duck Dynasty logo.
Price: $274.00

MOSSBERG MODEL 715T SERIES
Caliber: .22 LR with 10 or 25-round magazine. AR-style offered
in several models. **Barrel:** 16.25 or 18 inches with A2-style
muzzlebrake. **Weight:** 5.5 lbs. **Features:** Flattop or A2 style carry
handle. Available with several camo patterns including Mossy Oak
Brush, Muddy Girl, Realtree Max-5 finish with Duck Dynasty logo.
Price: Black finish $375.00
Price: Muddy Girl camo $430.00
Price: Mossy Oak camo $435.00
Price: Duck Commander $509.00

REMINGTON MODEL 552 BDL DELUXE SPEEDMASTER
Caliber: : .22 Short (20 rounds), Long (17) or LR (15) tubular magazine.
Barrel: 21" round tapered. **Weight:** 5.75 lbs. **Length:** 40" overall.
Stock: Walnut. Checkered grip and fore-end. **Sights:** Adjustable rear,
ramp front. **Features:** Positive crossbolt safety in triggerguard, receiver
grooved for tip-off mount. Operates with .22 Short, Long or Long Rifle
cartridges. Classic design introduced in 1957.
Price: $667.00

REMINGTON 597
Caliber: .22 LR, 10-shot clip; or .22 WMR, 8-shot clip. **Barrel:** 20".
Weight: 5.5 lbs. **Length:** 40" overall. **Stock:** Black synthetic or
camo coverage in several patterns. TVP has laminated, contoured
thumbhole stock. **Sights:** Big game. **Features:** Matte black metal
finish or stainless, nickel-plated bolt. Receiver is grooved and drilled
and tapped for scope mounts. Introduced 1997. Made in U.S.A. by
Remington.
Price: Standard model, synthetic stock $213.00
Price: Synthetic w/Scope $257.00
Price: Camo from $306.00
Price: Stainless TVP from $595.00
Price: Laminated stock, heavy barrel .22 WMR only $645.00

RUGER 10/22 AUTOLOADING CARBINE
Caliber: .22 LR, 10-shot rotary magazine. **Barrel:** 18.5" round tapered
(16.12", compact model). **Weight:** 5 lbs. (4.5, compact). **Length:**
37.25", 34" (compact) overall. **Stock:** American hardwood with pistol
grip and barrelband, or synthetic. **Sights:** Brass bead front, folding
leaf rear adjustable for elevation. **Features:** Available with satin black
or stainless finish on receiver and barrel. Detachable rotary magazine
fits flush into stock, crossbolt safety, receiver tapped and grooved
for scope blocks or tip-off mount. Scope base adaptor furnished with

Prices given are believed to be accurate at time of publication however, many factors affect retail pricing so exact prices are not possible.

70TH EDITION, 2016 ✦ **483**

each rifle. Made in U.S.A. by Sturm, Ruger & Co.
Price: Wood stock **$289.00**
Price: Synthetic stock **$289.00**
Price: Stainless, synthetic stock **$319.00**
Price: Compact model, fiber-optic front sight **$339.00**

RUGER 10/22 TAKEDOWN RIFLE
Caliber: .22 LR, 10-shot rotary magazine. **Barrel:** 18.5" stainless, or 16.6" satin black threaded with suppressor. Easy takedown feature enables quick separation of the barrel from the action by way of a recessed locking lever, for ease of transportation and storage. **Stock:** Black synthetic. **Sights:** Adjustable rear, gold bead front. **Weight:** 4.66 pounds. Comes with backpack carrying bag.
Price: Stainless **$409.00**
Price: Satin black w/suppressor **$429.00**

RUGER 10/22 SPORTER
Same specificaions as 10/22 Carbine except has American walnut stock with hand-checkered pistol grip and fore-end, straight buttplate, sling swivels, 18.9" barrel, and no barrelband.
Price: **$389.00**

RUGER 10/22-T TARGET RIFLE
Similar to the 10/22 except has 20" heavy, hammer-forged barrel with tight chamber dimensions, improved trigger pull. **Weight:** 7.5 lbs. **Stock:** Black or brown laminated hardwood, dimensioned for optical sights. No iron sights supplied. Introduced 1996.
Price: From **$550.00**
Price: Stainless from **$589.00**

RUGER 10/22VLEH TARGET TACTICAL RIFLE
Caliber: .22 LR. **Features:** Features include precision-rifled, cold hammer-forged, spiral-finished 16-1/8-inch crowned match barrel; Hogue OverMolded stock, 10/22T target trigger, precision-adjustable bipod for steady shooting from the bench; 10-round rotary magazine. **Weight:** 6-7/8 lbs.
Price: **$599.00**

RUGER SR-22 RIFLE
AR-style semiauto rifle chambered in .22 LR, based on 10/22 action. Features include all-aluminum chassis replicating the AR-platform dimensions between the sighting plane, buttstock height and grip; Picatinny rail optic mount includes a six-position, telescoping M4-style buttstock (on a Mil-Spec diameter tube); Hogue Monogrip pistol grip; buttstocks and grips interchangeable with any AR-style compatible option; round, mid-length handguard mounted on a standard-thread AR-style barrel nut; precision-rifled, cold hammer forged 16-1/8-inch alloy steel barrel capped with an SR-556/Mini-14 flash suppressor.
Price: **$669.00**

SAVAGE MODEL 64G
Caliber: .22 LR, 10-shot magazine. **Barrel:** 20", 21". **Weight:** 5.5 lbs. **Length:** 40", 41". **Stock:** Walnut-finished hardwood with Monte Carlo-type comb, checkered grip and fore-end. **Sights:** Bead front, open adjustable rear. Receiver grooved for scope mounting. **Features:** Thumb-operated rotating safety. Blue finish. 64 SS has stainless finish. Side ejection, bolt hold-open device. Introduced 1990. Made in Canada, from Savage Arms.
Price: 64 G **$221.00**
Price: 64 F **$175.00**
Price: 64 FSS **$254.00**
Price: 64 TR-SR **$348.00**

SMITH & WESSON M&P15-22 SERIES
Caliber: .22 LR. 10 or 25-round magazine. **Barrel:** 15.5", 16" or 16.5" **Stock:** 6-position telescoping or fixed. **Features:** A rimfire verson of AR-derived M&P tactical autoloader. Operates with blowback action. Quad-mount picatinny rails, plain barrel or compensator, alloy upper and lower, matte black metal finish. Many optional camo and color finishes available, including Tan & Black, Flat Dark Earth, Realtree APG camo, Pink Platinum, Purple Platinum, Harvest Moon Orange and others.
Price: Standard **$519.00**
Price: Pink, Purple, Platinum finish **$559.00**
Price: MOE Model with Magpul sights, stock and grip **$609.00**
Price: Performance Center upgrades, threaded barrel **$789.00**

THOMPSON/CENTER .22 LR CLASSIC
Caliber: .22 LR, 8-shot magazine. **Barrel:** 22" match-grade. **Weight:** 5.5 pounds. **Length:** 39.5" overall. **Stock:** Satin-finished American walnut with Monte Carlo-type comb and pistol gripcap, swivel studs. **Sights:** Ramp-style front and fully adjustable rear, both with fiber optics. **Features:** All-steel receiver drilled and tapped for scope mounting; barrel threaded to receiver; thumb-operated safety; triggerguard safety lock included. New .22 Classic Benchmark TGT target rifle variant has 18" heavy barrel, brown laminated target stock, blued with matte finish, 10-shot magazine and no sights; drilled and tapped.
Price: T/C .22 LR Classic (blue) **$396.00**
Price: T/C .22 LR Classic Benchmark **$505.00**

BROWNING BL-22

Action: Short-throw lever action, side ejection. Rack-and-pinion lever. Tubular magazines, with 15+1 capacity for .22 LR. **Barrel:** Recessed muzzle. **Stock:** Walnut, two-piece straight-grip Western style. **Trigger:** Half-cock hammer safety; fold-down hammer. **Sights:** Bead post front, folding-leaf rear. Steel receiver grooved for scope mount. **Weight:** 5-5.4 lbs. **Length:** 36.75-40.75" overall. **Features:** Action lock provided. Introduced 1996. FLD Grade II Octagon has octagonal 24" barrel, silver nitride receiver with scroll engraving, gold-colored trigger. FLD Grade I has satin-nickel receiver, blued trigger, no stock checkering. FLD Grade II has satin-nickel receivers with scroll engraving; gold-colored trigger, cut checkering. Both introduced 2005. Grade I has blued receiver and trigger, no stock checkering. Grade II has gold-colored trigger, cut checkering, blued receiver with scroll engraving. Imported from Japan by Browning.

Price: BL-22 Grade I/II, from..$620.00
Price: BL-22 FLD Grade I/II, from ....$660.00 to $750.00
Price: BL-22 FLD, Grade II Octagon $980.00
Price: Grade II Maple stock $780.00

HENRY LEVER-ACTION RIFLES

Caliber: .22 Long Rifle (15 shot), .22 Magnum (11 shots), .17 HMR (11 shots). **Barrel:** 18.25" round. **Weight:** 5.5 to 5.75 lbs. **Length:** 34" overall (.22 LR). **Stock:** Walnut. **Sights:** Hooded blade front, open adjustable rear. **Features:** Polished blue finish; full-length tubular magazine; side ejection; receiver grooved for scope mounting. Introduced 1997. Made in U.S.A. by Henry Repeating Arms Co.

Price: H001 Carbine .22 LR..$360.00
Price: H001L Carbine .22 LR, Large Loop Lever.....................$375.00
Price: H001Y Youth model (33" overall, 11-round .22 LR) $360.00
Price: H001M .22 Magnum, 19.25" octagonal barrel, deluxe
    walnut stock...$500.00
Price: H001V .17 HMR, 20" octagonal barrel, Williams Fire
    Sights..$500.00

HENRY LEVER-ACTION OCTAGON FRONTIER MODEL

Same as Lever rifles except chambered in .17 HMR, .22 Short/Long/LR, .22 Magnum. **Barrel:** 20" octagonal. **Sights:** Marble's full adjustable semi-buckhorn rear, brass bead front. **Weight:** 6.25 lbs. Made in U.S.A. by Henry Repeating Arms Co.

Price: H001T Lever Octagon $450.00
Price: H001TM Lever Octagon .22 Magnum..........................$550.00

HENRY GOLDEN BOY SERIES

Caliber: .17 HMR, .22 LR (16-shot), .22 Magnum. **Barrel:** 20" octagonal. **Weight:** 6.25 lbs. **Length:** 38" overall. **Stock:** American walnut. **Sights:** Blade front, open rear. **Features:** Brasslite receiver, brass buttplate, blued barrel and lever. Introduced 1998. Made in U.S.A. from Henry Repeating Arms Co.

Price: H004 .22 LR..$550.00
Price: H004M .22 Magnum $595.00
Price: H004V .17 HMR $615.00
Price: H004DD .22 LR Deluxe, engraved receiver.................$1,585.00

HENRY SILVER BOY

Caliber: 17 HMR, .22 S/L/LR, .22 WMR. Tubular magazine capacity: 12 rounds (.17 HMR and .22 WMR), 16 rounds (.22 LR), 21 rounds (.22 Short). **Barrel:** 20 inches. **Stock:** American walnut with curved

buttplate. **Finish:** Nickel receiver, barrel band and buttplate. **Sights:** Adjustable buckhorn rear, bead front. Silver Eagle model has engraved scroll pattern from early original Henry rifle. Offered in same calibers as Silver Boy. Made in U.S.A. from Henry Repeating Arms Company.

Price: .22 S/L/LR..$600.00
Price: .22 WMR..$650.00
Price: .17 HMR $675.00
Price: Silver Eagle..$850.00 to $900.00

HENRY PUMP ACTION

Caliber: .22 LR, 15-shot. **Barrel:** 18.25". **Weight:** 5.5 lbs. **Length:** NA. **Stock:** American walnut. **Sights:** Bead on ramp front, open adjustable rear. **Features:** Polished blue finish; receiver grooved for scope mount; grooved slide handle; two barrelbands. Introduced 1998. Made in U.S.A. from Henry Repeating Arms Co.

Price: H003T .22 LR..$550.00
Price: H003TM .22 Magnum..$595.00

MARLIN MODEL 39A GOLDEN

Caliber: .22, S (26), L (21), LR (19), tubular magazine. **Barrel:** 24" Micro-Groove. **Weight:** 6.5 lbs. **Length:** 40" overall. **Stock:** Checkered American black walnut; Mar-Shield finish. Swivel studs; rubber buttpad. **Sights:** Bead ramp front with detachable Wide-Scan hood, folding rear semi-buckhorn adjustable for windage and elevation. **Features:** Hammer block safety; rebounding hammer. Takedown action, receiver tapped for scope mount (supplied), offset hammer spur, gold-colored steel trigger. The 39 series certainly deserve the term "classic" since it has been in continuous production longer than any other rifle in the America, since 1922.

Price: $709.00

MOSSBERG MODEL 464 RIMFIRE

Caliber: .22 LR. **Barrel:** 20" round blued. **Weight:** 5.6 lbs. **Length:** 35-3/4" overall. **Features:** Adjustable sights, straight grip stock, 14-shot tubular magazine, plain hardwood straight stock and fore-end.

Price: $485.00
Price: SPX..$513.00

REMINGTON 572 BDL DELUXE FIELDMASTER PUMP

Caliber: .22 S (20), L (17) or LR (15), tubular magazine. **Barrel:** 21" round tapered. **Weight:** 5.5 lbs. **Length:** 40" overall. **Stock:** Walnut with checkered pistol grip and slide handle. **Sights:** Big game. **Features:** Crossbolt safety; removing inner magazine tube converts rifle to single shot; receiver grooved for tip-off scope mount. Another classic rimfire, this model was been in production since 1955.

Price: $723.00

ANSCHUTZ MODEL 64 MP

Caliber: .22 LR. Magazine capacity: 5 rounds. **Barrel:** 25.6 inch heavy match. **Weight:** About 9 pounds. **Stock:** Multipurpose hardwood with beavertail fore-end. **Sights:** None. Drilled and tapped for scope or receiver sights. **Features:** Model 64S BR (benchrest) has 20" heavy barrel, adjustable two-stage match-grade trigger, flat beavertail stock, weighs 9.5 pounds. Imported from Germany by Steyr Arms

Price: $1,399.00
Price: Model 64 S BR $1,539.00

ANSCHUTZ 1416D/1516D CLASSIC

Caliber: .22 LR (1416D888), .22 WMR (1516D), 5-shot clip. **Barrel:** 22.5". **Weight:** 6 lbs. **Length:** 41" overall. **Stock:** European hardwood with walnut finish; classic style with straight comb, checkered pistol grip and fore-end. **Sights:** Hooded ramp front, folding leaf rear. **Features:** Uses Match 64 action. Adjustable single-stage trigger. Receiver grooved for scope mounting. Imported from Germany by Steyr Arms.

Price: 1416D KL, .22 LR $1,099.00
Price: 1416D KL Classic left-hand $1,199.00
Price: 1516D KL, .22 WMR $1,169.00
Price: 1416D, thumbhole stock $1,599.00

ANSCHUTZ 1710D CUSTOM

Caliber: .22 LR, 5-shot clip. **Barrel:** 23.75 or 24.25" heavy contour. **Weight:** 6.5 to 7-3/8 lbs. **Length:** 42.5" overall. **Stock:** Select European walnut. **Sights:** Hooded ramp front, folding leaf rear; drilled and tapped for scope mounting. **Features:** Match 54 action with adjustable single-stage trigger; roll-over Monte Carlo cheekpiece, slim fore-end with Schnabel tip, Wundhammer palm swell on pistol grip, rosewood gripcap with white diamond insert; skip-line checkering on grip and fore-end. Introduced 1988. Imported from Germany by Steyr Arms.

Price: $2,089.00

BROWNING T-BOLT RIMFIRE

Caliber: .22 LR, .17 HMR, .22 WMR, 10-round rotary box Double Helix magazine. **Barrel:** 22", free-floating, semi-match chamber, target muzzle crown. **Weight:** 4.8 lbs. **Length:** 40.1" overall. **Stock:** Walnut, maple or composite. **Sights:** None. **Features:** Straight-pull bolt-action, three-lever trigger adjustable for pull weight, dual action screws, sling swivel studs. Crossbolt lockup, enlarged bolt handle, one-piece dual extractor with integral spring and red cocking indicator band, gold-tone trigger. Top-tang, thumb-operated two-position safety, drilled and tapped for scope mounts. Varmint model has raised Monte Carlo comb, heavy barrel, wide forearm. Introduced 2006. Imported from Japan by Browning. Left-hand models added in 2009.

Price: .22 LR, from................................$750.00 to $780.00
Price: Composite Target ....$780.00 to $800.00
Price: .17 HMR/.22 WMR, from ....$790.00 to $830.00

COOPER MODEL 57-M REPEATER

Caliber: .22 LR, .22 WMR, .17 HMR. **Barrel:** 22" or 24". **Weight:** 6.5-7.5 lbs. **Stock:** Claro walnut, 22 lpi hand checkering. **Sights:** None

furnished. **Features:** Three rear locking lug, repeating bolt-action with 5-shot magazine for .22 LR; 4-shot magazine for .22 WMR and 17 HMR. Fully adjustable trigger. Left-hand models add $150 to base rifle price. 1/4"-group rimfire accuracy guarantee at 50 yards; 0.5"-group centerfire accuracy guarantee at 100 yards. Options include wood upgrades, case-color metalwork, barrel fluting, custom LOP, and many others.

Price: Classic $2,245.00
Price: Custom Classic $2,595.00
Price: Western Classic $3,445.00
Price: Schnabel $2,395.00
Price: Jackson Squirrel..$2,355.00
Price: Jackson Hunter $2,195.00
Price: Mannlicher $4,395.00

CZ 452 LUX

Caliber: .22 LR, .22 WMR, 5-shot detachable magazine. **Barrel:** 24.8". **Weight:** 6.6 lbs. **Length:** 42.63" overall. **Stock:** Walnut with checkered pistol grip. **Sights:** Hooded front, fully adjustable tangent rear. **Features:** All-steel construction, adjustable trigger, polished blue finish. Imported from the Czech Republic by CZ-USA.

Price: .22 LR, .22 WMR $450.00

CZ 452 VARMINT RIFLE

Similar to the Lux model except has heavy 20.8" barrel; stock has beavertail fore-end; weighs 7 lbs.; no sights furnished. Available in .22 LR, .22 WMR, .17HMR, .17M2. Imported from the Czech Republic by CZ-USA.

Price: From $497.00

CZ 452 AMERICAN

Similar to the CZ 452 M 2E Lux except has classic-style stock of Circassian walnut; 22.5" free-floating barrel with recessed target crown; receiver dovetail for scope mounting. No open sights furnished. Introduced 1999. Imported from the Czech Republic by CZ-USA.

Price: .22 LR, .22 WMR $463.00
Price: Scout/Youth model w/16" barrel $312.00

CZ 455 AMERICAN

Caliber: .17 HMR, .22 LR, .22 WMR (5-round magazine). **Barrel:** 20.5". **Weight:** 6.1 lbs. **Length:** 38.2". **Stock:** Walnut. **Sights:** None. Intergral 11mm dovetail scope base. **Features:** Adjustable trigger. Six versions available including blue laminate with thumbhole stock, Varmint model with .866" heavy barrel, full-length Mannlicher walnut stock, and others. American Combo Package includes interchangeable barrel to switch calibers.

Price: from .... $421.00 to $565.00

DAVEY CRICKETT SINGLE SHOT

Caliber: .22 LR, 122 WMR, single-shot. **Barrel:** 16-1/8". **Weight:** About 2.5 lbs. **Length:** 30" overall. **Stock:** American walnut. **Sights:** Post on ramp front, peep rear adjustable for windage and elevation. **Features:** Drilled and tapped for scope mounting using special Chipmunk base ($13.95). Engraved model also available. Made in U.S.A. Introduced 1982. Formerly Chipmunk model. From Keystone Sporting Arms.

Price: From $171.00

Prices given are believed to be accurate at time of publication however, many factors affect retail pricing so exact prices are not possible.

RIMFIRE RIFLES Bolt Actions & Single Shot

HENRY MINI BOLT YOUTH RIFLE
Caliber: .22 LR, single-shot youth gun. **Barrel:** 16" stainless, 8-groove rifling. **Weight:** 3.25 lbs. **Length:** 30", LOP 11.5". **Stock:** Synthetic, pistol grip, wraparound checkering and beavertail forearm. Available in black finish or bright colors. **Sights:** William Fire sights. **Features:** One-piece bolt configuration manually operated safety.
Price: $275.00

MARLIN MODEL XT-17 SERIES
Caliber: .17 HRM. **Magazine capacity:** 4 and 7-shot, two magazines included. **Barrel:** 22 inches. **Weight:** 6 pounds. **Stock:** Black synthetic with palm swell, stippled grip areas, or walnut-finished hardwood with Monte Carlo comb. Laminated stock available. **Sights:** Adjustable rear, ramp front. Drilled and tapped for scope mounts. **Features:** Adjustable trigger. Blue or stainless finish.
Price: .... $269.00 to $429.00

MARLIN MODEL XT-22 SERIES
Caliber: .22 Short, Long, Long Rifle. Available with 7-shot detachable box magazine or tubular magazine (17 to 22 rounds). **Barrel:** 22 inches. Varmint model has heavy barrel. **Weight:** 6 lbs. **Stock:** Black synthetic, walnut-finished hardwood, walnut or camo. Tubular model available with two-tone brown laminated stock. **Finish:** Blue or stainless. **Sights:** Adjustable rear, ramp front. Some models have folding rear sight with a hooded or high visibility orange front sight. **Features:** Pro-Fire Adjustable Trigger, Micro-Groove rifling, thumb safety with red cocking indicator. The XT-22M series is chambered for .22 WMR. Made in U.S.A. by Marlin Firearms Co.
Price: From .... $221.00 to $340.00
Price: XT-22M .... $240.00 to $270.00
Price: XT-22MTSL (.22 WMR w/laminated stock)..................... $379.00

MEACHAM LOW-WALL
Caliber: Any rimfire cartridge. **Barrel:** 26-34". **Weight:** 7-15 lbs. **Sights:** none. Tang drilled for Win. base, 3/8" dovetail slot front. **Stock:** Fancy eastern walnut with cheekpiece; ebony insert in forearm tip. **Features:** Exact copy of 1885 Winchester. With most Winchester factory options available including double-set triggers. Introduced 1994. Made in U.S.A. by Meacham T&H Inc.
Price: From $4,999.00

MOSSBERG MODEL 817
Caliber: .17 HMR, 5-round magazine. **Barrel:** 21"; free-floating bull barrel, recessed muzzle crown. **Weight:** 4.9 lbs. (black synthetic), 5.2 lbs. (wood). **Stock:** Black synthetic or wood; length of pull, 14.25". **Sights:** Factory-installed Weaver-style scope bases. **Features:** Blued or brushed chrome metal finishes, crossbolt safety, gun lock. Introduced 2008. Made in U.S.A. by O.F. Mossberg & Sons, Inc.
Price: .... $212.00 to $253.00

MOSSBERG MODEL 801/802
Caliber: .22 LR, 10-round detachable magazine. **Barrel:** 18" free-floating. Varmint model has 21" heavy barrel. **Weight:** 4.1 to 4.6 lbs. **Sights:** Adjustable rifle. Receiver grooved for scope mount. **Stock:** Black synthetic. **Features:** Ergonomically placed magazine release and safety buttons, crossbolt safety, free gun lock. 801 Half Pint has 12.25" length of pull, 16" barrel, and weighs 4 lbs. Hardwood stock; removable magazine plug.
Price: Plinkster...$223.00
Price: Half Pint $223.00
Price: Varmint..$223.00

NEW ULTRA LIGHT ARMS 20RF
Caliber: .22 LR, single-shot or repeater. **Barrel:** Douglas, length to order. **Weight:** 5.25 lbs. **Length:** Varies. **Stock:** Kevlar/graphite composite, variety of finishes. **Sights:** None furnished; drilled and tapped for scope mount. **Features:** Timney trigger, hand-lapped action, button-rifled barrel, hand-bedded action, recoil pad, sling-swivel studs, optional Jewell trigger. Made in U.S.A. by New Ultra Light Arms.
Price: 20 RF single shot.......................................$1,800.00
Price: 20 RF repeater $1,850.00

ROSSI MATCHED PAIR SINGLE-SHOT/SHOTGUN
Caliber: .17 HMR rifle with interchangeable 12 or 20-gauge shotgun barrel. **Barrel:** 23" (rifle), 28" (shotgun). **Weight:** 5.25 to 6.25 lbs. **Stock:** Hardwood (brown or black finish). **Sights:** Fully adjustable front and rear. **Features:** Break-open breech, transfer-bar manual safety. Youth Model has .17 HMR or .22 LR rifle barrel with interchangeable .410 shotgun. Introduced 2001. Imported by BrazTech International.
Price: From $298.00
Price: Youth model from $245.00

RUGER 77/22 RIMFIRE
Caliber: .22 LR, 10-shot magazine; .22 WMR, 9-shot magazine. **Barrel:** 20" or 24" (stainless model only). **Weight:** 6.0 to 6.5 lbs. (20" bbl.); 7.5 lbs. (24" bbl.). **Length:** 39.25" overall (20" bbl.). **Stock:** Checkered American walnut or synthetic, stainless sling swivels. **Sights:** Plain barrel with integral scope mounting system complete with 1-inch Ruger rings. **Features:** Mauser-type action uses Ruger's famous rotary magazine. Three-position safety, simplified bolt stop, patented bolt-locking system. Uses the dual-screw barrel attachment system of the 10/22 rifle.
Price: Blue finish w/walnut or synthetic stock.........................$899.00
Price: Stainless steel w/walnut stock $969.00

RUGER 77/17 RIMFIRE
Caliber: .17 HMR, 9-shot rotary magazine. **Barrel:** 22" to 24". **Weight:** 6.5-7.5 lbs. **Length:** 41.25-43.25" overall. **Stock:** Checkered American walnut, laminated hardwood; stainless sling swivels. **Sights:** None. Integral scope mounting system with 1-inch Ruger rings. **Features:** Mauser-type action uses Ruger's rotary magazine. Three-position safety, simplified bolt stop, patented bolt-locking system. Uses the dual-screw barrel attachment system of the 10/22 rifle. Introduced 2002.
Price: Blue finish w/walnut stock..$899.00
Price: Stainless steel w/laminate stock $969.00

SAVAGE MARK II BOLT-ACTION
Caliber: .22 LR, .17 HMR, 10-shot magazine. **Barrel:** 20.5". **Weight:** 5.5 lbs. **Length:** 39.5" overall. **Stock:** Walnut-finished hardwood with Monte Carlo-type comb, checkered grip and fore-end. Camo or OD Green stock available. **Sights:** Bead front, open adjustable rear. Receiver grooved for scope mounting. **Features:** Thumb-operated rotating safety. Blue finish. Introduced 1990. Made in Canada, from Savage Arms, Inc.
Price: .... $228.00 to $280.00
Price: Varmint w/heavy barrel..$242.00
Price: Camo stock $280.00
Price: OD Green stock..$291.00

SAVAGE MARK II-FSS STAINLESS RIFLE
Similar to the Mark II except has stainless steel barreled action and black synthetic stock with positive checkering, swivel studs, and 20.75" free-floating and button-rifled barrel with detachable magazine. Weighs 5.5 lbs. Introduced 1997. Imported from Canada by Savage Arms, Inc.
Price: $336.00

SAVAGE MODEL 93G MAGNUM BOLT-ACTION
Caliber: .22 WMR, 5-shot magazine. **Barrel:** 20.75". **Weight:** 5.75 lbs. **Length:** 39.5" overall. **Stock:** Walnut-finished hardwood with Monte

Carlo-type comb, checkered grip and fore-end. **Sights:** Bead front, adjustable open rear. Receiver grooved for scope mount. **Features:** Thumb-operated rotary safety. Blue finish. Introduced 1994. Made in Canada, from Savage Arms.

Price: Model 93G $272.00
Price: Model 93F (as above with black graphite/fiberglass stock) $252.00
Price: Model 93 BSEV, thumbhole stock $627.00

SAVAGE MODEL 93FSS MAGNUM RIFLE
Similar to Model 93G except stainless steel barreled action and black synthetic stock with positive checkering. Weighs 5.5 lbs. Introduced 1997. Imported from Canada by Savage Arms, Inc.
Price: $336.00

SAVAGE MODEL 93FVSS MAGNUM
Similar to Model 93FSS Magnum except 21" heavy barrel with recessed target-style crown, satin-finished stainless barreled action, black graphite/fiberglass stock. Drilled and tapped for scope mounting; comes with Weaver-style bases. Introduced 1998. Imported from Canada by Savage Arms, Inc.
Price: $347.00

SAVAGE B-MAG
Caliber: .17 Winchester Super Magnum. Rotary magazine holds 8 rounds. **Stock:** Synthetic. **Weight:** 4.5 pounds. Chambered for new Winchester .17 Super Magnum rimfire cartridge that propels a 20-grain bullet at approximately 3,000 fps. **Features:** Adjustable

AccuTrigger, rear locking lugs, new and different bolt-action rimfire design that cocks on close of bolt. New in 2013.
Price: $359.00
Price: Stainless steel receiver and barrel...............$408.00

SAVAGE BRJ SERIES
Similar to Mark II, Model 93 and Model 93R17 rifles but features spiral fluting pattern on a heavy barrel, blued finish and Royal Jacaranda wood laminate stock.
Price: Mark II BRJ, .22 LR $519.00
Price: Model 93 BRJ, .22 Mag................................$527.00
Price: Model 93 R17 BRJ, .17 HMR $527.00

SAVAGE TACTICAL RIMFIRE SERIES
Similar to Savage Model BRJ series semiauto rifles but with matte finish and a tactical-style wood stock.
Price: Mark II TR, .22 LR $533.00
Price: Mark II TRR, .22 LR, three-way accessory rail $627.00
Price: Model 93R17 TR, .17 HMR $541.00
Price: Model 93R17 TRR, .17 HMR, three-way accessory rail $635.00

WINCHESTER MODEL 1885 LOW WALL HUNTER RIMFIRE
Caliber: .17 Winchester Super Magnum, .17 HMR, .22 LR, .22 WMR. **Barrel:** 24-inch octagon. **Weight:** 7.5 pounds. **Stock:** Oil finished Grade I walnut, checkered with Schnabel fore-end. **Sights:** Gold bead front, semi-buckhorn rear. **Finish:** Gloss blue. Single-shot lever-operated recreation of classic Model 1885 design.
Price: $1,470.00

ANSCHUTZ 1903 MATCH

Caliber: .22 LR, single-shot. **Barrel:** 21.25". **Weight:** 8 lbs. **Length:** 43.75" overall. **Stock:** Walnut-finished hardwood with adjustable cheekpiece; stippled grip and fore-end. **Sights:** None furnished. **Features:** Uses Anschutz Match 64 action. A medium weight rifle for intermediate and advanced Junior Match competition. Available from Champion's Choice.
Price: Right-hand..$1,195.00

ANSCHUTZ 64-MP R SILHOUETTE

Caliber: .22 LR, 5-shot magazine. **Barrel:** 21.5", medium heavy; 7/8" diameter. **Weight:** 8 lbs. **Length:** 39.5" overall. **Stock:** Walnut-finished hardwood, silhouette-type. **Sights:** None furnished. **Features:** Uses Match 64 action. Designed for metallic silhouette competition. Stock has stippled checkering, contoured thumb groove with Wundhammer swell. Two-stage #5098 trigger. Slide safety locks sear and bolt. Introduced 1980. Available from Champion's Choice.
Price: 64-MP R $1,100.00
Price: 64-S BR Benchrest..$1,327.00

ANSCHUTZ 2007 MATCH RIFLE

Uses same action as the Model 2013, but has a lighter barrel. European walnut stock in right-hand, true left-hand or extra-short models. Sights optional. Available with 19.6" barrel with extension tube, or 26", both in stainless or blue. Introduced 1998. Available from Champion's Choice.
Price: Right-hand, blue, no sights $2,595.00

ANSCHUTZ 1827BT FORTNER BIATHLON

Caliber: .22 LR, 5-shot magazine. **Barrel:** 21.7". **Weight:** 8.8 lbs. with sights. **Length:** 40.9" overall. **Stock:** European walnut with cheekpiece, stippled pistol grip and fore-end. **Sights:** Optional globe front specially designed for Biathlon shooting, micrometer rear with hinged snow cap. **Features:** Uses Super Match 54 action and nine-way adjustable trigger; adjustable wooden buttplate, biathlon butthook, adjustable hand-stop rail. Uses Anschutz/Fortner system straight-pull bolt action, blued or stainless steel barrel. Introduced 1982. Available from Champion's Choice.
Price: From about $3,195.00

ANSCHUTZ SUPER MATCH SPECIAL MODEL 2013

Caliber: .22 LR, single-shot. **Barrel:** 25.9". **Weight:** 13 lbs. **Length:** 41.7" to 42.9". **Stock:** Adjustable aluminum. **Sights:** None furnished. **Features:** 2313 aluminum-silver/blue stock, 500mm barrel, fast lock time, adjustable cheekpiece, heavy action and muzzle tube, w/ handstop and standing riser block. Introduced in 1997. Available from Champion's Choice.
Price: From about $3,995.00

ANSCHUTZ 1912 SPORT

Caliber: .22 LR. **Barrel:** 26" match. **Weight:** 11.4 lbs. **Length:** 41.7" overall. **Stock:** Non-stained thumbhole stock adjustable in length with adjustable buttplate and cheekpiece adjustment. Flat fore-end raiser block 4856 adjustable in height. Hook buttplate. **Sights:** None furnished. **Features:** "Free rifle" for women. Smallbore model 1907 with 1912 stock: Match 54 action. Delivered with: Hand stop 6226, fore-end raiser block 4856, screwdriver, instruction leaflet with test target. Available from Champion's Choice.
Price: $2,795.00

ANSCHUTZ 1913 SUPER MATCH RIFLE

Same as the Model 1911 except European walnut International-type stock with adjustable cheekpiece, or color laminate, both available with straight or lowered fore-end, adjustable aluminum hook buttplate, adjustable hand stop, weighs 13 lbs., 46" overall. Stainless or blue barrel. Available from Champion's Choice.
Price: Right-hand, blue, no sights, walnut stock..................$3,290.00

ANSCHUTZ 1907 STANDARD MATCH RIFLE

Same action as Model 1913 but with 7/8" diameter 26" barrel (stainless or blue). Length is 44.5" overall, weighs 10.5 lbs. Choice of stock configurations. Vented fore-end. Designed for prone and position shooting ISU requirements; suitable for NRA matches. Also available with walnut flat-forend stock for benchrest shooting. Available from Champion's Choice.
Price: Right-hand, blue, no sights $2,185.00

ARMALITE AR-10(T)

Caliber: .308 Win., 10-shot magazine. **Barrel:** 24" target-weight Rock 5R custom. **Weight:** 10.4 lbs. **Length:** 43.5" overall. **Stock:** Green or black composition; N.M. fiberglass handguard tube. **Sights:** Detachable handle, front sight, or scope mount available. Comes with international-style flattop receiver with Picatinny rail. **Features:** National Match two-stage trigger. Forged upper receiver. Receivers hard-coat anodized. Introduced 1995. Made in U.S.A. by ArmaLite, Inc.
Price: Black $1,912.00
Price: AR-10, .338 Federal $1,912.00

ARMALITE AR-10 NATIONAL MATCH

Caliber: .308/7.62 NATO. **Barrel:** 20", triple-lapped Match barrel, 1:10" twist rifling. **Weight:** 11.5 lbs. **Length:** 41". **Features:** Stainless steel flash suppressor, two-stage National Match trigger. Forged flattop receiver with Picatinny rail and forward assist.
Price: $2,365.00

ARMALITE M14A4(T)

Caliber: .223 Rem., 10-round magazine. **Barrel:** 24" heavy stainless; 1:8" twist. **Weight:** 9.2 lbs. **Length:** 42-3/8" overall. **Stock:** Green or black butt, N.M. fiberglass handguard tube. **Sights:** One-piece international-style flattop receiver with Weaver-type rail, including case deflector. **Features:** Detachable carry handle, front sight and scope mount (30mm or 1") available. Upper and lower receivers have push-type pivot pin, hard coat anodized. Made in U.S.A. by ArmaLite, Inc.
Price: From .... $1,318.00 to $1,449..00

ARMALITE M15 A4 CARBINE 6.8 & 7.62X39

Caliber: 6.8 Rem., 7.62x39. **Barrel:** 16" chrome-lined with flash suppressor. **Weight:** 7 lbs. **Length:** 26.6". **Features:** Front and rear picatinny rails for mounting optics, two-stage tactical trigger, anodized aluminum/phosphate finish.
Price: $1,107.00

BLASER R93 LONG RANGE SPORTER 2

Caliber: .308 Win., 10-shot detachable box magazine. **Barrel:** 24". **Weight:** 10.4 lbs. **Length:** 44" overall. **Stock:** Aluminum with synthetic lining. **Sights:** None furnished; accepts detachable scope mount. **Features:** Straight-pull bolt action with adjustable trigger; fully adjustable stock; quick takedown; corrosion resistant finish. Introduced 1998. Imported from Germany by Blaser USA.
Price: $4,400.00

BUSHMASTER A2/A3 TARGET

Caliber: 5.56mm, .223 Rem., 30-round magazine. **Barrel:** 20", 24". **Weight:** 8.43 lbs. (A2); 8.78 lbs. (A3). **Length:** 39.5" overall (20" barrel). **Stock:** Black composition; A2 type. **Sights:** Adjustable post front, adjustable aperture rear. **Features:** Patterned after Colt M-16A2. Chrome-lined barrel with manganese phosphate exterior. Available in stainless barrel. Made in U.S.A. by Bushmaster Firearms Co.
Price: (A3 type) $1,179.00

COLT M2012

Caliber: .308 Win. or .260 Rem. 5- or 10-round magazine. **Barrel:** 22" match-grade fluted, heavy or medium heavy, stainless or chrome-

moly. **Weight:** 8.5 to 13.2 lbs. **Stock:** Custom forged aluminum, custom Manners composite, or gray laminated hardwood. **Features:** Timney single-stage adjustable trigger, Cooper Firearms muzzle brake, matte black, gray or Coyote Tan finish.
Price: From .... **$2,796.00 to $3,195.00**

COLT ACCURIZED RIFLE
Caliber: .223 Rem. **Barrel:** 24" stainless match. **Features:** Features flattop receiver for scope mounting, stainless steel heavy barrel, tubular handguard, and free-floating barrel. Matte black finish. Weighs 9.25 lbs. Made in U.S.A. by Colt's Mfg. Co., Inc.
Price: Model CR6724 .... **$1,374.00 to $1,653.00**

OLYMPIC ARMS UM ULTRAMATCH AR15
Caliber: .223 Rem. minimum SAAMI spec, 30-shot magazine. **Barrel:** 20" or 24" bull broach-cut Ultramatch stainless steel 1x10" twist rate. **Weight:** 8-10 lbs. **Length:** 38.25" overall. **Stock:** A2 grip, A2 buttstock with trapdoor. **Sights:** None, flattop upper and gas block with rails. **Features:** Flattop upper, free-floating tubular match handguard, Picatinny gas block, crowned muzzle and factory trigger job. Premium model adds pneumatic recoil buffer, Harris S-series bipod, hand selected premium receivers and William Set Trigger. Made in U.S.A. by Olympic Arms, Inc
Price: UM-1, 20" Ultramatch **$1,332.50**
Price: UM-1P **$1,623.70**

OLYMPIC ARMS ML-2 MULTIMATCH AR15 CARBINES
Caliber: .223 Rem. minimum SAAMI spec, 30-shot magazine. **Barrel:** 16" broach-cut Ultramatch stainless steel 1x10" twist rate. **Weight:** 7-8 lbs. **Length:** 34-36" overall. **Stock:** A2 grip and varying buttstock. **Sights:** None. **Features:** The ML-2 includes bull diameter barrel, flattop upper, free-floating tubular match handguard, Picatinny gas block, crowned muzzle and A2 buttstock with trapdoor. Made in U.S.A. by Olympic Arms, Inc.
Price: ML-2 .... **$1,253.20**

OLYMPIC ARMS K8 TARGETMATCH AR15
Caliber: 5.56 NATO, .223 WSSM, .243 WSSM, .25 WSSM, 30/7-shot magazine. **Barrel:** 20", 24" bull button-rifled stainless/chrome-moly steel 1x9"/1x10" twist rate. **Weight:** 8-10 lbs. **Length:** 38"-42" overall. **Stock:** A2 grip, A2 buttstock with trapdoor. **Sights:** None. **Features:** Barrel has satin bead-blast finish; flattop upper, free-floating tubular match handguard, Picatinny gas block, crowned muzzle and "Targetmatch" pantograph on lower receiver. K8-MAG model uses Winchester Super Short Magnum cartridges. Includes 24" bull chrome-moly barrel, flattop upper, free-floating tubular match handguard, Picatinny gas block, crowned muzzle and 7-shot magazine. Made in U.S.A. by Olympic Arms, Inc.
Price: K8 .... **$908.70**
Price: K8-MAG **$1,363.70**

REMINGTON 40-XB RANGEMASTER TARGET
Caliber: 15 calibers from .220 Swift to .300 Win. Mag. **Barrel:** 27.25". **Weight:** 11.25 lbs. **Length:** 47" overall. **Stock:** American walnut, laminated thumbhole or Kevlar with high comb and beavertail fore-end stop. Rubber nonslip buttplate. **Sights:** None. Scope blocks installed. **Features:** Adjustable trigger. Stainless barrel and action. Receiver drilled and tapped for sights. Model 40-XB Tactical (2008) chambered in .308 Win., comes with guarantee of 0.75-inch maximum 5-shot groups at 100 yards. **Weight:** 10.25 lbs. Includes Teflon-coated stainless button-rifled barrel, 1:14" twist, 27.25-inch long, three longitudinal flutes. Bolt-action repeater, adjustable 40-X trigger and precision machined aluminum bedding block. Stock is H-S Precision Pro Series synthetic tactical stock, black with green web finish, vertical pistol grip. From Remington Custom Shop.
Price: 40-XB KS, aramid fiber stock, single shot **$2,863.00**
Price: 40-XB KS, aramid fiber stock, repeater **$3,014.00**
Price: 40-XB Tactical .308 Win. **$2,992.00**

REMINGTON 40-XBBR KS
Caliber: Five calibers from .22 BR to .308 Win. **Barrel:** 20" (light varmint class), 24" (heavy varmint class). **Weight:** 7.25 lbs. (light varmint class); 12 lbs. (heavy varmint class). **Length:** 38" (20" bbl.), 42" (24"bbl.). **Stock:** Aramid fiber. **Sights:** None. Supplied with scope blocks. **Features:** Unblued benchrest with stainless steel barrel, trigger adjustable from 1-1/2 lbs. to 3.5 lbs. Special 2-oz. trigger extra cost. Scope and mounts extra.
Price: Single shot **$3,950.00**

REMINGTON 40-XC KS TARGET
Caliber: 7.62 NATO, 5-shot. **Barrel:** 24", stainless steel. **Weight:** 11 lbs. without sights. **Length:** 43.5" overall. **Stock:** Aramid fiber. **Sights:** None furnished. **Features:** Designed to meet the needs of competitive shooters. Stainless steel barrel and action.
Price: **$3,067.00**

REMINGTON 40-XR CUSTOM SPORTER
Caliber: .22 LR, .22 WM. **Barrel:** 24" stainless steel, no sights. **Weight:** 9.75 lbs. **Length:** 40". **Features:** Model XR-40 Target rifle action. Many options available in stock, decoration or finish.
Price: Single shot **$4,500.00**

SAKO TRG-22 BOLT-ACTION
Caliber: .308 Win., 10-shot magazine, .338 Lapua, 5-shot magazine. **Barrel:** 26". **Weight:** 10.25 lbs. **Length:** 45.25" overall. **Stock:** Reinforced polyurethane with fully adjustable cheekpiece and buttplate. **Sights:** None furnished. Optional quick-detachable, one-piece scope mount base, 1" or 30mm rings. **Features:** Resistance-free bolt, free-floating heavy stainless barrel, 60-degree bolt lift. Two-stage trigger is adjustable for length, pull, horizontal or vertical pitch. TRG-42 has similar features but has long action and is chambered for .338 Lapua. Imported from Finland by Beretta USA.
Price: TRG-22 .... **$3,495.00**
Price: TRG-22 with folding stock **$6,075.00**
Price: TRG-42 .... **$4,445.00**
Price: TRG-42 with folding stock **$7,095.00**

SPRINGFIELD ARMORY M1A SUPER MATCH
Caliber: .308 Win. **Barrel:** 22", heavy Douglas Premium. **Weight:** About 11 lbs. **Length:** 44.31" overall. **Stock:** Heavy walnut competition stock with longer pistol grip, contoured area behind the rear sight, thicker butt and fore-end, glass bedded. **Sights:** National Match front and rear. **Features:** Has figure-eight-style operating rod guide. Introduced 1987. From Springfield Armory.
Price: About **$2,900.00**

SPRINGFIELD ARMORY M1A/M-21 TACTICAL MODEL
Similar to M1A Super Match except special sniper stock with adjustable cheekpiece and rubber recoil pad. Weighs 11.6 lbs. From Springfield Armory.
Price: **$3,555.00**

STI SPORTING COMPETITION
AR-style semiauto rifle chambered in 5.56 NATO. Features include 16-inch 410 stainless 1:8" twist barrel; mid-length gas system; Nordic Tactical Compensator and JP Trigger group; custom STI Valkyrie handguard and gas block; flattop design with picatinny rail; anodized finish with black Teflon coating. Also available in Tactical configuration.
Price: **$1,455.00**

TIME PRECISION .22 RF BENCH REST
Caliber: .22 LR, single-shot. **Barrel:** Shilen match-grade stainless. **Weight:** 10 lbs. with scope. **Length:** NA. **Stock:** Fiberglass. Pillar bedded. **Sights:** None furnished. **Features:** Shilen match trigger removable trigger bracket, full-length steel sleeve, aluminum receiver. Introduced 2008. Made in U.S.A. by Time Precision.
Price: **$2,833.00**

Prices given are believed to be accurate at time of publication however, many factors affect retail pricing so exact prices are not possible.

BENELLI ETHOS

Gauge: 12. 3" chamber. Magazine capacity 4+1. **Barrel:** 28" (Full, Mod., Imp. Cyl., Imp. Mod., Cylinder choke tubes). **Weight:** 6.5 lbs. **Length:** 49.5" overall (28" barrel). **Stock:** Select AA European walnut with satin finish. **Sights:** Red bar fiber optic front, with three interchangeable inserts, metal middle bead. **Features:** Utilizes Benelli's Intertia Driven system. Recoil is reduced by Progressive Comfort recoil reduction system within the buttstock. Cycles all 3-inch loads from light 7/8 oz. up to 3-inch magnums. Also available with nickel-plated engraved receiver. Imported from Italy by Benelli USA, Corp.
Price: $1,999.00
Price: Engraved nickel-plated (shown) $2,199.00

BENELLI LEGACY

Gauge: 12, 20, 28. 3" chamber (12, 20), 2 ¾" (28). **Barrel:** 24", 26", 28" (Full, Mod., Imp. Cyl., Imp. Mod., cylinder choke tubes). Mid-bead sight. **Weight:** 5.8 to 7.4 lbs. **Length:** 49-5/8" overall (28" barrel). **Stock:** Select AA European walnut with satin finish. **Features:** Uses the rotating bolt inertia recoil operating system with a two-piece steel/aluminum etched receiver (bright on lower, blue upper). Drop adjustment kit allows the stock to be custom fitted without modifying the stock. Introduced 1998. Ultralight model has gloss-blued finish receiver. Weight is 6.0 lbs., 24" barrel, 45.5" overall length. WeatherCoat walnut stock. Introduced 2006. Imported from Italy by Benelli USA, Corp.
Price: Legacy (12 and 20 gauge) $1,799.00
Price: Legacy (28 gauge) $2,039.00

BENELLI LEGACY SPORT

Gas-operated semiauto shotgun chambered for 12, 20 (2-3/4- and 3-inch) gauge. Features include Inertia Driven system; sculptured nickel finished lower receiver with classic game scene etchings; highly polished blued upper receiver; AA-Grade walnut stock; (A-grade on Sport II); gel recoil pad; ported 24- or 26-inch barrel, Crio chokes. Weight 6.3 (20 ga.) to 7.4 to 7.5 lbs.
Price: $2,439.00
Price: Legacy Sport II $1,899.00

BENELLI ULTRA LIGHT

Gauge: 12, 20, 28. 3" chamber (12, 20), 2 ¾" (28). **Barrel:** 24", 26". Mid-bead sight. **Weight:** 5.2 to 6 lbs. **Features:** Similar to Legacy line. Drop adjustment kit allows the stock to be custom fitted without modifying the stock. WeatherCoat walnut stock. Lightened receiver, shortened magazine tube, carbon-fiber rib and grip cap. Introduced 2008. Imported from Italy by Benelli USA, Corp.
Price: 12 and 20 gauge...$1,699.00
Price: 28 gauge..$1,799.00

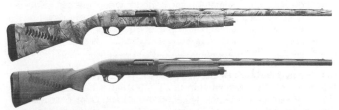

BENELLI M2 FIELD

Gauge: 20 ga., 12 ga., 3" chamber. **Barrel:** 21", 24", 26", 28". **Weight:** 5.4 to 7.2 lbs. **Length:** 42.5 to 49.5" overall. **Stock:** Synthetic, Advantage Max-4 HD, Advantage Timber HD, APG HD. **Sights:** Red bar. **Features:** Uses the Inertia Driven bolt mechanism. Vent rib. Comes with set of five choke tubes. Imported from Italy by Benelli USA.
Price: Synthetic stock 12 ga. $1,499.00
Price: Camo stock 12 ga. $1,549.00
Price: Synthetic stock 20 ga. $1,499.00
Price: Camo stock 20 ga. $1,599.00
Price: Rifled slug ....$1,469.00 to $1,589.00
Price: Left-hand 12 ga. $1409.00
Price: Left-hand model 20 ga. $1519.00

BENELLI MONTEFELTRO

Gauge: 12 and 20 ga. Full, Imp. Mod, Mod., Imp. Cyl., Cyl. choke tubes. **Barrel:** 24", 26", 28". **Weight:** 5.3 to 7.1 lbs. **Stock:** Checkered walnut with satin finish. **Length:** 43.6 to 49.5" overall. **Features:** Uses the Inertia Driven rotating bolt system with a simple inertia recoil design. Finish is blue. Introduced 1987.
Price: Standard Model $1,139.00
Price: Left Hand Model $1,229.00
Price: Silver $1,779.00

BENELLI SUPER BLACK EAGLE II

Gauge: 12, 3 ½-inch chamber. **Barrel:** 24", 26", 28" (Cyl. Imp. Cyl., Mod., Imp. Mod., Full choke tubes). **Weight:** 7.1 to 7.3 lbs. **Length:** 45.6 to 49.6" overall. **Stock:** European walnut with satin finish, polymer, or camo. Adjustable for drop. **Sights:** Red bar front. **Features:** Uses Benelli inertia recoil bolt system. Vent rib. Advantage Max-4 HD, Advantage Timber HD camo patterns. Features ComforTech stock. Introduced 1991. Left-hand models available. Imported from Italy by Benelli USA.
Price: Satin walnut $1,569.00
Price: Camo stock ....$1,680.00 to $1,899.00
Price: Black Comfortech synthetic stock $1,799.00
Price: Left hand, camo stock $1,999.00
Price: Left hand, Comfortech synthetic $1,899.00
Price: Turkey edition w/pistol grip stock................$1,999.00

BENELLI SUPER BLACK EAGLE II WATERFOWL EDITION

Gauge: 12, (3+1 capacity), chambered for 2 ¾", 3" and 3 1/4" ammunition. **Barrel:** 28". **Weight:** 7.3 lbs. **Length:** 49.6". **Features:** Lengthened and polished forcing cone, Rob Roberts Custom choke tubes, Realtree Max-4 camo finish, Hi Viz front sight, metal middle bead. From the Benelli Performance Shop.
Price: $2,669.00

BENELLI CORDOBA

Gauge: 20; 12; 3" chamber. **Barrel:** 28" and 30", ported, 10mm sporting rib. **Weight:** 7.2 to 7.3 lbs. **Length:** 49.6 to 51.6". **Features:** Designed for high-volume sporting clays and Argentina dove shooting. Inertia-driven action, Extended Sport CrioChokes, 4+1 capacity. Ported. Imported from Italy by Benelli USA.
Price: Field Models ....$2,069.00 to $2,099.00
Price: Performance Shop Model ....$2,719.00 to $2,829.00

BENELLI SUPERSPORT & SPORT II

Gauge: 20; 12; 3" chamber. **Barrel:** 28" and 30", ported, 10mm sporting rib. **Weight:** 7.2 to 7.3 lbs. **Length:** 49.6 to 51.6". **Stock:** Carbon fiber, ComforTech (Supersport) or walnut (Sport II). **Sights:** Red bar front, metal midbead. Sport II is similar to the Legacy model except has nonengraved dual tone blue/silver receiver, ported wide-rib barrel, adjustable buttstock, and functions with all loads. Walnut stock with satin finish. Introduced 1997. **Features:** Designed for high-volume sporting clays. Inertia-driven action, Extended CrioChokes, 4+1 capacity. Ported. Imported from Italy by Benelli USA.

Price: Supersport $2,199.00
Price: Sport II $1,899.00

BENELLI VINCI

Gauge: 12, 3-inch chamber. Gas-operated action. Features include modular disassembly; interchangeable choke tubes; 24- to 28-inch ribbed barrel; black, MAX-4HD or APG HD finish; synthetic contoured stocks; optional Steady-Grip model. Weight is 6.7 to 6.9 lbs. Tactical model available with 18.5-" barrel, Picatinny rail, pistol grip, ghost ring sight.

Price: .... $1,449.00 to $2,199.00

BENELLI SUPER VINCI

Gauge: 12 - 2-3/4", 3" and 3-1/2" chamber. **Barrel:** 26" and 28" barrels. **Weight:** 6.9-7 lbs. **Length:** 48.5"-50.5". **Stock:** Black synthetic, Realtree Max4 and Realtree APG. **Features:** 3+1 capacity, Crio Chokes: C,IC,M,IM,F. Length of Pull: 14-3/8". Drop at Heel: 2". Drop at Comb: 1-3/8". Type of **Sights:** Red bar front sight and metal bead mid-sight. Minimum recommended load: 3-dram, 1-1/8 oz. loads (12-ga.). Receiver drilled and tapped for scope mounting. Imported from Italy by Benelli USA., Corp.

Price: Black Synthetic Comfortech $1,799.00
Price: Camo $1,899.00

BERETTA A300 OUTLANDER

Gauge: 12, 3-inch chamber. **Capacity:** 3+1. Operates with 2 ¾" shells. **Barrel:** 28 inches with Mobilechoke system. **Stock:** Synthetic, camo or wood. **Weight:** 7.1 pounds. Based on A400 design but at a lower price. A300 Xtrema model is chambered for 3.5-inch 12-gauge Magnum.

Price: .... $775.00 to $850.00
Price: Xtrema $1,350.00

BERETTA A400 XPLOR UNICO

Self-regulation gas-operated shotgun chambered to shoot all 12-ga, loads from 2-3/4 to 3.5 inches. Features include optional Kick-Off hydraulic damper; 26- or 28-inch "Steelium" barrel with interchangeable choke tubes; anodized aluminum receiver; sculpted, checkered walnut buttstock and fore-end.

Price: $1,755.00
Price: With Kick-Off recoil reduction system.........................$1,855.00

BERETTA A400 XCEL SPORTING

Gauge: 12-gas operated, 3" chamber. **Barrel:** 28, 30 or 32". **Weight:** 7.5 lbs. **Stock:** Walnut and polymer. **Features:** In addition to A400 specifications and features, the Sporting model has aqua blue receiver. Optional Gun Pod electronic system gives digital read-out of air temperature, ammunition pressure, number of rounds fired.

Price: $1,745.00
Price: With Gun Pod $1,895.00
Price: With Kick-Off system...$1,845.00

BERETTA A400 ACTION

Gauge: 12, 20 (3") or 28 (2 ¾" chamber). **Barrel:** 28, 30 barrel. **Weight:** 5.3 (28 ga.) to 6.7 lbs. **Stock:** Walnut and polymer combination. **Features:** Gas-operating Blink operating system can reportedly fire 4 rounds in less than one second. Kick-Off hydraulic recoil reduction system reduces felt recoil up to 70 percent.

Price: $1,550.00
Price: With Kick-Off system...$1,655.00

BROWNING A5

Gauge: 12, 3 or 3.5-inch chamber. **Barrel:** 26, 28 or 30". **Weight:** 6.6 to 7 lbs. **Length:** 47.25 to 51.5". **Stock:** Gloss finish walnut with 22 lpi checkering, black synthetic or camo. Adjustable for cast and drop. **Features:** Operates on Kinematic short-recoil system, totally different than the classic Auto-5 long-recoil action manufactured from 1903-1999. Lengthened forcing cone, three choke tubes (IC, M, F), flat ventilated rib, brass bead front sight, ivory middle bead. Available in Mossy Oak Duck Blind or Break-up Infinity camo. Ultimate Model has satin finished aluminum alloy receiver with light engraving of pheasants on left side, mallards on the right. Glossy blue finish, Grade III oil-finished walnut stock,

Price: A5 Hunter $1,580.00
Price: A5 Hunter 3.5" $1,700.00
Price: A5 Stalker (synthetic) $1,420.00
Price: A5 Stalker 3.5" $1,580.00
Price: A5 Ultimate $1,920.00

BROWNING MAXUS HUNTER

Gauge: 12 ga., 3" & 3-1/2" chamber. **Barrel:** 26", 28" & 30" flat ventilated rib with fixed cylinder choke; stainless Steel; Matte finish. **Weight:** 7 lbs. 2 ozs. **Length:** 40.75". **Stock:** Gloss finish walnut stock with close radius pistol grip, sharp 22 lines-per-inch checkering, speed Lock Forearm, shim adjustable for length of pull, cast and drop. **Features:** Vector Prolengthened forcing cone, three Invector-Pluschoke tubes, Inflex Technology recoil pad, ivory front bead sight, One 1/4" stock spacer. Strong, lightweight aluminum alloy receiver with durable satin nickel finish & laser engraving (pheasant on the right, mallard on the left). All Purpose Hunter has Mossy Oak Break-Up Country Camo, Duratouch coated composite stock.

Price: 3" chamber...$1,550.00
Price: 3-1/2" chamber $1,700.00
Price: All Purpose Hunter $1,740.00

BROWING MAXUS SPORTING

Gauge: 12 ga., 3" chamber. **Barrel:** 28" & 30" flat ventilated rib. **Weight:** 7 lbs. 2 ozs. **Length:** 49.25"-51.25". **Stock:** Gloss finish high grade walnut stock with close radius pistol grip , Speed Lock forearm, shim adjustable for length of pull, cast and drop. **Features:** This new model is sure to catch the eye, with its laser engraving of game birds transforming into clay birdson the lightweight alloy receiver. Quail are on the right side, and a mallard duck on the left. The Power Drive Gas System reduces recoil and cycles a wide array of loads. It's available in a 28" or 30" barrel length. The high grade walnut stock and forearm are generously checkered, finished with a deep, high gloss. The stock is adjustable and one 1/4" stock spacer is included. For picking up either clay or live birds quickly, the HiViz Tri-Comp fiber-optic front sight with mid-bead ivory sight does a great job, gathering light on the most overcast days. Vector Prolengthened forcing cone, five Invector-Pluschoke tubes, Inflex Technology recoil pad ,HiViz Tri-Comp fiber-optic front sight, ivory mid-bead sight, one ¼" stock spacer.

Price: $1,760.00
Price: Golden Clays...$2,070.00

BROWNING MAXUS SPORTING CARBON FIBER

Gauge: 12 ga., 3" chamber. **Barrel:** 28" & 30" flat ventilated rib. **Weight:** 6 lbs. 15 ozs. - 7 lbs. **Length:** 49.25"-51.25". **Stock:** Composite stock with close radius pistol grip, Speed Lock forearm, textured gripping surfaces, shim adjustable for length of pull, cast and drop, carbon fiber finish, Dura-Touch Armor Coating. **Features:** Strong, lightweight aluminum alloy, carbon fiber finish on top and bottom The stock is

Prices given are believed to be accurate at time of publication however, many factors affect retail pricing so exact prices are not possible.

finished with Dura-Touch Armor Coating for a secure, non-slip grip when the gun is wet. It has the Browning exclusive Magazine Cut-Off, a patented Turn-Key Magazine Plug and Speed Load Plus. It will be an impossible task to locate an autoloading shotgun for the field with such shooter-friendly features as the Browning Maxus, especially with this deeply finished look of carbon fiber and the Dura-Touch Armor Coating feel. Vector Prolengthened forcing cone, five Invector-Pluschoke tubes, Inflex Technology recoil pad, HiViz Tri-Comp fiber-optic front sight, ivory mid-bead sight, one 1/4" stock spacer.

Price: **$1,550.00**

BROWNING MAXUS RIFLED DEER STALKER
Gauge: 12 ga., 3" chamber. **Barrel:** 22" thick-walled, fully rifled for slug ammunition only. **Weight:** 7 lbs. 3 ozs. **Length:** 43.25". **Stock:** Composite stock with close radius pistol grip, Speed Lock forearm, textured gripping surfaces, shim adjustable for length of pull, cast and drop, matte black finish Dura-Touch Armor Coating. **Features:** Stock is adjustable for length of pull, cast and drop. Cantilever scope mount, one 1/4" stock spacer. Available with Mossy Oak Break-up Country camo full coverage.
Price: **$1,520.00**
Price: Mossy Oak Break-Up Country camo **$1,640.00**

BROWNING GOLD LIGHT 10 GAUGE
Gauge: 10, 3-1/2". **Capacity:** 4 rounds. **Barrel:** 24 (NWTF), 26 or 28 inches. **Stock:** Composite with Dura-Cote Armor coating. Mossy Oak camo (Break-Up Country or Shadow Grass Blades). **Weight:** Approx. 9.5 pounds. Gas operated action, aluminum receiver, three standard Invector choke tubes. Receiver is drilled and tapped for scope mount. National Wild Turkey Foundation model has Hi-Viz 4-in-1 fiber optic sight, NWTF logo on buttstock.
Price: Mossy Oak Camo finishes...**$1,740.00**
Price: NWTF Model...**$1,870.00**

BROWNING SILVER
Gauge: 12, 3" or 3-1/2" chamber; 20, 3" chamber. **Barrel:** 12 ga.-26", 28", 30", Invector Plus choke tubes. **Weight:** 7 lbs., 9 oz. (12 ga.), 6 lbs., 7 oz. (20 ga.). **Stock:** Satin finish walnut. **Features:** Active Valve gas system, semi-humpback receiver. Invector Plus choke system, three choke tubes. Imported by Browning.
Price: Silver Hunter, 12 ga., 3.5" chamber............................**$1,360.00**
Price: Silver Hunter, 20 ga., 3" chamber, intr. 2008 ....**$1,200.00**
Price: Silver Sporting, 12 ga., 2-3/4" chamber,
　　intr. 2009 ....**$1,320.00**
Price: Silver Sporting Micro, 12 ga., 2-3/4" chamber,
　　intr. 2008 ....**$1,320.00**
Price: Silver Rifled Deer, Mossy Oak New Break-Up,
　　12 ga., 3" chamber, intr. 2008.....................................**$1,460.00**
Price: Silver Rifled Deer Stalker, 12 ga., 3" chamber,
　　intr. 2008 ....**$1,310.00**
Price: Silver Rifled Deer Satin, satin-finished aluminum
　　alloy receiver and satin-finished walnut buttstock
　　and fore-end **$1,360.00**

Price: Silver Stalker, black composite buttstock and
　　fore-end **$1,230.00**

CHARLES DALY MODEL 600
Gauge: 12 or 20 (3" chamber) or 28 (2 3/4") with magazine capacity of 5+1. **Barrel:** 26 or 28" (20 and 28 ga.), 26, 28 or 30 inches (12 ga.). Three choke tubes provided (Rem-Choke pattern). **Stock:** Synthetic, wood or camo. Comes in several variants including Field, Sporting Clays, Tactical and Trap. Left-hand models available. Uses gas-assisted recoil operation. Imported from Turkey.
Price: Field...**$523.00 to $633.00**
Price: Superior w/walnut stock (shown) **$597.00**
Price: Sporting...**$739.00**
Price: Tactical...**$685.00**
Price: Trap..**$769.00**

CHARLES DALY MODEL 635 MASTER MAG
Gauge: 12, 3.5-inch chamber. **Barrel:** 24, 26 or 28 inches. Ported. **Stock:** Synthetic with full camo coverage. Other features similar to Model 600 series.
Price: From **$595.00**

CZ MODEL 712/720
Gauge: 12, 20 (4+1 capacity). **Barrel:** 26". **Weight:** 6.3 lbs. **Stock:** Turkish walnut with 14.5" length of pull. **Features:** Chrome-lined barrel with 3-inch chamber, ventilated rib, five choke tubes. Matte black finish.
Price: 712 12 ga. ....**$499.00 to $699.00**
Price: 720 20 ga.....................................**$516.00 to $599.00**

ESCORT WATERFOWL EXTREME SEMIAUTO
Gauge: 12 or 20 ga., 2-3/4" through 3-1/2" chamber, multi 5+1 capacity. **Barrel:** 28". **Weight:** 7.4 lbs. **Length:** 48". **Stock:** Composite stock with close radius pistol grip; Speed Lock forearm; textured gripping surfaces; shim adjustable for length of pull, cast and drop; Realtree Max4 or AP camo finish; Dura-Touch Armor Coating. **Sights:** HiVis MagniSightfiber optic, magnetic sight to enhance sight acquisition in low light conditions. **Features:** The addition of non-slip grip pads on the fore-end and pistol grip provide a superior hold in all weather conditions. Smart-Valve gas pistons regulate gas blowback to cycle every round – from 2.75 inch range loads through 3.5 inch heavy magnums. Escorts also have Fast-loading systems that allow one-handed round changes without changing aiming position. Left-hand models available at no increase in price.
Price: Black/Synthetic **$551.00**
Price: Realtree Camo **$736.00**
Price: 3.5" Black/Synthetic **$649.00**
Price: 3.5" Realtree Camo **$815.00**

ESCORT SEMI-AUTO
Gauge: 12, 20; 3" or 3.5" chambers. **Barrel:** 22" (Youth), 26" and 28". **Weight:** 6.7-7.8 lbs. **Stock:** Polymer in black, Shadow Grass or Obsession camo finish, Turkish walnut, select walnut. **Sights:** Optional HiViz Spark front. **Features:** Black-chrome or dipped-camo metal parts, top of receiver dovetailed for sight mounts, gold plated trigger, trigger guard safety, magazine cut-off. Three choke tubes (IC, M, F) except the Waterfowl/Turkey Combo, which adds a .665 turkey choke to the standard three. Waterfowl/Turkey combo is two-barrel set, 24"/26" and 26"/28". Several models have Trio recoil pad. Models are: AS, AS Select, AS Youth, AS Youth Select, PS, PS Spark and Waterfowl/Turkey. Introduced 2002. Camo introduced 2003. Youth, Slug and Obsession camo introduced 2005. Imported from Turkey by Legacy Sports International.
Price: ....**$425.00 to $589.00**

FABARM XLR5 VELOCITY AR
Gauge: 12. **Barrel:** 30 or 32". **Weight:** 8.25 lbs. Gas-operated model designed for competition shooting. Features include a unique adjustable rib that allows a more upright shooting position. There

is also an adjustable trigger shoe, magazine cap adjustable weight system. Five interchangeable choke tubes. Imported from Italy by Fabarm USA.
Price: From .... $2,755.00 to $3,300.00
Price: FR Sporting .... $1,990.00 to $2,165.00
Price: LR (Long Rib)........................ $2,260.00 to $2,800.00

FRANCHI AFFINITY
Gauge: 12, 20. Three-inch chamber also handles 2 ¾ inch shells. **Barrel:** 26, 28 inches or 30 inches (12 ga.), 26 inches (20 ga.). 30-inch barrel available only on 12-gauge Sporting model. **Weight:** 5.6 to 6.8 pounds. **Stock:** Black synthetic or Realtree Camo. Left-hand versions available.
Price: Synthetic $849.00
Price: Synthetic left-hand action $899.00
Price: Camo $949.00
Price: Sporting $1,149.00

FRANCHI INTENSITY
Gauge: 12, 3.5" chamber. **Barrel:** 26", 28", 30" (IC, Mod., Full choke tubes). **Weight:** 6.8 lbs. **Stock:** Black synthetic or camo.
Price: Synthetic... $1,099.00
Price: Camo $1,199.00

FRANCHI FENICE
Gauge: 20 or 28. **Barrel:** 26", 28". **Weight:** 5.5 to 5.7. lbs. **Stock:** Oil finished, checkered AA walnut. **Features:** Light scroll engraving on silver finish receiver. Limited availability.
Price: Camo $1,359.00

FRANCHI 48AL FIELD AND DELUXE
Gauge: 20 or 28, 2-3/4" chamber. **Barrel:** 24", 26", 28" (Full, Cyl., Mod., choke tubes). **Weight:** 5.4 to 5.7 lbs. **Length:** 42.25" to 48". **Stock:** Walnut with checkered grip and fore-end. **Features:** Long recoil-operated action. Chrome-lined bore; cross-bolt safety. Imported from Italy by Benelli USA.
Price: Al Field 20 ga. $899.00
Price: Al Field 28 ga. $999.00
Price: Al Field Deluxe 20 ga. $1,149.00
Price: Al Field Deluxe 28 ga. $1,249.00

HARRINGTON & RICHARDSON EXCELL
Gauge: 12, 3" chamber. **Barrel:** 28", 22" (Turkey). Ventilated rib with four screw-in choke tubes (IC, M, IM, F). **Weight:** About 7 lbs. **Stock:** Black synthetic or camo. Imported by H&R 1871, Inc.
Price: Synthetic $499.00
Price: Waterfowl, camo finish $579.00
Price: Turkey, camo finish, 22" barrel, fiber optic sights........... $579.00

MOSSBERG 930
Gauge: 12, 3" chamber, 4-shot magazine. **Barrel:** 24", 26", 28", over-bored to 10-gauge bore dimensions; factory ported, Accu-Choke tubes. **Weight:** 7.5 lbs. **Length:** 44.5" overall (28" barrel). **Stock:** Walnut or synthetic. Adjustable stock drop and cast spacer system. **Sights:** Turkey Taker fiber-optic, adjustable windage and elevation. Front bead fiber-optic front on waterfowl models. **Features:** Self-regulating gas system, dual gas-vent system and piston, EZ-Empty magazine button, cocking indicator. Interchangeable Accu-Choke tube set (IC, Mod, Full) for waterfowl and field models. XX-Full turkey Accu-Choke tube included with turkey models. Ambidextrous thumb-operated safety. Uni-line stock and receiver. Receiver drilled and tapped for scope base attachment, free gun lock. Introduced 2008. From O.F. Mossberg & Sons, Inc.
Price: Turkey, from $782.00
Price: Waterfowl, from $782.00
Price: Combo, from $744.00

Price: Field, from... $672.00
Price: Slugster, from $645.00
Price: Turkey Pistolgrip; Mossy Oak Infinity camo $880.00
Price: Tactical; 18.5" tactical barrel, black synthetic stock and matte black finish $726.00
Price: SPX; no muzzle brake, M16-style front sight, ghost ring rear sight, full pistolgrip stock, eight-round extended magazine $938.00
Price: Home Security/Field Combo; 18.5" Cylinder bore barrel and 28" ported Field barrel; black synthetic stock and matte black finish $604.00
Price: Duck Commander Series .... $890.00 to $928.00
Price: High Performance (13 round magazine)..................... $974.00

MOSSBERG MODEL 935 MAGNUM
Gauge: 12; 3" and 3.5» chamber, interchangeable. **Barrel:** 22", 24», 26», 28». **Weight:** 7.25 to 7.75 lbs. **Length:** 45" to 49" overall. **Stock:** Synthetic. **Features:** Gas-operated semiauto models in blued or camo finish. Fiber optics sights, drilled and tapped receiver, interchangeable Accu-Mag choke tubes.
Price: 935 Magnum Turkey: Realtree Hardwoods, Mossy Oak New Break-up or Mossy Oak Obsession camo overall, 24" barrel $866.00
Price: 935 Magnum Turkey Pistolgrip; full pistolgrip stock $983.00
Price: 935 Magnum Grand Slam: 22" barrel, Mossy Oak Infinity camo overall $884.00
Price: 935 Magnum Flyway: 28" barrel and Advantage Max-4 camo overall $924.00
Price: 935 Magnum Waterfowl: 26"or 28" barrel, matte black, Mossy Oak New Break-up, Advantage Max-4 or Mossy Oak Duck Blind cam overall $725.00
Price: 935 Magnum Turkey/Deer Combo: interchangeable 24" Turkey barrel, Mossy Oak New Break-up camo overall $957.00
Price: 935 Magnum Waterfowl/Turkey Combo: 24" Turkey and 28" Waterfowl barrels, Mossy Oak New Break-up finish overall $957.00
Price: Duck Commander $986.00

MOSSBERG SA-20
Gauge: 20. 20" (Tactical), 26" or 28". **Weight:** 5.5 to 6 lbs. **Stock:** Black synthetic. Gas operated action, matte blue finish. Tactical model has ghost-ring sight, accessory rail.
Price: From .... $580.00 to $633.00

REMINGTON MODEL 11-87 SPORTSMAN
Gauge: 12, 20, 3" chamber. **Barrel:** 26", 28", RemChoke tubes. Standard contour, vent rib. **Weight:** About 7.75 to 8.25 lbs. **Length:** 46" to 48" overall. **Stock:** Black synthetic or Mossy Oak Break Up Mossy Oak Duck Blind, and Realtree Hardwoods HD and AP Green HD camo finishes. **Sights:** Single bead front. **Features:** Matte-black metal finish, magazine cap swivel studs. Sportsman Deer gun has 21-inch fully rifled barrel, cantilever scope mount.
Price: .... $804.00 to $929.00

REMINGTON MODEL 1100 CLASSIC
Gauge: 12, 20 or 28. Part of the Remington American Classics Collection honoring Remington's most enduring firearms. **Barrel:** 28" (12 ga.), 26" (20), 25" (28). Features include American walnut B-grade stock with classic white line spacer and grip caps, ventilated recoil pad the white line spacer and white diamond grip cap. Machine-cut engraved receiver has tasteful scroll pattern with gold inlayed retriever and "American Classic" label.
Price: $1,645.00

REMINGTON MODEL 1100 COMPETITION MODELS
Gauge: .410 bore, 28, 20, 12. **Barrel:** 26", 27", 28", 30" light target contoured vent rib barrel with twin bead target sights. **Stock:** Semi-

Prices given are believed to be accurate at time of publication however, many factors affect retail pricing so exact prices are not possible.

fancy American walnut stock and fore-end, cut checkering, high gloss finish. **Features:** Classic Trap has 30-inch barrel and weighs approximately 8.25 pounds. Sporting Series is available in all four gauges with 28-inch barrel in 12 and 20 gauge, 27 inch in 28 and .410. **Weight:** 6.25 to 8 pounds. Competion Synthetic model has synthetic stock with adjustable comb, case and length. Five Briley Target choke tubes. High-gloss blued barrel, Nickel-Teflon finish on receiver and internal parts. **Weight:** 8.1 pounds.

Price: Classic Trap $1,308.00
Price: Sporting Series, from $1,230.00
Price: Competition Synthetic: $1,279.00

REMINGTON MODEL 1100 TAC-4
Similar to Model 1100 but with 18" or 22" barrel with ventilated rib; 12 gauge 2-3/4"only; standard black synthetic stock or Knoxx SpecOps SpeedFeed IV pistolgrip stock; RemChoke tactical choke tube; matte black finish overall. Length is 42-1/2" and weighs 7-3/4 lbs.

Price: $1,015.00

REMINGTON VERSA MAX SERIES
Gauge: 12 ga., 2 3/4", 3", 3 1/2" chamber. **Barrel:** 26" and 28" flat ventilated rib. **Weight:** 7.5 lbs.-7.7 lbs. **Length:** 40.25". **Stock:** Synthetic. **Features:** Reliably cycles 12-gauge rounds from 2 3/4" to 3 1/2" magnum. Versaport gas system regulates cycling pressure based on shell length. Reduces recoil to that of a 20-gauge. Self-cleaning - Continuously cycled thousands of rounds in torture test. Synthetic stock and fore-end with grey overmolded grips. Drilled and tapped receiver. Enlarged trigger guard opening and larger safety for easier use with gloves. TriNyte Barrel and Nickel Teflon plated internal components offer extreme corrosion resistance. Includes 5 Flush Mount Pro Bore Chokes (Full, Mod, Imp Mod Light Mod, IC)

Price: Sportsman, from $1,046.00
Price: Synthetic, from $1,427.00
Price: Tactical, from $1,427.00
Price: Waterfowl, from $1,730.00
Price: Camo, from $1,630.00

REMINGTON MODEL V3
Gauge: 12, 3-inch chamber. Magazine capacity 3+1. **Barrel:** 26 or 28 inches. The newest addition to the Remington shotgun family operates on an improved VersaPort gas system, claimed to offer the least recoil of any 12-gauge autoloader. Operating system is located in front of the receiver instead of the fore-end, resulting in better weight distribution than other autoloaders, and improved handling qualities. **Stock:** Walnut, black synthetic, or camo. Designed to function with any 2¾ or 3-inch ammo. Made in the U.S.A. by Remington.

Price: Synthetic black..$895.00
Price: Walnut or camo $995.00

SKB MODEL IS300
Gauge: 12, 2-3/4 and 3-inch loads. Magazine capacity: 4+1. Inertia-driven operating system. **Barrel:** 26, 28 or 30 inches with 3 choke tubes IC, M, F. **Stock:** Black synthetic, oil-finished walnut or camo. **Weight:** 6.7 to 7.3 pounds. **Features:** Target models have adjustable stock dimensions including cast and drop. Made in Turkey and imported by GU, Inc.

Price: Synthetic $625.00
Price: Walnut or Camo Field $715.00
Price: Walnut Target $870.00
Price: RS300 Target with adjustable stock $1,000.00

STOEGER MODEL 3000
Gauge: 12, 2-3/4 and 3-inch loads. Minimum recommended load 3-dram, 1-1/8 ounces. **Magazine capacity:** 4+1. Inertia-driven operating system. **Barrel:** 26 or 28 inches with 3 choke tubes IC, M, XF. **Weight:** 7.4 to 7.5 pounds. **Finish:** Black synthetic or camo (Realtree APG or Max-4). M3K model is designed for three-

gun competition and has synthetic stock, 24-inch barrel, modified loading port.

Price: Synthetic $599.00
Price: Walnut or Camo $649.00
Price: M3K $699.00

STOEGER MODEL 3020
Gauge: 20, 2¾ or 3-inch loads. This model has the same general specifications as the Model 3000 except for its chambering and weight of 5.5 to 5.8 pounds.

Price: Synthetic...$599.00
Price: Camo $649.00

STOEGER MODEL 3500
Gauge: 12. 2 3/4, 3 and 3 1/2-inch loads. Minimum recommended load 3-dram, 1-1/8 ounces. **Barrel:** 24, 26 or 28 inches. Other features similar to Model 3000. Choke tubes for IC, M, XF. **Weight:** 7.4 to 7.5 pounds. **Finish:** Black synthetic or camo (Realtree APG or Max-4).

Price: Synthetic $679.00
Price: Camo $799.00

TRISTAR VIPER G2
Gauge: 12, 20; shoots 2-3/4" or 3" interchangeably. **Barrel:** 26", 28" barrels (carbon fiber only offered in 12-ga. 28" and 20-ga. 26"). **Stock:** Wood, black synthetic, Mossy Oak Duck Blind camouflage, faux carbon fiber finish (2008) with the new Comfort Touch technology. **Features:** Magazine cut-off, vent rib with matted sight plane, brass front bead (camo models have fiber-optic front sight), five round magazine-shot plug included, and 3 Beretta-style choke tubes (IC, M, F). Viper synthetic, Viper camo have swivel studs. Five-year warranty. Viper Youth models have shortened length of pull and 24" barrel. Imported by Tristar Sporting Arms Ltd.

Price: From $519.00
Price: Camo models from...$609.00
Price: Silver model................................. $639.00 to $689.00

WEATHERBY SA-SERIES
Gauge: 12 ga. & 20 ga., 3" chamber. **Barrel:** 26" and 28" flat ventilated rib. **Weight:** 6.5 lbs. **Stock:** Wood and synthetic. **Features:** The SA-08 is a reliable workhorse that lets you move from early season dove loads to late fall's heaviest waterfowl loads in no time. Available with wood and synthetic stock options in 12 and 20 gauge models, including a scaled-down youth model to fit 28 ga. Comes with 3 application-specific choke tubes (SK/IC/M). Made in Turkey.

Price: SA-08 Upland $799.00
Price: SA-08 Synthetic (New 2011) $629.00
Price: SA-08 Waterfowler 3.0 ....$799.00
Price: SA-08 Synthetic Youth $629.00
Price: SA-08 Deluxe...$829.00
Price: Element Deluxe w/inertia operated action, AA walnut **$1,099.00**

WINCHESTER SUPER X3
Gauge: 12, 3" and 3.5" chambers. **Barrel:** 26", 28", .742" back-bored; Invector Plus choke tubes. **Weight:** 7 to 7.25 lbs. **Stock:** Composite, 14.25"x1.75"x2". Mossy Oak New Break-Up camo with Dura-Touch Armor Coating. Pachmayr Decelerator buttpad with hard heel insert, customizable length of pull. **Features:** Alloy magazine tube, gunmetal grey Perma-Cote UT finish, self-adjusting Active Valve gas action, lightweight recoil spring system. Electroless nickel-plated bolt, three choke tubes, two length-of-pull stock spacers, drop and cast adjustment spacers, sling swivel studs. Introduced 2006. Made in Belgium, assembled in Portugal by U.S. Repeating Arms Co.

Price: Field $1,070.00
Price: Black Shadow .... $1,000.00 to $1,070.00 (3.5")
Price: Universal Hunter ....$1,160.00 to $1,230.00 (3.5")
Price: Waterfowl Hunter $1,200.00
Price: Sporting, Adj. comb $1,700.00
Price: Cantilever Buck $1,150.00
Price: Coyote, pistol grip composite stock $1,200.00
Price: Long Beard, pistol grip camo stock $1,270.00

BENELLI SUPERNOVA
Gauge: 12; 3.5" chamber. **Barrel:** 24", 26", 28". **Length:** 45.5-49.5". **Stock:** Synthetic; Max-4 , Timber, APG HD (2007). **Sights:** Red bar front, metal midbead. **Features:** 2-3/4", 3" chamber (3-1/2" 12 ga. only). Montefeltro rotating bolt design with dual action bars, magazine cut-off, synthetic trigger assembly, adjustable combs, shim kit, choice of buttstocks. 4-shot magazine. Introduced 2006. Imported from Italy by Benelli USA.

Price: $549.00
Price: Camo stock...$669.00
Price: Rifle slug model.......................... $829.00 to $929.00

BENELLI NOVA
Gauge: 12, 20. **Barrel:** 24", 26", 28". **Stock:** Black synthetic, Max-4, Timber and APG HD. **Sights:** Red bar. **Features:** 2-3/4", 3" chamber (3-1/2" 12 ga. only). Montefeltro rotating bolt design with dual action bars, magazine cut-off, synthetic trigger assembly, 4-shot magazine. Introduced 1999. Field & Slug Combo has 24" barrel and rifled bore; open rifle sights; synthetic stock; weighs 8.1 lbs. Imported from Italy by Benelli USA.

Price: Max-5 camo stock.....................................$559.00
Price: H20 model, black synthetic, matte nickel finish.............$669.00
Price: Tactical, 18.5" barrel, Ghost Ring sight........................$459.00
Price: Black synthetic youth stock, 20 ga. $469.00

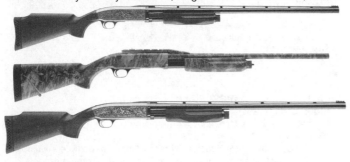

BROWNING BPS
Gauge: 10, 12, 3-1/2" chamber; 12, 16, or 20, 3" chamber (2-3/4" in target guns), 28, 2-3/4" chamber, 5-shot magazine, .410, 3" chamber. **Barrel:** 10 ga.-24" Buck Special, 28", 30" 32" Invector; 12, 20 ga.-22", 24", 26", 28", 30", 32" (Imp. Cyl., Mod. or Full), .410-26" barrel. (Imp. Cyl., Mod. and Full choke tubes.) Also available with Invector choke tubes, 12 or 20 ga.; Upland Special has 22" barrel with Invector tubes. BPS 3" and 3-1/2" have back-bored barrel. **Weight:** 7 lbs., 8 oz. (28" barrel). **Length:** 48.75" overall (28" barrel). **Stock:** 14.25"x1.5"x2.5". Select walnut, semi-beavertail fore-end, full pistol grip stock. **Features:** All 12 gauge 3" guns except Buck Special and game guns have back-bored barrels with Invector Plus choke tubes. Bottom feeding and ejection, receiver top safety, high post vent rib. Double action bars eliminate binding. Vent rib barrels only. All 12 and 20 gauge guns with 3" chamber available with fully engraved receiver flats at no extra cost. Each gauge has its own unique game scene. Introduced 1977. Stalker is same gun as the standard BPS except all exposed metal parts have a matte blued finish and the stock has a black finish with a black recoil pad. Available in 10 ga. (3-1/2") and 12 ga. with 3" or 3-1/2" chamber, 22", 28", 30" barrel with Invector choke system. Introduced 1987. Rifled Deer Hunter is similar to the standard BPS except has newly designed receiver/magazine tube/barrel mounting system to eliminate play, heavy 20.5" barrel with rifle-type sights with adjustable rear, solid receiver scope mount, "rifle" stock dimensions for scope or open sights, sling swivel studs. Gloss or matte finished wood with checkering, polished blue metal. Medallion model has additional engraving on receiver, polished blue finish, AA/AAA grade walnut stock with checkering. All Purpose model has

Realtree AP camo on stock and fore-end, HiVis fiber optic sights. Introduced 2013. Imported from Japan by Browning.
Price: Field, Stalker models......................................$700.00
Price: Camo coverage $820.00
Price: Deer Hunter $830.00
Price: Deer Hunter Camo..$870.00
Price: All Purpose $930.00
Price: Magnum Hunter (3.5")............... $800.00 to $1,030.00
Price: Medallion $830.00

BROWNING BPS 10 GAUGE SERIES
Similar to the standard BPS except completely covered with Mossy Oak Shadow Grass camouflage. Available with 26" and 28" barrel. Introduced 1999. Imported by Browning
Price: Mossy Oak camo...$950.00
Price: Synthetic stock, Stalker................................$800.00

BROWNING BPS NWTF TURKEY SERIES
Similar to the standard BPS except has full coverage Mossy Oak Break-Up Infinity camo finish on synthetic stock, fore-end and exposed metal parts. Offered in 12 gauge, 3" or 3-1/2" chamber, or 10 gauge; 24" bbl. has extra-full choke tube and HiViz fiber-optic sights. Introduced 2001. From Browning.
Price: 12 ga., 3" $950.00
Price: 3.5" $1,030.00

BROWNING BPS MICRO MIDAS
Gauge: 12, 20, 28 ga. or .410 bore, 24 or 26". Three Invector choke tubes for 12 and 20 gauge, standard tubes for 28 and .410. **Stock:** Walnut with pistol grip and recoil pad. Satin finished and scaled down to fit smaller statured shooters. Length of pull is 13.25". Two spacers included for stock length adjustments. **Weight:** 7 to 7.8 lbs.
Price: .... $700.00 to $740.00

BROWING BPS HIGH CAPACITY
Gauge: .410 bore. 3" chamber. 5-round magazine. **Barrel:** 20" fixed Cylinder choke; stainless Steel; Matte finish. **Weight:** 6 lbs. **Length:** 40.75". **Stock:** Black composite on All Weather with matte finish. **Features:** Forged and machined steel; satin nickel finish. Bottom ejection; dual steel action bars; top tang safety; HiViz Tactical fiber-optic front sight; stainless internal mechanism; swivel studs installed.
Price: Synthetic...$800.00

CHARLES DALY 300 SERIES
Gauge: 12, 20 or 28 gauge. Chambered for 3" and 2¾" shells (12 and 20), 2¾" (28 ga.). Model 335 Master Mag is chambered for 12-ga. 3½-inch shells. **Barrel:** 24, 26, 28 and 30 inches, depending upon specific model. Ventilated rib. Three choke tubes (REM-Choke pattern) are provided. **Stock:** Synthetic, walnut or camo. **Weight:** 7 to 8 lbs. Left-hand models available. Imported from Turkey.
Price: Field .... $365.00 to $495.00
Price: Tactical................................... $423.00 to $503.00
Price: Turkey $553.00

CZ 612
Gauge: 12. Chambered for all shells up to 3 ½ inches. **Capacity:** 5+1, magazine plug included with Wildfowl Magnum. **Barrel length:** 18.5 inches (Home Defense), 20 (HC-P), 26 inches (Wildfowl Mag). **Weight:** 6 to 6.8 pounds. **Stock:** Polymer. **Finish:** Matte black or full camo (Wildfowl Mag.) HC-P model has pistol grip stock, fiber optic front sight and ghost-ring rear. Home Defense Combo comes with extra 26-inch barrel.
Price: Wildfowl Magnum $428.00
Price: Home Defense .... $304.00 to $409.00

ESCORT PUMP SERIES
Gauge: 12, 20; 3" chamber. **Barrel:** 18" (AimGuard, Home Defense and MarineGuard), 22" (Youth Pump), 26", and 28" lengths. **Weight:** 6.7-7.0 lbs. **Stock:** Polymer in black, Shadow Grass camo or Obsession camo finish. Two adjusting spacers included. Youth model has Trio recoil pad. **Sights:** Bead or Spark front sights, depending on

model. AimGuard and MarineGuard models have blade front sights. **Features:** Black-chrome or dipped camo metal parts, top of receiver dovetailed for sight mounts, gold plated trigger, trigger guard safety, magazine cut-off. Three choke tubes (IC, M, F) except AimGuard/ MarineGuard which are cylinder bore. Models include: FH, FH Youth, AimGuard and Marine Guard. Introduced in 2003. Imported from Turkey by Legacy Sports International.

Price: $379.00
Price: Youth model...$393.00
Price: Model 87 w/wood stock...................................$350.00

HARRINGTON & RICHARDSON (H&R) PARDNER PUMP

Gauge: 12, 20.3-inch chamber. **Barrel:** 21 to 28 inches. **Weight:** 6.5 to 7.5 lbs. **Stock:** Synthetic or hardwood. Ventilated recoil pad and grooved fore-end. **Features:** Steel receiver, double action bars, cross-bolt safety, easy takedown, ventilated rib, screw-in choke tubes.

Price: From ....$231.00 to $259.00

IAC MODEL 97T TRENCH GUN

Gauge: 12, 2 ¾" chamber. Replica of Winchester Model 1897 Trench Gun. **Barrel:** 20" with cylinder choke. **Stock:** Hand rubbed American walnut. **Features:** Metal hand guard, bayonet lug. Imported from China by Interstate Arms Corp.

Price: $465.00

ITHACA MODEL 37 FEATHERWEIGHT

Gauge: 12, 20, 16, 28 (4+1 capacity). **Barrel:** 26, 28 or 30" with 3" chambers (12 and 20 ga.), plain or ventiltated rib. **Weight:** 6.1 to 7.6 lbs. **Stock:** Fancy grade black walnut with Pachmayr Decelerator recoil pad. Checkered fore-end made of matching walnut. **Features:** Receiver machined from a single block of steel or aluminum. Barrel is steel shot compatible. Three Briley choke tubes provided. Available in several variations including turkey, home defense, tactical and high-grade.

Price: 12, 16 or 20 ga. from $895.00
Price: 28 ga. from $1,149.00
Price: Turkey Slayer w/synthetic stock from...........$925.00
Price: Trap Series 12 ga..$999.00
Price: Waterfowl $885.00

ITHACA DEERSLAYER III SLUG

Gauge: 12, 20; 3" chamber. **Barrel:** 26" fully rifled, heavy fluted with 1:28 twist for 12 ga.; 1:24 for 20 ga. **Weight:** 8.14 lbs. to 9.5 lbs. with scope mounted. **Length:** 45.625" overall. **Stock:** Fancy black walnut stock and fore-end. **Sights:** NA. **Features:** Updated, slug-only version of the classic Model 37. Bottom ejection, blued barrel and receiver.

Price: $1,289.00

MAVERICK ARMS MODEL 88

Gauge: 12, 20.3" chamber. **Barrel:** 26" or 28", Accu-Mag choke tubes for steel or lead shot. **Weight:** 7.25 lbs. **Stock:** Black synthetic with recoil pad. **Features:** Crossbolt safety, aluminum alloy receiver. Economy model of Mossberg Model 500 series. Available in several variations including Youth, Slug and Special Purpose (home defense) models.

Price: $298.00

MOSSBERG MODEL 835 ULTI-MAG

Gauge: 12, 3-1/2" chamber. **Barrel:** Ported 24" rifled bore, 24", 28", Accu-Mag choke tubes for steel or lead shot. **Weight:** 7.75 lbs. **Length:** 48.5" overall. **Stock:** 14"x1.5"x2.5". Dual Comb. Cut-checkered hardwood or camo synthetic; both have recoil pad. **Sights:** White bead front, brass mid-bead; fiber-optic rear. Turkey Thug has red dot sight. **Features:** Shoots 2-3/4", 3" or 3-1/2" shells. Back-bored and ported barrel to reduce recoil, improve patterns. Ambidextrous thumb safety, twin extractors, dual slide bars. Mossberg Cablelock included. Introduced 1988.

Price: Turkey $600.00
Price: Turkey Thug $708.00
Price: Waterfowl $513.00
Price: Slugster $638.00
Price: Duck Commander $693.00

MOSSBERG MODEL 500 SPORTING SERIES

Gauge: 12, 20, .410, 3" chamber. **Barrel:** 18.5" to 28" with fixed or Accu-Choke, plain or vent rib. **Weight:** 6-1/4 lbs. (.410), 7-1/4 lbs. (12). **Length:** 48" overall (28" barrel). **Stock:** 14"x1.5"x2.5". Walnut-stained hardwood, black synthetic, Mossy Oak Advantage camouflage. Cut-checkered grip and fore-end. **Sights:** White bead front, brass mid-bead; fiber-optic. **Features:** Ambidextrous thumb safety, twin extractors, disconnecting safety, dual action bars. Quiet Carry fore-end. Many barrels are ported. FLEX series has many modular options and accessories including barrels and stocks. From Mossberg. Left-hand versions (L-series) available in most models.

Price: Turkey, from $466.00
Price: Waterfowl, from $537.00
Price: Combo, from $593.00
Price: FLEX Duck Commander......................................$835.00
Price: FLEX Hunting...$770.00
Price: FLEX All Purpose...$682.00
Price: Field, from $401.00
Price: Slugster, from $434.00

MOSSBERG MODEL 500 SUPER BANTAM PUMP

Same as the Model 500 Sporting Pump except 12 or 20 gauge, 22" vent rib Accu-Choke barrel with choke tube set; has 1" shorter stock, reduced length from pistol grip to trigger, reduced fore-end reach. Introduced 1992.

Price: $414.00
Price: Combo with extra slug barrel, camo finish....................$534.00

MOSSBERG 510 MINI BANTAM

Gauge: 20 & .410 ga., 3" chamber. **Barrel:** 18 1/2 " vent-rib. **Weight:** 5 lbs. **Length:** 34 3/4". **Stock:** Synthetic with optional Mossy Oak Break-Up Infinity, Muddy Girl pink/black camo. **Features:** Available in either 20 gauge or .410 bore, the Mini features an 18 1/2 " vent-rib barrel with dual-bead sights. Parents don't have to worry about their young shooter growing out of this gun too quick, the adjustable classic stock can be adjusted from 10 1/2" to 11 1/2" length of pull so the Mini can grow with your youngster. This adjustability also helps provide a proper fit for young shooters and allowing for a more safe and enjoyable shooting experience.

Price: From $466.00

Prices given are believed to be accurate at time of publication however, many factors affect retail pricing so exact prices are not possible.

70TH EDITION, 2016 ✛ **497**

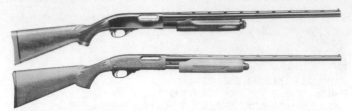

REMINGTON MODEL 870 WINGMASTER

Gauge: 12, 20, 28 ga., .410 bore. **Barrel:** 25", 26", 28", 30" (RemChokes). **Weight:** 7-1/4 lbs. **Length:** 46", 48". **Stock:** Walnut, hardwood. **Sights:** Single bead (Twin bead Wingmaster). **Features:** Light contour barrel. Double action bars, cross-bolt safety, blue finish. LW is 28 gauge and .410-bore only, 25" vent rib barrel with RemChoke tubes, high-gloss wood finish. Gold-plated trigger, American B Grade walnut stock and fore-end, high-gloss finish, fleur-de-lis checkering. A classic American shotgun first introduced in 1950.
Price: .... **$830.00 to $929.00**

REMINGTON MODEL 870 AMERICAN CLASSIC

Gauge: 12, 20 or 28 gauge. **Barrel:** 25" (28 ga), 26" (20 ga.), 28" (12 ga.) with ventilated rib and Rem Choke system. **Weight:** 6 to 7 lbs. Commemorating one of the most popular firearms in history, this model features a B-grade American walnut stock, a high polish blue finish, and machine-cut engraved receiver with gold filled banner reading "American Classic." Other features in keeping with those that were popular in the 1950s include ventilated recoil pad with white line spacer and a diamond grip cap.
Price: **$1,249.00**

REMINGTON MODEL 870 MARINE MAGNUM

Similar to 870 Wingmaster except all metal plated with electroless nickel, black synthetic stock and fore-end. Has 18" plain barrel (cyl.), bead front sight, 7-shot magazine. Introduced 1992. XCS version with TriNyte corrosion control introduced 2007.
Price: **$841.00**

REMINGTON MODEL 870 CLASSIC TRAP

Similar to Model 870 Wingmaster except has 30" vent rib, light contour barrel, singles, mid- and long-handicap choke tubes, semi-fancy American walnut stock, high-polish blued receiver with engraving. Chamber 2.75". From Remington Arms Co.
Price: **$1,098.00**

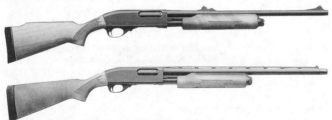

REMINGTON MODEL 870 EXPRESS

Similar to Model 870 Wingmaster except laminate, synthetic black, or camo stock with solid, black recoil pad and pressed checkering on grip and fore-end. Outside metal surfaces have black oxide finish. Comes with 26" or 28" vent rib barrel with mod. RemChoke tube. ShurShot Turkey (2008) has ShurShot synthetic pistol-grip thumbhole design, extended fore-end, Mossy Oak Obsession camouflage, matte black metal finish, 21" vent rib barrel, twin beads, Turkey Extra Full Rem Choke tube. Receiver drilled and tapped for mounting optics. ShurShot FR CL (Fully Rifled Cantilever, 2008)

includes compact 23" fully-rifled barrel with integrated cantilever scope mount.
Price: .... **$417.00 to $629.00**

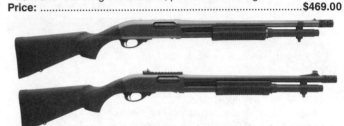

REMINGTON MODEL 870 EXPRESS SUPER MAGNUM

Similar to Model 870 Express except 28" vent rib barrel with 3-1/2" chamber, vented recoil pad. Introduced 1998. Model 870 Express Super Magnum Waterfowl (2008) is fully camouflaged with Mossy Oak Duck Blind pattern, 28-inch vent rib Rem Choke barrel, "Over Decoys" Choke tube (.007") fiber-optic HiViz single bead front sight; front and rear sling swivel studs, padded black sling.
Price: **$469.00**

REMINGTON MODEL 870 EXPRESS TACTICAL

Similar to Model 870 but in 12 gauge only (2-2/4" and 3" interchangeably) with 18.5" barrel, Tactical RemChoke extended/ported choke tube, black synthetic buttstock and fore-end, extended magazine tube, gray powdercoat finish overall. 38.5" overall length, weighs 7.5 lbs.
Price: **$601.00**
Price: Model 870 TAC Desert Recon; desert camo stock and sand-toned metal surfaces **$692.00**
Price: Tactical Magpul **$898.00**

REMINGTON MODEL 870 SPS SHURSHOT SYNTHETIC SUPER SLUG

Gauge: 12; 2-3/4" and 3" chamber, interchangeable. **Barrel:** 25.5" extra-heavy, fully rifled pinned to receiver. **Weight:** 7-7/8 lbs. **Length:** 47" overall. **Features:** Pump-action model based on 870 platform. SuperCell recoil pad. Drilled and tapped for scope mounts with Weaver rail included. Matte black metal surfaces, ShurShot pistol grip buttstock with Mossy Oak Treestand camo.
Price: **$829.00**
Price: 870 SPS ShurShot Synthetic Turkey; adjustable sights and APG HD camo buttstock and fore-end **$681.00**

REMINGTON 870 EXPRESS SYNTHETIC SUPER MAG TURKEY-WATERFOWL CAMO

Pump action shotgun chambered in 12-ga., 2-3/4 to 3-1/2 inch. Features include full Mossy Oak Bottomland camo coverage; 26-inch barrel with HiViz fiber-optics sights; Wingmaster HD Waterfowl

and Turkey Extra Full RemChokes; SuperCell recoil pad; drilled and tapped receiver.
Price: **$629.00**

REMINGTON 870 EXPRESS SYNTHETIC TURKEY CAMO

Pump action shotgun chambered for 2-3/4 and 3-inch 12-ga. Features include 21-inch vent rib bead-sighted barrel; standard Express finish on barrel and receiver; Turkey Extra Full RemChoke; synthetic stock with integrated sling swivel attachment.
Price: **$492.00**

REMINGTON 870 SUPER MAG TURKEY-PREDATOR CAMO WITH SCOPE

Pump action shotgun chambered in 12-ga., 2-3/4 to 3-1/2 inch. Features include 20-inch barrel; TruGlo red/green selectable illuminated sight mounted on pre-installed Weaver-style rail; black padded sling; Wingmaster HDTurkey/Predator RemChoke; full Mossy Oak Obsession camo coverage; ShurShot pistol grip stock with black overmolded grip panels; TruGlo 30mm Red/Green Dot Scope pre-mounted.
Price: **$710.00**

REMINGTON MODEL 887 NITRO MAG

Gauge: 12; 3.5", 3", and 2-3/4" chambers. **Barrel:** 28". **Features:** Pump-action model based on the Model 870. Interchangeable shells, black matte ArmoLokt rustproof coating throughout. SuperCell recoil pad. Solid rib and Hi-Viz front sight with interchangeable light tubes. Black synthetic stock with contoured grip panels.
Price: **$445.00**
Price: Model 887 Nitro Mag Waterfowl, camo **$594.00**

REMINGTON 887 NITRO MAG CAMO COMBO

Pump action shotgun chambered in 12-ga., 2-3/4 to 3-1/2 inch. Features include 22-inch turkey barrel with HiViz fiber-optic rifle sights and 28-inch waterfowl with a HiViz sight; extended Waterfowl and Super Full Turkey RemChokes are included; SuperCell recoil pad; synthetic stock and fore-end with specially contoured grip panels; full camo coverage.
Price: **$728.00**

STEVENS MODEL 350/320

Gauge: 12, 3-inch chamber, 5+1 capacity. **Barrel:** 18.25" with interchangeable choke tubes. Features include all-steel barrel and receiver; bottom-load and ejection design; black synthetic stock.
Price: Security Model **$276.00**

Price: Field Model 320 with 28-inch barrel **$251.00**
Price: Combo Model with Field and Security barrels **$307.00**

STOEGER P-350

Gauge: 12. Designed to fire any 12-gauge ammunition. **Capacity:** 4+1. **Barrel:** 18.5, 20, 24, 26 or 28 inches, with ventilated rib. **Weight:** 6.6 to 7 pounds. **Stock:** Black synthetic, or Realtree APG or Max-4 camo in standard stock configuration. Also available with vertical pistol-style handgrip.
Price: ....**$349.00 to $479.00**

WEATHERBY PA-08 SERIES

Gauge: 12 ga. chamber. **Barrel:** 26" and 28" flat ventilated rib. **Weight:** 6.5 lbs. -7 lbs. **Stock:** Walnut. **Features:** The PA-08 # Walnut stock with gloss finish, all metalwork is gloss black for a distinctive look, vented top rib dissipates heat and aids in target acquisition. Comes with 3 application-specific choke tubes (IC/M/F). Upland/Slug Gun combo includes 24" rifled barrel. Made in Turkey.
Price: PA-08 Upland **$449.00**
Price: PA-08 Upland/Slug combo............................**$649.00**
Price: PA-08 Turkey **$429.00**
Price: PA-08 Synthetic..**$399.00**
Price: PA-08 Synthetic Waterfowler..........................**$399.00**
Price: PA-08 Synthetic Turkey **$399.00**

WEATHERBY PA-459 TURKEY

Gauge: 12, 3-inch chamber. Barrel: 21.25 inches. Stock: Synthetic with Mothwing Spring Mimicry camo, rubber texturized grip areas. Vertical pistol grip. **Sights:** Ghost ring rear, fiber optic front. Picatinny rail. Features: Mothwing Spring Mimicry camo.
Price: **$549.00**

WINCHESTER SUPER X (SXP)

Gauge: 12, 3" or 3.5" chambers; 20 gauge, 3". **Barrel:** 18"; 26" and 28" barrels are .742" back-bored, chrome plated; Invector Plus choke tubes. **Weight:** 6 .5 to 7 lbs. **Stock:** Walnut or composite. **Features:** Rotary bolt, four lugs, dual steel action bars. Walnut Field has gloss-finished walnut stock and forearm, cut checkering. Black Shadow Field has composite stock and forearm, non-glare matte finish barrel and receiver. SXP Defender has composite stock and forearm, chromed plated, 18" cylinder choked barrel, non-glare metal surfaces, five-shot magazine, grooved forearm. Some models offered in left-hand versions. Reintroduced 2009. Made in U.S.A. from Winchester Repeating Arms Co.
Price: Black Shadow Field, 3" **$380.00**
Price: Black Shadow Field, 3.5" **$430.00**
Price: SXP Defender................................**$350.00 to $400.00**
Price: Waterfowl Hunter 3" **$460.00**
Price: Waterfowl Hunter 3.5" **$500.00**
Price: Turkey Hunter 3.5" **$520.00**
Price: Black Shadow Deer **$520.00**
Price: Trap..**$480.00**
Price: Field, walnut stock.........................**$400.00 to $430.00**

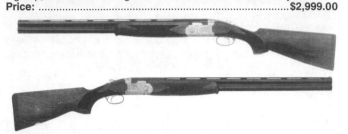

BENELLI 828U
Gauge: 12. 3-inch chambers **Barrels:** 26 or 28 inches. **Weight:** 6.5 to 7 lbs. **Stock:** AA-grade satin walnut, fully adjustable for both drop and cast. New patented locking system allows use of aluminum frame. Features include carbon fiber rib, fiber optic sight, removable trigger group, and Benelli's Progressive Comfort recoil reduction system.
Price: $2,999.00

BERETTA 686/687 SILVER PIGEON SERIES
Gauge: 12, 20, 28, 3" chambers (2-3/4" 28 ga.). .410 bore, 3" chamber. **Barrel:** 26", 28". **Weight:** 6.8 lbs. **Stock:** Checkered walnut. **Features:** Interchangeable barrels (20 and 28 ga.), single selective gold-plated trigger, boxlock action, auto safety, Schnabel fore-end.
Price: 686 Silver Pigeon Grade I...$2,350.00
Price: 686 Silver Pigeon Grade I, Sporting............................$2,400.00
Price: 687 Silver Pigeon Grade III...$3,430.00
Price: 687 Silver Pigeon Grade V..$4,075.00

BERETTA MODEL 687 EELL
Gauge: 12, 20, 28, 410. Premium grade model with decorative sideplates featuring lavish hand-chased engraving with a classic game scene enhanced by detailed leaves and flowers that also cover the triggerguard, trigger plate and fore-end lever. Stock has high-grade, specially selected European walnut with fine-line checkering, Offered in three actions size with scaled-down 28 gauge and .410 receivers. Combo models are available with extra barrel sets in 20/28 or 28/.410.
Price: $7,995.00
Price: Combo model...$9,695.00

BERETTA MODEL 690
Gauge: 12. 3-inch chambers. **Barrels:** 26, 28 or 30 inches with OptimaChoke HP system. Similar features of the 686/687 series with minor improvements. Stock has higher grade oil-finished walnut. Redesigned barrel/fore-end attachment reduces weight.
Price: $3,475.00

BERETTA MODEL 692 SPORTING
Gauge: 12, 3-inch chamber. **Barrels:** 30 inches with long forcing cones of approximately 14 inches. Receiver is ½-inch wider than 682 model for improved handling. **Stock:** Hand rubbed oil finished select walnut with Schnabel fore-end. Features include selective single adjustable trigger, manual safety, tapered 8mm to 10mm rib.
Price: $4,800.00
Price: Skeet $5,275.00

BERETTA DT11
Gauge: 12. 3-inch chambers. Competition model offered in Sporting, Skeet and Trap models. **Barrels:** 30, 32, 34 inches. Top rib has hollowed bridges. **Stock:** Hand-checkered buttstock and fore-end. Hand-rubbed oil, Tru-Oil or wax finish. Adjustable comb on skeet and trap models. Newly designed receiver, top lever, safety/

selector button. ACS (All Competition Shotgun) has adjustable rib, OptimaChoke HP system.
Price: From $8,999
Price: ACS $9,750.00

BERETTA SV10 PERENNIA
Gauge: 12, 20. 3-inch chambers. **Barrels:** 26 or 28 inches. **Weight:** 6.5 to 7.3 pounds. **Stock:** Oil-finished walnut with semi-beavertail fore-end, newly designed fore-end latching system. Kick-Off recoil reduction system is optional. Ejection system can be set to automatic or extractors only. Floral engraving. Perennia III model has higher-grade wood, removable trigger group, and more engraving. Also available in SV10 Prevail Sporting and Trap models.
Price: Perennia I $2,890.00
Price: Perennia III $3,950.00

BLASER F3 SUPERSPORT
Gauge: 12 ga., 3" chamber. **Barrel:** 32". **Weight:** 9 lbs. **Stock:** Adustable semi-custom, turkish walnut wood grade: 4. **Features:** The latest addition to the F3 family is the F3 SuperSport. The perfect blend of overall weight, balance and weight distribution make the F3 SuperSport the ideal competitor. Briley Spectrum-5 chokes, free floating barrels, adjustable barrel hanger system on o/u, chrome plated barrels full length, revolutionary ejector ball system, barrels finished in a powder coated nitride, selectable competition trigger.
Price: From $8,689.00
Price: Game Standard, from...$6,695.00

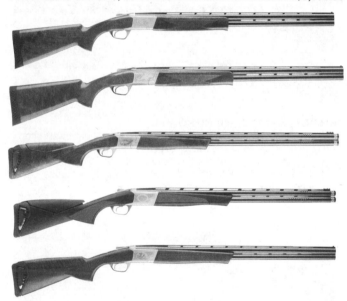

BROWNING CYNERGY
Gauge: .410, 12, 20, 28. **Barrel:** 26", 28", 30", 32". **Stock:** Walnut or composite. **Sights:** White bead front most models; HiViz Pro-Comp sight on some models; mid bead. **Features:** Mono-Lock hinge, recoil-reducing interchangeable Inflex recoil pad, silver nitride receiver; striker-based trigger, ported barrel option. Browning repositioned the Cynergy series with lower prices in 2015. Imported from Japan by Browning.
Price: Field Grade Model, 12 ga..$1,870.00
Price: Field, small gauges..$1,940.00
Price: Feather model, from $2,140.00
Price: Sporting, from..$2,400.00
Price: Sporting w/adjustable comb $2,670.00
Price: Camo, Mossy Oak Shadow Grass or Realtree Max 5.$2,000.00

Prices given are believed to be accurate at time of publication however, many factors affect retail pricing so exact prices are not possible.

SHOTGUNS Over/Unders

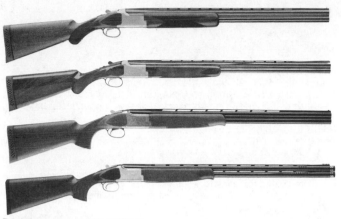

designed for the field, sporting clays, skeet and trap shooting. The models listed below are representative of some of the different models and variants. Many optional features are offered including high grade wood and engraving, and extra sets of barrels. Made it Italy and imported by Caesar Guerini USA.

Price: Ellipse	....	**$4,450.00**
Price: Ellipse Curve	....	**$6,900.00**
Price: Ellipse EVO Sporting	....	**$6,800.00**
Price: Magnus	....	**$4,600.00**
Price: Maxum	....	**$6,295.00**
Price: Forum	....	**$10,500.00**
Price: Woodlander	....	**$3,450.00**
Price: Invictus Sporting	....	**$6,850.00**

BROWNING CITORI SERIES

Gauge: 12, 20, 28 and .410. **Barrel:** 26", 28" in 28 and .410. Offered with Invector choke tubes. All 12 and 20 gauge models have back-bored barrels and Invector Plus choke system. **Weight:** 6 lbs., 8 oz. (26" .410) to 7 lbs., 13 oz. (30" 12 ga.). **Length:** 43" overall (26" bbl.). **Stock:** Dense walnut, hand checkered, full pistol grip, beavertail fore-end. Field-type recoil pad on 12 ga. field guns and trap and skeet models. **Sights:** Medium raised beads, German nickel silver. **Features:** Barrel selector integral with safety, automatic ejectors, three-piece takedown. Imported from Japan by Browning.

Price: Lightning, from	....	**$1,990.00**
Price: White Lightning, from	....	**$2,070.00**
Price: Superlight Feather	....	**$2,390.00**
Price: Lightning Feather, combo 20 and 28 ga.	....	**$3,580.00**
Price: Crossover Target	....	**$2,000.00**
Price: Micro Midas Satin Hunter w/13" stock	....	**$1,650.00**
Price: Gran Lightning 16 ga. (limited production)	....	**$2,700.00**
Price: 625 Sporting Golden Clays	....	**$4,800.00**

BROWNING 725 CITORI

Gauge: 12, 20, 28 or .410 bore. **Barrel:** 26, 28, 30". **Weight:** 5.7 to 7.6 lbs. **Length:** 43.75 to 50". **Stock:** Gloss oil finish grade II/III walnut. Features Include a new receiver that is significantly lower in profile than other 12-gauge Citori models. Other features include a mechanical trigger, Vector Pro lengthened forcing cones, three Invector-DS choke tubes, silver nitride finish with high relief engraving.

Price: 725 Field (12 or 20)	....	**$2,470.00**
Price: 725 Field (28 or .410)	....	**$2,540.00**
Price: 725 Feather (12 or 20)	....	**$2,550.00**
Price: 725 Sporting, from	....	**$3,070.00**
Price: 725 Sporting w/adjustable comb	....	**$3,530.00**
Price: 725 Skeet, from	....	**$3,140.00**
Price: 725 Trap, from	....	**$3,340.00**

BROWNING CITORI XT TRAP

Gauge: 12. **Barrels:** 30" or 32", Invector-Plus choke tubes, adjustable comb and buttplate. **Features:** Engraved silver nitride receiver with gold highlights, vented side barrel rib. Introduced 1999. Imported by Browning.

Price: XT Trap	....	**$2,650.00**
Price: XT Trap w/adjustable comb	....	**$3,000.00**

CAESAR GUERINI

Gauge: 12, 20, 28 gauge, also 20/28 gauge combo. Some models are available in .410 bore. **Barrels:** All standard lengths from 26 to 32 inches. **Weight:** 5.5 to 8.8 lbs. **Stock:** High grade walnut with hand-rubbed oil finish. **Features:** A wide range of over/under models

CONNECTICUT SHOTGUN A10 AMERICAN

Gauge: 12, 20, 28, 2 ¾" chambers, .410, 3-inches. Sidelock design. **Barrels:** 26, 28, 30 or 32" with choice of fixed or interchangeable chokes. **Weight:** 6.3 lbs. **Stock:** Hand rubbed oil finished, hand checkered at 24 lines per inch. Black, English or Turkish walnut offered in numerous grades. Pistol or Price of Wales grip, short or long tang. **Features:** Low profile, shallow frame full sidelock. Single-selective trigger, automatic ejectors. Engraved models available. Made in the U.S.A. by Connecticut Shotgun Mfg. Co.

Price: 12 gauge from	....	**$7,995.00**
Price: Smaller gauges from	....	**$9,045.00**

CONNECTICUT SHOTGUN MODEL 21 O/U

Gauge: 20, 3" chambers. **Barrels:** 26" to 32" chrome-lined, back-bored with extended forcing cones. **Weight:** 6.3 lbs. **Stock:** A Fancy (2X) American walnut, standard point checkering, choice of straight or pistol grip. Higher grade walnut is optional. **Features:** The over/under version of Conn. Shotgun's replica of the Winchester Model 21 side-by-side, built using the same machining, tooling, techniques and finishes. Low profile shallow frame with blued receiver. Pigeon and Grand American grades are available. Made in the U.S.A. by Connecticut Shotgun Mfg. Co.

Price: From	....	**$3,995.00**

CZ SPORTER

Gauge: 12, 3" chambers. **Barrel:** 30", 32" chrome-lined, back-bored with extended forcing cones. **Weight:** 8.5 lbs. **Length:** NA. **Stock:** Neutral cast stock with an adjustable comb, trap style fore-end, pistol grip and ambidextrous palm swells. No. 3 grade Circassian walnut. At lowest position, drop at comb: 1-5/8"; drop at heel: 2-3/8"; length of pull: 14-1/2". **Features:** Designed for Sporting Clays and FITASC competition. Hand engraving, satin black-finished receiver. Tapered adjustable rib with center bead and a red fiber-optic front bead, 10 choke tubes with wrench, single selective trigger, automatic ejectors, thin rubber pad with slick plastic top. Introduced 2008. Made in the Czech Repubic and imported by CZ-USA.

Price: G2 grade	....	**$2,497.00**
Price: Standard grade	....	**$1,899.00**

CZ CANVASBACK

Gauge: 12, 20, 3" chambers; 28 ga., .410 bore. **Barrel:** 26", 28". **Weight:** 7.3 lbs. **Length:** NA. **Stock:** Round-knob pistol grip, Schnabel fore-end, Turkish walnut. **Features:** Single selective trigger, set of 5 screw-in chokes, black chrome finished receiver. From CZ-USA.

Price: 12 or 20 ga.	....	**$827.00**
Price: 28 or .410	....	**$959.00**

CZ MALLARD
Gauge: 12, 20, 28, .410, 3" chambers. **Barrel:** 26". **Weight:** 7.7 lbs. Length: NA. **Stock:** Round-knob pistol grip, Schnabel fore-end, Turkish walnut. **Features:** Double triggers and extractors, coin finished receiver, multi chokes. From CZ-USA.
Price: $583.00

CZ REDHEAD
Gauge: 12, 20, .410 (3" chambers), 28 (2 3/4"). **Barrel:** 28". **Weight:** 7.4 lbs. Length: NA. **Stock:** Round-knob pistol grip, Schnabel fore-end, Turkish walnut. **Features:** Single selective triggers and extractors (12 & 20 ga.), screw-in chokes (12, 20, 28 ga.) choked IC and Mod (.410), coin finished receiver, multi chokes. From CZ-USA.
Price: Deluxe $953.00
Price: Mini (28, .410) $960.00
Price: Target $1,389.00

CZ SUPER SCROLL COMBO
Gauge: 20 and 28 combo. **Barrels:** 30 inches for both gauges with five choke tubes for each set. **Stock:** Grave V Turkish walnut with Schnabel fore-end, rounded grip. **Weight:** 6.7 pounds. **Features:** Ornate hand-engraved scrollwork on receiver, faux sideplates, triggerguard and mono-block. Comes in a custom-fitted aluminum case.
Price: $3,899.00

CZ UPLAND STERLING
Gauge: 12, 3-inch chambers. **Barrels:** 28 inches with ventilated rib, fiber optic sight, five choke tubes. **Stock:** Turkish walnut with stippled gripping surfaces. **Weight:** 7.5 pounds. Lady Sterling has smaller stock dimensions.
Price: $999.00
Price: Lady Sterling...$1,281.00

CZ WINGSHOOTER
Gauge: 12, 20, 28 & .410 ga., 2-3/4" chamber. **Barrel:** 28" flat ventilated rib. **Weight:** 6.3 lbs. Length: 45.5". **Stock:** Turkish walnut. **Features:** This colorful Over and Under shotgun has the same old world craftsmanship as all of our shotguns but with a new stylish look. This elegant hand engraved work of art is available in four gauges and its eye-catching engraving will stand alone in the field or range. 12 and 20 gauge models have auto ejectors, while the 28 gauge and .410 have extractors only. Heavily engraved scroll work with special side plate design, mechanical selective triggers, box Lock frame design, 18 LPI checkering, coil spring operated hammers, chrome lined, 5 interchangeable choke tubes and special engraved skeleton butt plate.
Price: 12 or 20 ga. $1,059.00

ESCORT OVER/UNDER
Gauge: 12, 3" chamber. **Barrel:** 28". **Weight:** 7.4 lbs. **Stock:** Walnut or select walnut with Trio recoil pad; synthetic stock with adjustable comb. Three adjustment spacers. **Sights:** Bronze front bead. **Features:** Blued barrels, blued or nickel receiver. Trio recoil pad. Five interchangeable chokes (SK, IC, M, IM, F); extractors or ejectors (new, 2008), barrel selector. Hard case available. Introduced 2007. Imported from Turkey by Legacy Sports International.
Price: From $641.00

FAUSTI CLASSIC ROUND BODY
Gauge: 16, 20, 28. **Barrels:** 28 or 30". **Weight:** 5.8 to 6.3 lbs. Length: 45.5 to 47.5". **Stock:** Turkish walnut Prince of Wales style with oil finish. Features include automatic ejectors, single selective trigger, laser-engraved receiver.
Price: 20 gauge...$4,950.00
Price: 16, 28 gauge, .410.................................$5,540.00

FAUSTI CALEDON
Gauge: 12, 16, 20, 28 and .410 bore. **Barrels:** 26, 28 or 30". **Weight:** 5.8 to 7.3 lbs. **Stock:** Turkish walnut with oil finish, round pistol grip. **Features:** Automatic ejectors, single selective trigger, laser-engraved receiver. Coin finish receiver with gold inlays.
Price: 12 or 20 ga. $1,999.00
Price: 16, 28, .410 ....$2,569.00

FN SC-1
Gauge: 12. 2-3/4" chamber. **Barrels:** 28 or 30 inches, ported with ventilated rib, Invector-Plus extended choke tubes. **Stock:** Laminated black or blue with adjustable comb and length-of-pull. **Weight:** 8 pounds.
Price: $2,449.00

FRANCHI INSTINCT SERIES
Gauge: 12, 20 with 3" chambers. **Barrels:** 26 or 28". **Weight:** 5.3 to 6.4 lbs. Length: 42.5 to 44.5". **Stock:** AA-grade satin walnut (LS), A-grade (L) with rounded pistol grip and recoil pad. Single trigger, automatic ejectors, tang safety, choke tubes. L model has steel receiver, SL has aluminum alloy receiver. Sporting model has higher grade wood, extended choke tubes.
Price: L $1,349.00
Price: SL $1,699.00
Price: Sporting..$1,899.00

KOLAR SPORTING CLAYS
Gauge: 12, 2-3/4" chambers. **Barrel:** 30", 32", 34"; extended choke tubes. **Stock:** 14-5/8"x2.5"x1-7/8"x1-3/8". French walnut. Four stock versions available. **Features:** Single selective trigger, detachable, adjustable for length; overbored barrels with long forcing cones; flat tramline rib; matte blue finish. Made in U.S. by Kolar.
Price: Standard $11,995.00
Price: Prestige..$14,190.00
Price: Elite Gold $16,590.00
Price: Legend $17,090.00
Price: Select...$22,590.00
Price: Custom ....**Price on request**

KOLAR AAA COMPETITION TRAP
Gauge: 12. Similar to the Sporting Clays gun except has 32" O/U /34" Unsingle or 30" O/U /34" Unsingle barrels as an over/under, unsingle, or combination set. Stock dimensions are 14.5"x2.5"x1.5"; American or French walnut; step parallel rib standard. Contact maker for full listings. Made in U.S.A. by Kolar.
Price: Single bbl. from $8,495.00
Price: O/U from $11,695.00

KOLAR AAA COMPETITION SKEET
Similar to the Sporting Clays gun except has 28" or 30" barrels with Kolarite AAA sub gauge tubes; stock of American or French walnut with matte finish; flat tramline rib; under barrel adjustable for point of impact. Many options available. Contact maker for complete listing. Made in U.S.A. by Kolar.
Price: Max Lite, from...$13,995.00

KRIEGHOFF K-80 SPORTING CLAYS
Gauge: 12. **Barrel:** 28", 30", 32", 34" with choke tubes. **Weight:** About 8 lbs. **Stock:** #3 Sporting stock designed for gun-down shooting. **Features:** Standard receiver with satin nickel finish and classic scroll engraving. Selective mechanical trigger adjustable for position.

Prices given are believed to be accurate at time of publication however, many factors affect retail pricing so exact prices are not possible.

Choice of tapered flat or 8mm parallel flat barrel rib. Free-floating barrels. Aluminum case. Imported from Germany by Krieghoff International, Inc.
Price: Standard grade with five choke tubes, from **$11,395.00**

KRIEGHOFF K-80 SKEET
Gauge: 12, 2-3/4" chambers. **Barrel:** 28", 30", 32", (skeet & skeet), optional choke tubes). **Weight:** About 7.75 lbs. **Stock:** American skeet or straight skeet stocks, with palm-swell grips. Walnut. **Features:** Satin gray receiver finish. Selective mechanical trigger adjustable for position. Choice of ventilated 8mm parallel flat rib or ventilated 8-12mm tapered flat rib. Introduced 1980. Imported from Germany by Krieghoff International, Inc.
Price: Standard, skeet chokes............................. **$10,595.00**
Price: Skeet Special (28", 30", 32" tapered flat rib,
  skeet & skeet choke tubes) **$9,100.00**

KRIEGHOFF K-80 TRAP
Gauge: 12, 2-3/4" chambers. **Barrel:** 30", 32" (Imp. Mod. & Full or choke tubes). **Weight:** About 8.5 lbs. **Stock:** Four stock dimensions or adjustable stock available; all have palm-swell grips. Checkered European walnut. **Features:** Satin nickel receiver. Selective mechanical trigger, adjustable for position. Ventilated step rib. Introduced 1980. Imported from Germany by Krieghoff International, Inc.
Price: K-80 O/U (30", 32", Imp. Mod. & Full), from.............. **$8,850.00**
Price: K-80 Unsingle (32", 34", Full), standard, from.......... **$10,080.00**
Price: K-80 Combo (two-barrel set), standard, from **$13,275.00**

KRIEGHOFF K-20
Similar to the K-80 except built on a 20-gauge frame. Designed for skeet, sporting clays and field use. Offered in 20, 28 and .410; 28", 30" and 32" barrels. Imported from Germany by Krieghoff International Inc.
Price: K-20, 20 gauge, from.................................. **$11,395.00**
Price: K-20, 28 gauge, from.................................. **$12,395.00**
Price: K-20, .410, from... **$12,395.00**

LEBEAU-COURALLY BOSS-VEREES
Gauge: 12, 20, 2-3/4" chambers. **Barrel:** 25" to 32". **Weight:** To customer specifications. **Stock:** Exhibition-quality French walnut. **Features:** Boss-type sidelock with automatic ejectors; single or double triggers; chopper lump barrels. A custom gun built to customer specifications. Imported from Belgium by Wm. Larkin Moore.
Price: From **$96,000.00**

MERKEL MODEL 2001EL O/U
Gauge: 12, 20, 3" chambers, 28, 2-3/4" chambers. **Barrel:** 12-28"; 20, 28 ga.-26.75". **Weight:** About 7 lbs. (12 ga.). **Stock:** Oil-finished walnut; English or pistol grip. **Features:** Self-cocking Blitz boxlock action with cocking indicators; Kersten double cross-bolt lock; silver-grayed receiver with engraved hunting scenes; coil spring ejectors; single selective or double triggers. Imported from Germany by Merkel USA.
Price: **$9,995.00**
Price: Model 2001EL Sporter; full pistol grip stock **$9,995.00**

MERKEL MODEL 2000CL
Similar to Model 2001EL except scroll-engraved case-hardened receiver; 12, 20, 28 gauge. Imported from Germany by Merkel USA.
Price: **$8,495.00**
Price: Model 2016 CL; 16 gauge **$8,495.00**

MOSSBERG SILVER RESERVE II
Gauge: 12, 3-inch chambers. **Barrels:** 28 inches with ventilated rib, choke tubes. **Stock:** Select black walnut with satin finish. **Sights:** Metal bead. Available with extractors or automatic ejectors. Also offered in Sport model with ported barrels with wide rib, fiber optic front and middle bead sights. Super Sport has extra wide high rib, optional adjustable comb.
Price: Field **$736.00**

Price: Field w/ejectors **$824.00**
Price: Sport **$905.00**
Price: Sport w/ejectors..**$1,019.00**
Price: Super Sport w/ejectors.....................................**$1,108.00**
Price: Super Sport w/ejectors, adj. comb **$1,216.00**

PERAZZI MX8/MX8 TRAP/SKEET
Gauge: 12, 20 2 ¾" chambers. **Barrel:** Trap: 29.5" (Imp. Mod. & Extra Full), 31.5" (Full & Extra Full). Choke tubes optional. Skeet: 27-5/8" (skeet & skeet). **Weight:** About 8.5 lbs. (trap); 7 lbs., 15 oz. (skeet). **Stock:** Interchangeable and custom made to customer specs. **Features:** Has detachable and interchangeable trigger group with flat V springs. Flat 7/16" vent rib. Many options available. Imported from Italy by Perazzi U.S.A., Inc.
Price: Trap from **$9,861.00**
Price: Skeet from **$9,861.00**

PERAZZI MX8
Gauge: 12, 20 2 ¾" chambers. **Barrel:** 28-3/8" (Imp. Mod. & Extra Full), 29.5" (choke tubes). **Weight:** 7 lbs., 12 oz. **Stock:** Special specifications. **Features:** Has single selective trigger; flat 7/16" x 5/16" vent rib. Many options available. Imported from Italy by Perazzi U.S.A., Inc.
Price: Standard, from **$9,861.00**
Price: Sporting, from **$9,861.00**
Price: SC3 Grade (variety of engraving patterns) from **$21,000.00**
Price: SCO Grade (more intricate engraving/inlays) from ...**$36,000.00**

PERAZZI MX12 HUNTING
Gauge: 12, 2-3/4" chambers. **Barrel:** 26.75", 27.5", 28-3/8", 29.5" (Mod. & Full); choke tubes available in 27-5/8", 29.5" only (MX12C). **Weight:** 7 lbs., 4 oz. **Stock:** To customer specs; interchangeable. **Features:** Single selective trigger; coil springs used in action; Schnabel fore-end tip. Imported from Italy by Perazzi U.S.A., Inc.
Price: From **$11,698.00**
Price: MX12C (with choke tubes) from **$12,316.00**

PERAZZI MX20 HUNTING
Similar to the MX12 except 20 ga. frame size. Non-removable trigger group. Available in 20, 28, .410 with 2-3/4" or 3" chambers. 26" standard, and choked Mod. & Full. Weight is 6 lbs., 6 oz. Imported from Italy by Perazzi U.S.A., Inc.
Price: From **$11,900.00**
Price: MX20C (with choke tubes) from **$13,700.00**

PERAZZI MX10
Gauge: 12, 2-3/4" chambers. **Barrel:** 29.5", 31.5" (fixed chokes). **Weight:** NA. **Stock:** Walnut; cheekpiece adjustable for elevation and cast. **Features:** Adjustable rib; vent side rib. Externally selective trigger. Available in single barrel, combo, over/under trap, skeet, pigeon and sporting models. Introduced 1993. Imported from Italy by Perazzi U.S.A., Inc.
Price: From **$11,900.00**

PERAZZI MX2000S
Gauge: 12, 20. **Barrels:** 29.5, 30.75, 31.5 inches with fixed I/M and Full chokes, or interchangeable. Competition model with features similar to MX8.
Price: **$12,500.00**

PERAZZI MX15 UNSINGLE TRAP
Gauge: 12. **Barrel:** 34 inches with fixed Full choke. **Features:** Bottom single barrel with 6-notch adjustable rib, adjustable stock, drop-out trigger. , or interchangeable. Competition model with features similar to MX8.
Price: **$8,395.00**

PIOTTI BOSS
Gauge: 12, 20. **Barrel:** 26" to 32", chokes as specified. **Weight:** 6.5 to 8 lbs. **Stock:** Dimensions to customer specs. Best quality figured walnut. **Features:** Essentially a custom-made gun with many options. Introduced 1993. Imported from Italy by Wm. Larkin Moore.
Price: From **$75,000.00**

RIZZINI OMNIUM
Gauge: 12, 20. **Barrels:** 26.5, 28 or 30 inches with choke tubes, ventilated rib. **Stock:** Walnut with pistol grip, Schnabel fore-end. **Features:** Entry level Rizzini over/under boxlock with blue or coin

finish, scroll engraving, automatic ejectors and single-selective trigger. Made in Italy by Battista Rizzini and distributed by Rizzini USA.
Price: From **$2,632.00**

RIZZINI S790 EMEL
Gauge: 20, 28, .410. **Barrel:** 26", 27.5" (Imp. Cyl. & Imp. Mod.). **Weight:** About 6 lbs. **Stock:** 14"x1.5"x2-1/8". Extra fancy select walnut. **Features:** Boxlock action with profuse engraving; automatic ejectors; single selective trigger; silvered receiver. Comes with Nizzoli leather case. Introduced 1996. Made in Italy by Battista Rizzini and distributed by Wm. Larkin Moore & Co.
Price: From **$14,600.00**

RIZZINI S792 EMEL
Similar to S790 EMEL except dummy sideplates with extensive engraving coverage. Nizzoli leather case. Introduced 1996. Made in Italy by Battista Rizzini and distributed by Wm. Larkin Moore & Co.
Price: From **$15,500.00**

RIZZINI UPLAND EL
Gauge: 12, 16, 20, 28, .410. **Barrel:** 26", 27.5", Mod. & Full, Imp. Cyl. & Imp. Mod. choke tubes. **Weight:** About 6.6 lbs. **Stock:** 14.5"x1-1/2"x2.25". **Features:** Boxlock action; single selective trigger; ejectors; profuse engraving on silvered receiver. Comes with fitted case. Introduced 1996. Made in Italy by Battista Rizzini and distributed by Wm. Larkin Moore & Co.
Price: From **$6,595.00**

RIZZINI ARTEMIS
Gauge: 12, 16, 20, 28, .410. Same as Upland EL model except dummy sideplates with extensive game scene engraving. Fancy European walnut stock. Fitted case. Introduced 1996. Imported from Italy by Fierce Products and by Wm. Larkin Moore & Co.
Price: From **$4,250.00**
Price: Artemis Light **$4,395.00**

RIZZINI S782 EMEL
Gauge: 12, 2-3/4" chambers. **Barrel:** 26", 27.5" (Imp. Cyl. & Imp. Mod.). **Weight:** About 6.75 lbs. **Stock:** 14.5"x1.5"x2.25". Extra fancy select walnut. **Features:** Boxlock action with dummy sideplates, extensive engraving with gold inlaid game birds, silvered receiver, automatic ejectors, single selective trigger. Nizzoli leather case. Introduced 1996. Made in Italy by Battista Rizzini and distributed by Wm. Larkin Moore & Co.
Price: From **$18,800.00**

SKB 590 FIELD
Gauge: 12, 20 with 3" chambers. **Barrel:** 26", 28", 30". Three SKB Competion choke tubes (IC, M, F). Lengthened forcing cones. **Stock:** Oil finished walnut with Pachmayr recoil pad. **Weight:** 7.1 to 7.9 lbs. **Sights:** NA. **Features:** Boxlock action, bright blue finish with laser engraved receiver. Automatic ejectors, single trigger with selector switch incorporated in thumb-operated tang safety. Youth Model has 13" length of pull. Imported from Turkey by GU, Inc.
Price: **$1,300.00**

SKB 90TSS
Gauge: 12, 20 with 2 ¾-inch chambers. **Barrel:** 28, 30, 32 inches. Three SKB Competion choke tubes (SK, IC, M for Skeet and Sporting Models; IM, M, F for Trap). Lengthened forcing cones. **Stock:** Oil finished walnut with Pachmayr recoil pad. **Weight:** 7.1 to 7.9 lbs. **Sights:** Ventilated rib with target sights. **Features:** Boxlock action, bright blue finish with laser engraved receiver. Automatic ejectors, single trigger with selector switch incorporated in thumb-operated tang safety. Sporting and Trap models have adjustable comb and buttpad system. Imported from Turkey by GU, Inc.
Price: Skeet **$1,470.00**
Price: Sporting Clays, Trap **$1,720.00**

STEVENS MODEL 555
Gauge: 12, 20, 28, .410; 2-3/4" and 3" chambers. **Barrel:** 26", 28". **Weight:** 5.5 to 6 lbs. **Features:** Five screw-in choke tubes with 12, 20, and 28 gauge; .410 has fixed M/IC chokes. Turkish walnut stock and Schnabel fore-end. Single selective mechanical trigger with extractors.
Price: **$694.00**

STOEGER CONDOR
Gauge: 12, 20, 2-3/4" 3" chambers; 16, .410. **Barrel:** 22", 24", 26", 28", 30". **Weight:** 5.5 to 7.8 lbs. **Sights:** Brass bead. **Features:** IC, M, or F screw-in choke tubes with each gun. Oil finished hardwood with pistol grip and fore-end. Auto safety, single trigger, automatic extractors.
Price: From ....**$449.00 to $669.00**
Price: Combo with 12 and 20 ga. barrel sets **$899.00**
Price: Competition **$669.00**

TRISTAR HUNTER EX
Gauge: 12, 20, 28, .410. **Barrel:** 26", 28". **Weight:** 5.7 lbs. (.410); 6.0 lbs. (20, 28), 7.2-7.4 lbs. (12). Chrome-lined steel mono-block barrel, five Beretta-style choke tubes (SK, IC, M, IM, F). Length: NA. **Stock:** Walnut, cut checkering. 14.25"x1.5"x2-3/8". **Sights:** Brass front sight. **Features:** All have extractors, engraved receiver, sealed actions, self-adjusting locking bolts, single selective trigger, ventilated rib. 28 ga. and .410 built on true frames. Five-year warranty. Imported from Italy by Tristar Sporting Arms Ltd.
Price: From **$630.00**

TRISTAR SETTER
Gauge: 12, 20 with 3-inch chambers. **Barrels:** 28" (12 ga.), 26" (20 ga.) with ventilated rib, three Beretta-style choke tubes. **Weight:** 6.3 to 7.2 pounds. **Stock:** High gloss wood. Single selective trigger, extractors.
Price: **$559.00**

WEBLEY & SCOTT O/U SERIES
Gauge: 12, 20, 28, .410. **Barrels:** 26, 28, 30", five interchangeable choke tubes. **Weight:** 5.5 to 7.5 lbs. **Stock:** Checkered Turkish walnut with recoil pad. **Features:** Automatic ejectors, single selective trigger, ventilated rib, tang selector/safety. 2000 Premium Model has higher-grade select walnut stock, color case hardening. 3000 Sidelock Model is a high-grade gun with 7-pin sidelocks, oil-finished premium-grade walnut stock with checkered butt, jeweled monobloc walls, and comes with high quality, fleeced line lockable case. Made in Turkey and imported by Centurion International.
Price: 900 Sporting **$1,250.00**
Price: 2000 Premium **$2,500.00**
Price: 3000 Sidelock **$6,000.00**

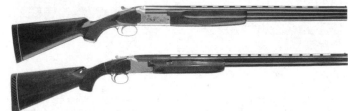

WINCHESTER MODEL 101
Gauge: 12, 2-3/4", 3" chambers. **Barrel:** 28", 30", 32", ported, Invector Plus choke system. **Weight:** 7 lbs. 6 oz. to 7 lbs. 12. oz. **Stock:** Checkered high-gloss grade II/III walnut stock, Pachmayr Decelerator sporting pad. **Features:** Chrome-plated chambers; back-bored barrels; tang barrel selector/safety; Signature extended choke tubes. Model 101 Field comes with solid brass bead front sight, three tubes, engraved receiver. Model 101 Sporting has adjustable trigger, 10mm runway rib, white mid-bead, Tru-Glo front sight, 30" and 32" barrels. Camo version of Model 101 Field comes with full-coverage Mossy Oak Duck Blind pattern. Model 101 Pigeon Grade Trap has 10mm steel runway rib, mid-bead sight, interchangeable fiber-optic front sight, porting and vented side ribs, adjustable trigger shoe, fixed raised comb or adjustable comb, Grade III/IV walnut, 30" or 32" barrels, molded ABS hard case. Reintroduced 2008. Made in Belgium by FN.
Price: Field **$1,900.00**
Price: Sporting **$2,300.00**
Price: Pigeon Grade Trap **$2,520.00**
Price: Pigeon Grade Trap w/adj. comb **$2,680.00**

ARRIETA SIDELOCK DOUBLE
Gauge: 12, 16, 20, 28, .410. **Barrel:** Length and chokes to customer specs. **Weight:** To customer specs. **Stock:** To customer specs. Straight English with checkered butt (standard), or pistol grip. Select European walnut with oil finish. **Features:** Essentially custom gun with myriad options. H&H pattern hand-detachable sidelocks, selective automatic ejectors, double triggers (hinged front) standard. Some have self-opening action. Finish and engraving to customer specs. Imported from Spain by Quality Arms, Wm. Larking Moore and others.
Price: Model 557 ....$6,970.00
Price: Model 570 ....$7,350.00
Price: Model 578 ....$8,200.00
Price: Model 600 Imperial $12,125.00
Price: Model 801 ....$19,850.00
Price: Model 802 ....$19,850.00
Price: Model 803 ....$15,000.00
Price: Model 931 ....$36,000.00

AYA MODEL 4/53
Gauge: 12, 16, 20, 28, 410. **Barrel:** 26", 27", 28", 30". **Weight:** To customer specifications. **Length:** To customer specifications. **Features:** Hammerless boxlock action; double triggers; light scroll engraving; automatic safety; straight grip oil finished walnut stock; checkered butt. Made in Spain. Imported by New England Custom Gun Service.
Price: $3,895.00
Price: No. 2 ....$5,895.00
Price: No. 2 Rounded Action $6,299.00

AYA MODEL ADARRA
Gauge: 12, 16, 20, 28, 410. **Barrel:** 26", 28". **Weight:** Approx. 6.7 lbs. **Features:** Hammerless boxlock action; double triggers; light scroll engraving; automatic safety; straight grip oil finished walnut stock; checkered butt. Made in Spain. Imported by New England Custom Gun Service.
Price: $4,800.00

BERETTA 486 PARALELLO
Gauge: 12 or 20, 3" chamber, or 28 with 2¾" chamber. **Barrel:** 26", 28", 30". **Weight:** 7.1 lbs. **Stock:** English-style straight grip, splinter fore-end. Select European walnut, checkered, oil finish. **Features:** Round action, Optima-Choke Tubes. Automatic ejection or mechanical extraction. Firing-pin block safety, manual or automatic, open top-lever safety. Imported from Italy by Beretta U.S.A.
Price: From $5,350.00

CIMARRON 1878 COACH GUN
Gauge: 12. 3-inch chambers. **Barrels:** 20 or 26 inches. **Weight:** 8 to 9 pounds. **Stock:** Hardwood. External hammers, double triggers. **Finish:** Blue, Cimarron "USA", Cimarron "Original."
Price: Blue .... $575.00 (20") to $594.00 (26")
Price: Original .... $675.00 to $694.00
Price: USA .... $832.00 to $851.00

CIMARRON 1881 HAMMERLESS
Gauge: 12. 3-inch chambers. **Barrels:** 20, 22, 26, 28 or 30 inches. **Stock:** Standard or Deluxe wood with rounded pistol grip. Single trigger, extractors, bead front sight.
Price: Deluxe ....$722.00 to $761.00

CONNECTICUT SHOTGUN MANUFACTURING CO. RBL
Gauge: 12, 16, 20. **Barrel:** 26", 28", 30", 32". **Weight:** NA. **Length:** NA. **Stock:** NA. **Features:** Round-action SxS shotguns made in the USA. Scaled frames, five TruLock choke tubes. Deluxe fancy grade walnut buttstock and fore-end. Quick Change recoil pad in two lengths.

Various dimensions and options available depending on gauge.
Price: 12 gauge $3,795.00
Price: 16 gauge $3,795.00
Price: 20 gauge Special Custom Model $7,995.00

CONNECTICUT SHOTGUN MANUFACTURING CO. MODEL 21
Gauge: 12, 16, 20, 28, .410. A faithful re-creation of the famous Winchester Model 21. Many options and upgrades are available. Each frame is machined from specially produced proof steel. The 28 and .410 guns are available on the standard frame or on a newly engineered small frame. These are custom guns and are made to order to the buyer's individual specifications, wood, stock dimensions, barrel lengths, chokes, finishes and engraving.
Price: 12, 16 or 20 gauge from $15,000.00
Price: 28 or .410 from $18,000.00

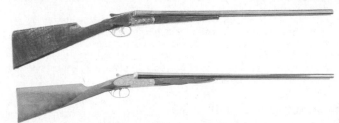

CZ BOBWHITE, SHARP-TAIL
Gauge: 12, 20, 28, .410. (5 screw-in chokes in 12 and 20 ga. and fixed chokes in IC and Mod in .410). **Barrel:** 26 or 28". **Weight:** 6.5 lbs. **Stock:** Turkish walnut with straight English-style grip and double triggers (Bobwhite) or conventional American pistol grip with a single trigger (Ringneck). Both are hand checkered 20 lpi. **Features:** Both color case-hardened shotguns are hand engraved.
Price: Bobwhite $789.00
Price: Bobwhite 28 or .410 ....$974.00
Price: Sharp-Tail $1,022.00
Price: Sharp-Tail Target $1,298.00

CZ HAMMER COACH
Gauge: 12, 3" chambers. **Barrel:** 20". **Weight:** 6.7 lbs. **Features:** Following in the tradition of the guns used by the stagecoach guards of the 1880's, this cowboy gun features double triggers, 19th century color case-hardening and fully functional external hammers.
Price: $922.00
Price: Classic model w/30" bbls. $963.00

EMF MODEL 1878 WYATT EARP
Gauge: 12. **Barrel:** 20". **Weight:** 8 lbs. **Length:** 37" overall. **Stock:** Smooth walnut with steel butt place. **Sights:** Large brass bead. **Features:** Colt-style exposed hammers rebounding type; blued receiver and barrels; cylinder bore. Based on design of Colt Model 1878 shotgun. Made in Italy by Pedersoli.
Price: $1,590.00

FAUSTI DEA SERIES
Gauge: 12, 16, 20, 28, .410. **Barrel:** 26, 28, or 30 inches. **Weight:** 6 to 6.8 lbs. **Stock:** AAA walnut, oil finished. Straight grip, checkered butt, classic fore-end. **Features:** Automatic ejectors, single non-selective trigger. Duetto model is in 28 gauge with extra set of .410 barrels. Made in Italy and imported by Fausti, USA.
Price: 12 or 20 ....$3,350.00
Price: 16, 28, .410 ....$3,990.00
Price: Duetto $5,300.00
Price: Round action $5,899.00

FOX, A.H.
Gauge: 16, 20, 28, .410. **Barrel:** Length and chokes to customer specifications. Rust-blued Chromox or Krupp steel. **Weight:** 5-1/2 to 6.75 lbs. **Stock:** Dimensions to customer specifications. Hand-checkered Turkish Circassian walnut with hand-rubbed oil finish. Straight, semi or full pistol grip; splinter, Schnabel or beavertail fore-end; traditional pad, hard rubber buttplate or skeleton butt. **Features:** Boxlock action with automatic ejectors;

double or Fox single selective trigger. Scalloped, rebated and color case-hardened receiver; hand finished and handengraved. Grades differ in engraving, inlays, grade of wood, amount of hand finishing. Introduced 1993. Made in U.S. by Connecticut Shotgun Mfg.

Price: CE Grade $19,500.00
Price: XE Grade $22,000.00
Price: DE Grade $25,000.00
Price: FE Grade $30,000.00
Price: 28/.410 CE Grade $21,500.00
Price: 28/.410 XE Grade $24,000.00
Price: 28/.410 DE Grade $27,000.00
Price: 28/.410 FE Grade $32,000.00

GARBI MODEL 101

Gauge: 12, 16, 20, 28. **Barrel:** 26", 28", choked to customer specs. **Weight:** 5-1/2 to 7.5 lbs. **Stock:** 14.5"x2.25"x1.5". Select European walnut. Straight grip, checkered butt, classic fore-end. **Features:** Sidelock action, automatic ejectors, double triggers standard. Color case-hardened action, coin finish optional. Single trigger; beavertail fore-end, etc. optional. Hand engraved with scroll engraving. Imported from Spain by Wm. Larkin Moore.
Price: From $14,650.00

GARBI MODEL 103A, 103B

Similar to the Garbi Model 101 except has Purdey-type fine scroll and rosette engraving. Model 103B has nickel-chrome steel barrels, H&H-type easy opening mechanism; other mechanical details remain the same. Imported from Spain by Wm. Larkin Moore.
Price: Model 103A. From.......................................$21,000.00
Price: Model 103B. From.......................................$28,360.00

GARBI MODEL 200

Similar to the Garbi Model 101 except has heavy-duty locks, magnum proofed. Very fine Continental-style floral and scroll engraving, well figured walnut stock. Other mechanical features remain the same. Imported from Spain by Wm. Larkin Moore.
Price: $24,100.00

MERKEL MODEL 47E, 147E

Gauge: 12, 3" chambers, 16, 2.75" chambers, 20, 3" chambers. **Barrel:** 12, 16 ga.-28"; 20 ga.-26.75" (Imp. Cyl. & Mod., Mod. & Full). **Weight:** About 6.75 lbs. (12 ga.). **Stock:** Oil-finished walnut; straight English or pistol grip. **Features:** Anson & Deeley-type boxlock action with single selective or double triggers, automatic safety, cocking indicators. Color case-hardened receiver with standard arabesque engraving. Imported from Germany by Merkel USA.
Price: Model 47E (H&H ejectors) $4,595.00
Price: Model 147E (as above with ejectors)............$5,795.00

MERKEL MODEL 47EL, 147EL

Similar to Model 47E except H&H style sidelock action with cocking indicators, ejectors. Silver-grayed receiver and sideplates have arabesque engraving, engraved border and screws (Model 47E), or fine hunting scene engraving (Model 147E). Limited edition. Imported from Germany by Merkel USA.
Price: Model 47EL $7,195.00
Price: Model 147EL $7,695.00

MERKEL MODEL 280EL, 360EL

Similar to Model 47E except smaller frame. Greener cross bolt with double under-barrel locking lugs, fine engraved hunting scenes on silver-grayed receiver, luxury-grade wood, Anson and Deeley boxlock action. H&H ejectors, single-selective or double triggers. Introduced 2000. Imported from Germany by Merkel USA.
Price: Model 280EL (28 gauge, 28" barrel, Imp. Cyl. and Mod. chokes)... $7,695.00
Price: Model 360EL (.410, 28" barrel, Mod. and Full chokes)... $7,695.00
Price: Model 280EL Combo $11,195.00

MERKEL MODEL 280SL AND 360SL

Similar to Model 280EL and 360EL except has sidelock action, double triggers, English-style arabesque engraving. Introduced 2000. Imported from Germany by Merkel USA.
Price: Model 280SL (28 gauge, 28" barrel, Imp. Cyl. and Mod. chokes)..$10,995.00
Price: Model 360SL (.410, 28" barrel, Mod. and Full chokes)..$10,995.00

MERKEL MODEL 1620

Gauge: 16. **Features:** Greener crossbolt with double under-barrel locking lugs, scroll-engraved case-hardened receiver, Anson and Deeley boxlock action, Holland & Holland ejectors, English-style stock, single selective or double triggers, or pistol grip stock with single selective trigger. Imported from Germany by Merkel USA.
Price: $4,995.00
Price: Model 1620E; silvered, engraved receiver $5,995.00
Price: Model 1620 Combo; 16- and 20-gauge two-barrel set $7,695.00
Price: Model 1620EL; upgraded wood $7,695.00
Price: Model 1620EL Combo; 16- and 20-gauge two-barrel set $11,195.00

MOSSBERG SILVER RESERVE II SXS

Gauge: 12, 20, 28. **Barrels:** 26 or 28 inches with front bead sight, five choke tubes. **Stock:** Select black walnut. **Weight:** 6.5 to 7.5 pounds. Side-by-side companion to over/under model with same Silver Reserve name. Blue barrels, silver receiver with scroll engraving. Single non-selective trigger with standard extractors.
Price: $1,067.00

PIOTTI KING NO. 1

Gauge: 12, 16, 20, 28, .410. **Barrel:** 25" to 30" (12 ga.), 25" to 28" (16, 20, 28, .410). To customer specs. Chokes as specified. **Weight:** 6.5 lbs. to 8 lbs. (12 ga. to customer specs.). **Stock:** Dimensions to customer specs. Finely figured walnut; straight grip with checkered butt with classic splinter fore-end and hand-rubbed oil finish standard. Pistol grip, beavertail fore-end. **Features:** Holland & Holland pattern sidelock action, automatic ejectors. Double trigger; non-selective single trigger optional. Coin finish standard; color case-hardened optional. Top rib; level, file-cut; concave, ventilated optional. Very fine, full coverage scroll engraving with small floral bouquets. Imported from Italy by Wm. Larkin Moore.
Price: From $40,900.00

PIOTTI LUNIK SIDE-BY-SIDE SHOTGUN

Similar to the Piotti King No. 1 in overall quality. Has Renaissance-style large scroll engraving in relief. Best quality Holland & Holland-pattern sidelock ejector double with chopper lump (demi-bloc) barrels. Other mechanical specifications remain the same. Imported from Italy by Wm. Larkin Moore.
Price: From $43,825.00

PIOTTI PIUMA

Gauge: 12, 16, 20, 28, .410. **Barrel:** 25" to 30" (12 ga.), 25" to 28" (16, 20, 28, .410). **Weight:** 5-1/2 to 6-1/4 lbs. (20 ga.). **Stock:** Dimensions to customer specs. Straight grip stock with walnut checkered butt, classic splinter fore-end, hand-rubbed oil finish are standard; pistol grip, beavertail fore-end, satin luster finish optional. **Features:** Anson & Deeley boxlock ejector double with chopper lump barrels. Level, file-cut rib, light scroll and rosette engraving, scalloped frame. Double triggers; single non-selective optional. Coin finish standard, color case-hardened optional. Imported from Italy by Wm. Larkin Moore.
Price: From $20,800.00

SKB 200 SERIES

Gauge: 12, 20, .410, 3" chambers; 28, 2¾-inches. **Barrel:** 26", 28". Five choke tubes provided (F, IM, M, IC, SK). **Stock:** Hand checkered and oil finished Turkish walnut. Price of Wales grip and beavertail fore-end. **Weight:** 6 to 7 lbs. **Sights:** Brass bead. **Features:** Boxlock with platform lump barrel design. Polished bright blue finish with charcoal color case hardening on receiver. Manual safety, automatic ejectors, single selective trigger. 200 HR target model has high ventilated rib, full pistol grip. 250 model has decorative color case hardened sideplates. Imported from Turkey by GU, Inc.

Price: 12, 20 ga...$2,100.00
Price: 28, .410...$2,250.00
Price: 200 HR 12, 20 ga.................................$2,500.00
Price: 200 HR 28, .410..................................$2,625.00
Price: 250 12, 20 ga.......................................$2,600.00
Price: 250 28, .410...$2,725.00

SKB 7000SL SIDELOCK

Gauge: 12, 20. **Barrel:** 28", 30". Five choke tubes provided (F, IM, M, IC, SK). **Stock:** Premium Turkish walnut with hand-rubbed oil finish, fine-line hand checkering, Price of Wales grip and beavertail fore-end. **Weight:** 6 to 7 lbs. **Sights:** Brass bead. **Features:** Sidelock design with Holland & Holland style seven-pin removable locks with safety sears. Bison Bone Charcoal case hardening, hand engraved sculpted sidelock receiver. Manual safety, automatic ejectors, single selective trigger. Available by special order only. Imported from Turkey by GU, Inc.

Price: From $6,700.00

STOEGER UPLANDER

Gauge: 12, 20, .410, 3" chambers; 28, 2-3/4 chambers. **Barrel:** 22", 24", 26", 28". **Weight:** 6.5 to 7.3 lbs. **Sights:** Brass bead. **Features:** Double trigger, IC & M choke tubes included with gun. Other choke tubes available. Tang auto safety, extractors, black plastic buttplate. Imported by Benelli USA.

Price: Standard..$499.00
Price: Supreme (single trigger, AA-grade wood) $539.00
Price: Longfowler (12 ga., 30" bbl.) $499.00

Price: Home Defense (20 or 12 ga., 20" bbl., tactical sights) ..$499.00
Price: Double Defense (20 ga.) fiber optic sight, accessory rail$499.00

STOEGER COACH GUN

Gauge: 12, 20, 2-3/4", 3" chambers. **Barrel:** 20". **Weight:** 6.5 lbs. **Stock:** Brown hardwood, classic beavertail fore-end. **Sights:** Brass bead. **Features:** Double or single trigger, IC & M choke tubes included, others available. Tang auto safety, extractors, black plastic buttplate. Imported by Benelli USA.

Price: .... $449.00 to $499.00

WEBLEY & SCOTT SXS SERIES

Gauge: 12, 20. **Barrels:** 28 inches, five interchangeable choke tubes. **Weight:** 6.5 to 7.5 lbs. **Stock:** Oil finished, hand-checkered Turkish walnut with recoil pad, splinter fore-end. **Features:** Automatic ejectors, single selective trigger, ventilated rib, tang selector/safety, charcoal case hardened receiver, English scroll engraving. 3000 Model is a high-grade gun with hand-rubbed oil-finished premium-grade walnut stock with checkered butt, jeweled monobloc walls, higher grade English scroll engraving, and comes with high quality, fleeced line lockable case. Made in Turkey and imported by Centurion International.

Price: Model 2000..$2,500.00
Price: Model 3000..$6,000.00

BERETTA DT10 TRIDENT TRAP TOP SINGLE

Gauge: 12, 3" chamber. **Barrel:** 34"; five Optima Choke tubes (Full, Full, Imp. Modified, Mod. and Imp. Cyl.). **Weight:** 8.8 lbs. **Stock:** High-grade walnut; adjustable. **Features:** Detachable, adjustable trigger group; Optima Bore for improved shot pattern and reduced recoil; slim Optima Choke tubes; raised and thickened receiver for long life. Introduced 2000. Imported from Italy by Beretta USA.
Price: $8,650.00

BROWNING BT-99 TRAP

Gauge: 12. **Barrel:** 30", 32", 34". **Stock:** Walnut; standard or adjustable. **Weight:** 7 lbs. 11 oz. to 9 lbs. **Features:** Back-bored single barrel; interchangeable chokes; beavertail forearm; extractor only; high rib.
Price: BT-99 w/conventional comb, 32" or 34" barrels **$1,430.00**
Price: BT-99 w/adjustable comb, 32" or 34" barrels **$1,680.00**
Price: BT-99 Golden Clays w/adjustable comb, 32" or
    34" barrels **$4,340.00**
Price: BT-99 Grade III ....**$2,540.00 to $2,840.00**

BROWNING A-BOLT SHOTGUN HUNTER

Gauge: 12 ga. 3" chamber. **Barrel:** 22". **Weight:** 7 lbs. 2 ozs. **Length:** 43.75". **Stock:** Satin finish walnut stock and forearm – checkered. **Features:** Drilled and tapped for scope mounts, 60° bolt action lift, detachable two-round magazine, and top-tang safety. Sling swivel studs installed, recoil pad, TRUGLO/Marble's fiber-optic front sight with rear sight adjustable for windage and elevation.
Price: $1,280.00

BROWNING A-BOLT SHOTGUN, MOSSY OAK BREAK-UP INFINITY

Gauge: 12 ga. 3" chamber. **Barrel:** 22". **Weight:** 7 lbs. 2 ozs. **Length:** 43.75". **Stock:** Composite stock and forearm, textured gripping surfaces, Mossy Oak Break-Up Infinitycamo finish • Dura-Touch Armor Coating. **Features:** Drilled and tapped for scope mounts, 60° bolt action lift, detachable two-round magazine, and top-tang safety. Sling swivel studs installed, rrecoil pad, TRUGLO/Marble's fiber-optic front sight with rear sight adjustable for windage and elevation.
Price: From $1,300.00

BROWNING A-BOLT SHOTGUN STALKER

Gauge: 12 ga. 3" chamber. **Barrel:** 22". **Weight:** 7 lbs. **Length:** 43.75". **Stock:** Composite stock and forearm, textured gripping surfaces, Dura-Touch Armor Coating. **Features:** Drilled and tapped for scope mounts, 60° bolt action lift, detachable two-round magazine, and top-tang safety. Sling swivel studs installed, rrecoil pad, TRUGLO/Marble's fiber-optic front sight with rear sight adjustable for windage and elevation.
Price: From $1,150.00

HARRINGTON & RICHARDSON ULTRA SLUG HUNTER/TAMER

Gauge: 12, 20 ga., 3" chamber, .410. **Barrel:** 20" to 24" rifled. **Weight:** 6 to 9 lbs. **Length:** 34.5" to 40". **Stock:** Hardwood, laminate, or polymer with full pistol grip; semi-beavertail fore-end. **Sights:** Gold bead front. **Features:** Break-open action with side-lever release,

automatic ejector. Introduced 1994. From H&R 1871, LLC.
Price: Ultra Slug Hunter, blued, hardwood **$291.00**
Price: Ultra Slug Hunter Youth, blued, hardwood, 13-1/8"
    LOP... **$291.00**
Price: Ultra Slug Hunter Deluxe, blued, laminated **$291.00**
Price: Tamer .410 bore, stainless barrel, black
    polymer stock **$193.00**

HARRINGTON & RICHARDSON ULTRA LITE SLUG HUNTER

Gauge: 12, 20 ga., 3" chamber. **Barrel:** 24" rifled. **Weight:** 5.25 lbs. **Length:** 40". **Stock:** Hardwood with walnut finish, full pistol grip, recoil pad, sling swivel studs. **Sights:** None; base included. **Features:** Youth Model, available in 20 ga. has 20" rifled barrel. Deluxe Model has checkered laminated stock and fore-end. From H&R 1871, LLC.
Price: $194.00

HARRINGTON & RICHARDSON ULTRA SLUG HUNTER THUMBHOLE STOCK

Similar to the Ultra Lite Slug Hunter but with laminated thumbhole stock and weighs 8.5 lbs.
Price: $401.00

HARRINGTON & RICHARDSON PARDNER AND TRACKER II

Gauge: 10, 12, 16, 20, 28, .410, up to 3.5" chamber for 10 and 12 ga. 16, 28, 2-3/4" chamber. **Barrel:** 24" to 30". **Weight:** Varies from 5 to 9.5 lbs. **Length:** Varies from 36" to 48". **Stock:** Walnut-finished hardwood with full pistol grip, synthetic, or camo finish. **Sights:** Bead front on most. **Features:** Transfer bar ignition; break-open action with side-lever release.
Price: Pardner, all gauges, hardwood stock, 26" to 32"
    blued barrel, Mod. or Full choke....................................**$206.00**
Price: Turkey model, 10/12 ga., camo finish
    or black...**$277.00 to $322.00**
Price: Youth Turkey, 20 ga., camo finish or black **$192.00**
Price: Waterfowl, 10 ga., camo finish or hardwood..................**$227.00**
Price: Tracker II slug gun, 12/20 ga., hardwood.......................**$291.00**

KRIEGHOFF K-80 SINGLE BARREL TRAP GUN

Gauge: 12, 2-3/4" chamber. **Barrel:** 32" or 34" Unsingle. Fixed Full or choke tubes. **Weight:** About 8-3/4 lbs. **Stock:** Four stock dimensions or adjustable stock available. All hand-checkered European walnut. **Features:** Satin nickel finish. Selective mechanical trigger adjustable for finger position. Tapered step vent rib. Adjustable point of impact.
Price: Standard grade Full Unsingle, from...........................**$10,595.00**

KRIEGHOFF KX-6 TRAP GUN

Gauge: 12, 2-3/4" chamber. **Barrel:** 32", 34"; choke tubes. **Weight:** About 8.5 lbs. **Stock:** Factory adjustable stock. European walnut. **Features:** Ventilated tapered step rib. Adjustable position trigger, optional release trigger. Fully adjustable rib. Satin gray electroless nickel receiver. Fitted aluminum case. Imported from Germany by Krieghoff International, Inc.
Price: $5,495.00

SHOTGUNS Bolt Actions & Single Shot

LJUTIC MONO GUN SINGLE BARREL
Gauge: 12 only. **Barrel:** 34", choked to customer specs; hollow-milled rib, 35.5" sight plane. **Weight:** Approx. 9 lbs. **Stock:** To customer specs. Oil finish, hand checkered. **Features:** Custom gun. Pull or release trigger; removable trigger guard contains trigger and hammer mechanism; Ljutic pushbutton opener on front of trigger guard. From Ljutic Industries.
Price: Std., med. or Olympic rib, custom bbls.,
fixed choke. **$7,495.00**
Price: Stainless steel mono gun **$8,495.00**

LJUTIC LTX PRO 3 DELUXE MONO GUN
Deluxe, lightweight version of the Mono gun with high quality wood, upgrade checkering, special rib height, screw-in chokes, ported and cased.
Price: **$8,995.00**
Price: Stainless steel model.................................. **$9,995.00**

ROSSI CIRCUIT JUDGE
Revolving shotgun chambered in .410 (2-1/2- or 3-inch/.45 Colt. Based on Taurus Judge handgun. Features include 18.5-inch barrel; fiber optic front sight; 5-round cylinder; hardwood Monte Carlo stock.
Price: **$669.00**

ROSSI SINGLE-SHOT
Gauge: 12, 20, .410. **Barrel:** 22" (Youth), 28". **Weight:** 3.75-5.25 lbs. Stocks: Wood. **Sights:** Bead front sight, fully adjustable fiber optic sight on Slug and Turkey. **Features:** Single-shot break open, 8 models available, positive ejection, internal transfer bar mechanism, trigger block system, Taurus Security System, blued finish, Rifle Slug has ported barrel.
Price: From **$171.00**

ROSSI TUFFY
Gauge: .410. **Barrel:** 18-1/2". **Weight:** 3 lbs. Length: 29.5" overall.
Features: Single-shot break-open model with black synthetic thumbhole stock in blued or stainless finish.
Price: **$205.00**

ROSSI MATCHED PAIRS
Gauge/Caliber: 12, 20, .410, .22 Mag, .22LR, .17HMR, .223 Rem, .243 Win, .270 Win, .30-06, .308 Win. **Barrel:** 23", 28". **Weight:** 5-6.3 lbs. Stocks: Wood or black synthetic. **Sights:** Bead front on shotgun barrel, fully adjustable front and rear on rifle barrel, drilled and tapped for scope, fully adjustable fiber optic sights (black powder). **Features:** Single-shot break open, 27 models available, internal transfer bar mechanism, manual external safety, blue finish, trigger block system, Taurus Security System, youth models available.
Price: Rimfire/Shotgun, from **$245.00**
Price: Centerfire/Shotgun **$345.00**

SKB CENTURY III TRAP
Single-shot, break-open 12 gauge with 2 ¾" chamber, SKB Competition Choke Tube System with three choke tubes. **Barrel:** 30 or 32 inches with lengthened forcing cone. **Stock:** Oil finished Grade II Turkish walnut, right or left-hand cast, Pachmayr SXT recoil pad. Adjustable comb and buttplate system is available. Imported from Turkey by GU, Inc.
Price: **$1,150.00**
Price: Adjustable comb **$1,300.00**
Price: Adjustable comb and buttstock **$1,430.00**

TAR-HUNT RSG-12 PROFESSIONAL RIFLED SLUG GUN
Gauge: 12, 2-3/4" or 3" chamber, 1-shot magazine. **Barrel:** 23", fully rifled with muzzle brake. **Weight:** 7.75 lbs. Length: 41.5" overall. **Stock:** Matte black McMillan fiberglass with Pachmayr Decelerator pad. **Sights:** None furnished; comes with Leupold windage or Weaver bases. **Features:** Uses rifle-style action with two locking lugs; two-position safety; Shaw barrel; single-stage, trigger; muzzle brake. Many options available. All models have area-controlled feed action. Introduced 1991. Made in U.S. by Tar-Hunt Custom Rifles, Inc.
Price: 12 ga. Professional model **$2,895.00**
Price: Left-hand model **$3,000.00**

TAR-HUNT RSG-16 ELITE
Similar to RSG-12 Professional except 16 gauge; right- or left-hand versions.
Price: **$2,895.00**

TAR-HUNT RSG-20 MOUNTAINEER SLUG GUN
Similar to the RSG-12 Professional except chambered for 20 gauge (2-3/4" and 3" shells); 23" Shaw rifled barrel, with muzzle brake; two-lug bolt; one-shot blind magazine; matte black finish; McMillan fiberglass stock with Pachmayr Decelerator pad; receiver drilled and tapped for Rem. 700 bases. Right- or left-hand versions. Weighs 6.5 lbs. Introduced 1997. Made in U.S.A. by Tar-Hunt Custom Rifles, Inc.
Price: **$2,895.00**

BENELLI M3 CONVERTIBLE
Gauge: 12, 2-3/4", 3" chambers, 5-shot magazine. **Barrel:** 19.75" (Cyl.). **Weight:** 7 lbs., 4oz. **Length:** 41" overall. **Stock:** High-impact polymer with sling loop in side of butt; rubberized pistol grip on stock. **Sights:** Open rifle, fully adjustable. Ghost ring and rifle type. **Features:** Combination pump/auto action. Alloy receiver with inertia recoil rotating locking lug bolt; matte finish; automatic shell release lever. Introduced 1989. Imported by Benelli USA. Price with pistol grip, open rifle sights.
Price: With ghost ring sights, pistol grip stock $1,589.00

BENELLI M2 TACTICAL
Gauge: 12, 2-3/4", 3" chambers, 5-shot magazine. **Barrel:** 18.5" IC, M, F choke tubes. **Weight:** 6.7 lbs. **Length:** 39.75" overall. **Stock:** Black polymer. **Sights:** Rifle type ghost ring system, tritium night sights optional. **Features:** Semiauto intertia recoil action. Cross-bolt safety; bolt release button; matte-finish metal. Introduced 1993. Imported from Italy by Benelli USA.
Price: from ....$1,239.00 to $1,359.00

BENELLI M4 TACTICAL
Gauge: 12, 3" chamber. **Barrel:** 18.5". **Weight:** 7.8 lbs. **Length:** 40" overall. **Stock:** Synthetic. **Sights:** Ghost Ring rear, fixed blade front. **Features:** Auto-regulating gas-operated (ARGO) action, choke tube, Picatinny rail, standard and collapsible stocks available, optional LE tactical gun case. Introduced 2006. Imported from Italy by Benelli USA.
Price: From $1,899.00

KEL-TEC KSG BULL-PUP TWIN-TUBE
Gauge: 12. **Capacity:** 13+1. **Barrel:** 18.5". **Overall Length:** 26.1". **Weight:** 8.5 lbs. (loaded). Pump action shotgun with two magazine tubes. The shotgun bears a resemblance to the South African designed Neostead pump-action gun. The operator is able to move a switch located near the top of the grip to select the right or left tube, or move the switch to the center to eject a shell without chambering another round. Optional accessories include a factory installed Picatinny rail with flip-up sights and a pistol grip.
Price: $990.00

MOSSBERG MODEL 500 SPECIAL PURPOSE
Gauge: 12, 20, .410, 3" chamber. **Barrel:** 18.5" 20" (Cyl.). **Weight:** 7 lbs. **Stock:** Walnut-finished hardwood or black synthetic. **Sights:** Metal bead front. **Features:** Available in 6- or 8-shot models. Top-mounted safety, double action slide bars, swivel studs, rubber recoil pad. Blue, Parkerized, Marinecote finishes. Mossberg Cablelock included. The HS410 Home Security model chambered for .410 with 3" chamber; has pistol grip fore-end, thick recoil pad, muzzle brake and has special spreader choke on the 18.5" barrel. Overall length is 37.5", weight is 6.25 lbs. Blue finish; synthetic field stock. Mossberg Cablelock and video included. Mariner model has Marinecote metal

finish to resist rust and corrosion. Synthetic field stock; pistol grip kit included. 500 Tactical 6-shot has black synthetic tactical stock. Introduced 1990.
Price: Rolling Thunder, 6-shot $537.00
Price: HS410 Home Security $502.00
Price: Tactical..$583.00 to $630.00
Price: 500 Blackwater SPX.......................................$478.00
Price: 500 Chainsaw pistol grip only; removable top handle ...$525.00
Price: JIC $435.00
Price: Road Blocker...$544.00

MOSSBERG MODEL 590 SPECIAL PURPOSE
Gauge: 12, 20, .410 3" chamber, 9 shot magazine. **Barrel:** 20" (Cyl.). **Weight:** 7.25 lbs. **Stock:** Synthetic field or Speedfeed. **Sights:** Metal bead front or Ghost Ring. **Features:** Top-mounted safety, double slide action bars. Comes with heat shield, bayonet lug, swivel studs, rubber recoil pad. Blue, Parkerized or Marinecote finish. Mossberg Cablelock included. From Mossberg.
Price: Special Purpose 9-shot................................$537.00
Price: Tactical Light Fore-End..............................$677.00
Price: Tactical Tri-Rail $640.00

MOSSBERG 930 SPECIAL PURPOSE SERIES
Gauge: 12 ga., 3" chamber. **Barrel:** 28" flat ventilated rib. **Weight:** 7.3 lbs. **Length:** 49". **Stock:** Composite stock with close radius pistol grip; Speed Lock forearm; textured gripping surfaces; shim adjustable for length of pull, cast and drop; Mossy Oak Bottomland camo finish; Dura-Touch Armor Coating. **Features:** 930 Special Purpose shotguns feature a self-regulating gas system that vents excess gas to aid in recoil reduction and eliminate stress on critical components. All 930 autoloaders chamber both 2 3/4 inch and 3-inch 12-gauge shotshells with ease—from target loads, to non-toxic magnum loads, to the latest sabot slug ammo. Magazine capacity is 7+1 on models with extended magazine tube, 4+1 on models without. To complete the package, each Mossberg 930 includes a set of specially designed spacers for quick adjustment of the horizontal and vertical angle of the stock, bringing a custom-feel fit to every shooter. All 930 Special Purpose models feature a drilled and tapped receiver, factory-ready for Picatinny rail, scope base or optics installation. 930 SPX models conveniently come with a factory-mounted Picatinny rail and LPA/M16-Style Ghost Ring combination sight right out of the box. Other sighting options include a basic front bead, or white-dot front sights. Mossberg 930 Special Purpose shotguns are available in a variety of configurations; 5-shot tactical barrel, 5-shot with muzzle brake, 8-shot pistol-grip, and even a 5-shot security / field combo.
Price: Tactical 5-Shot..$683.00
Price: Blackwater Series.......................................$865.00
Price: Home Security...$612.00
Price: Standard Stock..$787.00
Price: Pistol Grip 8-shot $883.00
Price: 5-shot Combo w/extra 18.5" barrel.......................$679.00

REMINGTON MODEL 870 PUMP AND MODEL 1100 AUTOLOADER TACTICAL SHOTGUNS
Gauge: 870: 12, 2-3/4 or 3" chamber; 1100: 2-3/4". **Barrel:** 18", 20", 22" (Cyl or IC). **Weight:** 7.5-7.75 lbs. **Length:** 38.5-42.5" overall. **Stock:** Black synthetic, synthetic Speedfeed IV full pistol-grip stock, or Knoxx

SHOTGUNS Military & Police

Industries SpecOps stock w/recoil-absorbing spring-loaded cam and adjustable length of pull (12" to 16", 870 only). **Sights:** Front post w/ dot only on 870; rib and front dot on 1100. **Features:** R3 recoil pads, LimbSaver technology to reduce felt recoil, 2-, 3- or 4-shot extensions based on barrel length; matte-olive-drab barrels and receivers. Model 1100 Tactical is available with Speedfeed IV pistol grip stock or standard black synthetic stock and fore-end. Speedfeed IV model has an 18" barrel with two-shot extension. Standard synthetic-stocked version is equipped with 22" barrel and four-shot extension. Introduced 2006. From Remington Arms Co.

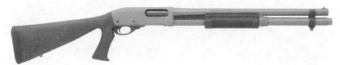

Price: 870 Express Tactical Knoxx 20 ga.	$555.00
Price: 870 Express Magpul	$898.00
Price: 870 Special Purpose Marine (nickel)	$829.00
Price: 870 Express Blackhawk Spec Ops	$638.00
Price: 1100 TAC-4	$1,015.00

REMINGTON 870 EXPRESS TACTICAL A-TACS CAMO

Pump action shotgun chambered for 2-3/4- and 3-inch 12-ga. Features include full A-TACS digitized camo; 18-1/2-inch barrel; extended ported Tactical RemChoke; SpeedFeed IV pistol-grip stock with SuperCell recoil pad; fully adjustable XS Ghost Ring Sight rail with removable white bead front sight; 7-round capacity with factory-installed 2-shot extension; drilled and tapped receiver; sling swivel stud.
Price: $720.00

REMINGTON 887 NITRO MAG TACTICAL

Pump action shotgun chambered in 12-ga., 2-3/4 to 3-1/2 inch. Features include 18-1/2-inch barrel with ported, extended tactical RemChoke; 2-shot magazine extension; barrel clamp with integral Picatinny rails; ArmorLokt coating; synthetic stock and fore-end with specially contour grip panels.
Price: $534.00

TACTICAL RESPONSE STANDARD MODEL

Gauge: 12, 3" chamber, 7-shot magazine. **Barrel:** 18" (Cyl.). **Weight:** 9 lbs. **Length:** 38" overall. **Stock:** Fiberglass-filled polypropolene with non-snag recoil absorbing butt pad. Nylon tactical fore-end houses flashlight. **Sights:** Trak-Lock ghost ring sight system. Front sight has Tritium insert. **Features:** Highly modified Remington 870P with Parkerized finish. Comes with nylon three-way adjustable sling, high visibility non-binding follower, high performance magazine spring, Jumbo Head safety, and Side Saddle extended 6-shot shell carrier on left side of receiver. Introduced 1991. From Scattergun Technologies, Inc.
Price: Standard model, from.................................$1,540.00
Price: Border Patrol model, from $1,135.00
Price: Professional Model 13" bbl. (Law enf., military only)...$1,550.00

TRISTAR COBRA

Gauge: 12, 3". **Barrel:** 28". **Weight:** 6.7 lbs. Three Beretta-style choke tubes (IC, M, F). **Length:** NA. **Stock:** Matte black synthetic stock and forearm. **Sights:** Vent rib with matted sight plane. **Features:** Five-year warranty. Cobra Tactical Pump Shotgun magazine holds 7, return spring in forearm, 20" barrel, Cylinder choke. Introduced 2008. Imported by Tristar Sporting Arms Ltd.
Price: Tactical...................................... $319.00 to $429.00

TRISTAR TEC12 AUTO/PUMP

Gauge: 12. 3-inch chamber. 20-inch ported barrel with fixed cylinder choke. Capable of operating in pump-action or semi-auto model with the turn of a dial. **Stock:** Pistol-grip synthetic with matte black finish. **Weight:** 7.4 lbs. **Sights:** Ghost-ring rear, raised bridge fiber-optic front. Picatinny rail.
Price: $689

WINCHESTER SXP EXTREME DEFENDER

Gauge: 12. 3-inch chamber. Pump action. **Barrel:** 18-inches with chrome-plated chamber and bore, "door breaching" ported choke tube. **Stock:** Adjustable military-style buttstock with vertical pistol grip. **Sights:** Ghost-ring rear integrated with Picatinny rail. Matte black finish.
Price: $560.00
Price: Marine Model with hard chrome metal finish $620.00

CHARLESTON UNDERHAMMER MATCH PERCUSSION PISTOL

Caliber: .36. **Barrel:** 9.5 in., browned octagonal, rifled. **Weight:** 2.25 lbs. **Length:** 16.75 in. overall. **Stocks:** Walnut grip. **Sights:** Blade front, open rear, adjustable for elevation. **Features:** Percussion, under-hammer ignition, adjustable trigger, no half cock. No ramrod. Made by Pedersoli. Imported by Dixie Gun Works.
Price: Dixie, FH0332 .... **$915.00**

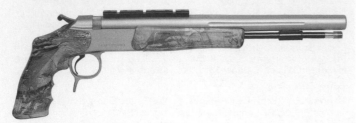

CVA OPTIMA PISTOL

Caliber: .50. **Barrel:** 14 in., 1:28-in. twist, Cerakote finish. **Weight:** 3.7 lbs. **Length:** 19 in. **Stocks:** Black synthetic, Realtree Xtra Green. **Ramrod:** Aluminum. **Sights:** Scope base mounted. **Features:** Break-open action, all stainless construction, quick-removal breech plug for 209 primer. From CVA.
Price: PP222SM Stainless/Realtree Xtra, rail mount **$318.00**
Price: PP221SM Stainless/black, rail mount **$378.00**

FRENCH AN IX, AN XIII AND GENDARMERIE NAPOLEONIC PISTOLS

Caliber: .69. **Barrel:** 8.25 in. **Weight:** 3 lbs. **Length:** 14 in. overall. **Stocks:** Walnut. **Sights:** None. **Features:** Flintlock, case-hardened lock, brass furniture, buttcap, lock marked "Imperiale de S. Etienne." Steel ramrod. Other Napoleonic pistols include half-stocked "AN XIII" and Gendarmerie with 5.25-inch barrel. Made by Pedersoli. Imported by Dixie Gun Works.
Price: Dixie Gun Works FH0890 .... **$740.00**
Price: Dixie Gun Works AN XIII FHO895................................. **$710.00**
Price: Dixie Gun Works Gendarmerie FHO954........................ **$665.00**

HARPER'S FERRY 1805 PISTOL

Caliber: .58. **Barrel:** 10 in. **Weight:** 2.5 lbs. **Length:** 16 in. overall. **Stocks:** Walnut. **Sights:** Fixed. **Features:** Flintlock. Case-hardened lock, brass-mounted German silver-colored barrel. Wooden ramrod. Replica of the first U.S. government made flintlock pistol. Made by Pedersoli. Imported by Dixie Gun Works.
Price: Dixie Gun Works RH0225 .... **$565.00**
Price: Dixie Gun Works Kit RH0411 .... **$433.00**

HOWDAH HUNTER PISTOLS

Caliber: .50, 20 gauge, .58 **Barrels:** 11.25 in., blued, rifled in .50 and .58 calibers **Weight:** 4.25 to 5 lbs. **Length:** 17.25 in. **Stocks:** American walnut with checkered grip. **Sights:** Brass bead front sight. **Features:** Blued barrels, swamped barrel rib, engraved, color case-hardened locks and hammers, captive steel ramrod. Available with detachable shoulder stock, case, holster and mold. Made by Pedersoli. Imported

by Dixie Gun Works, and individual models by Cabela's, Taylor's and others.
Price: Dixie, 50X50, PH0572 .... **$850.00**
Price: Dixie, 58XD58, PH09024 .... **$875.00**
Price: Dixie, 20X20 gauge, PH0581.. **$815.00**
Price: Dixie, 50X20 gauge, PH0581.. **$850.00**
Price: Dixie, 50X50, Kit, PK0952 .... **$640.00**
Price: Dixie, 50X20, Kit, PK1410 .... **$675.00**
Price: Dixie, 20X20, Kit, PK0954.. **$640.00**

KENTUCKY PISTOL

Caliber: .45, .50, .54 **Barrel:** 10.25 in. **Weight:** 2.5 lbs. **Length:** 15.4 in. overall. **Stocks:** Walnut with smooth rounded birds-head grip. **Sights:** Fixed. **Features:** Available in flint or percussion ignition in various calibers. Case-hardened lock, blued barrel, drift-adjustable rear sights, blade front. Wooden ramrod. Kit guns of all models available from Dixie Gun Works. Made by Pedersoli. Imported by Dixie Gun Works, EMF and others.
Price: .45 Percussion, Dixie, PH0440 .... **$375.00**
Price: .45 Flint, Dixie, PH0430 .... **$410.00**
Price: .45 Flint, Dixie, Kit FH0320 .... **$299.00**
Price: .50 Flint, Dixie, PH0935 .... **$435.00**
Price: .50 Percussion, Dixie, PH0930 .... **$395.00**
Price: .54 Flint, Dixie, PH0080 .... **$440.00**
Price: .54 Percussion, Dixie,PH0330 .... **$395.00**
Price: .54 Percussion, Dixie, Kit PK0436 .... **$283.00**
Price: .45 Flint, Navy Moll, brass buttcap,
Dixie, PK0436 .... **$610.00**
Price: .45 Percussion, Navy Moll, brass buttcap,
Dixie, PK0903 ....**$565.00**

LE PAGE PERCUSSION DUELING PISTOL

Caliber: .44 (Pedersoli), .45 (Armi, Chiappa). **Barrel:** 10.25 in. browned octagon, rifled. **Weight:** 2.5 lbs. **Length:** 16.6 in. overall. **Stocks:** Walnut, rounded checkered butt (Pedersoli), fluted butt (Armi). **Sights:** Blade front, open-style rear. **Features:** Single set trigger (Pedersoli), double set (Armi) trigger. Browned barrel (Dixie International). Bright barrel, silver-plated brass furniture (Armi). External ramrod. Made by Pedersoli, Armi, Chiappa. Imported by Dixie Gun Works.
Price: Dixie, Pedersoli, PH0431.. **$925.00**
Price: Dixie, International, Pedersoli, PH0231 ....**$1,250.00**
Price: Dixie, Armi, PH0310 .... **$627.00**

LYMAN PLAINS PISTOL

Caliber: .50 or .54. **Barrel:** 8 in.; 1:30-in. twist, both calibers. **Weight:** 50 oz. **Length:** 15 in. overall. **Stocks:** Walnut. **Sights:** Blade front, square-notch rear adjustable for windage. **Features:** Polished brass triggerguard and ramrod tip, color case-hardened coil spring lock, spring-loaded trigger, stainless steel nipple, blackened iron furniture. Hooked patent breech, detachable belt hook. Introduced 1981. From Lyman Products.
Price: 6010608 .50-cal.. **$409.95**
Price: 6010609 .54-cal...**$409.95**
Price: 6010610 .50-cal Kit **$349.95**
Price: 6010611 .54-cal. Kit..**$349.95**

MORTIMER TARGET PISTOL

Caliber: .44. **Barrel:** 10 in., bright octagonal on Standard, browned on Deluxe, rifled. **Weight:** 2.25 lbs. **Length:** 16 in. overall. **Stocks:** Walnut, checkered saw-handle grip on Deluxe. **Sights:** Blade front, open-style rear. **Features:** Percussion or flint, single set trigger, sliding hammer safety, engraved lock on Deluxe. Wooden ramrod. Made by Pedersoli. Imported by Dixie Gun Works
Price: Dixie, Flint, FH0316 ....**$1,175.00**
Price: Dixie, Percussion, PH0231 ....**$1,095.00**
Price: Dixie, Deluxe, FH0950 ....**$2,200.00**

BLACKPOWDER PISTOLS—Single Shot, Flint & Percussion

PEDERSOLI MANG TARGET PISTOL
Caliber: .38. **Barrel:** 10.5 in., octagonal; 1:15-in. twist. **Weight:** 2.5 lbs. **Length:** 17.25 in. overall. Stocks: Walnut with fluted grip. **Sights:** Blade front, open rear adjustable for windage. **Features:** Browned barrel, polished breech plug, remainder color case-hardened. Made by Pedersoli. Imported by Dixie Gun Works.
Price: PH0503.. $1,750.00

PHILADELPHIA DERRINGER
Caliber: .45. **Barrel:** 3.1 in., browned, rifled. **Weight:** .5 lbs. **Length:** 6.215 in. Grips: European walnut checkered. **Sights:** V-notch rear, blade front. **Features:** Back-hammer percussion lock with engraving, single trigger. From Pedersoli. Sold by Dixie Gun Works.
Price: Dixie, PH0913 .... $550.00
Price: Dixie, Kit PK0863 .... $385.00

QUEEN ANNE FLINTLOCK PISTOL
Caliber: .50. **Barrel:** 7.5 in., smoothbore. Stocks: Walnut. **Sights:** None. **Features:** Flintlock, German silver-colored steel barrel, fluted brass triggerguard, brass mask on butt. Lockplate left in the white. No ramrod. Introduced 1983. Made by Pedersoli. Imported by Dixie Gun Works.
Price: Dixie, RH0211... $470.00
Price: Dixie, Kit, FH0421 .... $470.00

REMINGTON RIDER DERRINGER
Caliber: 4.3 mm (BB lead balls only). **Barrel:** 2.1 in., blued, rifled. **Weight:** .25 lbs. **Length:** 4.75 in. Grips: All-steel construction. **Sights:** V-notch rear, bead front. **Features:** Fires percussion cap only – no powder. Available as case-hardened frame or polished white. From Pedersoli. Sold by Dixie Gun Works.
Price: Dixie, Casehardened PH0923 . ... $210.00

SCREW BARREL PISTOL
Caliber: .44. **Barrel:** 2.35 in., blued, rifled. **Weight:** .5 lbs. **Length:** 6.5 in. Grips: European walnut. **Sights:** None. **Features:** Percussion, boxlock with center hammer, barrel unscrews for loading from rear, folding trigger, external hammer, combination barrel and nipple wrench furnished. From Pedersoli. Sold by Dixie Gun Works.
Price: Dixie, PH0530 .... $210.00
Price: Dixie, PH0545 .... $165.00

TRADITIONS KENTUCKY PISTOL
Caliber: .50. **Barrel:** 10 in., 1:20 in. twist. **Weight:** 2.75 lbs. **Length:** 15 in. Stocks: Hardwood full stock. **Sights:** Brass blade front, square notch rear adjustable for windage. **Features:** Polished brass finger spur-style triggerguard, stock cap and ramrod tip, color case-hardened leaf spring lock, spring-loaded trigger, No. 11 percussion nipple, brass furniture. From Traditions, and as kit from Bass Pro and others.
Price: P1060 Finished... $244.00
Price: KPC50602 Kit $209.00

TRADITIONS PIRATE PISTOL
Caliber: .50. **Barrel:** 10 in., round armory-bright steel, 1:20 in. twist. **Weight:** 2.75 lbs. **Length:** 15 in. Stocks: Hardwood rounded bag-style grip with skull-crushing brass grip cap, fullstock. **Sights:** Square-notched rear adjustable for windage, brass blade front. **Features:** Flint, armory-bright polished lock, single trigger, polished brass triggerguard, stock cap and ramrod tip, color case-hardened leaf spring lock, spring-loaded trigger. From Traditions, and as kit from Bass Pro and others.
Price: P1430 Finished, flint $404.00
Price: KPC 5400 Kit, flint $330.00

TRADITIONS TRAPPER PISTOL
Caliber: .50. **Barrel:** 9.75 in., octagonal, blued, hooked patent breech, 1:20 in. twist. **Weight:** 2.75 lbs. **Length:** 15.5 in. Stocks: Hardwood, modified saw-handle style grip, halfstock. **Sights:** Brass blade front, rear sight adjustable for windage and elevation. **Features:** Percussion or flint, double set triggers, polished brass triggerguard, stock cap and ramrod tip, color case-hardened leaf spring lock, spring-loaded trigger, No. 11 percussion nipple, brass furniture. From Traditions and as a kit from Bass Pro and others.
Price: P1100 Finished, percussion $329.00
Price: P1090 Finished, flint $369.00
Price: KPC51002 Kit, percussion $299.00
Price: KPC50902 Kit, flint $359.00

TRADITIONS VEST POCKET DERRINGER
Caliber: .31. **Barrel:** 2.35 in., round brass, smoothbore. **Weight:** .75 lbs. **Length:** 4.75 in. Grips: Simulated ivory. **Sights:** Front bead. **Features:** Replica of riverboat gambler's derringer. No. 11 percussion cap nipple, brass frame and barrel, spur trigger, external hammer. From Traditions.
Price: P1381, Brass $194.00
Price: Dixie, White, PH0920 .... $210.00

TRADITIONS VORTEK PISTOL
Caliber: .50. **Barrel:** 13 in., 1:28 in. twist, Cerakote finish. **Weight:** 3.25 lbs. **Length:** 18 in. Stocks: Hardwood, black synthetic, Reaper Buck camo. Ramrod: Solid aluminum. **Sights:** LPA steel, 1-4X24mm scope. **Features:** Vortek break-open action with removable trigger group, quick-removal breech plug for 209 primer, over-molded stocks. From Traditions.
Price: P1-151178 Scope, select hardwood, Cerakote.......... $469.00
Price: P1-151178 No sights, select hardwood, Cerakote.......$374.00
Price: P1-151170 Scope, Black synthetic, Cerakote $419.00
Price: P1-151170 No sights, Black synthetic, Cerakote.......... $324.00

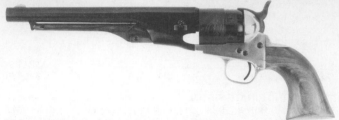

COLT ARMY 1860 PERCUSSION REVOLVER

Caliber: .44. **Barrel:** 8 in. **Weight:** 2.75 lbs. **Length:** 13.25 in. overall. **Grips:** One-piece walnut. **Sights:** Brass blade front, hammer notch rear. **Features:** Steel or case-hardened frame, brass triggerguard, case-hardened creeping loading lever. Many models and finishes are available for this pistol. Made by Pietta and Uberti. Imported by Cabela's, Cimarron, Dixie Gun Works, EMF, Taylor's, Uberti U.S.A. and others.
Price: Dixie, standard model with brass triggerguard RH0705 **$260.00**
Price: Dixie, standard model kit RK0965 .... **$234.00**
Price: Dixie, half-fluted cylinder cut for shoulder stock RH0125 ....
$234.00
Price: Dixie, 5.5 in. Sheriff's model RH0975 .... **$305.00**

COLT ARMY 1862 POLICE SNUBNOSE (THUNDERER) PERCUSSION REVOLVER

Caliber: .44, six-shot. **Barrel:** 3 in. **Weight:** 1.5 lbs. **Length:** 9.2 in. overall. **Grips:** Varnished birds-head walnut. **Sights:** Brass pin front, hammer notch rear. **Features:** Steel or case-hardened frame, steel triggerguard, no loading. Ramrod: Brass loading rod. Made by Uberti. Imported by EMF, Taylor's, Uberti U.S.A.
Price: Pietta CPPSNB44MYLC **$397.43**

COLT BABY DRAGOON 1848, 1849 POCKET, WELLS FARGO PERCUSSION REVOLVER

Caliber: .31. **Barrel:** 3 in., 4 in., 5 in., 6 in.; seven-groove; RH twist. **Weight:** About 21 oz. **Grips:** Varnished walnut. **Sights:** Brass pin front, hammer notch rear. **Features:** No loading lever on Baby Dragoon or Wells Fargo models. Unfluted cylinder with stagecoach holdup scene, cupped cylinder pin, no grease grooves, one safety pin on cylinder and slot in hammer face, straight (flat) mainspring. Made by Uberti. Imported by Cimarron, Dixie Gun Works, EMF, Uberti U.S.A. and others.
Price: from .... **$310.00 to $346.00**

COLT 1847 WALKER PERCUSSION REVOLVER

Caliber: .44 **Barrel:** 9 in. **Weight:** 4.5 lbs. **Length:** 15.7 in. overall. **Grips:** One-piece hardwood. **Sights:** Brass blade front, hammer notch rear. **Features:** Copy of Sam Colt's first U.S. contract revolver. Engraved cylinder, case-hardened hammer and loading lever. Blued finish. Made by Uberti, imported by Cabela's, Cimarron, Dixie Gun Works, EMF, Taylor's, Uberti U.S.A. and others.
Price: Dixie, standard model, blued steel RH0450 .... **$410.00**
Price: Dixie, standard model, blued steel kit RH0450 .... **$340.00**

COLT 1848 DRAGOON PERCUSSION REVOLVERS

Caliber: .44 **Barrel:** 7.5 in. **Weight:** 4.1 lbs. **Grips:** One-piece walnut. **Sights:** Brass blade front, hammer notch rear. **Features:** Copy of Eli Whitney's design for Colt using Walker parts and improved loading lever latch. Blued barrel, backstrap and triggerguard. Made in Italy by Uberti. Imported by Dixie Gun Works, Taylor's, Uberti U.S.A. and others.
Price: 1848 Dragoon, 1st-3rd models, ... **$385.00**
Price: 1848 Dragoon, 3rd. model, cut for stock RH0234 .... **$410.00**

COLT TEXAS PATTERSON PERCUSSION REVOLVER

Caliber: .36 **Barrel:** 9 in. tapered octagon. **Weight:** 2.75 lbs. **Length:** 13.75 in. **Grips:** One-piece walnut. **Sights:** Brass pin front, hammer notch rear. **Features:** Folding trigger, blued steel furniture, frame and barrel; engraved scene on cylinder. Ramrod: Loading tool provided. Made by Pietta. Imported by Dixie Gun Works.
Price: Dixie RH0600 .... **$560.00**

COLT NAVY MODEL 1851 PERCUSSION REVOLVER

Caliber: .36, .44, 6-shot. **Barrel:** 7.5 in. **Weight:** 44 oz. **Length:** 13 in. overall. **Grips:** Walnut. **Sights:** Post front, hammer notch rear. **Features:** Many authentic and non-authentic variations are offered that include, brass backstrap and triggerguard, steel or brass frame options, some have 1st Model square-back triggerguard, engraved cylinder with navy battle scene; case-hardened hammer, loading lever. Cartridge conversion pistols and cylinders are also available from Cimarron and Taylor's. Made by Uberti and Pietta. Imported by Cabela's, Cimarron, EMF, Dixie Gun Works, Taylor's, Traditions (.44 only), Uberti U.S.A. and others.
Price: Brass frame (Dixie Gun Works RH0100) **$240.00**
Price: Steel frame (Dixie Gun Works RH844) **$245.00**
Price: Confederate Navy (Cabela's) **$199.99**
Price: Cartridge conversion cylinders .38 Spl.
and .45 LC .... **$240-$300.00**

COLT SHERIFF MODEL 1851 PERCUSSION REVOLVER

Caliber: .44, 6-shot. **Barrel:** 5.5 in. **Weight:** 40 oz. **Length:** 10.5 in. overall. **Grips:** Walnut. **Sights:** Fixed. **Features:** Steel frame, brass backstrap and triggerguard; engraved navy scene; case-hardened frame, hammer, loading lever. Made by Uberti. Imported by EMF.
Price: PF51CH44512 Steel frame **$250.00**

COLT NAVY 1861 PERCUSSION REVOLVER

Caliber: .36 **Barrel:** 8 in. **Weight:** 2.75 lbs. **Length:** 13.25 in. overall. **Grips:** One-piece walnut. **Sights:** Brass blade front, hammer notch rear. **Features:** Steel or case-hardened frame, brass triggerguard, case-hardened creeping loading lever. Many models and finishes are available for this pistol. Made by Pietta and Uberti. Imported by Cabela's, Cimarron, Dixie Gun Works, EMF, Taylor's, Uberti U.S.A. and others.
Price: Dixie, standard model with brass triggerguard RH0841 **$315.00**
Price: Dixie, Sheriff's 5.5 in. barrel RK0975 .... **$205.00**

COLT POCKET POLICE 1862 PERCUSSION REVOLVER

Caliber: .36, 5-shot. **Barrel:** 4.5 in., 5.5 in., 6.5 in., 7.5 in. **Weight:** 26 oz. **Length:** 12 in. overall (6.5 in. bbl.). **Stocks:** Walnut. **Sights:** Fixed. **Features:** Round tapered barrel; half-fluted and rebated cylinder; case-hardened frame, loading lever and hammer; silver or brass triggerguard and backstrap. Made by Uberti. Imported by Cimarron, Dixie Gun Works, Taylor's, Uberti U.S.A. and others.
Price: Dixie Gun Works RH0422 .... **$340.00**

NAVY YANK PEPPERBOX

Caliber: .36, six-shot. **Cylinder-Barrel:** 3.1 in. **Weight:** 2.2 lbs.

Length: 7 in. overall. **Grips:** European walnut. **Sights:** Hammer notch rear. **Features:** Case-hardened frame, brass triggerguard, no loading lever or ramrod. Made by Pietta. Imported by Dixie, Taylor's.
Price: Pietta YAN36PP **$238.14**

DRAGOON PISTOL U.S. MODEL OF 1858 WITH DETACHABLE SHOULDER STOCK
Caliber: .58. **Barrel:** 12 in. **Weight:** 3.75 lbs., with shoulder stock 5.5 lbs. **Length:** 18.25 in. overall pistol. **Stocks:** Walnut pistol and shoulder stock. **Sights:** Flip-up blued steel rear, blade steel front. **Features:** Percussion, musket-cap nipple, case-hardened lock, brass furniture. Captive steel ramrod. Shoulder stock included. Made by Palmetto. Imported by Dixie Gun Works.
Price: Dixie Gun Works, with shoulder stock PH1000…......... **$600.00**

DANCE AND BROTHERS PERCUSSION REVOLVER
Caliber: .44 **Barrel:** 7.4 in., round. **Weight:** 2.5 lbs. **Length:** 13 in. overall. Grip: Two-piece walnut. **Sights:** Fixed. **Features:** Reproduction of the C.S.A. revolver. Brass frame and triggerguard. Made by Pietta. From Dixie Gun Works, Cabela's and others.
Price: Dixie Gun Works RH0120 .... **$343.00**

DIXIE WYATT EARP PERCUSSION REVOLVER
Caliber: .44 **Barrel:** 12 in., octagon. **Weight:** 46 oz. **Length:** 18 in. overall. **Grips:** One-piece hardwood. **Sights:** Fixed. **Features:** Highly polished brass frame, backstrap and triggerguard; blued barrel and cylinder; case-hardened hammer, trigger and loading lever. Navy-size shoulder stock requires minor fitting. Made by Pietta. From Dixie Gun Works, EMF.
Price: RH0130.. **$225.00**

GRISWOLD AND GUNNISON PERCUSSION REVOLVER
Caliber: .36 **Barrel:** 7.5 in., round. **Weight:** 2.5 lbs. **Length:** 13.25 in. Grip: One-piece walnut. **Sights:** Fixed. **Features:** Reproduction of the C.S.A. revolver. Brass frame and triggerguard. Made by Pietta. From Cabela's and others.
Price: Cabelas **$219.99**

LEACH AND RIGDON PERCUSSION REVOLVER
Caliber: .36. **Barrel:** 7.5 in., octagon to round. **Weight:** 2.75 lbs. **Length:** 13 in. Grip: One-piece walnut. **Sights:** Hammer notch and pin front. **Features:** Steel frame. Reproduction of the C.S.A. revolver. Brass backstrap and triggerguard. Made by Uberti. From Dixie Gun Works and others.
Price: Dixie Gun Works RH0611 .... **$340.00**

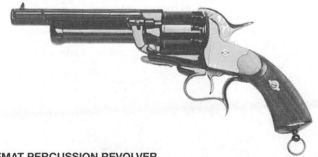

LEMAT PERCUSSION REVOLVER
Caliber: .44/20 ga. **Barrel:** 6.75 in. (revolver); 4-7/8 in. (single shot). **Weight:** 3 lbs., 7 oz. **Length:** 14 in. overall. **Grips:** Hand-checkered walnut. **Sights:** Post front, hammer notch rear. **Features:** Exact reproduction with all-steel construction; 44-cal. 9-shot cylinder, 20-gauge single barrel; color case-hardened hammer with selector; spur triggerguard; ring at butt; lever-type barrel release. Made by Pietta. From Dixie Gun Works.
Price: LeMat Navy with knurled pin barrel release **$925.00**
Price: LeMat Calvary with trigger spur and lanyard ring **$925.00**
Price: LeMat Army with cross pin barrel selector **$925.00**

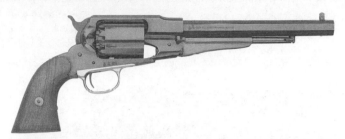

NEW MODEL 1858 REMINGTON ARMY PERCUSSION REVOLVER
Caliber: .36 or .44, 6-shot. **Barrel:** Standard 8 in., and 5.5 to 12 in. **Weight:** Standard 2 lbs. **Length:** Standard 13.5 in. Grips: Walnut, two-piece. **Sights:** Standard blade front, groove-in-frame rear; adjustable on some models. **Features:** Many variations of this gun are available. Also available as the Army Model Belt Revolver in .36 cal., a shortened and lightened version of the .44 model. Target Model (Uberti U.S.A.) has fully adjustable target rear sight, target front, .36 or .44. Imported by Cabela's, Cimarron F.A. Co., EMF, Taylor's, Traditions (.44 only), Uberti U.S.A. and others.
Price: Steel frame, Dixie RH0220 .... **$323.00**
Price: Steel frame kit, Dixie, oversized grips
and frame RV0440 .... **$245.00**
Price: Stainless steel Model 1858, Cabela's, Traditions **$399.99**
Price: Target Model, adj. rear sight (Cabela's, Traditions) **$499.99**
Price: Sheriff's Model, .44, steel frame (Cabela's, Traditions) . **$269.99**
Price: Brass frame Cabela's, Traditions,................................. **$279.99**
Price: Buffalo model, brass frame, .44-cal. (Cabela's) **$279.99**
Price: Buffalo model, stainless steel, .44-cal.
(Old South Firearms)... **$599.84**
Price: Traditions Redi-Pak, steel frame, accessories **$336.00**
Price: 1858 Target Carbine 18 in. barrel Dixie PR0338........... **$565.00**

NEW MODEL REMINGTON POCKET PERCUSSION REVOLVER
Caliber: .31, 5-shot. **Barrel:** 3.5 in. **Weight:** 1 lb. **Length:** 7.6 in. Grips: Walnut, two-piece. **Sights:** Pin front, groove-in-frame rear. **Features:** Spur trigger; iron, brass or nickel-plated frame. Made by Pietta. Imported by Dixie Gun Works, EMF, Taylor's and others.
Price: Brass frame, Dixie PH0407 .... **$243.00**
Price: Steel frame, Dixie PH0370.. **$288.00**
Price: Nickel-plated, Dixie PH0409 .... **$288.00**

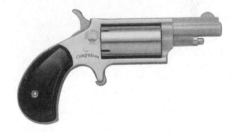

NORTH AMERICAN COMPANION PERCUSSION REVOLVER
Caliber: .22 **Barrel:** 1-1/8 in. **Weight:** 5.1 oz. **Length:** 4 in. overall. Grips: Laminated wood. **Sights:** Blade front, notch rear. **Features:** All stainless steel construction. Uses No. 11 percussion caps. Comes with bullets, powder measure, bullet seater, leather clip holster, gun rag. Long Rifle frame. Introduced 1996. Made in U.S. by North American Arms.
Price: NAA-22LR-CB Long Rifle frame.................................... **$241.00**

NORTH AMERICAN EARL PERCUSSION REVOLVER
Caliber: .22 **Barrel:** 4 in. **Weight:** 9.4 oz. **Length:** 7.75 in. **Sights:** Post front, notch rear. **Features:** All stainless steel construction. No. 11 percussion caps. Nonfunctional loading lever. Comes with bullets, powder measure, bullet seater, leather clip holster, gun rag. Introduced 1996. Magnum frame. Introduced 2012. Made in U.S. by North American Arms.
Price: NAA-1860-4-CB Magnum frame................................... **$316.00**

NORTH AMERICAN SUPER COMPANION PERCUSSION REVOLVER
Caliber: .22 **Barrel:** 1-5/8 in. **Weight:** 7.2 oz. **Length:** 5-1/8 in. Grips: Laminated wood. **Sights:** Blade font, notched rear. **Features:** All

Prices given are believed to be accurate at time of publication however, many factors affect retail pricing so exact prices are not possible.

70TH EDITION, 2016 ✦ **515**

stainless steel construction. No. 11 percussion caps. Comes with bullets, powder measure, bullet seater, leather clip holster, gun rag. Introduced 1996. Larger "Magnum" frame. Made in U.S. by North American Arms.

Price: NAA-Mag-CB Magnum frame **$251.00**

ROGERS & SPENCER PERCUSSION REVOLVER

Caliber: .44 **Barrel:** 7.5 in. **Weight:** 47 oz. **Length:** 13.75 in. overall. Stocks: Walnut. **Sights:** Cone front, integral groove-in-frame for rear. **Features:** Accurate reproduction of a Civil War design. Solid frame, extra-large nipple cut-out on rear of cylinder; loading lever and cylinder easily removed for cleaning. From Dixie Gun Works and others.

Price: **$450.00**

SPILLER & BURR PERCUSSION REVOLVER

Caliber: .36 **Barrel:** 7 in., octagon. **Weight:** 2.5 lbs. **Length:** 12.5 in. overall. Grip: Two-piece walnut. **Sights:** Fixed. **Features:** Reproduction of the C.S.A. revolver. Brass frame and triggerguard. Also available as a kit. Made by Pietta. From Dixie Gun Works, Traditions and others.

Price: Dixie RH0120... **$263.00**
Price: Dixie kit RH0300... **$233.00**

STARR DOUBLE-ACTION 1858 ARMY REVOLVER

Caliber: .44 **Barrel:** 6 in. tapered round. **Weight:** 3 lbs. **Length:** 11.75 in. Stocks: Walnut one-piece. **Sights:** Hammer notch rear, dovetailed front. **Features:** Double-action mechanism, round tapered barrel, all blued frame and barrel. Made by Pietta. Imported by Dixie Gun Works and others.

Price: Dixie RH460.. **$540.00**

STARR SINGLE-ACTION ARMY REVOLVER

Caliber: .44 **Barrel:** 8 in. tapered round. **Weight:** 3 lbs. **Length:** 13.5 in. Stocks: Walnut one-piece. **Sights:** Hammer notch rear, dovetailed front. **Features:** Single-action mechanism, round tapered barrel, all blued frame and barrel. Made by Pietta. Imported by Cabela's, Dixie Gun Works and others.

Price: Dixie RH460.. **$515.00**

BROWN BESS MUSKET, SECOND MODEL

Caliber: .75. **Barrel:** 42 in., round, smoothbore. **Weight:** 9 lbs. **Length:** 57.75 in. **Stock:** European walnut, fullstock. **Sights:** Steel stud on front serves as bayonet lug. **Features:** Flintlock using one-inch flint with optional brass flash guard (SCO203), steel parts all polished armory bright, brass furniture. Lock marked Grice, 1762 with crown and GR. Made by Pedersoli. Imported by Cabela's, Dixie Gun Works, others.

Price: Dixie Complete gun FR0810 .... $1,380.00
Price: Dixie Kit Gun FR0825 .... $1,050.00
Price: Cabela's Complete gun $1,100.00
Price: Dixie Trade Gun, 30.5-in. barrel, browned FR0665 .... $1,400.00
Price: Dixie Trade Gun Kit FR0600 .... $950.00
Price: Dixie Trade Musket , 30.5-in. barrel,
browned FR3170 .... $1,050.00
Price: Dixie Trade Musket Kit FR3370 .... $995.00

CABELA'S BLUE RIDGE RIFLE

Caliber: .32, .36, .45, .50, .54. **Barrel:** 39 in., octagon. **Weight:** 7.75 lbs. **Length:** 55 in. overall. **Stock:** American black walnut. **Sights:** Blade front, rear drift adjustable for windage. **Features:** Color case-hardened lockplate and cock/hammer, brass triggerguard and buttplate; double set, double-phased triggers. From Cabela's.
Price: Percussion $449.88
Price: Flintlock $599.99

CABELA'S KODIAK EXPRESS DOUBLE RIFLE

Caliber: .50, .54, .58, .72. **Barrel:** 1:48 in. twist. **Weight:** 9.3 lbs. **Length:** 45.25 in. overall. **Stock:** European walnut, oil finish. **Sights:** Fully adjustable double folding-leaf rear, ramp front. **Features:** Percussion. Barrels regulated to point of aim at 75 yards; polished and engraved lock, top tang and triggerguard. From Cabela's.
Price: .54-cal. $1,299.99

CABELA'S TRADITIONAL HAWKEN

Caliber: .50, 54. **Barrel:** 29 in. **Weight:** 9 lbs. **Stock:** Walnut. **Sights:** Blade front, open adjustable rear. **Features:** Flintlock or percussion. Adjustable double-set triggers. Polished brass furniture, color case-hardened lock. Imported by Cabela's.
Price: Percussion, right hand or left hand $499.99
Price: Flintlock, right hand $549.99

CVA OPTIMA V2 STAINLESS BREAK-ACTION RIFLE

Caliber: .50. **Barrel:** 28 in. fluted. **Weight:** 8.8 lbs. **Stock:** Ambidextrous solid composite in standard or thumbhole. **Sights:** Adj. fiber-optic. **Features:** Break-action, quick release breech plug, aluminum loading rod, cocking spur, lifetime warranty. Also available with exposed ignition as a Northwest Model.
Price: PR2029NM (.50-cal., Nitride stainless/Realtree Xtra,
thumbhole, scope mount) $448.00
Price: PR2023N (.50-cal., Nitride stainless/Realtree Xtra, fib. opt.
sight) $416.00
Price: PR2023NM (.50-cal., Nitride stainless/Realtree Xtra,
thumbhole, scope mount) $426.00
Price: PR2028SM (.50-cal, stainless/ Realtree Xtra,
scope mount) $400.00
Price: PR2022SM (.50-cal, stainless/Realtree Xtra,
fib. opt. sight) $378.00
Price: PR2022S (.50-cal, stainless/Realtree Xtra,
scope mount) $368.00
Price: PR2020SM (.50-cal, stainless/black, scope mount) $328.00
Price: PR2020S (.50-cal, stainless/black, fib. opt. sight)....... $318.00

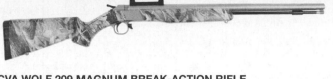

CVA WOLF 209 MAGNUM BREAK-ACTION RIFLE

Caliber: .50 **Barrel:** 24 in. **Weight:** 6.23 lbs. **Stock:** Ambidextrous composite. **Sights:** Dead-On Scope Mounts or Fiber Optic. **Features:** Break-Action, quick detachable breech plug for 209 primer, aluminum loading road, cocking spur, lifetime warranty. Also available with exposed ignition as a Northwest model.
Price: PR2112SM (.50-cal, stainless/Realtree
Hardwoods HD, scope mount) $309.00
Price: PR2112S (50-cal, stainless/Realtree
Hardwoods HD, fib. opt. sight) $301.00
Price: PR2110SM (.50-cal, stainless/black, scope mount) $261.00
Price: PR2110S
(.50-cal, stainless/black, fib. opt. sight) $253.00
Price: PR2110M
(.50-cal, blued/black, scope mount) $224.00
Price: PR2110
(.50-cal, blued/black, fig. opt. sight) $224.00

CVA APEX

Caliber: .45, .50. **Barrel:** 27 in., 1:28 in. twist. **Weight:** 8 lbs. **Length:** 42 in. **Stock:** Synthetic. **Features:** Ambidextrous with rubber grip panels in black or Realtree APG camo, crush-zone recoil pad, reversible hammer spur, quake claw sling, lifetime warranty.
Price: CR4013s (.45-cal., stainless/Realtree APG) $738.00
Price: CR4012S (.50-cal., stainless/Realtree APG)............. .. $695.00
Price: CR4011S (.45-cal., stainless/black)........................ ..$615.00
Price: CR4010S (.50-cal., stainless/black)........................ $615.00

CVA ACCURA V2 LR

Caliber: .50 **Barrel:** 27 or 30-in. **Weight:** 7.3 lbs. **Length:** 42 or 45-in. **Stock:** Synthetic. **Features:** Ambidextrous stock, quick release breech plug, crush-zone recoil pad, reversible hammer spur quake claw sling, lifetime warranty. Also available with exposed ignition as a Northwest model.
Price: PR3124NM (.50-cal, Nitride stainless/Realtree
Max-1 thumbhole, scope mount) $624.00
Price: PR3122SNM (.50-cal., stainless/Realtree
APG thumbhole) $608.00
Price: PR3116SM (.50-cal., stainless/Realtree HD
thumbhole, scope mount) $560.00
Price: PR3125N (.50-cal., Nitride, stainless/Realtree
HD, fib. opt. sight) $574.00
Price: PR3125NM (.50-cal., Nitride,stainless/black/RFealtree
HD, scope mount) $584.00
Price: PR3112SM
(.50-cal., stainless/Realtree APG, scope mount) $536.00
Price: PR3112S
(.50-cal, stainless/Realtree APG. fib. opt. sights) $526.00
Price: PR3110S (.50-cal, stainless/black, fib. opt. sights)........ $464.00

CVA ACCURA MOUNTAIN RIFLE

Caliber: .50. **Barrel:** 25-in. **Weight:** 6.35 lbs. **Length:** 40-in. **Stock:** Synthetic. **Features:** Ambidextrous stock, quick release breech plug, crush-zone recoil pad, reversible hammer spur quake claw sling, lifetime warranty
Price: PR3121SNM (.50-cal, Nitride stainless/Realtree
Max-1,scope mount) $584.00
Price: PR3120SM (.50-cal., stainless/black) $472.00

DIXIE 1803 HARPERS FERRY FLINTLOCK RIFLE

Caliber: .54. **Barrel:** 35.5 in., smoothbore. **Weight:** 9.5 lbs. **Length:** 29.5 in. overall. **Stock:** Halfstock, walnut w/oil finish. **Sights:** Blade front, notched rear. **Features:** Color case-hardened lock, browned barrel, with barrel key. Made by Euro Arms. Imported by Dixie Gun Works.
Price: FR0171 ....$1,050.00

DIXIE 1816 FLINTLOCK MUSKET

Caliber: .69. **Barrel:** 42 in., smoothbore. **Weight:** 9.75 lbs. **Length:** 56-7/8 in. overall. **Stock:** Walnut w/oil finish. **Sights:** Blade front. **Features:** All metal finished in "National Armory Bright," three barrelbands w/springs, steel ramrod w/button-shaped head. Made

by Pedersoli. Imported by Dixie Gun Works.
Price: FR0305 ....$1,460.00
Price: PR3180, Percussion conversion..................$1,425.00

DIXIE DELUXE CUB RIFLE
Caliber: .32, .36, .45. **Barrel:** 28 in. octagonal. **Weight:** 6.5 lbs. **Length:** 44 in. overall. **Stock:** Walnut. **Sights:** Fixed. **Features:** Each gun available in either flint or percussion ignition. Short rifle for small game and beginning shooters. Brass patchbox and furniture. Kit guns available in .32 or .36 calibers in percussion ($690) or flint ($710). From Dixie Gun Works.
Price: Deluxe Cub (.32-cal. flint) PR3130 ....$890.00
Price: Deluxe Cub (.36-cal. flint) FR3135 ....$890.00
Price: Deluxe Cub kit (.32-cal. percussion) PK3360................$690.00
Price: Deluxe Cub kit (.36-cal. percussion) PK3365................$690.00
Price: Deluxe Cub (.45-cal. percussion) PR0768....................$850.00
Price: Deluxe Cub (.32-cal. percussion) PR3140....................$850.00
Price: Deluxe Cub (.36-cal. percussion) PR3145....................$850.00

DIXIE EARLY AMERICAN JAEGER RIFLE
Caliber: .54. **Barrel:** 27.5 in. octagon, 1:24 in. twist. **Weight:** 8.25 lbs. **Length:** 43.5 in. overall. **Stock:** American walnut; sliding wooden patchbox on butt. **Sights:** Notch rear, blade front. **Features:** Flintlock or percussion. Conversion kits available, and recommended converting percussion guns to flintlocks using kit LO1102 at $209.00. Browned steel furniture. Made by Pedersoli. Imported by Dixie Gun Works.
Price: Percussion, PR0835 .... $1,295.00
Price: Flint, PR0835 .... $1,375.00
Price: Percussion, kit gun, PK0146 .... $1,075.00
Price: Flint, kit gun, PKO143........................... $1,075.00

DIXIE HAWKEN RIFLE
Caliber: .50 and .54. **Barrel:** 29.5 in. octagonal, 1:48 in. twist. **Weight:** 9 or 8.5 lbs. **Length:** 45.5 in. overall. **Stock:** European walnut, halfstock. **Sights:** Rear click adjustable for windage and elevation, blade front. **Features:** Percussion and flintlock, brass patchbox, double-set triggers, one barrel key. Flint gun available for left-handed shooters. Both flint and percussion guns available as kit guns. Made by Pedersoli. Imported by Dixie Gun Works.
Price: Percussion, .50 PR0502 .... $465.00
Price: Percussion, .54 PR0507 .... $450.00
Price: Flint, .50 FR1332 .... $525.00
Price: Flint, .50 left hand, FR1336 .... $525.00
Price: Flint, .50 left hand, kit, FR1345...................... $450.00

DIXIE JAPANESE TANEGASHIMA MATCHLOCK
Caliber: .50. **Barrel:** 53 in. **Weight:** 8.75 lbs. **Length:** 53 in. overall. **Stock:** Japanese cherry with drilled hole on bottom for wooden ramrod. **Sights:** Post front, block rear. **Features:** A replica of the snapping matchlock guns used in Japan from the 17th to 19th centuries. Brass lock with ball trigger, and brass lockplate and hammer. Pan has pivoting cover. Browned barrel. Case-hardened lock. Made by Miroku. Imported by Dixie Gun Works.
Price: Dixie MM0005 ....$1,100.00

DIXIE J.P. MURRAY ARTILLERY CARBINE
Caliber: .58. **Barrel:** 23.5 in. **Weight:** 8 lbs. **Length:** 39.5 in. **Stock:** European walnut. **Sights:** Blade front, fixed notch rear. **Features:** Percussion musket-cap ignition. Reproduction of the original Confederate carbine. Lock marked "J.P. Murray, Columbus, Georgia." Blued barrel. Made Euro Arms. Imported by Dixie Gun Works and others.
Price: Dixie, PRO173 . ...$1,100.00

DIXIE PEDERSOLI 1857 MAUSER RIFLE
Caliber: .54. **Barrel:** 39.75 in. **Weight:** 9.5 lbs. **Length:** 52 in. overall. **Stock:** European walnut. **Sights:** Blade front, rear steel adjustable for windage and elevation. **Features:** Percussion musket-cap ignition. Color case-hardened lockplate marked "Konigi.Wurt Fabrik." Armory bright steel barrel. Made by Pedersoli. Imported by Dixie Gun Works.
Price: Dixie PR1330 ....$1,595.00

DIXIE PENNSYLVANIA RIFLE
Caliber: .45 and .50. **Barrel:** 41.5 in. octagonal, .45/1:48, .50/1:56 in. twist. **Weight:** 8.5, 8.75 lbs. **Length:** 56 in. overall. **Stock:** European walnut, full-length stock. **Sights:** Notch rear, blade front. **Features:** Flintlock or percussion, brass patchbox, double-set triggers. Also available as kit guns for both calibers and ignition systems. Made by Pedersoli. Imported by Dixie Gun Works.
Price: Percussion, .45, PF1070................... $995.00
Price: Flint, .45, PF1060 .... $995.00
Price: Percussion, .50, PR3205 .... $995.00
Price: Flint, .45, PR3200 .... $995.00

DIXIE POTSDAM 1809 PRUSSIAN MUSKET
Caliber: .75 **Barrel:** 41.2 in. round, smoothbore. **Weight:** 9 lbs. **Length:** 56 in. **Stock:** European walnut, fullstock. **Sights:** Brass lung on upper barrelband. **Features:** Flintlock using one-inch flint. Steel parts all polished armory bright, brass furniture. Lock marked "Potsdam over G.S." Made by Pedersoli. Imported by Dixie Gun Works.
Price: Dixie FR3175 .... $1,495.00

DIXIE SHARPS NEW MODEL 1859 MILITARY RIFLE AND CARBINE
Caliber: .54. **Barrel:** 30 in., 6-groove, 1:48 in. twist. **Weight:** 9 lbs. **Length:** 45.5 in. overall. **Stock:** Oiled walnut. **Sights:** Blade front, ladder-style rear. **Features:** Blued barrel, color case-hardened barrelbands, receiver, hammer, nose cap, lever, patchbox cover and buttplate. Introduced 1995. Rifle made by Armi Sport (Chiappa) and carbine by Pedersoli. Rifle imported from Italy by Dixie Gun Works and carbine by Dixie and Cabela's.
Price: Rifle PR0862 .... $1,095.00
Price: Carbine (22-in. barrel, 39-1/4 in. long, 8 lbs.) PR0982 $1,400.00

DIXIE SMITH CARBINE
Caliber: .50. **Barrel:** 21.5 in., 3-groove, 1:66 in. twist. **Weight:** 7.75 lbs. **Length:** 39 in. **Stock:** Oiled walnut. **Sights:** Blade front, ladder-style rear. **Features:** Hinged breech that drops barrel to allow loading of pre-loaded brass or plastic cartridges fired by a musket cap. Blued barrel, color case-hardened receiver and hammer. Cavalry Carbine has saddle bar and ring, Artillery Carbine has sling swivel on buttstock and barrelband. Rifle made by Pietta. Imported from Italy by Dixie Gun Works.
Price: Dixie Cavalry Carbine PR0220 .... $925.00

DIXIE TRYON RIFLE
Caliber: .50. **Barrel:** 32 in. octagonal, 1:48 in. twist. **Weight:** 9.5 lbs. **Length:** 49 in. overall. **Stock:** European walnut, halfstock. **Sights:** Elevation-adjustable rear with stair-step notches, blade front. **Features:** Percussion, brass patchbox, double-set triggers, two barrel keys. Made by Pedersoli. Imported by Dixie Gun Works.
Price: Percussion, PR0860 .... $995.00
Price: Percussion, kit, PR0255 .... $890.00

DIXIE ZOUAVE RIFLE
Caliber: .58. **Barrel:** 33 in. **Weight:** 9.5 lbs. **Length:** 49 in. **Stock:** European walnut. **Sights:** Blade front, three-leaf military rear. **Features:** Percussion musket-cap ignition. Case-hardened lock and blued barrel. One-piece solid barrel and bolster. Made in Italy by Armi Sport. Imported by Dixie Gun Works, others.
Price: PF0340 ....$950.00

ENFIELD MUSKETOON P1861
Caliber: .58. **Barrel:** 33 in. **Weight:** 9 lbs. **Length:** 35 in. overall. **Stock:** European walnut. **Sights:** Blade front, flip-up rear with elevator marked to 700 yards. **Features:** Reproduction of the original cavalry version of the Enfield rifle. Percussion musket-cap ignition. Blued barrel with steel barrelbands, brass furniture. Case-hardened lock. Euro Arms version marked London Armory with crown. Pedersoli version has Birmingham stamp on stock and Enfield and Crown on lockplate. Made by Euro Arms, Pedersoli. Imported by Cabela's, Dixie

Prices given are believed to be accurate at time of publication however, many factors affect retail pricing so exact prices are not possible.

BLACKPOWDER MUSKETS & RIFLES

Gun Works and others.
Price: Cabelas, Pedersoli...............................**$900.00**
Price: Dixie Euro Arms PR0343 ....**$1,050.00**

ENFIELD THREE-BAND P1853 RIFLE
Caliber: .58. **Barrel:** 39 in. **Weight:** 10.25 lbs. **Length:** 52 in. overall. **Stock:** European walnut. **Sights:** Blade front, flip-up rear with elevator marked to 800 yards. **Features:** Reproduction of the original three-band rifle. Percussion musket-cap ignition. Blued barrel with steel barrelbands, brass furniture. Case-hardened lock. Lockplate marked "London Armory Co. and Crown." Made by Euro Arms, Armi Sport (Chiappa), Pedersoli. Imported by Cabela's, Dixie Gun Works and others.
Price: Cabela's, Pedersoli..............................**$930.00**
Price: Dixie Armi Sport/Chiappa PR1130 ....**$858.00**
Price: Dixie Euro Arms PR0340 ....**$1,200.00**

ENFIELD TWO-BAND P1858 RIFLE
Caliber: .58. **Barrel:** 24 in. **Weight:** 7.75 lbs. **Length:** 43.25 in. overall. **Stock:** European walnut. **Sights:** Blade front, flip-up rear with elevator marked to 1,000 yards. **Features:** Reproduction of the original two-band rifle. Percussion musket-cap ignition. Blued barrel with steel barrelbands, brass furniture. Case-hardened lock. Lockplate marked "1858 Enfield and Crown." Made by Euro Arms, Pedersoli, Chiappa. Imported by Cabela's, Dixie Gun Works and others.
Price: Cabela's, Pedersoli..............................**$930.00**
Price: Dixie Euro Arms PR1135 ....**$825.00**
Price: Dixie Chiappa 150th Aniv. Mod. PR0106 ......**$750.00**

KNIGHT BIGHORN
Caliber: .50. **Barrel:** 26 in., 1:28 in. twist. **Weight:** 7 lbs. 3 oz. **Length:** 44.5 in. overall. **Stock:** G2 straight or thumbhole, Carbon Knight straight or thumbhole or black composite thumbhole with recoil pad, sling swivel studs. **Ramrod:** Carbon core with solid brass extendable jag. **Sights:** Fully adjustable metallic fiber optic. **Features:** Uses four different ignition systems (included): #11 nipple, musket nipple, bare 208 shotgun primer and 209 Extreme shotgun primer system (Extreme weatherproof full plastic jacket system); vented breech plug, striker fired with one-piece removable hammer assembly. With recommended loads, guaranteed to have 4-inch, three-shot groups at 200 yards. Also available as Western gun with exposed ignition. Made in U.S. by Knight Rifles.
Price: Standard stock **$463.49**
Price: With maximum available options, scope.........**$774.99**

KNIGHT DISC EXTREME
Caliber: .50, .52. **Barrel:** 26 in., fluted stainless, 1:28 in. twist. **Weight:** 7 lbs. 14 oz. to 8 lbs. **Length:** 45 in. overall. **Stock:** Carbon Knight straight or thumbhole with blued or SS; G2 thumbhole; left-handed Nutmeg thumbhole. **Ramrod:** Solid brass extendable jag. **Sights:** Fully adjustable metallic fiber optics. **Features:** Bolt-action rifle, full plastic jacket ignition system, #11 nipple, musket nipple, bare 208 shotgun primer. With recommended loads, guaranteed to have 4-inch, three-shot groups at 200 yards. Also available as Western gun with exposed ignition. Made in U.S. by Knight Rifles.
Price: Standard **$530.99**
Price: With maximum available options, scope.........**$879.98**

KNIGHT HPX
Caliber: .50, .45-70 Govt. or .444 Marlin. **Barrel:** 26 in. as muzzleloader, 24 in. as centerfire. **Length:** 43.5 in./muzzleloader, 39.5 in./centerfire. Ignition: Full Plastic Jacket or bare 209 primer. **Stock:** Shadow gray laminated wood, G2 Camo or composite straight. **Weight:** 8 lbs./muzzleloader, 7.8 lbs./cartridge. **Features:** Break-open rifle with stainless steel action, quick-release trigger assembly, vented breech plug and stainless steel Dyna-coated barrel. **Ramrod:** Carbon core with solid brass extendable jag. **Sights:** Williams fiber-optic sights. Finish: Stainless steel. With recommended loads, guaranteed to have 4-inch, three-shot groups at 200 yards. Made in U.S. by Knight Rifles.
Price: : To be Introduced 2015-16, about....................**$900**

KNIGHT LITTLEHORN
Caliber: .50. **Barrel:** 22 in., 1:28 in. twist. **Weight:** 6.7 lbs. **Length:** 39 in. overall. **Stock:** 12.5-in. length of pull, G2 straight or pink Realtree AP HD. **Ramrod:** Carbon core with solid brass extendable jag. **Sights:** Fully adjustable Williams fiber optic. **Features:** Uses four different ignition systems (included): Full Plastic Jacket, #11 nipple, musket nipple or bare 209 shotgun primer; vented breech plug, striker-fired

with one-piece removable hammer assembly. Finish: Stainless steel. With recommended loads, guaranteed to have 4-inch, three-shot groups at 200 yards. Also available as Western gun with exposed ignition. Made in U.S. by Knight Rifles.
Price: Standard **$499.99**
Price: With maximum available options, scope.............**$759.99**

KNIGHT MOUNTAINEER FOREST GREEN
Caliber: .45, .50, .52. **Barrel:** 27 in. fluted stainless steel, free floated. **Weight:** 8 lbs. (thumbhole stock), 8.3 lbs. (straight stock). **Length:** 45.5 inches. **Sights:** Fully adjustable metallic fiber optic. **Features:** Bolt-action rifle, adjustable match-grade trigger, aluminum ramrod with carbon core, solid brass extendable jag, vented breech plug. Ignition: Full plastic jacket, #11 nipple, musket nipple, bare 208 shotgun primer. With recommended loads, guaranteed to have 4-inch, three-shot groups at 200 yards. Also available as Western gun with exposed ignition. Made in U.S. by Knight Rifles.
Price: Standard **$764.99**
Price: Maximum available options, scope...............**$1,119.99**

KNIGHT ULTRA-LITE
Caliber: .50. **Barrel:** 24 in. Ignition: 209 Primer with Full Plastic Jacket, musket cap or #11 nipple, bare 208 shotgun primer; vented breech plug. **Stock:** Black, tan or olive green Kevlar spider web. **Weight:** 6 lbs. **Features:** Bolt-action rifle. **Ramrod:** Carbon core with solid brass extendable jag. **Sights:** With or without Williams fiber-optic sights, drilled and tapped for scope mounts. Finish: Stainless steel. With recommended loads, guaranteed to have 4-inch, three-shot groups at 200 yards. Also available as Western version with exposed ignition. Made in U.S. by Knight Rifles.
Price: Standard **$899.99**
Price: Maximum available options, scope................**$1,149.99**

KNIGHT VISION
Caliber: .50. **Barrel:** 24 in. **Length:** 44 in. Ignition: Full Plastic Jacket. **Stock:** Black composite. **Weight:** 7.9 lbs. **Features:** Break-open rifle with carbon-steel barrel and all new machined steel action. With recommended loads, guaranteed to have 4-inch, three-shot groups at 200 yards. **Ramrod:** Carbon core with solid brass extendable jag. **Sights:** Weaver sight bases attached and Williams fiber-optic sights provided. Finish: Blued steel. Made in U.S. by Knight Rifles.
Price: To be determined, about **$450.00**

KNIGHT WOLVERINE
Caliber: .50. **Barrel:** 22 in. stainless steel, 1:28 in. twist. **Weight:** 6.9 lbs. **Length:** 40.5 overall. **Stock:** Realtree Hardwoods straight, CarbonKnight straight. **Ramrod:** Carbon core with solid brass extendable jag. **Sights:** Fully adjustable Williams fiber optic. **Features:** Ignition systems (included): #11 nipple, musket nipple, bare 208 shotgun primer; vented breech plug, striker fired with one-piece removable hammer assembly. Finish: Stainless steel. With recommended loads, guaranteed to have 4-inch, three-shot groups at 200 yards. Also available as Western gun with exposed ignition. Made in U.S. by Knight Rifles.
Price: **$499.99**
Price: Thumbhole stock **$479.99**

LHR REDEMPTION RIFLE
Caliber: .50. **Barrel:** 24 or 20 in. nitride finished, tapered barrel. **Weight:** 6.75 lbs. or 6.25 lbs. **Length:** 44 in. or 40 in. **Stock:** Walnut, black synthetic, G2-Vista Camo. Finish: Armornite nitride. **Features:** Break-open action, sliding hammerless cocking mechanism, optional pellet or loose powder, easy removable breech plugs retained by external collar, aluminum frame with steel mono-block to retain barrel, recoil pad. **Sights:** Williams fiber-optic sights furnished, drilled and tapped for scope. A similar model has five 21-in. interchangeable rifle barrels,

Prices given are believed to be accurate at time of publication however, many factors affect retail pricing so exact prices are not possible.

70TH EDITION, 2016 ⊕ **519**

a 20-gauge shotgun barrel and a 20-gauge rifled-slug barrel. Made in the U.S. by LHR Sporting Arms. Available through dealers or you may order from the factory.

Price: .50 ca. 24-in. barrel, black synthetic stock **$620.00**
Price: .50 cal. 24-in. barrel, G2 camo stock **$670.00**
Price: .50 cal. 24-in. barrel, walnut stock **$820.00**
Price: .50 ca. 20-in. barrel, black synthetic stock **$620.00**
Price: .50 cal. 20-in. barrel, G2 camo stock **$670.00**
Price: .50 cal. 20-in. barrel, walnut stock **$820.00**

LYMAN DEERSTALKER RIFLE

Caliber: .50, .54. **Barrel:** 24 in., octagonal, 1:48 in. rifling. **Weight:** 10.4 lbs. **Stock:** Walnut with black rubber buttpad. **Sights:** Lyman #37MA beaded front, fully adjustable fold-down Lyman #16A rear. **Features:** Percussion and flintlock ignition. Stock has less drop for quick sighting. All metal parts are blackened, with color case-hardened lock, single trigger. Comes with sling and swivels. Available in flint or percussion. Introduced 1990. From Lyman.
Price: 6033140 .50-cal. percussion **$565.00**
Price: 6033141 .54-cal. percussion **$565.00**
Price: 6033185 .50-cal. percussion stainless **$669.95**
Price: 6033146 .50-cal. flintlock blue **$614.95**
Price: 6033147 .54-cal. flintlock blue.................................... **$614.95**
Price: 6033148 .50-cal. flintlock left hand.......................... **$654.95**

LYMAN GREAT PLAINS RIFLE

Caliber: .50, .54. **Barrel:** 32 in., 1:60in. twist. **Weight:** 11.6 lbs. **Stock:** Walnut. **Sights:** Steel blade front, buckhorn rear adjustable for windage and elevation, and fixed notch primitive sight included. **Features:** Percussion or flint ignition. Blued steel furniture. Stainless steel nipple. Coil spring lock, Hawken-style triggerguard and double-set triggers. Round thimbles recessed and sweated into rib. Steel wedge plates and toe plate. Introduced 1979. From Lyman.
Price: 6031102/3 .50-cal./.54-cal percussion.......................... **$769.95**
Price: 6031105/6 .50-cal./.54-cal flintlock................................ **$829.95**
Price: 6031125/6 .50-ca./.54-cal left-hand percussion **$809.95**
Price: 6031137 .50-cal. left-hand flintlock **$670.00**
Price: 6031111/2 .50/.54-cal. percussion kit......................... **$625.00**
Price: 6031114/5 .50/.54-cal. flintlock kit............................ **$675.00**

LYMAN GREAT PLAINS HUNTER MODEL

Similar to Great Plains model except 1:32 in. twist, shallow-groove barrel and comes drilled and tapped for Lyman 57GPR peep sight.
Price: 6031120/1 .50-cal./.54-cal percussion.......................... **$769.95**
Price: 6031148/9 .50-cal./.54-cal flintlock **$824.95**
Price: 6031142 .50-cal left-hand percussion.......................... **$769.95**

LYMAN MUSTANG BREAKAWAY 209

Caliber: .50. **Barrel:** 26 in., 1:28 twist. **Ignition:** 209 primer. **Weight:** 7 lbs. **Stock:** Ultra Grade wood finish, checkered, rubber recoil pad. **Ramrod:** Solid aluminum. **Sights:** Fiber-optic front and rear. **Features:** Hammerless break-open action for 209 shotshell primer and up to 150-grain charges. Imported by Lyman.
Price: 6032113.. **$579.95**

LYMAN TRADE RIFLE

Caliber: .50, .54. **Barrel:** 28 in. octagon, 1:48 in. twist. **Weight:** 10.8 lbs. **Length:** 45 in. overall. **Stock:** European walnut. **Sights:** Blade front, open rear adjustable for windage, or optional fixed sights. **Features:**

Fast-twist rifling for conical bullets. Polished brass furniture with blue steel parts, stainless steel nipple. Hook breech, single trigger, coil spring percussion lock. Steel barrel rib and ramrod ferrules. Introduced 1980. From Lyman.

Price: 6032125/6 .50-cal./.54-cal. percussion........................ **$565.00**
Price: 6032129/30 .50-cal,/.54-cal. flintlock **$619.00**

PEDERSOLI 1776 CHARLEVILLE MUSKET

Caliber: .69. **Barrel:** 44.75 in. round, smoothbore. **Weight:** 10.5 lbs. **Length:** 60 in. **Stock:** European walnut, fullstock. **Sights:** Steel stud on upper barrelband. **Features:** Flintlock using one-inch flint. Steel parts all polished armory bright, brass furniture. Lock marked Charleville. Made by Pedersoli. Imported by Cabela's, Dixie Gun Works, others.
Price: Dixie Complete gun FR1045.. **$1,425.00**
Price: Dixie Kit Gun FK3440 .... **$1,140.00**
Price: Dixie French Model 1777 Complete gun FR0930 ...... **$1,450.00**
Price: Dixie French Currige An IX Charleville FR0157 .... **$1,450.00**

PEDERSOLI 1795 SPRINGFIELD MUSKET

Caliber: .69. **Barrel:** 44.75 in., round, smoothbore. **Weight:** 10.5 lbs. **Length:** 57.25 in. **Stock:** European walnut, fullstock. **Sights:** Brass stud on upper barrelband. **Features:** Flintlock using one-inch flint. Steel parts all polished armory bright, brass furniture. Lock marked US Springfield. Made by Pedersoli. Imported by Cabela's, Dixie Gun Works, others.
Price: Dixie Complete gun FR3210.. **$1,495.00**

PEDERSOLI 1841 MISSISSIPPI RIFLE

Caliber: .58. **Barrel:** 33 inches. **Weight:** 9.5 lbs. **Length:** 48.75 in. overall. **Stock:** European walnut. **Sights:** Blade front, notched rear. **Features:** Percussion musket-cap ignition. Reproduction of the original one-band rifle with large brass patchbox. Color case-hardened lockplate with browned barrel. Made by Pedersoli. Imported by Cabela's.
Price: Cabela's.. **$850.00**

PEDERSOLI 1861 SPRINGFIELD RIFLE

Caliber: .58. **Barrel:** 40 inches. **Weight:** 10 lbs. **Length:** 55.5 in. overall. **Stock:** European walnut. **Sights:** Blade front, three-leaf military rear. **Features:** Reproduction of the original three-band rifle. Percussion musket-cap ignition. Lockplate marked 1861 with eagle and U.S. Springfield. Armory bright steel. Made by Armi Sport/Chiappa, Pedersoli. Imported by Cabela's, Dixie Gun Works, others.
Price: Cabela's, Pedersoli.. **$980.00**
Price: Dixie Armi Sport/Chiappa PR3180 .... **$1,150.00**

PEDERSOLI BRISTLEN MORGES AND WAADTLANDER TARGET RIFLES

Caliber: .44, .45. **Barrel:** 29.5 in. tapered octagonal, hooked breech. **Weight:** 15.5 lbs. **Length:** 48.5 in. overall. **Stock:** European walnut, halfstock with hooked buttplate and detachable palm rest. **Sights:** Creedmoor rear on Morges, Swiss Diopter on Waadtlander, hooded front sight notch. **Features:** Percussion back-action lock, double set, double-phase triggers, one barrel key, muzzle protector. Specialized bullet molds for each gun. Made by Pedersoli. Imported by Dixie Gun Works.
Price: Percussion, .44 Bristlen Morges PR0165 .... **$2,995.00**
Price: Percussion, .45 Waadtlander PR0183 .... **$2,995.00**

PEDERSOLI COOK & BROTHER CONFEDERATE CARBINE / ARTILLERY/RIFLE

Caliber: .58. **Barrel:** : 24/33/39 inches. **Weight:** 7.5/8.4/8.6 lbs. **Length:** 40.5/48/54.5 in. **Stock:** Select oil-finished walnut. **Features:** Percussion musket-cap ignition. Color case-hardened lock, browned barrel. Buttplate, triggerguard, barrelbands, sling swivels and nose cap of polished brass. Lock marked with stars and bars flag on tail and Athens, Georgia. Made by Pedersoli. Imported by Dixie Gun Works, others.
Price: Dixie Carbine PR0830 .... **$1,100.00**
Price: Artillery/Rifle announced 2015 price to be determined
Price: Dixie Artillery Carbine PR0223 .... **$925.00**

Prices given are believed to be accurate at time of publication however, many factors affect retail pricing so exact prices are not possible.

BLACKPOWDER MUSKETS & RIFLES

PEDERSOLI COUNTRY HUNTER
Caliber: .50. **Barrel:** 26 in. octagonal. **Weight:** 6 lbs. **Length:** 41.75 in. overall. **Stock:** European walnut, halfstock. **Sights:** Rear notch, blade front. **Features:** Percussion, one barrel key. Made by Pedersoli. Imported by Dixie Gun Works.
Price: Percussion, .50 PR3155 .... $595.00

PEDERSOLI KENTUCKY RIFLE
Caliber: .32, .45 and .50. **Barrel:** 35.5 in. octagonal. **Weight:** 7.5 (.50 cal.) to 7.75 lbs. (.32 cal.) **Length:** 51 in. overall. **Stock:** European walnut, full-length stock. **Sights:** Notch rear, blade front. **Features:** Flintlock or percussion, brass patchbox, double-set triggers. Also available as kit guns for all calibers and ignition systems. Made by Pedersoli. Imported by Dixie Gun Works.
Price: Percussion, .32, PR3115 .... $695.00
Price: Flint, .32, FR3100 .... $750.00
Price: Percussion, .45, FR3120 .... $695.00
Price: Flint, .45, FR3105 .... $750.00
Price: Percussion, .50, FR3125 .... $695.00
Price: Flint, .50, FR3110 .... $750.00

PEDERSOLI KODIAK DOUBLE RIFLES AND COMBINATION GUN
Caliber: .50, .54 and .58 **Barrel:** 28.5 in.; 1:24/1:24/1:48 in. twist. **Weight:** 11.25/10.75/10 lbs. **Stock:** Straight grip European walnut. **Sights:** Two adjustable rear, steel ramp with brass bead front. **Features:** Percussion ignition, double triggers, sling swivels. A .72-caliber express rifle and a .50-caliber/12-gauge shotgun combination gun are also available. Blued steel furniture. Stainless steel nipple. Made by Pedersoli. Imported by Dixie Gun Works and some models by Cabela's and others.
Price: Rifle 50X50 PR0970 .... $1,495.00
Price: Rifle 54X54 PR0975 .... $1,495.00
Price: Rifle 58X58 PR0980 .... $1,495.00
Price: Combo 50X12 gauge PR0990 .... $1,350.00
Price: Express Rifle .72 caliber PR0916 .... $1,525.00

PEDERSOLI MORTIMER RIFLE & SHOTGUN
Caliber: .54, 12 gauge. **Barrel:** 36 in., 1:66 in. twist, and cylinder bore. **Weight:** 10 lbs. rifle, 9 lbs. shotgun. **Length:** 52.25 in. **Stock:** Halfstock walnut. **Sights:** Blued steel rear with flip-up leaf, blade front. **Features:** Percussion and flint ignition. Blued steel furniture. Single trigger. Lock with hammer safety and "waterproof pan" marked Mortimer. A percussion .45-caliber target version of this gun is available with a peep sight on the wrist, and a percussion shotgun version is also offered. Made by Pedersoli. Imported by Dixie.
Price: Flint Rifle, FR0151 .... $1,475.00
Price: Flint Shotgun FS0155 .... $1,425.00
Price: Percussion .45-cal. Whitworth rifle, PR0175$ 1,550.00
Price: Percussion Shotgun PS3160 .... $1,275.00

PEDERSOLI ROCKY MOUNTAIN & MISSOURI RIVER HAWKEN RIFLES
Caliber: .54 (Rocky Mountain), .45 and .50 in Missouri River. **Barrel:** 34.75 in. octagonal with hooked breech; Rocky Mountain 1:65 in. twist; Missouri River 1:47 twist in .45 cal., and 1:24 twist in .50 cal. **Weight:** 10 lbs. **Length:** 52 in. overall. **Stock:** Maple or walnut, halfstock. **Sights:** Rear buckhorn with push elevator, silver blade front. **Features:** Percussion, brass furniture, double triggers, two barrel keys. Made by Pedersoli. Imported by Dixie Gun Works, others.
Price: Rocky Mountain, Maple PR3430 .... $1,325.00
Price: Rocky Mountain, Walnut PR3435 .... $1,125.00
Price: Missouri River, .50 Walnut PR3415 .... $1,250.00
Price: Missouri River, .50 Maple PR3410 .... $1,475.00
Price: Missouri River, .45 Walnut PR3405 .... $1,250.00
Price: Missouri River, .45 Maple PR3080 .... $1,475.00

PEDERSOLI ZOUAVE RIFLE
Caliber: .58 percussion. **Barrel:** 33 inches. **Weight:** 9.5 lbs. **Length:** 49 inches. **Stock:** European walnut. **Sights:** Blade front, three-leaf military rear. **Features:** Percussion musket-cap ignition. One-piece solid barrel and bolster. Brass-plated patchbox. Made in Italy by Pedersoli. Imported by Cabela's, others.
Price: $930.00

RICHMOND 1861 RIFLE
Caliber: .58. **Barrel:** 40 inches. **Weight:** 9.5 lbs. **Length:** 55.5 in. overall. **Stock:** European walnut. **Sights:** Blade front, three-leaf military rear.

Features: Reproduction of the original three-band rifle. Percussion musket-cap ignition. Lock marked C. S. Richmond, Virginia. Armory bright. Made by Pedersoli, Euro Arms. Imported by Cabela's, Dixie Gun Works and others.
Price: Cabela's $950.00
Price: From Dixie Gun Works, Made by Euro Arms
PR0846 .... $1,150.00

REMINGTON MODEL 700 ULTIMATE MUZZLELOADER
Caliber: .50 percussion. **Barrel:** 26 in., 1:26-in twist, satin stainless steel, fluted. **Length:** 47 in. **Stock:** Bell & Carlson black synthetic or laminated wood. **Sights:** None on synthetic stocked model, Williams peep and blade front on laminated-wood model. **Ramrod:** Stainless steel. **Weight:** 8.5 lbs. **Features:** Remington single shot Model 700 bolt action, Reprimable cartridge-case ignition using Remington Magnum Large Rifle Primer., sling studs.
Price: 86960 .50-cal. synthetic black, no sights $999.00
Price: 86950 . 50-caliber laminated wood,
Willliams peep sights $949.00

THOMPSON/CENTER ENCORE PRO HUNTER
Caliber: .50 as muzzleloading barrel. **Barrel:** 26 in., Weather Shield with relieved muzzle on muzzleloader; interchangeable with 14 centerfire calibers. **Weight:** 7 lbs. **Length:** 40.5 in. overall. **Stock:** Interchangeable American walnut butt and forend, black composite, FlexTech recoil-reducing camo stock as thumbhole or straight, rubber over-molded stock and fore-end. **Ramrod:** Solid aluminum. **Sights:** TruGlo fiber optic front and rear. **Features:** Blue or stainless steel. Uses the frame of the Encore centerfire pistol; break-open design using triggerguard spur; stainless steel universal breech plug; uses #209 shotshell primers. Made in U.S. by Thompson/Center Arms.
Price: .50-cal Stainless/Black weathershield $599.99
Price: .50-cal Stainless/Realtree, weathershield $699.99
Price: .50-cal Stainless/Realtree AP,weathershield, scope,
case $1,099.99
Price: .50-cal Stainless/Black, weathershield, scope,
case $999.99

THOMPSON/CENTER IMPACT MUZZLELOADING RIFLE
Caliber: .50-caliber. **Barrel:** 26 in., 1:28 twist, Weather Shield finish. **Weight:** 6.5 lbs. **Length:** 41.5 in. **Stock:** Straight Realtree Hardwoods HD or black composite. **Features:** Sliding-hood, break-open action, #209 primer ignition, removable breech plug, synthetic stock adjustable from 12.5 to 13.5 in., adjustable fiber-optic sights, aluminum ramrod, camo, QLA relieved muzzle system.
Price: .50-cal Stainless/Realtree Hardwoods/,
Weather Shield, ... $329.99
Price: .50-cal Blued/Black/scope, case $369.99

THOMPSON/CENTER TRIUMPH MUZZLELOADER
Caliber: .50. **Barrel:** 28 in. Weather Shield coated. **Weight:** 6.5 lbs. **Stock:** FlexTech recoil-reducing. Black composite or Realtree AP HD camo straight, rubber over-molded stock and fore-end. **Sights:** Fiber optic. **Ramrod:** Solid aluminum. **Features:** Break-open action. Quick Detachable Speed Breech XT plug, #209 shotshell primer ignition, easy loading QLA relieved muzzle, Cabela's, Bass Pro. Made in U.S. by Thompson/Center Arms.
Price: .... $450.00 to $650.00

Prices given are believed to be accurate at time of publication however, many factors affect retail pricing so exact prices are not possible.

70TH EDITION, 2016 ◆ 521

THOMPSON/CENTER TRIUMPH BONE COLLECTOR
Similar to the Triumph but with added FlexTech technology and Energy Burners to a shorter stock. Also added is Thompson/Center's premium fluted barrel with Weather Shield and their patented Power Rod.
Price: .50-cal Synthetix/Realtree AP, fib. opt.... .... **$649.99**
Price: .50-cal Synthetic/scope/case................................... **$899.99**

TRADITIONS BUCKSTALKER
Caliber: .50. **Barrel:** 24 in., Cerakote finished, Accelerator Breech Plug. **Weight:** 6 lbs. **Length:** 40 in. **Stock:** Synthetic, G2 Vista camo or black. **Sights:** Fiber-optic rear. **Features:** Break-open action, matte-finished action and barrel. Ramrod: Solid aluminum.
Price: R72003540 .50-cal. Synthetic stock /blued............... **$219.00**
Price: R72103540 .50-cal. Synthetic stock/Cerakote **$254.00**
Price: R72103547 .50-cal. Synthetic stock/G2-Vista **$299.00**
Price: R5-72003540 .50-cal. Synthetic stock/blued, scope.... **$294.00**
Price: R5-72103547 .50-cal. Synthetic stock/Cerakote, scope. **$369.00**
Price: RY7223540 .50-cal. 13-in. pull, synthetic stock/ blued... **$219.00**

TRADITIONS CROCKETT RIFLE
Caliber: .32. **Barrel:** 32 in., 1:48 in. twist. **Weight:** 6.75 lbs. **Length:** 49 in. overall. **Stock:** Beech, inletted toe plate. **Sights:** Blade front, fixed rear. **Features:** Set triggers, hardwood halfstock, brass furniture, color case-hardened lock. Percussion. From Traditions.
Price: R26128101 .32-cal. Percussion, finished **$519.00**
Price: RK52628100 .32-cal. Kit, percussion, hardwood, Armory bright, unfinished brass **$438.00**

TRADITIONS DEERHUNTER RIFLE SERIES
Caliber: .50. **Barrel:** 24 in., Cerakote finish, octagonal, 15/16 in. flats, 1:48 in. twist. **Weight:** 6 lbs. **Length:** 40 in. overall. **Stock:** Stained hardwood or All-Weather composite with rubber buttpad, sling swivels. Ramrod: Synthetic polymer. **Sights:** Fiber Optic blade front, adjustable rear fiber optics, offset hammer spur. **Features:** Flint or percussion with color case-hardened lock. Hooked breech, oversized triggerguard, blackened furniture, PVC ramrod. Drilled and tapped for scope mounting. Imported by Traditions, Inc.
Price: R3200801 .50-cal. Flintlock, hardwood, fib.opt **$384.00**
Price: R2390801 .50-cal. Flintlock, left-hand, hardwood/blued, fib.opt. **$419.00**

TRADITIONS EVOLUTION BOLT-ACTION BLACKPOWDER RIFLE
Caliber: .50 percussion. **Barrel:** 26 in., 1:28 in. twist, Cerakote finished barrel and action. **Length:** 39 in. **Sights:** Steel Williams fiber-optic sights. **Weight:** 7 to 7.25 lbs. **Length:** 45 in. overall. **Features:** Bolt action, cocking indicator, thumb safety, shipped with adaptors for No. 11 caps, musket caps and 209 shotgun primer ignition, sling swivels. Ramrod: Aluminum, sling studs. Available with exposed ignition as a Northwest Gun.
Price: R67113350 .50-cal. synthetic black, Cerakote **$314.00**
Price: R67113353 .50-cal. synthetic Realtree AP camo...... ...**$374.00**

TRADITIONS HAWKEN WOODSMAN RIFLE
Caliber: .50. **Barrel:** 28 in., blued, 15/16 in. flats. **Weight:** 7 lbs., 11 oz. **Length:** 44.5 in. overall. **Stock:** Walnut stained hardwood. **Sights:** Beaded blade front, hunting-style open rear adjustable for windage and elevation. **Features:** Brass patchbox and furniture. Double-set triggers. Flint or percussion. From Traditions.
Price: R2390801 .50-cal. Flintlock.. **$519.00**
Price: R24008 .50-cal. Percussion **$479.00**
Price: KRC5208 .50-cal. Kit, percussion, hardwood/ Armory bright, unfinished brass **$374.00**
Price: R3300801 ,50-cal. Percussion, .50 cal., hardwood/blued **$324.00**

Price: R3200850 .50-cal. Flintlock,synthetic/blued, fib.opt........ .... **$329.00**
Price: R3210850 .50-cal. Flintlock, Cerakote, fib.opt........ .... **$314.00**
Price: R3210856 .50-cal. Flintlock/Realtree X-Tra, fib.opt........ .... **$404.00**
Price: R3300850 .50-cal. Percussion,synthetic, blued,fib.opt **$269.00**
Price: RKC53008 .50-cal. Percussion Kit, hardwood, Armory bright, unfinished brass **$299.00**

TRADITIONS KENTUCKY RIFLE
Caliber: .50. **Barrel:** 33.5 in., 7/8 in. flats, 1:66 in. twist. **Weight:** 7 lbs. **Length:** 49 in. overall. **Stock:** Beech, inletted toe plate. **Sights:** Blade front, fixed rear. **Features:** Full-length, two-piece stock; brass furniture; color case-hardened lock. Flint or percussion. From Traditions, Bass Pro and others.
Price: R2010 .50-cal. Flintlock,1:66 twist **$489.00**
Price: R2020 .50-cal. Percussion, 1:66 twist......................... **$429.00**
Price: KRC52206 .50-cal. Kit, percussion, hardwood/Armory bright, unfinished brass **$319.00**

TRADITIONS PA PELLET FLINTLOCK
Caliber: .50. **Barrel:** 26 in., blued, 1:48 in. twist., Cerakote. **Weight:** 7 lbs. **Length:** 45 in. **Stock:** Hardwood, synthetic and synthetic break-up, sling swivels. **Sights:** Fiber optic. **Features:** New flintlock action, removable breech plug, available as left-hand model with hardwood stock.
Price: R3800501 .50-cal. Hardwood, blued, fib.opt **$469.00**
Price: R3890501 .50-cal. Hardwood, left-hand, blued **$489.00**
Price: R3800550 .50-cal. Synthetic/blued, fib. opt................ **$434.00**
Price: R3810556 .50-cal. Synthetic/Cerakote, fib. opt.......... **$479.00**
Price: R3840556 .50-cal. Synthetic/Realtree Xtra., fib.opt **$510.00**

TRADITIONS PENNSYLVANIA RIFLE
Caliber: .50. **Barrel:** 40.25 in., 7/8 in. flats, 1:66 in. twist, octagon. **Weight:** 9 lbs. **Length:** 57.5 in. overall. **Stock:** Walnut. **Sights:** Blade front, adjustable rear. **Features:** Single-piece walnut stock, brass patchbox and ornamentation. Double-set triggers. Flint or percussion. From Traditions.
Price: R2090 .50-cal. Flintlock, 1:66 twist **$824.00**
Price: R2100 .50-cal. Percussion, 1:66 twist **$794.00**

TRADITIONS PURSUIT ULTRALIGHT MUZZLELOADER
Caliber: .50. **Barrel:** 26 in., chromoly tapered, fluted barrel with premium Cerakote finish, Accelerator Breech Plug. **Weight:** 5.5 lbs. **Length:** 42 in. **Stock:** Rubber over-molded Soft Touch camouflage, straight and thumbhole stock options. **Sights:** 3-9x40 scope with medium rings and bases, mounted and bore sighted by a factory trained technician. **Features:** Break-open action, Williams fiber-optic sights.
Price: R741140 .50-cal. Synthetic/Cerakote fib.opt...... **$344.00**
Price: R7411415 .50-cal. Synthetic/Cerakote/ Mossy Oak Infinity, fib. opt...... .... **$404.00**
Price: R741140NS .50-cal. synthetic/black Steel, no sights **$329.00**
Price: R7411415NS .50-cal. Synthetic/Cerakote, no sights **$389.00**
Price: R741140 .50-cal.Synthetic/Cerakote, 3x9 scope **$404.00**
Price: R741148NS .50-cal. Synthetic/Cerakote, Buck Camo... 3x9 scope... .... **$464.00**
Price: R74446NS .50-cal. Synthetic/Realtree Xtra stock and barrel, 3x9 range-finding scope....................**$539.00**

TRADITIONS TENNESSEE RIFLE
Caliber: .50. **Barrel:** 24 in., octagon, 15/16 in. flats, 1:66 in. twist. **Weight:** 6 lbs. **Length:** 40.5 in. overall. **Stock:** Stained beech. **Sights:** Blade front, fixed rear. **Features:** One-piece stock has brass furniture, cheekpiece, double-set trigger, V-type mainspring. Flint or percussion. From Traditions.

Prices given are believed to be accurate at time of publication however, many factors affect retail pricing so exact prices are not possible.

Price: R2310 .50-cal. Flintlock/hardwood stock $569.00
Price: R2320 .50-cal. Percussion/hardwood stock $504.00

TRADITIONS TRACKER 209 IN-LINE RIFLE

Caliber: .50. **Barrel:** 24 in., blued or Cerakote, 1:28 in. twist. **Weight:** 6 lbs., 4 oz. **Length:** 43 in. **Stock:** Black synthetic. **Ramrod:** Synthetic, high-impact polymer. **Sights:** Lite Optic blade front, adjustable rear. **Features:** Striker-fired action, thumb safety, adjustable trigger, rubber buttpad, sling swivel studs. Takes 150 grains of Pyrodex pellets, one-piece musket cap and 209 ignition systems. Drilled and tapped for scope. Legal for use in Northwest. From Traditions.
Price: R44003470 .50-cal. Synthetic/blued $184.00

TRADITIONS VORTEK STRIKERFIRE

Caliber: .50 **Barrel:** 28 in., chromoly, tapered, fluted barrel. **Weight:** 6.25 lbs. **Length:** 44 in. **Stock:** Over-molded soft-touch straight stock, removable buttplate for in-stock storage. **Finish:** Premium Cerakote and Realtree Xtra. **Features:** Break-open action, sliding hammerless cocking mechanism, drop-out trigger assembly, speed load system, accelerator breech plug, recoil pad. **Sights:** Optional 3-9x40 muzzleloader scope.
Price: R561140NS .50-cal. Synthetic/black Hogue Over-mold, Cerakote barrel $493.00
Price: R561146NS .50-cal. Synthetic/Realtree Xtra camo, Cerakote barrel $583.00
Price: R29564446 .50-cal. Synthetic Realtree Xtra camo stock and barrel, 3X9 scope.. $649.00

TRADITIONS VORTEK STRIKERFIRE LDR

Caliber: .50 **Barrel:** 30 in., chromoly, tapered, fluted barrel. **Weight:** 6.8 lbs. **Length:** 46 in. **Stock:** Over-molded soft-touch straight stock, removable buttplate for in-stock storage. **Finish:** Premium Cerakote and Realtree Xtra. **Features:** Break-open action, sliding hammerless cocking mechanism, drop-out trigger assembly, speed load system, accelerator breech plug, recoil pad. **Sights:** Optional 3-9x40 muzzleloader scope.
Price: R591140NS .50-cal, Synthetic/black Hogue Over-mold, Cerakote barrel, no sights $524.00
Price: R591146NS .50-cal Synthetic/Realtree Xtra camo, Cerakote barrel $614.00
Price: R29-594446 .50-cak, Synthetic Realtree Xtra camo on stock and barrel, 3X9 scope Cerakote barrel.......................... $693.00

TRADITIONS VORTEK STRIKERFIRE LDR NORTHWEST MODEL

Caliber: .50. **Barrel:** 28 or 30 in. chromoly tapered, fluted barrel. **Weight:** 6.25 or 6.8 lbs. **Length:** 46 or 48 in. **Stock:** Synthetic black, over-molded soft-touch straight stock, removable buttplate for in-stock storage. **Finish:** Premium Cerakote. **Features:** Break-open action, sliding hammerless cocking mechanism, drop-out trigger assembly, speed load system, accelerator breech plug, recoil pad.

Sights: Williams fiber-optic sights.
Price: R561140WA/R591140WA .50-cal. Northwest, synthetic/black, 28/30-in. Cerakote barrel .... $520/$559.00
Price: R561146WA/R591146WA .50-cal. Northwest, synthetic/ Realtree Xtra Camo, soft touch 28/30-in. barrel . $589/$619.00

TRADITIONS VORTEK ULTRALIGHT

Caliber: .50. **Barrel:** 28 in., chromoly, tapered, fluted barrel. **Weight:** 6.25 lbs. **Length:** 44 in. **Stock:** Over-molded soft-touch straight stock. **Finish:** Premium Cerakote, Realtree AP, Reaper Buck. **Features:** Break-open action, hammer cocking mechanism, drop-out trigger assembly, speed load system, accelerator breech plug, recoil pad. **Sights:** Optional 3-9x40 muzzleloader scope.
Price: R461140 .50-cal. Synthetic/black Hogue Over-mold, Cerakote barrel, fib. opt. $464.00
Price: R461143 .50-cal Synthetic/Realtree AP camo Hogue, Cerakote barrel, fig. opt.... ....$534.00
Price: R481148 .50-cal Synthetic/Reaper Buck camo, Cerakote barrel, fib. opt...,...........................$534.00
Price: R461140NS .50-cal. Synthetic/black Hogue Over-mold, no sights $449.00
Price: R461143NS .50-cal. Synthetic/Realtree AP camo Hogue, Cerakote barrel, no sights.......................$519.00
Price: R461148NS .50-cal. Synthetic/Reaper Buck camo, Cerakote barrel, no sights.......................$519.00
Price: R20-464443 .50-cal. Synthetic/Realtree AP camo stock and barrel, 2x9 rangefinder scope.............$634.00
Price: R25-464448 .50.cal. Synthetic/Reaper Buck camo stock and barrel, 2x9 rangefinder scope.............$634.00

TRADITIONS VORTEK ULTRALIGHT LDR

Caliber: .50. **Barrel:** 30 in., chromoly tapered, fluted barrel. **Weight:** 6.8 lbs. **Length:** 46 in. **Stock:** Over-molded soft-touch straight stock. **Finish:** Premium Cerakote, Realtree AP, Reaper Buck. **Features:** Break-open action, hammer cocking mechanism, drop-out trigger assembly, speed load system, accelerator breech plug, recoil pad. **Sights:** Optional 3-9x40 muzzleloader scope.
Price: R491140NS .50-cal. Synthetic/black Hogue Over-mold, Cerakote barrel, no sights..................................$479.00
Price: R491148NS .50-cal/Synthetic/Reaper Buck camo Hogue, Cerakote barrel, no sights..$554.00

TRADITIONS VORTEK ULTRALIGHT NORTHWEST MAGNUM

Caliber: .50. **Barrel:** 28 or 30 in. chromoly tapered, fluted barrel. **Weight:** 6.25 or 6.8 lbs. **Length:** 44 or 46 in. **Stock:** Over-molded, soft-touch, straight or thumbhole stock. **Finish:** Premium Cerakote and Realtree AP. **Features:** Break-open action, hammer cocking mechanism, musket-cap ignition, drop-out trigger assembly, speed load system, accelerator breech plug, recoil pad. **Sights:** Williams fiber-optic sights.
Price: R461140WA .50-cal. Synthetic/black Hogue Over-mold, Cerakote barrel, fib. opt. $469.00
Price: R461146WA .50-cal. Synthetic/Realtree AP, Hogue, Cerakote barrel, fib. opt.................................$529.00
Price: R481146WA .50-cal. Synthetic Thumbhole/Realtree Xtra camo, Cerakote barrel, fib. opt. $529.00
Price: R491140WA (LDR) , Synthetic/Black, Hogue, 30-in. barrel, Cerakote barrel, fib. opt $499.00

BAKER CAVALRY SHOTGUN

Gauge: 20. **Barrels:** 11.25 inches. **Weight:** 5.75 pounds. **Length:** 27.5 in. overall. **Stock:** American walnut. **Sights:** Bead front. **Features:** Reproduction of shotguns carried by Confederate cavalry. Single non-selective trigger, back-action locks. No. 11 percussion musket-cap ignition. Blued barrel with steel furniture. Case-hardened lock. Pedersoli also makes a 12-gauge coach-length version of this back-action-lock shotgun with 20-inch barrels, and a full-length version in 10, 12 and 20 gauge. Made by Pedersoli. Imported by Cabela's and others.
Price: Cabela's, Pedersoli..**$899.99**

CABELA'S HOWDAH HUNTER 20-GAUGE PISTOL

Gauge: 20. **Barrels:** Cylinder bored, 11.25 in. **Weight:** 4.5 lbs. **Length:** 17.25 in. **Stock:** American walnut with checkered grip. **Sights:** Brass bead front sight. **Features:** Blued barrels, swamped barrel rib, engraved, color case-hardened locks and hammers, captive steel ramrod. Available with detachable shoulder stock, case, holster and mold. Made by Pedersoli. Imported by Cabela's, Dixie Gun Works, Taylor's and others.
Price: Cabela's 20-gauge **$699.99**

KNIGHT TK-2000 TURKEY SHOTGUN

Gauge: 12. **Ignition:** #209 primer with Full Plastic Jacket, musket cap or No. 11. Striker-fired with one-piece removable hammer assembly. **Barrel:** 26 inches. **Choke:** Extra-full and improved cylinder available. **Stock:** Realtree Xtra Green straight or thumbhole. **Weight:** 7.7 pounds. **Sights:** Williams fully adjustable rear, fiber-optic front. **Features:** Striker-fired action, receiver is drilled and tapped for scope, adjustable trigger, removable breech plug, double-safety system. Made in U.S. by Knight Rifles.
Price: Standard...**$559.99**
Price: Thumbhole stock.. .**$579.99**

PEDERSOLI KODIAK MK III RIFLE-SHOTGUN COMBINATION GUN

Gauge: .50 caliber/12 gauge. **Barrels:** 28.5 in. **Weight:** 10.75 lbs. **Stock:** Straight grip, European walnut. **Sights:** Two adjustable rear,

steel ramp with brass bead. **Features:** Percussion ignition, double triggers, sling swivels, 12-gauge cylinder bored barrel. Blued steel furniture. Stainless steel nipple. Made by Pedersoli. Imported by Dixie Gun Works, and some models by Cabela's and others.
Price: Combo 50X12 gauge PR0990 ....**$1,350.00**

PEDERSOLI MAGNUM PERCUSSION SHOTGUN & COACH GUN

Gauge: 10, 12, 20 **Barrel:** Chrome-lined blued barrels, 25.5 in. Imp. cyl. and Mod. **Weight:** 7.25, 7, 6.75 lbs. **Length:** 45 in. overall. **Stock:** Hand-checkered walnut, 14-in. pull. **Features:** Double triggers, light hand engraving, case-hardened locks, sling swivels. Made by Pedersoli. From Dixie Gun Works, others.
Price: 10-ga. PS1030 .... **$1,125.00**
Price: 10-ga. kit PS1040 .... **$975.00**
Price: 12-ga. PS0930... **$1,125.00**
Price: 12-ga. Kit PS0940 .... **$875.00**
Price: 12-ga. Coach gun, 25.5-in. barrels, CylXCyl. PS0914 .... **$1,050.00**
Price: 20-ga. PS0334... **$1,100.00**

PEDERSOLI MORTIMER SHOTGUN

Gauge: 12. **Barrel:** 36 in., 1:66 in., cylinder bore. **Weight:** 9 pounds. **Length:** 52.25 in. **Stock:** Halfstock walnut. **Sights:** Bead front. **Features:** Percussion and flint ignition. Blued steel furniture. Single trigger. Lock with hammer safety and "waterproof pan" on flintlock gun. Lock marked Mortimer. Rifle versions of this gun are also available. Made by Pedersoli. Imported by Dixie.
Price: Flint Shotgun FS0155.....................................**$1,425.00**
Price: Percussion Shotgun PS3160.....................................**$1,275.00**

PEDERSOLI OLD ENGLISH SHOTGUN

Gauge: 12 **Barrels:** Browned, 28.5 in. Cyl. and Mod. **Weight:** 7.5 lbs. **Length:** 45 in. overall. **Stock:** Hand-checkered American maple, cap box, 14-in. pull. **Features:** Double triggers, light hand engraving on lock, cap box and tang, swivel studs for sling attachment. Made by Pedersoli. From Dixie Gun Works, others.
Price: PR4090 .... **$1,750.00**

AIRFORCE TALON P

AIRFORCE TALON P
Caliber: .25, single shot. **Barrel:** 12". **Weight:** 3.5 lbs. **Length:** 24.2".
Features: Quick-detachable air tank with adjustable power. Lothar
Walther 12" match barrel, optional combo packages available, 3,000
psi fill pressure and automatic safety. Air tank capacity-231 cc. Can be
charged using a high pressure air supply form a scuba tank or hand
filled with an air pump. Muzzle velocity adjustable from 500 to 900 fps.
Price: **$435.50**

ASG CZ P-09 AIR PISTOL
Caliber: .177 pellets and steel/plastic BB. **Barrel:** Rifled. **Power:**
Blowback. **Grips:** Checkered black plastic. **Sights:** Fixed. **Features:**
Polymer frame replica of the real CZ 75 family of handguns. **Velocity:**
426 fps.
Price: **$104.95**

ASG CZ P-09 BLOWBACK AIR PISTOL
Caliber: .177 pellets and steel/plastic BB. **Barrel:** Rifled and threaded
for barrel extension. **Weight:** 24.76 oz. **Length:** 8.07 inches. **Sights:**
Fixed. **Features:** Nylon and metal construction replica of the real CZ
75 family of handguns. **Velocity:** 492 fps.
Price: **$99.95**

ASG CZ SP-01 NON-BLOWBACK AIR PISTOL
Caliber: .177. **Barrel:** Rifled and threaded for barrel extension. **Weight:**
24.76 oz. **Length:** 8.07 inches. **Sights:** Fiber optics front and rear.
Features: Replica based on the CZ- 75 series pistols. **Velocity:** 380 fps.
Price: . . . . **$**

ASG CZ 75 BLOWBACK AIR PISTOL
Caliber: .177. **Barrel:** Rifled and threaded for barrel extension. **Weight:**
29.92 oz. **Length:** 7.32 inches. **Power:** CO2/Air blowback cartridge
stored in grip. **Sights:** Fixed. **Features:** Full metal construction and a
replica design based on the CZ- 75 line. **Velocity:** 325 to 361 fps.
Price: **$159.95**

ASG CZ 75 P-07 DUTY NON-BLOWBACK AIR PISTOL
Caliber: BB. **Barrel:** Threaded for barrel extension. **Weight:** 28.92 oz.
Length: 7.32 inches. **Power:** CO2/Air cartridge stored in grip. **Sights:**
Fixed. **Features:** Full construction and a replica design based
on the CZ- 75 line. **Velocity:** 361 to 394 fps.
Price: **$59.95**

ASG CZ 75 P-07 DUTY

ASG CZ 75 P-07 DUTY BLOWBACK AIR PISTOL
Caliber: BB. **Barrel:** Threaded for barrel extension. Weight: 28.92 oz.
Length: 7.32 inches. **Power:** CO2/Air cartridge stored in grip. **Sights:**
Fixed. **Features:** Metal slide and a replica design based on the CZ-
75 line. Velocity: 361 to 394 fps.
Price: **$120.95**

ASG CZ 75 P-07 DUTY DUAL TONE AIR PISTOL
Caliber: BB. **Barrel:** Threaded for barrel extension. **Weight:** 28.92 oz.
Length: 7.32 inches. **Power:** CO2/Air cartridge stored in grip. **Sights:**
Fixed. **Features:** Metal slide and a replica design based on the CZ-
75 line. **Velocity:** 325 to 361fps.
Price: **$119.95**

ASG CZ 75D COMPACT AIR PISTOL
Caliber: BB with capacity of 17. **Barrel:** Threaded for barrel extension.
Weight: 24.52 oz. **Length:** 7.28 inches. **Power:** CO2/Air cartridge
stored in grip. **Sights:** Adjustable rear sight and blade front sight.
Features: Replica design based on the CZ- 75 line. **Velocity:** 374 to
407 fps.
Price: . . . . **$**

ASG DAN WESSON 6" PELLET REVOLVER AIR PISTOL
Caliber: .177 Pellets. **Barrel:** Rifled. **Weight:** 36.76 oz. **Length:** 11.73
inches. **Power:** 12g CO2/Air stored in grip. **Sights:** Blade front and
adjustable rear sight. **Features:** Rifled barrel and comes with a
magazine capacity of 6 rounds and includes a speed loader and an
attachable rail for optics. **Velocity:** 426 fps.
Price: **$150.00**

ASG BERSA BP9CC

ASG BERSA BP9CC DUAL TONE BLOWBACK AIR PISTOL
Caliber: BB. **Weight:** 21.52 oz. **Length:** 6.6 inches. **Power:** 12g CO2/
Air stored in grip. **Sights:** Fixed 3-dot system. **Features:** Optical
safety lever included, threaded barrel with barrel extension tube and
accessory rail. **Velocity:** 350 fps.
Price: **$119.95**

ASG STI INTERNATIONAL DUTY ONE BLOWBACK AIR PISTOL
Caliber: Steel BB. **Weight:** 29.1 oz. **Length:** 8.66 inches. **Power:**
12g CO2/Air cartridge. **Sights:** Fixed. **Features:** Barrel threaded for
barrel extension tube, accessory rail and metal slide. **Velocity:** 367
to 400 fps.
Price: **$119.95**

ASG STEYR MANNLICHER M9-A1 AIR PISTOL
Caliber: Steel or plastic BB. **Weight:** 18.77 oz. **Length:** 7.36 inches.
Power: 12g CO2/Air cartridge located inside grip. **Sights:** Fixed.
Features: Non-Blowback design, accessory rail, metal slide and
offered in either dual tone or black finished. **Velocity:** 449 fps.
Price: **$44.95**

BEEMAN 2004 MAGNUM AIR PISTOL
Caliber: .177 **Barrel:** 7.4". **Weight:** 1.7 lbs. **Length:** 10" overall. **Power:**
Top lever cocking, single stroke pneumatic. **Grips:** Polymer. **Sights:**
Front and rear fiber-optic sights with red-dot sight. **Features:** Grooved
for scope mounting with dry-fire feature for practice.
Price: **$45.00**

BEEMAN 2004K AIR PISTOL
Caliber: .177 **Barrel:** 9.17". **Weight:** 2.1 lbs. **Power:** Pneumatic single-
shot. **Grips:** Polymer. **Features:** Comes with 250 count pellets and
safety glasses. 410 fps.
Price: **$55.00**

BEEMAN 2006 PNEUMATIC AIR PISTOL
Caliber: .177 **Barrel:** 7.4". **Weight:** 1.7 lbs. **Length:** 9.6" overall. **Power:**
Single-stroke pneumatic with over-lever barrel cocking. **Grips:**
Polymer. **Sights:** Front and rear fiber-optic sights with red-dot sight.
Features: Polymer frame, automatic safety, two-stage trigger and
built-in muzzle brake. 410 fps.
Price: **$55.00**

Prices given are believed to be accurate at time of publication however, many factors affect retail pricing so exact prices are not possible.

70TH EDITION, 2016 ⊕ **525**

BEEMAN P1 MAGNUM AIR PISTOL
Caliber: .177, 20. **Barrel:** 8.4". **Weight:** 2.5 lbs. **Length:** 11" overall. **Power:** Top lever cocking; spring-piston. **Grips:** Checkered walnut. **Sights:** Blade front, square notch rear with click micrometer adjustments for windage and elevation. Grooved for scope mounting. **Features:** Dual power for .177 and 20 cal.; low setting gives 350-400 fps; high setting 500-600 fps. All Colt 45 auto grips fit gun. Dry-firing feature for practice. Optional wood shoulder stock. Imported by Beeman.
Price: . . . . $530.00 to $565.00

BEEMAN P3 PNEUMATIC AIR PISTOL
Caliber: .177. **Barrel:** NA. **Weight:** 1.7 lbs. **Length:** 9.6" overall. **Power:** Single-stroke pneumatic; overlever barrel cocking. **Grips:** Reinforced polymer. **Sights:** Front and rear fiber-optic sights. **Features:** Velocity 410 fps. Polymer frame; automatic safety; two-stage trigger; built-in muzzle brake.
Price: $290.00

BEEMAN P11 AIR PISTOL
Caliber: .177 & .22. **Barrel:** Rifled. **Weight:** 1.7 lbs. **Length:** 9.6" overall. **Power:** Single-stroke pneumatic single shot; over-lever barrel cocking. **Sights:** Fiber-optic front and rear sights. **Features:** 2-stage non-adjustable trigger and automatic safety. **Velocity:** 600 fps in .177 caliber and 460 fps in .22 caliber.
Price: . . . . $614.95 to $634.95

BEEMAN P17 AIR PISTOL
Caliber: .177. **Barrel:** Rifled. **Weight:** 1.7 lbs. **Length:** 9.6" overall. **Power:** Single-stroke pneumatic single shot; over-lever barrel cocking. **Sights:** Fiber-optic front and rear sights. **Features:** This pistol was originally called the Marksman 2004. 2-stage non-adjustable trigger and automatic safety. A combo kit package is also available with a red dot sight or what the company calls a Sweet 17 Bundle which includes pellets and targets. **Velocity:** 410 fps.
Price: $44.99

BEEMAN 2008 CO2 AIR PISTOL
Caliber: .177. **Barrel:** Smooth bore. **Weight:** 2.0 lbs. **Length:** 8.5" overall. **Power:** CO2. **Sights:** Blade ramp front sight and fixed rear sight. **Features:** Manual safety. **Velocity:** 410 fps.
Price: $89.99

BEEMAN/FWB 103 AIR PISTOL
Caliber: .177. **Barrel:** 10.1," 12-groove rifling. **Weight:** 2.5 lbs. **Length:** 16.5" overall. **Power:** Single-stroke pneumatic, underlever cocking. **Grips:** Stippled walnut with adjustable palm shelf. **Sights:** Blade front, open rear adjustable for windage and elevation. Notch size adjustable for width. Interchangeable front blades. **Features:** Velocity 510 fps. Fully adjustable trigger. Cocking effort 2 lbs. Imported by Beeman.
Price: Right-hand $2,110.00
Price: Left-hand $2,350.00

BEEMAN HW70A AIR PISTOL
Caliber: .177. **Barrel:** 6-1/4", rifled. **Weight:** 38 oz. **Length:** 12-3/4" overall. **Power:** Spring, barrel cocking. **Grips:** Plastic, with thumbrest. **Sights:** Hooded post front, square notch rear adjustable for windage and elevation. Comes with scope base. **Features:** Adjustable trigger, 31-lb. cocking effort, 440 fps MV; automatic barrel safety. Imported by Beeman.
Price: $335.00

BENJAMIN MARAUDER PCP PISTOL
Caliber: .22 **Weight:** 2.7 lbs. **Length:** 18" overall. **Power:** Precharged pneumatic 3,000 psi multi-shot (8-round rotary magazine) bolt action. **Grips:** Synthetic. **Features:** Rifled, shrouded steel barrel, two-stage trigger, includes both pistol grips and a carbine stock and is built in America. 700 fps.
Price: $395.00

BENJAMIN MARAUDER WOODS WALKER PCP PISTOL
Caliber: .22 **Weight:** 2.7 lbs. **Length:** 18" overall. **Power:** Precharged pneumatic 3,000 psi multi-shot (eight-round rotary magazine) bolt action. **Grips:** Synthetic. **Sights:** CenterPoint Multi-Tac Quick Aim Sight. **Features:** Rifled, steel shrouded barrel, includes both pistol grips and a carbine stock. Two-stage trigger, Realtree AP camo finish and is built in America. Up to 700 fps.
Price: $510.00

BENJAMIN TRAIL NP BREAK BARREL PISTOL
Caliber: .177, single shot. **Weight:** 3.43 lbs. **Length:** 16" overall. **Power:** Nitro Piston with cocking aid for easier cocking. **Grips:** Synthetic. **Sights:** Fiber-optic front, fully adjustable rear. **Features:** Velocity to 625 fps. Rifled steel barrel.
Price: $95.00

BENJAMIN & SHERIDAN CO2

BENJAMIN & SHERIDAN CO2 PISTOLS
Caliber: .22, single shot. **Barrel:** 6-3/8", brass. **Weight:** 1 lb. 12 oz. **Length:** 9" overall. **Power:** 12-gram CO2 cylinder. **Grips:** American Hardwood. **Sights:** High ramp front, fully adjustable notched rear. **Features:** Velocity to 500 fps. Turnbolt action with cross-bolt safety. Gives about 40 shots per CO2 cylinder. Black or nickel finish. Made in U.S. by Crosman Corp.
Price: EB22 (.22) $118.59

BENJAMIN & SHERIDAN PNEUMATIC PELLET PISTOLS
Caliber: .177, .22, single shot. **Barrel:** 9-3/8", rifled brass. **Weight:** 2 lbs., 8 oz. **Length:** 12.25" overall. **Power:** Underlever pneumatic, hand pumped. **Grips:** American Hardwood. **Sights:** High ramp front, fully adjustable notch rear. **Features:** Velocity to 525 fps (variable). Bolt action with cross-bolt safety. Choice of black or nickel finish. Made in U.S. by Crosman Corp.
Price: Black finish, HB17 (.177), HB22 (.22) $133.59

BERETTA MODEL 84FS

BERETTA MODEL 84FS AIR PISTOL
Caliber: .177 & BBs models. **Barrel:** 3.6" **Weight:** 1.4 lbs. **Power:** CO2 valve system with blowback slide cycle action. **Sights:** Fixed. **Features:** Available in multiple combinations of sub-models in various finishes, are made to resemble the real Beretta handguns. **Velocity:** To 360 fps. Made by Umarex.
Price: . . . . $249.95 to $320.00

BERETTA MODEL PX4 AIR PISTOL
Caliber: .177. **Barrel:** 4.1" **Weight:** 1.6-lbs. **Power:** CO2 repeater. **Sights:** Blade front sight and fixed rear sight. **Features:** Semi-automatic, 16-shot capacity with maximum of 40-shots per fill. **Velocity:** To 380 fps.
Price: $99.99

BERETTA ELITE II CO2 & BB PISTOLS
Caliber: .177. **Barrel:** 4.8" **Weight:** 1.5-lbs. **Power:** CO2 repeater. **Sights:** Blade front sight and fixed rear sight. **Features:** Manual safety, semi-automatic, 19-shot capacity with maximum of 180-shots

Prices given are believed to be accurate at time of publication however, many factors affect retail pricing so exact prices are not possible.

per fill. **Velocity:** To 410 fps.
Price: . . . . **$49.99 to $60.00**

BERETTA PX4 STORM RECON CO2 PISTOL
Caliber: .177. **Barrel:** 4.1" **Weight:** 2.2-lbs. **Power:** CO2 repeater.
  Sights: Blade front sight and fixed rear sight. **Features:** Manual
  safety, semi-automatic, 16-shot capacity. **Velocity:** To 380 fps.
Price: **$200.00**

BERETTA 90TWO CO2 BB PISTOL & LASER
Caliber: .177. **Barrel:** 5.0" **Weight:** 1.99-lbs. **Power:** CO2 repeater.
  Sights: Blade front sight and fixed rear sight. **Features:** Manual
  safety, semi-automatic, 21-shot capacity. **Velocity:** to 375 fps.
Price: **$69.90**

BROWNING 800 EXPRESS AIR PISTOL
Caliber: .177. **Barrel:** Rifled 9" **Weight:** 1.5 lbs. **Length:** 18". **Power:**
  Single-shot break-barrel spring-piston single shot. **Sights:** Blade
  ramp front sight and adjustable rear sight. **Features:** Automatic
  safety, 11mm dovetail rail scope mounting possible, with Weaver
  mounts, cocking effort – 47-pounds. **Velocity:** 700 fps.
Price: **$168.00**

BROWNING BUCK MARK URX

BROWNING BUCK MARK URX AIR PISTOL
Caliber: .177 **Barrel:** 5.25" **Weight:** 1.5 lbs. **Power:** Single-shot break-
  barrel pellet pistol. **Sights:** Fixed. **Features:** Velocity to 360 fps.
  Made by Umarex.
Price: **$50.00**

COLT PYTHON

COLT PYTHON CO2 PISTOL
Caliber: .177 **Barrel:** 5.5" **Weight:** 2.6 lbs. **Power:** CO2 valve system
  with swing-out cylinder, removable casings and functioning ejector.
  Sights: Fixed. **Features:** Velocity to 400 fps. Made by Umarex.
Price: **$99.00**

COLT DEFENDER

COLT DEFENDER BB AIR PISTOL
Caliber: BB. **Barrel:** Smooth bore 4.3". **Weight:** 1.6-lbs. **Power:** CO2.
  Sights: Fixed with blade ramp front sight. **Features:** Semi-automatic,
  manual safety, 16-shot. **Velocity:** 410 fps.
Price: **$75.00**

COLT 1911 PELLET AIR PISTOL
Caliber: .177. **Barrel:** Rifled 5.0". **Weight:** 2.4-lbs. **Power:** CO2
  repeater. **Sights:** Blade ramp front sight and adjustable rear sight.
  Features: Semi-automatic, manual safety, 8-shot capacity. **Velocity:**
  425 fps.
Price: **$320.00**

COLT 1911 SPECIAL COMBAT CLASSIC BB AIR PISTOL
Caliber: BB. **Barrel:** Smooth bore 5.04". **Weight:** 2.05-lbs. **Power:**
  CO2 repeater. **Sights:** Blade front sight and adjustable rear sight.
  Features: Semi-automatic, manual safety, 20-shot capacity and also
  available in a Limited Edition NRA Model. **Velocity:** 400 fps.
Price: **$120.00**

COLT 1911 A1 CO2 PELLET PISTOL
Caliber: .177. **Barrel:** Rifled 5.0". **Weight:** 2.4-lbs. **Power:** CO2
  repeater. **Sights:** Blade ramp front sight and adjustable rear sight.
  Features: Semi-automatic, manual safety, 8-shot capacity. **Velocity:**
  425 fps.
Price: **$259.99**

COLT COMMANDER CO2 PISTOL
Caliber: .177. **Barrel:** Smooth bore 4.5". **Weight:** 2.1-lbs. **Power:** CO2
  repeater. **Sights:** Blade front sight and fixed rear sight. **Features:**
  Semi-automatic, manual safety, 18-shot capacity. **Velocity:** 325 fps.
Price: **$199.99**

COLT SINGLE ACTION ARMY CO2 REVOLVER
Caliber: .177. **Barrel:** Smooth bore 5.5". **Weight:** 2.1-lbs. **Power:** 12-
  gram CO2 repeater. **Sights:** Blade front sight and fixed rear sight.
  Features: Full metal revolver with manual safety. **Velocity:** 410 fps.
Price: **$149.99**

CROSMAN MODEL 1088

CROSMAN 1088 REPEATAIR PISTOL
Caliber: .177, 8-shot pellet clip. **Barrel:** Rifled steel. **Weight:** 17 oz.
  Length: 7.75" overall. **Power:** CO2 Powerlet. **Grips:** Checkered
  black plastic. **Sights:** Fixed blade front, adjustable rear. **Features:**
  Velocity about 430 fps. Single or double semi-automatic action. From
  Crosman.
Price: **$60.00**

CROSMAN 2240
Caliber: .22. **Barrel:** Rifled steel. **Weight:** 1 lb. 13 oz. **Length:** 11.125".
  Power: CO2. **Grips:** NA. **Sights:** Blade front, rear adjustable.
  Features: Ergonomically designed ambidextrous grip fits the hand for
  perfect balance and comfort with checkering and a thumbrest on both
  grip panels. From Crosman.
Price: **$69.00**

CROSMAN 2300S CO2 TARGET PISTOL
Caliber: .177 **Weight:** 2.7 lbs. **Length:** 16" **Power:** Single-shot, bolt
  action, CO2 Powerlet powered. **Sights:** Front fixed sight and Williams
  notched rear sight. **Features:** Meets IHMSA rules for Production
  Class Silhouette Competitions. Lothar Walter barrel, adjustable trigger,
  adjustable hammer, stainless steel bolt, 60 shots per Powerlet.
Price: **$254.00**

AIRGUNS—Handguns

CROSMAN 2300T CO2 TARGET PISTOL
Caliber: .177 Weight: 2.6 lbs. Length: 16" Power: Single-shot, bolt action, CO2 Powerlet powered. Sights: Front fixed sight and LPA rear sight. Features: Adjustable trigger, designed for shooting clubs and organizations that teach pistol shooting and capable of firing 40 shots per Powerlet.
Price: $160.00

CROSMAN 3576 REVOLVER
Caliber: .177, pellets. Barrel: Rifled steel. Weight: 2 lbs. Length: 11.38". Power: CO2. Grips: NA. Sights: Blade front, rear adjustable. Features: Semi-auto 10-shot with revolver styling and finger-molded grip design, 6" barrel for increased accuracy. From Crosman.
Price: $80.00

CROSMAN C11
Caliber: .177, 18-shot BB or pellet. Weight: 1.4 lbs. Length: 8.5". Power: 12g CO2. Sights: Fixed. Features: Compact semi-automatic BB pistol. Velocity up to 480 fps. Under barrel weaver style rail.
Price: $60.00

CROSMAN C41 CO2 PISTOL
Caliber: .177, 18-shot BB. Weight: 2 lbs. Length: 8.5" Power: 12g CO2. Sights: Fixed. Features: Compact semiautomatic BB pistol. Velocity up to 480 fps.
Price: $65.00

CROSMAN C-TT

CROSMAN C-TT
Caliber: BB, 18-shot magazine. Length: 8". Semi-auto CO2-powered repeater styled after Russian Tarev TT-30. Metal frame and polymer grip.
Price: $100.00

CROSMAN PRO77
Caliber: .177, 17-shot BB. Weight: 1.31 lbs. Length: 6.75". Power: 12g CO2. Sights: Fixed. Features: Compact pistol with realistic recoil. Under the barrel weaver style rail. Velocity up to 325 fps.
Price: Pro77CS $90.00

CROSMAN PUMPMASTER CLASSIC

CROSMAN PUMPMASTER CLASSIC PISTOL
Caliber: .22 Weight: 2 lbs. Length: 13.6" Power: Single-shot bolt-action pneumatic pump pistol. Sights: Front fixed sight and adjustable rear sight. Features: Control velocity with easy-pump forearm. Velocity up to 600 fps.
Price: $60.00

CROSMAN SURVIVALIST CO2 PISTOL
Caliber: .177, 20-shot BB. Weight: 1.1 lbs. Length: 6.9" Power: CO2-

powered. Sights: Fixed. Features: Compact semiautomatic, under-barrel Weaver-style rail and holster included. Velocity up to 495 fps.
Price: $40.00

CROSMAN T4
Caliber: .177, 8-shot BB or pellet. Weight: 1.32 lbs. Length: 8.63". Power: 12g CO2. Sights: Fixed front, windage adjustable rear. Features: Shoots BBs or pellets. Easy patent-pending CO2 piercing mechanism. Under the barrel weaver style rail.
Price: T4CS $90.00
Price: T4OPS, includes adjustable Red Dot sight, barrel compensator, and pressure operated tactical flashlight. Comes in foam padeed, hard sided protective case $167.99

CROSMAN VIGILANTE CO2 REVOLVER
Caliber: .177, pellets and BB. Barrel: 6" rifled steel. Weight: 2 lbs. Length: 11.38" Power: CO2-powered. Sights: Blade front sight and adjustable rear sight. Features: Semiauto 10-shot pellet clip and 6-shot BB clip with revolver styling and finger-molded grip design.
Price: $90.00

DAISY MODEL 717

DAISY POWERLINE MODEL 717 AIR PISTOL
Caliber: .177, single shot. Weight: 2.25 lbs. Length: 13-1/2" overall. Grips: Molded checkered woodgrain with contoured thumbrest. Sights: Blade and ramp front, open rear with windage and elevation adjustments. Features: Single pump pneumatic pistol. Rifled steel barrel. Crossbolt trigger block. Muzzle velocity 395 fps. From Daisy Mfg. Co.
Price: $200.00

DAISY AVANTI MODEL 747 TRIUMPH AIR PISTOL
Caliber: .177, single shot. Weight: 2.35 lbs. Length: 13-1/2" overall. Grips: Molded checkered woodgrain with contoured thumbrest. Sights: Blade and ramp front, open rear with windage and elevation adjustments. Features: Single pump pneumatic pistol. Lothar Walther rifled high-grade steel barrel; crowned 12 lands and grooves, right-hand twist. Precision bore sized for match pellets. Muzzle velocity 395 fps. From Daisy Mfg. Co.
Price: $264.99

DAISY POWERLINE 340 AIR PISTOL
Caliber: BB Features: Spring-air action, 200-shot BB reservoir with a 13-shot Speed-load Clip located in the grip.
Price: $24.99

DAISY POWERLINE 415 AIR PISTOL
Caliber: .177 BB. Weight: .93 lbs. Length: 8.6" overall. Grips: Molded checkered. Sights: Fiber optic front, fixed open rear. Features: CO2 powered, semi-automatic BB pistol, smooth bore steel barrel. Velocity: 495 fps. From Daisy Outdoor Products.
Price: $39.99

DAISY POWERLINE 5170

DAISY POWERLINE 5170 CO2 PISTOL
Caliber: .177 BB. Weight: 1 lb. Length: 9.5" overall. Sights: Blade

and ramp front, open rear. **Features:** CO_2 semi-automatic action, manual trigger-block safety, upper and lower rails for mounting sights and other accessories and a smooth-bore steel barrel. Muzzle velocity 520 fps. From Daisy Mfg. Co.
Price: $59.99

DAISY POWERLINE 5501 CO2 BLOWBACK PISTOL
Caliber: .177, BB. **Weight:** 1 lb. **Length:** 9.5" overall. **Sights:** Blade and ramp front, open rear. **Features:** CO_2 semi-automatic blow-back action, manual trigger-block safety, and a smooth-bore steel barrel. Muzzle velocity 430 fps. From Daisy Mfg. Co.
Price: $89.99

EAA/BAIKAL IZH-46M TARGET AIR PISTOL
Caliber: .177, single shot. **Barrel:** 10". **Weight:** 2.4 lbs. **Length:** 16.8" overall. **Power:** Underlever single-stroke pneumatic. **Grips:** Adjustable wooden target. **Sights:** Micrometer fully adjustable rear, blade front. **Features:** Velocity about 500 fps. Hammer-forged, rifled barrel. Imported from Russia by European American Armory.
Price: $690.00

EVANIX HUNTING MASTER AR6 AIR PISTOL
Caliber: .22. **Barrel:** 10" rifled. **Weight:** 3.05 lbs. **Length:** 17.3 overall. **Power:** Precharged Pneumatic. **Grips:** Checkered Hardwood. **Sights:** Adjustable rear, blade front. **Features:** 6 shot repeater with rotary magazine, single or double action, receiver grooved for scope, hammer block and trigger block safeties. **Velocity:** With 3,000 psi charge 922 fps to 685 fps (10-shot range starting with shot #1 to shot #10 using 11.9-grian RWS Hobby pellets) and 423 fps to 701 fps (10-shot range starting with shot #1 to shot #10 using 28-grain Eun Jin pellets).
Price: $659.99

GAMO MP-9 CO2 PISTOL
Caliber: .177, BB **Weight:** 3 lbs. **Power:** CO_2 cartridge. **Sights:** NA. **Features:** Blow-back semiautomatic replica of the B&T MP-9 9mm submachine gun. Shoots both pellets or BBs using the same magazine, Weaver-style tactical rails, ambidextrous compact design, foldable stock, 16-shot double magazine and manual safety. 450 fps.
Price: $159.95

GAMO P-900 IGT AIR PISTOL
Caliber: .177 **Weight:** 1.3 lbs. **Power:** CO_2 cartridge. **Features:** Break-barrel single-shot, ergonomic design, rubberized grip, rifled steel barrel and manual safety. 400 fps.
Price: $79.95

GAMO PT-25 BLOWBACK CO2 PISTOL
Caliber: .177 **Weight:** 1.5 lbs. **Power:** CO_2 cartridge **Features:** Semiautomatic design, iron sights, 16-shot double magazine, manual safety. 450 fps.
Price: $109.95

GAMO PT-25 BLOWBACK TACTICAL CO2 PISTOL
Caliber: .177 **Weight:** 1.5 lbs. **Power:** CO_2 cartridge **Sights:** Gamo red-dot. **Features:** Semiautomatic design, mounting rail on top and bottom, flashlight mounted on bottom rail, 16-shot double magazine, manual safety. 560 fps.
Price: $189.95

GAMO PT-85 BLOWBACK CO2 PISTOL
Caliber: .177 **Weight:** 1.5 lbs. **Power:** CO_2 cartridge **Features:** Semiautomatic design, iron sights, 16-shot double magazine, manual safety. 450 fps.
Price: $119.95

GAMO PT-85 BLOWBACK SOCOM CO2 PISTOL
Caliber: .177 **Weight:** 2.32 lbs. **Power:** CO_2 cartridge **Features:** Semiautomatic design, Quad rail included, 16 shot double magazine, manual safety. 560 fps.
Price: $139.95

GAMO PT-85 BLOWBACK TACTICAL CO2 PISTOL
Caliber: .177 **Weight:** 3.3 lbs. **Power:** CO_2 cartridge **Features:** Semiautomatic design, compensator, rifled steel barrel, manual safety, 16-shot double magazine, quad rail, laser and light Included. 560 fps.
Price: $269.95

HATSAN USA VORTEX PISTOL
Caliber: .177 lead pellets. **Power:** Gas piston powered single shot break barrel. **Features:** Rifled steel 10.2" barrel, overall length is 20" and weight is 3.9 lbs. Comes with a metal trigger blade and an anti-bear trap safety. **Sights:** TruGlo fiber optic front and rear sights. **Velocity:** 700 fps with lead pellets.
Price: $180.00

HATSAN USA PCP PISTOL
Caliber: .177, .22 & .25 lead pellets. **Power:** Precharged pneumatic. **Features:** Rifled steel 10.4" barrel, overall length is 16.3" and weight is 4.5 lbs. Comes with polymer grips and magazine holding 9-10 rounds depending upon the caliber. **Sights:** Fiber optic front and rear sights. **Velocity:** 710 to 870 fps with lead pellets depending upon the caliber.
Price: From $500.00

HAMMERLI AP-20

HAMMERLI AP-20 AIR PISTOL
Caliber: .177. **Barrel:** 9.84". **Weight:** 1.92-lbs. **Length:** 16.34". **Power:** Precharged pneumatic. **Sights:** Fully adjustable micrometer. **Features:** 2-stage adjustable set at 1.1-lbs. pull weight, single shot, bolt action single shot. **Velocity:** 492 fps.
Price: $1,100.00

MAGNUM RESEARCH DESERT EAGLE
Caliber: .177, 8-shot pellet. 5.7" rifled. **Weight:** 2.5 lbs. 11" overall. **Power:** 12g CO_2. **Sights:** Fixed front, adjustable rear. Velocity of 425 fps. 8-shot rotary clip. Double or single action. The first .177 caliber air pistol with BLOWBACK action. Big and weighty, designed in the likeness of the real Desert Eagle. Made by Umarex.
Price: $220.00

MAGNUM BABY DESERT EAGLE
Caliber: .177, 15-shot BB. 4" **Weight:** 1.0 lbs. 8-1/4" overall. **Power:** 12g CO_2. **Sights:** Fixed front and rear. Velocity of 420 fps. Double action BB repeater. Comes with bonus Picatinny top rail and built-in bottom rail. Made by Umarex.
Price: $59.99

MARKSMAN 200K AIR PISTOL
Caliber: .177 **Barrel:** Smooth bore 2.0" **Weight:** 1.5 lbs. **Power:** Spring-piston slide-action repeater capable of shooting pellets, darts or bolts. **Grips:** Checkered. **Features:** 18-shot BB reservoir and comes with holster, shooting glasses and ammo. **Velocity:** 200 fps.
Price: $34.99

MARKSMAN 1010 CLASSIC AIR PISTOL
Caliber: .177 **Barrel:** 8.81" **Weight:** 2.43 lbs. **Length:** 10" overall. **Power:** Spring piston capable of shooting pellets, darts or bolts. **Grips:** Checkered. **Sights:** Blade front and open rear. **Features:** 18-shot BB reservoir. 230 fps.
Price: $29.75

MORINI CM 162 EL MATCH AIR PISTOLS
Caliber: .177, single shot. **Barrel:** 9.4". **Weight:** 32 oz. **Length:** 16.1" overall. **Power:** Scuba air. **Grips:** Adjustable match type. **Sights:** Interchangeable blade front, fully adjustable match-type rear. **Features:** Power mechanism shuts down when pressure drops to a preset level. Adjustable electronic trigger.
Price: $1,075.00

REMINGTON 1911 RAC CO2 BB PISTOL
Caliber: BB .177 (4.5mm). **Barrel:** Smooth bore. **Weight:** 2.0 lbs. **Power:** 12 gram CO_2 cylinders. **Grips:** Synthetic. **Sights:** Fixed front and rear sights. **Features:** Polymer frame, semi-automatic 18-shot single action, manual safety, single action. **Velocity:** 320 fps.
Price: $139.99

RUGER MARK I

RUGER MARK I
Caliber: .177. **Barrel:** 6.5". **Weight:** 48 oz. **Sights:** Fiber optic front, open rear. Spring-piston operated pellet pistol up to 500 fps velocity with lead pellets, 600 fps with alloy. Made by Umarex.
Price: **$75.00**

SMITH & WESSON 586 & 686
Caliber: .177, 10-shot pellet. Rifled. **Power:** 12g CO2. **Sights:** Fixed front, adjustable rear. 10-shot rotary clip. Double or single action. Replica revolvers that duplicate both weight and handling. Made by Umarex.
Price: 586 4" barrel. Velocity - 400 fps **$300.00**
Price: 586 6" barrel. Velocity - 425 fps **$295.95**
Price: 685 6" barrel. Velocity - 425 fps **$300.00**

SMITH & WESSON M&P CO2 PISTOL
Caliber: .177, BB. **Barrel:** 4.24" smoothbore. **Weight:** 1.5 lbs. **Length:** 7.5" overall. **Power:** CO2-powered repeater. **Sights:** Blade front and ramp rear fiber optic. **Features:** Integrated accessory rail, drop-free 19-shot BB magazine, manual safety, double-action only, synthetic frame and available in dark earth brown or black color. 480 fps. Made by Umarex.
Price: (black) **$50.00**
Price: (dark earth brown) **$45.99**

SMITH & WESSON M&P R8 CO2 BB PISTOL
Caliber: BB. **Barrel:** Smooth bore 4.0". **Power:** CO2. **Sights:** Blade front sight and adjustable rear sight. **Features:** Manual safety and 8-shot capacity. **Velocity:** 410 fps.
Price: **$90.00**

SMITH & WESSON M&P 45 CO2 PISTOL
Caliber: .177. **Barrel:** Rifled 3.3". **Power:** CO2. **Sights:** Blade front sight and adjustable rear sight. **Features:** Manual safety, 8-shot capacity and also available in a combo kit package. **Velocity:** 370 fps.
Price: **$80.00**

SMITH & WESSON 327 TRR8 CO2 BB PISTOL
Caliber: BB. **Barrel:** Smooth bore 5.5". **Power:** CO2. **Sights:** Fiber optic front sight and adjustable rear sight. Scope mountable with Weaver mounts. **Features:** Manual safety and 6-shot capacity. **Velocity:** 400 fps.
Price: **$120.00**

SMITH & WESSON DOMINANT TRAIT (TRR8) CO2 BB PISTOL
Caliber: BB. **Barrel:** Smooth bore 5.5". **Power:** 12-gram CO2. **Sights:** Fiber optic front sight and adjustable rear sight. Scope mountable with Weaver mounts. **Features:** Manual safety and 6-shot capacity. **Velocity:** 400 fps.
Price: **$170.00**

STEYR LP10P MATCH AIR PISTOL
Caliber: .177, single shot. **Barrel:** 9". **Weight:** 38.7 oz. **Length:** 15.3" overall. **Power:** Scuba air. **Grips:** Adjustable Morini match, palm shelf, stippled walnut. **Sights:** Interchangeable blade in 4mm, 4.5mm or 5mm widths, adjustable open rear, interchangeable 3.5mm or 4mm leaves. **Features:** Velocity about 500 fps. Adjustable trigger, adjustable sight radius from 12.4" to 13.2". With compensator. Recoil elimination.
Price: **$1,400.00**

TECH FORCE 35 AIR PISTOL
Caliber: .177 pellet, single shot. **Weight:** 2.86 lbs. **Length:** 14.9" overall. **Power:** Spring-piston, underlever. **Grips:** Hardwood. **Sights:** Micrometer adjustable rear, blade front. **Features:** Velocity 400 fps. Grooved for scope mount; trigger safety. Imported from China by Compasseco, Inc.
Price: **$39.95**

WALTHER CP88
Caliber: .177. **Barrel:** 4" or 6". **Weight:** 2.5 lbs. **Length:** 7" or 9" overall.
Power: CO2. **Sights:** Blade ramp front sight and adjustable rear sight. **Features:** Manual safety, semi-auto repeater, single or double action and available in a compact version. **Velocity:** 345 to 450 fps.
Price: . . . . **$110.00 to $225.95**

WALTHER CP99 COMPACT
Caliber: .177, 17-shot steel BB semi-auto. **Barrel:** 3". **Weight:** 1.7 lbs. **Length:** 6-1/2" overall. **Power:** 12g CO2. **Sights:** Fixed front and rear. **Features:** Velocity of 345 fps. Realistic recoil, blowback action. Heavyweight steel construction. Built-in Picatinny mount. Made by Umarex.
Price: . . . . **$79.99 to $220.00**

WALTHER NIGHTHAWK
Caliber: .177. **Barrel:** Rifled 3.3". **Weight:** 1.47 lbs. **Length:** 7.0" overall. **Power:** CO2. **Sights:** Blade ramp front sight and adjustable rear sight. **Features:** Manual safety, repeater, double action only. **Velocity:** 400 fps.
Price: **$229.99**

WALTHER P38 PISTOL
Caliber: BB. **Barrel:** Smooth bore 4.75". **Weight:** 1.9 lbs. **Length:** 8-1/2" overall. **Power:** CO2. **Sights:** Fixed rear sight and blade front sight. **Features:** Semi-auto, manual safety, trigger pull weight – 8.3 lbs. **Velocity:** 345 fps.
Price: **$120.00**

WALTHER LP300 MATCH PISTOL
Caliber: .177 **Weight:** 1,018 g. **Length:** 236mm. **Power:** Recharged pneumatic single-shot pistol. **Grips:** Adjustable. **Sights:** Integrated front with three different widths, adjustable rear. **Features:** Adjustable grip and trigger. Made by Umarex.
Price: **$1,800.00**

WALTHER PPK/S
Caliber: .177, 15-shot steel BB. **Barrel:** 3-1/2". **Weight:** 1.2 lbs. **Length:** 6-1/4" overall. **Power:** 12g CO2. **Sights:** Fixed front and rear. **Features:** Velocity of 295 fps. Lookalike of one of the world's most famous pistols. Realistic recoil. Heavyweight steel construction. Made by Umarex.
Price: **$86.95**

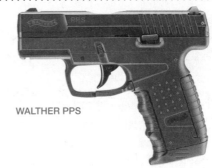

WALTHER PPS

WALTHER PPS PISTOL
Caliber: .177 **Barrel:** 3" **Weight:** 1.2 lbs. **Power:** CO2 valve system with blowback slide cycle action. **Sights:** Fixed. **Features:** Velocity of 350 fps. Metal replica frame and 18-round capacity. Made by Umarex.
Price: **$99.99**

WINCHESTER MODEL 11

WINCHESTER MODEL 11
Caliber: BB. CO2-powered pistol with 16-round removable magazine. **Weight:** 30 ozs. **Features:** Can be fired double or single action. Slide stays open after last shot. Dimensions and operating controls the same as 1911 pistol. Made by Daisy.
Price: **$154.99**

Prices given are believed to be accurate at time of publication however, many factors affect retail pricing so exact prices are not possible.

AIRFORCE CONDOR

AIRFORCE CONDOR RIFLE
Caliber: .177, .22 single shot. **Barrel:** 24" rifled. **Weight:** 6.5 lbs. **Length:** 38.75" overall. **Power:** Pre-charged pneumatic. **Stock:** NA. **Sights:** Intended for scope use, fiber-optic open sights optional. **Features:** Lothar Walther match barrel, adjustable power levels from 600-1,300 fps. 3,000 psi fill pressure. Automatic safety. Air tank volume: 490cc. An integral extended scope rail allows easy mounting of the largest air-gun scopes. Operates on high-pressure air from scuba tank or hand pump. Manufactured in the U.S.A by AirForce Airguns.
Price: (rifle with Spin-Loc Tank). $729.95
Price: (rifle with 4-16x50 scope and hand pump combo) . . . $1,124.95

AIRFORCE CONDOR SS AIR RIFLE
Caliber: .177, .20, .22, .25 **Barrel:** 18" **Weight:** 6.1 lbs. **Length:** 38.125" overall. **Power:** Pre-charged. **Sights:** Designed for a scope, but fiber-optic open sights are optional. **Features:** Pneumatic single-shot with 3,000 PSI fill pressure. Lothar Walther match-grade rifled barrel, air tank volume - 490cc. Sound-Loc technology helps to reduce the firing report. Air can be charged from either a scuba tank or replenished by a hand pump. The Condor SS is manufactured in the USA by AirForce Airguns. Adjustable power level from 600 to 1,300 fps.
Price: $717.00

AIRFORCE ESCAPE AIR RIFLE
Caliber: .22, .25 **Barrel:** 24" **Weight:** 5.3 lbs. **Length:** Adjustable 34.5" to 39" overall. **Power:** Pre-charged. **Sights:** Designed for a scope, but fiber-optic open sights are optional. **Features:** Pneumatic single-shot with 3,000 PSI fill pressure. Lothar Walther match-grade rifled barrel, air tank volume - 490cc. Air can be charged from either a scuba tank or replenished by a hand pump. Adjustable power level from 800 to 1,300 fps.
Price: (rifle with Spin-Loc tank) $679.95

AIRFORCE ESCAPE SS AIR RIFLE
Caliber: .22, .25 **Barrel:** 12" **Weight:** 4.3 lbs. **Length:** Adjustable 27.75" to 32.25" overall. **Power:** Pre-charged. **Sights:** Designed for a scope, but fiber-optic open sights are optional. **Features:** Pneumatic single-shot with 3,000 PSI fill pressure. Lothar Walther match-grade rifled barrel, automatic safety, air tank volume—213cc. Air can be charged from either a scuba tank or replenished by a hand pump. Adjustable power level from 500 to 1,200 fps.
Price: (rifle with Spin-Loc tank) $669.95

AIRFORCE ESCAPE UL AIR RIFLE
Caliber: .22, .25 **Barrel:** 18" **Weight:** 4.25 lbs. **Length:** Adjustable 28.5" to 33" overall. **Power:** Pre-charged. **Sights:** Designed for a scope, but fiber-optic open sights are optional. **Features:** Pneumatic single-shot with 3,000 PSI fill pressure. Lothar Walther match-grade rifled barrel, automatic safety, air tank volume—213cc. Air can be charged from either a scuba tank or replenished by a hand pump. Adjustable power level from 800 to 1,200 fps.
Price: (rifle with Spin-Loc tank) $629.95

AIRFORCE TALON AIR RIFLE
Caliber: .177, .20, .22, .25, single shot. **Barrel:** 18" rifled. **Weight:** 5.5 lbs. **Length:** 32.6". **Power:** Pre-charged pneumatic. **Stock:** NA. **Sights:** Intended for scope use, fiber-optic open sights optional. **Features:** Lothar Walther match barrel, adjustable power levels from 400-1,000 fps, 3,000 psi fill pressure. Automatic safety. Air tank volume: 490cc. Operates on high-pressure air from scuba tank or hand pump. Manufactured in the U.S.A. by AirForce Airguns.
Price: (rifle with Spin-Loc tank) $559.95

AIRFORCE TALON SS AIR RIFLE
Caliber: .177, .20, .22, .25 single shot. **Barrel:** 12" rifled. **Weight:** 5.25 lbs. **Length:** 32.75". **Power:** Pre-charged pneumatic. **Stock:** NA. **Sights:** Intended for scope use, fiber-optic open sights optional. **Features:** Lothar Walther match barrel, adjustable power levels from 400-1,000 fps. 3,000 psi fill pressure. Automatic safety. Chamber in front of barrel strips away air turbulence, protects muzzle and reduces firing report. Air tank volume: 490cc. Operates on high-pressure air from scuba tank or hand pump. Manufactured in the U.S.A. by AirForce Airguns.
Price: (rifle with Spin-Loc tank) $639.95

AIRROW MODEL A-8SRB STEALTH AIR RIFLE
Caliber: .177, .22, .25, 9-shot. **Barrel:** 20"; rifled. **Weight:** 6 lbs. **Length:** 34" overall. **Power:** CO2 or compressed air; variable power. **Stock:** Telescoping CAR-15-type. **Sights:** Variable 3.5-10x scope. **Features:** Velocity 1100 fps in all calibers. Pneumatic air trigger. All aircraft aluminum and stainless steel construction. Mil-spec materials and finishes. From Swivel Machine Works, Inc.
Price: About $2,299.00

AIRROW MODEL A-8S1P STEALTH AIR RIFLE
Caliber: #2512 16" arrow. **Barrel:** 16". **Weight:** 4.4 lbs. **Length:** 30.1" overall. **Power:** CO2 or compressed air; variable power. **Stock:** Telescoping CAR-15-type. **Sights:** Scope rings only. 7 oz. rechargeable cylinder and valve. **Features:** Velocity to 650 fps with 260-grain arrow. Pneumatic air trigger. Broadhead guard. All aircraft aluminum and stainless steel construction. Mil-spec materials and finishes. A-8S Models perform to 2,000 PSIG above or below water levels. Waterproof case. From Swivel Machine Works, Inc.
Price: $1,699.00

BAIKAL IZH-60 TARGET AIR RIFLE
Caliber: .177, single shot. **Barrel:** 18". **Weight:** 4.3 lbs. **Length:** 33" overall. **Power:** Spring piston single shot. **Stock:** Black synthetic. **Sights:** Post global front sight and adjustable rear sight. **Features:** Rifled barrel. Imported from Russia by European American Armory. **Velocities:** About 490 fps.
Price: $160.00

BAIKAL IZH61 AIR RIFLE
Caliber: .177 pellet, 5-shot magazine. **Barrel:** 18.5" rifled. **Weight:** 4.3 lbs. **Length:** 33" overall. **Power:** Spring-piston, side-cocking lever. **Stock:** Black synthetic. **Sights:** Adjustable rear, fully hooded front. **Features:** 11mm rail, Futuristic design with adjustable stock. Imported from Russia by European American Armory. **Velocity:** 490 fps.
Price: $165.95

BAIKAL IZH DROZD MP-661K BLACKBIRD AIR RIFLE
Caliber: .177 pellet, 400-round hopper. **Barrel:** Rifle 8". Bullpup design. **Weight:** 4.3 lbs. **Length:** 28" overall. **Power:** Uses 88-gram AirSource CO2 cylinder and 6 AA batteries. **Stock:** Futuristic black synthetic design with adjustable stock. **Sights:** Adjustable rear and post front sight. **Features:** Weaver scope mount and manual safety. **Velocity:** 490 fps.
Price: $350.00

BEEMAN HW100 S FSB PRECHARGE PNEUMATIC AIR RIFLE
Caliber: .177, .20 or .22. **Barrel:** 23.62". **Weight:** 8.6 lbs. **Length:** 42.13" overall. **Power:** Pre-charged pneumatic. **Stock:** Walnut Monte Carlo styled with checkering on the pistol grip & forend. **Sights:** None, but grooved for scope mounting. **Features:** 14-shot magazine, quick-fill cylinder, 2-stage adjustable match grade trigger and manual safety. Also this same basic rifle is available with a hardwood thumbhole stock called the Beeman HW100 T FSB Precharged Pneumatic. **Velocities:** 1,135 fps in .177 caliber, 865 fps in .20 caliber and 886 fps in .22 caliber.
Price: . . . . $1,769.95 to $1789.95

BEEMAN RS-2 DUAL CALIBER AIR RIFLE COMBO
Caliber: .177 & 22 single shot. **Barrel:** Rifled. **Weight:** 6.9-lbs. **Length:** 45.5". **Power:** Break-barrel, spring-piston, single shot. **Sights:** Fiber optic front and rear. **Features:** Come with a 4x32mm scope, rings and as soft carrying case. Switch barrel model with both a .177 and .22 barrel with 2-stage non-adjustable trigger and an automatic safety. **Velocity:** 1,000 fps in .177 caliber and 830 fps in .22 caliber.
Price: $179.99

BEEMAN BEAR CLAW THUMBHOLE AIR RIFLE
Caliber: .177. **Barrel:** Rifled 16.1". **Weight:** 8.5 lbs. **Power:** Spring-piston barrel cocking system. **Stock:** Stained European hardwood thumbhole ambidextrous (right or left hand) stock with rubber buttpad. **Sights:** 3-9x32mm scope. **Features:** Adjustable metal RS2 2-stage

trigger. **Velocity:** 1,000 fps.
Price: $219.99

BEEMAN MACH 12.5 AIR RIFLE
Caliber: .177, .22 **Weight:** 10.6 lbs. **Length:** 47.3" overall. **Power:** Single-shot break barrel spring system. **Stock:** Checkered European hardwood. **Sights:** 3-9x40mm AO/TT scope. **Features:** RS3 2-stage trigger, ported barrel with muzzlebrake. 1,400 fps (.177) and 1,200 fps (.22).
Price: $300.00

BEEMAN R1 SUPERMAGNUM AIR RIFLE
Caliber: .177, .20 or .22, single shot. **Barrel:** Rifled 19.75". **Weight:** 8.8 lbs. **Length:** 45.2" overall. **Power:** Spring-piston, barrel cocking, single shot. **Stock:** Walnut-stained beech, cut-checkered pistol grip, Monte Carlo comb and rubber buttpad. **Sights:** None. **Features:** 11mm dovetail grooved, 2-stage adjustable trigger with 36-lbs. cocking effort. The .22 caliber rifle is available in both right and left hand versions. **Velocities:** 1,000 fps in .177 caliber, 860 fps in .20 caliber and 765 fps in .22 caliber.
Price: . . . . $749.95 to $849.95

BEEMAN R7 AIR RIFLE
Caliber: .177, .20. **Barrel:** 13.5". **Weight:** 6.1 lbs. **Length:** 37" overall. **Power:** Break-barrel, spring-piston, single shot. **Stock:** Stained beech. **Sights:** None. **Features:** Receiver grooved for scope mounting; double-jointed cocking lever; fully adjustable trigger; checkered grip. This same rifle is also available in a R7 Elite Series Combo Package with includes a scope. **Velocities:** 700 fps in .177 caliber and 620 fps in .20 caliber. Imported by Beeman.
Price: . . . . $419.95 to $449.95

BEEMAN RAM COMBO AIR RIFLE
Caliber: .177 & .22. **Barrel:** 20". **Weight:** 7.9-lbs. **Length:** 46.5" overall. **Power:** Break-barrel, spring-piston, single shot. **Stock:** Black colored plastic. **Sights:** None. **Features:** 11mm dovetail grooved, 2-stage RS2 adjustable trigger, rubber buttplate and includes a 3-9x32mm scope. **Velocities:** 1,000 fps in .177 caliber and 850 fps in .22 caliber.
Price: $220.00

BEEMAN R11 MKII

BEEMAN R11 MKII AIR RIFLE
Caliber: .177, single shot. **Barrel:** 16.25". **Weight:** 8.6 lbs. **Length:** 43.5" overall. **Power:** Spring-piston, break-barrel, single shot. **Stock:** Walnut stock, adjustable buttplate and cheekpiece. **Sights:** None, but 11mm dovetail for scope mounting. **Features:** All-steel barrel sleeve and a 2-stage Rekord match grade adjustable trigger. **Velocity:** 925 fps. Imported by Beeman.
Price: $799.95

BEEMAN WOLVERINE CARBINE COMBO AIR RIFLE
Caliber: .177. **Barrel:** Twelve-groove rifled barrel. **Weight:** 8.5 lbs. **Length:** 45.5" overall. **Power:** Spring-piston break-barrel single-shot. **Stock:** All weather synthetic. **Sights:** 4x32mm scope. **Features:** 2-stage non-adjustable trigger, ventilated rubber buttplate and automatic safety. **Velocity:** 1,000 fps.
Price: $129.99

BEEMAN GUARDIAN COMBO AIR RIFLE
Caliber: .177. **Barrel:** Rifled. **Weight:** 5.85 lbs. **Length:** 37" overall. **Power:** Spring-piston break-barrel single-shot. **Stock:** Composite Monte Carlo with checkpiece. **Sights:** 4x20mm scope. **Features:** 2-stage non-adjustable trigger, soft rubber recoil pad and automatic safety. **Velocity:** 550 fps.
Price: $59.99

BEEMAN SPORTSMAN RANGER COMBO AIR RIFLE
Caliber: .177. **Barrel:** Rifled. **Weight:** 4.15 lbs. **Length:** 40" overall. **Power:** Spring-piston break-barrel single-shot. **Stock:** Composite thumbhole stock. **Sights:** 4x20mm scope. **Features:** Automatic safety and 11mm dovetail for scope mounting. **Velocity:** 480 fps.
Price: $79.99

BEEMAN SILVER KODIAK X2 COMBO AIR RIFLE
Caliber: .177 & .22. **Barrel:** Both barrels rifled. **Weight:** 8.75 lbs.

Length: 47.75" overall. **Power:** Spring-piston break-barrel single-shot. **Stock:** All weather synthetic with texture grip and forearm. **Sights:** None, but comes with a 4x32mm scope. **Features:** RS1 2-stage sporter trigger, automatic safety and ventilated rubber buttplate. **Velocity:** 1,000 fps.
Price: $169.99

BEEMAN HW97K AIR RIFLE
Caliber: .177, .20, .22. **Barrel:** 11.81". **Weight:** 9.2 lbs. **Length:** 44.25" overall. **Power:** Spring-piston, under-lever cocking. **Stock:** Walnut-stained beech; rubber buttpad. **Sights:** None. Receiver grooved for scope mounting. **Features:** Fixed barrel with fully opening, direct loading breech and an adjustable trigger. **Velocities:** 920 fps in .177 caliber; 820 fps in .20 caliber; and 750 fps in .22 caliber. Imported by Beeman Precision Airguns.
Price: . . . . $739.95 to $769.95

BEEMAN HW97K THUMBHOLE STOCK AIR RIFLE
Caliber: .177. **Barrel:** 11.81". **Weight:** 9-lbs. **Length:** 40.25" overall. **Power:** Under-lever, break-barrel, spring-piston, single shot. **Stock:** Black colored plastic thumbhole stock. **Sights:** None. **Features:** Muzzle brake, 11mm dovetail grooved, 2-stage adjustable trigger and rubber buttplate. **Velocity:** 930 fps.
Price: $729.95

BEEMAN HW97K ELITE SERIES COMBO AIR RIFLE
Caliber: .177, .20 & .22. **Barrel:** 11.81". **Weight:** 10.2-lbs. **Length:** 40.25" overall. **Power:** Under-lever, break-barrel, spring-piston, single shot. **Stock:** Stained beechwood in Monte Carlo styling. **Sights:** None. **Features:** Muzzlebrake, 11mm dovetail grooved, Rekord trigger and rubber buttplate. **Velocities:** 930 fps in .177 caliber, 820 fps in .20 caliber and 750 fps in .22 caliber.
Price: . . . . $849.95 to $889.95

BEEMAN HW97K BLUE AIR RIFLE
Caliber: .177, .20 & .22. **Barrel:** 11.81". **Weight:** 9.2-lbs. **Length:** 40.25" overall. **Power:** Under-lever, break-barrel, spring-piston, single shot. **Stock:** Laminated Monte Carlo styled. **Sights:** None. **Features:** Muzzlebrake, 11mm dovetail grooved, 2-stage trigger and rubber buttplate. **Velocities:** 930 fps in .177 caliber, 820 fps in .20 caliber and 750 fps in .22 caliber.
Price: . . . . $839.95 to $869.95

BEEMAN XCEL X2 AIR RIFLE
Caliber: .177. **Barrel:** 18". **Weight:** 6.9-lbs. **Length:** 46.5" overall. **Power:** Break-barrel, spring-piston, single shot. **Stock:** Hardwood Monte Carlo styled. **Sights:** None, but grooved for scope mounting. **Features:** Comes with a 3-9x32mm scope, ported muzzlebrake, automatic safety and an updated 2-stage adjustable trigger. **Velocity:** 1,000 fps.
Price: $290.00

BENJAMIN & SHERIDAN PNEUMATIC

BENJAMIN & SHERIDAN PNEUMATIC (PUMP-UP) AIR RIFLE
Caliber: .177 or .22, single shot. **Barrel:** 19-3/8", rifled brass. **Weight:** 5-1/2 lbs. **Length:** 36-1/4" overall. **Power:** Underlever pneumatic, hand pumped. **Stock:** American walnut stock and forend. **Sights:** High ramp front, fully adjustable notched rear. **Features:** Variable velocity to 800 fps. Bolt action with ambidextrous push-pull safety. Black or nickel finish. Made in the U.S.A. by Benjamin. Also manufactured under the Sheridan brand.
Price: Model 397 (.177) $170.00
Price: Model 392 (.20) $170.00
Price: Sheridan CB9 (.22) $200.00

BENJAMIN MARAUDER PCP AIR RIFLE
Caliber: .177, .22, .25 **Weight:** 8.2 lbs. **Length:** 42.87" overall. **Power:** Multishot bolt-action precharged pneumatic 3,000 psi hunting rifle. **Stock:** Hardwood or synthetic, ambidextrous with adjustable cheekpiece. **Features:** Shrouded rifled steel barrel, adjustable two-stage match-grade trigger with eight or 10-round magazine, ambidextrous bolt.
Price: .177, .22 . . . . $700.00
Price: .25 . . . . $750.00

Prices given are believed to be accurate at time of publication however, many factors affect retail pricing so exact prices are not possible.

BENJAMIN ROGUE .357 CALIBER
MULTI-SHOT

BENJAMIN ROGUE .357 CALIBER MULTI-SHOT AIR RIFLE
Caliber: .357, 6-shot mag (optional single-shot tray). **Features:** Electronic precharged pneumatic (ePCP), Bolt-action, 2-stage adjustable electronic trigger with dual electronic switches, Ambidextrous synthetic stock w/adjustable buttstock & sling swivel studs, 11mm, Adjustable power, Up to 900 fps (250 ft-lbs. max), 3000 psi (206 bar) max fill pressure (delivers full-power shots with as little as 1000 psi), Shrouded for stealthy hunting, Up to 20 shots at 100 ft-lbs. when filled to 3000 psi, Built-in manometer (air pressure gauge), Weaver bipod rail, LCD screen for EPiC controls on left side of gun, includes fill adapter. Made in the U.S. by Benjamin Sheridan Co.
Price: **$1,349.00**

BENJAMIN TITAN XS NP BREAK BARREL AIR RIFLE
Caliber: .177 **Weight:** 8.3 lbs. **Length:** 44.5" overall. **Power:** Single-shot Nitro Piston powered break barrel. **Stock:** Synthetic ambidextrous thumbhole. **Sights:** 4x32mm scope. **Features:** Rifled steel barrel, adjustable two-stage trigger, Picatinny mounting rail. 1,250 fps. 18 ft-lbs.
Price: . . . . **$ 232.00**

BENJAMIN TRAIL NITRO PISTON 2 BREAK BARREL AIR RIFLE
Caliber: .177, .22 **Weight:** 8.3 lbs. **Length:** 46.25" overall. **Power:** Break barrel single shot–Patent Pending Nitro Piston 2. **Stock:** Hardwood, black synthetic or Realtree Xtra camo. **Sights:** CenterPoint 3-9x32mm scope. **Features:** Clean Break Trigger (CBT), integrated sound suppression system. 1,200 fps in .177 and 1,400 fps in .22.
Price: .177 Trail NP Synthetic **$350.00**
Price: .22 Trail NP Synthetic **$350.00**
Price: .22 Trail NP Hardwood **$350.00**
Price: .22 Trail NP Realtree Xtra **$380.00**

BENJAMIN VARMINT POWER PACK BREAK BARREL
Caliber: .22 **Power:** Single-shot Nitro Pistol powered break barrel. **Stock:** Ambidextrous synthetic stock with raised cheekpiece. **Sights:** Red Class IIIa fast-acquisition laser. **Features:** Rifled steel barrel, two-stage adjustable trigger, Picatinny mounting rail, recoil-proof 90 lumen LED flashlight. 21 ft-lbs. 950 fps.
Price: .177 Trail NP Synthetic **$250.00**

BERETTA CX4 STORM

BERETTA CX4 STORM
Caliber: .177, 30-shot semiauto. **Barrel:** 17-1/2", rifled. **Weight:** 5.25 lbs. **Length:** 30.75" overall. **Power:** 88g CO2. **Stock:** Replica style. **Sights:** Adjustable front and rear. **Features:** 2-stage adjustable trigger with 8.5-lbs. pull weight, plastic buttstock, Weaver mounts and also available with a PS22 dot sight. **Velocity:** 600 fps. Made by Umarex.
Price: **$375.00**
Price: (with dot sight): **$400.00**

BROWNING LEVERAGE AIR RIFLE
Caliber: .177 & .22. **Barrel:** Rifled 18.9". **Weight:** 8.6-lbs. **Power:** Spring-piston under-lever. **Sights:** Fiber optic front sight and adjustable rear sight and comes with a Weaver Picatinny rail for scope mounting. **Features:** Automatic safety and ventilate rubber recoil pad & 5.2-lbs. trigger pull. **Velocity:** 1,000 fps (.177).
Price: **$230.00**

BROWNING GOLD AIR RIFLE
Caliber: .22. **Barrel:** Rifled 14". **Weight:** 8.4-lbs. **Power:** Spring-piston, break-barrel single-shot. **Sights:** Fiber optic front sight and adjustable rear sight and comes with an 11mm dovetail for scope mounting.

Features: Automatic safety, trigger – 4.0-pounds and adjustable buttplate. **Velocity:** 800 fps.
Price: **$300.00**

BSA MAGNUM SUPERSPORT AIR RIFLE, CARBINE
Caliber: .177, .22, .25, single shot. **Barrel:** 18-1/2". **Weight:** 6 lbs., 8 oz. **Length:** 41" overall. **Power:** Spring-air, barrel cocking. **Stock:** Oil-finished hardwood; Monte Carlo with cheekpiece, recoil pad. **Sights:** Ramp front, micrometer adjustable rear. Maxi-Grip scope rail. **Features:** Velocity 950 fps (.177), 750 fps (.22), 600 fps (25). Patented Maxi-Grip scope rail protects optics from recoil; automatic anti-beartrap plus manual tang safety. Muzzle brake standard. Imported for U.K.
Price: **$194.95**
Price: Carbine, 14" barrel, muzzle brake **$214.95**

BSA METEOR MK7 AIR RIFLE
Caliber: .177, .22, single shot. **Barrel:** 18-1/2". **Weight:** 15 lbs. **Length:** 47" overall. **Power:** Spring-air, barrel cocking. **Stock:** Oil-finished hardwood. **Sights:** Ramp front, micrometer adjustable rear. **Features:** Automatic anti-beartrap; manual tang safety. Receiver grooved for scope mounting. **Velocity:** 900 fps (.177), 600 fps (.22). Imported from U.K.
Price: **$199.99**

BSA R-10 MK2 PCP AIR RIFLE
Caliber: .17, .22 **Barrel:** 18" **Weight:** 7.3 lbs. **Power:** Pre-charged pneumatic (3,365 psi maximum fill pressure) bolt action. **Stock:** Oiled walnut Monte Carlo stock with right-hand raised cheekpiece and checkered grip and fore-end. **Sights:** No sights, aluminum 11mm dovetail grooves for scope installation. **Features:** Sling swivel studs, rifled steel hammer-forged free-floated fully shrouded barrel, two-stage adjustable trigger, adjustable buttplate, manual safety, 10-round capacity, up to 50 shots per fill in .17 and up to 45 shots per fill in .22 caliber. 1,000 fps in .17 and 900 fps in .22.
Price: **$1,299.99**

BSA SCORPION 1200 SE AIR RIFLE
Caliber: .177, .22 **Barrel:** 24" **Weight:** 8.75 lbs. **Power:** Pre-charged pneumatic (3,364 psi maximum fill pressure) bolt action. **Stock:** Synthetic ambidextrous stock with twin raised cheekpieces. **Sights:** No sights, aluminum 11mm dovetail grooves for scope installation. **Features:** Rifled steel hammer-forged free-floated barrel, 2-stage adjustable trigger, ventilated rubber buttplate, manual safety, 10-round removable rotary self-indexing magazine, built-in manometer (air pressure gauge). 1,200 fps in .17 and 1,000 fps in .22.
Price: **$980.95**

BSA SCORPION SE BEECH AIR RIFLE
Caliber: .17, .22, .25 **Barrel:** 18.5" **Weight:** 7.7 lbs. **Power:** Pre-charged pneumatic (3,365 psi maximum fill pressure) bolt action. **Stock:** Ambidextrous Monte Carlo Beech wood. **Sights:** No sights, aluminum 11mm dovetail grooves for scope installation. **Features:** Rifled steel hammer-forged free-floated barrel, 2-stage adjustable trigger, ventilated rubber buttplate, manual safety, 10-round removable rotary self-indexing magazine (10 round capacity in .17 and .22 and 8-round capacity in .25 caliber), with up to 40-shots per fill in .17 and up to 30 shots per fill in .22 and .25 calibers, built-in manometer (air pressure gauge). 1,000 fps in .17 caliber, 820 fps in .22 caliber and 700 fps in .25 caliber.
Price: **$879.99**

BSA ULTRA SE TACTICAL AIR RIFLE
Caliber: .17, .22, .25 **Barrel:** 12" **Weight:** 5.7 lbs. **Length:** 47.21" **Power:** Pre-charged pneumatic (3,365 psi maximum fill pressure) bolt action. **Stock:** Synthetic ambidextrous Monte Carlo stock with textured grip and forearm. **Sights:** No sights, aluminum 11mm dovetail grooves for scope installation. **Features:** Silenced, match-accurate barrel and a fully-checkered stock Match-grade cold-hammer-forged steel barrel, two-stage adjustable match-grade trigger, manual safety, built-in pressure gauge, rubber buttplate. 10-round capacity (eight rounds in .25 caliber).
Price: **$839.99**

CROSMAN CHALLENGER PCP COMPETITION AIR RIFLE
Caliber: .177 **Weight:** 7.1 lbs. **Length:** 41.5" overall. **Power:** Precharged pneumatic sporting class single-shot air rifle, which operates on either compressed air or CO2. **Stock:** Synthetic. **Sights:** Diopter front sight and Precision Diopter rear sight. **Features:** Rifled

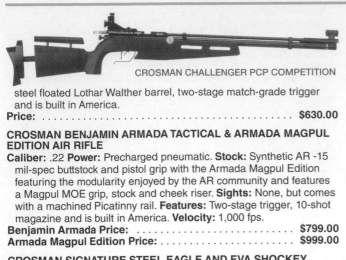

CROSMAN CHALLENGER PCP COMPETITION

steel floated Lothar Walther barrel, two-stage match-grade trigger and is built in America.
Price: **$630.00**

CROSMAN BENJAMIN ARMADA TACTICAL & ARMADA MAGPUL EDITION AIR RIFLE

Caliber: .22 **Power:** Precharged pneumatic. **Stock:** Synthetic AR -15 mil-spec buttstock and pistol grip with the Armada Magpul Edition featuring the modularity enjoyed by the AR community and features a Magpul MOE grip, stock and cheek riser. **Sights:** None, but comes with a machined Picatinny rail. **Features:** Two-stage trigger, 10-shot magazine and is built in America. **Velocity:** 1,000 fps.
Benjamin Armada Price: **$799.00**
Armada Magpul Edition Price: **$999.00**

CROSMAN SIGNATURE STEEL EAGLE AND EVA SHOCKEY SIGNATURE GOLDEN EAGLE AIR RIFLES

Caliber: .22 & .177. **Power:** Break Barrel with Nitro Piston 2 power plants. **Stock:** Synthetic all-weather stocks with soft touch grip inserts. **Sights:** None, but comes with a machined Picatinny rail and a 3-9x32mm CenterPoint scope on the Steel Eagle and a 4x32mm CenterPoint scope on the Golden Eagle. **Features:** Two-stage trigger. **Velocities:** Steel Eagle .22 caliber up to 1,100 fps and the Golden Eagle .177 caliber up to 1,400 fps.
Signature Steel Eagle Price: **$329.990**
Signature Golden Eagle Price: **$269.99**

CROSMAN BULLDOG TROPHY GAME AIR RIFLE

Caliber: .357. **Weight:** 8 lbs. **Length:** 36 inches. **Power:** Precharged pneumatic. **Stock:** Synthetic. **Sights:** Picatinny rail equipped. **Features:** Two-stage trigger, 26 inch rail above the barrel and a 5.5" accessory rail underneath. **Velocity:** Nearly 800 fps.
Price: **$999.99**

CROSMAN M4-177

CROSMAN M4-177

Caliber: .177 pellet or BB. Removable 5-shot magazine. **Weight:** 3.5 lbs. **Length:** 34". **Sights:** Windage-adjustable flip-up rear, elevation-adjustable front. **Features:** Rifled barrel, adjustable stock, pneumatic multi-pump operation gives up to 660 fps muzzle velocity. Bolt-action variation of AR-style rifle. Also available in kit form.
Price: **$75.00**

CROSMAN MARINES USMC MOS 0311 RIFLEMAN

Caliber: .177, BB **Weight:** 3.5 lbs. **Length:** 34". **Power:** Pneumatic multi-pump bolt-action variation of AR-style rifles. **Sights:** Dual aperture windage-adjustable flip-up rear sight and elevation-adjustable front sight. **Features:** Rifled barrel, adjustable stock, removable five-shot magazine and 350 BB reservoir. 660 fps with BBs and 700 fps with alloy pellets.
Price: **$100.00**

CROSMAN MODEL 664SB POWERMASTER AIR RIFLE

Caliber: .177 (single shot pellet) or BB, 200-shot reservoir. **Barrel:** 20", rifled steel. **Weight:** 2 lbs. 15 oz. **Length:** 38-1/2" overall. **Power:** Pneumatic; hand-pumped. **Stock:** Wood-grained ABS plastic; checkered pistol grip and forend. **Sights:** Fiber-optic front, fully adjustable open rear. **Features:** Velocity about 645 fps. Bolt action, cross-bolt safety. From Crosman.
Price: **$105.50**

CROSMAN MODEL 760 PUMPMASTER AIR RIFLE

Caliber: .177 pellets (single shot) or BB (200-shot reservoir). **Barrel:** 19-1/2", rifled steel. **Weight:** 2 lbs., 12 oz. **Length:** 33.5" overall. **Power:** Pneumatic, hand-pump. **Stock:** Walnut-finished ABS plastic stock and forend. **Features:** Velocity to 590 fps (BBs, 10 pumps). Short stroke, power determined by number of strokes. Fiber-optic front sight and adjustable rear sight. Cross-bolt safety. From Crosman.
Price: Model 760 . . . . **$48.00**

CROSMAN MODEL 1077 REPEATAIR RIFLE

Caliber: .177 pellets, 12-shot clip. **Barrel:** 20.4", rifled steel. **Weight:** 3 lbs., 11 oz. **Length:** 37" overall. **Power:** CO2 Powerlet. **Stock:** Textured synthetic. **Sights:** Fiber-optic front sight and fully adjustable rear. **Features:** Velocity 625 fps. Removable 12-shot clip. True semiautomatic action. From Crosman.
Price: **$90.00**

CROSMAN MODEL 2100 CLASSIC AIR RIFLE

Caliber: .177 pellets (single shot), or BB (200-shot BB reservoir). **Barrel:** 21", rifled. **Weight:** 4 lbs., 13 oz. **Length:** 39-3/4" overall. **Power:** Pump-up, pneumatic. **Stock:** Wood-grained checkered synthetic. **Features:** 755 fps with BBs and 725 fps with pellets. Cross-bolt safety; concealed reservoir holds over 200 BBs. From Crosman.
Price: Model 2100B **$69.99**

CROSMAN MODEL 2260 AIR RIFLE

Caliber: .22, single shot. **Barrel:** 24". **Weight:** 4 lbs., 12 oz. **Length:** 39.75" overall. **Power:** CO2 Powerlet. **Stock:** Hardwood. **Sights:** Blade front, adjustable rear open or peep. **Features:** Variable pump power; three pumps give 395 fps, six pumps 530 fps, 10 pumps 600 fps (average). Full-size adult air rifle. From Crosman.
Price: **$83.84**

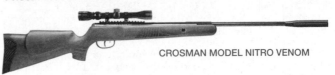

CROSMAN MODEL NITRO VENOM

CROSMAN MODEL NITRO VENOM AIR RIFLE

Caliber: .177, .22 **Weight:** 7.4 lbs. **Length:** 44.5" **Power:** Single shot Nitro Venom Piston design. **Stock:** Hardwood or synthetic ambidextrous stock with a raised cheekpiece and modified beavertail forearm. **Sights:** 4x32mm scope. **Features:** Precision rifled barrel with fluted muzzlebrake and sculpted rubber recoil pad. The rifle is equipped with a scope quick-lock mounting system for quick and easy optic mounting. 1,200 fps and 18 foot-pounds of energy (.177). 950 fps and 21 foot-pounds of energy (.22).
Price: .177 . . . . **$170.00**
Price: .22 . . . . **$180.00**

CROSMAN MODEL NITRO VENOM DUSK

CROSMAN MODEL NITRO VENOM DUSK AIR RIFLE

Caliber: .177 & .22. **Features:** Nitro Venom air rifle feature precision, rifled barrel with fluted muzzle brake and sculpted rubber recoil pad. The rifle is equipped with a CenterPoint 3-9x32mm precision scope and a quick-lock mounting system for quick and easy optic mounting. The ambidextrous hardwood stock with raised cheek piece and modified, beavertail forearm. Crosman Nitro Venom air rifle delivers serious hunting power with muzzle energy up to 21 fps and up to 1200 fps. Take one on a hunt to experience the power, stability and stealth of Nitro Piston® technology.
Price: .177 . . . . **$209.99**
Price: .22 . . . . **N/A**

CROSMAN MODEL TRAIL NP ALL WEATHER

CROSMAN MODEL TRAIL NP ALL WEATHER & LAMINATED HARDWOOD AIR RIFLES

Caliber: .177, .22 & .25, up to 1200 fps (.177), 950 fps (.22) & 900

Prices given are believed to be accurate at time of publication however, many factors affect retail pricing so exact prices are not possible.

fps (.25). **Weight:** 6.65 lbs. - 8 lbs. **Length:** 43" overall. **Features:** The Nitro Venom Dusk air rifle features a precision, rifled barrel with fluted muzzle break and sculpted rubber recoil pad. The rifle is equipped with a CenterPoint 3-9x32mm precision scope and a quick-lock mounting system for quick and easy optic mounting. The ambidextrous synthetic stock has a raised cheek piece and modified, beavertail forearm. Crosman Nitro Venom air rifles delivers serious hunting power with muzzle energy up to 18 fpe and up to 1200 fps.. Take one on a hunt to experience the power, stability and stealth of Nitro Piston® technology. The .22 caliber series is equiped with various harwood and laminated thumbhole and standard stocks and also models with bull barrels, imposing 23 ft-lbs of muzzle energy provides 16% more downrange energy than .177 cal. The new XL725 provides 24% more downrange energy than a .177 caliber offers. This is the most powerful Nitro Piston® break barrel available.

Price: .177 Trail NP **$247.00**
Price: .177 Trail NP XL 1500 . . . . **$247.00**
Price: .22 Trail NP All Weather **$247.00**
Price: .22 Trail NP Hardwood **$299.00**
Price: .22 Trail NP All Weather with Realtree APG **$279.95**
Price: .22 Trail NP All Weather 495fps **$299.00**
Price: .22 Trail NP Laminated Hardwood . . . . **N/A**
Price: .22 Trail NP XL 1100 . . . . **$359.00**
Price: .25 Trail NP XL 725 . . . . **$329.00**

CROSMAN MTR77 NP TACTICAL BREAK BARREL AIR RIFLE
Caliber: .177 **Weight:** 5.8 lbs. **Length:** 40" overall. **Power:** Single-shot Nitro Piston modern sporting rifle design. **Stock:** Textured synthetic all-weather tactical style. **Sights:** 4x32mm scope. **Features:** Rifled steel barrel, adjustable trigger and provides 18 foot-pounds of energy.
Price: **$200.00**

CROSMAN TR77 NPS TACTICAL BREAK BARREL AIR RIFLE
Caliber: .177 **Weight:** 5.8 lbs. **Length:** 40" overall. **Power:** Single-shot Nitro Piston. **Stock:** Compact, tactical-style, textured synthetic. **Sights:** 4x32mm scope. **Features:** Rifled steel barrel, 1,000 fps.
Price: **$160.00**

DAISY 1938 RED RYDER

DAISY 1938 RED RYDER AIR RIFLE
Caliber: BB, 650-shot repeating action. **Barrel:** Smoothbore steel with shroud. **Weight:** 2.2 lbs. **Length:** 35.4" overall. **Stock:** Wood stock burned with Red Ryder lariat signature. **Sights:** Post front, adjustable open rear. **Features:** Walnut forend. Saddle ring with leather thong. Lever cocking. Gravity feed. Controlled velocity. 350 fps. From Daisy Mfg. Co.
Price: **$39.99**

DAISY AVANTI MODEL 887 GOLD MEDALIST
Caliber: .177 **Barrel:** Lothar Walther rifled high-grade steel, crowned, 12 lands and grooves, right hand twist. Precision bore sized for match pellets. **Weight:** 7.3 lbs. **Length:** 39.5" overall. **Power:** CO2 power single shot bolt. **Stock:** Laminated hardwood. **Sights:** Front globe sight with changeable aperture inserts: rear diopter sight with micrometer click adjustment for windage and elevation. **Features:** Velocity to 500 fps. Crossbolt trigger block safety. Includes rail adapter. From Daisy Mfg. Co.
Price: **$499.00**

DAISY AVANTI MODEL 888 MEDALIST
Caliber: .177 **Barrel:** Lothar Walther rifled high-grade steel, crowned, 12 lands and grooves, right-hand twist. Precision bore sized for match pellets. **Weight:** 6.9 lbs. **Length:** 38.5" overall. **Power:** CO2 single shot bolt. **Stock:** Sporter-style multicolored laminated hardwood. **Sights:** Hooded front with interchangeable aperture inserts; micrometer adjustable rear peep sight. **Features:** Velocity to 500 fps. Crossbolt trigger block safety. From Daisy Mfg. Co.
Price: **$469.99**

DAISY MODEL 105 BUCK AIR RIFLE
Caliber: .177 or BB. **Barrel:** Smoothbore steel. **Weight:** 1.6 lbs. **Length:** 29.8" overall. **Power:** Lever cocking, spring air. **Stock:** Stained solid wood. **Sights:** TruGlo fiber-optic, open fixed rear. **Features:** Velocity to 275. Crossbolt trigger block safety. From Daisy Mfg. Co.
Price: **$29.99**

DAISY MODEL 753 ELITE

DAISY MODEL 753 ELITE
Caliber: .177, pellet. **Barrel:** Lothar Walther rifled high-grade steel barrel, crowned, 12 lands and grooves, right-hand twist. Precision bore sized for match pellets. **Weight:** 6.4 lbs. **Length:** 39.75" overall. **Power:** Recoilless single pump pneumatic, straight pull bolt. **Stock:** Full length match-style hardwood stock with raised cheek piece and adjustable length. **Sights:** Front globe sight with changeable aperture inserts, diopter rear sight with micrometer adjustable rear. **Features:** Velocity to 510 fps. Crossbolt trigger block safety with red indicator. From Daisy Mfg. Co.
Price: **$450.00**

DAISY MODEL 840B GRIZZLY AIR RIFLE
Caliber: .177 pellet single shot; or BB 350-shot. **Barrel:** 19", smoothbore, steel. **Weight:** 2.25 lbs. **Length:** 36.8" overall. **Power:** Single pump pneumatic. **Stock:** Molded wood-grain stock and forend. **Sights:** Ramp front, open, adjustable rear. **Features:** Muzzle velocity 320 fps (BB), 300 fps (pellet). Steel buttplate; straight pull bolt action; cross-bolt safety. Forend forms pump lever. From Daisy Mfg. Co.
Price: (840B Black) **$44.99**
Price: (840C Camo) **$49.99**

DAISY AVANTI MODEL 853 LEGEND
Caliber: .177, pellet. **Barrel:** Lothar Walther rifled high-grade steel barrel, crowned, 12 lands and grooves, right-hand twist. Precision bore sized for match pellets. **Weight:** 5.5 lbs. **Length:** 38.5" overall. **Power:** Single-pump pneumatic, straight pull-bolt. **Stock:** Full-length, sporter-style hardwood with adjustable length. **Sights:** Hooded front with interchangeable aperture inserts; micrometer adjustable rear. **Features:** Velocity to 510 fps. Crossbolt trigger block safety with red indicator. From Daisy Mfg. Co.
Price: **$399.00**

DAISY MODEL 10 AIR RIFLE
Caliber: .177 BB 400-shot repeater. **Barrel:** Smoothbore steel. **Weight:** 1.6 lbs. **Length:** 29.8" overall. **Power:** Lever cocking, spring air. **Stock:** Stained solid wood stock and forearm. **Sights:** Blade and ramp front, open fixed rear. **Features:** Cross-bolt trigger block safety. **Velocity:** 350 fps. From Daisy Outdoor Products.
Price: **$34.99**

DAISY 1938 PINK CARBINE AIR RIFLE
Caliber: .177 BB 650-shot repeater. **Barrel:** Smoothbore steel. **Weight:** 2.2 lbs. **Length:** 35.4" overall. **Power:** Lever cocking, spring air. **Stock:** Wood stock, painted pink. **Sights:** Blade and ramp front, adjustable open rear. **Features:** Saddle ring with leather thong. **Velocity:** 350 fps. From Daisy Outdoor Products.
Price: $39.99

DAISY POWERLINE MODEL 35 AIR RIFLE
Caliber: .177, BB. **Weight:** 3.1 lbs. **Length:** 34.5" overall. **Power:** Multi-pump pneumatic. **Stock:** Molded synthetic with checkering. **Sights:** Blade ramp front sight and adjustable rear. **Features:** Smoothbore steel barrel. 625 fps.
Price: **$39.99**
Price: (Camo) **$49.99**

DAISY POWERLINE® 500 BREAK BARREL
Caliber: .177 pellet, single shot. **Barrel:** Rifled steel. **Weight:** 6.6 lbs. **Length:** 45.7" overall. **Stock:** Stained solid wood. **Sights:** Truglo® fiber-optic front, micro-adjustable open rear, adjustable 4x32 riflescope. **Features:** Auto rear-button safety. Velocity to 490 fps. Made in U.S.A. by Daisy Mfg. Co.
Price: **$120.99**

DAISY POWERLINE® 800 BREAK BARREL
Caliber: .177 pellet, single shot. **Barrel:** Rifled steel. **Weight:** 6.6 lbs. **Length:** 46.7" overall. **Stock:** Black composite. **Sights:** Truglo fiber-optic front, micro-adjustable open rear, adjustable 4x32 riflescope. **Features:** Auto rear-button safety. Velocity to 800 fps. Made in U.S.A. by Daisy Mfg. Co.
Price: **$120.99**

DAISY POWERLINE® 880 AIR RIFLE
Caliber: .177 pellet or BB, 50-shot BB magazine, single shot for pellets. **Barrel:** Rifled steel. **Weight:** 3.7 lbs. **Length:** 37.6" overall. **Power:** Multi-pump pneumatic. **Stock:** Molded wood grain; Monte Carlo comb. **Sights:** Hooded front, adjustable rear. **Features:** Velocity to 800 fps. (BB). Variable power (velocity, range) increase with pump strokes; resin receiver with dovetailed scope mount. Made in U.S.A. by Daisy Mfg. Co.
Price: **$49.99**

DAISY POWERLINE® 901 AIR RIFLE
Caliber: .177. **Barrel:** Rifled steel. **Weight:** 3.7 lbs. **Length:** 37.5" overall. **Power:** Multi-pump pneumatic. **Stock:** Advanced composite. **Sights:** Fiber-optic front, adjustable rear. **Features:** Velocity to 750 fps. (BB); advanced composite receiver with dovetailed mounts for optics. Made in U.S.A. by Daisy Mfg. Co.
Price: **$60.99**

DAISY POWERLINE® TARGETPRO 953 AIR RIFLE
Caliber: .177 pellets, single shot. **Weight:** 6.40 lbs. **Length:** 39.75" overall. **Power:** Pneumatic single-pump cocking lever; straight-pull bolt. **Stock:** Full-length, match-style black composite. **Sights:** Front and rear fiber optic. **Features:** Rifled high-grade steel barrel with 1:15 twist. Max. Muzzle Velocity of 560 fps. From Daisy Mfg. Co.
Price: **$119.99**

DIANA MODEL 34 PREMIUM AIR RIFLE
Caliber: .177, .22 **Weight:** 7.5 lbs. **Length:** 46" overall. **Power:** Break-barrel single-shot. **Stock:** Monte Carlo stock with checkered forearm, pistol grip and soft rubber pad. **Sights:** Metal with interchangeable front sight inserts. **Features:** 1,000 fps in .177 and 800 fps in .22.
Price: **$479.99**

DIANA MODEL 52 AIR RIFLE
Caliber: .177, .22, .25 **Barrel:** 17.3" **Weight:** 9.4 lbs. **Length:** 45" overall. **Power:** Side-cocking, spring-piston design. **Stock:** Walnut stained beechwood with cheekpiece and fine checkering on forearm and pistol grip. **Sights:** Adjustable. **Features:** Two-stage adjustable trigger, rubber buttplate, 11mm scope rail. 1,150 fps in .177; 850 fps in .22, 610 in .25.
Price: **$649.99**

DIANA MODEL 56 TARGET HUNTER AIR RIFLE
Caliber: .177, .22, .25 **Weight:** 11.1 lbs. **Length:** 44" overall. **Power:** Recoiless spring gun. **Stock:** Monte Carlo stock with cheekpiece, adjustable rear buttpad for elevation, ambidextrous thumbhole design. **Features:** Upgraded metal safety catch, upgraded 2-stage all metal trigger assembly, muzzle stabilizer. 1,000 fps in .177; 900 fps in .22; 610 fps in .25.
Price: (.177 & .22). **$969.99**
Price: (.25). **$1,050.99**

DIANA MODEL 430 STUTZEN AIR RIFLE
Caliber: .177 & .22. **Barrel:** 15.4" rifled. **Weight:** 8.2 lbs. **Length:** 41" overall. **Power:** Break-barrel single shot. **Stock:** Thumbhole hardwood. **Features:** Scope rail, two-stage adjustable trigger, auto safety and rifled barrel. **Velocities:** 870 fps in .177 and 670 fps in .22.
Price: **$750.00**

DIANA MODEL 440 TARGET HUNTER AIR RIFLE
Caliber: .177, .22 **Barrel:** 15.4" **Weight:** 9 lbs. **Length:** 41" overall. **Power:** Break-barrel single shot. **Stock:** Thumbhole hardwood. **Features:** Scope rail, two-stage adjustable trigger, auto safety and rifled barrel. 870 fps in .177 and 670 fps in .22.
Price: **$650.99**

DIANA MODEL 470 TARGET HUNTER AIR RIFLE
Caliber: .177, .22 **Barrel:** 18" **Weight:** 9.4 lbs. **Length:** 45" overall. **Power:** Break-barrel single shot. **Stock:** Ambidextrous thumbhole hardwood, adjustable buttplate for elevation. **Features:** Upgraded two-stage adjustable trigger assembly with all-metal parts, rifled barrel. 1,150 fps in .177 and 930 fps in .22.
Price: **$725.50**

DIANA MODEL P1000 PCP AIR RIFLE
Caliber: .177, .22 **Weight:** 7.9 lbs. **Length:** 38" overall. **Power:** Precharged pneumatic airgun. **Stock:** Monte Carlo, two-piece hunting style. **Features:** 14-shot magazine, single-shot adapter, 300-bar steel cylinder, TO6-metal trigger with automatic safety, 11-mm top rail. 1,150 fps in .177 and 950 fps in .22.
Price: **$1,499.99**

DIANA MODEL P1000 PCP TARGET HUNTER AIR RIFLE
Caliber: .177, .22 **Weight:** 8.2 lbs. **Length:** 38" overall. **Power:** Precharged pneumatic airgun. **Stock:** Monte Carlo, two-piece hunting style. **Features:** 14-shot magazine, single-shot adapter, 300-bar steel cylinder, TO6-metal trigger with automatic safety, 11-mm top rail. 1,150 fps in .177 and 950 fps in .22.
Price: **$1,595.99**

DIANA MODEL PANTHER 31 PRO AIR RIFLE
Caliber: .177 & .22. **Barrel:** 15.6" rifled steel. **Weight:** 7.9 lbs. **Length:** 42" overall. **Power:** Break-barrel single shot. **Stock:** Ambidextrous synthetic with ridged texturing on forearm and pistol grip. **Features:** Scope rail, two-stage adjustable trigger, auto safety and rifled barrel. **Velocities:** 1,000 fps in .177 and 740 fps in .22.
Price: **$429.99**

GAMO BIG CAT 1250 HUNTER

GAMO BIG CAT 1250 HUNTER AIR RIFLE
Caliber: .177, .22 **Weight:** 6.1 lbs. **Power:** Break-barrel spring action. **Stock:** Ambidextrous all-weather black synthetic. **Sights:** 4x32mm scope. **Features:** Two-stage adjustable trigger, fluted polymer jacketed precision rifled steel barrel, rubber recoil pad. **Velocity:** .177 – 1,250 fps.
Price: **$199.95**

GAMO BIG CAT .25 CALIBER HUNTER AIR RIFLE
Caliber: .25. **Weight:** 6.1 lbs. **Power:** Break-barrel spring action. **Stock:** Ambidextrous all-weather black synthetic. **Sights:** 4x32mm scope. **Features:** Two-stage adjustable trigger, fluted polymer jacketed precision rifled steel barrel, rubber recoil pad. **Velocity:** 800 fps with PBA Platinum pellets.
Price: **$239.95**

GAMO BIG CAT 1400 AIR RIFLE
Caliber: .177 **Weight:** 6.61 lbs. **Power:** Break-barrel spring action. **Stock:** Ambidextrous all-weather synthetic. **Sights:** 4x32mm scope. **Features:** Two-stage adjustable trigger, fluted polymer jacketed precision rifled steel barrel, rubber recoil pad. 1,400 fps.
Price: **$199.95**

GAMO HORNET .177 CALIBER AIR RIFLE
Caliber: .177 **Weight:** 6.61 lbs. **Power:** Break-barrel spring action. **Stock:** Ambidextrous all-weather synthetic. **Sights:** 4x32mm scope. **Features:** Two-stage adjustable trigger, fluted polymer jacketed steel barrel, rubber recoil pad. **Velocity:** 1,000 fps with lead pellet.
Price: **$139.95**

GAMO BONE COLLECTOR BULL WHISPER AIR RIFLE
Caliber: .177, .22 **Weight:** 6.2 lbs. **Power:** Break-barrel spring action. **Stock:** Ambidextrous all-weather synthetic green and black colored. **Sights:** 4x32mm scope. **Features:** Two-stage adjustable trigger, fluted polymer jacketed precision rifled steel barrel, rubber recoil pad. 1,300 fps in .177; 975 fps in .22.
Price: **$289.95**

GAMO BONE COLLECTOR IGT AIR RIFLE
Caliber: .177 **Weight:** 6.1 lbs. **Power:** Break-barrel spring action. **Stock:** Ambidextrous all-weather synthetic green and black colored. **Sights:** 4x32mm scope. **Features:** Two-stage adjustable trigger, fluted polymer jacketed precision rifled steel barrel, rubber recoil pad. 1,300 fps.
Price: **$289.95**

GAMO BUCKMASTER SQUIRREL TERMINATOR AIR RIFLE
Caliber: .177 **Weight:** 6.1 lbs. **Power:** Break-barrel spring airgun. **Stock:** Ambidextrous all-weather synthetic. **Sights:** 4x32mm scope. **Features:** Two-stage adjustable trigger, turbo stabilizing system, fluted polymer jacketed rifled steel barrel, rubber recoil pad. 1,275 fps.
Price: **$229.95**

GAMO CAMO ROCKET IGT AIR RIFLE
Caliber: .177 **Weight:** 6.1 lbs. **Power:** Break-barrel spring action. **Stock:** Ambidextrous all-weather synthetic black thumbhole style.

Prices given are believed to be accurate at time of publication however, many factors affect retail pricing so exact prices are not possible.

Sights: Fiber optics front and rear and 4x32mm scope. **Features:** Two-stage adjustable trigger, fluted polymer jacketed precision rifled steel barrel, rubber recoil pad. 1,300 fps.
Price: **$248.95**

GAMO HUNTER AIR RIFLES
Caliber: .177. **Barrel:** NA. **Weight:** 6.5 to 10.5 lbs. **Length:** 43.5-48.5". **Power:** Single-stroke pneumatic, 850-1,000 fps. **Stock:** Wood. **Sights:** Varies by model **Features:** Adjustable two-stage trigger, rifled barrel, raised scope ramp on receiver. Realtree camo model available.
Price: Sport **$250.00**
Price: Pro **$300.00**

GAMO HUNTER EXTREME SE (SPECIAL EDITION) AIR RIFLE
Caliber: .177 **Weight:** 6.61 lbs. **Power:** Break-barrel spring action. **Stock:** Hardwood. **Sights:** 4x32mm scope. **Features:** Two-stage adjustable trigger, fluted polymer jacketed precision rifled steel barrel, rubber recoil pad. 1,650 fps.
Price: **$549.95**

GAMO RECON G2 WHISPER AIR RIFLE
Caliber: .177 **Weight:** 4.64 lbs. **Power:** Break-barrel spring action. **Stock:** Ambidextrous all-weather synthetic. **Sights:** Illuminated green dot. **Features:** Two-stage adjustable trigger, fluted polymer jacketed rifled steel barrel, rubber recoil pad. 750 fps.
Price: **$129.95**

GAMO SHAWN MICHAELS SHOWSTOPPER AIR RIFLE
Caliber: .177 **Weight:** 6.61 lbs. **Power:** Break-barrel spring action. **Stock:** Ambidextrous all-weather synthetic. **Sights:** 4x32mm scope. **Features:** Two-stage adjustable trigger, fluted polymer jacketed precision rifled steel barrel, rubber recoil pad. 1,400 fps.
Price: **$259.95**

GAMO SILENT CAT AIR RIFLE
Caliber: .177 **Weight:** 5.28 lbs. **Power:** Break-barrel spring action. **Stock:** Ambidextrous all-weather synthetic black thumbhole style. **Sights:** 4x32mm scope and fiber optics front and rear. **Features:** Two-stage adjustable trigger, fluted polymer jacketed precision rifled steel barrel, rubber recoil pad. 1,300 fps.
Price: **$259.95**

GAMO SILENT STALKER AIR RIFLE
Caliber: .177 **Weight:** 6.1 lbs. **Power:** Break-barrel spring action. **Stock:** Ambidextrous all-weather synthetic. **Sights:** 4x32mm scope. **Features:** Two-stage adjustable trigger, fluted polymer jacketed precision rifled steel barrel, rubber recoil pad. 1,300 fps.
Price: **$329.95**

GAMO SILENT STALKER WHISPER

GAMO SILENT STALKER WHISPER AIR RIFLE
Caliber: .177, .22 **Weight:** 6.61 lbs. **Power:** Break-barrel spring action. **Stock:** Ambidextrous all-weather synthetic. **Sights:** 3-9x40mm scope. **Features:** Two-stage adjustable trigger, fluted polymer jacketed precision rifled steel barrel, rubber recoil pad, flashlight with pressure switch. .177 – 1,300 fps and .22 – 975 fps.
Price: **$329.95**

GAMO VARMINT HUNTER AIR RIFLE
Caliber: .177 **Weight:** 7 lbs. **Power:** Break-barrel spring airgun. **Stock:** Ambidextrous all-weather synthetic. **Sights:** 4x32mm scope. **Features:** Two-stage adjustable trigger, fluted polymer jacketed rifled steel barrel, rubber recoil pad. 1,250 fps.
Price: **$249.95**

GAMO VARMINT HUNTER HP AIR RIFLE
Caliber: .177 **Weight:** 6.1 lbs. **Power:** Break-barrel spring action. **Stock:** Ambidextrous all-weather synthetic green. **Sights:** Laser and 4x32mm scope. **Features:** Two-stage adjustable trigger, fluted polymer jacketed precision rifled steel barrel, rubber recoil pad, flashlight with pressure switch. 1,400 fps.
Price: **$309.95**

GAMO VARMINT STALKER AIR RIFLE
Caliber: .177 **Weight:** 6.1 lbs. **Power:** Break-barrel spring action.

Stock: Ambidextrous all-weather synthetic black thumbhole style. **Sights:** 4x32mm scope. **Features:** Two-stage adjustable trigger, fluted polymer jacketed precision rifled steel barrel, rubber recoil pad. 1,250 fps.
Price: **$244.95**

GAMO WHISPER

GAMO WHISPER AIR RIFLE
Caliber: .177 **Weight:** 8 lbs. **Power:** Break-barrel spring action. **Stock:** Ambidextrous all-weather synthetic pistol grip style. **Sights:** 3-9x40mm scope. **Features:** Two-stage adjustable trigger, fluted polymer jacketed precision rifled steel barrel, rubber recoil pad. 1,100 fps.
Price: **$329.95**

GAMO WHISPER FUSION AIR RIFLE
Caliber: .177 **Weight:** 6.61 lbs. **Power:** Break-barrel spring action. **Stock:** Ambidextrous all-weather synthetic. **Sights:** 3-9x40mm scope. **Features:** Two-stage adjustable trigger, fluted polymer jacketed precision rifled steel barrel, rubber recoil pad, adjustable comb for height. 1,300 fps.
Price: **$309.95**

GAMO WHISPER FUSION PRO AIR RIFLE
Caliber: .177, .22 **Weight:** 6.61 lbs. **Power:** Break-barrel spring action. **Stock:** Ambidextrous all-weather synthetic. **Sights:** 3-9x40mm scope and fiber optics front and rear. **Features:** Two-stage adjustable trigger, fluted polymer jacketed precision rifled steel barrel, rubber recoil pad. .177 – 1,400 and .22 – 1,000 fps.
Price: **$329.95**

GAMO WHISPER G2 AIR RIFLE
Caliber: .177, .22. **Weight:** 6.3 lbs. **Stock:** Ambidextrous all weather synthetic. **Sights:** 4x32mm scope and fiber optics front and rear. **Features:** Two-stage adjustable trigger, turbo stabilizing system, fluted polymer jacketed rifled steel barrel, adjustable cheekpiece, rubber recoil pad. .177 - 1,250 fps and .22 - 975 fps.
Price: **$269.95**

HAMMERLI 850 AIR MAGNUM
Caliber: .177, .22, 8-shot repeater. 23-1/2", rifled. **Weight:** 5.8 lbs. 41" overall. **Power:** 88g CO2. **Stock:** All-weather polymer, Monte Carlo, textured grip and forearm. **Sights:** Hooded fiber optic front, fiber optic adjustable rear. Velocity of 760 fps (.177), 655 (22). Blue finish. Rubber buttpad. Bolt-action. Scope compatible.
Price: .177, .22 . . . . **$370.00**

HAMMERLI AR20 SILVER AND PRO AIR RIFLE
Caliber: .177. **Barrel:** Rifled 19.69". **Weight:** 8.75-lbs. **Length:** 43.66" overall. **Power:** Precharged pneumatic 350-shots maximum per fill. **Features:** 10-meter and 3-position designed, highly adjustable and ambidextrous and no safety. **Sights:** Front globe with aperture inserts and Diopter/micrometer adjustable rear sight. **Velocity:** 557 fps.
Price: . . . . **$995.95 to $1050.00**

HATSAN USA SPRING POWERED

HATSAN USA SPRING POWERED AIR RIFLES
Caliber: .177 **Power:** Spring powered. **Features:** Various models and designs available including combo packages with scopes. **Velocities:** 495 to 1,250 fps with lead pellets.
Price: Model 1000 Striker Combo **$150.00**
Price: Alpha Youth Muddy Girl (shown) **$180.00**
Price: Model 95 w/walnut stock **$199.00**
Price: Model 125 TH Combo **$267.00**

HATSAN USA CARNIVORE BIG BORE

Prices given are believed to be accurate at time of publication however, many factors affect retail pricing so exact prices are not possible.

70TH EDITION, 2016 ⊕ **537**

HATSAN USA CARNIVORE BIG BORE AIR RIFLE
Caliber: .30 & .357. **Power:** Precharged pneumatic. **Stock:** Synthetic with an adjustable comb, rubber recoil pad which adjusts vertically and angularly and a textured grip. **Weight:** 9.3 lbs. **Sights:** No sights but has a rail that will accept 11mm Weaver style scope bases. **Features:** Two stage adjustable Quattro trigger with gold plated blade, 255cc air reservoir, fully shrouded rifled 23" high-quality Turkish steel barrel, magazine capacity is 7-rounds in .30 caliber and 6-rounds in .357. **Velocities:** 860 fps in .30 caliber and 730 fps in .357 caliber.
Price: $799.00

HATSAN USA PCP AIR RIFLE SERIES
Caliber: .177, .22 & .25. **Power:** Precharged pneumatic. **Features:** Various models and designs available. **Velocities:** 1,070 to 1,250 fps with lead pellets.
Price: Model AT44PA..................................$554.00
Price: Model BT65 repeating rifle $851.00

HATSAN USA VORTEX SERIES

HATSAN USA VORTEX SERIES
Caliber: .177, .22 & .25 **Power:** Gas piston powered. **Features:** Various models and designs available including a scope. **Velocities:** 650 to 1,250 fps with lead pellets.
Price: From $220.00

HATSAN USA GALATIAN QE SERIES
Caliber: .177, .22 & .25. **Power:** Gas piston powered. **Stock:** Polymer stock with Monte Carlo cheekpiece with adjustable buttplate and comb. **Sights:** Fiber-optic both rear and front. **Features:** Integral silencer. Rifled steel choked barrel, metal trigger blade with magazine capacity ranging from 13 to 16 rounds depending upon the caliber. **Velocities:** 1,000 to 1,190 fps with lead pellets.
Price: From $950.00

MARKSMAN 2040 AIR RIFLE
Caliber: .177. **Barrel:** Smoothbore 10.5". **Weight:** 4-lbs. **Power:** Spring-piston pump action. **Stock:** Synthetic. **Sights:** Fiber optic front sight and adjustable rear sight. **Features:** Manual safety and 11mm dovetail for scope mounting. **Velocity:** 300 fps.
Price: $59.50

MARKSMAN ZOMBIE SPLAT BB AIR RIFLE
Caliber: BB. **Barrel:** Smoothbore 10.5". **Weight:** 1.6-lbs. **Power:** Spring-piston pump action. **Stock:** Synthetic. **Sights:** Fiber-optic front sight and adjustable rear sight. **Features:** Manual safety and 11mm dovetail for scope mounting. **Velocity:** 300 fps.
Price: $39.99

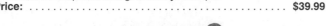

REMINGTON EXPRESS

REMINGTON EXPRESS AIR RIFLE/SCOPE COMBO
Caliber: .177, .22. **Weight:** 9.5 lbs. **Power:** Spring-piston system break-barrel action. **Stock:** Checkered hardwood or synthetic. **Sights:** Fiber-optic front sight and fully adjustable rear and 4x32mm scope. **Features:** Feel of a Remington Model 700 rifle, two-stage precision trigger, automatic safety. 1,000 fps and 16 ft-lbs of energy.
Price: Wood stock.....................................$189.99
Price: Synthetic stock $229.99

REMINGTON EXPRESS TYRANT AIR RIFLE/SCOPE COMBO
Caliber: .177, .22. **Weight:** 7.29 lbs. with scope. **Power:** Spring-piston system break-barrel action. **Stock:** Ambidextrous synthetic. **Sights:** No open sights, scope only- 4x32mm scope. **Features:** Includes 11mm optics dovetail groove, two-stage precision trigger with 4.5 lbs. pull weight, automatic safety and 27 lbs. cocking effort and 16" bull barrel. **Velocities:** 1,200 fps with alloy pellets and 1,000 with lead pellets.
Price: $169.99

RUGER AIR MAGNUM COMBO

RUGER AIR MAGNUM COMBO AIR RIFLE
Caliber: .177 & .22. **Barrel:** Rifled 19.5". **Weight:** 9.5-lbs. **Length:** 48.5". **Power:** Spring-piston system break-barrel action. **Stock:** Black colored synthetic. **Sights:** Fiber-optic front and back with 4x32mm scope and Weaver mounts. **Features:** Two-stage adjustable trigger with 3.5-lbs. trigger pull weight and rubber buttplate. **Velocities:** 1,400 fps with alloy pellets and 1,200 fps with lead pellets (.177) and 1,200 fps with alloy pellets and 1,000 fps with lead pellets (.22).
Price: $220.00

RUGER BLACKHAWK COMBO AIR RIFLE
Caliber: .177. **Barrel:** Rifled 18.7". **Weight:** 6.95 lbs. **Length:** 44.8". **Power:** Single-shot, Spring-piston, break-barrel action. **Stock:** Black colored synthetic. **Sights:** Fiber-optic front and back with 4x32mm scope and 11mm dovetail. **Features:** 2-stage adjustable trigger with 3.3-lbs. trigger pull weight and rubber buttplate. **Velocity:** 1,000 fps.
Price: $130.00

RUGER EXPLORER AIR RIFLE
Caliber: .177. **Barrel:** Rifled 15.0". **Weight:** 4.45-lbs. **Length:** 37.12". **Power:** Single-shot, Spring-piston, break-barrel action. **Stock:** Black colored synthetic. **Sights:** Fiber-optic front sight and micrometer adjustable rear sight. **Features:** 2-stage non-adjustable trigger and rubber buttplate. **Velocity:** 485 fps.
Price: $79.99

RUGER YUKON GAS-PISTON COMBO AIR RIFLE
Caliber: .177 & .22. **Barrel:** Rifled 18.7". **Weight:** 9.0-lbs. **Length:** 44.8". **Power:** Break-barrel, gas piston, single-shot. **Stock:** Hardwood. **Sights:** Fiber-optic front and adjustable rear sight and Weaver/Picatinny for scope. **Features:** 2-stage adjustable trigger with 3.3-lbs. trigger pull weight and rubber buttplate. **Velocity:** 1,250 fps with alloy pellets and 1,050 fps with lead pellets (.177).
Price: $220.95

RUGER BLACKHAWK ELITE AIR RIFLE
Caliber: .177. **Barrel:** Rifled 19.0". **Weight:** 7.8-lbs. **Length:** 44.75". **Power:** Break-barrel, spring-piston, single-shot. **Stock:** Black colored synthetic. **Sights:** None, but comes with 11mm dovetail base. **Features:** 2-stage trigger with 3.5-lbs. trigger pull weight and rubber buttplate. **Velocity:** 1,200 fps with alloy pellets and 1,000 fps with lead pellets.
Price: $120.00

RUGER TARGIS AIR RIFLE
Caliber: .177. **Barrel:** Rifled 18.7". **Weight:** 9.85-lbs. **Length:** 44.85". **Power:** Break-barrel, spring-piston, single-shot. **Stock:** Black colored synthetic with ventilated comb. **Sights:** Fiber-optic front sight and adjustable rear sight with Weaver/Picatinny rail system. **Features:** 2-stage trigger with 3.3-lbs. trigger pull weight and rubber buttplate. **Velocity:** 1,200 fps with alloy pellets and 1,000 fps with lead pellets.
Price: $176.00

STOEGER X50 AIR RIFLE
Caliber: .177, .22, .25 **Barrel:** 16.5" **Weight:** 8.9 lbs. **Power:** Break-action, spring and piston mechanism, single-shot. **Stock:** Matte

Prices given are believed to be accurate at time of publication however, many factors affect retail pricing so exact prices are not possible.

STOEGER X50

black lightweight synthetic or hardwood stock with nonslip rubber buttpad, and checkered grip panels and fore-end. **Sights:** 3-9x40mm scope and red fiber-optic front sight and fully adjustable rear sight with green fiber-optic inserts. **Features:** Automatic safety, two-stage adjustable trigger. .177 – 1,500 fps, .22 – 1,200 fp, .25 – 900 fps.
Price: $350.00

STOEGER X20S SUPPRESSOR AIR RIFLE
Caliber: .177 & .22. **Barrel:** 16.5" **Weight:** 7.0 lbs. **Power:** Break-action, spring piston, single-shot. **Stock:** Ambitious Monte Carlo synthetic with dual raised cheek pieces and textured pistol grip and forearm. **Sights:** No iron sights but comes with a 4x32mm illuminated red/green reticle CR1620 powered scope. **Features:** Automatic safety and two-stage adjustable trigger. **Velocities:** 1,200 fps in .177 (alloy pellets and 1,000 fps with lead) and 1,000 fps in .22 (allow pellets and 800 fps with lead).
Price: $300.00

STOEGER X20 WOOD BREAKBARREL AIR RIFLE COMBO
Caliber: .177 & .22. **Barrel:** 16.5" **Weight:** 7.0 lbs. **Power:** Break-action, spring piston, single-shot. **Stock:** Monte Carlo hardwood stock with dual raised cheek pieces and checkered grip and forearm. **Sights:** Fiber-optic front sight and adjustable rear sight and a 3-9x40mm AO scope. **Features:** Automatic safety and two-stage adjustable trigger. **Velocities:** 1,200 fps in .177 (alloy pellets and 1,000 fps with lead) and 1,000 fps in .22 (alloy pellets and 800 fps with lead).
Price: $200.00

STOEGER X5 AIR RIFLE
Caliber: .177. **Barrel:** 16.5" **Weight:** 5.7 lbs. **Power:** Break-action, spring piston, single-shot. **Stock:** Ambitious hardwood stock with dual raised cheek pieces or synthetic stock. **Sights:** Fiber optics with adjustable rear sight. **Features:** Automatic safety, two-stage nonadjustable trigger and 11mm dovetail. **Velocity:** 800 fps.
Price: $120.00

STOEGER ATAC GAS RAM AIR RIFLE
Caliber: .177 & .22. **Barrel:** 13.0" **Weight:** 9 lbs. **Power:** Gas ram GRT=Gas Ram Technology. **Stock:** Spacer adjustable to length, ambitious synthetic. **Sights:** No iron sights but comes with a 4-16x40mm AO scope. **Features:** AFC (airflow control) technology is a dual-stage noise-reduction system by Humbert CTTS, renowned silencer designer, automatic safety and two-stage adjustable trigger. **Velocity:** 1,200 fps in .177 (alloy pellets and 1,000 fps with lead) and 1,000 fps in .22 (alloy pellets and 800 fps with lead).
Price: $295.95

STOEGER X3 AIR RIFLE
Caliber: .177. **Barrel:** 14.5" **Weight:** 5.6 lbs. **Power:** Break-action, spring piston, single-shot. **Stock:** Ambitious hardwood stock. **Sights:** Fixed fiber-optic front sight with fully adjustable fiber optics rear sight. **Features:** Automatic safety, two-stage nonadjustable trigger and 11mm dovetail. **Velocity:** 550 fps with alloy pellets and 450 fps with lead pellets.
Price: $110.00

TECH FORCE 99 AIR RIFLE
Caliber: .177, .22, single shot. **Barrel:** 18", rifled. **Weight:** 8 lbs. **Length:** 44.5" overall. **Power:** Spring piston. **Stock:** Beech wood; raised cheek piece and checkering on pistol grip and forearm, plus soft rubber recoil pad. **Sights:** Insert type front. **Features:** Velocity 1,100 fps (.177; 900 fps: .22); fixed barrel design has an underlever cocking mechanism with an anti-beartrap lock and automatic safety. Imported from China by Compasseco, Inc.
Price: 177 or .22 caliber $255.00

TECH FORCE M8 AIR RIFLE & COMBO PACKAGE
Caliber: .177. **Barrel:** 9". **Weight:** 6.5 lbs. (rifle alone) **Length:** 40" overall. **Power:** Spring-piston, break-barrel, single-shot. **Stock:** Ambidextrous Monte Carlo hardwood stock with checkered grip and forearm. **Sights:** 11mm grooved dovetail for scope mounting. **Features:** Rifled barrel, automatic safety, rubber buttplate and

muzzlebrake for extra cocking leverage. Maximum Muzzle Velocity - 800 fps.
Price: (Rifle alone) $149.95
Price: (Combo Pkg. with 4x32 AO Scope): $195.95

TECH FORCE M12 AIR RIFLE & COMBO PACKAGES
Caliber: .177, .22 **Weight:** 6.85 lbs. (rifle alone) **Length:** 44.25" overall. **Power:** Spring-piston, break-barrel, single-shot. **Stock:** Ambidextrous Monte Carlo hardwood stock with checkered grip and forearm. **Sights:** 11mm grooved dovetail for scope mounting. **Features:** Rifled barrel, automatic safety, rubber buttplate and muzzlebrake for extra cocking leverage. Combo packages include a selection of riflescopes. **Velocity:** 800 fps.
Price: $199.99
Price: (Combo Pkg. with 3-9x32 AO Scope) $249.99
Price: (Combo Pkg. with 4-12x40 AO Scope. $279.99
Price: (Combo Pkg. with 4-12x40 AO/IR Scope). $299.99

TECH FORCE TF89 AIR RIFLE & COMBO PACKAGE
Caliber: .177, .22 **Barrel:** 17.9" **Weight:** 7.72 lbs. **Length:** 46.1" overall. **Power:** Spring pneumatic, single-shot. **Stock:** Beech wood checkered. **Sights:** Fixed front sight and adjustable rear. **Features:** Muzzlebrake, ventilated recoil pad, scope stop, grooved receiver for scope mounting, and cocking effort of 28 lbs. 1,100 fps.
Price: $225.00
Price: (Combo Pkg. with 3-12x44mm Scope) $279.95

TECH FORCE TF97 AIR RIFLE & COMBO PACKAGE
Caliber: .177, .22 **Barrel:** 16" **Weight:** 8 lbs. **Length:** 40" overall. **Power:** Spring pneumatic, under-lever, single-shot. **Stock:** Beech wood, Monte Carlo. **Sights:** Fixed front sight and adjustable rear. **Features:** Ventilated recoil pad, scope stop, grooved receiver for scope mounting, and cocking effort of 12 lbs. **Velocity:** 700 fps.
Price: $99.95
Price: (Combo Pkg. with 2-7x32mm Scope) $165.95

WALTHER LGV MASTER ULTRA AIR RIFLE
Caliber: .177 or .22. **Barrel:** 15.7" **Weight:** 10.1 lbs. **Power:** Super Silent-Vibration Reduction Technology spring operated. **Sights:** Tru-Glo® fiber-optic sights. **Features:** 1,000 fps with lead pellets. **Velocity:** 1,000 fps. Made by Umarex.
Price: $759.95

WALTHER LGV
COMPETITION ULTRA

WALTHER LGV COMPETITION ULTRA AIR RIFLE
Caliber: .177 **Barrel:** 15.7" **Weight:** 10.1 lbs. **Power:** Break-barrel spring-piston. **Sights:** Fiber-optic front sight and adjustable rear sight. **Features:** 2-stage adjustable trigger and 11mm dovetail rail. **Velocity:** 1,000 fps.
Price: $799.99

WALTHER LGV CHALLENGER AIR RIFLE
Caliber: .22. **Barrel:** 15.7" **Weight:** 8.4 lbs. **Power:** Break-barrel spring-piston. **Sights:** Fiber-optic front sight and adjustable rear sight. **Features:** 2-stage adjustable trigger, 11mm dovetail rail, single shot. **Velocity:** 700 fps.
Price: $630.00

WALTHER LGU AIR RIFLE
Caliber: .22. **Barrel:** 11.81" **Weight:** 9.5-lbs. **Power:** Under-lever spring-piston single shot. **Sights:** None. **Features:** 2-stage adjustable trigger with a pull weight of 1.97 lbs. and a cocking weight of 37 lbs. with a 11mm dovetail rail, single-shot. **Velocity:** 625 fps.
Price: $650.00

WALTHER LG400 ALUTEC COMPETITION AIR RIFLE
Caliber: .177. **Barrel:** 16.53" **Weight:** 9.26 lbs. **Power:** Precharged Pneumatic. **Sights:** Globe with aperture inserts front sight and Diopter/micrometer adjustable rear sight. **Features:** 5-way adjustable match trigger with trigger pull weight set at 0.11lbs. and adjustable buttplate. **Velocity:** 580 fps.
Price: $2,950.95

WALTHER LG400 ANATOMIC EXPERT AIR RIFLE
Caliber: .177. **Barrel:** 16.54" **Weight:** 9.04 lbs. **Power:** Precharged Pneumatic. **Sights:** Globe with aperture inserts front sight and

AIRGUNS—Long Guns

Diopter/micrometer adjustable rear sight. **Features:** 5-way adjustable match trigger with trigger pull weight set at 0.26 lbs. and adjustable buttplate. **Velocity:** 570 fps.
Price: **$3,750.00**

WALTHER LEVER ACTION

WALTHER LEVER ACTION
Caliber: .177, 8-shot lever action. **Barrel:** 19", rifled. **Weight:** 7.5 lbs. **Length:** 38" overall. **Power:** Two 12g CO2. **Stock:** Wood. **Sights:** Fixed front, adjustable rear. **Features:** Classic design. Velocity of 630 fps. Scope compatible. Made by Umarex.
Price: **$500.00**
Price: Nickel finish................................... **$600.00**

WALTHER 1250 DOMINATOR AIR RIFLE
Caliber: .177, 8-shot repeater. **Barrel:** 23.62", rifled. **Weight:** 8 lbs. **Length:** 40.94" overall. **Power:** Precharged Pneumatic. **Stock:** Wood. **Sights:** Adjustable for windage in front and adjustable rear sight. **Features:** Bolt action, manual safety, 2-stage adjustable trigger. Also available in combo package with a scope. **Velocity:** 1,200 fps.
Price: **$750.00**

WALTHER LG300 UNIVERSAL AIR RIFLE
Caliber: .177. **Barrel:** 16.54" rifled. **Weight:** 9.7 lbs. **Power:** Precharged Pneumatic. **Sights:** Post Globe front sight and Diopter/micrometer adjustable rear sight. **Features:** 2-stage adjustable trigger and adjustable buttplate. **Velocity:** 570 fps.
Price: **$1,759.95**

WALTHER LG300-XT JUNIOR AIR RIFLE
Caliber: .177. **Barrel:** 16.54" rifled. **Weight:** 7.72 lbs. **Power:** Precharged Pneumatic. **Sights:** Post Globe front sight and Diopter/micrometer adjustable rear sight. **Features:** 2-stage adjustable trigger and adjustable buttplate. **Velocity:** 570 fps.
Price: **$1,725.95**

WINCHESTER AIR RIFLE MODEL 77XS
Caliber: .177 BB and pellet; 50-shot BB repeater, single-shot pellet. **Weight:** 3.1 lbs. **Length:** 37.6" overall. **Power:** Multi-pump pneumatic air rifle. **Stock:** Composite. **Sights:** Blade and ramp front sight and adjustable rear sight with 4x32mm scope included. **Features:** Rifled steel barrel. From Daisy Outdoor Products. **Velocity:** 800 fps.
Price: (Black synthetic or wood stock) **$129.99**

WINCHESTER AIR RIFLE MODEL 500S
Caliber: .177 pellet. **Weight:** 4.85 lbs. **Length:** 39.375" overall. **Power:** Break-barrel spring air rifle, single-shot. **Stock:** Composite. **Sights:** Fiber-optic sights. **Features:** Rifled steel barrel. From Daisy Outdoor Products. **Velocity:** 490 fps (lead pellets).
Price: (Black synthetic or wood stock) **$119.99**

WINCHESTER AIR RIFLE MODEL 1100SS AND 1100WS
Caliber: .177 pellet. **Weight:** 9.1 lbs. **Length:** 46.25" overall. **Power:** Break-barrel spring air rifle, single-shot. **Stock:** Composite. **Sights:**

Fiber-optic front sight; micro-adjustable rear sight; 4x32mm scope. **Features:** Rifled steel barrel. Thumb safety engages when rifle is cocked. From Daisy Outdoor Products. **Velocity:** 1100 fps with alloy pellets.
Price: (Black synthetic or wood stock) **$129.99**

WINCHESTER AIR RIFLE MODEL 1250CS, SS, WS
Caliber: .177 pellet. **Weight:** 8.7 lbs. **Length:** 46.5" overall. **Power:** Break-barrel spring air rifle, single-shot. **Stock:** Composite. **Sights:** 1250CS and 1250S feature fiber-optic front sight; micro-adjustable rear sight (1250SS has no open sights). All models include a 3-9x32mm scope. **Features:** Rifled steel barrel, sling and folding bipod included (1250CS model only), thumb safety engages when rifle is cocked. From Daisy Outdoor Products. **Velocity:** 1250 fps (alloy pellets).
Price: (Camo synthetic with scope) **$219.99**
Price: (Black synthetic with scope, no front/rear sights) **$189.99**
Price: (Wood with scope) **$179.99**

WINCHESTER MODEL 1400 CS

WINCHESTER MODEL 1400 CS AIR RIFLE
Caliber: .177 **Weight:** 9 lbs. **Length:** 51.2" overall. **Power:** Break-barrel spring air rifle, single-shot. **Stock:** Camo composite. **Sights:** 3-9x32mm scope. **Features:** Rifled steel barrel with sound suppressor, thumb safety engages when rifle is cocked. 1,400 fps. Distributed by Daisy.
Price: **$229.99**

WINCHESTER AIR RIFLE .22 CAL. MODEL 1052
Caliber: .22 pellet. **Weight:** 8.2 lbs. **Length:** 46.25" overall. **Power:** Break-barrel spring air rifle, single-shot. **Stock:** Composite. **Sights:** No open sights with 4x32mm scope included. **Features:** Rifled steel barrel, sling included and thumb safety which engages when rifle is cocked. From Daisy Outdoor Products. **Velocity:** 1,000 fps with alloy pellets.
Price: **$199.99**

WINCHESTER MODEL MP4

WINCHESTER MODEL MP4 CO2 RIFLE
Caliber: .177, BB **Weight:** 5.8 lbs. **Length:** 46.5" overall. **Power:** CO2 semiautomatic with a 16-shot reversible rotary magazine. **Stock:** Composite collapsible. **Sights:** Flip-down front and adjustable flip-down rear sights. **Features:** Metal receiver, integral rail system with extended top rail, manual safety and rifled steel barrel, 700 fps. Distributed by Daisy.
Price: **$199.99**

Prices given are believed to be accurate at time of publication however, many factors affect retail pricing so exact prices are not possible.

THE 2016 GUN DIGEST
web directory

This is the 17th year of publication of the *Gun Digest* Web Directory. With every edition there are changes, additions and deletions to this ever-evolving reference.

The following index of web addresses is offered to our readers as a convenient jumping-off point. Considering that most of the web pages have hot links to other firearms related web pages, the Internet trail just goes on and on, once you've taken the initial step to go online. Half the fun is just exploring what's out there.

If the website you are searching for is not listed, simply type in the full name of the company or product, without spaces, between www. and .com—for example, www. krausebooks.com. The vast majority of current websites are based on this simple, self-explanatory format.

Another option is to go directly to one of the dominant search engines, such as Google (www.google.com) or Bing (www.bing.com), and enter the name of the company or product for which you are searching. This is also a good method of locating brand-new companies or those that may have changed their web address after this book was published.

Finally, make it a point to check out YouTube (www.YouTube.com) for videos on the subjects you are pursuing. Firearms enthusiasts and companies have posted many thousands of firearms-related videos—some good, some bad—but most are always interesting and informative. Many of the how-to gunsmithing videos, in particular, are excellent. Just be very specific when you type in the subject to be searched.

The general focus of our directory is on companies that have a proven track record of product success and have been in business for several years. A few additions represent products or companies that are worthy of checking out, even if they have just come onto the scene. Keep in mind that some websites, videos, blogs and forums contain information that is out of date or inaccurate. Such is the world of the Internet.

—*The Editors*

AMMUNITION AND COMPONENTS

2 Monkey Trading **www.2monkey.com**
2nd Amendment Ammunition **www.secondammo.com**
Accurate Reloading Powders **www.accuratepowder.com**
Advanced Armament Corp. **www.300aacblackout.com**
Advanced Tactical **www.advancedtactical.com**
Aguila Ammunition **www.aguilaammo.com**
Alexander Arms **www.alexanderarms.com**
Allegiance Ammunition **www.allegianceammunition.com**
Alliant Powder **www.alliantpowder.com**
American Derringer Co. **www.amderringer.com**
American Eagle **www.federalpremium.com**
American Pioneer Powder **www.americanpioneerpowder.com**
American Specialty Ammunition
    www.americanspecialityammo.com
Ammo Depot **www.ammodepot.com**
Ammo Importers **www.ammoimporters.com**
Ammo-Up **www.ammoupusa.com**
Applied Ballistics Munitions **www.buyabmammo.com**
Arizona Ammunition, Inc. **www.arizonaammunition.net**
Armscor **www.us.armscor.com**
ASYM Precision Ammunition **www.asym-ammo.com**
Atesci **www.atesci.com**
Australian Munitions **www.australian-munitions.com**
B&T (USA) **www.bt-ag.ch**
Ballistic Products Inc. **www.ballisticproducts.com**
Barnes Bullets **www.barnesbullets.com**
Baschieri & Pellagri **www.baschieri-pellagri.com**
Berger Bullets, Ltd. **www.bergerbullets.com**
Berry's Mfg., Inc. **www.berrysmfg.com**
Big Bore Express **www.powerbeltbullets.com**
Black Hills Ammunition, Inc. **www.black-hills.com**
BlackHorn209 **www.blackhorn209.com**
Brenneke of America Ltd. **www.brennekeusa.com**
Buffalo Arms **www.buffaloarms.com**
Buffalo Bore Ammunition **www.buffalobore.com**
Calhoon, James, Bullets **www.jamescalhoon.com**
Cartuchos Saga **www.saga.es**
Cast Performance Bullet **www.grizzlycartridge.com**
CCI **www.cci-ammunition.com**
Centurion Ordnance **www.centurionammo.com**
Century International Arms **www.centuryarms.com**
Cheaper Than Dirt **www.cheaperthandirt.com**
Cheddite France **www.cheddite.com**
Claybuster Wads **www.claybusterwads.com**
Combined Tactical Systems **www.combinedsystems.com**
Cor-Bon/Glaser **www.corbon.com**
Cutting Edge Bullets **www.cuttingedgebullets.com**
DDupleks, Ltd. **www.ddupleks.lv**
Defense Technology Corp. **www.defense-technology.com**

Denver Bullets **www.denverbullets.com**
Desperado Cowboy Bullets **www.cowboybullets.com**
Dillon Precision **www.dillonprecision.com**
Double Tap Ammunition **www.doubletapammo.com**
Down Range Mfg. **www.downrangemfg.com**
Dynamic Research Technologies **www.drtammo.com**
Dynamit Nobel RWS Inc. **www.dnrws.com**
E. Arthur Brown Co. **www.eabco.com**
EcoSlug **www.eco-slug.com**
Elephant/Swiss Black Powder **www.elephantblackpowder.com**
Eley Ammunition **www.eley.co.uk**
Eley Hawk Ltd. **www.eleyhawk.com**
Environ-Metal **www.hevishot.com**
Estate Cartridge **www.estatecartridge.com**
Federal Cartridge Co. **www.federalpremium.com**
Fiocchi of America **www.fiocchiusa.com**
Fowler Bullets **www.benchrest.com/fowler**
G2 Research RIP **www.g2ammo.com**
Gamebore Cartridge **www.gamebore.com**
GaugeMate **www.gaugemate.com**
Garrett Cartridges **hammerhead.creator@gmail.com**
Glaser Safety Slug, Inc. **www.corbon.com**
GOEX Inc. **www.goexpowder.com**
Graf & Sons **www.grafs.com**
Grizzly Cartridge Co. **www.grizzlycartridge.com**
Haendler & Natermann **www.hn-sport.de**
Hawk Bullets **www.hawkbullets.com**
Herter's Ammuniition **www.cabelas.com**
Hevi.Shot **www.hevishot.com**
High Precision Down Range **www.hprammo.com**
Hodgdon Powder **www.hodgdon.com**
Hornady **www.hornady.com**
HSM Ammunition **www.thehuntingshack.com**
Hull Cartridge **www.hullcartridge.com**
Huntington Reloading Products **www.huntingtons.com**
IMR Smokeless Powders **www.imrpowder.com**
International Cartridge Corp **www.iccammo.com**
Jagemann Technologies **www.jagemanntech.com**
James Calhoon **www.jamescalhoon.com**
Kent Cartridge America **www.kentgamebore.com**
Knight Bullets **www.benchrest.com/knight/**
Lapua **www.lapua.com**
Lawrence Brand Shot **www.lawrencebrandshot.com**
Lazzeroni Arms Co. **www.lazzeroni.com**
Leadheads Bullets **www.proshootpro.com**
Lehigh Defense **www.lehighdefense.com**
Lightfield Ammunition Corp **www.litfld.com**
Lomont Precision Bullets **www.klomont.com/kent**
Lost River Ballistic Technologies, Inc. **www.lostriverballistic. com**
Lyman **www.lymanproducts.com**
Magnum Muzzleloading Products **www.mmpsabots.com**

Magnus Bullets **www.magnusbullets.com**
Magtech **www.magtechammunition.com**
Maxam **www.maxam-outdoors.com**
Meister Bullets **www.meisterbullets.com**
Midway USA **www.midwayusa.com**
Mitchell's Mausers **www.mauser.net**
National Bullet Co. **www.nationalbullet.com**
Navy Arms **www.navyarms.com**
Nobel Sport **www.nobelsportammo.com**
Norma **www.norma.cc**
North Fork Technologies **www.northforkbullets.com**
Nosler Bullets, Inc. **www.nosler.com**
Oregon Trail/Trueshot Bullets **www.trueshotbullets.com**
Pattern Control **www.patterncontrol.com**
PCP Ammunition **www.pcpammo.com**
Pierce Munitions **www.piercemunitions.com**
Piney Mountain Ammunition
   www.pineymountainammunitionco.com
PMC **www.pmcammo.com**
PolyCase Ammunition **www.polycaseammo.com**
Polywad **www.polywad.com**
PowerBelt Bullets **www.powerbeltbullets.com**
PPU Ammunition **www.prvipartizan.com**
PR Bullets **www.prbullet.com**
Precision Reloading **www.precisionreloading.com**
Pro Grade Ammunition **www.progradeammo.com**
Pro Load Ammunition **www.proload.com**
Prvi Partizan Ammunition **www.prvipartizan.com**
Quality Cartridge **www.qual-cart.com**
Rainier Ballistics **www.rainierballistics.com**
Ram Shot Powder **www.ramshot.com**
Rare Ammunition **www.rareammo.com**
Reloading Specialties Inc. **www.reloadingspecialtiesinc.com**
Remington **www.remington.com**
Rio Ammunition **www.rioammo.com**
Rocky Mountain Cartridge **www.rockymountaincartride.com**
RUAG Ammotec **www.ruag.com/ammotec**
RWS **www.ruag-usa.com**
Samco Global Arms **www.samcoglobal.com**
Sauvestre Ammunition **www.centuryarms.com**
SBR Ammunition **www.sbrammunition.com**
Scharch Mfg. **www.scharch.com**
Schuetzen Powder **www.schuetzenpowder.com**
Sellier & Bellot **www.sellier-bellot.cz**
Shilen **www.shilen.com**
Sierra **www.sierrabullets.com**
Silver State Armory **www.ssarmory.com**
Simunition **www.simunition.com**
SinterFire, Inc. **www.sinterfire.com**
Spectra Shot **www.spectrashot.com**
Speer Ammunition **www.speer-ammo.com**

Speer Bullets **www.speer-bullets.com**
Sporting Supplies Int'l Inc. **www.wolfammo.com**
Starline **www.starlinebrass.com**
Stealth Gunpowder **www.stealthgunpowder.com**
Swift Bullets Co. **www.swiftbullets.com**
Tannerite **www.tannerite.com**
Tascosa Cartridge Co. **www.tascosacartridge.com**
Ted Nugent Ammunition **www.americantactical.us**
Ten-X Ammunition **www.tenxammo.com**
Top Brass **www.topbrass-inc.com**
Triton Ammunition **www.tritonammo.com**
Trueshot Bullets **www.trueshotbullets.com**
TulAmmo **www.tulammousa.com**
Velocity Tactics **www.velocitytactics.com**
Vihtavuori **www.vihtavuori.com**
Weatherby **www.weatherby.com**
West Coast Bullets **www.westcoastbullet.com**
Western Powders Inc. **www.westernpowders.com**
Widener's Reloading & Shooters Supply **www.wideners.com**
Winchester Ammunition **www.winchester.com**
Windjammer Tournament Wads **www.windjammer-wads.com**
Wolf Ammunition **www.wolfammo.com**
Woodleigh Bullets **www.woodleighbullets.com.au**
Xtreme Bullets **www.xtremebullets.com**
Zanders Sporting Goods **www.gzanders.com**

CASES, SAFES, GUN LOCKS AND CABINETS

Ace Case Co. **www.acecase.com**
AG English Sales Co. **www.agenglish.com**
All American Outdoors **www.allamericanoutdoorslic.com**
Dee Zee **www.deezee.com**
American Security Products **www.amsecusa.com**
Americase **www.americase.com**
Assault Systems **www.elitesurvival.com**
Avery Outdoors, Inc. **www.averyoutdoors.com**
Bore-Stores **www.borestores.com**
Boyt Harness Co. **www.boytharness.com**
Gardall Safes **www.gardall.com**
Campbell Industrial Supply **www.gun-racks.com**
Cannon Safe Co. **www.cannonsafe.com**
Fort Knox Safes **www.ftknox.com**
Franzen Security Products **www.securecase.com**
Frontier Safe Co. **www.frontiersafe.com**
Goldenrod Dehumidifiers **www.goldenroddehumidifiers.com**
Gunlocker Phoenix USA Inc. **www.gunlocker.com**
Gun Storage Solutions **www.storemoreguns.com**
GunVault **www.gunvault.com**
Hakuba USA Inc. **www.hakubausa.com**
Heritage Safe Co. **www.heritagesafe.com**

Hide-A-Gun **www.hide-a-gun.com**
Homak Safes **www.homak.com**
Hunter Company **www.huntercompany.com**
Kalispel Case Line **www.kalispelcaseline.com**
Liberty Safe & Security **www.libertysafe.com**
Morton Enterprises **www.uniquecases.com**
New Innovative Products **www.starlightcases.com**
Phoenix USA Inc. **www.gunlocker.com**
Plano Molding Co. **www.planomolding.com**
Plasticase, Inc. **www.nanuk.com**
Rhino Safe **www.rhinosafe.com**
Rotary Gun Racks **www.gun-racks.com**
Sack-Ups **www.sackups.com**
Safe Tech, Inc. **www.safrgun.com**
Secure Firearm Products **www.securefirearmproducts.com**
Securecase **www.securecase.com**
Shot Lock Corp. **www.shotlock.com**
SKB Cases **www.skbcases.com**
Smart Lock Technology Inc. **www.smartlock.com**
Snap Safe **www.snapsafe.com**
Sportsmans Steel Safe Co. **www.sportsmansteelsafes.com**
Starlight Cases **www.starlightcases.com**
Strong Case **www.strongcasebytnb.com**
Sun Welding **www.sunwelding.com**
Technoframes **www.technoframes.com**
Titan Gun Safes **www.titangunsafes.com**
Tracker Safe **www.trackersafe.com**
T.Z. Case Int'l **www.tzcase.com**
U.S. Explosive Storage **www.usexplosivestorage.com**
Versatile Rack Co. **www.versatilegunrack.com**
V-Line Industries **www.vlineind.com**
Winchester Safes **www.winchestersafes.com**
Ziegel Engineering **www.ziegeleng.com**
Zonetti Armor **www.zonettiarmor.com**

CHOKE DEVICES, RECOIL REDUCERS, SUPPRESSORS AND ACCURACY DEVICES

ACT Tactical **www.blackwidowshooters.com**
Advanced Armament Corp. **www.advanced-armament.com**
100 Straight Products **www.100straight.com**
Answer Products Co. **www.answerrifles.com**
AWC Systems Technology **www.awcsystech.com**
Briley Mfg. **www.briley.com**
Carlson's **www.choketube.com**
Colonial Arms **www.colonialarms.com**
Comp-N-Choke **www.comp-n-choke.com**
Elite Iron **www.eliteiron.net, Gemtech www.gem-tech.com**
Great Lakes Tactical **www.gltactical.com**
KDF, Inc. **www.kdfguns.com**
Kick's Industries **www.kicks-ind.com**

LimbSaver **www.limbsaver.com**
Mag-Na-Port Int'l Inc. **www.magnaport.com**
Metro Gun **www.metrogun.com**
Patternmaster Chokes **www.patternmaster.com**
Poly-Choke **www.poly-choke.com**
SilencerCo **www.silencerco.com**
Sims Vibration Laboratory **www.limbsaver.com**
SRT Arms **www.srtarms.com**
SureFire **www.surefire.com**
SWR Mfg. **www.swrmfg.com**
Teague Precision Chokes **www.teaguechokes.com**
Truglo **www.truglo.com**
Trulock Tool **www.trulockchokes.com**
Vais Arms, Inc. **www.muzzlebrakes.com**

CHRONOGRAPHS AND BALLISTIC SOFTWARE

Barnes Ballistic Program **www.barnesbullets.com**
Ballisticard Systems **www.ballisticards.com**
Competition Electronics **www.competitionelectronics.com**
Competitive Edge Dynamics **www.cedhk.com**
Hodgdon Shotshell Program **www.hodgdon.com**
Lee Shooter Program **www.leeprecision.com**
NECO **www.neconos.com**
Oehler Research Inc. **www.oehler-research.com**
PACT **www.pact.com**
ProChrony **www.competitionelectronics.com**
Quickload **www.neconos.com**
RCBS Load **www.rcbs.com**
Shooting Chrony Inc **www.shootingchrony.com**
Sierra Infinity Ballistics Program **www.sierrabullets.com**
Winchester Ballistics Calculator **www.winchester.com**

CLEANING PRODUCTS

Accupro **www.accupro.com**
Ballistol USA **www.ballistol.com**
Birchwood Casey **www.birchwoodcasey.com**
Bore Tech **www.boretech.com**
Break-Free, Inc. **www.break-free.com**
Bruno Shooters Supply **www.brunoshooters.com**
Butch's Bore Shine **www.butchsboreshine.com**
C.J. Weapons Accessories **www.cjweapons.com**
Clenzoil **www.clenzoil.com**
Corrosion Technologies **www.corrosionx.com**
Dewey Mfg. **www.deweyrods.com**
DuraCoat **www.lauerweaponry.com**
Emby Enterprises **www.alltemptacticallube.com**
Extreme Gun Care **www.extremeguncare.com**
G96 **www.g96.com**

Gun Butter **www.gunbutter.com**
Gun Cleaners **www.guncleaners.com**
Gunslick Gun Care **www.gunslick.com**
Gunzilla **www.topduckproducts.com**
Hollands Shooters Supply **www.hollandgun.com**
Hoppes **www.hoppes.com**
Hydrosorbent Products **www.dehumidify.com**
Inhibitor VCI Products **www.theinhibitor.com**
Jag Brush **www.jagbrush.com**
KG Industries **www.kgcoatings.com**
Kleen-Bore Inc. **www.kleen-bore.com**
L&R Ultrasonics **www.ultrasonics.com**
Lyman **www.lymanproducts.com**
Mil-Comm Products **www.mil-comm.com**
Montana X-Treme **www.montanaxtreme.com**
MPT Industries **www.mptindustries.com**
Mpro7 Gun Care **www.mp7.com**
Old West Snake Oil **www.oldwestsnakeoil.com**
Otis Technology, Inc. **www.otisgun.com**
Outers **www.outers-guncare.com**
Ox-Yoke Originals Inc. **www.rmoxyoke.com**
Parker-Hale Ltd. **www.parker-hale.com**
Prolix Lubricant **www.prolixlubricant.com**
ProShot Products **www.proshotproducts.com**
ProTec Lubricants **www.proteclubricants.com**
Rigel Products **www.rigelproducts.com**
Sagebrush Products **www.sagebrushproducts.com**
Sentry Solutions Ltd. **www.sentrysolutions.com**
Shooters Choice Gun Care **www.shooters-choice.com**
Slip 2000 **www.slip2000.com**
Southern Bloomer Mfg. **www.southernbloomer.com**
Stony Point Products **www.uncle-mikes.com**
www.topduckproducts.com
Triangle Patch **www.trianglepatch.com**
Wipe-Out **www.sharpshootr.com**
World's Fastest Gun Bore Cleaner **www.michaels-oregon.com**

FIREARM AUCTION SITES

Alderfer Austion **www.alderferauction.com**
Amoskeag Auction Co. **www.amoskeagauction.com**
Antique Guns **www.antiqueguns.com**
Auction Arms **www.auctionarms.com**
Batterman's Auctions **www.battermans.com**
Bonhams & Butterfields **www.bonhams.com/usarms**
Cowan's **www.cowans.com**
Fontaine's Auction Gallery **www.fontainesauction.net**
Guns America **www.gunsamerica.com**
Gun Broker **www.gunbroker.com**
Guns International **www.gunsinternational.com**
Heritage Auction Galleries **www.ha.com**

James D. Julia, Inc. **www.jamesdjulia.com**
Little John's Auctions **www.littlejohnsauctions.com**
Morphy Auctions **www.morphyauctions.com**
Poulin Auction Co. **www.poulinantiques.com**
Rock Island Auction Co. **www.rockislandauction.com**
Wallis & Wallis **www.wallisandwallis.org**

FIREARM MANUFACTURERS AND IMPORTERS

Accu-Tek **www.accu-tekfirearms.com**
Accuracy Int'l North America **www.accuracyinternational.com**
Adcor Defense **www.adcorindustries.com**
AIM **www.aimsurplus.com**
AirForce Airguns **www.airforceairguns.com**
Air Gun Inc. **www.airrifle-china.com**
Air Ordnance/Tippmann Armory **www.tippmannarmory.com**
Airguns of Arizona **www.airgunsofarizona.com**
Alexander Arms **www.alexanderarms.com**
America Remembers **www.americaremembers.com**
American Classic **www.americanclassic1911.com**
American Derringer Corp. **www.amderringer.com**
American Spirit Arms Corp. **www.gunkits.com**
American Tactical Imports **www.americantactical.us**
American Western Arms **www.awaguns.com**
Angstadt Arms **www.angstadtarms.com**
Anics Corp. **www.anics.com**
Anschutz **www.anschutz-sporters.com**
Answer Products Co. **www.answerrifles.com**
AR-7 Industries **www.ar-7.com**
Ares Defense Systems **www.aresdefense.com**
Armalite **www.armalite.com**
Armi Sport **www.armisport.com**
Armscor Precision Internationl **www.armscor.com**
Armscorp USA Inc. **www.armscorpusa.com**
Arrieta **www.arrietashotguns.com**
Arsenal Inc. **www.arsenalinc.com**
Atlanta Cutlery Corp. **www.atlantacutlery.com**
ATA Arms **www.ataarms.com**
Auto-Ordnance Corp. **www.tommygun.com**
Aya **www.aya-fineguns.com**
B&T (USA) **www.bt-ag.ch**
Baikal **www.imzorp.com**
Badger Ordnance **www.badgerordnance.com**
Ballard Rifles **www.ballardrifles.com**
Barrett Firearms Mfg. **www.barrettrifles.com**
Bat Machine Co. **www.batmachine.com**
Battle Arms Development **www.battlearmsdevelopment.com**
Beeman Precision Airguns **www.beeman.com**
Benelli USA Corp. **www.benelliusa.com**
Benjamin Sheridan **www.crosman.com**

Beretta U.S.A. Corp. **www.berettausa.com**
Bergera Rifles **www.bergararifles.com**
Bernardelli **www.bernardelli.com**
Bersa **www.bersa.com**
Bighorn Arms **www.bighornarms.com**
Blaser Jagdwaffen Gmbh **www.blaser.de**
Bleiker **www.bleiker.ch**
Bond Arms **www.bondarms.com**
Borden Rifles, Inc. **www.bordenrifles.com**
Boss & Co. **www.bossguns.co.uk**
Bowen Classic Arms **www.bowenclassicarms.com**
Breda **www.bredafucili.com**
Briley Mfg. **www.briley.com**
BRNO Arms **www.cz-usa.com**
Brown, E. Arthur **www.eabco.com**
Brown, Ed Products **www.edbrown.com**
Brown, McKay **www.mckaybrown.com**
Browning **www.browning.com**
BRP Corp. **www.brpguns.com**
BSA Guns **www.bsagunusa.com**
BUL Ltd. **www.bultransmark.com**
Bushmaster Firearms **www.bushmaster.com**
BWE Firearms **www.bwefirearms.com**
Cabot Guns **www.cabotguns.com**
Caesar Guerini USA **www.gueriniusa.com**
Caracal **www.caracal-usa.com**
Carbon 15 **www.professional-ordnance.com**
Caspian Arms, Ltd. **www.caspianarmsltd.com**
CDNN Sports **www.cdnnsports.com**
Century Arms **www.centuryarms.com**
Champlin Firearms **www.champlinarms.com**
Charles Daly **www.charlesdaly-us.com**
Charter Arms **www.charterfirearms.com**
CheyTac USA **www.cheytac.com**
Chiappa Firearms **www.chiappafirearms.com**
Christensen Arms **www.christensenarms.com**
Cimarron Firearms Co. **www.cimarron-firearms.com**
CK Arms/Freedom Gunworks **www.ckarms.com**
Clark Custom Guns **www.clarkcustomguns.com**
Cobalt Kinetics **www.cobaltarms.com**
Cobra Enterprises **www.cobrapistols.net**
Cogswell & Harrison **www.cogswellandharrison.com**
Collector's Armory, Ltd. **www.collectorsarmory.com**
Colt's Mfg Co. **www.colt.com**
Comanche **www.eagleimports.com**
Competitor Pistols **www.competitor-pistol.com**
Connecticut Shotgun Mfg. Co. **www.connecticutshotgun.com**
Connecticut Valley Arms **www.cva.com**
Coonan, Inc. **www.coonaninc.com**
Cooper Firearms **www.cooperfirearms.com**
Core Rifle Systems **www.core15.com**

Corner Shot **www.cornershot.com**
CPA Rifles **www.singleshotrifles.com**
Crickett Rifles **www.crickett.com**
Crosman **www.crosman.com**
C.Sharp Arms Co. **www.csharparms.com**
CVA **www.cva.com**
Cylinder & Slide Shop **www.cylinder-slide.com**
Czechp Int'l **www.czechpoint-usa.com**
CZ USA **www.cz-usa.com**
Daisy Mfg Co. **www.daisy.com**
Dakota Arms Inc. **www.dakotaarms.com**
Dan Wesson **www.danwessonfirearms.com**
Daniel Defense, Inc. **www.danieldefense.com**
Desert Eagle **www.magnumresearch.com**
Detonics USA **www.detonicsdefense.com**
Devil Dog Arms **www.devildogarms.com**
Diamondback **www.diamondbackfirearms.com**
Diana **www.diana-airguns.de**
Dixie Gun Works **www.dixiegunworks.com**
Double D Armory **www.ddarmory.com**
DoubleStar **www.star15.com**
DPMS, Inc. **www.dpmsinc.com**
DSA Inc. **www.dsarms.com**
Dumoulin **www.dumoulin-herstal.com**
EAA Corp. **www.eaacorp.com**
Eagle Imports, Inc. **www.eagleimportsinc.com**
Ed Brown Products **www.edbrown.com**
EDM Arms **www.edmarms.com**
EMF Co. **www.emf-company.com**
E.R. Shaw **www.ershawbarrels.com**
European American Armory Corp. **www.eaacorp.com**
Evans, William **www.williamevans.com**
Excel Arms **www.excelarms.com**
Fabarm **www.fabarm.com**
Fausti USA **www.faustiusa.com**
Flodman Guns **www.flodman.com**
FN Herstal **www.fnherstal.com**
FNH USA **www.fnhusa.com**
Forbes Rifle **www.forbesriflellc.com**
Franchi **www.franchiusa.com**
Franklin Armory **www.franklinarmory.com**
Freedom Arms **www.freedomarms.com**
Freedom Group, Inc. **www.freedom-group.com**
Galazan **www.connecticutshotgun.com**
Gambo Renato **www.renatogamba.it**
Gamo **www.gamo.com**
Gary Reeder Custom Guns **www.reedercustomguns.com**
Gazelle Arms **www.gazellearms.com**
German Sport Guns **www.german-sport-guns.com**
Gibbs Rifle Company **www.gibbsrifle.com**
Glock **www.glock.com**

Griffin & Howe **www.griffinhowe.com**
Gunbroker.com **www.gunbroker.com**
Guncrafter Industries **www.guncrafterindustries.com**
Gun Room Co. **www.onlylongrange.com**
Hammerli **www.carl-walther.com**
Hatsan Arms Co. **www.hatsan.com.tr**
Heckler and Koch **www.hk-usa.com**
Heizer Defense **www.heizerdefense.com**
Henry Repeating Arms Co. **www.henryrepeating.com**
Heritage Mfg. **www.heritagemfg.com**
High Standard Mfg. **www.highstandard.com**
Hi-Point Firearms **www.hi-pointfirearms.com**
Holland & Holland **www.hollandandholland.com**
H&R 1871 Firearms **www.hr1871.com**
H-S Precision **www.hsprecision.com**
Hunters Lodge Corp. **www.hunterslodge.com**
IAR Inc. **www.iar-arms.com**
Imperial Miniature Armory **www.1800miniature.com**
Inland Arms **inland-mfg.com**
International Military Antiques, Inc. **www.ima-usa.com**
Inter Ordnance **www.interordnance.com**
Israel Arms **www.israelarms.com**
ISSC, LLC **www.issc-austria.com**
Ithaca Gun Co. **www.ithacagun.com**
Iver Johnson Arms **www.iverjohnsonarms.com**
Izhevsky Mekhanichesky Zavod **www.baikalinc.ru**
James River Armory **www.jamesriverarmory.com**
Jarrett Rifles, Inc. **www.jarrettrifles.com**
Jesse James Firearms **www.jjfu.com**
J&G Sales, Ltd. **www.jgsales.com**
Johannsen Express Rifle **www.johannsen-jagd.de**
Jonathan Arthur Ciener **www.22lrconversions.com**
JP Enterprises, Inc. **www.jprifles.com**
Kahr Arms/Auto-Ordnance **www.kahr.com**
KDF, Inc. **www.kdfguns.com**
KE Arms **www.kearms.com**
Kel-Tec CNC Ind., Inc. **www.kel-tec.com**
Keystone Sporting Arms **www.keystonesportingarmsllc.com**
Kifaru **www.kifaru.net**
Kimber **www.kimberamerica.com**
Kingston Armory **www.kingstonarmory.com**
Knight's Armament Co. **www.knightarmco.com**
Knight Rifles **www.knightrifles.com**
Kolar **www.kolararms.com**
Korth **www.korthwaffen.de**
Krebs Custom Guns **www.krebscustom.com**
Kriss **www.kriss-usa.com**
Krieghoff Int'l **www.krieghoff.com**
KY Imports, Inc. **www.kyimports.com**
K-VAR **www.k-var.com**
Lanber **www.lanber.net**

Lantac-USA **www.lantac-usa.com**
Larue **www.laruetactical.com**
Lazzeroni Arms Co. **www.lazzeroni.com**
Legacy Sports International **www.legacysports.com**
Les Baer Custom, Inc. **www.lesbaer.com**
Lewis Machine & Tool Co. **www.lewismachine.net**
Linebaugh Custom Sixguns **www.customsixguns.com**
Lionheart **www.lionheartindustries.com**
Ljutic **www.ljuticgun.com**
LMT Defense **www.lmtdefense.com**
LRB Arms **www.lrbarms.com**
Lyman **www.lymanproducts.com**
LWRC Int'l **www.lwrci.com**
Magnum Research **www.magnumresearch.com**
Majestic Arms **www.majesticarms.com**
Marksman Products **www.marksman.com**
Marlin **www.marlinfirearms.com**
MasterPiece Arms **www.masterpiecearms.com**
Mauser **www.mauser.com**
McMillan Firearms **www.mcmillanfirearms.com**
MDM **www.mdm-muzzleloaders.com**
Meacham Rifles **www.meachamrifles.com**
Milkor USA **www.milkorusainc.com**
Miltech **www.miltecharms.com**
Mitchell's Mausers **www.mausers.net**
MOA Maximum **www.moaguns.com**
MOA Precision **www.moaprecision.com**
Montana Rifle Co. **www.montanarifleman.com**
Modern Weapon Systems **www.modernweaponsystems**
Mossberg **www.mossberg.com**
Navy Arms **www.navyarms.com**
Nesika **www.nesika.com**
New England Arms Corp. **www.newenglandarms.com**
New England Custom Gun **www.newenglandcustomgun.com**
New Ultra Light Arms **www.newultralight.com**
Nighthawk Custom **www.nighthawkcustom.com**
North American Arms **www.northamericanarms.com**
Nosler **www.nosler.com**
Nowlin Mfg. Inc. **www.nowlinguns.com**
O.F. Mossberg & Sons **www.mossberg.com**
Ohio Ordnance Works **www.ohioordnanceworks.com**
Olympic Arms **www.olyarms.com**
Osprey Defense **www.gaspiston.com**
Panther Arms **www.dpmsinc.com**
Para-USA **www.para-usa.com**
Pedersoli Davide & Co. **www.davide-pedersoli.com**
Perazzi **www.perazzi.com**
Pietta **www.pletta.it**
Piotti **www.piotti.com/en**
Pistol Dynamics **www.pistoldynamics.com**
PKP Knife-Pistol **www.sanjuanenterprise.com**

Power Custom **www.powercustom.com**
Precision Small Arm Inc. **www.precisionsmallarms.com**
Primary Weapons Systems **www.primaryweapons.com**
Professional Arms **www.professional-arms.com**
Proof Research **www.proofresearch.com**
PTR 91,Inc. **www.ptr91.com**
Purdey & Sons **www.purdey.com**
Pyramyd Air **www.pyramydair.com**
Remington **www.remington.com**
Republic Forge **www.republicforge.com**
Rhineland Arms, Inc. **www.rhinelandarms.com**
Rigby **www.johnrigbyandco.com**
Riverman Gun Works **www.rivermangunworks.com**
Rizzini USA **www.rizziniusa.com**
RM Equipment, Inc. **www.40mm.com**
Robar Companies, Inc. **www.robarguns.com**
Roberts Defense **www.robertsdefense.com**
Robinson Armament Co. **www.robarm.com**
Rock Island Armory **www.armscor.com**
Rock River Arms, Inc. **www.rockriverarms.com**
Rossi Arms **www.rossiusa.com**
RUAG Ammotec **www.ruag.com**
Ruger **www.ruger.com**
Sabatti SPA **www.sabatti.it.com**
Saco Defense **www.sacoinc.com**
Safety Harbor Firearms **www.safetyharborfirearms.com**
Samco Global Arms Inc. **www.samcoglobal.com**
Sarco **www.sarcoinc.com**
Sarsilmaz Silah San **www.sarsilmaz.com**
Sauer & Sohn **www.sauer.de**
Savage Arms Inc. **www.savagearms.com**
Scattergun Technologies Inc. **www.wilsoncombat.com**
SCCY Firearms **www.sccy.com**
Schmeisser Gmbh **www.schmeisser-germany.de**
SD Tactical Arms **www.sdtacticalarms.com**
Searcy Enterprises **www.searcyent.com**
Seecamp **www.seecamp.com**
Shaw **www.ershawbarrels.com**
Shilen Rifles **www.shilen.com**
Shiloh Rifle Mfg. **www.shilohrifle.com**
Sig Sauer, Inc. **www.sigsauer.com**
Simpson Ltd. **www.simpsonltd.com**
SKB Shotguns **www.skbshotguns.com**
Smith & Wesson **www.smith-wesson.com**
Sphinx System **www.sphinxarms.com**
Springfield Armory **www.springfield-armory.com**
SSK Industries **www.sskindustries.com**
Stag Arms **www.stagarms.com**
Stevens **www.savagearms.com**
Steyr Arms, Inc. **www.steyrarms.com**
STI International **www.stiguns.com**

Stoeger Industries **www.stoegerindustries.com**
Strayer-Voigt Inc. **www.sviguns.com**
Sturm, Ruger & Company **www.ruger.com**
Surgeon Rifles **www.surgeonrifles.com**
Tactical Rifles **www.tacticalrifles.com**
Tactical Solutions **www.tacticalsol.com**
Tar-Hunt Slug Guns, Inc. **www.tarhunt.com**
Taser Int'l **www.taser.com**
Taurus **www.taurususa.com**
Taylor's & Co., Inc. **www.taylorsfirearms.com**
Tempco Mfg. Co. **www.tempcomfg.com**
Tennessee Guns **www.tennesseeguns.com**
TG Int'l **www.tnguns.com**
Thompson Center Arms **www.tcarms.com**
Tikka **www.ticca.fi**
Time Precision **www.benchrest.com/timeprecision**
TNW, Inc. **www.tnwfirearms.com**
Traditions **www.traditionsfirearms.com**
Tristar Sporting Arms **www.tristarsportingarms.com**
Turnbull Mfg. Co. **www.turnbullmfg.com**
Uberti **www.ubertireplicas.com**
Ultralite 50 **www.ultralite50.com**
Ultra Light Arms **www.newultralight.com**
Umarex **www.umarex.com**
U.S. Armament Corp. **www.usarmamentcorp.com**
Uselton Arms, Inc. **www.useltonarmsinc.com**
Valkyrie Arms **www.valkyriearms.com**
Vektor Arms **www.vektorarms.com**
Verney-Carron **www.verney-carron.com**
Volquartsen Custom Ltd. **www.volquartsen.com**
Warrior **www.warrior.co**
Walther USA **www.waltherarms.com**
Weatherby **www.weatherby.com**
Webley and Scott Ltd. **www.webley.co.uk**
Westley Richards **www.westleyrichards.com**
Wild West Guns **www.wildwestguns.com**
William Larkin Moore & Co. **www.williamlarkinmoore.com**
Wilson Combat **www.wilsoncombat.com**
Winchester Rifles and Shotguns **www.winchesterguns.com**

GUN PARTS, BARRELS, AFTERMARKET ACCESSORIES

300 Below **www.300below.com**
Accuracy International of North America
 www.accuracyinternational.com
Accuracy Speaks, Inc. **www.accuracyspeaks.com**
Accuracy Systems **www.accuracysystemsinc.com**
Accurate Airguns **www.accurateairguns.com**
Advantage Arms **www.advantagearms.com**
AG Composites **www.agcomposites.com**

Aim Surplus **www.aimsurplus.com**
AK-USA **www.ak-103.com**
American Spirit Arms Corp. **www.americanspiritarms.com**
Amhurst-Depot **www.amherst-depot.com**
Apex Gun Parts **www.apexgunparts.com**
Armaspec **www.armaspec.com**
Armatac Industries **www.armatac.com**
Arthur Brown Co. **www.eabco.com**
Asia Sourcing Corp. **www.asiasourcing.com**
Barnes Precision Machine **www.barnesprecision.com**
Bar-Sto Precision Machine **www.barsto.com**
Bellm TC's **www.bellmtcs.com**
Belt Mountain Enterprises **www.beltmountain.com**
Bergara Barrels **www.bergarabarrels.com**
Beyer Barrels **www.beyerbarrels.com**
Bill Wiseman & Co. **www.wisemanballistics.com**
Bluegrass Gun Works **www.rocksolidind.com**
Bravo Company USA **www.bravocompanyusa.com**
Briley **www.briley.com**
Brownells **www.brownells.com**
B-Square **www.b-square.com**
Buffer Technologies **www.buffertech.com**
Bullberry Barrel Works **www.bullberry.com**
Bulldog Barrels **www.bulldogbarrels.com**
Bullet Central **www.bulletcentral.com**
Bushmaster Firearms/Quality Parts **www.bushmaster.com**
Butler Creek Corp **www.butlercreek.com**
Cape Outfitters Inc. **www.capeoutfitters.com**
Cavalry Arms **www.cavalryarms.com**
Caspian Arms Ltd. **www.caspianarms.com**
CDNN Sports **www.cdnnsports.com**
Cheaper Than Dirt **www.cheaperthandirt.com**
Chesnut Ridge **www.chestnutridge.com/**
Choate Machine & Tool Co. **www.riflestock.com**
Christie's Products **www.1022cental.com**
Cierner, Jonathan Arthur **www.22lrconversions.com**
CJ Weapons Accessories **www.cjweapons.com**
Colonial Arms **www.colonialarms.com**
Comp-N-Choke **www.comp-n-choke.com**
Custom Gun Rails **www.customgunrails.com**
Cylinder & Slide Shop **www.cylinder-slide.com**
Daniel Defense **www.danieldefense.com**
Dave Manson Precision Reamers **www.mansonreamers.com**
DC Machine **www.dcmachine.net**
Digi-Twist **www.fmtcorp.com**
Dixie Gun Works **www.dixiegun.com**
DPMS **www.dpmsinc.com**
D.S. Arms **www.dsarms.com**
eBay **www.ebay.com**
E. Arthur Brown Co. **www.eabco.com**
Ed Brown Products **www.edbrown.com**

EFK Marketing/Fire Dragon Pistol Accessories
www.efkfiredragon.com
E.R. Shaw **www.ershawbarrels.com**
ESS Solutions **www.esssolutions.com**
FJ Fedderson Rifle Barrels **www.gunbarrels.net**
FTF Industries **www.ftfindustries.com**
Fulton Armory **www.fulton-armory.com**
Galazan **www.connecticutshotgun.com**
Gemtech **www.gem-tech.com**
Gentry, David **www.gentrycustom.com**
GG&G **www.gggaz.com**
Great Lakes Tactical **www.gltactical.com**
Green Mountain Rifle Barrels **www.gmriflebarrel.com**
Gun Parts Corp. **www.e-gunpartscorp.com**
Guntec USA **www.guntecusa.com**
Harris Engineering **www.harrisbipods.com**
Hart Rifle Barrels **www.hartbarrels.com**
Hastings Barrels **www.hastingsbarrels.com**
Heinie Specialty Products **www.heinie.com**
High Performance Firearms/Hiperfire **www.hiperfire.com**
HKS Products **www.hksspeedloaders.com**
Holland Shooters Supply **www.hollandguns.com**
H-S Precision **www.hsprecision.com**
100 Straight Products **www.100straight.com**
I.M.A. **www.ima-usa.com**
Jack First Gun Shop **www.jackfirstgun.com**
Jarvis, Inc. **www.jarvis-custom.com**
J&T Distributing **www.jtdistributing.com**
John's Guns **www.johnsguns.com**
John Masen Co. **www.johnmasen.us**
Jonathan Arthur Ciener, Inc. **www.22lrconversions.com**
JP Enterprises **www.jprifles.com**
Keng's Firearms Specialities **www.versapod.com**
KG Industries **www.kgcoatings.com**
Kick Eez **www.kickeezproducts.com**
Kidd Triggers **www.coolguyguns.com**
King's Gunworks **www.kingsgunworks.com**
Knoxx Industries **www.impactguns.com**
Krieger Barrels **www.kriegerbarrels.com**
K-VAR Corp. **www.k-var.com**
L2D Custom Combat **www.l2dcombat.com**
LaRue Tactical **www.laruetactical.com**
Legend Armory **www.legend-armory.com**
Les Baer Custom, Inc. **www.lesbaer.com**
Lilja Barrels **www.riflebarrels.com**
Lone Wolf Dist. **www.lonewolfdist.com**
Lothar Walther Precision Tools Inc. **www.lothar-walther.de**
M&A Parts, Inc. **www.mapartsinc.com**
Magna-Matic Defense **www.magna-matic-defense.com**
Magpul Industries Corp. **www.magpul.com**
Majestic Arms **www.majesticarms.com**

MEC-GAR USA **www.mec-gar.com**
Mech Tech Systems **www.mechtechsys.com**
Mesa Tactical **www.mesatactical.com**
Michaels of Oregon Co. **www.michaels-oregon.com**
Midway USA **www.midwayusa.com**
Model 1 Sales **www.model1sales.com**
New England Custom Gun Service
   www.newenglandcustomgun.com
NIC Industries **www.nicindustries.com**
North Mfg. Co. **www.rifle-barrels.com**
Numrich Gun Parts Corp. **www.e-gunparts.com**
Osprey Defense LLC **www.gaspiston.com**
Pachmayr **www.pachmayr.com**
Pac-Nor Barrels **www.pac-nor.com**
Power Custom, Inc. **www.powercustom.com**
Precision Reflex **www.pri-mounts.com**
Promag Industries **www.promagindustries.com**
RCI-XRAIL **www.xrailbyrci.com**
Red Star Arms **www.redstararms.com**
River Bank Armory **www.riverbankarmory.com**
Riverman Gun Works **www.rivermangunworks.com**
Rock Creek Barrels **www.rockcreekbarrels.com**
Rocky Mountain Arms **www.rockymountainarms.com**
Royal Arms Int'l **www.royalarms.com**
R.W. Hart **www.rwhart.com**
Sage Control Ordnance **www.sageinternationalltd.com**
Sarco Inc. **www.sarcoinc.com**
Scattergun Technologies Inc. **www.wilsoncombat.com**
Schuemann Barrels **www.schuemann.com**
Score High Gunsmithing **www.scorehi.com**
Shaw Barrels **www.ershawbarrels.com**
Shilen **www.shilen.com**
Sims Vibration Laboratory **www.limbsaver.com**
Slide Fire **www.slidefire.com**
Smith & Alexander Inc. **www.smithandalexander.com**
Speed Shooters Int'l **www.shooter.com**
Sprinco USA Inc. **sprinco@primenet.com**
Springfield Sporters, Inc. **www.ssporters.com**
STI Int'l **www.stiguns.com**
S&S Firearms **www.ssfirearms.com**
SSK Industries **www.sskindustries.com**
Sun Devil Mfg. **www.sundevilmfg.com**
Sunny Hill Enterprises **www.sunny-hill.com**
Tac Star **www.lymanproducts.com**
Tactical Innovations **www.tacticalinc.com**
Tactical Solutions **www.tacticalsol.com**
Tactilite **www.tactilite.com**
Tapco **www.tapco.com**
Trapdoors Galore **www.trapdoors.com**
Triple K Manufacturing Co. Inc. **www.triplek.com**
Ultimak **www.ultimak.com**

Verney-Carron SA **www.verney-carron.com**
Vintage Ordnance **www.vintageordnance.com**
Vltor Weapon Systems **www.vltor.com**
Volquartsen Custom Ltd. **www.volquartsen.com**
W.C. Wolff Co. **www.gunsprings.com**
Weigand Combat Handguns **www.jackweigand.com**
Western Gun Parts **www.westerngunparts.com**
Wilson Arms **www.wilsonarms.com**
Wilson Combat **www.wilsoncombat.com**
Wisner's Inc. **www.wisnersinc.com**

GUNSMITHING SUPPLIES AND INSTRUCTION

4-D Products **www.4-dproducts.com**
American Gunsmithing Institute
   www.americangunsmith.com
Baron Technology **www.baronengraving.com**
Battenfeld Technologies **www.battenfeldtechnologies.com**
Bellm TC's **www.bellmtcs.com**
Blue Ridge Machinery & Tools
   www.blueridgemachinery.com
Brownells, Inc. **www.brownells.com**
B-Square Co. **www.b-square.com**
Cerakote Firearm Coatings **www.ncindustries.com**
Clymer Mfg. Co. **www.clymertool.com**
Dem-Bart **www.dembartco.com**
Doug Turnbull Restoration **www.turnbullrestoration.com**
Du-Lite Corp. **www.dulite.com**
DuraCoat Firearm Finishes **www.lauerweaponry.com**
Dvorak Instruments **www.dvorakinstruments.com**
Gradiant Lens Corp. **www.gradientlens.com**
Grizzly Industrial **www.grizzly.com**
Gunline Tools **www.gunline.com**
Harbor Freight **www.harborfreight.com**
JGS Precision Tool Mfg. LLC **www.jgstools.com**
Mag-Na-Port International **www.magnaport.com**
Manson Precision Reamers **www.mansonreamers.com**
Midway USA **www.midwayusa.com**
Murray State College **www.mscok.edu**
New England Custom Gun Service
   www.newenglandcustomgun.com
Olympus America Inc. **www.olympus.com**
Pacific Tool & Gauge **www.pacifictoolandgauge.com**
Penn Foster Career School **www.pennfoster.edu**
Pennsylvania Gunsmith School **www.pagunsmith.edu**
Piedmont Community College **www.piedmontcc.edu**
Precision Metalsmiths, Inc.
   www.precisionmetalsmiths.com
Sonoran Desert Institute **www.sdi.edu**
Trinidad State Junior College **www.trinidadstate.edu**

HANDGUN GRIPS

Ajax Custom Grips, Inc. **www.ajaxgrips.com**
Altamont Co. **www.altamontco.com**
Aluma Grips **www.alumagrips.com**
Barami Corp. **www.hipgrip.com**
Crimson Trace Corp. **www.crimsontrace.com**
Decal Grip **www.decalgrip.com**
Eagle Grips **www.eaglegrips.com**
Falcon Industries **www.ergogrips.net**
Herrett's Stocks **www.herrettstocks.com**
Hogue Grips **www.hogueinc.com**
Kirk Ratajesak **www.kgratajesak.com**
N.C. Ordnance **www.gungrip.com**
Nill-Grips USA **www.nill-grips.com**
Pachmayr **www.pachmayr.com**
Pearce Grips **www.pearcegrip.com**
Rio Grande Custom Grips **www.riograndecustomgrips.com**
Talon Grips **www.talongrips.com**
Trausch Grips Int. Co. **www.trausch.com**
Uncle Mike's **www.unclemikes.com**

HOLSTERS AND LEATHER PRODUCTS

Active Pro Gear **www.activeprogear.com**
Akah **www.akah.de**
Aker Leather Products **www.akerleather.com**
Alessi Distributor R&F Inc. **www.alessigunholsters.com**
Armor Holdings **www.holsters.com**
Bagmaster **www.bagmaster.com**
Bandara Gunleather **www.bandaragunleather.com**
Bianchi International **www.safariland.com/our-brands/bianchi**
Black Dog Machine **www.blackdogmachinellc.net**
Blackhawk Outdoors **www.blackhawk.com**
Blackhills Leather **www.blackhillsleather.com**
BodyHugger Holsters **www.nikolais.com**
Boyt Harness Co. **www.boytharness.com**
Brigade Gun Leather **www.brigadegunleather.com**
Center of Mass **www.comholsters.com**
Clipdraw **www.clipdraw.com**
Comp-Tac Victory Gear **www.comp-tac.com**
Concealed Carrie **www.concealedcarrie.com**
Concealment Shop Inc. **www.theconcealmentshop.com**
Coronado Leather Co. **www.coronadoleather.com**
Creedmoor Sports, Inc. **www.creedmoorsports.com**
Cross Breed Holsters **www.crossbreedholsters.com**
Deep Conceal **www.deepconceal.com**
Defense Security Products **www.thunderwear.com**
DeSantis Holster **www.desantisholster.com**
Diamond Custom Leather **www.diamondcustomleather.com**
Dillon Precision **www.dillonprecision.com**

Don Hume Leathergoods, Inc. **www.donhume.com**
Duty Smith **www.dutysmith.com**
Elite Survival **www.elitesurvival.com**
El Paso Saddlery **www.epsaddlery.com**
Fist **www.fist-inc.com**
Fobus USA **www.fobusholster.com**
Frontier Gun Leather **www.frontiergunleather.com**
Galco **www.usgalco.com**
Gilmore's Sports Concepts **www.gilmoresports.com**
Gould & Goodrich **www.gouldusa.com**
Hide-A-Gun **www.hide-a-gun.com**
High Noon Holsters **www.highnoonholsters.com**
Holsters.com **www.holsters.com**
Horseshoe Leather Products **www.horseshoe.org**
Houston Gun Holsters **www.houstongunholsters.com**
Hunter Co. **www.huntercompany.com**
JBP/Master's Holsters **www.jbpholsters.com**
Kirkpatrick Leather Company **www.kirkpatrickleather.com**
KJ Leather **www.kbarjleather.com**
KNJ **www.knjmfg.com**
Kramer Leather **www.kramerleather.com**
K-Rounds Holsters **www.krounds.com**
Levy's Leathers Ltd. **www.levysleathers.com**
Mernickle Holsters **www.mernickleholsters.com**
Michaels of Oregon Co. **www.michaels-oregon.com**
Milt Sparks Leather **www.miltsparks.com**
Mitch Rosen Extraordinary Gunleather **www.mitchrosen.com**
N82 Tactical **www.n82tactical.com**
Pacific Canvas & Leather Co. **paccanadleather@direct**way.com
Pager Pal **www.pagerpal.com**
Phalanx Corp. **www.smartholster.com**
Purdy Gear **www.purdygear.com**
PWL **www.pwlusa.com**
Safariland Ltd. Inc. **www.safariland.com**
Shooting Systems Group Inc. **www.shootingsystems.com**
Skyline Tool Works **www.clipdraw.com**
Stellar Rigs **www.stellarrigs.com**
Strong Holster Co. **www.strong-holster.com**
Tex Shoemaker & Sons **www.texshoemaker.com**
The Outdoor Connection **www.outdoorconnection.com**
Tuff Products **www.tuffproducts.com**
Triple K Manufacturing Co. **www.triplek.com**
Wilson Combat **www.wilsoncombat.com**

MISCELLANEOUS SHOOTING PRODUCTS

ADCO Sales **www.adcosales.com**
Aero Peltor **www.aearo.com**
American Body Armor **www.americanbodyarmor.com**
Ammo-Up **www.ammoupusa.com**
Battenfeld Technologies **www.battenfeldtechnologies.com**

Beamhit **www.swfa.com/beamhit-c8732.aspx**
Beartooth **www.beartoothproducts.com**
Burnham Brothers **www.burnhambrothers.com**
Collectors Armory **www.collectorsarmory.com**
Dead Ringer Hunting **www.deadringerhunting.com**
Deben Group Industries Inc. **www.deben.com**
Decot Hy-Wyd Sport Glasses **www.sportyglasses.com**
E.A.R., Inc. **www.earinc.com**
Gunstands **www.gunstands.com**
Howard Leight Hearing Protectors **www.howardleight.com**
Hunters Specialities **www.hunterspec.com**
Johnny Stewart Wildlife Calls **www.hunterspec.com**
Joseph Chiarello Gun Insurance **www.guninsurance.com**
Mec-Gar USA **www.mec-gar.com**
Merit Corporation **www.meritcorporation.com**
Michaels of Oregon Co. **www.michaels-oregon.com**
MT2, LLC **www.mt2.com**
MTM Case-Gard **www.mtmcase-gard.com**
Oakley, Inc. **www.usstandardissue.com**
Plano Molding **www.planomolding.com**
Practical Air Rifle Training Systems **www.smallarms.com**
Pro-Ears **www.pro-ears.com**
Quantico Tactical **www.quanticotactical.com**
Second Chance Body Armor Inc. **www.secondchance.com**
Smart Lock Technologies **www.smartlock.com**
SportEAR **www.sportear.com**
STRAC, Inc. **www.stractech.com**
Surefire **www.surefire.com**
Taser Int'l **www.taser.com**
Vyse-Gelatin Innovations **www.gelatininnovations.com**
Walker's Game Ear Inc. **www.walkersgameear.com**

MUZZLELOADING FIREARMS AND PRODUCTS

American Pioneer Powder **www.americanpioneerpowder.com**
Armi Sport **www.armisport.com**
Barnes Bullets **www.barnesbullets.com**
Black Powder Products **www.bpiguns.com**
Buckeye Barrels **www.buckeyebarrels.com**
Cabin Creek Muzzleloading **www.cabincreek.net**
CVA **www.cva.com**
Caywood Gunmakers **www.caywoodguns.com**
Davide Perdsoli & Co. **www.davide-pedersoli.com**
Dixie Gun Works, Inc. **www.dixiegun.com**
Elephant/Swiss Black Powder **www.elephantblackpowder.com**
Goex Black Powder **www.goexpowder.com**
Green Mountain Rifle Barrel Co. **www.gmriflebarrel.com**
Gunstocks Plus **www.gunstocksplus.com**
Gun Works **www.thegunworks.com**
Harvester Muzzleloading **www.harvestermuuzzleloading.com**

Honorable Company of Horners **www.hornguild.org**
Hornady **www.hornady.com**
Jedediah Starr Trading Co. **www.jedediah-starr.com**
Jim Chambers Flintlocks **www.flintlocks.com**
Kahnke Gunworks **www.powderandbow.com/kahnke/**
Knight Rifles **www.knightrifles.com**
Knob Mountain Muzzleloading
 www.knobmountainmuzzleloading.com
The Leatherman **www.blackpowderbags.com**
Log Cabin Shop **www.logcabinshop.com**
L&R Lock Co. **www.lr-rpl.com**
Lyman **www.lymanproducts.com**
Magkor Industries **www.magkor.com**
Middlesex Village Trading **www.middlesexvillagetrading.com**
MSM, Inc. **www.msmfg.com**
Muzzleloader Builders Supply
 www.muzzleloadersbuilderssupply.com
Muzzleload Magnum Products **www.mmpsabots.com**
Navy Arms **www.navyarms.com**
Northwest Trade Guns **www.northstarwest.com**
Nosler, Inc. **www.nosler.com**
October Country Muzzleloading **www.octobercountry.com**
Ox-Yoke Originals Inc. **www.rmcoxyoke.com**
Palmetto Arms **www.palmetto.it**
Pecatonica River **www.longrifles-pr.com**
Pietta **www.pietta.it**
Powerbelt Bullets **www.powerbeltbullets.com**
Precision Rifle Dead Center Bullets **www.prbullet.com**
R.E. Davis Co. **www.redaviscompany.com**
Rightnour Mfg. Co. Inc. **www.rmcsports.com**
Savage Arms, Inc. **www.savagearms.com**
Schuetzen Powder **www.schuetzenpowder.com**
TDC **www.tdcmfg.com**
Tennessee Valley Muzzleloading
 www.tennessevalleymuzzleloading.com
Thompson Center Arms **www.tcarms.com**
Tiger Hunt Stocks **www.gunstockwood.com**
Track of the Wolf **www.trackofthewolf.com**
Traditions Performance Muzzleloading
 www.traditionsfirearms. com
Turnbull Restoration & Mfg. **www.turnbullmfg.com**
Vernon C. Davis & Co. **www.stonewallcreekoutfitters.com**

PUBLICATIONS, VIDEOS AND CD'S

Arms and Military Press **www.skennerton.com**
A&J Arms Booksellers **www.ajarmsbooksellers.com**
American Cop **www.americancopmagazine.com**
American Gunsmithing Institute **www.americangunsmith.com**
American Handgunner **www.americanhandgunner.com**
American Hunter **www.nrapublications.org**

American Pioneer Video **www.americanpioneervideo.com**
American Rifleman **www.nrapublications.org**
Backwoodsman **www.backwoodsmanmag.com**
Blue Book Publications **www.bluebookinc.com**
Combat Handguns **www.combathandguns.com**
Concealed Carry **www.uscca.us**
Cornell Publications **www.cornellpubs.com**
Deer & Deer Hunting **www.deeranddeerhunting.com**
Field & Stream **www.fieldandstream.com**
Fouling Shot **www.castbulletassoc.org**
George Shumway Publisher **www.shumwaypublisher.com**
Grays Sporting Journal **www.grayssportingjournal.com**
Gun Digest, The Magazine **www.gundigest.com**
Gun Digest Books **www.gundigeststore.com**
Gun Dog **www.gundogmag.com**
Gun Mag **www.thegunmag.com**
Gun Tests **www.gun-tests.com**
Gun Video **www.gunvideo.com**
Gun World **www.gunworld.com**
Guns & Ammo **www.gunsandammo.com**
GUNS Magazine **www.gunsmagazine.com**
Guns of the Old West **www.gunsoftheoldwest.com**
Handloader **www.riflemagazine.com**
Handguns **www.handguns.com**
Harris Publications **www.harris-pub.com**
Hendon Publishing Co. **www.hendonpub.com**
Heritage Gun Books **www.gunbooks.com**
Krause Publications **www.krause.com**
Law and Order **www.hendonpub.com**
Man at Arms **www.manatarmsbooks.com**
Muzzle Blasts **www.nmlra.org**
Muzzleloader **www.muzzleloadermag.com**
On-Target Productions **www.ontargetdvds.com**
Outdoor Channel **www.outdoorchannel.com**
Outdoor Life **www.outdoorlife.com**
Paladin Press **www.paladin-press.com**
Police and Security News **www.policeandsecuritynews.com**
Police Magazine **www.policemag.com**
Primitive Arts Video **www.primitiveartsvideo.com**
Pursuit Channel **www.pursuitchannel.com**
Recoil Gun Magazine **www.recoilweb.com**
Rifle Magazine **www.riflemagazine.com**
Rifle Shooter Magazine **www.rifleshootermag.com**
Safari Press Inc. **www.safaripress.com**
Schiffer Publishing **www.schifferbooks.com**
Scurlock Publishing **www.muzzleloadingmag.com**
Shoot! Magazine **www.shootmagazine.com**
Shooting Illustrated **www.nrapublications.org**
Shooting Industry **www.shootingindustry.com**
Shooting Times Magazine **www.shootingtimes.com**
Shooting Sports Retailer **www.shootingsportsretailer.com**

Shooting Sports USA **www.nrapublications.org**
Shop Deer Hunting **www.shopdeerhunting.com**
Shotgun News **www.shotgunnews.com**
Shotgun Report **www.shotgunreport.com**
Shotgun Sports Magazine **www.shotgunsportsmagazine.com**
Single Shot Exchange **www.singleshotexchange.com**
Single Shot Rifle Journal **www.assra.com**
Skyhorse Publishing **www.skyhorsepublishing.com**
Small Arms Review **www.smallarmsreview.com**
Sporting Classics **www.sportingclassics.com**
Sporting Clays **www.sportingclays.net**
Sports Afield **www.sportsafield.com**
Sportsman Channel **www.thesportsmanchannel.com**
Sportsmen on Film **www.sportsmenonfilm.com**
Standard Catalog of Firearms **www.gundigeststore.com**
Successful Hunter **www.riflemagazine.com**
SWAT Magazine **www.swatmag.com**
Trapper & Predator Caller **www.trapperpredatorcaller.com**
Turkey & Turkey Hunting **www.turkeyandturkeyhunting.com**
Varmint Hunter **www.varminthunter.org**
VSP Publications **www.gunbooks.com**
Wildfowl **www.wildfowlmag.com**

RELOADING TOOLS

21st Century Shooting **www.21stcenturyshooting.com**
Ballisti-Cast Mfg. **www.ballisti-cast.com**
Battenfeld Technologies **www.battenfeldtechnologies.com**
Black Hills Shooters Supply **www.bhshooters.com**
Bruno Shooters Supply **www.brunoshooters.com**
Buffalo Arms **www.buffaloarms.com**
CabineTree **www.castingstuff.com**
Camdex, Inc. **www.camdexloader.com**
CH/4D Custom Die **www.ch4d.com**
Corbin Mfg & Supply Co. **www.corbins.com**
Dillon Precision **www.dillonprecision.com**
Forster Precision Products **www.forsterproducts.com**
Gracey Trimmer **www.matchprep.com**
Harrell's Precision **www.harrellsprec.com**
Holland's Shooting Supplies **www.hollandgun.com**
Hornady **www.hornady.com**
Hunter's Supply, Inc. **wwwhunters-supply.com**
Huntington Reloading Products **www.huntingtons.com**
J & J Products Co. **www.jandjproducts.com**
Lead Bullet Technology **www.lbtmoulds.com**
Lee Precision, Inc. **www.leeprecision.com**
L.E. Wilson **www.lewilson.com**
Littleton Shotmaker **www.littletonshotmaker.com**
Load Data **www.loaddata.com**
Lyman **www.lymanproducts.com**
Mayville Engineering Co. (MEC) **www.mecreloaders.com**

Midway **www.midwayusa.com**
Montana Bullet Works **www.montanabulletworks.com**
MTM Case-Guard **www.mtmcase-guard.com**
NECO **www.neconos.com**
NEI **www.neihandtools.com**
Neil Jones Custom Products **www.neiljones.com**
New Lachaussee SA **www.lachaussee.com**
Ponsness/Warren **www.reloaders.com**
Precision Reloading **www.precisionreloading.com**
Quinetics Corp. **www.quineticscorp.com**
RCBS **www.rcbs.com**
Redding Reloading Equipment **www.redding-reloading.com**
Russ Haydon's Shooting Supplies **www.shooters-supply.com**
Sinclair Int'l Inc. **www.sinclairintl.com**
Stealth Gunpowder **www.stealthgunpowder.com**
Stoney Point Products Inc. **www.stoneypoint.com**
Vickerman Seating Die **www.castingstuff.com**

RESTS— BENCH, PORTABLE, ATTACHABLE

Accu-Shot **www.accu-shot.com**
Battenfeld Technologies **www.battenfeldtechnologies.com**
Bench Master **www.bench-master.com**
B-Square **www.b-square.com**
Center Mass, Inc. **www.centermassinc.com**
Desert Mountain Mfg. **www.benchmasterusa.com**
DOA Tactical **www.doatactical.com**
Harris Engineering Inc. **www.harrisbipods**
KFS Industries **www.versapod.com**
Kramer Designs **www.snipepod.com**
Level-Lok **www.levellok.com**
Midway **www.midwayusa.com**
Rotary Gun Racks **www.gun-racks.com**
R.W. Hart **www.rwhart.com**
Sinclair Intl, Inc. **www.sinclairintl.com**
Shooting Bench USA **www.shootingbenchusa.com**
Stoney Point Products **www.stoneypoint.com**
Target Shooting **www.targetshooting.com**

SCOPES, SIGHTS, MOUNTS AND ACCESSORIES

Accumount **www.accumounts.com**
Accusight **www.accusight.com**
Advantage Tactical Sight **www.advantagetactical.com**
Aimpoint **www.aimpoint.com**
Aim Shot, Inc. **www.aimshot.com**
Aimtech Mount Systems **www.aimtech-mounts.com**
Alpen Outdoor Corp. **www.alpenoutdoor.com**
American Technologies Network, Corp. **www.atncorp.com**

AmeriGlo, LLC **www.ameriglo.net**
ArmaLaser **www.armalaser.com**
Amerigun USA **www.amerigunusa.com**
Armament Technology, Inc. **www.armament.com**
ARMS **www.armsmounts.com**
ATN **www.atncorp.com**
Badger Ordnance **www.badgerordnance.com**
Barrett **www.barrettrifles.com**
Beamshot-Quarton **www.beamshot.com**
BKL Technologies, Inc. **www.bkltech.com**
BSA Optics **www.bsaoptics.com**
B-Square **www.b-square.com**
Burris **www.burrisoptics.com**
Bushnell Performance Optics **www.bushnell.com**
Carl Zeiss Optical Inc. **www.zeiss.com**
CenterPoint Precision Optics **www.centerpointoptics.com**
Centurion Arms **www.centurionarms.com**
C-More Systems **www.cmore.com**
Conetrol Scope Mounts **www.conetrol.com**
Crimson Trace Corp. **www.crimsontrace.com**
D&L Sports **www.dlports.com**
DuraSight Scope Mounting Systems **www.durasight.com**
EasyHit, Inc. **www.easyhit.com**
EAW **www.eaw.de**
Elcan Optical Technologies **www.elcan. com**
Electro-Optics Technologies **www.eotech.com**
EoTech **www.eotech-inc.com**
Eurooptik Ltd. **www.eurooptik.com**
Field Sport Inc. **www.fieldsportinc.com**
GG&G **www.gggaz.com**
Gilmore Sports **www.gilmoresports.com**
Gradient Lens Corp. **www.gradientlens.com**
Guangzhou Bosma Corp. **www.bosmaoptics.com**
Hahn Precision **www.hahn-precision.com**
Hi-Lux Optics **www.hi-luxoptics.com**
HIVIZ **www.hivizsights.com**
Hollands Shooters Supply **www.hollandguns.com**
Horus Vision **www.horusvision.com**
Huskemaw Optics **www.huskemawoptics.com**
Insight **www.insighttechnology.com**
Ironsighter Co. **www.ironsighter.com**
KenSight **www.kensight.com**
Knight's Armament **www.knightarmco.com**
LaRue Tactical **www.laruetactical.com**
Laser Devices Inc. **www.laserdevices.com**
Lasergrips **www.crimsontrace.com**
LaserLyte **www.laserlytesights.com**
LaserMax Inc. **www.lasermax.com**
Laser Products **www.surefire.com**
Leapers, Inc. **www.leapers.com**
Leatherwood **www.hi-luxoptics.com**

Leica Camera Inc. **www.leica-camera.com**
Leupold **www.leupold.com**
Lewis Machine & Tool **www.lewismachine.net**
LightForce/NightForce USA **www.nightforceoptics.com**
LUCID LLC **www.mylucidgear.com**
Lyman **www.lymanproducts.com**
Lynx **www.b-square.com**
Matech **www.matech.net**
Marble's Gunsights **www.marblearms.com**
Meopta **www.meopta.com**
Meprolight **www.meprolight.com**
Mini-Scout-Mount **www.amegaranges.com**
Minox USA **www.minox.com**
Montana Vintage Arms **www.montanavintagearms.com**
Moro Vision **www.morovision.com**
Mounting Solutions Plus **www.mountsplus.com**
NAIT **www.nait.com**
Newcon International Ltd. **www.newcon-optik.com**
Night Force Optics **www.nightforceoptics.com**
Night Optics USA, Inc. **www.nightoptics.com**
Night Owl Optics **www.nightowloptics.com**
Nikon Inc. **www.nikonhunting.com**
Nitehog **www.nitehog.com**
North American Integrated Technologies **www.nait.com**
Novak Sights **www.novaksights.com**
O.K. Weber, Inc. **www.okweber.com**
Optolyth-Optic **www.optolyth.de**
Osprey Optics **www.osprey-optics.com**
Precision Reflex **www.pri-mounts.com**
Pride Fowler, Inc. **www.rapidreticle.com**
Premier Reticles **www.premierreticles.com**
Redfield **www.redfield.com**
Rifle Electronics **www.theriflecam.com**
Schmidt & Bender **www.schmidt-bender.com**
Scopecoat **www.scopecoat.com**
Scopelevel **www.scopelevel.com**
Shepherd Scope Ltd. **www.shepherdscopes.com**
SIG Sauer **www.sigsauer.com**
Sightmark **www.sightmark.com**
Simmons **www.simmonsoptics.com**
S&K **www.scopemounts.com**
Springfield Armory **www.springfield-armory.com**
Steiner **www.steiner-binoculars.com**
Sun Optics USA **www.sunopticsusa.com**
Sure-Fire **www.surefire.com**
Swarovski/Kahles **www.swarovskioptik.com**
SWATSCOPE **www.swatscope.com**
Swift Optics **www.swiftoptics.com**
Talley Mfg. Co. **www.talleyrings.com**
Steve Earle Scope Blocks **www.steveearleproducts.com**
Tasco **www.tasco.com**

Tech Sights **www.tech-sights.com**
Trijicon Inc. **www.trijicon.com**
Trinity Force **www.trinityforce.com**
Troy Industries **www.troyind.com**
Truglo Inc. **www.truglo.com**
Ultimak **www.ultimak.com**
UltraDot **www.ultradotusa.com**
U.S. Night Vision **www.usnightvision.com**
U.S. Optics Technologies Inc. **www.usoptics.com**
Valdada-IOR Optics **www.valdada.com**
Viridian Green Laser Sights **www.viridiangreenlaser.com**
Vortex Optics **www.vortexoptics.com**
Warne **www.warnescopemounts.com**
Weaver Scopes **www.weaveroptics.com**
Wilcox Industries Corp **www.wilcoxind.com**
Williams Gun Sight Co. **www.williamsgunsight.com**
Wilson Combat **www.wilsoncombat.com**
XS Sight Systems **www.xssights.com**
Zeiss **www.zeiss.com**

SHOOTING ORGANIZATIONS, SCHOOLS AND MUSEUMS

Amateur Trapshooting Assoc. **www.shootata.com**
American Custom Gunmakers Guild **www.acgg.org**
American Gunsmithing Institute **www.americangunsmith.com**
American Pistolsmiths Guild **www.americanpistol.com**
American Shooting Sports Council **www.assc.com**
American Single Shot Rifle Assoc. **www.assra.com**
American Snipers **www.americansnipers.org**
Assoc. of Firearm & Tool Mark Examiners **www.afte.org**
Autry National Center of the American West **www.theautry.org**
BATFE **www.atf.gov**
Boone and Crockett Club **www.boone-crockett.org**
Browning Collectors Association **www.browningcollectors.com**
Buffalo Bill Center of the West **www.centerofthewest.org**
Buckmasters, Ltd. **www.buckmasters.com**
Cast Bullet Assoc. **www.castbulletassoc.org**
Citizens Committee for the Right to Keep & Bear Arms **www. ccrkba.org**
Civilian Marksmanship Program **www.odcmp.com**
Colorado School of Trades **www.schooloftrades.edu**
Contemporary Longrifle Assoc. **www.longrifle.com**
Colt Collectors Assoc. **www.coltcollectors.com**
Cylinder & Slide Pistolsmithing Schools **www.cylinder-slide. com**
Ducks Unlimited **www.ducks.org**
4-H Shooting Sports Program **www.4-hshootingsports.org**
Fifty Caliber Institute **www.fiftycaliberinstitute.org**
Fifty Caliber Shooters Assoc. **www.fcsa.org**
Firearms Coalition **www.nealknox.com**
A.H. Fox Collectors Assoc. **www.foxcollectors.com**
Front Sight Firearms Training Institute **www.frontsight.com**

Garand Collectors Assoc. **www.thegca.org**
German Gun Collectors Assoc. **www.germanguns.com**
Gibbs Military Collectors Club **www.gibbsrifle.com**
Glock Collectors Assoc. **www.glockcollectors.com**
Gun Clubs **www.associatedgunclubs.org**
Gun Owners Action League **www.goal.org**
Gun Owners of America **www.gunowners.org**
Gun Trade Asssoc. Ltd. **www.gtaltd.co.uk**
Gunsite Training Center, Inc. **www.gunsite.com**
High Standard Collectors Assoc. **www.highstandard.org**
Hunting and Shooting Sports Heritage Fund **www.hsshf.org**
I.C.E. Training **www.icetraining.us**
International Ammunition Assoc. **www.cartridgecollectors.org**
IWA **www.iwa.info**
International Defensive Pistol Assoc. **www.idpa.com**
International Handgun Metallic Silhouette Assoc. **www.ihmsa.org**
International Hunter Education Assoc. **www.ihea.com**
Int'l Law Enforcement Educators and Trainers Assoc. **www. ileeta.com**
International Single Shot Assoc. **www.issa-schuetzen.org**
Ithaca Owners **www.ithacaowners.com**
Jews for the Preservation of Firearms Ownership **www.jpfo.org**
L.C. Smith Collectors Assoc. **www.lcsmith.org**
Lefever Arms Collectors Assoc. **www.lefevercollectors.com**
Mannlicher Collectors Assoc. **www.mannlicher.org**
Marlin Firearms Collectors Assoc. **www.marlin-collectors.com**
Mule Deer Foundation **www.muledeer.org**
Muzzle Loaders Assoc. of Great Britain **www.mlagb.com**
National 4-H Shooting Sports **www.4-hshootingsports.org**
National Association of Sporting Goods Wholesalers
www.nasgw.org
National Benchrest Shooters Assoc. **www.nbrsa.com**
National Defense Industrial Assoc. **www.ndia.org**
National Cowboy & Western Heritage Museum
www.nationalcowboymuseum.org
National Firearms Museum **www.nramuseum.org**
National Mossberg Collectors Assoc.
www.mossbergcollectors.org
National Muzzle Loading Rifle Assoc. **www.nmlra.org**
National Rifle Association **www.nra.org**
National Rifle Association ILA **home.nra.org/nraila**
National Shooting Sports Foundation **www.nssf.org**
National Skeet Shooters Association **www.nssa-nsca.com**
National Sporting Clays Assoc. **www.nssa-nsca.com**
National Tactical Officers Assoc. **www.ntoa.org**
National Wild Turkey Federation **www.nwtf.com**
NICS/FBI **www.fbi.gov**
North American Hunting Club **www.huntingclub.com**
Order of Edwardian Gunners (Vintagers) **www.vintagers.org**
Outdoor Industry Foundation
www.outdoorindustryfoundation.org
Parker Gun Collectors Assoc. **www.parkerguns.org**

Pennsylvania Gunsmith School **www.pagunsmith.com**
Pheasants Forever **www.pheasantsforever.org**
Piedmont Community College **www.piedmontcc.edu**
Quail & Upland Wildlife Federation **www.quwf.net**
Quail Unlimited **www.qu.org**
Remington Society of America **www.remingtonsociety.com**
Right To Keep and Bear Arms **www.rkba.org**
Rocky Mountain Elk Foundation **www.rmef.org**
Ruffed Grouse Society **www.ruffedgrousesociety.org**
Ruger Collectors Assoc. **www.rugercollectorsassociation.com**
Ruger Owners & Collectors Society **www.rugersociety.com**
SAAMI **www.saami.org**
Safari Club International **www.scifirstforhunters.org**
Sako Collectors Club **www.sakocollectors.com**
Scholastic Clay Target Program
www.sssfonline.org/scholasti-clay-target-program
Scholastic Shooting Sports Foundation **www.sssfonline.org**
Second Amendment Foundation **www.saf.org**
Second Amendment Sisters **www.2asisters.org**
Shooting for Women Alliance
www.shootingforwomenalliance. com
Sig Sauer Academy **www.sigsauer.com**
Single Action Shooting Society **www.sassnet.com**
Smith & Wesson Collectors Assoc. **www.theswca.org**
L.C. Smith Collectors Assoc. **www.lcsmith.org**
Steel Challenge Pistol Tournament **www.steelchallenge.com**
Students for Second Amendment **www.sf2a.org**
Sturgis Economic Development Corp.
www.sturgisdevelopment.com
Suarez Training **www.warriortalk.com**
Tactical Defense Institute **www.tdiohio.com**
Tactical Life **www.tactical-life.com**
Thompson/Center Assoc. **www.thompsoncenterassociation.org**
Thunder Ranch **www.thunderranchinc.com**
Trapshooters Homepage **www.trapshooters.com**
Trinidad State Junior College **www.trinidadstate.edu**
United Sportsmen's Youth Foundation **www.usyf.com**
Universal Shooting Academy
www.universalshootingacademy.com
U.S. Concealed Carry Association **www.uscca.us**
U.S. Fish and Wildlife Service **www.fws.gov**
U.S. Practical Shooting Assoc. **www.uspsa.org**
U.S. Sportsmen's Alliance **www.ussportsmen.org**
USA Shooting **www.usashooting.com**
Varmint Hunter's Assoc. **www.varminthunter.org**
Weatherby Collectors Assoc. **www.weatherbycollectors.com**
Winchester Arms Collectors Assoc.
www.winchestercollector. com
Women Hunters **www.womanhunters.com**

STOCKS, GRIPS, FOREARMS

10/22 Fun Gun **www.1022fungun.com**
Advanced Technology **www.atigunstocks.com**
AG Composites **www.agcomposites.com**
Battenfeld Technologies **www.battenfeldtechnologies.com**
Bell & Carlson, Inc. **www.bellandcarlson.com**
Boyd's Gunstock Industries, Inc. **www.boydgunstocks.com**
Butler Creek Corp **www.butlercreek.com**
Cadex **www.vikingtactics.com**
Calico Hardwoods, Inc. **www.calicohardwoods.com**
Choate Machine **www.riflestock.com**
Command Arms **www.commandarms.com**
C-More Systems **www.cmore.com**
D&L Sports **www.dlsports.com**
Duo Stock **www.duostock.com**
E. Arthur Brown Co. **www.eabco.com**
Fajen **www.battenfeldtechnologies.com**
Falcon Ergo Grip **www.ergogrips.com**
Great American Gunstocks **www.gunstocks.com**
Grip Pod **www.grippod.com**
Gun Stock Blanks **www.gunstockblanks.com**
Herrett's Stocks **www.herrettstocks.com**
High Tech Specialties **www.hightech-specialties.com**
Hogue Grips **www.getgrip.com**
Holland's Shooting Supplies **www.hollandgun.com**
Knight's Mfg. Co. **wwwknightarmco.com**
Knoxx Industries **www.blackhawk.com**
KZ Tactical **www.kleyzion.com**
LaRue Tactical **www.laruetactical.com**
Lewis Machine & Tool **www.lewismachine.net**
Lone Wolf **www.lonewolfriflestocks.com**
Magpul **www.magpul.com**
Manners Composite Stocks **www.mannersstocks.com**
McMillan Fiberglass Stocks **www.mcmfamily.com**
MPI Stocks **www.mpistocks.com**
Phoenix Technology/Kicklite **www.kicklitestocks.com**
Precision Gun Works **www.precisiongunstocks.com**
Ram-Line **www.outers-guncare.com**
Richards Microfit Stocks **www.rifle-stocks.com**
Rimrock Rifle Stock **www.bordenrifles.com**
Royal Arms Gunstocks **www.royalarmsgunstocks.com**
Speedfeed **www.safariland.com**
TacStar/Pachmayr **www.tacstar.com**
Tango Down **www.tangodown.com**
TAPCO **www.tapco.com**
Slide Fire **www.slidefire.com**
Stocky's **www.newriflestocks.com**
Surefire **www.surefire.com**
Tiger-Hunt Curly Maple Gunstocks **www.gunstockwood.com**
UTG Pro **www.leapers.com**

Wenig Custom Gunstocks Inc. **www.wenig.com**
Wilcox Industries **www.wilcoxind.com**
Yankee Hill **www.yhm.net**

TARGETS AND RANGE EQUIPMENT

Action Target Co. **www.actiontarget.com**
Advanced Interactive Systems **www.ais-sim.com**
Advanced Training Systems **www.atsusa.biz**
Alco Target **www.alcotarget.com**
Arntzen Targets **www.arntzentargets.com**
Birchwood Casey **www.birchwoodcasey.com**
Caswell Meggitt Defense Systems **www.mds-caswell.com**
Champion Traps & Targets **www.championtarget.com**
Custom Metal Products **www.custommetalprod.com**
Laser Shot **www.lasershot.com**
MGM Targets **www.mgmtargets.com**
MTM Products **www.mtmcase-gard.com**
National Muzzleloading Rifle Assoc. **www.nmlra.org**
National Target Co. **www.nationaltarget.com**
Newbold Target Systems **www.newboldtargets.com**
Paragon Tactical **www.paragontactical.com**
PJL Targets **www.pjltargets.com**
Porta Target, Inc. **www.portatarget.com**
Rolling Steel Targets **www.rollingsteeltargets.com**
Savage Range Systems **www.savagerangesystems.com**
ShatterBlast Targets **www.daisy.com**
Super Trap Bullet Containment Systems **www.supertrap.com**
Thompson Target Technology **www.thompsontarget.com**
Tombstone Tactical Targets **www.thombstonetactical.com**
Unique Tek **www.uniquetek.com**
Visible Impact Targets **www.crosman.com**
White Flyer **www.whiteflyer.com**
Western Range **www.westernrange.us**

TRAP AND SKEET SHOOTING EQUIPMENT AND ACCESSORIES

Atlas Trap Co **www.atlastraps.com**
Auto-Sporter Industries **www.auto-sporter.com**
Do-All Traps, Inc. **www.doalloutdoors.com**
Gamaliel Shooting Supply **www.gamaliel.com**
Howell Shooting Supplies **www.howellshootingsupplies.com**
Hunters Pointe **www.hunterspointetraps.com**
Promatic, Inc. **www.promatic.biz**
Trius Products Inc. **www.triustraps.com**
White Flyer **www.whiteflyer.com**

TRIGGERS

American Trigger Corp. **www.americantrigger.com**

Brownells **www.brownells.com**
Geissele Automatics, LLC **www.ar15triggers.com**
Huber Concepts **www.huberconcepts.com**
Jard, Inc. **www.jardinc.com**
Kidd Triggers **www.coolguyguns.com**
Shilen **www.shilen.com**
Spec-Tech Industries, Inc. **www.spec-tech-industries.com**
Timney Triggers **www.timneytriggers.com**
Williams Trigger Specialties **www.williamstriggers.com**

MAJOR SHOOTING WEBSITES AND LINKS

24 Hour Campfire **www.24hourcampfire.com**
Accurate Shooter **www.6mmbr.com**
Alphabetic Index of Links **www.gunsgunsguns.com**
Ammo Guide **www.ammoguide.com**
Auction Arms **www.auctionarms.com**
Benchrest Central **www.benchrest.com**
Big Game Hunt **www.biggamehunt.net**
Bullseye Pistol **www.bullseyepistol.com**
Firearms History **www.researchpress.co.uk**
Glock Talk **www.glocktalk.com**
Gun Broker Auctions **www.gunbroker.com**

Gun Blast **www.gunblast.com**
Gun Boards **www.gunboards.com**
Gun Digest **www. gundigest.com**
Guns & Ammo Forum **www.gunsandammo.com**
GunsAmerica **www.gunsamerica.com**
Guns Unified Nationally Endorsing Dignity **www.guned.com**
Gun Shop Finder **www.gunshopfinder.com**
Guns and Hunting **www.gunsandhunting.com**
Hunt and Shoot (NSSF) **www.huntandshoot.org**
Keep and Bear Arms **www.keepandbeararms.com**
Leverguns **www.leverguns.com**
Load Swap **www.loadswap.com**
Long Range Hunting **www.longrangehunting.com**
Real Guns **www.realguns.com**
Ruger Forum **www.rugerforum.com**
Savage Shooters **www.savageshooters.com**
Shooters Forum **www.shootersforum.com**
Shotgun Sports Resource Guide **www.shotgunsports.com**
Shotgun World **www.shotgunworld.com**
Sniper's Hide **www.snipershide.com**
Sportsman's Web **www.sportsmansweb.com**
Tactical-Life **www.tactical-life.com**
The Gun Room **www.doublegun.com**
Wing Shooting USA **www.wingshootingusa.org**

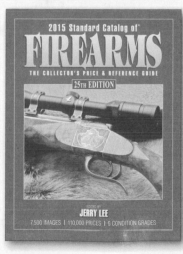

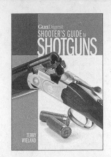

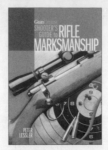

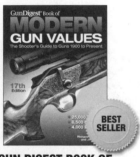

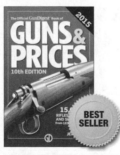

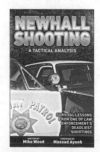

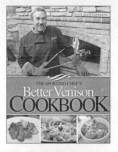

**THE SPORTING CHEF'S
BETTER VENISON
COOKBOOK**
U1948 • $24.99

COOKING GAME
U2929 • $9.99

BIG BUCK SECRETS
T4648 • $24.99

**WE KILL IT
WE GRILL IT**
V6707 • $9.99

**301
VENISON RECIPES**
VR01 • $10.95

**ADVENTURE
BOWHUNTER**
V9708 • $34.99

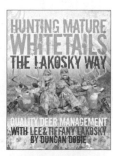

**HUNTING MATURE
WHITETAILS
THE LAKOSKY WAY**
W4542 • $29.99

**DEER & DEER
HUNTING'S GUIDE
TO BETTER
BOW HUNTING**
V6706 • $9.99

**STRATEGIES FOR
WHITETAILS**
WTLDD • $24.99

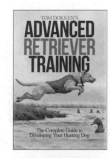

**TOM DOKKEN'S
ADVANCED RETRIEVER
TRAINING**
U1863 • $22.99

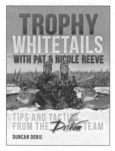

**TROPHY WHITETAILS WITH
PAT AND NICOLE REEVE**
U3680 • $31.99

**LEGENDARY
WHITETAILS**
W7618 • $29.99

GUT IT. CUT IT. COOK IT.
Z5014 • $24.99

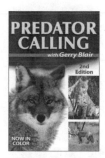

**PREDATOR CALLING
WITH GERRY BLAIR**
Z0740 • $19.99

THE RUT HUNTERS
U7573 • $31.99

GAME COOKERY
U7125 • $24.99

**THE MOUNTAIN MAN
COOKBOOK**
U9370 • $12.99

**TOM DOKKEN'S
RETRIEVER TRAINING**
Z3235 • $19.99

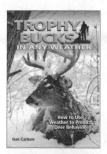

**TROPHY BUCKS
IN ANY WEATHER**
Z1781 • $21.99

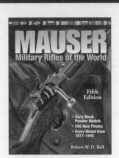
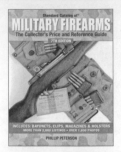
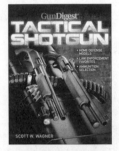
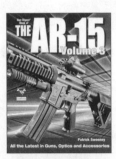
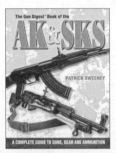

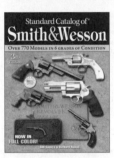
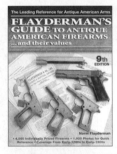

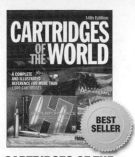
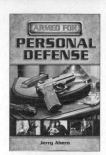

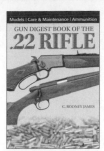

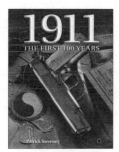
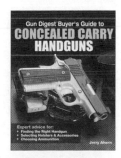
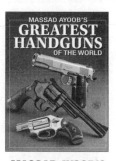
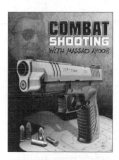
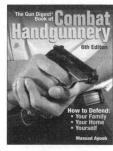

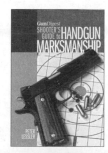
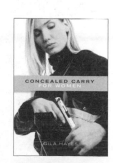

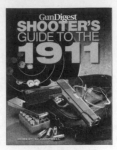

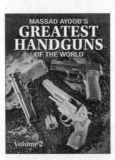
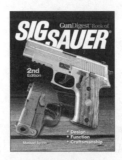

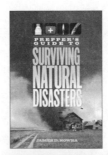

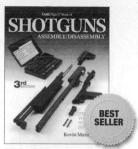
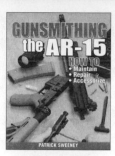
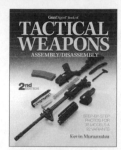
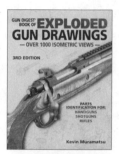

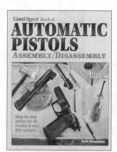
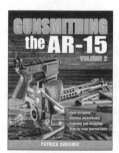

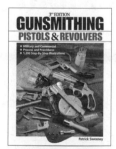

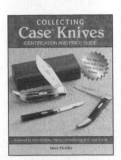

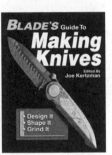

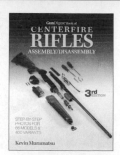

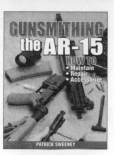
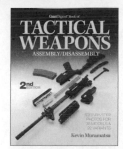
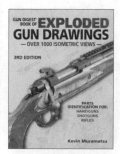

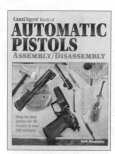
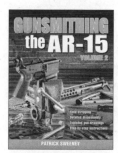

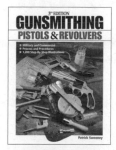

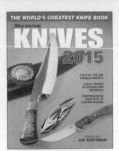

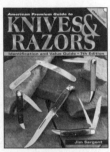
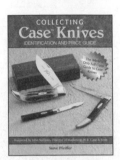